W9-CTH-651

Short Story Criticism

Guide to Gale Literary Criticism Series

For criticism on	Consult these Gale series
Authors now living or who died after December 31, 1959	*CONTEMPORARY LITERARY CRITICISM (CLC)*
Authors who died between 1900 and 1959	*TWENTIETH-CENTURY LITERARY CRITICISM (TCLC)*
Authors who died between 1800 and 1899	*NINETEENTH-CENTURY LITERATURE CRITICISM (NCLC)*
Authors who died between 1400 and 1799	*LITERATURE CRITICISM FROM 1400 TO 1800 (LC)* *SHAKESPEAREAN CRITICISM (SC)*
Authors who died before 1400	*CLASSICAL AND MEDIEVAL LITERATURE CRITICISM (CMLC)*
Black writers of the past two hundred years	*BLACK LITERATURE CRITICISM (BLC)*
Authors of books for children and young adults	*CHILDREN'S LITERATURE REVIEW (CLR)*
Dramatists	*DRAMA CRITICISM (DC)*
Hispanic writers of the late nineteenth and twentieth centuries	*HISPANIC LITERATURE CRITICISM (HLC)*
Native North American writers and orators of the eighteenth, nineteenth, and twentieth centuries	*NATIVE NORTH AMERICAN LITERATURE (NNAL)*
Poets	*POETRY CRITICISM (PC)*
Short story writers	*SHORT STORY CRITICISM (SSC)*
Major authors from the Renaissance to the present	*WORLD LITERATURE CRITICISM, 1500 TO THE PRESENT (WLC)*

ISSN 0895-9439

Volume 21

Short Story Criticism

Excerpts from Criticism of the Works of Short Fiction Writers

Drew Kalasky, Editor

Margaret Haerens
Jeff Hill
Marie Rose Napierkowski
Mary K. Ruby
Christine Slovey
Lawrence J. Trudeau
Associate Editors

GALE

an International Thomson Publishing company I(T)P®

STAFF

Drew Kalasky, *Editor*

...ens, Jeff Hill, Marie Rose Napierkowski, Mary K. Ruby,
Christine Slovey, Lawrence J. Trudeau,
Associate Editors

Debra A. Wells, *Assistant Editor*

Marlene S. Hurst, *Permissions Manager*
Margaret A. Chamberlain, Maria Franklin, *Permissions Specialists*

Susan Brohman, Diane Cooper, Michele Lonoconus, Maureen Puhl,
Shalice Shah, Kimberly F. Smilay, Barbara A. Wallace, *Permissions Associates*

Sarah Chesney, Edna Hedblad, Margaret McAvoy-Amato, Tyra Y. Phillips,
Lori Schoenenberger, Rita Velazquez, *Permissions Assistants*

Victoria B. Cariappa, *Research Manager*

Tamara C. Nott, Michele P. Pica, Tracie A. Richardson,
Norma Sawaya, *Research Associates*

Julia C. Daniel, Michelle Lee, Cheryl L. Warnock, *Research Assistants*

Mary Beth Trimper, *Production Director*
Deborah L. Milliken, *Production Assistant*

C. J. Jonik, *Desktop Publisher*
Randy Bassett, *Image Database Supervisor*
Robert Duncan, *Scanner Operator*
Pamela Hayes, *Photography Coordinator*

Margaret Haerens, Jeff Hill, Drew Kalasky, Julie Karmazin, Marie Rose Napierkowski,
Christine Slovey, Lawrence J. Trudeau, *Desktop Typesetters*

Library of Congress Catalog Card Number 88-641014
ISBN 0-7876-0753-3
ISSN 0895-9439

Printed in the United States of America
10 9 8 7 6 5 4 3 2 1

I(T)P™   Gale Research, an ITP Information/Reference Group Company.
ITP logo is a trademark under license.

Contents

Preface   vii

Acknowledgments   xi

Preface

A Comprehensive Information Source
on World Short Fiction

S hort Story Criticism (SSC) presents significant passages from criticism of the world's greatest short story writers and provides supplementary biographical and bibliographical materials to guide the interested reader to a greater understanding of the authors of short fiction. This series was developed in response to suggestions from librarians serving high school, college, and public library patrons, who had noted a considerable number of requests for critical material on short story writers. Although major short story writers are covered in such Gale series as *Contemporary Literary Criticism (CLC), Twentieth-Century Literary Criticism (TCLC), Nineteenth-Century Literature Criticism (NCLC),* and *Literature Criticism from 1400 to 1800 (LC),* librarians perceived the need for a series devoted solely to writers of the short story genre.

Coverage

SSC is designed to serve as an introduction to major short story writers of all eras and nationalities. Since these authors have inspired a great deal of relevant critical material, *SSC* is necessarily selective, and the editors have chosen the most important published criticism to aid readers and students in their research.

Approximately eight to ten authors are included in each volume, and each entry presents a historical survey of the critical response to that author's work. The length of an entry is intended to reflect the amount of critical attention the author has received from critics writing in English and from foreign critics in translation. Every attempt has been made to identify and include excerpts from the most significant essays on each author's work. In order to provide these important critical pieces, the editors sometimes reprint essays that have appeared elsewhere in Gale's Literary Criticism Series. Such duplication, however, never exceeds twenty percent of an *SSC* volume.

Organization

An *SSC* author entry consists of the following elements:

- The **Author Heading** cites the name under which the author most commonly wrote, followed by birth and death dates. If the author wrote consistently under a pseudonym, the pseudonym will be listed in the author heading and the author's actual name given in parentheses on the first line of the biographical and critical introduction.

- The **Biographical and Critical Introduction** contains background information designed to introduce a reader to the author and the critical debates surrounding his or her work.

- A **Portrait of the Author** is included when available. Many entries also contain illustrations of materials pertinent to an author's career, including holographs of manuscript pages, title pages, dust jackets, letters, or representations of important people, places, and events in the author's life.

- The list of **Principal Works** is chronological by date of first publication and lists the most important works by the author. The first section comprises short story collections, novellas, and novella collections. The second section gives information on other major works by the author. For foreign authors, the editors have provided original foreign-language publication information and have selected what are considered the best and most complete English-language editions of their works.

- **Criticism** is arranged chronologically in each author entry to provide a useful perspective on changes in critical evaluation over the years. All short story, novella, and collection titles by the author featured in the entry are printed in boldface type to enable a reader to ascertain without difficulty the works discussed. Also for purposes of easier identification, the critic's name and the publication date of the essay are given at the beginning of each piece of criticism. Unsigned criticism is preceded by the title of the journal in which it appeared.

- Critical essays are prefaced with **Explanatory Notes** as an additional aid to students and readers using *SSC*. An explanatory note may provide useful information of several types, including: the reputation of the critic, the intent or scope of the critical essay, and the orientation of the criticism (biographical, psychoanalytic, structuralist, etc.).

- A complete **Bibliographical Citation,** designed to help the interested reader locate the original essay or book, precedes each piece of criticism.

- The **Further Reading List** appearing at the end of each author entry suggests additional materials on the author. In some cases it includes essays for which the editors could not obtain reprint rights. Boxed material following the further reading list provides references to other biographical and critical sources on the author in series published by Gale.

Beginning with volume six, *SSC* contains two additional features designed to enhance the reader's understanding of short fiction writers and their works:

- Each *SSC* entry now includes, when available, **Comments by the Author** that illuminate his or her own works or the short story genre in general. These statements are set within boxes or bold rules to distinguish them from the criticism.

- A **Select Bibliography of General Sources on Short Fiction** is included as an appendix. This listing of materials for further research provides readers with a selection of the best available general studies of the short story genre.

Other Features

A **Cumulative Author Index** lists all the authors who have appeared in *SSC, CLC, TCLC, NCLC, LC,* and *Classical and Medieval Literature Criticism (CMLC),* as well as cross-references to other Gale series. Users will welcome this cumulated index as a useful tool for locating an author within the Literary Criticism Series.

A **Cumulative Nationality Index** lists all authors featured in *SSC* by nationality, followed by the number of the *SSC* volume in which their entry appears.

A **Cumulative Title Index** lists in alphabetical order all short story, novella, and collection titles contained in the *SSC* series. Titles of short story collections, separately published novellas, and novella collections are printed in italics, while titles of individual short stories are printed in roman type with quotation marks.

Each title is followed by the author's name and corresponding volume and page numbers where commentary on the work is located. English-language translations of original foreign-language titles are cross-referenced to the foreign titles so that all references to discussion of a work are combined in one listing.

Citing *Short Story Criticism*

When writing papers, students who quote directly from any volume in the Literary Criticism Series may use the following general forms to footnote reprinted criticism. The first example pertains to material drawn from periodicals, the second to material reprinted from books:

[1]Henry James, Jr., "Honoré de Balzac," *The Galaxy 20* (December 1875), 814-36; excerpted and reprinted in *Short Story Criticism,* Vol. 5, ed. Thomas Votteler (Detroit: Gale Research, 1990), pp. 8-11.

[2]F. R. Leavis, *D. H. Lawrence: Novelist* (Alfred A. Knopf, 1956); excerpted and reprinted in *Short Story Criticism,* Vol. 4, ed. Thomas Votteler (Detroit: Gale Research, 1990), pp. 202-06.

Comments

Readers who wish to suggest authors to appear in future volumes, or who have other suggestions, are invited to contact the editors by writing to Gale Research Inc., Literary Criticism Division, 835 Penobscot Building, Detroit, MI 48226-4094.

Acknowledgments

The editors wish to thank the copyright holders of the excerpted criticism included in this volume and the permissions managers of many book and magazine publishing companies for assisting in securing reprint rights. The editors are also grateful to the staffs of the Detroit Public Library, Wayne State University Purdy/Kresge Library Complex, the University of Michigan Libraries, and the Library of Congress for making their resources available. Following is a list of the copyright holders who have granted permission to reprint material in this volume of *SSC*. Every effort has been made to trace copyright, but if omissions have been made, please let Gale Research know.

COPYRIGHTED EXCERPTS IN *SSC*, VOLUME 21, WERE REPRINTED FROM THE FOLLOWING PERIODICALS:

Ararat, v. XXV, Spring, 1984. Copyright © 1984 by the Armenian General Benevolent Union. Reprinted by permission of the publisher.—*California History*, v. LXVIII, Winter, 1989. Reprinted by permission of the publisher.—*The Canadian Forum*, v. XXXIII, October, 1953 for a review of "Little Novels of Sicily" by Robert Weaver. Reprinted by permission of the author.—*Comparative Literature*, v. XXIX, Summer, 1977. © copyright 1977 by University of Oregon. Reprinted by permission of *Comparative Literature*.—*Critique: Studies in Modern Fiction*, v. VII, Spring, 1964; v. 8, Spring-Summer, 1966; v. XXI, 1979. Copyright © 1964, 1966, 1979, Helen Dwight Reid Educational Foundation. All reprinted with permission of the Helen Dwight Reid Educational Foundation, published by Heldref Publications, 1319 18th Street, N. W. Washington, DC 20036-1802.—*Encounter*, v. XXXIX, September, 1972 for "Miseries and Splendours of the Short Story" by Paul Theroux. © 1972 by the author. Reprinted by permission of the author.—*Forum Italicum*, v. 17, Fall, 1983. Copyright © 1983 by *Forum Italicum*. Reprinted by permission of the publisher.—*The Iowa Review*, v. 3, Fall, 1972 for an interview with Angus Wilson by Frederick P. W. McDowell. Copyright © 1972 by The University of Iowa. Reproduced by permission of Curtis Brown Ltd, London on behalf of the Estate of Angus Wilson.—*Italian Culture*, v. II, 1982. © 1982 Center for Medieval and Early Renaissance Studies. Reprinted by permission of the publisher.—*Italian Quarterly*, v. 1, Summer, 1957. Reprinted by permission of the publisher.—*Japan Quarterly*, v. 1, October, 1954. Copyright 1954, by the Asahi Shimbun. Reprinted by permission of the publisher.—*Journal of the Association of Teachers of Japanese*, v. 8, November, 1972. All rights reserved. Reprinted by permission of the publisher.—*Journal of the Short Story in English*, n. 16, Spring, 1991. © Université d'Angers, 1991. Reprinted by permission of the publisher.—*The Listener*, v. 95, March 4, 1976 for an interview with Angus Wilson by Robert Robinson. © British Broadcasting Corp., 1976. Reproduced by permission of Curtis Brown Ltd, London on behalf of the Estate of Angus Wilson.—*Literature and Psychology*, v. XXXV, 1989. © Editor 1989. Reprinted by permission of the publisher.—*London Magazine*, n.s. v. 5, March, 1966. © *London Magazine* 1966. Reprinted by permission of the publisher.—*London Review of Books*, v. 10, January 7, 1988 for "Last Words" by John Bayley. Appears here by permission of the *London Review of Books* and the author.—*Los Angeles Times*, August 25, 1969. Copyright, 1969, *Los Angeles Times*. Reprinted by permission of the publisher.—*MELUS*, v. 9, Winter II, 1982; v. 13, Spring-Summer, 1986. Copyright, MELUS, The Society for the Study of Multi-Ethnic Literature of the United States, 1982, 1986. Both reprinted by permission of the publisher.—*Neohelicon*, v. XVI, 1988. © copyright 1988 by Akademiai Kiado. Reprinted by permission of the publisher.—*The New Republic*, v. XCIX, May 24, 1939; v. 103, November 18, 1940; v. 137, November 25, 1957. Copyright 1939, 1940, 1957, The New Republic Inc. All reprinted by permission of *The New Republic*.—*New Society*, v. 38, October 28, 1976 for "In a Dark Wood" by Tony Gould. © *New Society*. Reprinted by permission of the publisher.—*The New Yorker*, v. XII, February 22, 1936 for "71 Varieties" by Clifton Fadiman; v. LXVII, April 29, 1991 for a review of *A Cat, A Man, and Two Women* by John Updike. Copyright © 1936, renewed 1964, 1992 by The New Yorker Magazine, Inc. © 1991 by the author. All reprinted by permission of the authors.—*New York Herald Tribune Books*, February 27, 1927; October 21, 1934; August 15, 1937. Copyright 1927, 1934, 1937, New York Herald Tribune Inc. All rights reserved. All reprinted by permission.—*The New York Review of Books*, v. 26, April 19, 1979. Copyright © 1979 Nyrev, Inc. Reprinted with permission from *The New York Review of Books*.—*The New York Times Book Review*,

COPYRIGHTED EXCERPTS IN *SSC*, VOLUME 21, WERE REPRINTED FROM THE FOLLOWING BOOKS:

PHOTOGRAPHS APPEARING IN *SSC*, VOLUME 21, WERE RECEIVED FROM THE FOLLOWING SOURCES:

A. E. Coppard
1878-1957

(Full name Alfred Edgar Coppard) English short story writer and poet.

INTRODUCTION

Coppard is recognized as an innovator of the English short story form. In an era when the norm for short fiction was the formula piece written for magazines, Coppard introduced a new model, rich in English rural traditions and poetic in mood and style. As a result of his influence, the short story was reappraised as a significant literary form.

Biographical Information

Born into a working-class family, Coppard grew accustomed to a life of hard work. When he was nine his father died, and he was removed from school and apprenticed to a London tailor. His education thereafter was self-acquired and included reading the works of such writers as Geoffrey Chaucer, William Shakespeare, John Keats, and Walt Whitman. When Coppard took a clerical position in Oxford, he befriended a number of literature students at the university, including Roy Campbell, William Butler Yeats, and Aldous Huxley; these acquaintances stimulated him to write. In 1919, having published several stories in literary journals, Coppard left his job and moved to a small cottage in the woods where he could write full time. His first collection of stories, *Adam and Eve and Pinch Me,* was published in 1921, with many more volumes of short fiction and poetry to follow. A collection of his works, *The Collected Tales of A. E. Coppard*, was published in 1948. Coppard died in 1957 at the age of seventy-nine, shortly before his autobiography, *It's Me, O Lord!*, was published.

Major Works of Short Fiction

Coppard's early prose style reflects the influence of Anton Chekhov and Guy de Maupassant, masters of the realistic short story, while his later works reveal a sophistication reminiscent of the stories of Henry James. His early works, which many consider his best, are particularly noted for their vivid depictions of peasant characters and rural settings, as evidenced by such acclaimed stories as "Ninepenny Flute" and "The Higgler." Coppard sought to recreate the oral tradition of the folk tale—the story heard rather than read—and his use of vernacular speech is considered deftly accurate yet lyrical. He is also noted for the air of fantasy and strangeness with which he infuses certain stories, such as "Silver Circus." The supernatural "Adam

and Eve and Pinch Me" and "Dusky Ruth" have been praised as being among his best writing.

Critical Reception

Although Coppard's popular audience grew slowly and remained fairly small, his early work was enthusiastically praised by reviewers and fellow writers who credited him with revitalizing and legitimizing the English short story. Coppard's reputation began to decline in the 1930s, however, with the publication of *Nixey's Harlequin,* which was thought by some to be inferior to his earlier works. Critics suggested that Coppard's stories were becoming pretentious and that his tendency toward rambling, unfocused narratives was becoming more pronounced. Still, most commentators agree that Coppard made great contributions to the short story form, particularly with his development of lyrical prose. C. Henry Warren, describing the poetical nature of Coppard's tales, wrote that "they are told with all the sensitiveness of a poet's power over word and image and they evoke one's imagination to a larger scope than their immediate theme, by unobrusively widening out from the particular to the universal."

PRINCIPAL WORKS

Short Fiction

Adam and Eve and Pinch Me 1921
Clorinda Walks in Heaven 1922
The Black Dog 1923
Fishmonger's Fiddle 1925
The Field of Mustard 1926
Silver Circus 1928
Nixey's Harlequin 1931
Polly Oliver 1935
Ninepenny Flute 1937
Ugly Anna and Other Tales 1944
Fearful Pleasures 1946
The Dark-Eyed Lady: Fourteen Tales 1947
The Collected Tales of A. E. Coppard 1948
Lucy in Her Pink Jacket 1954
Selected Stories 1972

Other Major Works

Hips and Haws (poetry) 1922
Pelagea (poetry) 1926
Yokohama Garland (poetry) 1926
The Collected Poems (poetry) 1928
Cherry Ripe (poetry) 1935
It's Me, O Lord! (autobiography) 1957

CRITICISM

Malcolm Cowley (essay date 1921)

SOURCE: A review of *Adam and Eve and Pinch Me*, in *The Dial*, Chicago, Vol. LXXI, July, 1921, pp. 93-5.

[*Cowley was a respected American writer, editor, and lecturer whose books of literary history and criticism include* Exile's Return *(1934) and* The Lesson of the Masters *(1971). Here, he praises Coppard's work for blending realism with fantasy and combining some of the characteristics of romance literature with a distinctly modern sensibility.*]

Some of the stories [in **Adam and Eve and Pinch Me**] are pure fantasy. Coppard begins: "In the great days that are gone I was walking the Journey upon its easy smiling roads and came one morning of windy spring to the side of a wood." He goes on to tell how he met Monk, "the fat fellow as big as two men but with the clothes of a small one squeezing the joints of him together," and how Monk walked with him on the Journey. How they met a man committing a grave crime, and a man committing a mean crime, and a man torturing a beast, and how Monk slew them all three. How they met with Mary and walked with

her till they came to a great mountain in a plain and near the top of it a lake of sweet water; there Mary told them her dream and left them very lonely in the world, and Zion still far away.

Elsewhere Coppard becomes an out-and-out realist, deriving obviously—but not entirely—from Maupassant and Chekhov. He tells the story of a little boy, the son of the village atheist, who wandered into church one Saturday after evensong because the place was cozy and beautiful. He fell asleep for an hour and when he woke the doors were locked. He put on the robe of a chorister; he ate the communion bread because he was hungry and drank great draughts of the communion wine. He uttered a rigmarole of prayer (Thirty days hath September; April, June, and November) and fell asleep on the soft carpet within the altar rail.

Evidently he is not, even here, utterly two-by-four; there is always a fourth dimension of poetry. That is the charm of his method. He is at his best when his stories, instead of marching off to an immediate blare of ghostly trumpets, begin with a matter-of-fact narration and slip quite insensibly over the borders of experience. The title story is like that; its hero comes back from a brilliant afternoon among the trees and dykes of his own fields to find that he has stepped unwittingly out of his body. **"Dusky Ruth,"** another tale, begins with a bald and exact description of an inn parlour in the Cotswolds; one reads on listlessly to find that the whole atmosphere has become suddenly charged with violent emotion. Coppard writes well enough to carry off these *tours de force*; his technique consorts well with his chosen subjects.

He uses both landscapes and people in obtaining his effects, and he uses them both in the same way. They are the materials with which he builds; he shapes them skilfully and dispassionately. Dusky Ruth, he says, "wore a light blouse of silk, a short skirt of black velvet, and a pair of very thin silk stockings that showed the flesh of instep and shin so plainly that he could see they were reddened by the warmth of the fire. She had on a pair of dainty cloth shoes with high heels, but what was wonderful about her was the heap of rich black hair piled at the back of her head and shadowing the dusky neck." This description is handled carefully, but with no more humanity than his description of the landscape of the Cotswolds, where "An odd lark or black bird, the ruckle of partridges, or the nifty gallop of a hare had been almost the only mitigation of the living loneliness that was almost as profound by day as by night." The prose here is closely related to that of the early Restoration, when the rolling grandeur of seventeenth century English was tempered with the sharpness and lucidity of the eighteenth. Again he has chosen a medium which falls in happily with the effects for which he is seeking.

The unity of his stories is emotional; it does not depend on time or space. The first few pages are spent in creating an emotion; the last in maintaining it; when the emotion dies, the story comes to an end, without much reference to plot or character. The result is sometimes an air of perverse incompleteness, and the psychoanalysts, to explain it, will refer hastily to their texts. To no avail, for Coppard's workmanship is not subconscious. The apparent difficulty is explained by the fact that his handling of a plot depends on aesthetic judgements and not on journalism or its recent ally, psychology.

The beauty which he attains (I use the word in its technical sense) is satisfyingly restrained; unlike his romantic forebears he has made the necessary compromise with the imperfections of the actual. In one story he tells how two gipsies found the body of a dead naked woman in the wood, "gone a bit dull like pearls look, but the fine build of that lady was the world's wonder." There was not a scratch or the sign of death on her anywhere, except for a little bird's dropping on her stomach. It is a weird and successful tale, and very modern in its treatment. If Madame Bovary had found that body sixty years ago, she would either have disregarded the one unpleasant detail, or else she would have allowed it to poison the experience. Coppard, on the other hand, makes a whole story turn on it. Madame Bovary, if she became an authoress, would never have staged a love scene, as that of Dusky Ruth was staged, in front of the four black handles of the beer engine. The only point of this discussion is the fact that two romantic generations resembled Emma Bovary much more than they resembled her creator; evidently Coppard has avoided their chiefest weakness.

In the same way he has avoided the *Bovarisme* of the present generation, which depends on neurosis rather than on a false romance. If Emma were a contemporary of ours, she would dissolve her vapours by attending fashionable psychiatrists, and would return home to write poems in free verse beginning "I am tired of . . ." or "I hate people who . . ." It is to her modern prototypes that we are indebted for the novel of nerves and for the development of the cult of the disagreeable. Coppard is not healthier, perhaps, but he is saner; he has nerves, but he does not allow them to be rasped continually.

In fact, he makes a habit out of not falling into pitfalls. He works in dangerous mediums; at any moment he might stumble into the bog of the Freudian novel or, on the other side, into the quicksands of Maeterlinck, but he keeps his feet on the firm way. To attain this surety he must either struggle a long time with his stories or else he tears up most of them. He is a careful workman and a sure workman, and a pleasant reminder that the short story, unlike the autobiographic novel, is not yet a dead form.

The Times Literary Supplement (essay date 1923)

SOURCE: A review of *The Black Dog*, in *The Times Literary Supplement*, No. 1119, June 28, 1923, p. 438.

[*In the following review, the critic finds fault with several stories in* The Black Dog, *yet admires many pieces for their distinctive portrayal of rural characters.*]

Among the diversely mannered tales which make up *The Black Dog*, the greater number will be found to develop the distinctive character of Mr. A. E. Coppard's two previous volumes. But the remainder serve no purpose more useful than a makeweight; for such stories as **"Simple Simon,"** **"Tanil,"** and **"The Man from Kilsheelan"** are excursions, admirably conducted, into regions of fantasy where there is nothing to nourish Mr. Coppard's earthly imagination. Whilst it is good to see a writer attempting to extend his range, the tales we have named are, in observation and sympathy, far behind the rest of the book, and smack of the literary apprenticeship.

The greater part of the book, however, testifies to a personality which is at the same time sensitive and robust. Mr. Coppard does not look outside the ordinary people of the villages for his characters, he does not choose idiots or introverts for his heroes, but he gives a vitality to country life which is strange to our usual vision of it. It is the strangeness which comes from suddenly seeing *with* people one has long been merely looking at. This gift of vision is intermittent, of course, but it is sure to appear whenever Mr. Coppard is writing of the country, and it is steadiest when his stories are in the open air. There is nothing sentimental in his treatment of the country; he does not idealize it, and has no illusions as to the wisdom of those who inhabit it. But sensuously it has deeply affected him, so that the emotions he describes stand out like motives from a rich texture, from a profound inheritance of memoried images. Such stories as **"The Black Dog"** and **"The Poor Man"** have a unity closer than that of plot or style (though sometimes style is immoderately loosened), the unity we look for in a poem and may call inadequately atmosphere, though it comes from within and is personal rather than objective. The title story relates the love of a country girl and a man of birth. With this simple situation Mr. Coppard is at his best. He has avoided making an idyll of it, yet it is idyllic, in an honest sort of way. The sensibility of the man, over-refined by the habit of wealth and town life, provides him with just the contrast he needs to bring out the full pungency of his sense of country life. Orianda had been companion to an old lady of title (at whose house Gerald met her) and gained a well-bred surface which concealed the natural ardour of her character. They go back to her home in the country, to an inn called "The Black Dog," kept by her father; and in that countryside the conflict of their temperaments is fought out. **"The Poor Man"** is a very different kind of tale, the story of a villager to whom a measure of success came too easily.

> I sang them the silly songs they liked [he says], and not the ones I cherished. I agreed with most everybody, and all agreed with me. I'm a friendly man, too friendly, and I went back on my life. I made nought of my life, you see; I just sat over the job like a snob codgering an old boot.

One day he is caught poaching, and could have put off the keeper with a false name and address, but at last, in a fury of self-assertion, stands up to his true character, and his life goes down in ruin and tragedy.

These two stories (with which **"The Handsome Lady"** and **"Mordecai and Cocking"** have much in common) are the fullest expressions of the peculiar blend of poetry and realism which distinguishes Mr. Coppard among his contemporaries and the direction in which we shall expect his gift finally to mature.

Hermon Ould (essay date 1925)

SOURCE: "A. E. Coppard's Stories," in *The Bookman,* London, Vol. LXVIII, No. 407, August, 1925, pp. 255-56.

[*In this review of* Fishmonger's Fiddle, *Ould notes the unusual vision of the world that is expressed in Coppard's stories and lauds the subtle craftsmanship of the author's work.*]

Mr. Coppard's stories are not, like so many short stories, the by-product of a novelist. He is primarily a writer of short stories, and so far as I am aware has never written a novel. By confining himself to a single form—I leave verse out of the reckoning—he has attained [in *Fishmonger's Fiddle*] a sureness of touch which is in striking contrast with the tentativeness of his first volume, *Adam and Eve and Pinch Me*. We now find no echoes of his preferences in literature: what he offers us is pure Coppard. His work is not, as Maupassant's is, objective. The world he paints is a world seen through his own whimsical-serious personality. If Maupassant was a perfect mirror in which was reflected a flawless representation of the section of life that came within his range of vision, Coppard is a somewhat bent and irregular window-pane, through which we are permitted to see a world, self-consistent but queerly changed, fantastically distorted in some directions and arbitrarily emphasised in others.

It is a tribute to his skill that we rarely pause to question the verisimilitude of his stories. The narrative, however improbable judged by normal experience, carries its own conviction, and it is only on those rare occasions when the author, detaching himself from his story, obtrudes his own person that we begin to doubt. A case in point is **"The Watercress Girl"**—a story which I thought was going to be the best of them all. In Mary McDowall Mr. Coppard draws a character of tragic power. She has flung vitriol into the face of her rival and is standing for her trial. I am not going to try to give a synopsis of the story, but will content myself with stating that towards its conclusion, the rival being out of the way, the lover comes back to Mary and is repulsed. So far one is convinced. The lover is pressing; Mary continues to resist. "I'll come again to-morrow," he says. "No, Frank, don't ever come any more," she replies. "Aw, I'm coming right enough," he cries.

"And I suppose we must conclude that he did," is Mr. Coppard's comment. Whereupon the whole thing collapses. When an author abdicates from godhead and confesses ignorance of the doings of his own creation, he immediately loses his hold on the reader. Expunge this last sentence, and **"The Watercress Girl"** would in my judgment be one of the best short stories of recent years.

It is not characteristic of Mr. Coppard, fortunately, to assume anything but omniscience. **"Fishmonger's Fiddle,"** which gives the book its title, is an incredible enough story of a man going into a fishmonger's shop with a 'cello under his arm and thereupon inconsequently arousing the romantic impulse in a girl who—when it comes to the point—has not the courage to reach out her hand for the boon which the gods are offering her. There are no "I supposes" about this. The tale is narrated as if it really happened and the reader is fain to believe. I almost wrote "the listener is fain to believe," for indeed most of the stories in this volume are like tales that are told aloud. They have the inconsequence and apparent irrelevancies of spontaneity, and it is only in retrospect that one realises how subtle is the art which has gone to their writing; for in truth there is little that is irrelevant in Mr. Coppard's work. The introduction of what appear to be irrelevancies is his way of filling your mind with the required atmosphere or of chaining your attention. It is not for nothing that he describes an incident like the following, although it has no obvious link with the story he is telling:

> A few cherries had spilled from one basket and lay on the ground. The little furry mouse had found them and was industriously nibbling at one. The higgler nonchalantly stamped his foot upon it, and kept it so for a moment or two. Then he looked at the dead mouse. A tangle of entrails had gushed from its whiskered muzzle.

You will get from this and similar passages what appears to be the Coppard attitude to life: It is a chancey, nonmoral affair, in which pointless suffering plays a large part, but humour and compassion will see you safely through it. *"Pour moi, un livre c'est un homme."* That can certainly be said of **"Fishmonger's Fiddle."**

C. Henry Warren (essay date 1927)

SOURCE: "The Modern Short Story," in *The Bookman,* London, Vol. LXXI, No. 424, January, 1927, pp. 236-37.

[*Here, Warren discusses some general misconceptions regarding modern short fiction and describes Coppard as "the one writer of to-day who is exploiting . . . the best possibilities of the short story."*]

That the prejudice of the reading public against the short story is rapidly passing is sufficiently evidenced in the recent experiments of two well-known English publishing houses. (I am not concerned here, of course, with the standardised magazine type of short story, whose only interest, apart from the speeding of an idle hour, would lie in the indication it offered of the psychology of the mass of modern readers.) The first of these experiments comes, with commendable audacity, from the house of Jonathan Cape, who has embarked upon a "Story Series," each volume of which is to consist of a bunch of short stories by a single author; and eight books of the series have already appeared. The second experiment comes from the house of Heinemann, in the shape of a beautifully produced volume of over a thousand pages, consisting of nearly two hundred of the "great" short stories of the world; and at the extraordinarily low price of eight and sixpence.

The prejudice against the modern short story is a little difficult to understand. So far as I grasp it, it seems to be based upon two grounds: (1) that the modern short story is gloomy, and (2) that it ends, so far as it can be said to end at all, unsatisfactorily.

I have seen dozens of letters to the editor of an enlightened weekly review (where one good story is printed in each number) bitterly protesting against the sombre nature of the fiction he publishes. "Give us," they say in effect, "as much of the gloomy state of affairs to-day as you like in your pages upon current events; but for mercy's sake give us lighter reading in your literary pages." The implication is that a man turns to art for an escape from the tragic nature of the life he is compelled to lead. Which is a fallacy. No man yet truly escaped from the tragedy of his life by rushing into a glittering orgy of "lighter reading." If modern life hurts you, you cannot really be rid of that hurt by running away from modern life; your only hope of release is by coming to some *understanding* of it. And who can help you to a better understanding than the artist? Would you place his position so low, once more, as the jester of olden times, and give him cap and bells and a painted bladder?

If the modern short story, then, has tended to be gloomy that is no reason for descrying it, unless of course that gloom is nothing finer than a morbid self-indulgence of the writer himself, intent only on working off his own black bile. If on the other hand the tragedy presented provides also an *interpretation,* we have every reason to be grateful; since through the seeing eye of the artist we have envisioned a harmony where before we saw only a chaos, and found a true escape at last in understanding.

So much for the first ground for prejudice. The second, though this may seem strange at first, is allied to it. To complain that the modern short story ends unsatisfactorily implies, I take it, that the reader likes a good honest plot. I sympathise with him, whilst at the same time reminding him that the short story is not necessarily the place for a plot at all, at least in the old sense of the word. For the modern short story is more akin to poetry than to the novel. Where ninety-nine writers can spread themselves attractively over three hundred pages of a novel, only one can discipline himself into the three thousand words of a short story; the short-story writer must be more strict in his selection, more sensitive, more loaded with vital images and, like the poet, more able to flash his interpretation in a single line. Also (and here lies the reason why he abandons the plot as such) he must realise that, since interpretation is his aim, and since no living interpretation is possible where the reader does not do half the work with the writer, he has to evoke the imagination rather than supply it. What he excludes therefore is as important a concern of his craft as what he includes. You have only to study the work of such recognised masters of the modern short story as A. E. Coppard, T. F. Powys, D. H. Lawrence,

Martin Armstrong, Liam O'Flaherty and John Metcalf to see how carefully they study this art of selection.

The result upon the reader of such methods as I have outlined is that, whereas the story with the slick plot may just as well be thrown away once you have robbed it of its only surprise, the modern selective story, wherein method and poetry have taken the place of plot, can be read over and over again and with a new enrichment every time.

The one writer of to-day who is exploiting to the full the best possibilities of the short story is Mr. Coppard. The title-story in his new book [*The Field of Mustard*] is a little masterpiece, his best yet, and as fine as anything Maupassant ever put his name to. The conversation of those three country women out gathering "kindling," revealing as it does not only their own pathetic histories but the way in which they echo the plight of all their multitudinous sisters, shows the fine insight into the peasant mind that is one of Mr. Coppard's greatest assets. His power of setting down peasant conversation, in all its raciness and native wit and rather inconsequent senselessness, is another; and such a piece of conversational writing as that in **"The Old Venerable,"** in which he reports the talk of an old man of the woods with an unsympathetic gamekeeper, makes one almost regret that Mr. Coppard should sometimes give his tales a more sophisticated setting in which he is not so clearly at home. It is significant that Mr. Coppard insists on calling his short stories "tales." In them is no intruding moral; their plot (if such it may be called) is quite as natural as the plots of everyday life itself; they mingle the rough and the smooth, the crude and the poetic, as life will capriciously do; they are told with all the sensitiveness of a poet's power over word and image and they evoke one's imagination to a larger scope than their immediate theme, by unobtrusively widening out from the particular to the universal. The best of the world's tale tellers have done no more. *The Field of Mustard* is (I use the word carefully) a beautiful book.

Punch (essay date 1927)

SOURCE: A review of *The Field of Mustard,* in *Punch,* Vol. CLXXII, February 23, 1927, pp. 223-24.

[In this essay, the critic praises Coppard for providing fresh interpretations of familiar themes.]

The bright art of the short story has at the moment no more talented exponent than Mr. A. E. Coppard. His tales, or *contes,* as we should have called them in the good old days when, having never heard of Tchehov, we all swore by Maupassant, are acceptable to the most fastidious of editors. All the stories in **The Field of Mustard** are well worth reading, and a good half of them are worth re-reading. It is not so much what he does as the cunning and lively way he does it. Take, for instance, his name-piece. Two women, returning home from gathering firewood, sit beneath a hedge and discuss a man whom they both have loved. Being no Classicist, I am not sure whether Lucian transcribed the equivalent colloquy, but certainly he might have done, for the models for it must have existed in his day and ages before. Judith, again, the heroine (to call her so) of what is perhaps the best story in the book, stoops to conquer and, as is the way of conquerors, destroys her victim and shirks the issue of her devastating condescension. That too seems a familiar situation; while Camilla and Olive, those spinsters in uneasy circumstances who travel the continent of Europe together, quarrel and are reconciled—they are as familiar as the dishes of the *table d'hôte* which constitute their staple diet. Mr. Coppart can take a trite or trivial theme and treat it with that touch of novelty which, since practically all plausible themes have been used times beyond measure, is all that we can reasonably ask of the story-teller, but which we do not often get. If he has any faults they are that his sense of irony sometimes runs away with him and that he succumbs too readily to the lure of the phrase. But he is a *raconteur* for whom to be thankful.

Ford Madox Ford (essay date 1927)

SOURCE: "Half Pixie and Half Bird," in *New York Herald Tribune Books,* February 27, 1927, p. 4.

[*Ford was a well-known English fiction writer and editor who published numerous novels in his career, including* The Good Soldier *(1915). Here, he expresses his admiration for Coppard's work and notes that the author's stories contain the same qualities found in the verse of several seventeenth-century British poets.*]

Mr. Coppard has been so long for me the White Hope of British literature that I can't get out of the habit of so regarding him, though there may well be others in Great Britain to-day. I am, however, so out of touch with the writers of my own country and for me the authors of to-day are so almost exclusively French or American that I may well be perpetrating an injustice to one or other English writer. Be that as it may, for me Mr. Coppard remains what I will call the one illuminated author of Great Britain. I use the word "illuminated" because, in thinking of this matter that is difficult to put into words, the rather idiotic phrase "the divine fire" came into my head just now.

I was walking the other day in Chicago in the corridor of a building whose carpet had an extraordinarily long silken pile. I suppose I must have dragged my feet, for when I touched the bell pull of the elevator it let out a distinctly visible spark and I received a quite sensible shock. And just as there are substances that will do that for you, so there are sentences—concatenations of words. I have always, I think, formed my judgment of a writer new to me by the first sentence of his that I read—or so nearly always as to make no difference—I receive from the aspect of the first half dozen words—if I am going to like the work of the writer for a long time—a certain sensation almost exactly equivalent mentally to that which one experiences on contact with some substance charged with electricity. And I remember with singular vividness the place and the time of my first contact with the work of Mr. Coppard And I do not know that the sensation is always an altogether agreeable one.

I was sitting in a garden on one of the extraordinary, lush hillsides of the South of England, on a fixed wooden bench under apple trees. The postman brought me a copy of *The Saturday Review*. I opened it immediately at the short story. In those days *The Saturday Review* contained a weekly *conte*: that was why I used to subscribe to it, for I am very little interested in what any journal has to say about events of the day or about "serious" literature. I experienced at once a distinctly disagreeable sensation. I was reading a sentence—a queer sentence about bananas—and I found myself saying to myself: "Damn it all, this fellow writes better than I do." Or rather it was perhaps that I thought I should have to extend myself if I wanted to write as well as that. I was, in short, instantly jealous of the talent of Mr. Coppard.

And reading **The Field of Mustard** I find that I remain jealous of the talent of Mr. Coppard. I wish people would not write better than I do.

Writing is, alas, a jealous occupation. I suppose one is lucky if one can live the sensation down. Sometimes one does. At any rate, I remember that the first English writer to whom I wrote for a contribution to the *Transatlantic Review* was Mr. Coppard.

I remember also sitting on the trunk of a tree beside this author in the deep, queer gloom of high beech woods He was talking about art—about a Japanese painter, Hokusai, I think. At forty the painter said that he was beginning to understand about painting; he expected to be perfect in his art at fifty; at fifty he cherished the same idea; at sixty and seventy, similarly, and at eighty he was still thinking that at ninety he would know how to paint. I suppose Mr. Coppard was drawing morals for his own self and his own art. I don't really know, because he was speaking not to myself but to some one else on his other side on that great tree trunk and I did not catch all that he said. But I was thinking to myself: What a queer creature this is, this brown, assured gypsy of the beech woods. But then—not gypsy; autochthonous; product of that soil; gnome, pixie . . . and I remember there came into my mind, I don't know why, the line that has always seemed to me to be rather inscrutable if not rather silly:

Oh lyric love, half angel and half bird.

Immediately, in the way the idle mind works, there came the phrase "Half pixie and half bird" . . . as descriptive of the being beside me on that tree trunk.

For Mr. Coppard is extraordinarily Celto-British with a touch of something altogether mysterious to him. (I am, of course, now talking of his art—but the description would suit his personality well enough.) For there are in England everywhere survivors of the little, dark, persistent races that were there before the Saxons and Danes; even before the druids. And these are the pixies!

So Mr. Coppard's stories, from *Clorinda Walks in Heaven* right down to the *Field of Mustard,* are pixie-gardens—little mazes in which the happy mind wanders until, with a little pop, it comes out somewhere where it least expected to be in the world. Yes, if one were a bird hopping along between the tiny box-hedges of an old Cornish vicarage garden—hopping round and round an old sundial, to the scent of lavender, coming out suddenly by the cucumber-frames when one confidently expected to emerge near the dog kennel—one would have much the emotions of a reader of the *Field of Mustard.* It is such beautiful, quaint and tricksy writing!

And it is impossible to say whence Mr. Coppard can derive. His career—as is the case with most writers of great human experience and insight into the hearts of women—had been romantically unliterary until he took it into his head to write stories. He had rolled his hump *un peu partont.* Then, suddenly he wrote stories—and much as was the case with Conard, suddenly found himself famous in England.

> **Mr. Coppard is concerned with moods, visions, legends, and with these primarily as they permit him to draw all possible variations of melody from the instrument of style. He is, first of all, a lover of words and rhythms—the large, orchestral rhythms of prose. He cultivates by turns the majestic harmonies and grave imaginative altitudes of the seventeenth century prosemen.**
>
> **—Ludwig Lewisohn, in "The Return of the Short Story," in The Nation, March 1, 1922.**

As a matter of fact, Mr. Coppard is almost the first English writer to get into English prose the peculiar quality of English lyric verse. I do not mean that he is metrical; I mean that hitherto no English prose-writer has had the fancy, the turn of imagination, the wisdom, the as it were piety and the beauty of the great seventeenth century lyricists like Donne or Herbert—or even Herrick. And that poetic quality is the best thing that England has to show. When the far-flung navies have melted away and the 4th of August, 1914, is forgotten there will remain "Full fathom five" . . . and "Sweet day, so cool" . . . and "Go, lovely rose." . . . And I should not wonder if there remained **"The Bogey Man"** or **"The Old Venerable"** from the *Field of Mustard.* I do trust, that Americans will read this book very widely, for they will here make acquaintance with a side of the English character that is very

little represented in this world and that is singularly attractive.

C. Henry Warren (essay date 1929)

SOURCE: "A Superb Tale Teller," in *The Bookman,* London, Vol. LXXVI, No. 451, April, 1929, pp. 36-7.

[*In this review of* Silver Circus, *Warren praises Coppard's perceptive portrayal of peasant characters. The critic also finds the book to be proof of Coppard's continuing development as a writer.*]

Mr. Coppard's tales made their first appearance shortly after the War. They obtained a hearing, shyly, almost furtively, in progressive periodicals with a very limited circulation. They were not proclaimed upon the housetops. A few discerning ones smiled, added the precious copies to their collections, and passed the good news on to others. Here was a man doing something new; here was a man who could give significance to an art that in England anyway was a kind of Cinderella among her sisters; here was a man for whom words still had something of the dew of the morning upon them. But the tales were not, by any stretch of the word, popular. Even Mr. Coppard's first book of collected stories appeared under the imprint of a private press.

All this is now changed. Within a few days of the appearance of [*Silver Circus*], his newest book, we were informed that it had run into a second printing. And collectors point with pride to their first editions of him. The change is not in Mr. Coppard; it is in the reading public. Men and women who, when Mr. Coppard was first writing, never dreamed of reading a short story that was not of the magazine type (something that tripped its meaningless way to a surprising *dénouement*—something to read on a railway journey and then throw away), are now reading this new kind of story with interest, if not yet with avidity. And the slow but positive increase in the demand has created in return a slow but positive increase in the supply. Where one collection of short stories was printed (and proclaimed a "drug on the market" at that), half a dozen or more are printed now. And all are the work of authors who have chosen this particular medium as carefully, as purposely as a poet chooses his. Indeed something of the poet is in every one of the best short story writers of to-day—A. E. Coppard, T. F. Powys, Liam O'Flaherty, H. A. Manhood and Sherwood Anderson (to mention only a few).

In no small measure Mr. Coppard is responsible in England both for this increased demand and for this increased supply. He has not only made a hearing for himself, he has made a hearing for others. *Silver Circus* is his sixth book of tales, and it is interesting to note with what fixity of purpose and sureness of inspiration he has followed the track he laid down in his first book, *Adam and Eve and Pinch Me.* The same fantasy is here, the same bold insight into peasant character, the same genius for so enlarging a simple theme that its cadences pass from particular to general, from local to universal. If one thing has changed—no, not changed, but grown—more than another, it is his amazing understanding of peasant character. The height of that understanding was reached in the title story of *The Field of Mustard*; and there is nothing in the present volume to surpass it—if indeed it can be surpassed. The other most noticeable development has been Mr. Coppard's progress from a tendency too frequently to indulge the purple patch, to a style that, for simplicity and directness and ease and sureness of attack, is like impossibly good conversation. As for his humour, it grows each year more delicious, more penetrating, more sly.

If the title tale was the best in his last volume, **"A Looking-Glass for Saint Luke"** is probably the best in this present volume. Mr. Coppard's mastery over the poetry of the vernacular is shown in his **"Darby Dallow Tells His Tale."** In **"That Fellow Tolstoy"** he pushes artifice as far as artifice should go—and no jot farther. Inventive fantasy and pathetic realism are nicely mixed in **"The Martyrdom of Solomon."** And **"Fine Feathers"**—but this remarkable tale has already been highly praised in these pages [*The Bookman* LXXI, No. 424, January 1927]. With **"The Field of Mustard," "The Higgler"** and **"A Looking-Glass for Saint Luke,"** it can be numbered among the superlative of Mr. Coppard's work; and *that* at once places it among the "great short stories" of modern English literature.

A. E. Coppard   (essay date 1931)

SOURCE: *The Writings of Alfred Edgar Coppard,* by Jacob Schwartz and A. E. Coppard, The Ulysses Bookshop, 1931, 73 p.

[*The following excerpt is taken from a work in which Coppard provides notes to accompany Schwartz's bibliography of the author's writings. Coppard here reacts to selected reviews and criticisms of his short story collections.*]

The reviews [of *Clorinda Walks in Heaven*] on the whole were . . . very friendly, and *The Outlook* began its notice with a headline, "The Critic Walks in Heaven", but there was certainly one justifiable protest from an Irish paper:

> To crowd two illegitimate births, five deaths, and one murder into nine short stories is something of a strain on one's patience in a country where there are plenty of things to breed pessimism.

I got a really colossal biff from the *Sunday Times*:—

> Mr. A. E. Coppard has done much better work aforetime, and, it is pretty safe to predict, will again do very much better work in the future than any contained in the volume of short stories entitled *Clorinda Walks in Heaven*. If there is any meaning whatever in the story which gives his volume its title, that meaning has altogether escaped one reader who has read it attentively and patiently twice through. The same may be said of

the longest story in the book, **'Craven Arms'**, the very title of which is an unfathomable mystery. Mr. Coppard presents the not unfamiliar figure of an obviously clever man who has fallen under bad influences, which have led him to the cultivation of a sort of sham exotericism of manner and style, a parody of profundity. The word of counsel of which he stands most in need is that he should find something to say worth saying, and say it in the plainest words he can find.

Although I admired its gusto I did not think the verdict a reasonable one. It is rather late in the day to interpret the "unfathomable mystery" of the title, **"Craven Arms,"** but I will do my best. I am aware that it is the name of many taverns up and down the land, that a great railway station is called after one of them, that there is an Earl of Craven who probably has a badge of heraldry; but this tale is not about a tavern, or a railway station, or an earl; it is about a man who shrank from marrying a girl he loved. I don't know how my "sham exotericism" managed to immerse the phrase in such profundity, but I do know that "craven" means "cowardly", and that "arms" are those appendages hanging from the shoulders with which we commonly embrace our girls. . . .

The reviews of [*The Black Dog*] were extraordinarily kind, although what was called my "variety", or ability to write different sorts of stories, aroused some adverse comment and I was urged to concentrate on country tales; only with such themes did I do myself justice, and so on. I can only answer that I do not believe in specialisation or formulæ in art. And I remembered that the *Saturday Westminster* said of my *Clorinda* volume that its country people had "an affectation of simplicity about them as though they were seen through the eyes of an intelligent week-ender". One reviewer of *The Black Dog* began: "I had the impression that Mr. Coppard was clever and that he was an admirer, to say the least of it, of Mr. D. H. Lawrence. The first story in the present book shook my faith in Mr. Coppard's cleverness while confirming my belief in his admiration for Mr. Lawrence".

I have to disclaim any liking for the work of this writer. Possibly it is a matter of temperament rather than of criticism that I find it unpalatable and boring. The charge of "cleverness" is a thing I can't argue about because I honestly do not understand its basis. *The Evening Standard* said: "Unlike most of his rivals in the same field who are choked with cleverness, he is not clever at all, and displays none of the tricks of the trade." *The Glasgow Herald* commented thus: "The style, like the matter, is unformed. Verbless sentences and unrelated participles are more suggestive of slipshod journalism than literary craftsmanship and grace". To *The Birmingham Post* *The Black Dog* was a beautiful idyll; to *The Yorkshire Post* it was the quintessence of half-bored half-cynical spirit. . . .

The title tale [of *Fishmonger's Fiddle*] was more than once criticised because "nothing really happened in it". But that was precisely the point of the tale. I made it clear that something was *trying* very hard to happen, and I know that often as much tragedy is involved in the things that do *not* happen as in more catastrophic climaxes.

The Times Literary Supplement (always immensely kind to me) said:

> Rural life, with its oddities and humours and raw melodrama, holds a special attraction for him; he has the air of knowing his characters in the flesh, as intimately as he knows the face of the sky and the moods of nature. The best of his tales have so strong a flavour of reminiscence—as though we were being told from memory at a fireside—that one can hardly, in the moment of reading, believe them to be fictions. . . . It is broadly true to say that Mr. Coppard's townbred sophisticated characters have less reality than his country folk.

The Outlook: "As for **Fishmonger's Fiddle,** I would be prepared to accept the 'cello joke and the lunch in the inn as allegorically significant if I could find a shadow of clue to the allegories. Either the secret of the symbolism is locked in Mr. Coppard's bosom—in which case he is playing a practical joke on his public—or, as seems more likely, he has ill-advisedly attempted to write simultaneously on two planes."

Symbolism? Allegory? Two planes? This is abracadabra to me. I am a writer of *fiction* about people who live and talk and do, without anything at the back of my mind other than what I conceive to be fitting for their presentation as interesting human beings.

The New Criterion, apart from its praise, pleased me very much by its critical recognition of my technique. "There is no affectation and the machinery of his method, for he is a most methodical worker, never disturbs the delicate charm of his finished work. The **"Fishmonger's Fiddle"** story is an interesting example of the purely abstract provoked by a minimum of definite physical fact. It is well chosen as the representative of the collection, the limits of which are strictly separated by a diversity of subject specially treated and fundamentally united by a single personal emotion." . . .

Once again [in **The Field of Mustard**] my "cleverness" seems to have distressed a reviewer:

The Queen: "Mr. Coppard is as clever as they make them—and, one suspects, knows it; but cleverness alone does not satisfy."

On the other hand, there was consolation in *The Spectator*: "His style, so simple and so natural, is beyond criticism."

There was another kind of charge in *Time and Tide*: "A too consistently coarse-mouthed and coarse-minded world. It may be said of Mr. Coppard's stories that every prospect pleases and only man is vile."

I caught a regular Tartar of a review—about my best book, too!—in the *New York Sun,* signed Cuthbert Wright.

New York Sun:

> His characters are all too real; we see them about us all day and every day, ubiquitous and unpleasant, in the street car, in the country store—and the plain truth of the matter is that we simply don't care what happens to them, either in reality or in Mr. Coppard's pages. Two lovers, under stress of poverty, decide to part for a season. The man makes a tragedy of it, but he is lying, and the woman knows it. Two old maids quarrel and make it up again. A man pretends to be in love with his best friend's wife; the best friend reciprocates and steals his own. A pig destroys a farmer's cabbage patch. A dreary procession—of bald men and old females, of 'namby-pamby unmasterful mortals', of people who have nothing to say, and who say it for twenty pages—passes before us. And at the end one is driven to cry, like M. Picabia, in his Dada days, Don't care! Don't care! Don't care!

> What is the reason for the boredom which rises to us from such books as this volume of Mr. Coppard's? Is it true that the sort of realism represented by such books is played out, and has in reality been dead for years? This, at least, is our hope.

As a counterblast to this there came tremendous praise from Ford Madox Ford in the *New York Herald Tribune* (Mar. 27, 1927), and I quote one short passage from it because it brought me a letter that was very difficult to answer:

> Mr. Coppard is almost the first English writer to get into English prose the peculiar quality of English lyric verse. I do not mean that he is metrical; I mean that hitherto no English prose writer has had the fancy, the turn of imagination, the wisdom, the as it were piety and beauty of the great seventeenth century lyricists like Donne or Herbert—or even Herrick. And that poetic quality is the best thing that England has to show. When the far-flung navies have melted away and the 4th of August 1914 is forgotten, there will remain 'Full fathom five' . . . and 'Sweet day, so cool' . . . and 'Go, lovely rose' . . . And I should not wonder if there remained **'The Bogey Man'** or **'The Old Venerable'** from **The Field of Mustard**.

A few weeks after reading that I felt almost too much like a character in one of my own stories, on receiving a letter from an admirer. He had been disconcerted to learn that his collection of my books was incomplete; he had searched through all his copies but could not find *Full fathom five* or *Sweet day so cool,* or *Go, lovely rose,* mentioned by Mr. Ford in his review. Where could he get them? . . .

From the reviews [of **Silver Circus**] I found I had not yet scotched the legend of my inability to write anything except "country" stories, although one critic quite unconsciously almost did the trick for me in *The Evening News*:

> The fact is that Mr. Coppard can do one kind of short story better than anyone else. Set him going in rural England, preferably not too far from the Thames Valley, and he will give you stories like apples, at once earthy and heavenly. The very swing of his sentences sets the old south-west wind blowing across the orchards. This is his great vein, and the further he gets away from it the worse he is. . . . The best tale here is **"The Presser."** If Mr. Coppard had given us a whole fat novel like **"The Presser"** we should have whooped for joy. Why didn't he?

I can only point out that I do not write fat novels, and that this particular tale is not about the Thames Valley or the wind blowing across the orchards; it is about a little boy working in the slums of Whitechapel.

The New York Times Book Review (essay date 1932)

SOURCE: "A. E. Coppard's Tales," in *The New York Times Book Review,* January 10, 1932, p. 7.

[*In this review, the critic argues that many of the stories in* Nixey's Harlequin *are inferior to Coppard's previous work because they digress from the main story line and fail to reach a satisfactory conclusion.*]

The ten stories gathered into [*Nixey's Harlequin*] by A. E. Coppard reveal an accentuation of both the faults and virtues of this brilliant English stylist, but chiefly the faults. There are a greater refinement of phrase and a delicacy of wit and a more profound etching of character; but there is also a more circumfuse narrative, a self-indulgent refusal to stick to the point and a marked reticence in working out human problems to their natural and necessary climax. Coppard refuses to follow the straight line, which is the essence of the short story. He unfolds his narrative capriciously, when there is a narrative; but more often he substitutes details of character for incident and a fine phrase for an ending. Among all the ten stories in this volume there is none that can compare in its power to move with **"The Jewel of Jeopardy"** or **"The Watercress Girl"**—to mention only two from former collections.

Coppard writes, as always, of the English middle classes, upper and lower, for whom he has a profound and compassionate understanding. His occasional peasants, such as the **"Gollan,"** are unconvincing. Of aristocrats, as he tells us in **"My Hundredth Tale,"** he knows nothing. His stories spring from the soil and life-stream of England—a simple, humble England which we know all too poorly. They are set amid greensward and hedgerows, in pubs and cottages, in sheds and stacks and sties, in villages and the lower courts of justice. And the maze of imagery which is the sole guide of Coppard's willful fancy springs direct from this setting.

A few of the stories, such as **"Wilt Thou Leave Me Thus?"** and **"The Limping Lady,"** are based upon surprise and originality in development. The latter reminds us, somehow, of an anecdote from Fielding, and is certainly the best of the collection. It concerns a poor woman who set up a rooming-house with the compensation money she got from her husband's death. She was gulled into giving free lodging to a former actress, whose grand airs recall all that she herself might have had from life. The unprofitable guest at last is shipped, but not without the surprising benefit of a ten-pound note. By contrast, some of the shortest stories concern nothing at all, and by measure of their failure to charm are merely silly. One of these, **"The Postoffice and the Serpent,"** is graced, and

so perhaps redeemed, by one of the finest of Coppard's many fine metaphors. He writes of a mountain "of no grand height, from the top of which, when the weather was kind, you could sniff the Atlantic and observe the Isles of Aran taking their ease in the sea like three great whales."

Finally, there is the strange and seemingly autobiographical **"My Hundredth Tale,"** in which Coppard does not retreat from the problems of mankind and from which he might, if he cared, gather evidence to refute every statement here made. This story shows that Coppard, one of the most gifted tellers of tales alive today, has a wider range than the subtle, charming, but diffuse and unexciting, vein to which he recently has chosen to limit himself.

Dorothy Brewster and Angus Burrell (essay date 1934)

SOURCE: "The Short Story and the Novelette: Anton Chekhov, Katherine Mansfield, A. E. Coppard, and Others," in *Modern Fiction,* Columbia University Press, 1934, pp. 348-403.

[*In the following excerpt, Brewster and Burrell illustrate Coppard's versatility in depicting a wide variety of character types and life experiences.*]

If one were asked what Mr. A. E. Coppard's sketches and stories and tales are about, one might for the moment be at a loss for an answer, so varied is his range of interest, and then one would say, "They're about life." That's what Mr. Coppard presents—life. This is, theoretically, what all writers do; but of many story writers one feels that their province is a little world of their own; that they have invented a much too pleasant and orderly garden and have attempted to fit life into these confines; and that their portrayal of life is debased and falsified. We are aware of a monotonous subject matter and an even more monotonous treatment. With Mr. Coppard we feel neither. We are astonished by his versatility, and delighted with his fresh and sometimes unusual handling. It is this wide variety of Coppard's interests that gives the impression of an unrestricted use of a very great range of the experiences of life.

His imagination plays over the human scene selecting all kinds of subjects. He is almost equally convincing whether he is writing of tragedy, melodrama, fantasy, high comedy, or low comedy. Perhaps what delights him most and what he presents with the greatest reality are the simple peasants of England, the farmers, the poachers, and their women. But he is equally skillful when he writes about more sophisticated men and women, old or young. He knows very odd people, some of them characters that remind one of Dickens. He writes of stage and circus people, of Cockneys, of artists and ex-artists, and of gypsies. And some of his most successful sketches are about children.

It is true that in his one hundred and more published tales there is a rather high percentage of stories shockingly tragic. They are not pleasantly tragic—remote and vitiated like so many contemporary stories of casual killings. Coppard provides no shock absorbers with his tales; for he too surely knows that one of the values of a story of this kind is its power to move the reader. He does not soften; he does not modify. What he does, at his best, as surely as Conrad (and in a much shorter space) is to make clear the motives for these tragic deeds. He makes them understandable; he accounts for them. But to make this point bear too much stress would be to do an injustice to Coppard. For in his work you will find stories that are mellow and pleasant and humorous.

He recounts a very absurd dream in **"Big Game."** Old Squance is an undertaker. But in the pleasant and healthy little village where he and his wife live very few people die, and to supplement his undertaking business he has the "more vital occupation of builder." But the cottages have been very well built in Tamborough, and so Mrs. Squance has to keep a little shop where she sells all sorts of notions. Mr. Squance is a mild man, yet he had gained for himself the reputation of being very heroic. It had to do with Mrs. Squance's dream.

> It seemed to be morning in her dream, early; it must have been early. She and Squance were at breakfast when what should walk deliberately and astoundingly into the room but a lion. Mrs. Squance, never having seen a lion before, took it to be a sheep dog, and she shouted, "Go out, you dirty thing!" waving a threatening hand towards it.

But Mr. Squance recognizes the animal and shouts "'Lion! lion!'"

> It had a tremendous head and mane, with whiskers on its snout as stiff as knitting needles, and claws like tenpenny nails; but its tail was the awfullest thing, long and very flexible, with a bush of hair at the end just like a mop, which it wagged about, smashing all sorts of things.

Mrs. Squance asks her husband if he has a pistol and when he says he has not, she says, "Then we're done." But she decides they're not done yet, and she tells her husband to hold him whilst she goes out for a pistol. The dream continues with the usual absurd dream difficulties. And when Mrs. Squance returns much later with the pistol, she finds that Mr. Squance has thrown the lion out of the window.

But that is not the end of the story. There is a moral, a charming modern instance of the "application" of the stories in the *Gesta Romanorum*. Mr. Coppard says that Mrs. Squance awakened "startled to find the window of their room actually smashed." She related these circumstances so many times as the years went on that "she herself at last vividly believed in the figure of old Ben as a lion-slayer."

His little sketch **"Luxury"** is a delightful and ingenious turning to literary account of a little incident that one feels has the true autobiographical touch. There are other sketches also, both of them dealing with children, **"Weep Not, My Wanton"** and **"Communion."** The first tells of a tinker, slightly drunk, walking along an English down with his little boy, upbraiding him for having lost a sixpence. The opening paragraph is a perfect setting of an English twilight summer evening. The only sounds are those of "anguish" from "a score of young boar pigs . . . being gelded by two brown lads and a gypsy fellow." The father's litany continues.

Coppard's imagination plays over the human scene selecting all kinds of subjects. He is almost equally convincing whether he is writing of tragedy, melodrama, fantasy, high comedy, or low comedy. Perhaps what delights him most and what he presents with the greatest reality are the simple peasants of England, the farmers, the poachers, and their women.

—Dorothy Brewster and Angus Burrell

What the father saw when he looked at his son was "a thin boy, a spare boy, a very shrunken boy of seven or eight years, crying quietly. He let no grief out of his lips, but his white face was streaming with dirty tears." The little boy does not speak, "and lifting his heavy hand the man struck the boy a blow behind with shock enough to disturb a heifer. They went on, the child with sobs that you could feel rather than hear."

Behind are the mother and their little daughter. The mother seemed "to have no desire to shield the boy or to placate the man." And soon they change places: the father takes the little girl, and when the mother joins the little boy and cries out, "'What's 'e bin doin' to yeh? Yer face is all blood!'" the little boy explains that it's nothing, it's only his nose, and gives his mother the sixpence. That is all, except the final paragraph of description of the countryside which finishes the picture.

> They went together down the hill towards the inn, which had already a light in its windows. The screams from the barn had ceased, and a cart passed them full of young pigs, bloody and subdued. The hill began to resume its old dominion of soft sounds. It was nearly nine o'clock, and one anxious farmer still made hay although, on this side of the down, day had declined, and with a greyness that came not from the sky, but crept up from the world. From the quiet hill, as the last skein of cocks was carted to the stacks, you could hear dimly men's voices and the rattle of their gear.

Of his story **"Willie Waugh,"** Miss Lillian Gilkes has written: "He can make the conversation of two English villagers over the loan of a saw convey a whole history of manners."

Sometimes Coppard gives us a story written in the conventional form that we are accustomed to, as in **"Fifty Pounds"** and **"Alas, Poor Bollington,"** in each of which there is the surprise ending. But we read neither of these stories so much for the form as for the very fine characterization and the imaginative invention achieved. Merely to outline the plots would give no sense of the qualities the stories possess. And the same may be said of many of Coppard's best tales: **"The Angel and the Sweep," "The Ballet Girl," "Judith," "The Old Venerable," "The Handsome Lady," "Dumbledon Donkey,"** and many others.

There is in Coppard's volume *Nixey's Harlequin* one long piece of fiction, **"My Hundredth Tale,"** that because of its personal interest we might discuss at some length. To say that this tale is strictly autobiographical would be very unsafe, yet in reading it we cannot help feeling that Coppard is treating himself as though he were one of his own characters. Fact and fiction are no doubt hopelessly intermingled; and perhaps Coppard is himself not always sure where fact stops and fiction begins, any more than Sherwood Anderson is in his *A Story Teller's Story.*

In **"My Hundredth Tale"** are some unforgettable pictures of a writer, Johnny Flynn by name; of his father, his mother, his friends, his loves. The story develops Flynn's later life, his troubles, uncertainties, reflections, and his sharply accented despair due to his inability to love with any peace. On this note he concludes, fearing that he is not a personality at all. He has lived in and with the passions of his characters so faithfully that now he can only counterfeit passion and no longer has any clear and definite personality. In his earlier sketch, **"Luxury,"** Coppard had given what one senses to be thinly disguised autobiography, but the man in that piece is clearly a fictionalized character. It is told in the third person, not, like **"My Hundredth Tale,"** in the first person. Where the mood of **"Luxury"** was light and bantering, Johnny Flynn's story is told in dead earnest . . .

> I am going to be garrulous [Flynn says], to say what I like, just anyhow. It will mean nothing to you, it may be tiresome to you, but to me it will be life, and my only heaven.

> Johnny is going to lay bare his inner substantiality.

When Johnny was ten he had a friend, Bill Brown, and Bill had a sister, Carlotta.

> She was shy and slender, with pale cheeks and pale hair that hung as beautifully from her crown as a waterfall from a rock. Whenever I kissed Carlotta she would turn her face gently away and not look at me, never look at me.

As a boy he visited the caravan of the gypsies, and was a special friend of the king and the queen. No wonder the fine figures of gypsies play frequent rôles in Coppard's tales. Johnny Flynn remembers the queen, a magnificent woman, "with a lovely brown Romany face and black curls as long and stiff as candles."

He was put to work helping a street vender, but that did not last long, though it left many impressions that he no doubt used later in his life as a writer. Then his father began to die, and an uncle, a "monumental mason" wanted to help him.

> At the back of his mind there was also the idea, dim but audacious, of arraying me as a child mute, in black, with gloves and a tall hat flounced with crêpe, for use as a special and novel attendant at infants' funerals.

There follows a magnificent narrative of the writer's recollection of his father's funeral.

For his South Downs he has such a passion as Emily Brontë had for the moors:

> I learned to run wildly up on these uplands, where the heart was never known to tire nor the limbs to fail; or I would lie and gaze at the lovely land, my mind flowering with thoughts that have borne no fruit. Fluid tender hours!

His friend Bill Brown excelled him in everything.

> I do suspect now that I did not love him at all, and that my emotion was but a reflection of another I indulged in, the timid silent worship of his timid silent sister, Carlotta.

He fell in love with other girls one after the other, "or with some together—it is so easy; fancy turns you round and about like a cock on a church, this way, that way." In each love affair his mother's divination toppled his idols. "How did she know that I had a queasy mind and was terrified by ugliness or vulgarity? I did not know it myself, then!" Very delightful reading it is—the way his mother does her toppling. There were Myra Stogumber, Violet Mutton—"Sacred Caesar, what a name!"—Honor Clapperton. And there was Rose Tilack, neat and clean, "but with a scatological mind that would have shamed a monkey."

Then John Flynn finished a book and

> its creation had been a tortuous delight. I had fashioned a group of people, imaginary persons, and filled them with passions and humours, with virtue, vulgarity, and laughter, with blood, bones, tears, bad temper, and love. Their emotions were not my own, they were spurious, and yet I had lived with these figments so closely, brooded over them so long, that I myself helplessly assumed the protean dooms I inflicted on them, suffering the foul and rejoicing at the fair when I permitted them a respite from my slings of outrageous fortune.

Flynn says that of all human characteristics he divined most keenly the thing called vulgarity. He had lived in it, he sprang from it. And the danger of one turned prig through reading and writing poetry was that, out of false shame, vulgarity might be denied. But with this quality of vulgarity, which Coppard uses very extensively, which he makes almost a business, he has done what he has done for melodrama. He came to know that vulgarity is the nourisher of existence, that in this soil flourished the emotions that impel human beings in every conceivable direction—toward low and vile exhibitions, but also toward piety and sacrifice, kindliness, and decency itself. It could lead to strength and health, as with Rabelais; and rarely did it lead to decay. Flynn (it is so difficult not to confuse him with Mr. Coppard) had felt of the herd, "hideous were their faces and forms and minds, vulgar their clothes and habits, their amiable jokes, their tears at funerals, their passions for food, politics, and propriety." From all of this he at first escaped to the fairer worlds of hills and imaginative dreaming. But there was too much health, too great vitality and sanity in Johnny Flynn to mope away his life and waste his gifts. A child of vulgar inheritance, he had two-fold the strength of its virtues. We find him casting off his shame and turning his distress to account; Johnny Flynn turned the light of his art upon hobgoblins that were his snobbish shames and he suddenly saw his own people as decent, kindly, no longer hideous. "I saw that those who ignorantly live may yet profoundly die." He reflects about the forest where he lives—"a floral bastion that leans and dreams in unimaginable beauty against the void." What is the purpose of the trees? To make chairs, "on which thc vast buttocks of the world may be seated to drink its tea or nurse its weeping child." And what is the purpose of the whole vulgar world? For the artist to record with fidelity and compassion and humor, so that a beauty emerges. Still Flynn was lonely because his world could not read his books.

He went for human companionship to London, where he found a desert; suburbs "that were as blank as the mind of Lot's wife." After some years, back to his town, and when he returned to his house in the forest he brought a woman with him. From this point the tale records three episodes of Johnny Flynn's love life, each thrilling, and each, in the end, unsatisfactory. Johnny finally takes stock, and then it is that he must believe he has lived so long with his characters that he has no clearly recognizable character of his own.

His life with Dove was wrecked by her jealousy of his writing. How well Coppard knows the vagaries of the heart! He hopes Dove will go away. "But there were other times that I thought I should die if she ever left me, just as I thought I would kill her if she did not, so incalculable are our wretched passions."

A fleeting episode with Carlotta and then she married her affianced tape manufacturer, though Johnny and Carlotta loved each other. His despair was largely mixed with wounded pride that Carlotta could give him up for a vulgarian. He was conscious of his superior quality, though he made never a claim to superiority of class. Thus for him Carlotta is another vulgar woman, as Dove had been. He vows to have no more traffic with such women; and the cry from his heart is that surely not all women are merely low.

In his unhappy examination of conscience, he believes he understands himself:

> I had lived so intently in my world of fictitious shadows, writing of people who had no existence, aping

emotions and postures that had no real play, counterfeiting violence and imitating peace, that when I touched this real thing of my own, imagination twirled up like a cloudy witness and warned me that I was lost indeed, that I was but a fiction-monger, a dealer in illusions and masquerade. I had lost myself in these shadows. I was a nonentity, my being was a myth. I had no love, I could only *pretend* a passion that had never stirred a ripple in my blood.

But this realization gave him a shock that produced a real emotion indeed, and then this realization and this emotion were digested and he spent five years writing books, until he came to a kind of valley of the shadow. This boredom and despair did not crush him; his great energy, his love of life were fighting for him. "If only the earth itself would burst like a rocket; if the sea would but leap into the sky and become a new Niagara, or the hills upheave their bosoms and twirl upon their own paps!"

Nothing happened. He went to London. There he met Livia, wealthy, perfumed, upper-class; they loved, and Livia returned to his forest with him. Livia turns out to be no cook and thoroughly untidy, with a passion for buns which Johnny hates. She goes away from time to time and gives Johnny breathing space. He thinks about love, that it is "mysterious, unprincipled, tender, fierce, sublime, brutish, delicate, and devastating, all fire and frailty, with less substance than a rainbow and eternally desirable."

Then Johnny, still miserably class-conscious in spite of his success as an artist, grows jealous. Livia is eluding him; he feels the cleavage in his heart. His fierce jealousy reaches a climax when he reads a letter about himself that Livia had written. There he finds himself called a vulgar, uncivilized man. A brief sharp quarrel and Livia leaves him. He says: "With the women of my own class love had been nipped by *their* deficiencies, with Livia it was ruined by my own . . . I am a lost ship waiting for a wind that will never blow again."

H. E. Bates (essay date 1941)

SOURCE: "Katherine Mansfield and A. E. Coppard," in *The Modern Short Story: A Critical Survey,* T. Nelson and Sons Ltd., 1941, pp. 122-47.

[*Bates was one of the masters of the twentieth-century English short story, and was also a respected novelist and contributor of book reviews to the* Morning Post *and the* Spectator. *His book* The Modern Short Story *(1941), is considered a useful introduction to the form. In the following excerpt from that title, Bates addresses conflicting elements of simplicity and sophistication in Coppard's writing style. He argues that Coppard's tendency toward the complexity associated with the writing of Henry James detracts from the earthy, folk-tale quality that makes his fiction interesting and innovative.*]

As the aftermath of one war resolved itself into the transitional period of preparation for another we were prom-

A page of manuscript for The Field of Mustard.

ised a renaissance in literature. After periods of national suffering, sacrifice, and victory, we were assured, the literature of a nation, fed on blood and glory, is seen to emerge with more virile splendour. Now, we heard, there will begin a notable period of poetry and drama, but most notably of poetry.

This renaissance, for reasons not hard to find, failed lamentably to mature. In the first place the sort of renaissance visualized was that in which the symbols of honour and glory would be the theme of songs sung on a major note; something was anticipated, I think, that would combine the martial patriotism of Kipling with that of the speech before Agincourt. In the second place, and most unfortunately, many poets could no longer sing, for the simple reason that they had been blown to bits. Those of their poet-comrades who did return saw before them a future of arid futility, for which there could be no expression in a major key and possibly no expression at all. It is not surprising, therefore, that the most popular poets of the immediate post-war period were Brooke, Noyes, Masefield, Drinkwater, and Housman, of whom only the last has any claim to be regarded as anything but a minor figure. The poetic renaissance was in fact a fiasco, just as the drama renaissance, if you cut out Shaw and O'Casey, was also a fiasco. The youngest generation of all, out of which the new poets were supposedly to emerge, found itself with voices that had broken too early, and heads that were old before their time. What they had to say was too much the sour fruit of frustration to find expression in

lyricism, and yet was too urgent to be wrapped up in the complacent folds of ordinary prose. That generation (the number of notable English and American short-story writers born between 1900 and 1910 will be found to be an interesting figure) needed and sought as a form something between lyric poetry and fictional prose. That form it found, and proceeded to develop as its own, in the short story.

It may be a coincidence, but if so it is an interesting coincidence, that immediately the Great War was over two important writers found their natural expression, as prose writers, solely and exclusively in the short story—an event for which there was no important English precedent except Kipling. I do not suppose these writers thought of themselves as innovators setting a fashion. Nevertheless their action in choosing the short story as a medium was the beginning of a fashion, if you can call it that, which in the next twenty years was to attract the following of scores of young writers for whom expression through poetry was not enough. Indeed it is not too much to say, I think, that Katherine Mansfield and A. E. Coppard, for all their faults and their debt to Tchehov, succeeded more than any other writers of their day in assisting the English short story to a state of adult emancipation. Before their time the short story in English had known imagination, as in Poe, ingenuity, as in Wells, masculinity, as in Kipling, humour and trickery, as in O. Henry, colour and irony, as in Crane, together with most of the virtues and vices of the novel; but with the possible exception of Conrad, himself only just coming into his own, it had been very little touched by poetry. Lyricism was kept outside it; poets, having their own medium, left it alone. But it will remain eternally to the credit of Katherine Mansfield and A. E. Coppard that both attempted to bring to the short story some of the fancy, delicacy, shape, and coloured conceit of the Elizabethan lyric—a comparison especially true in the case of Coppard—and that when they left it the short story had gained new vitality and new design and above all, perhaps, a certain quality of transparency.

To carry the comparison of these two writers any further would, I think, be unprofitable. Yet we may remark, before dealing with them separately, that both are the meeting-places of Russian and English influences—Katherine Mansfield combining Tchehov and Virginia Woolf (by way, perhaps, of Dorothy Richardson), Coppard combining Tchehov and, rather surprisingly, Henry James. Both had the satisfaction of being acclaimed, in the early twenties, as highly original writers—yet it would be truer to say, I think, that both were more remarkable as the means of transmitting certain influences than originating them. Neither disrupted, as Joyce did, the prose of their time; neither excited the moral and mystical controversies of *Ulysses* and *The Rainbow;* neither shook the foundations of society, like Samuel Butler. Yet after them, as after Joyce, Lawrence, and Butler, the things they touched could never be quite the same again. . . .

[A. E. Coppard] sprang suddenly into prominence in the years when *The Garden Party* was a vogue. Coppard, born in 1878, is reputed to share with Sherwood Anderson the legend of having had "a trunkful of fiction" waiting to be published when his first volumes of stories began to be issued by a private press. Certainly Coppard, who had spent some years of his life in business, had waited rather longer than most writers before opening up the literary shop. It is not surprising, therefore, that the first contents of that window should have had a certain maturity of finish. . . . Coppard's first window display, in fact, was like a show of well-made, bright-coloured handicraft: strong in texture, bold and fanciful in design, carefully finished, fashioned from excellent native materials which, like oak and wool, had their own sweet earthy and enduring flavour. For Coppard, like Sherwood Anderson, had recognized the beauty and value of indigenous materials.

Coppard's work is contained, except for a little verse, in a dozen volumes of stories. Of these only the first six or seven are outstanding; the work between *Adam and Eve and Pinch Me* and *Silver Circus* contains the cream of Coppard. In each of these volumes there meet a number of conflicting elements which are both the actual and the theoretical essentials of all Coppard's work: on the one hand realism, vivid factual description, earthiness, a home-brewed strength and simplicity; on the other hand fantasy, fairy-tale impossibility, exoticism, psychological trickery and hypothesis, sophistication; on the one hand buffoonery, punning, heartiness, bawdiness, good rounds of belly-laughter and low comedy; on the other hand a certain literary dandiness, pretty play of words, elaborate metaphorical crochet-work, a love of subtle conceits for their own sake. As time goes on the elements of the first group are forced into secondary place by the elements of the other; the home-brewed earthy simplicity is ousted by a kind of twilit fantasy; the trick of telling a tale rather than of writing a story reaches a stage where it is all too patently the result of a carefully elaborated theory.

For this too must be noted about the work of Coppard: his pieces are not stories but, as he is very careful to emphasize on every fly-leaf, tales. Behind this lies Coppard's theory that the art of telling stories, since it originates by the primitive camp-fires of unread peoples far back in time, is an oral and not a written one. In elaboration of this theory he would like to see tales once more told as if in the market-place, in the inn, at the street corner (as of course they are still told) with all the asides and insertions of common wit, buffoonery, bawdiness, and comment that accompany the spoken tale everywhere. Unhappily such a theory, worked out to a logical conclusion, would mean the end of writers, who would presumably only learn their tales by heart and recite them on suitable occasions to selected audiences. Such a method of tale-telling, having much in common with folk-lore, local legend, and the spoken parable (note that Coppard delights in allegory), would depend for its effect largely on pictorial simplicity, the use of homely metaphor, and the entire absence of literary language.

Unfortunately for Coppard's theory his work shows the strongest signs—increasing rather than decreasing as time goes on—that he is in reality a very literary writer, influenced in turn by other very literary writers, notably Henry James. Throughout Coppard's work may be observed, in fact, the consequences of a strange battle between tale-telling at its simplest and tale-telling at its most sophisticated. And in this battle Henry James is the major—and regrettably I think—the winning combatant.

This corruption of Coppard's work by sophisticated influences seriously detracts from what originally promised to be a very stout, yeoman achievement, very much of the English earth, closely akin to the lyric poetry of the Elizabethans. As Coppard began speaking, in the early twenties, through such volumes as *Clorinda Walks in Heaven*, *The Black Dog*, and *Fishmonger's Fiddle*, it was clear that a poet had taken up the short story, choosing as his backgrounds the countryside of middle England, the pubs, the provincial towns with their faded breweries and gloomy old-fashioned lawyers' offices, even the East End of London and the shops of tailors' pressers. A man with ripe powers of description, an uncanny knack of weaving a tale, a keen eye for lyrical colour, a sense of both humour and tragedy, Coppard had both strong and delicate gifts. The results excited attention, as they were bound to do, for Coppard's way was refreshing and the English short story had never known such pieces as **"Dusky Ruth," "The Poor Man," "The Higgler," "Fishmonger's Fiddle"**—stories as sturdy and sound in grain as oak, as delicate and oddly scented as hawthorn. Coppard's peculiar achievement in such stories was never subsequently surpassed. They had a flavour for which no one discovered a word until Mr. A. J. J. Ratcliff admirably described it as a "flavour of nutmeg."

But even so early as *Adam and Eve and Pinch Me,* Coppard may be seen succumbing to certain dangerous temptations. Quotations will best illustrate them:

> In the main street amongst tall establishments of mart and worship was a high narrow house. (**"Arabesque: The Mouse"**)

> But his fickle intelligence received a sharp admonitory nudge. (**"The Quiet Woman"**)

> He was of years calendared in unreflecting minds as tender years. (**"Communion"**)

> They were like two negative atoms swinging in a medium from which the positive flux was withdrawn. (**"Craven Arms"**)

> The gas-tube in the violence of its disappointment contracted itself abruptly, assumed a lateral bend, and put out its tongue of flame. (**"Fifty Pounds"**)

All these are casually selected examples of a style of writing which Coppard never learned was bad and consequently never learned to correct. The first three are examples of provincial journalese at its best, or worst, whichever you prefer; the fourth is a piece of pretentious word-play imposed on the main body of the story and meaning little or nothing; the metaphor of the gas-tube is atrocious.

Yet Coppard could also write:

> In front of them lay the field they had crossed, a sour scent rising faintly from its yellow blooms that quivered in the wind. (**"The Field of Mustard"**)

> He watched her go heavily down the stairs before he shut the door. Returning to the bed he lifted the quilt. The dead body was naked and smelt of soap. Dropping the quilt he lifted the outstretched arm again, like cold wax to the touch and unpliant as a sturdy sapling, and tried once more to bend it to the body's side. As he did so the bedroom door blew open with a crash. (**"The Higgler"**)

> The piazza was planted with palm trees, their trunks like vast pineapples, loaded with light saffron trusses— as large as wheat sheaves—of dates.

It seems incredible that the man who wrote the first group of sentences, each so unfitted to the essential structure of the short story, should also have written the second, in which every word is admirably distilled. Yet Coppard wrote with great care, piecing his stories together rather than writing them, noting down metaphors as they flashed on him, storing up oddities of description, odd names, odd situations, until a suitable niche was found for them in the final framework of the tale. All this gives his work the effect, at times, of being the product of an arts-and-crafts shop. Its apparent boisterous spontaneity is in reality studied; the shop window with its homespun cloth and rough carving has been set out by a West End hand. Coppard cannot escape, I think, the charge of pretentiousness even in some of his best work—yet that work, as seen in **"The Higgler," "Dusky Ruth," "Fine Feathers," "The Cherry Tree," "The Field of Mustard,"** is as English and as sturdily beautiful as the Cotswold Hills and the Buckinghamshire beech-woods that are so often the background of Coppard's tales. On these achievements, and a dozen or so like them, Coppard's reputation may safely rest. The worst of his work can never detract from their craftsmanship or their very English beauty.

Unlike Wells and Kipling, Coppard has no sociological axes to grind. He was interested only in the tale for the tale's sake; in his stories there is no social, religious, scientific, or imperialistic background or bias. Coppard was interested in what happened to people once they got on to the merry-go-round of emotion, and indeed his stories, half-real, half-fantastic, have something of the atmosphere of the fair-ground; behind the well-lit exteriors lurks a certain air of gipsyish fancy and romance, and it is interesting to note that Coppard for some years chose just that gipsyish mode of life, living as he did in an isolated caravan in the Buckinghamshire woods and writing many of his best stories there.

But Coppard, forty when the Great War ended, hardly belongs to the generation of writers that cut its teeth on bullets and found the future beyond 1920 a very sadly disrupted prospect. Coppard, though always regarded as a writer young in spirit, belongs essentially to the generation of Conrad and Maugham. His significance to the new generation lay in the fact that he alone of his generation sought his expression solely in the short story; Conrad chose as his primary medium the novel, Maugham the play and the novel; both, though excellent craftsmen in the shorter form, used it only as a supplementary and not exclusive means of expression. To young writers—and here I can speak very much from personal experience—the choice made by Coppard was an inspiration. To see the short story lifted from its place as an orphan of literature, handled at last as if it were an adult, and finally presented as a beautiful thing, strong in its own right, gave at least one very young writer of the 1920s great hope and encouragement, and I have no doubt it similarly affected others.

Punch (essay date 1944)

SOURCE: "Variations on an English Theme," in *Punch,* Vol. 206, No. 5382, March 29, 1944, p. 276.

[*In the following review of the collection* Ugly Anna and Other Tales, *the critic admires Coppard's rendering of rural England.*]

A. E. Coppard once wrote a story about a gentleman, a cook and a musical box. The musical box started to play, and for no particular reason the gentleman who had lived so staidly and respectably for years held out his hands to the cook and started waltzing round and round, down the steps and into the beyond. This story, with its troubling behaviour on the part of ordinary people, contains in miniature the genius of Coppard—freakish, tender, oddly penetrating, much imitated but inimitable. His new collection, *Ugly Anna*, is not different from what he has given us these twenty years, or perhaps it would be more grateful to say it is equally good, with no flaw in the crystal. Some of these stories are pure fantasy, such as **"The Drum,"** and **"Cheese,"** a new version of Coppard's favourite of the mouse-trap. But these are not the heart of his peculiar mystery, which consists in variations on the English theme. These characters who are animated by a life which is so grotesque, or tell with a reminiscent chuckle of such strange twists of fate—they are English of the English and recognizable from every country lane, rectory, pub and doorstep. "Under the turf lie the dead and gone neighbours, as close as may be allowed to the triangular green beside the post office and the old Swan tavern." From the dead neighbours and the living, the Jordans and the Merryweathers, Smulveys and Slowlys, Purdys and Cattermuts, Coppard spins his delicate tall stories. And from the homeliest (not the Basic) forms of the English language he spins his style. "The widow's last man had hung himself on a plum-tree, and that's a cold warning to any bachelor." . . . "The clock of time ticks you off, it ticks you off, and although Thaniel's hour had not yet struck he was being put, and not very gently either, on one side." Here is beauty, and with it goes a warning: "In some tales there is occasionally a little more than at first meets the eye, buried lightly as it were. It can't be helped, that's the way it goes."

William Peden (essay date 1948)

SOURCE: "Ruled by Force and Fudge," in *The Saturday Review of Literature,* Vol. XXXI, No. 13, March 27, 1948, pp. 18, 31.

[*Peden is an American critic and educator who has written extensively on the American short story and on such American historical figures as Thomas Jefferson and John Quincy Adams. In the following review of* The Collected Tales of A. E. Coppard, *Peden finds the collection exemplary of Coppard's best work, demonstrating "the variety of Coppard's interests and the flexibility of his technique."*]

Alfred Edgar Coppard was seventy in January last. Since 1920, his several volumes of carefully wrought tales and stories have won him a small but enthusiastic American audience. For the present volume, he has selected thirty-eight stories on which, seemingly, he wishes to let his reputation rest. The result is an important contribution to the literature of short fiction. A. E. Coppard has few equals among twentieth-century English short-story writers.

> **Coppard is a painstaking craftsman who has never bowed to contemporary trends, fashions, or fads. His short fiction is characterized by variety, vitality, and artistry.**
>
> —*William Peden, in* **Twenty-Nine Stories,** *1960.*

The variety of Coppard's interests and the flexibility of his technique are well demonstrated in the present volume, including as it does ghost stories and tales of the supernatural, tales of fantasy and whimsy, symbolic and allegorical sketches, and carefully-plotted realistic and naturalistic stories. It is as a writer of fantasy that Coppard is best known in America; his most frequently anthologized piece is probably **"Adam and Eve and Pinch Me,"** a chimerical story of Jaffa Codling's visions. Coppard's real forte, however, lies in full-length characterization, and among his best works are realistic stories like **"The Poor Man," "Fine Feathers," "Ninepenny Flute," "A Little Boy Lost," "The Hurly Burly,"** and **"The Field of Mustard."** In stories such as these the author's sympathies are always with his major characters, somber though their destinies may be. The world of those stories is one governed by fate or coincidence rather than by reason; in it, the accidents of heredity and the effect of environment are more instrumental than virtue or wisdom or perseverance. It's a sinful world, as one of its inhabitants comments, ruled by force and fudge.

Typical is the lot of Phemy in the poignant **"The Hurly Burly."** Phemy is a good woman in the sense that Hardy's Tess is a good woman, patient, hard-working, essentially honest. Yet her life is a succession of disappointments and frustrations, prematurely shortened by hard work, highlighted by a loveless marriage, and blasted by accident (she dies of bloodpoisoning caught from a diseased cow while milking with a cut finger). On her deathbed, reflecting upon the meaninglessness of her life, she asks, "Nurse, what was I born into the world at all for?"

Few if any of Coppard's characters find the answer to Phemy's question. Homer Dodd, for example (in **"Fine Feathers"**), is a clerk, ambitious, not untalented. As the years strip from him his dreams and illusions, he too recalls the past. "It's bad," he concludes; "Why, I might just as well have been born a fool." Old Dick (in **"The Venerable"**) seeks his salvation in the litter of pups his spaniel Sossy presents him. But Sossy is killed, meaninglessly. "Fizzled and mizzled I am now," Old Dick says, "and that's fact." And he drowns the pups and with them what little the years have left of his self-respect and hope. Dan Pavey (in **"The Poor Man"**) stakes *his* hopes of redemption on his illegitimate son. The boy drowns; Dan's mind dies with his son. To the evils of what one character calls this "abdominal futility" of life are added the injustices imposed by caste and class. The central character of the long **"My Hundredth Tale"** (which may or may not be as close to autobiography as anything in this volume) is ruined by his attachment with a woman of a higher class. Honor, states this tailor's son who became a successful novelist, is a fortune the vulgar cannot win, an idea repeated in several stories including **"Judith," "Fine Feathers,"** and **"The Poor Man."**

A highly skilled craftsman, A. E. Coppard exploits fully the devices of the professional storyteller, including the elements of shock and surprise. Yet he very rarely employs them for their own sake as he does in the meretricious **"The Man from Kilsheelan."** Similarly with his almost constant use of symbolism. Only in isolated stories, like the overwritten **"The Fair Young Willowy Tree"** or **"The Green Drake,"** does he use the symbol as an end in itself. Usually Coppard's symbolism is a major element in his stories, adding in effect an additional dimension to his narrative level. And he uses detailed, concrete symbols to heighten the effect of many a story, at the same time transporting the reader from a world of reality to one of unreality or nightmare. In **"Arabesque— The Mouse,"** for example, we have the analysis of a half-crazed Russian obsessed with memories of his mother who had bled to death after losing both hands in an accident. This Russian, having set a trap for a mouse, fails to kill the animal. Instead, "the thing crouched there holding out its two bleeding stumps humanly, too stricken to stir."

If he is first of all a teller of tales, Coppard is next a poet and an artist. Passages of real lyric beauty appear and reappear in his stories; the final effect of much of his work is closer to that evoked by poetry than by prose. Many of these stories deserve to be read and remembered long after many of Coppard's more publicized contemporaries are forgotten.

Wilson Follett (essay date 1948)

SOURCE: "Panoplied in Their Original Magic," in *The New York Times Book Review,* April 4, 1948, p. 5.

[*Below, Follett offers a laudatory review of* The Collected Tales of A. E. Coppard.]

Casting a ballot for A. E. Coppard always seems the combination of a manifest duty with a really acute pleasure. I cast my own first one for **Adam & Eve & Pinch Me** in 1921, some months before that first disclosure of a new talent was published in America. The excitement of that discovery is still vivid. Of course that title-story is in [**The Collected Tales**]—as it must be in any selection of its author's tales, were the number but six instead of thirty-eight.

The thirty-eight, a winnowed selection (by Coppard himself) of volumes published from 1921 to 1944, proffer the not inferior excitement of rediscovery and corroboration. They read equally well if you start with the last story—**"Fifty Pounds,"** one of the most conventional—and read backward to the front cover, or if you start with **"The Higgler"** and follow through seriatim, or if you forage at random. For the stories are not arranged chronologically, or by kinds, or (so far as I can perceive) on any system except that of interesting sequences and curious contrasts.

If a confirmed Coppardian were to go through all the volumes, checking to the number of thirty-eight the stories that he could not possibly spare, I expect he would find a coincidence of 75 per cent or better between his own nominations and these. It is, by this test or any, a volume for the permanent library—the best of one of the best of the writers between the two wars. For **"The Man from Kilsheelan"** and **"Father Raven"** and **"Dusky Ruth"** and the rest have kept, after years or decades, the freshness of the Book of Ruth or of the story of Judith (whose story, indeed, Coppard retells, *mutatis mutandis,* in this very collection). They are panoplied in all the original magic.

The secret of that magic? The late Ford Madox Ford, always a great one for providing the one and only explanation of the inexplicable, thought he had found it in "the peculiar quality of English lyric poetry" that Coppard was almost the first to get into his prose. But explaining a magician is as nearly impossible as explaining any other spell—say, that of a painting or of a Chopin nocturne.

This Coppard will take "a young sailor just off the sea" into a tavern on a summer evening. All you know about the sailor is that he has a bundle under his arm and has come from Sitka. All you know about the tavern is that "there was hearty company, and sawdust on the floor." But in three sentences you know that nothing could stop you from following that young Archy Malin out into the night in whatever direction he goes, and that he is going into a world all wonderful and strange and sown (as another not negligible writer of tales once said) with graves that yawn in pathways leading to the light.

You are committed to him for better or worse, through thick and thin; you dog him, a shadow among other shadows, "under a now risen moon over a darker bay," both more real than you, until, "half full of beer and melancholy," he passes into "a waft of curious perfume" and the heart of an adventure that may be a dream after all. You never know exactly what has been done to you, and still less can you draw up a diagram of how it has been done. The "something invisible" that plucked the handkerchief from Archy Malin's fingers has first plucked from you your propensity to question, to compare, to entertain reservations. This experience is absolute. There is no mathematical rationale of necromancy.

Coppard's own brief prefatory comment, addressed to the nature of the short story as compared with the novel, tells us nothing very new or unfamiliar; it merely restates familiar theory in a Coppardian way. In practice he supplied one of the two major influences of the last generation upon fiction of the shorter forms in the English language. The other was Katharine Mansfield's, which the American short story of the last two decades has elected prevailingly to follow. In all the transmissible attributes of solidity and shape, it might have got farther faster if it had followed Coppard's. But that would not have given it the endowment of magic, which is not for followers of anything.

Frank O'Connor (essay date 1963)

SOURCE: "The Price of Freedom," in *The Lonely Voice: A Study of the Short Story,* The World Publishing Company, 1963, pp. 170-86.

[*O'Connor was an Irish short story writer whose fiction is known for its realistic portrayal of life in Ireland and its detached yet sympathetic humor. O'Connor's critical commentary is distinguished by his insistent probing into the connections between society and individual talent as well as his attempt to analyze the creative process of the writer he is examining. In the essay below, O'Connor examines Coppard's preoccupation with personal freedom and financial security, concerns that the critic asserts affected Coppard's writing technique and inspired his recurring themes.*]

The saddest thing about the short story is the eagerness with which those who write it best try to escape from it. It is a lonely art, and they too are lonely. They seem forever to be looking for company, trying to get away from the submerged population that they have brought to life for us. Joyce simply stopped writing short stories. D. H. Lawrence rode off in one direction; A. E. Coppard, that other master of the English short story, in another, but they were all trying to escape.

No doubt, they all had much to escape from. . . . [Lawrence and Coppard were both] members of the English working class, and—in the manner of members of the English working class—resented it. Coppard's poverty was of a darker sort than Lawrence's because it was not until he was already a young man that he acquired any education and, with it, the chance of escape that education gives. He loved Oxford as Newman and Arnold loved it, but he went there as a clerk, not as a student. Yeats's description of Keats—"his face and nose pressed to a sweetshop window"—harsh as it is, describes Coppard for me. Apprenticed at the age of nine to a Whitechapel tailor, he had a cruel childhood, and described it in a group of stories in which he calls himself "Johnny Flynn"—the name by which in later life he was known to his family and friends. In these stories there is a terrible note of anguish and self-pity, as in the child's prayer: "O God, make him give me a penny tonight, only a penny; make him give me a penny, please God. Amen." The prayer was not answered, and I suspect that Flynn never forgave God or the English upper classes for it.

The child's prayer for the penny later becomes the prayer of the grown writer in **"Luxury"** for personal security and personal freedom.

> The garden is all right, and literature is all right, only I live too much on porridge. It isn't the privation itself, it's the things privation makes a man do. It makes a man do things he ought not want to do, it makes him mean, it makes him *feel* mean, I tell you, and if he feels mean and thinks mean he writes meanly, that's how it is.

It isn't how it is, and I don't think it ever made Coppard write meanly, though once, enraged by a poor book of his, I called his preoccupation with money "an unearned income complex." All the same, I don't think one can understand his work without keeping it in mind.

The other thing—the preoccupation with personal freedom—he shared with many of his generation, who have been denigrated and partly rehabilitated as "Georgians." Coppard was a Georgian in the same way that Robert Frost, Edward Thomas, Edmund Blunden, and a score of others were Georgians, and he shared their obsession with personal freedom—freedom from responsibilities, freedom from conventions—particularly sexual conventions; freedom from duties to state and church, above all, freedom from the tyranny of money. It was a healthy and necessary reaction, as the almost inordinate sense of responsibility in the work of C. P. Snow in our own time is a healthy and necessary reaction.

And in those days a very little money was enough to set a writer free for serious work. There were still plenty of reviews that would pay a guinea for a critical article, and a single man could live for quite a while on a guinea. In spite of their latter-day admirers, the young writers were not violently attracted by rabbits and pheasants, but there were always untenanted mills or barges on the Thames, and one could rent a beautiful Elizabethan cottage (without water or light) for a few pounds a year, and in those English villages that had been dead for two generations one had the most beautiful background in the world and a personal freedom that was an adequate substitute for life in the Latin Quarter. Coppard rented a cottage, lived in a caravan, and set off on walking tours through Europe. He

was a fine stylist and could have made a fortune as a writer of popular travel books: **"Mr. Lightfoot in the Green Isle"** and **"Rummy"** can always make an Irishman homesick, and few writers did Italy so proud.

> Full and bright the moon, but it did not seem to light up the gulf; the water had no sparkle, there was only a gloomy movement of purple bulk. All the eastern heaven in the direction of Leghorn was menaced by a cloud as high and wide as ten thousand mountains, and every few minutes it was ripped by lightning that made no sound. But the white villas by the sea glimmered carelessly in the moonlight; the fine trees, the olives, the palms, were still, and you knew of the water only by the white foam squandering round the rocks. At one station perched on a ledge of mountain Beamish could see down into a courtyard below him; there was a clothes line stretched across the yard, and on the line a pair of trousers inside out—how white the pockets were!—was hanging to dry. Immense and clear on the wall of a palazzo near by, the shadow of an ancient empty lantern hoisted above a gateway was thrown by a neighbouring street lamp. It was half past nine, though the clock tower showed but a quarter to four, and the town seemed empty, lifeless, soundless, stone quiet, until the train moved again. Then the trousers on the line began to toss violently in a sudden thrust of wind, and the lantern shadow on the wall was waving to and fro.
> [**"The Wildgoose Chase"**]

In the early books of stories, particularly *The Black Dog* (1923) and the magnificent *Fishmonger's Fiddle* (1925), the sense of personal freedom creates the feeling of a country being looked at again in an entirely new way. It even creates the feeling of the form itself being handled in a new way. Most storytellers see the short story first as a convention that appeals to them: the convention of Chekhov, the convention of Maupassant—in America nowadays, the convention of Joyce—and it is only as their work develops that they create a convention of their own. Coppard knew Chekhov and Maupassant backward, but he never settles for one convention rather than the other, or indeed for any convention other than his own need to grip the reader by the lapel and make him listen.

As a result, his formal range is remarkable—greater I should say than that of any other storyteller. A story like **"The Field of Mustard"** might be an exercise in the manner of Chekhov; others suggest Maupassant; others still seem to be folk tales like those of Hardy: **"At Laban's Well"** could be a prose version of a poem by Robert Frost, while **"Mr. Lightfoot in the Green Isle"** is merely a skittish description of a walking tour in Ireland which might have appeared in a travel magazine. In the publisher's advertisement for *The Dark-Eyed Lady* (1947), there is a passage that, for all its unendurable archness, must have been written by Coppard himself, since it defines so clearly his attitude to the art of storytelling. "His tales have appeared in all sorts of journals and magazines, from those designed for the lofty, beetling brow to those for the ignoble noddle—all's one to this writer." It is ironic that the author of such stories should never have become popular, but this sentence, like all truthful statements of a writer's aims, defines not only Coppard's range but his limitations.

In the early books of stories, particularly *The Black Dog* (1923) and the magnificent *Fishmonger's Fiddle* (1925), the sense of personal freedom creates the feeling of a country being looked at again in an entirely new way. It even creates the feeling of the form itself being handled in a new way.

—Frank O'Connor

One can trace his feeling of freedom even better in his tendency to prefer quality—in the painter's sense of the word—to design. What this meant in practice to Coppard was that whenever a character entered a restaurant or a railway carriage there should be someone or something there for him to observe, even when this distracted from the character's own preoccupation. He might have just visited the hospital where his sweetheart was dying or the prison where his only son was awaiting execution, but having a bit of Coppard in him, he could never resist a momentary interest in an old gentleman with a passion for Hittite. This is perfectly true and within the experience of everybody. Some nervous weakness drives us to cheerful irrelevancies even when we are anticipating what we know perfectly well will be the end of the world for us.

Technically what it means is that to write a story resembling the best of Coppard we should have to carry a notebook and jot down the details of every moment of interest and pleasure—the appearance of a house of landscape, the effects of lighting, the impression of characters glimpsed in passing, with their actual words. Then we should have to work these notes into the texture of whatever story we happened to be writing until every paragraph tended to be a complete work of art, like the paragraph I have quoted from **"The Wildgoose Chase."**

Like Whitman, watching the live oak in Louisiana, "I know I could not do it," but that, I suspect, is how the great early Coppard stories were written. In these the surface of the story is always exquisitely rendered—the glimpses of landscape, the snatches of conversation overheard, the odd names of villages and people, the illiterate shop signs— even the comments in the visitors' book in country inns. I am sure that Coppard actually noted something like the entry in the visitors' book that "recorded the immense gratification of the Dredging Department of the London and So-and-So Railway" and the gratitude of the Plaistow policemen—"To satisfy thirty-one policemen is no mean fete. We are confident there is no more comfortable hostile place to put up than at Tumble Down Dick's." I feel sure he had seen something like the person's sign that

read "Moore the Marryer—Christenings Done Here" and the ironmonger's that read "Kitchen Late Kettle," for, in Hardy's lovely words, "He was a man who used to notice such things." It is even revealed to me that I remember an Irish village where the butcher named Kidney advertises himself as "Kidney for Meat," a detail that would have made Coppard happy for a week and that would inevitably have appeared in a story.

The landscape, too, seen in sudden vivid flashes like jottings from a painter's notebook is surely the moment caught and held in a brilliant sentence or two. "Oppidan was startled by a flock of starlings that slid across the evening with the steady movement of a cloud." Or the picture of sheep being driven to the pool:

> The sound of all the trotting feet was like a passing shower and, pressed together in a solid phalanx as they galloped, nothing else could be distinguished except the black ears of sheep dancing like dark waves on a rushing river of milk.

But though Coppard may have thought that he wrote for every sort of magazine and in every sort of manner, there was one kind of story that he wrote again and again as though he were in the grip of some inner compulsion. That is the story in which the motivation is given by some woman's secretiveness. Clearly, some personal experience was responsible for the way Coppard came back to the subject again and again, and even, in his later, more garrulous stories, recovered much of his mastery when he handled it afresh.

The early ***Adam and Eve and Pinch Me*** (1921) contains **"Dusky Ruth,"** one of his most beautiful and characteristic stories. It describes a walker—as it might be Coppard himself—who comes to an inn in the Cotswolds where he meets an attractive barmaid. After some dalliance she agrees to come to his room that night, but when she does so she bursts into tears, and, instead of making love to her, the walker spends his time comforting her for some secret grief he never understands. Next morning as he leaves the inn she gives him a radiant smile, and the meaning of this, too, eludes him.

If Somerset Maugham had told that story, the woman's smile would have left us in no doubt of his meaning, the meaning of the old song:

> He that will not when he may
> He shall not when he wold.

But this, of course, is not Coppard's meaning at all. He was fascinated primarily by women's secretiveness: it is the theme of most of his great stories, and I fancy one could almost trace his decline as a writer by confining oneself to the stories in which it recurs. In *Fishmonger's Fiddle* (1925), which is probably Coppard's finest book, it occurs in several forms. **"The Watercress Girl"**—a wonderful story comparable with the best of Chekhov's— describes how Mary McDowall has a love affair with Frank Oppidan and gradually finds him cooling. A baby is born to her and dies, unknown to Frank, who is planning to marry a girl called Elizabeth with a little money. "To Mary's mind that presented itself as a treachery to their child, the tiny body buried under a beehive in the garden. That Frank was unaware made no difference to the girl's fierce mood; it was treachery." Once more, the passion exists only because Mary has kept the child's birth a secret from Frank, and because of that she can throw vitriol at Elizabeth and destroy her looks for ever.

Her words when she is sentenced are the perfection of "quality" in Coppard's work—the few broken phrases that serve to distinguish Mary from every other passionate woman in the world. Here we are far from Flaubert, Maupassant, and the cab horse. Even the punctuation seems deliberate, as though Coppard had invented it to describe the heavy breathing of a hunted woman in an English country courthouse. "'Twas he made me a parent, but he was never a man himself. He took advantage; it was mean, I love Christianity." If that did not come straight out of Coppard's collection of press cuttings it should have; it has an air of absolute authenticity.

The ending of the story is equally authentic. On Mary's release from jail Frank arrives, intending to "mark" her as she has marked Elizabeth, but the revelation that he has been a father changes him as it changes Mary. Her secret is no longer her own and hatred for Frank drops away.

The theme of **"The Higgler,"** a more famous story, is the same. The girl in this, who has a little fortune of her own, loves the Higgler, but is too shy and secretive to hint at it to him, so she forces her mother, who disapproves of him, to act as matchmaker. The Higgler, knowing the old lady's business head, concludes that her daughter is a bad bargain and marries instead a stupid girl without a penny. In both stories we catch a glimpse of Coppard's preoccupation with money, but a glimpse only, for it is kept in its proper place as part of the necessary condition of life.

But in **"The Little Mistress"**—an enchanting story—money, which has been a mere incidental in the other stories, intrudes, and with it an excess of what I have already described as "quality." It describes how a flighty woman with a devoted and long-suffering husband discovers that her ugly maid is reading the letters she receives from her lover and gradually grows to despise him and her own infidelity, which—if I understand the story correctly—is attractive to her mainly because of the mystery with which she surrounds it. But Francesca isn't only well-to-do; she seems to share Coppard's delight in the irrelevant and unexpected until even a careful reader begins to forget the number he started with. While she and Goneril, the flighty and the virtuous girl, discuss the meaning of life, a horse is being shod in the stable nearby, and the smith and carter discuss the meaning of horses at inordinate length.

"What was that you was a-going to say, Archie?"

"To say, Ted?" the carter questioned, "to say? What *was* I a-going to say?"

"Ah, I can't tell you, Archie. Only God Almighty could do that, but it were summat about this 'ere hoss, I believe."

At this point the reader is strongly tempted to ask what it was that Coppard was a-going to say.

But the typical Coppard situation is that of **"A Wildgoose Chase,"** from which I have already quoted the beautiful description of the Italian Riviera. In this story, Martin Beamish, a man with an inherited income of "six or seven hundred a year" (notice the casual way in which the figure is thrown off) decides to separate from his wife for a period "without restrictions." This has apparently been a dream of Beamish's for many years, as it has, perhaps, been that of other husbands, but Beamish is fortunate in having the "six or seven hundred a year" that it takes. The experiment does not work out too well. "Exulting in his escape—how simple it was!—and retrieving so whatever it was he had wanted to retrieve, he made only a modest use of the occasion because he had no clear idea of what he wanted to be at except to be going, going, going . . ." so he ends up at the British Museum, reading archaeology. By the time he tires of it his wife has gone to the Riviera where she is apparently studying something other than archaeology. This is too much for him and he follows her. After a few days she agrees to come back with him and he nobly decides to ignore the issue of the other man, if any. But by the time they reach Dijon he has revealed that he thinks she merely invented the other man to bring him to heel, and his wife leaves him for good and all.

It is a beautiful story and true of most of us. Athalie's "mystery" is the essence of her beauty. Lost, she becomes alluring again, rediscovered she becomes a bore, but when her mystery is violated and she flees, she becomes again all the beauty in the world.

All the beauty in the world—and for a miserable six or seven hundred a year!

In *The Field of Mustard* (1926) the money problem seems to get even more out of hand. The title story—one of Coppard's masterpieces—describes two poor country women, both of whom have had love affairs with a frolicsome gamekeeper: years later, when both are broken by life, they reveal the truth to each other, but the revelation no longer means anything to them. "O God," sighs one in words that have the poignancy of Mary McDowall's cry from the dock, "cradle and grave is all there is for we." But **"Olive and Camilla"** handles the theme in a much less satisfactory way. These two girls have lived together for years, apparently quite content with each other's company, until Olive takes to drink and the gardener, and the fact emerges that all through their relationship the men Olive had thought of as suitors were really Camilla's lovers. Like the Beamishes of **"A Wildgoose Chase"** the two girls are in comfortable circumstances for if, at the beginning of the story "Olive had enough money to do as she modestly liked" while Camilla "had nothing except a grandmother," the grandmother obligingly dies of dropsy "and left her a fortune." I am afraid I heave a deep sigh over that "fortune"; it is even worse than Beamish's "six or seven hundred a year" and worlds removed from the little bit of money that attracts the Higgler and Frank Oppidan. "His face and nose pressed to a sweetshop window" is a line that comes more strongly to mind. The reader may even forgive my rude description of it as "an unearned income complex."

The treatment is even more casual. It is a fine story, but I have to put my finger on passage after passage in which Coppard's mania for quality has run away with him and played hell with the design. I know that in earlier stories he has made fun of it, but the digressions were sufficiently amusing to justify the joke. In **"Olive and Camilla"** the joke has gone too far. It begins with a discussion of suicide and we are told the story of the "cook in Leamington who swallowed ground glass in her porridge, pounds and pounds, and nothing came of it," and then it continues with the scene in the railway carriage when a soda water bottle bursts and drenches Olive. She has to change and, of course, leaves her corsets behind—a shameless digression developed with shameless inconsequence.

> Camilla firmly declared that the young Frenchwoman who had travelled with them in the morning must have stolen them.
>
> "What for?" asked Olive.
>
> "Well, what do people steal things for?" There was an air of pellucid reason in Camilla's question, but Olive was scornful.
>
> "Corsets!" she exclaimed.
>
> "I knew a cripple once," declared Olive, "who stole an ear trumpet."

No doubt one of these days a graduate student will prepare a dissertation on Coppard which will show that the loss of Olive's corsets is symbolic of her forthcoming loss of virtue and he will have no difficulty in explaining the cook's swallowing of ground glass and the cripple's theft of the ear trumpet, but all the same I find myself reaching out for a very soft black pencil. It is not, God knows, that I want to eliminate the thing that delights me in Coppard, the accidental and incidental, the queer people in the dining room when the hero walks in, the noises and the feeling of a real and beautiful world outside in which the parson describes himself as "Moore the Mar-ryer" and the ironmonger's shop is that of "Kitchen Late Kettle." It is because all the characters are being taken out and replaced by Coppard himself; because the wonderful sense of personal freedom that for a time penetrated and leavened the dull mass of Necessity has begun to get out of hand and the necessary daily bread has started to blow up into a thin feathery pastry. To be quite so much at ease with the logic of circumstance—the power of things, which the Spanish poet tells us can do more than Hercules himself—is to be a thoroughgoing romantic, and, what is more, a romantic with an independent income. Olive and Camilla are delightful girls, but I wish

someone would attach a few weights to them: they do so badly need a job in an office to keep them quiet between nine and five.

Nine and five for unmarried women, seven and twelve—with time off—for the others, the hours they must offer to Necessity are those one wants to fill in in so many fine Coppard stories. Take **"Emergency Exit"** (1935). It is the tale of a rich girl (naturally), who, finding herself pregnant by an Italian gentleman who doesn't attract her (of course), emigrates to Canada (where better?), and sets up house with a military officer named McNair whom she does not marry (why should she?). "We did intend to, really, at some time," she says, "but we kept putting it off and putting it off until in the end it did not seem worth while; and a year or two ago we separated, finally" (just like that!). Elizabeth returns to England with her ten-year-old son and stays in the home of her mother and aunt who believe her to be married to McNair, and falls in love with a painter called Vicary Vines who lives in a cottage not unlike the cottage the liberated Coppard might have lived in. Before Elizabeth can marry Vicary she must, so to speak, kill off the husband who is not a husband, but in the end, her son so dislikes the thought of her remarriage that we are left with the impression that she probably returns to the supposedly dead McNair, who has come to England to look her up.

It is obvious that Coppard is deeply attracted by the woman and admires the perfect freedom of her behavior, even to her irritation when Vicary Vines shows himself shy of entering her bedroom, but it never seems to have occurred to him that from the point of view of the suspicious reader what he seems to be admiring is a very large income indeed, or that the reader might ask himself exactly how Elizabeth would have behaved if her income had been say, half what it was; or even how she would have behaved if only she had the responsibility of earning her own living, or—as an extreme hypothesis—how she would have behaved if she had to support an invalid father. Freedom and necessity—those two poles between which we mortals must live—are getting far too close to the old poles of wealth and poverty we know from Victorian romances. That there is a relationship between them no sensible man would deny; that they are identical is an idea that experience rejects. One begins to do sums, equating conduct with cash, and arrives at such conclusions as that for five hundred pounds one can afford an illegitimate child, for one thousand pounds a lover on the Riviera, for fifteen hundred pounds bigamy, and for a clear two thousand bigamy and a love affair with an American Indian.

> God what a little accident of gold
> Fences our weakness from the wolves of old!

Scawen Blunt was right, but at least the wolves in his poem are real wolves, not expensive life-sized specimens from a toyshop menagerie. For all his wealth and all his love affairs, Blunt got himself into a real Irish jail.

This is one of the problems of literature in the period after the First World War, and it is a particular problem with

Coppard, though it becomes clear only when he is no longer capable of breathing all his genius into it. And it is at this point that I begin to wonder whether Coppard's favorite subject is not one best suited to comedy, or even farce; whether, in fact, the particular sort of freedom he longs for is really personal freedom at all and not merely a new form of the old naturalistic compulsion that put a man's nose to the grindstone and never admitted the possibility of his raising it again. Coppard, like Lawrence, being a man of the people, knew what the grindstone was, and when he describes people of his own class, like Frank Oppidan and the Higgler, each with his dream of a nice girl with a little money, the personal freedom Coppard had himself achieved gave him a new perception of the possibilities of their lives; but when he turned it on people of the leisured classes it tended to become a romanticism of wealth and position. With Lawrence this doesn't really matter: the man was a flaming romantic anyhow, and I find myself reading those later stories in which he represents himself as a benevolent god, gamekeeper, gypsy, stallion, or sunlight come on earth to relieve wealthy women of their sexual frustrations as fairytales, legends, prose poems—anything on God's earth except a representation of human life and destiny. But the thought of Coppard as god or gamekeeper only makes me laugh. I see him squatting on a fence after he had introduced me to a nice girl who had had an unhappy love affair with a modern poet and hear him say—referring back to an earlier argument of ours—"And you think I'm unfair to modern poetry!"

In this metamorphosis Coppard's greatest virtues become faults in their own right. His uncanny perception of a woman's secretiveness, her mystery, the thing that lures men, continues, but the mystery gradually seems to require a larger and larger income to support it in the style to which it is accustomed, until the dullest, plainest housewife begins to seem more attractive. The quality—the packing of the story with fascinating though largely irrelevant detail—becomes more irritating, as though Coppard were not really performing an impudent pirouette but indulging some nervous tyranny. Freedom and necessity are not abstractions but different poles of the human condition, and too much emphasis on one can only result in some inhuman form of the other.

I should be surprised if life in the communist states which attracted Coppard so much did not result in some new sort of personal eccentricity, some sort of erratic behavior that merely caricatured the behavior of men and women in some country where—theoretically at least—they are free.

Doris Lessing (essay date 1972)

SOURCE: Introduction to *Selected Stories* by A. E. Coppard, Jonathan Cape, 1972, pp. vii-xii.

[*A Persian-born English novelist, short story writer, and dramatist, Lessing is known as a powerful contemporary writer working primarily in the realist tradition. Her works display a broad range of interests and focus on such specific topics as racism, communism, feminism, and mysticism. In the following excerpt from Lessing's introduction to* Selected Stories, *she offers a personal reminiscence of Coppard.*]

[The stories in *Selected Stories*] are as fine as any we have. In friends' houses, on the shelves where the books stay which will be kept always, you find Coppard. Talking to people, not necessarily literary, who have read their own way into literature, and who use books for nourishment and not debate, Coppard's tales are found to be treasures. He wrote a good many, some now in collections hard to come by. They are not widely known or quoted. Yet that they can have a general appeal was proved when recently they were adapted for television: like Lawrence, Coppard tells a good story.

He was an exquisite craftsman, and wrote well-made tales. But their shape was that of the growth of people or events, so that watching one unfold, you have to cry 'What else? Of course!' as you do in life. Coppard's work owes everything to this quality of knowing how things must be, how they have to work out. He understands growth. Nowhere are cataclysms or marvels, not so much as the whiff of a foreign port or an exotic person. If there's a sailor, then he has come back from somewhere and will be off again.

There is a steadily flowing stream in English writing that is quiet, low in key. To this belong E. M. Forster's tales, some of Kipling, and of H. E. Bates, many of D. H. Lawrence; here too belong the poems of W. H. Davies and most of Walter de la Mare. They are English, full of nature and the countryside, straying very little into towns and streets. Thinking of Hardy, also a country writer, helps to see a difference. Sorrow and rebellion rage in Hardy; nothing of the kind in Coppard, who doesn't believe in tragedy. He was one of the people who helped me to understand that very English man, my father, whose relationship to the countryside he was brought up in was like Coppard's. It is a sparrow's-eye view, sharp, wry, surviving, and not one that can quarrel with the savage economies of the field or the hedgerow.

I was lucky enough to meet Mr Coppard. It happened that we were once two weeks together on a delegation to the Soviet Union, which was a miniscule effort, common then, towards peace between nations. There were six of us, under conditions which made us get to know each other pretty well, one being that we were all working so hard sightseeing, and talking about what we saw, and violently disagreeing, that we slept very little. What came out strong in him was his inability to play the role 'writer'. He didn't like making speeches, he didn't like formal occasions, or conferences or big statements about literature. He did like talking half the night to an old pre-revolutionary waiter about Tolstoy, or examining the plants that grew beside the field in a collective farm. He liked flirting in a gentle humorous way with the beautiful girl doctor at the children's holiday camp. At a formal dinner he was talking to the young poet who spent much time tramping around the country by himself: Coppard knew England through walking over it.

He was a small man, light in build. At that time he was seventy-two, but looked sixty, and with a boyish face. Characteristically he would stand to one side of a scene, in observation of it, or quietly stroll around it, his face rather lifted, as it were leading with his chin, his nose alert for humbug, or for the pretensions of the rich or the powerful—about which he was not passionate but mildly derisive. The thing was, he did not have it in him to be solemn. His favourite writer was Sterne, his book *Tristram Shandy,* he was amused by philosophers and had his poets by heart.

Walter Allen   (essay date 1981)

SOURCE: "T. F. Powys, Coppard," in *The Short Story in English,* Oxford at the Clarendon Press, 1981, pp. 176-80.

[*Allen is an English novelist of working-class life and a distinguished popular historian and critic of the novel. Below, he discusses "The Higgler," "Dusky Ruth," and "The Field of Mustard," as examples of Coppard's best work.*]

A late starter as a writer, Coppard did not publish his first collection of tales until he was forty-five. He was entirely self-educated, having been apprenticed to a tailor in Whitechapel at the age of nine. When he was thirty he became a clerk at an ironworks in Oxford, where he cultivated and was cultivated by a number of dons and undergraduates and began to write. For a time he made his home in a caravan, and in his best work one can feel the sense of freedom, the exposure to nature and country life, that must have been his on escaping into a gipsy-like existence. Some of his best stories seem to come out of this, as for example **'The Higgler'**, probably his best-known story.

The higgler, Harvey Witlow, is a young man just back from the war, and wondering what to do about Sophie Daws, who expects him to marry her. Prospecting for trade, he is exploring part of the moor new to him when he comes across a little farm:

> It had a small rickyard with a few small stacks in it; everything here seemed on a small scale, but snug, very snug; and in the field were hundreds of fowls, hundreds, of good breed, and mostly white. Leaving his horse to sniff the greensward, the higgler entered a white wicket gateway and passed to the back of the house, noting as he did so a yellow wagon inscribed ELIZABETH SADGROVE. PRATTLE CORNER.

Efficient yet unfussy and unbuttoned, easy and well-mannered, that is a good example of Coppard's prose; behind it there is a personality and a human voice speaking.

Witlow calls on Mrs Sadgrove, who is a widow with a daughter.

> Beautiful she was: red hair, a complexion like the inside of a nut, blue eyes, and the hands of a lady. He saw it all at once, jacket of bright green wool, black dress, grey stockings and shoes, and forgot his errand, his mother, his fifty pounds, Sophy—momentarily he forgot everything.

He is recalled to himself when Mrs Sadgrove sells him fifteen score of eggs, two dozen pullets, and a young goose. He drives home rejoicing.

He begins a regular trade with Mrs Sadgrove. Soon, when he calls, he is given a cup of tea. He helps when the bees swarm. He buys the cherry crop. But he can get nowhere with the girl.

> Harvey would try a lot of talk, blarneying talk or sensible talk, or talk about events in the world that was neither the one nor the other. No good. The girl's responses were ever brief and confused. Why was this? Again and again he asked himself that question. Was there anything the matter with her? Nothing that you could see; she was a bright and beautiful being. And it was not contempt, either, for despite her fright, her voicelessness, her timid eyes, he divined her friendly feeling for himself.

He is invited to Sunday dinner and after dinner strolls round the farm with Mrs Sadgrove. She asks him if he will marry her daughter, telling him that Mary will inherit the farm and five hundred pounds when she is twenty-five. Yet she puts no pressure on him. The outcome of each visit is the same; he wonders about the mystery, suspecting a dodge on the part of Mrs Sadgrove which Mary does not know about. Suddenly he marries Sophy and gives up calling at Prattle Corner. His luck changes. Sophy and his mother quarrel endlessly; he can find nowhere that will take the place of Mrs Sadgrove's farm as a source of the goods he must buy for trade; his horse dies. As a last resort he decides to call on Mrs Sadgrove and see if she will lend him some money. But when he arrives at Prattle Corner he finds Mary alone. Her mother has died the night before and the girl, unaided, has been trying without success to lay her out. Witlow takes over; the account of the laying out is a most memorable piece of writing.

As they are leaving the corpse he asks her whether she knew that her mother had suggested he should marry her.

> 'I've often wondered why,' he murmured, 'why she wanted that.'
>
> 'She didn't,' said the girl. . . .   The girl bowed her head, lovely in grief and modesty. 'She was against it, but I made her ask you. . . . Mother tried to persuade me against it, but I was fond of you—then.'

The story ends:

> He drove away into deep darkness, the wind howling, his thoughts strange and bitter. He had thrown away a love, a love that was dumb and hid itself. By God, he had thrown away a fortune, too! And he had forgotten all about the loan! Well, let it go; give it up. He would

give up higgling; he would take on some other job; a bailiff, a working bailiff, that was the job that would suit him, a working bailiff. Of course there was Sophy; but still—Sophy!

What happens in 'The Higgler' is unpredictable; the story is as wayward as life itself. Nothing seems to have been arranged or contrived by the author. Coppard is at his best when writing about women. He responds to their moods, and whether or not he understands them does not matter for the response is all. There is 'Dusky Ruth', which appeared in 1921 and was a piece, according to [H. E.] Bates, such as the English short story had not seen before. In a Cotswold town a walker meets an attractive barmaid. He makes an assignation with her, and she duly comes to his room at night but 'she was crying there, crying silently with great tears, her strange sorrow stifling his desire', so that he spends the night comforting her. When he leaves the inn next morning to go on his way she greets him 'with a curious gaze, but merrily enough', and her 'shining glances follow him to the door, and from the window as far as they could view him'. Again, in relation to the heroine, reader and central character are in similar positions.

Of all Coppard's stories of women the finest is probably 'The Field of Mustard', in which two country women, 'sere and disvirgined women', come together after an afternoon gathering kindling in their common memory of a gamekeeper they loved years ago, ' . . . a pretty man. Black as coal and bold as a fox.'

I find in Coppard at his best, as in these stories, something very close to Hardy. They are as it were natural and apparently effortless equivalents to lyric poems and are not marred at all by the faults that beset Coppard when he is not at his best, faults that Bates, in *The Modern Short Story*, sums up as 'a certain literary dandiness, pretty play of words, elaborate metaphorical crochet-work, a love of subtle conceits for their own sake'.

James Gindin (essay date 1985)

SOURCE: "A. E. Coppard and H. E. Bates," in *The English Short Story 1880-1945: A Critical History*, edited by Joseph M. Flora, Twayne Publishers, 1985, pp. 113-41.

[*In the following essay, Gindin discusses similarities between the works of Coppard and H. E. Bates. He also details the prominent themes and techniques employed in Coppard's fiction.*]

In 1971 Granada Television produced a series of dramatic adaptations entitled *Country Matters* from some of the stories of A. E. Coppard and H. E. Bates. Critically successful and highly popular in England, *Country Matters* was later exported to the United States and shown on the Public Broadcasting Service stations. The series both drew on and reinforced a connection between the two writers in

the general critical and public consciousness, which thought of them as practitioners of the short-story form dealing unpretentiously with rural English life and representing something both ordinary and quintessentially English. From the perspective of *Country Matters*, the two writers were regarded as virtually synonymous despite the fact that Alfred Edgar Coppard (1878-1957) was more than a quarter of a century older than Herbert Ernest Bates (1905-74). The difference in age was somewhat obliterated because Coppard, a self-educated clerk, did not begin to write seriously until toward the end of World War I; and his first volume of short stories was published in 1921. Bates had his first novel, *The Two Sisters*, accepted for publication in December 1925 when he was only twenty years old. Both writers had numerous volumes of short stories published in the late 1920s and 1930s (Bates also saw publication of novels, novellas, essays, a book on the short story, children's books, and a few poems; Coppard four volumes of poetry). For a considerable length of time they shared the same publisher, Jonathan Cape. Both continued writing during and after World War II, still appealing to many readers while seeming to others anachronistic, insulated, or sentimental. Bates himself, in 1971, in the second volume of his autobiography, made the connection between the two writers both evaluative and explicit, contrasting his and Coppard's capacity for rendering English life judiciously and justly with the "lumps of offal" produced by the young writers of the 1950s and 1960s [*Autobiography*, Vol. 2, *The Blossoming World*, 1971].

More significantly, both Bates and Coppard were articulate defenders of the technique of the short story as distinguished from other forms of fiction. Both recalled Turgenev, a master of the shorter form, as a model, an acknowledgment of influence they shared with writers as diverse as James, Conrad, Ford, and Galsworthy. For Bates and Coppard, Turgenev initiated the focus on unity and compression in the short story, although Bates added the almost equivalent influences of Chekhov, Maupassant, and Crane. In 1948, in a preface for an American collected edition of his tales, Coppard maintained that the short story was not simply a compressed or stripped-down version of the novel but, rather, a form altogether different in nature and origin. The story originated in folk tales and oral transmission, its unity most frequently inhering within the mind or consciousness of a single character. In this, Coppard asserted, he was following the principles of another of his masters, Henry James. Later, in his autobiography [*It's Me, O Lord!*, 1957], written shortly before his death and published posthumously, Coppard repeated his reverence for James, although he did not always incorporate the master's technical dictates in his stories. For example, James followed the notion, deriving from Turgenev, that a storyteller began with a character and invented episodes to bring out the character's significance. Coppard said that he worked in the opposite direction, beginning with the episode and finding or inventing a character to illustrate it. He added that the episodes derived from his own experience but were not literally true and thus had merely "the sensation of truth." Coppard applied his interpretation of the short story to his autobiography, which is a series of anecdotes, impressions, and opinions, with no attempt at a coherent version of self; he claimed at the very beginning that autobiography, in its selection, omission, and exaggeration, is a form of fiction like the short story.

Bates considered the short story less as anecdote than Coppard did. Concentrating on the elements of unity and compression, Bates saw the short story as the effectively distilled novel—even praising his own powers of compression by rather grandiosely claiming that he got more "atmosphere" in a sentence than Thomas Hardy characteristically managed in a page. In his later years, Bates acknowledged his debt to Coppard; in the third and final volume of his autobiography [*The World in Ripeness,* 1972] he wrote that Coppard had once told him that the story could learn a great deal from cinematic art in the use of quick cuts, close-ups, and other techniques with a sharp pictorial impact, an influence that Bates asserted had appeared more visibly and consciously in his fiction as he had grown older. For both, the effect of the story was primarily visual. Bates, however, dissented from some of Coppard's opinions and preferences. He cited their disagreement over Stephen Crane, whose work Bates had admired since his school days, and he thought that Coppard was a fine writer except when he was "unwise enough to take that most elephantine of bores, Henry James, as the chief of his models" [*Autobiography,* Vol. 1, *The Vanished World,* 1969]. In 1940, in a short critical book on the short story, Bates stressed compression and unity as the salient features of the form and described Coppard's work as uneven, claiming that some of his stories were among the best, some among the worst, of recent English examples. He praised Coppard for avoiding any suggestion of Kipling's "loud vulgarities" that sounded like Wagner's music (opinions that Coppard shared, although in more explicitly political terms). In his critical book, Bates omitted entirely any reference to Henry James, neither discussing him as an influence on Coppard nor as an original practitioner of literary technique.

Although both advocated and illustrated many of the technical elements in fiction—the unity, the compression, the selection, the restriction to a single point of view, that are characteristic of what has come to be defined as "modernism"—neither Bates nor Coppard can accurately be called a "modernist" writer. "Modernism" can cover a range that includes writers as diverse as Joyce, Lawrence, Kafka, Chekhov, Katherine Mansfield, and Virginia Woolf, but generally and accurately excludes both Bates and Coppard. In part, this may be a judgment, a statement that Bates and Coppard are writers of the second rank. More appropriately, however, it is a descriptive statement about the kind of fiction they wrote and the ways in which they regarded their work. Seldom did Bates or Coppard, especially the latter, consciously place exclusive reliance on symbol or metaphor to convey what could otherwise not be conveyed. Rather, they generally wrote anecdotes or described situations, or defined characters or relationships, with directness and understatement, with no explicit sense that these represented or suggested anything further (in fact, both sometimes explicitly blocked off such

suggestion, although neither may have suppressed quite as much as he seemed to think he had). Their fiction radiates the plain man's point of view, the refusal to make more of something than it is. And, in this point of view, they both, explicitly and implicitly, unlike the "modernists," acknowledged no special role or function for the artist, who is as vulnerable or imperfect as anyone else and has nothing of the seer about him, no quality of revelation or representation that is deeper or more significant than that of any other viewer. The disagreement between Coppard's view of Henry James and Bates's is less a disagreement about the nature of fictional art than one about the particular achievement of James. Bates saw in James a high priest of the metaphorical art he rejected; Coppard saw in him only a careful and scrupulous shaper of life whom he endorsed as he would never have venerated a votary of high art. For both Bates and Coppard, the function of the writer, particularly within the short story, was to present life as effectively as he could, not to embroider, but simply to depict the vagaries of the particular. And, in this, both implicitly denied the writer had any special insight; they regarded as pretentious and inflated the making of the particular into the representative—a characteristic that the literary culture has come to associate with "modernism." This is more than a difference in setting, rural as against cosmopolitan, or in voice, the plain man as against the artist. Rather, it is a difference about the way fiction reflects and relates to human experience. . . .

Coppard's ruralism is often restricted to setting, a thick texture of detail that surrounds a story or an anecdote about people. **"The Hurly Burly"** begins with a young servant on a farm working and organizing the place efficiently and economically while her young master is in jail. When he is released, he, grateful, marries her but continues to regard her as a servant, placing increasingly large demands on her until she dies from overwork. The emotional force of the story, which Coppard emphasizes, is in her incredibly self-destructive devotion and the injustice of the relationship between owner and servant. The richness of the story, however, is in the detail, the routines of farm life, which Coppard observes carefully but does not seem to integrate into the emotional drama. Sometimes, his stories of rural or natural people do integrate setting and drama more closely and effectively, as in **"The Watercress Girl,"** in which the young girl who cultivates and sells watercress grown in a swamp expresses her feelings and passions directly, apart from any of the conventions of society. Jilted by her lover, she throws acid in her rival's face. Her honest passion, in a story that makes no moral judgment whatever, reunites her with her lover in an example of the stark brutality of rural life. At other times, Coppard's veneration for natural simplicity carries the charm of the deliberately trivial. In one of his best-known and earliest stories, **"Arabesque—The Mouse,"** an indolent, sensitive, and melancholy man sits reading Russian novels and recalling the dead mother he loved and the loved girl who left him. He also feels guilty about the traps he sets to kill the mice who invade his house and ruminates with misery over each mouse corpse. As the story becomes an ingenious and funny debate between the necessity for and the aversion to killing mice, it leaves the heavy and melancholy suggestions of Russian novels and lost loves satirized, undeveloped, and unrelated to experience. In some of his fiction, Coppard uses nature not just to show country character or the hard direct brutality of rural life. Nature also conveys elements of mystery, of living, unknown presences, as in **"Ahoy, Sailor Boy!,"** in which a sailor returning to England senses a frightening and attractive female ghost among the winds, moors, and forests of his native land. Nature is animistic and evocative, in a manner somewhat reminiscent of John Cowper Powys, although in Coppard never philosophically worked out. Nor in **"Ahoy, Sailor Boy!"** does the use of the ghost invite any of the psychological speculation implicit in James's ghost stories. The animistic Coppard can become trivial, Disneyfied, as in **"The Fair Young Willowy Tree,"** in which the growing female willow tree falls in love with and whispers sweet sentiments to the tall telephone pole placed near her. After several years, the willow's growing branches begin to entangle the telephone wires and the willow is chopped down by insentient man. Coppard as mystic or animist can easily descend into sentimentality; he is generally far more effective in his delineation of country people than he is in describing nature or deriving any meaning from it.

. . . . .

Coppard, in his autobiography, used his years as the oldest child in a destitute family on parish relief (when A. E. was only nine, his father died, leaving a wife and three younger daughters) to explain a permanent hatred for all policemen and parsons. . . .

In some of Coppard's stories, the anticlericalism is the whole point, as in **"Abel Staple Disapproves,"** an anecdote in which a solid, sensible farmer and his conventional brother in law are in a pub writing a memorial for the farmer's wife who has just died. The farmer wants no hymn or religious reference included, but his brother-in-law disagrees. They toss a coin to decide; the farmer loses and is resigned to his defeat by cant. Other Coppard stories are reverse mini-allergories, like **"Father Raven,"** in which a pastor, vouching for all, leads his flock to heaven to find himself the only one barred because of his false pledge; or **"Clorinda Walks in Heaven,"** in which a dead spinster on her journey to a rather whimsically conveyed heaven sees a parade of men, all the suitors she denied and thwarted. Sometimes the shaft of the anecdote is aimed particularly at the Protestant clergy. In **"Purl and Plain,"** an amiable and jovial old Catholic father and a stuffy, self-righteous young Protestant curate await the birth of a child of a mixed marriage, the Catholic to baptize the baby if a boy, the Protestant if a girl. The child is a girl, but the parents, having noted the difference between the representatives of the two religions, change their minds and decide to baptize the child as a Catholic. In another slight tale, **"Christine's Letter,"** a rigidly religious young Protestant appeals to his wife, who has run off and become a waitress, to return. Yet, the letter itself makes clear that she has run off because she could no longer stand his arid sanctimony.

The
BLACK DOG
and other stories by
A. E. COPPARD

JONATHAN CAPE
ELEVEN GOWER STREET LONDON

Title page from The Black Dog, *1923.*

Even in some of Coppard's more fully developed and effective stories, religion, particularly Protestantism, is the life-denying villain. Tracing the career of a farm boy who, enchanted with the stage, joins a traveling troop, **"Ring the Bells of Heaven"** establishes his healthy farm background and even his unrequited love as ultimate aids in his career, having provided him with experience in expressing emotion, but the fundamentalist religion he must abandon is nothing but a barrier. One of Coppard's most moving stories, **"Fishmonger's Fiddle,"** centers on the character of a young woman jilted by her husband and forced by circumstance to live with her puritanically religious aunt and uncle. When she later falls in love with a strange itinerant musician who plays a cello in a fish shop, she realizes that she must suppress her own desire out of gratitude to the aunt and uncle she resents. Her hopes and her failure are conveyed with a searching and convincing complexity. Another story of complex characterization, **"The Poor Man,"** depicts an iconoclastic rustic with a great talent for singing who annoys the puritanical local rector because he is a numbers runner and acknowledges and keeps the illegitimate son he loves. By encouraging the police to arrest the rustic for poaching, the rector helps precipitate the disaster that ruins the rustic's life. Such stories, whether simple or complex, convey Coppard's protest against religion as a force that inhibits or denies humanity.

In his own life, Coppard illustrated the "Plain Man Speaking"—that no-nonsense view of the ordinary Englishman. He entitled his autobiography *It's Me, O Lord!* and provided a subtitle, "An abstract and brief chronicle of some of the life with some of the opinions of A. E. Coppard written by himself." Opinions on issues other than religion, such as quick attacks on capitalism or the pompous follies of government, appear but are never developed or explained. Coppard's fiction always carries the voice of direct and involved statement and has none of Bates's tone of measured detachment. Coppard's autobiography praises or damns directly; it gives lists of those he hated, but almost never provides any justification. He claims to have loved Chaucer, Shakespeare, Milton, Wordsworth, Keats, Browning, early Tennyson, Whitman, Bridges, Masefield, Housman, Yeats, Hardy, Beethoven, and folk music. On the other hand, he had no tolerance at all for Donne, Dryden, Swift, Samuel Johnson, Thackeray, Byron, Shelley, Bach, Mozart, El Greco, or Van Gogh. Coppard always thought of himself as liberal or radical, an unquestioned point of view implicit in the fiction and explicit in the autobiography. He regarded the Boer War as the greatest example of English injustice in his lifetime. In 1950, when he was over seventy, he organized the Authors' World Peace Appeal, which sent a delegation of writers to Russia to try to help ease cold war tensions and alert the public to the dangers of nuclear combat between the United States and the Soviet Union. Coppard organized a steering committee that included Doris Lessing, Alex Comfort, Cecil Day Lewis, Compton Mackenzie, Herbert Read, and Naomi Mitchison. At the peak of the committee's influence, in 1951 and 1952, Dylan Thomas and Christopher Fry were also members. Despite what became, in literary circles at least, the orthodoxy of some of Coppard's opinions, he continued to think of himself as something of an iconoclast, a point of view that often conveyed a quality of quirky charm. For successive issues of *Who's Who,* covering many years, he listed his only recreation as "resting." . . .

Since he was often a writer of sketches and anecdotes, a great deal of Coppard's fiction originates in the autobiographical. A number of stories begin with descriptions of lower-class green-grocers' and other shops in a seaside town, seen by a very poor young boy, that directly recall Coppard's experience in Brighton in the mid-1880s. "**The Cherry Tree**" is a sketch of two young girls who ingeniously pare the housekeeping money to get their poor widowed young mother a bottle of stout and some cherry-tree seeds, an echo of her rural past, for her birthday. "**The Presser**" uses the character of young Johnny Flynn, often a surrogate for Coppard himself in the early stories, working as a messenger in a tailor's shop in London. In this sketch, Johnny, frightened by the brutality he sees in the East End streets, is also constantly hungry because his puritanical aunt demands all his wages as the price for his room and board yet nearly starves him; but Johnny is fond

of the kindly employer and the lively, direct workers in the sweatshop, all of whom reflect the solidarity of the deprived. In this, as in other short sketches, Coppard's description of urban settings achieves a vitality and specificity sometimes missing from his rural scenes.

Other vignettes seem to chronicle Coppard's experience in resigning his clerkship to write. "**Luxury**" is a rather trivial sketch in which a poor man, having given up everything to write in a country cottage, is enraged by what he sees as his own foolishness. He gives three of his precious bananas to schoolboys who wander by, and, eating the fourth and last banana himself, decides to continue trying to write. "**Alas, Poor Bollington,**" describes a man, living alone in the country, who thinks that he has left his wife, whereas she thinks that she had left him. When they talk this over, four years later, they conclude that he was the one who had really left, and she refuses to see him ever again. Although the conclusion seems simplified and contrived, the early parts of the story, before the confrontation, contain some interesting and complex suggestions about guilt and jealousy.

Some of Coppard's stories and sketches concentrate on the theme of sexual freedom. In "**My Hundreth Tale,**" a long and overwritten story, Johnny Flynn, now a writer living alone in the woods, recalls all his past mistresses. Many were too direct and "vulgar" for his taste; he was too "vulgar" for the last, considerably younger than he. The only conclusion he derives is that no love affair lasts. In another story, "**Nixey's Harlequin,**" the narrator is resentful that another man in the village has the same name he has; he is nonplussed when that name is discovered on the list of twenty-two lovers found recounted in the diary of a married woman who has died. Coppard's point is that the narrator should have been flattered rather than annoyed by the mistake. Here, as often, Coppard venerates promiscuous married women. Less theory ridden and mechanical, and more effective, is "**The Field of Mustard,**" a sharply direct and compressed vignette of hard-working women gathering in the harvest and talking of their past illicit loves.

The theme of sexual freedom is also central to some of Coppard's most thoroughly developed and complex stories, which achieve considerable sympathy for the somewhat unconventional characters they depict. "**Olive and Camilla**" deals with two middle-aged spinsters who travel together, build adjacent houses in the country, and see each other frequently. Their affection, they come to realize, is based as much on rivalry as on closeness, as much on recalling tales of past and lost heterosexual love as on priding themselves on their capacity to live without men. "**The Little Mistress**" concentrates on a sensitive, playful, rather fey young woman married to a big, bluff doctor considerably older than she. The wife fires a series of servants, reflecting her own restless and changing affections, even as she corresponds flirtatiously with a young single man off in the colonies. Finally, the wife finds satisfaction by keeping a servant who has had an illegitimate child and allowing the servant to read her correspondence, solely vicarious satisfactions for both of them.

The story carries a delicate and convincing sensitivity reminiscent of some of Katherine Mansfield's.

Another effectively sensitive slice of experience is **"Doe,"** in which a middle-aged former bachelor tells his old friend, a vicar with a parish in a rural slum, about his past. As a bachelor, under temporary economic stress and wanting only to write, he had fired the maid who devotedly worked for him. With no other alternatives, she became a prostitute. Discovering this years later, he reclaimed her and married her, but, although both tried, the marriage failed, the habits and perspectives of the prostitute having become too ingrained. After the woman sickens and dies, her widower decides to move in with the vicar, sharing his difficult and impoverished life—the widower using the vicar as the acceptable listener to a guilt he cannot assuage, the vicar using the widower for some sense of experience he himself has never had, the two amiable and dependent on each other in their talk and their constant differences about belief in God and salvation. These stories, so diverse in other ways, all illustrate what Frank O'Connor, in his admiring and discerning criticism of Coppard's work, called both his principal fault and principal virtue, a "pre-occupation with personal freedom" [*The Lonely Voice: A Study of the Short Story,* 1963].

A number of Coppard's anecdotes or sketches are about ironic reversals of circumstance, characters defeated by what they most desired or defined themselves by. For example, the young runner in **"The Third Prize,"** who needs money and wants to marry, wins the local race and, because of a mistake on the part of officials, collects the prize money twice. Feeling guilty about his greed, he gives one prize to an itinerant blind singer. He then loses the other prize to the charlatan who had arranged the mistake in the first place and threatens the runner with exposure and possible imprisonment if he does not hand over the money. In **"Dusky Ruth,"** a man meets a lovely, mysterious barmaid at a Cotswold inn. Surprised that she is willing to go to bed with him, he is eager until, just as they are about to make love, he suspects that she may be the wife of a murderer, and immediately freezes. The sense of mystery he sought is more than he can handle. Sometimes, in more ambitious and longer stories, like **"Silver Circus,"** the ironic reversal turns into unconvincing melodrama. In this rare fictional excursion outside England, a Viennese porter whose wife has left him is persuaded, for money, to simulate a tiger in a circus reenactment of a fight with a simulated lion. The role of the lion, of course, turns out to be played by the man the porter's wife is now living with. Discovering his identity within the fight, the tiger kills the lion, although it hardly matters to the reader which kills which.

Another story of ironic reversal of circumstance is **"A Broadsheet Ballad."** It concerns two sisters who have apparently been made pregnant by the same young farmer. He decides to marry the younger sister, although her pregnancy is revealed as a sham designed to win the farmer from her spoiled and demanding older sister. Insofar as the story deals with emotions, jealousies, and sibling ri-

valries, it is effective, but Coppard devises a melodramatic plot to make the story fit the frame of the "country ballad" and to underline the unexamined theme of primitive country justice. The younger sister is found murdered. The reader knows the older sister did it, but circumstances point toward the young farmer. The girls' father, fonder of his older daughter, suppresses evidence so that the farmer hangs for the crime he did not commit. In the primitive country terms in which Coppard distances himself from his material, presenting it with no indication of an authorial point of view, the crime of murder equals the crime of trifling with a proud girl's affection.

Coppard often uses class issues as a principal theme, sometimes in simple sketches or anecdotes, like **"Ninepenny Flute,"** in which a young working-class man obtains a broken flute, repairs it, and defends it in a pub fight. The sketch goes no further, but the voices and the attitudes in the pub emerge authentically. Similarly, **"The Ballet Girl"** is a slight, rather charming tale of a naive young bookmaker's boy in Oxford, sent, as a joke, by his employers to one of the colleges to collect a bill due from an improvident and loutish gentleman. The boy talks his way into and out of situations, is gulled on fools' errands, but, after numerous escapades and parties, emerges from the college with a young girl who dances in the local ballet and "rather" loves him for his freedom from pomp or snobbery.

In a more involved and complicated story, **"Judith,"** the young lady of the local manor house, whose husband is away, as he often is, injures her leg while hunting. The diffident local schoolmaster carries her back to the manor, and the two gradually fall in love. On the night they consummate their love, a local man is murdered. The schoolmaster, having been seen sneaking away from the manor house at dawn, is accused; he lies to protect the lady's reputation and is convicted for a murder he did not commit. The lady, wracked by guilt, writes a long and truthful account of why he lied and then tries to commit suicide. Still in a coma when discovered by her doctor and her returning husband, her letter not believed, she is judged to be sacrificing herself to save the schoolmaster, and he is executed. After her gradual recovery, the lady can no longer recall her letter, which the doctor has burned. The story is a delineation of her vague, class-born guilts and evasions, her buried half-perceptions and her resolves to forget, her dimly seen apprehension about the protections and injustices of class, rather than a story of false accusation and noble sacrifice.

A more consistently successful story is **"The Higgler,"** in which a veteran of World War I, a traveling trader in poultry, eggs, and fruit, manages to survive economically until he stops by a prosperous farm and buys all its eggs and chickens. The farm is run by an intelligent middle-class widow and her educated daughter, and the business connection with the "higgler" continues profitably for both. The woman invites the "higgler" to dinner regularly, and the relationship develops into one of mutual attraction. The woman would marry him, but the "higgler" is fearful about trespassing on class boundaries and feels he can never marry outside his class. He stops visiting the farm entirely and quickly marries his working-class former mistress, but neither the marriage nor the business prospers. Becoming desperate a few years later, he returns to the farm to request a loan. The woman has just died, and the "higgler" discovers that her daughter, whom he had thought would, as a university graduate, particularly abhor the match, had approved all along. The central issue of class guilt and intransigence is conveyed with sensitivity, understatement, and copious detail about both the working farm and the working trade.

Another story, very different in tone although written with equal skill and sharp detail, is **"Fine Feathers."** In this, young Homer, a clerk in a rural brewery, refuses to follow his father as gardener to the local squire. He criticizes "the three R's of squirearchy—reeving, riding, and rent-collecting." At the same time, Homer is entranced with ideas of gentility, and determines to buy himself an elegant dress suit. Saving money to buy the suit takes fifteen years, his purchase delayed by his father's death and the need to support his mother, as well as by his sister's pregnancy and subsequent marriage. He finally does buy the suit, and is pleased when he thinks the squire's daughter has invited him to a ball at the manor. He arrives, proudly dressed in his finery, to discover that he and the squire's daughter had misunderstood each other and that he had been asked only to help with the serving. It is the only time he wears the suit, for he soon has to sell it to help his sister support her children when her husband's latest store fails. As Homer ages, living out his life as the clerk in the brewery, with almost no social life, the suit remains his obsession, his failed vision of a grander life, a defiance of class. Here, the triviality is Homer's rather than Coppard's. Coppard supplies a perspective of sympathy for the wasted life, the life narrowed by obsession and by class values internalized to a point that subsumes either support or defiance, that sets the terms in which experience itself is apprehended.

The sensitivity, directness, and sympathy of some of Coppard's socially conscious fiction and his concern for personal and sexual freedom explain the considerable popularity of his fiction despite its uneven quality. In addition, his language and visual description are usually compressed and evocative. Ford Madox Ford may have been exaggerating, as he often was, when he wrote that Coppard was "almost the first English writer to get into English prose the peculiar quality of English lyric verse" [*New York Herald Tribune,* March 27, 1927], but Ford was underscoring a terse and earthy linguistic power that many others have noted and responded to.

For Coppard, . . . working in the shorter forms of fiction was more comfortable. In his autobiography, a form he said he disliked because it was so sprawling, Coppard wrote that he liked to see "all round and over and under my tale before putting a line of it down on paper." For him, the writing of fiction was less a form of self-examination or self-discovery than an exercise of control. This severe control enabled Coppard to write effective vignettes, skillfully turned ironic anecdotes, charming arguments for

a particular way of life or freedom from convention, and to do so with a sharply compressed verbal acuity. Although Bates's work demonstrates greater range of subject matter, variety of perspectives and tones, more precise description and a more continuously productive industry, he, too, was most comfortable within the cultivation of reticence, his own version of severe and compressed control. He could, at times, for example, show understanding of the phenomenon of the English male, inhibited and detached; but more often such revelation was truncated by the security of his narrator's detachment. In the work of both Coppard and Bates, the control and understatement often produce engaging and effective fiction; both merit respect and appreciation for what they achieved. Neither can be charged with intellectual or emotional pretense. Yet the risk of being pretentious, in fiction, may sometimes be worth taking, may reveal discoveries about both the self and the exterior world that carefully self-imposed reticence helps to block off. To some extent, the limitation visible in the work of Coppard and Bates is a limitation in the form of the short story itself, the concomitant of its length, simultaneously its virtue and its flaw. Yet it is also a limitation that the greatest of the short story writers, Joyce, Lawrence, Chekhov, and Mansfield, in their capacity to reveal fully both their worlds and their perspectives, have managed to transcend. Coppard and Bates can well be appreciated both within and despite the comfortable limitations they seldom transcend.

FURTHER READING

Bibliography

Schwartz, Jacob and Coppard, A. E. *The Writings of Alfred Edgar Coppard.* London: The Ulysses Bookshop, 1931, 73 p.
    Bibliography of the author's works published before 1931, with a forward and notes by Coppard.

Criticism

Feinstein, Elaine. "Ghostly Gardens." *London Magazine* 12, No. 3 (August-September 1972): 157-60.
    Review of *Selected Stories* which lauds Coppard's "fresh instinctive genius."

Gould, Gerald. Review of *The Black Dog,* by A. E. Coppard. *The Saturday Review* (London) CXXXVI, No. 3532 (July 7, 1923): 20.
    Praises Coppard's writing style and method, characterizations, and original themes.

Jaffe, Adrian H. and Scott, Virgil. "A. E. Coppard: 'Adam and Eve and Pinch Me'." In *Studies in the Short Story,* pp. 390-403. New York: William Sloane Associates, 1949.

Suggests approaches to studying the themes and symbolism of Coppard's "Adam and Eve and Pinch Me." Also provides study questions.

Jehin, A. *Remarks on the Style of A. E. Coppard.* Buenos Aires: Talleres Graficos Contreras, 1944, 15 p.

Thorough study of Coppard's techniques of contrast, inversion, and transposition.

Latimer, Margery. "Not to be Analyzed." *The New York Herald Tribune Books* 1, No. 51 (September 6, 1925): 5.

Review of *Fishmonger's Fiddle* which argues that Coppard's stories are too stylistically complex to be analyzed and should be simply enjoyed.

O'Brien, Edward J. "'The Higgler' by A. E. Coppard" and "Commentary." In *The Short Story Case Book*, pp. 542-549. New York: Farrar & Rinehard, 1935.

Reprints Coppard's story with thematic and stylistic commentary on facing pages.

Review of *Silver Circus*, by A. E. Coppard. *Punch* CLXXVI (April 10, 1929): 392.

Faults some of stories in *Silver Circus* for a lack of purpose and "a sort of literary facetiousness."

"Mr. Coppard's Tales." *The Times Literary Supplement*, No. 1,221 (June 11, 1925): 397.

Review of *Fishmonger's Fiddle* that praises the simplicity and concreteness of Coppard's stories.

West, Geoffrey. "The Artist and the World Today." *The Bookman* LXXXVI, No. 512 (May 1934): 92-6.

Solicits opinions from various writers, including Coppard, on the apparent state of economic, social, political, and spiritual crisis in the world in 1934.

Additional coverage of Coppard's life and career is contained in the following sources published by Gale Research: *Contemporary Authors*, Vol. 114; *Twentieth-Century Literary Criticism*, Vol. 5; *Yesterday's Authors of Books for Children*, Vol. 1.

Jean Rhys
1890-1979

(Born Ella Gwendolen Rees Williams) West Indian-born English short story writer, novelist, and autobiographer.

INTRODUCTION

Rhys's works combine personal experience with emotional and psychological insight to examine the nature of relations between the sexes. Her novels and short stories typically focus on complex, intelligent, sensitive women who are dominated and victimized by men and society. Alone and alienated, these women are unable or unwilling to learn from past mistakes, achieve emotional and financial independence, or gain control of their lives. Although Rhys was called "the best living English novelist" by Alfred Alvarez in 1974, she spent most of her career writing in relative obscurity. Her early works, dating from 1927, were largely ignored or forgotten until her novel *Wide Sargasso Sea* was published in 1966; the critical and popular success of this work occasioned new interest in her entire output. Rhys's early work has subsequently been reprinted and studied extensively. Critics have praised her spare, understated prose, realistic characterizations, dreamlike imagery, and ironic, often embittered tone in her stories, which depict the plights of her characters while evoking sympathy for their situations.

Biographical Information

Rhys's biography is central to any interpretation of her work, as her writings are, by her own admission, largely autobiographical. She was born in Roseau, Dominica, in the Lesser Antilles, where as a young girl she received religious training in a convent. Many of Rhys's stories are infused with her childhood memories of the island. At the age of seventeen she emigrated to England, briefly attending school in Cambridge before pursuing a failed career as a chorus girl. In 1919 she married journalist Jean Lenglet and lived throughout continental Europe. Rhys moved to Paris in the early 1920s with her husband and their newborn daughter. While in Paris Rhys worked at various jobs, pursued occasional writing opportunities, and in 1924, through a literary connection, met author and editor Ford Madox Ford. When Lenglet was jailed in 1925 for dubious business practices, Rhys was taken in by Ford, who published her earliest writings in his *Transatlantic Review* and sponsored publication of her first collection of short fiction, *The Left Bank and Other Stories.* Four novels followed, but World War II interrupted Rhys's career and she fell into obscurity. Many of her readers assumed she had died. She was "rediscovered" in 1949 by actress Selma Vaz Dias, who sought her permission to adapt her novel *Good Morning, Midnight* as a dramatic monologue. Encouraged by the knowledge that her work had not been

forgotten, Rhys produced *Wide Sargasso Sea*, the novel considered her masterwork, and two more short story collections. Rhys was awarded the W. H. Smith Literary Award, the Heinemann Award of the Royal Society of Literature, and the Council of Great Britain Award for Writers. She died in England in 1979, leaving her autobiography incomplete.

Major Works of Short Fiction

Rhys's stories consistently explore feminine consciousness and illustrate the complexities of relationships between women and men. The lives Rhys portrays are bleak, with desperation at their cores. The women are lonely outsiders, financially and emotionally at the mercy of callous men. The central characters in all Rhys's fiction appear to be versions of Rhys herself, with little attempt at disguise, and the plots seem lifted directly from her own often chaotic life. Her Bohemian existence in Paris during the 1920s, for example, provided the material for *The Left Bank*, a collection that contains thinly veiled allegories of the author's own alienation, weaknesses, and failed relationships. As Rhys aged, her stories began to examine the effects of growing old; several pieces in *Sleep It Off, Lady* treat the loneliness and isolation that may accompany aging. The central women in "Rapunzel, Rapunzel," and the title story in the collection, for instance, are humiliated by the other characters simply because they are elderly. Thomas Staley has observed a progression through the stories in this collection in which life is traced "from youth and adolescence to adulthood and, inevitably, to old age."

Critical Reception

Rhys's work has been uniformly praised for its economically lucid prose, its realism, its vivid imagery, and for Rhys's stylistic mastery of her material. Critics have also paid close attention to the repression of her female protagonists, their curious inability to rescue themselves, and the author's consistently pessimistic world view, as well as themes of aging, race, and colonialism. Although Rhys's stories commonly focus on women's issues, many commentators have noted that the concerns they express affect all of society, men as well as women. As Staley has remarked, Rhys's work "explores with compassion and a rare intelligence the panic and emptiness of modern life."

PRINCIPAL WORKS

Short Fiction

The Left Bank and Other Stories 1927
Tigers Are Better-Looking 1968
Sleep It Off, Lady 1976
Jean Rhys: The Collected Short Stories 1987

Other Major Works

Postures (novel) [also published as *Quartet*] 1928
After Leaving Mr Mackenzie (novel) 1931
Voyage in the Dark (novel) 1934
Good Morning, Midnight (novel) 1939
Wide Sargasso Sea (novel) 1966
My Day (autobiographical sketches) 1975
Smile Please (unfinished autobiography) 1979
The Letters of Jean Rhys (correspondence) 1984
Jean Rhys: The Complete Novels (collected novels) 1985

CRITICISM

A. Alvarez (essay date 1974)

SOURCE: "The Best Living English Novelist," in *The New York Times Book Review*, March 17, 1974, pp. 6-7.

[*In the following appreciative survey of Rhys's works, Alvarez maintains that the "purity of Miss Rhys's style and her ability to be at once deadly serious and offhand make her books peculiarly timeless."*]

When Jean Rhys published her first book, a collection of short stories called **The Left Bank,** in 1927, it came with an enthusiastic preface by Ford Madox Ford. He was presumably rather less enthusiastic about her first novel, *Quartet,* which appeared the next year. It is the story of a young woman, left penniless when her husband is sent to prison, who drifts into an affair with an older man, egged on by his crushingly understanding and emancipated wife. Writing of **The Left Bank,** Ford had praised his protegée's "passion for stating the case of the underdog." It turned out that the underdog heroine had an uncanny eye for the hypocrisies and secret brutality of those on top and an equal gift for expressing, without dramatics, the pain and confusion of her own condition. Ford himself was the model for the novel's unspeakable Mr. Heidler.

Three more novels followed in the 1930's: *After Leaving Mr. Mackenzie* in 1930, *Voyage in the Dark* in 1934, and *Good Morning, Midnight* in 1939. Then silence. Like one of her heroines, Miss Rhys went to earth, or just went under, and the books went out of print. It was nearly 20 years before she was traced, after the B.B.C. broadcast a dramatized version of *Good Morning, Midnight.* She was living in Cornwall and had accumulated, in her two decades underground, the extraordinary stories which made up the collection **Tigers Are Better-Looking.** She was also writing, and compulsively rewriting, another novel, *Wide Sargasso Sea,* which was finally published in 1966. It is a masterpiece, but so in its different way is *Good Morning, Midnight,* which had sunk with remarkably little trace. This time, however, Miss Rhys got the recognition she had deserved for so long—though none too soon. She is now 79. . . .

To my mind, she is, quite simply, the best living English novelist. Although her range is narrow, sometimes to the point of obsession, there is no one else now writing who combines such emotional penetration and formal artistry or approaches her unemphatic, unblinking truthfulness. Even the narrowness works to her advantage. She knows every detail of the shabby world she creates, knows precisely how much to leave out—surprisingly much—and precisely how to modulate the utterly personal speaking voice which controls it all, at once casual and poignant, the voice of the loser who refuses, though neither she nor God knows why, to go down. Because of this voice, the first four novels read as a single, continuing work. They have the same heroine—although she goes by different names—the same background of seedy hotels and bedsitters for transients in Montparnasse and Bloomsbury, and they recount the single, persistent, disconnected disaster of a life in which only three things can be relied on: fear, loneliness and the lack of money.

Money, above all, is the permanent anxiety, the spring that moves the plots and people. When the heroines have it, they blow it recklessly on clothes and drink, knowing it won't last, anyway. Without it, they twist like cornered animals and humiliate themselves by begging from contemptuous family or ex-lovers, or by sleeping with men they don't want. When Mr. Mackenzie stops Julia Martin's allowance, blood money to end an affair, she has to face London again and her impoverished, acidly genteel uncle and sister. ("Norah herself was labelled for all to see. She was labelled 'Middle class, no money.'") She drifts into an affair with the not quite spontaneous, vaguely stunted Mr. Horsfield, then out of it again—Mr. Horsfield buys the ticket—back to the familiar demimonde of Paris, with no money, no future and no longer even sure of her looks.

In *Good Morning, Midnight,* Sasha Jansen is older, already in her forties, and the plot is reversed. She has been holed up in London trying to drink herself to death when she is rescued by a friend and packed off to Paris to recuperate and buy herself clothes. But her Paris is haunted: her baby died there; her marriage broke up; affairs have torn her to shreds. There are bars she can't enter, hotels she daren't pass, and at every moment of inattention the past comes back at her in piercing detail. Her world is unstable and superstitious, as threatening and volatile as nitroglycerin. So she drifts, holding herself in, absurdly prone to tears, until she is picked up by a gigolo who is deceived by her old fur coat into thinking she has money. Together they perform a kind of parody mating dance, at once cynical and anguished, in which each seeks to use the other as an instrument for a revenge on life. They end, of course, more injured than before. But then, what else is possible, since they are both walking wounded?

"'Look,' he says, still speaking in a whisper. He throws his head up. There is a long scar, going across his throat. Now I understand what it means—from ear to ear. A long, thick, white scar. It's strange that I haven't noticed it before.

"He says: 'That is one. There are others. I have been wounded.'

"It isn't boastful, the way he says this, nor complaining. It's puzzled, puzzled in an impersonal way, as if he is asking me—me, of all people—why, why, why?"

This one question—why?—reverberates all through Miss Rhys's work. She is far too shrewd to try to provide an answer other than the inevitable one: "This happened and then that happened." In other words, that's how things are. She is also far too pure an artist to allow herself the luxury of self-pity. Like the gigolo, she is "puzzled in an impersonal way." So the moments of drama and confrontation—when the subterranean terror and despair seem about to burst through—remain strictly moments, done briefly, without comment or fuss, from the outside. Her mind flicks away from them, quick as a fly, and settles on some small detail off to one side: her makeup is wrong, the light falls oddly, a bell rings, a car hoots, or a cliche comes to life. ("Now I understand what it means—from ear to ear.") And this, as she does it, is far more unnerving than any full-throated howl of anguish could ever be. She is like the girl in the Max Beerbohm story who looks life straight in the face out of the very corners of her eyes.

She is like a Beerbohm heroine in other ways, too. Miss Rhys's apparently autobiographical heroines have been, in their time, chorus girl, mannequin, artist's model, even a part-time prostitute. In other words, they are in the Muse business, the stunning, vulnerable girls who, when Miss Rhys began writing, more usually inspired books than wrote them. At the beginning of *Voyage in the Dark* the 19-year-old virgin chorus girl is reading *Nana;* at the end she like Nana, is on the game, but chillingly and without any of Zola's unearned polemic. This makes the world Miss Rhys creates seem strangely unprecedented, glassy clear yet somehow distorted, as though she were looking up at things from the bottom of a deep pool. She makes you realize that almost every other novel, however apparently anarchic, is rooted finally in the respectable world. The authors come to their subjects from a position of strength and with certain intellectual presuppositions, however cunningly suppressed. She, in contrast, has a marvelous artistic intelligence—no detail is superfluous and her poise never falters as she walks her wicked emotional tightrope—yet is absolutely nonintellectual: no axe to grind, no ideas to tout.

She also writes from a position of weakness: as though orphaned, her women have no one to fall back on, no money, no will to get on, and one skin too few to protect them against the endlessly hostile world. Julia Martin, like all the others, is "too vulnerable ever to make a success of a career of chance."

Yet that is the only career she has ever had, drifting from man to man, loan to loan, injury to injury, waiting appalled until her looks finally fail and there is nothing left. In the money or out of it, the heroines have a certain chic, a certain emotional style, but they are never respectable and the middle-class world knows this and treats them accordingly. "If all the good, respectable people had one face," says Julia, "I'd spit in it." But inevitably it is they who end spitting in hers.

Miss Rhys is particularly expert in the chill hypocrisy of the English. "I got the feeling," says a foreigner in one of her postwar stories, "that I was surrounded by a pack of timid tigers waiting to spring the moment anybody is in trouble or hasn't any money. *But tigers are better-looking, aren't they?*" This sense of being an outsider unwillingly involved in the intricate social games the British play is constant in Miss Rhys's work. Perhaps this is because she spent the first 16 years of her life on the West Indian island of Dominica, where her Welsh father was a doctor, her mother a Creole. The dream of a tropical paradise as irretrievably lost as her innocence haunts *Voyage in the Dark.* But it was another quarter of a century before she was able to face it head-on.

Wide Sargasso Sea is her only novel to be set in the past and with a heroine not immediately identifiable with the author, except in her being, like all the others, one of those who are defeated as though by natural right. Antoinette Cosway is a 19th-century Creole heiress, inbred, hovering on the border-line between innocence and decadence, at once besotted by her exquisite West Indian island and menaced by it, as her mother has been menaced by their freed slaves and eventually driven out of her mind by them. An Englishman, stone cold and destructive as all Miss Rhys's Englishmen are, marries Antoinette for her dowry, betrays her and glassily drives her mad in her turn. His name is not given, but the book ends at Thornfield Hall, the scene of *Jane Eyre*. Antoinette, in fact, has become the first Mrs. Rochester, crazy and shut away in an attic, her own tenuous life merely an obstruction to other, sturdier lives, waiting her release by fire.

It is a hallucinatory novel, as detailed, abrupt and undeniable as a dream, and with a dream's weird and irresistible logic. It is also the final triumph of Miss Rhys's stylistic control, her persistent search for a minimal sensuous notation of distaste. Despite the exotic setting and the famous, abused heroine, there is no melodrama. Her prose is reticent, unemphatic, precise, and yet supple, alive with feeling, as though the whole world she so coolly describes were shimmering with foreboding, with a lifetime's knowledge of unease and pain.

The purity of Miss Rhys's style and her ability to be at once deadly serious and offhand make her books peculiarly timeless. Novels she wrote more than 40 years ago still seem contemporary, unlike those of many more popular authors. More important, her voice itself remains young. She was about 30 before she began to write—apparently having other things on her mind before that—yet the voice she created then, and still uses, is oddly youthful: light, clear, alert, casual and disabused, and uniquely concerned in simply telling the truth.

Nancy J. Casey (essay date 1974)

SOURCE: "The 'Liberated' Woman in Jean Rhys's Later Fiction," in *Revista/Review Interamericana*, Vol. 4, No. 2, 1974, pp. 264-72.

[*In the essay below, Casey explores the development of strong female characters in Rhys's later short fiction.*]

Jean Rhys is best-known for her *Wide Sargasso Sea,* a novel that places her among West Indian writers for its concern with the alienation of the Creole after the Emancipation of 1833. Yet *Wide Sargasso Sea* is also significant in its rejection of the traditional belief in the superiority of men even in the most apparently equal male-female relationships that marks her works before World War Two. Within the same year as the publication of this novel, two scarcely known short stories—**"I Spy a Stranger"** and **"Temps Perdi"**—appeared that strike down even more fiercely at female submission to male dominance.

Critics tend to agree that the strength of Jean Rhys's early work is its harshly realistic portrayal of women too weak to move with a fast, cruel, masculine world. E. W. Mellown, Jr., in one of the few lengthy studies of Miss Rhys's fiction, discusses the four early novels as a body of work dealing with a woman at the mercy of her sexual desires [in *Contemporary Literature*, XIII, Autumn, 1972]. He points out that from the youthful Anna Morgan (*Voyage in the Dark*) to the aging Sasha Jansen (*Good Morning, Midnight*), Miss Rhys describes "woman in one of her archetypal roles"—that is, as I understand Professor Mellown's article, woman as a slave to her sexual appetites.

The strength of Jean Rhys's early work is its harshly realistic portrayal of women too weak to move with a fast, cruel, masculine world.

—*Nancy J. Casey*

Yet despite the sordid life that each of these women in the early works endures, neither narrator nor protagonist questions the wisdom of rushing headlong after sex, love, and marriage. Only the reader recognizes the woman's ironic situation in these spare, straightforward tales. But in **"I Spy a Stranger"** and **"Temps Pardi,"** Miss Rhys creates a character who, after a life of the sexual determinism Professor Mellown describes, rejects love, men, and most all other human beings as well. The early novels remain merely powerful examinations of the existence of the underdog. These two short stories suggest a drastic response to the traditional, destructive, male-dominated relationships that the Annas and Sashas take for granted. I think that an understanding of the route Miss Rhys's fiction has taken is incomplete without these recent works, for they represent a strength of will and an honest appraisal of self missing in the protagonists of her pre-war novels.

I

Titles of books to be written ten years hence, or twenty, or forty, or a hundred:—*Woman an Obstacle to Insect Civilization? The Standardisation of Woman. The Mechanisation of Woman, Misogyny*—well, call it misogyny—*Misogyny and British Humour* will write itself. (But why pick on England . . . It's no worse than some of the others). *Misogyny and War, The Misery of Women and Evil in Man or the Great Revenge that Makes all other Revenges Look Silly*. My titles go all the way from the sublime to the ridiculous.

I could have made my collection as long as I liked; there is any amount of material. But why take the trouble? It's only throwing myself against the wall again.

These are titles of books fabricated by Laura, an English woman forced home from Europe by the Second World War. At the time of the story—**"I Spy a Stranger"**—she lives in a small English town, where she is persecuted by townspeople who think she is a spy.

Laura has been unable to contact her friends in Europe. To forget them, and to protect herself against the hostility around her, she keeps to her room, reads, and collects newspaper clippings in a notebook. Ricky, her landlord and the husband of her cousin, Mrs. Hudson, turns against Laura as anonymous threatening letters turn up. The night of an air-raid, Laura listens to records in her room without turning out her lights. After the raid, the warden warns the Hudsons about Laura, then searches her room and confiscates her notebook. Eventually the notebook is notorious, because no one knows exactly what its purpose is, but everyone thinks it subversive. Soon even Mrs. Hudson believes Laura is crazy, and arranges to send her to a sanitarium where she might get a "rest." Unable to understand the woman, Mrs. Hudson watches her leave with indifference and relief.

Miss Rhys employs an omniscient, third person narrator in this story, who relates the episode of Laura through both Mrs. Hudson's and Laura's eyes. A conversation between Mrs. Hudson and her sister, Mrs. Trant, that spans the length of the story, reveals the observer's view of Laura's behavior. The narrator's interspersing of the excerpts from Laura's notebook that Mrs. Trant and Mrs. Hudson read, reveals Laura's mind and her understanding of the Hudsons' treatment of her. Without the second point of view, the reader would accept Mrs. Hudson's conclusion that Laura is mad. Ricky comments that "'The old girl's got no sense of humour at all, has she? . . . And she's not very sociable'." He misunderstands her seclusion, her incessant letter-writing and reading. In her notebook, Laura explains this behavior:

> After I realised I was not going to get answers to my letters the nightmare finally settled on me. I was too miserable to bear the comments on what had happened in Europe—they were like slaps in the face.

> I could not stop myself from answering back, saying that there was another side to the eternal question of who let down who, and when. This always ended in a quarrel, if you can call trying to knock a wall down by throwing yourself against it, a quarrel. I knew I was being unwise, so I tried to protect myself by silence, by avoiding everybody as much as possible. I read a great deal, took long walks, did all the things you do when you are shamming dead.

We catch hints here that the xenophobic residents of the village suspect Laura because she does not support wholeheartedly England's righteousness in the war with Germany. Laura is no traitor; she simply does not wish to choose sides in the struggle. The war is not political or nationalistic for her, but a source of suffering because it has wrenched her from her friends and her chosen way of life. Laura's stake in the war is personal. The Englishman's is ideological. This shifting of the narrator's attention, then, enables the reader to see Laura both as the world knows her, and as she knows herself.

Laura's connections with protagonists of past narratives by Miss Rhys are clear. She has lived abroad—in France and Eastern Europe—most of her life, because she hates England with its "unforgiving sky" and its "mechanical quality":

> When I bought a ticket for the Tube, got on to a 'bus, went into a shop, I felt like a cog in a machine in contact with others, not like one human being associated with other human beings. The feeling that I had been drawn into a mechanism which intended to destroy me became an obsession.

Her aversion to England is as intense as that of Sasha Jansen, who feels suffocated by London. Laura delights in the color and texture of fabrics and objects, as do the earlier women. In her notebook she records her belongings: scarves, "reels of coloured cotton," jewelry, a cigarette-case, postcards. Like Marya Zelli (*Quartet*), she wonders why some people are "expert in mental torture," but "pretend blandly that it doesn't exist? Some of their glib explanations and excuses are very familiar. I often think there are many parallels to be drawn between—." Of course, Laura's experience at the Hudsons' would reinforce her belief in human cruelty, yet I cannot help but think as I read this statement that Laura never completes, that she refers to an affair similar to Marya Zell's with her married lover, H. J. Heidler. To escape her unhappiness, Laura reads incessantly and takes long walks—"all the things you do when you are shamming dead." Her comment is a haunting reminder of Sasha Jansen, who wants to close the lid of the coffin over herself. Finally, Laura's hysterical screaming and swearing as she is taken off to the sanitarium foreshadows the same behavior in Antoinette Cosway (*Wide Sargasso Sea*).

Despite these obvious similarities, Miss Rhys takes an entirely new tack in this short story. Previous heroines cling to the ideal of marriage and family, or at least of the comfort of an occasional lover. Anna Morgan is young enough to believe that she will someday marry one of her short-term flames. Marya Zelli has married, and although she rejects her husband, she does not reject love, but assumes that Heidler will fill in the gap that her husband leaves. Julia Martin (*After Leaving Mr. Mackenzie*) regrets the loss of her dream of husband and home, because a traditional marriage, even after her years of moving from man to man, seems the best way of life. Sasha Jansen shakes off her fear of human contact to go to bed with the strange man next door. She, at least, does not reject the chance of temporary warmth. Laura, however, has rejected almost all human contact. She has loved in the past, as her jottings in her notebook make clear: ". . . the ring he gave me . . . the blue envelope on which he wrote. . . ." In the early days of her stay with the Hudsons, Laura seeks her friends in Europe: all affection in her is not dead. Yet her strongest friendship is with a woman she calls Blanca, who speaks acidly of the "extraordinary attitude" of Englishmen towards women. This woman, obviously independent and scornful of men, influences Laura, for Laura moves beyond the subservience to men of the Annas and Sashas, to a defiance that is entirely new. I think it worth quoting an entire passage from this short narrative, because it is a startling comment on the problem of men stated, I suspect, long before women's liberation became fashionable:

There is something strange about the attitude to women as women. Not the dislike (or fear). That isn't strange, of course. But it's all so completely taken for granted, and surely that is strange. It has settled down and become an atmosphere, or, if you like, a climate, and no one questions it, least of all the women themselves. There is *no* opposition. The effects are criticised, for some of the effects are hardly advertisements for the system, the cause is seldom mentioned, and then very gingerly. The few mild ambiguous protests usually come from men. Most of the women seem to be carefully trained to revenge any unhappiness they feel on each other, or on children—or on any individual man who happens to be at a disadvantage. In dealing with men as a whole, a streak of subservience, of servility, usually appears, something cold, calculating, lacking in imagination.

But no one can go against the spirit of a country with impunity, and propaganda from the cradle to the grave can do a lot.

I amuse myself by making a collection of this propaganda. . . .

Laura not only decries the suppression of women by men, but also the willingness of women to *repress themselves*. Lois Heidler (*Quartet*) is typical of this repressed woman in that she supposedly winks at her husband's affair—because she believes herself emotionally superior to jealousy—then turns on his mistress with a cruelty that devastates Marya. Each of the protagonists I have noted, until Laura, plays along with this system. Because they cannot be human beings in their own right, these women take what affection they can from a man, and when he dumps them, take what money he will give. Theirs is a shameful existence totally dependent on the good will of former lovers. Laura recognizes that most women, whether they are adventuresses, or wives, suffer humiliation because they must cater to men. She asks Mrs. Hudson how she can "breathe after a lifetime of this"—"this" being her domestic routine with husband, cottage, and next-door neighbors. Mrs. Hudson and Mrs. Trant do not understand fully Laura's horror of women's lowly position: "'Do you know,' said Mrs. Hudson, 'there are moments—don't laugh—when I see what she meant? All very exaggerated, of course'." She fears the truth of Laura's statement and backs away from it. Her sister rejects it outright. She worries about her daughter—a "moody . . . fanciful, and self-willed" girl who likes Laura—because it is a "bad sign" when a girl likes unpopular people. Mrs. Trant has been gulled by the birth-to-death propaganda that Laura abhors. If she can cow her daughter with the same propaganda, she will do so. Men have suppressed her, she has repressed herself, and now she must in turn suppress her daughter. Laura's imaginary titles of books of the future leaves both women cold, then, because they think, or hope, that Laura's statements about the oppression of women are madness.

Miss Rhys offers a curious pun on the name of Emily Brontë that crystallizes her attitude toward women in this narrative and in *Wide Sargasso Sea* as well. Mrs. Hudson tells her sister that the man next door has a dog he calls Brontë. As a joke, he pretends to kick it, saying "Here's Emily Brontë or my pet aversion'." He does his act in Laura's presence. She flies at him; Ricky accuses her of having no sense of humour. It is significant that Miss Rhys refers to Emily Brontë in this work, and to Charlotte Brontë in *Wide Sargasso Sea*. Emily Brontë is unsympathetic to the brutality of Heathcliff, while her sister rationalizes the obtuse behavior of Rochester and the submission of Jane Eyre to him. *Wide Sargasso Sea* destroys Charlotte Brontë's gentle, sympathetic study of the master of Thornfield Hall, his mad wife in the attic, and his plain-Jane governess. She exposes Rochester's insensitivity; she reveals the tortured woman who is his wife. It is consistent, then, that Laura in her ramblings about the persecution of women should defend Emily Brontë, for the latter apparently represents to her a classical writer in line with her own thinking. Kicking the dog symbolizes relegating women to their "proper" place in society.

It is unfortunate that **"I Spy a Stranger"** remains relatively unknown, for it provides a departure from Miss Rhys's earlier assumption that the traditional roles for women are worth seeking. As I read this story my hands shook, because I realized that after years of rationalizing her protagonists' under-dog existence, Miss Rhys rejects it as inadequate. In **"I Spy a Stranger,"** and **"Temps Perdi"** as well, she portrays a woman who has given up any hope of happiness with another human being. She lives isolated by her own choice.

II

"Temps Perdi" is a three-part study of an old, unnamed woman living more in the past than in the present. In Part One, she describes her life at "Rolvenden," a house on the east coast of England. She recalls in Part Two her life in Vienna, where she roamed the streets and beer halls with several Japanese officers and their French interpreters and secretaries. In Part Three, the woman remembers her visit after many years to the Caribbean island, Dominica, where she was raised. As a child she had heard about the reservation where the last of the Carib Indians live, and convinces Nicholas, the overseer of Temps Perdi, an estate near the Carib Quarter, to take her there. In the final paragraph of the story, the woman says that when she leaves "Rolvenden," she will write the words "temps perdi"—Creole for "wasted time"—on the looking-glass: "Somebody might see them who knows about the days that wait round the corner to be lived again and knows that you don't choose them, either. They choose themselves."

Miss Rhys returns to the contrast between the Caribbean and England in this narrative, although she does not suggest, as she does in *Voyage in the Dark* and *Wide Sargasso Sea,* that the tropical environment affects the woman's ability to adjust to England. This woman does hate England, however. She remarks, as the snow falls, that it was better the first time she saw it: ". . . it was a marvel, the only thing in England that hadn't disappointed me." Everything in England is beige and dull. A comparison of her descriptions of her English house and her Caribbean island quickly reveals her disparate attitudes:

> "Rolvenden". . . . There is nothing in the house that you can say is ugly; on the other hand there is nothing that you can say is beautiful, impulsive, impetuous or generous. All is sparse, subdued, quiet and negative. . . .

> Everything [at Temps Perdi] had run wild, but there was still hibiscus growing by the stone garden walls and butterflies made love over the thorny bougainvillea. . . . But the white-cedars at the end of the garden—the lowest about eighty feet high—had dropped their leaves and were covered with flowers, white flowers very faintly tinged with pink, so light and fragile that they fell with the first high wind. . . .

She uses no such lush imagery to describe England. In fact, she never says exactly what "Rolvenden" looks like, as though it were insignificant. Her powers of metaphor and her sense of pattern and color emerge only in contemplation of the tropical environment that produced her.

This Caribbean background suggests her resemblance to Anna Morgan. The tuneless piano in the woman's house reminds her of Creole songs and a Cuban circus act she saw as a child. Anna also recalls her past in the West Indies as she hears the fading tinkle of a piano in the slums of London. The woman of **"Temps Perdi"** echoes the woman in Miss Rhys's previous work in her response to a young woman's ecstatic declaration of love for everyone and everything: "'And then you wake up,' I thought." In her old age, she, like Sasha Jansen, runs and hides—"a real Carib"—until death comes with its "own anaesthetic." Yet this woman fears books as much as the other woman cherished them for their usefulness in blotting out the world. "I am almost as wary of books as I am of people. They also are capable of hurting you, pushing you into the limbo of the forgotten. They can tell lies—and vulgar, trivial lies. . . ." She demands truth in a way that Sasha Jansen or Julia Martin never would have. When two men from the village deliver coal to "Rolvenden," the woman notes their "silent, sly, shy laughter. I can imagine what they would have said about me if I had asked them indoors." That familiar tendency to attribute her perceptions of herself to someone else crops up again. But she catches herself, as earlier characters in Miss Rhys's fiction have not: "That's an exaggeration. They don't think or say anything that I would imagine they would think or say. Speak for yourself and no falsities. There are enough falsities; enough harm has been done."

The falsity this woman wishes most to correct is that women must submit to men. She, like Laura in **"I Spy a Stranger,"** has learned after all her years of suffering and catering to men, that she must be independent. In **"I Spy a Stranger,"** Laura writes in her notebook of the "extraordinary attitude" of Englishmen toward women. Miss Rhys picks up this thread, and combines it with the attitudes of Japanese, German, and West Indian men, in **"Temps Perdi."** The woman remarks in Part One that the English soldiers in the cottage near hers wash up with "venom" in the colorful bathrooms. Her implication is that these men, involved in warfare, trample on the pink, black, green, and blue that women have designed. Her attack on men becomes stronger when she remembers her days in Vienna. Captain Yoshi, after showing a photograph of his wife in European dress, declares that "Madame Yoshi is a most fortunate woman. Madame Yoshi *knows* that she is a most fortunate woman'." Yoshi then pulls out pictures of his children, but only discusses his daughters, not his son. "Too sacred?" the narrator wonders. Later, one of the secretaries reveals that the Japanese greatly admire the German military strength, and the excellent way in which the Germans and Englishmen treat women—not like the French, who "love women too much." The other secretary adds that she saw an Englishman redden when he unthinkingly called a woman, a "woman." He quickly corrected himself, calling her a "person." Although the narrator does not comment, her inclusion of this material is no mistake. English, German, and Japanese men alike seek to dominate women, to bestow their favour on them, to treat them coolly, as though they were not creative, energetic persons in their own right. Ironically, despite her bitter "And then you wake up," the narrator at this point in her life was herself a slave to this male dominance, as her strong recollections of the many dresses she could have worn only to please men make apparent. Finally, when she visits Salybia, the protagonist talks eagerly with Nicholas about the secret language of the Carib women that the men do not know. Here, at least, are women with a weapon against their own men. But in the village a black policeman brushes off the deaths of "two or three Caribs" in a riot as if they were dogs. "It might have been an Englishman talking," the narrator observes. Indeed, a recurrent theme in Jean Rhys's work is the failure of the European or Englishman to understand the native West Indian. The pretty, crippled Creole girl—half Carib, half some undisclosed strain—who poses eagerly for sightseers, symbolizes this West Indian exploited by outsiders, for she is the product of a Carib woman's submission to a European man. She symbolizes, furthermore, the woman prostituted for her good looks and willingness to please. Again, the narrator does not comment, but against the background of her portrayal of male dominance in England and Europe, this exposure of the same crime on her beloved island rounds out with bitterness her condemnation of men.

What then does a woman who has suffered exploitation do? Like the Carib whose picture she describes, the narrator is helpless against the enemy—people, especially men. Her solution, then, is not to submit as does the pretty Creole girl—who is only *half* Carib—but to be a "savage person—a *real* Carib. They run and hide." And so she chooses the chill of "Rolvenden" as her retreat from human cruelty. There she has time to reflect on her life, which, as she suggests in the title, has been a wasted time when she struggled to capture dreams that she finally learns are not worth the fight. With hope and spontaneity gone, she is an old shrew, without fear, waiting for death.

Tony Gould (essay date 1976)

SOURCE: "In a Dark Wood," in *New Society,* Vol. 38, No. 734, October 28, 1976, p. 209.

[In the following review, Gould admires the stories in Sleep It Off, Lady, *observing that each "has something to say and says it with utter simplicity and stark economy."]*

"It's as if I'm twins," says a young woman in one of the stories in Jean Rhys's new collection. And the author elaborates: "Only one of the twins accepted. The other felt lost, betrayed, forsaken, a wanderer in a very dark wood. The other told her that all she accepted so meekly was quite mad, potty."

This passage contains the essence of Jean Rhys's vision. The universe lours, the sky is the "colour of no hope," people are simultaneously smug and dangerous to know, nothing is quite what it seems—yet what can you do but accept? Did not Christ say, "Blessed are the meek: for they shall inherit the earth"?

Sleep It Off, Lady is all we have come to expect from this remarkable writer, now in her eighties. None of the stories is more than a few pages long, but each one has something to say and says it with utter simplicity and stark economy. Their uniqueness lies in the peculiar blend of innocence and experience which is Jean Rhys's hallmark.

In the story, **"Goodbye Marcus, Goodbye Rose,"** is the twelve year old girl an innocent victim? She goes out for walks with the old sea-captain, who talks of love and whose hand once "dived inside her blouse and clamped itself around one very small breast." Should she tell? Of course she doesn't, and only partly for fear of being blamed. She examines her own behaviour and decides that "he'd seen at once that she was not a good girl—who would object— but a wicked one—who would listen. He must know. He knew. It was so." Whether she was innocent or not is finally irrelevant. The experience has given her a new view of herself, and that is what counts.

It has been said of Jean Rhys that her voice remains young, and certainly some of her best stories are told from a child's standpoint. But perhaps the most memorable one in this collection is the title story, which describes the death of a lonely old woman. Even in this, the voice is young. The infirm and frightened old lady is that twin who is "lost, betrayed, forsaken, a wanderer in a very dark wood." The twin who accepts is, of course, the artist Jean Rhys. That is her secret, her ability to view her other self—at any stage of life—quite dispassionately. This is the truth. There it is. It is so.

A. C. Morrell (essay date 1979)

SOURCE: "The World of Jean Rhys's Short Stories," in *World Literature Written in English,* Vol. 18, No. 1, April, 1979, pp. 235-44.

[In the following essay, Morrell examines Rhys's world view as presented in four short stories that span her career.]

Jean Rhys's world, as seen in her three volumes of short stories, is a unified one. In every story a central consciousness, whether narrator, implied narrator, or protagonist, perceives and responds to reality in essentially the same terms. Rhys has said of her work: "I start to write about something that has happened or is happening to me, but somehow or other things start changing." One might argue that thus is all fiction forged. But in Rhys's work, the autobiographical beginnings are responsible for this central consciousness which we may take to be Rhys's own; the other things that "start changing" are her patternings of experience into a coherent world-view. Rhys is not at all interested in creating individual characters. She does create again and again a society of types acting out the attitudes and assumptions which keep that society intact. Her stories have the strong cumulative effect of a sorrowful, scornful anatomy of essential evil.

I will examine the four stories **"In a Café," "Goodbye Marcus, Goodbye Rose," "Till September Petronella,"** and **"I Used to Live Here Once."** These range from the beginning to the most recent part of Rhys's writing career; they are set variously in Paris, Dominica, London, and the English countryside; they include her two modes, i.e., episode and complete story; the last three show stages in the development of Rhys's typical female character from childhood to adulthood to late middle age; and these four together outline the ideas and themes which comprise Rhys's work. With the exception of the first, **"In a Café,"** in which the narrator is a cynical observer of what she later explores in depth, each portrays a central consciousness struggling to fulfill her desires or reaching out for understanding from others. She fails and is failed by them. She subsides into the only attitude or role she is allowed as others reject or merely use her. By the end of each story, the social order, in which outcasts are necessary to carry the burden of guilt for the rest, has been perpetuated.

Stories like **"In a Café"** make up the bulk of the 1927 *The Left Bank* volume and were not chosen for republication in the 1968 *Tigers are Better-Looking* or the 1976 *Sleep It Off, Lady.* Stories in the later volumes are less scornful, more detailed and sympathetic analyses. However, **"In a Café"** is a good early example of Rhys's central consciousness as observer rather than participant, it fully prefigures her later arrangements of ideas, and is skillfully wrought.

In this café, the musicians are "middle-aged, staid," and go wonderfully well with the café itself. They are capable of playing in "the serene classic heights of Beethoven and Massenet." The patrons are dignified whether they are business men and their "neat women in neat hats," or artistic types accompanied by "temperamental ladies . . . [wearing] turbans"; the atmosphere is peaceful and conduces to philosophic conversation. The alliance of respectable manners and religious certainty is made plain in this satiric comment:

. . . The atmosphere of a place that always had been and always would be, the dark leather benches symbols of something perpetual and unchanging, the waiters, who were all old, ambling round with drinks or blotters, as if they had done nothing else since the beginnings of time and would be content so to do till the day of Judgement.

Into this eternity of calm steps a vulgar Hermes, ancient phallic pillar and artificer of music, to sing about the "grues" of Paris. His song is accompanied by the piano in a "banal, moving imitation of passion"; it tells the pathetic story of the making of a "grue," of her warm-heartedness, finally of the despicable, now decorously married, hero who passes her by in the street when she is reduced to utmost misery. The patrons are embarrassed: women look into their mirrors and rouge their lips; men drink their beers thirstily and look sideways. The song is applauded tumultuously. This jolting of the habitual world of the café is brief. A calm, self-assured, fair-haired American girl buys two copies of the song. The staid, respectable atmosphere is resumed with the request for the American song "Mommer loves Popper. Popper loves Mommer," the title of which the pianist chalks up "for all the world to see."

This is Jean Rhys's world. The implied contrast between the two songs is ironic. The singer cares as little for the "grues" as do the café patrons: like a pimp, he capitalizes upon the economic condition of certain unfortunate women, and upon the "necessities" of monied, respectable men. As prostitutes are not mentioned in polite circles, he has caused a tremor of guilty unease certain to sell his song. The idea of the "grues" has been again sentimentally indulged; the individual woman is still invisible. Conventional sentiment is restored with "Mommer loves Popper": the world goes on.

"Goodbye Marcus, Goodbye Rose" is part of the latest, 1976, volume *Sleep It Off, Lady*. It relates an episode in twelve-year-old Phoebe's life. An elderly Englishman, Captain Cardew, intrudes himself into her peaceful childhood world of Dominica, shattering her secure illusions and providing her with new ones. Until his wife Edith objects to his friendship with the child, and they return to England, Captain Cardew rids himself of a temptation by giving in to it. He first clamps his hand around "one very small breast," remarking, "Quite old enough." Subsequently while walking with Phoebe he restricts himself to:

. . . ceaseless talk of love, various ways of making love, various sorts of love. He'd explain that love was not kind and gentle, as she had imagined, but violent. Violence, even cruelty, was an essential part of it. He would expand on this, it seemed to be his favourite subject.

During the narrative section of the story, Phoebe's response to all this is confused. She is pleased to be taken for walks by Captain Cardew because he treats her "as though she were a grown-up girl." She is perfectly passive under his onslaught. She remains still when the Captain grabs her breast, thinking only that he is making a great mistake, is being absentminded and will take his hand away without really noticing what he's done. She says nothing about the incident; nobody would believe her, or if they did, she'd be blamed. She knows he ought not to talk as he does to her, is shocked and fascinated, but cannot bring herself to speak, afraid that she will only manage "babyishly 'I want to go home.'" Phoebe is caught between two worlds, neither of which is secure: in the familiar world of childhood, she will be blamed for wrongdoing; in the "adult" world of Captain Cardew she fears not being "quite old enough." This paralysis lasts until the Cardews leave the island. Alone, Phoebe attempts to make sense of her experience.

The progression of Phoebe's thoughts, which form the conclusion of the story, is startling in its inexorable rejection of everything she has believed or been heretofore. The stars are no longer her "familiar jewels" but are "cold, infinitely far away, quite indifferent." Sure Captain Cardew behaved as he did because he "knew" she was not a good girl, she examines ideas of wickedness. Wasn't it more difficult to be wicked than good? Didn't Mother Sacred Heart say "that Chastity in Thought Word and Deed was your most precious possession?" that a chaste woman would have "a thousand liveried angels" to lackey her? Phoebe relinquishes the promised angels as she had the stars and experiences a sense of "some vague irreparable loss." She now understands the connection between chastity and economic security. Before, she had envied the girls who put up their hair, went to dances, and married "someone handsome (and rich)." Anxiety about whether one would be chosen in marriage is reflected in the child's rhyme:

If no one ever marries me
And I don't see why they should
For nurse says I'm not pretty
And I'm seldom very good . . .

That was it exactly.

Only a few weeks ago, like other girls, she made secret lists of her trousseau and named her future children. Now children, as well as heavenly jewels and angelic servants, are relinquished:

Now goodbye Marcus. Goodbye Rose. The prospect before her might be difficult and uncertain but it was far more exciting.

The lewd chatter of an old man has introduced Phoebe to the whole world of loveless sex and she accepts it buoyantly.

In **"Goodbye Marcus, Goodbye Rose"** two possibilities for women are presented to Phoebe. One is the respectable, conventional life she has been taught to expect: in it, chastity is a woman's sole guarantee of marriage, jewels, servants, children, freedom, and respectability. On the practical level, Phoebe is mistaken to believe this way is not possible for her: her virginity is intact. Intuitively, however, she is correct: her chastity is gone forever. Her great mistake is to believe that the life reserved for wicked, unchaste women is her, or anyone's alternative. The Cardews are "respectable" people; yet the brutality of the Captain's sexual attitudes touches his wife intimately. The supposed two worlds are one. In her turn Edith Cardew punishes Phoebe:

> "Do you see how white my hair's becoming? It's all because of you." And when Phoebe answered truthfully that she didn't notice any white hairs: "What a really dreadful little liar you are!"

The social web of appearance ("For nurse says I'm not pretty"), respectability, religion, and economic necessity traps equally the chaste and the unchaste, the respected and the outcast.

"**Till September Petronella**" is from Rhys's middle volume, *Tigers are Better-Looking,* of 1968. It features Petronella, who could well be Phoebe ten years later, alone in London. The action of this story is more complex and extended than that of the other three. Petronella receives a telegram from the painter Marston, inviting her to spend a couple of weeks in the country. Also at the cottage are the music critic Julian and his girlfriend Frankie, who is, like Petronella, an artist's model; the two couples eat, drink, and make clever-cynical conversation. The next day, Petronella and Marston are treated with suspicion by country people, the four drink a lot of wine, become rude and quarrelsome. Marston weeps because Petronella won't sleep with him, Julian insults her, and she runs away. A farmer gives her a lift in exchange for sex; he takes her to a pub, back to the cottage for her suitcase, then to Cirencester where she catches the train back to London. There, Petronella meets a stranger, a young man named Melville. They go to Hyde Park then on to what seems to be a hotel suite for dinner and sex. He drops her off at her bedsitting room, where she sits alone waiting for the church clock to strike. In this story, unexplained actions seem random and meaningless. The significance of "**Till September Petronella**" is revealed in Petronella's vague halfthoughts, in what is said, and in the gradual accumulation of symbolic detail.

The most important refrain in the story is Petronella's missing her French friend Estelle, who has recently returned to Paris. Estelle "walked the tightrope so beautifully," that is, managed a life similar to Petronella's with more ease. Estelle's bed-sitting room was more like something out of a long romantic novel than a Bloomsbury room. She brought brightness and friendship to Petronella's life; it was after she left that Petronella "hit a bad patch." She remembers Estelle at significant moments. Her sympathetic understanding was a contrast to Marston's unfathomable demand that Petronella be "gay." Back in London, she doesn't want to return to her house because: "'When I pass Estelle's door . . . there'll be no smell of scent now.'" On her way to dinner with Melville she is reminded of pleasant evenings with Estelle, who very practically insisted on the necessity to eat one good meal a day. But the illusion that Estelle is walking alongside

her vanishes: "'I shall never see her again—I know it.'" Finally, back at the Bloomsbury house, Petronella passes the door of Estelle's room: "not feeling a thing as I passed it, because she had gone and I knew she would not ever come back."

As Petronella accepts the loss of her only friend she acquiesces to what people expect of her. An artist's model, dependent upon her looks (for as long as they might last) for a living, semi-suicidally depressed and very poor, Petronella has, in losing Estelle, lost the self-respect which might have kept her from part-time prostitution. She has successfully avoided the unattractive Marston for some time: Julian's and Frankie's opinion that she has been leading him on for his money drives her away from the cottage. But it is as if they have clarified reality for Petronella. In their loveless world, she might as well get what she can, however she can. Her response to Marston will be different in September.

After her sexual encounter with the farmer, which is implied rather than stated, Petronella's thoughts and words are mainly repetitions. She is started on this track when the farmer says of her what others have said: "Well, you look as if you'd lost a shilling and found sixpence." On the train to London, she repeats Marston's words to herself: "Never mind . . . never mind, never mind. . . . Don't look so down in the mouth, my girl, *look gay.*" She kisses herself, now, in the cool glass as she had before kissed a plaster cast of a Greek head. When Melville offers her the taxi, she associates him with the farmer: *"'You have it,' he said. The other one said, 'Want a lift?'"* As she and Melville drive along, Petronella thinks of her landlord's reaction when she received Marston's invitation: "There's a good time coming for the ladies. There's a good time coming for the girls." In Hyde Park, as he evaluates the poetic phrases she quotes to him, Petronella judges Melville and every man in the terms Julian had used about her: "How do they know who's fifth-rate, who's first-rate and where the devouring spider lives?" To describe her experience at the hotel with Melville she amends Marston's opinion of steak:

> "I've been persuaded to taste it before," Marston said. "It tasted exactly as I thought it would. . . ." But Marston should have said, "it tastes of nothing, my dear, it tastes of nothing. . . ."

To keep herself awake in the taxi, Petronella sings for Melville the same song she had sung for the farmer: "Mr. Brown, Mr. Brown, Had a violin. . . . " She then tells him about her failure to be graduated from the chorus to a speaking part because she could not remember how to say the one line she had been taught: "Oh, Lottie, Lottie, don't be epigrammatic." At her house, Melville promises to write. Petronella quickly repeats what the farmer had said girls want: "Do you know what I want? I want a gold bracelet with blue stones in it. Not too blue—the darker blue I prefer." As she quips, "The pleasure was all mine," Melville repeats her lost line: "Now Lottie, Lottie, don't be epigrammatic." Alone in her room, Petronella recalls the girls in the dressing room on the night she'd fluffed her line saying to her, "What a waste of good tears!" and says aloud to herself: "Oh, the waste, the waste, the waste!" As she sits waiting for the church clock to strike, we realize that time has stopped for her. Having finally learned her lines, Petronella has stepped into a state of suspended animation; henceforth she will only be able to repeat, in words and actions, what she has been taught.

This is a fully-realized story unified by time, place, and symbols. It begins in Petronella's room and ends there two days later. References to the arts provide the allusive backbone of meaning: the barrel organ plays *Destiny, La Paloma,* and *Le Rêve Passe*; Petronella becomes immersed in long romantic novels; Julian whistles the second act duet from the opera *Tristan;* a reference is made to Samson and Delilah; the picture in Marston's studio is *The Apotheosis of Lust;* Petronella has kissed a plaster cast of a Greek head, then her own reflection, ironically recalling Pygmalion; a man named Peterson wrote a play about Northern gods and goddesses and Yggdrasil; Marston quotes poetry about unrequited love; in the pub there are three pictures of Lady Hamilton; and a club is called the Apple Tree, a reference to Adam and Eve, and perhaps a satiric allusion to Galsworthy's tale "The Apple Tree." These are like signposts in a foreign country in a language Petronella has begun to understand. By incorporating these references, Rhys is making a point about the mythical, religious, and artistic bases of behaviour in the culture to which Petronella must adapt.

"I Used to Live Here Once" is the last story in the latest volume, *Sleep It Off, Lady,* of 1976. It is a tiny story, less than two pages long, which, because of its location in Rhys's *oeuvre* gives the impression of a finale. It relates a brief, emotionally significant incident during Jean Rhys's return after many years of exile to her old home in Dominica.

The character in **"I Used to Live Here Once"** balances between memory and the present until the final sentence, which is like the fall of a tightrope-walker. "She" is "extraordinarily happy" walking alone, recognizing the setting and noticing changes. When she approaches the boy and girl on the lawn of her old home she calls "Hello" several times to them, says "I used to live here once" and "her arms went out instinctively with the longing to touch them." The boy gazes expressionlessly at her, says to the girl, "Hasn't it gone cold all of a sudden. D'you notice? Let's go in . . ." and she watches them running from her. The last sentence is: "That was the first time she knew."

What she knows is that she has brought on the cold. Her strangeness inspires mistrust if not fear in children; they cannot know they represent to her the long-ago relinquished Marcus and Rose. And there can be no return home to her warm and colourful West Indian world.

There is another, a symbolic, reading of this episode. The stepping stones across the river, variously safe and treacherous, represent a dangerous passage through life. It is as if the character has died in that life and is crossing the

eternal river searching for her lost heaven. As she walks the broad road feeling "extraordinarily happy," dangers past, she looks up at the blue glassy sky, which is strange to her, unremembered, as if she has entered a new sphere. The description "glassy" is a warning hint: glass is manmade, hard. Still she goes on, and with great excitement looks at the house she has been wanting to see. It is white and "worn stone steps" lead up to it. At the top are two very fair children. But as she approaches them, asserting that she belongs here too, they flee from a draught of cold as if she were a ghost they cannot see. If this was the heaven she had struggled and travelled to reach again, she has just been cast out by the angels, doomed to remain in the limbo of death in life she has known. I accept this reading as Rhys's final comment on life and the life to come. It is all too likely that, heaven being manmade, painted white and peopled by angels in whom "white blood is asserting itself against all odds," there, as here, the orderly and respectable citizen will be preferred to the chaotic yearning consciousness of the exile. This is what "she" and Rhys know: to be an outcast in life is to be an outcast for eternity. This bleakly poetic final vision is the most fitting culmination of Rhys's world-view.

I have mentioned that Jean Rhys writes two types of stories, the episode and the completed experience. The effect on the reader of the first is like watching ripples radiate out from a stone thrown into still water. **"Goodbye Marcus, Goodbye Rose"** and **"I Used to Live Here Once"** are intensely observed, economically presented brief periods in a life, which expand in meaning after reading until we understand the whole of the characters' lives and the attitudes of the society which produced them. **"In a Café"** and **"Till September Petronella"** are complete stories which present the organization of a whole world: their effect on the reader is that of looking at a mandala. The circle image also applies to Rhys's stories as a whole and describes her world-view.

The central, organizing consciousness contributes much to the overall impression of oneness. This consciousness is Rhys's own; each female character represents a fragment of it. Each is alone, and learns, if she can, the same lesson about her relation to the world. One might almost say that Rhys has told the same story 46 times, only finding different characters, settings, and symbols to convey her meaning. I do not mean by this to slight the real range and diversity of Rhys's stories. Her compelling rendering of the exact spirit of each place and her haunting references to earlier literature deserve separate studies.

Her stories insistently expose the position of the lone woman in any society, whether West Indian, French, or English. Money, the need to have it, is very important. Most of Rhys's female characters have little or no training, no family, no secure position. As Marston says:

> What's going to become of you, Miss Petronella Grey, living in a bed-sitting room in Torrington Square, with no money, no background and no nous?. . . Is Petronella your real name?

Indeed, these women have no real name, no separate identity; money is only one aspect of that. Young Phoebe's coming from a secure family does not protect her.

It is not by chance that Phoebe, Petronella, and all the others are exiles or outcasts. Especially in **"In a Café,"** **"Goodbye Marcus, Goodbye Rose,"** and **"Till September Petronella"** show staid middle-class men casually using vulnerable and unfortunate females and, incidentally, the disdain and cruelty of women who intend never to be in that position. Phoebe and Petronella and all their sisters are altered by men's treatment of them; in the future they will behave so as to fulfill the men's and society's original intention for them.

Rhys's world-view is uncompromising: the making of scapegoats is society's first and necessary evil. The so-called "respectable" men, the Captain Cardews, the Parisians in the cafe, Petronella's farmer, as well as her "unacceptable" but rich artistic friends, project their sexuality outside of their comfortable religious, family, and social establishments onto designated outcasts. These men are destroying an aspect of themselves inimical to society's smooth functioning: this is why Rhys's lone women are dismissed by polite society and ultimately destroyed. Stray, "wicked" women are shown to be necessary to the perpetuation of the "decent" world. **"I Used to Live Here Once"** flatly dismisses sanguine hopes for a more tolerant future, whether placed in a new generation or in a life hereafter and thus completes the circle of social relations which is Jean Rhys's central preoccupation.

Jean Rhys with Elizabeth Vreeland (interview date 1979)

SOURCE: An interview in *The Paris Review*, No. 76, 1979, pp. 219-37.

[*In the following interview, which was conducted shortly before her death, Rhys discusses her life and writing career.*]

[Rhys]: We moved here [to Devon] because I wanted a place of my own. We bought it—my late husband and I—sight unseen because anything was better than rooms. That's all we'd been in. A room is, after all, a place where you hide from the wolves. That's all any room is. It was difficult here at first. The gales came through the crevices. The mice were everywhere. A frog in the bathroom. Then when I first came here, I was accused of being a witch. A neighbor told the whole village that I practised black magic. I got very cross, but gradually it all died down.

[Vreeland]: *What a shock it must have been when you first arrived from the West Indies.*

Of course, I hated the cold. England was terribly cold when I first came there. There was no central heating. There were fires, but they were always blocked by people trying to get warm. And I'd never get into the sacred circle. I was always outside, shivering. They had told me when I left Dominica that I would not feel the cold for the first year—that my blood would still be warm from the tropic sun. Quite wrong!

Where did you go to school?

It was at Cambridge, the town, not the University. The east wind comes right across from . . . Russia, I suppose. I used to lie in bed and shiver and shiver, wondering why I'd ever dream of wanting to see daffodils and snowflakes. Then the maid would bring me this hot water bottle. It was very sweet of her. Oh, I found England bitterly cold.

And the people?

I didn't find them terribly warm. I was so unhappy in England. I was delighted to get away.

Where did you go after Cambridge?

I left school early because I wanted to become an actress. While I was studying at the Royal Academy of Dramatic Arts in London, my father died in the West Indies. My mother wrote me that she couldn't afford to keep me at school. But I didn't want to go back to Dominica. I knew I'd miss my father too much. So I joined the chorus of a show on tour around England.

How did your family in Dominica react?

There wasn't much they could do about it. Anyway I believe in fate.

But you could have gone back. You did have the choice.

I suppose so. But I wanted to be an actress. I was a very bad actress, but that's what I wanted to be. I do believe that life's all laid out for one. One's choices don't matter much. It is really a matter of being adapted. If you can adapt, you're all right. But it's not always easy if you're born not-adapted, a bit of a rebel; then it's difficult to force yourself to adapt. One is born either to go with or to go against.

In your first written but not your first published novel, Voyage in the Dark, *the heroine is also born in the Antilles. She becomes a chorus girl who travels about the dreary towns of the English provinces, is deflowered by a rich Englishman who cares for her, who then abandons her. Did you write it as a form of purgation?*

I wrote it because it relieved me. I never wrote for money at the start. I wrote the makings of *Voyage in the Dark* long, long ago. I wrote it in several exercise books and then I put it away for years. Someone described the result as "unpublishably sordid but with great sensitiveness and persuasiveness"—so I went on to other things. Then, twenty years later, fate had it that I tackle it again. I hadn't really written a book; it was more or less a jumble of facts. From the notes I'd done ages before I managed to put together *Voyage in the Dark.*

And is it still your favorite?

I suppose so. Because it came easiest.

The contrast of the sunny Caribbean landscape with the bleak English one is very moving in Voyage in the Dark. *Mango trees; hammocks; mauve shadows; purple sea, and the fight not to have a dark patch under your arms while putting on your gloves . . . the business of being a lady. One gets brilliant flashes of what it must have been like.*

It's all a bit romanticised. Now I'm trying to do it again as it really was. For my memoirs. I hope I've succeeded. It may be a bit dull, perhaps.

But the colors weren't romanticised, and the smells . . .

No, it's a very beautiful place, Dominica, and that wasn't romanticised. The mountains are lovely; but it hasn't got any nice beaches, none of those lovely white beaches the tourists love. It's a volcanic island . . . the beaches are black.

When I was excited about life, I didn't want to write at all. I've never written when I was happy. I didn't want to. . . . When I think about it, if I had to choose, I'd rather be happy than write.

—*Jean Rhys*

What did you do all those years when you weren't writing?

When I was excited about life, I didn't want to write at all. I've never written when I was happy. I didn't want to. But I've never had a long period of being happy. Do you think anyone has? I think you can be peaceful for a long time. When I think about it, if I had to choose, I'd rather be happy than write. You see, there's very little invention in my books. What came first with most of them was the wish to get rid of this awful sadness that weighed me down. I found when I was a child that if I could put the hurt into words, it would go. It leaves a sort of melancholy behind and then it goes. I think it was Somerset Maugham who said that if you "write out" a thing . . . it doesn't trouble you so much. You may be left with a vague melancholy, but at least it's not misery—I suppose it's like a Catholic going to confession, or like psychoanalysis.

Did you keep a journal?

Not exactly. I wrote things down. Not each day. More in spurts. I would write to forget, to get rid of sad moments. Once they were written down, they were gone.

Is it always a sadness for you to write?

No. Writing can also be very exciting. When you're really in the mood to write, you write without apparently wanting to. But it doesn't always happen that way. Sometimes it's a struggle, and it's very tiring.

What is the story of the publication of **The Left Bank***?*

It's an odd story. My first husband was a poet, half-French half-Dutch. He had been on the Disarmament Commission in Vienna after the first World War. There were two Japanese officers in the Allied Commission. But one was supposed to speak French and couldn't, and the other was supposed to speak English and couldn't. So they both got secretaries who were in fact interpreters and translators, and that was the job my husband got, to the one who was supposed to speak English, Mr. Miyaki. Someone in his office became interested in my writing and showed my stories to Ford Madox Ford. Ford cared terribly about writers. If he thought anyone had any good in him at all, he'd go to any lengths to help, pulling every string he could to help. He did that for any amount of people. He really got D. H. Lawrence started, and a lot of the writers who are not so well known.

In his introduction to **The Left Bank***, Ford praised your "singular instinct for form," which he says is "possessed by singularly few English writers and almost no English women writers."*

The things you remember have no form. When you write about them, you have to give them a beginning, a middle, and an end. To give life shape—that is what a writer does. That is what is so difficult.

Were there others beside Ford who helped you as you started to write?

The whole atmosphere of Paris helped, and I learned to read French pretty well. All that no doubt had an influence on me. But Ford helped me more than anybody else: "Do this!" "Don't do that!" He insisted on my reading French books and I think they helped me a lot. They had clarity. Ford always said that if you weren't sure of a passage to translate it into another language. If it looked utterly silly, one got rid of it. English can be so imprecise. Ford published several of my stories in the *Transatlantic Review,* and he helped me with money. He really helped. It was he who found the publisher for **The Left Bank.** After that there was a quarrel and I never saw him again. He went to America to live.

Hemingway takes a lot of swipes at him in A Moveable Feast.

I think it's a spiteful book. He bullies everybody. Ford wasn't at all the way Hemingway described him.

Then he wasn't pretentious and snobbish and evil-smelling . . . ?

Not at all. And back then Hemingway wasn't catty. He always seemed to me as if he were enjoying himself terribly. He was a very nice-looking young man. But in that book, he was disparaging about everybody—Fitzgerald, Gertrude Stein, everybody. I didn't like it at all.

An actress recently asked to play Marya in a film version of Quartet *hesitated because she said she found it dated— dated in that today Marya would have some other option than having to live* à trois *with the Heidlers. She could take a job. . . .*

In those days, if you were English, or supposed to be English, and you were in Paris and didn't know French well, it was pretty well impossible. I mean what job could you get? One of the things the Heidlers tell Marya when she goes there is that they'll find her a job. "Come stay with us for a little bit. Sooner or later we'll pull a string and find you a job." That was how they convinced her. In England you could get some sort of job, but in Paris it wasn't so easy. You might get a job as a mannequin, or in a shop, but then you wouldn't know the prices, or anything. Of course, it did all happen in the twenties.

It happens today. Three people in a trap.

Yes, much the same sort of thing, perhaps, slightly changed. I think, that as usual, people will do what they have to do. That's where fate comes in.

Why did you leave Paris finally and settle back in England?

I was told "You must go to London to sell *Quartet.*" I didn't want to particularly, but everyone said I must; so in the end I did. I went right to London, then back to Paris for a short time to write *After Leaving Mr. Mackenzie,* and then I came back to England, remarried and stayed.

In After Leaving Mr. Mackenzie, *Julia Martin finds herself alone and broke in Paris in such an apathy that she can only lie in bed, allowing her decisions to be made by chance: "If a taxi hoots before I count to three, I'll go to London, if not, I won't."*

Don't you think that by the time she arrived at that stage, she was rather tired? I mean you can get very tired. And then it is rather a temptation to just lie down and see what happens.

And pull the covers over your head.

That's right. I did that as a child. I was so afraid of cockroaches and centipedes and spiders.

They're so large in the Indies.

But that was nothing like my fear of *obeah.* That's West Indian black magic. I remember we had this *obeah* woman as a cook once. She was rather a gaudy kind of woman, very tall and thin and always wore a red handkerchief on her wrist. She once told my fortune and a lot of it has come true. My life was peopled with fears. I think that's one of the reasons I don't go back. Maybe my big reason.

But you wrote a wonderful story about going back to your convent school there after twenty-five years.

I did go back once. For a very short time. But all my nuns had gone. Everything's very changed. I'm trying to do an autobiography now and I find it very difficult to remember when I was a child in the West Indies.

You wrote that you have such a great memory . . . that you can shut your eyes and remember conversations . . .

That's what I've tried to do, but it's a very long time ago now.

You write in Quartet *that when you tell lies people think it's a* cri de coeur, *and then when you tell the truth, nobody believes you.*

That's always so. I've noticed that. They believe the lies far more than they believe the truth.

Then you really haven't a problem of veracity with your childhood in the book.

If I had a problem I doubt that anybody would contradict me. I don't think anybody's alive to contradict me. I try to be more or less truthful, though I suppose the whole thing's a bit romanticized.

You wrote in Voyage in the Dark *that the fantastic is what you don't do, and the real is what you do.*

I suppose the fantastic is what you imagine, but as soon as you do a fantastic thing, it's no longer fantastic, it becomes real.

And the difference between romance and reality?

Reality is what I remember. You can push onto reality what you feel. Just as I felt that I disliked England so much. It was my feeling which made me dislike it. Now I make a lot of the nice part of the Indies, and I've sort of more or less forgotten the other part, like going to the dentist who only came to the island every now and again. I'm trying to write the beauty of it and how I saw it. And how I did see it as a child. That's what I've been toiling at. It's such a battle. I can't waste much more time on it.

Have you written of your relations with the black people in Dominica?

That's very complicated because at the start I hated my nurse. A horrid woman. It was she who told me awful stories of zombies and *sucriants,* the vampires; she frightened me totally. I was a bit wary of the black people. I've tried to write about how I gradually became even a bit envious. They were so strong. They could walk great distances, it seemed to me, without getting tired, and carry those heavy loads on their heads. They went to the dances every night. They wore turbans. They had lovely dresses with a belt to tuck the trains through that were lined with paper and rustled when they moved. Then, my chief worry was that I was expected to get married. I thought, my God, what will I do? At first I doubted that I'd ever get a proposal. Then I knew I was *bound* to marry, otherwise I'd be an old maid which would be perfectly awful. That worry made one very self-conscious. But the black people didn't worry a hoot about that. They had swarms of children and no marriages. I did envy them that.

Did you have young friends who were black?

No, it was more divided then. There were a lot of colored girls at the convent I went to. I didn't always like them—but I was kind of used to them.

Was the incident real in The Wide Sargasso Sea *when you go swimming in a pool in the woods with the black girl, Tia?*

That might have happened. But the girl never stole my dress as we bathed. That was fiction.

Although you are one of five children, one gets the feeling you had a lonely childhood.

Yes, I never saw much of them. They left early and came to England. One brother went to India and spent his life there. I didn't see him at all. The other wandered about rather. He went to Canada and Australia and East Africa, then he went back to the West Indies. In Australia he got married, came to London, fell down the stairs and died. I don't think he was drunk or anything. My other brother said, "Just like Orin, he would die in a melodramatic way."

You say your motto is "not harrowing." What does this phrase mean for you?

Don't surprise or amaze or make me angry, or make me sorry about something. Lots of words that used to be quite common one doesn't hear any more. It's sad about words which meant quite a lot. I mean a word like "splendid." Nobody says a thing is "splendid." You never say a thing is splendid, or a person is splendid. Do you? Splendor's gone. Magnificent is gone.

How do you work now?

I can't write any more. My hand is unsteady, so I have a very nice girl who comes along twice a week, sometimes three times, and I dictate to her. It was difficult at the start.

Do you ever try dictating into a tape recorder?

No, because mechanical things always go wrong with me. If they possibly can, they do. If there is a thought or an idea that has been worrying me, I try to write it out, and try very hard to make it clear. Then when she comes I can dictate it to her. Of course it's by no means the same thing as writing.

Is it an all-consuming occupation when you feel you must write?

It seems as if I was fated to write . . . which is horrible. But I can only do one thing. I'm rather useless, but perhaps not as useless as everyone thinks. I tried to be an actress—a chorus girl—and the whole thing ended when I was handed a line to say: "Oh Lottie, don't be epigrammatic." But, when the cue came, the words just disappeared. That was that. I was interested in beauty—cosmetics—but when I tried to make a face cream, it blew up.

Someone wrote that you have been fighting oblivion since the twenties, do you think this true?

I'm not fighting oblivion now. I'm fighting . . . eternity? I feel very isolated. I'm not sure men need women, but I'm sure that women need men. But then loneliness is a part of writing, isn't it? Though week after week, if you never see anyone, it can become rather trying. If there's a knock at the door, I expect some wonderful stranger. I fly to the door. But it's only the post man. I've got myself a bit depressed over this autobiography. When I began it I wrote a lot about the years after I came to England and I was more or less grown up, and of being in France, and [a] lot of that. And then I got this idea that I wanted to write about the West Indies as they were, as I remembered them. And I find it very difficult, also I feel that nobody's going to believe me.

Has anyone seen it?

My editor's seen a sort of rough copy of it and she likes it, but it wasn't right. And I haven't got it quite right yet. Another worry is that I can't seem to find a title.

Did you always have a title before you started a book?

I've always known it before, but this time I can't. I've got a title, but the publisher's not pleased with it. They want to call it *Smile Please,* but I want to call it *And the Walls Came Tumbling Down.* That's what I feel is happening. Of course, I don't know. I only know what I read in the papers.

You write in After Leaving Mr. Mackenzie *that it is always places you recall in your memory, not people. Is that still the case?*

That was a character in the book who says that. I remember some places very well, but I think I remember people better.

Was Paris your favorite place to be?

In the twenties Paris was a very interesting place. Of course, I was delighted to get away from England. I like Paris. I made friends. Whenever I had some money, I'd shoot back to Paris. Paris sort of lifted you up. It's pink, you know, not blue or yellow; there's nothing like it anywhere else.

You went back after you wrote Good Morning, Midnight.

Oh yes, I went back in 1939, just before the war. The publisher was awfully pleased with the book. He rang me up to tell me how pleased he was, and I was very hopeful. But then war was declared, almost immediately, and they didn't want books . . . I was forgotten and I gave up writing.

Absolutely?

I didn't write for a long time. And then I wrote some short stories. And then there was this thing about doing *Good Morning, Midnight* on the BBC radio. And then I started *The Wide Sargasso Sea.*

Where did the idea come from of reconstructing Bertha's life—the Jane Eyre heiress who sets fire to the house and jumps from the parapet?

When I read *Jane Eyre* as a child, I thought, why should she think Creole women are lunatics and all that? What a shame to make Rochester's first wife, Bertha, the awful madwoman, and I immediately thought I'd write the story as it might really have been. She seemed such a poor ghost. I thought I'd try to write her a life. Charlotte Brontë must have had strong feelings about the West Indies because she brings the West Indies into a lot of her books, like *Villette.* Of course, once upon a time, the West Indies were very rich, and very much more talked about than they are now.

How about films of your books?

Films are always going to happen but then they never do. They had an option on *The Wide Sargasso Sea.* They even went out to the West Indies to see where they were going to shoot it and even picked the house. Now I'm very skeptical. The director and the scriptwriter went out, that was several years ago . . . They made all sorts of arrangements, but some backer pulled away. They seem to think it would be a very expensive film. I really don't see why.

Whenever you have costumes or houses that burn up, it's expensive, and you have two *houses that burn up.*

But extras are very cheap. I suppose they have to take photographers, cameras, people . . . costs rather a lot, but I don't see that it would be too much more expensive than any other.

Have you any desire to go to Paris?

I'll never go back now. I went back to the West Indies and I hated it. No, I think "Never Go Back" is a good motto.

There's a title for your book. Never Go Back.

But that's just what I'm doing. I *am* going back.

What are you reading now?

I'm reading a book of Daphne du Maurier. She's a good writer; I like the man who wrote *From Russia with Love* . . . Ian Fleming. He's one who can take you away from everything if you're bored and sad. Some books can really

take you away. It's marvelous. Thrillers are my great thing now. I must say Americans dream up such awful horrors. But I'd like to get away myself. I'm always thinking of some place to run away to, like the desert, or Morocco. But I haven't got a car; so I can't drive. It means I'm always stuck here. But you know, one gets into a groove.

But why not go to Morocco this winter?

Do the women still wear veils there?

Yes, many still do.

They aren't very kind to women in Morocco, or perhaps that is exaggerated. One thinks of it as being exaggerated.

Au fond, *I think women really run things there, though it would not seem as if they do.*

They are just as smart in France. It really doesn't look as if they are running things. But they often have control of the money. Not always, but often.

You once wrote in The Lotus *that people live much longer than they should, especially women.*

I'd planned to die at thirty, and then I'd push it on ten years, forty, and then fifty. You always push it on. And then you go on and on and on. It's difficult. Too much trouble. I've thought about death a great deal. One day in the snow I felt so tired. I thought, "Damn it, I'll sit down. I can't go on. I'm tired of living here in the snow and ice." So I sat down on the ground. But it was so cold I got up. Oh yes, I used to try to imagine death, but I always come up against a wall.

And the book, that's the reason to go on now, no?

But you know I'm beginning to feel that I don't want to do a mental striptease any more. Which would mean tearing up all I've written. I don't mind writing about when I was a child, but I don't quite know why I should go on writing so much about myself. I've had rather a rum life, but I was thinking the other day, would I go through it all again. I think not. I guess I write about myself because that's all I really know.

Thomas F. Staley   (essay date 1979)

SOURCE: "The Later Writing," in *Jean Rhys: A Critical Study,* University of Texas Press, 1979, pp. 121-31.

[*In the following excerpt, Staley examines the depiction of feminine consciousness in Rhys's later short fiction.*]

Wide Sargasso Sea was both a critical and popular success and its publication had spectacular and far-reaching, if belated, effects on Rhys's literary career. For the first time—after over forty years—her work came to the attention of a substantial number of readers. On the basis of their success with *Wide Sargasso Sea,* her publisher brought back into print virtually all of her earlier work, and the steady sales encouraged Penguin to publish her work in paperback. By the early seventies all of her work was available in both hardcover and paperback. Her critical reputation from the middle sixties through the seventies has grown steadily. Critics have pointed primarily to her strong originality and her remarkable insight into the feminine psyche, and lying beneath most of the praise, is the collective recognition that Rhys simply writes like nobody else; her talent and intelligence encompass dimensions not found elsewhere in the modern English novel. The increasing interest in her work is to some extent a result of the growing attention that has been paid to women artists and of the recognition of women generally, but this development accounts only in part for her reputation. It is not only because readers are more attuned to the feminine consciousness that Rhys has gained such wide attention, but, more significantly, it has come to be recognised that her work explores with compassion and a rare intelligence the panic and emptiness of modern life and it does this within the consciousness of the female.

Since the publication of *Wide Sargasso Sea,* Rhys has thus far published three books. The first, *Tigers Are Better-Looking,* appeared in 1968. A volume of short fiction, it includes nine stories from *The Left Bank,* a segment from Ford's original introduction, and eight additional stories, all of which had appeared in various periodicals throughout the 1960s. *Sleep It Off, Lady* (1976), a second collection of short stories, brings together a group of mostly unpublished stories, but many of them predate, at least in initial composition, the eight new stories in *Tigers Are Better-Looking.* A third volume, *My Day* (1975), is a privately printed gathering of three 'pieces', autobiographical sketches really. Given the careful composition and seemingly endless rewriting that Rhys does before reaching a final draft, these three volumes represent a substantial amount of work, especially when we consider the author's great age and delicate health. This later work does not exceed her earlier achievement, but, in fact, seems to parallel it on a smaller scale except for the last stories in *Sleep It Off, Lady,* with no slackness or diminution of her original powers. The later stories are characterised by those same qualities of subtle brilliance, acute observation, clarity of focus (in most of them), and that remarkable balance and sense of proportion which all of her mature work possesses. Furthermore, the new stories from *Tigers Are Better-Looking* and *Sleep It Off, Lady* represent her full development as a short-story writer. More ample in theme and range of sympathy, they also reveal a versatility and technical mastery of the genre that was only initiated in *The Left Bank.*

The first, longest, and one of the best stories in *Tigers Are Better-Looking,* '**Till September Petronella**', deals with a young model, Petronella Gray, who lives in a bleak Bloomsbury bed-sitter and plans to spend a fortnight in the country with Marston, a young painter. Also staying in the cottage are his friend, Julian, a music critic, and Julian's current lover, Frankie. After one night there Petronella, no longer able to withstand the tensions in the house and Julian's verbal assaults, returns to London. The story is remarkable for its depiction of the surface and underlying tensions at this neurotic gathering. From the beginning the theme is clearly revealed and relentlessly pursued. The group at the cottage and the events described portray a war—as old and as brutal as any other—between the sexes. This story is closely related in theme to an uncollected story of Rhys's which appeared in *Penguin Modern Stories 1* (1969), '**I Spy a Stranger**', which also demonstrates the polarisation of the sexes, in a condition where men and women are natural adversaries. Images of the battlefield abound in '**I Spy a Stranger**' and reflect the war that goes on between the sexes.

Although much younger, Petronella reminds us of Laura in '**I Spy a Stranger**' in that she is like those women who draw male animosity simply by their presence, and in Petronella's case it seems she is unable to defend herself against men. As Petronella unpacks her things when she first arrives Frankie discusses with her the biological inferiority of women, and from there radiate the lines drawn in this war of social and sexual relationships between men and women. And even after Petronella exits through a window, events confirm that there is really no escape from the battle.

The title itself confirms and adds further ironic dimensions to the story's theme. Dates seldom appear in Rhys's work especially as they relate to historical events, but here a date confers important meaning to the story itself. After having stolen away from the cottage, Petronella is driven into town by a farmer, and while she waits for him to carry on some business in town before taking her to pick up her things at the cottage and putting her on a train to London, she sits in a pub eating tea and cakes. As she looks around the 'small, dark, stuffy room', her eyes come upon two calendars: 'One said January 9th, but the other was right—July 28th, 1914. . .' (ellipses in text). In only a few short weeks the war of guns and trenches would begin, and for the reader the desperate quality of life that Petronella lives is made all the more ominous, and a trim and more catastrophic ironic meaning is given by the title. September, when her 'friends' return from the country, far from bringing any relief, will only confirm the underlying human barbarism on a grander and more violent scale.

Of Rhys's earlier heroines Petronella is closest to Anna Morgan of *Voyage in the Dark.* She seems to be an extension of the Anna whom the doctor at the end of the novel following the abortion confidently predicted would be 'ready to start all over again in no time'. The careful composition of place at the beginning of the story, with its description of Petronella's Bloomsbury surroundings as she is preparing to leave for the country, characteristically frames the attitude of the heroine as it describes her world. The landscape itself pulses with feeling as Petronella prepares to quit this confining life for a brief period. She had, as so frequently happens to Rhys's heroines, 'struck a bad patch', and 'she hated those streets, which were like a gray nightmare in the sun'. Instead of being an escape from the bleak Bloomsbury world, Petronella's brief visit to the country brings out more clearly than ever to her the hopelessness of her situation, but, at the same time, the experience confirms for her the need to defend one's self against the enemy. Viewed on one level, the story can be seen as an indictment of easy masculine chauvinism and sexist attitudes which dominate most male—female relationships: as Petronella's experience reveals, a woman cannot afford innocence in this world, but neither is its loss a guarantee of survival if male aggression is indiscriminate. But at its deeper reaches the story explores the underside of behaviour and feeling as human beings knowingly and unknowingly torment each other, and the ultimate helplessness of women against male aggression.

Petronella is the Rhys feminine type that we have seen throughout her novels: intuitive, capable of bitter humour toward herself and those around her, trapped in a depressing environment, dependent upon and vulnerable to men and yet somehow steeled against what she knows will be eventual abuses. Petronella has not yet progressed very far along that inevitable downward spiral of life already travelled by Rhys's older heroines, who are wise in their knowledge of men but at the same time long for love; Petronella is young enough to build some defenses, but by the end of the story she is aware that ultimately they too will fail.

The four male characters in the story have been outlined for us in previous novels; they too embody in various ways (on a smaller scale, of course) the dominant male types and display the male attitudes toward women found in Rhys's novels. The weak Marston longs for a passionate relationship and yet fears it. He is not overtly cruel, but pathetic in his weakness that allows others to endure pain while he retreats into his private neurotic world. Marston allows Julian to attack and ridicule Petronella because males stand together against women no matter how antipathetic they are to each other. In Rhys's work it seems the stronger the male personality, the greater the capacity for human cruelty. The arrogant and hollow Julian draws strength from engaging in ridicule and cynicism. His tormented personality obviously seeks release through his mean verbal onslaughts at Frankie and Petronella. He is an example of the bullying male who, having exploited women, through guilt or perversity has a sadistic desire to show them up as insincere and even villainous. Such an image of the female is necessary to justify his own uses of them. Petronella sees clearly his malignancy and spiritual emptiness: his 'beautiful eyes were little mean pits and you looked down into them into nothingness'. The confident farmer who picks Petronella up along the road after she has escaped the cottage, and later takes her back to get her things and eventually puts her on the train for London, expresses more directly his attitude toward women. He sees his pleasures satisfied by what he believes is a fair and open exchange. With easy assurance he draws his stereotype of the male-female relationship, and the place women hold in his eyes: '"They like a bit of loving, that's what they like, isn't it? A bit of loving. All women like that. They like it dressed up sometimes—and sometimes not, it all depends. You have to know, and I know. I just know."' And with that talent for flat, cutting irony which we see so frequently in

Rhys's heroines, Petronella replies: '"You've nothing more to learn, have you?"'

The final male figure, Mr Melville, the young man whom she meets in a taxi upon arriving back at Paddington, is also a familiar Rhys type. Melville combines bravado with nervousness. Although not nearly so fully drawn, he reminds us, in his stops and starts with Petronella, of Horsfield in *Mr Mackenzie*. His advances, obvious but not without a leering charm, cause the bitter events at the cottage momentarily to recede from her thought. However, she recalls Marston's advice the night before: '"Take my advice and grow another skin or two and sharpen your claws before it's too late. *Before it's too late,* . . . mark those words. If you don't, you're going to have a hell of a time."' It is this advice and the nullifying effects of the entire visit, with its underlying tensions and Julian's ridicule and abuse, that prompt her to bare her 'claws'. She deals with Melville as directly as the combative Frankie dealt with Julian:

> 'We must see each other again.' he said. 'Please. Couldn't you write to me at—' He stopped. 'No, I'll write to you. If you're ever—I'll write to you anyway.'

> . . . 'Do you know what I want? I want a gold bracelet with blue stones in it. Not too blue—the darker blue I prefer.'

> 'Oh, well.' He was wary again. 'I'll do my best, but I'm not one of these plutocrats, you know.'

> 'Don't you dare to come back without it. But I'm going away for a few weeks. I'll be here again in September.'

But as she returns to her room she is aware that it is a Pyrrhic victory, only one slight victorious confrontation in a losing war.

The theme of survival always complements the theme of suffering and helplessness in Rhys's fiction, and **'Till September Petronella'** is no exception. Rhys's considerable sympathy for her female victims of continued male exploitation not only diminishes what could be mere morbidity, but offers insight into and understanding of the ways women battle against impossible odds. It is in this shadow of hopelessness that Rhys discovers a vitality in her heroines, such as Petronella, that exposes essential truths of human nature. Her stories frequently complement and draw attention to the themes of her novels, but stories such as **'Till September Petronella'** with its subtle unity of tone and brilliant arrangement of detail remind us that Rhys's achievement does not lie exclusively with the novel.

Most of the remaining new stories in this collection recall both in setting and theme Rhys's earlier work. **'The Day They Burned the Books',** for example, is set in the West Indies. It is a story of adolescent understanding and tenderness set against the caprice and ignorance of the adult world. Rhys has treated this subject before in such stories as **'Again the Antilles',** but in this story she exposes a vengeful ignorance of which a child is the victim. **'Let**

Them Call It Jazz' returns to the exile in its woeful portrait of a West Indian woman immigrant whose only real possession is a melody she has composed in her head, which is taken from her for five pounds. She is left thinking: 'I don't belong nowhere really, and I haven't money to buy my way to belonging.' **'Outside the Machine'** is a curious and interesting story, for it treats a subject that emerges frequently but is usually subdued in Rhys's fiction: women's relationships with each other. And this story ends on a note of kindness, of one woman toward another, that is indeed rare in Rhys's world. **'A Solid House',** set in London during the blitz, also explores the tensions which emerge in the complex relationships women have with each other.

The most dramatically intense of the new stories is the last, **'The Sound of the River',** a haunting and fearful account of a man and a woman who have rented a remote cottage next to a river. The woman, who narrates the story, is temporarily moved out of her obsessional and premonition-laden private world by the horrible reality of the man's death. After he had tried one night to comfort her and quell her obsessive fears, he had appeared to drift off to sleep. But when the narrator awakens to see the sun for the first time during their stay, she realises that the man is dead, that he died the night before and that she had lain next to him throughout the night. She comes to realise, too, that reality itself is every bit as disturbing and menacing as those fears locked inside of us. The river is analogous to the rhythm and turmoil of life and its passing as it moves in its endless course.

The stories in *Sleep It Off, Lady* can be seen collectively to form a kind of thematic coda, or retrospective chorus, to all of Rhys's previous work. If the less successful ones leave the reader with the feeling that this is material written long ago that for one reason or another was discarded, the majority confirm the clarity of focus that has always marked her work as well as that certainty of feeling within that narrow world she draws upon for her subject matter. The mood and view of the world that hovers over all of her work is securely present in the stories in this volume. The progression of the sixteen stories, moving from youth and adolescence to adulthood and, inevitably, to old age, from Dominica to London, Paris and, finally, to Devon, are recognisable to the reader as an echo of Rhys's previous fiction. We can also see in these stories a retrospective progression that reveals a life as well as a substantial art. The last story, **'I Used to Live Here Once',** gathers up many of the qualities and attitudes characteristic of Rhys's art in its richly symbolic depiction of the ultimate separation that occurs between not only youth and age but between all human beings because of their fears and conflicting needs. It charts the perilous journey one takes in life to arrive at that point of impotent wisdom and awful knowledge.

The last four stories in *Sleep It Off, Lady,* treating as they do the loneliness and frequent humiliation of old age, reveal in their depth of feeling and intensity Rhys's sustained powers of observation and sympathetic understanding of her characters. Rhys's treatment of the dreadful circum-stances of these aged victims reminds us in an uncanny way of the themes and outlook found in her stories of childhood disillusionment—as though the very old and very young share the same vulnerability and the world itself looks upon them with the same sense of exclusion, but they in turn see, precisely because they are outsiders, the whole enterprise of life with a clarity of vision that penetrates the vulnerable facade of hypocrisy and prejudice which society erects to protect itself. Actually it is in the vision of these outsiders and victims that we come closest to Rhys's own view of the world and to her central thematic concerns. The most fully realised stories in *Sleep It Off, Lady* are those which treat the lost innocence of youth as it becomes aware of the adult world and the aged as they attempt to cope in a world insensitive to them.

The first story in the volume, **'Pioneers, Oh, Pioneers',** concerns the fate of Mr Ramage, a young Englishman who comes to Dominica to buy an estate, as 'remote as possible'. He weds a coloured girl of dubious reputation and attempts to 'go native'. But to cross such a cultural gap is impossible. His behaviour is regarded as highly eccentric by both the natives and the white population. He is bitterly maligned by the whites and finally killed by the blacks. On the periphery of these events, but central to the story's theme, is the young girl Rosalie's identification with and sympathy for Ramage.

In the opening scene Rosalie and her young friend observe the absurd figure cut by an elderly Englishwoman who rides up the mountain in the heat in her heavy, dark riding habit and carries a huge chunk of ice, held by a blanket, that drips on her knee. In its absurdity and humour, this scene foreshadows the more important but equally ludicrous scene which seals Ramage's fate with the white community. Rosalie defends the old woman by saying, 'she wants her drinks cold', while her friend dismisses her as crazy. However, behaviour such as the old woman's is acceptable because it is merely identified as evidence of the legendary eccentricities within the English character.

But eccentricity on the part of the white man who identifies with the natives is labelled as barbaric by the majority of the whites and occasions less tolerant reaction. In a marvellously funny scene, Mr Eliot and his wife are out looking at some young nutmeg trees and have stopped to heat water for tea when they run into Ramage 'coming out from under the trees. He was burned a deep brown, his hair fell to his shoulders, his beard to his chest. He was wearing sandals and a leather belt, on one side of which hung a cutlass, on the other a large pouch. Nothing else.' They are both shocked by the spectacle of this naked Englishman, but Mrs Eliot, with a degree of sophistication never seen before in the Islands says, '"Mr Ramage, the kettle is just boiling. Will you have some tea?"' But this little episode as recounted by Mr Eliot to the white settlement seals Ramage's fate, and he is hounded by both the natives and the whites until he is killed.

Rosalie sympathises strongly with Ramage and reveals in her sympathy a union with him which predicts her own fate. Her sensitivity will make her as vulnerable to the world as Ramage's eccentricities have made him. She is one of those women about whom Rhys will write again and again, whose special qualities of feeling inevitably lead to suffering and torment. Rather than finding support for their feelings, women such as Rosalie are repeatedly victimised by men and shunned by other women.

The second story in the volume, **'Goodbye Marcus, Goodbye Rose',** deepens the theme of the lost innocence of childhood and focuses more emphatically on the intrusion of the adult world and its dramatic and far-reaching effects. The young girl in the story, Phoebe, is left at the conclusion of the tale with her entire outlook on life shaken, but her experience has become for her an awakening, a kind of rite of passage into adulthood:

> Well there was one thing. Now she felt very wise, very grown-up, she could forget these childish worries. She could hardly believe that only a few weeks ago she, like all the others, had secretly made lists of her trousseau, decided on the names of her three children. Jack. Marcus. And Rose.
>
> Now goodbye Marcus. Goodbye Rose. The prospect before her might be difficult and uncertain but it was far more exciting.

Although something is destroyed, and 'some vague irreparable loss saddened her', there is something to be gained, 'the fun of being grown-up and important, of doing what you wanted instead of what you were told to do, would start'.

This manifest change in Phoebe's life is brought about by her encounter and subsequent visits with an old sea captain who takes her on long walks and one day places his hand on her breast. He does not fondle her, nor does Phoebe feel any sexual pleasure, but the psychological effect upon her is profound. She feels violated, seduced, but gradually she begins to feel as well that she has been initiated into another realm of experience, and somehow set apart from her friends, and, because it is also secret, separated from her family and drawn into a strange union with the randy old captain. Phoebe sees more of Captain Cardew, and during their long walks together he delights in telling her of love and passion; Phoebe is drawn to an identification with him that is no less intense because she senses something wicked in him and thus in herself. What we see in both of these stories is not only the way the intrusion of the adult world erases the protective cover of childhood from the young heroines, but, more importantly, the way in which these experiences, indirect in the first story, reveal to Rosalie and Phoebe particular sympathies within themselves to values and sensibilities which are opposed to those of the social world in which they were brought up. Rhys's account of these early experiences, although published much later, seem to prefigure the more developed and ultimately more self-destructive female sensibilities that we see in the heroines of her novels. Without making too much of these short works, the reader, nevertheless, gets the feeling that they are brief explo-

rations into the early formation of a particular female consciousness that gradually sets itself apart from the established values and behaviour expected of women. These are young women who will choose ultimately to accept the consequences in a quest for freedom. And they somehow know full well from the beginning the nature of their risk, but because they do not know men they really have no sense of how perilous their journey will become.

The range of Rhys's subject matter has never been wide, but her understanding of what it is to have been a woman in this century is comprehensive.

—Thomas F. Staley

While the early stories in *Sleep It Off, Lady* take us backward in a way, the last four stories extend the range of Rhys's own sympathies as she treats with considerable feeling and power the inevitable humiliation and loneliness that comes to the elderly near the end of their lives. These stories are remarkable for their intensity and depth of feeling; they also possess a closeness to the experience in style and utterance that the other stories in the volume, for all their polish, seem to lack. As the characters in subsequent stories grow older and approach death the narrative voice seems to reside more deeply in the experiences as they unfold and become increasingly horrible. In **'Rapunzel, Rapunzel'** the narrator, who is herself elderly, lies next to an old woman, Mrs Peterson, in a convalescent home and watches admiringly as she brushes her hair. She realises that, 'she must have taken great care of it all her life and now there it all was, intact, to comfort and reassure her that she was still herself'. A few days later a barber comes in and Mrs Peterson requests a trim and a shampoo. The barber with 'a large pair of scissors' nearly cuts all of her beautiful hair to the roots, and tells her, 'You'll be glad to be rid of the weight of it, won't you dear?' With a few clips of the scissors Mrs Peterson is robbed, not of her vanity, but of the last comfort and ressurance she had left, and shortly thereafter she dies. Told from the point of view of the narrator-observer, who can identify with the old woman, the story's brutally sad ending achieves enormous meaning. Rhys's irony is brilliantly effective because it is dependent on the narrator's cold recognition of the callousness with which Mrs Peterson is stripped of her last symbol of self-respect. And the narrator's own protective devices are revealed in the closing lines of the story, which make us all the more aware of the narrator's own struggle for life—a struggle all the more intense because of the nearness of death and rejection by the living. Rejection in one form or another lies deeply within these stories of old age. The title story, **'Sleep It Off, Lady',** the most dramatically intense of the stories, traces the fears and obsessions of the elderly to a horrible conclusion. And the last story, **'I Used to Live Here Once',** mentioned earlier, offers a concluding vision of the inevitable separation between those who, to use the story's own symbolism, have crossed the stream and those who have not. A terrifying vision really, but the power of Rhys's art has always resided in her ability to see most clearly those things within us that separate and drive us apart.

The range of her subject matter has never been wide, but her understanding of what it is to have been a woman in this century is comprehensive. Written in a style that brings form and content into a harmonious whole rarely equaled in modern fiction, her work reveals in its humour, sympathy, and understanding a fully realised and significant portrait of the female consciousness in the modern world.

Peter Wolfe (essay date 1980)

SOURCE: "The Short Fiction," in *Jean Rhys,* Twayne Publishers, 1980, pp. 32-66.

[*In the following excerpt, Wolfe discusses the similarities between Rhys's short fiction of the 1960s and her later work.*]

That Jean Rhys's uncollected fiction and the stories in the recently published collection *Sleep It Off, Lady* resemble her collected work of the 1960s shows clearly in the subjects, characters, and techniques of **"I Spy a Stranger."** This story, which came out in *Art and Literature* [Vol. 8, Spring 1966] returns to the British pastime of picking on underdogs; in **"A Solid House,"** Jean Rhys called this practice "witch-hunting." The object of the witch-hunt in **"Stranger"** hasn't a chance; as a middle-aged intellectual spinster with a background in foreign travel, she is a natural victim of her neighbors' war hysteria. The harshness of her fellow boarders outdoes that described in both [**"The Lotus"**] and **"House."** The most embattled, **"Stranger"** could also be the best of the three tales. Its people react to the war more believably than those in **"House,"** and the nonappearance of its main character calls forth a bolder technique than does **"Lotus."** The whole story consists of two women gossiping. One, Marion Hudson, takes charge of the conversation; her sister, Mrs. Trant, exists to break up the recitation by asking the right questions.

Mrs. Hudson is complaining about the hubbub caused in her neighborhood recently by her cousin Laura. One anonymous letter warned her to "get rid of that crazy old foreigner, that witch of Prague," who has been staying with her. (In 1969, Jean Rhys told the *Sunday Observer* [June 1, 1969] that one of her neighbors had called *her* a witch.) Concurring with the British wartime sport of baiting foreigners, Mrs. Hudson asks Laura, who has been away from England long enough to be mistaken for foreign, to go to London. "It's no use thinking you can ignore public opinion," she says, reminding Laura that, having only come back home as a last resort, she should not complain about being the butt of local gossip. This gossip, she admits to her sister, started with an ugly remark dropped by a Mr. Fluting, which Laura responded to in kind. The outcome

of the incident could have been predicted: even though Fluting started the trouble, Laura, who is less able to defend herself, pays more dearly for it.

Mrs. Hudson takes this unfairness in stride, even though its victim is her cousin. The traditional British distrust of intellect expresses itself in her reference to Laura's "cracky ideas." Cracky ideas to Mrs. Hudson mean Laura's dismay over the war—its origin, meaning, and impact on friends trapped on the Continent. Laura has written letters, scoured newspapers, and ordered books from London to get information about these subjects. In the meantime, she has taken to her room and put together a war scrapbook consisting of "headlines and articles and advertisements and reports of cases in court and jokes." Though upset by the war, she has nonetheless tried to make sense of it. This courage marks her out for cruelty. After her neighbors drive her to her room, they resent her for keeping to herself. She can do no right:

> She had some good clothes when she first came and she used to make the best of herself. "These refugees!" he'd say, "all dressed up and nowhere to go." Then she got that she didn't care a damn what she looked like and he grumbled about that. She aged a lot too. "Ricky," I said, "if you do your best to get people down you can't blame them when they look down, can you?" Sometimes I wonder if she wasn't a bit right.

The bitterness intensifies. The police confiscate her scrapbook, only to return it as harmless. But Ricky, Mrs. Hudson's querulous son or husband, wants it destroyed, anyway. Nor is he alone. Nobody understands the pressures Laura lives with. Nobody can afford to; it would mean suspending prejudice and challenging the majority. Mrs. Hudson admits that Laura is steady, helpful, and generous: "She paid well and she was good about helping me in the house, too. Yes, I was quite pleased to have her—at first." The qualification spells the difference between recognition and action: to like unpopular people is dangerous. Regardless of who is to blame, Laura has enemies. Anyone who sides with her will also invite enemies.

Trouble comes after the source of trouble has been removed—Laura having agreed to go away. The worst air-raid to hit the town has upset the townsfolk. Nobody wonders whether the air-raid has upset her, too. She is too valuable as a victim. Even though she is leaving, Mrs. Hudson's Ricky storms, "That's enough now. She's as mad as a hatter and I won't stand for it a day longer. She *must* get out." He is determined to hurt her. Under the pretext that her blackout curtain has been leaking light, he and Fluting try to have her arrested as a spy. (The cowardly Ricky also threatens to kick her door in until the door's sturdiness changes his mind.) Although their scheme fails, it does wound her heart. The only compassion she receives comes from a stranger, Dr. Pratt. A kindly local physician, he is nevertheless called "old-fashioned" and "obstinate as the devil" for saying that Laura should not be on her own. Seeing her whipped gladdens Ricky, who takes her to the cab waiting to cart her away. "Come along, old girl," he says cruelly, "It's moving day." When she protests, he responds with cheerful brutality—hitting and kicking her all the way out of the house.

The move to the sanitorium dooms her. "A large, ugly house with small windows," some of them barred, the sanitorium *is* ugly, Mrs. Hudson admits. But it costs far less than the one Dr. Pratt recommended. It also has a golf course, adds Mrs. Hudson with manufactured cheer, looking to clear herself for staying away from the rest home on visiting day. Avoiding Laura comes easily to her because it means avoiding guilt. It is also Mrs. Hudson's standard practice. So little has she cared about her cousin that she never bothered to know if Laura plays golf. In an indirect confession of guilt, she ends the story with the groundless hope that golf is, in fact, Laura's game.

The wartime setting of the first part of **"Temps Perdi"** (1967) recalls both **"Stranger"** and **"A Solid House."** The fragmented, imagistic story also recalls the early **"Vienne"** in its episodic structure and Japanese characters. In fact, it repeats some phrases and ideas nearly *verbatim* from the earlier work. The action does not begin in Vienna, though. At the start, the narrator is living alone in Rolvenden, a house belonging to an English school teacher who left the area in order to escape the Blitz. The war has insinuated itself into the daily lives of those who stayed behind. The two houses flanking Rolvenden in this "time of smash and grab" have been taken over by the army, and tanks rumble through the local streets. A snowfall cheers the lonely narrator, sending her mind back to a Cuban high-wire act she saw years before on her small Caribbean island. But the festive memory only comforts her briefly. Yanking her back to the dreary present is the fear that some villagers have been taking her coal. The gay, colorful tropics have yielded to the biting East Anglia winter, where neighbors steal and where everything—faces, clothes, furnishings—is colored beige.

But no confrontation with a whey-faced thief occurs. In a Proustian motif hinted at in the story's title, a smell wafts her back to Vienna. Part II, "The Sword Dance and the Love Dance," begins immediately. The officers of the Japanese commission from "Vienne" have come back with names and personalities. One, "the tallest, handsomest, and best-dressed" of the commission, likes to dance; another, who lost an eye in the Russo-Japanese War, hates all white people—except the Germans, whom he esteems as the future leaders of Europe. The narrator's husband has also gained definition; Pierre works as Hungarian interpreter to the Japanese. Neither he nor his wife makes much happen, though. Some political and military gossip promises to generate drama. But, instead, it flattens into an inventory of the narrator's wardrobe. A further train of associations leads to a reference to the Caribs, a mysterious West Indian tribe the narrator visits in Part III, "Carib Quarter."

"Carib Quarter" explains the Creole patois term, "Temps Perdi," as "wasted time, lost labor." The explanation reveals little. Right after it, the action, what little there is, takes over. Accompanied by a handsome black man named Nicholas, the narrator goes to Salybia, the Carib enclave.

As the story's title suggests, the visit falls short of her expectations—expectations created by books, illustrations, and hearsay. If the Caribs have a secret language and live off buried treasure, as legend claims, they keep the information to themselves. The day brings no uplift. The narrator reaches Salybia by riding through scrubland on a morose, bony horse. The most notable Carib she meets is the town's main attraction, a beautiful girl who cannot walk. Every visitor to the Quarter photographs this symbol of wingless beauty and gives her some coins. But the crippled girl never intended to become a tourist attraction. She tells the narrator that, though she enjoys the attention, she came back to Salybia to spend time with her dying mother.

The remark dumps the narrator where she was at the outset: "It is at night that you know old fears, old hopes, that you know unhappiness, turning from side to side under the mosquito-net, like a prisoner in a cell full of small peepholes." **"Temps Perdi"** is a looking-glass story. The West Indian who migrated to England returns to the tropics to find the same dreariness and dislocation that have always plagued her. Her travels have taught her that life everywhere is a prison. People are trapped behind mosquito nets, in remote outposts, or by crippling diseases. What looks like an escape is merely the substitution of one cage for another. The narrator has no more freedom at winter-swept Rolvenden than amid the glitter and glow of Vienna. But her entrapment does not include us. As in **"Vienne,"** wayward plotting and dim character portraits keep us outside the narrator's psychological cage.

The narrative focus sharpens in **"Sleep It Off, Lady"** (1974), Jean Rhys's latest and perhaps best short story. The work embodies several familiar motifs: cruel neighbors whittling down a spinster who lives alone; old age as a crime; a sympathetic but ineffectual doctor. Jean Rhys distances this material with great skill; her Miss Verney, the aging woman broken by neglect and derision, tries people's patience as grievously as those two other tipplers, Lotus Heath and Selina Davis [**"Let Them Call It Jazz"**]. Miss Verney seems doomed from the start. Like **"House"** and **"Stranger,"** the story begins with two women talking. Jean Rhys launches her theme by beginning, "One October afternoon Mrs. Baker was having tea with a Miss Verney." The indefinite article before her name calls Miss Verney's identity into question. This is intended: the younger Letty Baker has both a first name and a husband; by contrast, Miss Verney is cut off from life's best chances by being single, by her sex, and, finally, by her age, which is "well over seventy." But deprivation has not immobilized her. She has a project: to tear down an ugly old shed squatting on her property. The project makes sense: "It was an eyesore," we learn of the shed. "Most of the paint had worn off the once-black galvanised iron. . . . Part of the roof was loose and flapped noisily in windy weather and a small gate off its hinges leaned up against the entrance." But nobody will tear the shed down for her. The intimation that the hideous, sagging wreck will outlast *her* makes Miss Verney panic. The panic heightens when the shed acquires a totem—Super-rat, an imaginary or real rat she spots while emptying a small yellow dustbin. The fear symbolized by the color yellow (a constant in Jean Rhys) grips Miss Verney. Even after a local man mines the shed with rat poison, the rat mocks her with his presence; he thrives in the shed, intends to stay, and wants Miss Verney to know it.

Having committed us to Miss Verney imaginatively before telling us of her alcoholism, Jean Rhys can safely have the man who put out the poison attribute the rat to her heroine's tippling. This insult draws Miss Verney further into her obsession and further away from other people. As she withdraws from others, she understands less about the world around her and becomes more frightened. She shuts her windows; bolts the windows and doors of the shed; takes special pains storing and disposing of food, like cheese and pork products, that could attract a rat; cleans her house fanatically. Then she takes to eating less while drinking more. Naturally, her health declines along with her social image. A doctor who knows the dangers of loneliness as well as Dr. Pratt of **"Stranger"** advises her to get a telephone and to avoid heavy lifting. The visit to the doctor gives her hope. She feels younger, stronger, more relaxed; as soon as her phone is installed, she will invite Letty Baker to tea. Then she remembers to empty the little yellow dustbin. The chore does not faze her. The big bin that holds her rubbish is standing in its proper place near the shed, heavy stones on its lid to foil Super-rat, who seems to have been outsmarted.

Heartened, Miss Verney makes the mistake of removing the rocks holding down the dustbin lid. Although she succeeds, the subsequent effort of lifting her small pailful of paper, bread scraps, and eggshells knocks her down and clamps her to the cold earth. She still cannot move by nightfall, and none of the passers-by hear her cries for help. Frozen against the freezing darkness, she watches the road empty of people. Then she spots a twelve-year-old neighbor looking at her from her parents' gate. But Undine, or Deena, dismisses her pleas with the words, "Sleep it off lady." The cold-hearted girl who loves cold weather and whose namesake in European folklore lacks a soul then turns soullessly away. The next morning Miss Verney is found by a postman bearing a package of books for her. But she profits as little from the communication and interchange the book-bearing postman symbolizes as from her undelivered telephone. That evening she dies.

In ascribing her death to heart failure, her doctor never discovers its meaning. But this insult to Miss Verney is only one of several. She cannot avoid waste, decay, and vermin. The trash that spills from her little yellow dustbin festoons her body like a funeral wreath. And why shouldn't it? Her neighbors see no moral difference between her and the trash she lies in. The woman who had planned to come out of her lonely shell sprawls in a litter of eggshells, symbolizing her maimed rebirth. Miss Verney spends her last waking moments awaiting the assault of Super-rat. The slow romantic decline suggested in a line from Tennyson's "Ulysses" she recites, "After many a summer dies the swan," does not apply to her any more than the various symbols of communication that call atten-

---

Ford Madox Ford on Rhys's passionate style:

When I, lately, edited a periodical, Miss Rhys sent in several communications with which I was immensely struck, and of which I published as many as I could. What struck me on the technical side—which does not much interest the Anglo-Saxon reader, but which is almost the only thing that interests me—was the singular instinct for form possessed by this young lady, an instinct for form being possessed by singularly few writers of English and by almost no English women writers. I say 'instinct,' for that is what it appears to me to be: these sketches begin exactly where they should and end exactly when their job is done. . . .

I tried—for I am for ever meddling with the young!—very hard to induce the author of the *Left Bank* to introduce some sort of topography of that region, bit by bit, into her sketches. . . . But would she do it? No! With cold deliberation, once her attention was called to the matter, she eliminated even such two or three words of descriptive matter as had crept into her work. Her business was with passion, hardship, emotions: the locality in which these things are endured is immaterial. So she hands you the Antilles with its sea and sky—'the loveliest, deepest sea in the world—the Caribbean!'—the effect of landscape on the emotions and passions of a child being so penetrative, but lets Montparnasse, or London, or Vienna go. She is probably right. Something human should, indeed, be dearer to one than all the topographies of the world. . . .

Ford Madox Ford, in a preface to The Left Bank and Other Stories, *by Jean Rhys, 1927. Reprint. Books for Libraries Press, 1970, pp. 7-27.*

---

tion to her hopelessness. Degradation is her lot. Dismissed as trash, she is done in by the job of emptying trash, and she dies amid trash. She could have spilled out of her dustbin with the other debris.

A remarkable achievement for an eighty-year-old, **"Sleep It Off, Lady"** proves that, though basically a novelist, Jean Rhys can also do justice to the more exacting demands of the short story. Works like it, **"Illusion,"** and **"Petronella"** come often enough in her career to show that some of her best work belongs to the genre. Although she sometimes misfires, her voice in the short stories is usually strong and clear, and her grasp of femininity, extraordinary.

Sleep It Off, Lady (1976) brings back many of the characters, settings, and attitudes of Jean Rhys's other fiction. Just as note-worthy is her ability, in her latest book, to write freshly and gracefully about grubby, formless lives. The exiles, outcasts, and dropouts peopling the book would escape notice but for the careful attention Jean Rhys gives them, her honesty and accuracy of observation creating poetical effects out of prosaic materials. Plot, style, and mood fuse easily in these bleak little encounters; one of the most touching, skilfully pointed stories in the book is only a page and a half long.

Several of the others have appeared in the (London) *Times, Mademoiselle,* and the *New Yorker*. Many have titles that are either ironic (**"Pioneers, Oh Pioneers," "On Not Shooting Sitting Birds"**) or flat (**"Heat," "Night Out 1925"**). Most include some item of autobiography—a young West Indian girl with a doctor for a father, a West Indian *émigrée* forced to drop out of London's Academy of Dramatic Art because her father dies, an elderly woman living alone in Devonshire. Then there is the book's careful organization. The stories look at Jean Rhys chronologically, from her island girlhood through her years in London and Paris; before providing a short parting glimpse at Dominica, the book inserts a group of stories about old people set in provincial England. But the stories trace a realistic curve from childhood to old age. A retired naval captain in **"Goodbye Marcus, Goodbye Rose"** and an old nun who dies at the end of **"The Bishop's Feast"** make age a force in the West Indian group of tales opening the book. Similarly, childhood counter-weights age in the last two stories. Besides twelve-year-old Deena, old Miss Verney's horrible neighbor in **"Sleep It Off, Lady,"** Jean Rhys includes two little white children in **"I Used to Live Here Once,"** the last story in the book. The story merits discussion. In it, Jean Rhys returns in spirit, through her anonymous heroine, to the Caribbean home she had revisited physically in the third story of the book. **"The Bishop's Feast,"** a description of her first homecoming in twenty-five years. She is standing by a river, symbolic of the border she has just crossed, and looking at the local landmarks. A car parked in front of her family's summer home is but one incongruity in a parade of familiar and unfamiliar things. Then the drama starts. Two children she speaks to on a "rough lawn" disregard her; at her third greeting, one of them complains of a sudden chill in the air. Then they both go home. Their turning from the heroine to go indoors makes her see that the chill that touched them came from her. Having brought a chill to the tropics, she must be dead. Jean Rhys's tactic of delaying this recognition till the story's last sentence, "That was the first time she knew," makes for a powerful climax; the "rough lawn" where the aged heroine's recognition takes place refers to the loss of innocence and the shedding of illusions marking the passage from one stage of being to the next. Though given less than 500 words of foreshadowing, this passage touches our hearts.

The first brace of stories, to which **"I Used to Live Here"** refers, all take place around the turn of the century. The date of **"Pioneers"** is November 1899; **"Heat,"** the fourth story in the book, is set 8 May 1902, the day Mont Pelée erupted, razing the city of St. Pierre in Martinique; some letters in the next story, **"Fishy Waters,"** date the action March 189—. The book's second story, **"Goodbye Marcus, Goodbye Rose,"** varies the pattern subtly. Twelve-year-old Phoebe entices Captain Cardew, a handsome old battle veteran who has come to the West Indies to retire. Normally soft-spoken and reserved, the veteran officer slides his hand inside Phoebe's blouse, cupping her small breast, and soon starts telling her tales dealing with the violence and cruelty of sexual love. "The only way to get rid of a temptation was to yield to it," Cardew tells his wife. Phoebe is that temptation; she is gotten rid of. At twelve, she is already old enough to turn a man's head, even unintentionally. Her charms have made her a prey to danger. They have also cost Cardew his tropical idyll, his wife insisting that he take her promptly to England.

The Cardews' setback typifies the plight of English settlers in the Caribbean, be they planters, merchants, or retirees. As Edward Rochester shows in *Wide Sargasso Sea,* Europeans do not adapt easily to the tropics. The loneliness, the hanging heat, and the distrust of both the law and the police shared by the local blacks wreck the peace of white colonists. Often, trouble comes from other whites; British migrants to the West Indies have inherited the national disposition to hypocrisy evident in *Quartet* and *Mr. Mackenzie* while neglecting their nation's tradition of personal freedom. The title, **"Pioneers, Oh Pioneers,"** refers ironically to the westering spirit—the wish to start anew in the new world. The story's chief character, Mr. Ramage, arrives in Dominica "a handsome man in tropical kit, white suit, red cummerbund, solar topee." Two years in the islands change him completely. Shedding his imperialist trappings, he lets his beard and hair grow, stops wearing clothes, and marries a local black girl, an act that frets his British counterparts. (The Socialist carpenter from England, Jimmy Longa, also forfeits the benefits of white society by moving into a black district in **"Fishy Waters."**) Then his wife leaves him under conditions mysterious enough to make the local, black-operated newspaper suspect that he killed her. A "fiery article" sends a mob of black vigilantes to his home. The morning after their raid he is found dead. Though his shotgun is nearby, his death remains a mystery, along with his wife's disappearance and the outcome of the vigilante raid itself:

> A crowd of young men and boys, and a few women, had gone up to Ramage's house to throw stones. . . . A man had shouted "White zombi" and thrown a stone which hit him. He went into the house and came out with a shotgun. Then stories differed wildly. He had fired and hit a woman in the front of the crowd. . . . No, he'd hit a little boy at the back. . . . He hadn't fired at all, but had threatened them. It was agreed that in the rush to get away people had been knocked down and hurt, one woman seriously.

Jean Rhys's refusal to clear up the confusion extends an argument stated in **"Temps Perdi"** and *Wide Sargasso Sea:* Europeans cannot make sense of the tropics. If they veer from social norms, they cannot survive. His fellow whites snub Ramage because he does not attend church, dances, or tennis parties. Then the blacks savage him as soon as they see that his lack of white support will let them get away with it. As in her novels, the society that breaks the individual in Jean Rhys consists of broken individuals.

Displacement and homelessness also permeate **"Overture and Beginners Please,"** the sixth tale in the book and the first one set in England. The nameless West Indian heroine is spending the Christmas holidays in a Cambridge boarding school emptied of its students; her only English relative, an aunt, whose mean, carping ways recall Anna

Morgan's stepmother in *Voyage in the Dark,* has not invited her to spend the holidays. The story, which covers more time than any other in the book, then shows its heroine, a hit in a school play, joining the chorus line of a traveling musical comedy troupe. In the next story, **"Before the Deluge,"** the heroine is an actress from the outset. Yet here, it is not she, but a colleague, an English soprano of twenty-four, who grieves (because her career falls flat). This stroke of misdirection imparts a lesson. Gloom can touch anybody in *Sleep It Off, Lady,* the unknown contents of an attic in **"Who Knows What's Up in the Attic?"** pointing up the possibility of the surprising amid the everyday. The commonplace houses danger in **"Fishy Waters"** and **"The Insect World."** The latter story features a London spinster of twenty-nine during the Blitz. No wonder she has hallucinations and nightmares: German bombs have flattened the street next to hers; the prospect of reaching her thirtieth birthday without a husband, at one time a vague worry, has become a real threat. Allowing herself to be talked into buying a dress whose color and size are both wrong and then not eating when hungry, she has lost her will. This shattering of her inner and outer defenses has made her see people as skin-burrowing insects.

"Fishy Waters," the longest work in the book, is one of several stories ending with a final and irreversible separation. (As has been seen, **"Goodbye Marcus, Goodbye Rose"** recounts the events forcing Captain and Mrs. Cardew from Dominica.) The separation can come from a false start, a plan that miscarries, or a prospective friendship that never develops. **"On Not Shooting Sitting Birds"** makes the failed connection sexual. To please a London man on her first date with him, the heroine makes up a hunting story which she sets in the Dominican woods. The Londoner's riveting on a detail that means nothing to her causes a misunderstanding that spoils the evening. The date ends soon afterwards, both awkwardly and abruptly. Two Paris-based stories dealing with the failure to connect sexually after a sexual connection promises to develop are **"Night Out 1925"** and **"The Chevalier of the Place Blanche,"** both of which end with would-be lovers exchanging final goodbyes.

Sex touches **"Rapunzel, Rapunzel"** more subtly. The irreversible farewell of this tender story involves the butchering of the long silky hair of an Australian patient in a convalescent home near London. Mrs. Peterson's beautiful hair conveys her womanly identity. Although Rapunzel's letting-down of her hair saved her in the fairy tale, the shearing of Mrs. Peterson's brings disaster. To the narrator's sympathetic, "Don't worry, you'll be surprised how quickly it'll grow again," she answers, with prophetic finality, "No, there isn't time." Then, to nobody in particular, she says, "Nobody will want me now." Life starts draining from her immediately. That night, after a violent spell of coughing and vomiting, she leaves the convalescent home. Was she taken away to die? Did her remark, "Nobody will want me now," mean that the promise of rousing male lust was all that kept her alive? Jean Rhys invites these questions with great compassion, the narrator noting of Mrs. Peterson, with whom she had quarreled

earlier, "I can't say that we ever became friendly." The narrator does not reserve her heart for friends; that Mrs. Peterson has suffered entitles her to sympathy. A different sort of dead-end, freshened by an expansion of moral vision, comes in the West Indian story of a litigation, **"Fishy Waters."** The wife of the prosecution's star witness in a child abuse case believes her husband of many years guilty of having abused the child himself. Her belief is never confirmed or refuted. The story ends in darkness and estrangement as the English couple, the Penrices, agree to leave Roseau as soon as they can.

The story also blends different storytelling techniques. There are many ways to tell a story, and in **"Fishy Waters"** Jean Rhys moves smoothly between several of them. Some letters to the editor of a local newspaper about the upcoming trial yield to a letter Maggie Penrice writes to a friend in England about the defendant; next comes the trial, including both the give-and-take between lawyers and witnesses and the judge's summing-up and verdict; finally, a short passage of domestic realism describing Maggie's uneasiness over the trial and Matthew's determination to leave the island ends the story. Although broken into several sequences, each of which features a different voice and mood, the story holds solid. This unity comes not only from the strong central incident—the alleged beating and torture of little Jojo—but also from the plot-twist at the end, in which Jimmy Longa, the hard-drinking working man, is replaced as Jojo's abductor by respectable Matthew Penrice. Jean Rhys maintains both unity and excitement, moreover, without introducing either Jojo or Longa, the story's two main characters for most of the way.

Other stories in *Sleep It Off, Lady* call for different strategies. For instance, **"Night Out 1925"** observes the unities of setting, time, and action. This tightly executed story recounts a visit to a private club in Paris featuring "a crowd of girls in varying stages of nakedness" who do sexual whirligigs with each other for a fee. Again, Jean Rhys refocuses her narrative elements in a marvelous stroke of misdirection, the scantily clad girls serving as plotting devices rather than as developed characters. As with Julia Martin's dreary visit to a London nightclub with Mr. Horsfield in *Mr. Mackenzie,* the barhopping couple in **"1925"** show that a man and a woman who cannot enjoy each other while out on the town do not belong together. The failure of the partying couple imparts a strong aura of futility. As has been said, they have no reason to spend any more time together.

Desolation of this kind runs through the book. The color yellow, symbolizing fear in Jean Rhys, appears often: describing a sun-stopped shopping street in Roseau in **"Pioneers,"** the curtain of a boarding school dormitory in **"Overture,"** some May grass in **"Attic,"** and poor Miss Verney's dustpail in the title story; yellow-gray, the hue of an English sky in December in **"Overture,"** is actually called the color of despair. This negativity, however, need not engulf or crush, thanks to Jean Rhys's balance, understanding, and sympathy. Though ending in confusion and bitterness, **"On Not Shooting Sitting Birds"** shows that setbacks can be shrugged off. Once again, Jean Rhys's conjury uncovers, at the end, the story's narrative focus in an unexpected place: reading the story prepares us to read it with the insight it deserves. Its main detail, apparently an incidental, is the pink underwear the West Indian heroine buys before her first date with a man she has found attractive. The failure of the dinner date disappoints, without saddening, the heroine. As the story's last paragraphs show, the letdown, though regrettable, does not trouble her sleep. Her new pink underwear, which is mentioned three times in the three-page story, keeps its romantic promise. What is more, as the word, "perhaps," shows, the heroine will acquiesce even if this promise fails to materialize straightaway. It might be argued, similarly, that Jimmy Longa learns from his West Indian troubles in **"Fishy Waters"** and that the Cardews stand a good chance for happiness after leaving the Caribbean in **"Goodbye"**:

> I felt regretful when it came to taking off my lovely pink chemise, but I could still think: Some other night perhaps, another sort of man.
>
> I slept at once.

James R. Lindroth　(essay date 1984)

SOURCE: "Arrangements in Silver and Grey: The Whistlerian Moment in the Short Fiction of Jean Rhys," in *The Review of Contemporary Fiction,* Vol. 5, No. 2, 1984, pp. 128-34.

[*In the following essay, Lindroth studies the symbolic use of color in Rhys's short stories.*]

The ultra-refined aestheticism of Whistler's Peacock Room or his "Arrangements" provides a key to Jean Rhys's short fiction since, like Whistler's compositions, those of Rhys display a world of exquisitely modulated light. Her language of color, like Whistler's, is narrow, achieving its effects as much by the withholding of hues and tones as by their inclusion. Her scale, like that of the painter, is often small, revealing form and meaning through subtle color notation rather than through bold, dramatic strokes; moreover, even when choosing the larger design, Rhys, like Whistler, tends to project harsh psychological realities into spaces from which everything has been excluded except delicate arrangements of color: silver and grey, yellow and black, green and gold.

Two such color arrangements, offering good examples of this Whistlerian technique in the way they dominate the story's background and final moment, can be found in the title story of *Tigers Are Better-Looking,* a collection first published in 1968. The unfinished comparative, the device of the title [**"Tigers Are Better-Looking"**], is a trope for Rhys's elliptical method. Snobs, lying in wait for those deemed socially unacceptable, are the metaphorical predators the missing term is meant to signify. Unexpectedly, they are not only withheld from the title but from the story, vacating a space filled instead with the symbolic

colors of the tiger. Not withheld are the harsh realities of a lover's desertion, followed by a pub brawl, police arrest, and a sordid night in jail for the story's bereft protagonist. Finally, however, the physical and psychological distress deriving from these events is dissipated and the ugly world aesthetically transformed by the color arrangement at the story's end.

Mr. Severn, a London journalist who lives in Bloomsbury, awakes one morning to discover a note left by his departed lover. The note introduces the comparison of the social predators to tame tigers, explains the departure as a flight from this predatory society, and ends with the ironic question revealing a mixture of fear and contempt: "But tigers are better-looking, aren't they?" Rhetorically, the question functions as *bon mot,* giving the victim a measure of revenge and at the same time demonstrating the cleverness sparking Severn's love and, now with its withdrawal, his desolation. More artful still, the lover's haikulike question, through its emphatic "tigers," makes present the pattern of yellow and black, colors which become the symbolic correlatives of Severn's subsequent distress.

Severn attempts to fill in a predictable way the void opened by his lover's departure. He picks up two London street girls, takes them to a pub, and begins to drink himself into oblivion. Color reemerges as Severn, his mind reverberating with his lover's *bon mot,* illustrates it by drawing outrageous yellow figures on the table's white cloth: "Pictures, pictures, pictures. . . . Faces, faces, faces. . . . Like hyaenas, like swine, like goats, like apes, like parrots. But not tigers, because tigers are better-looking, aren't they?" These yellow drawings, called obscene by an indignant waiter whose complaint leads to Severn's violent ejection, furnish one component of the tiger pattern, the other appearing with the black eye Severn receives in the ensuing fracas on the street outside the pub.

With the yellow muted and the black lightened to grey, silver, and white, these colors recombine to mark a psychic transformation at the end of Severn's journey from ugliness to beauty. Rhys gives symbolic emphasis to Severn's passage through the streets upon his release from jail by withholding physical data. In place of vivid, impressionistic detail we are given abstraction: number instead of shape and color. The numbers, though, are an equation symbolizing movement through psychological time as well as physical space: "Two hundred and ninety-six steps along Coptic Street. One hundred and twenty round the corner. Forty stairs up to his flat. A dozen inside it. He stopped counting." This withholding of physical, sensuous detail prepares for a psychic regeneration precipitated by the aesthetic "whole" the light presents when Severn opens the door to his apartment: "It was one of its good times, when the light was just right, when all the incongruous colours and shapes became a whole." A window, outlined in silver, presents a color frame for this whole, a space filled with subtle modulations of silver, grey, white, and yellow. Specifically, the arrangement consists of the "yellow-white" of a brick wall, accented by several grey pigeons; a "silvered drainpipe"; a chimney with a "mysterious hole in the middle through which" shows "the grey, steely sky"; other chimneys of "every fantastical shape, round, square, pointed"—all framed by "silver oilcloth curtains." Luxuriating in the beauty of this aesthetic whole, Severn forgets the distress of the lover's departure, of the previous evening's events, of his own impoverished state; within the context of this exquisitely lighted space he feels the world transformed and himself renewed.

Rhys's method of filtering harsh psychological realities through these delicate arrangements of color operates in all of the short fiction from the earliest stories, collected under the title *The Left Bank* (1927), to the last collection, *Sleep It Off, Lady* (1976). **"Tea with an Artist"** is an early story offering a particularly ingenious illustration of the method. Verhausen, the artist of the story's title, is typical of other Parisian artists of the 1920s in that he is prolific but poor; he is unlike most in that he refuses to sell or even display his pictures, considering them constituents of his psychic landscape. The story's title keys the reader to an extraordinary occurrence: Verhausen admits a stranger to his artistic inner sanctum with an invitation to afternoon tea. Through its suggestion of tea as ritual, the title also emphasizes arrangement as a central figure, given further emphasis through the placement of color in space.

In Verhausen's studio the unframed pictures unexpectedly have been turned to the wall so that the space is organized around patches of blank canvas, with the effect achieved not by the presence of richly sensuous color but its absence. Again, as in a Whistler "Arrangement," Rhys arrests the spectator as much by the colors withheld as those presented. The greyish white of these canvases now becomes the background against which another striking, as yet unpainted, picture emerges. This is the picture of the table set for tea. Like the canvases, it is a rectangle, but placed in a horizontal rather than vertical plane; like them, it is white—more specifically it is blank space organized around color, the blue of cups and saucers and the yellow of "thickly buttered" slices of gingerbread.

The vertical plane of the blank canvas backs organizing the background space is repeated in the "straight-backed chairs" framing the table, while the "blue eyes" of the artist echo the blue of the china. The purity of the blue against white against grey is preserved by the withholding of color in a description of Verhausen's clothes, spotted not with food evoked by its color but through an abstraction: "Mr. Verhausen looked exactly as he had looked in the cafe, his blue eyes behind the spectacles at once naive and wise, his waistcoat spotted with reminiscences of many meals." Through the abstract noun "reminiscences," Rhys preserves the color harmony of her scene and transforms the vulgar and distasteful into the formally distant.

With the entrance of the artist's mistress, carrying a bag of green-groceries, the quotidian threatens the artist's arrangements, not only of the canvases, table, and tea but the still more striking arrangement of one of his pictures: "A girl seated on a sofa in a room with many mirrors held a glass of green liqueur. Dark-eyed, heavy-faced, with big,

sturdy peasant's limbs, she was entirely destitute of lightness and grace. But all the poisonous charm of the life beyond the pale was in her pose." In the picture, the mirrors, the glass of green liqueur, and the sofa on which the girl has been carefully posed hold the quotidian at bay; outside of the picture the same girl becomes "heavy, placid and uninteresting." As harsh as the physical reality is the psychological: this dull girl wholly dominates Verhausen's life outside his pictures, where the niggardly price paid for vegetables becomes a source of deep pleasure.

Two artichokes, picking up the green of the liqueur, and a yellow dog, amplifying one of the color motifs of the tea, suppress this harsh reality and restore the emphasis on arrangement of color and form. At the beginning, a yellow dog accents the mauve shadows transforming the dirty streets leading to Verhausen's studio; at the end the color motif is again sounded with the notation of the same yellow dog's absence. Seen within the context of the color arrangements, the two artichokes, whose mention brings the conversation between Verhausen and his mistress to a close, emerge as striking green forms. Another notation of compositional form, looking back to the way Verhausen has earlier touched his canvases with "loving, careful hands," brings the story to a close. The speaker's last memory is of the woman's big hands, the way they touched Verhausen's cheek demonstrating "in that movement knowledge, and a certain sureness: as it were the ghost of a time when her business in life had been the consoling of men." Through this final emphasis on pairs of framing hands, Rhys duplicates the aesthetic transformation of the mundane achieved by Verhausen in his picture of the girl holding the glass of green liqueur, and the story ends not with the ugliness of the everyday but with a Whistlerian reverie.

"Sleep It Off, Lady" presents blue and pink as the color correlatives of the worlds of dream and hallucination. First, Miss Verney, a seventy-year-old spinster struggling to support life under the burden of an increasingly threatening reality, has a death-dream in which a galvanized iron shed is transmuted into a "dark blue coffin." Next, malicious neighbors falsely charge her with an alcoholic fantasy structured around a large pink rat. In a similar manner, green and yellow evoke the real world but filtered through an exquisitely refined Whistlerian sensibility. This filtering process transforms the physical reality at the center of Miss Verney's life, the ugly iron shed no contractor will remove, as a series of color notations. Eschewing any attempt to draw it in terms of geometric shapes and volumes, Rhys evokes the shed as color. The "once-black" exterior, now "greenish," encloses a largely waste space whose focal point is an "almost dark" mass of shadows at its far end. Not only does Rhys employ color notation to suggest the physical reality of the shed but Miss Verney's psychological responses as well. For example, when a huge rat, walking with a monarch's solemnity, emerges from these shadows, there begins between the rat and the woman a contest for continued possession, not just of the shed, but of life, since from one perspective the rat embodies the threat of the blue coffin's enveloping darkness. Once again the filtering process transforms the literal focal points of the rat's attention—the ugly detritus of food scraps and waste originating in the cottage—into a series of color notations: the yellow containers and a bin and plastic pail that Miss Verney employs to hold and transport this detritus from cottage to shed. Her fear upon seeing the rat for the first time is evoked as a rush of color, the yellow pail dropping from her paralyzed fingers to the shed floor.

Yellow and green also reinforce an organizing trope of weight, heaviness alternating with lightness. The iron shed, its implacable material essence bodied forth in the dominant green of its once-black exterior, prepares for the figure of weight with which the story concludes, the paralytic heaviness of the stricken woman's body. Linking the two figures of unmoving and immovable weight is the ritual with the yellow pail, carried each day between the cottage and the shed. Here Miss Verney empties the contents into a large dustbin, its lid held down by two large stones, which have effectively baffled the rat's nightly forays. Her ritual interrupted when she discovers that the bin, along with the stones, has been left in the road, Miss Verney puts down the yellow pail and attempts to restore order. The figure of weight is intensified as she struggles to retrieve the second stone from the road: "After a few steps she felt that she had been walking for a long time, for years, weighed down by an impossible weight, and now her strength was gone and she couldn't any more." Rhys shifts from heaviness to extraordinary lightness back to heaviness as Miss Verney drops the stone, picks up the yellow pail whose buoyancy is emphasized through its contents of "paper, eggshells, stale bread," and collapses: "She was sitting on the ground with her back against the dustbin and her legs stretched out, surrounded by torn paper and eggshells. Her skirt had ridden up and there was a slice of stale bread on her bare knee." Paradoxically, as frail and light as the yellow pail, eggshells, and paper, yet as immobile in her paralyzed state as the green iron shed, Miss Verney presents a powerful image of human mortality. Like the contents of the yellow pail, she has been reduced to waste, made vulnerable to the depredations of the most loathsome of scavengers, yet her last moments are framed by colors that filter the ugliness.

Yellow is once again the dominant color of **"The Sound of the River."** In this potentially macabre story, a woman goes to sleep next to her lover, dreams of the wind in the telegraph wires, and awakes in the yellow sunlight to discover her lover a corpse. On the day before this bizarre event, fear permeates the atmosphere of the woman's mind, and Rhys employs her language of color to evoke it. Reduced to its chief color coordinate, a "yellow-breasted" bird becomes a "flash of yellow in the rain," and then Rhys composes a symbolist poem identifying fear with the bird's flash of yellow: "Fear is yellow. You're yellow. She's got a broad streak of yellow. They're quite right, fear is yellow." The atmosphere of yellow fear becomes the background for the portrait of the death-stalked man, a portrait evoked rather than represented. As in a Whistler lithotint, the lover's face is noted with line and shadow, diverting attention from eyes to "deep hollows" beneath them, hollows accentuated by the vertical lines of the nose's "thin bridge" and of cheekbones over which the skin has

been "stretched taut." Just as yellow sunlight and the lover's corpse dominate the woman's morning, so do yellow moonlight and the lover's death-haunted face dominate the previous evening's darkness.

At the core of this darkness is color transformation: The fast-flowing river, brown and "broken-surfaced" in the daylight, becomes in the moonlight an unbroken stream of silver, "frozen" looking and "curiously metallic." Transformation, illustrated through the remarkable change of brown into silver, is the story's major trope, given additional emphasis in a poem Rhys parenthetically interjects in the narrative: "You're not my daughter if you're afraid of a horse. You're not my daughter if you're afraid of being seasick. You're not my daughter if you're afraid of the shape of a hill, or the moon when it is growing old. In fact you're not my daughter." With its poetic envelope of repeated statements and its theme of fear, this first poem anticipates the second both in form and content; however, unlike the second, it offers transformation—the girl's transformation from protected daughter into rejected stranger—as a powerful complement to the theme of fear.

This transformation is repeated in the yellow sunlight with the entrance of a hostile coroner whose suspicions transform the woman from protected mistress into putative murderer. Questioning the time elapsed between her discovery of her lover's corpse and her call for help, he forces her to retreat deeply into poetic reverie. Her defense, understandable only in poetic terms, lies in the transformation of the river from silver soundlessness into living presence. Suddenly filling the empty house where she had gone to seek help, the sound of the river paralyzes her as she stands before a locked door making the telephone inaccessible. It is with the poetic explanation reverberating through her mind, an explanation no coroner would accept, that the story concludes: "I was late because I had to stay there listening. I heard it then. It got louder and closer and it was in the room with me. I heard the sound of the river. I heard the sound of the river." In a stylistic variation from the two earlier poems, Rhys opens the envelope so that the repeated statements form the poem's emphatic climax instead of its frame. And here, as in some of Whistler's "Nocturnes," even the silver and yellow of the moonlit river give way to darkness and silence.

Transformation, as might be expected from its title, is also central to **"Rapunzel, Rapunzel"**; however, its major trope is not transformation but disappearance. It is not a replica of Rapunzel's golden hair around which the story is organized, but its absence. White, the absence of color, is the story's dominant tone, introduced in the first lines through the evocation of a vision: "During the three weeks I had been in the hospital I would often see a phantom village when I looked out of the window instead of the London plane trees. It was an Arab village or my idea of one, small white houses clustered together on a hill. This hallucination would appear and disappear and I'd watch for it, feeling lost when a day passed without my seeing it." More than a vision, the white of the Arab houses is part of Rhys's color language, a vocabulary of style that functions both as form and symbol. Formally, the white of the house anticipates the color of the Rapunzel surrogate's hair. This surrogate, transformed from the beautiful young girl with long golden hair into an aged lady, is evoked through her "slim back," the perspective from which the narrator most consistently views her, and her "long, silvery white, silky" hair.

A second transformation, implicit in the hallucinatory disappearance of the original white houses, occurs when the aged lady, who spends hours each day rhythmically brushing her hair, accepts the offer of a "man's barber" to trim it: "He dried her hair gently. Then he picked it up in one hand and produced a large pair of scissors. Snip, snip, and half of it was lying on the floor." As strong as the image of transformation is, that of absence is most emphatically underscored when the barber, having cut the hair, departs with it: "He went off carrying the hair that he had so carefully collected in a plastic bag." The trope of transformation is complemented by the trope of disappearance. The white houses disappear, half the aged lady's hair disappears "under the dryer," and finally the barber makes the hair's disappearance permanent through his departure with it in a plastic bag.

A mirror reappears but only to emphasize the hair's absence, its irrevocable disappearance. Through the mirror, nakedness—the absence or disappearance of clothes—functions not as a component of the sensual but as a statement of the aged lady's new vulnerability. The aged lady's "naked" face reflected in "her handglass" becomes a synecdoche for a spiritual and emotional nakedness and presages her complete disappearance, first behind a screen making absent all but her voice, sobbing, "'I'm so sorry, I'm so sorry,'" and then from the room itself. This final disappearance finds its emphatic statement in the white sheets of an empty bed. A color displacement, substituting the yellow of a book for Rapunzel's hair, further emphasizes the stark whiteness of the bed and the missing woman's hair:

> I'd be leaving the convalescent home the day after tomorrow. Why wasn't I thinking of that instead of a story read long ago in the Blue or Yellow fairy book (perhaps the Crimson) and the words repeating themselves so unreasonably in my head: "Rapunzel, Rapunzel, let down your hair"?

Rapunzel's abundant golden hair, the means of her escape, calls attention to the absence of color in the aged lady's hair and to the disappearance of the hair itself. The deletion of the word "yellow" from the line emphasizes not only the loss of color but the impossibility of escape from the home, from age, from the human predicament.

"Till September Petronella," the first story in *Tigers Are Better-Looking,* begins with the white of a dress and colors withheld: those of a second "striped dress," the "colour of the carpet," which, although unstated, Petronella associates with her mood of depression, and the color of "one of those long, romantic novels, six hundred and fifty pages of small print" evoking a life so rich and sensuous that it expands in the consciousness imprinting it-

self so indelibly that when one sees a particular color one thinks, "'This colour reminds me of that book.'" The white of the opening prepares for the addition of grey in the comparison of London streets to "a grey nightmare in the sun" and through the interpolation of a poem on age's greyness: "'I'll never let my hair go grey. I'll dye it black, red, any colour you like, but I'll never let it go grey. I hate grey too much'."

The second scene, set in the English countryside, also begins with white, an English gentleman's "long, white face" accented by "his pale-blue eyes." Yellow and green, the colors respectively of honeysuckle and the "jug" it is in, dominate Petronella's country bedroom; these colors are repeated as Petronella stares out of the window at two still trees under a still moon, and in a blue and silver variation as she dreams of attending the opera: "I could imagine myself in a box, wearing a moonlight-blue dress and silver shoes." The white of the gentleman's face is repeated in a lady friend's hands, "too white for her face," and contrasted to "long, calm black hair." White combines with green as Petronella again stares out of the window, this time at "sheep feeding in the field" framed by elm trees, and the white of the gentleman's long face is repeated in the white of a plaster cast, "the head of a man, one of those Greek heads," that Petronella remembers having kissed "because it was so beautiful." This white is intensified both by the ideographic white of its "blind eyes" and through the contrasting "black" bars on an "iron bedstead," which "grin" in the strong sunlight.

In the next scene, the red of poppies in a garden is echoed in the red of a young woman's frock and the "red and blue handkerchief" with which she ties her hair. The blue of the white-faced gentleman's pale-blue eyes is matched by a second gentleman's blue shirt set off by grey trousers. Drawing together the red, green, and black of the previous scenes, the white-faced gentleman now appears in "black silk pyjamas with a pattern of red and green dragons." An afternoon row in which Petronella is insulted is framed by white, the "white glare" of the sun through the window at lunch and the white glare marking Petronella's flight into the countryside: "It was pretty country, but bare. The white, glaring look was still in the sky." Softening the white glare is the grey of a dove, and, of course, the grey, cooing dove becomes a symbolic analogue of Petronella Gray.

Silver, grey, and black inform a moment from Petronella's past life as an aspiring actress. Framing this moment of failure, occurring when she cannot successfully read her single line, "'Oh, Lottie, Lottie, don't be so epigrammatic,'" are the stage manager in his "'grey-striped trousers . . . black tail-coat and top hat and silver side-whiskers'" and Petronella in a "'yellow dress and a large straw hat and a green sunshade'." Running through the story is a trope of blankness, a trope emphasized by the story's dominant white, made particularly emphatic through the colorless, white face as an analogue of blankness. The trope becomes most explicit in Petronella's remembrances of the moment of failure in the theater: "'I rehearsed it and rehearsed it, but when it came to the night it was just a blank'"; and it is this "dreadful blankness" that Petronella laments at the story's end: "'Oh, the waste, the waste, the waste!'"

The blank void of the unspoken, the unrealized, and the unlived is not only emphasized by these words but symbolically underscored by the picture of Petronella at her window. Just as Rhys makes white emphatic through the withholding of color, so does she make the window a symbol of blankness by withholding all physical details of the world onto which the window looks. Like the blank, blind eyes of the white plaster cast that Petronella has kissed, the window is also blank and blind. A basic part of Rhys's language of color, the white of these blank, unfilled spaces not only symbolizes the intense moments of failure in the life of Petronella Gray but empty moments in the lives of all of the characters who so remarkably appear in her delicately colored arrangements.

Arnold E. Davidson (essay date 1985)

SOURCE: "From *The Left Bank* to *Sleep It Off, Lady*: Other Visions of Disordered Life," in *Jean Rhys*, Frederick Ungar Publishing Co., 1985, pp. 113-33.

[*In the following excerpt, Davidson discusses the importance of Rhys's short fiction within her overall body of work.*]

Jean Rhys, it will be remembered, wrote short stories as well as novels. Her first book was *The Left Bank and Other Stories*. Her last creative works were two collections of short fiction, *Tigers Are Better-Looking* and *Sleep It Off, Lady*. These three volumes bracket her five novels, but they also parallel them, for both the first stories and the final ones evince, as I will subsequently demonstrate, Rhys's characteristic craft and control and are surprisingly effective in capturing, often in very short compass, the same idiosyncratic view of life that informs her longer fictions. *The Left Bank* is therefore (and despite some weaknesses in the stories—which are hardly surprising in a writer's first work) more than just a promise of better things to come, and neither are the last two volumes a reworking of old material on a smaller scale and a sign of diminishing artistic power. All of Rhys's stories can stand alone. But they stand more firmly in conjunction with the novels and, taken with the novels, they both fill out and more fully specify this author's vision of her world.

To start with the first volume, *The Left Bank* is, as its title suggests, partly grounded in Paris and on the wrong (or right—it all depends on one's point of view) side of the Seine. But the locale of these stories is not so restricted as that. As Ford Madox Ford observes in his preface to the collection, "every great city has its left bank." Furthermore, the longest tale, **"Vienne,"** is set not just in that city but also in Budapest and Prague, while at least a few of the stories, such as **"Again the Antilles,"** obviously takes place in the West Indies, and a few others—for example, **"Hunger"**—could well take place anywhere in the

world. Indeed, the setting for all the stories is, in one sense, universal. They portray not so much different physical places but a pervasive state of dispossession and disjunction that can sometimes be discerned in even the most outwardly regulated of individual lives. Thus the narrator of the first selection in the volume, **"Illusion,"** is called upon to take some clothes to the hospital for a sick acquaintance and thereby discovers that plain, proper, and always soberly garbed Miss Bruce has for years bought gorgeous gowns but only to hide them in the back of her closet.

All of Rhys's stories can stand alone. But they stand more firmly in conjunction with the novels and, taken with the novels, they both fill out and more fully specify this author's vision of her world.

—Arnold E. Davidson

The art of **"Illusion,"** it might also be noted, is appropriately underplayed. Neither the first mistaken vision nor the latter amended one is at all emphasized, and the narration at first seems to be little more than simple objective reporting: "Miss Bruce was quite an old inhabitant of the Quarter. For seven years she had lived there, in a little studio up five flights of stairs. She had painted portraits, exhibited occasionally at the Salon." This opening portrait of the painter as a middle-aged lady is sustained not by the fact of her profession but by a few attendant quirks—how little Miss Bruce's "British character" is touched by "the cult of beauty and the worship of physical love" going on "all round her." And at the end of the story, despite her secret being known, she is still the same person. Dining again with the narrator, she briefly dismisses the secret gowns and then notices a striking neighbor: "Not bad hands and arms, that girl!' said Miss Bruce in her gentlemanly manner." It is hard to say whether this ending makes her more pathetic or less.

The other stories in the volume are generally simple in technique (direct first-person or third-person narration) but they vary widely in scope and effect. For example, the shortest tale in the book, the two page **"In the Luxemburg Gardens,"** tells of a young man who quickly passes from "meditating on the faithlessness of women" to attempting another pickup, as apparently reported by the Garden itself (the Garden has witnessed many such scenes). **"Trio"** is also most brief, a three-page sketch describing three blacks thoroughly and quite incongruously enjoying themselves in a Paris restaurant, but it resonates with larger implications when the narrator notes, in the final sentence, how the scene observed reminds her of her own lost Antilles. **"Vienne,"** however, at some sixty pages, is almost a novelette. The retrospective narrator of this work weaves, through what only at first might seem a series of disconnected memories, a persuasive picture of life at the edge in the Europe of the twenties—individuals straying beyond the boundaries of the law in countries approaching the verge of social collapse.

As even the titles suggest—**"In a Café," "Mannequin"**—a number of the selections in *The Left Bank* are almost slice-of-life sketches. Some of these are clearly sliced so as to serve up obvious indications of social injustice and brutality. **"From a French Prison,"** for example, centers on an old man and a small boy (perhaps his grandson) who, visiting an inmate, are as hopelessly caught in the rules of the prison as is the prisoner in the prison itself. Or, in **"The Sidi,"** we see an Arab imprisoned (perhaps unjustly) and then callously killed through violence and neglect while he is awaiting trial. Or still other stories briefly show different sides of the same suffering, as when **"Hunger"** (a first-person meditation on how it feels to go five days without food) is immediately followed by **"Discourse of a Lady Standing a Dinner to a Down-and-out Friend"** (a first-person musing on how awkward it is when an acquaintance does not manage her life better).

Other works, however, are more oblique and problematical renderings of inescapable human limitations and also of the partial transcending of those limitations. Thus the probably mad painter in **"Tea with an Artist"** cannot bring himself to part with any of his paintings, but he does impressive work. His wife, a former prostitute, has the soul of a peasant. He knows that she will sell or simply burn all of the paintings the moment he is dead. Yet the two of them, in their odd way, are happy, and she, with her total indifference to his art, has, paradoxically, become its best subject. And even more problematic is Dolly Dufreyne of **"In the Rue de l'Arrivée."** This protagonist tries to drink herself into a mental stupor as an escape from her despair at recognizing how low she has already sunk. Having sunk still lower and going home drunk, she is accosted by a fellow denizen of the lower depths whom she insults for trying to pick her up. When she receives sympathy instead of a countering insult, she begins to see, with "extraordinary clearsightedness," that only the "hopeless" and the "unhappy" can be "starkly sincere" and thus samples "some of the bitter and dangerous voluptuousness of misery." Only the fact that we are also told that she was "weeping gently but not unhappily" swings this delicate balance of small victory and utter defeat a little to the positive side.

But perhaps the most successful early tale is **"Vienne."** This last story in *The Left Bank,* like the first one, turns full circle but in a larger and more complicated circle. The narrator begins with the fact that, except for a "few snapshots," Vienna has all "slipped away." She goes on to remember her life there with her husband and their small circle of acquaintances, particularly noting the love affairs of one friend and the different women he took until one more capable woman thoroughly took him. She recollects her rise in the world, as her husband's financial dealings—which he would not at the time discuss with her—succeeded, and how she found him considerably more voluble in Budapest when his bubble schemes had burst and, well into his employer's money, he faced the prospect of prison; how she talked him out of the suicide he melodra-

matically but not too seriously contemplated; how they made their way across the frontiers of countries preparing for war or revolution; how, in Prague, they went for one last ride in their fancy car (which was already sold), while she hoped that he would understand, would crash it, and she would "scream with laughter at old hag Fate because I was going to give her the slip," but he only—the story's end—returned them to their hotel.

Of course the retrospective narration has indicated from the first that **"Vienne"** will not end with the protagonist's demise. But it makes no triumph out of her continuing survival either. Indeed, the death she did not gain in the last paragraphs allows her precisely those other limited possessions—the "few snapshots"—that she can still claim in the story's beginning. A life redeemed only by a few photographs is still very much in question, which is to say that, in prospect and retrospect, the narrator valorizes the death that eluded her. But matters are not that simple either; the deeper irony in **"Vienne"** is that the story itself becomes both an extension and an analogue of those early noted photographs. Mixing memory and desire, the narrator transforms the disconnected sketches which make up her account into a series of moving pictures that are equally the record of her possession and her loss.

"La Gross Fifi" from *The Left Bank* also merits brief assessment both for its intrinsic quality (Thomas Staley finds it "the most sustained narrative in the collection") [in *Jean Rhys,* 1979] and for the way in which it anticipates other stories that Rhys will publish some fifty years later. Roseau, the narrator of the work, is a young woman at loose ends in the south of France. She is staying in a disreputable resort hotel, is in the process of being left by the latest man in her life, and is ambivalently acquainted with a few more proper vacationers whose petty hypocrisies assure her that she does not want to belong to their world but whose cutting cliquishness also attests that being excluded carries its disadvantages too.

The center of the story, however, is Francine (Fifi) Carly, and a very imposing center she is—vastly overweight, rakishly overdressed, forty-eight, and frequently attended by a strikingly handsome gigolo just half her age. Roseau has to explain to one of her English acquaintances, a young husband who has joined her for a drink in her hotel restaurant, that, no, "the gentleman" with Fifi is not her son, and then she also has to explain just what it is that he is: "Don't you know what a gigolo is? They exist in London, I assure you. She keeps him—he makes love to her. I know all about it because their room's next to mine!" But if Roseau can hear Fifi in love, Fifi can also hear Roseau in loneliness. That same night the older woman, prompted by the younger woman's weeping, comes into her room, tenderly undresses her and puts her to bed, maternally comforts and counsels her, and becomes a kind of improper friend in obvious contrast to the proper ones.

Fifi's advice is simple and to the point: "One nail drives out the other nail." Roseau is still young and beautiful. Fifi will help her to find another man perhaps more "chic" than the last one. That advice is soon given more point by the fact that it might well apply to Fifi too, who definitely is not young and beautiful. The next morning, when Fifi's gigolo returns after having been away all night, Roseau hears the two of them quarreling bitterly and then passionately making up. A week later, however, he is gone again, this time for a longer time. "Fifi in ten days grew ten years older," and not just because she has been abandoned but also because of the not-so-covert sneers and jeers that the abandonment elicits from all the proper people who never approved of Fifi and her gigolo in the first place.

The story ends with the gigolo returned again, with Fifi "radiant" at the "triumph" of the second reconciliation and agreeing to celebrate the event by an excursion to Monte Carlo, with Roseau reading in the next day's newspaper of "YET ANOTHER DRAMA OF JEALOUSY." A young man has killed his older mistress. "Questioned by the police he declared," the account states, "that he acted in self-defense as his mistress, who was of a very jealous temperament, had attacked him with a knife when told of his approaching marriage." The following morning Roseau decides that she must leave the hotel. As she is packing, she comes across a book of French poetry that Fifi had earlier given her and reads one passage that particularly appealed to Fifi: *"Maintenant je puis marcher légère, / J'ai mis toute ma vie aux mains de mon amant,"* which was earlier translated in the story as "I can walk lightly for I have laid my life in the hands of my lover." Roseau then weeps "heartbroken" for "poor Fifi" until "she imagined that she saw her friend's gay and childlike soul, freed from its gross body, mocking her gently for her sentimental tears," whereupon "she dried her eyes and went on with her packing."

The story closes on that problematic note. There is something suspect, for Roseau, when she weeps, and there is something suspect, for the reader, when she stops. This contradictory and inconclusive ending is not resolved by arguing, as does Peter Wolfe, [in *Jean Rhys,* 1980] that a crucial line from the poem underlies Roseau's tears: *"J'ai mis toute ma vie aux mains de mon amant,"* this critic maintains, "tells [Roseau] that she could never love as wildly or as beautifully as Fifi." Taken in context, however, the line hardly validates wild love. Fifi did put her life in the hands of her lover, and the story graphically attests to what end. He threw her—her love and her life—away; first and figuratively by leaving her for another woman, second and finally by murdering her when she made a fuss about it (and of course he murdered her, for even if she had attacked him—which is highly unlikely given what we have already seen of Fifi—once he had taken the knife from her he certainly does not have to stab her to death to keep her from injuring him). A better reading is Staley's suggestion that "the power of the story resides in Roseau's implicit recognition that her life is somehow anticipated by Fifi." In short, it is herself that Roseau weeps for, and it is also Roseau who knows that those tears are futile. There is a Fifi in her future; the most that she can do is be ready to meet, with something of Fifi's elan, an older, sadder version of herself. One nail drives out another in more ways than one.

The youthful author of **"La Gross Fifi"** creates a character who reads in an older other woman something of what her own fate will probably be. Some fifty years later Jean Rhys can acknowledge just how valid that early written reading was. "Old age, she admits," paraphrased at the conclusion of Judith Thurman's 1976 profile, [in *Ms.,* January 1976] "is as terrible as she always knew it would be." And at the conclusion of her career she can write firsthand about what she then knew firsthand. Some of the most impressive stories in both *Tigers Are Better-Looking* and *Sleep It Off, Lady* as well as the final tales in each volume (not considering the selections from *The Left Bank* reprinted in *Tigers Are Better-Looking*) are studies of old age and impending death in which Rhys graphically portrays the burgeoning ills that declining flesh is necessarily heir to.

One of the best of these late works is the penultimate tale in *Sleep It Off, Lady,* a tale which also provides that volume with its title. The protagonist of [**"Sleep It Off, Lady"**] is Miss Verney, an elderly spinster of "certainly well over seventy" who lives alone in a small rural cottage. She is at first mostly content with that arrangement but is perturbed by a singularly ugly shed that comes with her property and that, decrepit and dilapidated as it is, still threatens to outlast her. She is even more perturbed when she discovers that a large rat has taken up residence in the shed. She observes the rat walk regally across its dominion (*"I'm the monarch of all I survey. / My right, there is none to dispute"*), and soon discovers just how valid the Gilbert and Sullivan claim that she voiced for the creature actually is. Certainly she cannot dispute the rat's rights, while everyone disputes hers. The local builder who first agrees to tear down the shed simply does not come at the promised times, which presently conveys to the old lady the clear message that he has no intention of doing the job. A representative from a larger firm in a nearby town comes once but only to assure her that he knows better than she what it is that she should do. The shed might be used as a garage by the next residents, and she doesn't want to decrease the value of her property, does she? A local man first puts out poison and then wonders aloud, when that doesn't work, if perhaps the rat weren't pink. The neighbors know that Miss Verney drinks.

The rat that occupies her shed soon occupies, in a different sense, her cottage too. Morbidly afraid of the animal, she tries not to think of it, but nevertheless it dominates her life. She almost barricades herself in her house; is careful about how she opens even a window; and "spent hours every day sweeping, dusting, arranging the cupboards and putting fresh paper into the drawers"—as if a rat on the premises well might be the immediate result of even the smallest oversight in one's housecleaning. She even dreams about the rat at night. Thus preoccupied, her life changes. She no longer goes for walks or visits with her neighbors. She eats less and drinks more. Her health suffers, which soon brings her to a doctor's attention. He prescribes pills, a telephone, and no strenuous work.

She is still buoyed up by even this small sign of concern. The next day she has, she thinks, put the rat behind her and looks forward to installing a telephone, to talking again with her acquaintances. Then, late in the day, she remembers that she has not yet taken the garbage out. But the bin is not where it should be and neither are the heavy stones used to keep the lid on (and the rat out). Struggling to get everything in its proper place, she suffers some kind of a stroke, collapses, and discovers that she cannot move even after she has recovered consciousness. Helpless on the ground, "surrounded by torn paper and eggshells," she can only call for help. Her predicament is noted only by the ominously odd daughter—a girl who never plays or smiles—of a neighbor. Asked to have her mother call for help, the girl answers: "It's no good my asking mum. She doesn't like you and she doesn't want to have anything to do with you. She hates stuck up people. Everybody knows that you shut yourself up to get drunk." The "horrible child" concludes, "Sleep it off, lady," and went "skipping away." Miss Verney can only lie in the deepening darkness waiting for the advent of "Super Rat." She is discovered unconscious the next morning and dies soon after of, the doctor concludes, shock and cold and her heart condition. "Very widespread now—a heart condition."

These last words, presumably the doctor's, ironically sum up the impetus of the whole story of this protagonist dispossessed. In the present tense of the narration Miss Verney was given no past, no abiding story to speak of, nor was she allowed even the distinguishing mark of a noticed first name. Her death too is robbed of substance and dignity and not just by its grotesque circumstances and brutal cause but also by the way it is so readily reduced to something apt, appropriate, expected, and dismissed. Furthermore and as Wolfe rightly emphasizes, the protagonist's demise perfectly symbolizes her society's view that the proper place for the aged is some figurative dust bin. The prevalence of that view tells us, of course, just how validly the doctor spoke even as he definitely misdiagnosed who it was that suffered from that widespread heart condition.

Or we might briefly consider the three late stories in *Tigers Are Better-Looking* as studies of characters at the end of their tether. In **"The Lotus,"** for example, an older woman living in a dank basement apartment tries to claim a small place in the lives of a young couple higher up in the building and the world. The husband is willing to patronize Lotus Heath as an amusing "old relic of the past," but his wife will not tolerate the other woman and drives her away with crude insults such as comments on her "awful" odor of "whisky" mixed with "mustiness." Later that same night Lotus goes out drunk and naked into the street. She is soon picked up by the police who return her to the building and try to find out something about her. Questioned, the young man claims to know "nothing" of the disreputable woman and neither, he asserts, does anyone else. And he is, of course, quite right, but not in the sense imagined. The story ends with the husband back in his quarters "admiring the way Christine [had] ignored the whole sordid affair" and preparing to make love to his "lovely child" of a wife. Time will inevitably acquaint these two with just what it was that troubled Lotus Heath.

The subsequent **"A Solid House"** takes place during the London Blitz, but the protagonist, identified only as Teresa, is much more affected by the slow collapsing of her own life than by any falling German bombs. She had earlier sought death through an overdose of (probably sleeping) pills only to dream ("But were they dreams?") of a journey through a landscape that—with a still and leaf-clogged river, an "empty and dilapidated house," a rocking horse beneath a tree, and two oddly emblematic statues of a man and woman—was as poetically evocative of death as the journey described in Emily Dickinson's "Because I Could Not Stop for Death." When her suicide fails, she takes refuge in another dwelling. Correlative to that surviving life is the structure in which it continues, "the solid house of the story's title [that] stands in a bomb-gutted city and lodges frightened, broken tenants. Presiding over this establishment is Miss Spearman, a sharp, angular, and nearly deaf old woman from whom Teresa imagines she might learn "the real secret" of "how to be exactly like everybody else" and thereby survive in the world. But Miss Spearman's "sidelines" are secondhand ladies' clothes and secondhand spiritualism. She has no serviceable secrets to impart, nor is there a place in the house for Teresa, who at the conclusion of this subtly rendered and imagistically effective tale is figuratively turning again towards the suicide that earlier eluded her.

The protagonist in the last of these three stories, **"The Sound of the River,"** survives no better. An older couple vacationing in a cottage near a river are trying to be happy despite the continuous rain and the woman's pervasive forebodings—forebodings that prove true one morning when she discovers that the man lying beside her has died during the night. The nightmare that this protagonist awoke to on that "first fine day" continues, in a kind of Kafka sense, as she runs, seemingly without moving, to the nearest telephone to call a doctor; finds the neighbor away and the room in which he keeps his telephone locked; finally breaks into the room to reach a doctor who obviously does not believe her story when he arrives on the scene and pointedly wonders why he was summoned so tardily and did she not really know in the night that what she "thought . . . was a dream" was actually the man dying. Yet Staley still suggests that "the woman, who narrates the story, is temporarily moved out of her obsessional and premonition-laden private world by the horrible reality of the man's death." His death, however, hardly makes her world less private nor proves her premonitions false, and by the same token of that death she has been consigned to a rather more threatening public world (the suspicions of the doctors) than the one she previously inhabited.

Even the death described in **"Sleep It Off, Lady"** might seem preferable to the enduring portrayed in these three grim tales. Yet any comforting consideration that the end of life should mark the end of suffering too is countered by **"I Used to Live Here Once,"** a two-page sketch that, coming immediately after the title story, concludes *Sleep It Off, Lady*. This appropriately final work in Rhys's fictional canon tells of a woman who, returning to what used to be her home, tries vainly to speak to two children playing in the yard. She is finally noticed but only as a sudden chill that sends the children "running across the grass to the house." And "that was the first time she knew." In eternity she has become what she was in time, a disturbing presence preferably overlooked. In short, what she is is a pathetic, yearning ghost. As A. C. Morrell, in "The World of Jean Rhys's Short Stories," [in *World Literature Written in English,* 18, 1979], rightly observes: "The bleakly poetic final vision is the most fitting culmination of Rhys's world-view."

The stories in the last two collections do not, however, all focus on the old, the dying, or the dead. They do not all center on unrelieved human setbacks and suffering either. **"Outside the Machine,"** for example, concludes with one woman patient in a hospital giving another, who is being turned out with no money and before she is ready to take care of herself, an unexpected gift of cash. If the sum is not enough to buy the recipient back "to life again," it is still "enough for a week or perhaps two" and is most welcome. Or **"Let Them Call It Jazz"** ends on an even more muted note of triumph. Selina Davis, a black from the West Indies who is not at all at home in London (and a narrator whose "bubbling, colorful language" is one of Rhys's "great triumph[s]" as a short story writer [Wolfe, *Jean Rhys*]) has finally found a small place for herself but that place has cost her her chief possession. The Holloway song (which she learned in Holloway prison) has been taken from her for a song. Some one heard her whistle it at a friend's apartment, set it down, sold it, and out of gratitude gave her five pounds. The gift at first galls: "For after all, that song was all I had. I don't belong nowhere really, and I haven't money to buy my way to belonging." But soon Selina realizes her grief is all "foolishness," for "even if they played it on trumpets . . . no walls would fall so soon. 'So let them call it jazz,' I think, and let them play it wrong. That won't make no difference to the song I heard." While the five pounds can make a small difference to her: "I buy myself a dusty pink dress with the money."

Such gains, small as they are, are rare in Rhys's fiction. The predominant direction of all the stories, including those in *The Left Bank,* is down. The characters who follow that downward course are also almost all women. As Morrell observes, Rhys's "stories insistently expose the position of the lone woman in any society, whether West Indian, French, or English." That position is tenuous at best and particularly so, as Rhys shows in her late tales, for the elderly woman who has lost her youth and beauty, the capital whereby a woman is supposed to purchase a place in the world. Indeed, the plight of Rhys's older protagonists is simply the logical extension of the problems faced by their younger sisters in the other short stories and the novels. In this sense the fiction is all of a piece. "It is [Rhys's] recurrent, almost obsessive theme, that women are permanent and perpetual victims of masculine society" both in its "individual" manifestations and its "institutionalised" ones. Rosalind Miles's generalizations [in *The Fiction of Sex: Themes and Functions of Sex Difference in the Modern Novel,* 1974] apply as much to the stories as the novels and aptly emphasizes the social implications of the former as well as the latter.

So if the stories "expose the position of the lone woman in . . . society," that isolated woman also exposes the society.

Society is portrayed in most of the stories as stripped down (or stripping down) to some of its barer brutalities. Chief among these brutalities is a violence against women that is so endemic it need not even be recognized as violence. Thus in **"Rapunzel, Rapunzel,"** from *Sleep It Off, Lady,* a patient in a hospital, an older woman obviously proud of her "long, silvery white, silky hair," asks the visiting barber to just trim the ends, but he practically shears her and then callously comments, "You'll be glad to be rid of the weight of it, won't you dear?" His motive is merely to show that he can do unto her whatever he pleases and can charge her for the injury too. Bereft of what was most important in her life, she suffers a total collapse, weeps continuously, and perhaps even dies (the issue is left deliberately unclear) at the end of the story. Or the violence can be more pointed and its motives much more obvious, as when another hospital patient, a chorus girl and one of the minor characters in **"Outside the Machine,"** briefly describes for the other patients a recent theatrical brouhaha. A stagehand had tried to kiss one of the dancers; she had smacked him; he had hit her back; the dancers insisted the man be fired; they had to strike before he was let go; and consequently, this narrator concludes, the stagehands so "hate us" that "we have to go in twos to the lavatory." Later in the story a parson visits the hospital and preaches to the patients on the virtues of forbearance and the vices of rebellion. "God is a just God," he insists, and "man, made in His image, is also just. On the whole. And so, dear sisters, let us try to live useful, righteous and God-fearing lives in that state to which it has pleased Him to call us. Amen." The stagehands' hatred and the preacher's homily expound equally the same text.

Other violences are also present in Rhys's world but are more glancingly observed. As already implicitly suggested, racial animosities underlie **"Let Them Call It Jazz."** Selina, suddenly evicted by her Notting Hill landlord, is no doubt another innocent casualty of the Notting Hill riots of 1958. Several of the stories set in the West Indies, such as **"The Day They Burned the Books"** from *Tigers Are Better-Looking* or **"Pioneers, Oh, Pioneers"** from *Sleep It Off, Lady,* also turn on racial tensions. Or war is seen in other tales. **"A Solid House,"** set, as noted, in World War II, begins with Teresa and Miss Spearman waiting out a bombing raid. I would also here observe how effectively **"Till September Petronella"** (one of the best stories in *Tigers Are Better-Looking*) is inobtrusively dated as taking place towards the end of July and in 1914. World War I will break out in one more week. Full mobilization for that wasteful combat will begin. The various young men who were pledged to reappear, come September, in Petronella's empty life will likely find that they have other dates to keep. Mass killing can also be done quite naturally. The most graphic destruction portrayed in Rhys's fiction is in **"Heat,"** the brief account in *Sleep It Off, Lady* of "Mont Pelée's eruption and the death of some 40,000 people."

The volcano that destroyed the Martinique city of St. Pierre is beyond control by man. Man's own violence, however, is another matter. But that latter violence is rationalized or denied by its perpetrators, not condemned or controlled. In other words, hypocrisy runs a close second to violence in all of the stories, and in some of them the contest is too close to call. For example, in **"Fishy Waters"** from *Sleep It Off, Lady,* the brutal assault on a very young black girl brings a disreputable white man to trial. Guilty of a smaller violence against the girl (he had threatened to saw her in half when her screams disturbed him), he is deemed guilty of the larger violence too. But after the trial the wife of the proper witness whose testimony convicted the other man begins to realize that her husband was probably the guilty party. And hypocrisy is even more central in the title story in *Tigers Are Better-Looking,* a story that itself takes its title from a brief passage early in the work: "I got a feeling that I was surrounded by a pack of timid tigers waiting to spring the moment anybody is in trouble or hasn't any money. *But tigers are better-looking aren't they?*" The tiger may eat you but it won't pretend that it is your friend first, as did Heather in this tale when she took her new acquaintances to a bar where they could be taken (and she presumably receive part of the take). The tiger has the courage of its hungry convictions and does not calculate the state of your pocketbook (as do various characters in the story as well as the police) before it springs.

The beast that springs in Jean Rhys's stories is no tiger at all but simply the world in which her characters live; the spring is typically some forced recognition of the nature of that world. So here too the short fictions supplement the longer ones to give us other versions of the Rhys heroine and other justifications for how she came to be like that. Indeed, one of the best justifications for the Rhys heroine is **"Goodbye Marcus, Goodbye Rose,"** and I will accordingly conclude with this emblematic tale from *Sleep It Off, Lady* that effectively sets forth, both in the text and beyond it, the disconcerting validity of Rhys's vision.

The title of the story perfectly sums up the denouement of its problematic plot. Phoebe, a twelve-year-old West Indies girl, has been strangely taken up by a visiting Captain Cardew, a "very handsome old man" and a former military "hero." He gives her boxes of chocolates, takes her on long walks, and in general treats her "as though she were a grown-up girl." In fact, on one of their excursions, he informs her that she will "soon . . . be old enough to have a lover," and immediately his "hand dived inside her blouse and clamped itself around one very small breast." Phoebe cannot cope with that action (she imagines that it is a "mistake" that he will rectify without even noticing) nor is she comfortable with his subsequent attentions that take the form of long discourses on the varieties and the violence of love. She knows that if she talked to anyone about the captain she would be both blamed and not believed. She does not know how to extricate herself without seeming babyish. She is also fascinated as well as shocked and is drawn into a complicity in this sick courtship, which soon ends with the Captain's wife condemn-

ing the girl for all that has happened and then arranging to return with her husband to England. Phoebe, left to figure out for herself what it all means, can only deduce that everything has somehow been her fault, "that he'd seen at once she was not a good girl—who would object—but a wicked one—who would listen. He must [have known]." At the end of the story she is trying to accommodate herself to this new conception of herself. So goodbye to the preteen dreams of a proper marriage and the children that she was going to have. **"Goodbye Marcus. Goodbye Rose."** As the children's song that she then remembers reminds her, marriage appertains only to the good. She must prepare for a different future, the prospect of being bad.

We have seen, at the conclusion of the story, how Phoebe has come to alter radically her design—admittedly a child's design—for her own life. But whether or not she abides by the revised plan is a question that cannot be answered, even though it is clear that Phoebe's conceptions of what might constitute a bad life are just as jejeune and innocent as were her immediately prior conceptions of what might constitute a good one. The story, in short, does not extend beyond the text. The criticism of it, however, does, and what is particularly revealing about that criticism is the way that it shows the tale suffering a violence at the hands of its commentators which is roughly comparable to the violence Phoebe endures at the hands of Captain Cardew. What the three critics who have written in some detail on this story all attest to, as much as does the story itself, is the social privileging, the institutionalizing, of male violence. That violence need not even be admitted as violence as long as it remains relatively discreet. Thus the captain knows that if his actions are private and stop somewhat short of actual rape, the girl is not likely to complain and will not likely be believed if she does. And Phoebe, as previously noted, knows so too. We see the latitude allowed to the captain and we see the girl blamed for his claiming it.

The man clearly abuses the trust, the body, and the soul of a child. Nevertheless, one recent critic concludes: "The lewd chatter of an old man has introduced Phoebe to the whole world of loveless sex and she accepts it buoyantly." [Morrell]. Yet what choice does she have—to accept buoyantly or to accept drowningly? And neither does her apparent willingness prove her full consent. That is the captain's logic but a logic by which, it should also be noted, he does not abide. He acts before he asks and has no intention, as the above formulation would have it, of doing her a favor. Or consider how another critic observes that "Phoebe entices Captain Cardew," that the story "recounts the events forcing Captain and Mrs. Cardew from Jamaica," but "that the Cardews stand a good chance for happiness after leaving the Caribbean," [Wolfe]. This sounds almost as if the conniving young girl took advantage of the trusting old man, whose tropic vacation was thereby cut short but who hopefully, and through no fault of Phoebe's, will probably suffer no permanent damage such as the collapse of his marriage. This same critic, incidentally, elsewhere observes that "the tropics corrode mainland codes of conduct," so that "English people and their home-grown values come to grief in late Rhys tales . . . [such as] **'Goodbye Marcus, Good-bye Rose.'** The poor man would have never acted that way in England; the West Indies weather is somehow responsible. Rhys knows better what the Captain's home-grown values really were.

Equally dubious is [Staley's] claim that even though Captain Cardew admittedly "places his hand on [Phoebe's] breast, he does not fondle her." That simply does not wash. This third critic, noting that "the randy old captain . . . delights in telling her of love and passion," further evinces the same skewed perspective and almost praises the old boy for still being so full of life. Nor can we accept his postulation that "Phoebe is drawn to an identification" with Captain Carew because "she senses something wicked in him and thus in herself." Such an argument turns a powerless complicity into a willing cooperation and even, as in the first formulation, a welcome voyage of self-discovery. It ducks the pertinent question of what he is by dubiously discussing what she is and making her primarily responsible for her own victimization.

For this last critic, the story reveals to Phoebe that she has "values and sensibilities which are opposed to those of the social world in which [she was] brought up." This is true but not in the sense implied. Phoebe sees, in her fumbling way, how bankrupt are the social codes that make her violation possible. To put Phoebe somehow at fault, to attempt to valorize the ethos she is abandoning, only proves how right she was to repudiate it. In short and to conclude, this text especially demonstrates that Rhys's radical revaluing of her society can leave even her critics stumbling behind her and it also shows that such revaluing characterizes the stories every bit as much as it does the novels.

Kathleen Chase (essay date 1988)

SOURCE: A review of *The Collected Short Stories,* in *World Literature Today,* Vol. 62, No. 3, Summer, 1988, p. 497.

[*Here, Chase praises Rhys for her ability to "bring to keen life the spiritual and physical atmosphere of the locales and eras she is writing about."*]

Jean Rhys's stories fall into three groups: those written in the twenties, those from the sixties, and those written or completed when Rhys was an octogenarian. Some are slight, some less than two pages. Others are rather puzzling, but all are offbeat and highly original—in short, completely sui generis. They are "sad . . . told in a voice of great charm," states Diana Athill [in her introduction to *Jean Rhys: The Collected Short Stories*], but they are not all sad. Some are wryly ironic, whereas others are light-hearted. A great many of them are set in Paris, others in London, still others in Dominica in the West Indies, where Rhys was born. (Her parents were British, and when she

was sixteen she went to London to live; after her first marriage she left for the Continent).

Spare and bare (with exceptions) as the stories are, they manage, uncannily, to bring to keen life the spiritual and physical atmosphere of the locales and era she is writing about, whether it be backstage with mannequins or chorus girls, inside a prison or hospital, in a Bloomsbury bedroom or sitting room, or in a Viennese café (in **"Vienne,"** a well-rounded longer story). We relive the torment and the *difficulté d'être* of all the single, lonely, unprotected women seeking to make up, in a round of drinks, for a life wasted and unfulfilled. We see the Carribbean, "the deepest, the loveliest in the world"—though paradise did have its evil serpents. Two places were dear to the heart of Jean Rhys: Paris and Dominica. England was cold, dark, and disenchanting to her.

Of the later stories, **"Till September Petronella"** was originally a long novel. "I cut and cut," Rhys wrote in a letter. "Most aren't real short stories, more like . . . parts of a novel." *Tigers Are Better Looking* and *Sleep It Off, Lady* are the titles of the two published books in which these stories are incorporated. **"Temps Perdi"** (Creole patois for "wasted time," not lost time) grips one with its deft space-time transitions and quiet, nostalgic recollections of the West Indies: "The days that wait for you around the corner to be lived again"; "It had a sweet sound sometimes, the patois. I can't get the words out of my mind, Temps Perdi." Nor, I believe, will the reader.

Laura Neisen De Abruña (essay date 1988)

SOURCE: "Jean Rhys's Feminism: Theory Against Practice," in *World Literature Written in English,* Vol. 28, No. 2, Autumn, 1988, pp. 326 36.

[*In the following excerpt, De Abruña argues that Rhys's views, as demonstrated in her fiction, were anti-feminist.*]

Despite recent attempts by feminist critics to read all of her fiction as a portrait of oppressed women, Jean Rhys's "heroines" are unco-operatively anti-feminist. They dislike and fear other women, while hoping for love and security from men who, they anticipate, will finally reject them. Her women—Anna, Marya, Julia, Sasha, and Antoinette—expect, often fatalistically, that these relationships will fail; and their predictions become self-fulfilling prophecies that legitimize their fears and preserve them from responsibility. The only exception to this is *Wide Sargasso Sea* (and, to a lesser extent, *Voyage in the Dark*). . . .

Critics have considered Rhys a spokesperson for society's oppressed, a satirist of sexism, and a champion of all those persecuted by a mechanistic and conformist, cold northern European environment. Louis James [in *Jean Rhys,* 1978], for example, praises Rhys's sensitivity to prejudice:

Although Jean Rhys is not a self-consciously political writer, few novelists have made a more effective exposure of sexist exploitation. Few, if any, have revealed so vividly the way in which economic and social dependence undermine a woman's psychic being.

Helen Nebecker [in *Jean Rhys, Woman in Passage: A Critical Study of the Novels of Jean Rhys,* 1981] suggests that Rhys intended to expose the need for love as "woman's eternal delusion." According to Nebecker, Rhys's presentation of men shows a developing awareness that the role assigned him by Victorian culture oppressed him as well, so that Mackenzie's or Heidler's hatred and fear of women comes from their demands for emotional and financial security. Rhys's women expect the men to play the roles of "God the Father or Christ the Savior in their lives." Ironically, Ford Madox Ford began this type of interpretation in his introduction to Rhys's **Left Bank and Other Stories** with his remark that Rhys had a "terrific—an almost lucid—passion for stating the case of the underdog."

Since the 1970s there has been a plethora of books and articles, inspired by this type of criticism, that praise Rhys's fiction as feminist or social statement. Despite this, the evidence in the fiction itself, in her autobiography *Smile, Please,* and in the recently published letters shows that Rhys's "theories" about woman's place in society were anti-feminist. We know that when she read a review of her work that was even mildly feminist, she laughed and tore it up. Often she seems hostile to other women; they are part of an unexamined and unexplained paranoia that pervades her fiction and autobiographical writings. Except in her last novel, Rhys's fictional women never seek a solution for their isolation in relationships with other women. Either the thought does not occur to them, or the women they meet are more ruthless, vicious, and competitive than the men. Thus, in complete isolation, Sasha and Julia are left with the debilitating problems of dependancy, feelings of rejection and self-pity, delusions of persecution, self-defeating exaggerations of unfortunate circumstances, and passivity—all covered up with alcoholism, depression, or, in Sasha and Antoinette's cases, anger.

The compassion for the "underdog" cited by Ford, James, Nebecker, and others is, disconcertingly to feminist critics, a compassion for individuals, perhaps like Rhys herself, who suffer from apparently irremediable wrongs, starting in childhood, and who will continue to live frustrated, bitter lives. As Marsha Cummins has pointed out [in *World Literature Written in English* 24, 1984], Rhys's characters do not rebel against the partriarchy because they have internalized its value system and therefore become "other" to themselves. They not only accept society's rejection of them, but also anticipate it. Her characters' paranoid expectations are then legitimized, and the women can feel themselves to be innocent, irresponsible victims. Far from wanting to thwart the system, these women want to belong to it, to be accepted, to be the pampered, hothouse exotics luxuriating in its material goods. The young narrator in **"Mixing Cocktails"** (*The Left Bank*) says:

> I long to be . . . Like Other People! The extraordinary, ungetatable, oddly cruel Other People, with their way of wantonly hurting and then accusing you of being

thin-skinned, sulky, vindictive or ridiculous. All because a hurt and puzzled little girl has retired into her shell.

Marya, in *Quartet,* says something very similar: "I don't want anything black or miserable or complicated any more. I want to be happy, I want to play around and have good times like—like other people do." Much of this sense of isolation is reflected in Rhys's writing, which was autobiographical and therapeutic, a rewriting of her early feelings of alienation from her mother and of rejection after her first affair. As Carole Angier has said [in *Jean Rhys,* 1985], Rhys always felt isolated from other people, despite her envy of their comfort:

> The only ones she could really understand and feel for were the ones who were most like her: women who were anxious or unhappy, and anxious and unhappy in the same ways as she was. . . . To the end she preferred the company of men, and went on hoping that the end of her isolation would come from them.

Her relationships with her family were strained, and even at the age of nine, Rhys felt that she was different and hated herself. She seems to have been afraid of her mother—a trapped, lonely, and reserved woman who was uninterested in her. In her autobiography, *Smile, Please,* Rhys remembers: "Even after the new baby was born there must have been an interval before she seemed to find me a nuisance and I grew to dread her. Another interval and she was middle-aged and plump and uninterested in me". Rhys's father, a British immigrant to Dominica, felt exiled and homesick. Although Jean remembers him as kind and gentle, he was often preoccupied and ignored the children. Left with the nurse Meta, Jean was prey to the older woman's superstitions. Meta, Jean says, showed her a world of "fear and distrust" in which she was still living, even in her eighties.

Depressed after Lancelot Smith jilted her and bought her off with monthly cheques, and after a botched illegal abortion, the twenty-year-old author bought two exercise books and filled them with the material for her novel *Voyage in the Dark.* In this and in her other novels—*Quartet, After Leaving Mr. Mackenzie, Good Morning, Midnight,* and *Wide Sargasso Sea*—Rhys wrote and rewrote the story of a West Indian woman rejected first by her mother and subsequently and fatefully by her lovers.

If much of Rhys's fiction was partly a therapeutic process for her individual problems, where does this put feminist critics who wish to point out the role, literary and psychological, played by women in Rhys's fiction? Even if we find that, despite Rhys's intentions, significant analysis of her characters can still be made from the feminist perspective, we must at least begin our analysis by acknowledging the gap between Rhys's "theories" about women and her practice of presenting them in her fiction. I would argue two things: first, that Jean Rhys was not a feminist or even a modern writer—and, two, that despite Rhys's bad intentions, she often manages to create something better than the intended exposé of mankind's cruelty and intolerance. She showed the hopeless existence of passivity and the courage needed for women, in her fiction about the Caribbean, to continue their lives despite racism and xenophobia. Her analysis of British imperialism gives some interesting portraits of its racism, intolerance, and xenophobia. Here Rhys is at her best—when going beyond self-pity to find outside sources for feelings of alienation in the realities of West Indian life in the nineteenth and twentieth centuries.

For Rhys's characters, the world is a hostile place in which other people are intolerant and jealous and always looking for a reason to pull someone down. In **"Mixing Cocktails"** (*The Left Bank*), the young girl learns an early lesson in intolerance:

> Humanity is never content just to differ from you and let it go at that. Never. They must interfere, actively and grimly between your thoughts and yourself—with the passionate wish to level up everything and everybody.

The fiction has many examples of one human's gratuitous cruelty to another. In the story **"Sleep It Off, Lady"** (*Sleep It Off, Lady*), young Deena watches as seventy-year-old Miss Verney has a heart attack while emptying her garbage. Instead of helping the elderly woman who is flat on her back, skirt up, and humiliatingly festooned with garbage, Deena calls her "stuck up" and tells her to "sleep it off." In this and in other stories, Rhys's imagery suggests that society is a collection of wild animals preying on one another; everyone needs someone to attack and insult. As Hans writes in **"Tigers Are Better-Looking"** (*Tigers Are Better-Looking*): "I got the feeling that I was surrounded by a pack of timid tigers waiting to spring the moment anybody is in trouble or hasn't any money." But tigers, he says, are better-looking than humans, and they do not insult their prey after the attack. People, the narrator of **"The Lotus"** (*Tigers Are Better-Looking*) suggests, "laugh when you're unhappy"; and Marya of *Quartet* complains of the same treatment: "I've realized, you see, that life is cruel and horrible to unprotected people. I think life is cruel. I think people are cruel."

Both Julia in *After Leaving Mr. Mackenzie* and Sasha in *Good Morning, Midnight* believe that strangers in restaurants and in the tube eye them and pass judgements on their age, their drinking, and their shabby clothes. None of these characters believes that her discomfort might be coming from her imagination. They prefer the myth that their male lovers and their powerful friends, like lawyers and businessmen, control society and have infinite power to hurt and defeat them. That Jean herself shared these beliefs is evident from *Smile, Please* and her letters and conversations with novelist David Plante, who helped her write the autobiography. Since *Smile* was written when Jean was in her eighties, it is clear that she never mastered her feelings of persecution. She still saw others as "trees walking"; and even as an octogenarian, by then an alcoholic for over thirty years, she raged, when drunk, about her hatred of people, the enemies, who wanted to rob her of her Dominican memories:

> "And what is Dominica like now? They say there are no roses in Dominica now. There were, I remember them. They gave such a scent to the air." She suddenly shouted, "Lies! Lies!" She bared her teeth. "A pack of lies. And who cares? Who does anything? Terrible things people do. Getting rid of roses in Dominica. I hate the word "people." She spat the word out. "People! I hate people! I hate everyone. I think they are all enemies" [David Plante, *Difficult Women: A Memoir of Three: Jean Rhys, Sonia Orwell, Germaine Greer*, 1984].

Because of their dominant position in society, the men in Rhys's fiction seem responsible for most of the victims' problems. The fiction shows us many men who either dislike or actually hate women. In **"The Insect World"** (*Sleep It Off, Lady*), for example, Audrey buys a book in which the former owner has written "Women are an unspeakable abomination." Mr. Sawyer, from **"The Day They Burned the Books"** (*Tigers Are Better-Looking*), came to live on an unnamed Caribbean island. Although he hated the climate and the people, and everything about the island, he married a mulatto woman and filled their house with English books. When drunk, he abused her verbally and sometimes physically as well, pulling her hair out one night at a dinner party and taunting her: "You damned, long-eyed, gloomy half-caste, you don't smell right." Rhys gives his hatred no motivation, so that we sympathize with Mrs. Sawyer when she burns his books, the symbol of his intolerance. White males are needlessly cruel to Selina Davis, the mulatto West Indian who moves to London looking for work, only to find that everything is stolen from her, even the one song she learns in prison. Again, in **"A Solid House"** (*Tigers are Better-Looking*), Teresa opens her cigarette case to find it empty. The tobacconist always refuses to serve women whenever there is a shortage and seems very pleased to have an excuse for rudeness. At least, Teresa thought, his hatred is undisguised:

> His open hatred and contempt were a relief from all the secret hatreds that hissed from between the lines of newspapers or the covers of books, or peeped from sly smiling eyes. A Woman? Yes, a woman. A woman must; a woman shall or a woman will.

The apparent reason for male dislike of women in Rhys's fiction is the connection between money and gender. All of the women in Rhys's novels take money from their lovers—Anna reluctantly, Julia, Marya, and Sasha much less so. Since Antoinette's money goes directly to Rochester after their marriage, even she is economically dependent on a male. The money seems to make the women the passive property of their lovers and to create a humiliating bond. None of them has the belief that she owns herself or that she could work for some independence. In her autobiography, Rhys spoke of her own beliefs as similar:

> It seems to me that the whole business of money and sex is mixed up with something very primitive and deep. When you take money directly from someone you love it becomes not money but a symbol. The bond is now there. The bond has been established. I am sure the woman's deep-down feeling is "I belong

to this man, I want to belong to him completely." It is at once humiliating and exciting.

Most of Rhys's characters have a divided consciousness of this self-destructive attitude. On the one hand, they feel lost and betrayed yet hopeful that the right male will rescue them; on the other hand, they realize that their submissiveness and passivity are essentially wrong, even though they feel powerless to change their situations.

In Rhys's fiction, the hatred of men for women does not engender feelings of solidarity among the women. On the contrary, in a typically "underdog" manner, they scapegoat one another. Dislike of other women takes three forms in the fiction: the young women are portrayed as vicious; the sexually mature women as competitive and ruthless, and older women as reminders of the humiliations of aging. In the story **"Trio"** (*The Left Bank*), Rhys presents a Martinique girl of fifteen flirting with an older man who is probably her father:

> She had exactly the movements of a very graceful kitten, and he, appreciative, would stop eating to kiss her . . . long, lingering kisses, and, after each one she would look around the room as if to gather up a tribute of glances of admiration and envy—a lonely, vicious little thing.

In *Good Morning, Midnight* the young girls at a restaurant table pick out Sasha to ridicule and ask one another loudly what an old woman like that is doing there. Sasha feels that they have attacked her as part of a game in which young women show themselves to advantage by laughing at an older woman. Surprisingly, Sasha accepts their evaluations and questions her right to exist since she is old, alien, and a stranger. The hostility that Rhys's younger heroines experience is more destructive because unexpected. Frankie, the upper class woman of **"Till September Petronella"** (*Tigers Are Better-Looking*), tries to humiliate Petronella by calling her down as a cheap chorus girl. In *Voyage in the Dark* Anna Morgan is shocked by the way other women look at her:

> But I was thinking it was terrifying—the way they look at you. So that you know that they would see you burnt alive without even turning their heads away; so that you know in yourself that they would watch you burning without even blinking once.

For their own protection, they believe, some of Rhys's women become anti-feminist. Lois and Marya, in *Quartet*, both know that they are Heidler's victims; yet they make the mistake of attacking one another instead of turning on Heidler, who began the menage à trois for his simple amusement.

Because they fear that age will rob them of their attractiveness to men, who are their only resource, Rhys's victims often project this fear in a loathsome hatred of elderly women. Petronella hopes that she will never have to age and swears that she will dye her hair any colour to avoid grey. Sasha hates herself because, at age forty, she

feels useless. Audrey, of **"The Insect World"** (*Sleep It Off, Lady*), wants older women to disappear so that they will not remind her of her fate:

> In front of her stood an elderly woman with dank hair and mean-looking clothes. It was funny how she hated women like that. It was funny how she hated most women anyway. Elderly women ought to stay at home.

One reason for these attitudes is the equation of beauty with one's potential to be loved. The hunger to be beautiful and the obsessions for clothes and comfort that beset many characters are cloaks for their thirst to be loved, which, Rhys says, is "the real curse of Eve." Rhys believed that her culture had impressed upon all women that marriage was a woman's mission in life and that you were a failure if you did not attain this goal.

However, Rhys did not believe in love in any optimistic way. She seems to find in it something cruel and violent, even though she never gave up hope in it. The contradiction is cleared up by a statement in *Smile, Please* in which she claimed that she believed in love but not in humanity: "Because I believe that sometimes human beings can be more than themselves." That love is also cruel and violent is part of Rhys's philosophical position. She believed that the beautiful is something that human beings can only degrade and corrupt but never understand. As she wrote in a letter to Diana Athill, "Perhaps there is violence in *all* magic and *all* beauty" [*The Letters of Jean Rhys*, 1984].

In some of Rhys's fiction love and lust are entangled in the woman character's mind, especially if she is young or confused. In **"Goodbye Marcus, Goodbye Rose"** (*Sleep It Off, Lady*), the elderly Captain Cardew takes twelve-year-old Phoebe on walks around the island. She is flustered by his continual, obsessive talk of love and ways of making love:

> He'd explain that love was not kind and gentle, as she had imagined, but violent. Violence, even cruelty, was an essential part of it. He would expand on this, it seemed to be his favourite subject.

He then thrusts his hand into her shirt and clamps it on her breast. The girl is sure that she is at fault and decides that no one will marry her because she has jeopardized her chastity. As Helen Nebecker has pointed out, something sinister has also occurred to Anna Morgan, who fantasizes that "I only dreamt it, it never happened." Many of Rhys's women are affected by the confusion of love with sex; but after each disaster they get up and stagger on, never realizing their mistake, waiting to be finished off by the next affair.

One exception to Rhys's anti-feminist fiction is her last novel, *Wide Sargasso Sea*, in which she goes beyond victimization by giving us an account of Antoinette's childhood experiences and linking them with the social and historical problems of West Indians in the Caribbean during the 1830s and 1840s. In many ways, all of Rhys's heroines have a colonial sensibility. This extends the importance of her fiction because there is a parallel between the way the British treat the creole immigrants in England and the way colonials in general are treated. . . .

Because she asserts herself within the limited context offered her, Antoinette is one of the lucky Caribbean women in Rhys's fiction. Problems are not resolved in her earlier novels *Quartet, Voyage in the Dark, After Leaving Mr. Mackenzie,* and *Good Morning, Midnight,* or in her collections of short stories **The Left Bank, Tigers Are Better-Looking,** and **Sleep It Off, Lady.** The women in these novels and short stories are more typical of creole and Afro-Caribbean women presented in other Caribbean literature. They feel like outsiders in a cold country and a hostile culture. They remember the warm, relaxed atmosphere of the islands with a sense of nostalgia, of regret, and of tremendous confusion in identity. For all of the women characters examined here—Marya, Julia, Sasha, Antoinette, Audrey, Petronella, Selina, Anna, and Miss Verney—confusion in identity is the inheritance of prejudice directed against women who are figurative, if not literal, outsiders.

Veronica Marie Gregg (essay date 1990)

SOURCE: "Jean Rhys on Herself as a Writer," in *Caribbean Women Writers: Essays from the First International Conference,* edited by Selwyn R. Cudjoe, Calaloux Publications, 1990, pp. 109-15.

[*In the following excerpt, Gregg compiles letters and autobiographical sources in which Rhys comments on the craft of writing.*]

Writing gave shape and meaning to Jean Rhys's life: "Until I started to write, and concentrated on writing, it was a life in which I didn't quite know what was going to happen" [interview with Mary Cantwell, *Mademoiselle,* October 1974]. Rhys brought unswerving commitment and a relentless capacity for hard work to her writing. In an interview in her later years [with Thomas Staley, in *Jean Rhys: A Critical Study,* 1979], she referred to her reclusive lifestyle: "I don't see how you can write without shutting everything else out."

In conversations with David Plante Rhys emphasized the sacrifices demanded of her craft:

You have to be selfish to be a writer . . . monstrously selfish [in *Paris Review* 76, 1979].

Nothing ever justifies what you have to do to write, to go on writing. But you do, you must, go on.

Trust only yourself and your writing. You will write something marvellous if you trust yourself and don't give up. . . . People think they can sit down and write novels. Nonsense. It isn't done that way. It is not a part-time occupation, it's your life.

Only writing is important. Only writing takes you out of yourself [David Plante, *Difficult Women: A Memoir of Three: Jean Rhys, Sonia Orwell, Germaine Greer,* 1982].

You should know it all. You should know . . . all the big, big writers. . . . All of writing is a huge lake. There are great rivers that feed the lake, like Tolstoy and Dostoevsky. And there are trickles, like Jean Rhys. All that matters is feeding the lake. I don't matter. The lake matters. You must keep feeding the lake. It is very important. Nothing else is important. . . . But you should be taking from the lake before you can think of feeding it. You must dig your bucket in very deep. . . . What matters is the lake and man's unconquerable mind [*Paris Review*].

Implicit in this statement is Rhys's recognition of the connections between reading and writing and the writer's duty to study her precursors, a responsibility that demands rigorous intellectual application. Yet she also suggests that she is an amanuensis:

I'm a pen. I'm nothing but a pen.

And do you imagine yourself in someone's hand?

Of course. Of course. It's only then that I know I'm writing well. It's only then that I know my writing is true. Not really true as fact. But true as writing. That's why I know the Bible is true . . . the writing is true, it *reads* true. Oh to be able to write like that! But you can't do it. It's not up to you. You're picked up like a pen, and when you're used up you're thrown away, ruthlessly, and someone else is picked up. You can be sure of that: someone else will be picked up [*Paris Review*].

Rhys's persistent preoccupation with this aspect of her work is also revealed in her letters:

I don't believe in the individual Writer so much as in Writing. It uses you and throws you away when you are not useful any longer. But it does not do this until you are useless and quite useless too. Meanwhile there is nothing to do but plod along line by line [Jean Rhys, *Letters, 1931-1966,* 1984].

In responding to criticism that her work was dated, Rhys argued that such an opinion was invalid, insisting that a work of art must be grounded in the material and the particular world in which the writer lives:

Books and plays are written some time, some place, by some person affected by that time, that place, the clothes he sees and wears, other books, the air and the room and every damned thing. It *must* be so, and how can it be otherwise except his book is a copy? [*Letters*].

Rhys's observations point to her awareness of the essential dichotomy of the artistic enterprise—the particular individual rooted in time and place, her vision informed by a particular reality, and the recognition of the impersonal nature of art. She expresses the nature of art as inspiration or language—impersonal and ecumenical—and its contradictory complement, solitary meditation. The artistic enterprise consists not in suppressing the personality but in opening it up and converting it into what Octavio Paz in *Peras del Olmo* describes as the point of intersection between the subjective and the objective. This conjunction results in the "destruction" of the artist even as she endures within the work of art. What will endure is not the writer but the artistic product and the language. Yet the work of art cannot exist without its creator, who continues to sacrifice herself to the artistic process in trying to achieve the perfect work:

> I usually dislike my books, sometimes, don't want to touch them. But the Next One will be a bit better. I am always excited and forget all failures and all else [*Letters*].

In a career spanning more than fifty years, Rhys insisted repeatedly upon the connection between simplicity and artistic truth: "I have written upon the wall, 'Great is truth and it shall prevail.' Simplify—simplify—simplify" (ca. 1939). She believed that even artists operating within the conventional framework of English society were often challenged by the need to tell their truth but bowed to the domination of the prevailing ideology. Referring to English society as a kind of ant civilization, she pointed to the connection between art and life and the damaging constraints which convention imposes upon literature:

> I believe that if books were brave enough the repressive education [of the ant civilization] would fail but nearly all English books and writers slavishly serve the ant civilization. Do not blame them too much for the Niagara of repression is also beating on them and breaking their heart. [British Library, Folio 152].

In the 1950s, a period in which Rhys produced little, she continued to read extensively. In a letter to fellow writer Morchard Bishop she reacts fiercely to what she perceives as a dangerous attempt to control and coerce the production and reception of works of art:

> I read a letter in the *Observer* last Sunday from some editor . . . promising to accept a story up to the standard of *Boule de suif* [by Maupassant]. Well I should damned well think he would. And Hemingway's [*The Old Man and the Sea*]. Why not add Prosper Mérimée's *Carmen* for good measure. . . .
>
> Poor *Boule de suif.* They won't let her rest. . . .
>
> The thing is, I very much doubt whether any story seriously glorifying the prostitute and showing up not one but several English housewives, to say nothing of two nuns!—their meanness, cant and spite—would be accepted by the average editor or any editor.
>
> And *La Maison de Tellier* [Maupassant]—well imagine. . . .

Of course I may be quite wrong. . . . But I do read a lot and have a very definite impression that "thought control" is on the way and ought to be resisted. But will it be resisted?

> Why say as Mr. Green does, "I demand a positive and creative view of life"? What is that? And why demand a view of life? Not his business, surely.
>
> It's all very well to talk about *The Old Man and the Sea,* but what about *Hills Like White Elephants* or *A Way You'll Never Be.* . . . Would those be up to his "positive and creative" standard? [*Letters*].

Rhys's ideological position and working aesthetic is to create "books written in short, simple sentences depending for the effectiveness on the intensity of the feeling of the author" ("The Bible Is Modern," n.p.). A study of the process of her literary composition, emendations of manuscripts, replacements of one stylistic variant with another, suppressions, and elaborations can further elucidate the way she uses form as ideology.

In her letters (often to impatient editors or to Selma Vaz Dias, who "rediscovered" her and adapted some of her work) Rhys repeatedly refers to the labor involved in her artistic creation: "I do toil, you know, and even a short story is written six times or more before I am satisfied. . . . Of course some things have to be done over and over before the words are in the right place" (Letter to Vaz Dias, December 1963).

Rhys discloses that to get the right word in the right place she must search for each word individually; "I [think] very hard of each word in itself" (Plante). Rhys's strategy recalls that of her mentor, Ford, who insists that the writer's mind has to choose each word and her ear has to test it until she has it right. The insistence on the *mot juste* extends even to Rhys's finished work. When Vaz Dias adapts *Good Morning, Midnight,* the author advises her that every word must be exact:

> This is about the end of *Good Morning, Midnight.* . . . It's fine—except that . . . I don't think "rustle" is the right word for a man's dressing gown. . . . Taffeta rustles and so do stiff silks, I suppose, but wouldn't a man's dressing gown be a heavy silk? Please don't think me pernickety but every word must be exact [*Letters*].

Before giving permission for the reprinting of her early works after the success of *Wide Sargasso Sea,* Rhys was "very anxious to make a few alterations in *Postures* which they are going to publish as *Quartet.* . . . These alterations are all cuts of words or sentences." *Of Voyage in the Dark* she observes, "the revisions . . . are small but important, making it a better book for now, 1964" [*Letters*].

In her lifetime, Rhys was acutely aware of the attitudes of critics and commentators to her work. She reacted with outrage when she thought that she was denigrated because she was a woman:

I think that the Anglo-Saxon idea that you can be rude with impunity to any female who has written a book is utterly *damnable*. You come and have a look out of curiosity and then allow the freak to see what you think of her. It's only done to the more or less unsuccessful and only by Anglo-Saxons. Well . . . if it were my last breath I'd say *hell to it* and to the people who do it [*Letters*].

In her fiction, Rhys's scathing attack on British society's attitude to women is rendered especially in **"I Spy a Stranger,"** a short story written during World War II. The piece bears affinities with the works of Virginia Woolf (*Three Guineas* and *A Room of One's Own*), Dorothy Richardson, and Katherine Mansfield.

Despite similarities of techniques, styles, motifs, and thematic concerns, Jean Rhys does not fit easily or completely within the body of modernist writing or women's fiction of her generation. Jean D'Costa points to the difficulties created by Rhys's particular voice [in "Jean Rhys, 1890-1979," in Daryl Dance, ed., *Fifty Caribbean Writers,* New York, Greenwood Press, 1986]:

A reader new to Rhys usually puzzles over her viewpoint looking both ways across the channel and the Atlantic, she seems for and against both perspectives. Her insider-outsider's treatment of England, France and the Caribbean gnaws at comfortable ethnocentricisms. . . . Looking for some kind of familiar ground, the reader tries to fit Rhys into available models of contemporary fiction, and fails. . . . She belongs to no recognizable school; fits into no ready-made slot.

Rhys's fiction belongs, as she did, to worlds whose mutual understanding has "the feeling . . . of . . . things that . . . couldn't fit together." The dissonances of seemingly different worlds inform the Rhysian novel, finding coherence in her art. . . . All her work is charged with a sense of belonging in many wheres at once.

As a white female West Indian, her cultural heritage would have bequeathed an odd double vision born of the place of the white West Indian in her native land. She was white but not English or European, West Indian but not black. She was taught the language and customs of a land she had never seen, England, while living in and being shaped by the reality of the West Indies. Her sense of belonging to the West Indies would necessarily be charged with an awareness of being part of another culture. The ambiguity of being an insider/outsider in both the metropolis and the colony shaped Rhys's apprehension of the world and was further complicated by the complexity of the West Indian society in which she lived—the ambivalences inherent in the color-class relationship and the simultaneous existence of different cultural modes, Creole, black, and indigenous. The interaction among the groups was regulated by strict social and political norms, but at a psychosocial level the relationship was syncretic. In Dominica, the Creole culture consisted of a blend of French and English, further complicating the social and historical setting. Out of this reality and as a means of rendering her vision of the world, Rhys developed an ideology of secular individualism and

psychological privacy combined with a self-image of isolation expressed through "the solitary, observing, experiencing self" which is present in all her fiction.

The relationship between her personal history and the nature of her art is mediated by the writing itself. In talking about herself as a writer, she observes:

I can't make things up, I can't invent. I have no imagination. I can't invent character. I don't think I know what character is. I just write about what happened. Not that my books are entirely my life—but almost . . . *Though I guess the invention is in the writing*. . . . But then there are two ways of writing. One way is to try to write in an extraordinary way, the other in an ordinary way. Do you think it's possible to write both ways? . . . I think so. I think what one should do is write in an ordinary way and make the writing seem extraordinary. One should write too about what is ordinary and see the extraordinary behind it [Plante, emphasis added].

If Rhys uses her life as a pretext for art, she insists repeatedly that life and a book are very different. Among her major strategies are pastiche and parody. . . . In analyzing the functions of parody and pastiche in contemporary English writers, Robert Burden offers a useful definition [in *The Contemporary English Novel,* 1979], which applies to my understanding of Rhys's attitude to the literary traditions, styles, and principles of Europe and to her relationship with them:

One of the fundamental purposes of parody in literature has long been that of literary criticism; that is to say, the literary technique of parody often preempts the activity of the would-be literary critic by offering within the text degrees of self-interpretation. It focuses on the limitations, personal or historical, of past forms; it often does this by suggesting the obsolescence of "previous" styles. . . . Parody is distinguished as a mode of imitation in a subversive form. This distinguishes it from pastiche, which implies a non-subversive form of imitation, which depends on systems of borrowing: a patchwork of quotations, images, motifs, mannerisms or even whole fictional episodes which may be borrowed, untransformed, from an original in recognition of the "anxiety of influence." Pastiche may be the result of the conscious recognition of influence and of the fact that the condition of writing is in fact a condition of re-writing. . . . It may be used to stress the ironic awareness that language, literary forms, themes and motifs regularly come to the writer in, so to speak, second-hand form.

In the Rhys canon, pastiche and parody represent a built-in discourse with the European literary tradition and the ideological framework that defines, constricts, and to some extent distorts her as woman, artist, and West Indian.

The use of pastiche and parody is combined with the relentless honing of language to "deconstruct" the literature and language to which she is heir and to expose their absences and render her own ideological and critical position. In using and criticizing the literary resources of Europe while aiming for the simplest and clearest form of expression, Rhys creates a space for her work and for the works of later writers who also experience a "nothingness" in terms of the metropolitan canon.

Writing was the imperative of Jean Rhys's life. In her bleakest moments, she drew courage from the role writing played in her life:

> I must write. If I stop writing my life will have been an abject failure. It is already that to other people. But it could be an abject failure to myself. I will not have earned death [*Smile Please,* 1976].

Lucy Wilson (essay date 1990)

SOURCE: "European or Caribbean: Jean Rhys and the Language of Exile," in *Literature and Exile,* edited by David Bevan, Rodopi, 1990, pp. 77-89.

[*In the following excerpt, Wilson explores the impact of Rhys's exile on her work.*]

The question of identity in Jean Rhys' life and fiction is inextricably bound to the condition of exile that shaped her perceptions and those of her characters. Rhys was truly a woman without a country. England, where she lived for most of her adult life, was a cold, unreceptive place for the writer. Recognition came too late to compensate for a lifetime of loneliness and financial difficulty. The question of Rhys' West Indian roots is even more problematic. The daughter of a Welsh father and a white Creole mother, Rhys felt exiled even before she moved to England because she was cut off from the black community in Dominica. Thus Rhys suffered from what Amon Saba Saakana describes as "the mental condition of double alienation" [in *The Colonial Legacy in Caribbean Literature,* 1987]. Doubly dispossessed, Jean Rhys differs from black West Indian exiles who, as George Lamming points out [in *The Pleasures of Exile,* 1960], "could never have felt the experience of being in a minority".

Jean Rhys is both Prospero *and* Caliban, a descendant of white colonisers but also, as a woman, colonised and excluded by the patriarch's language. "Carib Indian and African slave, both seen as the wild fruits of Nature, share equally that spirit of revolt which Prospero by sword or language is determined to conquer" [Lamming]. In her own way, Rhys also shares that revolutionary spirit: she wrests Prospero's language from him, inverts and subverts it in her fiction, and turns the empty space between two worlds into a privileged place, the exile's domain, by means of what Edward Said calls a "contrapuntal" awareness.

The uniquely literary nature of exile has been examined by Said, Andrew Gurr, and Michael Seidel, among others. According to Gurr, [in *Writers in Exile: The Identity of Home in Modern Literature,* 1981] exile has had an "enormously constructive" effect on writers who were born in the colonies and fled to the metropolis, since it creates in

them "a stronger sense of home" and thus "a clearer sense of [their] own identity" than is available to their metropolitan counterparts. Questioning this essentially romantic view, Said writes [in *Harper's Magazine,* September, 1984.]: "To think of exile as beneficial, as a spur to humanism or to creativity, is to belittle its mutilations. . . . For exile is fundamentally a discontinuous state of being. Exiles are cut off from their roots, their land, their past." Yet Said recognises the literary nature of exile, in that the unreality of the exile's new world resembles fiction. Furthermore, the exile's double or contrapuntal vision can lead to a restored and enhanced identity and even a more meaningful life.

Michael Seidel [in *Exile and the Narrative Imagination,* 1986] similarly views the exilic condition as a paradigm for narrative strategy:

> . . . for narrative performs not only as an experiential rival but as an aesthetic substitute or supplement. Exilic imagining in this sense is both the mirror and the "other" of narrative process; mimesis becomes an alien (or allegorical) phenomenon that establishes fictional sovereignty on fictional ground. . . . The narrative imagination inhabits exilic domain where absence is presence, or, to put it the other way around, where presence is absence.

While Seidel focuses "on exile as an enabling fiction" and not on the actual conditions or politics of exile, the autobiographical nature of Jean Rhys' fiction accommodates such a double perspective. And the purely aesthetic concerns expressed by Seidel do not address the real pathos of exile, the extent to which exiles, and women in particular, are often relegated to a position of powerlessness in their adopted land. This is the essence of Jean Rhys' vision. In her novels and stories, matters of race, gender, class, and ethnicity are intensified by the contrapuntal vision of exile, which highlights the interplay of power structures within British, West Indian, and Continental societies. . . .

[In] two of Rhys' short stories, . . . the exile's privileged perspective, combined with a semi-documentary style, reconstructs an image of Europe after World War I that in some ways resembles Christopher Isherwood's pre-World War II Germany in *The Berlin Stories,* especially the distanced yet nonjudgmental point of view that distinguishes both authors' vignettes. In **"Vienne",** England displaces Dominica as the "absent presence", for this story parallels experiences in Rhys' life that occurred several years after the events recalled in *Voyage in the Dark.* The pregnant narrator, Francine, and her husband Pierre are thinly disguised versions of Rhys and her first husband, Jean Lenglet, when they lived on the Continent during the years following the Great War, an exciting time when many people were involved in the dangerous but highly profitable business of currency exchange.

Francine's exilic perspective approaches the "scrupulous subjectivity" described by Edward Said as the ideal stance for the exile:

If the exile is neither going to rush into an uncritical gregariousness nor sit on the sidelines nursing a wound, he or she must cultivate a scrupulous (not indulgent or sulky) subjectivity. . . . For there is considerable merit to the practice of noting discrepancies between various concepts and ideas and what they actually produce.

But **"Vienne"** is one of Rhys' early stories, and as such it is tainted by "uncritical gregariousness". A Japanese officer is a "poor dear" and an English translator a "marvellous person"! There is an indulgent chattiness to Francine's insistence—"I mustn't cry, I won't cry"—that is absent from a much later version of this episode in **"Temps Perdi",** and a comparison of these two stories attests to the development and refinement of Jean Rhys' contrapuntal or exilic vision over a period of approximately forty years. A third story, **"I Spy a Stranger"**, from the same period as **"Temps Perdi"**, shows how the subject of misogyny accrues added political significance with the advent of World War II. All three stories overlap in terms of Rhys' life experiences, and consequently, when examined together, they disclose the exilic imagination as it develops both in historic time and in narrative space.

In **"Vienne"** and **"Temps Perdi"**, misogyny is seen as a common denominator among the German, the Japanese, and the English officers who frequent Sacher's Hotel in Vienna during the summer of 1921. In the earlier story, Francine explains with characteristic directness that:

> Hato [a Japanese officer] was a great joy. He despised Europeans heartily. They all did that, exception made in favor of Germany—for the Japanese thought a lot of the German army and the German way of keeping women in their place. They twigged that at once. Not much they didn't twig.

When Rhys retells this story in **"Temps Perdi"**, a Japanese officer's affinity for Germanic misogyny is presented less directly. The nameless narrator recalls the typist Simone's reconstruction of Captain Yoshi's confidences:

> "Well", I said, "He looked as if he were telling you all his secrets."

> "He was", Simone said, "he was. Do you know what he was saying? He was saying how much he admires the Germans. He said they'll soon have the best army in Europe, and that they'll dominate it in a few years. . . . He said the French love women too much. He said only the Germans know how to treat women. The Germans and the English think the same way about women, he said, but the French think differently. He said the English and the French together won't last another year, and that they are splitting up already."

Although less direct in terms of narrative structure, the **"Temps Perdi"** passage is more far-reaching than the one from **"Vienne"**, since at a distance of forty years Rhys associates the Germans' attitude toward women with their later attempt to dominate Europe militarily.

There are other significant differences between the two stories. The youthful Francine in **"Vienne"** has internalised Prospero's attitudes; she uses the language of the patriarchy when she describes women in terms of their "podgy hands", "thick ankles", and "enormous" feet—women being equal to the sum of their bodily parts. Her goal for her own appearance is to achieve a doll-like look by means of make-up and "stuff dropped in [her eyes] to make the pupils big and black". The much older narrator in **"Temps Perdi"** recalls her youthful preoccupation with pretty dresses, but the passages critical of other women's appearance have been expunged.

Rhys launches a direct attack on misogyny in **"I Spy a Stranger"**, which is also written in the first person, although the character who corresponds to Francine of **"Vienne"** and the nameless narrator in **"Temps Perdi"** is here not the narrator but rather her cousin Laura. Like Francine, Laura has lived in Central Europe, returning to England only when she was "forced to". In her exercise-book, Laura writes about being unable "to bear the comments on what had happened in Europe . . . the eternal question of who let down who, and when", a passage that recalls Francine's despair when Pierre admits "that he had lost money—other people's money—the Commission's money—Ishima had let him down". Laura's cousin, Marion Hudson, is pressed by her husband and her irate neighbours to expel Laura from the Hudson household and force her to return to London, now that the blitz is over. Laura's unsociable, bookish ways, but especially her Central European connections, have turned public opinion against her. Laura is suspected of "trying to pass information on to the enemy", and her exercise-book is confiscated by the police as evidence.

While the exercise-book reveals no evidence that Laura is a spy, it does contain the most blistering condemnation of English misogyny to be found in all of Rhys' fiction. Laura recalls:

> . . . those endless, futile arguments we used to have when we all knew the worse was coming to the worst. The world dominated by Nordics, German version—what a catastrophe. But if it were dominated by Anglo-Saxons, wouldn't that be a catastrophe too? Then, of course, England and the English. . . . There is something strange about their attitude to women as women. Not dislike (or fear). That isn't strange of course. But it's all so completely taken for granted, and surely that is strange. It has settled down and become an atmosphere, or, if you like, a climate, and no one questions it, least of all the women themselves. There is *no* opposition. The effects are criticized, for some of the effects are hardly advertisements for the system, the cause is seldom mentioned, and then very gingerly. The few mild ambiguous protests usually come from men. Most of the women seem to be carefully trained to revenge any unhappiness they feel on each other, or on children—or on any individual man who happens to be at a disadvantage. In dealing with men as a whole, a streak of subservience, of servility, usually appears, something cold, calculating, lacking in imagination.

But no one can go against the spirit of a country with impunity, and propaganda from the cradle to the grave can do a lot.

Laura amuses herself in the exercise-book by inventing titles for future books:

> *Woman an Obstacle to the Insect Civilization? The Standardization of Woman, The Mechanization of Woman . . . Misogyny and British Humour. . . . Misogyny and War, The Misery of Woman and the Evil in Men or the Great Revenge that Makes all other Revenges Look Silly.*

Through Laura, Jean Rhys has aligned herself with Caliban, with the black slave and the Carib Indian who have been "colonised by language, and excluded by language". In England, Rhys, like George Lamming's exiled Caliban:

> . . . does not feel the need to understand an Englishman, since all relationships begin with an assumption of previous knowledge, a knowledge acquired in the absence of the people known. This relationship with the English is only another aspect of the West Indian's relation to the *idea* of England.

Rhys' "*idea* of England" is complicated by the fact that in her life and her fiction, England represents both the "present absence"—in *Voyage in the Dark*, Anna Morgan's dark, frowning London houses "all alike all stuck together"—and the "absent presence"—Francine's imagined place of refuge from the terrifying events that force her and Pierre to flee from Hungary when Pierre's mismanagement of other people's money gets them in trouble with the law. Anna, exiled in England, longs for the West Indies; Francine, adrift in Central Europe, insists: "We must go to London". Pierre warns her not to count on help from her English friends, but Francine persists. As the two later stories reveal, Pierre was right. For the older version of Francine in **"Temps Perdi"**, England is "the land of the dead"; and in **"I Spy a Stranger"**, Laura has discovered that "coming back to England was the worst thing [she] could have done, that almost anything else would have been preferable".

England, for Jean Rhys, was "perhaps the greatest disappointment of her life and one she never stopped resenting." But as an emblem of the exilic condition, the *idea* of England plays a crucial role in the unfolding of Rhys' contrapuntal vision. Like *Voyage in the Dark,* **"Temps Perdi"** juxtaposes England and the West Indies, though structurally the works are quite different. Whereas Anna Morgan's West Indian memories and English experiences overlap in the text as in her mind, the narrator in **"Temps Perdi"** separates her experiences in England, on the Continent, and in the West Indies. In the process, she travels through time and space to a mythical place where women speak a secret language.

Section One of **"Temps Perdi"** is itself divided into two time frames. The narrator, apparently fairly advanced in years, recalls her stay, at some point in her past, in an

English country house whose coldness in turn reminds her of Vienna. Section One thus slips gracefully into the second section—"The Sword Dance and the Love Dance"—set in Vienna shortly after World War I. Section Two ends with the narrator's remark that the liberating effect of memory will turn her into "a savage person—a real Carib", a phrase that provides the transition into Section Three: "Carib Quarter".

The third section describes the narrator's brief return visit to the West Indies and to an estate called Temps Perdi, which in the Creole patois "does not mean, poetically, lost or forgotten time, but, matter-of-factly, wasted time, lost labor". This section contains both: the "wasted" effort of the narrator's disappointing visit to Salybia, the Carib Quarter, and the "lost" time of a (probably apocryphal) account of the "original West Indians", who presumably inhabited the islands before the Caribs came from the South American mainland and the Spaniards from Europe. According to a book once read by the narrator, the male members of this aboriginal people were killed by the Spaniards and the Caribs, or deported to Haiti:

> But the book, written by an Englishman in the 1880s, said that some of the women, who had survived both the Spanish and the Caribs . . . had carried on the old language and traditions, handing them down from mother to daughter. This language was kept a secret from their conquerors, but the writer of the book claimed to have learned it.

Local West Indian custom holds that the Carib women have inherited this "language that the men don't know".

Jean Rhys was limited by her exilic condition. A white girl in a black society that she envied and longed to be a part of, a West Indian in the imperial English system that reinforced her sense of powerlessness as both a colonial and a woman: Rhys perceived both worlds as though from a very great distance.

—Lucy Wilson

Despite the narrator's disclaimer regarding the nineteenth-century author's excess of imagination, this idea of an all-female aboriginal language is emblematic of the exile's true "home"—a language untainted by Prospero's value because it predates the white man's rule. The language of the patriarchy reinforces the distance between persons of different race, creed, class, or sex. Even within a group, feelings of difference and hostility are maintained by means of language, as in the distinction made throughout *Voyage in the Dark* between women and girls, ladies and tarts, virgins and non-virgins. By keeping women divided among themselves, the language of Prospero protects its interests.

But the secret language of the Carib women has had the opposite effect: it has forged a bond among women that has survived incursions from two continents, linking generations of mothers and daughters in a conspiracy of eloquent silence.

Whether this secret language does or ever did exist among the Carib women is beside the point; its significance within the context of Jean Rhys' life and work should be clear. Toward the end of **"Temps Perdi"**, the narrator lies "caged under a mosquito net" thinking: "Now I am home, where the earth is sometimes red and sometimes black. Round about here is ochre—a Carib skin." Rhys' home is neither the West Indies of her "lost" childhood nor the England of her many and sometimes "wasted" adult years. Home for Jean Rhys is a language like "a Carib skin", a mosquito net of language that protects and confines the writer, "a prisoner in a cell of small peepholes". Safe within the Carib body of her text, Jean Rhys is also limited by her exilic condition. A white girl in a black society that she envied and longed to be a part of, a West Indian in the imperial English system that reinforced her sense of powerlessness both as a colonial and as a woman: Rhys perceived both worlds as though from a very great distance and felt herself cut off from other people. But this contrapuntal point of view is for Rhys, as it is for Edward Said and other exiles, a source of power and inspiration: "Exiles cross borders, break barriers of thought and experience (. . .). Seeing 'the entire world as a foreign land' makes possible originality of vision."

In a poem about the novelist [in *Collected Poems 1948-1984,* 1986], Derek Walcott describes the child Jean Rhys, whose sigh transcends the barriers between two cultures:

> And the sigh of that child
> is white as an orchid
> on a crusted log
> in the bush of Dominica,
> a V of Chinese white
> meant for the beat of a seagull
> over a sepia souvenir of Cornwall,
> as the white hush between two sentences.

A fragile white flower of the Caribbean transplanted to the cold brown English soil, Jean Rhys made her home in neither place. Rather, she lived and continues to thrive in a linguistic space, the "white hush between two sentences".

FURTHER READING

Bibliography

Mellown, Elgin W. *Jean Rhys: A Descriptive and Annotated Bibliography of Works and Criticism.* New York: Garland Publishing, 1984, 218 p.
> Exhaustive reference work with citations through the early 1980s; includes a useful introduction.

Biography

Angiers, Carole. *Jean Rhys.* London: André Deutsch, 1990, 762 p.
> A thorough biography that explores Rhys's life in relation to her work.

Criticism

Auchincloss, Eve. Review of *Sleep It Off, Lady* in *The Washington Post Book World* (7 November 1976): G1-G2.
> Praises "urgent creative intelligence," which Rhys uses to "transmute observation and experience into utterly original works of art."

Borinsky, Alicia. "Jean Rhys: Poses of a Woman as Guest," in *The Female Body in Western Culture*, edited by Susan Rubin Suleiman, pp. 288-302. Cambridge, Mass.: Harvard University Press, 1986.
> Examines the ways in which Rhys's female characters are defined by their surroundings.

Gardiner, Judith Kegan. "'The Grave,' 'On Not Shooting Sitting Birds,' and the Female Esthetic." *Studies in Short Fiction* 20, No. 4 (Fall 1983): 265-70.
> Analyzes female creativity as evidenced in short stories by Katherine Anne Porter and Rhys.

Hagley, Carol R. "Ageing in the Fiction of Jean Rhys," *World Literature Written in English* 28, No. 1 (Spring 1988): 115-25.
> Contends that Rhys's exploration in her fiction of "the ill-treatment of women in a male-dominated world" reflects her wider concern with "the alienation and exploitation of human beings anywhere regardless of age or sex."

James, Louis. *Jean Rhys.* London: Longman, 1978, 74 p.
> Critical survey of Rhys's fiction.

Jebb, Julian. "Sensitive Survivors." *The Times*, London (30 March 1968): 21.
> Review of *Tigers Are Better-Looking* that proclaims Rhys "a twentieth-century master."

Kloepfer, Deborah Kelly. *The Unspeakable Mother: Forbidden Discourse in Jean Rhys and H. D.* Ithaca, N. Y.: Cornell University Press, 1989, 191 p.
> Study of language in Rhys's fiction.

O'Connor, Teresa F. "Jean Rhys, Paul Theroux, and the Imperial Road." *Twentieth Century Literature* 4, No. 4 (Winter 1992): 404-14.
> Examines "The Imperial Road," an unpublished story by Rhys, and its relationship to two of Theroux's stories.

Suárez, Isabel Carerra, and Esther Álvarez López. "Social and Personal Selves: Race, Gender and Otherness in Rhys's 'Let Them Call It Jazz' and *Wide Sargasso Sea*." *Dutch Quarterly Review of Anglo-American Letters* 20, No. 2 (1990): 154-62.

Finds "great parallelisms" in "the effects of a hostile social environment on the psychological evolution" of the central characters of the two works by Rhys.

Thompson, Irene. "The Left Bank Apéritifs of Jean Rhys and Ernest Hemingway." *The Georgia Review* XXXV, No. 1 (Spring 1981): 94-106.
    Compares the Paris-based writing of contemporaries Rhys and Hemingway, including their separate relationships with Ford Madox Ford.

Tyler, Ralph. "Luckless Heroines, Swinish Men." *The Atlantic* 235, No. 1 (January 1975): 81-4.
    A critical review of *Tigers Are Better-Looking* that focuses on Rhys's obscurity and rediscovery.

Additional coverage of Rhys's life and career is contained in the following sources published by Gale Research: *Concise Dictionary of British Literary Biography, 1945-1960*; *Contemporary Authors,* Vols. 25-28R, 85-88; *Contemporary Authors New Revision Series,* Vol. 35; *Contemporary Literary Criticism,* Vols. 2, 4, 6, 14, 19, 51; *Dictionary of Literary Biography,* Vols. 36, 117; and *Major 20th-Century Writers.*

William Sansom
1912-1976

English short story writer, novelist, travel writer, and author of children's books.

INTRODUCTION

Often compared with the work of Czech writer Franz Kafka, Sansom's short stories are distinguished by minute descriptions of setting and character and by their depictions of people who are faced with extreme situations outside their normal experience. The author's precise writing and meticulous attention to language have been praised by numerous critics who laud the descriptive qualities and interesting uses of verbal rhythm in his tales. Sansom has also produced several collections of innovative "travel stories" that set fictional stories in exotic locations and emphasize the scenic surroundings of the area.

Biographical Information

Sansom was born in London in 1912 and received his education at Uppingham School in the Rutland region of England. Aiming toward a career in international banking, he spent two years traveling and studying languages in Europe, before accepting a position with the British branch of a German bank in 1930. Five years later, he became a copywriter for an advertising agency, where he worked with the poet Norman Cameron. During World War II, Sansom was a fireman with the National Fire Service, combatting infernos created by German bombing attacks on England. This work became one of the primary subjects of Sansom's early fiction, as well as his first published book, a nonfiction account that he penned with two other writers. In 1944 Sansom became a full-time writer, publishing his first fiction collection the same year. After the war, he produced works in various genres in addition to short fiction, composing film scripts, travel essays, novels, children's books, a biography of French writer Marcel Proust, and other titles. He continued his prolific output of books until his shortly before his death in 1976.

Major Works of Short Fiction

Several of Samson's favorite themes and techniques are evident in his earliest stories, many of which are published in *Fireman Flower, and Other Stories*. The typical Sansom character in these pieces is alone, contemplating an astonishing twist that suddenly confronts him or her. In the course of the story, the protagonist becomes an acute observer at a crucial moment, recording both the events

that transpire and the responses that result. Sansom's first published story, "The Wall," is an example, depicting a crew of fire fighters as a burning wall crashes down upon them. Rendering such scenes in microscopic detail and unnatural clarity, Sansom's painstaking construction evokes a sense of nonparticipation or unreality in the reader as the sensuous details slow the action to an almost dream-like pace. A similar attention to particulars is evident in volumes such as *South* and *The Passionate North*, though here Sansom's vivid imagery evokes the exotic locales in which the stories are set. These tales are closely related to the author's nonfiction works in the travel genre and have been described by Sansom as "a bastard out of the liaison of two distinct literary wishes—to describe a place (travel book) and to tell a story (fiction)." One of the best-known of these travel stories is "Three Dogs of Siena," which records the thoughts and adventures of three canines as they explore a new town.

In many of Sansom's stories that date from the 1950s, male-female relationships are a central feature. "A Contest of Ladies" recounts the misadventures of a man who attempts to woo a beauty contestant. In the end, they are wed, but the marriage promises revenge more than love.

The subject of marriage is also treated in "Life, Death," where a young man must give up the artistic aspects of his fish-market job in order to better provide for his wife-to-be. "Life, Death" also offers evidence of Sansom's rhythmic use of language, a tool he employs to enhance the characterization of the first-person narrator. Many of Sansom's later stories, collected in *The Ulcerated Milkman* and *The Marmalade Bird,* also treat romantic and family relationships, while the story "The Ulcerated Milkman" turns on the unusual friendship that develops between two hospital patients.

Critical Reception

Sansom's technical abilities and descriptive skills are conceded by most reviewers, with many giving extensive praise to these qualities. American fiction writer Eudora Welty has been one of the proponents of Samson's work, declaring that "the flesh of William Sansom's stories is their uninterrupted contour of sensory impressions. The bone is reflective contemplation." Less appreciative critics have found that Samson's short fiction has several drawbacks. First, the lavish description can become too detailed, overwhelming and slowing the story. Second, the author's characterization has been criticized on the grounds that the people in his stories seem two-dimensional, appearing more as artificial set pieces than authentic human beings. Finally, several critics have complained that the author, especially in later stories, tends to explain too many of his ideas and is unwilling to let readers make their own connections. Despite these reservations, Sansom has been recognized as one of the important short fiction writers to emerge from England after World War II. William Peden has concluded that "the highest praise one can give Sansom is that even at his less-than-best, he is fun to read. And to reread. His continuing sense of 'wonderment at life' is contagious."

PRINCIPAL WORKS

Short Fiction

Fireman Flower, and Other Stories 1944
Three 1946
The Equilibrand 1948; included in *Among the Dahlias*
Something Terrible, Something Lovely 1948
South 1948
The Passionate North 1950
A Touch of the Sun 1952
Lord Love Us 1954
A Contest of Ladies 1956
Among the Dahlias, and Other Stories 1957
Selected Short Stories 1960
The Stories of William Sansom 1963
The Ulcerated Milkman 1966
The Vertical Ladder, and Other Stories 1969
The Marmalade Bird 1973

Novels

The Body 1949
The Face of Innocence 1951
A Bed of Roses 1954
The Loving Eye 1956
The Cautious Heart 1958
The Last Hours of Sandra Lee 1961; also published as *The Wild Affair*
Goodbye 1966
Hans Feet in Love 1971
A Young Wife's Tale 1974

Other Major Works

Jim Braidy: The Story of Britain's Firemen [with James Gordon and Stephen Spender] (nonfiction) 1943
Westminster in War (nonfiction) 1947
It Was Really Charlie's Castle (juvenilia) 1953
The Light That Went Out (juvenilia) 1953
Pleasures Strange and Simple (travel essays) 1953
The Icicle and the Sun (travel essays) 1958
Blue Skies, Brown Studies (travel essays) 1961
Away to It All (travel essays) 1964
Grand Tour Today (travel essays) 1968
A Book of Christmas 1968; also published as *Christmas*
The Birth of A Story (nonfiction) 1972
Proust and His World (biography) 1973
Skimpy (juvenilia) 1974

CRITICISM

Ronald Mason (essay date 1947)

SOURCE: "William Sansom," *Modern British Writing,* edited by Denys Val Baker, The Vanguard Press, Inc., 1947, pp. 281-91.

[*In the essay below, Mason focuses on the stories in* Three, *contending that these works demonstrate Sansom's attempt to unify parallel strains of realism and allegory in his work.*]

Elaborate yet compact, the specimens so far published of this arresting writer have begun to shape themselves into a pattern calling for examination by critics wary for important developments in modern literature. It is naturally early to make ambitious claims for Sansom's work; but he is, in his way, prolific, he keeps his name regularly before the public in the reviews which those sympathetic with his general aims are most likely to read, and he is establishing a reputation as a writer who is guarding and cherishing a distinctive province of his own with an almost solicitous exclusiveness. It will not be long before someone with the gift will parody him aptly and effectively; and that is as much a tribute as a criticism. Character and distinction come seldom so early to a young author, and they throw even his early productions into refreshing relief against the competence level of the literary reviews.

It may be that writers of imaginative fiction are not common enough in this country nowadays, death and the contemplative life having knocked the bottom out of most progressive work in that field in the last twenty years. For this reason, perhaps, the appearance of a writer with courage enough to exploit an imaginative individuality from the start may be deceptive; and it is possible that a critic who leaps to herald an important innovation may simply be betraying his own inability to distinguish between a swan and a goose in the silence where all birds are dead and yet something pipeth like a bird. Whether Sansom's work would catch the eye in an age rich in imaginative fiction is not really relevant; the point is that it happens to catch the eye today.

Up to and, I think, including the publication of his most recent book of stories, *Three*, he has contrived at present to do little more than to state his case. And although, as I will explain in a moment, there are passages in **Three** where his peculiar imagination does seem at last to have moved out of a static into a dynamic condition and to have achieved moments of really significant artistic illumination, yet he has not penetrated effectively past the necessary experimental stage. By wisely tempering ambition with caution, he has escaped the disasters to which a more ambitious writer like Rex Warner has laid himself open; but avoiding Warner's clumsinesses has involved missing Warner's undoubted triumphs. Sansom's imagination is clearly enough of somewhat the same order as Warner's; and they both owe much of their expressive form to Kafka. Here the resemblance ceases; for Warner, working broadly with a fine imaginative clarity, reduces large generalities to dramatic and artistic compass, while Sansom battens on the familiar symbol and enlarges it to proportions calculated to overpower and capture the imagination by unfamiliarity. That is the first stage well accomplished in his remarkably interesting progress; and though it seemed difficult for him at one time to do any more than consolidate the position he had daringly achieved, his recent work has hinted at wider developments which may have great value in the future. Any ultimate importance that his writing may have will depend on his use, at this crucial point, of his mastery of realism, in imaginative contexts which until lately have been beyond his reach; and any conclusions drawn, without the essentially preliminary nature of even his best work in mind, are bound to be conjectural.

His work is based on a sure foundation of exact and telling realism; his eye for detail is photographic and his skill in selection sure. His mastery of realist narrative is apparent in the greater part of his shorter pieces, and is excellently illustrated in the opening of the sketch **"Steam Tugs and Grey Tape."** As, however, I regard this basic quality of realism as fundamental to Sansom's imaginative achievement, I would prefer to take by way of illustration two much more considerable pieces, oddly similar to each other as it happens: the famous showpiece **"The Wall,"** even

now possibly his best-known sketch, and the more recent **"Building Alive,"** which appeared a few months ago in *Horizon*. Both of these pieces squeezed the last drop of imaginative suggestiveness out of the reportage which was the stock-in-trade of so many of the more alert writers of the late 'thirties and early 'forties. Two of the best pieces of straight reporting that the war produced, they are lifted out of the region of ordinary journalism by Sansom's power of injecting emotional value into a scene that is ordinarily without it, or in the present instances into those parts of the scenes that do not usually contain it. In these short sketches it is the falling wall, or the bombed and tottering house, that is instinct with horrifying life, not the groups of men in danger of being crushed by them. The moment of Sansom's imagination that saw the thing as living and the men as passive and powerless subordinates has been extended and amplified into a prime factor of his inspiration. This brilliant reversal of the design of familiar activity has determined, whether consciously or not, the form of his more important later writings.

The part that Sansom's duties in the Fire Service have played in forming the chief characteristics of his writing can, I suppose, be easily exaggerated; but it is clear that its uniform routine and its surrealist duties provided him with ready-made material for his specialized imagination, offering him at a crucial stage in his development the rare good fortune of a necessary routine familiarity with some activity that, whether he liked it or not, excited his creative faculties beyond any other contemporary experience. The result is that in his stories, far more than in any official or semi-official write-ups, films or pictures, the precarious and monotonous intricacies of this Service find their most imaginative rendering.

Here, of course, he finds worthy companions. Stephen Spender's connection with the N.F.S. has been less conspicuously productive of this kind of literature, probably because his imagination is more sensitive to the variety of impressions in normal day-to-day existence and hardly needs an abnormal set of connations to inflame it to creative pitch; but Henry Green, who had already revealed in *Living* and *Party Going* an original power of infusing dynamic life into strictly localized settings like factories or railway-stations, was able to a build the Fire Service into the background of several sketches, and most particularly into his remarkable novel *Caught*; and his use of it in this way points to a very clearly defined distinction between his view of modern life and Sansom's. Green, for all the paraphernalia of realistic description in *Caught,* is interested less in the technicalities than in the psychological relationships between his characters; and we remember Piper and Pye and Shiner Wright the more vividly perhaps, but no more certainly, for having seen them in their routine context. Sansom is radically different. He is not interested in character for its own sake as Green is; he picks out in his characters' minds only those few instants in which they are being immediately reacted upon by some impersonal power, fire or water or steam, by which they are in danger of being controlled. In this way Green's more orthodox picture of human action against the background of the blitz is replaced by a disturbing vision of dwarfed human insignificance before the elemental onset of fire or explosion or vertigo or pressure of water. Smoke billows up, flames crackle, pumps roar, jets play, walls fall; and in the eyes and mind of the helpless firemen the imagination transfers the terrifying dynamism to the inanimate object. **"The Wall"** can be taken as the perfect example and epitome of Sansom's instinctive imaginative approach to contemporary activity; and he has repeated this unashamedly enlarged realism in later studies, notably, **"In the Morning"** and **"The Boiler Room,"** in both of which the destructive power latent in certain objects, a storage tank full of petrol and a boiler on the point of bursting, supplies the motive force for what little human action there is.

Sansom clearly finds a diabolical fascination in the machinery which clutters up our particular corner of modern existence. The trailer-pumps which chug through his stories, the hoses that snake and coil through them, the dynamos that hum and the ladders that sway, are all given lurid life in the flickering flames and drifting smoke, crashing walls and blazing roofs. Life with Sansom is a kind of animated Wadsworth landscape dancing devils' tattoos in a fearsome reek that Wadsworth's flat functionalism never visualized. Perhaps a more illuminating comparison is with Graham Sutherland; and the calling shapes and beckoning shadows dire, which his view of our age has impelled Sutherland to mass into his pictures, are closely enough akin to Sansom's mechanical familiars to make the artist express in his own medium very much what the writer expresses in his. Incidentally, for a very suggestive rendering in pictorial form of the central impression left by Sansom's collected stories, I would recommend Keith Vaughan's design on the jacket of *Fireman Flower*, a composition that incidentally owes something to Sutherland's influence. And, as an indication of Sansom's sympathetic affinities as well as of his critical apprehensions of them, his recent study in *The Windmill*. . . of the grotesque cartoonist Grandville is particularly revealing.

I dwell on Sansom's preoccupation with this suggestive symbolism because it is to be regarded as symptomatic of the profound unease that he shares, perhaps unusually sensitively, with all sensitive people today. His work is not the result of the superimposition of an ability to write upon a happy idea or two, which occurred to him while fighting fires; it is the precise and logical projection by an unusually vivid imagination of an instinctive feeling that in the machine and its unpure destructive power man has met his match. The physical dwarfing of Sansom's humans in face of their terrifying and masterful machines is an exact representation of the spiritual dwarfing of mankind in face of the overpowering onset of scientific and industrial progress. It is not an original thought, of course, and it is not even a particularly profound one, but it happens to be felt on their pulses by many artists and writers; and the way that Sansom has chosen to express in imaginative form what he has felt intuitively is original enough to make his development of it of real and suggestive value. The mystery and horror of the result is a perfectly genuine reflection of the mystery and horror of many aspects of the present stage of civilization.

This symbolism by way of inflated realism is Sansom's most effective trick. It is derivative, of course, in part from the surrealists, in part through Kafka and Warner. That does not matter very much. What will matter is his creative use of this genuine apprehension of a modern historical fact. At present he has done little more than record it, a duty valuable in itself but naturally incomplete in the hands of a creative artist who is aware that knowledge is merely a prelude to an imaginative use of it.

His awareness of a necessity to develop in more directions than one was apparent in his first published collection of short stories and sketches, *Fireman Flower*, in which he included, besides the grim and challenging studies in realism, a number of more ambitious pieces which suggested that he began quite early to feel forward, in a deliberate attempt to widen his range of effectiveness. In these pieces his own accomplished realism was too generously diluted with Kafka symbolism for the ultimate profit of the finished product; and whereas on his own ground no writer is more economical and pointed, in these attempts he has allowed the access of fantastic technique, not perfectly under control, to push some of his most carefully designed structures out of shape. In this way **"The Forbidden Lighthouse," "In the Maze,"** and the long title-story, **"Fireman Flower,"** succeeded in being little more than interesting essays in variations on Kafka (coupled in the first-named story with Freud, in the second with Warner, and in the third with Sansom himself). In these studies he confined his vital realism to exact and dispassionate description, while, for incident and development, he strayed away into a fantasy with fewer roots in the actual than are essential for its healthy expansion. The failure was especially disappointing in **"Fireman Flower"** itself, where, of all places, Sansom could have been expected to bring off an experimental essay in symbolism and make good an advance of supreme importance in his own development as a writer; but here, in his own chosen and familiar context, the touch was surprisingly sluggish, and the whole piece was deficient in both the poise and the "bite" that marked the best of his earlier work. It was a pity, because in **"Fireman Flower"** there were more than traces of imaginative understanding most valuably matured, both in the selection of episodes and in the culminating paragraph: a deliberate set-piece of lyricism expressive of a genuine poetic apprehension of the reconciliation of opposites implicit in a true vision of beauty; but in spite of that, **"Fireman Flower,"** itself, remained merely a bundle of tantalizing hints of an extended constructive ability that as yet was a potentiality rather than a fact.

Yet there was one story in this first volume where he did succeed in coordinating his divided technique; and in this single instance he was able to exploit his mastery of realism in conjunction with an adequate expression of his fantastic imagination. He boldly advanced beyond his conquered territory and successfully expanded his theme into regions where he was for once able to express a poetic and intuitive vision, with real creative insight; and in the remarkable short story **"The Long Sheet,"** he cleverly braked down his symbolic transports to the dimensions of parable—parable securely enough based on reality, but employing as its medium a fantastic and unusual subject and form. He called up in aid of his fancy all his considerable powers of elaborate and logical realism; and the result is an object-lesson in controlled allegory, emerging in the last section in a neat and convincing intellectual statement inevitable in its context, and entirely in accord with the imaginative presentation of the whole. Here he fused realism and fantasy in so cogent and successful a form that **"The Long Sheet"** still ranks as perhaps the most suggestive and important of all his stories yet published.

It is evident that in Sansom there exist two parallel imaginative strains whose coordination is a major technical problem. Of the pure realism I would add no more to my general opinion, that its value is as a foundation only on which important work can be raised, were it not that he appears to regard it still as a self-sufficient unit in his work by continuing to publish such pieces as **"Building Alive"** and **"Cat up a Tree."** I confess that the inclusion of the later piece in *Three,* vigorous and vivid as it is, surprised me; since, unless, he made a deliberate choice of the three items out of separate elements in his own work, it represents a vein of competence that he has worked over so many times before that it can be of no more than passing interest to those who look for adventure rather than for repetition in Sansom's work. On the other hand, the strain of pure allegory, which obviously attracts him deeply, is tenuous, unless it can be controlled and nourished at the source by Sansom's acute observation of material reality, and, which is even more important by a balanced critical view of life. Detached pieces of allegorical bravura like **"The Kiss"** are admittedly minor *tours de force,* but they rank as elaborate prose poems whose chief value lies more in their capacity to record intuitive moments than in any qualities of larger illumination.

In three long pieces all published within the last few months, Sansom has made perhaps his most sustained effort since **"The Long Sheet"** to face up to the business of unifying these two parallel strains into a powerful, single, imaginative instrument. One of these, *The Equilibriad,* appeared separately in the sixth series of *English Story*; the other two form the solid and significant bulk of *Three*.

It is one of the signs of a serious creative writer that he does not remain long in the consolidation of his achieved visions, but having absorbed them makes use of them in traveling forward to fresh experiments and experiences. These latest stories indicate that Sansom has by now extracted all the valuable juice from the N.F.S., or realistic, phase of his career, and is carrying his profits into even more suggestive fields. He still cannot do without his infernal machines (witness that recent remarkable essay in tension, **"The Little Room,"** and the last story in *Three,* **"The Invited,"** which is set among engine-sheds and their complicated surroundings); but his interest is wider and more catholic, and he is deliberately altering his focus and bringing the intricacies of living humanity into his line of vision—where before he was only concerned with the intricacies of humanity's lurid modern setting. This harbors

enormous possibilities; for if Sansom can, in due course, anatomize Frankenstein as he has faithfully anatomized his terrifying invention, then there is no more promising writer working today—although I must not omit the inevitable truism that the anatomization of humanity requires far subtler mechanism than Sansom has yet shown signs of employing. Nevertheless, these later stories are uncommonly stimulating, not only for their technique but for the evidence they provide of that balanced view of life—that long view—which I demanded as a foundation for significant allegory; **"The Equilibriad,"** especially, is a study of rare subtlety and originality which man is no longer seen as in conflict with the impersonal forces of scientific or industrial development, but in his even more tragic and inconclusive conflict with the evasions and ambiguities of his own nature. If it is not consciously or unconsciously derived from a mood akin to that in which Kafka wrote "The Transformation," then the coincidence is unusual, since the emphasis here, as in the earlier work, is on man's everlasting and ever-unsuccessful quest for contact and responsiveness among his fellows; and if Kafka's story is the more poignant, it is only because Sansom's is perhaps rooted deeper in the intellect than in the imagination—a condition still common with him. A similar theme is followed in far greater detail and with the coloring, unfamiliar in Sansom, of economic, and class, consciousnesses to exaggerate the eternal disunities in the **"The Invited,"** the last story in *Three*. There has been here an access of power along with the access of vision; the elaborate realism no longer stifles the larger breath of humane sympathy and understanding, and this admirable extension of the familiar Sansom vein into the region of illuminating commentary is heartening evidence of his sure progress towards a completer and more comprehensive insight.

But the welcome increase in the scope of his control is nowhere more apparent than in **"The Cleaner's Story."** Here for the first time he sees human beings in more than one dimension; as individuals, as well as units, as embodiments of arbitrary idiosyncrasies as well as relevant factors in the social conflict that for many is the only intelligible symbol of the universal conflicts that form the central inspiration of Sansom's writing, and which he is now able to perceive on so many planes. He has abrogated neither his realism nor his symbolism, but has reinforced them both with a new satiric lightness; and by the simple and brilliant device of telling his story from the mouth of a cleaner of the floor of a café, has contrived to intensify the illumination of his scene just as the vividness of the colors in a landscape are intensified if you look at them upside down. Observant, humorous, perceptive, this striking short story is unlike anything he has ever done before, but yet seems to embody, on inspection, the most valuable of all the characteristics that I have noted in my progress through his earlier work—faithful realism, intensity of atmosphere, and enlargement of detail to a symbolical significance. So far from being at a tangent from his former course, it completes much of his preliminary development and suggests potentialities as yet foreign to him.

The farthest limits of his realism have already begun to shade into the nearer regions of an imaginative literature in which he holds out the highest promise. His way now lies through an intensification of his realism to a kind of supercharged state at which it can combine with his powerful allegorical imagination, to generate and radiate a creative force of its own. This high-pressure suggestiveness, transferred into wider fields of fantasy and reinforced by his welcome access of social and humanitarian vision, may hold unpredictable possibilities for the future of imaginative fiction. It remains to be seen whether he can do at full length what he has perfected in little; and whether, from a nightmare miniaturist, he can mature into a powerful and imaginative creative artist equal to the demands of a particularly exacting civilization.

Alice S. Morris (essay date 1956)

SOURCE: "Characters without Will," in *The New York Times Book Review,* March 25, 1956, pp. 4, 24.

[*In this review of* A Contest of Ladies, *Morris argues that the story writer's usual concerns with plot development don't interest Sansom because his works are "entertainments" and "extravaganzas" that "come off best when quick and to the point."*]

In the fifteen stories that make up *A Contest of Ladies,* William Sansom again exhibits a gift for dazzling verbal prestidigitation. For surely, as has been remarked in the past, Mr. Sansom's sly and energetic legerdemain marshals the English language into magical bursts of freshness and improvisation. In these new stories, as in those of his earlier collections, whatever mood Mr. Sansom is after he stunningly evokes: the macabre, the malevolent, the boisterous, the farcical. His sense of place—Strasbourg, Marseilles, the Costa Brava, an English countryside—is impressively conveyed; and his mists, thunderstorms and blazing suns alert the reader to the immediacies of weather.

For all this high skill in bringing to life an atmosphere and a setting, the stories strangely fail themselves to come to life. The upper hand Mr. Sansom holds eventually overwhelms them. His characters are permitted no will of their own: only Mr. Sansom's own. Like microbes placed on slides under a microscope, he prods them into positions, or situations, of an amused and sardonic devising. Although they may assume various entertaining postures in the process, they are too often the extravagant postures of corpses or puppets.

In fairness to Mr. Sansom, the usual concerns of the storyteller—the development of a human situation, the illumination of some facet of human experience—are matters outside his interest. He is a man of conceits, of diverting and sometimes flashy notions. His stories are more accurately entertainments, or outright extravaganzas, and these come off best when quick and to the point.

"The Big Stick," a regalement on the complex art of being a second-rater; **"A Roman Holiday,"** about a vacationing draper's clerk happily recalled to the joys of his calling by a view of saintly statues odd-angled against the Roman sky; **"A Country Walk,"** in which a city type with tweedy aspirations is hounded into panic by some normal manifestations of nature—these brief, artful exercises make engaging reading.

The longer tales—**"A Contest of Ladies," "Happy Holiday Abroad," "An Interlude"**—lead one very far for rather little. While, page by page, they hold out whole cornucopias of witty and splendid observation, the delights, heaven knows how, tend to pall. Mr. Sansom's conceit, or whim, crumbles slowly under the elaboration and the reader is left with the feeling that he's been had.

Horace Gregory wrote once in the Book Review: "Somewhere in William Sansom exists the best, the most unpredictable writer of short fiction that England has produced since the death of D. H. Lawrence." It still, somewhere in William Sansom, does.

John B. Vickery (essay date 1961)

SOURCE: "William Sansom and Logical Empiricism," in *THOUGHT,* Vol. XXXVI, No. 141, Summer, 1961, pp. 231-45.

[*Vickery is a Canadian-born educator and critic. In the following essay, he asserts that many of Sansom's short stories are philosophical, addressing "the nature of mind and the nature of reality."*]

The fiction of William Sansom, like the poetry of Empson, has by and large not made the transatlantic crossing with any great success nor has it aroused any sustained critical interest. The explanation does not lie in his having written too little to provide a basis for judgement, for he is the author of five novels (*The Body, The Face of Innocence, A Bed of Roses, The Loving Eye,* and *The Cautious Heart*), eight volumes of short stories (*Fireman Flower, Something Terrible, Something Lovely, South, The Passionate North, A Touch of the Sun, Lord Love Us, A Contest of Ladies,* and *Among the Dahlias*), and several novelles (*Three, The Equilibriad*) as well as children's stories and essays. Nor can the critical indifference be ascribed to a lack of sympathetic and influential readers. Persons as diverse as Horace Gregory, Eudora Welty, and Norman Holmes Pearson have been enthusiastic about Sansom's fictive skill, but their praises have not led to any serious or sustained attempt at interpretation.

Actually the critical lag which his work has suffered from stems perhaps from a threefold cause. To some American reviewers his characters lack humanity and moral earnestness in conception, while to others his style is seriously flawed by idiosyncratic mannerisms. And for still others his work can be dismissed because it lacks a thematic depth or, rather, because the theme has become style itself. Clearly these views are both interrelated and symptomatic of a critical limitation in American literary circles that is no less serious for being so widespread. But this is not the place to explore the significance of Sansom's implicit identification with writers like Frederick Buechner, Truman Capote, and Sacheverell Sitwell as an elegant trifler, nor to ponder the mystery of a provincial moralism concerning style which apparently exempts only Katherine Anne Porter from stricture.

More pertinent at the moment is the isolation of that factor which renders Sansom's work important and very nearly unique in contemporary British literature. Put most simply, the controlling mode of Sansom's art at its best, and I have no wish to deny the commercial trickery or the sophomoric cleverness of some of his work, is neither impressionism nor verbal exoticism but philosophic. Consequently, he is part of what may be called a Continental rather than an English or American tradition. This is not to say that the English or the Americans do not have a philosophic tradition but only that it is of a different order. The traditional philosophical concern of the English and American writer has been with the overlapping areas of social and individual morality which philosophy calls ethics. This is the point on which Jane Austen, George Eliot, Hawthorne, Dickens, Dreiser, Fitzgerald, and many others focus when their works broaden out to universality. In contrast, the Continent has a tradition of philosophic fiction which one might call more nearly professional. This is so not only because many of its authors have had academic training in philosophy but also because its manifest content is such that intensely literate philosophers like Gustav Bergmann and John Wisdom (who actually refers to Sansom in one of his essays) can immediately recognize conscious imitations of philosophic problems, both perennial and contemporary. Attention is not concentrated exclusively on the ethical dimension; metaphysics, epistemology, logic, ontology, and phenomenology, all are involved in the fictional universe.

Today the most obvious examples of this tradition are those writers loosely identified as existentialists. In *Nausea,* for example, Sartre adumbrates those concepts of being and nothingness, of the *en-soi* and *pour-soi* that appear in purer form in his philosophical works, which in their turn abound in dramatically concrete analyses of human psychology appropriate to the novel. Similarly, Mme. de Beauvoir's novels are phenomenological samples of her *Ethics of Ambiguity,* while Camus' *Noces* and *The Stranger,* like many of Sansom's stories, appraise the ontological status of sensations. But the existentialists are not the only representatives of this tradition. Their forerunner, André Malraux, with his use of anguish and absurdity as metaphysical facts, is in its mainstream, as is Raymond Queneau, whose *Exercises in Style* and *The Skin of Our Dreams* wittily play with the epistemological problems of perception. Herman Hesse is a major figure here by virtue pre-eminently of his *Magister Ludi* in which he elegiacally chronicles the function of ontological theories as games and vice versa. So too is Robert Musil, who makes the notion of substance central to his *The Man without Qualities* and in so doing subjects it to a logical analysis that reflects his awareness of the *Wiener Kreis.* Certainly earlier and perhaps better known in this country is Thomas Mann for whom, as *The Magic Mountain* and *Doctor*

Faustus in particular demonstrate, history is the dialectic of metaphysical systems seen as operant in the individual. And balancing the portentous sobriety of Mann is Kafka, the metaphysical comedian, who erects in novels like *The Trial* and *The Castle* multivalued logical structures designed not to eliminate ambiguity but, as Bertrand Russell said in *Principia Mathematica,* to control it. The lone American to participate in this tradition is Henry James, whose status as the supreme epistemological novelist has frequently been obscured by his use of society and its manners as the medium of his analyses. Even Melville, who might ordinarily be thought of as the most philosophic of American writers, really only registers his awareness of philosophy. Rarely does he, in Gilbert Ryle's phrase, "do a bit of it," a point dramatized by *The Confidence Man*'s avoidance of a solution to its central philosophic problem.

Sansom does in fact belong to this Continental tradition but in a characteristically British fashion, for his outlook more nearly resembles that of the contemporary empiricist and analytic philosophers of Oxford and Cambridge (particularly striking since he is a nonuniversity man) than that of the older Continental rationalist or today's existentialist. This can be seen by turning to some of his short stories and tracing out their primary themes, which are unabashedly and at least semideliberately philosophic in nature. These themes are too numerous and complex to deal with here, involving as they do analyses of time, perception, consciousness, the emotions, authority and the individual, qualities such as perfection, and relations such as sameness and differences. Essentially, however, Sansom's philosophic problems are generated by his attraction to two questions: the nature of mind and the nature of reality. And of these, the former is ultimately seen to be the ground of the latter. This is grippingly dramatized in **"One Sunny Afternoon,"** in which a man alone in his home, resting, is drawn by a survey of his past and future to feel the imminence of an unpredictable event. Yielding himself to fancies, he finds his premonition "projected out of imagination into the full reality of predicament." Then a maniac, who, it turns out, has just murdered his wife and baby, slips into the room to terrorize Axmann. The previously imagined, formless menace has taken on shape and he is confronted with "realizing it, while its reality grew greater and greater." This is a motif that Sansom elaborates countless times in a variety of guises: the birth of reality through the mating of imagination and will.

Yet since he is a writer rather than a philosopher, he does not formulate this relation as an initial proposition to be elaborated and proven. Instead his characters begin with the naive realism of the man in the street who asserts, as does the lone character in **"My Tree,"** that "I cannot ever believe that the tree has not its own true identity, its own exact size, its independence of my miserable self." They are disabused of this notion and launched on the philosopher's quest—which is really Sansom's central theme, matched only by that of the philosophical life in his later collections of stories—by the occurrence of an impossible event which violates nature's law. Representative here is the opening story in his first collection, where a man looking through a green liqueur glass lowers it only to find that "the green gloom persisted . . . the quinquina glass had left its imprint on the world." Sensuous impressions as well as mental acts like imaging are, then, in Sansom's world, capable of creating reality.

The philosopher's quest for adequate explanations is inaugurated because, for one thing, as the narrator of **"Beauty and Beast"** recognizes, "our simple minds like things to match up." And for another thing, as the tourist learns from the topiarist in the allegorical **"In the Maze,"** "'My brain, alone of all my organs, is never still. My brain is the eternally active limb'." One possible solution entertained by the mind is the denial or doubt of the unusual event's actually having occurred. Thus, in **"The Witnesses"** the narrators are uncertain whether the fireman really saw the pump operator attempting to kill him. The brain is described as "the unreliable agent" while other external factors are noted which might have contributed to the fireman's illusion. And yet this attitude is never permitted to stand as a final solution in Sansom's stories, for it is essentially an evasion of those paradoxes metaphysics is designed to resolve. It is instructive that the example here adduced deals only with an improbable not an impossible event. When the latter does appear, the mind's instinctive attitude is to deny, but Sansom makes the event itself so sensuously immediate, so disarmingly "given," that the mind cannot withhold assent to the reality of the event. **"A Saving Grace"** dramatizes this process nicely through the rather hoary means of a ghost story. Here, however, the emphasis is not upon the action of the story but on the psychology of the narrator, who self-consciously analyzes his reaction to the ghosts' appearance to reveal its underlying rationale: "you admit that somewhere, beyond your instant understanding, there is a reason quite logical for his visitation. . . . You must assume your own ignorance, you give him a lien on a place, certain but as yet uncertified, in the scheme of things." In this, as in **"The Windows,"** the highly cerebral quality of Sansom's characters is underscored. Not only do they possess minds but also the reader and they are made particularly aware of their mental operations. Thus, frequently they both narrate the events and simultaneously react to their consciousness of their minds functioning.

Confronted by the apparent fact that some forms of reality are impossible and yet occur, the mind may react in one of two major ways in its search for an explanation. One attempt to solve the apparent violation of natural law is to plunge into traditional forms of superstition and to postulate magic as an operative force in the universe. This is what Niccolo, the old keeper of the Pitti Palace, does in **"Afternoon"** when his attempts to seize the street urchin encroaching upon his beloved museum are frustrated by the boy's ability "to slide back a full metre" out of his grasp without ducking, side-stepping, or twisting away. To him, it is "a most placid, magical escape . . . the first magic in all his life that he had seen." Of a similar order is **"Poseidon's Daughter,"** which opens with a description of the wind that evokes the primordial past standing just behind the present in Greece. In the course of the narrative the impression that the present scene on the

Tyrrhenian beach possesses a mythical and legendary matrix is subtly intensified until it compels man to accept it as a world of total possibility: "A legendary sea—it was difficult not to look round suddenly and think: 'Anything can happen here'."

Such a primitive mode of thought is particularly likely in countries such as Greece and Italy where ancient customs and beliefs persist tenaciously, but it is also possible, with adaptations, in urban industrialized areas and its populace. **"Venice"** raises this only as a speculative possibility, a tentative entertaining of an apparently outmoded concept such as witchcraft. But in **"The Boiler Room"** the implicit danger of the boilers for the two stokers is seen in the description of the machines as looking "like huge dormant pachyderms, enclosed by a bright fence, truncated featureless monsters, but alive." Here we have a glancing revelation of the unconscious impression the boilers make on a mind and its attempt to formulate a mythology for the machine age based on the superstitious legends of the past.

The preceding method of "explaining" reality's idiosyncrasies is, of course, antiphilosophic insofar as it promulgates reasons whose probability is of no higher order than the events they are supposed to explain. A witty exposé of the consequences of such an approach is presented in **"Three Dogs of Siena,"** a contemporary beast fable. The dogs are the embodiment of "ever-searching minds" eager for life or reality and the problem or challenge they pose is that of knowledge, of introspective psychology—how to know what they are thinking. When they confront a group of men about to perform a Sbandierata, an elaborate flourish of flags, we witness the impact on the dogs of a new and unusual sight. In their behavior we are to read, with wry chagrin, the characteristically human reaction to the existential puzzle. First, there is the "germ of hysteria," then a plethora of inaccurate interpretations inspired by their wonder and conditioned by their use of analogy and the attempt to relate the new phenomena to their previous experience. Giant birds, eagle-giants, snakes, fire, and "animated sharp-toothed cloths," all are postulated as values to be assigned the unknown variable, the flags; but all are wrong, as the kicks received by the dogs attest. These same kicks also provide a mediate explanation of the flags, one whose "meaning was absolute" because given, not sought, and because existentially inescapable rather than logically inferred.

When the mind turns to the various forms of "rational" explanation, it does so, as Aristotle announces in the opening sentence of the *Metaphysics,* because "all men naturally desire knowledge." Hence, he goes on, they value the senses, especially sight, for it "*reveals* many distinctions." In one of the stories already referred to, it is precisely the sight of a tree that sparks a man's desire to make knowledgeable distinctions: "why does it stand there? What is it? Why do I own it? To what purpose? These are questions that can longer be avoided . . . the smaller topics of living pale and disappear beside such fundamental questions." From this, it is clear that the fundamental questions for Sansom's characters are those of purpose or cause, essence, properties, those, in short, asked by the metaphysician. And just as Aristotle stresses the delight and love men feel for the senses because they are conducive to knowledge, so Sansom shows how the topics, questions, and unknown answers mentioned above become a genuine passion and obsession with men aroused to thought by sensations. Indeed, it is precisely in this arousal of thought by sensations that Sansom's style, at least one form of it, has a major reason for being.

Yet Sansom is not really a nineteenth-century British rationalist for whom the goal of life is the disinterested acquisition of truth. He sees the search for explanations as motivated also by the conflict within the individual of possibilities and improbabilities so extreme as to be virtual impossibilities. The tension generated in the mind by extreme instances of what is conceivable to the imagination and to common sense is a most acute form of metaphysical malaise, as Ludwig Wittgenstein, John Wisdom, and others have shown. Among Sansom's characters, in effect, it frequently entails an apparent denial of the law of contradiction. They live in a world obedient to what his editors call Leibniz's Law of Continuity which codifies their perception that a thing both is and is not.

Such a state, constituting as it does the logical version of schizophrenia, drives the mind to seek a resolution of the tension. Its characteristic action after its initial confrontation with incertitude is to leap to identify and catalogue a fact and then to attempt an explanation by elaborating reasonable and probable hypotheses. Thus, Pietro of **"Poseidon's Daughter,"** while underwater fishing, harpoons what he thinks is a concealed octopus. But as he hauls it in, it suddenly appears as a "human body floating slowly up towards him hanging there on the surface—a body with streaming hair, a woman's body. Before he could recognize its features, he knew it was his wife." Immediately he assumes it is his sick wife, who either deliberately or in her sleep has leapt from their cliff home to her death. Yet the danger and limitations of such essentially "scientific" and probable hypotheses are immediately pointed out when the body proves to be that of a man, not a woman, and when he discovers his wife alive though poised precariously from where he had imagined her falling. These are farther underscored by the fact that after a storm "no body had been washed up anywhere" so that ultimately he is left with the unanswered question: "could he be certain that he ever saw anything—that it was not some private vision?" Thus, the attempted solution results not only in the reassertion of the original problem but also in the raising of an additional metaphysical question—whether this action of the mind proves it to be its own cause or whether it is subject to some external and superhuman power.

Out of this multiplicity of possible explanations which many of Sansom's characters are led to advance in support of their observations and actions, the author develops another of his major themes, the problematic character of truth and observation. **"The Witnesses"** raises as its central issue the credibility of any eyewitness. It does so by the bizarrely witty device of making the witnesses the eyes themselves of the character who is led to his death by his own brain. Like the Gestalt psychologist, Sansom throws doubt on the possibility of objectively rendering experience. The story **"Afternoon"** shows that different values are attached to an event because of the scope of the perspective from which it is viewed and concludes that the wider the scope, the less the value. Complications arise also from the fact, sharply realized in **"A White Lie,"** that "in moments of emotion the mind still finds time to angle off on the most ordinary material considerations." That the mind is a selector as well as a reflector leads, we learn from **"Tutti Frutti,"** to a moral question by observation of what it has omitted from its calculations.

Similarly, **"Through the Quinquina Glass"** poses the problem of human perception; of what Kohler has called the place of value in a world of facts. Here, however, the stress is not so much on the possibility as on the care necessary in formulating a description of what we see. The narrator's point of view is one of philosophical or epistemological parsimony and his notion of the logically valid statement is reminiscent of the so-called physicalist thesis of the early Carnap and of what contemporary philosophers like A. J. Ayer and Morris Lazcrowitz have dubbed the "strong" (as opposed to "weak") verification theory of meaningfulness. This he expounds to a friend in the fashion of the true analytic philosopher, that is, by means of anecdote and example: "We see a man cleaning a car—and we say to ourselves 'There is a man cleaning a car.' But perhaps that man is really wondering whether he should propose marriage to his girl. That, of course, is of more moment than cleaning a car. So what we are seeing is in truth a man wondering about a proposal—not a man cleaning a car. We should be more humble in our judgements: We should say, at the most, 'There is a man'."

And yet even this limited statement is subject to doubt and error as the narrator of **"The Ballroom"** proves when his eyes say "abruptly the room had poured full of children" only to refute this a moment later with "this was after all no room full of girls, it was of course one child only, one child reflected in a dozen mirrors," a child whom the conclusion reveals as an elderly recluse, Miss Amery. Thus, he reflects that knowledge about a secret process, such as a human life, is an impossibility: "Whatever is found, people can only suppose how life was actually lived: nobody *knows*." It can never be reconstructed "for sure," that is, verified by observation which itself is verifiable and certain.

With the concomitant and concerted actions of reality and the mind to refute the proffered explanations, Sansom limns in additional themes: first, the part played in man's life by fate and coincidence and, second, the nature of the mind as an organism ceaselessly activated by the presence of the irreconcilable. The first of these is carefully delineated with ironic ambiguity in **"Tutti Frutti."** Ohlsson, arriving in Nice desirous of romantic adventure, demonstrates, according to Sansom, that sufficient hope can occasion the realization of its wish, dream, or fairy tale. Yet as Ohlsson's accident indicates, fate or coincidence—

and the two are frequently indistinguishable in these stories—can interfere and destroy the opportunity created by the mind. Of even greater speculative subtlety is **"A Small World"** which deals with the apparently accidental plane crash in a London suburb that kills a husband and wife. The theme is that "of independent and possibly capricious movements and effects over the new great distances that have made the world so small. Possibly capricious—but possibly interwoven beyond the wildest dreams of prescience, possibly the first faint blueprinting of the system scorned as fate." It is in just this plenitude of possibilities that the ambiguity inherent in the metaphysical structure of Sansom's world resides. Like Mme. de Beauvoir, he sees ambiguity as possessing a metaphysical core that thereby inevitably projects it into human affairs, into the realm of ethics.

The other theme, that of the mind's ceaseless endeavors to absorb the impossible event into a coherent pattern, runs throughout a number of the stories. It is the central problem attempted by many and finally solved by the narrator in **"Beauty and Beast."** In the presence of a startling fact—"a very beautiful woman married to an unusually ugly man"—minds immediately begin their complicating action which, in this case, consists of ascribing elaborate motives to explain the unusual relation. But the explanations of society are useless: "nothing was explained. She remained a mystery." The narrator alone possesses genuine knowledge of the situation, for he knows the "why" as well as the "what." It is just this quality that distinguishes the Sansom hero from the rest of his characters and accounts for the frequency with which he is cast as the contemplative or retrospective narrator. In reality, he is Aristotle's artist of the *Metaphysics,* and thus, as an artist, he naturally enough narrates with the stylist's eye. Aristotle, we remember, declares the artist is wiser than the man of experience because he knows the cause. In his stories, Sansom frequently employs as a basic situation the man of experience endeavoring to become the artist by learning the cause of events, actions, and thoughts.

On simple problems, seen from a limited or short-range viewpoint, or subject to privileged communication (as in **"Beauty and Beast"**), Sansom's hero may turn up what we would ordinarily call a cause. But more frequently the author involves his characters in complex and incredible situations of Kafka-like inexplicability; and when he does, the tales become allegories in which all attention is focused as much on the mind's habit of allegory as on the meaning. In effect, such stories as **"The Peach-House Potting-Shed," "The Forbidden Lighthouse," "In the Maze," "The Long Sheet,"** and **"Fireman Flower"** are allegories on allegory. The central effect in them is to render the notion of causality as problematic and difficult as Hume did for subsequent philosophers with his famous analysis. Sansom's approach to the problem is, however, precisely the reverse of Hume's though the net result of both is to curtail an easy reliance on the concept. Where Hume argues that causality has no existence as a logical relation, Sansom deluges the mind with possible causes in order to demonstrate the impossibility of ascertaining causes in any specific situation.

"The Death of Baldy" formulates this view in its very first paragraph: "cause and occasion multiply, it is difficult to fix on any single action that affects our lives. Or affects our deaths. When finally the axe comes down on the bared neck—can one ever call that an axe? Not rather the impress of past action? And the thought that led to that action? And the state of mind that caused the thought?" And after an extensive narrative and reflective analysis, virtually coterminous with the story itself, the conclusion is once again ambiguity—the precise cause of Baldy's death cannot be formulated. **"From the Water Junction"** is even more explicit in its assessment of the causal question. Since "there is no end to these possibilities and no means by which their validity call be measured," the issue of why "the three pale long-legged boys had made their home on the subterranean quays of the water-junction" is held to be "not of the first importance." "Let it suffice," says the author, that such a situation existed. Questions of this sort, about causation, can be formulated and so are valid as such, but empirically they are incapable of truth or falsity since the infinity of possibilities scarcely permits of an unequivocal answer.

The impossibility of utilizing the concept of causation in explanatory hypothesis affords the mind, according to Sansom, three alternatives, each of which it entertains in the course of the philosophical quest. First, there is the rational man's equivalent of the irrational postulate of magic—the obsessive assertion of an explanation without regard for its correspondence to reality. That this is not simply a stubborn refusal to pay the empirical piper and to dance to his tune is seen in **"The Little Fears."** This is the story of a man obsessed by the fear of being murdered and of his account of the three incidents which he construes as attempts on his life. Its theme is the mind's capacity to interpret events in a manner that is coherently true but does not correspond to actuality. Here, then, in embryonic and simplified fashion, is the philosopher who embraces the so-called coherence theory of truth in which the criterion is self-contained consistency and deductive validity. Though the narrator approaches it, he is not insane, and for this reason he is incapable of settling comfortably into his conviction. Instead, the ingenuity and critical acuteness that inspired this theory persist so that its details can never be fixed permanently, and the search for the completed theory continues: "Again and again I achieve certainty, only to find it reversed, incontrovertibly reversed by a simple, unseen readjustment of first premises! Incontrovertible—rather, controversive, for even the reversal itself becomes then insecure, the reversal may be reversed in the fawning of a new perspective. Permutations then extend without horizon . . . error, error, error." Knowledge is dissolved by recurrent mental acts into a momentarily changing phenomenon.

The second alternative derives from the first in that the only resort where the coherence theory is inviolable is insanity, that form of mental life which alone can mount a sustained denial of actuality. Because he is not insane, only obsessed, the narrator of **"The Little Fears"** moves toward the second alternative when he carries his Cartesian analysis of the grounds of knowledge to its ultimate conclusion: "I know nothing. Knowledge has become an apparition—insubstantive and only of ephemeral wonder." This alternative is reached by Fireman Flower in the story bearing his name. It is ostensibly the tale of a volunteer fireman in London during World War II and his efforts to reach the source of a particular fire. Actually it is an allegorical account of a metaphysical quest that ends, somewhat like Hesse's *Journey to the East,* with the recognition that the quest was illusory but necessary. More specifically, it celebrates the philosopher's emancipation from traditional metaphysics and recognition of its function as an illuminating puzzle.

From the very outset, Flower finds himself making inferences and hypotheses which both phenomenal and logical reality force him to modify or to reject. At length ambiguity and existence's apparent denial of the law of contradiction force him to accept the second alternative, namely, that the world of thought is a chaos. Conflicting interpretations or impressions in the mind, when irresolvable, produce disorder too in reality, in the phenomeno-logically given: "It was this dead light, this duet of life and the denial of life that first impressed Flower with the true quality of the chaos into which he had ventured." In effect, such a view of thought is not so much a philosophy as an abandonment of philosophy, which in itself entails self-contradiction (i.e., "'Thought is chaotic,' says a thinking creature" can be rendered meaningful only by the use of the philosophical concept of a meta-language; hence, philosophy must be invoked in order to abandon it).

If the first alternative approximates the coherence theory of truth of the great formal idealist philosophers, then the use of metaphysical speculation to deny the rational character of thought, as in the second alternative, is clearly reminiscent of the nineteenth-century romantic philosophers like Schopenhauer and Nietzsche. That many minds often do accept this last view either completely or intermittently Sansom tacitly recognizes by the attention he devotes to characters whose motives are dominated by emotions. These persons have structured their emotions into patterned actions of such complexity that in reality they illustrate a metaphysics of passion which Sansom chronicles and analyzes with all the subtlety and dispassionateness of Aquinas or Spinoza. Stories like **"The Little Room," "Pas de Deux," "A Woman Seldom Found," "An Interlude," "The Forbidden Lighthouse," "Time and Place,"** and **"A Waning Moon"** are engrossing studies of what Spinoza called the *conatus* of the human organism.

But just as philosophers become disenchanted with the irrational as a controlling concept, so Sansom's prototypical hero, the questing mind, moves on to a new concept with which to resolve those problems which contemporary thinkers call "philosophical puzzles" or "metaphysical surprises." Thus, for Fireman Flower the symbolic chaos of the burning warehouse can be dispelled by pushing on to the center of the fire. In the process, what is sought ceases to be the cause but instead becomes the essence of the fire. But once it does, the mind discovers that the problem has not been made any simpler: it realizes in

principle the multiplicity of aspects, the complexity of any substance and with this the difficulty of determining its essence. This realization, however, has to be confirmed by the actual philosophical enterprise of isolating by exploratory analysis the essence of a concept. Hence, Fireman Flower undergoes a series of dream-like, surrealistic experiences virtually each one of which leads him to think "'At last I have come face to face with the essence of things! Here is the abstract! . . . Here is reason!'"

And yet the result of his successive failures is not despair nor a distortion of the evidence as had resulted in the case of the concept of causality. He discovers that the illusion of the concept of essence is derived from the mind, from its anticipation, expectation, and desire that the illusion be the reality. A metaphysic that isolates an aspect or quality as the essence of its subject inevitably leads to philosophic puzzles and paradoxes. These, however, constitute what John Wisdom has called one aspect of philosophical progress, namely, provocation. They provoke the mind into its analytic, questioning mode which is the antithesis of traditional metaphysical systems that claim to offer certitude. This is so for two reasons. First, the analytic mode never provides categorical or complete answers; it prefers what Karl Popper calls the piecemeal approach which it knows is essential to the freed mind. Flower grasps this point first when he sees that "freedom from doubt has nothing whatsoever to do with pure freedom. Freedom from doubt, the greatest deception of all!" The second point, that philosophical analysis is a form of therapy, Flower grasps only at the end of the story. When he breaks through to the roof high above the fire, he symbolizes his escape from what Cornford calls the individual's "myth-historia," those ingrained attitudes and habits of language which one employs without thought, without conceiving of a possible alternative mode.

The analytic unraveling of puzzles results in an understanding of metaphysical errors, of what Gilbert Ryle calls "category-mistakes," and of the anxiety which motivated the philosophic quest together with the reasons for that state of mind. All this Flower achieves when he looks down on the warehouse, its surroundings, and his companions and smiles, "his awareness of all things warming him." Now, at last, he is capable of a truly analytic definition of "essence": the totality of existence—the antinomies of the "single rusted nail" and "the Giaconda smile," the "cat's head in the gutter" and "the breasts of Joan"—-apprehended with love and hence accepted unreservedly. Thus, he endorses the view of the great logician, Willard Quine, whose essay "On What There Is" tells us that the answer is "everything." At this point, Sansom's philosopher hero sees the validity of Wittgenstein's assertion: "Philosophy simply puts everything before us, and neither explains nor deduces anything. . . . The work of the philosopher consists in assembling reminders for a particular purpose."

The truly interesting and rewarding feature of this conclusion and of Sansom's stories in general, however, is not to be found in the endorsement of logical empiricism and linguistic analysis which they seem to carry. For these are but one of several philosophies confronting the modern mind. Actually the value or rather one of the values of Sansom's fiction is his demonstration of philosophy's capacity to be effectively drawn into literature, to permeate it with that challenge the intelligence hurls at itself when man is most earnestly seeking the truth. This is not to say that Sansom commands our attention because he puts some intellectual bulk in our literary diet or immunizes us with high seriousness against the frivolities of drugstore fiction. Instead, like the *Phaedo,* he shows us that there really is an absorbing drama of the intellect and that abstractions and concepts are central for man's emotional life as well as for his intellectual existence. Ideas are not pallid, anemic, static entities existing apart from the so-called real world, but just the reverse—they are at the very core of the world man has made for himself, and in large measure they are responsible for the particular nature that world assumes.

Elizabeth Bowen (essay date 1963)

SOURCE: An introduction to *The Stories of William Sansom,* The Hogarth Press, 1963, pp. 7-12.

[*Bowen was an Anglo-Irish fiction writer and critic. Her novels and short stories are often compared with the fiction of Virginia Woolf and display similar stylistic control and subtle insight in the portrayal of human relationships. Bowen is also noted for her series of supernatural stories set in London during World War II. Here, she asserts that two of Sansom's greatest strengths are his ability to convey hallucination and to depict scenes. She also comments on Sansom's ability to achieve "a compulsive hold on the reader."*]

Rare is the writer with command of his powers who absolutely cannot write a short story—if he so desire, or if (as may happen) it be desired of him. Few there must be who have not, at one time or another, wanted to try the hand at this form, or found themselves seized by an idea which could be embodied in no way other than this. The writer not sooner or later tempted to try everything, if only to prove to himself that he cannot do it, must be exceptional; might one not say, defective? Incidental short stories of writers by nature given to greater space, or by need bound to the synthesis of the novel, generally warrant attention and give pleasure. Some have the *éclat* of successful command performances. Few quite misfire. Few fail to merit the author's signature or to bear the particular stamp he gives any work. Yet such stories, recognizably, are by-products. One does not feel that they were inevitable. In this, they differ essentially from stories by the short-storyist *par excellence:* the short-storyist by birth, addiction and destiny. Such is William Sansom.

William Sansom, I do not need to point out, has extended himself into other fields. One could say he has experimented *with* extension, and that there has, moreover, been no experiment he has cause to regret. His by now six novels are in a position, a foreground, of their own. And of his equal command of the 'short novel' (novelette or *novella*) has he not given us examples? His two travel books exercise a sharp, sensuous fascination: of their kind and in their own manner they are unrivalled. He has mastered the essay; he has manifested a gift for writing for children. It could be that these his other achievements eclipse, for some of his readers, his short stories—as achievements, these others have been substantial and dazzling. Yet the short story remains (it appears to me) the not only ideal but lasting magnet for all that is most unique in the Sansom art.

Here is a writer whose faculties not only suit the short story but are suited by it—suited and, one may feel, enhanced. This form needs the kind of imagination which is able to concentrate at high power and is most itself when doing so. The tension and pace required by the short story can be as stimulating to the right writer of it as they are intimidating to the wrong one: evidently they are stimulating to William Sansom. That need to gain an immediate hold on the reader (a hold which must also be a compulsive one) rules out the writer who is a slow starter: the quick starter, reacting, asks nothing better. There is also the necessity to project, to make seen, and make seen with significance—the short story is for the eye (if the mind's eye). Also the short story, though it high-lights what appears to be reality, is not—cannot wish or afford to be—realistic: it relies on devices, foreshortenings, 'effects'. In the narration there must be an element of conjury, and of that William Sansom is an evident master.

Though all the short stories written by William Sansom are not, I find, present in this collection, the thirty-three which are present have been well chosen. (That a reader should be so conscious of those missing testifies to the power those pieces had to stamp themselves on the memory and, indeed, haunt it.) Those here are, one must concede, outstanding examples of their different kinds. Kinds? One had better say, types of subject—pedantic though that sounds. The wider a storyist's range, the more unavoidable it becomes that one should classify when attempting to take stock of his whole output. From his wartime London, N.F.S. and fly-bomb period, we have, for instance, those two masterpieces, **"The Wall"** and **"Building Alive."** Portrayal of the terrible, or of the nature of terror, reaches three of its highest levels in **"The Vertical Ladder," "How Claeys Died"** and **"Among the Dahlias."** Comedy, canine in one case, human in the other, overflows with a cheering rumbustiousness from **"Three Dogs of Siena"** and **"A Contest of Ladies."** That extra dimension of oddness added to humans by their being in a pub or bar, or even in a hotel with the bar closed, appears in **"Displaced Persons"** (another masterpiece), **"Eventide"** and **"A Game of Billiards."** Of the pursuit of man (or woman) by a fatality, not to be given the slip or shaken off, there are several examples in stories here, the most memorable, and grimmest, being **"Various Temptations."** The resignation-reconciliation theme (very pronouncedly a Sansom one when he writes of courtship, engagements to marry, or marriage) carries to their conclusions two other stories, **"A Waning Moon"** and **"Question and Answer."**

Two of the greatest, at times awesome and certainly most curious powers of this writer appear in two kinds of story not mentioned yet. Where it comes to conveying hallucination, I know few if any who can approach him. (Kipling, possibly, though in another manner?) The fewness of 'pure' hallucination stories in this collection to me is a matter of regret—above all, I hope that this does not mean that this author is reneging on this power? We have, however, the wondrous **"A Saving Grace"** . . . The other group, to be identified with the other power, are what one might nominate the great scenic stories: those in which what in the hands of another writer could be called 'background' or 'setting' steps forward, takes over, dominates like a tremendous insatiable star actor, reducing the nominal (human) protagonists to 'extras', to walkers-on. In such Sansom stories, who, what, why and how people are is endlessly less important than where they are. How this can be made to come off, and come off triumphantly, is evident in **"My Little Robins,"** **"Time and Place,"** **"Gliding Gulls,"** **"Episode at Gastein,"** **"A Country Walk,"** and, to a great extent, two stories already spoken of in another context (or, under another heading) **"A Waning Moon"** and **"Question and Answer"** . . . **"Pastorale"** is debatable: in a sense, the couple in it defeat the landscape.

To a point, all Sansom stories are scenic stories. Corsica, maritime Provence, Scandinavia, the Highlands of Scotland, the Isles of the West and the past-haunted, mountainous Austrian spa are far from being the only robbers. In this formidable and dismaying world of the Sansom art, no 'inanimate' object is inanimate—mutely, each is either antagonist or accomplice. Influences and effluences are not only at work; they seem the determinants—to a point where mock could be made of human free will. The human is not only the creature of his environment, he becomes its plaything. For the moment, that moment, perhaps, only? But a Sansom moment, given extraordinary extension, so that during it hands may move round round the clock face, the sun set then rise, or leaves be torn from a calendar, is a Sansom story.

This writer's timing, with its expansions and contractions (as though he were playing on an accordion, or squeezebox) is one of the instances of the trickiness he so well uses—trickiness which (I suggested earlier) a short story not only licences and justifies but demands.

The need for the writer's obtaining compulsive hold on the reader (that is, the reader's imagination) has been referred to. Few, if any, are the occasions when the writer of the stories in this collection allows you or me to slip through his fingers. I suggest that what rivets one to a Sansom story is a form of compulsion, rather than "interest" in the more usual, leisurely or reflective sense. The characters, the men and women protagonists, are not in themselves 'interesting'—or at least to me. In the main they are pallid; the few more coloured ones (like Miss Great-Belt, the Danish beauty-contestant in **"A Contest of Ladies"**) are, often, handsome wound-up automata, jerking through their small ranges of looks and gestures. The fatalism shown by most of these people is, one feels, neither desperate nor romantic; rather, it is the outcome of

an incompetence which may shade off at any moment into sheer impotence. These people do not appeal to us, or attract our sympathies. But to say that they 'fail' to do so would be misleading. Why? Because it has not for a single instant been their creator's intention that they *should* (interest, attract or appeal to us, I mean). The enormous suspense element in a Sansom story is generated in no ordinary way. Since we care little for, or about, these people, do we greatly care what happens to them? Why, no! Then how are we held? We are held not by what happens but by how it happens. The substance of a Sansom story is sensation. The subject is sensation. The emotions are sensations of emotion. The crisis (to be depended upon to be 'sensational' in the accepted sense) is a matter of bringing sensation to a peak where it must either splinter or dissolve because it can no more. Or it may, sometimes, simply, ironically and altogether subside. . . . We accompany, thus, the nominal Sansom 'character' throughout the ups-and-downs of fear, or infatuation, or suspicion, or daydream-success, or amazement, or apprehension, or whatever it be. We ease off during the intermissions, let-ups and pauses allowed by the malady or the ordeal (or, it may be, the delight) only to quiver under the shock of renewed assault.

Held we are: either rooted, like the firemen looking up at the falling wall in **"The Wall,"** or gummed, like the youth scaling the gasometer in **"The Vertical Ladder."**

A Sansom story is a *tour de force*. Readers who dislike, mistrust or resent that should turn to something other than this volume. In me these stories induce, also, suspense of another kind, call it sympathetic suspense—will they come off? It is staggering how they do. Their doing so is anything but a matter of fortuity. Nothing here is slapdash or 'got away with'. The writer has taken, and shown himself right in taking, a succession of calculated risks. He is not writing *for* effect, he is dealing *in* it, and masterfully. For his purposes, vocabulary is clearly very important—vocabulary in the literal sense, in the matter of words, yes; but also there has to be a complete command of the vocabulary of the senses. To have knowledge of, to be able to call up into what in the story is actuality, to be able not merely to convey to the reader but impose on him (almost, inflict on him) smells, tastes, sounds rendered complex or curious by acoustics or echoes, differences (as though under the touch) of surfaces, gradations of light and its watery running off into shadow—this was essential for the writer of the Sansom stories. Equally, the writing of these stories, these particular stories, as they come to us, must have been an essential for William Sansom—burdened, he would have otherwise been, with a useless faculty.

Weather is part of the vocabulary. 'The day slate-dark, the air still, the cindertrack by the cottages without life in a watered middle-day light'—is the overture to **"Something Terrible, Something Lovely."** The visage of the house in **"A Saving Grace"** (the house from out of whose open door one by one the dead are to proceed, the dog and all, to group themselves smilingly on the lawn, as though for a photograph), is framed in 'the hour before dusk . . . when the hot afternoon is grown old and cool'. There are, again and again, in **"A Country Walk,"** those weather-passages betraying the terrible animosity of Nature. Such as:

> The shadow of a cloud was passing over the map, it came towards him like a fast-moving tide, heaving the hills as it came.

> A simple matter? Not so simple. He watched it, he began to judge whether it would envelop him or not. It came at a fast windblown pace, eating up the fields, blotting out life like the edge of a dangerous sea moving in.

> The whole countryside grew more inimical. Every deep acre of this ancient sleeping earth breathed a quiet, purposeful life—and it was against him. Not now the simple material conflict with animals—the grave earth itself and the green things growing in collusion with it took on presence and, never moving, breathed a quiet hatred on to the mineral air.

Animals, birds also are part of the vocabulary—they seem, at the moments of their emergences, long to have existed *within* it, behind all words. Corsican robins, the lion at liberty in the middle of the dahlia-edged path, and those dogs of Siena—Enrico, Osvaldo, Fa. And, in the Hampstead garden, 'isolated at the very top of a tall sapling, crouched on the tapering end of this thin shoot so that it bent over under the weight like a burdened spring . . . a huge dazed cat'.

The Stories of William Sansom speak for themselves. A peril of introduction is that it can go on for too long. So this breaks off, though there could be more to say.

Times Literary Supplement (essay date 1963)

SOURCE: "Sansom and Delilah," in *The Times Literary Supplement,* No. 3193, May 10, 1963, p. 340.

[*Here, the critic comments on Sansom's wide variety of subjects and the stylistic flexibility he displays throughout his writing.*]

The name of William Sansom first became familiar at a time when, in the little mushroom-magazines sprouting overnight from the literary soil of World War II, the short story flourished. It was the heyday of *Horizon* and *Penguin New Writing* (in both of which Mr. Sansom's initial stories appeared): also the period of the Kafka boom, when no Bloomsbury or Chelsea bedsitter was complete without a copy of *The Castle* or *The Trial* and the Soho cafés resounded with misquotations from Kierkegaard. Shortly after, with the liberation of France, M. Sartre and Existentialism became the vogue instead (offering, as they did, not only a philosophy and a way of life in accordance with the prevalent psychological climate, but a uniform as well); these were in turn replaced by Mr. Beckett and M. Ionesco, whose examples—*malgré eux*—now provide excuses for wilful obscurantism in our embryo dramatists similar to those which Kafka's work provided for his enthusiastic imitators of the early 1940s.

The esoteric world created by Kafka naturally appealed to amateurs who, unable either to delineate character or describe everyday life, trusted that readers might be deluded by nebulous atmosphere and cryptic dialogue into believing their work fraught with a symbolic meaning which it did not actually possess. Writers such as Rex Warner, who in *The Wild Goose Chase* and *The Aerodrome* used Kafkaesque settings and situations for purposes of social and political allegory, and Ruthven Todd, with his poetic novels *Over the Mountain* and *The Lost Traveller,* belong of course to quite another category.

The pages of the ephemeral highbrow reviews were filled by contributors of this sort, whose names are nowadays for the most part forgotten; but Mr. Sansom, though strongly influenced at the outset by the author of *The Great Wall of China,* was never really of their number. As if to prove this, he has included in his own omnibus selection of stories few of his prentice pieces, and none belonging to the genre mentioned above (such as **"The Long Sheet"** whose publication in *Horizon* attracted the attention of critics and public alike). An admirable lack of nostalgic sentiment is shown by his refusal to include, also, the title-story of his first collection **Fireman Flower**: in fact, of the stories printed here, only **"The Wall"**, **"Building Alive"** and **"Cat Up a Tree"** have a background recalling the author's wartime service in the A.F.S. Even stories more remotely touched with the Kafkan influence, but fully able to stand on their own merits (**"The Inspector"** and **"Through the Quinquina Glass"**, for instance) are excluded; **"The Vertical Ladder"**, on the other hand is quite rightly in, as foreshadowing a type of terror-tale—perhaps deriving from Poe—which Mr. Sansom has since made peculiarly his own: a single individual involved in a dangerous predicament largely due to his or her obstinacy: Ruth falling into the slate quarry after an hysterical flight brought on by a row with her husband in **"A Waning Moon"**; and poor urban dog-faced Harris, caught up in a tangle of thorns on the edge of a precipice during **"A Country Walk"**, and bent double by rheumatic fever for the rest of his life in consequence, are later examples of this trend; as Miss Elizabeth Bowen's introduction puts it, in "the great scenic stories", "the human is not only the creature of his environment, he becomes its plaything".

Reading variations on this theme such as **"To the Rescue!"**, **"Among the Dahlias"** (in which an inoffensive, rather endearing businessman is confronted on a path at the Zoo by an escaped lion, with a sequel not to be revealed here), or **"A Game of Billiards"** (the protagonist trapped in the upstairs of a grim Victorian pub, and forced to act as marker to a madman playing an invisible opponent with an imaginary ball), one remembers Mr. Sansom's brilliant essay on Poe; and the opening paragraphs of **"Various Temptations"**, published in *Penguin New Writing,* concerning a psychopathic murderer, befriended by a lonely neglected girl, are both reminiscent and worthy of his great predecessor:

His name unknown he had been strangling girls in the Victoria district. After talking no one knew what to them by the gleam of brass bedsteads; after lonely hours standing on pavements with people passing; after perhaps in those hot July streets, with blue sky blinding high above and hazed with burnt petrol, a dazzled head-aching hatred of some broad scarlet cinema poster and the black leather taxis; after sudden hopeless ecstasies at some rounded girl's figure passing in rubber and silk, after the hours of slow crumbs in the empty milk-bar and the balneal reek of grimtiled lavatories? After all the day-town's faceless hours, the evening town might have whirled quicker on him with the death of the day, the yellow-painted lights of the night have caused the minutes to accelerate and his fears to recede and a cold courage then to arm itself—until the wink, the terrible assent of some soft girl smiling towards the night . . . the beer, the port, the meatpies, the bedsteads?

This extract amply illustrates Mr. Sansom's method, in which colour, weather, season are evoked in turn, and all the reader's senses subtly played upon, until the necessary ambience is established. (Miss Bowen claims for Mr. Sansom "a complete command of the vocabulary of the senses":

To have knowledge of, to be able to call up into what in the story is actuality, to be able not merely to convey to the reader but impose on him (almost, inflict on him) smells, tastes, sounds rendered complex or curious by acoustics or echoes, differences (as though under the touch) of surface, gradations of light and its watery running off into shadow—this was essential for the writer of the Sansom stories,

she continues, with a striking affinity of style to that of the subject of her essay.) In the above-quoted passage—and in his occasional use of the unfamiliar adjective ("balneal") he has stylistic affinities with transatlantic contemporaries like Eudora Welty and Ray Bradbury: especially the former.

"Various Temptations", however, comprises a pity and understanding which Poe seldom achieved (apt as he was to concentrate on the business of arousing horror alone), and Mr. Sansom is only incidentally a latter-day "master of the macabre". In **"Impatience"**, an account of the rivalry between two Soho barbers who are also "razor-men" in another sense, violent tension is blended with comedy; **"A Last Word"** (describing a different kind of rivalry, this time between two elderly misers in Fulham) and "Outburst" (a shop assistant in a school outfitter's driven by his customers to the limits of endurance) combine both humour and pathos; the Corsican bird-killing engineer in **"My Little Robins"** (one of the three surviving stories from the volume *South*: demonstrating once again Mr. Sansom's wisdom as a selector of his own work, since he is at his best on British soil) presents a figure built up of the comic and sinister in equal portions, whose peaked képi, blue dungarees, and black glasses are properties left over from the author's Kafkan past: marking, so to speak, the exact point from which he began to emerge as an entirely different type of writer.

Miss Bowen, herself a short-story writer of distinction, naturally contributes a valuable appraisal of his art and of the form in general (if we exclude her use of the horrid word "storyist" to describe those who practise it), making the correct sharp distinction between the practitioners whose stories are mere by-products of their longer works and the comparatively few, like Sansom, "whose faculties not only suit the short story but are suited by it—suited and, one may feel, enhanced. . . . the short story", she adds, "though it highlights what appears to be reality, is not—cannot wish or afford to be—realistic: it relies on devices, foreshortenings, 'effects'. . . . an element of conjury", of which she quite rightly declares Sansom to be a master. While few readers of the present selection will be found to disagree with this statement, many, on the other hand, may quarrel with her view—admittedly personal—that his protagonists "are not in themselves 'interesting'. . . . often handsome wound-up automata, jerking through their small ranges of looks and gestures". As a refutation, one has only to instance those denizens of the "Dilly", Cuthbertson and the Dropper, or Messrs. Cadwaller and Horton, those "brothers in thrift . . . each mumbling on a long jutting, petulant, prognathous jaw" in **"Impatience"** and **"A Last Word"**: all four of whom are as animated and accurately observed as any creation of Mr. V. S. Pritchett; the "nominal" Sansom character belonged, surely, to that earlier, outgrown phase defined above.

The previously mentioned stories give some idea of the variety and flexibility of which he became capable; yet his true preoccupation, his real forte, lies in yet another direction: exemplified by two long stories in particular, **"On Stony Ground"** and **"Episode at Gastein",** and their respective protagonists. In the former case the narrator, who wears a woollen kidney-band, enters the garden-accessory department of a London store to buy seed for his two window-boxes and is immediately captivated by the girl assistant who serves him: their courtship is enacted ritualistically against a spotlit altar of "sticks, axe-handles, fresh rakes. Stiff sacks of bone-meal . . . big tins of blight control and liquid manure", and finally founders when he kisses her in the street encumbered with an umbrella on one arm and a parcel looped with string round his other finger (having been compelled to invent a country garden to excuse his frequent visits to the fertilizers and pest-syringes). **"Episode at Gastein"**—almost a short novel, taking place as the title suggests at a spa amid steam and flying spray, in thermal baths and public rooms of skyscraper hotels—relates the attempts of Ludwig de Broda, an aging comfortably-off Austrian "Bobby" (or "knut"), to ensnare with a view to marriage an orange-haired Viennese fifteen years his junior, who is herself on the look-out for a husband. De Broda's campaign fails because, like that of his English counterpart, it is too carefully planned; and (again as in **"On Stony Ground"**) he loses his Laure to a younger man more direct in his approach.

Mr. Sansom's unromantic heroes are handicapped by an innate defeatism: Fred Morley (another "old bachelor": in this author's work they, and benedicts, abound) the retired music-hall actor in **"A Contest of Ladies"**, who has his private house decorated like an hotel and entertains a bevy of international beauty-queens there, only succeeds in getting married because he allows the girl in question to take charge of the situation. In this she is, however, unusual for a Sansom heroine, since as a rule they are inscrutable enchantresses, passive Delilahs—ordinary enough underneath: their mysterious inscrutability exists only in the eye of the admirer—waiting quietly to be wooed and won. (The phrase is used advisedly, for there is something Victorian about Mr. Sansom's suitors: one of his novels, *The Cautious Heart,* ends with a marriage-proposal being accepted, and in another, *The Loving Eye,* an actual wedding-breakfast provides the climax.) A vitiating influence emanates from these quiet, reserved young women: a sapping of masculine strength results, though they do not themselves take up the shears; even plain hapless Olara in **"Various Temptations"** shares this ability to castrate the will, allowing her temporarily to tame the tiger slumbering inside Ron Raikes the strangler.

None the less, it cannot be denied that their would-be lovers enjoy the process; a pointer to the attitude they adopt may be found in the first sentence of a story called **"The Girl in the Bus"** (which despite this preamble has a happy marital outcome):

> Since to love is better than to be loved, unrequited love may be the finest love of all. If this is so, then the less requited the better. And it follows that the most refined passion possible for us must finally be for those to whom we have never even spoken, whom we have never met.

These sentiments would certainly be endorsed by Matthew Ligne, the Kensington householder whose *Loving Eye,* in the novel of that name, spies upon his inamorata at an opposite window for over a hundred pages before he dares make her acquaintance. Matthew, close on forty, unmarried of course and financially well fixed, suffers from "incipient eczema" and an abdominal ulcer: even for a Sansom hero he is an extremely slow starter; the Marylebone drinking-club pianist who tells (sometimes in the present tense) the story of his *Cautious Heart* is less inhibited in that he goes to bed quite soon with his Turkish-Irish lady, but finds it hard otherwise to make headway owing to the constant intrusions of one of those hearty, shiftless minor public schoolboys (whose raffish locutions Mr. Sansom renders so accurately), a petrol-sniffing addict and compulsive thief to whom the girl is asexually devoted.

Matthew and the pianist make it in the end, however, and the novels close, respectively, in the manner earlier outlined: with the "boys" both safely in the net. ("The resignation-reconciliation theme", as Miss Bowen calls it, "very pronouncedly a Sansom one when he writes of courtship, engagements to marry, or marriage.") Mr. Sansom meanwhile has given us a masterly parade of the metropolitan seasons, rain or shine, and a living cross-section of the types who walk the city streets. He is especially adept at that strange form of circumlocution beloved of the saloon-bar habitué (on which the late

Patrick Hamilton was possibly the principal authority) and at the dead-pan facetious pronouncement (ably analysed and demonstrated in **"On Stony Ground"**: "Mauvais in parts, like the reverend ovoid.").

In the sphere of the novel, he has never quite surpassed his early study of obsessional jealousy, *The Body,* and in *The Last Hours of Sandra Lee* his delight in the convolutions of office-party vocabulary caused him to spin out an acceptable novelette to a length which its material could not sustain; but—though **"Gliding Gulls and Going People"**, **"Displaced Persons"** and **"Pastorale"** are pieces of reportage which might be better replaced by the inexplicably omitted **"Murder"** and the more recent **"Lorelei of the Roads"**—readers of this selection cannot fail to salute his out standing gifts. **"Life, Death"**, the tale of an art-fishmonger's personal tragedy, creating its own completely new species of demotic poetry, is an unquestionable small masterpiece and few living writers in the English language can so delicately sketch for us the act of "falling in love" and its consequences grave or gay.

Eudora Welty (essay date 1963)

SOURCE: "Time and Place—and Suspense," in *The New York Times Book Review,* June 30, 1963, pp. 5, 27.

[*Welty is a highly-respected American fiction writer and critic, whose works include the novel* Losing Battles *(1970) and* The Collected Stories of Eudora Welty *(1980). In this review of* The Stories of William Sansom, *Welty notes the "wonderful set-pieces of description in the book" and declares that Sansom can "hardly be surpassed" in this regard.*]

Since the appearance of his first book of stories, **Fireman Flower,** 20 years ago, the enormously talented English writer, William Sansom, has been warmly read and warmly admired for his stories, novels and travel pieces in this country. This is a welcome collection of 33 of his stories, here presented with an excellent appreciation by exactly the right fellow-writer, Elizabeth Bowen.

One sees different things, or sees familiar qualities differently, in re-reading at a stretch a good writer's work. One gets to know better the long thoughts, the cast of mind, the range and play of mood, the feelings that have lain deeper for their weight and reserve than the faster-flowing ones that color the separate stories and impart the first effervescence.

The flesh of William Sansom's stories is their uninterrupted contour of sensory impressions. The bone is reflective contemplation. There is an odd contrast, and its pull is felt in the stories, between the unhurriedness of their actual events and their racing intensity. In fact their speed is most delicately regulated to suspense. The suspense, which is high, has not a positive, but a negative, connection with the pace at which things happen. Things happen slowly, even in slow-motion, but the suspense mounts fast and high because all the while it has been compressed within. And it is the suspense that the stories are really about.

The wall, in **"The Wall,"** takes three pages to fall. The story is three pages long. The wall that falls is the story, and those three pages are the length of excruciation that we can bear. We have been given the measure.

For conveying in the short story how places, hours, objects, animals, human beings in their behavior look and feel, and wound, this writer can hardly be surpassed. One after the other here are the wonderful set pieces of description that characterize his work, the flourish of flags in Siena, the masterpiece of a centerpiece of fresh, dead fish in a Marseilles restaurant—but to start naming them is not to be able to stop.

"How Claeys Died," "Various Temptations," "Episode at Gastein," "Three Dogs of Siena," "Among the Dahlias"—here are his best-known stories, sinister, comic, tragic. Here is **"A Saving Grace,"** a true original among ghost stories. What a marvelous conviction it brings, that there is an affinity quite unassailable between what is dead and gone and what has been altogether foolish and delicious, a connection delicate and wistful (if slow to arrive) between human memory and a certain hilarious, vaudeville quality that living life will ask for till death comes.

In Sansom's humor lie both caprice and tolerance; his wit is in splendid partnership with fantasy. And his comic stories do not go on for long without the element of threat, or peculiar danger.

—Eudora Welty

Here are the fine comic stories. How did Patten meet his wife? **"A Game of Billiards"** tells us. Patten got caught in the deserted billiard room of the upstairs floor of his pub on his way to the "Gentlemen's" by a score for an imaginary game of billiards with an imaginary opponent. Patten had indeed day-dreamed of being closeted with a madman some day, and has always imagined that "he would crumble instantly. But now—surprisingly—it was the opposite. He felt capable, alert, strong. After all, the rehearsals had been of some use." But the game goes on, and how is Patten ever going to get out? And then the door of the billiard room is opened by mistake: a girl is looking for the "Ladies'." "She stood like the embodiment of all heroic rescue—the figure of sudden salvation, the sworded angel . . . in her pink dressy blouse and her blue serge skirt." She isn't really the one who sounds the alarm for the rescue, she only takes his signaling for a friendly direction. But back safe in the pub, whom does Patten see first, to tell his story to? "It was his saviour in the satin blouse."

In Mr. Sansom's humor lie both caprice and tolerance; his wit goes along in splendid partnership with fantasy. And his comic stories do not go on for long without the element of threat, or peculiar danger.

The stories of scenes are well represented here. These are highly complex and extremely accomplished works of art. Time and place, in the stories, not only exist to an intense degree—they create the characters out of themselves, and then belabor or nourish or trick or lure or teach or obliterate or exalt them.

In **"A Waning Moon,"** we go into the giant, metallic, malevolent outside of the Western Highlands from the claustrophobic and malevolent inside of a trailer with a husband and wife on holiday. The story is at once terrifying in the true nightmare sense and comic—for a certain length of time—in the domestic sense. How Mr. Sansom can write about place! It is so marvelous, for example, to see the slate hillside in this story marbled in moonlight and the marble chips moving and turning out to be goats.

In **"Pastorale,"** a loving pair traveling in remote wilds on the Corsican coast, who have been completely absorbed in each other, feeling no need to even say "Thank you" or smile, are suddenly confronted by the sight of the Calanches: "precipitous cliffs of fierce red granite, a steep convulsion of weird rock . . . figures deep in thought about themselves, their stone thoughts cowled and draped with red stone . . . An aeolian music sang round them, but it was too ancient a sound for human ears." The lovers shudder at last and run back to their bedroom. They are, it seems, town-dwellers.

In **"Time and Place,"** a man and woman who are, on the contrary, nothing to each other, self-sufficient fellow guests of a hotel, take a casual walk into the Highlands and are caught in a Scotch mist: "The circular blindness . . . and wherever they looked it was circular and perpetual, round and round, and round overhead. It seemed, too—but gently, slowly—to be thickening still and closing in. But perhaps that was the illusion of their eyes training for some point of definition—any mark for their human eyes." What can they do in the long run but lie down together on his mackintosh and wait for the mist to lift? Back in the hotel, of course, a mere nodding acquaintance is resumed—or rather avoided.

In these scenic stories, as in the war stories, there lies an element of allegory. It is the situation itself, which he sees as already existing as he began the story, that has inspired or directed or driven Mr. Sansom. One feels the surer of this because all of a given story's attributes, aspects and elements, from its title on, are each in their own way parts of one whole; and this whole has been conceived, one needs hardly say, as a work of art.

"A World of Glass" happens in Trondheim—where everybody wears dark glasses; there is the landscape of snow and icicles and ice-bound lakes, the clarity, the frozen beauty, transparency, and cruelty. And we learn that the story is, in fact, the story of an eye, the eye of a young girl, a lifelong resident of this city; the eye is then revealed as being glass; her blindness is revealed to have been caused by glass, a broken bottle in the hand of her husband, a deed of unseeing drunkenness. And there are also elements of reflection, of things in reverse: Trondheim's architecture is false Greek in the snowbound north.

The narrator himself is not a simple tourist. He is an actor who must disguise himself to hide his famous identity. It is with the blind young girl, the victim, he tells us, that eventually he explores and examines this strange city—it has become all but an abstraction—"through her eyes." And before he can leave he is arrested for assault. He attacks a tourist he sees there from his own country, and punishes a perfect stranger. The scene, the characters—*both* the characters, the prevailing figures of speech, the action, the words of dialogue, the title, the whole conception is this, and to make this, a world of glass, the glass eye. And it all reveals very well another vein, perhaps the deepest, of Mr. Sansom's feeling: the need, in every place and every thing, for the human element.

William Sansom has never been anything less than a good writer. I think as time passes his writing becomes more flexible without losing its tightness of control; the flexibility is its own sign of such sureness. And what is perhaps more unusual among writers so good, his work with time seems to have gained, not lost, spontaneity.

The very act and mystery of writing a story is central to his work, this reader believes. And which came first, the work or the mystery that brought it about? One wonders how he might have even escaped the allegory form of **"Fireman Flower,"** for instance, given the raw experience of firefighting in wartime London out of which it came. He makes us wonder how often, indeed, as life works it out, is the allegory not the literal, the literal not the allegory. In fact, it is pretty much like the two snapshots of her sailor son, who is growing a beard, that the lady bartender in **"Eventide"** shows her customer. The cleanshaven one she puts on the bar for him to see.

"'That's how he is really,' said the woman and then showed him the other photograph, of a similar young sailor, but with a beard.

"'And that's how he really is.'"

James Dean Young (essay date 1964)

SOURCE: "William Sansom: Unwroughter," in *Critique: Studies in Modern Fiction,* Vol. VII, No. 1, Spring, 1964, pp. 122-25.

[*In the following essay, Young is critical of Sansom's work because of a "failure of an appropriate point of view" in the stories, the author's "overdependence on syntactic qualification," and his "intrusive use of statements of meaning."*]

Some things go without saying, but fiction is not one of them. William Sansom is a writer much published in the past fifteen years; the thirty-three stories in *The Stories of William Sansom* span those years in a rough chronological way, with the last story, probably the earliest, making a return to the beginning. The arrangement is chronologically arbitrary, as if the important thing to see was the development of the writer, and finally merely arbitrary, suggesting that perhaps he has not developed at all.

Sansom is not a writer to whom one can be indifferent. When a number of years ago, somewhere in the slough of graduate school, I read an earlier volume of his stories, I thought that I would not have to read Sansom again. But he has continued to publish—novels, stories, travel books—so that I had an uneasy feeling that perhaps I had been wrong, remembering J. B. Priestley's unarming aside: "unlike many writers and all politicians and editors, I am often wrong." Perhaps I had been, so I began reading the collection, half wanting to change my opinion, if only the stories would change my mind. The reputation and the reviews I knew. Eudora Welty has praised him publicly over the years; Elizabeth Bowen presently in the introduction. The reputation is, of course, divided; no one is indifferent. The praise is, as far as one can judge, real praise; the damning almost always condescension—as if the stories needed putting down. And so they do.

My only real objection to the stories, although it is manifested in three different ways, is that the meaning is always explicitly stated; it is never made implicit. This particular strategy appears in the stories in a failure of an appropriate point of view, in an overdependence on syntactic qualification, and finally in an intrusive use of statements of meaning, establishing the meaning of the story independently of the narrative. All but seven stories are told by an omniscient narrator, discussing the characters and events in the third person. Not one of the exceptions makes a meaningful use of first-person focus. This lack of functional interest in the point of view causes, I should think, the working up of significance through adjectives and other modifiers, as in this paragraph near the beginning of **"Pastorale"**:

> Against such earthen textures the pearl-pale car shone with a princely lustre; the chromium flashed precious silver, the clean canvas of its hood sat reefed like Parisian cloth, the luggage of yellow pigskin and gold clasps told the tale of Pullman seats and luxury. At the wheel sat a young lean dark man; the sun flashed on his oiled hair, on the platinum watch glittering from his soft glove, on the white card he now studied. The woman at his side, her face like a soft white nut in its rich brown hat, peered over—and then, with eyes screwed, looked up at the house above in disbelief.

I am unconvinced that the scene means what he says it does, and this doubt causes me to be unconvinced that it could appear as he describes it. In fact, it must *not* be so if he has had to labor so hard in writing it up.

Let me illustrate the third aspect with two brief examples. The story entitled **"The Girl on the Bus,"** so that I will not be misunderstood, might not have been a bad story; it focuses on a single moment—almost split second—with great intensity, but the original moment, finally so blown up, expanded, and made much of, cannot take the meaning which Sansom insists on. The story begins: "Since to love is better than to be loved, unrequited love may be the finest love of all." Now, that is rather clever—for the beginning of an essay. Once said, can one go on to write a story that will mean just that? The narrator confesses that he finds the story of "my friend Harry" engaging, producing the effect of prefacing a joke with "this is the funniest thing I've ever heart." The story can hardly live up to its narrator's publicity. Other inanities of narration: "It would be useless to describe her." (Either do it or not, but do not excuse yourself for either.) "Now if you knew Harry as I know Harry, you would know that Harry then began to worry." (Unfortunately, that is not quite the way the song goes.) "Life is so very various, nothing has quite such a unique importance as we give it." (To which I said amen, but proceeded to watch Sansom give the events of this story more significance than either they or I could bear.)

My second example is **"Three Dogs of Siena,"** which begins, too, with its essay-like first paragraph, clever, witty, and a little pompous: "What we would call the 'mongrels' of Italy are more than an essay in democratic procreation: they are an unceasing pleasure to the eye of those who love the individual, the purely creative rather than the creatively pure, the fresh." After viewing the three dogs closely (not quite, alas, from their points of view) and after sharing their inspection of the strange town and the stone tablet of Romulus and Remus, with significance almost established, Sansom becomes the editorial narrator, impatient with us that we might have been inattentive to what he has presented. So he comments: "Such, then, were the minor encounters of these three eager lovers of life. Before the following day, we saw them again twice. . . . No, they were not to be touched by such ceremonies of stone—they went in search of life." So we are told what we must think and forced to back off. "The Italians love their dogs as they love life—but they also love ceremony, and in all ceremony there is the touch of death." Complete and explicit, this kernel of idea might have resulted in a real story. Instead, the commentary prevents the rendering; the statement of significance inhibits the writing of the events in a way that would make them become meaningful.

One should say something about the seriousness with which Sansom has been taken. Mr. John Vickery has written recently of Sansom's connections with "logical empiricism," persuasively, I suppose, if one accepts the proposition. It is that "Sansom's fiction demonstrates the capacity of philosophy to permeate literature with that challenge the intelligence hurls at itself when man is earnestly seeking the truth." Well, that may be. The proposition certainly says more about philosophy than it does about literature; stories might be seen as being permeated with the intelligence hurling challenges at itself, but in what way are they also good stories? Mr. Vickery deals with some thirty-two stories in developing his thesis; he discusses only two of the stories in the present collection, although he mentions four others. Could Sansom really care this much about refutation?

Sansom rarely suggests in his stories that he knows how the meaning of a piece of fiction arises, that a story is not a piece of exposition but an object of art, that its significance comes from the way whatever is told is said. Sansom is always telling us, always insisting on the meaning, never letting it alone. As far as I can tell in reading these stories, aside from a certain efficiency and cleverness, he does not care how the stories are told at all; he does not seem to have discovered the necessity of relation between the matter of a story and its manner, nor to have learned that the significance of a story lies in their connection. I should like to think that I have accounted for the terrible feeling of dissatisfaction, of incompleteness, which I had while reading through this volume. It is sad to see a man with energy, inventiveness, and experience never discovering that what he has been doing should be an art, that the meaning of a story arises from the presented form and not from the interpreted subject. It is sad because it reveals a man with real talent who has not discovered any way to use it. Sansom's stories are written, but they are not made; nothing achieves a meaning; everything is forced, interpreted, slapped with meaning and allowed to die, unwrought, in the imagination.

Peter F. Neumeyer (essay date 1966)

SOURCE: "Franz Kakfa and William Sansom," in *Wisconsin Studies in Contemporary Literature,* Vol. VII, No. 1, Winter-Spring, 1966, pp. 76-84.

[*In the following essay, Neumeyer discusses how Sansom's use of detail and setting, as well as the mood and intent of his stories, was influenced by the writings of Franz Kafka.*]

It has occasionally been recognized that there is a debt on the part of William Sansom to the writing of Franz Kafka, though the debt seems never to have been very precisely defined, nor the distinctions between the two authors very clearly drawn. Now, especially in the light of a letter from William Sansom himself, and in view of the fact that Sansom's style has changed considerably from what it was when the comparisons first were made, it would seem the occasion to re-examine the nature of the debt at the time it was incurred.

The similarities critics claim to have seen range from the superficial to the deep and all-permeating. Thus Walter Allen, some years ago, accused Sansom of "exploitation of mannerisms" of Kafka—of grafting onto his own works the "externals" of Kafka's stories. Allen said that "Mr. Sansom is coming very close to parody," and that his writing never rises above the level of pastiche.

William York Tindall has suggested that there is a similarity in "manner," and that both Sansom and Kafka rely on a Freudian frame of reference:

> The short stories in William Sansom's *Fireman Flower* (1944) are the closest approximations to Kafka. These

delirious visions of firemen in the intricate warehouse, of maze, potting-shed, and their occupants, and of the leg-roasting beauty seem portentous allegories but, like dreams, remain unclear. Fear is the principal emotion; the machinery is Freud's and the manner is persuasively matter-of-fact.

Ronald Mason, in the language of critical cautiousness, saw a similarity in "mood" and intent when he said of Sansom's story, **The Equilibriad,** that it was consciously or unconsciously derived from a mood akin to that in which Kafka wrote "The Transformation." In the view of Mason, the use of this "mood" has led, in both authors, to emphasis on "man's everlasting and ever-unsuccessful quest for contact and responsiveness among his fellows."

Edwin Muir, who because of his translations with Willa Muir is largely to be credited for the English recognition of Kafka that began about 1930, has also seen a similarity between Kafka's writing and that of Sansom. Muir's contention, going rather deeper than the previous comments, and reflecting his own poetical and religious inclination, is that it is the uses of the timeless and the archetypal that Sansom derived from Kafka. This timelessness would not have been considered by Muir to be irreconcilable with what Tindall considers matter-of-factness, for Muir too pointed out the precision of detail, the "interesting invention," the "circumstantiality" in the writing of Kafka.

All these views—Allen's claim that there are surface similarities, Tindall's claim that there is a Freudian substructure, and Muir's finding in both authors a predilection for "archetypal" situations—go some way toward defining the relationship between the two writers. But more needs to be said, both by way of examining the precise manner in which the surface or stylistic similarities operate, and also by way of suggesting the underlying affinities and disparities in the perspectives of the two authors.

As the advocates of Kafka's debt to Dickens show they well know when they cite the relevant entry in Kafka's diaries, it is only common sense to look first at an author's own acknowledgement of his literary debts. To my knowledge, such a published statement did not exist in the case of William Sansom. It seemed a reasonable first step, therefore, to ask Mr. Sansom himself what he felt his literary relations to Kafka to be, and we may thank him for his gracious and explicit reply. His statement should shed light directly on the intent of Mr. Sansom, and indirectly, and by refraction, on Kafka. To the questions of how much he thought he had been influenced by Kafka, Mr. Sansom answered as follows:

> I would not say that my work now is influenced much by Kafka—except in so much as his visual eye had the same peculiar clarity as the surrealists whose way of looking at things, of *isolating* objects or movements, etc., has always influenced me very strongly! (I am really a painter *manqué*). However, there are stories in my first book of short stories called **Fireman Flower** which do show partly his influence.

One must make in my case one distinct statement—I was influenced by his form rather than his content. I loved his unfussy, clear, sinuous prose. I loved his continual humility and doubt. I loved his clear way of positioning say a room, and its exact properties—where the window was where the door, without too much damned decoration. His rooms are like bare, beautifully constructed theatrical abstractions: wonderfully clear and *there*. Fourthly, his people who were symbols of people, mysterious, not puppets but tremendous shadows, bigger than real people and again unfussed by chatty observations irrelevant to the theme.

At that time I was writing 'philosophically.' That's the easiest word. And the statements I wished to make were allied to the writings and teachings of Lao Tsze, who engrosses me. So none of the content was Kafka. But I would agree there were parts of his form which instructed me. At the same time, I was much impressed by Rilke's *The Diary of Malte Laurids Brigge,* in which there are episodes of a similarly removed-from-reality-but-thus-having-extra-reality quality. In fact, the Rilke I liked and do like more than Kafka. It may interest you to peek into this book again. I should think it most likely a simple coincidence that the writing is sometimes similar in its disembodied, overembodied way.

Of K's work, I cannot point to any particular part. Although the *Metamorphosis* always seems to come first to mind; and the extraordinary *tour de force* of *Amerika*.

In addition to confirming, in some measure, the opinions of Tindall, and even Muir, the letter is helpful in that it suggests a method by which we may look at Kafka and Sansom together. We might note, first, the clarity of Kafka's "visual eye," and his "isolating" of objects, and we might then consider in what way that relates to the elevating or the increase in meaning of the stories—the manner in which it has to do with the "tremendous shadows, bigger than real people."

If the mere isolating of objects were art, every mechanical draftsman would be an artist, and—with all respect to the experimenters in "pop art"—so would be the designers of our billboards. But the specific rendering is, after all, only the first step, and the picture and the stories don't take on their import for us until, to use Sansom's phrase again, they begin to cast their tremendous shadow. And it is only (if the extension of the metaphor may be forgiven) when the life-giving rays of the creative artist shine on the earthbound object, that its shadow lengthens, that it grows, and that it acquires a life and a meaning greater than itself. That Kafka's creations seemed infused with such a life is what attracted Sansom. And that Kafka really did, quite literally, see the world in terms of meanings and implications beyond the mere existence of the objects immediately perceived is a fact for which we have evidence.

In a letter to Milena Jesenska, Kafka wrote "I can take a joke, too, but with me everything can also become a threat," and as if by way of specific clarification, Kafka wrote in a letter to his sister:

The clock is ticking, I have got used even to the ticking of the clock, I don't hear it very often, besides, and that generally when I am doing something particularly praiseworthy. In fact the clock has certain personal relations to me, like many things in the room, save that now, particularly since I gave notice—or, more accurately, since I was given notice, . . . they seem to be beginning to turn their backs on me, above all the calendar. . . .

In the stories of Kafka, too, the homely, the orderly, the mundane and unexceptional objects seem to take on extended meanings, and the most trivial moments of daily life are impregnated with portentous implications: a pair of rusty scissors, a coal bucket, a suitcase, a man returning to an empty house, a man overtaking a girl on a walk. The objects and situations are simple, clear and unornamented, but their import is enormous, and it seems to grow still, as we look on. As Herbert Tauber has said, even "Landscapes . . . symbolize states of mind, houses and rooms are symbols of personality. . . ."

When Sansom looked to Kafka, then, he did see, and he did avail himself of the technique of meticulously etched delineation of the objects described. But that is only the beginning, the means, for the end sought was the transcendence, the implication, the meaning beyond the object itself. And just as Tauber has claimed for Kafka, so Sansom too used setting to symbolize state of mind, and particularity to prefigure enormous suggestion.

In the early story, **"The Boiler Room,"** for instance, two brutalized O'Neill-type characters, their tempers building up under the pressure of close contact and trivial provocation, explode, close in mortal combat with clinker and sharp coal shovel. Paralleling their state of mounting and finally bursting tension, the boiler they were to tend also undergoes constantly increasing internal pressure until, finally, at the height of the men's combat, the piercing warning whistle sounds and the boiler is about to burst.

The clarity of outline and the exploiting of implication Sansom has combined with a third quality of Kafka that he has not mentioned in the letter, but that also goes some way to helping imbue the objects and the circumstances with significance. With Kafka, Sansom shares a peculiar perspective—and the word must be taken almost literally, as is suggested by Sansom's calling himself a "painter manqué." As the paintings of Mantegna shock even the modern viewer with their recumbent corpses that one views as though one lies at the soles of their feet, and as Kafka seeks to make us view from the position of mouse or dog—or from spheres of existence not susceptible to analysis—so, too, we see through Sansom's eyes from high on crumbling walls, from low on the ground, or, hugely and distortedly, from the dentist's chair, "the wink of a bright instrument, a white arm . . . braced dark against the sky . . ." (**"A Visit to the Dentist"**). We sense with the patient the magnification we, ourselves, always feel of all dental operations within our skull as Sansom tells of "the sensitive tongue . . . at work, licking like a ferrety tentacle at this big hard new thing in his mouth." The hole the patient

saw briefly where once a tooth had been is made hugely our own, "a deep dark hole as red as a dark plush curtain." And in the central situation of the story, as is characteristic of Kafka's and Sansom's writing, an ominous and doomladen cloud seems to overtake the unpretentious protagonist, a shy, middle-aged botanist who has made a visit to the city to obtain new dentures. In a condition bordering on shock, he goes to a restaurant afterwards. During the vaguely evil comedy of errors that follows, the most innocent gestures and comments of the modest hero are mistaken for improper advances on the waitress and the woman at the neighboring table. A large man in the restaurant, "a humourless man measuring him, a man who liked to order things, a cold straightener-up, the kind who would take your car to pieces or jump at the chance of directing traffic, who loved his little power seriously . . ." hits the botanist in the mouth, shattering the new teeth. The dreamlike compulsion and inevitability with which the protagonist sinks farther and deeper into quicksand of irremedial disaster, entirely impotent to help himself, is of course comparable to the futile attempts of K to arrive at the castle and to the pre-determined ineffectuality of Joseph K in seeking to help himself. We cannot say, really, whether in the Sansom story the incident is important, whether it means more than the surface happenings that are depicted—but we sense fearfully that it *might* be, for we have felt anxiously with our tongue the gaping hole in our mouth, and we have seen the magnified white arm against the sky. White against black gives a sharp, clear picture, and the fact that the arm is against the sky means, at the very least, that we saw it from a view other than that of the dispassionate observer. With the clarity of outline, with the change of perspective, Sansom has made us inhabitants of his world of ambiguous bodings of disaster. Sometimes, it must be said, the catastrophe does not materialize, and the cloud passes by, just as is the case with Kafka's little girl "eclipsed by the shadow of the man behind overtaking her. And then the man has passed by and the little girl's face is quite bright."

The small sketch, **"Steam Tugs and Gray Tape,"** shares and exemplifies clearly these same characteristics of circumstantiality and ominousness. Sansom describes how his fire-fighting unit delivered a van-load of furniture from a bombed-out house to a local collecting point. As the furniture is unloaded, what appears to be "a thick brown oiled liquid" flows from one of the beds. This liquid is bugs—vermin. The narrator and his co-workers attempt to persuade the official in charge of the collection depot that it would be criminal to store the infested bed with the uncontaminated furniture. The official, however, is impervious to any logic other than that seemingly demanded by his orders. "But it's down 'ere, ain't it?" he says, and against that fact, argument proves vain.

The narrator and his colleagues refuse to carry the bed farther than the vestibule. In large white letters they write "Bugs" on the bed. Sansom concludes:

> As we left I took a last glance back at the little gray clerk. The door was closing. He still stood by the bed, edging perhaps a little nearer to it, ledger in hand,

with his two henchmen still snuffling like shadows behind. He stood watching the door, waiting for it to close.

Again, the events are prosaic, matter of fact, and if one's imagination is not macabre, one need see nothing sinister in the clerk's "edging perhaps" closer to the verminous bed. The clerk need not *necessarily* have an unholy understanding with the filthy animals—but on the other hand, with Sansom, as with Kafka, "everything can also become a threat."

"The Peach-house Potting Shed" is one of Sansom's finest stories. It is significant for our purposes as indicating how related in theme the writing of Sansom and that of Kafka can be, and the extent to which the likeness goes beyond the grafting of "externals" of which Walter Allen spoke. In this story, the universe of a lonely gardener is his garden. His orders come by mail from a mysterious and removed Estate Office, and never does he see anyone from that place. He fears for his job, until one day he is informed by mail that a gentleman will occupy the estate too. The two never meet until, as though by a nightmare tempest, they are driven into each other's arms. The arbitrary, omniscient, impersonal, and all-powerful Estate Office is so obviously of the same city as the Gate of the Law and as the Castle, and the gardener and the gentleman, so close and yet never communicating, are so clearly of the desperate family of Joseph K and Gregor Samsa, that the author can hardly be thought to have wanted to conceal his debt. These similarities are, however, not "externals"; they are mirrorings of a view of man's essential isolation. They represent a view which Sansom shares with Kafka. They are not decoration.

Some years ago, Albert Votaw spoke of "the literature of extreme situations" when he wrote:

> Modern literature has come more and more to deal with lonely men in extreme situations—that is, in situations in which the use of power is so radically unbalanced that communication becomes virtually impossible. The relationships between master and slave, between torturer and victim, replace the collaboration of equals, which was the material of previous literatures.

Kafka is recognized as one of the fathers of this hopeless, but courageous, literature of desperation, the literature of the unequal struggle. Camus's exegesis of the myth of Sisyphus is the shibboleth for the apostles of the lonely man in the age in which God is dead. And one of Sansom's earliest, and best known stories, **"The Long Sheet"** (in which men are condemned for eternity to wring a sheet bone dry, only to have it wet completely the moment they think their task ended), is as clear a statement of the same philosophy as Kafka's obsessively repeated anecdote of the man at the Gate of the Law. On the other hand, a distinction must be made between Sansom and Kafka even in these early stories.

What distinguishes many of the early Sansom stories from virtually all of Kafka's writing is a difference in the point of view. We assume that Kafka is K, or Samsa, and we are incredulous when we read in the reminiscences of Brod or Janouch that Kafka was jovial, kindly, sociable, modestly gregarious. The crises of Kafka's characters seem to us to be the crises of the author himself. Sansom, on the other hand, is a very different case. Usually (not always) he is the observer, humorous, ironic, admittedly sometimes sinister. But never does he seem irremediably and inextricably entwined in his material. This may simply be Sansom's artistic shortcoming, but it remains, nonetheless, a difference. "Ho! Ho! Ho! snorted a little fly, bucking like a foal," Sansom begins a story. In the next paragraph he says, "I never heard it speak. That, of course, was my imagination." And somewhat later he addresses the same fly, "little black pegasus in motor goggles." Even in the existential **"The Long Sheet"** Sansom is telling the story from the outside, not as a participant. Kafka never maintained such a degree of artistic distance. The letter repetition in the code name, Samsa (the insect of "The Metamorphosis"), is hardly meant to conceal. While Kafka is generally taken to be, himself, within the nightmare of which he writes, and while the soul-states of his lonely creatures are assumed to be echoings of the cry from the heart of Franz Kafka himself, Sansom seems, by contrast, a raconteur—an ironic one, at that—enjoying the artistic effect of the human perplexity.

With the general tenor of the earlier comments on Sansom and Kafka, then, we may agree. Sansom does borrow technique from Kafka—specifically the technique of meticulous and unornamented delineation of the object described. And Sansom's landscapes do symbolize (or echo) states of mind, as do Kafka's (and as may be said do those of Edmund Spenser and Thomas Hardy, too). And from Sansom's sharply outlined objects, a dark shadow of suggestion seems to extend and to cast over the most trivial items and fleeting moments a burden of import, and often of menace, far greater than the mere empirical existence of the objects would seem to necessitate. And, finally, in his earlier stories Sansom shared Kafka's preoccupation with the lost and anchorless condition of man in a world without landmarks, in which the waves are so enormous as to overwhelm the most resolute of the puny efforts of a mortal. But always Sansom's unease seems to have been a less compulsive one, as is shown by his frequent persona, the bemused bystander. Moreover, we should note that Sansom has said (and even a cursory glance at his writings will show the statement to be true) that his work now is not much influenced by Kafka. That, too, is understandable, for though Kafka (and Brecht), who asked strangely final questions, and who postulated absurd non-answers, were the two German writers who had a considerable English following in the mid-nineteen forties, their influence began to wane by the nineteen fifties. Perhaps some of their non-answers became less absurd. Or perhaps even their questions became absurd.

Philip Toynbee (essay date 1966)

SOURCE: A review of *The Ulcerated Milkman*, in *London Magazine*, n.s. Vol. 5. No. 12, March, 1966, pp. 80-3.

[*Here, Toynbee expresses concern that Sansom's "extreme virtuosity may be sliding into the kind of professionalism which irons out all the natural wrinkles and awkwardness of a writer's imagination."*]

Ever since he began writing, around the beginning of the last war, Sansom has been very much his own man. It is true that his first stories were written under the influence of Kafka, but that choice of influence by a young English writer at that time was itself an individual and almost eccentric act of abasement. It did not prove, in the event, to be a particularly significant one; for Sansom soon moved away from the allegorizing fantasies of his early stories to a sort of wayward and highly personal realism. He has chosen, ever since, to look at the familiar but to look at it with such a raking and transforming eye that the familiar, in Sansom's books, has taken on qualities and aspects which it had never displayed before.

Another thing that needs to be said is that this very independent writer has always seemed to be more concerned with how to write than with what to write about. That may be the wrong way of putting it. It might be truer to say that he has always had a natural talent for vigorous and original expression, and that his material has really exercised his attention *more* than his manner, simply, because there was no material which he felt to be naturally his own. If this is so, it is important to recognize that it makes Sansom a very rare bird indeed among the various and noisy flocks of the last twenty-five years. At a time when a new novelist could make a name for himself, not for any new quality in his writing, not for any freshness of vision or originality of language, but simply because he had written the first novel ever about life in a dental supply factory on the Trent, William Sansom has always been remarkable for the quality of his writing, rather than the terrain of his investigation.

The danger which always threatens a writer of this unusual kind is that he may become a mere mannerist, a virtuoso of the pen, a high-wire acrobat who poises with upraised hands for our applause after every daring sentence or paragraph. I believe there have been moments in his career when Sansom has been particularly conscious of this danger, and particularly conscious of the need to find something specific and important to say. I have felt, when reading some of his earlier novels and stories, that he must have constantly repeated to himself before breakfast, 'Every day in every way my heart gets bigger and bigger. Every day in every way. . . .' Something heavy, and alas, at times sticky, had been heaved across the natural grain of his talent and deflected him in the direction of an almost studied sentimentality. This has usually been accomplished by a stubborn choice of 'normal' human types for his characters—as if he had become intolerably afflicted by some taste in himself for the abnormal, the macabre, the morbid.

But if there is, after all, such a thing as natural Sansom material then I am fairly sure that it lies closer to Ten Rillington Place than to Rosebud Cottage. What really attracts his imagination, I should have thought, is the strangeness that lies within the familiar; the eccentricities that always lie at the heart of the conventional. He shares large tracts of territory with Henry Green: both writers have shown the same fascinating flair for looking at what we thought we knew too well from strange angles which reveal unguessed-at shapes and colours. I doubt whether Sansom has ever written a better book than his early novel, *The Body;* for here he found both a theme and a social territory which were perfectly suited to his natural vision and technique. Jealousy in the suburbs! And with no hint of condescension or social malice in the treatment; a passionate and almost obsessed concern with a passionate obsession. The point is that in a book like [*The Ulcerated Milkman*] Sansom had no reason at all to fear that he might be missing 'significance' by being too peripheral in his concern, too bizarre in his imagination. Jealousy is a central human concern; the social field in which it was shown in operation was no eccentric enclave but entirely 'normal' and 'contemporary'.

What really attracts [Sansom's] imagination is the strangeness that lies within the familiar; the eccentricities that always lie at the heart of the conventional. He has the same flair for looking at what we thought we knew too well from strange angles which reveal unguessed-at shapes and colours.

—Philip Toynbee

What all this adds up to is that Sansom is far from being a predictable, or a reliable, writer. He is constantly reproaching himself for being too much this or too much that; constantly trying to right an imaginary balance. And his newest danger of which he is probably more aware than anybody else, is that his extreme virtuosity may be sliding into the kind of professionalism which irons out all the natural wrinkles and awkwardness of a writer's imagination. The *openings* to his stories have always been important—sometimes too selfconscious for comfort but more often beautifully deft, without any displeasing intrusiveness of skill or vocabulary. In his new volume of stories the skill sometimes seems almost mechanical:

> 'They were hopping about the pavement on their little ladders, using them like stilts, window-cleaners all in the clear spring sunshine.'

> The trick here lies, of course, in that single mildly arresting, mildly comical inversion—'window-cleaners all'.

> 'The album lies before me. The old man in the shop sold it for a pound. But its value is untold, though we shall now try to tell something about it.'

Here a reader is hooked by the little play on the cliché-word 'untold', and by the sophisticated 'story-telling' frankness of the artful narrator. And so on. Perhaps the trouble is that 'artful' has too often become 'crafty'.

But a more serious doubt springs from the debilitating anecdotage of some of these stories. The first one, for example—**"A Mixed Bag"**—describes how a husband is compelled by his wife to search in their dustbin for a cheque which she may or may not have thrown away by mistake. It is plain to me that the reason why the story got itself written is that Mr Sansom was fascinated by the contents of dustbins, and longed to flex his literary muscles by describing them. 'But Beale tossed such thoughts and the letter away and addressed himself to the moment, to a scrabble of wet brown paper, a very clean-looking screw-up of candle-smooth, greaseproof wrapping, dry big fluff of hoover-dust, the peelings of a number of potatoes. From all this and from what lay deeper beneath, rose a smell, not malodorous but near to the mysterious smell of rotten grass-cuttings, bringing memories of the ends of gardens, of nettle beds and shadowy composts.'

This, and all the rest of the description, is splendid; but I suppose Mr Sansom felt that it couldn't be served up on its own, as a mere fragment of prose or, still worse, as an 'essay'. So he has tagged on to the dustbin's contents a foolish little episode of the husband finding in the dustbin a love-letter written by his wife. We know too little of husband or wife to find this interesting; all it does is to try, unsuccessfully, to compel all that excellent rubbish to serve some extraneous and 'human' purpose.

At his worst—**"The Little Sailor"**—Mr Sansom attempts a direct assault on our emotions, abandoning all his talents for subtlety and indirection in an all-out tear-jerker. The sailor is dying of thirst in his drifting lifeboat: the boat is blown towards land and then away again. 'But the sailor never knew. His eyes had closed on the vision of the tree, and his heart, overwhelmed, had ceased to beat.' No, no! We had suspected the worst when we first saw the word 'little', and indeed Mr Sansom has given us a dreadful little lump of melting sugar in the worst manner of Hans Andersen.

Other sketches—like **"News from Chelsea"**—are mildly amusing pieces of social observation. Others—**"The Lorelei of the Roads"**—are brilliant reminders of Mr Sansom's macabre inventive power, but not, perhaps, its best exemplifiers. Another—**"Old Man Alone"**—is an almost tragic example of a marvellous possibility missed. The theme is the horrifying, but entirely realistic one, of an old man who lives alone falling down and breaking his thigh and lying incapacitated on the floor through many tormented and hallucinated hours. This is a made-to-order Sansom theme, and yet it seems to me that he almost wilfully bungles it by two disastrous errors. In the first place he makes much too flagrant and greedy a demand for our initial sympathies by making his old man a nobly pathetic ex-soldier. We feel—and I resent—the writer's impatience to engage our sympathies in the shortest possible space: he is trying to get his hooks into us. The second fault of the story is that here, again, Mr Sansom has been unable to resist a foolishly neat ending. The old

man, rescued and in hospital, reads a complaining letter from his emigrant daughter which ends with the words: 'You see Dad, accidents will happen, not like in your safe old stuffy London. . . .'

Yet in between that ending and that beginning how much there is to remind us that the writer who is nodding through so much of this volume is possessed of an imaginative skill which makes most of his juniors seem very drab and tawdry indeed. And there is at least one story here in which the full Sansom band is performing at full blast. In **"Hot and Cold"** we confront two fishmongers lying in deck-chairs in the backyard of the shop during a heatwave. They get bored with drinking beer, and soon their horseplay leads to the younger one stretching himself out naked on the slab and the other one packing ice all round him. That is, in a sense, all that happens; but how much is suggested (without any hooks being used on us) of stale lives suddenly illuminated by humour and imagination; of odd desires lying just below the surface of normality; of human relations suddenly vibrating like a seismograph.

Mr Sansom has nodded before. We can be reasonably sure that he will wake himself up again before his next book, and discover a new material fit for the exploitation of his hungry and still unsatisfied talents.

Paulette Michel-Michot (essay date 1971)

SOURCE: "A High-Water Mark," in *William Sansom: A Critical Assessment,* Société d'Édition Les Belles Lettres, 1971, pp. 145-76.

[*In this excerpt from her book-length study of Sansom, Michel-Michot analyzes the stories in* Lord Love Us, *concluding that the collection is especially interesting because of "the way reality is heightened into art."*]

Sansom finds his true self in the collection **Lord Love Us**. Here fancy is let loose but does not dwell on the sinister or the macabre as it did in many of the early stories, it is free to roam just for the fun and the beauty of it. Sansom succeeds in rendering the quality and the intensity of a moment's delight and the irrepressible zest that urges many of his protagonists to revel in their joy and delight. The characters are simple and ordinary people who have retained the power to marvel and to create or discover beauty in the most ordinary things. It is characteristic of these stories, however, that this moment of joy and delight—in some of the stories, resulting from the very act of creating—suddenly comes to a stop; the happiness and the glory are shattered, which by contrast heightens the previous joy and makes the protagonist mourn for the death of his happiness, and the reader for the death of beauty. In some stories, however, the pathos associated with transitoriness, with the death of happiness and beauty, is overdone and becomes sheer sentimentality. Sansom's style in this collection is another source of delight: his fancy is 'on-the-loose', he coins new words, revivifies worn-out expressions, hackneyed phrases or quotations, he puns on everything and is literally driven by his love of words. He creates an extraordinary rich hybrid between prose and verse, which reveals his love of, and delight in, words—the material of his art—and his sharp ear for music and rhythm. In this collection Sansom comes forth as an artist in language. Yet none of these stories is quite faultless, for at some point Sansom goes wrong either by pretending he has something to say, a theme, besides rendering the quality of a moment or by overdoing the pathos; sometimes, too, the language fails to be the beauty-making power that turns most ordinary things into a source of delight and beauty. Four of the five stories analysed in this chapter present Sansom's artists at work, and the last one is a humorous attack on the anti-artist.

"Life, Death" [first published in *Contact* in 1950] tells the story of a young fishmonger's happy life, of the new happiness love brings him, and the tragic end of his love. The fishmonger is a simple, innocent boy, whose greatest joy in life is to display the fish on his slab; he does his job with great gusto, with an eye for shape and colour, in fact he turns it into an art. One day a young girl standing in his queue shyly asks for two herrings. On that day the boy's world is turned upside down; he has her picture in his eye all day. Soon the boy starts giving the girl two extra herrings without the cashier's knowing it; and the girl accepts them blushing, without a word. The boy is happier than ever before; his slab is his world, his joy, and the girl, coming every day, brings more sun to his life. Their silent conspiracy eventually brings them together and they soon get engaged. They need money before they can get married, so that the boy decides to try for manager. From then on the boy is no longer happy with his slab and with the present: "it was tomorrow I wanted." Weeks go by with the usual ups and downs. One day the boy wants his father to meet Lil. He is rather apprehensive, for Lil is shy and "Dad as stern as Dads can be"; but quite unexpectedly Lil "opens like a flower, all sudden she starts to chat and laugh and play the pretty goat. And soon she has [his] dad on the reins." This is a revelation for the boy. Eventually the boy goes up for manager and they get married in Spring. Lil gives him a "little nipper" and there is "glory all around". But after a year "two of us died. Two left the three, two just wilted—but for why?—and died, Lil and our nipper passed away." The boy has gone back to his slab but life has never been the same since: "there's shade about for me," he says, and he can only ask: "Why, if *you* can tell me, such happy days? Why with happy days such shade?"

This story conveys the fishmonger's irrepressible love of life and beauty, his simple happiness and his zest when he works at his slab, and, when his heart is lifted up by love, his ability to curb his irrepressible spirits—he stops slipping her extra fish, he abandons his slab to work in a dark depot and saves hard on caramels, his only vice—and finally his higher happiness when he lives with Lil and his "little nipper" with "glory all around".

Everything the fishmonger says and does is the expression of his power to work magic on ordinary things. When he works at the slab his greatest joy is to display the fish.

Illustration by Lynton Lamb for the story "Life, Death," in Sansom's Lord Love Us.

The fish, which for others is just fish or a means of making money, becomes in his hands a material for a work of art. He plays with shape and colour and creates delightful pictures, fresh and colourful. When Lil comes into his life and brings love and more joy to it his heart is lifted up and sings. The day he first sees her he is so disturbed that he "sells helter-skelter where you please". He lifts the most ordinary things and events from the commonplace, the two extra herrings he gives Lil become a silent declaration of love, and he feels happy for he "had dared speak a first word to [his] love, though this was with wink and hand"; "dark Milly" comes to look like a foreign god, "one with six arms taking offerings in her fat hole and chinking wealth and prayer all day"; the way the girl pronounces the name of the cinema. "Gawmont", becomes for him the supreme proof that they would be happy together—"She never said that Gomont. And I knew from this she had no lah-da, she was one with me, we would go well together, she and I." His innocent liking for caramels becomes an expensive vice and he turns it into an opportunity to curb himself, to resist temptation; in the process his vice is endowed with value for it offers him a chance of working for his happiness. When Lil meets his father "she opens like a flower" and she makes him "as proud and happy as kings can be." Though his happiness is not unmixed, for he has to work in a place he does not like, he takes the rough with the smooth and works in the prospect of perfect happiness and with the sense of working for it. This duller yet promising life takes him naturally to his wedding day. The event is evoked with an almost pastoral freshness which recalls the simple ballad tunes and suggests that he has retained his zest for life and his refreshing innocence. At the beginning of the story the boy is working in *sunshine* and expresses his *sheer joy,* now he lives with his Lil and the "little nipper" "with *glory* all around"; he has achieved a different and higher kind of happiness. At the end of the story, however, the glory and happiness are suddenly shattered, his zest for life smothered, he moves in a vacuum and his outward gaiety is but a poor decoy for the void in him; even his slab does not bring him joy. The sudden and cruel destruction of his happiness makes us all the more aware of its beauty and value, and, just as the boy is left in a big void, the reader is left to mourn for the death of a beauty which has been conveyed to him in such an irresistible way.

The story is not told by an omniscient third person but by the fishmonger himself, so that the expression itself reflects his gusto and inventiveness; it has the richness and the simplicity of the fishmonger's attitude to life, it is both rich and colloquial. At the beginning of the story the boy explains what his life is like:

> It was my happy job to set the fish for show. I'd take a turbot say for central, a heavy fellow white and round. Then red lobsters, I'd ring my lobsters round that turbot, all their noses in, to make the petals of a flower. Then I'd take a cut of haddock, place this fellow by the turbot's head. I don't know why I put that haddock at the head more than at tail or sides. I don't know what I did not half the time. But it always came out right. I've that eye for colour: and I'd parsley my lobsters, green to red.

The reader is there with him, watching him compose the picture, The I-form, a word like "say" and the succession of short sentences create an impression of immediacy. Each sentence corresponds to a gesture or an attitude: first the choice of a fish—"Then red lobsters"—then the place it is given—"I'd ring my lobsters round that turbot, all their noses in"—and finally the effect to be created—"to make the petals of a flower". Nothing is preconceived, the boy's gestures and thoughts naturally follow the inspiration of the moment. The vocabulary is simple, even elementary; so are the sentences, yet the whole is endowed with extraordinary freshness, joy, spontaneity and beauty; for it is the boy's fantasy and love for what he is doing that can turn fish into flowers, and it is his simple unsophisticated way of talking about it that makes the reader marvel at the scene he is watching. Chaos—a heap of fish—is not organized from without to fit into a rigid frame but is turned into a work of art developing according to its own inward laws (shape and colour of the material) and expanding over the whole slab. The way the boy arranges his slab is the very expression of his creative imagination; the slab becomes a thing of beauty, the picture is colourful, the boy joyful and endowed with a natural sense of humour:

> But my long fish, you'll say? My three H's, rule of three and thumb, haddock and hake and halibut? My pike if you like? Yes, they'd all come in—they'd come in squaring up the rest, they'd come for squaring up. I'd put a lemon in a big pike's mouth, lemon to teeth, and sometimes there'd be mullet like coral and bream as pink-brown babies. And soles with their faces all one side—a tearful sight.

Just as he can turn fish into flowers he humorously turns school abstractions like the three R's and the rule of three into humorous and fanciful principles of composition. The reader's interest in the fish is as keen as the boy's, and he comes to wonder, yes, indeed, what about his long fish? Yet the reader is not so much interested in the boy's fish as fascinated by his inventiveness and sense of composition; what he wonders is rather 'what will he devise for them?' The answer comes as if soothing an anxiety, "they'll *all* come in", none will be excluded, all are worth figuring on the slab picture. The repetition of "come in" and "squaring up" suggests the way things fit into place in the boy's mind: in a flash he sees what is to be done, then he realizes the long fish's contribution to the whole, "they'd come for squaring up". The finality of the squaring up effect is at once swept away by the boy's inventiveness flaring up again; this frame is soon adorned. The boy's expression follows the same course: the words come to his lips freely, spontaneously, and one feels that it is only afterwards that he becomes aware of the effect he has achieved. He gives a new and humorous freshness to worn-out expressions such as "lemon to teeth". His inventiveness and sense of composition are infinite, his slab and the way he arranges it the very image of the boy himself, of his creative and beauty-making power, and of his extraordinarily fresh approach to things, people, and life in general. All this is conveyed in very simple words, in very simple sentences which follow the rhythm of the boy's inspiration and thinking, and give full play to his imagination and to his unexpected and humorous associations. Readers of Sansom are familiar with his supple style, but this is the first time he moves away from the elaborate towards the fresh, the simple, the unsophisticated and the colloquial.

Sansom shows a remarkable sensitiveness and a great gift for conveying the freshness of the boy's emotions and approach to life in a simple yet poetic and rhythmic prose. The sudden appearance of Lil into his life, the effect she has on him, making him start a firework with his fish, and the record of the long winter he passes saving money are significant examples. . . .

The boy's reaction when his happiness is shattered reflects the same simplicity and a natural puzzlement at something which passes his understanding:

> Then it came that two of us died. Two left the three, two just wilted—but for why?—and died. Lil and our nipper passed away. A year alone we were together, then they died.

The archaic *then it came that* is another resonance from ballad poetry; then the emphasis is on the unity of the family abruptly broken by death. The rhythm is not harsh but jerky, interrupted again and again, which suggests the tearing to pieces of the family, and the boy's puzzlement. The latter is allowed to break through in the question "but for why?", which throws a kind of innocent pathos on the whole. The mixture of the 'traditional' and simple style ("then it came that") with the common speech ("but for why", "our nipper"), which in fact blows fresh force into worn-out situations, revivifies the poetic diction and makes the archaic and the colloquial blend naturally. Similarly, at the end of the story Sansom moves away from the ballad pathos, and, more effectively and acutely than tears, the fishmonger's "No I'm not broke, I'll crack a joke . . ." makes us feel his loss and the terrible void in him. The joy and creativeness which came bubbling out from within are now turned into outward gaiety hiding a terrible void, and the lack of tears makes the loss, the void and the pain all the more acute.

Compared with **"Tutti Frutti"** for instance, this story reveals an important development in the story-teller's art. **"Tutti Frutti"** is forced, the intention to select and to oppose is too obvious and too deliberate, the symmetry is contrived, whereas in **"Life, Death"** the reader is irresistibly carried along both by the protagonist's zest and by the way the story is told. Compare, for instance, the sudden blow to each of the protagonists: in **"Tutti Frutti"** Sansom's resort to the unconscious fails to carry conviction in relation to what happens actually, he mixes the unconscious urge to self-destruction suggested in the death-scene with accident; the event, the fall through the window, is felt to fit artificially into Sansom's preconceived scheme. In **"Life, Death"** on the other hand the blow comes out of the blue and shatters the protagonist's happiness, and as such it has the same shattering effect on us as on the protagonist himself. Yet at the end, though Sansom avoids the cheap sentimentality to which the death of the boy's happiness could have led, there is something wrong: the boy's question "why, if *you* can tell me, such happy days? Why with happy days such shade?" is quite superfluous and in a way irrelevant, for Sansom introduces here a new idea—the question suggests the answer 'such is life'—which bears no relation to what he has presented in the story, for the boy's creativeness, his zest for life and beauty, and his power to work magic on ordinary things are certainly an uncommon gift.

It is worth noticing that the gusto, the fantasy and the creativeness of the fishmonger both at his slab and in life are the same as Sansom's when writing the story: he plays with words just as the boy plays with fish, following the inward pressure of the moment, arranging them so as to create beauty and delight. And Sansom's gift for revivifying worn-out expressions, clichés or traditional 'poetic' diction by introducing common-speech phrases is similar to the boy's beauty-making power.

We find a less successful expression of the same theme in **"Trouble in Wilton Road, Victoria"** [first published in *Encounter* in 1954]: the rendering of a particular moment and of the protagonist's emotion, then the blow coming out of the blue, and finally the sudden shattering of the happiness and of the beauty. As in **"Life, Death,"** the interest of the story lies in the protagonist's fanciful expression of his joy and creative zest and in the pictures he gives of the simple and happy life he leads with his wife. Donald is another type of artist: whereas the fishmonger plays with shapes and colours when he arranges the fish on his slab, Donald indulges in non-figurative compositions when he lays the table. But the success of this story is marred by the general and vague comments Sansom seems to be making about art and artistic creation. Once more he pretends he has something big to say whereas all his art and talent are in the rendering of Donald's intense creative joy.

[In **"A Change of Office"**] Sansom presents something—here the dark magic, the riot, the exuberant and fanciful kind of life that goes on in parks, seen and experienced by a heightened imagination—only to reject it afterwards, but not until we have really been intoxicated with it. The protagonist of this story is Sansom's poet.

The narrator, a park keeper, explains why he won't have anything more to do with parks. Parks are not the quiet places one might think they are; he presents the riot, the disturbance, the endless demands put on him by all the living creatures in the park. On the whole he has no trouble with the "parkly birds and beasties" except for the day when seven swans came up off the water and were at him. The kids, on the contrary, are always after him asking him to fish their toys and sailboats out of the ponds; and off he is with his trousers rolled up to get them out. Children are a nuisance but grown-ups are worse still: "Masters of scouts about? Parsonson-the-loose? A problem there you'd say? Ten out of ten, you're right." When he is in his little house he is always disturbed by people who take it for the gents or the ladies. Very often he has to turn himself into a policeman to prevent young cripples in their wheelers—who ride "faster than their legs would never carry them"—from "crash[ing] and smash[ing] the rest of their poor bodies up to pieces". "And then there's dogs and tarts and tics, and tommies at their nursing maids, sergeants in a mess with ladies barely in distress." All this life 'on-the-loose' in the park is conveyed, as these short quotations show, in a highly exuberant and fanciful way. This picture of riot, of disturbance, of the endless demands on the keeper, is meant to convey how much the man can stand, for all this disorder is normal for him, it makes up his ordinary daylife. But what is to come is still worse. One evening while he is peacefully at home drinking his 'Biddy'—too much 'Biddy' in fact—he begins to hear things and then sees with horror that the animals of the nearby zoo have escaped and have turned his park into "a blooming Noah's Ark". His heightened imagination builds up a highly fanciful picture:

> I'm fairly diddled, willies I have and where the willies are there's no way out. Rhinos come in to chaver up my lino? So help me Egbert. Vultures a-perch on Mrs Pankhurst's bust? Gazelles in my Gazebo? Hippos abroad? Lord cut the duck from under me, there's monkeys making houseboat out of boathouse, and of me, and what great secretary bird has laid an eggsir down our birdglade? What's in the gnus tonight? What hartebeestes are making hockey of my fair green lawn? And who's to say the lions are not a-squat about our Redwood tree to play Trafalgars? Who's to constrict the boas, the boars, the boring of the mandrills bumming sunsets to the moon—the humming-birds a battle with my bumblebees, them leopards dropping spots about, I'd knock their daylights out of all of them if only it was not the night.

The vision is hallucinatory and exhilarating, so are the style and the metaphors; fancy is let loose to build up a picture of "Dame Nature Red in Tooth and Claw", which contrasts with the conventional idea one may have of parks. The park keeper gets into an armour and, in a mad escape, runs into the railings round his house. The next morning a policeman finds him with his head caught between the railings; the copper, a representative of law and order. . . .

So the park keeper retreats from the world of imagination, fantasy and magic to the world represented by the copper: "And you, my Billy boy, have had a night—there's not an animal in sight!"; "And it was true." the park keeper adds. From the very beginning of his mad escape the park keeper moves towards limitations: he first puts an armour on, i.e. puts a screen between life and himself, then he runs into the railings, which in fact turns him into a prisoner standing behind bars, and now he accepts the copper's admonitory return to mundane reality. So, escaping the fanciful and hallucinatory world of imagination, he makes himself a prisoner of a stricter order which imposes limitations on him but at the same time gives him a sense of safety.

In this story the park keeper remembers and eventually renounces the direct experience of a life which does not know any limitation; he chooses not to be troubled by it and accepts with the copper a simple, problemless, codified existence, a penny-in-the-slot way of life. Whatever one's interpretation of this story it is rich in many ways. It is not only pleasant, it is exhilarating. Sansom masterly succeeds in creating this sense of boundless life, of fancy 'on-the-loose', both in the picture the park keeper gives of the life that goes on in the park and in the way he conveys it, i.e. in his language and style. Just as the fishmonger is Sansom's painter, one may say that the park keeper is his poet. He loves words, the material of his art, he manipulates them in every possible way and uses them with a zest that urges him to revel in all kinds of associations just for the fun of it. The park keeper's 'terrible' vision of the animals going freely in the park and himself finally standing behind bars is a good example of Sansom's *savoir faire;* he remembers that he has an old armour and decides to put it on to venture outside his house:

> Never you mind! The way in there is my way out, I said, that coat of mail shall see the ending of this pretty tale, the sky can rain hyena dogs and jungle cats, aye it can hail down polar-bears for all I care—once I'm the inner man within the man of tin its toodle-oo to this, I'll show the Zoo who's who!

> I got it out and in I got—and then to still the willies took another glass of good red Bid, I raised my lid and quaffed down deep inside so I could scoff at what went on without . . . giraffes playing Tee-Vee masts upon our Knoll? Don't make me laugh! Them goats they make the leather off of shamming they've come to clean my windows off? Of course! And, pardon my cough, wild boars can jaw their heads off, ostriches bury theirs like croquet hoops about the lawns, hoopoes can loop the loop for all I care and cassowaries emulate

the late lamented dodobird, gorillas play at thrillers, otters can odorise the roses, ant-eaters nose about my pants of rin-tin-tin, elephants tie their baggage in forgetmeknots, zebras make mare-bones bare against the night—what do I care, for drawing my pistol full and deep with Bid against the creeps and taking in hand my shooting-stick, my shotless cannon-cane, I fling my portal wide and out into the baleful dark I stride—wishing myself a fond good knight.

But pistolful of Bid or not, the moment I come out my willies overcome me, fair turned up I am, my heart was never made of steel although the rest was, metal man or no I'm off my mettle now—I bang my lid down taking to my heels and like an old tin kettle on the blow I'm racing for the railing, looking nor this-a-way nor that, all that I'm for is getting going while the going's good, to be out of the wood as fast as a true tin soldier could. . . .

Sansom's skill, ingenuity and endless tricks both illustrate and enrich the suggestive power of this passage. Though he is literally driven by his love of words and puns he succeeds in making it significant and illustrative of the thing conveyed. Sometimes the 'fireworks' is so extravagant and the puns, associations of all kinds, alliterations and rhymes follow one another at such at such a rate that one gets either breathless or intoxicated.

Unfortunately, Sansom does not know where to end his story. . . .

[The park keepers] retreat safe beneath the ground with "never a green thing near [his] eye" could have come naturally after the copper episode and his own discovery that this was midsummer's night. . . .

But these are mere details compared with the delight one takes in reading the story, Sansom's "Midsummer Night's Dream", for the fantasy is catching and the reader is taken along at such a speed that it is not until he starts thinking it over that the defects appear, and even then he does not really mind.

'Caffs', pools and bikes are sources of intense joy for the protagonists of [**"Caffs, Pools and Bikes,"** first published in *Punch* in 1953]. One of them speaks for the lot, his joy is theirs and soon becomes the reader's. What he likes best is to go on his bike to the garage 'caff' where he meets his friends—ordinary workers like himself—and where they make their pools. Just as the fishmonger and Donald turn ordinary things into material for a work of art, these ordinary fellows discover beauty and poetry in the most ordinary, even ugly or disgusting, things. The reader responds to this presentation of beauty and of the delight the protagonists take in it as to a work of art, i.e. thoroughly enjoying things from which he would probably recoil in real life. This suggests the problem of art and of its disinterestedness. Sansom excels in creating the aesthetic distance that enables the reader to rejoice in the thing created. The protagonists' joy and delight are catching, their zest and power to discover beauty irresistible.

The atmosphere at the 'caff' is cheerful, simple and cordial. The things Cyril orders are cheap and common: tea, custard tart and the cheapest cigarettes one can find are his cup of tea. Then they are ready for a tret, they get down to their pools, a most serious occupation. Their gestures and attitude are the expression of their effort and concentration: they bite their nails, "[scratch] their nappers off", "Suck-a-stub frowns come creeping on their faces". They give themselves up to the task more completely than they ever do at night school. Making pools is *the* thing, not for what it can bring them if they win but for the joy they experience in making them. Their cogitations about the chances of the various football teams become either singing or humorous combinations of names:

Wanderers or *Wednesday*? *Spurs* prevail on *Arsenal*? Where will *Orient* be come *Saturday*—gone *west*?

Making pools appeals to them and as such is apt to stir their imagination. In a similar way an articulated lorry driving into the petrol station for filling up is another opportunity for heightening up the conventionally repulsive. This scene is a glorification of the beauty of the ordinary and explodes the myth of pastoral beauty. Pastoral beauty is replaced by the magic of cities, of petrol fumes and "smells of good clean grit" instead of "messy leaves." Everywhere in the garage, up on the wall or down on the compo floor, there are things of beauty for those who can discover them.

After presenting this paradise the narrator steps out of the scene, takes some distance with it and considers the danger that threatens the boys' happiness: what will happen if they ever win the jack-pot? Money is a corrupting agent and a cheat; it will be "Goodbye Caff! Goodbye to all such simple joys!" Money will induce the winner to do things he does not like. While he enjoyed meeting friends at the usual 'caff', drinking cheap fizzy drinks and making pools, the ordinariness was only superficial, for underneath there lay treasures of happiness and of beauty; now with "sixty thousand sitting in the bank" the situation is reversed and his wealth is a poor mask for his inward misery and dissatisfaction. . . .

The winner will go the way all flesh goes, he will end up with prostitutes for second-hand experience and will pay dearly for an unsatisfactory and frustrating way of life:

> Along comes the boy that's won his div and then it's 'Pleasetermeetyer!' 'Charmed I'm sure'—no cure for that but champagne to your supper, when a cup of tea is all you're after, caviare it's got to be, a ritzy car and then you're taken for the kind of ride you never had upon a bike, hot lips and hearts of ice, that is the price we'll pay the day we win—wages of virtue to pay the price of sin.

Prostitutes, champagne, caviare, a ritzy car are the 'hot lips', the glittering appearance, the glorious envelope of a cold heart. Money means the death of his simple warmheartedness and of his happiness, for it won't bring him any satisfaction or real pleasure. The interest of this passage does not lie in the moral comment on the corrupting power of money but in the way this is conveyed: as ordinary things have been lifted out of the commonplace, now wealth and luxury are deflated with the same zest and exuberance. The language is inflated in a humorous and fanciful way; commonspeech expressions are parodied in the use Sansom makes of them—"after all we are human, only that", "the way all flesh goes", "tonight's the night", "div"—they are given a false glittering radiance full of expectancy which suddenly vanishes with "pleasetermeetyer", only to leave a keen sense of frustration. The rhythm of the whole passage takes the reader to the end in one stretch: up to "pleasetermeetyer" then down by fits through a series of ups and downs, for as soon as the 'promising' champagne, caviare, etc. are mentioned they appear as frustrating or unwanted 'pleasures'. The passage ends on a pun on the expression 'to be taken for a ride', and on the 'hot lips and hearts of ice' image, which, on the one hand, carries forth the preceding ride image and conveys the difference between his former and his present happiness, while, on the other, it illustrates the kind of love he will experience in the arms of "scarlet-hearted judies". The change is then epitomized in "wages of virtue to pay the price of sin", which is a funny twisting of "the wages of sin is death"!

After this there follows a brief evocation—on the theme of "oùsont les neiges d'antan"—of the beauties to which the winner will no longer be responsive, a nostalgic mourning for the delight he took in the simple things that surrounded them. . . .

[But the sound of a bike] brings him back to a heightened present, to the boys turned into a horde who answer the call; starting their engines, they are ready to leave for their own world of beauty and joy which, however, contains a threat to their happiness, for the blue dreams are dreams of pure monoxide. As they start their engine there is a sense of impending danger; they bring a tremendous force into being, which reminds us that by filling their pools they also initiate a process that can hit them back. Unfortunately this is not the end of the story; the last metaphor is not allowed to speak for itself: the narrator becomes sententious and passes general comments on the human condition which are rather out of place in the context. . . .

Apart from [a few] minor faults this story is typical of what Sansom can do, i. e. present the quality of an emotion—the joy and intense delight of this set of people able to discover beauty in the things that make up their everyday life, their anticipated mourning for the happy past and for the death of beauties which have for them the freshness and enrapturing power of pastoral beauty.

The heightening of reality into art is achieved, and the aesthetic distance is preserved, by Sansom's impressionistic technique and metaphorical use of language, by the rhythm and suppleness of his style. . . .

The way the protagonist speaks, the kind of things he eats, drinks and smokes is symbolic of the quality of 'the material' his life is made of; yet it is lifted out of the ordinary by the rhythm, the simplicity, the over-all sense of delight and irrepressible zest. To elevate petrol smells, "odours of oils", etc. to create a world of new and fresh sensations and to make the reader respond freshly to the scene he deflates the traditional pastoral beauty—"no messy leaves"—and he uses its conventional 'poetic' language in relation to his 'unpoetic' subject:

> while on our air that smells of good clean grit (no messy leaves) *the richer smell* of petrol *sits,* odours of oil and smoking rubber *weave a spell* about our motors . . . while *raise your eyes* and there's the picture of a speed-ace racing round an advert for an additive, or drop them in a *peacock pool* of petrol staining the bone-grey compo floor with all its *rainbow glory,* drop them brother, an *adore.*

These words contribute to transfer the freshness and wonder conventionally associated with pastoral beauty on to his 'unpoetic' subject; thereby Sansom both revivifies the traditional poetic diction and heightens the world of city noises and smells into a world of beauty and delight.

The story as a whole is a metaphor conveying the magic of the ordinary, the heightening of reality into art. It also images the perfect response to art, i.e. the aesthetic enjoyment taken in the artistic achievement, the thing created, independently of the reactions and sensations the real thing could arouse in real life. The process is carried one step further, for, after presenting the delight and the beauty Sansom moves on to another facet of the aesthetic response, i.e. the mourning for the death of beauty. **"Life, Death"** and **"Trouble in Wilton Road, Victoria"** image the creative imagination of the impressionistic artist playing with shapes and colours and of the non-figurative artist playing with rounds and squares, and convey their delight in creating beauty with quite ordinary material. **"Caffs, Pools and Bikes"** renders the intense delight not so much in creating as in discovering and enjoying the beauty that lies in most ordinary things. . . .

[**"Time Gents, Please,"** first published in *Time and Tide* in 1951] is a humorous 'debunking' of the 'Old Boy' myth. The protagonists are "fixtures and [live] by Fixtures." They always meet under the clock of Victoria Station, which shows an exactness and a preoccupation with time which the story proves to be completely empty and formal, for in fact they are people who have run out of touch with the times, with real life. They stick to the old ways and days: they play cricket in a very gentleman-like and amateurish way, and go to Old Boy dinners; they try to make time stand still, but in doing so they become Time's fools. One day they are beaten by a ladies' team at cricket, a game they consider strictly for men, and, at the end of the story, their final defeat is given a big bang, the clock falls on them. The interest of the story is not social, it lies in the way Sansom succeeds in catching those 'fixtures' and in confronting them with the times (their jobs, a cricket ladies' team) as opposed to time (the clock and their formal preoccupation with time).

Sansom first satirizes them by showing the narrow and shallow realm of their experience:

Farquhar and Urquhart. . . . Those were their names, and cricketing their pleasure. Cricket, and junketing with Old Boys; in between-times, once or twice a year an evening out—cheers, chaps!—upon the beer.

The conciseness and the economy are the very expression of their limitations. They do not have interesting jobs—the school tie won't do any more even if the pretence is there—other chaps have come up to take the place of the Old Boys. They have some sort of hackneyed jobs out of which they do not get any satisfaction; they are careless about them but slick enough to cover up their blunders by using the deceitful modern advertising clichés:

> Yet to turn a penny, all the older ways aslump, each had had to join a job of up-and-coming kind. Thus you might hear the fellows say, vaguely but with meaning: 'Farquhar's in a radio way, Urquhart's in Dry cleaning.'

'Meet you under the Clock, old boy?'

'Meet you under the Clock!'

> Click the two receivers went! And each would glance at the smaller clock in each's little office—Friday the day, the next day Saturday Off—as if to urge along the weary hours. Then Farquhar'd sigh and sell a superhet, and Urquhart miles away would shrink a blouse. 'Fabriolize your shrunks.' he'd later say: and Farquhar'd make a megacycle pay. . . .

The humour lies in the fanciful exaggeration of both situation and expression.

Longing for the Saturday as they do, these men might be expected to come alive when they take their pleasure:

But come the Saturday you'd see them grey of bag, of buttoned blazer blue, pork-pie greenly set aloft, brown of each shining shoe—you'd see them gruff a timely greeting, on time and under Time, watches shot from cuff comparing times with Time above. 'Time for a quick one?' 'No time like the present.' Each with a small green ticket wet in hand would wet each whistle—then the train, the drowsing day of cricket. . . .

Sansom's knack at minimizing the life of a phrase images the life-killing attitude of the Old Boys, their wish to make time stand still and to preserve the status quo.

Sansom is really good at catching these fixtures. He makes them speak only in clichés either from the advertising world or from the Old Boys jargon. Yet these set phrases appeal to Sansom's love of words and he uses them in unexpected ways, so that, at times and for our delight, the satire and the metaphor run wild:

> Thus their life they whiled away as Farquhar went his radio way while Urquhart drily cleaned. Urquhart wrote out little cards: 'May we have your shirt, Sir?' Farquhar'd sell A.I.T.Vs.—A.C.D.C. 'they're a cert, sir.' 'Fires shaped like electric fans, fans like electric

fires!' 'Renovated, cleaned and spotted, worn or torn wear, we're the Dyers!' 'Buy our brand-new Telewhizz, bright with visual hiccup! Buy fluorescent lamp, my little plastic pick-up!' 'De luxe, de Luxe! There are no flukes! Give us your dirty garment! The pleasure's ours, the risk is yours, if it's ruined there's no harm meant!'

Here again Sansom has caught both the tone and the method of modern advertising by which you sell things by gimmicks, and he deflates in the most exhilarating way the smiling robbery of modern commercial advertising methods. The same process takes place when the Magpies—one recognizes in the name a non-professional Old Boy type of team—meet a ladies' team:

> A Ladies' team! Blazers and blouses, stockings and skirts! The principle, sir, it's *that* that hurts!

But the girls "went in to slaughter 'em". The narration of the match is another opportunity for Sansom to run wild in the most enjoyable way, and to deflate the reserved, polite Old Boy countenance:

> Brawned as bloody Amazons! Baleful as Bacchantes! Thrills and chills and spills and frills—the flashing of their panties! Bails to the right of them, balls to the left—slogging for sixes and sevens! Body line! Filthy swine! Got'er! You rotter! Never were two elevens ever more, ruseful, accuseful, abuseful. . . . Howzat? and howzis—here's one for your trousis! And here, where it hurts, is one for your skirts. . . . Cricket that day lost its greenswardly chastity! Weep for the willow on that very nasty day!. . . .

One of the things Farquhar and Urquhart could rely on is lost for ever: cricket, a game strictly for men, is now invaded by women. The shock and the shame of it all! for they are beaten by the women Now what they long for is their "weekday workday days". They fall back on something that is nothing, on their uninteresting jobs. . . .

But the humour, fanciful and unbridled, mainly arises from Sansom's use of clichés and catch-phrases, from his knack at playing on words and coining new ones. In the opening paragraph, for instance:

> They referred to that great clock that hangs above the platforms at Victoria, grimy old trystwatch dear to denizens of the Surreyed South as is the Strand to citizens returned from Empires in the East.

Trystwatch is a play on wristwatch and tryst, and refers to the clock at Victoria, which in fact is used for meetings. Surrey, turned into an adjective, *Surreyed,* comes to life as a metaphor for the wealthy stockbrokers traditionally residing in Surrey. Sansom also turns adjectives into verbs:

> you'd see them *gruff* a timely greeting.

> later out they'd *brisk* . . .

He revitalizes the words and gives them a new freshness. Or he telescopes two words and keeps the connotations of both: when they go to an Old Boy dinner they go "up the stairs of tilish gilt Pagoni's, where—how beautiful the stagly ones!—they'd . . ." *Tilish* suggests *stylish* and *tiled* but the words are reduced and the picture evoked is deflated into *tilish gilt.* The same kind of thing happens with *stagly*: a stag party is an all-male party but reading *stagly* one cannot help thinking of a stag, a creature whose force and virility are reduced in the Old Boys to mere pretence and self-delusion.

Sometimes Sansom's puns have not such rich connotations, they consist mainly in word associations, e.g. "and after that [the cricket match], a dinner for the Old Oakhampton Boys! A willow, then an oak. Hamptonians all!" Or, when the two old boys go to the gents to change their clothes after the cricket match for the Old Boys' dinner: "Then they wrestle there alone with ties, with butterflies and other flies"—meaning of course trousers' fastening.

The numerous puns, play on words, coined words, telescopic words are rich with connotations or simply exhilarating. The reader is hurried on by the numerous examples of alliteration and assonance and by the rhythm of Sansom's prose, which very often breaks into rhyming verse. The clichés—either from ordinary life, commercial advertising or Old Boy jargon—besides imaging the protagonists' way of talking, are a source of delight for the reader. The fantasy Sansom works into them, the effect of unexpectedness he creates and his own sense of revelry in words are irresistible. He resorts not only to conversational clichés but to hackneyed literary phrases such as the concealed references to "The Charge of the Light Brigade" and to Henley's "Invictus" "bloody but unbowed". He manages to give these phrases a twist which contributes to the humour of the story, and which makes of these insipid characters the funniest and most unheroic of people.

As in the other stories Sansom does not end with the big bang. It is as though he did not want his story to verge on tragedy, which in fact it does not just because of the tone he has used throughout; after the fall of the clock he goes on in a mock-heroic style to tell us that the story has a "faintly happy ending":

> never more would those our heroes stand beneath the Clock. That clock was fallen, they were fallen too. Fate struck a crushing happy ending. Neither was killed.

The anti-heroic note, e.g. "they both spent a year in a hospital bed" and "each of them married a nurse", comes as an anticlimax, but the humour fails to come off. Contrary to what we have had so far, this is just the kind of things we had expected. This story gives us another example of Sansom's failure to end his story at the right moment and on the right note, but it is also a brilliant example of his zest for words, of his irresistible joy in manipulating them in the most unexpected way—using at the same time all the resources of spoken language and of a literary heritage, which, for obvious reasons, is mainly Victorian.

This is the most delightful collection in Sansom's work. As the analysis has shown the interest lies in the way reality is heightened into art: a fishmonger displaying fish on a slab becomes an impressionist artist playing with shapes and colours, a man laying the table an artist indulging in non-figurative designs, a park keeper becomes a poet recalling a past experience with something of both the heightened imagination and the obsession of a Coleridge for instance. The repulsive sphere of petrol smokes, motor bikes and lorries, the ordinary world of ordinary workers meeting in pubs and making their pools, become sources of intense joy and beauty. This beauty-making power can operate on *any* object; the meanest thing and the cheapest emotion can give Sansom the impulse to create, or can be a source of delight and wonder; in this Sansom is partly like Wordsworth, who conveys the beauty of the most common flower.

The obvious delight which Sansom takes in writing these stories is catching and of the same order as the joy his artist protagonists take in creating. They follow their love of colour patterns or game of squares and rounds as Sansom follows his fantasy or his love of words, which drive him on and on drawing delightful arabesques. The pleasure in the thing made is what matters, not what it means or what it tells us about life. Sansom has not much to say about life though at times he pretends he has and thereby mars the effect of his stories. What matters is the delight, the joy in creating or in discovering the beauty and wonder that lies in most common things. The reader enjoys the thing made as he responds to a work of art, to the beauty of the thing achieved independently of that of the real thing in real life.

The success of the stories and the delight the reader takes in them—in spite of their limitations—lie in the irresistible fantasy of Sansom's style and language.

—Paulette Michel-Michot

The success of the stories and the delight the reader takes in them—in spite of their limitations—lie in the irresistible fantasy of Sansom's style and language. Fancy is let loose for the fun of it. His love of words drives him to irrepressible associations, he plays with them at different levels, he is intoxicated and sometimes intoxicating. Meaning does not matter so much as the pure fun of manipulating words in every possible way, with the result that he often revivifies worn-out expressions and language in general. . . .

Sansom exploits not only all the possibilities of spoken language—from working-class idiom, children's language and nursery rhymes to the Old Boy jargon—but also those of literature. His stories are full of literary echoes: his way of writing sometimes evokes that of poets, which is significant of Sansom's approach to language. The park keeper's

heightened imagination, for instance, reminds one of Coleridge seeing domes in air, and his shudder at all green things in the park of The Ancient Mariner's at all the slimy things. He sometimes alludes directly by quoting (cf. Tennyson's Nature Red in Tooth and Claw) or indirectly to a particular poem or phase—The Charge of the Light Brigade is suggested in the cricket match in **"Time Gents, Please"**, implying both the slaughter and the passing of the old order. Or he intentionally misquotes a phrase: Henley's pompous and heroic "My head is bloody but unbowed" is altered to "bloody but not unbowed my head"; the meaning is completely reversed and conveys the defeat of the old order and of its pretence.

Just as Sansom imitates and parodies particular ways of speaking, he also imitates and parodies particular literary styles and dictions. In **"Life, Death"**, for instance, the evocation of the fishmonger's wedding—"Until a month in Spring my lovely Lil I naved . . ."—reminds one of ballads and of the naïveté that is associated with such poetry. The style is consciously literary and is meant to evoke resonances from that kind of poetry; yet Sansom revivifies the traditional poetic diction by introducing common-speech idioms and colloquialisms. In **"A Change of Office"** he imitates eighteenth-century nature poetry at its most conventional and by putting the description in the copper's mouth and opposing it to the park keeper's rich, fanciful and dangerously exuberant view of nature, thereby making it representative of a turn of mind and of a style of life—law and order v. fancy and freedom.

Just as any object gives Sansom the impulse to create, any form of language, spoken or written, is turned to serve his purpose, whether he imitates, stylizes or parodies it. His dexterity and ingenuity are a source of delight; the reader is carried along from one surprise to another marvelling at the effect achieved.

The success of the stories rests on the transfiguring power of the language and style, so that when either fails the whole is dangerously threatened. In **"The Mistletoe Bough"** and **"Friends"** (beginning and end), for instance, the sentimentality of the situation is not redeemed by the language, on the contrary, the style is in the same key and contributes to make both the situation and the emotion still cheaper. Quite at the other end, when Sansom's imagination is 'on-the-loose', he is at times so irresistibly driven on by his love of words and the prospect of playing with them that he soars in such long stretches of fanciful associations and puns that the reader eventually gets breathless, and though these passages are often exhilarating, he sometimes resents the exaggeration and the wildness.

It is not surprising that fantasy should take charge, for this has often happened in the earlier stories. The difference is that instead of showing us the terror and the nightmare that lie beneath the calm and ordinary surface of things and people, here Sansom reveals the magic, the freshness and the beauty of it all. Instead of having the story told by an omniscient narrator, who sometimes failed to view the situation from the inside, Sansom here gives the word to the protagonist himself, so that we get the story "straight from the horse's mouth". This approach is no doubt more congenial to Sansom's talent: his urge to create and his fantasy are not hindered by technical problems of structure and presentation; the story follows the arabesque patterns drawn by his, or the protagonist's, roaming fancy. Yet, instead of accepting this lyrical structure, Sansom sometimes comments and thereby spoils the beginning and/or end of some of the stories (e.g. **"Life, Death", "Time Gents, Please"**).

That Sansom has found in these stories both a subject and an approach congenial to his talent is confirmed by the fact that *The Loving Eye,* which appeared in the same year, has the same kind of qualities as **Lord Love Us** and is his best novel. The exuberance of the protagonist—is allowed to roam across a series of back-gardens to a window which becomes the source of both his joys and his pains.

Though none of the stories is faultless, the collection is delightful. They are irresistible illustrations of Sansom's creative zest, making of every little commonplace thing a source of endless delight, which develops in arabesque form following the fanciful curves of his heightened imagination and of his sharp ear for language. This collection reveals Sansom the poet, the magician, the word-craftsman, and is a high-water mark in his career.

Lila Chalpin   (essay date 1980)

SOURCE: "The Short Stories," in *William Sansom,* Twayne Publishers, 1980, pp. 105-30.

[*Chalpin is an educator and critic. In the following excerpt from her book on Sansom, she groups the author's stories into several categories and analyzes representative pieces. The critic also summarizes the changes in Sansom's writing that resulted in a move from the "brief epigrammatic" style of his early career to the later tales that reflect "the angst of contemporary life and his own mature view of the human condition."*]

Compared with his novels, which are uneven in form, [Sansom's] short stories are uniformly successful. He has himself expressed greater enjoyment in writing short stories than novels. They seem to be more suitable to his watchful eye and do not demand the depth of exploration of human psyche. Stories also capture these words of his: "A writer lives best, in a state of astonishment. Beneath any feeling he has of the good or the evil of the world lies a deeper one of wonder. . . ."

While the ambiguities of illusion versus reality found in *Fireman Flower* remain a viable theme, Sansom explores many other themes. I have selected stories representative of recurrent themes on revenge, fear and violence, marriage, friendship and death, challenges to Sansom, societal issues, and two stories that are his favorites. These themes are often refracted by Sansom's narrator who is both detached and romantic. Usually the detached side of his

personality wins because he would rather yearn for something or someone and be unfulfilled than forced into active participation in life.

I   STORIES OF REVENGE

A story that combines the theme of revenge with humor is **"A Contest of Ladies,"** the title story from a collection published in 1956. It is about a May-December relationship.

Fred Morley, an eccentric, wealthy bachelor finds himself host to six beauty queens who have come to his home in a Channel Island resort town for a beauty contest. Immediately he picks out Miss Great-Belt of Denmark as the most beautiful and most disaffected by his charms.

At the same time he is enjoying the intimacy of the beauty queens, he observes their strange beauty routines.

> He had found Miss Clermont-Ferrand sitting with her head in her beautiful hands and each elbow cupped in the half of a lemon. Across the landing there had whisked a blue kimono topped by a face plastered livid dry pink, with hollows it seemed where the eyes might be and naked lips huge now as a clown's, a face terribly faceless—too late he had seen that this might be Miss Great-Belt. Then Miss Rotterdam, in a bathing dress, had come bumping across the landing on her bottom, and vanished into the bathroom: no hands nor legs, she had explained *en route*—a question of stomach muscles. Miss Sauerkraut liked to lie on the balcony on half a ping-pong table, head-downwards. Miss Civitavecchia he had found carefully combing the long black beards that hung from her armpits, a peninsula specialty; unlike Miss Amsterdam who took no such Latin pride in the strong growth of dark hair that covered most of her—it seemed that whenver he asked for her the answer came: "Upstairs shaving."

Sansom revels in the comic description of external beauty and is at his best in this story when describing that aspect of women. Five years later, when he returns to this subject in *The Last Hours of Sandra Lee,* he no longer handles it with the same lightness.

While Fred subtly arranges a dinner date with Miss Great-Belt, he takes two other queens out at noon. But Miss Great-Belt never appears at their rendezvous. Later when he confronts her at home, she casually gives the excuse that to dine and sit all night in a cramped theater box with the contest coming up the next morning is not appealing.

To Fred's hurt response at her breaking the date, she chastises him for his licentious behavior in taking advantage of the women at his home.

> "Well *really.* You spend the morning with not one but *two* of these . . . these *women* upstairs. And then you expect to spend the evening with *me?* What do you think I am? What next? Shall I tell you what *you* are— you're an old satyr, that is what. A wolf! With pointed ears! With hoofs!"

She delivers the word "hoofs" with a mouth shaped for "whoofing" down whole houses. Fred does not take this accurate portrayal of himself gracefully. He vows revenge. And he can carry it out easily because, unbeknown to her, he is one of the judges of the beauty contest.

The next day at the contest hall, Miss Great-Belt loses all her composure when she sees Fred in the judges' stand. Her first reaction is anger at herself for being so stupid as to tell him off. Then she condemns him as a monster for not having told her that he would be a judge. But her fears are allayed by the thought that he will be sorry for his deception and, because deep-down he is really in love with her, he will vote for her. She also feels that even if he does not, there are four other judges who will surely see how much more beautiful she is than the other women.

But she is wrong. Fred not only votes against her but persuades everyone to do so also. His vanity has been too bruised by her attack to vote objectively.

When she hears the decision, she is wildly upset. She thinks of setting his house on fire, accusing him of rape, and assaulting him. But then she decides on a calmer, more vengeful act: she will flirt with him, woo him, and marry him. And she does.

Fred is triumphant at the end and innocent of his bride's vengeance. But the reader is aware of the lifelong tortures Miss Great-Belt will invent for him. The ending is contrived, though it does make an interesting reversal of the usual power-struggle between man and woman. Sansom has given her the ability to see Fred as he is and the self-confidence to do battle against him. On the one hand, these abilities seem to warrant her abandonment of Fred and progress to another more worthy challenge. But, on the other hand, Sansom may well be describing the love-hate magnetism of two people bent on winning each other at whatever the cost.

Another story of revenge, **"A Last Word,"** published in *A Contest of Ladies* and later in *The Stories of William Sansom,* succeeds in being humorous even though it ends in a funeral. The revenge is between a landlord, Henry Cadwaller, and his tenant, Horton.

Cadwaller is parsimonious and Horton proves to be his main irritant both as a tenant and a friend; thereby, Horton becomes the stimulus of Cadwaller's life. When Cadwaller sets the overflow-holes in the bathtub three inches lower to save on water bills, Horton covers them with a sponge so he can enjoy a full tub. Cadwaller serves his guests food half-raw to save gas but Horton constantly sends his food back to the cook to be burnt! Although Cadwaller has made a no-cooking rule in the rooms, the odor of cooking always seeps through Horton's door. Try as Cadwaller does, he never finds a gas-ring, for Horton cooks beneath a tent of sheets on an electric blanket.

As they age together, they become companions, lunching together or going to a pub together. At lunch if one is served a larger helping, there are nasty words. Eventually they learn to order different dishes and suffer only if they see huger helpings at other tables. In the pub, Cadwaller orders three mild beers, inexpensive and worthwhile in terms of drinking time. Horton orders a small whiskey in a large glass, enjoying Cadwaller's discomfiture over all the free soda water that goes with the whiskey.

Compared with his novels, which are uneven in form, [Sansom's] short stories are uniformly successful. He has himself expressed greater enjoyment in writing short stories than novels. They seem to be more suitable to his watchful eye and do not demand the depth of exploration of human psyche.

—Lila Chalpin

From his thrift of walking around in shoes with soles "the size of the yolk of a flat-fried egg," Cadwaller contracts bronchitis. He refuses fires and hot-water bottles so that, in effect, he kills himself. Bereft of his adversary, Horton appears to others as an old little boy left out of the game with no one to play with. He is seen digging up a bush in the garden before Cadwaller's funeral. His shoulders shake and everyone wonders if he is weeping.

At the end of the short funeral service, Horton is the last one to place his bush on the grave. People see him walk away, a solitary figure "into the years of loneliness. . . . Nobody . . . saw the giant chuckle beneath Mr. Horton's bowed shoulders: nobody knew the true nature of his last tribute, his bloom, his last word, *Rubus Idaeus,* the common raspberry."

Thus Horton gains revenge over his companion by the humorous transformation of a school boy's "raspberry" cheer into an adult horticultural pun. The ending like the rest of the story has a subtle and comic effect that are superior to some of the moralistic endings of Sansom's earlier stories.

II   STORIES OF FEAR AND VIOLENCE

While Sansom deplored violence in the media because he felt man was nine-tenths parrot, he occasionally wrote about men full of physical violence or with the potential for it. Although **"Various Temptations"** originally appeared in *Something Terrible, Something Lovely* in 1948 and **"Among the Dahlias"** in *Among the Dahlias* in 1957, and both were chosen eventually by Sansom for his collection *The Stories of William Sansom* in 1963, they share a common theme. Both are concerned with a willing victim who passively awaits victimization. Several years later, Muriel Spark, another fine British writer, also chose this theme in her novella *The Driver's Seat.*

Clara in **"Various Temptations"** and Doole in **"Among the Dahlias"** appear to be ordinary people content with their humdrum lives. Then into their lives comes an over-whelming force: in **"Various Temptations,"** the force is an insane strangler; in **"Among the Dahlias,"** the force is a lion let loose from his cage in the zoo.

Each character meets her/his fate with a certain perversity. Clara, a plain woman and invisible mender by occupation, lies in her lonely bed with the window open. She is invisible to most people not only by virtue of her occupation but by virtue of her common, bland appearance. She knows a strangler has already murdered four women in her neighborhood. But since the newspapers equate the strangler with Jack the Ripper, who chose prostitutes as his victims, Clara feels both comforted and rejected.

> . . . Clara put the paper down—thinking, well for one thing she never did herself up like those sort, in fact she never did herself up at all, and what would be the use? Instinctively then she turned to look across to the mirror on the dressing-table, saw there her worn pale face and sack-coloured hair, and felt instantly neglected; down in her plain-feeling body there stirred again that familiar envy, the impotent grudge that still came to her at least once every day of her life—that nobody had ever bothered to think deeply for her, neither loving, not hating, nor in any way caring.

Similarly Doole, on his lunch hour, strolls through the zoo and encounters an uncaged lion. He thinks,

> O, God, please save me. . . . If only it could speak, if only like all these animals in books it could *speak,* then I could tell it how I'm me and how I must go on living, and about my house and my showroom. . . . I'm not just meat, I'm a person, a club-member, a goldfish-feeder, a lover of flowers and detective-stories—and I'll promise to reduce that profit on fire-surrounds, I promise from forty to thirty percent. I'd have to some day anyway, but won't make excuses any more. . . . Two separate feelings predominated: one, an athletic, almost youthful alertness—as though he could make his body spring everywhere at once and at superlative speed; the other, an over- powering knowledge of guilt—and with it the canny hope that somehow he could bargain his way out, somehow expiate his wrong and avoid punishment. He had experienced this dual sensation before at moments in business when he had something to hide, and in some way hid the matter more securely by confessing half of his culpability.

He is desperate to be spared so he is willing to admit to anything.

Clara is "chosen" by Ron Raikes, the strangler. He enters through her window and wins her sympathy by sitting on her bed and talking to her. Even he, with his killer instincts, senses something is wrong. She is not struggling for her life and thus does not agitate him to quell her. She also appears to be unattractive.

He moves in with her, living in her sitting room, and soon they plan to marry. When she returns one day with a surprise birthday present for him, two ties, six yards of white

material for her bridal gown, and a box of thin red candles, she muses on Ron's strange attractiveness. He seems interested in his own safety but also is preoccupied with her as no one ever has been. Starved for attention, she willingly risks her life. Subconsciously she knows he is dangerous. Consciously, she decides, just this once for his surprise birthday tea, to make herself look pretty. And here is her fatal error. She paints her lips with a thick scarlet smear. She hears Ron opening the door and lights a red candle to give a festive air. To him, she now resembles the kind of women who have been his victims. He observes that

> . . . her face seemed to be charged with light, expressive, and, in its new self-assurance, predatory. It was a face bent on effect, on making its mischief. Instinctively it performed new tricks, attitudes learnt and stored but never before used, the intuitive mimicry of the female seducer. . . . The trouble roasted on his brain.

He ends his observation by leaning toward her as if to clown and kiss her. Instead, he takes the ties she has brought as a gift and strangles her.

On the other hand, Doole, in **"Among the Dahlias,"** is never attacked by the lion. . . .

Doole suffers rejection, rejection by a lion who does not consider him fit to devour. Why is Doole disappointed that he has not been chosen as a victim? Evidently his mundane life, like Clara's, holds no excitement for him. He feels alone and undesirable.

The ending is a teaser. Doole partly recovers his nerve and begins to look at himself in the mirror with an eye to self-improvement. He has his teeth fixed, visits a Turkish bath regularly with the intention of losing his old self by sweating, and he begins to run long distances regularly. Does he do it to run away from himself or from something?

In both stories, Sansom mixes pathos with comedy. Clara is overjoyed to be wanted by someone, even if that someone is a criminal known for strangling women. Her gaiety at the end of the story as she assumes Ron is clowning but is actually strangling her diminishes into little noises. These noises suggest both frightened resistance and disbelief. Doole never became more actively involved in life than after rejection by the lion. His meanness as a businessman used to distract him from self-realization. But once his life has been spared he no longer is able to lose himself in his usual pettiness. He appears to be forever after confronted with the big question of why the lion found him wanting. . . .

Fear and violence are combined within the persona of the same individual in **"The Man with the Moon in Him,"** published in *Among the Dahlias*. A nameless man, affected by the full moon, goes out for a lonely walk. He follows a heavily painted girl up the stairs to a train. But he does not follow her into the train. Instead, he waits for the doors to slam shut and for the train to depart. Then he takes out a pencil stub from his pocket. With it he writes quickly in the white space of an advertisement in large letters a single obscene word.

Then he drops the stub into his pocket. In between arrivals and departures of trains, he repeats the act of writing the obscene word on other advertisements. At one point, he is defacing a poster of a girl in a low-cut dress. His stub slips from his hand and falls near the live-voltage rail. Frustrated, he leaves the station.

Soon he sees a young woman smelling of soap and scent. He follows her through a park. As she disappears behind a bush, holding a package of fish she has just purchased, he leaps at her from behind.

> . . . She made no sound but for a little sob deep inside her open mouth. The fish in its newspaper fell squashed between them. He butted her face up with his chin and looked close into her eyes. . . . She stared up at him with the innocence of a child about to be struck . . . with all the strange love of victim for assailant.

Her look and attitude so disarm him that his hands drop to his sides. As she presses her pocketbook on him, he says gauchely the first thing that enters his mind: "'A pencil . . . could you please lend me . . . a pencil?' before she fell, in a dead faint, to the ground."

Sansom has deftly transposed a primitive man who is repressed and bored into a marshmallow. The comic effect brings relief after the tension that has been built, and the twist of violence diminishing into fear rather than fear accelerating into violence, as in the works of Poe, is a clever device.

III   Stories of Marriage

While most of Sansom's novels focus on romance and young married couples, his short stories from 1957 on, concomitant with his own aging process, deal with middle-aged crises. He can render the bristle of two people concisely and effectively. Elizabeth Bowen views the underlying theme of these stories as one of resignation and reconciliation. Often the catalyst is a forbidding landscape that both alienates the couple and brings them together.

"A Waning Moon," although originally published in *The Passionate North,* a travel book, was included in *The Stories of William Sansom* because it is a vivid example of the conflict of a middle-aged couple with themselves, each other, and the landscape. The story opens with a woman's scream in the night in a deserted place. Nearby is a caravan or mobile home with a man inside.

Through flashback Sansom recounts how the woman, Ruth Rose, came to be screaming out for help. She and her husband are on a caravan holiday in the Highlands. In the beginning, the moon was full but some nights later it is on the wane and its weakening force seems to affect the atmosphere. It affects the couple, too. They argue as they make camp in the darkness.

As they settle in, he goes out for water while she cooks supper. When he returns, they discuss what they can decipher of the dark landscape around them. She says it looks like scree, jagged and loose. While eating dinner he writes in his journal that they are in slate-quarrying country. Tension mounts as he withdraws into his notebook and Ruth pours herself a large glass of whiskey. She goads him further.

> . . . Draining the whiskey she raised again her voice and repeated and repeated what she knew he had heard before. Beginning to move with it too, swaying on her seat, thumping the table, turning on with one flat sharp stroke the wireless switch, flooding thus the caravan with sound against his silence—so that again he moved his hand wearily across his forehead. And suddenly she wrenched herself up, pulling at the same time the table-cloth, crashing down plates and food and the mess of gravy, shaking the caravan, screaming. . . . She took up a tea-pot and threw it against the wall, and as so much sound and violence crashed away out of her that same very need for finality overtook her own senses, the known act was flushed over with hysteria, the room took charge mounting into a headache and a blackening of light—until she could only get to the door and fling open and, screaming, bundle down the steps into the night air.

The atmosphere assumed the shape of anger in this anthropomorphic paragraph. It sends Ruth out into the misty land where she wanders through a forbidden gate. She finds herself bounded by a precipice and a still mineral lake to which she is magnetically drawn. Whether she slips into the quarry-lake or, in a trance, jumps in is unknown.

As she hits the icy water, her scream reaches her husband's ears as he sits sulking inside the caravan. He rushes to her rescue and, at great peril, saves her from drowning. When she recovers her senses, she rebukes him with her old bitterness. He tries to calm her down and steer her away from the lake. But he is suddenly struck by a violent thought. No one saw him go there. He could loosen his grip on her and let her fall back into the quarry. "He . . . looked for the last time round that basin of loneliness. Then, quite suddenly, she raised her free hand and made a gesture to move the hair from her eyes, to smooth open her brow. A movement well-known to him, simple, a gesture both efficient and helplessly feminine."

This feminine gesture saves her and him. Despite his wife's temper, he feels compassion for her and knows they must live out their lives together and accept the loneliness they feel at times as part of the human condition. Sansom makes the husband believable. He is a man with a sense of proportion. But Ruth, in her jealous isolation, resembles some of the shrill characters from his novels. Her jealousy and temper tantrums endanger her life. Once saved from drowning, she displays no capacity to relent or change; thus she becomes a stereotype of a virago.

"The Dangerous Age," published in *Among the Dahlias,* is an amusing story about a middle-aged couple whose problem begins when the wife, Janet Orde, decides that, with the onslaught of middleage, she must create some illusions of youth. She changes all the bright bulbs in their home to forty-watt bulbs. This softens her wrinkles and assures her that her husband, Bertram, will not be tempted by the dangerous age to philander.

When Bertram comes home, his reactions to the new ambience are not what she expected.

> "Funny," he said, "feels a bit foggy in here. Didn't notice it outside. Chimney been smoking?"
>
> "No, dear."
>
> "Well, I don't know," he said. He looked round the room, sniffing, his teeth bared in that ever-fixed smile. Then he went over to the wine-cupboard. Fingering for glasses, he stumbled in the corner among darkly shiny walnut. "I'm going blind," he muttered. . . .
>
> Quite brightly, as if it had just occurred to her, she added:
>
> "I've changed the bulbs—did you notice? The lights are softer."
>
> "So *that's* it!" he said and looked over to his own chair. "But can we read?"
>
> "It's these dreadful headaches," she said, turning her big dark eyes on him, letting her mouth quiver a little. "These bright lights *split* my head right open."

Bertram is sympathetic and privately resolves to buy himself a spotlight reading lamp. But he does not.

Increasingly he finds it difficult to read at home. Since he is too vain to buy glasses, he holds the reading matter in his hands but finds his thoughts wandering dangerously.

> He was sitting, with the yellow lights, with Janet's flat bosom, with the frilled beige blouse, the long droop of pearls.
>
> "You look like an old dog," he said to her silently, "a collie." And in the next second, thought: "But you're my own dear collie, my Janet whom I courted at sweet twenty-three.". . . He was very fond of Janet.

While he contemplates pursuit of other women, Janet feels that the lowered lights have made her look more beautiful. She does not realize that he can no longer see her except as a blur in that darkened, dead room.

One day when Bertram mistakenly picks up a golfball for his sherry glass, he decides to get eye glasses. Janet greets his decision with mixed feelings. She figures that, if his eyes are weakening, then even in sharp daylight she will be protected from too sharp scrutiny.

Getting glasses spurs him to seek a new woman because glasses are further proof of his disintegration. So he gath-

ers up courage and meets a Miss Eglinton in a railway station. Eventually he is lying to Janet about needing to work late at the office. Janet believes him and derives comfort from knowing he is earning extra money for the future in case he goes blind. The story ends with the following ironic lines: "Alone among her soft furnishings she suddenly felt like Lucrezia Borgia. Deliciously. But guiltily too."

Sansom's tone in this story is controlled and objective. He pokes fun at Janet for sacrificing reality for the illusion of youth and he pokes fun at Bertram for sacrificing his youthful vigor and fidelity, pre-lowered-lights stage of life, for the reality of middle-aged decline. Janet's illusion *becomes* Bertram's reality. Ironically, each seems satisfied with the exchange. Their middle-aged battle of the sexes is gently mocked with very comical results. . . .

Another story of marriage written later in Sansom's life is **"Love at First Sight,"** published in *The Marmalade Bird.* It is very short and focuses on the love Richard and Mona Lister feel for each other at first sight aboard ship on a holiday. What is unusual about this view of a married couple is Sansom's laying bare the illusion each had about the other and showing them in search of that person for the rest of their lives.

Mona first sees Richard's face framed in a porthole, eyes gazing intently at hers as she stands on a higher deck. To her, his eyes are "visionary, rhapsodic, lost." To him, her face is also framed by a porthole and fits his particular dream of a girl.

They meet and marry. And Richard never again looks so beatific as he did that first time. The tender sensibility of the blush he had shown is not to be found in the Richard she married. "He was predatory and materialistic, an engineer by profession though, of course, . . . he had . . . his romantic moments." What Mona does not know is that at the time she saw him, he was in the men's room passing water and idly looking through the porthole. Unlike the couples from Sansom's earlier romantic stories and novels, the Listers do not live happily ever after. Duped by their initial reactions, they never achieve the soulful intimacy they thought each would give the other.

IV   STORIES ABOUT FRIENDSHIP AND DEATH

The Ulcerated Milkman, published in 1966, contains the short story of the same name, **"The Ulcerated Milkman,"** which is one of Sansom's most comic and pathetic stories. Unfortunately, it has never been included in any other collections published outside of England.

Bradshaw, the protagonist, is a milkman who loathes milk while exhorting others to drink it. He goes from doorway to doorway praying for a plague of "great tits." Meanwhile the milk company announces a contest. For the milkman who increases sales the most in a three-month period, there will be a prize of a motor scooter. He works hard at winning but begins to spit blood from ulcers.

Soon he is hospitalized and told the cure for his ulcers is—milk! Disgruntled, nostalgic for stout, he and Brown, the elderly patient in the next bed, eat semolina and junket with milk while reciting a litany of potatoes *à la français* and other forbidden foods. They vie with each other to produce menus spicy, hot, and dangerous to their health.

After Bradshaw returns from an X-ray, he tells Brown about a dream he had while drugged. It is a humorous dream blending both forbidden foods and women, particularly the pretty nurses. . . .

The nurses appear to him as bunnies and everyone seems more privileged than he and Brown. Brown is appreciative of Bradshaw's humor and imagination. But the reverse is not true. Bradshaw takes Brown's presence for granted. As Bradshaw's health improves he becomes insensitive to Brown's feelings. Brown's fantasies about foods irk Bradshaw because they are no longer forbidden to him.

One day Brown has a violent hemorrhage and is taken out of the room. Bradshaw does not see him leave because he is making the rounds of the rooms to boast about the motor scooter he has won in the contest. When he returns to the room and learns that Brown has died, he is remorseful for his rudeness.

As he returns to normal life and delivers milk on his scooter, he thinks of the hospital as the place of golden days and wishes he could drive old Brown down to the coast on his free days.

Michel-Michot feels the balance of tragedy with comedy in this story "is disturbing because it does not emerge from the story itself but is contrived by Sansom to bring into relief the other side of reality at all costs." But she is perhaps overlooking the unreality patients feel in hospitals and the ensuing euphoria of feeling better that makes them egotistical. Sansom, having had ulcers himself, understands these feelings well. The emptiness Bradshaw faces when he recovers and realizes his loss of a dear friend seems entirely realistic and plausible. Thus the story is memorable for its depiction of a tender relationship between men.

V   A Story Sansom Regretted Having Written

One story Sansom regretted ever writing is **"The Last Ride,"** published in *Among the Dahlias*. It is about a beloved uncle's funeral at a crematorium. The narrator is Nennie, a niece of Uncle Jack, who is considered the "queer one" of the family. Proof of her queerness, she feels, is in her looking forward to Uncle Jack's cremation. ". . . Although she had been deeply affected when Uncle Jack died, she had cried herself to sleep, she felt in some other compartment of her strange mind that he was still alive and intent on giving them all an interesting and unusual day out. She knew he was dead all right, but half her mind was still able to think otherwise."

While the priest is praying over the coffin, Nennie believes Uncle Jack would have roared at the solemnity of all the friends and relatives gathered round. But, when the priest finishes and the coffin moves off mysteriously of its own accord toward the brass doors that swing open to receive it, everyone sighs with either relief or sadness.

> The dead coffin of its own accord came to life and moved off. Dreams of furniture on the move became real, the dreadful advance of wardrobes came for a moment true. The coffin slid off by itself on a secret mechanical voyage. The great brass doors opened like the petals of a hungry plant to receive their long polished food foot by foot—until only the last of it remained, and then this too disappeared, and Uncle Jack had gone at last. With ruthless finality, the gates closed.

Nennie is tempted to applaud the "entertainment." Everyone looks uncomfortable. That night in her diary Nennie writes about Uncle Jack's last gay ride with appreciation.

In retrospect, Sansom felt that the story had questionable morals but did not elucidate. Whether his own mother's recent death had caused him to criticize **"The Last Ride"** or whether the story had been criticized by others for its callousness is open to conjecture.

VI   Challenges

Sansom enjoyed challenges. He once read in a brochure about a school of writing whose cardinal rule of good writing was never write a story on the theme of false teeth. He thought this was absurd. Hence he wrote not one story about false teeth but two! And both are bizarre.

"A Visit to the Dentist" appears in *Among the Dahlias* (1957) and **"The Biter Bit"** appears in *The Marmalade Bird* (1973). The sixteen-year lapse in time between these stories reveals much about Sansom's tenacity or perversity!

"A Visit to the Dentist" is the story of a middle-aged man named Pemberton who leaves his dentist's office with a new bridge of plastic teeth. He is still partly drugged as he wanders into an expensive-looking, dimly lit restaurant for coffee. As he muddles through the gory events that have just transpired in the dentist's office, he realizes with horror that he has one particularly strong dislike—objects made from plastic.

> He noticed that the brown brittle electric light sockets soon split, he had broken his fingernails trying to open a plastic-sealed medicine carton, somebody had once sent him a set of occasional cups and saucers whose very touch and unusual lightness had inspired something near to horror in him. And now, he reflected, as he sat in this strange restaurant, he had a plastic device in his mouth for life. . . .

He offends the waitress, upsets a stand of cakes, and hears himself whistle out rather than speak words. In his muddled, drugged state he mistakes a customer's poodle for a cat and calls it nice pussy. (Sansom can never resist the double meaning of pussy!)

As the drug starts to wear off, he sees that the restaurant appears to have many stylish women in it, all with poodles. As a burly male customer accuses Pemberton of insulting his lady friend, Pemberton tries to explain that he is not drunk. A humorous exchange occurs as the big man says, "Well, I can rumble your type all right," and Pemberton, misunderstanding, says, "Rumble? This is all Greek to me. . . . And I haven't my Liddell and Scott handy."

The man angrily asks if Pemberton is being funny, obviously not understanding that Liddell and Scott is a reference book. To make matters worse, Pemberton snatches for another reference book that may be more familiar and says, "Well, let's say my Baedeker."

This sends the place into an uproar as his words are construed as his wanting to go to bed with the woman escorted by the big man. A fight ensues, Pemberton is punched in the mouth, and the new bridge breaks. With blood in his mouth, he hails a cab to return the broken denture to the dentist before closing time.

This story dwells on the embarrassment occasioned by the dentures, the pain at the dentist's office, and difficulty of a middle-aged man in adjusting to a new way of speaking and viewing himself. In contrast, **"The Biter Bit"** dwells on the acceptance of dentures by an older man and a practical joke played on him by two young men.

"The Biter Bit" is an extended anecdote about a young man, Thomas John, who likes to visit joke shops specializing in "grotesque masks, greenish gloves in the form of terrible claws, giant-toed false feet to slip over your shoes, bandaged fingers running with blood, even stick-on 'pus-topped' boils . . . itching powder, stink-bombs . . . carefully curled brown snakes of 'Naughty Doggie' dirt . . . tell-tale cat-sick, and a pneumatically controlled plate-wobbler."

When Thomas John and Ted are told a story by old Paddy, who is really only fifty, about taking out his dentures in mid-ocean and tossing them into the water but catching them before they fell, they spur him to reenact the trick over a nearby river. As is expected, Paddy takes out the dentures, tosses them toward the river, and fails to catch them in time. They see the dentures float away and sink. No search can bring them back.

So Thomas John goes to the joke shop and buys an upper set of false teeth. The boys contrive to take Paddy fishing, and while he dozes they tie the dentures to his line. When he awakens he is delighted to discover the dentures. Mud and all, he pops them into his mouth and declares that they fit better than ever!

Thomas John proves to be a poor loser because Paddy's naive delight in the teeth makes him feel ashamed. This shame and the ensuing irritation Thomas develops toward Paddy, even after he has confessed the trick, is not convincing. How much more interesting this story would have been had Sansom examined the character of a practical

joker rather than pad it with lists of joke-shop items and the history of dentures! . . .

After reading these two stories on dentures, I conclude that the brochure that warned against trying to write an interesting story about false teeth was right! Although Pemberton is a more interesting man than Thomas John, both men are manipulated into situations for the sake of a pun rather than insight into character. Sansom should have declined the challenge of the brochure!

VII   LATER STORIES ON SOCIETAL THEMES

Although Sansom tried to write of the effects of the Welfare State and middle-class affluence in his few novels (*The Last Hours of Sandra Lee, Goodbye,* and *A Young Wife's Tale*), he never felt comfortable with the results. However, in the last eight years of his life, he successfully depicts the problems of contemporary life in several short stories. In *The Marmalade Bird,* his last collection, there are four such stories.

The first story **"Down at the Hydro,"** depicts the flirtation of an elderly colonel with a married woman at an expensive dieters' resort. Lying in their gazebos, starving on salads, enduring sitz baths and massages, and, above all, experiencing rejuvenation, the characters and their fellow dieters feel justified in expending a great deal of money for someone else to discipline them into thinness. In addition, the dieters are treated to lectures on the efficacy of mineral waters and enemas.

Sansom catches not only the tone of the Hydro but also the attitude of "patients" with the gentle comic spirit of Bunin.

> It had set a pace of some intimacy. No one would go so far as to say they were all one big family, nor did the staff say so. There was surprisingly little archness in the attitude of the staff. Someone indeed had labelled the huts "gazebos," but mostly because once there had been a old gazebo thereabouts. And there was a habit of likening patients to their cars: "Your engine's clogged and tired—isn't it just natural to come in for a decoking?" But this was, after all, perhaps the easiest way to get at the average contemporary mind. Though the allusion sometimes misfired, as indeed with Deirdre Mackay herself, who had been caught out with a petit beurre one morning. Without preamble, the nurse had said: "Somebody's taking their car out of the garage too soon!"

The analogy of humans to cars demonstrates the theme of a flaccid society that has sacrificed its humanity for the efficiency of technology. The members of this society willingly allow themselves to be victimized by the image-builders of the business world in preference to exerting free will and determining their own condition.

The second story **"Mamma Mia,"** is a brief sexual encounter between a young Italian migratory worker and a middle-aged working-class widow. This story demonstrates the sexual permissiveness of the age better than *A Young Wife's Tale* because Sansom is telling the story objectively without intruding his usual moral judgment.

When the widow, Mrs. Brown, becomes pregnant, she becomes the object of jokes about immaculate conception. But she ignores them and ". . . as jokes will create truth, there were some who even began to believe it: the old girl looked so queenly, almost holy with her little dark-eyed babe beside her."

She never attempts to find Piero and he, for his part, retains the mellow memory of a warm, giving woman who illustrated the loveliness of English women. Thus Sansom handles not only illicit sex but illegitimate children with a light touch in keeping with contemporary society's less condemnatory views.

The third story **"A Day Out,"** is a breathless account of a cockney family's outing in their car. The roads are crowded with other affluent workers, roadside restaurants, and signs. The son of the family, who is the narrator, gets particular pleasure out of stopping in the men's room to pull off and on his new nonwool synthetic shirt and watch the sparks fly. He and his siblings drink many Cokes on their bumper-to-bumper excursion and voice continual amazement at the new sights in the amusement park, the new supermarket, and the new merchandise. Near the end of the jolly outing, his mother tells him to pull over to the side so his father can throw up and not dirty the car.

For a brief moment, the narrator looks up at the stars, his first glance at something that is not man-made. He thinks,

> . . . The whole sky's soft like velvet and d'you know, even with all them other cars passing, when I look up at that sky it all feels dead quiet. Up there, I think, it's going on for ever . . . silver stars like pepper dust going on forever and ever and ever . . . and I feel so lonely I want to cry . . . it's so bleeding beautiful like. . . . Still we don't want to go on about *that* sort of thing. . . . Did the whole sixty-one miles in under five hours . . . a right good day had by all.

Through the clichés of this young man's vocabulary Sansom implies a great deal. The new rich enjoy their material possessions with the gusto that the advertising world advocates. The price they will pay cannot be reckoned, but the meaningless conversations of the family forebode a disintegration of meaningful relationships of man to man and man to nature.

The fourth story **"The Day the Lift . . . ,"** describes the entrapment of a prosperous businessman, A. B. Bowlsend, in an elevator. Before he enters the elevator, he is reviewing in his mind the blessings of suburban life and his family of a wife and two daughters. After he finds himself trapped in the elevator with a strange man who does not panic, Bowlsend becomes hysterical. He screams and attracts the attention of Healey, the man he has come to do business with.

Once rescued, Bowlsend is mortified when Healey asks where the woman is who screamed. He is upset that Healey only offers him a glass of water and treats the matter lightly. Finding it hard to admit that he was only in the

elevator a quarter of an hour, he rewards himself by stopping on the way home at a pub for a large brandy.

Once home, he does an about-face on family plans. He tells them,

> . . . We are *not* going to the Wapham marina. Waste of time and money. It's time we all stiffened up a bit. Ought to be thankful we're alive, not spend the time always wanting more of this, more of that. And you Marlene [his teenage daughter], you're to be back home at eleven o'clock tonight. And every night, see?

While Bowlsend is comical in his posturing, his experience conveys Sansom's message well. Prosperity must be used in conjunction with the Puritan ethic of discipline; otherwise man will be incapable of surviving the vicissitudes of life.

VIII   Sansom's Two Favorite Stories

"Life, Death," originally published in *Lord Love Us* in 1954 and in *The Stories of William Sansom* in 1954, and **"The Bonfire,"** published in *The Marmalade Bird* in 1973, are two favorite stories of Sansom's. They are interesting to examine because they were written at the beginning and end of his career. Also, they handle the subject of death in a masterful prose style.

"Life, Death" is a simple story told as if it were a ballad. A fishmonger falls in love with a shy customer, woos her, weds her, and loses her and their baby to death. He tells his story in the first person. From his enthusiastic outpouring of words, he creates a happy picture of an artist-fishmonger's work. For example.

> Now I had my white coat and my blue apron, and how I'd jam my straw on pleased to great the trade. But first I finish off—now I'd got my central. Mackerel, trouts and my red-spotted plaice-lings—those coloured fellows I would take next. Striped mackerels I'd make into a ring, and place a crab within. Two rings I'd make, one each side to balance. Then stars of rainbow trout, all wet colours one each side to balance. Then stars of rainbow trout, all wet colours of the rainbow dew. But my plaice—my good brown plaice with the bright red dabs, these I'd bend tail to head, tail to head so they'd make a round, and I'd set them plumb in the middle below the big turbot, for a braver-marked fish would be hard to find.

This arrangement of fish is a piece of conceptual art that awakens Sansom's sensibilities. Michel-Michot likens the fantasy and creativity of the fishmonger at work to Sansom at work: "He plays with words just as the boy plays with fish, following the inward pressure of the moment, arranging them so as to create beauty and delight. And Sansom's gift for revivifying worn-out expressions, clichés, or traditional 'poetic' diction by introducing common-speech phrases is similar to the boy's beauty-making power.". . .

The ending, after the loss of his wife and daughter, resembles the traditional lament of ballads.

They've gone, I said, my loved ones are gone. Please only give me back my slab—and they, who knew, did that. But I tell you this, my slab never is the same again, there's a shade about for me.

The boy has become a man. He has risen to be manager of the fish store in order to provide a good life for his family. Once he loses them, he yearns for the comfort of his old clerking job at the slab, for his ambition has died. Like the traditional lament, the story ends with his altered condition in life and his need to talk forever about his terrible loss.

"The Bonfire" was placed by Sansom significantly at the end of his last collection, *The Marmalade Bird*. He regarded it as one of his best pieces of writing, particularly in its ending. Suprisingly, **"The Bonfire"** returns to the subject of fire with its dangerous entrapment. Sansom proves he has not exhausted this subject. The protagonist, however, differs from the protagonist of the fireman stories in his advanced age and house-proud attitude. But Wilkins, the protagonist, is just as conscientious as Fireman Flower.

The story begins with the wife, Mrs. Wilkins, looking at her husband's bruised knees and asking him what gigantic secretary has been sitting on them lately. Wilkins looks at his bruised knees and wonders if wishing to have his new typist sit on them actually caused telepathic bruises; he replies that all he has been doing is breaking sticks for a bonfire at the end of the garden.

He prides himself on making a fire by the boy-scout method, which makes him feel as if he has mastered the elements. But his wife is upset by the bruises this method causes and she says, "That garden'll be the death of you. . . . Last week lumbago, now bruises. All those scratches from the roses. Poets have died from the prick of a thorn."

Her prognostication almost comes true. As Wilkins walks to the end of his garden, Sansom reverses the familiar design of a realistic rendering of the scene. The man is passive; "things" become active. Against the end-wall lies the blackened bonfire patch with its wild mysteriousness.

> He . . . felt it to be some sort of sacred grove. It was darkly shadowed by neighbouring trees, which also let through curiously bright shafts of sunshine like occasional beams of sunlight in a church . . . and gave the whole quietly sleeping place a pagan, holy look. But sleeping? It rather seemed to be waiting, watching. "It'll be the death of you," echoed back to him as he felt once again the quiet threat of so much darkly green growth, and he threw down his boxes and paper almost like a challenge. "Just try," he told the poisoned nettles. Each nettle grew exactly upright, its pointed leaves arrowed downwards, intense with held action.

Then suddenly his prayers are answered. A gust of wind blows the flame out. No sooner does this happen than Wilkins scoffs at his foolishness about calling the grove sacred. As if a higher force reads his mind, a small rim of red sparks begins to eat away at the sheet of newspaper.

With practicality he decides to remove his trousers and rid himself of the thorns that are pinioning him. But the trouser legs are too tight-fitting to remove easily. He stands up, fly unzipped, trouser tops flapping above the knee, feeling absurd. As the flame burns secretly like a magic curse, he feels helpless as a child. He hears an ominous crackling and Sansom describes its effect with a crescendo worthy of Proust.

> A smell sweet as childhood rose up to Wilkins' nose, the remembered smell of paper and kindling sticks from a fire grate. Wee Willie Wilkin, child, boy, youth and now large strong provident man held fast in a trap built by himself, built with care of dry things and air for the maximum efficient flame, topped by a climber dug up with equal care for a more efficient flowering of garden, yet now a thick-tentacled dry octopus reaching out to grip and hold him.

His indignation at the realization that he has carefully entrapped himself causes him to gain extraordinary strength. He frees one leg to kick the fire out but the other leg is still pinned by thorns and his trousers which are halfway down his legs.

He is still in danger of burning to death. The heat hits him and he finally cries weakly for help. The fire hits his face and body. His body convulses and he wrenches himself free, dragging the rose with him. He rolls about on the lawn in his smoldering clothes and collapses.

His wife comes to the rescue with a wheelbarrow which she uses to drag him away from the fire. The last two lines of the story, which Sansom said "wrote themselves," are:

> Then she stood quite still, a figure of sudden peace, and quietly watered her husband.

> And the bonfire burned on, not so high now, but settling down to eat up all the year's succession of events, the winter's storm-broken branches, brown ferns and greyed chrysanthemums, the dried daffodils of spring, early irises, prunings, a large reaping of weeds, the first dead roses of summer.

The husband blends into the landscape that he formerly thought he was master of. The wife waters him as she would a smoldering object. The visual effects of this scene are superb.

So is the last touch of the first dead roses of summer. The scent is pervasive. Roses suggest serenity, a symbol of the Virgin Mary. They also suggest perfection, which is what Wilkins aspires to in his garden. Paradoxically, the roses have thorns which not only actively subjugate this house-proud man but also nearly cause him to lose his life.

In this last published short story of Sansom's, he reveals both his early interests and those that came later. His early interests centered around the natural element of fire and the way in which it disabused a character of his notion of reality. His later interests centered around human adjustment to the vicissitudes of life.

One of his ardent critics, John Vickery, has made comments on early stories that are applicable to **"The Bonfire."** In "William Sansom and Logical Empiricism" Vickery says,

> . . . [We] find the questions of Sansom's characters are those of purpose or cause, essence, properties, those, in short, asked by the metaphysician. . . . So Sansom shows how the topics, questions, and unknown answers [irritate his mind and force him to rely on unknowns]. . . .

Sansom's characters learn that they cannot eliminate ambiguity. They must learn to live with frustrations and their own mediocrities. But to a degree, as in Wilkins's finding superhuman strength to wrench himself free of the fire, they can control their lives. A neosurrealist work results from this juxtaposition of the commonplace with the horrific. The resolution between the ideals of Wilkins and his reaction to nightmare forces is a matter of equilibrium which Sansom creates in this story in a masterly fashion.

IX   SUMMARY OF THE SHORT STORIES

Throughout his thirty years of writing, Sansom gathered strength in the short-story form. His first stories were brief, epigrammatic, and moved quickly. They were in harmony with the nervous, fragmented life of the 1940s. Reflecting the influence of Poe and Grandville, these stories dwelled on the bizarre with no irrelevancies or digressions. His use of language to emphasize mood was right from the start lyrical and polished.

During the second decade of his writing career, his short stories began to sparkle with wit and irony. They also became less surrealistic and more romantic. The resolutions of the plots, when the stories were plotted and not sketches or slices of life, were neither comic nor tragic. The protagonist was allowed a certain freedom of action but not the kind of freedom that permits him to control his destiny or integrate himself back into society. Reflecting the influence of Proust, these stories dwelled on explicit details of setting that subtly defined character. Like Proust, Sansom evoked the feelings of déjà vu with his ability to make the reader abruptly conscious of past sensations. Thus, he captured the mystery in the relationship between the sexes as he was rarely able to do in his novels. At times his stories reflect the influence of Bunin in their simple factual framework containing less explicit detail but letting feelings speak for themselves. Images solidify and move of their own motion. The themes pertain less to illusion and reality and more to the necromancy of love, time, and death.

During the last decade of his writing career, his short stories reflected the angst of contemporary life and his own mature view of the human condition. So versatile was he by the end of his life that he could call upon the bizarre effects of his early stories, the witty and romantic effects of his later stories, and the wisdom of his middle age to write a variety of stories. The vigor and sophistication of his last stories are entirely consistent with the excellence of all his previous stories, proving Elizabeth Bowen's description of him as "a short-storyist par excellence, a short-storyist by birth, addiction and destiny."

Clare Hanson   (essay date 1985)

SOURCE: 'The Free Story,' in *Short Stories and Short Fictions, 1880-1990,* The Macmillan Press Ltd, 1985, pp. 132-39.

[*In this essay, Hanson discusses Sansom's early stories and analyzes the manner in which the author uses 'dreamlike and horrific' elements but ties them to everyday reality.*]

William Sansom began his career in an advertising agency, writing 'formula stories' in his spare time. What he saw during the blitz in London changed his idea of what a story should be and altered the course of his life and career. The fictions which he wrote in the war period won great acclaim, and still form the basis of his reputation, though he subsequently published novels and travel books as well as further collections of stories. It has been suggested earlier that the short fiction form was well suited to convey the disorientation of life in the war period, and the excellence of the work produced by Sansom and Bowen in particular indicates that the form was certainly favoured at this time for reasons other than the mundane one of paper shortages.

Like [Elizabeth] Bowen, Sansom focuses on the effects of war on the civilian population, but his fictions are unlike hers in being more overtly disruptive. His work has frequently been compared with that of Kafka, and he has also been labelled a Surrealist. But these are not, ultimately, valid comparisons, for both Kafka and the Surrealists started from the premise that the 'barrier of the real' had already been broken. Sansom moves form the real to the dreamlike and horrific, but uses distorted images which still bear some relation to a commonly perceived, everyday reality: he does not attempt to cross into a no-man's land beyond the real. His war fictions contain hallucinatory and distorted images, but this is to make the point that war in its modern form is the ultimate distortion, a violation of almost all the normal impulses of life. Sansom's treatment of the London blitz may in this respect be compared with that of Thomas Pynchon in *Gravity's Rainbow* (1973).

'Fireman Flower' is the title-story from Sansom's first collection (1944), and the fiction reflects and creates a state of mind as we, with Fireman Flower, attempt to construct a private order out of the monstrous disorder of a large urban fire. The fire is an uncontained image for the war, and as Fireman Flower journeys through it Sansom uses various techniques to indicate his increasing dismay and disorientation. The narrative opens with a carefully specific description of a London night scene which might almost have come from Elizabeth Bowen:

> At the time he was riding to a most important fire. Looking out from the back of the van he could see how clean the streets had been washed by the night. . . . Sometimes, on an acute camber, a silver thread of petrol fountained from a pin-hole in the petrol tank cap. There was little other movement. The vehicle raced evenly forward. The fireman saw only the dark linoleum road slipping backwards: or, if he raised his eyes, the departing rows of houses, the terraces, the crescents, regular, eyeless, washed grey by the moonlight.

As the fireman draws nearer to the fire and his nervousness increases we see one way in which he attempts to control his fear, using the apparent rationale of official orders to combat the situation:

> My task is succinctly—to discover the kernel of the fire. I must disregard the fire's offshoots, I must pass over the fire's deceptive encroachment . . .
>
> . . . we are all engaged upon this job of the fire, and we are all equipped similarly with both the incentive to complete the job and the weapons with which to work.

The absurdity of such an attempt to impose a rational structure on an irrational situation is conveyed through Flower's stilted diction, which does not have the stamp of truth or belief. His alienation and inability to come to grips with the situation are further indicated through his distorted perception of scenes which are swiftly cut down to size by the narrator:

> Yet here was this immense edifice standing quite alone! And Flower's pump was now racing up a broad highway that led straight towards the great central door, a road that dramatized the building's tremendous isolation, the aloof building that reared so hugely against the nightblue sky, alone on its firelit plain, unencumbered by the city, a black castle flecked with orange flames that crashed from its windows and among its high turrets like the flames in a fairy tale.
>
> But it was neither castle nor cathedral. It was a black-bricked warehouse of hideous design.

When Flower finally arrives at the fire, we move with him through a montage of phantasmagoric scenes, in each of which he seeks the cause or meaning of the fire. At first he sees the movement of men around the fire as part of a rational exercise with a rational goal. A fellow fireman endorses this view:

> We cannot think to control what is beyond our sphere of command. However, up to that point they have worked out for us an excellent routine, with which we have always been satisfied, which has in the past proved its worth, and which for these reasons is beyond question.

Flower is at first seduced by this account, but then begins to question the motives and goals of the 'they' who are in overall control. What had at first seemed rational now seems to have no solid basis in fact or reason, and Flower has to reject this as a 'story-book' view of the fire. He next experiences the fire as imaging the triumph of the senses over the intellect. Floating in a warm, scented bath (the fire hoses are playing over crates of broken perfume bottles) he is almost able to approve this development:

> Can sensuality, after all, be no forlorn dead-end, but instead a highway from which great things can be obtained? They say—'Food, a roof and a mate—only with these provided can one be free to start thinking on aware planes.' In that case, possibly the finer the roof, the sweeter the food, the subtler the mate—possibly these refinements may stimulate rather than divert?

But, again, he is swiftly disillusioned, and, panicking, runs backwards, literally and metaphorically, to scenes from his former life. Their cosy familiarity first attracts and then repels him, as he begins to form the idea that hope for mankind must lie in change and in the future. He turns from the past to thoughts of his fiancée:

> Pink patchouli and the odious whalebone—how could I love these when there are Joan's fresh cheeks, Joan's clean sunbed? That is the struggle, though . . . the wrestling of security with hope, of the womb with the bright dirigible, of safety with the will to create!

The logical consequence is that Flower is moved to reject the past and accept all that the future may bring, particularly in terms of the development of machinery and technology. He thus begins to see the war as a necessarily destructive period out of which will come new possibilities for mankind:

> Life as he had known it had been broken down. From the elements a new world had been moulded. Iron, fire, brick, smoke, and water from the huge hydrants were patterned into a new choreography that enlivened fiercely the blood and the spirit.

But almost immediately after Flower has expressed his Nietzschean feelings of joy-in-destruction, he is distracted by a new scene, and once again a visual phenomenon changes the direction of his thought. A wall behind him crumbles and brings a new transformation through the humble agent of flour (there is surely a pun here—Flower's imagination has a similar power to transform mundane reality):

> Like milky lava it had spread down from ceiling height, fanning majestically to either side and far out across the floor. Now it had set in a sheer wall of oiled ice, lucently marvellous, smooth, polished, yet intimating from within that it would be soft and wet to touch. The high white walls, the white-crusted girders, the duning and the silting of those soft flourbeds, and now finally the flow of the great pellucid glacier merged into a

harmony of massed shape and tactile wonder that radiated some limitless composure of beauty unaffected by dramas and associations, pure.

And again Flower turns his back on an understanding he has won, and changes his mind about the true meaning of the fire. This new scene has a beauty which stirs him to a deeper, more mystical 'explanation' of the fire:

> Here the harmony soothes, yet elates. Here is a limitless spiritual ideal . . . here must be the real kernel of the fire, where joy and melancholy become one sensation, where one can trace the web of this great fire to the finely balanced pattern at its very center.

Then the text continues, characteristically, 'But just as he was thinking this, Flower glanced over his shoulder', and we are offered yet another change of perspective. Flower suddenly tires of all his attempts to understand the fire, and in reaction to the strain climbs up to the top of the building, where he can breathe the night air. By chance, he finds the true 'source' of the fire lying at his feet: a 'random, reasonless rocket'. All Flower's attempts to divine the causes of the fire come to this, and as he accepts, as he must, the random nature of this particular drama, his sympathies extend into a simple love of all things that exist, however random or arbitrary their existence may seem to be:

> Then he turned towards the numberless roofs that stretched far away into the distance, and with a great quiet love he let himself grow aware of them, of the sleeping chimneys that told of armchairs beneath, of windvanes that knew all weathers, of curved cherubs upon the mansards of palaces, of low leaking roofs where the garret washing still dripped.

The fiction ends with a celebration of the random and fortuitous nature of human perception and experience. It is this which links Sansom so closely to Bowen and to Pritchett.

'The Wall', also from the collection *Fireman Flower,* works in a rather similar way. In this short fiction Sansom makes specific reference to the photographic and cinematic techniques which had helped to free his fiction from conventional narrative appearances. The unnamed narrator, for example, 'photographs' the first terrifying sight of a wall on fire, about to fall towards him: the whole scene is depicted as in a freeze frame. As the wall actually begins to crumble, the narrator, mesmerised, still sees the scene in photographic or cinematic terms:

> Although at this time the entire hemispherical scene appeared static, an imminence of movement could be sensed throughout—presumably because the scene was actually moving. Even the speed of the shutter which closed the photograph on my mind was powerless to exclude this motion from a deeper consciousness.

'The Wall', like **'Fireman Flower'**, is concerned with the relationships between illusion and reality, chance and

design. Sansom's later fictions have less urgency than those dealing with the war, and have less immediate impact, but deal sensitively with the less exotic crises of life under normal civilian circumstances. **'Nevermore Without End'** (1950), for example, documents an inevitable and expected change in feeling between two lovers who meet again after three years' separation. They strive in vain to re-create old feelings:

> Close as they walked—they walked like brother and sister. They walked abreast, he remembering vaguely that to take an arm is not to cling to an arm, and that lovers who cling walk always in some way turned a little in towards each other. He tried this.

Their love is linked closely to climate and scene: it has blossomed in the cold beauty of a Copenhagen winter, but seems impossible to recover in the easy diffuseness of summer.

'Gliding Gulls and Going People' (also from 1950) is still more relaxed in form than **'Nevermore Without End'**. It is structured around a boat trip amongst the wild scenery of Northern Scotland. In a wide-angled shot, as it were, we first see a solid mass of human beings waiting to embark on their excursion; then ten characters are singled out in close-up. Completely unconnected with each other, they none the less form an intriguing cross-section of the boat's clientéle.

The boat trip is fairly overtly a metaphor for life itself: a round trip which the passengers are continually struggling to enjoy. They try to seize certain moments from time, to arrest and possess them, but fail precisely because of their acquisitively grasping attitude. They find it difficult to be open to the landscape, to really see it for themselves—perferring to see 'what on a hundred calendars had been dreamed and painted for them'. One man even passes the journey reading his Boswell, in preference to actually looking at the Hebrides as they pass before him.

If the journey is a metaphor for life, there is also a fairly direct comparison between the human beings on the boat and the gulls over and above it. The gulls move in an apparently purposeless fashion, bumping against each other, then flying off for no apparent reason; concerted in their activity only in the struggle for food. Similarly on board the ship people move around aimlessly, making no real contact in their chance encounters, united only in their need for food. At one point Sansom rudely juxtaposes the beauty of the landscape and the indifference to it exhibited by the passengers as much as by the voracious gulls:

> as everybody turned from their places to the companionway and the blind bowels of the dining saloon, so Eigg and Rum came magnificently at last into full view.

> And the ship, naked of sightseers, ploughed past them. . . . All around, mountains and misted horizon and metal-green sea would have lain as empty in those days as now. . . . Gigantic mountainous Rum came to

port—and at last the Cuillins topped in vertiginous cloud towered terribly to starboard.

Yet no-one saw. Even the gulls, questing open-eyed round, had swooped to the sea and were pecking the first plate-emptyings thrown out in the ship's wake.

The comparison of gulls and people suggests a distaste for humanity which emerges more distinctly elsewhere in this fiction. So Sansom describes a young man trying to decide which girl to pick up in the following predatory terms: 'And those eyes under their short lids, bitter and ambitious, lustful, swivelled warily between the two grouped and the one sitting. Where was the better chance?' Human beings are presented as selfish, inward-looking and avaricious—but within their limitations they are still searching for happiness. The landscape, in this particular fiction, offers a beauty beyond the self which the passengers have at least the wit to lament as it passes beyond their grasp:

Islands reaching out towards some place irrevocable, a place that only might have been, and now in visionary moment at end of day shown somehow as a real possibility. Perhaps for the first time many of those people began to look at what was passing with moved hearts, with curious regret . . .

. . . For the first time the journey is seen as it is, for the first time it is felt to be sliding away forever from grasp. Never again, nevermore. Evanescent as the water at the ship's keel, the white ephemeral wake, water that marks the passage, white and wide, that melts and vanishes in personless flat green.

'Gliding Gulls and Going People' is in many ways an exemplary free story—episodic, Impressionist, founded, in Elizabeth Bowen's key phrase, on vision rather than feeling. And the more we examine the free story the more apparent it becomes that vision, in both senses of the word, is central to this form of short fiction. In discussing technique, Bowen, Pritchett and Sansom refer in turn to 'vision', 'the glance', 'the eye of the painter'; they also make frequent comparisons with photographic and cinematic art. It is as though their fictions are predicated on the idea of the eye/I as a camera: thus these fictions not only have a very strong visual impact, but depend philosophically on the notion of reflection rather than (self) reflexion. The fundamental assumption is that fiction can reflect and illuminate objective reality: subjective bias can emerge only to a limited extent through choice of shading or camera angle.

The 'free story' has never had a programme and its exponents have, by definition perhaps, rejected the impulse to aesthetic prescription. None the less, the free story has established itself as a very definite, and very popular, form of short fiction: one might even argue that it has been *the* dominant short form in this century. When we examine most contemporary 'short story' anthologies, we find that free stories tend to form the backbone of the collection. In particular, . . . the form has proved attractive to writers who are also novelists, . . . It is surely time for the free story to emerge from the critical shadows, to be recogn-

ised as a form distinct from modernist and postmodernist short fiction on the one hand, and the short story or tale on the other.

William H. Peden (essay date 1988)

SOURCE: "The Short Stories of William Sansom: A Retrospective Commentary," in *Studies in Short Fiction,* Vol. 25, No. 4, Fall, 1988, pp. 421-31.

[*Peden is an American critic and educator who has written extensively on the American short story and on American historical figures such as Thomas Jefferson and John Quincy Adams. Here, he argues that Sansom's work is underappreciated and praises the "almost uncanny blending of the real and the fantastic" in the author's tales, as well as Sansom's ability to evoke a scene.*]

The product of one of the most undervalued and least appreciated major twentieth-century fiction writers, William Sansom's short stories were never widely read or appreciated in the United States. And since his death in 1976, they have been virtually ignored. Seldom anthologized or written about, they are now out of print and poorly represented in the libraries of most North American colleges and universities. . . .

Sansom's first published story, **"The Wall,"** grew out of an incident in which he had participated during his wartime service with the Fire Brigade: "for the first time I said to myself: I must write down something absolutely true." Picked up by a friend by chance, **"The Wall"** was sent to Cyril Connolly's *Horizon:* "I myself would never, never have thought of submitting the MS to so very august a body," Sansom said later; "I had no literary pretensions, thought *Horizon* and such far above me." Published in July, 1941, the story was an "overnight success, and its reception set me off writing like a racing engine." More and more of his stories began to appear in periodicals like Penguin *New Writing* and *Transformation;* and in 1944 Sansom's first collection of short fiction, *Fireman Flower and Other Stories,* was published.

"**'The Wall,'**" Sansom commented many years later in *The Birth of a Story,* "was not calculated to please people, but to please the truth." Narrated by one of four fireman hosing down a burning building during the London blitz, **"The Wall"** seems as much reportage as fiction. Beginning with its terse opening sentence—"It was our third job that night"—it creates the effect of an interview: "I suppose we were drenched," "I suppose we were worn down and shivering," "I suppose our hands and our faces were black," "my eyes only digested" the sudden collapse of the wall and the death of one of the fireman, and so forth. (The dust jacket of the original English version refers to it simply as a "description of an actual firefighting experience.") But **"The Wall"** is actually far removed from conventional realism. Through the limited vision of the narrator, and the skillful use of repetition, Sansom manges to achieve an almost lyrical, ballad-like effect. **"The Wall"** is more prose poem and fable than reportage, and is close kin to Kafka, from whom Sansom learned to keep his "fables, as is vital with fantasy, with their feet close to the ground. Realism, in fact, of a different kind."

"Fireman Flower" similarly illustrates Sansom's almost uncanny blending of the real and the fantastic. We are introduced to the narrator, Fireman Flower, "riding to a most important fire," but the story is "allegorical," as Sansom states in his prefatory note to the collection. With the firefighters we soon are embarked on a trip into a world of fantasy and the unreal, a journey of surrealistic sequences—some effective, some ludicrous—ranging from a scene in a perfumed bath where the firefighters are "smiling, laughing, . . . joking, . . . even dancing," to a rather silly climax in a "deserted" and "moonlit" room where Fireman Flower meets an old friend.

If **"Fireman Flower"** suffers, however, from being overlong, **"Saturation Point"** is impressive in its brevity. Vividly visual, it is a remarkable excursion into the Surreal and the Absurd, centering in a gigantic commandant with a penchant for "kicking-in the brains of old men," and a beautiful striptease artiste who slices "a long cut of meat from her . . . leg" as the fantasy ends with an unseen chorus chanting: "Gaulette's leg has been roasted! . . . Gaulette has had her leg roasted for the commandant's table!"

Following the publication of *Fireman Flower,* Sansom travelled extensively and wrote copiously. The results are impressive: *Three,* a collection of two novellas and one short story, was published in 1946; *Something Terrible, Something Lovely,* in addition to *South* and *The Equilibriad,* was in print two years later. Of these, *Something Terrible, Something Lovely* is one of the best among all his collections: twenty-one remarkable stories, tales, and narrative sketches ranging from conventional realism to grotesque farces, malodramas, and strange excursions into a world of warped personalities and surreal inscapes. With few exceptions they display the adroit story-telling and the marvelous evocation of scene that were to become Sansom's hallmarks. And throughout, Sansom handles words the way a lapidary handles precious gems—lovingly, with fascination and elegance, evoking a later critic's comment that Sansom uses the language "as though he had invented it."

Among the realistic stories, the title piece is one of the best in the entire Sansom canon. Two girls, Nita, age nine, and her eight-year-old cousin, are talking: "It was the boys done it. . . . We'll do it back to the boys." Do *what,* the reader wonders. Something *terrible?* Something *awful?* Knowing Sansom's penchant for the violent, the grotesque, the *unspeakable*—like the thing emerging from the beach that terrifies the protagonist of **"Crabforth,"** something that "appeared to be the head of a worm" but turns out to be quite different—the reader of **"Something Terrible, Something Lovely"** feels a growing fear of dread, horror, and the unknown, until finally he is allowed to discover just what it was the boys did and what the girls do in revenge.

"Various Temptations" is similarly effective, a suspense narrative of a psychopathic murderer and his victims. From its opening sentence—"His name unknown, he had been strangling girls in the Victoria district"—the story rises to such a degree that the climax comes as a relief rather than a horror.

In similar moments of crisis—sometimes physical, tangible, external; at other times metaphysical, emotional, or imagined—Sansom's characters see things in a new light. Their angle of vision, what Stephen Crane called the "cylinder of vision," is altered. They see, like Sansom, the wonder or terror or amazement of life. **"Journey into Smoke,"** another of Sansom's fireman stories, is essentially realistic, yet soars far beyond reportage into a surreal world of horror. **"Building Alive"** is similarly a metaphor of doom alive with a stir of haunting echoes, a kind of hallucinogenic *trip.* At the other extreme, **"A Saving Grace"** is one of the most unusual "ghost stories" in twentieth-century fiction, a portrait of a house and the benevolent ghosts who occupy it. **"The Little Room,"** in contrast, is a nauseatingly memorable story of the final agonies of an incarcerated nun:

> . . . now . . . as a swimmer out of her depth she began to struggle, her forebrain gone, . . . thoughtless but to move, the instincts alone in charge. The naked head lurched. . . . , her arms weaved slow frog movements, weakening at each thrust. Before long they stopped moving altogether.

It became Sansom's custom to write nine or ten months each year, and to spend the remaining two or three months travelling. The result was a series of articles in magazines like *Holiday,* several travel books, and—eventually—short stories which he called "literary bastards" that could "best be offered as a series of 'landscapes with figures' . . . about places as much as people." The first of these, *South: Aspects and Images from Corsica, Italy, and Southern France* is just that. "Pastorale," one of the best of the *South* pieces, is typical. The first-person narrator, a peripatetic and ubiquitous voyeur not unlike Sansom himself, observes the actions of a wealthy couple at a *pension* in Corsica, a couple "sufficiently young in marriage still to be interested in themselves . . . They never look at other people. They are absolutely incurious of the world about them." One afternoon, while walking through the wild terrain to the towering mountains, the narrator secretly observes the pair—lovers "sure of each other's affection and without need for . . . reassurance." But then, as the sky darkens and the towering mountains "started to glow, to burn, to blaze with hot red light," the story, or rather the *meaning* embedded within the narrative, opens up, unfolding like the petals of a flower, and reveals the quintessential nature of the pair. The setting, in effect, *creates* the story; stated another way, mood, tone, and atmosphere *are* the story.

"Poseidon's Daughter," on the other hand, is part narrative, part myth, part mood. Pietro, a diver from a small town in Southern Italy, is attacked by *something;* he harpoons it; he realizes with horror that his victim is the body of his wife, whom he'd left asleep at home. From here, the story proceeds with mounting terror and horror—a tour de force, to be sure, but an effective one.

Sansom is essentially a teller of tales, a spinner of magical webs, an explorer of a domain of dreams, nightmares, the surreal and the bizarre.

—William H. Peden

Perhaps the best of the *South* pieces, and among the most memorable in Sansom's voluminous canon, is the saga of the **"Three Dogs of Siena,"** a plotless little masterpiece of three dogs—one from Naples, one from Genoa, one from Venice—owned by three brothers who have returned to their birthplace to attend the wedding of their sister. The dogs take over the city, investigating "without doubt, the need to find evidence of their own existence," and in a climactic scene of Tuscan revelry and medieval pageantry, the dogs are kicked by a drummer:

> . . . the kicks had not hurt, but the meaning was absolute. . . . Life, it seemed, was over; trotting was done. No more now but to sit in doorways, to sit and wait. Calmly to await the cold breath. They had been touched by the city, they had been permitted to see beyond the veil. No more to do but wait, satisfied, content, half-dead already.

The 1950s were the most productive and the most important decade in Sansom's career as a short story writer: *The Passionate North* was published in 1950, *A Touch of the Sun* in 1952, *Lord Love Us* in 1954, *A Contest of Ladies* in 1956, and *Among the Dahlias* in 1957. Each collection is characterized by the variety, stylistic elegance, and narrative expertise that had become his hallmarks. Here we are in the presence of a writer who has achieved mastery of his own particular province: a world more often than not bizarre, threatening, full of surprises, in which "all the senses are involved, sound, sight, smell, touch, taste plus such ancillary divisions as colour and, where apposite [sic], a reference to an evocative piece of music" [William Sansom, *The Birth of a Story*, 1972]. His stories are "aglow with a rare narrative excitement and a magical quality of suspense; in the vividness of his communication of sensory perceptions, and in his sometimes uncanny creation of mood and atmosphere" [William Peden, "The Tightrope Walkers," *The Virginia Quarterly Review*, Summer 1956], Sansom has few peers.

Consider the range and artistry of a new representative stories from the Fifties. The protagonist of **"Episode at Gastein"** in *A Touch of the Sun*— aristocratic, disenchanted Ludwig de Broda—is spiritually akin to Joseph Conrad's men of "universal detachment" or the lost Hans Castorp of *The Magic Mountain* (not coincidentally, Sansom's de Broda is a great admirer of the novels of Tho-

mas Mann). Enchanted—but rejected—by a woman half his age, de Broda is convincing both as an individual and as a symbol of a sick and moribund society. The climactic scene in which he contemplates suicide in a steaming bathtub while the winds of an Austrain winter sigh and scratch at his window is not *un*-tragic, but it is tragedy tinged with the Absurd.

"What risks, what terrible risks are taken at each moment of existence," comments the central character of **"Murder,"** an effective tour de force of a chimney sweep and a man who imagines that the sweep is murdering his wife. The comment is relevant to many of Sansom's stories of the Fifties, be they serious, comic, or serio-comic. Fear or the threat of violence—real or imagined—is a common chord among many of Sansom's most impressive stories. Characteristic is **"The Smile,"** a bizarre metaphor of man-woman relations. A suspicious husband, a twentieth-century counterpart to Coleridge's Ancient Mariner, has a compulsion to pour out to utter strangers the story of his past wrong-doings. He buttonholes a passerby and tells him strange details concerning his relations with his wife ("when I met her she was leading quite a life. Cabaret. Dancer. Wasn't above making a bit with the customers either") and describes in detail the fantastic fidelity test to which he had subjected her. This is all sick, very sick, and anticipates the "Sick" or "Black" humor of the Sixties. As is true of so many of Sansom's impeccably wrought stories, tales, and narrative sketches, there hovers above **"The Smile"** unspoken vibrations of corruption, of the terrifying *unknowableness* of human relations, and an unwinking awareness of human susceptibility to failure: what Conrad termed the "fascination of the abominable."

Quite, quite different—indeed unique among Sansom's collections—*Lord Love Us* was published in 1954, the year of his marriage to Ruth Grundy. Highly experimental in technique, essentially light-hearted and joyous, and ranging from the frivolous to the semi-comic to the serious to the warmly amusing or the sentimental, *Lord Love Us* is a collection of prose poems, anecdotes, and narratives differing so markedly from its predecessors that it must have come as a shock to readers unaware of the fact that Sansom had both written and illustrated children's books. Unfortunately, but not surprisingly, *Lord Love Us* is the least-known of Sansom's short-fiction collections, and it is not unsurprising that amongst all his works it was his favorite.

It's a small book, just over a hundred pages including illustrations. The title of the collection is revelatory, particularly when one finds out that the book contains no story entitled "Lord Love Us." Sansom, so often a prober of the dark, the suppressed, and the unwholesome, seems to love all the dwellers in this small segment of his created universe—a universe depicted with an exuberance of language, word play, and verbal experimentation reminiscent of Joyce. Listen to these recollections of a retired zoo keeper:

> Them birds come pecking my eschscoltzias? Wooooo
> I would cry and up the prettilings would fly . . . Bees

in my budleia? Buzz as you please, my bumbly bees, bumble my budleia's buds off—who's to know but who's the poorer? In the end you'll buzz me no more. (**"A Change of Office"**)

Similar word play—along with Sansom's continuing sense of the wonderful in the non-exceptional, of simple pleasures and sorrows—characterizes these stories and sketches, whether he is writing about the death of a goldfish (**"The Mistletoe Bough"**) or the reflections of a good-natured man: "Know what I like?. . . . I like to get the old bike out, and make it down to the pub. . . . Living is what you make of it—don't make too much is all I say!" (**"Caffs, Pools, and Bikes"**) With the same touch, he can write a warm-hearted satire on cricket (**"Time Gents, Please"**), or a relatively conventional narrative of a young man reflecting on how he won a sack race but "lost his lovely Pam" (**"The Sack Race"**). And then there are **"Friends,"** about the death of a blind man's dog, and the best of them all, **"Life, Death"**—the conventional raised into art—a magically lovely piece narrated by a fishmonger, concerning the death of his wife and their infant child: "Why, if *you* can tell me, such happy days? Why with happy days such shade?"

With *A Contest of Ladies* (1956), we return to more familiar Sansom territory. The fifteen stories, some of them originally published in the 1940s but hitherto uncollected, range from the ordinary to the grotesque, from the commonplace to the melodramatic. And many of them are tainted with the odor of corruption and decay ("Hour of sundowners. Hour when the human beast, old moon-monkey, awakes to the idea of night. Hour of day's death and dark's beginning, uneasy hour of change.").

The title story, really a novella, is characteristic. A decadent retired actor accidentally plays host to half a dozen international "beauties" assembled at a "rakish seaside resort" where the actor, Morley, has a large house decorated to resemble a hotel. The narrative is simple: the Danish entry, Miss Great-Belt, eventually marries Morley. What is remarkable about **"A Contest of Ladies"** is the sense of decay, corruption, and absurdity that permeates what can perhaps best be described as a semi-comic, semi-sick twentieth-century morality play. The description of the "ladies" at their "beauty chores" becomes a ritual of the grotesque and the horrible:

> Lilac flesh, . . . purple lips, night-shade eyes; . . . it became a circumambulation of the dead . . . , a dream parade of maidens killed before their time [the reader is inevitably reminded of the somnambulistic nudes of Delvaux]. . . . Moles took on a new presence. . . . Bruises . . . showed clearer and clearer, . . . and the yellowing armpits took on a new and virulent . . . life.

"A Country Walk," on the other hand, begins conventionally enough: a Londoner who has been living in Sussex decides to go for a walk. But from this low-keyed opening, the story soon becomes something quite different. The Londoner is bewildered and eventually oppressed by a series of incidents beginning with the ordinary and

culminating in the surreal: a bird's rising from a bush, or the barking of a dog, is followed by a piglet that assumes the dimensions of a monster. The walker panics. Feeling trapped by the encroaching vegetation, he collapses:

> Drenched through and in shock, . . . he developed rheumatic fever, and it bent him double for the rest of his life. Formerly, people would have said that darker forces than nowadays we recognize had cast a spell on him that night. What is a spell? Was it so?

The question is left unanswered, as it is in **"Death in the Sunday City"** or **"The Ballroom,"** both Poe-esque in their meticulous evocation of mood and their richly pictorial quality and convincing in their own terms of fable and fantasy, nightmare and illusion. Reminiscent of Poe, too, is **"Pas de Deux,"** another dance-of-death fable that may irritate one kind of reader and delight yet another.

But perhaps the most impressive of the *Contest of Ladies* stories is **"A Woman Seldom Found."** As in so many of Sansom's best pieces, the opening scene is deliberately prosaic: "Once a young man was on a visit to Rome." Sophisticated, bored, and convinced that "life was largely illusion," he encounters a veiled woman, tastefully dressed and apparently very beautiful. She invites him to her "large and elegant mansion." They drink, embrace; she leads him to her bedchamber. Naked, she draws him to her; he has failed to turn off the chandelier. And here the similarity to conventional slick fiction ends. "Don't worry, lover," she says, and reaches out her hand, which grows larger and larger, "stretched out through the bedcurtains, across the long carpet . . . until at last its giant fingers were at the door." What follows can mean various things to various readers: Illusion vs. reality? *La Vida es Sueño*? A "trip" into the realm of the surreal, of nightmare, of madness? The reader is free to choose.

Though somewhat less impressive than its three immediate predecessors, *Among the Dahlias* (1957) contains three or four stories that are among Sansom's best. The title story—part comedy, part farce, part commentary on man's susceptibility to fear—concerns a Mr. Doole. Forty, pink-faced, and plump ("It was easy to imagine him in a bathing suit; one knew he had thin, active legs."), he loves animals and often visits the zoo. Not overly susceptible to fears, but not free from them either, Mr. Doole, walking contentedly among the bird-runs, is suddenly frozen with terror: "some thirty feet away stood a full-maned lion." What ensues, and the ultimate fate of Doole *and* the lion, is narrated in wry good humor with a very sombre undercurrent. Suffice it to say that neither man nor beast is the same after the chance, or is it an inevitable, encounter.

"A Visit to the Dentist" similarly exists in a realm between the comic and the un-comic, between the ordinary and the surreal. The protagonist, like Mr. Doole, is a quiet, unassuming man in his forties who has just left his dentist's office minus five teeth. A "man of small passion," he makes a modest quest to have a cup of tea before returning to the peace and quiet of his small villa at Kew— a quest which ends in a bewildering and amusing series of mistakes, embarrassments, and harassments. It is a circular journey from nowhere to nowhere, at once absurd and pathetic. Another middle-aged protagonist, Paul, of *The Equilibriad,* a victim of myasthenia, is apprehensive and haunted by forebodings of monotony and frustration. His is a strange monodrama, a love-hate relationship with his cousin Ada, four years his junior ("I see how I savoured my humiliation," she tells him; "I love to be debased."). At the end, Paul is alone again, sharing with the reader the uncertainty of whether or not any of the events really happened. Like more than a few of Sansom's pieces written during these middle years, the story ends enigmatically: "As his eyes grew accustomed again to the room, . . . he saw that Ada was no longer there. . . . She had left, . . . abandoning him with the hook hanging around his neck, leaving him to work his own grapple with mumbling of his own mouth."

In the nine years between the publication of *Among the Dahlias* and *The Ulcerated Milkman* (1966), Sansom devoted more and more of his energy to novels and travel books. Though not one of his best collections, *The Ulcerated Milkman* contains four or five memorable stories. "A Mixed Bag" is a thoroughly engaging and good-natured story of infidelity, narrated unerringly from start to finish. "Don't Smoke on the Apron" is an equally competent but more conventional story of infidelity with an O. Henryish fillip of an ending. And "Old Man Alone" convincingly creates the physical and mental anguish of an aged solider who is immobilized following a fall in his two-room flat.

"Like Yesterday," perhaps the best of *The Ulcerated Milkman* stories, is ingeniously and convincingly narrated by a writer who purchases an album of old postcards in a secondhand shop and from it reconstructs the love affair, courtship, and marriage of the writer of the cards—a happy marriage followed by the birth of a child and a series of disasters. "November passes," the narrator comments. "And so, it seems, does poor little Jacko. He died . . . in a shabby room in a shabby . . . street." Warmhearted without degenerating into sentimentality, stories such as "Like Yesterday" repudiate the frequently made contention that Sansom is a writer who has no sensitivity and no concern for individuals beyond their usefulness as illustrations of entertaining or intriguing ideas.

In spite of intermittent illnesses and a diminishing readership, Sansom never lost his love for the short story or his "wonder, amazement, [and] . . . astonished interest" in people. This wonderment and interest illuminate the sixteen stories in his last major collection, *The Marmalade Bird,* published in 1973, three years before his death. It's a good book, and some of the best individual stories are glimpses into the world of private terrors, real or imagined, that had always been Sansom's particular province.

"The Day the Lift . . . ," for example, depicts a few dreadful moments experienced by a man whose "life was nicely ordered . . . ; nothing could be upset but conceptions of order and punctuality . . . which he valued and hung to." Nothing, that is, except the stalled elevator in which he is trapped. During a few moments of panic, Sansom tells us everything we need to know about the man's life—at the same time creating the feel, the smell, the very *essence* of his prison. The reader temporarily shares the man's steadily-mounting terror.

The central character of "A Strange Meeting," ironically and appropriately named Love, similarly creates his own cage and his own moments of waking nightmare. Weekending with friends in Surrey, Love goes for a walk before dinner; it's a strange evening, with "lilac-coloured clouds" rolling "sadly across an unusual yellowish sky . . . in a land lost in place and time, immeasurably desolate." Narrow lanes, he reflects, are "seldom safe," and an ensuing series of events lead to a climax as hilarious to the reader as it is embarrassing to Mr. Love and his hosts.

Among the more conventional pieces, "Down at the Hydro" is one of the best in the entire Sansom canon, a convincing account of a brief romance between an elderly retired colonel and a married woman who come together briefly at a health spa (as always, Sansom creates the setting superbly). And "The Almighty Test" is a delight. As much essay as conventionally structured short story, it is a pleasantly acerbic commentary on the rigors of an English Christmas at home: mother, "pale and shuddering, down to the kitchen to check over" the details that kept her awake through the night; the children at long last quiet, "unapproachable, . . . tight-lipped and tense with acquisition"; the turkey, tasting of "tender string; . . . the stuffing . . . apparently digested by the bird itself; the pudding would not light, the mince pies . . . all pastry"— all to be followed by the invasion of drunken friends and strangers. It's a small classic by a writer who never lost his zest for life and for fiction, closing his career as a short-story writer as effectively as he had begun it three decades before with *Fireman Flower.*

Despite his productivity, Sansom maintained an admirably high level of craftsmanship. He is a magician, a magus— at his best when he transmutes essentially realistic or non-exceptional characters and situations into high adventure, myth, or romance. Always, he insisted, his stories had their origins in actuality: "if you start making things up, you get into very deep water . . . you get all messed up." With few exceptions, Sansom's best short stories are firmly rooted in recognizable settings; it's a truism to repeat that he has few rivals in his *visual* renderings of place. His evocations of the smells and sights and sounds of specific places—whether they be a Venetian restaurant, a spa in the Austrian Alps, a dingy street in Soho—are superb: no one, as V. S. Pritchett once put it, "can describe a door like William Sansom." Yet despite this evocation of the real, Sansom was seldom willing to remain long within the realms of conventional realism: he is essentially a teller of tales, a spinner of magical webs, an explorer of a domain of dreams, nightmares, the surreal, and the bizarre.

As with most extremely prolific writers, it is best to take Sansom's stories and tales in relatively small quantities: who would want to watch a magician perform for twenty-four hours at a stretch? Sansom has his weaknesses, to be sure: a tendency occasionally to create puppets rather than individual human beings, a fondness for the too-facile ending, and an over-reliance on the story-within-a-story framework.

But perhaps the highest praise one can give Sansom is that even at his less-than-best, he is fun to read. And to reread. His continuing sense of "wonderment at life" is contagious. His stories are alive with excitement, suspense, and a magic seldom found in contemporary fiction. Like Keats, he has opened magic casements and left us with unforgettable glimpses—humorous, tragic, comic, banal, terrifying, delightful—into a world uniquely his own, the likes of which will probably not be seen again. As such, William Sansom is a writer to be cherished, a "caretaker to keep the lost domain of Arnheim green, and to prevent the crack in the House of Usher from closing."

FURTHER READING

Criticism

Anand, Mulk Raj. A review of *Fireman Flower, and Other Stories. Life and Letters Today* 41, No. 82 (June 1944): 178-80.
　　Reviews Sansom's first collection, addressing the allegorical aspects of the stories.

Hardwick, Elizabeth. "Three Stories." *Partisan Review* XIV, No. 3 (May-June 1947): 320-21.
　　Finds both strengths and weaknesses in Sansom's writing in *Three*.

Krim, Seymour. "Short Stories by Six." *Hudson Review* III, No. 4 (Winter 1951): 626-33.
　　Praises the "sensuous pleasure" and "zestfulness" of *South,* but complains that the stories are overly descriptive and too similar to one another.

Lane, Margaret. A review of *A Contest of Ladies. London Magazine* 3, No. 6118 (20 November 1957): 608-09.
　　Observes that once Sansom has worked through the humor in his stories, he doesn't seem inclined to further shape his material.

Morris, Alice S. "Living Landscapes." *The New York Times Book Review* LV (10 September 1950): 4.
　　Notes that Sansom's subject in *South* is the individual reacting to unfamiliar situations and that the author acts as a "dispassionate analyst" in recording their experiences.

———. "Pathways to Horror." *The New York Times Book Review* LIX (10 October 1954): 5, 28.
　　Assesses *Something Terrible, Something Lovely* and views Sansom as a "daring and inventive" writer who is unable or unwilling to allow his characters to "live."

Nemerov, Howard. "Sansom's Fictions." *The Kenyon Review* XVII, No. 1 (Winter 1955): 130-35.
　　Reviews the collections *The Passionate North* and *Something Terrible, Something Lovely.* Nemerov concedes Sansom's "brilliance" but expresses disappointment that the stories are "preordained" and "of a forced significance."

O'Brien, Kate. A review of *Three. The Spectator,* No. 6142 (15 March 1946): 280-82.
　　Compliments Sansom's "very positive and even aggressive style" while noting several flaws in the book.

Sansom, William. *The Birth of a Story.* London: Chatto & Windus/Hogarth Press, 1972, 122 p.
　　The author explains how he wrote and revised his story "No Smoking on the Apron."

Swados, Harvey. "The Long and Short of It." *Hudson Review* X, No. 1 (Spring 1957): 159.
　　Reviews *A Contest of Ladies* briefly, lauding Sansom's linguistic skills but faulting him for being a writer "without heart."

Additional coverage of Sansom's life and career is contained in the following sources published by Gale Research: *Contemporary Authors,* Vols. 5-8R, 65-68; *Contemporary Authors New Revision Series,* Vol. 42; *Contemporary Literary Criticism,* Vols. 2, 6; *Dictionary of Literary Biography,* Vol. 139; and *Major 20th-Century Writers.*

William Saroyan
1908-1981

(Also wrote under pseudonyms of Archie Crashcup and Sirak Goryan) American short story writer, dramatist, novelist, autobiographer, essayist, screenwriter, and songwriter.

INTRODUCTION

Saroyan is known for his short fiction that is considered sentimental, nostalgic, and optimistic in its celebration of the potential of the human spirit and of the simple pleasures in life. The son of Armenian immigrants, Saroyan wrote of the lighter side of the immigrant experience in America, with special emphasis on the humor and importance of family life, which are central to Armenian culture. Most of his works are set in the United States and reveal his appreciation of the American dream and his awareness of the strengths and weaknesses of American society.

Biographical Information

Saroyan was born in Fresno, California, to Armenian immigrants. His father died when he was three years old, and he and his three siblings were placed in an orphanage in Oakland, California. In 1915 they were reunited with their mother in Fresno. While a teenager he dropped out of school and moved to San Francisco, where he worked at various jobs and eventually became a telegraph operator. In 1928 he published his first short story in *Overland Monthly and Outwest Magazine*. Determined to become a full-time writer, he published his first collection of short stories, *The Daring Young Man on the Flying Trapeze, and Other Stories*, in 1934. This work was very successful, and he produced several subsequent collections of short fiction. In 1939 he began a prolific career as a playwright. Saroyan wrote in various genres, including juvenile fiction and autobiography, as well as gaining notoriety as a public figure. He died of cancer in Fresno in 1981.

Major Works of Short Fiction

Saroyan's first collection, *The Daring Young Man on the Flying Trapeze*, is his most critically and commercially popular book of short fiction. The title story concerns a young writer struggling with his role in a materialistic world. The protagonist makes an attempt to carry on in a hostile environment but eventually welcomes death. Saroyan introduces one of his notable themes in this story—the importance and magnificence of life in the face of death—a theme he would use over and over in his work. In "A Cold Day" Saroyan uses an epistolary form to describe his harsh working condition to Martha Foley, the editor of *Story* magazine. The narrator of "Seventy Thou-

sand Assyrians," a young man of Armenian heritage, discovers his barber, Badal is an Assyrian, whose people, like the Armenians, have been driven from their land and are in danger of extinction altogether. He acknowledges his bond with Badal and contrasts the endurance of their two lives against the ominous fate of their respective homelands and people.

Critical Reception

Saroyan's work has been widely reviewed but until recently has not received serious critical analysis. In structure and in philosophy commentators find his writing simplistic, an attribute for which he has been both praised and scorned. Many critics cite Saroyan's refusal to adapt his writing to changes in American life as a significant factor in the decline of his literary reputation. Moreover, commentators maintain that many of his stories are formulaic and overly sentimental. He has also been derided for the discursive, self-indulgent nature of his short fiction. Despite these opinions, Saroyan remains a well-respected writer and his works are widely read. Critics assert that his special talent lay in his ability to create poetic, humorous characters and situations and in his appreciation of the simple pleasures in life.

PRINCIPAL WORKS

Short Fiction

The Daring Young Man on the Flying Trapeze, and Other Stories 1934
Inhale and Exhale 1936
Three Times Three 1936
*The Gay and Melancholy Flux: Short Stories 1937
Little Children 1937
Love, Here is my Hat and Other Short Romances 1938
The Trouble with Tigers 1938
Peace, It's Wonderful 1939
3 Fragments and a Story 1939
My Name is Aram 1940
The Insurance Salesman, and Other Stories 1941
Saroyan's Fables 1941
Best Stories 1942
48 Saroyan Stories 1942
Thirty-One Selected Stories 1943
Dear Baby 1944
The Saroyan Special: Selected Short Stories 1948
The Fiscal Hoboes 1949
The Assyrian, and Other Stories 1950
Love 1955
The Whole Voyald, and Other Stories 1956
After Thirty Years: The Daring Young Man on the Flying Trapeze (short stories and essays) 1964
Best Stories of Saroyan 1964
An Act or Two of Foolish Kindness: Two Stories 1977
The Man with the Heart in the Highlands, and Other Early Stories 1989

Other Major Works

The Hungerers: A Short Play (drama) 1939
The Time of Your Life (drama) 1939
Three Plays: My Heart's in the Highlands, The Time of Your Life, Love's Old Sweet Song (dramas) 1940
The Human Comedy (novel) 1943
The Adventures of Wesley Jackson: A Novel (novel) 1946
A Decent Birth, a Happy Funeral (drama) 1949
The Twin Adventures: The Adventures of Saroyan: A Diary; The Adventures of Wesley Jackson: A Novel (novels) 1950
Rock Wagram (novel) 1951
The Bicycle Rider in Beverly Hills (autobiography) 1952
The Laughing Matter (novel) 1953
Mama I Love You (novel) 1956
Papa You're Crazy (novel) 1957
The Cave Dwellers (drama) 1958
The Slaughter of the Innocents (drama) 1958
Here Comes, There Goes, You Know Who (autobiography) 1962
Boys and Girls Together (novel) 1963

Not Dying (autobiography) 1963
One Day in the Afternoon of the World (novel) 1964
Two Short Paris Summertime Plays of 1974: Assassinations and Jim, Sam and Anna (dramas) 1979

*Contains stories from *Inhale and Exhale* and *Three Times Three*.

CRITICISM

Burton Rascoe   (essay date 1934)

SOURCE: "Saroyan on the Flying Trapeze," in *New York Herald Tribune Books,* October 21, 1934, p. 9.

[*Rascoe was an American literary critic who contributed to such influential periodicals as the* American Mercury, Bookman, Esquire, New York Herald Tribune Books, *and* Newsweek. *In the following review of* The Daring Young Man on the Flying Trapeze, and Other Stories, *he declares Saroyan "an extraordinary talent" and lauds his promise as a writer.*]

Our breath is bated while we await the progress and development of the extraordinary talent which produced the title story of [*The Daring Young Man on the Flying Trapeze, and Other Stories*]. Will young Mr. Saroyan, we ask, ever get outside himself for more than a sustained instant and cease to marvel at himself as at an animated forked radish, wistful, sentient and beset in a pumpkin and spinach universe? And will we like him then, quite as much as now, when he becomes aware that other people exist and begins to ask himself why it is that this one does that and why that one says thus and so? Will we like him quite as well when we are finally privileged to see some of those "short stories" we learn from this book that he is incessantly writing?

What we have here is not a collection of short stories but an adolescent diary of a young man whose freshness and originality has the smack of genius. But what we have also is some experimental work in prose orchestration by a young man unusually clever, who is definitely resolved to achieve emotional effects on paper whether they are of emotions he has felt or merely emotions he believes people are capable of feeling. He is, in fact, a technician, mastering his keyboard with conscientious practice, employing grace notes with self-satisfaction and not above faking a passage neatly if put to it.

The title story made something of a sensation when it first appeared in the magazine, *Story.* Its appeal, it must be admitted, was somewhat factitious. It is the interior monologue of a starving young writer. It is a record of the stream of ideas. Impressions, sensations of an articulate and mentally well-nourished youth from the moment he wakes up in a cheerless hall bedroom one morning, through his breakfastless day in search of employment, along with his fears of actual death by starvation until, after a hopeless search, he returns to his room.

Bewildered, he stood, beside his bed, thinking there is nothing *to do but sleep*. Already he felt himself making great strides through the fluid of the earth, swimming away to the beginning. He fell face down upon the bed, saying, I ought first at least to give the coin to some child (a penny he had found). A child could buy any number of things with a penny.

Then swiftly, neatly, with the grace of the young man on the trapeze, he was gone from his body. For an eternal moment he was all things at once: the bird, the fish, the rodent, the reptile and man. An ocean of print undulated endlessly and darkly before him. The city burned. The herded crowd rioted. The earth circled away, and knowing that he did so, he turned his lost face to the empty sky and became dreamless, unalive, perfect.

Now, strictly speaking, from a technical point of view, Mr. Saroyan boggles his intention in this story. And the reason he boggles his intention is that he has two of them, one literary in the meaner sense and the other honest. In fever, in physical exhaustion, in hunger, in a toxic condition produced by alcohol or any other toxic agency, there is a heightened consciousness, a febrility that makes one's ordinary sensitivity to one's surroundings seem slothful and phlegmatic. While reading **"The Daring Young Man on the Flying Trapeze"** we who have experienced any of these states of being know that Mr. Saroyan is trying to vocalize the febrility of hunger and still keep that vocalization within the pattern of one man's actions between shaving in the morning and going to bed at night, sustained meanwhile only by black coffee, nicotine and the adrenal stimulus of a hate reaction to a condition, personified by "a thin, scatterbrained, miss of fifty" and by "a conceited young man who closely resembled a pig," who took his unsuccessful applications for a job. But Mr. Saroyan's other intention is to make you like Mr. Saroyan and feel sorry for him, Mr. Saroyan, to the exclusion of other young men who have tribulations in this world. He wants you to feel that Mr. Saroyan is a very superior young man especially deserving of your sympathy. And the reason he gives in support of his superiority is that he can write. He romanticizes the condition of being a writer—unbearably, to one who has been harassed by a lot of conditions, not the least of which is that of being a writer.

The most poignant line of the piece, indeed, is "He was a living young man who was in need of money with which to go on being one, and there was no way of getting it except by working for it: and there was no work." That is the whole of the tragedy and the part that does not concern Mr. Saroyan alone. The tragedy of the depression has been that there has been no work for men who are eager to work and capable of working. The point is that there are many living young men who are in need of money with which to go on being living young men and there is no way of their getting money except by working for it, and there has been no work for them. But here we are made to drum up a special grief that the depression made things unpleasant to a brilliant young writer. This is a plea for a bit of mothering on the part of the public and I have

no doubt that it will be generously forthcoming. But whether to Mr. Saroyan's advantage as a writer remains a question.

What, then, are Mr. Saroyan's qualities as a writer? He is excited, eager, clever, honestly introspective, narcissistic wistful, humane, tender and the very reverse of naïve while affecting naïveté. He is an original. I see no traceable influence upon him except that of Sherwood Anderson, the untutored, homely honesty of whose early writings Mr. Saroyan has apparently absorbed. Although he employs the interior monologue, it is not Joycean; it has more of the quality of midnight jottings in a diary under the ecstatic wakefulness induced by coffee, youthfulness and self-confidence.

To date, if we are to judge by these stories, Mr. Saroyan is receptive. He receives the world with aliveness, if not with passion, and cultivates his ego with a happy spirit that is not without a touch of arrogance. He hates cruelty in any form. He loves human pride and human dignity. He knows, as he reveals to us in his sketches of Karl and Josef and Irving that there are certain cultural factors and inheritances which account for traits in character and that there are certain propulsions as there are in the Harry, the money-maker, which are sadly inexplicable and humanly valuable without seeming to be so. There is evidence, in isolated observations in these sketches, that a new, refreshing and interesting talent is in the first experimental stages of creation. It is an impatient talent, too willing to dub in false passages rather than wait for the authentic expression: but it is an apollonian and eager talent, entertaining us and leaving us expectant.

Louis Kronenberger (essay date 1934)

SOURCE: "Saroyan High Jinks," in *The New York Times Book Review,* November 4, 1934, p. 7.

[*A drama critic for* Time *from 1938 to 1961, Kronenberger was a distinguished historian, literary critic, and author highly regarded for his expertise in eighteenth-century English history and literature. In the following review of* The Daring Young Man on the Flying Trapeze, and Other Stories, *he acknowledges Saroyan's talent but maintains that he has yet to prove himself as a writer.*]

Mr. Saroyan's first short stories aroused considerable attention when they appeared, some months ago, in magazines; and his first book **The Daring Young Man on the Flying Trapeze, and Other Stories,** will unquestionably arouse more. He appears on the scene ready, as it were, to take a bow. There is nothing retiring or hesitant about him; he writes in what might be termed the autobiographical grand style. Under the guise of writing short stories he will let you know what he thinks of everything from Hemingway to the NRA. In the act of writing a short story he will let you know how he thinks a short story should be written. With the slightest turn of the wrist he will abandon his hero or heroine and wax talkative about Saroyan.

His ego, in the present volume, is his undoing. For, though he offers no proof as yet of being an important writer, there can be no question of his having talent. He writes with an ease and dexterity and, at times, with a freshness that one seldom encounters in a first book by a 26-year-old author; he is bursting with personality; and he reveals enough cleverness to startle both the stodgy and the hardboiled. But unfortunately he doesn't possess a jot of humility or, what is more important in literary matters, of restraint. He talks shamelessly about himself whenever he chooses, and this habit, besides being irritating in itself, offers much too little in return for irritating us. And for a personality that, however pungent, is still a mass of impudent contradictions and fleeting poses one can have little affection or esteem.

It would perhaps be irrelevant to say of Saroyan as a short-story writer that he has not learned his trade. For he seems to have no intention of writing the short story as we commonly think of it. A good two-thirds of the "stories" in this book are nothing but pegs on which Saroyan can hang his ideas and opinions, his personal reminiscences and reflections on life. Even the best thing in the book, **"Seventy Thousand Assyrians,"** is a kind of Shandyesque performance in which, while pretending to do one thing, Saroyan actually does another. In **"Seventy Thousand Assyrians,"** however, his evasion is a success; and success need not apologize for itself. But in numerous other instances Saroyan's high jinks lead to failure. Such pieces as **"A Curved Line," "Love, Death, Sacrifice, and So Forth," "Three Stories," "Dear Greta Garbo,"** and even the relatively superior **"Aspirin Is a Member of the NRA,"** are all instances of gross self-indulgence where Saroyan thought he could get away with a kind of uncritical ad-libbing. As a matter of fact such caperings make it much harder for the reader to give the good things in the book their due.

> **Saroyan is bursting with personality; and he reveals enough cleverness to startle. . . . But unfortunately he doesn't possess a jot of humility or, what is more important in literary matters, of restraint.**
>
> *—Louis Kronenberger*

The good things are of two kinds: stories like **"Seventy Thousand Assyrians," "Myself Upon the Earth"** and **"The Daring Young Man on the Flying Trapeze,"** which, though full of faults and immaturities, reveal a genuine gift for writing and a genuine feeling for something in life; and stories like **"Harry," "The Man With the French Postcards"** and **"Fight Your Own War,"** which, though essentially no more than clever, are handled with skill and straightforwardness. In those stories Saroyan has either

held his "personality" in check or shaped it toward a sound end. The rest of the time he has either ranted or wisecracked, or both.

It will be too bad if Saroyan goes on pampering himself. So far he has not proved that he has anything to say, but he has made it clear that he has his own way of saying things, that he has his own way of looking at things, and that he is little indebted to others for his ideas. Hidden inside his clowning are the makings of a rare quality in writing—buoyancy; hidden inside his slaps at the world is a very serviceable quality—punch. But unless he cares more for the passing moment than for the future, he must abide by the same laws that other writers have been willing to follow, and must settle down to the hard task not of saying he is good but of proving it.

Clifton Fadiman   (essay date 1936)

SOURCE: "71 Varieties," in *The New Yorker*, Vol. XII, No. 1, February 22, 1936, pp. 67-9.

[*Fadiman became one of the most prominent American literary critics during the 1930s with his insightful and often caustic book reviews for the* Nation *and the* New Yorker *magazines. In the following excerpt from a review of* Inhale and Exhale, *he expresses a preference for Saroyan's description of characters and incidents over pondering on a grand scale: "I must confess that when Saroyan is being most himself and telling us all about the World and Life and Time and Death, I don't understand him."*]

These 71 stories [in *Inhale & Exhale*]—no doubt Mr. Saroyan could have made them 571 or 5,071—are not, of course, stories at all. They're pretty much the sort of thing you remember from *The Daring Young Man on the Flying Trapeze.* You may not think them worth doing, but you have to admit that only the prodigious Saroyan can do them at all. So here they are, 71 lengths or chunks of Saroyan, 71 exercises in sensibility, 71 monologues, prayers, jokes, conversations, lectures, sermonettes, travel sketches, anecdotes, diary extracts, self-adjurations, and letters to the editor. Saroyan scurries around within the field of his temperament, and when he's finished with a scurry he calls it a story. Even his temperament doesn't stay put: it's about as predictable as the next move of Mr. Robins in **"Jumbo."** He might start anywhere, and does; end anywhere, and does. His mind, fresh, agile, and acrobatic, darts about like a water bug; and it is not perhaps too unkind to prolong the analogy by suggesting that, like the water bug, it lives on surface tension. It needs practically no support. Give Mr. Saroyan a word, a memory, and a whole battery of undifferentiated and spontaneous emotions is called into play. The slightest collision with an idea, and he is off like the wind. He is the greatest hit-and-run writer in the history of American letters.

"I was glad the world was there; so I could be there too. I was alone, so I was sad about everything, but I was glad too. It is the same anyway. I was so glad about everything I was sad." Now, what are you going to do with a man who feels like that and writes like that? What is he talking about? Don't try to pin me down, gentlemen. It may be something pretty big. It may be something awfully trivial. How do you check up? Saroyan is his own court of last resort. Tell him it's nonsense, and he'll agree, with charming alacrity. But he will add that it's *his* nonsense, and that anyway, you're reading it, aren't you? And he's got you there. You are reading it.

You may get tired of the dull sound of Saroyan steadily pounding his chest in the Whitman manner and bellowing that he's in love with Life, that he's simply crazy about Life, that Life, folks, is better than Death. Still, he *is* in love with it, no faking, and not many writers of our time are. And just because he's quite persuaded that Life (whatever that is) is superior and preferable to Death, his prose, some of it acquires a crazy, incoherent vitality all its own. I doubt that this vitality has anything to do with literature—I mean literature of the pre-Saroyan epoch—but there it is, all set to give you a tingling sensation, very much like a nickel-in-the-slot electric battery.

Since *The Daring Young Man,* Saroyan has become a required taste. I think with exceptions below noted I'll beg off. I fear, after all, I'm not what is known as a vanguard critic. For I must confess that when Saroyan is being most himself and telling us all about the World and Life and Time and Death, I don't understand him. When he is being most profound and old-Russian (by the way, who would ever have thought that the old Slavic yearn would come back to us fifty years later via Armenia and San Francisco?), I don't understand him. I don't understand his purple passages at all at all, and I would like to remind him timidly that most such passages have a sign on them reading Dead End. No, 438 pages of spontaneity are too much for this dusty, academic mind. Perhaps an ingrained puritanism prevents me from enjoying the spectacle of 71 masterpieces being created one after the other without the slightest effort. That sort of thing should be left to the Deity. *C'est Son métier.* In general, I like Mr. Saroyan and I like many of his feelings, but only occasionally do his feelings and himself and English prose connect simultaneously in a way that makes sense to me.

But once in a while they do connect, and then, while I can't join the cult lock, stock, and barrel, I will cheer as violently as anyone for this surprising young Near-Eastern Far-Westerner. When, as in **"The Broken Wheel"** (a beautiful story), he is recalling simply and gravely some queer memory of his valiant childhood, I think he's a wonder. And I like the lighthearted, sardonic way in which he writes funny stories, such as the hilarious **"Our Little Brown Brothers the Filipinos."** Let him but write out of a hot, fused core of fine feeling, as he does in **"The Armenian & the Armenian,"** and he's irresistible. Tie him down to a specific person or incident, and he offers something strange and lovely. In fact, I think he's a flop only when he's being a Great Writer. But that seems so often.

Harold Strauss   (essay date 1936)

SOURCE: "Mr. Saroyan Continues to Write Very Much as He Pleases," in *The New York Times Book Review,* February 23, 1936, pp. 4, 13.

[*During his years with the publishing firm Alfred A. Knopf, Strauss edited works by Kobo Abe, Junichiro Tanizaki, Yukio Mishima, and Yasunari Kawabata, thereby playing an important role in the introduction of modern Japanese literature to American readers. In the following review of* Inhale and Exhale, *he judges Saroyan "the most prolific and uneven of writers."*]

A storm of conflicting opinion is usually raised by any mention of William Saroyan, whose meteoric advent on the literary scene dates from the publication last year of **The Daring Young Man on the Flying Trapeze**. And there is good reason for the conflicting opinion, for Saroyan is the most prolific and uneven of writers; he spouts one story after another, apparently without revision, without self-criticism, without adherence to any one style. Indeed, he says "Style is necessary only when one has nothing to say, or a lie to tell." In **Inhale & Exhale** alone there are seventy-two stories of such startling unevenness that one can support or deny any thesis by its text.

His huge output, good, bad and indifferent, is at least a token of tremendous vitality. Saroyan writes as one talks, with complete unrestraint, freely, abundantly. In all his many styles he has that litheness and life that suggests perpetual motion. By instinct he is a philosopher of the flux, an anti-intellectual who refuses to believe in fixed principles, no matter how empirical. And yet he is forever perversely striving to find some order in the universe. He says bluntly that "life is art arranged." Nevertheless, his curious psychology has not induced him to seek a disciplined order within himself.

We cannot, at this early point in Saroyan's career, take a lack of discipline too seriously. It is a fault of immaturity common in all the young contributors to the little advanced guard of magazines scattered over the country. Actually Saroyan, although he has been forced to wide public attention, is still in his little-magazine stage. There are other signs of his immaturity: a lack of variety of theme springing from a paucity of experience; marked self-consciousness; a feeling of unbalance and strain, and a tendency to engage in high-sounding generalities in realms to which his experience does not extend.

In the stories themselves one can trace the exact line marking off experience from fantasy. In many dealing with his boyhood, he is rich and suggestive. Any youthful impression, any recollected moment of suffering, is enough to set him off. He tells how he learned about the laws of private property by stealing five pears (**"Five Ripe Pears"**), about the meaning of war (**"The War"**), about the sudden growing up of school friends (**"The Death of Children"**), about how he learned to like getting his hair cut (**"The Barber Whose Uncle Had His Head Bitten off by a Circus Tiger"**) and about how he smashed his bicycle

("**The Broken Wheel**"). And there is much about "my brother, Krikor."

When Saroyan does not plunge into vacuous generalities about life and art and society and economics, the stories in this volume shape together into a sort of loose autobiography. They probably are arranged with this in mind. After the boyhood stories comes a series about the monotony of small-town life and the hunger for experience. Then another group about adolescence and the attempts to escape monotony through drinking and gambling (there is relatively little sex). There is a group about his literary success and his first introduction to the world of stuffed shirts, and a final group written during a recent tour of Russia and Scandinavia. The more easily Saroyan himself can be substituted for the protagonist of the story, the better that story is likely to be.

By far the most common theme is an attack on the moral concepts resulting from the ownership of property. Saroyan has a hatred for those whose lives are ruled by their possessions. His attitude, however, has nothing of the Socialist in it. He is much closer to St. Francis in his passion for freedom from the obligations of possession. Sometimes he handles this theme humorously, as in the story "**Raisins,**" in which he tells how a whole countryside devoted itself to raisin-grape growing during the "have-you-had-your-iron-today" period and then, when the bottom dropped out of the market, had itself to subsist on raisins. But more often the theme is treated with passion and indignation, as in "**The Oranges,**" "**Two Thousand and Some Odd Dollars,**" "**Prelude to an American Symphony,**" or "**I Can't Put Two and Two Together.**" The Franciscan attitude is carried through to the group of stories about Russia, which points the moral that "people act the same under communism as under anything else, except a tombstone."

Certain other themes recur. Several stories deal with the terrified desire of lost souls to crawl back into the womb. The stories about gambling, the significance of which we have already pointed out, are plentiful. The best of these are "**Two Days Wasted in Kansas City,**" "**The Horses and the Sea**" and "**Little Miss Universe.**" But best of all is that small group in which Saroyan, like Ben Hecht at his best, dramatizes a little incident that a city editor would box as a human-interest story. One of these ("**Our Little Brown Brothers the Filipinos**") concerns a Filipino wrestler who refuses to abide by the referee's decision and holds the ring all night against half of the town's police force. Another ("**A Night of Nothing**") concerns a strange happening at a dance marathon. These stories Saroyan handles with a rich combination of humor and pathos. And finally there is a minute but excellent group concerning the groping attempts of lonely souls to find solace in love. "**Secrets of Alexandria,**" about a movie pick-up, and "**The Mother,**" about an illegitimate pregnancy, are so superb that one regrets Saroyan's usual avoidance of this theme.

Saroyan's is a troubled, unformed but genuine talent. If we are irritated by his intentionally and elaborately mixed

metaphors, by the banalities which he wishes to have us accept as humor ("Steve knew nothing. He was a philosopher"), by his freakish verbal jugglings, we are likely to rise to a pitch of excited appreciation of the very next page. To the present reviewer this is sufficient reason to subject his work to the severest possible analysis. Analysis, but not judgment, for Saroyan should not be judged until he reaches maturity. Meanwhile, his talent is no frail thing to be crushed by a word of criticism.

Alfred Kazin (essay date 1937)

SOURCE: "The Art of Mr. Saroyan," in *New York Herald Tribune Books,* August 15, 1937, p. 4.

[*A highly respected American literary critic, Kazin is best known for his essay collections* The Inmost Leaf *(1955),* Contemporaries *(1962), and* On Native Grounds *(1942), a study of American prose writing since the era of William Dean Howells. In the following enthusiastic review of* Little Children, *he commends Saroyan's evocation of childhood and notes that the book is appealing despite its shortcomings.*]

Mr. Saroyan is one of these rare writers (not always the most gifted but usually the most delicate) who can write only of themselves, but mould and even destroy the outer frame of sentimental autobiography. A Saroyan story is not so much a chronicle as it is a tender, even a timid, evocation of a world in which other little men may snicker or weep. There are immigrants in it, children, wistful heroism and swaggering failure; there is a pattern drawn and followed; but what counts is the faint glow of half-muttered (we mustn't say too much) or tremulously understood (we mustn't boast too much) pity or terror or tenderness.

Mr. Saroyan despises any attempt to understand that world. He suffers in and with it, for that is the mark of his participation. In the end there will be a smiling stammer for every one who stumbles from one communal assault to another.

The little children [of *Little Children*] are California boys and girls, plucked out of memory and guided by the prankish Joe or Dewey who is Mr. Saroyan himself. Mr. Saroyan can spin back all the dumb torments of an American boyhood, the wonder at speed, the tickle of envy, the thumbing of loud magazines, the fiddling with mechanics, the business of looking open-mouthed with rapture at pigtails in the third row, always sitting with the girls and always haughty. And when the boy grows up he bows at the shrine of Western Union and from four to twelve knocks importantly at exotic houses, meanwhile ignoring his homework, getting called down by teacher, and taking pigtails for that first, that terribly disappointing walk and ice cream treat.

Growing older the boy is surprised by the folly of dying, the stupidity of getting rich and fat, like Katz in "**The**

Man Who Got Fat," who was such a good telegraphist, such a joy to watch as he clicked the keys, but who got the itch to go up in the world and then became fatter and fatter, more nervous, smoking and drinking all the time with worry.

Sometimes the little children laugh. But when they do, like the infant Hamlet in **"Laughing Sam,"** it is because they must not weep. If they are very, very young, like the kid in **"The First Day of School,"** or the little boy and girl in **"The Cat,"** drawing their initials in the fresh sidewalk cement and then skating away to a life beyond childhood, there is a threat against their laughter, the faint promise of adolescent shock or lingering dissolution. Tragedy as such is unknown; but instead a warm, sometimes overcomplacent sadness, not uncomfortable to bear, but a fact of life, like an ugly man's features or shrewishness or a bad memory, something that each man acknowledges in turn, hoping with familiar desperation that there will be adjustment or expiration.

For here every one is a child of good will, and there is neither villainy nor external cruelty. The fact that men are like children, and that children are at once naïvely fortunate and unfortunate, is the theme; but it is all to the good, we suppose, that the theme arouses darting emotions, that Mr. Saroyan knows enough to keep to the tone of naïveté. The falling and rising music encompasses all the rest. Here a waif is remembered for himself; there he is absorbed in the beat and the stress of atmospheric music. Great literature? Hardly. A ridiculous tour de force? Even less. Mr. Saroyan is a note-taker and a note-giver; he is not a novelist. What he is able to produce is something minute, but not necessarily perishable. He cannot extend, integrate, plan as a whole; his characters are walking, talking, dreaming moods whose speech is announcement rather than expression. Mr. Saroyan does all the talking for them, and it does not matter that you can hear him whisper stage directions. When he is impudent and turns cute, he is childish; but in this book the swagger and the shrill eccentricity are not too much in evidence. Concede everything, limit him, box him off; there is still something about Mr. Bill Saroyan that belongs to us.

C. John McCole   (essay date 1937)

SOURCE: "That Daring Young Man, Mr. Saroyan," in *Lucifer at Large,* Longmans, Green and Co., 1937, pp. 257-73.

[*In the following essay, McCole provides a highly critical assessment of Saroyan's originality as a writer.*]

Mr. William Saroyan has not only evoked perdition upon all the short-story professors by telling them they can go take "a jump in the river," but he has also hurled all their baggage-load of techniques into the river after them. As a matter of fact, long before Mr. Saroyan ever thought of becoming a writer he had decided that the only thing for

him to do, would be to make his own rules. For one thing, his own rules might be easier to follow.

Some day, perchance, the literary historian might find it interesting to remember that William Saroyan's first break with the professors took place one afternoon when our future author was at the somewhat unpromising age of eleven. He had been sent home from school that day because he had talked out of turn; he had become "pretty sore" about the whole affair; and, then and there, he had formulated the first of his own rules. And what was it? Avoid all rules! For he found that people make laws for their own protection anyway: and, so, "to hell with them."

This is definite enough at least. But still more definite was the way in which Saroyan—after swearing to avoid all literary theory—then set about the business of elaborating more theory. "Several months" of mature deliberation elapsed, however, before he had arrived at the second of his canons: Forget all about Poe and O. Henry and all other writers and just "sit down and write." (He admits that he himself has even been able to "stand and write.") But it was not until he had formed his third guiding literary principle that his genius was given its fullest scope: the writer, he said, should learn to handle a typewriter so that he can "turn out" stories as fast as can Zane Grey.

This third principle was particularly effective. For example, when the editors of one of our better-known story magazines encouraged the young writer by accepting his **"The Daring Young Man on the Flying Trapeze,"** they received for several months afterwards at least one story, and sometimes two, a day from their unknown contributor! Standing and sitting, typing and typing, Mr. Saroyan was at work.

He had arrived at authorship. What is more, and although he was only in his twenties, he found himself at that particular stage of authorship where he could offer advice to his young contemporaries. Learn to breathe as deeply as possible, he told them. Learn to get the real taste of food, to sleep soundly, to be fully alive, to "laugh like hell," to get *really* angry. For "You will be dead soon enough."

In the meantime William Saroyan himself was very much alive. We began to hear a good deal about him. His father, we learned, had been born in Armenia, had been a teacher, and an unpublished writer in New York City; and had finally gone West to try his hand at grape-farming in the rich Fresno vineyards of California, where the son was born in 1908. The young man's grandmother—Saroyan has pictured her in one of his tales—was a born storyteller; with her countless legends of a curiously interesting past she furnished an inspiration and a source for much of the work our author was later to do.

Saroyan began to write, at first in Armenian, and later in English. He began to be published; he found himself famous; and his publishers found him prolific. But still he refused, despite his carefully formed rules and gratuitous advice, really to consider himself as a writer. ". . . I am not a writer at all," he says in **"Myself Upon the Earth."**

". . . I write because there is nothing more civilized or decent for me to do."

Mr. Saroyan's publishers, however, disagree with their young author. Not only is he a writer, and a great one, they say, but he "can well afford to disdain the sure-fire tricks of an old trade." Now and then, it is true, one of "the professors" has raised his voice in mild remonstrance against this total abandonment of tradition. Thus, some time ago Dr. Ernest Brennecke, of Columbia University, pointed out that many of Saroyan's tales are not short-stories at all. But such criticism does not disconcert Saroyan, as witness his reply to Dr. Brennecke: "What the hell difference does it make what you call it just so it breathes?" And to that incontrovertibly logical interrogation, there can, of course, be no answer.

· · · · ·

It doesn't make the least difference what we call Saroyan's work. But it does make a difference whether or not we understand it, whether we join the hallelujah chorus of his admirers because we are honestly convinced of the literary value of his work, or merely because everyone else is praising him. Certainly Saroyan's work does breathe, though at times a bit stentorously. It is compellingly vigorous; some of it has captured at least a certain grace. Also we must grant that its author handles subjective states of feeling with a penetrating sympathy; and that his sardonic undertones are often effective. But to say all this is not, I repeat, really to understand Mr. Saroyan's work or his position.

An understanding of that position must at the outset take into account a two-fold surrender which Saroyan has made. For one thing, he has abandoned himself to the idea that to be different is to be original. For another, he has subscribed to the mistaken belief that intensity is to be identified with vitality, that it is a valid substitute for artistry, and that it can be secured by inventing startlingly new techniques and loudly proclaiming one's independence from tradition and freedom from self-conscious craftsmanship. As a result of these convictions, William Saroyan has thrown most of the traditional rules of literary art into the river. What is more, he has then completed the job by jumping into the river himself. And that river, as I shall show in a moment, is the river of the Bergsonian flux.

In all of this I do not mean, of course, to say that Saroyan is a conscious pupil of Bergson's—as a matter of fact, were Saroyan to see that learned Frenchman splashing about in the vortex of his flux philosophy, he would probably think of him as only another one of the plaguy professors. (And, so, "to hell with" him!) Nor do I mean to lay the blame for all our present-day flux philosophy at Bergson's inviting door. Aldous Huxley's "stream of life" theory, William James' conception of the "stream of thought," the whole school of our stream-of-consciousness novelists—all these must share the responsibility. But I do mean to say that William Saroyan has immersed himself in at least the overflow of all these philosophies; and though Bergson is not, I think, the principal villain in the piece, an interesting parallel can be drawn between his philosophy and the technique of the young American—a parallel which may reveal many of the latter's shortcomings as a thinker and as an artist.

That he is prolific cannot be denied. The "one-story-a-day author," he has been called; Harold Matson, his literary agent, lost his breath trying to keep up with his client! And out in his uncle's vineyards in the San Joaquin Valley, where Saroyan now lives when not in Hollywood, he is still doing as many as four stories a week; while more than a hundred of his tales have already been published. I mention this to show how obviously impossible it is for me here to inquire into the subject matter of all these stories. But I do deem it advisable to discuss a few of them very briefly by way of establishing a basis for my later discussion.

"The Daring Young Man on the Flying Trapeze"—which is the title story of his first volume—tells of an impoverished young writer who haunts the employment agencies and libraries, tries desperately to get a story written, and dies of starvation before he can finish it. "Then, swiftly, neatly, with the grace of the young man on the trapeze, he was gone from his body. For an eternal moment he was all things at once: the bird, the fish, the rodent, the reptile, the man. An ocean of print undulated endlessly and darkly before him. The city burned. The herded crowd rioted. The earth circled away, and knowing that he did so, he turned his lost face to the empty sky and became dreamless, unalive, perfect."

"War" describes a group of children, of foreign descent, fighting on the streets and reminding the narrator of the way in which nations fight because "the little boys seemed so very innocent and likeable, and whole nations seemed so much like little boys . . ." "1,2,3,4,5,6,7,8" describes a romance which a young telegraph operator has with a girl, another operator, hundreds of miles away; and derives its curious title from a pattern of rhythm which the central character recognizes in some phonograph tunes he hears. "Aspirin Is a Member of the N.R.A." is a bitterly ironic tale of a young man who lived for months in a Manhattan hall-bedroom; and during that time took dozens of aspirins to quiet the pain in his head, while he listened to the radio announcement that "Aspirin is a member of the N.R.A." "It made me laugh," he reflects, "to hear that. But it is the truth . . . Aspirin *is* helping to bring back prosperity . . . It isn't preventing anything, but it is deadening pain."

A few of the stories—and especially the title one—from *The Daring Young Man on the Flying Trapeze* represent curiously imaginative, dexterous, and swiftly sure studies in interesting subjective states. And yet, and despite the critical blurb which attended the appearance of this volume, that is about all that can be said for it. It was a rocket, but it has burned out. I even think that most of us felt it growing cold while reading it.

Of *Inhale & Exhale* (1936) the same cannot be said. The flame is at least appreciably brighter here; there is a little heat as well as light. There is not only the appearance of virtuosity; there is, as well, more range and some little humor, a quality in which the first volume is almost entirely lacking. And humor may help! One thinks of the Scotchman's advice to the surgeon who was tending his wife: "Try her wi' a joke ance, Doctor."

In *Inhale & Exhale* an occasional frugal joke works wonders—and is much more effective than Mr. Saroyan's sardonic scalpel. It relieves the monotony of its author's megalomania; and proves a welcome leaven to a bread that is otherwise often bitter. One can, for example, laugh at the tale of the boxer who, in **"Our Little Brown Brothers the Filipinos,"** refused to leave the prize ring until he had been declared winner—and who could not, until then, be budged by a hundred policemen! In **"Solemn Advice to a Young Man About to Accept Undertaking as a Profession"** there are amusing reminiscences of a mortician trying to sell an overly economical widow an expensive coffin for her husband who had just died and left her a comfortably large insurance. **"My Picture in the Paper"** humorously records the bewilderment of the author when, after the appearance of his first volume, publicity began to seek him out. And others of the stories offer interesting and whimsical accounts of Saroyan's brother, his sister, other members of his family, and his life in various California vineyards.

So far so good. The book has its merits—and of these the critics have told us in sycophantic unison. I need not repeat them here. But I do think it time that we now note some of Saroyan's defects, of which the critics have *not* told us—at least with any amount of clarity or confidence.

. . . . .

The melancholy flux. The general tone of *Inhale & Exhale* is suggested by the opening paragraph of the first story: "Everything begins with inhale and exhale, and never ends, moment after moment, yourself inhaling and exhaling, seeing, hearing, smelling, touching, tasting, moving, sleeping, waking . . . until it is now, this moment, the moment of *your* being . . . and I remember having lived among dead moments, now deathless because of my remembrance, among people now dead, having been a part of the flux which is now only a remembrance . . ."

This same curiously strange philosophy permeates the entire volume, though more characteristically perhaps is it to be noted in the story which is entitled **"The Gay and Melancholy Flux"**—from which I take this revealing passage: "One day you were born, O God Almighty, you were lucky that day, and I don't care how miserable you've been ever since . . . Therefore, *while* is the world. I mean, *word,* not world, though either will do. *While* is the holy word. The word of God and man and earth and universe. While one thing, another. While sun and warmth, darkness and cold . . . While everything, nothing. While nothing, everything. While now, never. Forever and forever."

"What's the meaning of all the noise?" Referring to **"The Gay and Melancholy Flux,"** the author is led to observe

that it is the craziest story he has ever read, and to wonder what all the noise it makes is really about! Those who are familiar with Henri Bergson's *Creative Evolution* will find, however, a parallel which may throw some light on the matter.

Compare, for example, the two Saroyan passages which I have quoted above, with this selection from the brilliant Frenchman who is one of the sponsors of our school of "flux" writers: Life is a "current passing from germ to germ through the medium of a developed organism. It is as if the organism itself were only an excrescence, a bud caused to sprout by the former germ endeavoring to continue itself in a new germ. The essential thing is the *continuous progress* indefinitely pursued, an invisible progress, on which each visible organism rides during the short interval of time given it to live." Having noted the similarity between the two authors, let us now inquire somewhat more carefully into the work of the Frenchman that we might pursue our comparison further.

The "beneficent fluid." According to Bergson, the real function of man's intelligence is to touch reality and to live reality; but to do both only to the extent that they concern ourselves and our own work—the furrow that *we* happen to be plowing, as he puts it. Let happen what will to the furrows in all neighboring fields.

For this job he tells us that we gain strength from a certain "beneficent fluid"—an ocean in which we find ourselves—that is life's wonder itself. But whenever we immerse ourselves in reality, we note, of course, thousands of incidents which seem absolutely unrelated to our past and to our future, until we come to realize that all of this discontinuity finds some design in a background which is really continuous. At first, therefore, each psychic experience seems to be but a swell of water: it is up to us to see each of these swells as part of the ocean.

Thus all individual experience merges into a flow or a flux; you cannot always tell, as a matter of fact, just what part of the ocean is yours: which of your experiences are distinct and valid, and which are not. That makes no difference. For the individual's mental state swells anyway while he tries to swim. In much the same way as a snowball does by *rolling upon itself!* —Such is Bergson's figure.

In this process the most that the individual can do is to reunite all these scattered and flowing elements by imagining itself a "formless ego." Individuality must become, I might suggest, a sort of very necessary spool, on which "it threads the psychic states which it has set up as independent entities." For our intellects can form clear ideas of only one thing: immobility. And when we think, we "think matter"—ideas play a very small part in our existence: our whole past we see chiefly as a series of impulses and tendencies. These discontinuous impulses and tendencies become, then, the only parts of the swelling ocean of flux that we can really distinguish.

"Waves coming and going." By these tokens it will be noted that the author whose work finds a parallel with all

William Saroyan, 1934. According to his son, Aram, "This was perhaps Saroyan's favorite photograph of himself as a young man. He considered the dour expression to be true to his deeper nature." (Photograph by Willard Van Dyke)

the flux theories, thinks of life as being significant chiefly because it changes its colors with a chameleon-like swiftness. He does not try to name or understand the interesting animal, though he is fascinated by its swiftly changing spots. He sees in the flux of living nothing but a vast movement, unimpeded by any certainty, and carrying him along on the crest of its waters as they flow forever into some unfathomable darkness.

The writer who has absorbed the overflow of this philosophy can, I repeat, only look upon himself as a sort of forlorn figure—can only imagine himself the "formless ego" of which Bergson speaks—seated in a very shaky boat upon a current. He is carried along the stream with breathless rapidity; he sees no buoys or light-houses of tradition to guide him; and he recognizes only the necessity of keeping, somehow or another, in the flux itself. To use the words which Mr. Saroyan's publishers employ in speaking of their young author: "He takes a headlong plunge into the vivid life about him . . ." He does not have to learn to swim in his medium at all: "It cannot be said of William Saroyan that he has forged steadily and cautiously ahead by dint of a long apprenticeship in his medium."

So it is, that Saroyan has so willingly disregarded all rules: they do not help with the swimming, with the comprehending of life, anyway!

To carry my comparison further, let me quote again from Bergson: "We are at ease only in the discontinous, in the immobile, in the dead. *The intellect is characterized by a natural inability to comprehend life*." And Mr. Saroyan expresses the same idea in these words: "All that I have learned is that we breathe, and remember . . . and it begins nowhere and it ends nowhere, and all that I know is that we are somehow alive, all of us in the light, making shadows, the sun overhead, space all around us . . . and the sea sullen with movement like my breathing, waves coming and going . . ."

Life is one grand toothache. Mr. Saroyan speaks, we will observe, of the sea being *sullen* with movement. And, indeed, the life portrayed in his tales is, for the most part, an unpropitious expanse of unbearable and dismal pain. A very few of his stories are, it is true, divertingly humorous. But an unpleasant majority of them reflect life, to use Masefield's figure, as "a long headache in a noisy street."

In **"Laura, Immortal,"** for example, we have a typical illustration of this. A man returns to his old home only to find, as he describes it, "the desolation of my life from the first moment of its reality, on backward to the first moment of reality in the life of man." Confronted by the sum of all human desolation, he stands before the house, praying and weeping and cursing until his heart makes "a violence in the earth." Again, in **"The World & the Theatre,"** a boy suffering from toothache, says: ". . . a man doesn't begin to live before he begins to die, and I wasn't bawling about the pain of the tooth, I was bawling because I knew."

Our author continually admits the varied wonder of life. But of what use is this wonder when it becomes only a sweet confection, leaving him, when he nibbles at it, with a great toothache, a feeling of desolation that causes him to gnash his teeth, curse, and—to quote from the above mentioned character—make with his own heart a violence in the earth?

Life is an "evasion of death." The current of life reflected in the short stories of this young American is not only sullen and painful. It is also without direction; it is meaningless and purposeless; it completely engulfs the pitiable figure in his little bark upon it—or trying to swim in it, if you prefer the Bergsonian figure. When there is "loud laughter, and dancing" we are immediately made to feel that both serve but to make us forget how purposeless our progress is—to cover up the Nihilism in which we drift continually. "There is no beginning and no end. You get yourself born somehow or other, but that's no beginning, that's more like an end, but it isn't even an end. Nothing is, nothing ever could be . . ." Thus speaks the central character in **"The Gay and Melancholy Flux."**

And Bergson? We can have, he tells us, only a feeling of our own evolution and "of the evolution of all things in pure duration"—a feeling which forms but "an indistinct fringe that fades off into darkness." We can keep swimming, but it will do us no good. As one of the other Saroyan characters observes, it is impossible to win with "Dice or anything else. You lose . . . You only get to try . . ." Life is just an "evasion of death." "We are just killing time now, waiting to get back into the emptiness." In other words, we keep swimming though we realize we are only swimming toward some maelstrom up the river.

A "weak woeful clod of clay." Man will be sucked into this maelstrom, though in the meantime he is permitted to make a brief "shadow" in the sun upon the water. He is not, as William Saroyan sees him, much more than a "weak woeful clod of clay" who finds this business of trying to be a Christian a damnably distressing affair. His church is "so purely ornamental" and so annoyingly "statistical about the soul." As an individual, man resembles "a lie for the next generation." He is "a document, the subject of bad poems." And, finally, "There is no dignity anywhere, not even among peasants . . ."

On thumbing one's nose at the universe. It should be remembered that the most important shadow which the stream-of-life author can cast before him, would seem to be his own. To exist we must change, and "to change is to mature, to mature is to go on creating oneself endlessly," says the author of *Creative Evolution*. Man wishes, of course, to observe, but "he wishes above all things to observe himself," echoes the author of *The Daring Young Man on the Flying Trapeze*. Each one of us "is interested in himself, as an experiment . . ."

We might think of this point of view with the help of the following figure. While the author is being whirled along in his currents, he is not likely to be tempted into an understanding, into a true understanding, of the problems of the other people in the flux: "He lives, and he lives within himself, which is the universe." As a consequence he has little time for quiet moments of beauty, or for the most significant problems which confront the human race.

It will be noted that Saroyan illustrates this attitude by refusing almost entirely to grapple with any of the deeper problems of humanity. He touches upon them, I admit. But he does not clarify them; and he refuses, above all, to hope for any solution to them: when a life-preserver, in the form of common human experience, is thrown out to him he persists in stubbornly pushing it away, though it might often be a helpful thing to cling to. It does not always pay to reject human tradition altogether.

But William Saroyan does almost just that. The real way to become a philosopher, he argues, is not to be found in profiting by the sum of human wisdom, but rather by intensifying personal attitudes. He even becomes quite practical in illustrating this point of view by suggesting a nice little poker game as the best place in which to become a philosopher. Sit down, deal when it's your turn, take an occasional swig of whiskey. *That* will teach you about our universe! Ten hours of this and you will know more about the world than any six scientists could ever know! Above all, you will learn enough about the universe to realize that but one gesture is necessary in explaining it—and "that gesture a comical one."

Creating oneself endlessly. Clinging to Mr. Saroyan like a Nessus-shirt is another one of the Bergsonian ideas, already referred to: the idea that "to change is to mature, to mature is to go on creating oneself endlessly." Now when Mr. Dooley observed that the trouble with our knowledge is not that we haven't learned enough, but that we have learned so many things that "jest ain't so," he uttered a remark that applies nicely to the young William Saroyan gazing about the world in wild-eyed surmise and turning out stories—projections of intense personal impulses and attitudes—at the rate of almost one a day.

For to change is *not* necessarily to mature. Nor does it follow that we mature by an endless creation of ourselves. The artist matures by *transfiguring* experience—by deriving from it, to quote Saroyan's "big brother," Thomas Wolfe, "the palpable and living substance of his art."

But most of the Saroyan stories are *transcripts* of experience—usually of traumatic experience—rather than transfigurations of it. Indeed, it is to be noted that he has little skill in creating any character other than an *alter ego*: all of his characters speak and feel exactly alike. The "art" of his work is not the result of a richly endowed mind focusing a highly creative intelligence upon life and distilling from it some rarely concentrated beauty. It is the result of a mind caught in the flux of life, with little time to fuse experience with imagination, and forced to compensate itself by highly magnifying its own ego.

On his Bergsonian bark, and seeing only his own shadow upon the water, he tries feverishly to distract himself too often with the mere flotsam and jetsam carried along by the current.

"A thing of many fragments." William Saroyan tells us that a novel is "a thing of many fragments held together by the frequent perishing and frequent resurrection of a brave and stubborn man"; and by way of giving point to this theory he generously concedes that Christ actually lived a novel that is "almost a first-rate" one. He has not himself as yet essayed the writing of a novel; but, significantly enough, his stories are just such "fragments"—fragments held together by their author's frequent perishing in disillusionment and his resurrection into an intensely passionate, but uncontrolled, exaltation. (Even his publishers, it is to be noted with interest, refer to his *"fever of exaltation."*)

Perhaps it is this effect of violent contrast in Saroyan's moods which makes many of his admirers think him powerful: as warmth may even be mistaken for heat by a man who has just come out of the cold. For, although in some of his stories he rises to a genuine feeling, he usually fails to sustain that feeling: vulgarisms, blasphemies, crude or annoyingly incompetent writing, characters that expectorate and curse on every page—these matters distract from the effect of real beauty and often leave its object just another piece of wreckage on the stream.

A fresh voice in our literary wilderness. It must be conceded that many of his techniques are effective. The method, for example, employed in **"1,2,3,4,5,6,7,8"** advances the narrative swiftly by alternating the speech in the first and third persons; the individualized technique in **"The Daring Young Man on the Flying Trapeze"** lends, I think, both urgency and freshness to the story; his handling of subjective moods is often not without verve and a sort of hard, cold brilliancy.

Too often, however—and we might as well admit it—he is *neither* original *nor* effective. He can ape Faulkner in such passages as the following: *"I am now almost seventeen and I have lived all these years upon the earth,* thinking, *no matter what happens, I shall be somewhere upon this earth forever,* thinking, *it is because of Maria, because I love her and am now walking to her,* thinking, *tomorrow all of us will turn away from the fields, our earth, and go to our houses, waiting for their wrath."*

In **"Secrets of Alexandria,"** and other tales, he uses headlines to get effects in a cinematographic manner which Dos Passos long ago proved would get at least one effect—that of an "art" surprisingly suggestive of the morning newspaper. And like the same author, he has hit upon routine descriptions of brothel scenes, etc., that have become a formula with him.

Many of his cynicisms were uttered long ago by Dreiser even before that confused writer began pouring out his tired soul into numerous autobiographies. Some of the shadows which he casts are merely those of Freud and Lawrence elongated into grotesque fancies. He omits punctuation; but so do a score of other published writers—and a million who are not yet published, though it is beginning to seem that they will be. In short, I think Saroyan's claims to originality have been egregiously exaggerated.

Also, I think unjustified his claim to being considered a "fresh" voice. He pretends to throw overboard all "rules" of writing. He does throw most of them overboard—with the exception of his own. We are told that he is free from that kind of literary self-consciousness which so often fails in producing anything truly creative. As a matter of fact, Mr. Saroyan is nothing if he is not self-conscious. He is self-conscious in the very way in which he is continually assuring us that he is not self-conscious. He is supposed to be creating a more intense art form, when he and his school are actually turning what was formerly a perfected form of art, into an intense projection of personal experience—making of it an immense proving ground for experimentation.

Emotional somersaults. Meanwhile, he threatens, unless his future work shows an advance over that so far published, to perish in the sea of his own egoism, endlessly trying to create himself, to keep himself afloat by depending upon fevered strokes of irony. His *Three Times Three* (1937)—the most recent Saroyan book at the moment of this writing—is a collection of nine "stories" as fevered and formless as those in his previous volumes.

Real irony, of the classic kind, might help him. But Mr. Saroyan's irony does not happen to be of the classic kind. It is rather what Jean Paul Richter described as "hot baths of sentiment alternating with cold douches of irony." Writing on another author than Saroyan, Alan Reynolds Thompson refers to such emotion as "a device of emotional somersaults . . . because it is the revulsion of the author's intelligence against his own romantic sentiments, and because it thus differs essentially from the classic irony which is based on the objective observation by a normal individual of extravagances in others."

Perhaps that is it. Perhaps the author of *The Daring Young Man on the Flying Trapeze* has been merely performing emotional somersaults!

Harlan Hatcher　　(essay date 1939)

SOURCE: "William Saroyan," in *English Journal,* Vol. XXVIII, No. 3, March, 1939, pp. 169-77.

[*An American educator who served for over fifteen years as the president of The University of Michigan, Hatcher published works about the modern novel and modern drama as well as histories of the Great Lakes region. In the following excerpt, he contends that the strengths and weakness of Saroyan's short fiction are directly related to his personality and outlook on life.*]

Saroyan has kept himself in the spotlight almost continuously by his singular penchant for writing to the letter columns of the papers and magazines to protest criticisms of him by reviewers as his collections of stories keep coming from the press. Six volumes have already appeared in four years, magazines of all sorts are currently carrying his work, and there is no sign of the well going dry. That is to say, Saroyan has been before us long enough, and has accumulated a corpus of published work extensive enough, to warrant a critical examination and stock-taking. What is it all about?

First of all, it is chiefly about one William Saroyan, born in California of Armenian immigrants in 1908, how he has been growing up in the beautiful, mad, and tragic world before and after Hoover, what he has done and thought, and how it feels to be Mr. Saroyan inhaling and exhaling, meeting people, intoxicated with the awareness of his own separate ego in "the gay and melancholy flux," and fascinated by the fun of making comments on all that engages his restless attention by tapping away on the keys of a typewriter. His writing is intensely personal and contains a fairly complete autobiography, though it is important and only fair to remember that, since he usually employs the first person, even when writing of other characters, it is easy to mistake the created character for Saroyan himself.

Saroyan's own personality so completely dominates his writing, even when he tries to draw characters other than himself, that it becomes the first problem to be reckoned with. In the six collections published to date there are certain stories in which it is true that the author is excessively self-conscious, sometimes tricky, fond of posing, pleased with his own cleverness, and blatantly sardonic about the ways of the world which he observes with the beguiling naïveté of one who has just discovered it all for the first time in the history of the races of men. These particular qualities are offensive to many people—especially reviewers, who like to lecture him about them—and are responsible for the general opinion that has already taken hold of Saroyan's reputation and labeled him half-genius, half-phony. There are some grounds for this judgment, although they are easily exaggerated. In his perceptive, Whitman-like piece called **"Myself upon the Earth,"** for example, included as the third story in his first collection, he wrote:

> I do not want to say the wrong thing. I do not want to be clever. I am horribly afraid of this. I have never been clever in life, and now that I have come to a labor even more magnificent than living itself I do not want to utter a single false word. For months I have been telling myself, "you must be humble. Above all things, you must be humble." I am determined not to lose my character.

That statement, of course, carries within it its own charming contradiction, and a humble Saroyan would not be William Saroyan whose writing we like. But, even assuming its truth, we turn to the facetious and boisterously clever preface to the collection and read:

> I immediately began to study all the classic rules, including Ring Lardner's, and in the end I discovered

that the rules were wrong. . . . so I wrote some new rules.

I wrote Number One when I was eleven and had just been sent home from the fourth grade for having talked out of turn and meant it.

Do not pay any attention to the rules other people make, I wrote. They make them for their own protection, and to hell with them. (I was pretty sore that day.) . . .

My third rule was: Learn to typewrite, so you can turn out stories as fast as Zane Grey.

It is one of my best rules.

This side of Saroyan's personality, the simple explanation for which may be referred to the psychologists, is no doubt responsible also for the critical weakness which urges him to reprint some of his incredibly trivial pieces instead of allowing them to be generously forgotten in ephemeral magazine issues. But these irritations and mistakes of a boy suddenly famous in his mid-twenties, with his picture in the paper "along with a story about me and my writing," must not be permitted to obscure the fairly substantial number of rare and individual "stories" or the fresh young voice of this gifted writer.

Saroyan's first work was unique, perfectly timid (how important in our day!), and particularly refreshing. We had just come through the narrows of the depression in 1932-33. Each new sign of "recovery," however timorous, was publicized with rejoicing. The new and uninspired proletarian novels were flooding the market place. Then, at the beginning of 1934, Saroyan captured the newspaper headlines with his restrained and beautifully articulated story of the jobless young man who starved to death in a San Francisco rooming house, with a single brightly polished penny on the table proclaiming "In God We Trust, Liberty, 1923," and some sheets of Y.M.C.A. paper on which he had begun to pen his "Application for Permission To Live." The story had utilized in an individual manner the new techniques for exploring the subconscious in sleep and wakefulness, it showed the tragic surrender of the young man crazed and sick with hunger, and it used the circus symbol of the flying trapeze, with exactly the right degree of irony, to enlarge the implications and to point the climax:

> *Through the air on the flying trapeze,* his mind hummed. Amusing it was, astoundingly funny. A trapeze to God, or to nothing, a flying trapeze to some sort of eternity; he prayed objectively for strength to make the flight with grace. . . . Then swiftly, neatly, with the grace of the young man on the trapeze, he was gone from his body. . . . The earth circled away, and knowing that he did so, he turned his lost face to the empty sky and became dreamless, unalive, perfect.

In the more than two hundred Saroyan stories which have followed this beginning, few have reached the level of

"The Daring Young Man," but many have used variants of the same theme. It is safe to say that nobody has spoken with greater poignancy and understanding of the dreams and sufferings of the impoverished young people in the 1930's than William Saroyan. He knows from firsthand personal experiences, as well as from observation, what it is like to be without the price of a date, a movie, a hamburger and coffee, or a week's rent of a dingy room. "You hear a lot of sad talk about all the young men who died in the Great War," he says in **"Aspirin Is a Member of the N.R.A."** "Well, what about this war? Is it less real because it destroys with less violence, with a more sustained pain?"

Some of Saroyan's best work is in this more serious vein. He writes about the dreams that disturb lonely young men in the furnished rooms. Sometimes it is poetry, random phrases remembered in dives and booking joints while they are "listening to the talk of another man, waiting for national recovery, *time to murder and create.*" Sometimes the depressed dreamer projects himself into the surroundings for which he longs and creates a house with a yard, trees, and flowers, a lovely girl at the door, and a fine job that will make a millionaire of him. For a brief moment it is all intensely real. In one especially good story with the title **"1, 2, 3, 4, 5, 6, 7, 8,"** this longing for a sympathetic girl and romance gets itself identified with the haunting counterpoint of a cheap jazz record which he plays over and over on his phonograph. The eight swift chords beat on in his head with unaccountable persistence until they come to signify the approach of the same lonely desire of the girl at the other end of the teletype machine. Then, one sad day, the music and the girl, but not the longing, went away; so, also, in Saroyan restlessness, did the boy, "helplessly, weeping for this girl and the house, and sneering at myself for wanting more of life than there was in life to have." In another called **"The Job,"** in the latest collection, *The Trouble with Tigers,* he writes of the bond of sentiment that unites through desperation two jobless and wandering boys, and of their code which compels the one who found a job to give support to his friend, and the more imperative code of self-respect which sends the friend on his way with the farewell, "All the luck in the world, kid, you'll need it."

All these stories make impressive reading. Though they tell of desperation and failure, they manage to keep to Saroyan's large thesis that "man has great dignity, do not imagine that he has not." They are well supported by another group, also in the serious vein, in which he writes about children and adolescence with a passionate closeness to experience that is almost as near as we can hope to get in words to the thing itself. He knows what it is like to sell papers on a street corner; to peddle oranges and curse poverty; to cut school for a day to wander about the country for no reason that he can explain to a schoolteacher; to lie in bed weeping for childhood's melancholy, far-off things; to smart under the vulgar personal remarks of grandmothers, uncles, and other relatives who notice his physical transitions; and the thousand and one impressions that make those early years so bewildering. In stories like **"The World & the The-**

atre," "Resurrection of a Life," "Laura, Immortal," "The Oranges," in *Inhale & Exhale*; "And Man," in *The Daring Young Man*; several in the collection called *Little Children*; and the top-notch "The Man with His Heart in the Highlands" in *Three Times Three*, Saroyan has made a genuine contribution to our short-story literature.

In still another group of stories that are more nearly personal essays, Saroyan has written of himself upon the earth and how he thinks and feels about it. Some of them are rather magnificent in the Emerson-Whitman manner, and some are only a little less impressive in the Byronic pose. These are the pieces that have excited most of the controversy among the reviewers. In them he tells himself about Man, Eternity, Death, Brotherhood, Literature, Love, Nothingness, the Great American Novel, and other large subjects. In **"Myself upon the Earth"** he says:

> The earth is vast. And with the earth all things are vast, the skyscraper and the blade of grass. . . . I am a story-teller, and I have but a single story—man. I want to tell this simple story in my own way, forgetting the rules of rhetoric, the tricks of composition. I have something to say and I do not wish to speak like Balzac.

In **"The Tiger"** he has his young author say:

> You see, when I write English I write Chinese, Japanese, Italian, French, and every other language. You see, I said, I am a writer. I write in every language, in English. . . . So far I have written only one word—God. . . . I wrote over two million false words before I achieved this one word.

He hopes to add two more words: *is* and *Love*. And in a characteristic and revealing passage in **"A Cold Day"** he reminds himself:

> Do not deceive. Do not make up lies for the sake of pleasing anyone. . . . Simply relate what is the great event of all history, of all time, the humble, artless truth of mere being. . . . The man you write of need not perform some heroic or monstrous deed in order to make your prose great. Let him do what he has always done, day in and day out, continuing to live. Let him walk and talk and think and sleep and dream and awaken and walk again and talk again and move and be alive. It is enough. There is nothing else to write about. You have never seen a short story in life. . . . Your own consciousness is the only form you need. Your own awareness is the only action you need.

This is a noble purpose with which no one could quarrel. But it is easier to announce the goal than to achieve it. It is not at all surprising that the author sometimes fails to arrive, or that he sometimes contents himself by staying at home entirely and talking about getting ready to commence to start. When he finds it hard to get going, he talks about his room, his typewriter, his cousin, his uncle, or Ezra Pound, or of his contempt for the phony and the trickster whom he can spot with uncommon accuracy in life or in the movies. That is, he is ill-content when he is

not writing. When un-Saroyan authors would go into meditation to clarify and arrange their materials and wait for something to say, William Saroyan sits at his typewriter and writes about sitting at his typewriter without anything to say. When he runs down, he goes right on: "I don't feel like writing any more. How can anybody begin to mention everything." He ends **"Myself upon the Earth"** with these words:

> Day after day I had this longing, for my typewriter. This is the whole story. I don't suppose this is a very artful ending, but it is the ending just the same. The point is this: *day after day I longed for my typewriter.*

> This morning I got it back. It is before me now and I am tapping at it, and this is what I have written.

In like manner, Saroyan, who is weak in invention but strong in perception, often does not construct his story; he merely blueprints it, puts up a scaffold, and contends that these appurtenances are more interesting than the finished structure. The people who stand for hours watching the steam shovels dipping dirt at Sixth Avenue and Forty-seventh Street will not be concerned with the smooth operation of the completed subway. William Saroyan is really too clever about it, even when he is good—as he usually is. His last collection, *The Trouble with Tigers,* has three of his good ones in this manner: **"A Scenario for Karl Marx," "O.K. Baby, This Is the World,"** and **"We Want a Touchdown."** The second of these, incidentally, carries the Saroyan philosophy:

> The picture begins with this young doctor holding up a new-born baby by its legs and slapping life into it. The young doctor says, O.K. baby, this is the world, so inhale and exhale and be with us a while. They're not going to be kind to you out there because nobody was kind to them, but don't hate anybody. There's nobody to hate. You're going to be pushed around, and so forth and so on. That's the idea. He tells the baby how it is and what to expect and the story begins.

And in **"We Want a Touchdown"** he begins by telling his readers that he was, "by a great margin, the noisiest" writer that ever broke into print and then outlines a novel around one of those elaborate metaphors which he often uses so effectively, in this case the oval stadium, "holiest of all shapes," with the people looking *down* upon the field, the symbol of the world. "Sure, I said. If I were to concentrate on the theme I could do something great."

In this sentence Saroyan has offered a fair criticism of much of his writing. He plunges on headlong, trying to get the right word said about everything as he rushes by, and believing that, if you get that word said, everything is all right henceforth. He has tried to lunge at the human garden and grab the secrets of what grows there. Like other writers he has felt the barrier erected by words between perception and the report, and he has tried to tear through to greater immediacy. He therefore seldom takes time to construct a formal work, to tell an "artistic" story, or to follow the rules. He makes one story by throwing in crude, jagged-edged fragments of life on the wing, and then writes another to justify and explain his procedure and express his contempt for form. Some of his pieces are carried solely by their troubled impetuosity, as though he took seriously his own advice to a writer:

> Try to learn to breathe deeply, really to taste food when you eat, and when you sleep, really to sleep. Try as much as possible to be wholly alive, with all your might, and when you laugh, laugh like hell, and when you get angry, get good and angry. Try to be alive. You will be dead soon enough.

In fact, those words contain a summarizing truth about Saroyan. This sensitive but turbulent spirit who was kicked about in his youth by poverty and made to feel his separateness because he was Armenian; who writes with filial tenderness of his father, the unpublished writer and vine-grower of California, a man of great cultivation who had been a teacher of repute in his homeland but had fled it for political reasons and toiled as a janitor in New York to get money to bring the family to America; this young man, fulfilling in his own career toward acceptance and fame the ambition of his father, seems determined not to be embittered by experience and to let nothing escape until he can note it down in words. Inhale and exhale, and let the words fall into any shape they please, even if the result is sometimes, as Saroyan admits, some of "the worst prose ever written." His style, therefore, is like breathing and comes out now smooth and melodious, as some of the quoted examples show, and now in yells, in detached oaths and phrases from the street, and in the jerky rhythm of a man out of breath entirely. His sentence structure has been known to drive English teachers mad and to make Saroyan himself very happy. But there is always something behind the arrangements of the words. Here are two final examples of the unconnected, catalogue style in which he specializes, the first from **"Woof Woof"** and the second from **"The Tiger"** in *The Trouble with Tigers*:

> That's what money is. Forty-eight cents, forty-nine cents, woof woof, fifty cents, a cheap room in a decaying building on a main street, a hard bed containing eighty-five, eighty-six, woof woof, lice.

> After April came May and after New Orleans New York. Then June and the sea, Atlantic. Then Europe and the cities there, and I mean death, the tiger following each who lives, brother.

It must be obvious that with such a personality, interested in these materials, holding these views, and living in these dispersed times, one must reconcile one's self to accept what the author has to give and not complain too harshly because this tremendous talent is undisciplined and lacking in form and concentration. For his talent is genuine in its own genre, and his style, profane and raucous, impassioned and lyrical by turns, shows the beauty and the amorphousness that fits in with himself and the distracted discontinuity of his age.

Otis Ferguson (essay date 1939)

SOURCE: "It Reads Like Fiction," in *The New Republic*, Vol. XLIX, No. 1277, May 24, 1939, pp. 78-9.

[*In the following excerpt from a review of* Peace, It's Wonderful, *Ferguson comments on the fragmentary quality of the stories and on the progress Saroyan has made as a writer since publishing his earliest fiction.*]

The twenty-seven new Saroyans in this seventh book [*Peace, It's Wonderful*] show the author's growth in discipline and ease in the form (for example, he doesn't have to write that he is a great writer until page 117, an almost final triumph over doubt). Saroyan's form isn't that of the plotted story, where things happen from a beginning through a middle toward an end. Nothing "happens": he jumps full-tilt into the middle and full-tilt out, like a kid hopping a truck. Though he has done much with it, it is not particularly his: it is the artful form of no-form that has served so well for the expression of the last ten, fifteen years, translating an attitude, a thing, a person seen, an incident or mood or wisecrack, into the running terms of fiction. Static in development, its motion is toward a completed effect in feeling. It is halfway between excerpts from a novel—the form which gathers and carries all effects like a river—and the familiar essay, which is an entire effect in itself.

Saroyan's natural, vivid prose style and that exuberant appetite of his ran wild at first, resulting mainly in cock-a-doodle-doo. But he has been getting out from under that gradually, developing control of subject and a sterner selection, by trial and error and prolific work. He still can get such a jag on over his own words that he imagines them to have said something ("crazy, absurd, magnificent . . . ridiculous and beautiful fight"); and the life-is-death-how-vast-I'm-laughing mysticisms still enter here and there to confound reason (**"Comedy Is Where You Die and They Don't Bury You Because You Can Still Walk"**). But **"The Same as Twenty Years Ago"** and **"The Warm, Quiet Valley of Home"** are so bright and complete in their mood as to be almost a new kind of writing; **"The Year of Heaven"** and **"Piano"** and the one about the new Jack London stand out too. The fact is that, whatever the proportion of actually good single pieces, there is a reader's continuity in this book—probably because of the world Saroyan makes for himself, lives and works in. It is a cockeyed world, but very close to the common things and people of the countryside; the book somehow makes you feel good about them.

Edmund Wilson (essay date 1940)

SOURCE: "The Boys in the Back Room: William Saroyan," in *The New Republic*, Vol. 103, No. 21, November 18, 1940, pp. 697-98.

[*Wilson, considered America's foremost man of letters in the twentieth century, wrote widely on cultural, histori-*

cal, and literary matters. Perhaps his greatest contributions to American literature were his tireless promotion of writers of the 1920s, 1930s, and 1940s, and his essays introducing the best of modern literature to the general reader. In the following essay, Wilson perceives a decline in the quality of Saroyan's fiction after The Daring Young Man on the Flying Trapeze, and Other Stories: *"[A] columnist is what William Saroyan seems sometimes in danger of becoming—the kind of columnist who depends entirely on a popular personality, the kind who never reads, who knows nothing in particular about anything, who merely turns on the tap every day and lets it run a column."]*

The story becomes monotonous; but you have to begin by saying that Saroyan, too, derives from Hemingway. The novelists of the older generation—Hemingway himself, Dos Passos, Faulkner, Wilder—have richer and more complex origins, they belong to a bigger cultural world. But if the most you can say of John O'Hara is that he has evidently read Ring Lardner as well as Hemingway, the most you can say of Saroyan is that he has also read Sherwood Anderson (though he speaks of having looked into a book which he bought for a nickel at a bookstore and which was in Swedish and had pictures of churches). When you remember that Lardner and Anderson were among the original ingredients in Hemingway, you see how limited the whole school is.

But what distinguishes Saroyan from his fellow pupils is the fact that he is not what is called hard-boiled. What was surprising and refreshing about him when he first appeared was that, though he told the familiar story about the wiseguy who went into the bar, and I said and the bartender said and I said, the story was not cruel, but represented an agreeable mixture of San Franciscan bonhomie and Armenian Christianity. The fiction of the school of Hemingway had been full of bad drunks; Saroyan was a novelty: a good drunk. The peculiar spell exerted by his play, *The Time of Your Life,* consisted in its sustaining the illusion of friendliness and muzzy elation and gentle sentimentality which a certain amount of beer or rye will bring on in a favorite bar. Saroyan takes you to the bar, and he creates for you there a world which is the way the world would be if it conformed to the feelings instilled by drinks. In a word, he achieves the feat of making and keeping us boozy without the use of alcohol and purely by the action of art. It seems natural that the cop and the labor leader should be having a drink together; that the prostitute should be a wistful child, who gets married by someone that loves her; that the tall tales of the bar raconteur should turn out to be perfectly true, that the bar millionaire should be able to make good his munificent philanthropical offers: that they should be really Jack the Giant-Killer and Santa Claus; and that it should be possible to croak the vice-crusader, who is trying to make everybody unhappy, as harmlessly as the devil in a children's "extravaganza."

These magical feats are accomplished by the enchantment of Saroyan's temperament, which induces us to take from him a good deal that we should not take from anyone else.

With Saroyan the whole thing is the temperament: he hardly ever tries to contrive a machine. The good fairy who was present at his christening thus endowed him with one of the most precious gifts that a literary artist can have, and Saroyan never ceases to explain to us how especially fortunate he is: "As I say, I do not know a great deal about what the words come to, but the presence is always anxious that I take time out to say something. I say, What's there to say? And the presence says, Now don't get funny; just sit down and say something; it'll be all right. Say it wrong; it'll be all right anyway. Half the time I *do* say it wrong, but somehow or other, just as the presence says, it's right anyhow. I am always pleased about this. My God, it's wrong, but it's all right. It's really all right. How did it happen? Well, that's how it is. It's the presence, doing everything for me. It's the presence, doing all the hard work while I, always inclined to take things easy, loaf around, not paying much attention to anything, much, just putting down on paper whatever comes my way."

> **Saroyan has a natural felicity of touch which prevents him from being offensive or tiresome in any of the more obvious ways; and his stories and soliloquies at their best have the quality of the spontaneous songs of one of those songwriters who finds the right melody for his feelings without knowing anything about music.**
>
> **—Edmund Wilson**

Well, we don't mind Saroyan's saying this, because he is such an engaging fellow; and we don't mind his putting down on paper whatever comes his way. It is true that he has a natural felicity of touch which prevents him from being offensive or tiresome in any of the more obvious ways; and his stories and soliloquies at their best have the quality of the spontaneous songs of one of those songwriters who finds the right melody for his feelings without knowing anything about music. But Saroyan is entirely in error in supposing that when he "says it wrong," everything is really all right. What is right in such a case is merely this instinctive sense of form which usually saves him—and even when he is clowning—from making a fool of himself. What *is* wrong, and what his charm cannot conceal, is the use to which he is putting his gifts. It is a shock for one who very much enjoyed *The Daring Young Man on the Flying Trapeze* to go back to reading Saroyan in his latest collection, *The Trouble with Tigers*. There is nothing in the book so good as the best things in *The Flying Trapeze,* and there is a good deal that is not above the level of the facility of the daily columnist. In fact, a columnist is what William Saroyan seems sometimes in danger of becoming—the kind of columnist who depends entirely on a popular personality, the kind who never reads, who knows nothing in particular about anything, who merely turns on the tap every day and lets it run a column.

It is illuminating to compare this inferior stuff with the contents of a less well known collection published in California. This volume, *Three Times Three,* seems to have been consecrated to miscellaneous pieces which the author regards as not having quite come off. The result is something a great deal more interesting than the slick and rather thin stuff of *Tigers*. One of these pieces, **"The Living and the Dead,"** of which Saroyan rightly says that it is not so good as it ought to be, seems to me, miscarry though it does, one of the best things Saroyan has written. The scene with the Armenian grandmother after the departure of the money-collecting communist is of a startling and compelling beauty. This theme of the foreign-born asserting in modern America the virtues of an earlier civilization is one of the principal themes in Saroyan; whenever it appears—as in the short story called **"70,000 Assyrians"**—it takes his work out of the flat dimensions of the wiseguy watching life in the bar; and here it is sounded with poignant effect. This is followed by an admirable scene, in which the young man walks out on the street and sees a child crying at a window, and reflects that for "the children of the world eternally at the window, weeping at the strangeness of this place," where the Communist must always look forward to a perfected society of the future, where his grandmother must always look backward to a world that has gone with her youth and that could never really have been as she remembers it, it is natural for them to escape to the "even more disorderly universe" of drunkenness, a state sad enough in itself. But the whole subject, with its three motifs, required a little doing; and Saroyan, as he admits, did not do it. He would have had to be more serious, and he would have had to work the thing out with care; and he knows that he can get away with an almost infinite number of lesser pieces without having their second-rateness complained of.

Kipling said one very good thing about writing: "When you know what you can do, do something else." Saroyan *has* tackled in his plays something larger and more complicated than his stories; but these plays seem to be yielding to a temptation to turn into columns, too. The three which have been produced and published have many attractive and promising features in a vein a little like J. M. Barrie's; but George Jean Nathan, in the November *American Mercury* gives rather a disquieting account of no less than five more Saroyan plays which have already been tried out. There was a report that Mr. Nathan had been attempting to get Saroyan to acquaint himself with a few of the classics of the theatre, and it sounds as if the attempt had come to nought.

In the meantime, Saroyan goes on with his act, which is that of the unappreciated genius who is not afraid to stand up for his merits. This only obscures the issue. Most good artists begin by getting bad reviews; and Saroyan has been rather remarkably fortunate. Let him set his mind at rest. Everybody who is capable of responding to such things appreciates what is fine in his work. The fact that a number of people who do not know good theatrical writing from bad do not enjoy Saroyan is no excuse for the artist to neglect his craft. He will be judged not by his personality act or by his ability to get produced and published—

which he has proved to the point of absurdity; but by work that functions and lasts.

With his triumph there has crept into Saroyan's work an unwelcome suspicion of smugness. One had always had the feeling with his writing that, for all its amiability and charm, it has had behind it the pressure of a hard and hostile environment, which it has required courage to meet, and that this courage has taken the form of a debonair kidding humor and of a continual affirmation of the fundamental kindliness of people—a courage which, in moments when it is driven to its last resources and deepest sincerity, calls upon its assurance of the loyalties of straight and simple people—Armenians, Czechs, Greeks—surviving untouched by the hatreds of an abstract and complex world. In Saroyan the successful playwright, for whom this pressure has been partially relieved, there seems to be appearing an instinct to exploit this theme of loving-kindness and of the goodness and rightness of things; and there is perhaps a just perceptible philistinism. If Saroyan, in his latest play, *Love's Old Sweet Song,* has hit upon precisely the right way to make fun of *Time* magazine, he has, on the other hand, in his parody of *The Grapes of Wrath,* come close to the familiar complacency which declares that the unemployed are unemployable. This is the path that leads to Eddie Guest, William Lyon Phelps and Dr. Frank Crane; and let not Mr. Saroyan deceive himself: no writer has a charmed life.

Henry Seidel Canby   (essay date 1940)

SOURCE: "Armenian Picaresque," in *The Saturday Review of Literature,* Vol. 23, No. 10, December 28, 1940, p. 5.

[*Canby was a professor of English at Yale University and one of the founders of the* Saturday Review of Literature, *where he served as editor in chief from 1924 to 1936. He was the author of many books, including* The Short Story in English *(1909), a history of that genre which was long considered the standard text for college students. In the following review of* My Name Is Aram, *Canby hails the artistry of Saroyan's accounts of a young Armenian boy in America who experiences are strongly colored by his heritage.*]

I intend to be enthusiastic about this book, and so I should like to make it clear, first of all, that I am no bought-and-sold admirer of Mr. Saroyan. I didn't much like *The Daring Young Man on the Flying Trapeze,* thought it too clever by half, thought that Mr. Saroyan, on the stage and off it, was one of the characteristic products of Broadway bred to Hollywood out of (often) Chicago—precocious, smart-alecky, over-sophisticated, under-educated—a late Greek, Europeanized-Oriental production, sure to be amusing, and sure to be forgotten. I may have been right, or all wrong. Whatever I thought, *My Name Is Aram* has converted me to a belief in William Saroyan as a contributor to American literature and made me feel that I ought to reassess him from the beginning up.

For the book, in its highly original way, has linked itself to one of the most fertile lines of the American literary tradition; while at the same time adding a new element of the utmost importance for an imaginative study of America as America is. It is an Armenian book, charged with the Christianized orientalism of the Armenians, rich in the highly humorous contrasts of their ideal of living in a California environment, written with the naïve blend of spirituality and realistic cynicism that one finds in Arabic popular literature. And at the same time it is intensely American. It belongs on the same shelf with Aldrich's *Story of a Bad Boy,* with *Tom Sawyer* and *Huckleberry Finn* (particularly the latter), and with Tarkington's *Penrod.* One could write an essay on changing American *mores* in a small boy's America that has not, after all, so much changed, by comparing, chapter by chapter, **My Name Is Aram** and *Huckleberry Finn.* Mark Twain stuffed the prejudices, the folk lore, the freedom, and the ideals of the Mississippi valley into his books; Saroyan has depicted the pioneer generation of the native born of foreign stock, adjusting themselves to America with rude aggressiveness, and complex imaginations and immense energies—youngsters perfectly at home in a California that looks them over with shocked surprise. Both books give us types to think about, and if Saroyan works in shallower soil and keeps nearer the surface, he scarcely is less amusing and often as evocative of a boy's imagination.

The events in this little book are all boys' events: there are fishing parties, and the large adventures of Aram (who knew he could drive a car just by looking at it) with the millionaire Indian, who, being also an imperfectly adjusted American, took his immense pleasure in seeing a small boy have a good time. There is Aram's back-strapping experience when he mixed in an American love affair, his adventures with a country choir, his adventures on a first trip to a big city. They are all trivial in themselves, and perfectly delightful. But the solid Armenian life background, with its sets of values and its characters entirely different from what we think of as Californian, are not trivial; and the personality of this Americanizing Armenian who becomes under your eyes, as you read, a new race, puzzling his grandparents even more than his school teachers, is not trivial at all. I prefer the adjectives perceptive, humorous, imaginative, original. I should vote, indeed, for this story of an Armenian boyhood as the most truly American book of the year.

Edwin Berry Burgum   (essay date 1944)

SOURCE: "The Lonesome Young Man on the Flying Trapeze," in *The Virginia Quarterly Review,* Vol. 20, No. 3, Summer, 1944, pp. 392-403.

[*In the following excerpt, Burgum perceives that Saroyan's depiction of disillusioned, alienated Americans has evolved.*]

William Saroyan has reached the top of the ladder scarcely ten years after his first steps in learning to please the public. His achievement has not been the triumph of a vulgar opportunism. One can be sure (from reading "Sweeney in the Trees") that money has meant little to him; and if he has been tempted by fame, as his frequent references to his genius suggest, it is only that fame has seemed the proof of his being a likeable person. Writing has been the decoy by which he has sought to bring people closer to him. It has been the medium through which he could make more people the more intimately aware of his friendly spirit.

The mellowness of success has long since tranquillized his style, which had originally been less confident and more demanding. But it was clear from the start that he was a born writer. His first published pieces were the letters he wrote the editor of *Story* magazine informing him of his genius and his plans as a possible new contributor. Their impulsive mingling of truth and fantasy about himself whetted appetites that had been dulled by a surfeit of sophistication. Their request for recognition was an ingenuous and flattering assumption that the reader possessed both the good nature and the moral integrity to recognize and to further merit. It was obvious that a new comet had appeared on the literary horizon. At the same time it was agreeable to note that this rare personality was not portentous, as Thomas Wolfe had earlier proved, uncastrated and impossible to corral, but a whimsical animal, one eye already cocked on the halter. There were piquant and comforting signs of his not demanding to remain one of the eccentrics of literature. The note of desperation in his appeal was nothing more than a prayer for escape from such an isolation. Saroyan wrote about himself because his competence as a writer was the first problem to be gotten rid of. Until he had the assurance of being accepted, it hardly paid to bother with any more objective theme.

For the time being he felt very lonely. But because he was absorbed by his own depression, he could hardly realize how typical he was. For it was the era of the great depression. Other youths felt down and out because they wanted to work and could find no jobs. Saroyan felt friendless because his job was writing and nobody yet knew it since he had not yet started to publish. Like any other worker without experience, he had only the potentialities of his personality to offer. And he offered them boldly, because he was desperate, hesitantly because he was still unsure of himself, but winsomely because that was the way he was made.

But that was the way the average young American was reacting in the early thirties, when we were for the first time shaken loose from the certainties Americans had taken for granted since the founding of the Republic. The girls might turn to reading *Gone with the Wind* in every leisure hour for at least one winter, and fancy themselves back in the boom of the Reconstruction period. Boys like Saroyan failed to get beyond the title. They were beginning to doubt the promise of American life. Individual initiative, pell-mell for the pot of gold, was useless when the rainbow itself had disappeared. For the first time they were not sure of anything. Instead of the stable ground of the American way, they found themselves to their consternation on the flying trapeze. And it was revealed to them that that was where most Americans had always been without knowing it, only now it was swinging more wildly than ever. They were very anxious and lonely there, pitched this way and that by the changing course of events, the sudden closing of the banks and the unexpected opening of the WPA. They oscillated between depression and hope as belief spluttered out like a defective electric bulb. Such was the world of the young Saroyan. He was one of the crowd that had suddenly become aware of the helplessness of individualism and began groping for attachments they had not missed before. But all they found was a common frustration through which they could not break even to reach one another.

Saroyan's best expression of this profound change in the national temper bears the awkward title of **"1,2,3,4,5,6,7,8."** A young man is working for the telegraph company. It is a cruel, impersonal corporation, the employees of which are forbidden to use the wires for their personal consolation. Nevertheless, this youth on one dull Sunday does get a "hello" message from the main office where it turns out there is a girl as lonely as he. Previously, in the empty hours off duty, he had played Brahms on a squeaky portable Victrola in his rooming house, and escaped into the maternal embrace of art. But he had really enjoyed most a trifling dance hall tune of the day, which was so satisfactory an opium of the senses that he often hummed its theme to himself as "1,2,3,4,5,6,7,8." Indeed that was the best way to hear it, since his landlady objected to the racket set up by the machine, even though he always turned it off by eleven. Now, fortunately, he need no longer sing his tune. He can go walking in his spare time with this girl. And they fall in love because they are both so lonely working for the telegraph company. They plan the inevitable little house. But they love each other too much to admit they are only singing a new version of "1,2,3,4,5,6,7,8." They love each other too much for frankness. And so one Sunday when the telegraph machine fails to spin its usual message, the youth does not fear a breakdown in the efficient equipment of the company, but knows that his girl is no longer there. She has been unable to torment herself any longer with a bliss that can promise no fulfillment. So the youth discards his broken fantasy by giving his portable Victrola to his landlady, and seeks to keep in spiritual communion with his girl's demand for reality by leaving his job also and moving out of town into the certainty of the unknown.

So distraught was this youth that in telling his story he oscillates between the first and the third persons. Clearly he (or his creator who is identical with himself though the name is Romano) is trying to objectify his own unhappiness. He must project it from him into the third person because he cannot bear to carry it around with him and squarely acknowledge it as his own. The moving style of the story (which is, I think, the best Saroyan has written) is the esthetic reward of this psychological situation. Its nuance in expressing very real emotional conflicts results from the need to give them at least a superficial control. When Romano walks away from his conflicts by leaving the town behind, he also secures their temporary purgation.

For Saroyan the real purgation came with the success of his stories. From now on he writes habitually in the third person. If he uses the first, he is no longer conscious of describing himself, but only of following a customary device to make other people come more alive. In his later stories he is more objective than Hemingway. He feels no need to force inner conflicts to an issue, and project casehardened words like bullets in a slow-motion film. Saroyan's words were well oiled even in his misery. Now they flow as smoothly as though one of his Greek waiters were saying, "That's life," over a bottle of beer off duty. He tells his stories as such a waiter would tell them for himself, if he were more articulate, had an ear for the vivid sentence, and knew when to stop repeating himself. Such an artistry charms the respectable white-collar reader. It takes him into that hazardous land beyond the limits of his experience, and shows him he has nothing to be afraid of there. It permits his democratic idealism to resume its innocent play. For these new people of Saroyan's, who are unaware of being inspected, seem quite reconciled to their station, admirably frugal in making the best of anything. The stories of Saroyan, in his middle period, draw apart the curtain on the lower classes and show them to be no menace at all.

A deeper insight might demur that Saroyan's is a superficial view of our underprivileged masses, or that he presents them as they used to be before the CIO, or that he is concerned with only the detritus of the labor movement. But Saroyan has become a success, and the immediate response of his emotions, like a benevolent octopus, colors the world about him. His vision is reversed, and he sees that other people are really as good-natured as he has become. Since there must be some distinction between genius and the commonplace, he doubtless would agree with us that his new people are shallow. But that is a minor matter. They are well-intentioned, though sometimes stupid and generally happy-go-lucky. They may be reckless, but they have little of either money or surplus energy to spend. They are not material for either tragedy or psychoanalysis. With amazement (through one of those unexpected associations the analysts are fond of) one realizes that Saroyan has resurrected a less boisterous, a paler, version of the "good nigger" of Joel Harris and the old vaudeville stage in his easy-going, unskilled, white-faced workers, from the lower strata of our foreign born, Armenian, Greek, Italian. It turns out (from the point of view of theme as opposed to style) not to have been Wolfe who has been gelded, but Farrell and Maltz and proletarian literature generally. Even the fringe of racketeers is not fearsome as in Hemingway. They are only a little careless like the Mexicans in early Steinbeck. Their heart is not in the business, which, after all, is little more than a harmless game, played with the negligible small change of capitalism.

Formerly Saroyan's characters knew that they were lonely and homeless, and rebelled. Now they no longer know it because they have got used to substitutes for home and

Saroyan and his son, Aram, in 1953.

friendship in the casual habitual idle hours at the neighborhood bar or the chance acquaintances in the familiar diner. They are the "rejected children" of our psychologists, who compensate by making acquaintances easily and who come to feel at home in the instability of drift. If they lose one job, they will probably get another. If they fail to get another, they will probably find some similarly jobless girl to commiserate with them. If they squabble or blow off their mouths, the offense is tempered by its being the customary diction of their class and by the certainty that quarrels evaporate as quickly as they form. They take life as it comes, indifferent to our official codes of respectability (by which they seem never to have been infected in their grammar school education), believing tenderly in a romantic love they never see consummated, disciplined indeed by finding it to be another of life's failures, cultivating the simple garden in which they for the time being find themselves, as Voltaire advised. If they have their dreams, they are reconciled to knowing in advance that they will not come true. But they do not understand that what they take for reality (arms around some girl whose last name they do not know) is little more than a dream in relation to the destiny of the country. That greater world of ideals and advancement, caught from Sunday sermons and tabloid newspapers, has left no mark upon their con-sciousness. They accept it as another world from theirs. But its remoteness has deprived them of ambition and self-confidence. The apathy that cushions their good humor measures their vague awareness of their inability to grasp the traditional ideals of American manhood.

Yet it is this disillusionment on the periphery of consciousness that determines the mood of every one of these stories. It is what makes all the characters so talkative. They talk to keep the truth from themselves. It is what leads one story to spin a design of mock ecstasy out of the clichés of idealism in **"Ah Life, Ah Death, Ah Music, Ah France,"** and another to rekindle the flash in the pan of O. Henry's trick conclusions. It is what leaves most of the stories up in the air, concluded by a mere verbalism of hope ("Somehow or other she knew that he would get a piano someday, and everything else too"), or by a verbalism of pathos ("Go ahead and laugh. What else can you do") in a world where everything changes and nothing concludes. Rarely, as in **"The La Salle Hotel in Chicago,"** the buried resentments break through the defenses that had become habitual. Saroyan's style then becomes hysterical, his emergent thoughts anarchistic, but the end is the same. The anarchist, like a true Saroyan character, walks away from the difficult situation, and the other men ask, "What the hell was he shouting about anyway?" If one must think, it is better to forget the future, leave the present, and remember **"The Warm Quiet Valley of Home."** With a little beer and an old Ford, it can sometimes be done. Once there, the irresponsible joy and the unconfirmed dreams of childhood return to wipe out any possibility of mature perception. And one loses there, too, even the dubious perspective of irony when the old folks reconstruct once more their old illusion of the warmer, more distant home in Armenia. Veneration for the dead dim heroes of medieval Armenia distills a peace which passes the feeble compensations of daily life. It is something from which one is not forced to walk away.

Joseph Remenyi   (essay date 1944)

SOURCE: "William Saroyan: A Portrait," in *College English,* Vol. 6, No. 2, November, 1944, pp. 92-100.

[*In the following essay, Remenyi offers a portrait of Saroyan, emphasizing the influence his character and predilections had on his writing.*]

To create, stated Henrik Ibsen, means to set judgment upon one's self. This romantic definition of creativeness does not cripple the need of classical balance. By applying Ibsen's definition of creativeness, William Saroyan's works explain much of himself. They reveal an extrovert using writing as a means for his most intense expression; thus he can keep pace with a pragmatic and incongruous world which is rather indifferent to the carefree design of an imaginative fervor. Born thirty-five years ago in the Fresno section of California, in a home close to a vineyard district, and brought up in Armenian immigrant surroundings, possessing a background that knew strangeness, sorrow, poverty, and joy, his growth was conditioned by emotions and experiences which, without the assistance of his native tenderness, combined with a religious heritage, might have made him a clever cynic in an age of elbow-philosophy and unscrupulous indirectness. Even so, his dexterity and boisterous temper sometimes bring him to the level of destiny's court jester or to that of an emotional materialist of the moment; and the hullabaloo or the sheer claptrap of his art and the fact that he is likely to be the Baron Münchhausen of intimate pleasures strengthen one's doubt in his absolute sincerity. His fertile though repetitive imagination should be exhausting to himself; he never runs the risk of being objective. His positive attitude is related to the glory of living. The tone of many of his sketches echoes the voice of the traditional European *feuilleton*; the kind of sketchy short story that Continental newspapers used to publish for the superficial inspiration and entertainment of the readers. Saroyan's "modernity" does not make them less trivial. On the other hand, their suggestiveness makes them artistically somewhat more authentic, though not necessarily more genuine. For example, in one of his better stories, entitled **"The Pomegranate Trees,"** one encounters the following dialogue:

Pomegranates, my uncle said, are practically unknown in this country.

Is that all you're going to plant? I said.

I have in mind, my uncle said, planting several other kinds of trees.

Peach trees? I said.

About ten acres, my uncle said.

How about apricots? I said. . . .

This is, indeed, mannerism with the pretense of naturalness. The "I said" tires one with the same results with which a snob of simplicity ceases to be funny after a certain time. Saroyan suggests a verbal game that makes fun of unaffectedness.

From all this, as a general statement, what conclusion should one reach as to the outstanding traits of this writer? He is an overrated or belittled romanticist; an actor, sometimes a ham actor, impressed with his own histrionic emotionalism, his own parody, but also an uplifter, a moralist who does not dare to preach. He rationalizes the chill of life with a deceiving tenderness; it is like introducing an oriental lantern into an occidental darkness. In his book entitled *The Modern Short Story,* the English writer H. E. Bates aptly states: "Saroyan is the Eastern carpet-seller in a foreign country armed with the gift of the gab, a packet of psychological conjuring tricks, and a bunch of phoney cotton carpets from which, unexpectedly, he now and then produces a genuine Ispahan." Edmund Wilson in his "The Boys in the Back Room" recognizes the illusionism of Saroyan, in the following manner: "Saroyan takes you to the bar, and he creates for you there a world which is the way the world would be if it conformed to the feelings instilled by drinks." There is warmth in this writer, a communicative emotional heat. Yet his enthusiasm for goodness and sweetness and spiritual nobility is coupled with a confusing irony—his most important gun against a conventional world. Sometimes he has a discerning eyesight; whatever foresight he has it is that of the self-advertiser, the clowning funmaker whose objective seems to compel a colorless and cruel world to succumb to the joyfulness and ingeniousness of a man by the name of William Saroyan.

In referring to Saroyan's romanticism, one is right in asking whether it is exciting because of its artistic merit or because of its too often dwarfish originality. He does not give the impression of an uprooted writer; yet he does not give the impression that he is a writer with roots. His assumed world in which his contrived characters move is only seemingly unassuming. A grimace is likely to be an aggressive defense mechanism. His gadabout sensitiveness seems the godchild of pride which uses humility and irony for self-realization. He is the Jacobin who plots not against an existing government but against a life that postpones joy and happiness. In his play, *The Time of Your Life,* the following is said: "In the time of your life, live so that in that good time there shall be no ugliness or death for yourself or for any life your life touches." He speaks like a holy Epicurean, and it is important to see the physiognomy of the oppressed spirit in these words; of the spirit that inherited memories of persecution and humiliation, and in whom the reality of freedom (with all its American trimmings) initiated the kind of courage that made him fall in love with life as he thinks it should be lived. He goes to extremes of affirmation, because he thinks that current life in its negation of happiness is even more extreme. His maudlin or nervy infallibility is manifested in glibly expressed advices that he likes to offer to people. It is like playing dice with the obvious. In the postscript of his *Three Plays,* entitled "The One Easy Lesson," Saroyan uses the following cheerful plain talk: "Eat simple food and drink the kind of liquor you seem to like most, and if you see a pretty face, smile and let her know there's still love of poetry in the world. Don't study the books, unless you are still under twenty. If you are under twenty, study *all* the books, but don't forget yourself." One could quote pages from other writings of Saroyan which are as adolescent in their pretentiousness; their dominant characteristics are generalities which show about as much wisdom as if some one would say that water is wet. This reminds me of the diluting method of this writer; there are few "best-seller" writers anywhere who can make of a thin plot or of a superficial situation a story or a situation of "meaning" in the same manner as it is done by Saroyan. He has a rather quantitative than qualitative talent; too frequently it seems like a travesty of vitality.

Saroyan's romantic outlook consists of three salient motives and manifestations. There is a puzzling Eastern inheritance related to his family, to his childhood, and indirectly to immigrant life in general; there is his definite relationship to our American civilization, as an American without the trace of a foreign accent; and there is his narcissism, his lollipop emotionalism, and his ironic shrewdness which seems the acid test of his immunity to theories, to class discrimination, and to other cumbersome interferences of a practical world. Unfortunately, there is little progress in the maturing judgment of this writer; there is too much disregard of good taste as an artistic and psychological attribute; there is childish indifference to greatness in others, for example, by naming his first novel *The Human Comedy,* considering what this title means to Balzac.

William Saroyan, a cross-breeding of sincerity and twistedness, is especially significant as a sentimentalist in comparison with his American contemporaries who are "hard-boiled" writers. Sherwood Anderson's grotesque sense of intimacy affected him; but today's writers of nonconforming evil and ruthlessness seem outside the orbit of his art. Critics have pointed out that Saroyan's uncompromising attitude about the goodness of human nature is his most conspicuous romantic trait. Even his nonsense sometimes suggests a tender and gentle sense. His affinity with common humanity shows that a wounded heart can make evil useless and goodness useful.

The paradoxical Saroyan understands the activity of silence; he understands how important truisms are in the life of little people. In this respect he implies some relationship to Chekhov, with the difference, however, that the Russian writer represents maturity in the very best sense of the word, whereas Saroyan's interest in oversimplified psychology shows his incurable adherence to a youthful storm-and-stress level of the mind. Nevertheless, here and there, he knows how to articulate silence in an almost musical sense, indicating sensitiveness that is moving in its effect. For instance, in his sketch entitled **"And Man,"** one meets a faithful expression of youthful loneliness. Of course, by its very nature, a quotation is incomplete in relation to the complete impression of a work of art; yet the following paragraph should prove Saroyan's aptitude for articulating silence.

> During the summer I sometimes stopped suddenly before a mirror to look at myself, and after a moment I would turn away, feeling disgusted with my ugliness, worrying about it. I couldn't understand how it was that I looked utterly unlike what I imagined myself to be. In my mind I had another face, a finer, a more subtle and dignified expression, but in the mirror I could see the real reflection of myself, and I could see that it was ugly, thick, bony, and coarse. I thought it was something finer, I used to say to myself. I hadn't bothered before about looking at myself. I had thought that I knew precisely how I looked, and the truth distressed me, making me ashamed. Afterwards I stopped caring. I am ugly, I said. I know I am ugly. But it is only my face.

The sketch begins with the admission that the confessor was fifteen and ends with the following utterance of self-mastery:

> I had seen the universe, quietly in the emptiness, secret, and I had revealed it to itself, giving it meaning and grace and the truth that could come only from the thought and energy of man, and the truth was man, myself, moment after moment, and man, century after century, and man, and the face of God in man, and the sound of the laughter of man in the vastness of the secret, and the sound of his weeping in the darkness of it, and the truth was myself and I was man.

He learned "to walk through the silence of the earth," and, in fairness to the author, it must be said that in this sketch and in some others his cultivated sentimentality functioned with emotional authenticity and made of his self-centeredness, of a purely human fact, an artistic reality. But even these citations fail to reveal a flawless artist; unnecessary words hunt each other, and their pathos violates creative discipline, and they also suggest a forced note of frankness.

Often his romanticism echoes up-to-date bohemianism; he is lavish in his romantic identification with those who ridicule life's gloom with love. Murger's Rodolphe and Mimi reappear in the world of an American *avant garde* writer; this writer of uncritical impulses is less "modern" than an automobile or an airplane, despite the confusion that he caused on the American stage and on the American literary market place and despite his flirtation with expressionism and surrealism.

Saroyan is a prolific writer. He is passionately in love with publicity, with humanity, and with himself. A zigzag brightness of the spirit illuminates the output of his writings; sometimes it is intoxicating brightness. Yet he writes too much; too much sunshine makes clouds desirable. Too much twinkling of the eye makes one wonder whether one can see. Of the seventy-one stories and sketches in **Inhale and Exhale,** many are nothing but extended aphorisms and parables. He simplifies moods or situations; but that is precisely what epigrams do. He does not seem to know the difference between slapstick comedy and real mirth; his lack of self-criticism might be interrelated to his lack of composition. His drifting imagination co-operates with the acrobatic gleams of self-consciousness; his spontaneity is limited because of a problematical reasoning intelligence. The burlesque performance of his writing is often pointless because there is no focusing intelligence to support it. He uses the method of hackney originality; after writing a short story, he transforms it into a one-act play and finally into a lengthy play. Other writers did this too; Arthur Schnitzler, for instance, Anatole France, and Luigi Pirandello. As a matter of fact, it does not indicate inferior inventiveness because a writer uses a theme in various genre; in Saroyan's case, however, so much writing is but subtle or shouting bluff. It does not result from the writer's incapacity to do a better job but from the same psychology that one finds in ardent gossipers; even without rumors they cannot stop talking. Saroyan is gossiping about goodness, and this seems the main reason why he monopolizes the publishing and theatrical world with an uncritical gusto.

The prolificness of Saroyan and his writing technique imply an unstableness, owing to the fact that he is the son of immigrant parents. Saroyan is neither a pessimist nor an optimist. He is the symbol of a conflict conquered by self-centered and projected happiness, but unconquered in the tiring effort of "belonging" externally to the American world. The happiness that he consciously and spontaneously spreads prevents him from being a searcher of truth in a philosophical sense; but the very fact that he refers to his Armenian origin in a willy-nilly manner, the very fact that his imaginative expressions had to accept an American coloring in order to be recognized as American contributions to literature, signifies the same kind of self-consciousness that one has when one wears a new suit for the first time. Saroyan is not class-conscious, but he is conscious of an America that was a host to his parents, who were Armenian immigrants. He wants to have the ease and freedom of an American host; hence the hospitality of his too numerous publications and plays, and hence the zeal to be unique, to be original, to be interesting even in manner, which is, after all, the technique of substance. He is, indeed, like a host who entertains his guests with all sorts of tricks because he is afraid they might leave his place too soon.

The pity and absurdity that emanate from his sketches, stories, and plays seem to require the kind of verbal pyrotechnics which critics and the public associate with his art. I said that Saroyan is not uprooted but that he has no roots either. He is creating his own roots while he creates his own art. Probably it is due to this immense task that there is scarcely ideological or artistic growth in his work. The arabesque characteristics of Knut Hamsun's *Hunger* or the mosaic richness of the early stories of Maxim Gorki were significant substantial and technical phases in the evolution of these writers. But the spiritual naïveté and craftiness of Saroyan and his experimentalist technique, his perspective as an artist of writing, have not changed very much since *The Daring Young Man on the Flying Trapeze* appeared, and this was in the year 1934. What was then youthful remained youthful; what was artistically ripe remained artistically ripe; what was irritating remained irritating; and what was sophomoric and meaningless remained so.

Because Saroyan is an artist, though a minor one, in his indignation against an ugly world and in his attachment to goodness he does not follow the directive of sentimental righteousness. He is not a crusader; he is essentially an unchained lyricist (not a poet), who cannot dismiss the cruelty of the world with a light gesture and who cannot accept the aberrations of politicians and other poker-faced pillars of society as inevitable debaucheries of human fate. He sees goodness from the inside. It is mobile goodness; its energy is not that of an ostentatious or hysterical reformer but that of a soul recognizing beauty in *Homo sapiens*. Children and adults, dreamers and failures of humanity, raconteurs and timid people, tramps, "wise guys" and practical citizens, sailors, saloon-keepers, and escapists, live in this merry-go-round world of Saroyan. His sensibilities are not complicated; his judgment is an imaginative sequel to a commonplace existence. His purposeful vagueness has occasionally the charm of measured spontaneousness and playfulness.

Saroyan often stands on his head and thus looks at the world; he can be droll and dull, but it is really not difficult to understand him. He may not be able to suggest everything he would like to suggest; this improviser of stories and plays may not be strong in structure-building, but he offers warmth and color that is sometimes trustworthy. In his notes about his plays he says: "The message of each play comes from the world—which the writer regards as the only and therefore the best place known to man. The comedy, tragedy, absurdity and nobility of these plays come from people whom the author regards as beautiful." One may argue about this omnipotent recognition of beauty in human nature, but one cannot deny the writer's ability to make of his ethics the kind of psychological experience which, precisely because of its meagerness of ideas and because of its temperamental glow, might give the movies an opportunity to supply the audiences with better pictures. Audiences, like women, enjoy flattery; Saroyan's flattery has at least a certain artistic quality.

He shares his subjectivity with everybody; he can talk in terms of the people though he talks about himself. **"The Daring Young Man on the Flying Trapeze"** is the story of a poverty-stricken young writer; what makes him distinct is his relationship to Saroyan, his appealing Armenian rambling in an American metropolitan community. It is rather difficult to pick a significant part from the pensive and wild sentences of this story, but this should suffice:

> He rose in an elevator to the seventh floor, moved down a hall, and, opening a door, walked into the office of an employment agency. Already there were two dozen young men in the place; he found a corner where he stood waiting his turn to be interviewed. At length he was granted this great privilege and was questioned by a thin, scatterbrained miss of fifty.

> Now tell me, she said; what can you do?

> He was embarrassed. I can write, he said pathetically.

> You mean your penmanship is good? Is that it? said the elderly maiden.

> Well, yes, he replied. But I mean that I can write.

> Write what? said the miss, almost with anger.

> Prose, he said simply.

> There was a pause. At last the lady said:

> Can you use a typewriter?

> Of course, said the young man.

> All right, went on the miss, we have your address; we will get in touch with you. There is nothing this morning, nothing at all.

In his collections of stories and sketches, in *Inhale and Exhale; Peace, It's Wonderful; Love, Here Is My Hat; Little Children; Three Times Three; The Trouble with Tigers,* there is much poor, downright bad material. However, some of his short romantic stories, despite the silly explanatory notes of the writer, reach the readers' hearts. They are presumptuous, they are screwy, they have a kidding quality, they are lively. Even their emptiness seems to be hunting for feeling.

Saroyan has an aptitude for unexpected titles. Women's hats, sometimes, make their heads interesting. It has been said that if Coleridge's *The Ancient Mariner* had been called *The Old Sailor,* the fame of the poem might have suffered. Saroyan's inclination for unusual titles is undeniable. His *My Name Is Aram,* a collection of fourteen stories and sketches, is partly in demand because of the intriguing title of the book. The stories, similarly to other stories of Saroyan, deal with boyhood memories, with relatives, but also with friends and strangers. The environment of the tales is the Armenian district in Fresno, California. In these stories Saroyan shows us fools and practical people, distorted and delightful characters. The following "confession" is revealing: "As to whether or not the writer himself is Aram Garoghlanian, the writer cannot very well say. He will, however, say, that he is not, certainly *not,* Aram Garoghlanian." This teasing statement seems organically related to the "practical joker" in Saroyan.

If he would only learn how to revise his work. This applies to his first novel, *The Human Comedy* (this time he failed as an expert in catchy titles), as well as to his plays. Saroyan's pleasure in having written *The Human Comedy* is evident on every page. It is the wartime story of a California family by the name of Macauley. The adults and the children of the family are, in a psychological sense, known to the reader from earlier stories. Mrs. Macauley, Homer, who at the age of fourteen is very much in the stream of life, his boss, the manager of the telegraph office, the operator, Grogan, Ulysses, the four-year-old brother of Homer, and the rest of the characters are convincingly human. There is *deus ex machina* clumsiness in the novel; there are defects that defeat the purpose of coherence and psychological inevitableness; it is a sketchy novel, humorous, gentle, though on the border line of sentimentality, in parts definitely trite.

His plays, the one-acts and the longer ones, are the kind of dramas and comedies that one cannot sit through quietly; one either leaves the theater or is grateful for a queer and amusing evening. His *Razzle Dazzle* volume contains sixteen short plays, with an introductory note by the writer. Lope de Vega wrote over a thousand plays, but most of them were rejected by posterity. Saroyan has to watch his prolificness. His best plays are published in two volumes, entitled *Three Plays: First Series* and *Three Plays: Second Series,* The final evaluation of *My Heart's in the Highlands,* of *The Time of Your Life,* or of *The Beautiful People* has not been made. There are critics who consider Saroyan's plays cockeyed or extravagant; others consider them whimsical, lovable, extraordinary. In my opinion there is a great deal of affected honesty and obscureness in these plays; but the good qualities of Saroyan are also observable. Some of the plays seem mere attempts at newness—*épater le bourgeois* in twentieth-century America. In the Preface to *The Time of Your Life* Saroyan proclaims this credo: "A play is a world, with its own inhabitants and its own laws and its own values." How romantic a definition! It almost suggests the caricature of an aesthetic creed because it has been so often stated.

In summing up the artistic and psychological significance of William Saroyan, it seems logical to ask whether his preoccupation with singing, loving, bustling common sense, and nonsense indicates a real concern with the fundamentals of human nature. He is still a young man; this broadcaster of human sentiments and whims is still principally a promise rather than a realization, though part of his work has some creative merit. Despite the mobility of his spirit, he has a static idiom; despite his strongly personal tone, he suggests universal appeal, for which he has not as yet found his form. Will he find it? I do not say that he should polish his expression, but I would say that he should find his expression. For the time being he has not found it. Is he searching for it, or is he satisfied with the ease with which moods dance on the floor of his imagination?

He must learn how to grow up without betraying his childlike wonderments. He is in the army now; his virginal conceit of the heart might be affected by it, and I mean favorably. Inasmuch as the army means discipline, it is possible that this experience will also generate in him the need of artistic discipline. Of course, it is possible that in his deepest self Saroyan always recognized the need of creative discipline but that he lacked the ability to make use of this awareness. Leibnitz' *Best World of All Existing Worlds* induced Voltaire to write *Candide*; Saroyan is not Voltaire, neither is he Ella Wheeler Wilcox, but he is an agent of artistic sensibilities which sometimes permit him to reach the object of a more or less reliable creative expression.

Sic itur ad astra. Vergil's path to greatness seems unknown to him; yet he is eager to examine imponderables in his own fashion, therefore in harmony with that classical tradition of literature which sacrifices temporariness for eternal verities. In his mind he is an Armenian regionalist, born and reared in California, enjoying the wide horizons of the American scene; throughout his work one senses the potential qualities of a romantic sensibility, reduced, however, to the experience of exaggerated and exaggerating self-love which confuses and interferes when the detachment of creative understanding and conscientiousness is required.

Dan S. Norton   (essay date 1944)

SOURCE: "Mr. Saroyan—Still His Own Hero," in *The New York Times Book Review,* November 19, 1944, pp. 3, 36.

[*In the following review, Norton finds the stories in* Dear Baby *trite.*]

William Saroyan has had another affair with his heart, and he calls the little one ***Dear Baby***. It is somewhat underweight (117 pages) and not so lusty as the others have been, but it's a Saroyan, all right. It has the smile on its lips, the lump in its throat, the tear in its eye, and the bag full of tricks—the same old tricks.

The twenty pieces in ***Dear Baby*** have been written over a period of ten years. The earliest was published in 1935, the year after Saroyan made the first public announcement of his genius in ***The Daring Young Man on the Flying Trapeze***. But the book is no publisher's potpourri of things left over after a young writer went to war. On the contrary, it is a special Saroyan potpourri, with each piece newly revised and some retitled. Probably what Saroyan says of one of the sketches (he is disguised, at the moment, as a bald-headed man named Donald Kennebec who has just written the sketch) is also his opinion of the book: "I feel that I have effectively utilized the material; that I have shaped it into a work which, if anything, will enhance my already considerable fame."

While once again Saroyan holds the mirror up to Saroyan, perhaps we can discover what makes him famous. It might be his versatility. In a typical collection like ***Dear Baby*** he offers, in addition to several short stories, a dissertation on the innocence of grapes, a travelogue, a humorous

and mystical essay, a fable about a financial mouse, a number of symbolic sketches (choose your own symbols), and five rhapsodic soliloquies. And Saroyan is not only versatile but also prolific. His performance has been as various as vaudeville and almost as continuous as the movies.

Yet his fecundity and his versatility are not in themselves the reasons for his fame. In spite of the fact that he has written a great deal, he is really not a writer but a character. I don't mean someone in a book or play (except of course a Saroyan book or play); I mean someone who is called a character by other people. We Americans are so fond of this kind of character that although we prefer a genuine one like Brigham Young, we are willing to accept a synthetic one like Salvador Dali.

Instead of using his books to show us the world, Saroyan has used them to invent a character for himself. That is why most of the people who read ***Dear Baby*** will be looking for Saroyan rather than stories, and that is why all the lyric pieces in the book are about Saroyan in the grip of emotion, not about the emotion that grips Saroyan. The writer of successful lyrics gives his feelings form so that they live outside himself. Saroyan's rhapsodic soliloquies are mere lumps of consciousness, poked here and there in a tentative way but not shaped into anything clear and permanent. They are apt to be muddy Wordsworth (**"How It Is to Be"**) or inchoate Keats (**"The Hummingbird That Lived through Winter"**).

Now, as long as some people take pleasure in a phenomenon like Lucius Beebe, I see no reason why Saroyan should be discouraged from being a character, since that is what he wants to be. But while his fame increases, his interesting talent as a writer is obscured. If, for example, it were not part of his act to be the boy philosopher who presents a sentimental education in every paragraph, the title story in ***Dear Baby*** might not be an unhappy marriage between Hemingway and *Good Housekeeping,* and **"Sailing down the Chesapeake"** might be an excellent piece of fiction.

But perhaps it is unfair to criticize ***Dear Baby*** in this fashion. If we must judge it according to the artist's intention, we must judge it as a portrait of the artist. In this book Saroyan has not matured, but he has solidified. Without changing, he has become what he aspired to be. First of all he is conscientiously unpredictable. Because every genius is a paradox, Saroyan has worked for eleven years to be accepted as the arcane Armenian, and in ***Dear Baby*** (once again in the character of Donald Kennebec) he celebrates his partial success: "I have at times been spoken of by certain women who follow the course of contemporary literature as enigmatic and unpredictable, but after all I am a writer."

This paradoxical genius is permanently young, and he is careful to show all the contempt of youth for rules and matters of fact. "Now, if hummingbirds come into the world through some other means than eggs," he says, "I ask the reader to forgive me. The only thing I know about Agass

Agasig Agassig Agazig (well, the great American naturalist) is that he once studied turtle eggs.". . . The fact that
Saroyan has been playing this same disarming trick ever
since he started writing may cause some readers to be less
amused than they were eleven years ago. But one can't be
sure. Many of us like a trick first because it is novel and
thereafter because we know what to expect. If this weren't
true, what would happen to radio comedians?

Behind the double talk and the boyish pranks and the
razzle-dazzle is the real Saroyan, the cosmic kid. While
he is pulling our hat down over our eyes he is whispering
the secret of the universe in our ears. There's a message
in his madness, and the message is that life is love and
that wisdom belongs to the heart. In *Love, Here Is My
Hat,* an early Saroyan collection, the boy and girl of one
of the stories went to a movie. "It was a lousy movie, and
the idea was to prove that love and love alone is what the
world is seeking. So it was a good movie too. You could
tell how much of it was lousy: the rest of it was good: it
was people wanting to be together, so it was good."

This description fits Saroyan's own Hollywood valentine,
The Human Comedy, and *Dear Baby* also, but it over-
looks one vital point. In a story or play or movie the idea
cannot be separated from its expression. The idea is false
if it is presented falsely. That's the trouble with the message from the daring young seer with the sibylline leaves.
It is not profound and simple; it is cheap and simplified.

If you are interested in Saroyan, you will find him in *Dear
Baby*. But if you are interested in honest fiction, *Dear
Baby* can't give you anything but love—the kind you can
get for a nickel from any juke box.

William Peden   (essay date 1950)

SOURCE: "Saroyan with Trumpet & Tremolo," in *The
Saturday Review of Literature,* Vol. 33, No. 4, February
4, 1950, pp. 15-16.

[*Peden is an American critic and educator who has written extensively on the American short story and on such
American historical figures as Thomas Jefferson and John
Quincy Adams. In the following review of* The Assyrian,
and Other Stories, *he states that the title story is respectable, though the remaining pieces are such that "even
[Saroyan's] most ardent admirers are likely to be quite
unhappy."*]

William Saroyan's contribution to the American short story is a considerable one indeed. He brought to the American literary scene freshness of vision, simplicity, spontaneity, and gaiety. He possessed a sympathetic understanding of little people, a distinctly personal literary style, and
a contagious sense of humor. He exerted a beneficial influence against the pretentious, the overwritten, the too-
fancily-plotted short story. Like Mark Twain, he opened
the windows and aired the room at a time when fresh air
was badly needed.

Saroyan at his least successful, however, can be very, very
inadequate, and his newest collection of short stories [*The
Assyrian, and Other Stories*] is one about which even his
most ardent admirers are likely to be quite unhappy. It
seems safe to venture that most of these pieces would
never have seen print had their author been Joe Doakes
rather than William Saroyan. Most of these short stories,
to put the matter simply, are not very good.

The Assyrian is a long piece of work, almost a novelette,
about a famous American writer of Assyrian descent who
at fifty is washed up, dying on his feet, confronted and
terrified by loneliness, torn by the conflicting demands of
a Dickensian sentimentality and a bleak cynicism. *The
Assyrian* attempts to analyze the problem of the artist as
a man of good will in a world he never made or is incapable of understanding. It tries to bridge the uncrossable
gap separating the protagonist's concept of what life ought
to be and the way his life has been lived. This is a big
theme, of course, one with which the intellectual has wres-
tled for centuries. As Saroyan says in his introduction,
The Assyrian is the one story in the collection which really
takes a chance, the story Saroyan needed most to write.
But it is too diffused, too episodic, too much enmired in
talk to be successful as a short story. It is, however, deserving of respect.

Unfortunately, the same thing cannot be said of most of
the others. Two or three stories, specifically **"The Pars-
ley Garden"** and **"The Theological Student,"** show flashes of Saroyan's insight and narrative deftness. They tend,
however, to be dwarfed by items such as **"The Third Day
After Christmas,"** a tale of a warmhearted barkeep and
a homeless waif, which are characterized by a boozy sentimentality far removed from genuine emotion. Others, like
"The Poet at Home," tend to be unpleasantly cute, cute
to the point of erecting a very high wall between the story
and all but the most pixieish reader.

This collection includes an essay on writing which is more
interesting than most of the fiction it introduces. "The
Writer on the Writing" is primarily an engaging account
of how and when some of the stories came to be written,
of how much money they made or failed to make. More
important are Saroyan's remarks on writing as an art which
can be gladly, happily achieved and still be good art, or
his belief in the necessity for writing and the importance
of the artist in society. At times sincere and modest, at
times flippant and arrogant, this essay encourages one to
believe that Saroyan, unlike the Assyrian, is very far from
finished, has not really "had it," after all.

William Peden   (essay date 1956)

SOURCE: "Saroyan Parade," in *The New York Times Book
Review,* February 19, 1956, p. 26.

[*In the following review, Peden judges the stories of* Love
highly uneven in quality.]

Love consists of some thirty short stories and narrative sketches originally issued in magazines ranging from *Story* and the *Yale Review* to the *Pasadena Junior College Magazine*. This collection again illustrates the fact that Saroyan still tends to be his own worst literary enemy. The best of these stories are very good, but others are quite the opposite.

At its best a Saroyan story is a delight—fresh, vigorous and perceptive. He has always been extremely successful in depicting children; several of these pieces possess all the warmth, insight and humor which made *My Name Is Aram* so notable. Equally recognizable as a Saroyan type is the ubiquitous "young writer seeking material for a tale." We find this character betting his last dollar on a worthless horse, or selling his beloved phonograph records because "being of the time, I wanted money"; in a more pensive mood he reflects upon death while gazing at some marathon dancers, or rents an apartment for a beautiful (and pregnant) young woman he happens to meet one day on a street corner.

This Saroyan character can utter both profound truth or nonsense out of either corner of his mouth. A man of surging emotions, he erupts into violence or dissolves into self-pity with equal alacrity. Behind everything he sees decay, loneliness and death; but, in the meantime, there are love and music and the miracle of life. Saroyan's adults, like his children, are always passionately alive.

Any kind of extreme individuality, however, when not kept under control, is likely to degenerate into eccentricity and eventually becomes a bore. Some of the stories in *Love* are so mannered or so repetitious as to be almost intolerable. Even Saroyan's most sympathetic readers may regret the inclusion of stories such as **"Solemn Advice to a Young Man About to Accept Undertaking as a Profession"** or **"Jim Pemberton and His Boy Trigger."** These are not only mediocre stories; they are very bad Saroyan.

Margaret Bedrosian   (essay date 1982)

SOURCE: "William Saroyan and the Family Matter," in *MELUS*, Vol. 9, No. 4, Winter II, 1982, pp. 13-24.

[*In the following excerpt, Bedrosian examines the sense of waning community felt by ethnic individuals in Saroyan's fiction.*]

In one of his numerous autobiographies, William Saroyan once wrote of his dead father's failure to express the emotional truth of his life through aborted literary attempts. Now, over a year after his own death, these words offer one of the aptest commentaries on Saroyan's writing as well:

> He hadn't made it. But as if as a special favor to me he had kept a record of it, of the failure, the loss, and the finality. . . .

In a sense the writing was my own, and I didn't like it. It just wasn't tough enough for the truth of us, of this world, and I wished it had been.

What we discover in the work of this most famous and prolific of Armenian-American writers is a lifelong tension between the forces of good-humored acceptance and the more insistent voice of his own experience as the orphaned son of an Armenian immigrant. For as Saroyan frequently informs his readers, his father didn't do him any favor by dying of an appendicitis attack when the boy was only three. Subsequently his mother was forced to find work as a live-in maid and placed her four children in a San Francisco orphanage, where for the next five years William's chief exposure to family and ethnicity depended on occasional weekend picnics overlooking the Bay. It was only after this initial uprooting that he came to what critic Howard Floan has identified [in *William Saroyan*] as his "best materials," "Fresno, home, family, and difference." Instinctively relating his own knowledge of homelessness to his first encounter with Armenian music, Saroyan found the sources of a resilient philosophy:

> It was different. Even so, wasn't it mine even more than any other song I had ever heard or had ever whistled? Wasn't it more *deeply* mine? It *seemed* to be. *Well, walk, walk, walk, walk, wounded homeless, unkillable homeless, well, walk, walk, walk, walk.*

This passage is pivotal in understanding Saroyan's relationship to his ethnic group, an affinity based less on the shared values of communal life than the common experience of "wounded homelessness," of belonging to a dying race, of having been abandoned by one's father into a world devoid of security and rest.

This was an attitude he had portrayed movingly in his 1934 short story, **"Seventy Thousand Assyrians."** Here Saroyan depicts the Assyrians as the one ethnic group whose claim to world attention fell even below that of the Armenians, a people who can't "even dream any more" about an independent existence as Arabs kill them piecemeal on their native grounds and intermarriage subverts their distinctive identity in America. The moral of this bittersweet tale is that the fragility of his national ties has freed the humble Assyrian barber to join the race of man, "the part that massacre does not destroy." Stripped of any chauvinistic pride, Theodore Badal is "himself seventy thousand Assyrians and seventy million Assyrians, himself Assyria, and man, standing in a barber shop, in San Francisco, in 1933, and being, still, himself, the whole race." But though the punctuated cadence ends this story on a note of proud self-sufficiency, we have to heed Saroyan's earlier caution to the reader: "Readers of Sherwood Anderson will begin to understand what I am saying after a while; they will know that my laughter is rather sad."

It is true. Saroyan's laughter *is* sad, because the "tougher truth" of his family's and ethnic group's struggles stands at the back of his celebrations of earthy Armenian homelife, where flat bread and sun ripened grapes may nurture individual quests into a chancy world, but can't lighten the journey. Throughout, the thrust of Saroyan's life and art came from a radical existentialism, isolated from communal solace. It was an orphan's creed, sinewy and streetwise, marbled with a rigidity that rejects self-pity and forgives slowly.

The sharp edges of this worldview emerge most painfully in three works of fiction Saroyan wrote in mid-career in the early 1950s: a novella entitled *The Assyrian,* and two novels, *Rock Wagram* and *The Laughing Matter.* Expressed with increasing intensity through these works is the sense that the melancholy that plagues the "dying race"—whether Armenian or otherwise—has seeped into the protagonist's soul, where it can only find a healthy outlet in swift motion—flying, gambling, racing. When at rest, the main character finds himself in spiritual limbo, unable to adopt the ethos of his ancestors and equally incapable of creating a viable personal code. Thus in the middle of his writing career Saroyan returned to the theme of his earliest short story, **"The Daring Young Man on the Flying Trapeze"** (1933), in which the young man's refusal to be saved from starvation by the Salvation Army coupled with his steady motion to the end forms his chief claim to heroism. But, whereas the daring young man was only responsible for his own life, the middle-aged protagonists of the later period face crises of family life, where the models of their ethnic past remind them of their domestic shortcomings. With each successive work, we find the ethnic group serving a dual function, not only mirroring the central character's spiritual uprootedness, but exhorting him to pursue family ideals beyond his grasp.

In *The Assyrian,* the novella that begins the 1950 collection of stories with that name, Paul Scott re-examines the profiles of his life as he prepares to meet his approaching death. What little we know of his life falls into the typical Saroyan pattern: Scott is a zestful gambler, deriving from the swift throw of the dice a keen sense of personal freedom, the satisfaction of beating the odds against defeat, of riding through inner turmoil on a tide of luck only confident timing and daring can compel. He has come to Lisbon, Portugal on another gamble, climaxing a lifelong search for an elusive connectedness and transcendence. In the process of following his brief meditation on his past amidst the backdrop of this gracious city, where civility soothes his restlessness, the reader finds the key to Scott's character in the constant push against constraint, social and otherwise:

> He had always gone too far, but he had always come back, too. He had always plunged overboard, and then taken a swim, sometimes silently, desperately, knowing that he was struggling for his life, for another chance to find out how far he could go, struggling silently and proudly; sometimes indifferently, scarcely struggling at all, apparently only waiting.

But the cost of compulsively defying boundaries can be disease. Early in the story, Scott traces the root of his malaise to "bitterness about himself": "He knew he didn't care about anybody else in the world, not even [his daugh-

ter] if the truth were told, he cared only about himself, and always had." In both these passages, the repetition of "always" underscores Scott's isolation as a form of now-instinctive self-protection.

The anger and shame of Scott's self-recognition will recur in the later works, accompanied by the central character's ambivalent tie to his ethnic heritage, wherein the members of a small, dying race urge family bonding. In *The Assyrian,* Paul Scott has responded to his call, having early on sided with "the tired side," "the impatient and wise side," hidden in him like a life spring until he reaches puberty. He has even learned the strange language "as if it were a secret shared by only a handful of people miraculously salvaged out of an extinct race." He ends his description of adolescent self-discovery with the same paradoxical notion that marks **"Seventy Thousand Assyrians"**: "He began to understand how superior he must be to most other people in that his very race was finished and had no need to clamor for irrelevant rights of any kind". But the skeptical reader can't help but respond, "What is more relative than the term 'irrelevant'?" For though Scott feels pride at the Assyrians' miraculous escape from extinction, the relief hasn't lifted him emotionally. Like Theodore Badal, the melancholic Scott confronts himself as essentially alone, asking himself "How does anybody have a friend?"

Before he leaves Lisbon, Scott dines with a fabulously wealthy Assyrian, an old man of 91. The meeting between the two men shows that the spiritual fatigue ascribed to the ethnic group is as much projection as actual description: one doesn't have to renounce life with one's people. Thus we find in Curti Urumiya a man vigorous in appetites, as mentally alert as ever, fully aware that the game of life—like the game of intrigue surrounding his business moves—should at least amuse. Unlike Scott, seeking freedom from his "tiresome" self, the old man radiates psychological well-being, relishing the hours like the delicacies his Greek cook prepares daily. Accordingly, he views his ethnic identity as an aesthetic dimension of his life and rebuts Scott's disavowal of specific national ties ("Being alive is nationality enough for anybody") with vital self-assertion:

> . . . the other little bit sometimes, in some cases, seems to make being alive just a little more fun. For instance, I have for many years felt that I have . . . outwitted the foolishness of life, and I must confess it makes me very happy. I mean, I survived, although my race didn't.

Reinforcing this notion of ethnicity as an aesthetic value, the two men's use of Assyrian reminds us of the modern re-enactment of an ancient religious rite. The deepest spiritual communion these two wanderers "of the same family" can achieve is to speak their common language. Like priests respectful of ritual time, they reach "a silent agreement that they [will] begin to speak that language without test or preparation, at the proper moment." As they taste the sounds of the old tongue, rescuing each word like a precious relic from the sea of modern European languages around them, we witness the closest analogue to a religious ceremony in this existential space. But since these secret words no longer symbolize ideals applicable in the contemporary world, the language is ultimately reduced to the status of an artifact, briefly uniting connoisseurs like once functional art, without permanently bonding them.

Significantly, it isn't long after this that, feeling death twinges and the old restiveness, Scott ignores a doctor's orders to stay put and boards a plane going east. He carries into death the same willed loneliness that's always urged him "to be done" with the social pretenses, to keep moving:

> He'd had it and he was satisfied. "I never gave a shit for any of it anyway," he thought. "There was always a little rhythm anyway, and there still is. I got out here all right, and I'll get on the plane all right, too, the same as the other travelers going east, and I'll get there, too."

David Stephen Calonne   (essay date 1983)

SOURCE: "I Want to Live While I Am Alive," in *William Saroyan: My Real Work Is Being*, The University of North Carolina Press, 1983, pp. 28-46.

[*Calonne is an American educator and critic. Assessing Saroyan's short story collections published in the second half of the 1930s, he determines that these works reflect an affirmation of life in an inhospitable, divisive modern world.*]

For Saroyan, it is clear, living itself is the highest value; he violently opposes any system, belief, or authority which seeks to thwart the unfolding of the individual's inner self. He depicts a modern world which is mired in illusion, which has forgotten the spiritual dimension of experience. In *The Trouble with Tigers* he describes humanity as "this mangled tribe, this still unborn God"; thus the deepest potentials inherent in life have yet to be realized by many people. The essential divinity of humanity is still tragically submerged, and the function of the artist is to reveal this hidden inner realm. To ignore this divine impulse within is to destroy one's potential for achieving authentic selfhood and psychological maturity.

In the six volumes that appeared after *The Daring Young Man,* this central idea is revealed in a variety of thematic formulations. Although it would be a distortion to identify each book with the exposition of a single theme, certain general patterns may be discerned. In the seventy-one stories of *Inhale and Exhale,* Saroyan offers a comprehensive treatment of all the [themes introduced in his first collection], with the addition of pieces written during his travels to Europe and Russia. *Three Times Three* illustrates Saroyan's deepening concern with the place of art in modern life; *Little Children* focuses on the world of childhood, while *Love, Here Is My Hat* presents charac-

ters seeking wholeness through relationships. Finally, both *The Trouble with Tigers* and *Peace, It's Wonderful* reflect the approach of World War II. In each story collection, Saroyan again directs his attention to the chaos of a turbulent world.

Perhaps the most significant aspect of Saroyan's growth as a writer during this period was his exploration of art and its relationship to the process of becoming one's true self. He returns repeatedly to the role of the artist in contemporary society, developing and refining his ideas in a number of different contexts. One of his most powerful portraits of the artistic sensibility came out of personal experience—his meeting with Jean Sibelius in July 1935. In **"Finlandia,"** from *Inhale and Exhale,* Saroyan contemplates the composer and the genius of his music.

> All I wanted was music. No dialectics. Just the simple old-fashioned fury of one man alone, fighting it out alone, wrestling with God, or with the whole confounded universe, throwing himself into silence and time, and after sweating away seven pounds of substance, coming out of the small room with something detached, of itself, alive, timeless, crazy, magnificent, delirious, blasphemous, pious, furious, kindly, not the man, not all men, but a thing by itself, incredibly complete, an incision of silence and emptiness, and then sound and the shapes of things without substance. Music. A symphony.

The experience of great music was to become an integral part of Saroyan's life as a writer, and it is in **"Finlandia"** that he first explored its aesthetic dimensions. He remarked in *Razzle-Dazzle* that "I am a writer who is a composer. You will see music in all of my writing—the form and quality of music in all of it." For him, as for Rilke, "Gesang ist Dasein"—singing is being.

In **"Finlandia,"** the artist is depicted creating in isolation, "wrestling with God," achieving the order which is a symphonic work. The composer has created "something detached, of itself, alive, timeless"—a new reality whose harmonious structure makes the disintegrated self whole. Through the composition of music, Sibelius has made contact with a metatemporal realm, with an eternal energy which exists continuously in the present. The narrator/Saroyan feels "closer in spirit to him [Sibelius] than any writer" because the composer moves in a dimension beyond words, beyond the mind's linear, "logical," idea-bound limitations. Sibelius lives in being and recreates it immediately in sound, an experience which the writer can only approximate through language. . . .

"Finlandia" is important in Saroyan's development, for it is here that he begins to evolve a coherent aesthetic philosophy; as his career progressed, it became evident that art was central to his quest for meaning and personal wholeness. . . .

For him, as for Nietzsche, art is the highest metaphysical activity of man. It gives us a feeling of connection to power, meaning, truth, holiness—to the deepest hidden reaches of life's mystery. The meaninglessness of the "real world" and the disorder of experience are precisely what he seeks to overcome, indeed to redeem, through art.

In the story **"The World and the Theatre,"** for example, a ten-year-old boy has begun to grow disgusted with the unrelieved pain of the Depression, a time when "there was no work in the packing-houses and everybody was out of work and in need of money and all kinds of people were too proud to go down to the city and get some free groceries and maybe a little money and these people were all starving to death." Rather than endure passively the agonies that surround him, the boy discovers the world of vaudeville: "To hell with the outside, I said. To hell with the streets and all the things I see there. It was warm in the theatre and the stage was flooded with light. The scene was a city block, but it wasn't like any city block I had ever seen. It was like a city on another earth, all bright and fine, full of light, a good place to be and live."

This is the occurrence of the great divide: the realization by the child that art and life, reality and imagination, "inside and outside," are twin, contiguous realms of experience—the world and the theater. The vision of the theater as a fragile, enclosed space protecting the vulnerable temporarily from the unrest outside is a conception of the place of art which . . . pervades Saroyan's dramatic philosophy. For the unnamed boy of this story, the theater is an entrance into an imaginative world which supplies momentarily an affirmative picture of life's unrealized possibilities. Just as Sibelius's music made possible a vision of "the shapes of things without substance," so the theater has opened the boy's imagination to a world "full of light."

In his next book, *Three Times Three,* Saroyan continued to explore the role of the artist in a difficult time. The story **"Baby"** is divided into fifteen sections; each gives a brief lyrical sketch of some aspect of the American experience. In section three, Saroyan again divides existence into two realms: "The surface life and the inward one, the inward one waiting patiently for another century. It will come. Horror cannot exist forever. The inward life will lift its broken body out of the nightmare and breathe." The nightmare here is both the Depression and the oncoming fury of World War II, and we meet again the lost of *The Daring Young Man*: "The street of America is a long street, and the lost who walk along this street are many."

In section eight, the narrator launches into autobiography, and it becomes clear that again we are hearing the voice of Saroyan himself—the young artist who wants to change the world, who wants to see the resurrection of an America now lashed by the tempest of economic and spiritual collapse: "I will show them God in themselves, I said. I will teach them to remember. I will talk to them in the language of revelation." Saroyan identifies the expansive energy of America with his own youthful aspirations as a writer; both are full of unrealized potential, a groping earnestness, and burdened with an awareness that the old world is in its death throes.

The function of the artist in **"Baby"** is revelatory; he must show a reverence for the miraculous nature of life which pushes outward toward new birth even in the darkest time. . . .

There is also in **"Baby"** a new, free, syncopated rhythm, a rhythm which was to catch the ear of later American writers.

> Sang baby. O maybe. Sang motors and wheels till Saturday night in America, and a hundred thousand jazz orchestras sang *So come sit by my side if you love me,* and the sad-eyed, weary-lipped Mexican girl silenced Manhattan uproar with soft, velvet-petaled singing of darkness and death, O heart there is no end to the river's flowing. Sang locomotive north through snow to Albany and west to Chicago, O baby maybe.

We hear the freedom of music in this passage, with its alternating onrushing excitement and brief, staccato, elemental sentences. The alliterative use of "s" is also apparent when it is read out loud. This rhapsodic urgency is, as we have seen, a central aspect of Saroyan's literary style. It is the language of being, attempting to catch in its quick energetic movement some of the texture, mystery, and flux of experience. It is the obsession of the artist to "get to the probable truth about man, nature, and art, straight through everything to the very core of *one's own* being."

Saroyan's desire to achieve unification of the warring opposites of self and world through his paratactic style illustrates his typically Romantic attitude concerning the place of language in the transformation of consciousness. . . .

As we see in **"Baby,"** the artist must express the fluid self in fluid forms. For Saroyan, "a writer is great insofar as he is simultaneously artful and artless, a swift-moving inhabitant of both the inevitable and visible world and the uncreated but creatable, uncharted, invisible, fluid, limitless but nevertheless real other world." This is a precise description of the twin realms outlined in **"Baby"**: the "surface life and the inward life." Although the world the artist depicts is "uncharted" and "invisible," it is nevertheless available to consciousness and must be poetically, lyrically invoked through rhythmic, musical language.

It should be clear, then, why Saroyan became a literary godfather to the Beat Generation, and specifically to Jack Kerouac and his fellow writers. In this early prose, Saroyan was a true innovator, spawning a fresh new style—a fusion of jazz, Whitman, the quick tempo of American life, popular songs, and the oral tradition of Armenian literature. It is precisely this *oral,* musical dimension of Saroyan's prose-poetry, along with its emphasis on immediate, passionate experience, which appealed so powerfully to the Beats: his words are meant to be *heard.* It has been pointed out by Lawrence Lipton that Beat literature "is the spoken word committed to writing. It is oral in structure. . . . The printed poem is not the poem. It is only the 'score' of the poem, just as in music the score is not the music. It has to be *played back.*" Literature for both Saroyan and the Beats should be as immediate, visceral, improvisatory, and spontaneous as the experience of hearing great music. It must be realized, like life itself, in *performance;* then it will *breathe.*

"Baby" is noteworthy both for its stylistic innovations and for its search for the "inward life." Other pieces included in **Three Times Three** also emphasize that the writer's task is to help both himself and his public attain inner wholeness: "Maybe art is a correction of errors, within the artist, in the world, in man, in the universe." But most important, Saroyan here begins to organize his insights concerning the artistic experience into an organic whole. In **"Life and Letters"** he considers the relation of "real" time to time as we perceive it when we read a work of literature.

> In letters time is not the same thing that it is in life, not the same thing that it is in the universe, time in letters is not daybreak, day, noon, afternoon, evening, and night. In letters time is altogether an inexplicable and magnificent thing, and in so small a thing as a mere short story time can become so tremendous an intensification of experience that the reader, God bless him and keep his eyes unastigmatic, will have lived more richly, more greatly, more swiftly, more meaningfully, and more magnificently than he could ever have had the wit or daring or madness to live in the light of day, in the world.

In the world of literature, our awareness of time is mysteriously altered; "real" time is transcended and our experience is intensified through the artful compressions of the short story form. The successful work of art captures a sense of timelessness, and it is evident here that Saroyan again conceives of literature as an expander of consciousness in the Romantic mode. As we have seen in **"Finlandia,"** he sees art as opening the mind to a more significant realm of awareness, onto a "place of reality" where the self is free joyously to exfoliate. The description of time in short stories applies equally well to his other work—especially. . . to such plays as *The Time of Your Life*.

Also emphasized is the idea that life for the artist is a continuing process of inner exploration; it is "an inward progression of an inward time, an inward growth of an inward world or universe, an inward purification of the inward identity, and an inward strengthening of the inward body." In reading a great work of art, therefore, our own "inward lives begin to accelerate" in the same way as does the writer's. The writer triumphs over time by creating "the growth of immortality in another." The reader's experience of time is not only "intensified" but also "accelerated" as he makes contact with the same world the writer inhabited at the moment of composition.

"Quarter, Half, Three-Quarter, and Whole Notes" continues Saroyan's discussion of literature and the nature of the creative personality in a series of brief sentences and paragraphs. The isolation of the artist is accepted as a prerequisite for successful inner journeyings: "There is only one way to write a story and only one way to write one sentence and that is to be pious and simple and inwardly isolated; above all things inwardly isolated. When you move through the mob you must move through it alone; otherwise there is a chance that your vision will be blurred."

Samuel Beckett, with whom Saroyan shares many spiritual and philosophical concerns, has also written about the solitude of the artist in his study *Proust*: "For the artist, who does not deal in surfaces, the rejection of friendship is not only reasonable, but a necessity. Because the only possible spiritual development is in the sense of depth. The artistic tendency is not expansive, but a contraction. And art is the apotheosis of solitude." Saroyan's "inward isolation" is Beckett's "solitude"; it is a solitude in which the artist cultivates an inner strength and resolution of purpose—a strength which may be dissipated through an exclusive immersion in social life.

The creation of integral works of art can come about only when the self has achieved a measure of balance and integration. In **"Quarter, Half, Three-Quarter, and Whole Notes,"** Saroyan uncovers the primary link between life and art.

> It is essential for anyone alive to establish a personal method of living and to impose personal limitations: one must possess one's identity fully and vigorously and steadily, if one hopes to dominate time rather than be dominated by it. The year is empty because the moment was empty, and the moment *need* not be empty. There must be no evasion. Evasion occurs when one performs acts not pertinent to the ultimate object of one's activity in life, which is to achieve personal wholeness, and to give the material world reality and order. A story (or any other work of art) does not occur when one does the actual writing: it began to occur when one began to live consciously and piously. The writing, which is the least of it, follows inevitably.

Achieving "personal wholeness" through writing is directly connected to the level of authenticity the artist has attained. The impulse to live "consciously" and fully again links Saroyan to Whitman, whose poetry charts the continuing process of the self's quest for unity: the world is complete for the man who is himself complete. In addition, to live successfully in time and not be burdened by it one must "possess one's identity fully." In life, then, one transcends time through being in control of the self; in art, time is overcome through the magic of literary construction and technique.

A final piece dealing with the artistic process is to be found in *Peace, It's Wonderful*. In **"The Sweet Singer of Omsk,"** Saroyan writes another autobiographical story (he mentions himself by name) about his daimon: "I admit it. I am possessed. Most of the time not violently so. But often enough. Not haunted, mind you. The presence is not an evil one. It is often angry and bitter and furious, but most of the time it is warm and friendly and amiable and gentle and courteous, and at times a little gallant, even. It is a good presence, and in varying degrees it is with me always." Saroyan tells us that "very often I do not know what I write, what I say. I simply write, something perhaps more significant than I know, which falls in place by itself, rather strangely."

The "presence" is of course the Muse, and Saroyan echoes the Romantic conception of the artist as a kind of instrument through which the energy and fire of divine creativity are expressed. The artist is essentially passive during this process. Stravinsky has said that "I am the vessel through which *Le Sacre du Printemps* passed," and it is clear Saroyan feels similarly about his writing. André Gide's remark that "the true artist is always half-unconscious of himself, when he is producing" also comes to mind: at their most inspired, artists are aware that their work is being done for them—by the Muse, the unconscious, the daimon, "the presence." Hence Saroyan writes: "I have always suspected that what I am doing is not the work of one man." The speed with which some of Saroyan's best works were written (*The Time of Your Life* was finished in six days) supports the notion that "the presence" played a central role in his artistic creation.

The stories so far considered thus contain a coherent exposition of Saroyan's developing aesthetic philosophy. Great art is a process by which the individual can achieve true being: it is a way into expanded states of consciousness. As has been shown, he discounts "outer travelling" for "the more places you reach the more you understand that there is no geographical destination for man." Rather, "home" can best be reached in "the world of one man at a time: the inner, the boundless, the ungeographical world of wakeful dream." It is precisely this "ungeographical world" which many of Saroyan's characters so ardently seek, and from which they are so terribly alienated.

> **The incurable loneliness of the human heart is illustrated in many of Saroyan's early stories; his characters must learn to accept the fact that breaking through completely to another human being is an illusory dream. The search for communication leads them to an even deeper awareness of their own essential organic apartness. . . .**
>
> —*David Stephen Calonne*

Although Saroyan's advocacy of this inner world is powerful and for the most part convincing, art's absolutes ultimately have little impact on the ceaseless struggles of everyday life. Although art, as we have seen, offers an opportunity for inner wholeness to some of Saroyan's characters—through the music of Sibelius, the pleasures of the theater, or the ecstasy of literature—just as many are cut off, alienated from the true, vital sources of spiritual sustenance. The irony is that the transcendence that they seek often seems accessible only through language, through the splendors and therapeutic qualities of Saroyan's poetic prose. The search for love and wholeness in the "real world" is often frustrating and unfulfilling—the yearning remains unappeased.

"At Sundown" from *Inhale and Exhale,* for example, is another Andersonian story of youth's longing for love and understanding: "And I remember dimly this strange longing I once had which soon became tragic, quietly in the heart where all great tragedies occur." The incurable loneliness of the human heart is illustrated in many of Saroyan's early stories; his characters must learn to accept the fact that breaking through completely to another human being is an illusory dream. The search for communication leads them to an even deeper awareness of their own essential organic apartness as the grandeur and intensity of romantic expectation are deflated by reality. . . .

The quest for love is closely associated in Saroyan's imagination with the search for home, for a place of rest and calm. Being human means exhausting one's self in the effort to reach home, to be more than "puny and weak and mortal." In **"The Trains"** from *Love, Here Is My Hat,* we return to the concept of travel as a metaphor for the journeyings of the human spirit as it seeks serenity. Joe Silvera, a twenty-four-year-old painter, has returned to his hometown of Fresno after an absence of seven years. Yet he does not *feel* at home, and he spends hours looking out the window, watching the trains come and go.

> He would watch for the appearance, far in the south, of the crack passenger trains from Los Angeles. And listen for their cry of arrival: the whistle desolating and full of human anguish, like the ungodly anguish of the heart after possessing flesh and losing spirit; and the last minute haste, the roar, the fire and smoke; and then, almost meaninglessly, sadly, the slow stop, the tentative pause, the swift-ending moment of rest; and then the going again, unlike the movement of the spirit, the train going from city to city, place to place, climate to climate, configuration to configuration. Unlike the going of the spirit, which traveled ungeographically, seeking absurdly magnificent destinations: all places, the core of life, the essence of all mortality, eternity, God. And, he thought bitterly, seeking everything else, in one big bright package.

The human heart is continuously dissatisfied, restless, seeking ultimate consummation. It is not content to arrive at geographical *places* in time and space; it seeks not the superficial, but the very mystery of existence.

Joe Silvera realizes, with Thomas Wolfe, that you can't go home again. Indeed, he begins to wonder whether home is merely a word signifying nothing, whether his spirit wants a magic which exists outside human existence. . . .

The quest for self-integration through love is often frustrating, for, as Yeats put it, "Love has pitched his mansion in the place of excrement." In **"War and Peace"** we meet Sammy, a twenty-year-old San Fransciscan whose pained introversion is rooted in a violent sexuality. He is helplessly attracted to women and afraid of their power over him. Like Sam Wolinsky of **"Seventeen,"** Sammy is wracked by animal need and channels his lust into a love for reading. Sammy's mother worries about his intense self-involvement, and the young man resents her wanting him to be a "good boy. He'd like to tell her he stank from being a good boy." Sammy is plagued by the feeling that he is ugly, a "small evil-looking animal which breathes

Carol Marcus, to whom Saroyan was married and divorced twice. Their relationship reportedly was tempestuous.

and wants glory." He leaves the house for the evening and considers visiting a brothel, but, unlike Sam Wolinsky, he holds back, realizing that "he could always buy with money the one thing of life which has its beauty and magnificence in being given." He returns home and immerses himself in Tolstoy's *War and Peace,* returning to the unhappy womb of his mother's house and to the escape of literature.

Neither Joe Silvera nor Sammy, however, is a special case: they are humanity in microcosm, for they "want what everybody wants and never gets." They desire, as we are told in **"The Poor Heart,"** "the enormity and abundance that isn't ever steadily part of this life." The human heart with its infinite longings and unappeasable appetite for wholeness cannot be satisfied by the things of the material world, and its yearning for a deeper reality is often frustrated. The last story in *Love, Here Is My Hat,* **"Am I Your World?"** ends with the sobering words: "It's kind of funny the way a man can stay alive when everything but his body is dead; when everything but comedy is dead and buried, when the whole world is a cemetery." Saroyan's characters *do* stay alive, however. If many are "so inwardly violent and bewildered, so marvelously lonely," it is because they are poets of feeling whose real inner life

depends on the sweet shudder of response felt from another human heart.

This desire of Saroyan's characters to establish communion with themselves and others exemplifies the phrase. . . : I want to live while I am alive. They want life above all things, and the real struggle is not only interpersonal; rather, they are up against the spiritual aridity of their age. *Peace, It's Wonderful* contains one of Saroyan's most powerful statements on estrangement in the modern world, **"Noonday Dark Enfolding Texas."** Traveling through El Paso by train, the narrator experiences a wasteland, a landscape devoid of meaning and hope: "It was a dead city, it was part of a dead world, a dead age, a universe dying, aching with loneliness, gasping for breath. That is the thought that frightens you. That makes you want life the worst way." The world is yearning for a new birth, a new consciousness, a new way of being; the omnipresence of death and decay makes the narrator's commitment to authentic living all the stronger.

The story ends darkly with a vision of humanity reminiscent of T. S. Eliot's "hollow men."

> I went down to the street and began walking through the beautiful, ugly, dying city. The girls were like the girls of all places, only different. They were Texas, but different from ever before. They were Texas in the sudden darkness of noonday; enfolded in the dark; sealed in the far away dream. One of them was the one I was seeking, and knew she was, so that, even in that desolation, there was meaning at last to write home about. Afterwards, on the train, going away from Texas, rolling out of the dream, I listened to the men in the smoker roaring with the lonely laughter of the living, and suddenly I began to cry, roaring with laughter, because I knew we were all dead, didn't know it, and therefore couldn't do anything about it.

This death-in-life is the ultimate estrangement, the terror of the human soul trapped in static isolation. The real tragedy is that these men (and the narrator includes himself among them) do not realize that they are dead, that their inner selves are suffocating.

For Saroyan, this lack of self-knowledge and absence of authentic communication between human beings leads to the ultimate estrangement: the insanity of political and social upheaval, the idiocy of war. Warnings of impending catastrophe can be found in his earliest work; for example, *Inhale and Exhale* contains an autobiographical sketch, **"The Little Dog Laughed to See Such Sport,"** which he wrote in London in 1935.

> So before the war starts (and everybody alive, from the cab driver to the Professor of Economics, at Columbia, will tell you the war will soon start), I want to tell the world that I am not interested. I am completely bored with the war. It has nothing to do with me. I have no quarrel of such a ridiculous nature, although I have quarrels enough. I want nothing of it. I refuse to accept its reality. Kill yourselves all you like. Do it artfully, with the finest guns and gases invented.

Saroyan was forced finally to "accept the war's reality," although he attempted in books like *The Human Comedy* and *The Adventures of Wesley Jackson* to soften its horror. It was extremely difficult for him to acknowledge that death had triumphed over life, that there was a spirit of evil in the world, that his dreams of universal brotherhood had been shattered. The character and mood of his writing changed following the war; he found it more problematical to sustain a poetic and lyrical attitude toward life's possibilities. Just as World War I literally sickened D. H. Lawrence, Saroyan was also finally unable to assert that the war had nothing to do with him.

War is the triumph of a mob consciousness which levels distinctions between people and fails to recognize the sanctity of individual life. In *Three Times Three,* the failure of the masses to achieve self-realization is discussed. In the introductory note to **"Public Speech,"** Saroyan writes:

> I sincerely wish I could believe with the Communists that there is hope for the masses, but I cannot. I honestly believe there is hope for man, for one man at a time, and I honestly believe that, with all the encumbrances of the world, all the viciousness, all the deceit and cruelty, man's only hope of salvation is himself; he is his salvation. God is. . . . The masses aren't ready, I'm afraid, for the shock of genuine knowing, and not spiritually equipped to face the inward tragedy which occurs with genuine knowing. I don't think the Communists are either.

In the text of the piece, the speaker tells his audience that "all who live are born out of flesh, and living is private." Again it is humanity's inner world which Saroyan seeks to celebrate and protect from the encroachment of any system, capitalist or communistic, which denies individual freedom: "I hate all who seek to complicate that which parades the earth in barefoot simplicity: the living of the inhabitants of the earth."

Although Saroyan points out that the majority of humanity is not prepared for true self-knowledge, this should not be construed as an elitist remark. By "genuine knowing," Saroyan means the achievement of authentic being—and by this definition, few of any age can be counted as successful. Yet this stage of development also brings with it an "inward tragedy"—perhaps the knowledge that the quest for balance is a lonely and difficult one. To really grow as a person requires great struggle and anguish; but to remain as one is—static, undeveloped, dead—requires no effort. Political solutions to the problems of inner growth are fraudulent because the struggle for "genuine knowing" is ultimately a private, individual, interior quest.

According to Saroyan, it is precisely this fearful consciousness insisting on the mythologies of nationalism and governments which is responsible for the world's chaos. His anarchic, life-affirming passion reaches a rhetorical climax in **"The People, Yes and Then Again No"** from *The Trouble with Tigers*: "This is your world and it is my world, and it is not real estate, and not nations, and not governments; it is this accidental place of mortality; it is

this pause in time and space. It is this chance to breathe, to walk, to see, to eat, to sleep, to love, to laugh. It is not financial statistics. It belongs to this mangled tribe, this still unborn God, man." The noblest and best qualities of people are yet to appear; but they will emerge as humanity grows out of psychological and spiritual infancy. If this tribe is "mangled," it yet has a chance to become whole.

Later in his career, Saroyan wrote: "When I speak of the human race I speak of the *concealed* human race, the *still* concealed human race, which is trying to come out from under, as it has been trying for a million years or more." The struggle of life is man's struggle to express the limitless potential that lies buried within the individual soul. Life is not a matter of quantifiable data, of "statistics"; there is no algebra of the spirit. Rather, life is a vast mystery which should be revered and celebrated. Because people do not realize this, the human race is yet unborn, still in the womb of evolutionary development.

Humanity's potential for peace and brotherhood and life's awful stark actualities are contrasted in Saroyan's writings of the period. In four of the pieces of *The Trouble with Tigers,* we sense the oncoming tide of death. In **"O.K. Baby, This Is the World,"** the Fascists make their approach to Madrid; **"Everything"** discusses the war in China; Mussolini's armies invading Abyssinia form the background of **"Citizens of the Third Grade."** In **"The Tiger,"** Saroyan states the controlling theme of the book: "The room cold and the moment clear and cold and tragic. The presence. The word, unwritten. The tiger, unseen. Brother, I mean death. The red headline across the emptiness of time."

The war's impact on life in America can also be seen in three stories from *Peace, It's Wonderful*. In **"The Greatest Country in the World,"** a Czechoslovakian and his fourteen-year-old son quarrel when the boy suggests that Germany will overcome his father's homeland through its superior military capabilities. **"The War in Spain"** depicts a naive eighteen year old convinced of the romance of combat who leaves to become a soldier. And in **"The Best and Worst People and Things of 1938,"** two men in a bar discuss the tragic state of the world. One nominates Hitler as "Heel Number One of the Year." The ultimate mood these stories convey is aptly and concisely expressed by the Scandinavian longshoreman of **"The Monumental Arena"**: "There is a mistake in some place of our life."

Yet the final story in the book, **"The Journey and the Dream,"** refrains from despair or nihilism and ends in a kind of prayer urging pity and hope. The narrator of the story has been gambling and drinking all night, and in the morning, he tells us that

> when I walked into the street I was laughing because it was so good to be in the world, so excellent to be a part of the chaos and unrest and agony and magnificence of this place of man, the world, so comic and tragic to be alive during the moment of its change, the sea, and the sea's sky, and London, and London's

noise and fury, and the cockney's lamentation, the King's palace, the ballet at Covent Garden, and outside Covent Garden the real ballet, and France, and the fields of France, and Paris, and the streets of Paris, and the stations, and the trains, and the faces, and the eyes, and the grief, and Austria, and Poland, and Russia, and Finland, and Sweden, and Norway, and the world, man stumbling mournfully after God in the wilderness, the street musicians of Edinburgh crying out for God in the songs of America, dancing after Him down the steep streets, the tragic dream stalking everywhere through day and night, so that when I walked into the street, I was laughing and begging God to pity them, love them, protect them, the king and the beggar alike.

Here is Saroyan's typical fusion of laughter and tragedy, of tears and ecstasy. Man is hungering after spiritual illumination, "stumbling mournfully after God in the wilderness," still estranged from himself and the world. Yet the narrator is also laughing, laughing through loneliness, pain, grief. Finally he hugs the world's chaos to his soul and achieves the joy of acceptance.

Jules Archer   (essay date 1984)

SOURCE: "More Letters from Bill," in *Ararat,* Vol. XXV, No. 2, Spring, 1984, pp. 124-28.

[*Archer is an American author known for his histories and biographies intended for a young adult audience. In these studies, he avoids glossing over unpleasant aspects of history and presents famous figures realistically, depicting not only their strengths but also their failings and weaknesses. In the following excerpt, Archer recounts correspondences in which Saroyan discussed writing and his career.*]

My friend Arnie Bennett and I were nineteen when we discovered Bill Saroyan. The year was 1934, when the Dionne quintuplets survived and Chancellor Dollfuss of Austria didn't. Struggling for publication, we avidly read magazines like Whit Burnett's *Story,* a showcase for the best and brightest.

Lending me an issue, my friend said, "There's a story in it that will knock you out. Tell me what you think of it."

I read the whole issue. When we met again, I told him I was speechless. The story was fantastic. I'd never read anything like it, this side of Walt Whitman. The guy was a genius, and we had to do something to help him get famous.

When we began to discuss specifics, Bennett looked increasingly puzzled. "What the hell are you talking about?" he exclaimed. "There was nothing like that in the story."

It was my turn to look puzzled. "Well, what story did you mean? There was only one that was really amazing."

"The story by George Milburn, of course."

"Oh, that was good, but it couldn't hold a candle to that piece by a guy named William Saroyan, called '1 2 3 4 5 6 7 8'. Didn't you think it was fantastic?"

"That was one of the stories I didn't read."

"Read it," I said, pressing the issue into his arms.

He read it. When we met again, his eyes glowed when he talked about it. "You're right, Jules. We've got to do something for him. The guy *is* a genius. I'm going to write him a letter telling him we're going to whoop it up for him as the most original voice in America today."

So Arnie wrote the first letter. I don't have a copy of it, but I have a copy of Saroyan's reply, written on cheap yellow second sheets, dated June 12, 1934.

"A thousand thanks, Bennett," he wrote.

It is splendid to know that one's work is liked by the young. I am very glad you saw "1 2 3 4 5 6 7 8": let me try to explain about the song: it is possible to write about almost anything, and if one works hard enough it is possible sometimes to write *greatly* about anything. The song is "Meditation" by Massenet, from the opera *Thais,* as recorded by Paul Ash and his Granada Orchestra: Brunswick, record number 2783-A. The record is rather old, I think; and you might be able to pick it up at some record exchange store, or you might be able to find it among the old and forgotten records of a friend. In the story of the young telegraph clerk and the music and the dream of an artful life I meant to show that endings take place in life more subtly than in art, and that if art is to grow and not continue to be repetition, the artist must make some attempt to get into his subject matter and force himself to say what is truthful, no matter how unconventional and unusual his work of art may turn out to be.

But I hate to talk about such things: actually it is impossible to speak of what goes on within a writer while he is writing. Poe, in explaining his composition of "The Raven," was either spoofing or kidding himself: He explained everything but his genius, which is the only thing.

Please forgive me for taking so long to answer your letter. One thing or another has kept me going and coming for several weeks, and this is the first chance I have had to take time out for a letter or two.

My sincerest good wishes to each of you: Jules and yourself. I will tell you something: at your age or for that matter at any age life is just a trifle more important than letters: living is just a bit more important than writing. When you devise an artful style of living you devise also an artful style of writing. Most writers make the mistake of trying to perfect their writing before trying to perfect their living: the results are generally sad.

Tennis is swell. Lately, though, I have had to give it up. I used to play quite a lot. What I liked about the game was its liveliness: the bouncing of a ball and one's being in opposition to a bouncing ball. Also its precision. In the story, though, I was mostly spoofing Hemingway.

It is probably true: very often I do not write short stories. I do not have to: I can get by with murder almost. *The American Mercury* is printing another story soon, called **"Ah-Ha."** If the story is a story, then it is perhaps one of the most original to appear in America in years and years. If it is not a story, it certainly is remarkable prose, of some sort. The story is very short: a little over two pages of *Mercury* print, but it says more than two dozen of the usual run of stories. (Pardon me: I'm not bragging.)

You didn't ask for advice, but I am going to make a few suggestions anyway. Live first: write afterwards. By living I do not mean taking a boat and going to China. I mean keeping your ears and eyes and heart open: getting it all into you. Refuse to become an artist: remain, that is, a man: someone alive, nothing more. Artists are bores. They are conceited and generally stupid. Take little seriously: I mean little that is outside of yourself. Take very seriously those experiences within yourself which you know to be vital and good.

There is hardly anything more to say. In other words, be. Verb. You yourself. Being is doing. All right. Let it stand.

When my story appears in *The American Mercury* will you drop the editor a very brief note, if you like the story. Make it very brief, though. If you feel like it, send me a picture of yourself and Jules: and, if you like, something each of you have written. But don't worry about writing, and don't be in a hurry. If you have something to say, and I believe you have, it will be said inevitably.

Random House is publishing a book of my stories some time this year: *The Daring Young Man on the Flying Trapeze and Other Stories*. If you are in the money when the book is announced, I would appreciate it greatly if you would send to the publishers for a first edition. If the first edition is sold out soon enough after publication, I believe the book will sell fairly well. If you can make any other sort of fuss about the book, by all means do so: I mean it would probably help a lot. And when I get to New York I'll get in touch with you and we'll talk things over: if I ever get to New York again.

Many thanks again, and good wishes to each of you.

If we had been enthusiastic about Saroyan before, that letter set us on fire. I took over the correspondence. On June 20th I wrote him a long, effusive letter that let all my emotions hang out to a "kinsprit," to use Christopher Morley's term. Saroyan's words had touched us to the core. We saw him as the purest, most honest spirit in modern letters.

"It is 11:15 and I ought to get to bed, but I would rather write to you," I wrote him.

I have just torn up a rough draft of a letter about four typewritten pages long. I tore it up because in it I told you how your letter to Arnie almost cost me my job, about my acquaintances—postmarked—in the literary field, about the dime I gave the bum at the opera house on account of you, and because I referred to Francis Thompson, Gertrude Stein, and Schnitzler. I couldn't decide whether or not I was showing off, so I tore it up.

You are wrong about *The Philosophy of Composition*. There is no reason why Poe should have deceived his readers. I think you have twisted his genius to fit your own theory.

Look, Saroyan—living is fine. I mean, you've got to live to write. But aren't books living? Isn't Dostoyevsky an adventure? Anyhow, Arnie says the chief distinction between someone like you and ourselves is that you begin with the premise that you have something to say and must say it, while we begin with the assumption that we want to write. When I think of you, Saroyan, I get literary constipation and write worse than usual.

I told Arnie I was afraid to criticize you in my first letter because I was sure you wouldn't think me sympathetic. It's always easy to condemn something new on the grounds of precedent. You see, I was going to throw in your face Irving Babbitt's theory that a genius which is nothing more than an outpouring of undisciplined emotion is not really great. It is personal, without craftsmanship, and therefore limited art. Also, that your type of story is easily duplicated—the fate of all work created with little effort—and therefore worth less than a story by George Milburn or Albert Halper. When I read what I have just written, it disgusts me. I hate to think that it might be true. I'm too crazy about your stuff to want to find fault. I've already spread the gospel by introducing **"70,000 Assyrians"** to five people, and mentioning it in my English class. They are all agreed that it is fine stuff, but cannot concur on a verdict of story or essay.

Arnie and I will be among the first subscribers to *The Daring Young Man,* in spite of the fact that we never buy new books . . . The *Mercury* story will be boosted as innocently as we can manage, and any other break we can give you, you can depend upon us to do it. We are afraid, however, that you are a writer's writer, and you know what that means.

Some questions: How much money have you left of all you've earned since *The Daring Young Man*? What does 'Aspirin Joins the NRA' mean? What do you look like? What do you do for a social and sex life? (Arnie and I hoped you went out with whores, and in the next breath, hoped you didn't.) do you honestly despise the literati? And what's wrong with *Arrowsmith*?

I have a friend who's your age, Saroyan. He's a clever, talented young man of twenty-six, and he's had about the lousiest breaks of any writer I ever read about. We call him Midas, because everything he touches turns to brass. He is so soul-sick, he has utterly renounced good writing—after finishing a particularly fine story—and has declared his intentions of writing and selling only junk. He has been everything from an assistant stage manager with a group theatre to a radio writer, and the net result is that he is hopelessly in debt to his mother, and completely despondent. Cornel De Jong, whose book *Bella Fulla Straw* is a financial flop, must now either get a job or starve. Milburn, until the angels descended with a Guggenheim Fellowship, was up against it badly. Saroyan, why should a young man tear his guts open for the privilege of pouring perfume on a garden of weeds? Saroyan, why shouldn't I write conventional, readable stories and eat regularly? Why shouldn't my friend? How many unheeded Saroyans are still starving and freezing in cities like San Francisco, and in towns and in the country? Saroyan, the rose that once has blown forever dies.

In a week or so Arnie and I will forward pictures and a short story each. Have you photographs you can spare?

I will close this letter with a quotation, but I will not tell you where it is from. I think it is beautiful: ". . . . Keats, half-chewed in the jaws of London and spit dying on to Italy. . . ." It is 12:00 and I am tired, Good night, Saroyan.

Forty-eight years later that letter would crimson my cheeks, but remembering that I was only nineteen and as honest as I could be at that ambivalent age, I can make paternal allowances for the literary excesses of youth. And so, verbatim.

On June 26, 1934, Saroyan replied with a letter that I often quote to classes I teach on writing at the University of California, Santa Cruz, Extension, because it has lost nothing of its validity in the intervening years.

"Many thanks, Archer, for your fine letter," he replied.

I wish you hadn't destroyed the other one. Unwitting I meant: in regard to Poe. Certainly he didn't lie. But he failed to explain his genius. I meant this. I think my story **"Ah-Ha"** comes closest in spirit to Poe than anything printed in this country. Angoff [*Mercury* editor] describes it as nightmarish. Well, that's all right, too. I didn't quite get how my letter to your friend Bennett nearly cost you your job. Why? Also: don't be afraid of showing off. Every man who ever got around to being great started by showing off. Me, too. Max Baer, too. It's the overture. One outgrows it, but it's necessary. If you think you are good, say it loudly, and often. Living and writing are the same thing. Anything I say I say for myself: there can be no arguments. I speak only for myself. You must feel free to criticize my work as much as you feel the need to: your privilege. I assure you I won't mind. I do a bit of criticising myself: of my own work.

Tell me about your English class. What school? How do you like it. How old are you?

I have earned very little money writing. I have about a dollar and thirty cents in cash at the moment. The title

is **"Aspirin is a Member of the NRA."** It comes from the radio program, Bayer Aspirin is a Member of the NRA. It means that contemporary management of public affairs is basically evasive: pain is eased, but future pain is not avoided. I look like hell. My social life is extremely simple: part of the time I talk with the unemployed around Howard Street, and part of the time I visit the rich at their homes: Fairmont Hotel, etc. For a whole picture. **"The Poor and The Rich"** is a recent story, not yet sent out. Most of my stuff hangs around until I feel like wasting postage. Sometimes a story never goes out. Years ago when I sat down to write, I sat down to write for myself: no thought of even wanting to be printed. It is a wise method. No headaches. My sex life is also simple: I take what I can get, provided I feel inclined. My relations with whores are generally platonic: I do not like to mix art with business and with whores the act is business, and when it isn't fake, so I stick to art. Whores are the loveliest of people when selected with care. See my story **"Sleep In Unheavenly Peace."** I honestly dislike those who think they are artists and nothing else. *Arrowsmith* I did not read; I saw a movie of it. I don't know what's wrong with it. What is? Sinclair Lewis, perhaps?

Cleverness and talent mean nothing: everybody is clever, and talented. It is no easier to write and sell junk than it is to write and sell other kinds of writing. Your friend isn't going to have an easy time. Tell me about him. Writing should never be a profession. I mean this. I'll starve forever, but I won't be amazed. I knew this when I started out to write. There are worse things than not having lots of money. De Jong, I think, deserves to be given a decent break. I hope he has some luck: sorry to hear his book flopped. Now get this straight: mine will flop, too. It's in the cards. But I'm not worrying. Let it flop. If I am offered any sort of a prize or fellowship I shall have to ask those who hand out the doughnuts to eat them themselves. My sympathies are with the unknown writer; always. I think, in his way, he is doing the real writing of America. I am the unknown writer who got around to a bit of mediocre recognition by standing on his head and saying, "Take a letter to America." I need no introduction. I am unknown from coast to coast. There ought to be ten thousand good writers starving in America.

My old man died when I was two and a half. I live with my mother and sister when I am in Fresno. Send along the photographs and stories. Return the photograph I am enclosing. Good wishes all around.

That letter just about flipped us out. Arnie Bennett and I lost no time in sending short stories to our idol. And we set about writing threatening letters to magazine editors, warning that any issues they put out without a Saroyan story would be ignored as beneath notice. When **"Ah-ha Ah-ha"** appeared in the *American Mercury,* I wrote editor Charles Angoff, "Is it possible the *Mercury,* Zombie-like, has come back to life?" He replied, "I agree with you that it is a superb job."

He showed my letter to Saxe Commins, a Random House editor, who wrote and told me about their forthcoming edition of Saroyan's first book, *The Daring Young Man on the Flying Trapeze,* a collection of his short stories.

"We are confident in our prediction," he declared, "that his volume will win recognition from critics and public alike." I replied that he already had my order, and the orders of Arnie Bennett and another friend, waiting to be filled.

I wrote Saroyan in part, "'There ought to be ten thousand good writers starving in America' was inspiring enough to make me temporarily abandon a well-rounded plot for the S.E.P. in favor of something I've put off off for two years; a story of life in a large law office and its effect upon adolescents. Slightly proletarian by suggestion. I know about this."

On August 1st he sent me a card: "I meant to write to you and Bennett long ago, but one thing out here lead [sic] to another. I went away for a while, and when I came back there was a lot of work to do, and consequently this delay. . . . I have read about half of your story: so please do not mind. The writing is good and the story holds one's interest. This is just to let you know I haven't forgotten you fellows and will write when I get a chance. Say howdy to Bennett. See the next issue of *Story*; and if you have cash, send for a copy of my book."

I replied telling him what Arnie and I were doing to whoop it up for the book. On August 12th he wrote me,

> You are a pal, and I'm damn grateful, though you have a right to feel that I am no such thing, which isn't so. I have actually been dizzy with all sorts of complications, and I have done hardly any work, hardly any letter-writing. . . . Please be patient, though. Getting a first book off the press is one of the toughest things I can think of, and when you get one off the press I think you will agree with me. A while back I managed to write some stories and sold one to *Vanity Fair*, called **"Little Caruso"**: it is fine American humor, and it will appear in a couple of months. Thanks for writing Angoff; his reply seems swell. And thanks for getting your third friend to send in an advance order, too: that is doing a fellow a favor. I'll do the same for you some day, and no fooling. You fellows will be coming along soon, I'm sure, and I feel pretty proud of knowing you beforehand: I mean, proud too that you know me beforehand. Say hello to Bennett, and write again. Good wishes.

Our little fan club continued bombarding magazine editors with letters hailing each new Saroyan story as it appeared. I wrote him recording our efforts, and editors' responses, along with my own evaluations of the stories. In my next letter I told him that no other modern writer had the power to stir me to my depths as he did.

On October 2nd he sent me a card: "I feel miserable: I haven't written you a decent letter. . . . Many thanks for your last letter: and for the ballyhoo on my behalf. I think I understand how you feel. All of us are still a bit young. Ten years or twenty from now I'll have an idea or two. Bill."

In October when I read my autographed copy of ***The Daring Young Man,*** my astonishment, admiration and enthu-

siasm knew no bounds. The impact of reading a whole book of his stories left me despairing of my own small talent. . . .

On October 16th a third friend, Herman Baron felt impelled to write to Saroyan, and received this reply:

> You three fellows are really whooping it up for me in a big way in the big city, and I'm much obliged to you: and what's more nothing could please me more than to know that young men, guys who are alive, find something in my stuff. This means plenty to me. So I feel proud of the letters from Arnold and Jules and you. Yesterday I returned that gangster photograph of myself, signed for you, but I didn't mean to be in such a hurry, though it actually was yesterday: therefore this note. I won't try to explain the two stories you didn't get because explanations are a nuisance: they do stand, though young fellow, and my saying this (of course) in no way is meant to ignore your own attitude toward them. So: don't be worried. Rhapsodic? Don't worry about that either. When you must be rhapsodic (and all young writers must or else don't deserve to be known as either young or writers), be rhapsi (tough word that:), be rhapsodic, that's all. Refer to Prelude to an American Symphony: New Masses: soon. Very rhapsodic, but what of it? Well, many thanks again for reading my stuff and writing to me: and very good wishes to you, to Jules, and to Arnold.

On October 20th Saroyan wrote me, "In much haste: many thanks for finding so much in the stories you have read. I am returning the gangster photograph, signed. . . . Please do not feel bad because I cannot take time out to talk about the stories you mailed me. They show much that is admirable, but some need of growth, technical: I mean, you and Bennett must learn to stand over your subject matter and make it behave: must be the boss."

When I wrote Saroyan again, I sent him copies of all the reviews of the book I could get, and discussed them. On November 8th he wrote me: "The reviews make me laugh. Thus & Thus & Thus: & the whole business comes to nada. I am answering the ones who are burned up because my book is going over quietly. (Quietly? Well, it's quiet where I am. I'm not in New York.) *The Nation & The New Republic* take vicious socks at my chin & make me laugh louder than ever & if they print my answers all of us will have a lot of fun. Which is one of the reasons why it is pleasant to have had a book printed. Send me any clippings (reviews) that come your way & any information you get about the book. I appreciate it very much. Bill."

I sent him some more reviews, and on November 20th he wrote me: "Many thanks for the letters & clippings. . . . I have no argument with any critics: they can think what they like. I just write and let it go at that. Sure Armenians are terrible, as per custom: along with all other people. Who cares? A good artist elevates them and embellishes their vices, alters them etcetera. Art, the great deceiver. (Not altogether of course.) Tell Bennett I can't write a letter just now. Working steadily etcetera. So long."

When Saroyan came to New York to make the rounds of the cocktail circuit, he phoned me. "Jules," he sighed, "I wanted to get together with you and Arnie and Herman, but do you know what's happened to me? They've turned me into a social lion. I perform at all these goddam literary affairs, and they've made me sicker than a dog. I can't even hold my head up. All I want to do is crawl into bed and sleep. But I had to call you and tell you I'm thinking of you guys, and maybe if I can get out of this rat race we can finally meet."

But we never did. Saroyan's star shot sky-high, and the demands on his time were overwhelming. I never stopped thinking of him, of course. Three years later I wrote him again at his 348 Carl Street address in San Francisco.

He replied,

> I remember you. What's happened to that little gang? Now that you're 23 (and I suppose the others are about the same age) this is the time where you'll have a better chance to get going. That's how it was with me. Anyhow. Did I tell you I was dying of ptomaine that time we talked over the phone in N.Y.? Well, maybe that's what it was. Anyhow, I lived, I guess. I got a letter from your friend Pearl Gutfeld a while back and although lately I haven't been answering every letter I get I decided to answer hers, because there is always the chance that if I don't I'll be hurting somebody who shouldn't be, so if I can take time out I do and write an answer. My first book will always be an exciting when [sic], no matter when read. I looked it over again after the letter from Miss Gutfeld and was kind of impressed. That's what I meant when I said I read it for somebody young because even if you aren't young when you read it it somehow makes you go back to when you were young: that was what I meant to do, unconsciously anyhow, and it happened, which means I was very lucky, and I was. My new books are better, but different; they'd naturally have to be. In my opinion I am one of the most important writers in the world, which of course is going to make you laugh; it makes everybody else laugh when I tell them so, but it's the truth. They'll know as time goes on. I know now; that's the difference.

> I have two more books accepted, making six. The stuff is all very fine and practically the only stuff in print I care to read: that's how you can be sure of your reading, by writing it yourself; after four or five years what you wrote you wrote four or five years ago becomes especially fine because it becomes isolated, self-sustaining, by itself whole, and you know the years haven't been lost, though you yourself have grown and naturally changed; the change is subtle, sharply remembered things gradually becoming extremely dimly remembered, so that when you read, you live again. That probably explains some of what you ask in your letter. Hope you have a nice time in Europe; you're lucky to be going. I went all right; it was great; also worked in Hollywood a short while (read this issue *Story* about that). I note there are some more questions to answer, so I'll go over to a new page. I only write what I wrote, as the saying is. I never draw up a campaign. The others can do that and earn fame and fortune, which I don't need as badly as they do. When

> I write a novel it will be there: and a play too. I don't even promise to write another story; but it happens, as a rule. See **"The Pomegranate Tree"** in *The Atlantic Monthly* in the next issue or the one after. You ought to examine the book I published in Hollywood: **Three Times Three**: you can get it at one or another of the shops on Fifth Avenue. It's a good book for people who write. Dutton's has it, I'm sure. I remember seeing two copies there this August; it's a cinch they haven't sold them. Read **The Man With the Heart in the Highlands,** **"The Living and The Dead"**; read the whole book." . . .

That was my last contact with Bill Saroyan. I made no further effort to continue our linkage. I liked to discover geniuses when they were unknown. Once their genius was recognized, and they were universally hailed, I lost interest and moved on to new discoveries. But Bill Saroyan continued to play a crucial part in my development as a writer. At least, the young, dynamic Saroyan did. Forgive my heresy, but I came to feel that his best work had been done in those unspoiled, go-to-hell years. In my opinion he was never able to top himself when young, an untrammeled spirit.

In the thirties my father, a man wise beyond his years, told me, "Jules, you'll never be another Saroyan—a genius. You'll be a fine, competent writer. But no genius. You know why? You've never known poverty, never suffered enough."

He was right. I published over sixty books, and more than a thousand magazine articles and stories. Fine. Competent. But definitely no works of genius. But what the hell, how many Saroyans are there in any generation?

Walter Shear   (essay date 1986)

SOURCE: "Saroyan's Study of Ethnicity," in *MELUS*, Vol. 13, Nos. 1-2, Spring-Summer, 1986, pp. 45-55.

[*In the following essay, Shear studies Saroyan's treatment of ethnicity in the stories in* My Name Is Aram.]

At one time William Saroyan was America's most famous ethnic writer—more famous than ethnic, perhaps. In the late 1930s and early 1940s Saroyan exploded onto the literary scene as a true wunderkind, the writer who was singlehandedly revolutionizing the form of both the short story and the drama. He was the man who refused the Pulitzer Prize and argued with Louis B. Mayer over the issue of artistic integrity. As a literary personality, he had an instinctive desire to be a part of the American cultural scene, to feel that he counted on such a stage. Yet at the same time he felt apart from it, hating the entrepreneurs of culture and his writing rivals with such a passion he was often dismissive of the popular mainstream culture of his day. In these moods he was apparently satisfied with his own artistic ego and his quieter working out in his fiction of his own cultural dilemma.

Saroyan's ethnic writing, which is in essence his emotional record of what it means to be a member of the Armenian subculture, is scattered throughout the corpus of his work, appearing in almost every form his protean talent produced—short story, novel, novella, memoir, essay. While his later fictional works (especially his novels) tended to regard ethnic existence as a problem—sometimes as a state racked by irreconcilably conflicting values—his earlier work, while not always optimistic, tended to emphasize a seemingly immortal quality in his ethnic heritage and the capacity of recent immigrants for adjustments. In one of his earliest stories, the mother tells her family in Armenian, "It is no use to cry. We have always had our disappointments and hardships and we have always come out of them and always shall."

The Saroyan book which investigates most intensively the relationship between the young ethnic and the mainstream culture is a collection of short stories written fairly early in his career, *My Name Is Aram*. Its analysis of the ethnic's position is deceptively elaborate and thus this aspect of the book has often been overlooked. The only two literary critics who have studied the book in detail stress its wavering between romantic allegiances and realistic constraints. Howard Floan points to the conflicting claims of "dream and reality" in the stories, while David Stephen Calonne believes the romantic elements dominate since the central character's "activities celebrate the triumph of freedom over restraint, of the intense over the quotidian" [Floan, *William Saroyan;* Calonne, *William Saroyan: My Real Work is Being*]. While not dismissing these considerations, I will concentrate on the book's analysis of the relationship between the ethnic community and the mainstream culture and its examination of the social interaction within each group. In his investigation Saroyan employs a second generation ethnic, the Armenian-American boy, Aram, as narrator and a schematic division of the arenas of social action into: 1. an official world of status and socially-defined relationships; and 2. a community evoked and defined by personal relationships. These two overriding frames are, in most stories, paralleled and given public enhancement by the social divisions between the American mainstream world and the Armenian ethnic world. To avoid rejecting the values of any group, Saroyan opens the plot form of these stories so that at the end of each there is a suggestion of continuance rather than conclusion. Saroyan dramatizes his ethnic society as a total system functioning according to particular principles, but he views it as depending on inconsistencies for its operation.

Saroyan's official world is partly defined by those Calonne refers to as "the mediocre instruments of society's institutions," but in a broader sense it is that arena where one comes to terms with one's social role. The personal world is characterized by a free and innocently irresponsible activity of the human spirit, an expression which seems connected with the ethnic's desire to articulate another kind of community. In general the characters in the stories exhibit a persistent concern for one another's personhood, a caring that may be related to the social conditions of the 1930s, but which seems more particularly tied to the social uncertainties in the position of the American ethnic. Whatever the reason, the characters often respond to each other by developing and elaborating attitudes of seriousness and mock-seriousness which successfully avoid risking anyone's personhood. The stories show people taking care of one another in a psychological sense, a nurturing that is reflected figuratively in the concern for health and physical condition which is a pervasive motif for the stories.

As the official world and the personal community interact, what they demonstrate is the necessity for lying (or keeping silent)—that is, for temporarily suppressing the claims of one world so the other might occupy center stage. In this manner each world can proclaim its status without contradicting the other world. The first story of the collection, **"The Summer of the Beautiful White Horse,"** directly confronts the problem of consistency and honesty. On seeing his cousin Mourad with a new white horse, Aram is dumbfounded because theirs is a proud and honest family and "I *knew* my cousin Mourad couldn't have *bought* the horse, and if he couldn't have bought it he must have *stolen* it, and I refused to believe he had stolen it." As the quotation implies, logic is not much help. At first it seems to cancel itself out. Then it seems to conclude that Mourad and Aram must be in some jeopardy, for obviously the horse is stolen. But again worldly logic is suspended as the boys' enthusiasm for the horse is such that they avoid facing the legal (official) view. In the same spirit of suspension, John Byro, when he sees the situation, only hints at his own position as owner—to show his good will for the name of the family and to avoid a direct, official confrontation. This intermittent concern with consistency works. Finally it is personal concern—not any official logic of right and wrong—which unites Byro again with his horse. Later, in **"Locomotive 38, the Ojibway,"** the Indian title character also suppresses a fact, his ability to drive, in order for Aram to have the fun of actually experiencing some of his aspirations. Both the Indian and Byro, an Assyrian, seem to have an instinctive feeling for the world of these Armenian boys.

The world of personal relationships is invariably activated by a nonethnic official society, but it is also generated by structures in the ethnic group, where social relationships are, because of the eroding authority within the group's social structures, always contingent, always in need of some improvisation. For the ethnic, therefore, the personal seems to be inevitably effacing the official. While this can seem a natural condition to the children, it evokes pathos in the adults. Since it is only contingently official, the Armenian ethnic society seems in the American social order defined by the more personal interactions of an extended family, a group which in its affections and its tendency to accept people for what they want to be seems to imply a version of the family of humankind. It has in common with the personal world a feeling of being psychologically inside, at a remove from conventional American society.

The major family is the Garoughlanian because the main character—the first person narrator in all the stories—is Aram Garoughlanian. It is a family who, we are told, "come by all their wisdom naturally, from within," a condition that accents the tie between family identity and personal idiosyncrasy. As a boy (in most of the stories he is between 10 and 14), Aram is still spontaneously a member of both Armenian and American societies and thus can function as a kind of understanding go-between. From his Armenian background, he has inherited a feeling for the personal world, for characters like his cousin Mourad who "enjoyed being alive more than anybody else who had ever fallen into the world by mistake." But he also understands how the official world operates and its non-Armenian rationality. For example, he and Joey accept their strappings at school because they've broken the rules and they want to "be fair and square with the Board of Education." Most often Aram is not a protagonist, but rather a witness to the drama of the fears, dreams, and inclinations of others.

Typically, the stories concern what doesn't happen—how Aram's uncle fails to raise pomegranates, how another uncle doesn't get a job, how his cousin doesn't get in trouble for stealing a horse, how two people don't fall in love, etc. What doesn't happen is not failure, however—the personal world, say, defeated by a more ruthless and indifferent official world. And it is in this respect that the forms of the stories can be considered open; that is, the narratives deliberately evade the kind of final closures implied by a triumph of personal desire or a rejection of an official sort. Further, the characters retain their role as agents even though their aims may not be achieved, for their agency consists chiefly in the improvising of relationships to the official world and thus guaranteeing the continuity of existence on a personal level.

Instead of hostilely confronting each other and concluding with someone's sense of failure, both the mainstream world and the Armenian world open with a feeling of multiplicity and freedom. Aram is not imprisoned by old country perspectives, but neither does he reject his heritage. Because of this, he comes to understand the necessity of some distance between the official world and the personal world, to see that an authentically-lived existence in one world creates more freedom in the other. When Aram humorously comes to the realization that he is losing the 50 yard dash and that his fellow racers are not simply there to contribute to his triumph, he is finally released from the bondage imposed by his egotistically subjective response to the I-must-triumph-over-my-competitors paradigm of the official world. At the end of **"The Summer of the Beautiful White Horse,"** when the boys realize that John Byro is not going to press charges against them, all three come to share in the recognition that personal dreams can in the right human context become fundamental claims.

Within the context of the ethnic world, the figure of the family patriarch is used to dramatize an official force transformed into a purely personal effect. Uncle Khosrove, the most prominent of these types, is the loudest in a series of uncles and grandfathers who pour out their stylized version of a wisdom calculated to regulate family activities. Theirs, however, are no longer iron, absolute commands.

In fact, the strength of the orator's insistence seems only to signify a corresponding fading of official status. Although these characters are overtly accepted and acknowledged as authority figures, no member of the family follows their advice completely.

Because of their diminished status, these characters bring out most strongly the juggling of logic, the social manipulation of what is recognized and what is not, that results from the interaction between external convention and internal evaluation. For example, Uncle Khosrove's publicly stated attitude toward games, that one should not take winning or losing too seriously, seems a recognition that personal attitudes should never be bound tightly to one's objective fate as a game player. But he pretends to a stoicism he does not possess: he is in fact the worst loser in the world. The fact that he "himself lost *his* life when he lost a game" demonstrates the lack of personal command which results from the precarious nature of his present social status. There is a kind of logic in the fact that this inconsistency between idea and behavior leads directly to Khosrove's most intensely personal relationship, that with the Arab, who comes to represent the loss of everything external. The narrator imagines that the Arab, by losing a game of *tavli* to his uncle (thus officially opening the possibility for a personal relationship), comes to a recognition of status: the Arab "understood *who* my uncle Khosrove was—without being told."

The uncle and the Arab come to enjoy a silent communion. As Aram's mother explains, "They understand one another and don't need to open their mouths." When Aram seeks an objective fact, the Arab's name, Khosrove screams as if he is being murdered, reacting as if the relationship to be preserved must remain totally private. What the two friends share is the old social world—literally, the old country—now gone but still alive personally, reduced to an unspoken understanding. When the Arab dies, Aram concludes, "He died an orphan in an alien world, six thousand miles from home." As Calonne notes, the gap between their old world, personal, silent communion and Aram's leafing through American advertisements becomes a symbolic image for "the developing gulf between the two generations," and thus, for a kind of pathetic failure of the personal in this version of the ethnic family.

The context of the old world and the new world is used more overtly in **"Old Country Advice to the American Traveler,"** where Uncle Garro gives advice to the younger Uncle Melik about the dangers of travel on a train.

> "Several moments after the train begins to move . . . two men wearing uniforms will come down the aisle and ask you for a ticket. Ignore them. They will be imposters."

> "How will I know?"

> "You will know. You are no longer a child."

A man, Garro says, will offer a cigarette. Don't take it, he advises. "The cigarette will be doped." He further envisions a young woman intentionally bumping into Melik. This woman will be a whore.

On the actual journey, Melik not only finds that none of this happens, he himself offers another young man a cigarette, goes out of his way to sit with a young lady, starts a poker game, and has a wonderful trip. Yet at the end of the story he tells Uncle Garro that he has followed his instructions. The story ends with Garro saying, "I am pleased that *someone* has profited by my experience." There is an obvious irony in the events, and yet the reversing of much of the advice does not cancel it esthetically. It remains the embodiment of the old world of Garro, still *his* experience. In an important sense the difference in characters, and in their relationship to the new world, means that each has his own truth.

The personal comes to have several shades of meaning in this collection. Most of the patriarchs are smaller scale variants of Uncle Khosrove, "an enormous man with a powerful head of black hair and the largest mustache in the San Joaquin Valley, a man so furious in temper, so irritable, so impatient that he stopped anyone from talking by roaring, *It is no harm; pay no attention to it*". With its massive, total dismissal of the external world, his seems the voice of pure psychic energy, the voice of completely internal power. However, the family reaction to Khosrove tends to imply that such articulation is really a kind of reaching after lost official power. The ranting intensity in his official role tends to seem that of an imprisoned voice, to become a personal comment on present status. In these stories, which are largely paced by dialogue, many of the characterizations are basically voices. All articulate a felt relationship to the ethos of their world, but while some convey a strong sense of active agency, others suggest an isolated self and like the silence of the "poor and burning Arab" convey the pathos of those deprived of or denied social status. They remind us that to come to the New World is to lose most of one's former social status.

Several of the stories are direct examinations of the community as the arena for weighing personal desire. Using Aram's low-keyed concern, the early stories of the volume analyze critically, but sympathetically, qualities of the dream of the self. In **"The Summer of the Beautiful White Horse"** the typical (and typically impossible) boy's dream of riding a horse is permitted to happen through an almost miraculous suspension of feelings about property rights. John Byro, the owner of the horse, is an outsider to some extent ("an Assyrian who, out of loneliness, had learned to speak Armenian"), but he comes to a kind of understanding as he looks at the returned horse. "I do not know what to think. . . . The horse is stronger than ever. Better tempered too." Somehow the horse being stolen had been a good experience for all involved.

The following story, **"The Journey to Hanford,"** features a playful interaction between two comic extremes: 1. Aram's grandfather, who orates—in such a way, again, as to imply a diminished official force—the practical view of life; and 2. Uncle Jorgi, who is tolerated by the family but

Stylized photo of Saroyan.

considered a fool because his only ambition is to play a zither. The prominent refrain in the story is the grandfather's complaint about unrealistic writers: "When you read in a book that a man who sits all day under a tree and plays a zither and sings is a great man, believe me, that writer is a liar"; "When you read in a book . . . that a woman is truly a creature of wonder, that writer has turned his face away from his wife and is dreaming. Let him go." It is soon apparent that even though he may be articulating the truths of realism, his comments are essentially psychological declarations of his status.

There is little response to the statements and the story's plot also features an evasion of conflict. Uncle Jorgi is sent to Hanford to get a job, the journey here, like those in other stories, being the movement to the world beyond the ethnics. With little suspense, it transpires that Jorgi is saved from having to work, though it is Aram who has to explain to this naïve zither-player that the farmer has lied to him about all the watermelons being harvested: "He didn't want to hurt your feelings. He just said that because he knew your heart wouldn't be in your work."

The story ends with the harmony of the family restored, the two philosophies reconciled because appearances indicate that at least Jorgi has tried to get work. Aram observes, "When I came back to the parlor the old man was stretched out on the couch, asleep and smiling, and his son Jorgi was singing hallelujah to the universe at the top of his beautiful, melancholy voice."

In **"The Pomegranate Trees"** a foolish dream of Uncle Melik, to grow pomegranates in vast quantities and sell them to an eager public, comes, as one expects, to failure. And yet, through the casual dialogue between Aram and his uncle in which each comes to learn gradually, sympathetically about the other and about the world around them, the experience comes to have a value of its own. The marvelous quality of the story is its concealment of the exact time the uncle knows the dream is doomed and the underplaying of the moment, finally, when the two realized that in a crucial sense this failure doesn't matter.

Not simply a pretty lie, the personal dream evokes the psychological debt connected with social dignity or status. (One begins to owe a consistency of identity to others and to a degree their expectations become demands for some assimilation of their values.) **"My Cousin Dikran, the Orator"** concentrates on the uncertain mixture of the precious and the precarious in the ethnic's movement into mainstream society. Here public speaking is the sign of the emergence from a more private tribal identity. Aram observes a farmer leap to his feet to make his pledge: "Gone are the days of poverty for this tribe from the lovely city of Dikranagert—the five Pampalonian brothers—twenty-five cents." After having made this overt commitment to a common cause, the farmer goes home, "his head high, and his heart higher. Poor? In the old days, yes. But no more." Though the amount is paltry by mainstream standards, the new-found pride in identity is the essential value. Although the actions here are restricted to the ethnic community, the people, by officially indicating what they feel they have become, are risking themselves in the movement from their old-country identity. A more public dream, life in a new society, can now be lived and shared.

As the story develops, the emphasis shifts to Dikran, a second generation figure, and the same kind of social movement is traced, this time one step closer to assimilation into the American mainstream. Here, however, the story is much more critical of the movement. Aram's family is pleased when the boy Dikran (aged 11) becomes adept at giving speeches. Nonetheless, the patriarch of the family is still dissatisfied, because all the boy's knowledge is from books, impersonal. Dikran's speech at the school program is "the best thing of its kind—the best of the worst kind of thing"—for the boy concludes that the World War, in which several million were killed, was a good thing for the world. In spite of his pride in the boy's achievement in an American ritual, the old man feels he must speak to the boy out of what he knows: "Continue your investigation of the world from books, and I am sure, if you are diligent and your eyes hold out, that by the time you are sixty-seven you will know the awful foolishness of that remark [about the war]—so innocently uttered by yourself tonight." Certified social achievement is a good thing, but in this case the status of the elder in the ethnic community permits personal sensitivity to have the final word by articulating a truer wisdom.

The stories **"A Nice Old-Fashioned Romance with Love Lyrics and Everything"** and **"The Circus"** concentrate on characters working out the social fictions which their roles in the official world force upon them. Both utilize favorite materials of Saroyan's, the classroom and the confrontation between students and teachers. Here and elsewhere in Saroyan the American classroom is another arena where one's personal behavior can win a form of status, providing one can manipulate official structures. In **"The Circus"** the narrative is always uncomfortably on the verge of a serious confrontation as the boys openly challenge the rules by fleeing from school (instead of sneaking out). They imagine that their punishment this time may involve the removal to a more indifferent (more absolutely official) environment, the reform school. But at the end the institutional patriarch (the principal, old man Dawson) turns more personally understanding, whipping them with more blows, as required for such an offense, but with a gentler stroke. He also pays tribute to their bizarre concern for him: "I'm awfully grateful to you boys . . . for modulating your howls so nicely this time. I don't want people to think I'm killing you."

In **"A Nice Old-Fashioned Romance"** Aram is accused, unjustly, of writing on the blackboard a poem, saying that his teacher, Miss Daffney, is in love with Mr. Derringer, the principal in this story. The fact that Aram is actually innocent means nothing because to both teacher and principal his past behavior in the classroom makes him guilty. His punishment, however, is not the issue; rather the question in the story is whether the two authority figures will be able to acknowledge that the poem in fact objectifies their secret feelings. The story ends with Miss Daffney's removing herself from the scene, apparently because of her inability to make what is an obvious truth into a sufficiently public feeling that it might form the basis for a positive bond.

One of the complications in the story occurs when Miss Daffney surprises Derringer beating a chair instead of Aram. As she suspects, a small deal between the principal and the boy has been negotiated. Derringer wants Aram to be more "gracious" about Miss Daffney's appearance in "his" poems. Aram, who has not written the poems, sees a chance to strike a personal bargain on the level of the official lie. "If you punish me," he tells Derringer, "then I won't be gracious." Derringer agrees not to punish him, but so that no one gets suspicious, he gets Aram to howl while he straps the chair. Miss Daffney, bursting in on this private scene, regards Derringer's action as a falsification of his school role (and perhaps as a personal betrayal of her as well). In this instance, however, as she might have figured out, turning the social ritual into a more personal relationship is not a bad idea, for it also opens the possibility for the surfacing of some feelings of affection in the sorting out of what is going on.

As is the case in several other stories, the movement around and about the official social situation creates the playfulness of a game situation. The advantage of turning a social situation into a kind of game is that all parties can see that the official rules and outcomes are not the absolutely confirming measurements they can seem. Characters involved are more apt to appreciate the ingenuity, the active intention, and the persistence of the other person. They are inevitably moved to an attempt at understanding. The great danger is the tendency of the ego to draw the official world into its private domain, as is the case with Uncle Khosrove's attitude toward the games. At one time Aram, encouraged by Lionel Strongfort's advertisements, imagines himself becoming the most powerful man in his neighborhood. Not until he has alarmed his relatives, irritated his neighbors, provoked advice from his Uncle Gyko and stories from his grandmother, and lost the key race to the other boys does he begin to understand that the dream in this case cannot be more. Sometimes the greater strength of external reality is simply in the fact that, while it cannot be exceeded, it can be naturally and democratically shared.

In this story Uncle Gyko is an adult mirror of Aram's ego dreams. Believing that the secret of greatness is "the releasing within one's self of those mysterious vital forces which are in all men," Gyko deludes himself that he is getting wisdom from God. In fact, as Aram informs us, he gets all his ideas from "the theosophy-philosophy-astrology-and-miscellaneous shelf at the Public Library." His concluding advice for Aram is the great secret of the private world—but also, as Aram eventually sees, its supreme delusion: "We are a great family. We can do anything." In this story, and throughout the book, Saroyan's fascination with the desire to achieve is tempered by his witty awareness of the terms the world dictates to its social inhabitants.

Heinrich Straumann has remarked that a prominent and ultimately unfortunate strain in Saroyan's work is a tendency to try to escape from reality. It is perhaps the most formidable kind of negative criticism of Saroyan since it implies that his weakest work is his most characteristic. The argument of this paper is that Saroyan is essentially a modernist in that he regards his fictional reality as multifaceted and that his awareness of the claims of the ethnic community pushed him in this direction. His aim in *My Name Is Aram* is to show how his main character, possessed both of a heritage of values and an active imagination, senses himself moving psychologically between an old order and a new possibility. Much of the maneuvering is done through conversation, a crucial activity which keeps the characters alive to their environment as a community and invaluable to one another as individuals. And it is further enriched by humor, that detached awareness of the individual that both sets of ethos, ethnic and mainstream, are, as cultures, inherently peculiar.

Even though Saroyan has said that the characters are based on his own memories, their dialogue seems less remembered talk than improvisation, the sketching out in the writing process of an increasing communal awareness and an increasing communal crisis. The book seems based primarily on Saroyan's recollections of people's infinite capacities for manipulating their conventions. In it he creates, through a rhythmically comic interchange of internal values and social perspectives, a version of how culture might work. He ultimately suggests, through the narratives' postponing and suspending of judgements on people, that some measurement systems are valuable only when they function intermittently.

Gerald W. Haslam   (essay date 1987)

SOURCE: "William Saroyan," in *A Literary History of the American West,* Texas Christian University Press, 1987, pp. 472-81.

[*Haslam is an American educator, short story writer, and novelist. In the following essay, he traces the courses of Saroyan's literary career and critical reception.*]

Few American writers tumbled as dramatically from critical acclaim as did William Saroyan. There were many reasons, not the least of which was his personality. Because, as Saroyan's son Aram has argued, the writer came to personify "what might be called the mythic potential of his particular social-historical moment." Saroyan's self-centered, sometimes abrasive character became perhaps more important than his writing in the eyes of some. William Saroyan was, during the first half of his career, as much a public figure as an artist, and the confusion of those two roles made it easy to ignore his literary accomplishments once his notoriety faded.

In fact, the artist's psychological contradictions are finally much less important than the quality of his art and, from his first published volume (*The Daring Young Man on the Flying Trapeze and Other Stories,* 1934) until his last (*Obituaries,* 1979)—both of which were cited as among their years' best books—Saroyan was an authentic, singular American genius. He was also, as Bob Sector has pointed out, "his own biggest fan."

Another factor in the Fresno native's fall from critical grace was the adversarial relationship he had developed with critics. He wrote in 1940:

> . . . I acknowledge the *partial* truth and validity of every charge brought against my work, against myself personally, and against my methods of making my work public. What is lacking in their criticism is the fullness and humanity of understanding which operates in myself, in my work, and in my regard for others. . . . Consequently, it is difficult for them to make sense in themselves that which is complicated and unusual for them. What should enlarge them because of its understanding, drives them more completely behind the fort of their own limitations.

Little wonder he was a prime candidate for literary ostracism.

Today, with the author's personality no longer a factor, Saroyan's work is enjoying critical reevaluation. His work, not his ego or pugnaciousness or reclusiveness, is at issue, and it stands up very well indeed. As David Kherdian recently observed:

His writing had a quality of innocence and eagerness and wonder about a moment—any moment of living— that made us feel more alive ourselves—more alive, that is, than we actually were, but for this very reason it made us yearn and stretch and seek a way to grow.

And H. W. Matalene has asserted that "the place of William Saroyan in the history of the American theater still seems as secure as he always told us it would be."

After World War II, the Californian fell with a thud out of critical fashion. Not only were the books he published slammed, but his earlier achievements were ignored or slighted, making him a kind of literary nonperson. Even in his native West his accomplishments were neglected; he was not listed in the annual bibliographies published by *Western American Literature,* although much of his best writing was set in the West. *My Heart's in the Highlands, The Time of Your Life,* and *Hello Out There,* Saroyan's three finest plays, employed distinctly western settings and tones, as even negative critics acknowledged. William Saroyan was very much a writer of his time, of his place, and of his dynamic cultural blend, Armenian-American.

Add to those distinguished dramas stories such as **"The Daring Young Man on the Flying Trapeze," "The Pomegranate Trees,"** and **"Seventy Thousand Assyrians,"** novels *The Human Comedy, The Adventures of Wesley Jackson,* and *Tracy's Tiger,* as well as memoirs such as *The Bicycle Rider in Beverly Hills, Not Dying,* and *Obituaries,* and it appears that few twentieth-century American authors produced a richer, more diverse body of work. Saroyan straddled the worlds of high and folk culture. He was an artist of unique and powerful gifts, marred by an apparent lack of discipline, but one who moved both regional and ethnic expression to new heights.

Mary McCarthy, writing in *Partisan Review* in 1940, pinpointed a source of both Saroyan's greatest art and perhaps some of his problems with the literary establishment. "He still retains his innocence," she observed,

> . . . that is, he has had to fight off Ideas, Movements, Sex, and Commercialism. He has stayed out of the literary rackets—the Hollywood racket, the New York Cocktail-party racket, and the Stalinist racket, . . . What is more important, the well of inspiration, located somewhere in his early adolescence, has never run dry.

When he died on May 19, 1981, in Fresno, Saroyan had won both the New York Drama Critics Circle Award and the Pulitzer Prize for *The Time of Your Life* (the first writer to be so doubly honored), an Academy Award for *The Human Comedy,* and the California Gold Medal for *Tracy's Tiger.*

William Saroyan emerged as a writer during the Great Depression, while America was in the throes of a national loss of faith and questioning of values. Although many critics had trouble accepting his optimistic, original stories, readers did not. He was powerfully pro-human. He talked and wrote about the human spirit. That Saroyan also did such things as turn down his Pulitzer Prize certainly did little to raise his stock among insiders. His behavior, like some of his writing, seemed downright unliterary. As novelist Herbert Gold wrote following Saroyan's death, "He didn't want to be the greatest Armenian-American writer in the world. He wanted, very boyishly, just to knock everyone's eyes out with beauty and fun and delight."

Born in Fresno in 1908, Saroyan was placed in an Oakland orphanage at the age of three following the death of his father, a poet and ordained minister. Four years later, his family reunited and returned to Fresno where he grew up. Experiences that would later resurface as rich literary material in such books as *Little Children* (1937) and *My Name Is Aram* (1940) marked the remainder of Saroyan's childhood. He worked at odd jobs, rubbing elbows with a lively group of people of all ethnic types, developed earthy rural values, and was always assured of the support of his extended family and the Armenian community. He did not graduate from high school.

Small wonder that Saroyan's work evidences little social or intellectual pretension. He has also refused to be limited; in **"Seventy Thousand Assyrians"** his protagonist says: "I am an Armenian . . . I have no idea what it's like to be an Armenian . . . I have a faint idea what it's like to be alive. That's the only thing that interests me greatly." That is, while everything he writes is influenced by his Armenian and poor, small-town and western heritage, that influence emerges from within rather than being imposed from without. When he tells his truth well enough, it is everyone's.

In 1928, while working in San Francisco, Saroyan published a story in *Overland Monthly and Outwest Magazine* and decided to make writing his career. Six years later his first book, **The Daring Young Man on the Flying Trapeze and Other Stories,** was published. It was a fresh, zany, ironic, and highly individualistic collection. "Try to be alive," the author advised in his preface. "You will be dead soon enough." If the collection exhibited many of the considerable strengths that were to mark Saroyan as a cutting-edge artist unconcerned with established literary forms, many of those same innovative tales were viewed by critics as undisciplined. Saroyan's response to Eric Bentley's complaint about careless writing perhaps sums up his attitude: "One cannot expect an Armenian to be an Englishman."

Whatever its source—the writer's ethnicity, his San Joaquin Valley upbringing, his distrust of established tastemakers—Saroyan showed during the 1930s a vivacity and originality that seemed exactly correct for those grim times. "I cannot resist the temptation to mock any law which is designated to hamper the spirit of man," he wrote in an early story. Critics of that period, burdened by polemic proletarian positions or still awakening to the power of naturalism, didn't know how to treat this brash westerner; Nona Balakian asserts, Saroyan was "inevitably misunderstood or belittled."

By the beginning of World War II, Saroyan estimated that he had written more than five hundred tales. His craft progressed so that not only great talent but considerable skill marked his writing, and he began to evidence a profound sense of place in his fiction. Increasingly in his writing—especially in the superb *My Name Is Aram*—Saroyan returned to Fresno and California's San Joaquin Valley for both setting and subjects. In so doing, he produced some major western American literature. Howard Floan, noting the artistic growth these valley stories demonstrated, points out that in his early tales the young people of Saroyan's stories had been essentially undiluted projections of himself. In *Little Children* and *My Name Is Aram* the writer uses such characters to greater effect, for the stories are not self-centered, "they are about the immigrants of Fresno and the San Joaquin Valley, the people recalled from his boyhood days whose images gave him the impetus to extend himself beyond the lyricism of his early tales to the more dramatic later ones. . . . If Saroyan had not discovered the literary uses of Fresno and the Valley, he could not have given us the best of his short stories—nor his plays." He was, then, very much a western writer.

Saroyan's plays demonstrate even more clearly than his stories the importance of the oral tradition and his ethnic heritage in his work. He explained:

> Everything I write, everything I have ever written, is allegorical. This came to pass inevitably. One does not choose to write allegorically any more than one chooses to grow black hair on his head. The stories of Armenia . . . are all allegorical, and apart from the fact that I heard these stories as a child . . . I myself am a product of Asia Minor, hence the allegorical and the real are closely related in my mind.
>
> In fact all reality to me is allegorical. . . .

When in 1939 he converted a short story, **"The Man with the Heart in the Highlands,"** into the play *My Heart's in the Highlands,* he demonstrated not only his comfort with spoken language, but his allegorical bent. The play was successful and even his detractors agreed that the Californian had provided a radical departure from usual theatrical fare. Both George Jean Nathan and John Mason Brown considered it the finest Broadway play of the 1938-39 season.

The following year Saroyan produced one of the classic plays of the modern American theatre, *The Time of Your Life.* It confirmed what the author's earlier dramatic work had hinted, that he was as original and irreverent on stage as he was in print. Balakian points out that "nothing quite so informal and spontaneous had happened on the American stage before Saroyan came along." Audiences were well advised to attend Saroyan's remarks about allegory if they sought to understand his dramas. The theatre became a major outlet for Saroyan's work. *The Beautiful People, Jim Dandy: Fat Man in a Famine,* and *The Cave Dwellers* (his last Broadway production, in 1957), among others, all illustrated his quest, stated earlier in a short story:

"If I want to do anything I want to speak a more universal language, the heart of man, the unwritten part of man, that which is eternal and common to all races."

From the beginning—as early as the publication of **"The Daring Young Man on the Flying Trapeze"**—Saroyan evidenced a freedom from conventional literary modes of reality that marks him today as an early exemplar of what has been called Magical Realism. Merged levels of consciousness, powerful intuition, an insistence upon what is perceived rather than what is expected, little concern for chronological time, these and other elements led Edmund Wilson to praise "These magical feats" which he said "are accomplished by the enchantment of Saroyan's temperament, which induces us to take from him a good many things that we should not accept from other people." Another giant of American criticism, John Mason Brown, proclaimed that "Saroyan has managed to widen the theatre's horizons by escaping from facts and reason. . . ." Saroyan himself explained his gift this way:

> . . . I do not know a great deal about what words come to, but the presence says, Now don't get funny; just sit down and say something; it'll be all right anyway. Half the time I *do* say it wrong, but somehow or other, just as the presence says, it's right anyhow. I am always pleased about this.

During World War II, the Californian produced two of his most successful novels, *The Human Comedy* and *The Adventures of Wesley Jackson,* the latter a picaresque version of army life with a somewhat hard edge which Wilson admired. The former book began as an award-winning screenplay, over which Saroyan battled with Metro-Goldwyn-Mayer, trying to buy it back, then retreated to write a play, *Get Away Old Man,* that dramatized the conflict. It opened on Broadway in 1943. If Saroyan got the final word, MGM seems to have managed the final laugh: the play flopped.

Saroyan emerged as a writer during the Great Depression, while America was in the throes of a national loss of faith and questioning of values. Although many critics had trouble accepting his optimistic, original stories, readers did not. He was powerfully pro-human. He talked and wrote about the human spirit.

—*Gerald W. Haslam*

Following the war, Saroyan went into a critical tailspin. Disillusioned by his military experience—he served in the Army—tax problems, and the collapse of his marriage to Carol Marcus, his mood and literature darkened. By his own admission, he drank too much and gambled too much. "Three years in the army and a stupid marriage had all but knocked me out of the picture and, if the truth is told, out of life itself." His son's biography, *William Saroyan* (1983), offers the other side of the story.

He gradually brought his drinking and gambling under control, and once more began producing high-quality work. But, critically at least, it was too late. As Matalene points out:

> . . . One senses that critics have been less interested in discovering and teaching Saroyan's message than they have been in congratulating themselves for having been so democratic as to have admitted to the canon of recognized literature the work of an uneducated, penniless Armenian from Fresno—at least for as long as he seemed amusing.

He no longer seemed amusing, and he was dropped like the outsider he always was, one of the less savory and defensible episodes in American literary history.

During the final years of his life he produced several probing, sometimes delightful memoirs, the first of which, *Not Dying* (1963), led Herbert Mitgang to observe in *The New York Times*: "A hardboiled romantic, Saroyan shows that he can be more in the vanguard than many of the official literary-map personages in *Esquire*; that he'll be around long after this year's hipsters have become next year's squares."

Often Saroyan's mood was morose in his later works; he seemed preoccupied by death. Of *Not Dying* he observed, "I haven't laughed once in the writing of this book."

William Saroyan had always been concerned over the degree to which artificiality dominates reality in human experience, a situation he thought literary critics apotheosized. Ironically, in the biography which offers his ex-wife's and his children's perspectives on the author's life, Saroyan's son Aram asserts that the truth of his father's character remains obscure, while "his legend, dating back to the earliest part of his carrer, continues to dominate popular consciousness of both his literary career and public image."

A more balanced assessment of Saroyan has been offered by his friend and associate James H. Tashjian, editor of *The Armenian Review*. "No question: William Saroyan was a battlefield on which Ormuzd and Ahriman fought relentlessly—good versus evil," he wrote in his preface to *My Name Is Saroyan* (1983), explaining:

> . . . There is little question that Saroyan's personal conduct was in direct contradiction of his father's rigid code—Saroyan gambled and gamboled, he was flaky and notoriously unreliable, he drank heavily on occasion, wenched and was twice divorced—all misvirtues. . . . But he was, at the same time, a dedicated pacifist, a ridiculer of the goosestep, a foe of peonage and patronage. He was impatient of dissimulation, generous and charitable . . . and was respectful of all religions.

William Saroyan was a flawed, passionate man, a complicated mixture of virtue and vice whose great talent magnified all aspects of his personality. Tashjian makes one

other major point, observing that "Saroyan is only 'enigmatic' to those who cannot . . . understand what his Armenian heritage meant to him."

Both Aram Saroyan and Tashjian agree that a major element in William Saroyan's makeup was the early death of his father, Armenak, a subject he returned to, both directly and indirectly, throughout his literary career. It "forged in him a basic Oedipal urge—to find the father who had left him," Tashjian points out. "This was to grow into a veritable passion in his manhood. It colored his thoughts and his carrer." Perhaps the most touching of such work is "Armenak of Bitlis" (*Letters from 74 rue Taitbout*, 1969), which recounts a visit to his father's grave in San Jose, then leads the author to recount a sterile meeting with his own son in New York. It is a powerful piece that illustrates well the writer's continuing abilities.

Sham remained a continuing theme. Early in his carrer Saroyan had lamented the influence of tastemakers such as literary critics this way:

> It's wonderful to get up in the morning and go out for a little walk and smell the trees and see the streets and the kids going to school and the clouds in the sky. . . . This is a nice world. So why do they make all the trouble?

Late in his career, once he had become somewhat reclusive, his tone changed. "Can a society which has thrived on lies be expected to survive?" he asked. He answered himself this way: "Possibly, but the people of that society can't be expected not to be grotesque." In some places, his style turned preachy and verbose.

Still, flashes of the old spirit surfaced. In a 1978 interview with Herbert Gold, Saroyan remarked, "I'm growing old! I'm falling apart! And it's VERY INTERESTING!" He worked out of one of two tract houses in Fresno which he had bought in the 1960s—he also kept an apartment in Paris—and rode around his hometown on a bicycle. An eleven-year-old neighbor remembered, "I saw him ridin' with no hands and everything, lots of times." He was a great favorite of neighborhood children, and they were favorites of his.

Bella Stumbo, in the *Los Angeles Times,* added that "He refused all interviews with the press (on the grounds that the 'knotheads' asked him stupid questions), and even turned down invitations to the White House in later years." Shortly before his death, Saroyan called the Associated Press to leave a posthumous statement: "Everybody has got to die, but I have always believed an exception would be made in my case. Now what?"

Following Saroyan's death, a memorial service was held in Paris. His Holiness Vazken I, the Catholicos of all Armenians, eulogized the author, calling him "the prodigy of the nation, the vehicle through which three millennia of Armenian experience was perhaps most perfectly expressed." The Catholicos concluded by observing that "William Saroyan's writing, his humanism, speaks not just about or to Armenians but to all people."

As usual, Saroyan himself merits the last word. The final sentence of the final volume published during his lifetime, what Herbert Gold calls "his wonderful late book, *Obituaries,*" reads: "I did my best, and let me urge you to do your best, too. Isn't it the least we can do for one another?"

FURTHER READING

Bibliography

Foard, Elisabeth C. *William Saroyan: A Reference Guide.* Boston: G. K. Hall, 1989, 207 p.
    Extensive secondary bibliography about Saroyan and his work.

Biography

Floan, Howard R. *William Saroyan.* New York: Twayne, 1966, 176 p.
    Critical biography. Floan attempts to "define the unique quality of [Saroyan's] imagination, to account for his enormous popular appeal and for the obvious staying power of this appeal."

Foster, Edward Halsey. *William Saroyan.* Boise, Idaho: Boise State University, 1984, 51 p.
    General biographical and critical monograph on Saroyan.

Lee, Lawrence, and Gifford, Barry. *Saroyan: A Biography.* New York: Harper & Row, 1984, 338 p.
    Biography drawn from conversations with Saroyan's friends and associates, journalistic research, and Saroyan's own autobiographical writings.

Saroyan, Aram. *William Saroyan.* New York: Harcourt Brace Jovanovich, 1983, 168 p.
    Presents a personal perspective on Saroyan's life and work.

Criticism

Ararat XXV, No. 2 (Spring 1984): 1-140.
    Special issue devoted to Saroyan's life and work.

Balakian, Nona. "The World of William Saroyan." In *Critical Encounters: Literary Views and Reviews, 1953-1977,* pp. 162-76. Indianapolis: Bobbs-Merrill, 1978.
    Positive assessment of Saroyan's fiction. Balakian contends that "it is only when one reads Saroyan continuously over a period of time that one can come to a true estimate of his stature as a writer, apart from the particular things one loves in him."

Calonne, David Stephen. *William Saroyan: My Real Work is Being.* Chapel Hill: University of North Carolina Press, 1983, 185 p.
    Book-length critical study of Saroyan's fiction, dramas, and autobiographical work.

Carpenter, Frederic I. "The Times of William Saroyan's Life." In *American Literature and the Dream,* pp. 176-84. New York: Philosophical Library, 1955.
    Traces the thematic and stylistic development of Saroyan's fiction.

Fisher, William J. "What Ever Happened to Saroyan?" *College English* 16, No. 6 (March 1955): 336-40, 385.
    Derides Saroyan's later work as pretentious, lazy, and vitriolic.

Foster, Edward Halsey. *William Saroyan: A Study of the Short Fiction.* New York: Twayne Publishers, 1991, 174 p.
    Full-length critical analysis of Saroyan's short fiction.

Kronenberger, Louis. "Mr. Saroyan's Performance." *The Nation,* Vol. CXXXIX, No. 3618 (7 November 1934), 541-42.
    Caustic review of *The Daring Young Man on the Flying Trapeze, and Other Stories.*

Phillips, William. "Big City Primitive." *The Nation* 145, No. 8 (21 August 1937): 203-04.
    Unfavorable review of *Little Children.*

Rahv, Philip. "Narcissus." *Partisan Review* II, No. 6 (January-February 1935): 84-6.
    Marxist critique of *The Daring Young Man on the Flying Trapeze, and Other Stories.*

Rolo, Charles J. "The Dangers of Playing Safe." *Atlantic Monthly* 185, No. 4 (April 1950): 85-6.
    Derides the formulaic stories comprising *The Assyrian.*

Strauss, Harold. "Mr. Saroyan Speaking." *New York Times Book Review* (3 January 1937): 14.
    Offers a laudatory review of *Three Times Three.*

"Barbaric Yawp." *Time* XXVII, No. 9 (2 March 1936): 79-80, 82.
    Provides a mixed review of *Inhale and Exhale.* The critic asserts that Saroyan's collection "still has something to say but is not yet sure of how to say it."

"Armenian American." *Time Literary Supplement,* No. 1812 (24 October 1936): 859.
    Considers autobiographical aspects of *Inhale and Exhale.*

Additional coverage of Saroyan's life and career is contained in the following sources published by Gale Research: *Contemporary Authors,* Vol. 103; *Contemporary Authors,* Vols. 5-8 (rev. ed.); *Contemporary Authors New Revision Series,* Vol. 30; *Contemporary Literary Criticism,* Vols. 1, 8, 10, 29, 34, 56; *Dictionary of Literary Biography,* Vol. 86; *DISCovering Authors; Major 20th-Century Authors; Something about the Author,* Vols. 23, 24; and *World Literature Criticism.*

Jun'ichirō Tanizaki
1886-1965

Japanese novelist, novella and short story writer, dramatist, essayist, and memoirist.

INTRODUCTION

Tanizaki wrote memorably on beauty, eroticism, and obsession, but his treatment of these potentially sensational themes was never gratuitous. Rather, he used the emotional intensity of passion, cruelty, and degradation as a means of expressing the humanity of his characters in a dramatic way. Though early in his career he was influenced by writers and cultures of the West, Tanizaki eventually came to reject Westernization and turned to Japanese history, culture, and literature for inspiration and subject matter.

Biographical Information

Born in the cosmopolitan city of Tokyo in 1886, Tanizaki grew up during the Meiji era (1867-1912), when many centuries-old institutions of Japanese society—notably the *shogun* (military governor), the *samurai* (warrior aristocracy), and the feudal system—suffered elimination or significant reform. Furthermore, Western ideas, arts, laws, customs, schooling, and business methods were welcomed into the country at an unprecedented rate. In 1908 Tanizaki entered Tokyo University but quit his studies in 1910, having written "Shisei" ("The Tattooer"), the best known of his early short stories. In the decade that followed, he devoted himself to writing, particularly dramas. At this early stage in his career, Tanizaki revelled in Western thought and practices and advocated them in his writings. However, in 1923 he moved from Tokyo to a region near Osaka where the older culture and conservative values of Japan predominated, and his writings reflect a corresponding change in his outlook. For example, Tanizaki not only produced a highly-regarded version of Lady Murasaki's eleventh-century masterpiece *Genji monogatari* (*The Tale of Genji*), translating the novel from classical to modern Japanese, he also used earlier periods in Japanese history as the backdrop for such works as *Bushūkō hiwa* (*The Secret History of the Lord of Musashi*) and *Shōshō Shigemoto no haha* (*The Mother of Captain Shigemoto*). In the essay *In'ei raisan* (*In Praise of Shadows*) he pines for the purity and the subtle, suggestive beauty of traditional Japan, attributing the loss of these national characteristics to modernization and the influence of the West. Tanizaki died in 1965.

Major Works of Short Fiction

The most significant of the Western writers by whom Tanizaki was influenced were Edgar Allan Poe and Os-

car Wilde. Like these authors, Tanizaki displayed an interest in the relation of the grotesque to the beautiful. He also shared their emphasis on plot and the creation of a fictional world based on fantasy and subconscious obsessions. Tanizaki's works differed from the Japanese literature of his time, which was dominated by naturalism and the confessional "I-novels." Nearly all of his fiction explores the sexual obsessions and perversions of the protagonist. The typical male hero is obsessed by the beauty of an unattainable woman and he suffers acutely because of this obsession. For Tanizaki, beauty is never far from pain; humiliation, rejection, and masochism commonly form the base of the protagonist's erotic pleasure. The story "The Tattooer" reveals many of Tanizaki's standard themes. Here, a tattooer derives dual gratification from his art: he takes pride in the images he creates on canvases of flesh but also gains sadistic pleasure from inflicting pain with his needle. The tattooer becomes obsessed with an extraordinarily beautiful young woman of whom he has only once had a partial glimpse. Upon encountering her several years later, he convinces her that he should be allowed to create his greatest design upon her skin. Completion of the tattoo signals her symbolic conversion to *femme fatale,* and the artist submissively becomes her first victim. In the novellas *Yoshino kuzu* (*Arrowroot*) and *The Mother of Captain Shigemoto*, as with many of Tanizaki's works, the theme of yearning for unattainable beauty is often developed through the protagonist's quest for the ideal mother-figure. Similarly, "Shunkinshō" ("A Portrait of Shunkin") demonstrates the elevated position given to women by men in Tanizaki's fiction. In this story, a former servant devotes his life to the care of a blind and disfigured woman who refuses to return his love because of his lower social standing. Furthermore, he voluntarily blinds himself both to share her handicap and to honor her request that he not look upon her scarred face. Some of the more perverse subjects evident in Tanizaki's fiction are incorporated into *The Secret History of the Lord of Musashi*. This novella, set in sixteenth-century Japan, depicts the sexual deviation and treachery of the warlord Terukatsu. Aroused by the practices of warriors who take decapitated heads and severed noses from enemies slain in battle, he surreptitiously disfigures his lover's husband by cutting off his nose during the night. Terukatsu then encourages his lover to believe that her now-noseless husband was earlier responsible for her father's murder—an act performed by Terukatsu himself! According to Edmund White, "The cause of Terukatsu's double-dealing is his own bizarre obsession; what he most longs to see is a sadistic woman make love to a noseless man."

Critical Reception

While critics have occasionally labeled Tanizaki's works indecent, most commentators acknowledge the highly literary quality of his fiction, which features carefully wrought language and images, classical and modern influences, and penetrating portrayals of emotion and human nature. Donald Keene has stated: "No one would turn to Tanizaki for wisdom as to how a man should live his life, but anyone seeking the special pleasure of literature and an echo in even his most bizarre works of eternal human concerns could hardly find a superior writer."

PRINCIPAL WORKS

Short Fiction

Bushūkō hiwa [*The Secret History of the Lord of Musashi*] (novella) 1931
Yoshino kuzu [*Arrowroot*] (novella) 1931
Ashikari (novella) 1932
Neko to Shōzō to futari no onna [*A Cat, a Man, and Two Women: Stories*] 1936
Shōshō Shigemoto no haha [*The Mother of Captain Shigemoto*] (novella) 1950
Seven Japanese Tales 1963
The Reed Cutter and Captain Shigemoto's Mother (novellas) 1994

Other Major Works

Chijin no ai [*Naomi*; also translated as *A Fool's Love*] (novel) 1924
Tade kuu mushi [*Some Prefer Nettles*] (novel) 1929
Manji [*Quicksand*] (novel) 1930
Bunshō tokuhon [*A Style Reader*] (criticism) 1934
In'ei raisan [*In Praise of Shadows*] (essay) 1934
*Genji monogatari [*The Tale of Genji*] (modernized version) 1939-41
Sasameyuki [*The Makioka Sisters*] (novel) 1943-48
Kagi [*The Key*] (novel) 1956
Yōshō jidai [*Childhood Years*] (memoir) 1957
Fūten rōjin nikki [*The Diary of a Mad Old Man*] (novel) 1962

*The original, composed in classical Japanese by Murasaki Shikibu, dates to the early eleventh century.

CRITICISM

Stanley Edgar Hyman (essay date 1966)

SOURCE: "A Japanese Master," in *Standards: A Chronicle of Books for Our Time*, Horizon Press, 1966, pp. 179-83.

[*A longtime literary critic for the* New Yorker, *Hyman rose to a prominent position in American letters during the middle decades of the twentieth century. He is noted for his belief that much of modern literary criticism should depend on knowledge received from disciplines outside the field of literature; consequently, many of his best reviews and critical essays rely on his application of theories gleaned from such disciplines as cultural anthropology, psychology, and comparative religion. In the following essay, Hyman praises the wide appeal of the short fiction comprising* Seven Japanese Tales, *maintaining that "however native Tanizaki's fiction might be, it is also securely with the tradition of European literature."*]

My favorite painting in all the world is one that I have never seen. It is "Portrait of Taira Shigemori" by the medieval Japanese painter Takanobu, and it is in a private collection in Tokyo. I know it from a color reproduction in André Malraux's *The Voices of Silence,* and every time I look at it again I am left breathless with wonder and delight. I feel (as Malraux meant me to feel) that this painting communicates perfectly to me across great barriers of time and culture.

Some Japanese prints, less powerfully, give me the same experience, but Japanese literature does not. The poetry seems to me entirely untranslatable, reading in English as faint rubbings of vanished poems. The few Japanese novels that I have read tended to leave me with a vague feeling of having missed the point. When she dyes a syllable of his name on her kimono, or he gives her the smaller segments of the tangerine, it is enormously significant, is it not? But significant of what, exactly?

In 1963 I picked up Junichiro Tanizaki's *Seven Japanese Tales,* translated by Howard Hibbett. Before I had finished the first tale, **"A Portrait of Shunkin,"** I knew that I was in the presence of a master, and that, however native Tanizaki's fiction might be, it is also securely within the tradition of European literature. I had the sense of immediate communication that the Takanobu portrait gives me.

I was a little late coming to him. Tanizaki (now dead) was then 77; he had been publishing for more than 50 years; he was said to be Japan's greatest living writer; and he was a strong candidate for the Nobel Prize. Three of his novels have been published in this country: *Some Prefer Nettles* in 1955, *The Makioka Sisters* in 1957, and *The Key* in 1961. After reading all except the first, I am lost in admiration for Tanizaki's talents and variety.

Two of the novellas in *Seven Japanese Tales* are master pieces. My favorite, **"A Portrait of Shunkin"** (1933), is like nothing else I have ever read. It is the story of a female monster and her devoted slave. Shunkin is a blind samisen virtuoso and Sasuke is a former servant of her family and pupil of hers, who himself becomes a samisen master. He cares for her, runs her school, and they live together and have children. She will not marry him because of his social inferiority, however, and the children are sent out for adoption.

The novella rises to two related horrors. In the first, Shunkin, probably in revenge for her sadistic and rapacious treatment of pupils, is disfigured by an unknown attacker, who throws a kettleful of boiling water on her face as she sleeps. Shunkin makes Sasuke promise never to look at her ravaged face, and he keeps his promise by blinding himself with a sewing needle. These awful deeds, which arouse the sort of pity and terror that the self-discovery and self-blinding of King Oedipus do, result in a love of serene beauty. When Sasuke tells Shunkin of his act, she for the first time feels respect and love for him, and they embrace, weeping. "I am inclined to think," the narrator comments, "that the destruction of her beauty had its compensations for Shunkin in various ways. Both in love and in art she must have discovered undreamed-of ecstasies."

There are a number of exotic Japanese customs in the novella, but Tanizaki's craft makes the details of nightingale singing or lark soaring, Shunkin's hobbies, seem as reasonable and familiar as my own pursuits. They are not put in for local color; they function symbolically in the story. The nightingales, which must be taken from the nest in infancy and carefully trained to sing artificial calls, perfectly symbolize the exactions of art; and Shunkin's prized lark, which soars up and never returns, bears with it her sight, her beauty, and her life.

The horror and ecstasy of the novella are kept in perfect tension by a narrator, a masterly creation, who endlessly questions, speculates, and doubts. Thus we see Sasuke's

fanatic joy in sacrifice through the eyes of a man who cannot comprehend it (Melville uses the same device in "Bartleby the Scrivener" and "Benito Cereno"). The narrator's skepticism at the end of the story is perfect: "It seems that when the priest Gazan of the Tenryu Temple heard the story of Sasuke's self-immolation, he praised him for the Zen spirit with which he changed his whole life in an instant, turning the ugly into the beautiful, and said that it was very nearly the act of a saint. I wonder how many of us would agree with him."

The other superb novella in the book is **"The Bridge of Dreams"** (1959). It is another disturbing and perverse study of devotion, now in a recurring chain. The narrator's father is so devoted to his first wife that he gives his second wife her name and turns the second into a facsimile of the first; the second wife loves her husband so devotedly that when she has a child by him she sends it out for adoption, so that her predecessor's son may retain all her maternal love. The narrator, Tadasu, loves his stepmother (who has entirely merged with his mother in his mind) to the point of marrying, after his father's death, in order to have someone to take care of his stepmother; after she dies he divorces his wife and takes his half-brother, who "looks exactly like Mother," to live with him.

The story is thus a succession of ingrown triangles. These relationships are perverse and symbolically incestuous: Tadasu suckled at his mother's breasts until he was four; his stepmother encourages him to continue the habit, and he suckles at her dry breasts until he is 13; when her baby is sent away, Tadasu, then 19, sucks the milk from her breasts. He suffers "an agony of shame" until he realizes that his father must have arranged it all. In this perversity, again, there is great beauty. The various trios sit by the garden pond to enjoy the cool of the evening, with one mother or another dangling her feet in the water while father or son drinks beer, happy and at peace in their web of ties.

The symbolic resonance that birdsong brings to **"A Portrait of Shunkin"** is obtained here by poetry and one odd symbol. The novella begins on a poem, "On reading the last chapter of *The Tale of Genji*," written by one or the other of Tadasu's mothers. Other poems are quoted about the stream, or are inscribed on the gates of Heron's Nest (their house), or are mounted on the transom, or come to the narrator's mind in connection with some feature of the house. The effect is to cover Heron's Nest with a patina of order and beauty, so that the perverse attachments of the members of the family can be recognized as the corruption of traditional virtues.

The odd symbol is a "water mortar," a hollow bamboo tube under the pond's inlet, designed to clack regularly as it fills and empties. As an infant sleeping at his mother's breast, Tadasu heard the clack of the water mortar in his dreams; it is disconnected when his father is dying, and is started up again after the funeral. It seems to symbolize the security and reassurance that are the goals of the characters' neurotic attachments.

Ultimately, though, the water mortar remains mysterious, a voice not quite explainable by either hydraulics or psychoanalysis. All the mysteries of this uncanny novella remain: we never learn what the real reason is for anything, or which mother wrote the poem, or even whether Tadasu's wife killed his stepmother, as he suspects that she did. The title symbol, the bridge of dreams, is at once the title of the last chapter of *Genji* (where it represents Life), the footbridge over the pond at Heron's Nest, and Father's dying words (which well represent his Faustian ambition, handed on to the others, to bridge love across death).

The best of the other stories, **"A Blind Man's Tale"** (1931) is a historical novella about the warlord civil wars of the sixteenth century; its theme is likewise devotion, the life-long loyalty of the narrator, a blind minstrel and masseur, to his noble lady. The other four are short, and much less impressive. They are: **"The Tattooer"** (1910), **"Terror"** (1913), **"The Thief"** (1921), and **"Aguri"** (1922). I think that, as was the case with Chekhov, Tanizaki needs the roominess of the larger form for his highest artistry.

The two novels that I have read further display Tanizaki's range. *The Makioka Sisters* is an excellent novel of a sort that does not very much interest me, the long realistic family chronicle. Its action is the struggle to get the third sister, Yukiko, properly married; when that is achieved the novel ends. Meanwhile Tanizaki has taken us through "the most disastrous flood in the history of the Kobe-Osaka district," "the worst typhoon" to hit Tokyo "in over ten years," and the China Incident. The book communicates the very texture of Japanese life, and that is the trouble. When, on their honeymoon, Teinosuke asks his wife Sachiko to name her favorite fish, and she names sea bream, this is not some powerful symbol of her aspirations, as are Shunkin's nightingale or Tadasu's water mortar; it is just her taste in fish.

The Key is something else again. Hardly longer than a novella, it is a sensual and melodramatic story, told in His and Hers diaries, of a professor's debauching of his innocent wife, so successfully that she kills him to live with her lover, who will be married for convenience to her daughter. Ikuko is another monster, another Shunkin, but here we watch the process of manufacture.

Tanizaki's theme is not really devotion, but devotion curdled into neurotic fixation. In the fashion of Japanese culture, he is very matter-of-fact about the body. What is quite remarkable is the way Tanizaki combines this with a sense of the body's mystery. There is no matter-of-factness, but a burning sensuality, in the professor's photographing his wife naked in *The Key,* published when the author was 70, or in Tadasu at his stepmother's breasts in **"The Bridge of Dreams,"** published when the author was 73.

In this respect, as in many others, Tanizaki reminds me of the Leskov of "Lady Macbeth of the Mtensk District." If one cannot be Tolstoi or Dostoevsky, it is not too bad to be Leskov.

Donald Keene   (essay date 1971)

SOURCE: "Three Modern Novelists: Tanizaki Junichirō," in *Landscapes and Portraits: Appreciations of Japanese Culture,* Kodansha International Ltd., 1971, pp. 171-85.

[*Keene is an American educator, translator, and critic with a special interest in Japanese literature. In the following excerpt, he examines recurring motifs in Tanizaki's short fiction.*]

The writings of Tanizaki Junichirō are apt to surprise equally by their exceptional diversity of subject and manner, and by their equally exceptional consistency of themes. The diversity is likely to attract our attention first. Tanizaki derived materials for his novels from the distant past of the Heian and Muromachi periods, from the war chronicles of the sixteenth century and the popular fiction of the early nineteenth century. Still other works were closely based on personal experience. His inspiration was usually Japanese, but at the outset of his career he was influenced especially by Baudelaire and Poe, as he later recalled with some shame: "It is not my intention to debate here whether having been influenced by the West was beneficial or harmful to my writings, but no one knows as well as I— to my great embarrassment—in what extremely superficial, indeed mindless ways this influence revealed itself." Apart from European influence, two journeys to China, his only travels abroad, added an exotic touch to some of his writings and provided the basis for harshly objective comments on Japan. Tanizaki used his materials freely, whether Japanese or foreign, sometimes producing carefully documented historical tales, sometimes works that, despite their factual appearance, are almost entirely of his invention.

Tanizaki's methods of narration embrace almost every variety of technique, including the normal third-person account; the first-person confession; the mixed contemporary and historical style in which the narrator (often Tanizaki himself) intrudes at times into the telling of a story from the distant past; and the novel composed of letters or diaries. The diversity of Tanizaki's work is suggested moreover by the remarkably contrasting shapes and appearances of the first editions of his books, each intended to produce a distinct impression by its format, type, binding and even paper as well as the content.

So great is the variety of works Tanizaki wrote in the half-century between 1910 (the year of his début with **"The Tattooer"**) and 1962 (the year of *Diary of a Mad Old Man*) that it is only on reflection that we perceive the striking consistency of themes throughout the works composed over this long period. Most conspicuous was his utter preoccupation with women. His novels are filled with superbly evoked portraits of women, but with rare exceptions he seemed uninterested in depicting male characters. This is true, of course, of much modern literature in Japan; the men, in fiction at least, tend to be weak-willed and negative, no match for the women. Tanizaki created some characters that might be described as alter egos of himself—Sadanosuke in *The Makioka Sisters* comes most quickly to mind—but he failed to impart to them his own immense masculine energy and purpose. It seems improbable that Tanizaki was incapable of drawing such a character; rather, his absorption with women was so great as to make him see in men only the mirrors or slaves of his female characters.

The characteristic male in a Tanizaki novel is an abject figure whose greatest pleasure is to be tortured by the woman he adores. This is true whether the hero is a figure of the distant past or a contemporary. This masochistic worship of women, this glorification of demonical women who reduce men to grovelling slaves, is certainly not a heritage of the traditional Japanese literature. We cannot imagine Prince Genji craving to be trodden on by Murasaki or finding his greatest pleasure in waiting on her like a servant, but this is precisely true of Seribashi in *Ashikari* or Sasuke in **"A Portrait of Shunkin."** Of course, women are frequently depicted in the old literature as monsters of jealousy or deceit, and Saikaku's heroines (like Tanizaki's) sometimes exhaust their partners by excessive sexual demands; but although the worship of cruel women may have in fact existed in traditional Japan, Tanizaki was undoubtedly indebted to Western influence for literary expression of this phenomenon.

Tanizaki's first important story, **"The Tattooer"** (1910), concludes with the tattooer Seikichi becoming the victim of the work of art he has created. The girl into whose back he has etched a monstrous spider flashes a smile of triumph as she realizes she now is capable of trapping men within her terrible web. One theme, first given expression in the same story, was to persist through all of Tanizaki's later writings: Seikichi is first attracted to the girl by catching a glimpse of her naked foot. We are told: "To his sharp eyes a human foot was as expressive as a face. . . . This, indeed, was a foot to be nourished by men's blood, a foot to trample on their bodies."

An extreme expression of Tanizaki's foot-fetishism, as he himself called it, was **"Fumiko's Feet"** (1919). In this story an old man, infatuated with the beautiful feet of his young mistress, asks a young painter to draw her portrait in a pose that best reveals her feet. When he himself is bed-ridden and too feeble to play with the girl's feet in his accustomed manner, he asks the willing painter to roll like a dog at Fumiko's feet and allow himself to be trampled by her. The old man dies blissfully happy because during his last moments Fumiko's foot has been pressed against his forehead.

Almost every work of Tanizaki's has passages revealing his fascination with women's feet. In the play *The Man with the Mandoline* the hero, a blind man, drugs his wife so that he can fondle her feet while she sleeps. Sometimes, as in **"A Portrait of Shunkin,"** it is the woman who insists on warming her feet against a man's face or chest, sometimes it is the man who longs desperately to feel the weight of a cruel woman's feet. In Tanizaki's last major work *Diary of a Mad Old Man* (1962), the tottering old man gets down on his hands and knees in the shower-room for the privilege of cramming his daughter-in-law's

toes into his mouth. In the same work the foot-fetishism that runs through Tanizaki's entire career is given its grand finale in the description of the tombstone that the old man erects almost at the cost of his life: it is a reproduction of his daughter-in-law's footprint, enlarged to heroic size, and meant to stand in triumph forever over the abject old man.

A related aspect of foot-fetishism and the craven masculine surrender to the female, the desire to abase himself before her, is the man's fascination with her excreta. I can hardly recall a Western novel that even mentions the heroine's going to stool, but this is a frequent, almost obsessive theme in Tanizaki's works. *The Makioka Sisters* (1942-47) alone contains more detailed and graphic references to bowel movements than one would find in a whole library of Western novels, and the last sentence of the work is the unforgettable: "Her diarrhoea never did stop that day, and even after she boarded the train it still continued." In **"A Portrait of Shunkin"** the attentions of Sasuke to his mistress Shunkin in the lavatory are lovingly described. In *Secret Stories of the Lord of Musashi* (1935) the hero manages to find his way to the beautiful princess by creeping up through the hole in her toilet. In *The Mother of Captain Shigemoto* (1950) the ninth-century courtier and lover Heijū falls madly in love with a palace lady who refuses him. Determined to cure himself of his passion, he decides to obtain possession of her chamber pot, supposing that when he sees that the contents are exactly like those of a quite ordinary person's chamber pot he will be disillusioned. He snatches away the pot from a lady-in-waiting and carries it home. But he cannot bring himself to open the covered leather box, not because he is afraid of being disgusted, but because he wants to savor the pleasure. "He took it in his hands again, lifted it up and looked at it, put it down and looked at it, turned it around, tried calculating the weight of the contents. At last, with great hesitation, he removed the lid, only for a balmy fragrance like that of cloves to strike his nostrils." He probes the contents, more and more astonished by the exquisite fragrance. Instead of being disillusioned he is now frantically determined to become intimate with so extraordinary a woman. Carried away by his delight, "he drew the box to him and sipped a little of the liquid in the contents."

Tanizaki's absorption with the excretory processes was not confined to his fiction. In his essay "In Praise of Shadows," for example, he devotes pages to describing the traditional Japanese toilets, which he finds infinitely more agreeable than the gleaming Western vessels. He declares, "It may well be said that the most elegantly constructed works of Japanese architecture are the toilets." In another essay, "All About Toilets" (1935), he writes, "A certain nostalgic sweet remembrance accompanies the smell of a toilet. For example, when someone who has been away from home for a long time returns after an absence of years, when he goes into the toilet and smells the odor he knew long ago, it brings back better than anything else memories of his younger days, and he really feels the warmth of 'I'm home!'" But in excreta as in feet Tanizaki insists that they belong to a beautiful woman. The steam from another man's urine on a cold day definitely does not please him.

Even a superficial acquaintance with the literature of psychoanalysis reveals how intimately connected fetishism is with the reiterated mentions of the excretory processes. Here is Freud on the subject: "Psychoanalysis has cleared up one of the remaining gaps in our understanding of fetishism. It has shown the importance, as regards the choice of a fetish, of a coprophilic pleasure in smelling which has disappeared owing to repression. Both the feet and the hair are objects with a strong smell which have been exalted into fetishes after the olfactory sensation has become unpleasurable and been abandoned." Various of the followers of Freud have pointed out that fetishism is associated with a clinging to the mother and the strong desire to identify with her, and with a castration anxiety. Case after case is reported of foot-fetishists whose memories of their mothers are lovingly entwined with fecal smells. But it is not within my powers to psychoanalyze Tanizaki; suffice it to say that Tanizaki's fetishism and coprophilia both seem to be associated with the longing for the mother, which is a powerful though intermittent theme in his works.

The heroines of Tanizaki's novels generally suggest in appearance what he wrote of his mother, who was small (less than five feet tall), delicate of features, well-proportioned rather than frail. On the whole Tanizaki had less to say about the faces of his women than their feet. The features are classical, we are told, but they are deliberately blurred, as in the description of Oyu-san in *Ashikari:* "There was something hazy about Oyu-sama's face, as if one saw it through smoke. The lines of her features—the eyes, the nose, the mouth—were blurred as if a thin veil lay over them. There was not one sharp, clear line." The narrator in **"A Portrait of Shunkin"** tells us, "There is a photograph of her at thirty-six which shows a face of classic oval outline and features so delicately modeled they seem almost ethereal. However, since it dates from the eighteen-sixties, the picture is speckled with age and as faded as an old memory. . . . In that misty photograph I can detect nothing more than the usual refinement of a lady from a well-to-do Osaka merchant family—beautiful, to be sure, but without any real individuality." In a late work **"The Bridge of Dreams"** (1959), again, we are told, "I cannot recall my first mother's features distinctly . . . all I can summon to my mind's eye is the vague image of a full, round face. . . . All I could tell from the picture was that she wore her hair in an old-fashioned style." The clearest identification of this dimly perceived beauty with his own mother was given by Tanizaki in the story **"Yearning for My Mother,"** written in 1918, the year after his mother's death. When he finds her in his dream she is insubstantial, hardly more than a beautiful shadow.

The function of the male in Tanizaki's stories is to worship this unearthly creature. In *Ashikari* Seribashi's slavish devotion to Oyu-san not only keeps him from presuming to have physical relations with her, though sometimes they share the same bed, but even from having relations with his own wife. In **"The Bridge of Dreams"** the narrator's attachment to his stepmother, who has blended completely in his mind with the mother he lost when a small child, is so great that even after he is married he "was always careful to take precautions against having a child—that was the one thing I never neglected." The young man in this story still suckles at his stepmother's breast at the age of eighteen, and there is more than one hint that he has sexual relations with her. He marries only to provide the stepmother—whom he always refers to as Mother—with a devoted servant, and when the stepmother dies he immediately gets rid of his wife, preferring to live in his memories.

But if this mother figure is gentle and dimly perceived even when in her presence, she is often cruel. The fear that the mother may refuse the child her love apparently belongs to the same complex of phenomena associated with foot-fetishism I have already mentioned, but in Tanizaki's stories the cruelty of the beloved woman becomes a source of allure. For his male characters it is not enough to grovel before a beautiful woman, to kiss her feet and even to crave her excreta; he must feel she is cruel. The old man in *Diary of a Mad Old Man* describes his ideal of a beautiful woman: "Above all, it's essential for her to have white, slender legs and delicate feet. Assuming that these and all the other points of beauty are equal, I would be more susceptible to the woman with bad character. Occasionally there are women whose faces reveal a streak of cruelty—they are the ones I like best. When I see a woman with a face like that, I feel her innermost nature may be cruel, indeed I hope it is." The fascination Naomi, the heroine of *A Fool's Love,* exerts over the hapless hero lies as much in her cruelty as in her exotic beauty. Shunkin is conspicuously cruel to Sasuke, referring to him contemptuously as a servant. Even a seemingly compliant and inarticulate Kyoto lady, Ikuko in *The Key* (1956), will betray and destroy her husband. Indeed, the cruelty of a woman, her delight in observing pain, is often what first attracts a man to her. The hero of **Secret Stories of the Lord of Musashi** is captivated as a boy when he sees a beautiful young woman smile as she carefully cleans and dresses a severed head. He is in particular driven to an ecstasy of delight when he sees her tending a head from which the nose has been cut, a *mekubi*, or "female head," an obvious reference to castration. The whole life of the future Lord of Musashi is determined by that sight, and he desires nothing more than to recreate the scene, if possible becoming the severed head over which the smiling young woman bends. Oyu-san in *Ashikari* is certainly not a monster, but she demands not only obedience but utter sacrifice from her slaves. At the end of *Manji* (1930) Mitsuko destroys the health of her two worshippers by insisting that they drink heavy sedatives each night before going to bed, to insure that they will not be unfaithful to her. Such examples of cruelty only serve to inflame the men who wait on these beautiful women. Even if cruelty destroys a man's body it can only foster his passion.

Men sometimes figure in the novels in the role of consort to the queen bee, destined to be discarded once they have fertilized the women they worship. But in *Manji* the males are contemptible and even unnecessary. Sonoko is satisfied with her homosexual love for Mitsuko and has no use for her husband; Mitsuko, for her part, though tied to the feckless young man Watanuki, derives her greatest pleasure from the adoration of Sonoko, another woman. In other stories, however, the male is necessary, if only to provide the woman with a suitable object for her sadistic impulses. Kikkyō in *Secret Stories of the Lord of Musashi* is drawn to Terukatsu because he alone can enable her to wreak vengeance on her husband, Norishige. Terukatsu supposes that once he has performed the service demanded of him—cutting off Norishige's nose and destroying his castle—Kikkyō will surrender herself to him, but he discovers that the queen bee, her object attained, has no further interest in her abettor.

The woman usually express no particular preference in men, as if their features made no difference. It is true that Itsuko in *The Key* is attracted by Kimura's young body, but there is never any suggestion that she loves him or values him as anything more than the instrument of her lust. For that matter, though Itsuko is repelled by her husband's body, she is not averse to intercourse with him, providing he is sufficiently active. Tanizaki, reflecting the sentiments of his female characters, seldom describes the faces of the males. One of his rare descriptions of a man's face, Watanuki's in *Manji,* is not so much a portrait as a forewarning of his treacherous character. Sonoko, though at first she finds Watanuki attractive, is quickly disenchanted.

But if handsome male features do not seem to interest women, ugliness is no obstacle. Kikkyō is more devoted to Norishige after his nose is cut off (his mouth has already been made into a hare-lip, and one ear has been shot off) than when he was whole. In *Diary of a Mad Old Man* the old man does not wish his daughter-in-law to see him when he removes his false teeth and looks, in his own words, exactly like a monkey, but she insists that it does not make any difference. Indeed, the indifference of Tanizaki's women to men suggests the indifference of a cat to human beings. Perhaps it was no accident that Tanizaki throughout his life was fascinated by cats.

I have so far described themes that remained astonishingly constant in Tanizaki's writings for over fifty years. My examples have been chosen from every period of his career, and many others might be adduced. I think that these are the basic themes of his books, but the last impression I would like to give is that his writings are monotonous or that he failed to respond in any way to the enormous changes that occurred in Japanese society. At one level at least Tanizaki's writings present an evolving set of ideas about traditional Japan and the West. This is expressed even in the preferences in women of his different heroes. For example, Jōji, the hero of *A Fool's Love* (1925), seems to embody Tanizaki's own feelings of about 1915. Jōji is enslaved by the European-looking beauty of Naomi (whose very name sounds foreign), so much so that he feels ashamed of his own typically Japanese features. At the end of the novel they are living in the foreign section of Yokohama, and he has accepted her demand that she have the right to entertain foreign male friends without interfer-

ence from him. The implied condemnation of this surrender to the cult of Western beauty suggests that Tanizaki himself was no longer so susceptible. This is developed in *Some Prefer Nettles* (1929) into a rediscovery of traditional Japanese beauty. Kaname, the hero, is attracted by the West, particularly by the worship of women as goddesses, but in the end he finds himself succumbing to the quiet charms of an old-fashioned Kyoto woman. Tanizaki's former adulation of Western things is replaced by a new appreciation of traditional Japanese culture. In the decade after *Some Prefer Nettles* he gives us a collection of portraits of typically Japanese women, each composed and classical of face but harboring the ferocity of a tigress. The period was brought to an appropriate close with Tanizaki's translation into modern Japanese of *The Tale of Genji,* bringing new life to its great gallery of beautiful women.

It may have been the anxieties of war, perhaps even a fear that as the result of the war that began in 1941 Japan would be changed beyond all recognition, that drew Tanizaki back from the past to modern Japan, the Japan of the 1930's. With something of the elegiac spirit of a chronicler recording (lest people forget) the last days of Rome before the barbarian invasions, he recreated in *The Makioka Sisters* the city of Osaka in days of peace and luxury. The military authorities were right when they decided in 1943 that *The Makioka Sisters* was subversive, for in this novel Tanizaki indicates that Western elements had become precious parts of the lives of cultivated Japanese and were no longer merely affectations or passing crazes as in the days of Tanizaki's youth. The youngest sister, Taeko, is condemned for her waywardness, an excess of Western freedom, it is true, but the inarticulate Yukiko, a typically old-fashioned Japanese beauty, shows to best advantage in Western clothes.

The conflict between East and West in the minds and lives of the Japanese has now become the most hackneyed of all themes, the first one that leaps in pristine freshness into the mind of every maker of documentary films or television producer. But for Tanizaki this subject, which had absorbed him in the 1920's, lost all appeal and interest after the war. In the last novels the so-called conflict completely melts away. Tanizaki is no longer obsessed by his preference for the past. Utsugi, the old man of *Diary of a Mad Old Man,* has nostalgic remembrances of his mother, but he delights in the up-to-the-minute costumes of his daughter-in-law, Satsuko. Quite unlike the Tanizaki of *In Praise of Shadows*, Utsugi is eager to tear down the old, Edo-style house he grew up in and to erect instead a bright new Western-style house where he can live more independently of his wife. In the end he builds a swimming pool in the garden big enough for Satsuko to practice synchronized swimming. Old man Utsugi has accepted Western things as inevitable and even attractive elements in Japanese life. Like all the heroines of Tanizaki novels, Satsuko has a dazzlingly white complexion—in *In Praise of Shadows* Tanizaki had lovingly dwelt on his fascination for white skin, not the matter-of-fact white of a European woman's, but the mysterious, glowing ivory of a Japanese face—but she shows to advantage when sunburned. Satsuko's feet, of course, are important, but their shape is rather unlike that of Tanizaki's earlier heroines, for she has always worn shoes. Satsuko bathes in a tiled shower, rather than in the scented wooden tub Tanizaki lovingly described in *Some Prefer Nettles,* but this does not make her less desirable to her eager father-in-law.

Tanizaki's early period as a writer was certainly marked by infatuation with the West. About 1918, he tells us, "I had come to detest Japan, even though I was obviously a Japanese." He dreamed especially of the kind of women he saw in foreign films. "What I sought were lively eyes, a cheerful expression and a clear voice, a body that was healthy and well-proportioned, and above all, long straight legs and adorable feet with pointed toenails cased in snugly fitting high-heeled shoes—in short, a woman with the physique and clothes of a foreign star." Tanizaki was in the mountains at Hakone at the time of the Great Earthquake of 1923. He was deeply worried about his family, but "almost at the same instant joy welled up inside me and the thought, 'How marvellous! Tokyo will become a decent place now.'" He had visions of a new Tokyo: "Orderly thoroughfares, shining, newly-paved streets, a flood of cars, blocks of flats rising floor on floor, level on level in geometrical beauty, and threading through the city elevated lines, subways, street cars. And the excitement at night of a great city, a city with all the amusements of Paris or New York, a city where the night life never ends. Then, and then indeed, the citizens of Tokyo will come to adopt a purely European-American style of life, and the young people, men and women alike, will all wear Western clothes. This is the inevitable trend of the times, and whether one likes it or not, this is what will happen."

> **The more complex side of Tanizaki's writing, expressed in countless variations, imparted a distinctive quality, sombre, grotesque or comic, that contributed much to the greatness of the man I consider to have been the finest modern Japanese novelist.**
>
> *—Donald Keene*

Tanizaki could hardly have been a better prophet of what in fact did take place in Tokyo. However, after the earthquake he decided to move to the Kansai, and gradually his attitudes began to change. He discovered that "I loved the old Japan as a form of exoticism, in precisely the sense that a foreigner treasures the prints of Hiroshige." He visited Nara and Kyoto, again just like a foreign tourist. Gradually he shifted to a more positive appreciation of Japanese culture as it survived in the Kansai, and to an increasing distaste for Tokyo, which he considered a shoddy imitation of the West. Yokohama, where Tanizaki had in earlier days enjoyed dancing with foreign women, became in *A Fool's Love* the symbol of the unhealthy Japanese mania for the West. In contrast, the world described in *In Praise of Shadows,* is essentially that of Osaka, a city where the merchant class created a solid and substantial culture capable of resisting Westernization better than Tokyo, a city where the descendants of the old inhabitants had been pushed aside by latecomers, peasants attracted to the big city. . . .

Ashikari (1932), also a story of the Kansai, is a narration within a narration. Tanizaki, the antiquarian, visits Minase, the site of the palace of the thirteenth-century Emperor Gotoba. In a manner reminiscent of Merimée describing Roman ruins in Spain as a prelude to his story of Carmen, but more subtly, Tanizaki passes from the present-day loneliness of Minase to the Minase evoked by the poets, and then to the Minase of fifty years ago as Seribashi, the man he accidentally encounters, relates the story of Oyu-san. The use in this story of Kansai dialect would have been a mistake, for it would have called attention to the narrator, and it is essential that he be the transparent medium for the story who vanishes at the end. Tanizaki's intent in this story is quite the opposite of the usual kind of historical fiction. He wrote: "My wish has been to avoid imparting any modern interpretations to the psychology of Japanese women of the feudal period, but instead to describe them in such a way that I will recreate what those long-ago women actually felt, in a manner that appeals to the emotions and understanding of modern people." By preserving a distance between himself and his characters he kept intact the understated reserve that he felt to be an essential element especially in the women of the Kansai region. Some critics at the time evidently objected to this remoteness, but Tanizaki defended himself in a postscript written to **"A Portrait of Shunkin"** (1934): "In response to those who say that I have failed to describe what Shunkin or Sasuke are really thinking, I would like to counter with the question: 'Why is it necessary to describe what they are thinking? Don't you understand their thoughts anyway from what I have written?'"

Even at the height of Tanizaki's absorption with the Kansai, the last preserve of traditional Japan, he returned at times to more overt descriptions of his abiding, perverse inclinations. *Secret Stories of the Lord of Musashi,* as the title indicates, belongs to an entirely different world. It deals with a man, rather unusually for Tanizaki, and is set in the Kantō during the sixteenth century. The theme, suitably announced in a preface written in stiff, formal Chinese, is the distorted sexual passion of the hero. Terukatsu, unlike the passive males of *Manji, Ashikari* or **"A Portrait of Shunkin,"** is a martial leader, and his exploits are worthy of his heroic age. But, as Tanizaki reminds us in the preface, the sexual lives of heroes are often surprising. Terukatsu, for all his martial prowess, is a masochist who craves the cruelty of a beautiful woman. In this respect he shows his kinship with Seribashi, Sasuke and old man Utsugi.

Tanizaki employed a favorite technique in this work: he describes finding various old accounts of Terukatsu, and attempts to piece them together into a biography, emphasizing the aspects of his life that normally do not appear in typical accounts of the lives of great generals. The novel opens superbly. Terukatsu, a boy of thirteen, is initiated into the world of manhood by being led to a room in a besieged castle where women are washing, arranging and fastening name-tags to the heads of enemy dead. The scene, filled with a morbid, glowing quality, ranks with Tanizaki's finest achievements, and indeed with anything written in this century. Tanizaki may have derived inspiration from *Oan Monogatari,* an account of her experiences in Ogaki Castle at the time of the Battle of Sekigahara in 1600 by a young woman of the warrior class. But all that *Oan Monogatari* contains that is relevant is this single passage: "I remember that the heads which had been taken by our side were collected in the keep of the castle, each one with a tag attached to it. . . . There is nothing to be afraid of in a head. I sometimes went to sleep among all the heads with their carnal smell." Tanizaki may have been less influenced by the text than by the contemporary illustration that shows women in elaborate kimonos preparing the severed heads.

Terukatsu in later life not only enjoyed witnessing the spontaneous, indefinable cruelty of women, he even sought to provoke it, especially in women of the mildest dispositions. His wife O-etsu, an innocent girl of fifteen, is given to such girlish pleasures as hunting fireflies. In later life she takes orders as a nun and is known for her piety and saintliness. But in an unforgettable scene of the novel Terukatsu compels the priest Dōami (one of his biographers) to go down into a hole in the floor, leaving only his head exposed above the floor level, and to pretend that he is a severed head. Terukatsu, having made O-etsu drunk, tests her courage by asking if she will cut off Dōami's nose. She professes her willingness, though he eventually requires her only to drill a hole in Dōami's ear. She performs this service gladly, laughing all the while. When O-etsu recovers from her inebriation she recalls with mortification her wanton behavior. Terukatsu for his part is satisfied at having thus converted his angelic wife into a monster of cruelty, but this achieved, he loses interest in her.

Tanizaki intended to continue *Secret Tales of the Lord of Musashi* beyond its present conclusion, and even prepared a rough outline of subsequent developments. Although this project was never realized, he referred to it even in his late years, sometimes promising to return to this novel after he had completed his revised translation of *The Tale of Genji.* It is a pity he did not; even so, it ranks as one of his masterpieces.

The three complete translations of *The Tale of Genji,* the first of which appeared in 1938, and the third in 1965, the year of his death, unquestionably brought this great novel within the reach of the Japanese reading public—earlier critics had complained that it was easier to read in English translation than in the original—but we must regret the novels Tanizaki might have composed had he not chosen to devote years of his life to this task. Surely there can be no question of his having run out of things to write. After the first version of *The Tale of Genji,* in fact, Tanizaki wrote *The Makioka Sisters,* by far his longest novel and

perhaps his best (though atypical because of the peculiar wartime circumstances of composition). Between the first and the second Genji translations Tanizaki also wrote such important works as *The Mother of Captain Shigemoto,* and between the second and third translations he wrote two of his most popular works, *The Key* and *Diary of a Mad Old Man. . . .*

It is fitting that Tanizaki's last novel, *Diary of a Mad Old Man,* like the last works of many other great artists, should have been comic. This does not mean that his earlier works are unrelievedly serious. *Secret Stories of the Lord of Musashi,* despite its macabre themes, is humorous in its description of the relentless pursuit of Norishige's nose, and some short works, like *The Cat, Shōzō and the Two Women* (1936), are amusing throughout. But *Diary of a Mad Old Man* is in its self-satire a wonderfully comic work, and at the same time true to Tanizaki's deepest feelings as *The Key* is not. It is as if Tanizaki, still intrigued by the old themes of his writings, is now able also to see them at such a distance that they appear comic. It is a captivating book, marred only by the weak ending. Probably this was because the logical ending, the death of the old man, was the one subject Tanizaki at this stage of his life could not treat with humor.

In 1934 Tanizaki wrote of himself, "I am basically uninterested in politics, so I have concerned myself exclusively with the ways people live, eat and dress, the standards of feminine beauty, and the progress of recreational facilities." No doubt this is how he chose to see himself, sometimes at least. But the more complex side of his writing, expressed in countless variations, surely imparted a distinctive quality, sombre, grotesque or comic, that contributed much to the greatness of the man I consider to have been the finest modern Japanese novelist.

Anthony H. Chambers (essay date 1972)

SOURCE: "Tanizaki Junichirō's Historical Fiction," in *Journal of the Association of Teachers of Japanese,* Vol. 8, No. 1, November, 1972, pp. 34-44.

[*An American educator and critic, Chambers is considered an expert on the work of Tanizaki. In the following excerpt, he determines the influence of Japanese history and culture on Tanizaki's short fiction.*]

It is clear that in his early years Tanizaki Junichirō was strongly attracted to the West, that he adopted Western dress, lived in Western-style buildings and associated with foreigners in Yokohama. He was also intrigued by China: following a trip to China in 1919 he surrounded himself with Chinese bric-a-brac and posed for photographs in Chinese costume. He was also taken by the exoticism of Kyoto and Osaka; for Tanizaki, born and reared in Tokyo, a trip to Kansai was almost like a trip to a foreign land. Always drawn to the exotic, he seems not to have been much interested in the modern Japan of his youth; but from his childhood he was fascinated by Japan's past, and following the 1923 earthquake, when he was forced by conditions in Tokyo to live for a time near Osaka, he indulged his interests and seems to have found new meaning in Japanese tradition. He did not return to live in Tokyo as he originally planned, but stayed on in the Osaka area, where he studied the Japanese past and wrote a number of historical novels and novellas.

All of this is familiar enough to anyone who has read English translations of Tanizaki's works and the biographical sketches provided on their jackets. Less familiar, however, and more difficult to deal with, are the questions of how Tanizaki viewed the Japanese past, what his attitudes toward and tastes in Japanese tradition were, why he chose to write historical fiction, and what he hoped to accomplish by doing so. This [essay] represents an initial attempt to answer these questions.

It might be useful to begin with some brief, general answers. Of all the periods of Japanese history, it was the Heian Period which Tanizaki found most congenial. He was also an enthusiastic connoisseur of the plebeian arts of the Tokugawa Period: kabuki, the puppet theater, music and dance. He was far less fond of that part of Japanese tradition inspired by Confucian and Buddhist morality; in particular, the drab, didactic literature written under Confucian influence was not at all to his taste. It was in large part in reaction to the Confucian tone of much of Japanese literature that Tanizaki wrote historical fiction. He believed that literature should be beautiful, not didactic, and that the beauty most appropriate to modern Japanese readers was the eternal, unchanging beauty of Japanese tradition. Finally, he sought to breathe vitality into Japanese history through the portrayal of women and romance—subjects neglected by Confucian historians—and through what might almost be called exposes of the past.

It is not difficult to imagine why Tanizaki was so drawn to the Heian Period. In Japan, as Tanizaki wrote, "reliance on women is held to be the opposite of manliness; and the concept of 'woman' is relegated to a position diametrically opposed to everything sublime, eternal, solemn and pure." "Why did women come to be despised," he asks, "and looked upon as slaves following the establishment of military government and the emergence of *bushido*? Why was kindness to women considered a lapse into effeminacy, unbefitting a warrior?" In contrast to this, one of the most persistent themes in Tanizaki's writings is "woman worship." His male characters, when they emerge as individuals at all, are almost invariably abject and masochistic woman worshippers whose primary object in life is to be dominated, even mistreated, by the women they love. From this fact, from his autobiographical writings and from the testimony of those around him, it is safe to assume that Tanizaki himself was a "woman worshipper." The Heian Period is the only well documented era of Japanese history that shared Tanizaki's attitudes toward women, and hence it was the period with which he could most readily identify. "Women did not rule over men in the aristocratic society of the Heian Period," he wrote, "but they had the same freedom as men, and the attitude of men toward women was not tyrannical as in later ages: women were

treated courteously and gently, at times as the most beautiful and precious things in the world."

It was for somewhat different reasons that Tanizaki was fond of kabuki and the puppet theater, and of shamisen music. He developed a liking for kabuki and the shamisen in his childhood, when he was able to catch strains of shamisen music floating from neighboring houses, and when his mother took him regularly to the kabuki theater. A taste for the puppet theater came more slowly. Initially Tanizaki was bored by the puppets and disgusted by the slobbering narrators; the process of his conversion is memorably described in *Tade Kuu Mushi* (*Some Prefer Nettles*). One suspects that ultimately it was the color and exuberance of the plebeian Tokugawa arts that appealed to Tanizaki. . . .

Complementing Tanizaki's sympathy for the Heian Period and for the plebeian Tokugawa arts is a strong antipathy for the sterility and didacticism of the Confucian tradition, and for the Japanese naturalist writers whose works paradoxically share some of the same unattractive qualities. [In *Kokubungaku: Kaishaku to Kanshō,* Volume 34, 1969] Hashimoto Yoshiichirō describes Tanizaki as "the most persistently antimedieval of novelists" and suggests that Tanizaki's veneration for women was a primary reason. As Hashimoto points out, "Buddhism and Confucianism, the religious and moral systems that held sway over medieval and Tokugawa Japan, taught contempt for the female form." A doctrine less compatible with Tanizaki's inclinations can scarcely be imagined. Further, Tanizaki found the stiff lifelessness of Confucian writings insufferable; and he deplored the effect of Confucian influence on Japanese letters. "We will never know," he lamented, "how many geniuses were lost to so-called 'light literature' thanks to the notion, current during the feudal period, that novels and the theater were for the diversion of women and children and were not suitable entertainment for samurai. A man of letters like Rai Sanyō for example, had he not been confined by this thinking, would probably have written political or historical novels with some human warmth rather than the overly stiff *Nihon Gaishi*." As Albert Craig has pointed out [in *Personality in Japanese History,* 1970], the Confucian canons of history that guided writers like Sanyō "demanded the recording of those aspects of life that would serve as a moral mirror for posterity, not the details that would make them come alive." Tanizaki found the antitheses of Confucian didacticism in the great Heian romances, of which he wrote that the story unfolds of itself, through the actions and words of the characters; and the author, objectively relating the happiness and misery of the characters, causes the reader to taste these emotions as if they were his own.

If Confucian didacticism was not to Tanizaki's taste, neither was the drabness of the Japanese naturalist writers, who were also in their own way, reacting to the Confucian tradition. He argued that the fascination of the naturalists and their successors with minute details of everyday life was the result of Western influence and that it represented altogether too narrow a view of the role of literature. Tanizaki's taste called for a richer, more imaginative fabric than his contemporaries were willing to produce. At one point his aversion to the droning monotony of the naturalists grew so strong that he rejected all realistic literature out of hand: "I have gotten into a bad habit recently. I cannot bring myself to write or read anything which takes real facts for its material, or which is even realistic. This is one reason that I make no attempt to read the works by contemporary authors that appear in the magazines every month. I'll scan the first five or six lines, say to myself 'Aha! he's writing about himself,' and lose all desire to go on reading." Disinclined to read the work of most of his contemporaries, Tanizaki turned to historical fiction and to the exoticism of foreign literature. "Generally I find myself reading things that have nothing to do with the present. When I read historical novels, nonsense tales, even realistic novels of fifty years ago or contemporary Western novels far removed from Japanese society, I can enjoy them as so many imaginary worlds." In the course of this reading Tanizaki apparently came to the conclusion that there was a serious lack of historical fiction in Japan, and for a time he had ambitions of helping to fill the gap. He was deeply impressed by *Quo Vadis,* and in the late 1920's dreamed of writing a long historical novel along the same lines, set perhaps in Kamakura or Ashikaga Japan, and full of courtiers, beautiful women and priests, involved in deep and complicated relationships and undergoing vast changes.

Tanizaki Junichirō is praised by some Japanese as the greatest writer among them, damned by others as a sentimental reactionary. He is in any case extremely famous, and one can hope that some day he will be better known abroad than he is now.

E. G. Seidensticker, in Japan Quarterly, *October-November, 1954.*

Thus Tanizaki's desire to write historical fiction represented on one hand an urge to escape from the drab realism of his contemporaries into a more romantic and aesthetically pleasing world, and on the other hand, an ambition to rectify what he considered a serious lack in modern Japanese literature—a desire to portray the Japanese past as it really was.

For turning his back on the colorless recording of day-to-day life and for looking to the Japanese past for comfort and inspiration, Tanizaki was denounced as a reactionary and an escapist. Apparently such criticism did not bother him. It was his view that modern Japanese writers, under Western influence, were constantly striving to accomplish something new, to discover beauty in new forms, to contribute to a better society. He saw himself, on the other hand, as a writer who attempted no more—and no less—than to equal the artistry of his predecessors. More than once he pointed out that traditionally an Oriental writer or artist strives not to express his own individuality and to discover new beauties unexpressed by his teachers, but to attain to the same heights reached by those before him. Beauty, he wrote, is single and unchanging in eyes of the Oriental artist, and that single beauty has been sung repeatedly by Eastern poets through the ages. In Tanizaki's mind, one aspect of the unchanging beauty of Japanese tradition was feminine beauty. There is in Japan, he maintained, a tradition of the "eternal woman": "Men in ancient times did not love a woman's personality, nor were they attracted by the particular beauty of individual women. Just as the moon is always the same moon, it must have seemed to them that there is a single, universal, eternal 'woman'." A clearer statement of the concept comes in *Some Prefer Nettles,* during Kaname's first visit to the puppet theater: "The classical beauty was withdrawn, restrained, careful not to show too much individuality, and the puppet here quite fitted the requirements. A more distinctive, more colorful figure would only have ruined the effect. Perhaps, indeed, to their contemporaries all the tragic heroines . . . had the same face. Perhaps this doll was the 'eternal woman' as Japanese tradition had her." Tanizaki saw himself as part of the great anonymous stream of artists who return "again and again, age after age, to an ultimate, unchanging beauty." "I have come to feel that the work of an artist is not simply to do something uncommon, to display his individuality: it is all right if one differs from the ancients only slightly, if one's self is revealed only in the minutest point. In fact, I see nothing wrong in becoming completely absorbed in the great accomplishments of the past and not showing one's individuality at all."

No one has ever accused Tanizaki of failing to leave his individual imprint on his works; but in such works as *Yoshino Kuzu, Ashikari,* "**Mōmoku Monogatari,**" "**Shunkinshō,**" and *Shōshō Shigemoto no Haha* he does seem to have striven for a classical repose, a misty suggestiveness, of the sort that characterizes *The Tale of Genji.* It was this approach that Tanizaki, during his middle years, felt to be most appropriate for himself as a modern writer. He maintained that the function of Japanese literature always "has been to make the reader forget the pain and harshness of everyday life," and nothing is more soothing than the comfortable familiarity of tradition. As long as people pursue happiness by struggling for ever better worlds, he argued, there can be no end to inordinate desires. One position may be to find meaning in endless progress and development; but an equally valid position is to seek a quiet spot in the midst of all the motion. Tanizaki asks why the warriors of the Ashikaga Period spent their leisure in such serene pastimes as poetry, the tea ceremony and nō. His answer leaves no room for doubt: "Nothing short of these traditional arts could provide sustenance for their hearts." . . .

A number of examples could be given to show how Tanizaki in his own writings sought to recapture the shadowy, suggestive beauty of Japanese tradition. The exquisite firefly hunt of *Sasameyuki (The Makioka Sisters)* comes immediately to mind. The reader is not allowed to "witness" the hunt itself: the events of the expedition flow dreamily, impressionistically through Sachiko's mind as she lies in bed, waiting for sleep to come. Here indeed the eaves are deep and the walls dark, the useless decoration stripped away. Another example, and one of Tanizaki's greatest accomplishments, is the last chapter of *Shōshō Shigemoto no Haha* (*The Mother of Captain Shigemoto*), in which Shigemoto is reunited with his mother after a separation of many years. The meeting takes place on a hazy, moonlit night, on a hillside at the foot of Mt. Hiei, far from the streets and mansions of the city. Shigemoto first becomes aware of his mother's presence when he dimly sees her dressed in white and picking yellow roses under a solitary cherry tree, illuminated by the warm flow of the moon. Nothing is new in this scene: cherry blossoms and hazy moonlight are images used with exasperating frequency in classical Japanese literature, and the theme of the child longing for his mother, while characteristic of Tanizaki's works, is also central to *The Tale of Genji*. But Tanizaki's combination of these traditional elements is perhaps unique, and he succeeds brilliantly in what he set out to do: "to arouse fresh, strong feelings in the reader while following in the footsteps of the ancients."

In almost all his writings Tanizaki sought to embody the traditional Japanese sense of beauty, which he believed was uniquely suited to Japanese temperament and physiology, for he believed that nothing else could soothe and comfort modern Japanese living in the bright lights of the Twentieth Century.

—Anthony Chambers

Tanizaki's embrace of traditional aesthetics was one aspect of his reaction to the drab writings of his contemporaries and to Confucian didacticism. Another was his desire to breathe life into the past, to give it flesh and color—in short, to restore what Confucian writers had deemed unsuitable. In Tanizaki's view, the honest depiction of sex and romantic love, and of their effects, was lacking in the traditional accounts of Japanese history, and he argued that one of the most beneficial effects of Western influence on Japanese literature was "the liberation of love, or more precisely, the liberation of sexual desire." Armed with the tools provided him by Western example and with his own imagination, Tanizaki could proceed to rewrite Japanese history by investing it with the sex and romance that must have been there but which were systematically omitted by the historians. "It goes without saying," he wrote, "that there is a romance of one kind or another in the life of every historical hero, and that by portraying this aspect without reserve an author could convey a real sense of humanity."

Tanizaki must have felt that part of his task was to provide the past with women. As has been pointed out above, Confucian and Buddhist precepts hold women to be infe-

rior creatures, scarcely worthy of serious attention. This attitude is reflected in the writing of Japanese history, and was a great irritation to Tanizaki. "I frequently think that I would like to write a historical novel based on some person of the past, but I am always frustrated by the difficulty of forming a clear picture of the women who surrounded him. . . . Since ancient times Japanese family genealogies, from that of the Imperial Family down, have given comparatively detailed accounts of the activities of men, but when a woman appears she is simply noted as 'girl' or 'woman,' normally with no indication of the years of her birth or death, or even of her name. In other words, there are individual men in our history, but there is no such thing as an individual woman." The "eternal woman" of whom Tanizaki wrote was eternal and unchanging only on the surface; underneath she must have been in a turmoil of suppressed emotions. Tanizaki describes his intentions this way: "My wish has been to recreate the psychology of Japanese women of the feudal period just as it was, without imposing modern interpretations, and to portray it in a way that will appeal to the emotions and understanding of modern readers. . . . Even a woman who appeared to be chaste and pure no doubt felt an immoral love, unperceived by others; jealousy, hatred, cruelty and other depraved passions must have passed faintly through her heart. But it is extremely difficult to portray convincingly a woman who never gave the slightest outward sign of these feelings, whose entire life was lived inside herself."

Thus Tanizaki knew that the task he set for himself was a difficult one, and it must be said that he did not always succeed in it. His most convincing female characters are without question the four Makioka sisters, but they of course are not ladies of feudal Japan. Three feudal women might be mentioned: Shunkin of **"Shunkinshō,"** Lady Oyū of *Ashikari,* and Lady Oichi of **"Mōmoku Monogatari."** All of these women are portrayed with enough depth to set them apart as individuals; and Shunkin in particular, a brilliant and sadistic musician, is far from being the gentle, unselfish, withdrawn "eternal woman" of Japanese tradition. But more than the character of these ladies, it is the style, plot and atmosphere of these three works that linger in the reader's mind. To the Western reader, in any case, the women of Tanizaki's historical function are insubstantial.

The work in which Tanizaki succeeds most brilliantly in bringing the past to life is *Bushūkō Hiwa* (*The Secret History of the Lord of Musashi*), and he accomplishes it by following his own prescription—that an author can convey a sense of humanity by portraying the romance in the life of a historical hero. Oddly enough, the central character of the work is a man, and though women play an important part in his life, they are not the vivid creations one might expect from reading **"Shunkinshō."**

The hero of *The Secret History* is Terukatsu, a sixteenth-century leader of great ability and courage. But Tanizaki does not tell the story of Terukatsu's heroic exploits; rather, he concentrates on exposing Terukatsu's secret desires and motivations.

The novel opens when Terukatsu is thirteen and he is allowed to watch several ladies grooming enemy heads—taken in battle—for presentation to the lord of the castle. The scene makes a profound impression on the boy, particularly the sight of a beautiful young woman preparing a head from which the nose has been cut. Terukatsu experiences a masochistic desire to be such a head and to enjoy the sensation of being handled by the beautiful lady. This desire develops into a lifelong obsession.

Naturally such a perversion can be acted upon only vicariously. Young Terukatsu slips into the enemy camp determined to take a noseless head and present it to the lady in the castle. He succeeds in taking the nose of the enemy commander himself, but has to flee without the head. Later he has an affair with the same commander's daughter who, haunted by her father's noseless spirit, seeks revenge in kind on her own husband, Norishige, whom she suspects of being responsible. Terukatsu is only too glad to help; the goal and finally the reality of a noseless Norishige are precisely what Terukatsu needs to satisfy his sadomasochistic desires and to give the sharpest edge to his affair with the lady.

This partial summary of the plot of **The Secret History** is enough to show Tanizaki's intent. History—albeit fictitious history—is put to the limelight, and the secret obsessions of its heroes are revealed for the first time: history is not always what it seems to be. The work closes with these words: "If one peruses the *Tsukuma Gunki* and other official histories, keeping in mind that there was this secret side to the Lord of Musashi's sex life, many unexpected discoveries will undoubtedly be made. It is in this hope that I have written these pages." Most important is that Terukatsu, Norishige, and the other characters of the novel are very much alive, and through them Tanizaki brings the whole period of civil wars to life.

In works like **The Secret History of the Lord of Musashi,** then, Tanizaki tried to restore to Japanese history the vitality that had been stifled by Confucian historians. In **"Shunkinshō"** he provided Japanese history with strong, individual women. And in almost all his writings he sought to embody the traditional Japanese sense of beauty, which he believed was uniquely suited to Japanese temperament and physiology, for he believed that nothing else could soothe and comfort modern Japanese living in the bright lights of the Twentieth Century.

Makoto Ueda (essay date 1976)

SOURCE: "Tanizaki Jun'ichirō," in *Modern Japanese Writers and the Nature of Literature,* Stanford University Press, 1976, pp. 54-84.

[*Ueda is a Japanese educator and critic. In the following excerpt, he examines Tanizaki's treatment of beauty in his fiction.*]

Tanizaki Jun'ichirō (1886-1965) was never known as a literary theorist or critic. Always confident in his mission as a novelist, he had no urge to write a defense of literature or a social justification of the novel. Not a fast writer, he usually wanted to spend as much of his time as possible on writing fiction; he found little time for reading or evaluating the works of his contemporaries. And yet, by the end of his long literary career, he had produced a sizable number of writings that reveal his ideas on the nature of literature. There is, for instance, *The Composition Reader,* in which he said what he considered to be a good prose style and how one could go about attaining it. *In Praise of Shadows* and several other essays eloquently expound his ideal of beauty in life and art. Though he could seldom be induced to write reviews, his few essays in this genre, especially those on Sōseki's *Light and Darkness* and Kafū's *During the Rains,* leave no doubt that he could have become an exceptionally perceptive critic. His quarrel with Akutagawa on whether or not a novel should have a plot was one of the liveliest literary controversies of the time. In his fiction, too, aesthetic questions are often directly woven into the texture of the work, as in the well-known **"Tattoo,"** *Some Prefer Nettles,* and **"The Portrait of Shunkin,"** not to mention such lesser-known stories as **"Creation"** and **"Gold and Silver."**. . .

Tanizaki's concept of beauty is eloquently expounded in his celebrated essay *In Praise of Shadows.* As the title indicates, the essay expresses his admiration for a shadowy and crepuscular style of beauty in both life and art. He prefers a Japanese-style washroom because it is darker than others inside; he is fond of lacquerware because it is most attractive in a dimly lighted room; he likes Japanese houses because of their large, drooping roofs; he is fascinated with the nō actors' gorgeous costumes that perfectly match the dusky stage. Why did he like shadows so much? His answer was that Orientals had always liked them, and that he was an Oriental. As for why Orientals liked them, he gave two reasons: Orientals were by nature passive, and had learned to live with darkness instead of trying to conquer it as Occidentals did; and Orientals, with their darker skins, had automatically cultivated a sense of beauty befitting their complexion. But the essay is much more than a comparative study of Eastern and Western ideals of beauty. It is written with enthusiasm, leaving no doubt that the author is far more fascinated than the average Oriental with this dusky ideal of beauty. In his youth, Tanizaki had in fact been an ardent admirer of the West and of Western female beauty. The main reason why he admired shadows so much was that they breed fantasies.

Support for this interpretation can be found throughout *In Praise of Shadows.* The author intimates that he likes to "sink into meditation" in the dim light of a Japanese-style washroom. He also observes that Japanese soup, lying silently at the bottom of a lacquered bowl, makes one want to meditate rather than eat. He likes Japanese yō kan jelly because, looking on it, he feels as if it had "absorbed sunlight deep under its translucent jadelike surface and were emitting a dim light as in a dream." He loves to see gold lacquer work by candlelight because its surface glitters in the dark and creates "a strangely luminous dreamworld" with its reflections. He likes to see a Japanese woman under the same circumstances, and imagines that in old Japan a high-ranking noble-woman must have spent many hours of the night sitting in a huge tatami-matted room lighted by a candle, its dim, rainbow-colored light filling the atmosphere like dense fog. He adds that

> . . . people of today, long accustomed to the light of electric lamps, have forgotten there once was this type of darkness. Particularly in the house, the "visible darkness" makes one feel as if something imperceptible were wavering in it, and readily invokes fantasies in one's mind, so that it is more likely to induce a sense of mystery than the darkness outdoors. No doubt it was in such darkness that goblins and weird spirits hovered about; and weren't these women, who lived darkly behind so many doors and drapes and screens, also goblins after their fashion? I can imagine how tightly the darkness enfolded them, closing in on them through every opening in their clothes, downward along the neck, upward along the arms and legs. Or perhaps they emitted that darkness from within their bodies, through their blackened teeth or through their dark hair, as a ground spider spins its web.

In Praise of Shadows ends with the author's declaration that he would try to call back, through the art of fiction, the world of shadows that was so rapidly disappearing with the modernization of Japan. He did what he prom-

---

An excerpt from "The Tattooer"

Deep in his heart the young tattooer concealed a secret pleasure, and a secret desire. His pleasure lay in the agony men felt as he drove his needles into them, torturing their swollen, blood-red flesh; and the louder they groaned, the keener was Seikichi's strange delight. Shading and vermilioning—these are said to be especially painful—were the techniques he most enjoyed.

When a man had been pricked five or six hundred times in the course of an average day's treatment and had then soaked himself in a hot bath to bring out the colors, he would collapse at Seikichi's feet half dead. But Seikichi would look down at him coolly. "I dare say that hurts," he would remark with an air of satisfaction.

Whenever a spineless man howled in torment or clenched his teeth and twisted his mouth as if he were dying, Seikichi told him: "Don't act like a child. Pull yourself together—you have hardly begun to feel my needle!" And he would go on tattooing, as unperturbed as ever, with an occasional sidelong glance at the man's tearful face.

But sometimes a man of immense fortitude set his jaw and bore up stoically, not even allowing himself to frown. Then Seikichi would smile and say: "Ah, you are a stubborn one! But wait. Soon your body will begin to throb with pain. I doubt if you will be able to stand it. . . ."

Jun'ichiro Tanizaki, in Seven Japanese Tales,
translated by Howard Hibbett,
Alfred A. Knopf, 1963.

---

ised. Most of Tanizaki's later works create such a world, a twilight world inhabited by people who thrive on darkness. Many important happenings occur at night in *The Secret Tale of the Lord of Musashi, Ashikari, The Mother of Captain Shigemoto,* and *The Key.* All of the events that happen in **"A Blind Man's Tale," "A Portrait of Shunkin,"** and *From the Notes of an Old Tale* are reported by blind men, living in darkness. The narrator of *The Diary of a Mad Old Man* is not blind, but he is nearing eighty years of age and his eyesight and other faculties are considerably weaker than an average person's. Among Tanizaki's later works virtually the only major novel not dominated by the world of shadows is *The Makioka Sisters.* But even here, daylight seldom enters. The four Makioka sisters were born and brought up behind the many doors and screens of a gloomy old house in Osaka. Of the four, Yukiko, the novel's heroine, has a particularly downcast appearance and an unusually introverted personality. She perfectly complements the traditional Japanese house, with its lack of interior lighting; indeed, at the end of the novel the author marries her to a viscount's son who, after many years of wandering in the West, has rediscovered the beauty of traditional Japan.

As is evident from the above-cited passage, shadows were also a prime factor in Tanizaki's concept of ideal female beauty. He adored women who looked their best by candlelight. He did not like women who passed for beautiful in today's Japan—the type of women who competed in Miss Universe contests—because "their facial features are too clear-cut and too self-sufficient to encourage dreamers." His ideal woman, he explained, had less distinctive features, creating an indefinable impression like a hazy spring moon. Many of the heroines in Tanizaki's later works can be viewed as personifications of this ideal. The heroine of **"The Portrait of Shunkin,"** for example, has a face that, although exquisitely beautiful, is without individuality or any definite appeal. The principal female character in *Ashikari* has the features of a typical Japanese beauty, except that there is "something misty" about her face. Likewise, Yukiko in *The Makioka Sisters* has features less clear-cut than those of any of her three sisters, and is all the more attractive because of it. In each case, the heroine's face stimulates the onlooker's imagination by not being expressive of her inner feelings. It is a face capable of refusing the command of the conscious mind: it hardly shows an emotion, unless it is rooted deep in the subconscious. Yukiko, for instance, betrays no sign of happiness even when, at long last, a marriage is successfully arranged for her. Tanizaki liked a face of this type precisely because it so much resembled a mask.

In this respect, the theme of crepuscular beauty becomes a connecting link between Tanizaki's earlier and later heroines. His earlier ones are generally distinguished by their ruthless, possessive qualities, and his later ones by their calm beauty. But all of them have clouded, enigmatic features that mask the secret stirrings of the subconscious. And the subconscious knows neither good nor evil, but only the promptings of desire. Tanizaki's earlier heroines remain beautiful even as they follow their darkest impulses, paying little heed to the daytime world of public morality. Their beauty, as critics pointed out at the time (and as Tanizaki himself agreed), is daemonic. The heroines of **"Tattoo," "A Spring Time Case,"** *Because of Love,* **"An Idiot's Love,"** and *The Whirlpool* all have this quality. The only major difference between them and the later heroines is that the former show what is hidden in their minds' secret depths. But the two types of heroine are sisters under the skin, just as the serenely beautiful heroine of *The Makioka Sisters,* all surface appearances to the contrary, in some ways resembles her more daemonic younger sister.

Among the types of daemonic beauty, Tanizaki seems to have been most attracted to the beauty of cruelty. This is probably because he thought of the human subconscious as basically destructive. Women, whose beauty came to full flower only at the expense of their male admirers, were naturally cruel; men, for their part, were never happier than when they were physically abused by the women they adored. One of Tanizaki's favorite film actresses was Simone Signoret, especially after he saw her play the role of a murderess in *Les Diaboliques*; he admired her for her "large, smutty-looking face and lusterless, tired skin, for the impression she gave of being a ruthless, fearless, cunning woman." Many of Tanizaki's earlier heroines have this ruthless quality, and are beautiful because of it. In his later works, the heroine of *The Diary of a Mad Old Man* comes closest to this type; in fact, she is directly compared with Simone Signoret.

Tanizaki's predilection for the beauty of cruelty also found expression in his fondness for members of the cat family. He once remarked that of all animals he would most like to have a leopard as a pet because it was "beautiful, lithe, elegant, as genteel as a court musician and as merciless as a devil." The same is true of his early heroines. Of course, he could not keep a leopard at home; he therefore kept cats instead. His love of cats is reflected in his short novel *The Cat, Shōzō, and Two Women,* which must rank as one of the world's finest cat stories.

Tanizaki also found mothers beautiful but daemonic. Maternal beauty in itself had no evil connotations for him. But when he related it to the child's latent sexual drive, he thought that it took on a distinctly equivocal aspect. Once, when Tanizaki was asked what woman struck him as being supremely beautiful, he answered that it was his late mother, as he remembered her, not in her last days, but as a young, beautiful woman. Such a young, beautiful mother is the heroine of his short story **"Longing for Mother,"** in which the son, looking at the mother closely, cannot help feeling "a mysterious, daemonic eeriness" in her. "Her powdered face," he says, "created an impression of coldness rather than of beauty or loveliness." The hero of **"Arrowroot Leaves in Yoshino,"** pining for his late mother, wishes that she were a fox, an animal with supernatural powers in Japanese folklore. For Captain Shigemoto, too, his mother was a shadowy person who never showed herself outside the darkness of a dimly lighted room. When, after many years of searching, he as last meets her, he first takes her to be the spirit of an old

cherry tree that is blossoming with "daemonic beauty" above her.

To conclude, Tanizaki's literary aesthetic centers on the beauty of half-light, of dusky visions that vibrate in the imagination. Living in the age of electricity, he nevertheless tried to create a world of shadows by means of literature. He preferred his world to be dimly lit because it permitted the weird creatures of the subconscious to come out into the open. In the kingdom of Tanizaki's fiction, women markedly outweigh men in importance, because he thought of them as creatures of darkness, belonging to the subconscious. Female beauty as worshiped by Tanizaki inevitably becomes equivocal: a woman who treats her lover sadistically or who seduces her son is always pictured as supremely beautiful. But this is logical, because for Tanizaki beauty and the grotesque are one and the same. The logic, of course, is that of the subconscious, the dark abode of Freudian goblins.

Like the West's modernists, Tanizaki asked big questions, and thought he should be able to answer them. Hopelessly bourgeois in taste and unquestioning about his questioning self, Tanizaki was meticulous in language, scandalously curious about sexual politics, masterful in storytelling, and boldly risk-taking in appearing vulgar and sex-crazed right up to his death in 1965 at age 79.

Masao Miyoshi, in "Beauty and Sadness Now," in **The Nation,** *New York, April 4, 1994.*

Noriko Mizuta Lippit (essay date 1977)

SOURCE: "Tanizaki and Poe: The Grotesque and the Quest for Supernal Beauty," in *Comparative Literature,* Vol. XXIX, No. 3, Summer, 1977, pp. 221-40.

[*In the following excerpt, Mizuta Lippit analyzes the thematic and stylistic influence of Edgar Allan Poe on Tanizaki's short fiction.*]

Students of Tanizaki usually agree that, like other Taisho writers, he began his career under the spell of the West: the influence of Poe, Baudelaire, and Oscar Wilde, among others, is reflected in many of his early works. It is agreed, however, that the influence of the Japanese literature of the seventeenth and eighteenth centuries, especially the erotic and sadistic stories in Kusazoshi and Kabuki plays, was also strong. According to the orthodox view, the influence of the western writers became superficial by the end of the Taisho period. Drawn to both East and West,

Tanizaki, after a period of severe internal conflict between the two attractions, turned completely to the world of classical Japanese literature, and made a conscious artistic endeavor to link his later works with his Japanese heritage. My purpose here is to consider whether the western influences were indeed superficial and to examine Poe's influence on Tanizaki's later development, when he attempted to create his Japanese Byzantium.

Tanizaki Junichiro, one of the major modern Japanese writers, was born in 1886 in the old section of Tokyo and died in 1965 at the age of 79. He left behind thirty volumes of collected works which include novels, plays, tales, essays, and three versions of his translation into modern Japanese of *The Tale of Genji*. Such works as *A Fool's Love, Some Prefer Nettles, The Makioka Sisters, The Key,* and *The Diary of a Mad Old Man* were translated into English, and some were long-standing best sellers in the United States. The western reader will remember him best for the controversy aroused by *The Key* (1956), the sensual story of a perverted old man who schemes to throw his wife into the arms of his young assistant in order to arouse his ebbing sexual interest. In *The Diary of a Mad Old Man* and *Seventy-Nine-Year-Old Spring*, written following *The Key*, Taniazki turns to the theme of perverted eroticism. These erotic books, dealing with man's carnal desire and desperate effort to retain his waning sexual force in old age, have been criticized for approaching pornographic literature.

Most of his works, in fact, were controversial, and critics do not agree in their assessment of them or of Tanizaki himself as a writer; they do agree, however, on the perfection of his novelistic skills in creating a self-sufficient, polished world of beauty. In most of his works, especially those of his middle period, Tanizaki fastidiously excluded the social, economic, and political life of Japan, creating a literary space untouched by the forces of life in modern Japan. Often drawing material from Japanese history or old Japanese legends, he created a "pleasure dome" which is "out of space, out of time."

It is only natural that proletarian writers and such existentialist writers as Ōe Kenzaburo criticize the lack of basic ideology and relevance to modern existence in Tanizaki's works. On the other hand, critics like Ito Sei argue that to regard the conditions of the flesh, such as erotic desire for life, as a determining factor in human life is an ideology in its own right, and defend Tanizaki as a writer whose major theme was man's struggle to attain the sense of life at the risk of moral and social integrity. With critical assessment so polarized and many critical questions unresolved Tanizaki will no doubt continue to be the subject of many critical studies in the future.

Tanizaki's creative works can be divided roughly into three periods; the first ends with *Some Prefer Nettles* in 1928, and the third starts with *The Key* in 1956. It is in the first period, from the 43rd year of Meiji to the 3rd year of Showa (1910-1928), that western influences, including that of Poe, were most evident; we can find many themes, expressions, descriptions, and stories reminiscent of Poe

and of such writers as Baudelaire, Wilde, Zola, and Thomas Hardy.

Some critics have emphasized the influence of Wilde on Tanizaki, underestimating that of Poe. The importance of Wilder's influence is undeniable. Tanizaki tries to separate art from life, placing art above life. Because of his characters' antimoralistic and antisocial pursuit of sensual pleasure, justified for the sake of artistic creation, the term "diabolism" has been widely applied to Tanizaki's early works. Yet Tanizaki's diabolic aesthetes do not suffer from the serve remorse or pangs of conscience experienced by Dorian Gray. In Tanizaki's works, there is no struggle against conscience, against a firmly established social and religious orthodoxy.

In Taisho Japan there was no orthodoxy of religion nor was there a fully developed and established bourgeoisie against whose moral principles and hypocrisy writers had to rebel. Above all, the writers lived in a protected literary circle called *Bundan*, a greenhouse in which they were free to experiment with any new foreign ideas. Tanizaki's famous and quite autobiographical work, **"The Sorrow of the Pagan Outcast"** (**"Itansha no Kanashimi,"** 1917), in which the hero sadistically ignores the affections of his family and friends in order to be true to his artistic sensibility and creative urge, appears to be the puerile rebellion of an adolescent; likewise, the masochistic self-torture which he calls "the sorrow of the pagan outcast," appears quite sentimental, since the orthodoxy against which he rebels at the risk of self-destruction is in fact quite obscure.

Instead, Tanizaki's heroes' diabolic pursuit of sensuous pleasure proves to be a distorted effort to attain a sense of life through the pursuit of unattainable feminine beauty, the pursuit of the absolute. Throughout Tanizaki's works, the search for a sense of life through the masochistic pursuit of an unattainable woman is a major theme. Tanizaki's heroes feel a deep sense of alienation that spurs them to perverted efforts to recover from it. Tanizaki's grotesque expresses these efforts to overcome alienation: it is not merely an exercise in decadent aestheticism. Indeed, the grotesque that expresses the heroes' pursuit is an appropriate style. In Tanizaki, as well as in Poe, the grotesque does not refer merely to this perverted pursuit, but also to the narrative form or perspective, which is ironic and tragicomic. Furthermore, Tanizaki developed, in his later period, his own myth of eternal woman, a myth that justifies the heroes' grotesque efforts at self-recovery. By developing his own myth, Tanizaki created his own world of romanticism. In these respects Tanizaki's works are fundamentally similar to Poe's.

The major themes of Tanizaki's early works are the fear of death, the sado-masochistic pursuit of feminine beauty, the discovery of perversity or cruelty in human nature, and the relation of art to these themes. As a young man Tanizaki himself suffered from a strange nervous condition manifested in sudden seizures of fear, especially fear of trains. In many of his tales, he describes this as a fear of persecution, a fear of madness and death. The narrator of **"The Fear"** (**"Kyōfu,"** 1913) explains that his heart starts beating rapidly the minute he enters a moving vehicle. The drumming of his heart increases in speed and intensity, and he feels as if all his blood were rushing to his head, with his body about to burst into pieces or his brain into madness. This immediately reminds us of the descriptions in Poe's "The Imp of the Perverse" and "The Tell-Tale Heart," where the narrators burst out into self-destructive confessions of their crimes, urged on by the ever growing sound of their hearts.

In "My Adolescent Days" ("Seishun Monogatari," 1932), Tanizaki says that he could not exalt death or madness as did Takayama Chogyu, a romantic writer of a decade earlier; instead, when he read Poe, Baudelaire, Strindberg, and Gorki, anxiety and fear permeated his nervous system, distorting his senses and his emotional responses to things. The fear of the explosion of his body and brain could be ignited at any time and place by the slightest sensory stimulus, for it had no concrete external source. He calls the period in which he suffered from this fear a period of inferno. In many of his tales he describes it in terms of the dizziness felt when standing at the verge of an abyss, a sensation of extreme fear and pain that might culminate in the total loss of his sanity.

The fear is clearly that of death and persecution, yet Tanizaki, unlike Poe, gives death itself a very small role in his works. Furthermore, the fear of death is actually the fear of his own urge toward self-destruction. The fear, therefore, can be called a "pleasurable pain" and its source is entirely internal. The hero's urge toward self-destruction is indeed the work of what Poe called the "imp of the perverse." In fact, to evoke this state of pleasurable pain, of the abysmal terror of self-destruction, is the purpose of the protagonists' diabolic actions in almost all of Tanizaki's works and is their major theme.

This sensation of pleasurable pain is directly related to the other themes of this period, the discovery of the perversity or cruel love of destruction in human nature, and the sadomasochistic pursuit of feminine beauty. Many of Tanizaki's tales were obviously inspired by Poe's crime and detective stories, tales in which the heroes commit, with the utmost cruelty, crimes that are almost gratuitous. These tales include **"Gold and Silver," "The Criminal," "An Incident at Yanagiyu,"** and **"The Cursed Play."**

Many devices and techniques used by Poe appear in these tales, including the Dupin-narrator relationship later popularized in that of Sherlock Holmes and Dr. Watson. In most cases, the heroes' extreme sadism, the analytical precision with which they murder and hide the corpse, and their observations on criminal psychology vividly reveal their fascination with evil and gratuitous cruelty and their concern with making murder a work of art. The discovery of one's own perversity is related to the theme of the double; Tanizaki wrote several tales, such as **"A Story of Tomoda and Matsunaga,"** in which he deals explicitly with the double and doppelgänger.

Yet the sadism of the heroes is often masochistic. In **"The Devil at Noon"** (**"Hakūchyukigo," 1918**), the hero, after witnessing a grotesque murder carried out by a beautiful woman, offers to be murdered by the same woman. He asks a friend to witness the scene of his own cruel death. **"A Harlequin"** (**"Hokan," 1911**), a masterpiece of the early period, is the story of a man who takes uncontrollable pleasure in humiliating himself and in pleasing others by allowing them to control and manipulate him. His effort to exist only in the consciousness of others, in which condition the pain he feels gives him a strong sense of his own self and body, is a classic case of masochism. The hero feels a strong sense of himself, a unity of consciousness, by existing only in the other's image of himself.

Tanizaki's grotesque world of perversity is obviously similar to Poe's. In the latter's crime stories, the heroes commit sadistic, gratuitous crimes which are often followed by self-destructive confessions. Such crimes appear in "William Wilson," "The Tell-Tale Heart," "The Black Cat," "The Cask of Amontillado," and "The Imp of the Perverse." In "The Black Cat," the hero perceives the ominous otherness in the cat's eyes and murders it brutally. The same pattern appears in "The Tell-Tale Heart," in which the hero is provoked to cruel murder by the old man's vulture-like eye. The heroes of "The Black Cat" and "The Imp of the Perverse" explain their acts of perverse evil as the result of the human impulse for self-torture.

> Yet I am not more sure that my soul lives, than I am that perverseness is one of the primitive impulses of the human heart . . . This spirit of perverseness, I say, came to my final overthrow. It was this unfathomable longing of the soul *to vex itself*—to offer violence to its own nature—to do wrong for the wrong's sake only—that urged me to continue and finally to consummate the injury I had inflicted upon the un-offending brute.

The act of evil for evil's sake is as masochistic as it is diabolic: the pure evil is directed against himself, to vex his own soul so that he can be immersed in the immediacy of pain and terror. In the spontaneous experience of pain and terror, the nonreflecting consciousness kills the reflecting consciousness and thus the hero is immersed in the sense of himself, of his immediate body and subjectivity. The criminal action is an extreme method the hero adopts to cultivate artificial sensuous intoxication through self-torture. Murder is an attempt to eliminate the split in his consciousness caused by the ominous eye, to restore the wholeness of his consciousness.

In "The Premature Burial" and "The Pit and the Pendulum," the heroes, by their own imagination, induce sensations of the utmost terror and pain of death. "A Descent into the Maelström" and "MS. Found in a Bottle" also describe the heroes' experience of the ecstasy and terror of self-annihilation, their experience of an abysmal descent into nothingness. Thus, both in Poe and Tanizaki, the diabolism is actually directed toward the heroes themselves as a method of inducing pain and ecstasy and of intoxicating the reflecting consciousness in the immediacy of pain.

In Tanizaki, the themes of the discovery of perversity in human nature and the masochistic desire for self-destruction are intertwined and are, furthermore, related to his other major theme, the pursuit of the *femme fatale*. **"Secrets of Lord Bushu"** (**"Bushuko Hiwa,"** 1931), set in medieval Japan, is the most successful dramatization of the relations among these themes. One night in his youth, Lord Bushu was taken by a devilish old lady to the attic of a castle. There, women were preparing severed enemy heads to be brought before the lord of the castle for identification. In the dark room filled with a nauseating odor, he had the sensation of looking deeply into an abyss which had suddenly opened in his mind, and felt dizzy with terror and expectation. The young boy was particularly struck by the beauty of the hands of one beautiful young girl, hands which handled the heads. A faint smile appeared on her face when she handled an especially ugly head, one without the nose, and looking at her, he felt himself in an extreme state of excitement that led him to a hitherto unexperienced ecstasy. The ugliness and the grotesqueness of the severed head brought out the sublimity in the girl's cruel beauty and he found himself wishing earnestly that he were that severed head. He later finds that the beautiful wife of his master is secretly planning to remove her husband's nose as an act of revenge. Discovering this secret wish of the lady, Lord Bushu swears to be her servant and succeeds in rendering her husband an ugly cripple without a nose. He has intense moments of ecstasy when he imagines the man with an ugly, noseless face making love to a beautiful woman.

> **Tanizaki emerges not as a "pagan outcast," but as the legitimate heir to both the Japanese literary tradition and to the western tradition of romanticism, in both of which the grotesque plays an essential role.**
>
> —*Noriko Mizata Lippit*

Here the sadism of the lord is actually masochistic, and it becomes clear that the three major themes of this early period—the fear of death, the discovery of the abyss (the perversity of one's own nature), and the fear of absorption in it—are directly related to Tanizaki's heroes' masochistic pursuit of the *femme fatale*. Indeed, the pursuit of the *femme fatale* is itself, for Tanizaki, a theme which deals with man's urge for self-torture and self-destruction. In **"The Devil"** (**"Akuma,"** 1912), the hero is tortured by a physically attractive and cruel woman, while at the same time threatened by a mysterious, devilish man who swears to take revenge on him because of his relationship with her. Although extremely frightened by him, the hero continues his self-humiliating pursuit of the woman. In **"The Devil: A Sequel"** (**"Zoku Akuma,"** 1913), he encourages the man to murder him and is indeed murdered by him.

Both the woman and the man are devils, yet the true devil is the "imp of the perverse," his self-destructive urge. Both are only agents of his inner desire, and he deliberately manipulates them to torture himself. In all of Tanizaki's stories in which the fatal woman is the main theme, the heroes are involved in drawing out the diabolic nature of beautiful women, thus molding them into ideal women, black widow spiders which devour males after sexual ecstasy. The creation of the cruel, beautiful woman is the externalization of the hero's inner desire and in actuality she is his puppet. This can be seen most readily in *A Fool's Love* (*Chijin no Ai*, 1924).

The hero of the novel falls in love with a western-looking waitress and encourages her to be more bold in displaying her beauty and sexual attraction. She begins to have many love affairs, yet the more cruel her treatment of him becomes, the more ecstatic the pleasure he finds in being with her. The creation of the fatal woman in order to be tortured by her is also the main theme of such other major works of the early period as **"Tattoo"** (**"Shisei"**), *Jyōtaro* and **"Until Forsaken"** (**"Suterareru Made"**). In the later period, such major works as **"A Portrait of Shunkin"** (**"Shunkinshō"**), *Ashikari* and *The Diary of a Mad Old Man* (*Futen Rojin Nikki*) are only extensions of these early works.

Tanizaki's heroes, however, do not pursue beautiful women for the sake of erotic fulfillment. Rather, they pursue an unattainable absolute, the symbolic essence of feminine beauty. In the early period, the beauty is typically revealed in human flesh, but it is human flesh as an *object d'art* which refuses normal erotic communication: Tanizaki's heroes find the essence of feminine beauty in women's feet.

In **"Tattoo,"** the author says that the beautiful is the strong and the ugly the weak. The heroes long for the beauty that rejects them absolutely as ugly and weak, precluding any possibility of normal human relationships. Thus, beauty is elevated to the position of an absolute, an almighty existence. This is inevitable, for the pursuit of beauty, like the commitment to evil, is self-torture. Tanizaki's characters are involved in such fetishism, besides the involvement in women's feet, as licking a handkerchief dirtied by the woman's mucous, drinking a loved one's urine, and so forth. The pursuit of the unattainable beauty and the pursuit of the ugly are essentially the same.

Tanizaki separates art from life and from morality (goodness) in order to associate beauty with evil. In **"Unicorn"** (**"Kirin,"** 1910), which shows the strong influence of Oscar Wilde, Tanizaki presents a Chinese emperor who is torn between his aspiration to become a virtuous ruler and his desire to become a slave to his beautiful and brutal empress; he finally yields to the empress, whom he calls the devil. The pursuit of pleasure and beauty must lead to the pursuit of evil, for the true pleasure the heroes seek is that of self-persecution. The fear of death described by Tanizaki's heroes is based on their psychic dread of life, their sense of alienation; their masochism is a means of objectifying their fear. Yet Tanizaki's hero is the creator of the sadistic persecutor; she is the externalization of his inner desire and is almost his double. Thus he is the schemer responsible for the whole situation: he is the persecutor as well as the victim. In this sense, Tanizaki's hero becomes a God, the creator of his own, self-contained world.

In both Tanizaki and Poe, art plays a significant role in this grotesque endeavor to restore the sense of life. We have seen that the creation of an ideal fatal woman is itself an art. In **"Tattoo"** (1910), a sadistic young tattooer, who enjoys watching the pain he causes his customers, finds an innocent young girl with beautiful feet in whom he recognizes hidden powers of evil. Pouring all his psyche into his art, he tattoos on her back an enormous female black widow spider, thus transforming her into a diabolical woman. She then declares that the tattooer will be her first victim. Here it is the tattooer's art that turns the innocent girl into a diabolical woman, thus fulfilling his secret masochistic desire to be devoured by a beautiful and cruel woman. Art is both the secret agent for creating evil and the means of inducing a masochistically ecstatic state of consciousness.

The similarity to Poe's art here is obvious, although in Poe's case the diabolical women do not have the same fleshly eroticism. Poe's dreamers create their own "bower of dreams," the "arabesque" room, by decorating it with their art of interior decoration. The arabesque room is meant to induce a dreaming consciousness in the inhabitant's mind; there he indulges in his grotesque dreams of transcendence by destroying his own and his lover's physical being or sanity. The agents of the hero's grotesque imagination, evoked by his art, are Poe's vampiric women with supernal beauty.

The similarity and difference between the concepts of art of the two authors can best be illustrated by comparing Tanizaki's **"The Golden Death"** (1914) with Poe's "The Domain of Arnheim"; **"The Golden Death"** is almost entirely based on Poe's tale. In both tales, the narrator tells of his friend, extravagantly rich and poetic in nature, who attempts the creation of an earthly paradise. In both tales the narrator's visit to the paradise forms the climax, and in both paradises the narrator finds that the original nature has been transformed by art, creating an extremely bizarre and bewildering earthly paradise, that is, a grotesque and arabesque one. It was both Poe's and Tanizaki's pleasure dome, which their art, by correcting nature, created. For both writers, art proves to be superior to nature; it is not nature but art that saves the heroes.

In Poe's "The Domain of Arnheim," the narrator's visit to the paradise strongly suggests his actual dreaming. The river journey is actually an inner journey, the imaginative fulfillment of his dream. At the end of his journey, the "arabesque canoe" which had taken the narrator to the inner gate of the paradise descends rapidly into a huge amphitheater. This tale, like, "The Fall of the House of Usher" and in fact like most of Poe's tales, is a dramatization of the myth he presents in *Eureka*. *Eureka* presents Poe's myth of the fall of man and nature from the Original Unity—primordial nothingness—and their return through self-annihilation and the destruction of earthly reality. The poet in *Eureka* is endowed with the power to initiate the return movement to Original Unity. The task of Poe's artists is to dream of glorious, "golden" death, to convert the void into a space filled with meaning.

The grotesque and arabesque are for Poe a means of entering into a darkly radiant world of dreams through destruction of the body and of reality. As Poe's keen irony dramatizes in his tales, this attempt at grotesque transcendence appears mad and comical from the perspective of rational intelligence. Poe's ironic grotesque presents the grotesque, transcendental hero as both tragic and comic, as both *Eureka*'s archetypal poet and an insane, perverted man.

In **"The Golden Death"** the end of the hero's dream is also death. Yet the purpose of his art is not to cause death itself, but to bring about a state of extreme sensuous intoxication, so extreme as to risk self-destruction. Tanizaki's paradise is more voluptuous and erotic than Poe's, filled with the statues of centaurs, animals, and beautiful naked women. In the midst of the ecstasy created by the effect of the paradise, the hero dies, covering his entire body with golden powder. He himself becomes a most glorious, shining part of his paradise, a work of art.

The narrators of both tales are objective observers who witness the heroes' grotesque endeavors to create their own paradises. While Poe's narrator gradually becomes involved in the drama of the hero and at the end becomes almost his double, Tanizaki's narrator remains a rational man who escapes from the intoxicating effect of the paradise. Although he calls the hero a great artist, the narrator maintains the distance between the rational reader and the grotesque hero. In Tanizaki too, the dual or ironic point of view which regards the hero both as absurd and mad and as a positive artist is present.

Indeed, both Poe and Tanizaki frequently use the uninvolved, third-person narrator to describe the hero's grotesque effort. In Poe's stories the uninvolved narrator becomes involved. Thus, at the climax, the hero's drama is experienced by the narrator as his inner experience. In the works in which Poe uses a first-person narrator, the hero is split between a rational self and an irrational one; the narrator-hero, representing the rational self, describes the grotesque drama of the irrational self, a drama which the narrator-hero says that he himself finds difficult to comprehend. This skillful use of the narrator is a device to express the ironic, dual perspective inherent in Poe's grotesque; the serious and rational appear comical and absurd, while the mad and perverted appear tragic.

Although Tanizaki uses the uninvolved third-person narrator with great skill, the tales narrated by the hero himself do not always maintain the ironic point of view successfully. The reader is called upon to take the hero's grotesque drama seriously and with sympathy, which immediately raises the question of the drama's social, moral, and ideological relevance. It is only in *The Diary of a Mad Old Man* that Tanizaki, dramatizing man's tragicomic struggle for life, uses the ironic perspective successfully. In this work he reveals an almost terrifying spirit of irony and self-mockery. In his middle period, however, Tanizaki turned to the world of dream and imagination in his effort to create a self-sufficient romantic world, one that could give structure to his hero's grotesque pursuit of a sense of life.

While Poe had a myth that justified the poet's grotesque endeavor at destructive transcendence through his art, Tanizaki had no such cosmic myth. Tanizaki's heroes, therefore, are not transcendental heroes, but mad aesthetes who indulge in sensuous ecstasy to the point of death. Poe was a romantic who perceived the deterioration of the isomorphic relations between the order of mind and that of the body, and who believed in the power of imagination to transcend the phenomenal world to reach a higher level of reality where the split between subject and object is eliminated.

Tanizaki, on the other hand, did not yet have his own myth to explain metaphorically his view of the universe— his view of the source of man's alienation and of the life and task of the artist, and his vision of the ideal reality. Although in his youth he defined himself as a romantic writer who believed in the "poetic intuition" which perceives the world beyond phenomenal reality (a world he grasped in Platonic terms), it is difficult to call Tanizaki's early works romantic in the absence of a myth which creates a self-sufficient world of dream and legitimizes the theme of grotesque recovery from alienation. While Poe's mythopoeic thrust to create his own universe resulted in the creation of the beautiful, mathematically balanced universe of *Eureka,* in which the Poet is finally absorbed, Tanizaki had to depend on his skill of expression to convince the reader of the validity of his hero's grotesque endeavor. Asking the reader to hold in abeyance the question of morality, Tanizaki sought to appeal only to the reader's aesthetic sense. In this endeavor, the novel was not quite an appropriate form, and in the middle period his works gradually moved toward the world of romance.

While Poe's exploration of the sado-masochistic attempt to attain a sense of life and of the endeavor in grotesque art to induce dreaming consciousness presents features of human experience that are meaningful and interesting from the existential-phenomenological point of view, Poe dramatized them in his own fantasy world. He also had a myth that justified them externally as legitimate endeavors for man's return to Original Unity.

Tanizaki's middle period starts, in my opinion, with his awareness of the need to create a self-sufficient world of dream and beauty in which the question of morality and relevance to reality will be temporarily suspended. Without such a world, his exploration of grotesque eroticism might prove to be merely sensational.

This problem concerned all of the writers of the grotesque. Until the middle of the nineteenth century, the grotesque had been considered pejoratively, for it explored the realm of the ugly, the fantastic, and the subconscious, including man's fears and secret desires. During the romantic age, when artists saw the grotesque aspects of objective reality, the grotesque came to be regarded as closely related to the artist's reaction to and conception of reality. Even then, the grotesque was approved only half-heartedly; it is only in the modern period that the grotesque becomes recognized, through the works of Dostoevski, Kafka, Faulkner, Pinter, and Beckett, among others, as a highly significant symbol, style, form of imagination, and structural basis for literary works. Poe, by placing the origin and function of the grotesque in his romantic myth, was the first writer to clarify the link between Gothic terror and the romantic quest, thus integrating Gothic literature into the tradition of western romanticism. The idea of grotesque, destructive transcendence occupies the central place in his myth.

Tanizaki's turning to the world of classical Japanese culture reflects the same concern as that of the writers of the grotesque with the legitimacy of the grotesque world he creates. It is, like Coleridge's adoption of the medieval ballad form, a device to draw a magic circle around the hero and his exploration. It also reflects his mythopoeic desire to create his own dreamworld, which first became evident at this time.

Some Prefer Nettles, the novel that marks the end of Tanizaki's first period, already presents his effort to draw a magic circle, to create a myth of ideal feminine beauty that would enable him to pursue the theme of the masochistic search for a sense of life as the theme of man's search for unattainable ideal beauty. In his early writings, beautiful, diabolic women were the object of the hero's desire and the hero wanted to be tortured by them. Tanizaki describes the essence of such women as "white flesh." In this period, the woman is a living creature with white flesh, and it is the beauty and pleasure of the flesh itself that intoxicates the hero. Yet gradually, this white flesh is transformed into a white woman, an eternal woman who becomes the object of the hero's aspiration.

The eternal woman is first of all unreachable. In **"The Sorrow of the Mermaid" ("Ningyo no Nageki,"** 1919), Tanizaki says that the mysterious beauty of the mermaid, a beauty that absorbs the whole existence of the hero, is fully revealed in her immense, unfathomable eyes. Her "divine orbs" look as if they are gazing at eternity from the depth of her soul. The reader will be reminded of Poe's description of Ligeia's eyes, eyes which make the hero feel the approach of the full knowledge of eternity. The mermaid is unattainable for human beings, but she is the only source of excitement for the hero, who is tired of all the pleasures of this world. This unattainable beauty gradually takes a more distinct form in Tanizaki's later works as both the beauty of eternal maternity, from which the hero is alienated, and that of the classical Japanese court lady hidden behind a thick screen.

By identifying the fatal woman as a mother figure, and transforming the hero's masochistic longing for the fatal woman into man's longing for his lost mother, Tanizaki explains the origin of the hero's alienation and gives universality and human relevance to his hero's masochistic drama. Poe's longing for his mother and for a mother figure is well known. So is Tanizaki's attachment to his own mother, whom he describes as a beautiful woman. Yet unlike Poe, Tanizaki's creation of eternal motherhood and its beauty is a conscious literary device; Tanizaki as a man evidently did not suffer from a mother complex. The essence of unattainable feminine beauty is symbolized in a persona of a mother figure.

At the same time, Tanizaki came to identify ideal beauty with the beauty of the classical Japanese court lady, whose white face glows faintly in a dark, screened room like the fluorescent glow of fireflies at night. Glimpsed only momentarily, she is inaccessible, a dream woman existing only in one's imagination and separated in time and space. Although the essence of her beauty is also whiteness, it is no longer white flesh, but whiteness itself. Tanizaki's fatal woman thus emerges as an archetypal Japanese court lady as well as an archetypal mother.

There is no doubt that Tanizaki rediscovered the beauty of Japanese culture and literature, yet the claim that Tanizaki, abandoning his western influences, returned to the classical world is misleading. Instead, Tanizaki created his own dreamworld and eternal woman, as exotic to him as their western counterparts, out of classical Japanese culture. The court life he presents in *The Mother of Captain Shigemoto* (1949) and the medieval life in *Secrets of Lord Bushu* are distinctively Tanizaki's own creations rather than historically accurate representations. Tanizaki himself explains enviously in "Ave Maria" (1923) that the myth of the eternal woman and the worship of woman do not exist in Japanese culture. Thus he creates his own goddess to rule over his self-sufficient dreamworld, a mythical world or one which functions as a substitute for myth. The eternal mother as goddess, as the symbolic essence of his dreamworld, is most vividly expressed in *The Mother of Captain Shigemoto,* the masterpiece of his middle period. Captain Shigemoto's mother, who has lived in his dream, finally appears at the end of the novel shining faintly in the darkness with a circle of light around her. Tanizaki's return was not to classical Japanese culture but to the primordial and infantile area of human consciousness, to the realm of the subconscious and dreams.

Some Prefer Nettles (*Tadekuu Mushi,* 1928) explains how this autonomous dreamworld is created. The protagonist Kaname is torn between his attraction to a Eurasian prostitute, who powders her legs to make them completely white, and his father-in-law's old-fashioned, doll-like mistress, who is carefully groomed to suit the old man's anachronistic taste. In this transitional novel, the hero is torn between his desire for white flesh and his longing for whiteness, the eternal beauty of woman.

With his mistress, Ohisa, Kaname's father-in-law lives an aesthete's life in complete retirement, re-creating a type of life of old Edo. They frequent the Bunraku theater and Kaname, while watching the white face of a crying doll move faintly across a distant stage, comes to realize that the essence of Ohisa's beauty is that eternalized by the Bunraku puppet. Tanizaki writes:

> The Ohisa for whom his secret dream searched might not be Ohisa at all, but another, a more Ohisa-like Ohisa. And it might even be that this latter Ohisa was no more than a doll, perhaps even now quiet in the dusk of an inner chamber behind an arched stage doorway. A doll might do well enough, indeed.

After this novel, Tanizaki turned to the world of classical literature and beauty and recreated his ideal feminine beauty in historical figures and in historical settings. Such masterpieces as *Yoshinokuzu, Ashikari,* "A Portrait of Shunkin," "The Story of a Blind Man" ("Mōmoku Monogatari"), *The Mother of Captain Shigemoto,* "The Bridge of Dreams" ("Yume no ukihashi") were written one after another.

In these novels, the desire for white flesh disappears almost completely (although still lurking below the surface) and the hero's longing for the essence of feminine beauty is dramatized as his longing for an unattainable mother figure or for a superior woman with classic Japanese beauty. The hero's self-torture, born out of his longing for the unattainable, is intense, yet by fathoming this pain, the hero obtains a deep, soul-satisfying pleasure, a complete ecstasy. The eternal women in these stories are only extensions of the beautiful and cruel women of supernal beauty who tortured the heroes in the early works. Thus Tanizaki created his own world of romance by creating his own romantic myth of supernal beauty. Tanizaki also developed stories of sado-masochistic torture in historic Japanese settings, using the rich tradition of the grotesque in Japanese literature.

Poe's supernal beauty is also unattainable. Poe's myth of the Poet's return to the original unity presents a drama of the Poet in search of the beauty which exists only in the original paradise, the origin of life itself. Poe's ideal woman is doomed to die. Both Ligeia and Eleonora, whose beauty symbolizes man's original state of harmony and his aspiration for it, die and thus become unattainable for the heroes. They may even have existed only in their dreams. Following their aspiration for supernal beauty, the heroes enter the path to self-annihilation, returning to the original condition of nothingness.

Supernal beauty is attained only through self-destruction. The grotesque in Poe is a symbol of decadent human nature and reality, the result of the Fall, as well as a symbol which points towards transcendence of the decadent. In Tanizaki too, the grotesque serves not merely to induce sensuous pleasure, but as a means of entering his dreamworld, of returning home. It is a means of the hero's assuring his sense of life, a sense which he cannot obtain in the modern, industrial world. The origin and function of Tanizaki's grotesque, too, are legitimized by his creation of a romantic world of dream.

Some Prefer Nettles is often considered a dramatization of the conflict between Tanizaki's attraction to the beauty and culture of the West and those of the East. With this novel, the period of western influence on Tanizaki appears to end, and since his major works all explore the world of classical beauty, critics argue, as I have noted, that the western influence on Tanizaki was not lasting. Rather, however, the novel dramatizes the shift of the hero's pursuit of white flesh to whiteness itself, a shift from the world of reality to the world of romance, to the self-sufficient world of romantic dream. Poe's influence on Tanizaki appears, then, not merely in Tanizaki's early choice of the themes that were to characterize his literary career, but also in the creation of the romantic world that began with this shift.

Tanizaki was fascinated by the Gothic themes presented in the writings of Baudelaire, Wilde, and Poe, such as the ties between love and cruelty, pleasure and pain, and domination and humiliation, and tried to dramatize them in his own language and in the natural settings of Japanese life. Tanizaki's later turning to the world of classical beauty did not mean that he had discarded these themes and western influences. On the contrary, he developed these same themes more fully and uniquely within the tradition of Japanese culture.

More importantly, Tanizaki developed the Gothic themes into romantic themes: Tanizaki's insistent dramatization of man's sense of self-estrangement from "home," of his vision of and aspiration for eternal femininity, and of his grotesque, desperate effort to regain it, finally results in the creation of a self-contained, romantic world of his own. Based on Japanese tradition, Tanizaki created his own literary space and his own myth of the ideal woman to enable himself to develop his Poesque romantic theme of the self-destructive pursuit of a sense of life.

Tanizaki's literary world develops, therefore, from a mere description, however interesting, of man's perverted effort to attain a sense of life, a world that reflects his Edo taste or Gothic taste, to a romantic world in which man's alienation from the original harmony and his struggle to regain it become a major theme. The grotesque is not only integrated into his romanticism, but also emerges as a positive, although paradoxical, symbol which points toward the ideal reality. Poe's influence on the formation of his world is significant—especially Poe's concept of supernal beauty, his hero's tragicomic drama of search for it, and the role of the grotesque in this drama.

Toward the end of his life, Tanizaki returned to present reality from the world of romance and seemed to resume his earlier pursuit of the theme of erotic desire for white flesh, especially in *The Key* and *The Diary of a Mad Old Man*. Yet this time the heroes are old men, nearing death, who have already lost their sexual power. Their longing for white flesh is symbolic and not physical; the white flesh is almost a symbol of desire for life itself. Their longing for erotic desire is actually a longing for a life-giving force.

In Tanizaki's later works, eros, life, and death are linked to each other; life can be experienced only as a sense of life, and in man's pursuit of a sense of life he encounters the terror of death. Eros is a beautiful, sublime, and grotesque life-force, which brings life to death. In the old men's desperate, masochistic, erotic desires, Tanizaki presents man's tragicomic, grotesque yet sublime struggle for life. This is essentially the same struggle Poe dramatized in his tales of the grotesque and systematized in his romantic myth. Tanizaki proves in these novels that the themes which preoccupied him in his early days were indeed his own. Tanizaki's early exposure to Poe's world of "negative romanticism," with its central concept of grotesque transcendence, cannot be irrelevant to the ultimate development of his own world of romanticism in the Japanese literary tradition. While Tanizaki's Japanese romantic world is unique, it is not incompatible with the western romantic tradition. Thus Tanizaki emerges not as a "pagan outcast," but as the legitimate heir to both the Japanese literary tradition and to the western tradition of romanticism, in both of which the grotesque plays an essential role.

The long career of Junichirō Tanizaki offers a spectacle of unity in the utmost diversity. From his early "diabolist" tales through the traditionalist underpinnings of his middle period to the erotic realism of his last novels, Tanizaki's preoccupations remain the same: the secret ritual, the obsessive desire, the nostalgia so profound that it defines an entire existence.

Geoffrey O'Brien, in a review of **The Secret History of the Lord of Musashi and Arrowroot,** *in* **The Village Voice,** *April 27, 1982*.

J. Thomas Rimer (essay date 1978)

SOURCE: "Tanizaki Junichirō: The Past as Homage. 'A Portrait of Shunkin' and 'The Bridge of Dreams'," in *Modern Japanese Fiction and Its Traditions: An Introduction,* Princeton University Press, 1978, pp. 22-37.

[*An American-born educator and critic, Rimer specializes in Japanese literature. In the following excerpt, he offers the stories "Shunkinshō" ("A Portrait of Shunkin") and "Yume no ukihashi" ("The Bridge of Dreams") as evidence that Tanizaki's fiction is modern yet heavily influenced by traditional Japanese themes and literature.*]

For many readers, the work of Tanizaki Junichirō remains the most absorbing in modern Japanese literature, and in many ways, for its period, the most contemporary in spirit. Tanizaki examined the foibles and obsessions of his time with an elegant and ironic spirit that continues to give his work a surprising freshness. Yet an analysis of his writing indicates a powerful interest on his part in the themes and techniques of older Japanese literature. His perception of these older traditions, and his use of them, help provide the richness of texture that gives his narratives their grace and their weight. . . .

Tanizaki's life spanned the entire modern period. He began writing early in the century, often, it is said, under the "Satanic" influences of Edgar Allan Poe and Oscar Wilde. Fascinated by Western culture, he enjoyed visiting the foreign shops, stores, and hotels in Tokyo and nearby Yokohama, and he witnessed the destruction of that "modern" civilization he so appreciated when Tokyo burned after the great earthquake of 1923. Tanizaki left to live in a quiet area in the vicinity of Osaka, the large industrial city near Kyoto, the old capital. He wrote a considerable number of works during the increasingly difficult period of the 1930s; during the Second World War he finished composing what is perhaps his masterpiece, the long and evocative novel *Sasame yuki* (*Thin Snow*) as a tribute to the world he saw crumbling around him. In the vastly different postwar era he continued to produce novels as provocative as *Kagi* (*The Key*) in 1956, and, in 1962, the novel that provides a last ironic look at himself and his generation, *Fūten rōjin kikki* (*The Diary of a Mad Old Man*).

For Japanese readers of his generation, Tanizaki's works often seemed scandalously "modern." He himself commented that his extensive reading of Western literature (by which he may have meant such writers with a Naturalist bent as Ibsen, Zola, and Strindberg) gave him the ability to portray the liberation of sexual desire. Tanizaki seems to have meant that he had been liberated to portray a new set of relationships between men and women. Women in his work often became fierce and demanding creatures; if not quite jealous goddesses, they certainly remain larger than life. His male characters often find themselves most comfortable when groveling at their feet. In this respect, Tanizaki's celebrated short story **"Shisei"** (**"The Tattooer"**), written in 1910, can serve as a paradigm for much of his later work. When the beautiful heroine is about to have a spider tattooed on her body, the tattooer warns her of the pain involved. "I can bear anything for the sake of beauty," she replies simply. The thrust of much of Tanizaki's work is suggested by the overtones of that one sentence. His ability to push his reader into a peculiar psychological state, as well as his highly developed dramatic sense (he was a promising playwright early in his career) remained enormous assets for him throughout his creative life.

For all his interest in overtures toward sex and psychology, Tanizaki was always careful to stress the ultimate importance of careful literary construction. In 1927, he provided an explicit statement of the value of such methods in his own literary work, in the midst of a literary debate with Akutagawa Ryūnosuke, the author of *Rashūmon* and other celebrated stories. Tanizaki speaks as though he were a musician, explaining the importance of a fugue:

> According to Akutagawa, I am excessively given to novel, fanciful plots. I wish to write only of the perverse, the fantastic, what excites the masses. This is not good. This is not what a novel should be. There is no artistic value in plot interest. Such, I think, is Akutagawa's general view. Unfortunately I disagree. Plot interest is, described differently, the way in which a work is assembled, interest in structure, architectural beauty. It cannot be said that this is without artistic value. . . . It is of course not the sole value, but I myself believe that among the literary forms the novel is that which can possess the greatest sense of structural beauty. To do away with plot interest is to throw away the special prerogatives of the form known as the novel.

Those readers who seized on the more outrageous aspects of Tanizaki's thematic concerns (some would term them obsessions) failed to take note of the means by which their interest was inevitably caught and sustained in those narratives. The means Tanizaki often chose owe much to traditional Japanese literature.

In **"Shunkinshō"** (**"A Portrait of Shunkin"**), Tanizaki explores to the full the psychological relationships between master and slave. The composition of such a work of fiction, with its eerie artistic and erotic insights, would doubtless have been impossible in Japan before the twentieth century; but its creation in 1933 would also have been impossible without a desire to render a certain literary homage to the past.

The narrative is presented in the first person by a learned man of this century with a taste for the traditional arts. He attempts to assemble various documents in order to recreate, and to understand, the life of Shunkin, the blind daughter of a rich Osaka merchant in the early nineteenth century, who became an expert player on the samisen. The narrative focuses on the relationship between Shunkin and the young boy Sasuke, who, having joined the family to learn a merchant's trade, is eventually assigned as a servant and pupil to the difficult daughter. The story chronicles the relationship between this extraordinary pair, from childhood and adolescence through adulthood, when Shunkin herself becomes a teacher. The two live together as mistress and servant until the beautiful Shunkin, scalded on the face by an unknown assailant, is able, through her own first experience with humility, to begin to accept Sasuke as her equal. Sasuke's own sacrifice is to blind himself, so as never to see the scarred face of his beloved. They finish out their lives together in the embrace of mutual darkness.

"Shunkin" is an extraordinarily rich narrative that can intrigue and move the reader in a variety of ways. The subject matter itself stands as a particularly powerful example of Tanizaki's predilection for creating forceful and autocratic women for his central characters. Sasuke, who is reduced to a kind of psychological slave, fondles her feet, takes her to the lavatory, and performs every conceivable function (including the sexual) to insure her comfort and well-being. Shunkin is not grateful. Tanizaki uses his psychological study of the relationship between the two, his literary manifestation of the special closed world in which they live, to suggest that the relationship between "Teacher" and "Taught" operates in any human situation. Although in **"Shunkin"** all such elements seem pushed to extremes, the characters remain believable: the reader, perhaps to his discomfort, is forced to recognize that he finds himself in familiar territory, no matter how purposefully exotic the trappings.

Tanizaki's own taste and learning create in **"Shunkin"** a document that reveals much about the quality of life in the late Tokugawa period. The various distinctions between social classes and the general compartmentalization of life are carefully delineated. All of society seems a series of airless rooms. Art (in this case the musicality of Shunkin) in such a social context, suggests Tanizaki, may have provided the most delicious of dangers, since it cut across all social distinctions and barriers—as it does in a number of important moments in the novella. The deepest level of thematic structure in **"Shunkin"** reveals Tanizaki's convictions concerning the necessary rigors of all art: only unrelenting efforts, and often the most painful ones, can produce any genuine results. Once attained, however, the continuing sacrifice seems justified. For Tanizaki, beauty is never far from pain.

When Sasuke begins to learn the samisen, he studies at night, in a dark closet, so as not to disturb the other sleeping apprentices. His difficulties are enormous.

> . . . Sasuke would wait until he was sure they were sound asleep then get up and practice in the closet where the bedding was kept. The attic room itself must have been hot and stuffy, and the heat inside the closet on a summer night almost unbearable. But by shutting himself up in it he could muffle the twang of the strings and at the same time avoid the distraction of outside noises, such as the snoring of his roommates. Of course he had to sing the vocal parts softly and pluck the strings with his fingers, instead of with a plectrum: sitting there in the pitch-dark closet, he played by his sense of touch alone.

Later, Shunkin's very abuse spurs Sasuke on to greater skills:

> "You're such a weakling!" she told Sasuke scornfully. "You're a boy, and yet you can't stand the least thing. It's all because of your crying that they blame me and think I'm being cruel to you. If you really want to become an artist you've got to grit your teeth and bear it, no matter how much it hurts. If you can't, I won't be your teacher."

> After that, however badly she abused him, Sasuke never cried.

Only after Sasuke has blinded himself can he feel that he has attained a proper level of understanding:

> Always before, even while they were making love, they had been separated by the gulf between teacher and pupil. But now Sasuke felt that they were truly united, locked in a tight embrace. Youthful memories of the dark world of the closet where he used to practice came flooding into his mind, but the darkness in which

he now found himself seemed completely different. Most blind people can sense the direction from which light is coming: they live in a faintly luminous world, not one of unrelieved blackness. Now Sasuke knew that he had found an inner vision in place of the vision he had lost. Ah, he thought, this is the world my teacher lives in—at last I have reached it!

Shunkin as well only achieves the highest pinnacle of her art through suffering. The narrator comments on this fact:

> How ever blessed with talent, she could scarcely have attained the ultimate mastery of her art without tasting the bitterness of life. Shunkin had always been coddled. Though severe in her demands on others, she herself had never known hardship or humiliation. There had been no one to humble her. But then Heaven had subjected her to a cruel ordeal, endangering her life and smashing her stubborn pride.

Indeed, Tanizaki ultimately suggests, the beauty of the lives of these two people seems to lie in their suffering, however perversely inspired.

In constructing **"Shunkin,"** Tanizaki solves with consummate skill the chief artistic problem such an account proposes: he has made the fantastic world of the heroine credible. In this regard, the unnamed narrator plays a key role, although his presence contributes little of real importance to the theme of the story. He serves rather as a bridge between the commonplace world of the reader and the bizarre world of Tanizaki's heroine. The narrator begins by explaining that he has become quite interested in the musician Shunkin and that he has managed to visit the grave-site of the woman and her pupil Sasuke, also a fine musician. He goes on to tell the reader that he has located an old biography of Shunkin and a dim photograph of her as well. He has also spoken with an old woman who knew the pair when she was very young. The narrative that follows is constructed of juxtapositions of portions of that biography, along with statements made by the old woman, plus an extensive commentary provided by the narrator himself. Some statements contradict each other. Often the narrator speculates on the psychological meaning of the actions outlined in the biography. Raising questions about aspects of the meaning of the events makes the reader more willing to assume that the events actually took place; such questions act as a device to cast over the somewhat fabulous and hallucinatory narrative a thin semblance of ordinary reality.

For example, after an extraordinary account of the birth of Shunkin's illegitimate child, during which Shunkin's wanton cruelty toward Sasuke is first revealed, Tanizaki halts the flow of narrative so that his narrator can make the following comment.

> Why did Shunkin treat Sasuke in this fashion? To be sure, Osaka people have always been more concerned about questions of family background, property, and status, when it comes to marriage, than those to Tokyo: Osaka is famous for its proud old merchant families—

and how much prouder they must have been in the feudal days before Meiji! A girl like Shunkin would doubtless have regarded Sasuke, whose family had served hers for generations, as someone immeasurably beneath her. Then too, with the typically embittered attitude of a blind person, she must have been determined not to show any weakness, or let anyone make a fool of her.

I suppose she felt that she would be insulting herself irreparably by taking Sasuke as her husband. Probably she was ashamed of sleeping with an inferior, and reacted by behaving coldly toward him. Then did she consider him nothing more than a physiological necessity? As far as she was aware of her own feelings, I dare say she did.

The narrator's speculations here seem to provide the reader only a partial explanation for Shunkin's cruel behavior. In previous sections of the narrative, Tanizaki has already let the reader see further into the real nature of Shunkin than the narrator himself seems prepared to do. There seems something more, something terrible to state, that the narrator cannot quite bring himself to envision. Yet the reader quickly realizes that he can sense certain depravities in the couple's relationship. Forced to take cognizance of his own ability to recognize the presence of such abnormalities, the reader is shocked at himself and his own reactions. Tanizaki, of course, has sought all these results.

Sophisticated as the use of such a narrative technique may be in developing a contemporary psychological portrait of Shunkin and Sasuke, such methods owe some debt to earlier traditions. The first person narrator is perhaps the oldest organizing device used in what might be termed traditional Japanese fiction. . . . In **"Shunkin,"** Tanizaki avoids the use of an omniscient narrator. The reader is shown his attitudes, foibles, tastes, curiosities. His personality is sketched to the extent that he can help propel the narrative along; yet his personal characteristics are not sufficiently obtrusive that they risk distracting the reader's attention from the couple. This reflective solo voice, so much a part of the traditional Japanese modes of narrative, is here fitted with great skill into a framework in which the device functions to produce precisely the complex effect desired.

A narrative constructed from so many diverse elements requires some kind of overall unity to which the various parts of the story can be related. Tanizaki adopts a number of strategies to bring this unity about. One involves the use of images and objects that recur again and again in his narrative. Such symbolism is a familiar enough device for Western readers. Blindness, for example, serves as one unifying image helping to link various levels of meaning.

Sasuke is first drawn to darkness when he learns to play at night:

> . . . Sasuke never felt inconvenienced by the darkness. Blind people live in the dark like this all the time, he thought, and Shunkin has to play the samisen the same way. He was delighted to have found a place for himself

in that dark world of hers. Even afterward, when he could practice freely, he was in the habit of closing his eyes whenever he took up the instrument, explaining that he felt he had to do exactly as Shunkin did. In short, he wanted to suffer the same handicap as Shunkin, to share all he could of the life of the blind. At times he obviously envied them.

"A Portrait of Shunkin" thus becomes, in one sense an account of how Sasuke's wish was eventually granted. The language of the narrative is filled with diverse images of blindness as the story progresses.

Tanizaki's most poetically effective symbols, however, are those of birds. Shunkin keeps caged nightingales and larks. When she listens to them sing, her spirits brighten. She often takes her caged larks to the roof of her house and, in accordance with custom, lets them out of their cages to soar into the sky and sing. The birds normally soon return, but, at the end of the story, her favorite lark does not come back. Shunkin falls into a despondency that eventually brings about her death. The birds have one meaning for her, but another for the reader, who comes to see Shunkin as a caged bird who finds the only release possible in her music. The lyrical images of the birds singing in flight may seem to provide too obvious a parallel to the blind samisen player. But they function well within the context of the atmosphere of the story.

An allied technique Tanizaki employs shows a great reliance on traditional Japanese aesthetics. No Western critical term serves to define such a device. He chooses one moment, one revelation, when the thrust of the whole narrative, its largest significance, seems suggested in a critical central moment. Such a moment creates, in modern prose, precisely that sense of *aware,* that deep sensitiveness to things, so highly prized by traditional Japanese writers. The whole is rendered visible by the revelation of one small element. The narrative microcosm that fulfills this function in **"Shunkin"** takes place at a party to which Shunkin (accompanied by Sasuke) has been invited by a wealthy young student. The gathering is boisterous. All the guests are fascinated by the beauty and *hauteur* of the blind woman. Suddenly, an untoward incident occurs:

> That afternoon while they were all out strolling in the garden Sasuke led Shunkin among the plum blossoms, guiding her slowly from tree to tree and stopping before each of them. "Here is another!" he would say, as he held her hand out to stroke the trunk. Like all blind people, Shunkin depended on her sense of touch to make sure that something was really there; it was also her way of enjoying the beauty of flowers and trees. But when one of the jesters saw her eagerly caressing the rough bark of an old plum tree with her delicate hands, he cried out in a queer, shrill voice: "Oooh, I envy that tree!" Then another jester ran up in front of Shunkin, threw himself into a grotesque pose, arms and legs aslant, and announced: "I'm a plum tree too!" Everyone burst out laughing.

Up until now the pressures of vulgar humanity have been carefully excluded from the story. Until this moment, the reader has unwittingly come to inhabit the closed world of Shunkin and her companion. Now the reader is shocked into the realization that, whatever the nature of Shunkin's cruelty and obsessive demands for excellence, she is a great artist. And now she is being made fun of. The reader's sympathies for her are crystallized, fully engaged. They remain so for the rest of the narrative. This means of creating *aware* in prose, of producing a shock of realization which can suggest the significance of a narrative and so push it forward, finds many antecedents in Japanese fiction, stretching back to *The Tale of Genji,* that classical text which most occupied Tanizaki during the course of his own artistic career. He read and studied that work continuously, and first translated it into modern Japanese before the war.

"Shunkin" is an altogether modern piece of writing and indeed seems a thorough vindication of James's dictum quoted earlier, "What is character but the determination of incident? What is incident but the illustration of character?" Yet it owes much to the Japanese past, not only for the choice of subject matter but because of the author's occasional use of traditional literary methods. **"Yume no ukihashi"** ("The Bridge of Dreams"), however, a later story written in 1959, after Tanizaki's profound involvement with *Genji,* seems an even more effective literary experiment, for here Tanizaki attempts a recreation of some of the themes from Lady Murasaki's novel, paying homage (albeit in his own way) to the classic, while maintaining with great flair his own literary identity.

More than any other work of Tanizaki, **"The Bridge of Dreams"** seems difficult to summarize. The peculiar power of the story lies in the creation and in the sustaining power of a special atmosphere. At a climactic moment, the young man Tadasu, who narrates the entire account in the first person, cries out, "I was back in the dream world that I had longed for, back in the power of the old memories that had haunted for so many years." As a small child, Tadasu lived in an elegant and secluded house in Kyoto with his father and his mother Chinu. His mother died when he was five, and his father remarried another woman so like his own first mother that the child's memories become completely confused and blurred. He reestablishes the same relationships with his new mother, some of them abnormal and erotic. When Tadasu is eighteen, his father dies and asks his son to take his place, marrying another girl his own age for the sake of appearances. This bizarre relationship continues until the demise of his second mother, who is bitten by a centipede and dies. Tanizaki's tangle of erotic relationships may seem perverse and arbitrary when subjected to such summary treatment. They are, however, part and parcel of the atmosphere of the story. And the atmosphere is the subject of, and the justification for, the entire narrative.

Tanizaki has created a world as close to that of the court depicted in *The Tale of Genji* as might be possible in a twentieth-century setting. The reference to *Genji* is clear from the title of the story, **"The Bridge of Dreams,"** itself the name of the very last book of Lady Murasaki's novel. Indeed Tanizaki's story opens with a quotation, a poem written by one of the mothers on the subject of *Genji.* The house in which Tadasu is brought up seems to exist in a timeless world. The descriptions of the rooms and gardens have nothing contemporary about them. The sense of the past is always powerful; indeed it is the present that seems ambiguous and arbitrary. Tanizaki creates his links with the present through his characters, who cool their beer in the garden pond and, reluctantly, visit a physician when care is needed. But the world of the house, with its silences, the occasional *koto* music, and the sound of the old-style bamboo clapper in the pond, seems as complete as that of those secluded chambers in which so many of the characters of *Genji* live and, occasionally, die.

Tanizaki's treatment of his characters and of their interrelationships provides an equally effective reworking of certain themes in *Genji,* Tanizaki's musical variations on an earlier theme. That theme, so skillfully developed by Murasaki, concerns the love shown by several important male characters for their mothers, or, perhaps one should say stepmothers. Murasaki relates the discovery by these male characters of this love to their own ability to understand themselves. More often than not, Lady Murasaki uses the theme to show the eternal appeal of certain types of beauty and to suggest the interdependence of all human affection. The emotional and moral world of *Genji,* created when it was, contains much that suggests an ultimate openness and innocent good will in many kinds of human relationships. For Tanizaki, living in the twentieth century, the recreation of a modern version of this earlier world brings with it a strong odor of decadence and decay. This too, for Tanizaki, is beautiful, and such are the elements that make up his own contribution to the world of *Genji.*

Along with the theme of loving one's mother, muted and etherealized in Murasaki, eroticized in Tanizaki, is a second theme common to both narratives, that of children concealed and discovered. Again, in Lady Murasaki's novel, this motif is often used (along with its value as a plot device) as a means by which a character can achieve self-definition and self-enlightenment. For Tanizaki, the lost child serves rather as a means to permit the others (especially Tadasu) to turn ever more inwards upon themselves. Some Japanese writers and critics have pointed out that Tanizaki is, in fact, a moralizer; to the extent that a foreign reader may agree that this might be the case about so atmospheric a story as **"The Bridge of Dreams,"** such a penchant for moralizing might be seen in Tanizaki's discreet suggestion (certainly nowhere stated) that he is depicting a culture that has lived too long.

Tanizaki's care in selecting every proper detail in order to create the atmosphere he desires shows his literary skill and learning at its best. The story is filled with references to *Genji* and the whole history of Kyoto, just as *The Tale of Genji* itself is filled with earlier literary and cultural references. A discussion on calligraphy, one of the arts most prized in Lady Murasaki's novel, opens Tanizaki's story. Poems by Kamo no Chōmei are mentioned; and indeed Chōmei himself, who, in his *Hōjōki (An Account of My Hut*) created a celebrated (and fictionalized) account of his own retirement, seems a perfect prototype for Tadasu, who is keeping a record of his own spiritual existence. Rai Sanyō (1780-1832) and Ishikawa Jōzan (1583-1672), two other learned writers and poets from the Tokugawa period, are also cited, expanding the world of taste and learning in which the characters of the story live. Even when Tadasu leaves the house in search of the mysterious younger brother he has never seen, his trip takes him to villages in the countryside famous in classical literature through references in *The Tale of the Heike* and the medieval *nō* plays. Indeed, the only thoroughly modern element in the story is the occasional intrusion of the doctor, who heralds births and deaths. His appearance always seems startling and usually (despite his personal kindness) disagreeable.

Tanizaki's most elusive homage to *Genji* may lie in his tacit adoption of certain of Lady Murasaki's attitudes. In the earlier novel, the world created by the author is one inhabited by the women of the court, retired from the world, who have the leisure to dream and to reflect. Largely cut off from the world of politics and court activity, they learn of events outside their purview slowly and imperfectly. Tanizaki has made his main character a man, but, despite the change in sex, Tadasu remains far more a part of the world of his strange home than he does of any world at large. Both he and Shunkin exist in terms of the atmospheres surrounding them. Toward the end of **"The Bridge of Dreams,"** the reader is casually informed that Tadasu graduated from high school and studied law at the university, but elements from the outer world have nothing to do with what he perceives to be his real existence. Tanizaki has remained quite faithful to Lady Murasaki in this respect.

What is more, Tanizaki has absorbed and made use of one of Lady Murasaki's major literary devices, and one so appropriate to the atmosphere in which she lived and wrote: that of indirection. In *The Tale of Genji,* the truth about the various characters and their mutual relationships are revealed in pieces; the reader comes to know the truth, or a variety of truths, quite slowly. Overarching relationships—physical, psychological, or spiritual—are slowly suggested as the narrative moves forward. The reader of Lady Murasaki's novel thus comes to be enlightened in somewhat the same fashion that he might hope to be in real life.

In **"The Bridge of Dreams,"** indirection and reticence make it possible for Tadasu to tell his story. Before the final revelation of his relations with his second mother and of his marriage of convenience to the daughter of the family gardener, Tadasu makes the following statement.

> I have tentatively given this narrative the title of "The Bridge of Dreams," and have written it, however amateurishly, in the form of a novel. But everything that I have set forth actually happened—there is not one falsehood in it. Still, if I were asked why I took it into my head to write it all, I should be unable to reply. I am not writing out of any desire to have others

read this. At least, I don't intend to let anyone see it as long as I am alive. If someone happens across it after my death, there will be no harm in that; but even if it is lost in oblivion, if no one ever reads it, I shall have no regret. I write for the sake of writing, simply because I enjoy looking back at the events of the past and trying to remember them one by one. Of course, all that I record here is true: I do not allow myself the slightest falsehood or distortion. But there are limits even to telling the truth; there is a line one ought not to cross. And so, although I certainly never write anything untrue, neither do I write the whole of the truth. Perhaps I leave part of it unwritten out of consideration for my father, for my mother, and for myself. . . . If anyone says that not to tell the whole truth is in fact to lie, that is his own interpretation. I shall not venture to deny it.

Tadasu's words are, at least in part, an ironic reworking of the well-known passage in *The Tale of Genji* in which Genji defines the art of fiction:

> I have a theory of my own about what this art of the novel is, and how it came into being. To begin with, it does not simply consist in the author's telling a story about the adventures of some other person. On the contrary, it happens because the storyteller's own experience of men and things, whether for good or ill—not only what he has passed through himself, but even events which he has only witnessed or been told of—has moved him to an emotion so passionate that he can no longer keep it shut up in his heart. Again and again something in his own life or in that around him will seem to the writer so important that he cannot bear to let it pass into oblivion. There must never come a time, he feels, when men do not know about it.

Tanizaki's passage reflects something of Murasaki; but, more than that, Tadasu's words reveal certain artistic principles involved in the composition of much Japanese poetry and prose. ". . . I certainly never write anything untrue, neither do I write the whole of the truth." Such a principle of adhering closely to the "truth" of one's natural materials but shaping them to the ends of art is one alive in the earliest poetic diaries and is still visible in contemporary fiction. Instinctive selectivity from all the possible materials that the observation of life might offer: in the art of Tanizaki, at least, reticence and taste join together at this point to produce, not verbal photographs, or confessions, but literary evocation.

"A Portrait of Shunkin" and **"The Bridge of Dreams"** will surely strike a Western reader as contemporary in their explicitness and profound in their artistic concerns. And the stories explain themselves. No footnotes on Japanese culture are required to penetrate these peculiar worlds that Tanizaki has created. The author's mastery of the intimate connections between character, incident, and atmosphere permit each element of these stories to reinforce the others; each word of the text seems inevitable, exquisitely appropriate. Nevertheless, Tanizaki's work satisfies profoundly because behind his own personal accomplishment lies a long literary heritage to which his art pays the ultimate compliment of constant reference.

Donald Keene (essay date 1984)

SOURCE: "Tanizaki Jun'ichirō," in *Dawn to the West, Japanese Literature of the Modern Era: Fiction, Vol. 1,* Holt, Rinehart and Winston, 1984, pp. 720-85.

[*In the following excerpt, Keene provides an overview of Tanizaki's short stories.*]

Tanizaki's earliest writings, mainly poems in Chinese on historical subjects, appeared in the literary magazine circulated among students at his middle school. An essay published in 1902 startled his classmates by the assurance and vocabulary with which he criticized "oriental" pessimism. His insistence on joy as an essential element in human life was the first evidence of the hedonist disposition for which he would be famed. A few months later he went beyond oriental philosophy to write an essay in which he invoked the names of Dante, Carlyle, and Shakespeare in his discussion of "Moral Concepts and Aesthetic Concepts."

Tanizaki's first story appeared in the same magazine. **"Shumpū Shūu Roku"** (**"Account of Spring Breezes and Autumn Rain"**), published in 1903, suggests the Ken'yūsha in its title [the Ken'yūsha was a group of young writers who gathered around Ozaki Kōyō and produced much popular literature], and the language recalls not only Ozaki Kōyō but Kōda Rohan and Higuchi Ichiyō, predictable influences on a precociously gifted boy writing at this time. Despite the ornate language, unimaginable in a seventeen-year-old of a half-century later, and the self-conscious allusions to Buddhist texts and works of European philosophy, the story is unaffected and even moving. It relates how Tanizaki, returning home with the prizes he had won as the best pupil in elementary school, is informed by his father that he will not be able to go on to middle school. The father insists that education is not necessary for success; many men of humble birth and small education have amassed great fortunes. The boy bursts into tears.

What manner of tears were they? Tears of gratitude for the solicitude of my father? No. Tears of indignation over the heartlessness of the world? No. Ah, those were tears of grief that because I could not go to middle school I would have to find work in some business establishment.

Ever since I was a small child I had disliked military men most of all human beings, and businessmen next. Even supposing a man achieves a worldwide reputation and his exploits resound through the nation, can one say that what he does accords with the way fit for human beings if he robs others of their lives or sheds blood with a sword? Even supposing a man amasses an immense fortune and can abandon himself to uninterrupted days of a spring of opulence, surely there is no point in his having been born a man if he makes this dreamlike existence no more than a dream.

Beneath the surface of this ponderously balanced prose we find a first statement of Tanizaki's dislike of the military and businessmen, which remained with him through his life, though it was certainly not typical of most ambitious and patriotic boys of his age. But the boy Tanizaki was properly Confucian in his feelings of remorse over being the kind of unfilial son who worries more about his education than about providing for his parents who were rapidly growing old in their struggle to make ends meet. The story concludes:

My heart has become iron. My heart has died. Without wild passion, without anguish, without gods, without Buddha, without tears, there remains only an object like a cold stone in the abyss of my soul. Have I attained the calm immobility of a philosopher of the Epicurean school? I do not know my own heart.

These lines were followed by a tanka, which rather cryptically describes the frost on the moss at the Oka Temple glowing like lapis.

Tanizaki had convincingly described a painful memory of his childhood. Another painful occurrence came soon afterward. He was enabled to continue his education by his teacher, who found for him a job as a *shosei*, a kind of combination houseboy and tutor, in the family of a restaurant proprietor. His humiliation at being treated like a servant would be remembered not only in the autobiographical story **"Shindō"** (**"The Boy Prodigy,"** 1916), but even in the very late volume of short essays *Tōsei Shika Modoki* (*In the Manner of a Modern Storyteller,* 1961), evidence of how deeply his resentment lingered within him. Tanizaki worked as a shosei from 1902 to 1907, when he was unceremoniously expelled from the household after a love letter he had addressed to a maid was intercepted. He daily suffered minor annoyances; for example, the lady of the house, intending to test his honesty, included one more banknote than she had listed on the deposit slip when she sent him to the bank. But his classmates found him an exceptionally lively and cheerful, as well as gifted, student and he generally ranked at or near the top of his class in the best middle school of Japan.

In March 1905 Tanizaki was promoted from the First Middle School to the First High School. He enrolled in the division of English Law, presumably in the hopes of convincing the family who were still employing him as a shosei that he was serious about getting ahead, in the manner expected of Meiji youths. But his enthusiasm for literature had by no means waned and he continued to be active in the school literary societies. His stories, published in the high school magazine, described such personal experiences as his tribulations as a shosei and his first love affair. . . .

Tanizaki entered the Tokyo Imperial University in 1908, after his graduation from high school. This time he enrolled in the Department of Japanese Literature, always known as a haven for students who chose not to study. He had made up his mind to become a writer, and his attitude toward classes was cavalier. He seemed indifferent also to the plight of his family, who were suffering not only because he failed to contribute to their support, but because they still had to provide him with food and a bed. His father had no choice but to pawn the family belongings, and there were so many family quarrels over money that his mother was often hysterical.

Tanizaki neglected his studies to the point of rarely appearing at the university. He took to frequenting the licensed quarters, and before long contracted a venereal disease. He had established himself in the eyes of family and friends as an egregiously unfilial son. But he discovered the one remedy for his disgrace: while recuperating from nervous exhaustion at a friend's house in the country in 1909 he began to write for publication. This was the height of the popularity of Naturalism, but Tanizaki from the outset of his career displayed disdain for this school of writing and preferred to describe unusual people and events. He established his reputation (though its worth was not immediately recognized) with the short story **"Shisei"** (**"The Tattooer"**), published in the November 1910 issue of *Shinshichō* (*New Thought Tides*), a Tokyo University literary magazine. Years later (in 1956) Tanizaki, recalling the circumstances of the composition of **"The Tattooer,"** stated that he had originally placed the story in a contemporary setting, but had shifted the period back to the Tokugawa era because the story did not work as a modern piece. This remark suggests how Tanizaki would use the past in his writings. He had no desire to make the figures of the past come alive by attributing to them contemporary attitudes in the manner of authors of popular historical fiction, nor did he (like Mori Ōgai) attempt to preserve absolute fidelity to the facts, nor (unlike Akutagawa Ryūnosuke) was he dependent on the past for his materials. Tanizaki chose to set works in the past because this gave him greater scope for his imagination. Actions that might seem exaggerated or even absurd if attributed to contemporary people were believable of people who lived in the past, when life was more brightly colored and unfettered by social conventions of the present.

Junichirō Tanizaki was a worshiper of women. He worshiped his mother; he worshiped Kannon, the Buddhist goddess of mercy, and his third wife, Matsuko, and probably many other women too. The men in his fiction are, if anything, even more extreme than their creator in their worship of the female sex.

Ian Buruma, in "Fatal Attractions," in **The New York Times Book Review,** *February 13, 1994.*

After Tanizaki completed the first draft of **"The Tattooer,"** his first thought was to show it to Izumi Kyōka. At this time, when Naturalism of the most prosaic variety was the prevalent literary mode, only Kyōka continued to include in his works supernatural or irrational elements associated with the writings of the past. Tanizaki's world was closer to reality than Kyōka's, but the early works resemble Kyōka's in their rejection of the cold glare of common sense. **"The Tattooer"** is entirely a work of fiction, and whether or not the background is historically accurate is of no importance; what remains in the reader's mind is the intense coloration and the unhealthy, decadent atmosphere. Seikichi, the tattooer, is first attracted to a girl when he catches a glimpse of her naked foot. We are told: "To his sharp eyes a human foot was as expressive as a face. . . . This, indeed, was a foot to be nourished by men's blood, a foot to trample on their bodies." Tanizaki's foot-fetishism is often coupled with the ideal of the beautiful but cruel woman. In this instance the tattooer is at the enslaved by the girl after he has transformed her by tattooing a monstrous spider on her back; as his first glimpse of her foot presaged, she has become a heartless creature destined to trample on many men. Tanizaki's taste for the perverse, the sinister, the ingeniously wrought, which he shared with Kyōka, runs through his career. In his last novel, *Fūten Rōjin Nikki* (*Diary of a Mad Old Man,* 1962), he described his perfect woman: "Above all, it's essential for her to have white, slender legs and delicate feet. Assuming that these and all the other points of beauty are equal, I would be more susceptible to the woman with bad character."

Another early story, **"Shōnen"** (**"Children,"** 1911), tells of a group of small boys and one girl who play at various games involving sado-masochism. "Cops and Robbers" is given a distinctive twist by the extreme savagery with which the "robber" is punished. The narrator, observing the expression of pain when the "robber" is trampled on—so fiercely that his face is twisted out of shape—experiences a pleasurable sensation more intense than any he has previously known. The next game is that of "Wolf and Traveler." This time the narrator is the victim, and when another boy stamps on his face, he once again experiences strange pleasure. During the next game, "The Human Being and the Three Dogs," the narrator, as one of the dogs, licks the soles of the human being's feet and sucks at the toes. This scene prefigures one in *Diary of a Mad Old Man,* written a half-century later, in which the old man, kneeling in the shower, takes his daughter-in-law's foot and crams her toes into his mouth. The most memorable of the games the children play is the last. Up until this point the girl, Mitsuko, has always had to play the part of a victim, but this time she makes the boys her slaves. They gladly trim her toenails, clean the insides of her nose, and even drink her urine. Mitsuko, though only a child, is another example of the cruel woman who fascinated Tanizaki throughout his life. . . .

"Kirin" (**"The Kylin,"** 1910) . . . ostensibly drew its materials directly from Chinese sources, but it strikingly resembles Tanizaki's other sado-masochistic stories. Confucius and a small band of disciples arrive in the dukedom of Wei, where Duke Ling lives in the utmost splendor with his consort, Nan-tzu. When the arrival of the sage is reported, the duke summons him, hoping that Confucius will teach him to reign in a manner consonant with his magnificent palace and his incomparably beautiful consort. Confucius is tempted with promises of every kind of earthly delight if he consents to stay and teach there. Confucius, who desires nothing more than suitable employment with a ruler, says that he is willing to spend the rest of his days in Wei, providing that the duke genuinely desires to foster the happiness of his people. The duke assures him that this is the case, and before long he has become so absorbed with the pursuit of virtue that he neglects Nan-tzu. When she reproaches him, he declares:

> It is not that I do not love you. I have always loved you like a slave serving his master, or like a human being worshiping a god, but from now on I shall love you as a husband loves his wife. It has been my function to purchase happiness for you, whatever the cost to my country or to my own wealth or to my people or even my life. But the sage has taught me that there is more important work for me to do. The beauty of your body has always been my greatest strength, but the sage's mind has given me an even greater strength.

The slavish worship of beautiful women is so frequent a theme in Tanizaki's writings that the duke's assertion that an even more powerful force exists in the world is bound to startle anyone familiar with Tanizaki's work. Nan-tzu derides the duke's attempts to free himself from her charms, and declares that she will make Confucius her captive. At this point the reader is likely to foresee that Nan-tzu will achieve precisely what she predicts, regardless of what history has to say about the iron-clad virtues of Confucius, but her attempts to seduce him are rebuffed. Instead of feeling disappointment, however, she is more and more intrigued by this strange man who can resist all temptation. Finally, she offers as the pièce de résistance the spectacle of what has happened to people who have been punished for having spoken ill of her or for having attracted the duke's attention. Women who have aroused Nan-tzu's jealousy have had their noses cut off, both feet amputated, and they are bound with iron chains. The loving attention Tanizaki bestows on his descriptions of the maimed and tortured is characteristic of this period of his career, as is the comment: "Nan-tzu's face as she gazed rapturously at the sight was as beautiful as a poet's, as dignified as a philosopher's." She menaces Confucius with a similar fate, her eyes as gentle as ever, her words as cruel, but he remains obdurate. In the end, the duke, though by now he detests Nan-tzu, returns to her bedchamber, unable to leave her. Confucius and his disciples are obliged once more to set out on their weary travels.

"**The Kylin**" is written in a severe, at times pedantic language, which indicates that Tanizaki, if he had so chosen, could have written in the manner of Kōda Rohan or Mori Ōgai, giving new life to the Chinese classics. But his choice of materials was quite dissimilar, and the fin-de-siécle atmosphere is closer to Flaubert's *La tentation de St. Antoine* or Wilde's *Salomè* than to Chinese sources. The beautiful, cruel woman wears the trappings of traditional Chinese ladies, whether in the perfumes that scent her mouth and hair or the exotic foods and other treasures with which she tempts Confucius, but she belongs to the same race as the other cruel women in Tanizaki stories.

The duke is able, thanks to Confucius, to overcome his tendency to grovel, but philosophy is no match for lust: Confucius, as he leaves Wei, declares, "I have never yet met a man who loved virtue as much as he loved sex," an authentic quotation from the Master.

"**The Kylin**" attracted even more attention than "**The Tattooer.**" By March 1911, when *Shinshichō* ceased publication, four or five stories by Tanizaki had appeared and had received favorable notice from such eminent figures as Ueda Bin and Mori Ōgai. [According to Nomura Shōgo in *Denki Tanizaki Jun'ichirō*] Kikuchi Kan recalled that university students had read "**Children**" with consuming interest. Tanizaki, encouraged by this success, left the university in July 1911. He had decided to become a writer, and consoled himself with the reflection that Ozaki Kōyō had also left Tokyo University without obtaining a degree.

In October 1911 Tanizaki published in *Mita Bungaku*, the literary magazine of Keiō University, the novella *Hyōfū* (*Whirlwind*), which he wrote at the request of the editor, Nagai Kafū. The story is of a young artist who, exhausted by his indulgence with a Yoshiwara prostitute, decides to free himself of his passion by traveling to the north of Japan on a sketching tour. He is obsessed with sex, even to the point of desiring a leper he meets in the train, but he manages to fight off the call of his blood until he returns to the Yoshiwara. In the intense excitement of release from his self-imposed austerity, he dies in his mistress's arms. This issue of *Mita Bungaku* was banned by the police because of Tanizaki's story, and *Whirlwind* was not reprinted until 1950. Tanizaki subsequently exercised great care when writing about erotic subjects, lest he run afoul of the censors again, but *Whirlwind* was by no means his only story to be banned.

Not long after this setback Tanizaki's career was given an immense boost: Takita Choin, the editor of *Chūō Kōron*, a man celebrated as a discoverer of literary talent, paid a visit to Tanizaki, then living with his family in a squalid tenement. Takita had been so impressed by "**Children,**" *Whirlwind*, and another story that he requested a contribution for the November issue of his magazine. Tanizaki wrote in response the story "**Himitsu**" ("**A Secret**"). It is not one of his most expertly crafted works, but it is entirely original, a believable (or intermittently so) account of a man who decks himself in woman's finery and pretends to be a woman. The story not only abounds in crazily imaginative details, but is full of humorous situations. In one scene the narrator is so successful in his disguise as a woman as to attract the notice of everyone at the theater, but to his chagrin he finds that he is no match for a real woman who is even more fashionably dressed. On closer examination he realizes that the woman was formerly his mistress, and this discovery naturally complicates his reactions even further. This is a minor work, but the author is unmistakably Tanizaki.

Recognition from Takita assured Tanizaki of favorable auspices under which to begin a career, and he took full advantage of them. He was able to write what he pleased for the best magazines and newspapers, and his fee for each page of manuscript was regularly higher than that received by any other writer. Even if he was often ignored or slighted by "serious" critics, his position in the literary world was unassailable.

In November 1911, about the time that **"A Secret"** appeared, Nagai Kafū published an article on Tanizaki in *Mita Bungaku*. It was highly laudatory, beginning with such statements as: "Tanizaki Jun'ichirō has succeeded in exploiting a domain of art that nobody else in the Meiji literary world has hitherto been able to, or even desired to exploit. To put it in other terms: Tanizaki Jun'ichirō possesses to the full certain rare qualities and abilities that none of our many other writers today possesses." Kafū listed in particular three characteristics of Tanizaki's writings: a mysterious depth produced by carnal dread, an intense pleasure savored by way of reaction to physical cruelty; entirely city-oriented concerns; and the perfection of style.

Kafū's praise expressed in part his distaste for Naturalist literature, but as a description of Tanizaki's early writings it was remarkably perceptive. He said in later years that he had been moved to write this essay by the plea of the publisher of Tanizaki's first collection of short stories, who feared that the book might otherwise be banned by the police. In any case, Kafū's praise raised Tanizaki to the rank of an important writer. Tanizaki was naturally deeply grateful, and Kafū remained his sensei until Kafū's death. Tanizaki had been the despair of his family, but thanks to Kafū he had suddenly revealed himself as a filial son who justified by his success the money spent on his education. Tanizaki and Kafū never became close friends, probably because both were difficult and demanding men, but each respected the other's art.

In December 1911 Tanizaki's first collection of short stories, *The Tattooer,* appeared. It contained in addition to the title story six other works including **"The Kylin,"** [the one-act play] *Shinzei,* **"Children,"** and **"A Secret."** It was considered for the prize awarded by the Ministry of Education for the finest work of literature of the year, an indication of the respect he had come to command. Soon afterward Tanizaki was asked to write his first newspaper serial and other commissions followed. Many of his writings of this period are, however, inferior. Perhaps the most notable is **"Akuma"** (**"The Devil,"** 1912), which boasts a specially revolting episode: a young man, captivated by a certain woman, manages to steal her handkerchief. She has a bad cold, and the handkerchief is dirty, but after savoring its odor to his heart's content the man "began to lick it like a dog." The narrator comments: "This was the taste of snot. I felt as if I were licking some suffocatingly carnal odor, but only a faint, salty taste lingered on my tongue. Presently, however, I began to discover something curiously sharp in taste, almost intolerably captivating. This secret, strange paradise lurked on the reverse side of the world of human pleasure."

This kind of writing, and no doubt also the title of the story, earned for Tanizaki the sobriquet of "Diabolist" (*akuma shugisha*). He came to detest this expression, but

he did little to prove that it was mistaken. His flamboyant sexual activities and his chronic lack of funds caused him to go in hiding from his creditors more than once. His writing suffered, but he recalled in a letter to his brother Wilde's remark that he had put all his genius into his life and only his talent into his works. Tanizaki added, "Almost the same thing could be said about my life from last year to this summer. I do not wish to describe it in further detail, but at any rate I do not very much regret anything about my life to the present. As far as I am concerned, the *life of art* is more important than the *art of life*." In 1916 he wrote in the same vein:

> For me art came first and life second. At first I strove to make my life accord, insofar as possible, with my art, or else to subordinate it to my art. At the time I was writing **"The Tattooer," "Until One Is Deserted,"** and *Jōtarō*, this seemed to be possible. And I managed to carry on my pathological life of the senses in the greatest secrecy. When eventually I began to feel that there was a gap between my life and art that could not be overlooked, I planned how I might, at the very least, make as advantageous use of my life as possible for my art. I intended to devote the major part of my life to efforts to make my art complete. I chose to interpret my marriage also as being, ultimately, a means of making my art better and deeper. In this manner I continued to place art before life. But today the two— leaving their respective importance aside—have for the time become separate. In my mind I think of art, but in my heart I yearn for the beauty of the devil. And, when I look back over my life, I am intimidated by the tocsin of humanity. I who am cowardly and deceitful have always had a tendency to wander off onto side roads, unable to persist in the struggle between these two contradictory purposes.

When Tanizaki wrote these lines he feared that in becoming a father the "second self" who was his child might deprive him of some of his vital force. He confessed that even after the first month he still felt no affection for the baby and supposed that he never would. He had made up his mind that if he had a second child he would give it away in adoption. Such remarks could hardly have endeared him to most Japanese readers, who no doubt interpreted them as further proof of his "Diabolism." His insistence on the precedence of his art over his way of life suggested not the consecration of the artist who gives up his daily pleasures in order to perfect his art but the author who immerses himself in debauchery with the ostensible aim of being able to write more convincingly about human passions. Tanizaki's name was often coupled with that of Oscar Wilde as an advocate of art for art's sake who denied that literature had any other function except to be beautiful. Tanizaki certainly read Wilde and occasionally quoted him, but the connections between the two men were neither deep nor pervasive. . . .

[Tanizaki] disliked the persona of the suffering intellectual who believed himself to be the conscience of the Japanese nation, and he preferred to write about his distorted pleasures. His private life at the time when he was writing *Jōtarō* [published in 1914] was turbulent. He behaved abominably toward his wife, perhaps because she was insufficiently vicious; and even though he had written that he had married in order to deepen his art, he soon afterward openly stated that marriage had been a mistake. His writings, though much praised and even the subject of a special issue of *Chūō Kōron* in April 1916, were mainly a means to earn the money needed for his extravagances. Many years later, when a Complete Works (*zenshū*) was prepared in 1957 under his supervision, Tanizaki insisted on leaving out most of his writings of this period, expressing his strong dislike for them. Several were also disliked by the censors and banned; the play *Kyōfu Jidai* (*The Age of Fear,* 1916), a work of sadistic cruelty, outdid *Hamlet* in that *every* character was dead at the conclusion!

It is not surprising that Tanizaki's works of the "bad" period should have been a source of embarrassment to him in later years, and they represent an awkward hurdle for the commentator to vault between the brilliant early stories and the period that began in 1925 with *Chijin no Ai* (*A Fool's Love*). But the badness of the bad period can be exaggerated: even the works Tanizaki refused to include in the 1957 Complete Works are by no means devoid of interest. For example, **"Konjiki no Shi"** (**"The Golden Death,"** 1914), the story of a young man's narcissistic fascination with his own beauty and intelligence, presents Tanizaki's conception of beauty in a particularly striking manner, for all its faults of construction and characterization. His insistence on the body—"a people which despises the flesh will never produce great art"— echoes views expressed in *Jōtarō*, and there are even virtually identical passages in both works on the relative effectiveness of different arts to communicate beauty. In **"The Golden Death,"** however, such views are not merely thrown off in passing but developed into the central theme of the story. Okamura, the hero, has expended his vast fortune to create a visual paradise composed of elements borrowed from the architecture, sculpture, and gardens of the entire world. He guides the narrator to his masterpieces—sculptures that consist of living people, proof of his thesis that no beauty can surpass that of the human body. At the end Okamura takes part in an extravaganza that features hordes of beautiful men and women who are costumed as bodhisattvas and lohans. Okamura himself appears as the Buddha, his body entirely covered with gold leaf. After a night of drinking and dance he dies because the gold leaf has choked his pores.

In 1970, the year of his own death, Mishima Yukio devoted almost the whole of an essay on the art of Tanizaki to **"The Golden Death."** Mishima felt sure that one could perceive even in a failure like **"The Golden Death"** the marks of genius; "or, rather, one can often discover in such works both the characteristic qualities of the author and important themes that he never developed in his later works." Despite obvious influences from Poe and Baudelaire, the extraordinary individuality of this story for its time cannot be doubted. The discussions of art between Okamura and the narrator if more fully developed might have become a rare Japanese prototype of the *roman idéologique*. Mishima believed that Okamura's death enabled him to achieve a unity between his life and art, but

that Tanizaki rejected suicide: "That is to say, anyone who attempts to make of himself a work of art will be tempted repeatedly by the desire to commit suicide; to go on living thus means relinquishing the attainment of beauty, or, to put it in other words, relinquishing the important premise of the discussions of art in **'The Golden Death.'"** Mishima attributed the failure of the story to its period, a time when Japanese culture had lost any semblance of a unifying order. Okamura's garden of delights was filled with copies of Michelangelo and Rodin sculptures, *tableaux vivants* of Giorgione and Cranach paintings, the art of Rome, China, Esoteric Buddhism, and so on—a conglomeration of East and West that faithfully reflected the confusion in the aspirations of intellectuals of the time and that suggested to Mishima nothing so much as the Tiger Balm Garden in Hong Kong. Mishima's essay demonstrates how much can be found in even the works of Tanizaki's "bad" period, though Mishima's interest, it might be argued, was not unconnected to his own decision to commit the kind of death that would achieve a unity between his life and art. . . .

Tanizaki's trip to China, [in the autumn of 1918], ostensibly inspired by his fondness for the Chinese classics, gave rise to a few travel accounts, but did not deeply affect his writings. His main object seems to have been sensual pleasures. A second trip to China, in 1926, was more serious; Tanizaki met various Chinese intellectuals with whom he would keep in touch until the close of his life, including Kuo Mo-jo and T'ien Han.

One eternal motif in Tanizaki's varying works was the study of the self under the pressure of some great destructive power inherent in human nature.

M. Ueda, in a review of Seven Japanese Tales, *by Junichiro Tanizaki, in* Pacific Affairs, *Winter 1964-65*.

Tanizaki's interest in foreign countries was oriented elsewhere than China. The curious, anecdotal story **"Dokutan"** (**"The German Spy"**), published in 1915, describes Tanizaki's first European friend, a shiftless Austrian from whom he learned French conversation. As a boy Tanizaki had not been much interested in the West, and had never felt impelled to come any closer to Western people than reading about them in fiction. He was ready to admit that some novels and plays written in the West possessed deeper content than similar works by Japanese, but he was sure that he himself wanted to become a distinctively Japanese artist. He recalled in **"The German Spy,"** "I was particularly unmoved by Western painting and music. Even while our gentlemen of letters were making a great fuss over Gauguin and trumpeting the cause of exoticism, I was of the opinion that any Japanese who was interested in pursuing exotic art would do better to direct his attention to China or India." He went on:

Two or three years later, however, I reached a point where I could not but shake off such stupid ideas. I discovered that, as a modern Japanese, there were fierce artistic desires burning within me that could not be satisfied when I was surrounded by Japanese. Unfortunately for me, I could no longer find anything in present-day Japan, the land of my birth, which answered my craving for beauty. There was neither the overripe civilization of the West nor the intense barbarity of the South Seas. I came to feel violent contempt for my surroundings, and at the same time I began to think that I would have to observe more deeply, more intimately, the West, whose art was so infinitely greater than our own. I would have to seek from the West objects to satisfy my craving for beauty, and I was suddenly overcome with passionate admiration for the West. Western paintings and music had hitherto left me indifferent, but now they made me tremble with excitement at every contact. For example, the paintings of the Impressionist school, which I knew only from color or collotype reproductions, overwhelmed me by their powerful, intense character, so unlike the manner of expression of Japanese paintings, which are distinguished only by manual dexterity and totally lack content or stimulation. I could hear Western music only on the rare occasions when it was performed by Japanese, or in excerpts on phonograph records, but how directly and how grandly it sang of the sorrows and joys of human life as compared to the etiolated, somnolescent sounds of the samisen, or the curiously perverse, retrogressive, superficial *hauta, jōruri,* and the like. Japanese vocalists sing in voices trained to produce unnatural falsetto tones, but Western singers sing boldly and with impetuousness, like birds or wild beasts, sending forth their natural voices so ardently they risk bursting their throats or caving in their chests. Japanese instrumental music produces a delicate sound like the murmur of a little stream, but Western instrumental music is filled with the grandeur of surging waves and has the intense beauty of the boundless oceans.

Once I had become aware of these truths, I felt an uncontrollable desire to learn everything there was to be known about the countries of Europe that have given birth to these many astonishing works of art, and about the various aspects of the daily lives of the superior race of men living there. Everything labeled as coming from the West seemed beautiful and aroused my envy. I could not help looking at the West in the same way that human beings look up to the gods. I felt sad that I had been born in a country where there seemed to be no possibility that any first-rate art could ever be nurtured. I grieved in particular over my misfortune that, having been condemned to the fate of being born in Japan, I had chosen to make my life as an artist, rather than as a politician or a military man. And I made up my mind that the only way to develop my art fully was to come into ever closer contact with the West, if only by an inch closer than before, or even by totally assimilating myself into the West.

In order to satisfy this craving I would go abroad if possible—no, going abroad would not be enough; the best and only way was to move there permanently, resolved to become one with the people of that country and to have my bones buried in its soil.

There could hardly be a more wholehearted affirmation of the West than Tanizaki professed in **"The German Spy."** Of course, it can be argued that this is a work of fiction, and that the sentiments do not necessarily reflect Tanizaki's beliefs, but the tone carries conviction, and similar sentiments are found in other works of the time. . . .

The writings toward the end of Tanizaki's "bad" period were among the worst of his entire career. Perhaps it was dissatisfaction with his own novels and short stories that induced him to turn to the theater. None of his plays was really successful, though *Okuni to Gohei* (*Okuni and Gohei,* 1922) was effective. Indeed, only a few works of the period were of significance for his oeuvre. One was **"Haha wo kouru ki"** (**"Longing for Mother,"** 1919), written a year and a half after the death of his mother. It describes in the form of a dream the search of a small boy for his lost mother. The theme was one particularly close to Tanizaki's heart and would be treated again and again until the final statement in **"Yume No Ukihashi"** (**"The Bridge of Dreams,"** 1959). Tanizaki, though famed for his portraits of women, was even more successful in describing children, whether in recollections of his own childhood or fictitious characters. **"Longing for Mother,"** a curious mixture of fantasy and nostalgia, is not wholly convincing, but it is certainly more moving than the plays. Another story of special significance to the student of Tanizaki's career, though not of great literary distinction, is **"Fumiko no Ashi"** (**"Fumiko's Feet,"** 1919), an early and extreme example of Tanizaki's foot fetishism. An old man, infatuated with the beautiful feet of his young mistress, asks a painter to draw her portrait in a pose that best displays her feet. When the old man is bedridden and too feeble to play with the girl's feet in his accustomed manner, he asks the willing painter to roll like a dog at Fumiko's feet and allow himself to be trampled by her. The old man dies blissfully happy because during his last moments Fumiko's foot has been pressed against his forehead. . . .

Tanizaki's worshipful love of Nezu Matsuko inspired most of his best writings, beginning with **"A Blind Man's Tale."** The central situation in many of these works is that of a man who serves a beautiful but cruel woman. He does not dislike her cruelty; indeed, this is an important part of her attraction. Tanizaki's two wives had been gentle. That no doubt was why he lost interest in them and why he was so determined that Matsuko would remain cruel, in his imagination if not in fact. Even after they were married in 1935 (the divorce from [his second wife] Tomiko took place in 1933, when he and Matsuko were already living together), he addressed letters to Matsuko in the deferential language of a servant petitioning a haughty mistress.

"A Blind Man's Tale," the second of a series of historical stories, is related throughout in the first person, rather in the manner of *Manji,* but the distinctive quality of the narration is supplied not by dialect but by the archaic language and, above all, by the deferential tone, appropriate in a blind masseur who is relating long-ago events to the nobleman he is massaging. The visual appearance of **"A Blind Man's Tale"** also was intended to suggest the accounts written in the late sixteenth century with long, unbroken paragraphs consisting of strings of kana only occasionally interrupted by Chinese characters. The original edition was in an old-fashioned format, and the box, endpapers, and title page were of handmade paper from Kuzu. This was the first of many books by Tanizaki that appeared in formats intended in some way to match the contents.

"A Blind Man's Tale" is the story of how a masseur, a gifted samisen player, served the peerlessly beautiful sister of the warlord Oda Nobunaga. Naturally in a work of this period there are descriptions of battles and deeds of treachery, but the quality that marks it as a work by Tanizaki is the masseur's slavish devotion to his mistress, whose body he knows from his hands, though he can never aspire to be more than a humble servant. This is not quite the same as the masochism of Tanizaki's earlier stories, but stemmed from the craving he mentioned in [a September 1932] letter to Matsuko to worship a noble woman. The sixteenth-century battles are of interest to Japanese familiar with the names of the people involved, but even readers born outside these traditions can hardly fail to be moved by the portrait Tanizaki drew of Yaichi, the blind man. Surely there is little indebtedness to Western literature in this work, though Tanizaki may have owed something to Ozaki Kōyō's *Darkness in the Heart*. . . .

Perhaps what distinguished Tanizaki's works most conspicuously from those of other major Japanese writers of the twentieth century was his absorption with writing itself. . . . His success in creating a body of writings that perpetuated Japanese traditions, after so long having immersed himself in completely untraditional activities, did not represent a change in direction so much as a deepening of his art in the way he found most feasible and congenial. No one would turn to Tanizaki for wisdom as to how a man should live his life, nor for a penetrating analysis of the evils of modern society, but anyone seeking the special pleasure of literature and an echo in even his most bizarre works of eternal human concerns could hardly find a superior writer.

Deborah DeZure (essay date 1989)

SOURCE: "Tanazaki's 'The Bridge of Dreams' from the Perspective of *Amae* Psychology," in *Literature and Psychology*, Vol. XXXV, Nos. 1 & 2, 1989, pp. 46-64.

[*In the following excerpt, DeZure perceives evidence of* amae, *a psychological syndrome particular to the Japanese, in the characters of the story "Yume no ukihashi" ("The Bridge of Dreams").*]

"The Bridge of Dreams" by Jun'ichiro Tanizaki is the confessional memoir of a young man, Tadasu, and his relationships with his mother and stepmother. The tale traces the development of his obsessional dependency needs in relation to them and culminates in his social and economic deterioration and his demoralization. For western readers, it calls to mind Marcel's involvement with his mother in Proust's *Remembrance of Things Past* and generally suggests a Freudian Oedipal Complex. But the tale is not occidental, and to characterize it quite so neatly in western terms is to misread and oversimplify the psychological dynamics Tanizaki portrays. The tale does exemplify personality syndromes particular to Japan, referred to collectively as the psychology of *amae*; and its unique application clarifies ambiguities of characterization, form, and imagery.

Takeo Doi, a Japanese psychiatrist, characterizes various dimensions of personality indigenous to the Japanese as the psychology of *amae*. *Amae* has no specific equivalent in English but does encompass a cluster of related western psychoanalytic constructs, among them: indulgent love, reciprocal dependence, denial of separation, passive love, passivity, loss of self, and, in its more neurotic forms, mother fixation and obsession.

Doi writes:

> The prototype of *amae* is the infant's desire to be close to its mother, who, it has come vaguely to realize, is a separate existence from itself. Then one may perhaps describe *amae* as, ultimately, an attempt psychologically to deny the fact of separation from the mother . . . *Amae* psychology works to foster a sense of oneness between mother and child. In this sense, the *amae* mentality could be defined as the attempt to deny the fact of separation that is such an inseparable part of human existence and to obliterate the pain of separation . . . Wherever the *amae* psychology is predominant, the conflicts and anxiety associated with separation are conversely lurking in the background. . . . Since *amae* would seem to arise first as an emotion felt by the baby at the breast towards its mother . . . it corresponds to that tender emotion labeled by Freud "the child's primary object choice." [*The Anatomy of Dependence*, trans. John Bester]

This infant desire to depend upon the mother figure is reinforced by Japanese cultural patterns of maternal indulgence, late weaning, prolonged co-sleeping among children and their parents, and a societal value which prizes dependence over autonomy. The "desire to depend and presume upon another's benevolence" [David Y. H., "Asian Concepts in Behavioral Science," *Psychologia*, 25, No. 4, 1982], one of the connotations of *amae*, is carried over into diverse elements of Japanese adult life from its first manifestations in the infant's relationship with his mother. This culture-bound pattern of behavior and feeling is widely recognized in Japan and pervades dimensions of language, psychology, politics, law, and the arts. It is, therefore, relevant to explore Japanese literature with the insights of *amae*.

AMAE PSYCHOLOGY APPLIED TO CHARACTER ANALYSIS: TADASU, PROTAGONIST AND NARRATOR

Tadasu's mother obsession appears to be an extension into adulthood of a yearning to *amae* with his mother.

Amae psychology shapes not only Tadasu's behavior and character development but is also the basis of the formal structure of his "confessional," the emotional development of the other major characters with whom Tadasu relates, and the imagery he employs in narrating his memoir.

The tale is structured by a prototypic infant desire for a mother. Three scenes portray Tadasu suckling at his mother's breast. Each time the suckling reinforces this infantile need in Tadasu. The three episodes have great significance for the development of character and events and are the most dramatic moments in the memoir.

The prototypic *amae* experience occurs in Tadasu's childhood with his real mother:

> Sometimes I fretted and lay awake for a long time, pleading, "Let me sleep with Mama!"

> Then Mother would come to look in on me. "My, what a little baby I have tonight," she would say, taking me up in her arms and carrying me to her bedroom . . . She lay down next to me just as she was, not taking off her sash, and held me so that my head nestled under her chin. The light was on, but I buried my face inside the neck of her kimono and had a blurred impression of her being swarthed in darkness. The faint scent of her hair, which was done up in a chignon, waffled into my nostrils, seeking out her nipples with my mouth, I played with them like an infant, took them between my lips, ran my tongue over them. She always let me do that as long as I wanted without a word of reproach. I believe I used to suckle at the breasts until I was a fairly large child, perhaps because in those days people were not at all strict about weaning their children. When I used my tongue as hard as I could, licking her nipples and pressing around them, the milk flowed out nicely. The mingled scents of her hair and milk hovered there in her bosom around my face. As dark as it was, I could still dimly see her white breasts . . . often my dreams were penetrated by the distant clack of the water mortar, far beyond my sheltered windows.

After this first description of memories of breast feeding before age five, we are aware of Tadasu's strong attachment to his mother. Their relationship, however, is still within the normal cultural bounds of late weaning in Japan and exemplifies indulgence of male children by their mothers. Tadasu ends his description of this memory by announcing that his mother died when he was five. The decisive aspect of this memory, therefore, is his association of his close relationship with his mother and her subsequent death, which in turn led to the frustration of his need to *amae*. This separation from the mother he loved is the trauma which fixates Tadasu's infantile attachment and need to *amae* with a mother or mother figure and determines much of his personality.

The second breast feeding episode occurs when Tadasu is an adolescent. His stepmother invites him to share her bed and suckle from her milkless breasts:

> . . ."What a funny little boy you are! Now, hurry up and see if you can find the milk!"

> I drew the top of her kimono open, pressed my face between her breasts, and played with her nipples with both hands. Because she was still looking down at me, a beam of light shone in over the edge of the bedclothes. I held one nipple and then the other in my mouth, sucking and using my tongue avidly to start the flow of milk . . . But as hard as I tried, it wouldn't come. . . . I wouldn't let go of her breasts, and kept sucking at them. I knew it was hopeless, but still enjoyed the sensation of rolling around in my mouth those firm little buds at the tips of her soft, full breasts.

> . . . Once again by some strange association, I seemed to drift among the mingled scents of hair oil and milk that had hovered in my mother's bosom so long ago. That warm, dimly white dream world—the world I thought had disappeared forever—had actually returned.

> . . . When I reached the age of twelve or thirteen, I began sleeping alone at night. But even then I would sometimes long to be held in my mother's bosom. "Mama, let me sleep with you!" I would beg. Drawing open her kimono, I would suck at her milkless breasts, and listen to her lullabies. And after drifting peacefully asleep I would awaken the next morning to find that in the meantime—I had no idea when—someone had carried me back and put me to bed alone in my small room. Whenever I said: "Let me sleep with you!" Mother was glad to do as I wished, and Father made no objection.

Just as the first episode was followed by the associated pronouncement that his mother died when he was five, this episode, too, is followed by a significant association: "Within half a year, though I hadn't forgotten my real mother, I could no longer distinguish sharply between her and my present one . . . Gradually the two images merged." Thus, with the second episode, Tadasu is no longer able to distinguish between reality and illusion. This confusion reveals his ambiguous vision of the world and the people in his life.

Indulgence of male children is by no means unusual in Japan. Doi quotes Daisetsu Susuki as writing, "The mother enfolds everything in an unconditioned love. There is no question of right or wrong. Everything is accepted without difficulties or questioning." However, it is clear from the second episode that the breast feeding initially took place at the initiative of the mother and not on request of the son. Moreover, asking Tadasu to suck when there was no milk was a bizarre form of enticement. From this episode, it appears that the mother herself is maladjusted. Whatever her motives are, or those of the passive and indulgent father, they no longer reflect characteristic Japanese practices.

The third episode takes place on the veranda when Tadasu is eighteen. His stepmother, having given birth to a son, offers Tadasu milk from her swollen breasts:

> "I wonder if you remember how to nurse," she went on. "You can try, if you like." Mother held one of her

breasts in her hand and offered me the nipple. "Just try it and see!" I sat down before her so close that our knees were touching, bent my head toward her, and took one of her nipples between my lips. At first it was hard for me to get any milk, but as I kept suckling, my tongue began to recover its old skill. I was several inches taller than she was, but I leaned down and buried my face in her bosom, greedily sucking up the milk that came gushing out. "Mama," I began murmuring instinctively in a spoiled, childish voice.

I suppose Mother and I were in each other's embrace for about half an hour. At last she said: "That's enough for today, isn't it?" and drew her breast away from my mouth. I thrust her aside without a word, jumped down from the veranda, and ran off into the garden.

. . . Mother's state of mind was a mystery to me, but my own actions had been equally abnormal. The moment I saw her breasts there before me, so unexpectedly revealed, I was back in the dream world that I had longed for, back in the power of the old memories that had haunted me for so many years. Then, because she lured me into it by having me drink her milk, I ended by doing the crazy thing I did. In an agony of shame, wondering how I could have harbored such insane feelings, I paced back and forth around the pond alone. But at the same time that I regretted my behavior and tortured myself about it, I felt that I wanted to do it—not once, but over and over again— if I were lured by her that way—I would not have the power to resist.

This episode of breast feeding, with the statement of intense shame and impotence to resist, completes Tadasu's development in relation to his mother. The shame Tadasu bears remains with him; the powerlessness to deny his mother and his own desires for her determine his actions in the future.

Thus, the prototype of *amae,* the closeness of mother and child manifest in the act of breast feeding, structures the character development of the narrator and, therefore, structures the tale itself as a memoir of his life. . . .

[That *amae* does not end suggests] the ongoing nature of Tadasu's quest for a mother and the continuation of his feelings of yearning, shame, and confusion as established in the breast feeding episodes. As the tale ends, we are told of his latest attempt to recapture his mother by bringing his brother, Takeshi, to his home becuase Takeshi resembles the stepmother. And, as the memoir ends, it is dated, "the anniversary of Mother's death," suggesting the continuity of his obsession in which telling the story of his life is used as a way to re-live once more his closeness with his mothers. This is confirmed by Tadasu's statement of purpose in writing: "I write for the sake of writing, simply because I enjoy looking back at the events of the past and trying to remember them one by one."

In Jungian terms, Tadasu has a mother complex. It reveals itself most clearly in the emphasis placed upon his mother figures as the central characters in the memoir. We learn almost nothing of Tadasu's life at school. We are told of no friends; and we hear that after his father's death, Tadasu receives no guests but Sawado and her family. In short, Tadasu is friendless and alienated from society; if he functions in the outside world, he clearly gives it no attention in his memoir.

Tadasu's mother complex is apparent in other ways. Physically, Tadasu prefers to identify with his mother, not his father. He writes, "She used to say I looked exactly like him, not like my mother, that made me unhappy too." In evaluating Sawado, all of his reactions are relative to his feelings for his mother: for example, "Mother's strength and firmness made her [Sawado] seem retiring, by contrast." Tadasu marries to provide his mother with a servant. He takes Takeshi, his brother, to live with him to be near one who resembles his stepmother and to fulfill his wish, "simply to go on living as long as possible with Takeshi, my one link with Mother."

Tadasu's mother complex is an obsession. Doi identifies a number of pathological conditions associated with an obsession, all of which relate to *amae* psychology. One of these, *hitomishiri,* is the way a baby comes to distinguish its mother from other people, objecting when other people hold him, calming down only in his mother's arms. If a child's *hitomishiri* is too strong, the child will make no move to leave its mother and tends to shy away from strangers.

Tadasu exemplifies *hitomishiri.* As a child, he cried incessantly for his mother and would not be quieted until she came to him. After her death, when Okane, his nurse, tried to comfort him, he "cried about in bed. 'I don't want you to sing for me. I want Mama!' Kicking off the covers, I howled and wept." At times his father would try to comfort him, but Tadasu rejected him because of his father's intolerable "masculine smell."

Doi writes about *hitomishiri:*

> Where the individual is by birth extremely sensitive or where the mother's personality or other environmental factors have hindered a good relationship with the mother during the early stages, the individual it seems never transcends the experience of *hitomishiri* which continues into adulthood.

The frustration of *amae* which Tadasu experiences is a function of his mother's death and of a father whose own sense of loss made it impossible to comfort his son or to serve as an adequate love object substitute. Therefore, coupled with Tadasu's fixation at a stage of *hitomishiri,* Tadasu lives with feelings of the frustration of *amae* (*shinkeishitsu*) and the feelings of shame associated with them.

The frustration of *amae* has many other effects, including the tendency to form an inadequate sense of self (*jibun ga nai*). Doi points out that if the need to share *amae* with a mother has been unsatisfied or if the primary love object is denied to the child, satisfactory feelings of self are impossible to attain. This is because the loss of the world to which one belongs is normally experienced as a loss of the self. Tadasu suffers from this sense of inadequacy. Tadasu defines himself through his identification with others, most notably his mothers. He acknowledges his passivity and lack of initiative. He accepts all demands and acquiesces in all decisions made about his life (with, of course, the outstanding exception of his indulged desire to sleep with and presume upon his mothers). In the end, he chooses to live his life for his mother's sake and ultimately for her memory. In short, he totally denies his own *jibun* as an active, asserting being.

Associated with an inadequate sense of self is the tendency to project. Tadasu frequently projects attitudes and motives to his mothers and his father, which enables him to deny responsibility for his actions. He attributes to others the feelings he is afraid to acknowledge because of his weak sense of self. After he suckles with his mother at age eighteen, Tadasu rationalizes and projects responsibility for the act onto his parents. For example, "possibly knowing he [father] hadn't long to live, he was trying to create a deeper intimacy between mother and me so that she would think of me as taking his place and she made no objection." Tadasu is merely the passive one who obeys the will of others and is dependent upon them. Doi concludes that a man who has a *jibun* is capable of checking *amae,* while a man who is at the mercy of *amae* has no *jibun.* Tadasu is clearly the latter.

At more aggressive moments, Tadasu's projection transforms itself into a sense of being victimized (*higai*). In anger at his mother and father for the shame of nursing at his mother's breast at eighteen, his first thoughts are, "I hardly think Mother would have tried to tantalize me so shamelessly without his permission." Ultimately, Tadasu expresses feelings of regret, *kuyama,* defined by Doi as "to regret something that has happened over which one has no control, or about which it is too late to do anything." After Tadasu suckles in the third episode and acknowledges that he has no self control, he has feelings of deep regret. Once again, this kind of regret Tadasu's impotence and *jibun ga nai.*

The frustration of *amae* leads to feelings of loneliness and insatiable yearning. The word *loneliness* appears a number of times in the memoir, both in relation to Tadasu and to his father. The term is used to end the tale when Tadasu offers a final explanation for all that has gone before:

> Because my real mother died when I was a child, and
> my father and stepmother when I was some years older,
> I want to live for Takeshi until he is grown. I want to
> share with him the loneliness I knew.

Another more tentative interpretation of the effect of frustrated *amae* on Tadasu is related to homosexuality. Doi suggests that closeness to the mother and frustration of *amae* in some cases lead to homosexuality. As the tale ends, Tadasu tells us that he will never marry again and turns his attention to a young boy, his brother. Tadasu is reluctant to acknowledge Sawado's beauty and tells us

that only others think of her as beautiful. Further, his identification with his mother rather than his father suggests the classic Freudian cause of homosexuality. While there is no overt reference to either bisexuality or homosexuality, the closing passage is suggestive of a final denial of women in his life.

THE ARCHETYPE OF *Amae* PATHOLOGY

The frustration of *amae* in the lives of the Japanese has led to the development of an archetypical pattern. This pattern, seen in Japanese literary figures like Yoshitsune, includes many pathological factors already cited by Doi. In early life, the frustration of *amae* and a sense of denial fixate the character in a stage of infantile dependence. Life is thereafter permeated with an emotional yearning. The archetypical character is often sensitive and yet can exhibit cruelty or contradictory behavior. The character will often presume upon others. Most importantly, he is compulsively driven to be self-destructive. Eventually, the character resigns himself to his loss and from continued frustration becomes increasingly passive and apathetic.

The archetypical pattern fits Tadasu's life in many ways. Tadasu was denied *amae* in his early childhood by the death of his mother and the inability of his father to *amae* with him. Tadasu's yearning for *amae* continues throughout his life. His behavior toward his mothers is one of extreme indulgence and presumption. His sensitive nature, as demonstrated in his acute sensory description and awareness, is contrasted with his selfishness and cruelty as revealed in his plan to marry Sawado and use her for his mother's purposes. Clearly, Tadasu's relationship with his stepmother is self-destructive though he pursues it as if without choice.

Tadasu becomes increasingly passive and dependent on others, particularly mother figures. Tadasu acknowledges his passivity when he writes, "not that I was determined to steal Takeshi away from them and bring him home again. I am not the sort of person to do a thing like that on my own initiative."

Tadasu is the subordinate in his home although he is a married man, already about twenty years old, and the only male figure. Tadasu writes, ". . . . since I was still going to school and was still a dependent . . . Mother was in charge of all the household accounts." At an earlier point, when his father tells him to marry for his mother's sake and give away his child should he ever have one, Tadasu makes no objections. He passively agrees. Tadasu tells us that he was always careful to ensure that he never conceived a child, thereby fulfilling his father's wishes even after both his stepmother and father are dead. At the end of the tale, presumably because of the scandal of incest, Sawado's family forces him into a divorce settlement in which he loses his estate. Once again, it appears that he accepted these events with resignation. Finally, he ends up working as a bank clerk in the bank once owned by his father, a clear demotion and fall from power and status. In all these ways, Tadasu's passivity exemplifies the results of a frustrated need to *amae* and reflects the Japanese archetypical pattern of *amae* pathology.

THE FATHER

Tadasu's personality and behavior are in many ways clearer than those of his father and stepmother about whom he tells us. Veiled by Tadasu's tendency to project and distort, his selective inattention, and his ambivalence towards his parents, the father and stepmother are enigmatic figures. In addition, the ambiguity in characterization is due to Tadasu's inability to distinguish between reality and illusion. The motives for the parents' actions are presented to us as questions in the mind of Tadasu, questions which he cannot answer because he is incapable of decisiveness and is torn by conflicts of trust-mistrust and shame.

The father was an insular man who "liked a quiet life." His main respites were his wife and the solitude of his home and garden to which he seldom invited guests. The father presents a contrast to the grandfather who was active and financially more successful, living in the hub of Kyoto business and social life. We are told that the grandfather's teahouse, built for entertaining, was no longer in use. From these few background facts, we may infer that perhaps Tadasu's father also suffered from some pathology of *amae* which made him adverse to strangers and capable of only limited communication.

The father's life appears to center around his first wife. Except for an "appearance at his bank now and then . . . [he] spent most of his time at home with her." Tadasu makes a point of telling us that his father's love and attention for his mother were so strong and undivided that they excluded him:

> All my father's love was concentrated on my mother. With this house, this garden and this wife, he seemed perfectly happy.

This suggests that Tadasu felt frustrated *amae* with his father even before the loss of his real mother. If Tadasu had already felt rejected by his father, we can more readily understand his inordinately close relationship with his first mother and interpret, in part, his excessive need for her as a response to his father's distance.

However, numerous references to the father reveal his concern and interest in his son. Tadasu's memories include many episodes of eating at home, dining out, and feeding fish with his mother and father. Although no feelings of warmth towards the father are to be found in these descriptions, they do suggest some domesticity and a family relationship.

The most significant clue to the father's personality is his direct admission to Tadasu that "Her death was a terrible blow to me—I couldn't get over it." The father states that he is remarrying only because the woman resembles his first wife. He has a persistent, pathological need to think of his second wife as his first wife. Here, then, is the basis for the crucial influence of the father on the son. Because of the father's need to believe that his present wife is his first one, he projects that need onto Tadasu. The father manipulates others to ensure that Tadasu thinks of the stepmother as his first mother. This served to ensure the security of the father's own fantasy, his bridge of dreams which denied the reality of death. Tadasu's acceptance of this illusion further assured the perpetuation of the fantasy. Thus, Tadasu writes, "No doubt father had instructed my present mother how to behave and was trying his best to confuse me about what my mothers had said or done so that I would identify them in my mind." A further example is that the father changes his second wife's name to Chinu, the name of his first wife.

In a second way, the father projects his needs—this time onto his wife. He assumes that his wife has a need to see him reincarnated in Tadasu. Therefore, the father says to Tadasu on his deathbed:

> "Everyone says you resemble me. I think so myself. As you get older you'll look even more like me. If she has you, she'll feel as if I am still alive. I want you to think of taking my place with her as your chief aim in life, as the only kind of happiness you need."

There is no evidence to confirm that, in fact, the mother wants Tadasu as a reincarnation of her husband, but rather preferred to maintain him as a young lover quite distinct from her husband. It is really only the father's need which is reflected here. Consistent with the father's life struggle to shun death by creating illusions, the father structures this last bridge of dreams to perpetuate his own life on earth.

The father's inability to accept his wife's death may well have had its roots in a personality maladjustment established before her loss. His social isolation would suggest this. Nonetheless, his wife's death is the factor which dramatically alters his ability to function and eventually leads him along a self-destructive path.

As the father progresses in his self-destructive behavior, his motives become increasingly unclear. Tadasu states that his father had no objections to Tadasu lying with his stepmother during his adolescence. This raises questions about the father's motives, but it still does not seem necessarily insidious or perverse. However, we learn of other more questionable acts: the father probably knew that Tadasu was suckling from the stepmother at age eighteen; the father gave away his second son; and, on his deathbed, the father asks Tadasu to take his place with his second wife. We must, therefore, view the father's motives as pathological, harmful to himself as well as others. This calls to mind the title of another Tanizaki novel, *Some Prefer Nettles,* because the father appears to be masochistic.

The issue is further complicated by the geisha past of the mother, also presented in a veil of mystery. In the father's apparently self-destructive behavior, he may have been responding in some way to her immoral past. Tadasu suggests that perhaps the father's fatal illness has driven him to resignation. The doctor's prohibition against sexual relations may also have affected the father. Whether or not the father willfully desired to destroy his son, the father did so at the expense of his wife and his own personal shame.

The father also exemplifies the archetypical pattern of *amae* pathology which, in turn, explains some of his enigmatic behavior. In the end, the father succumbs to total passivity in the face of a wife who succeeds in demoralizing him and his son. This is born out by Tadasu's references to his father as one who "made no objections," which demonstrates an essentially passive attitude to other's actions. The father also states that he is resigned to death. Most significantly, the father is locked into a compulsive self-destructive need to recapture the illusion of his first wife, even if it means living vicariously through the delusion and arousal of his own son.

THE STEPMOTHER

The stepmother's personality is even more complex and ambiguous than the father's. Not only are we unclear as to her motives, we also cannot be sure at times that Tadasu is speaking about her, rather than the first wife. For example, we do not know for sure which mother wrote the poem at the beginning of the tale. The spectrum of possible interpretations for the stepmother begins at one extreme in which she is a perverted, lascivious, former geisha who indulges herself with father and son. At the other extreme she can be understood as the passive subordinate of a sick, self-destructive husband who orders her to carry on perverse activities in order to satisfy his obsession with his first wife; she patiently tends her husband during his illness and treats Tadasu with the indulgent love of a Japanese mother.

The ambiguity which surrounds this character is typified by Tadasu's inability to decide why she and his father sent the baby away. Tadasu makes numerous conjectures about her motives, ranging once again from characterizing her as a demonic whore to a self-sacrificing mother, which is, in fact, the range of Tadasu's confused images of his mother figures. At one point, Tadasu writes that possibly the stepmother sent the baby away for Tadasu's sake (as confirmed by the father's words on his deathbed). At another point, Tadasu thinks that sending the baby away gave the stepmother more of an opportunity to entice him. It is implied that perhaps her activities and status as a former geisha or her role as a second wife had something to do with her decision. Sokichi Tsuda indicates, however, that ordinarily Japanese stepmothers are particularly covetous of their own real children because only they are bound in obligation to their parents. Therefore, the stepmother would not be likely to give the baby away. Her husband's imminent death or his prohibition from intercourse may have affected her decision. And, last, if the most extreme of the rumors is true, that Takeshi is Tadasu's own son, then sending the baby away could be seen as an act of shame or denial.

Any combination of these interpretations is possible. The evidence, however, points heavily in the direction of her incestuous activities, although not to the extreme position that Tadasu is the father of the baby. We are told early in the tale that the stepmother, "preferred the thick, fleshy Konoe line . . . which probably reveals her personality"; which is to say, it reflects her sensuous nature. She was a geisha; and whether or not she had been officially married before, she was divorced after three years for an unknown reason. Tadasu writes that he was reluctant to ask Okane about his stepmother's past because he was afraid of what he might discover. We do not, however, know what aroused Tadasu's suspicions. One might conjecture about the feelings of rejection the stepmother felt as a result of that first marriage. There are suggestions of her excessive physical self-indulgence, if not bisexuality. She spends most of her time getting massaged by Tadasu and Sawado. Sawado is said to massage the stepmother alone at night in the stepmother's bed. The stepmother's selfishness is clear when Tadasu discusses his marriage and she replies, "You're not getting married for their benefit—it's enough if you and I and Sawado are happy." The order of pronouns is significant here; it characterizes the stepmother's interference between Tadasu and Sawado as a married couple.

For Tadasu, as for Tanizaki in other works, feet are used repeatedly as the symbol of female sensuality. Tadasu writes about his real mother:

> Mother would sit at the edge of the pond and dangle her feet in the water, where they looked more beautiful than ever. She was a small, delicately built woman with plump, white little dumpling like feet which she held quite motionless as she soaked them in the water letting the coolness seep through her body . . . Even as a child I thought how pleasant it would be if the fish in our pond came playfully around her beautiful feet, instead of coming only when we fed them.

Foot imagery itself contains the dual association central to Tadasu's confusion; that is, the feet are both sensual and maternal.

In remembering his stepmother, Tadasu writes,

> As I looked at her feet through the water, I found myself remembering my real mother's feet. I felt as if they were the same; or rather to put it more accurately, whenever I caught a glimpse of my mother's feet, I recalled that those of my own mother, the memory of which had long ago faded, had had the same lovely shape.

The sensuous nature of the stepmother's feet is confirmed by the daughter-in-law who perceives them as a source of envy and jealousy. This reaction to the stepmother's feet provides one of the few clues to Sawado's feelings towards her mother-in-law. When the mother invites Sawado to dangle her feet, too, Sawado responds, "Your feet are so pretty! . . . I couldn't possibly show ugly ones like mine beside them!"

Preoccupation with feet and feet fetishes, evident in Tadasu's attachment to the memory of his mother's feet, have been associated with mother complexes. Donald Keene states [in *Landscapes and Portraits,* 1971]:

Psychoanalysis has cleared up one of the remaining gaps in our understanding of fetishism . . . Both the feet and hair are objects with a strong smell which have been exalted into fetishes after the olfactory sensation has become unpleasurable and been abandoned. Various of Freud's followers have pointed out that fetishism is associated with a clinging to the mother and a strong desire to identify with her, and with castration anxiety . . . Tanizaki's fetishisms . . . seem to be associated with longing for the mother which is a powerful intermittent theme in his works.

For Tadasu, feet represent sexuality and his mothers, and each memory of breast feeding refers to the hair of his mothers.

THE QUESTION OF INCEST

Whether Tadasu did, in fact, commit incest with his stepmother is a significant ambiguity central to understanding what happens to Tadasu after his father's death. We first hear rumors of incest from Okane, although she need not be believed. Okane does, however, represent the community at large and its responses to the behavior of this secluded Kyoto family. There are other more significant factors which suggest that incest did occur. First, the tale is a confessional written for a reason which Tadasu will not share with us. As if attempting to expiate his guilt by writing down his deeds and their causes, he tries to purge himself. Just at the time in the narrative when Tadasu would have begun having sexual relations with his stepmother, he intrudes into the text to tell us that lies of omission may follow because

There are limits even to telling the truth. There is a line one ought not to cross. And so, although I certainly never write anything untrue, neither do I write the whole of the truth.

Other than incest, there is no action logically emanating from the text itself which Tadasu could be withholding from the reader. In addition, Tadasu tells us that he, "went to suckle at Mother's breast more than once," at the age of eighteen and after. He also writes that "unable to forget the days when mother had given her breasts to me, I now found my sole pleasure in massaging her." After his father's death, he tells us that his stepmother thrives so well that, "Mother was almost too plump as if now that father was dead her worries were over." And, finally, we are not told (because, as Tadasu states, "it is too painful to relate") the reason for his divorce and the settlement in favor of Sawado and her family.

Tadasu's guilt could have stemmed solely from his confused incestuous desires and his shame about breast feeding with his mother as an adult. However, incest itself is the natural conclusion of the events described and is consistent with the degree of pathology associated with the stepmother, the son, and the father.

SHAME AND GUILT

Shame is a significant aspect of **"The Bridge of Dreams"** which affects the form of the work, specifically, the point of view. The tale itself is written as an "I" memoir. It is a confessional of Tadasu's abnormal life, a life for which he bears great shame. He writes,

I am not writing out of a desire to have others read this. But even . . . if no one ever reads it, I shall have no regret.

Tadasu himself calls the work a "novel"—referring perhaps to an I-novel (*shishosetsu*). The tale concerns a man who is self-indulgent, preoccupied both by an obsession and by his resultant shame associated with the obsession. He is excessively introverted and sensitive with a tendency to distort reality. The formal manifestation of this sense of shame lies in the use of a subjective "I" or first person narrator.

Helen Merrill Lynd notes that the experience of shame cannot be expiated. It carries the weight of "I cannot have done this. But I have done it and I cannot undo it, because this is I." It is pervasive . . . ; its focus is not a separate act, but a revelation of the whole self. The thing that has been exposed is what I am. For this reason, the shame of Tadasu is not expiated by his confessional, but continues to his last words which indicates that his shame is ongoing.

Shame is central to Tadasu's behavior and attitudes about himself. Tadasu frequently uses the term *shame* in reference to his own sense of shame as well as to his parents' shamelessness. The most dramatic statement of his shame follows the third episode of breast feeding. He writes,

In an agony of shame, wondering how I could have harbored such insane feelings, I paced back and forth around the pond alone. But at the same time that I regretted my behavior and tortured myself for it, I felt that I wanted to do it—not once, but over and over. I knew that if I were placed in those circumstances again—if I were lured by her again that way—I would not have the will power to resist.

Tadasu's shame was dramatically revealed to him by acting out his long-felt incestuous desires. It led to his recognition of his total lack of self-control. He saw himself as unalterably "abnormal" without the desire or ability to change.

Tadasu's feelings of shame are related, in part, to his disappointed trust in his parents and their limited trust in him. Tadasu writes of his stepmother, "Did our sudden encounter give her the impulse to embarrass and upset me?" and "I hardly think Mother would have tried to tantalize me so shamelessly without his permission". Her shamelessness placed the burden of shame on Tadasu. As explained above in reference to *jibun ga nai*, a loss of self experienced as a result of parent's death creates a sense of shame in the one who has been abandoned. The father's inability to *amae* with Tadasu further confirmed the boy's feelings of inadequacy and shame. Later in life, Tadasu questions why his parents did not confide in him about the decision to send Takeshi away. For Tadasu, it is a sign of their mistrust. Tadasu often remarks that his parents think of him as a child, although he is already grown. This, too, confirms his feelings of shame.

Shame, then, as the emotional state resultant from frustrated *amae*, pervades the narrative world of this tale. Characterization reveals a confused, ambiguous portrayal of people and relationships. Point of view is limited to a subjective first person narrator using a confessional tone. The theme suggests the illusive nature of reality where people are caught in a confused world of dreams, sexuality, and death.

John Updike (essay date 1991)

SOURCE: A review of *A Cat, a Man, and Two Women*, in *The New Yorker*, Vol. LXVII, No. 10, April 29, 1991, pp. 101-02.

[*A perceptive observer of the human condition and an extraordinary stylist, Updike is considered one of America's most distinguished men of letters. Best known for such novels as* Rabbit Run *(1960),* Rabbit Redux *(1971),* Rabbit Is Rich *(1981), and* Rabbit at Rest *(1990), he is a chronicler of life in Protestant, middle-class America. In the following review, Updike comments on the bizarre events depicted in* A Cat, a Man, and Two Women *(Neko to Shōzō to futari no onna).*]

In the long title story [of *A Cat, a Man, and Two Women*], we are not surprised that the hero, the plump and ineffectual Shozo, loves his pet cat, Lily, more than he loves either his wife, Fukuko, or his exwife, Shinako, but we *are* surprised to have the love detailed with such unabashed physicality. Shozo feeds Lily by making her tug at a little marinated mackerel held in his mouth; his watching wife reflects, "It might be all very well to like cats, but it was going too far to transfer a fish from master's mouth to cat's." At the other extreme of intimacy, the odor of cat excrement mixes with his fondness, and he remembers with a curious relish the moment when, during a tussle, the "breath from her bowels" blew straight into his face. He brags to his wife, "Lily and I are so close we've smelled each other's farts!" When the cat gets into bed with him, "he would . . . stroke that area of the neck which cats most love to have fondled; and Lily would immediately respond with a satisfied purring. She might begin to bite at his finger, or gently claw him, or drool a bit—all were signs that she was excited."

In one of the two shorter stories bound in with this piece of feline erotica, **"Professor Rado,"** we are not too startled when the taciturn professor, in a moment reminiscent of Proust or of Tanizaki's *The Key,* is seen through a window being caned by a lightly clad maidservant, but this just foreshadows the real voyeuristic treat, in which the professor is spied kneeling at the feet of a beautiful tall leper he has long admired from afar. Ecstatically he fits her deformed foot with an artificial toe, and she, her voice distorted by her diseased nose, tells him it doesn't

hurt a bit. Masochism, O.K., and necrophilia, we've heard of that, but leprophilia?—it isn't even in the dictionary!

[In the introduction to his translation of *A Cat, a Man, and Two Women,* Paul McCarthy] offers in his introduction a helpful cultural observation: "Japanese society is characterized by quite clear-cut divisions between the public persona and the private life; between *tatemae* (what is outwardly expressed) and *honne* (what is actually thought and felt)." Voyeurism, the glimpse through a chink in *tatemae* into the depths of *honne,* recurs in Tanizaki, and a sense of mutual spying through the enshrouding forms of decorum permeates his stately masterpiece, *The Makioka Sisters.* His characters suggest potbellied stoves whose cast-iron exteriors conceal the fire that makes them hot. His stories have the propulsive fascination of hidden menace, and his characters keep deepening, pushing the story into new corners. Shinako, Shozo's rejected first wife, captures Lily in a spiteful maneuver but comes to love her much as her ex-husband did, and rapturously shares her bed with her. Lily, it should be said, is no simple indigenous cat, but "of a European breed," and "European cats are generally free from the stiff, square-shouldered look of Japanese cats; they have clean, chic-looking lines, like a beautiful woman with gently sloping shoulders." Thus Tanizaki, in 1935 on the verge of his six-year patriotic labor of translating *The Tale of Genji* into modern Japanese, gently burlesqued the infatuation with things Western that he had sympathetically dramatized in his novel of 1924, *Naomi.*

The cat story ends puzzlingly: Shozo, discovering that his former wife has reconstituted his loving relationship with Lily, flees, "as if pursued by something dreadful," just when a Western reader expects a happy reconciliation on the basis of a shared passion. Nor does the ending of the second shorter story, **"The Little Kingdom,"** take us where we thought we were going. The reader, foreseeing a power struggle between a fifth-grade teacher, Kaijima, and a mysteriously magnetic student, Numakura, who organizes all the other students into a little kingdom of unquestioning allegiance, petty theft, and commerce in an invented currency, instead sees the poor instructor almost resistlessly succumb to the student's spell, as illness and poverty drag him and his family down. The students' little kingdom proves to be the only realm wherein he can acquire milk for his baby, and the bitter irony of this comes upon us without warning. In Tanizaki, the bizarre reaches out to possess reality; perverse sexual obsession is just his most usual instrument for demonstrating how precariously society's façades and structures contain the underlying *honne.*

Nobuko Miyama Ochner (review date 1993)

SOURCE: A review of *The Secret History of the Lord of Musashi* and *Arrowroot,* in *Southern Humanities Review,* Vol. 27, No. 1, Winter, 1993, pp. 86-91.

[*In the following review, Miyama Ochner explores the mother fixation portrayed in* Arrowroot *(Yoshino kuzu) and the perversion of the title character in* The Secret History of the Lord of Musashi *(Bushūkō Hiwa).*]

Tanizaki is often regarded as having remarkably consistent themes despite the wide range of his subject matter, settings, and style. As a writer who is profoundly interested in the workings of the subconscious, he treated such recurrent themes as the femme fatale, foot fetishism, sadomasochism, longing for mother, coprophilia, and predilection for crepuscular beauty. Except foot fetishism, these themes appear in the two short novels [*The Secret History of the Lord of Musashi* and *Arrowroot*]. . . .

Another of Tanizaki's recurrent themes . . . is the child's longing for its mother. Tanizaki's own mother was a well-known beauty. In 1919, after his mother's death, he published **"Longing for Mother,"** a poetic fantasy in which the narrator dreams of searching for his lost mother and encountering her as an unrecognizably young and attractive woman. This theme of longing for mother underlies the novel *Arrowroot,* in which the narrator's friend named Tsumura searches for the relatives of his long-deceased mother in an effort to learn about her background. The longing-for-mother theme is given an important twist in this novel, because Tsumura finds and falls in love with a cousin who resembles his mother, and eventually marries her. In other words, the image of the mother and that of the wife overlap—an important thematic link in the eleventh-century classic *The Tale of Genji,* in which the hero continually seeks the love of women resembling his dead mother. The influence of this classic tale by Murasaki Shikibu on Tanizaki is quite clear, for Tanizaki spent seven years (1935-1942) on translating the fifty-four chapters of *The Tale of Genji* into modern Japanese, not once but three times. (A direct result of Tanizaki's immersion in *The Tale of Genji* is his long novel *The Makioka Sisters,* 1943-1948, a nostalgic portrayal of the affluent Osaka merchant family in decline; this novel is often called the modern *Tale of Genji.*)

The Secret History of the Lord of Musashi is set in the sixteenth century, during the period of the so-called "Warring States," a time of constant warfare among samurai lords. In his first historical fiction, Tanizaki uses the device of a modern-day narrator gathering his material from diverse historical sources to tell the story of the unusual sexual life of the warlord. In the case of *The Secret History,* these sources are all fictitious, but the manner of their use gives the air of authenticity to the novel. This narrative technique is used also in other works (such as **"A Portrait of Shunkin"**).

The story focuses on the sexual deviation of the hero, from its awakening in his boyhood to its grotesque development in his adulthood. As a young boy, he is sent to his father's overlord as hostage and experiences a siege by enemy forces. It was standard practice during the medieval period in Japan to take enemy heads as proof of one's conquest. The boy witnesses a group of women cleaning, dressing, and tagging severed heads of the enemy for inspection. He is mesmerized particularly by the faint, unconsciously cruel smile of a beautiful young woman as she looks upon the heads, and he wishes to become a severed head himself, to be handled and smiled at. The morbid, masochistic pleasure he experiences becomes the most intense when he sees a head without the nose. Evidently, warriors sliced off the noses of the enemies instead of their heads when they had too much to carry, to identify and claim their trophies later. The boy becomes obsessed with the noseless head, and when he sneaks into the enemy camp and kills the sleeping general, he takes the general's nose. The siege ends abruptly, and the cause of the general's shameful death is kept a secret. The boy reaches adulthood, is now called Terukatsu, and continues to serve the overlord. Some years later, Norishige, the son of the overlord, marries Lady Kikyō, the daughter of the dead enemy general. A series of shooting accidents occurs to Norishige, in which he eventually loses a part of his upper lip and an ear. It becomes clear to Terukatsu that someone is trying to shoot off Norishige's nose, and he senses the revenge of Lady Kikyō for her father's ignominious death. Terukatsu offers his services to the lady and becomes her accomplice. One night Norishige is attacked and his nose is sliced off. Terukatsu becomes the lady's lover and derives sexual stimulation from the sight of the comically pathetic noseless Norishige. Lady Kikyō's hidden malice and cruelty toward her husband are projections of Tanizaki's image of the Japanese woman of the feudal period—a woman who has a virtuous appearance yet harbors thoughts of an illicit love, hatred, cruelty, and so forth.

When Terukatsu becomes the lord of the province of Musashi and marries, he tries to recreate the sadistic pleasure by having a servant pose as a noseless head; however, his wife's refusal to participate in this game puts an end to his plan after the first attempt. His marriage thus turns out to be disappointing, so Terukatsu attacks Norishige's domain and captures his former overlord and lady, to try to regain Lady Kikyō's attention. However, the novel ends somewhat abruptly with Lady Kikyō turning into a virtuous and loving wife to Norishige and thus frustrating Terukatsu's scheme. The story is told through a mixture of narration and exposition, with restraint and humor. Much of the humor is generated by the "clown" figure of the harelipped and noseless Norishige, whose increasingly severe speech impediment is ably, if not with scientific accuracy, captured in English translation as, for instance: "I affeal hoo you hymhahy as a samurai" (I appeal to your sympathy as a samurai).

Arrowroot (the original title: *Yoshino kuzu,* or, Yoshino arrowroot) is set in the modern times of the 1930s. It is at once a simpler and a more complex work than *The Secret History.* It is simpler in terms of "plot": the writer-narrator visits Yoshino, an area rich in history and legends, in search of material for fiction, in the company of a friend named Tsumura, who searches for his dead mother's relatives there and finds a cousin, whom he marries. Abounding in scenic descriptions, the work may thus be described as a travel sketch. The novel is complex in terms of interlocking imagery, associations, and multiple layers of time.

The frame of the novel is the narrator's recollection of his trip to the mountains of Yoshino twenty years earlier, in the early 1910s. In addition to this return to the narrator's personal past, various literary associations and historical legends surrounding Yoshino also point to several time periods in the past. These include the narrator's memories of earlier trips to Yoshino as well as a Kabuki play associated with the location (dating back to the eighteenth century); the narrator's viewing of the drum Hatsune, said to be made with a fox skin—the drum which purportedly belonged to Lady Shizuka, a paramour of the tragic hero Yoshitsune (twelfth century) and who is depicted in both the Kabuki play and Nō plays (fourteenth century). In Tsumura's memory, his mother is associated with the music "The Cry of the Fox," which is in turn associated with the folktale-based story of the fox, Kuzunoha (Arrowroot Leaf), assuming the human form, marrying a man and giving birth to a child, yet having to return to the animal realm. The longing-for-mother theme is evident in this fox/mother story as well.

In addition to such intricate linking of literary allusions, the work is imbued with the special aura of the mountains of Yoshino, which served as the natural fortress and hiding place for the Southern Court during the fourteenth and fifteenth centuries, when the imperial line split into two factions and maintained an uneasy rivalry, finally ending in the victory of the Northern Court. These multiple layers of time resonate with one another and give depth to the narrative.

One of the characteristics of Tanizaki's writings is richness of sensory details. An excellent example is seen in *Arrowroot,* when the narrator and his friend are offered ripe persimmons: "A large, conical persimmon with a pointed bottom, it had ripened to a deep, translucent red, and though swollen like a rubber bag, it was as beautiful as jade when held up to the light. . . . Tsumura and I each devoured two of the sweet, syrupy persimmons, reveling in the penetrating coolness from our gums to our intestines."

Anthony Hood Chambers (essay date 1994)

SOURCE: "*Arrowroot*" and "*Captain Shigemoto's Mother,*" in *The Secret Window: Ideal Worlds in Tanizaki's Fiction,* Council on East Asian Studies, Harvard, 1994, pp. 7-15, 93-105.

[*In the following excerpt, Chambers maintains that the protagonists in* Arrowroot *and* The Mother of Captain Shigemoto Mother *create imaginary, idealized worlds that are revealed to the reader by means of narrative devices.*]

In one of the most moving plays of the Bunraku and kabuki repertory, a white fox assumes the form of a beautiful woman (a power that foxes were believed to have), marries a gentleman named Abe no Yasuna, and gives birth to a son. They are happy together until the fox's true identity comes to light, making it impossible for her to go on living with her husband and son. She slips away late at night to return to her lair; but before she goes, she lovingly tucks in her son and writes a farewell poem on the shōji near his bed:

> Koishikuba tazunete miyo
> > Izumi naru Shinoda no mori no urami
> > > kuzunoha

> If you miss me come and search
> > Shinoda Forest in Izumi among the wistful
> > > arrowroot leaves.

The play, known as *Kuzu no ha* (*Arrowroot Leaves*), is one of the most famous expressions in Japanese culture of a child's longing for his mother.

Kuzu no ha was also the working title of a story Tanizaki struggled over for some years in the late 1920s and finally published in 1931 as *Yoshino kuzu* (*Arrowroot*). It was slow to take shape. Tanizaki had written fifty pages before he started over with a new setting (autumn instead of spring) and a new focus, a young woman making paper in the village of Kuzu. By December 1929, the story line had evolved into something resembling that of the final version, but progress was still slow. He wrote to his editor:

I have been having so much trouble writing that I have started over once again, this time in epistolary form. That is why I am behind schedule. . . .

This is the outline of the story. The main character's late mother in these letters was once a prostitute in Shimmachi. Even now, his mother's relatives are farmers in the mountains of Yoshino. He marries their daughter. To find the family, he takes a number of old redemption certificates and love letters from the storehouse and studies them.

The writing was interrupted early in 1930 by "complications" at home, which led to the sensational announcement in August that Tanizaki's wife Chiyo would divorce him and marry his friend Satō Haruo. In any case, Tanizaki was dissatisfied with what he had written so far. He confessed to his editor, "I have reread my 'Kuzu no ha' and am not impressed. I would like to rewrite it as a children's story and publish it in a magazine that caters to women or children." Instead, he continued his research, visiting Shinoda Forest and combing second-hand shops for courtesans' letters and apprenticeship papers. During a stay on Mount Yoshino in the fall of 1930, he reviewed primary sources on the history of Yoshino, hiked to the sites he mentions in the novella, and wrote most of the final version. The result is one of his most subtle and complex works.

Arrowroot has two important characters: Tsumura, a pampered, romantic youth from Osaka, and his friend, a skeptical Tokyo writer, the narrator. The narrator's initial motivation for accompanying Tsumura to Yoshino is a desire to learn more about "the secret history of the Southern Court," about which he wants to write a book. Tsumura, for his part, is driven there by a longing to recapture his lost childhood. As the narrator grows in sensitivity and understanding, he loses interest in his historical research and grasps the centrality of Tsumura's dream, so that the two quests gradually merge into one.

Tsumura's story emerges little by little, and the novella is half read before one grasps his centrality. His relationship with the narrator resembles that between the *shite* (protagonist) and the *waki* (side-man) of a nō play: the *waki* usually appears on stage first and fixes the attention of the audience, but his main function is to set the scene for the *shite*, provide a foil for him, and encourage him to tell his story. As the focus of **Arrowroot** shifts and narrows, the central question turns out to be, "Then what is the purpose of this trip?," as the narrator asks Tsumura at the beginning of the last chapter, fulfilling his role as *waki* by eliciting the heart of the story from the *shite*. Tsumura, about to unveil his last secret, replies, "Well, there is something I haven't told you about yet."

In addition to the *waki-shite* relationship, **Arrowroot** adapts the *jo*, *ha*, and *kyū* (introduction, agitated development, quick close) structure and rhythm of the nō and other genres of Japanese performing arts. In a representative nō play, the *waki* makes his entrance in the *jo* and explains why he has come to the site of the drama. The *shite* enters during the first part of the *ha* and hints of his past in an emotional narration. In the second section of the *ha*, the *waki* and the *shite* discuss the history of the site; and in the third section of the *ha*, the *shite* relates past events at the location. The pace gradually quickens as the play moves from one section to another. These divisions correspond with Tanizaki's chapters. The *jo* consists of the narrator's commentary on the Heavenly King and his decision to accompany Tsumura to Yoshino in "The Heavenly King." The *ha* begins with the travel account that takes the two men from Nara to Natsumi in "Imoseyama." This lyrical chapter, studded with literary allusions, is a *michiyuki*—a poetic litany, common in Japanese theater, of the sights and impressions of a journey. The *michiyuki* helps suspend disbelief by lulling the reader into a world apart—from the immediate, everyday world of Tokyo, via the old capitals of Kyoto and Nara, to a timeless setting in the depths of the Yoshino mountains, a dream world where Tsumura can establish his own "reality" and unfold his mystery to increasingly receptive narrator and readers. The *ha* continues with the visit to the Ōtani house in "The Drum Hatsune" and Tsumura's disclosures in "The Cry of the Fox" and "Kuzu." In the *kyū*, "Shionoha," the narrator and Tsumura go to Kuzu together, the narrator hikes into the mountains, and finally the narrator is reunited with Tsumura and Owasa.

The narration flows from the secondary narrator (Tsumura), to the primary narrator, and finally to the reader. This degree of distancing is particularly effective in creating the narrative "shadows" that Tanizaki advocated, because the action is far enough removed to afford the reader's imagination room to grow. The shadows are deepened by the chronology: the narrator is recalling a trip already twenty years in the past, and Tsumura's reminiscences go back another twenty years. Chronological distancing also enhances the story's plausibility, as Itō Sei has pointed

out: "The narrative begins with the actuality of the narrator—in other words, with the present—and works gradually back into the past. In the process, the sense of present reality is extended to a sense of reality in the tale of the past. It is the technique of a picture scroll that begins with the present and moves back in time as it is unrolled" [*Tanizaki Jun'ichirō no bungaku*].

Tsumura's search for his mother's village is ordinary enough; but by placing it in rich geographical, historical, legendary, and literary contexts, Tsumura endows it with a splendor and universality that induce the narrator and the reader to participate in his world with him. Even a reader who is not already familiar with Yoshino lore will recognize the fundamental appeal of spring blossoms and autumn foliage; an ancient, exciting history; folkloric archetypes, such as "mysterious mountain recesses," "the sacred jewel hidden deep in a cave," and magical foxes; and, above all, a child's quest for his lost mother. Tsumura universalizes his story by cloaking it in these elements. The village of Kuzu becomes the prototype of all hometowns lost or forgotten in the rush of modernization; Tsumura's search for his mother embodies longings that everyone feels.

The associations that bring a setting alive are abundant in Yoshino. Recalling **Arrowroot** thirty-two years after its publication, Tanizaki contrasted Tokyo (the narrator's home) with Yoshino:

> Cherry-blossom viewing in Tokyo is simply a matter of sitting in a tea room behind bamboo screens, eating dumplings, roast taro, and hard-boiled eggs, and drinking bottled Masamune. In the shadow of these flowers are no Yoshitsune, Wakaba-no-Naishi, Shizuka, Tadanobu, or Genkurō the fox, no Hatsune drum or Hiodoshi armor. Blossom viewing without these associations did not seem to me like blossom viewing at all. . . . There is no fantasy in the Tokyo blossoms. But when I went to see the famous blossom sites in western Japan I felt as though I might somewhere meet the phantom of Wakaba-no-Naishi or Lady Shizuka, and at times I even felt as if I had turned into a fox or into Gonta and was wandering about, lured [as on the stage] by the sound of a drum or a whistle.

References to the history of the Southern Court and the legendary Heavenly King dominate the introductory section of **Arrowroot**. The narrator mentions the nō play *Kuzu* and the fourteenth-century chronicle *Taiheiki* and lists the books he has used in his research. The most important associations in the rest of the novella are with fox legends in the plays *Yoshitsune senbonzakura* (*Yoshitsune and the Thousand Cherry Trees*) and *Arrowroot Leaves*, and in the song "Konkai" ("The Cry of the Fox").

The relatively short *michiyuki*, which follows the introductory section, is particularly rich in allusions. The most important allusion is to the fox Genkurō (a character in *Yoshitsune and the Thousand Cherry Trees*), who is drawn to Minamoto Yoshitsune's mistress Shizuka and to her drum Hatsune, because his parents' skins have been used to make it. The subject of the fox and the drum is broached gradually. When Tsumura first mentions *The Thousand Cherry Trees* and Hatsune, the narrator pulls the narrative back to a factual, concrete level by quoting from the nō play *Futari Shizuka* (*The Two Shizukas*) and *Yamato meisho zue* (*Famous Places in Yamato, Illustrated*), and then only cautiously refers to Yoshitsune and Shizuka. The effect is to pace the emergence both of Tsumura as the central character and of the principal theme of the novella.

In the exposition section, extended allusions to *The Thousand Cherry Trees*, the fox Genkurō, *Arrowroot Leaves*, and "The Cry of the Fox" bring the fox theme to the center of attention. There is also an allusion to a celebrated ninth-century love poem:

> Satsuki matsu hanatachibana no ka o kageba
> mukashi no hito no sode no ka zo suru

> The orange blossoms that wait for early summer
> Bear the fragrance of the sleeves of the one of
> old.
>
> (*Kokinshū* no. 139, anonymous)

This is the only allusion in the novella that is unrelated to Yoshino, which suggests that Tanizaki chose it especially for its thematic relevance. The allusion comes when Tsumura is thinking about his mother, and so contributes to a theme that has been developing with the fox allusions—that Tsumura's filial longing for his mother is also a romantic longing.

The Genkurō-Shizuka story has special significance for Tsumura because he believes that there are romantic overtones in the relationship between the fox and Shizuka. This is not as far-fetched as it sounds. Though the fox (in the form of Yoshitsune's retainer Tadanobu) and Lady Shizuka are in a servant-master relationship, the *michiyuki* of *The Thousand Cherry Trees* is choreographed to look like a lovers' journey. Tanizaki elaborated on this idea many years later:

> Since it is the hand of a beautiful woman that holds the drum, there is no feeling of cruelty. Indeed, the child fox might well feel anger at the heartlessness of human beings; but if I, with my masochistic inclinations, were that child fox, I would on the contrary feel all the more affection for Shizuka and wish to serve her the more loyally.

According to Tsumura's interpretation, then, Genkurō the fox is romantically attracted to Shizuka because he associates Shizuka with the longing he feels for his mother; and the fox's situation becomes a metaphor for Tsumura's own. In his mind the concepts of "mother," "fox," "beautiful woman," and "lover" are intimately associated. In this context, Tsumura describes an aspect of his psychology that is frequently encountered in Tanizaki's male characters:

> I am convinced that, from the first time I heard the song ["The Cry of the Fox"], my imagination saw more

than just my mother. The figure I saw was my mother, I think, and at the same time, my wife. And so the image of my mother that I held in my little breast was not that of a matron, but that of an eternally young and beautiful woman.

One could hardly ask for a clearer statement of the fantasy that Tsumura shares with other Tanizaki men. The man is both child and husband; the woman, both mother and lover. As Tsumura says of *Arrowroot Leaves*, "the father and the son are of one mind in their love for the mother."

It is not quite enough, however, for Tsumura to put his longings in a universal context. Before the narrator can identify with them, he must set aside the modern rationality of a deracinated Tokyo writer and learn to appreciate legends and fantasies. He is more than just a *waki*, because his growing sensitivity is a central theme of ***Arrowroot***.

At first the narrator sees no need to go to Yoshino at all: "I had completed my research on everything that could be investigated from a distance, and if Tsumura had not prodded me, I surely would never have set out for those mountain recesses. I had so much material that my imagination would take care of the rest, even without a visit to the site. In fact there are certain advantages to proceeding that way." Tsumura, on the other hand, stresses that there is more to Yoshino than the history of the Southern Court.

Tanizaki's stories begin ostensibly as classical tales of noble figures, richly embroidered with literary accounts and poetry of the time. Unmistakably, though, Tanizaki's obsessive themes are woven in. They are erotic, at least in part, but for Tanizaki sex is the great metaphor for humanity's immortal longings and mortal abasement.

Richard Eder, in "Confession as the Ultimate Deception," in **The Los Angeles Times Book Review,** *February 27, 1994.*

The narrator's attitude begins to change as soon as he reaches the Yoshino River. Gazing upstream from the bridge at Mutsuda toward Imoseyama (and toward Tsumura's ancestral village), he remembers having seen this view before as a child, his mother holding him, "young and impressionable, on her lap" and whispering in his ear. Visiting Yoshino again in his youth, he "leaned once more on the bridge railing and thought of my dead mother as I gazed upstream." A less romantic type than Tsumura, he has not dwelled on memories of his mother, but they have reasserted themselves nonetheless "at unexpected times," when he has recalled the view from the bridge "with a pang of nostalgia." In hiking upstream with Tsumura, then, the narrator, too, is pursuing memories of his mother, perhaps without realizing it.

Presently the narrator reverts to the skeptic. When Tsumura mentions *Yoshitsune and the Thousand Cherry Trees*, the narrator thinks of Koremori and the famous Tsurube sushi-shop scene, which he dismisses as fiction, despite its importance to the residents of Shimoichi. Tsumura is more interested in the scenes that involve Shizuka's drum Hatsune than he is in the sushi scene, and he wants to visit a family in Natsumi that claims to possess the drum. Again the narrator is skeptical, even pedantic: there is no historical evidence that Shizuka was ever in Yoshino, he says, and the forebears of the Ōtani family were probably inspired by *The Two Shizukas* (which is set in Natsumi) to identify their drum as Shizuka's. As it turns out, the narrator is right—the drum appears not to be authentic. But Tsumura is undeterred. He is interested not in the literal facts, but in the idea—the tradition, the fantasy, the mystery—of Shizuka and the fox.

The Ōtani family also has a scroll that purports to be a history of Natsumi, but it, too, is dubious. Rather than helping to establish the true history of the region, the clumsy document ironically serves to remind the narrator of the importance of tradition and symbolism. The head of the Ōtani family believes that Shizuka left her drum there, and he believes in the scroll. The "truth" does not matter—the drum and the scroll symbolize the past glory of his family; they are the focal points of his respect for the past and they help him to find meaning in the present. Thus the narrator's faith in historical "fact" and his skepticism of tradition are weakened. History, as Tsumura has told him, is not everything; dreams about the past are important.

The journey up the river is a sensory delight. The narrator, accustomed to finding stimulation in books, finds it here in the "cold white" paper on the shōji, the "glossy, ripe coral surfaces" of persimmons glowing in the afternoon sun, the "sounds of a blacksmith's hammer and the *sah-sah* of a rice polisher," and especially in the ripe persimmons that he eats at the Ōtani house. Ultimately it is the persimmons that make the deepest impression on the narrator—"I filled my mouth with the Yoshino autumn," he recalls. In their rich vitality, they embody the non-cerebral world that he is learning to appreciate. Savoring Yoshino with all of his senses has reawakened this bookish writer, estranged in Tokyo from the Japanese heartland, to the roots of his culture. He is ready now to listen to Tsumura's story.

Tsumura has clung to his dreams even when the facts justify skepticism. He has no clear memories of his mother but cherishes a vague image of her playing "The Cry of the Fox" on the koto. It does not matter that it was probably his grandmother, not his mother, whom he remembers. When he is shown a koto that belonged to his mother, the instrument excites his imagination, even though it may not be the koto he remembers. It is the fantasy that the koto stimulates that is important, not the precise identity of the koto or of the woman whom he remembers

playing it. Similarly, Tsumura's fox-mother fantasies are stimulated by the discovery that his maternal grandfather actually worshipped a fox—a real fox—that lived near his house in Kuzu; but there is no fox when Tsumura arrives in Kuzu. Even Aunt Orito remembers little. She may even have forgotten her sister's name. The visit to Kuzu, in short, produces hardly any concrete information about Tsumura's mother: there is no fox, the koto is questionable, Orito's memory is unreliable. But none of this matters to Tsumura. On the contrary, the absence of facts is fuel for his fantasies.

Near the end of the novella the narrator sets out one last time in pursuit of facts, but his expedition deep into the Yoshino mountains beyond the village of Kuzu produces only fatigue and disappointment. He finds it impossible to learn the truth about the Heavenly King, despite his original confidence, and abandons his project. "Sannoko may be the site of legends," he concludes, "but not of history." As the narrator emerges from the mountains, leaving history behind, he sees Tsumura and Owasa crossing toward him on a suspension bridge. "The bridge swayed slightly under their weight and the sound [*ko-n, ko-n*] of their wooden sandals echoed in the valley." In Japanese convention, "*ko-n, ko-n*" is the sound of the fox's bark. With this haunting image, at once visual, aural, and romantic, the fox formerly venerated by Tsumura's grandfather comes back to life in the person of Tsumura's rediscovered "fox-mother," Owasa. Just as the persimmons upstage history and the senses eclipse the intellect, Tsumura's fantasies culminate in a marriage of archetypal happiness, while the narrator's research comes to nothing, except the story he has told.

. . . . .

Japan in the late 1940s was picking up the pieces, groping for a new identity under a foreign occupation, the nation's self-confidence shaken and its military tradition discredited. The Korean War, which helped to spark Japan's economic recovery, was in the future. Food was still being rationed; black markets were thriving. It was in these years of deprivation that Tanizaki emerged as the preeminent figure in Japanese letters with the complete publication of *The Makioka Sisters*, his receipt of the Order of Culture from the emperor in November, 1949, and the publication in 1949-1950 of *Shōshō Shigemoto no haha* (*Captain Shigemoto's Mother*)—his first piece of fiction after *The Makioka Sisters*. "This may be Mr. Tanizaki's greatest masterpiece," wrote Masamune Hakuch. "*Shigemoto's Mother* makes it clearer than ever that Mr. Tanizaki is a consummate writer" ["Kaisetsu," in Tanizaki's *Shōshō Shigemoto no haha,* 1953]. The critic Kamei Katsuichir wrote that *Shigemoto's Mother* "encompasses all the elements of Tanizaki's writing, it is their ultimate crystallization" ["*Shōshō Shigemoto no haha* oboegaki," *Bungei*, May, 1956].

Captain Shigemoto's Mother was the last novel Tanizaki wrote for newspaper serialization. He began negotiations with the Osaka *Mainichi Shinbun* after he had completed *The Makioka Sisters* in May 1948. At first he planned to serialize the sequel to *The Secret History of the Lord of Musashi*, postponed since 1933, but instead he decided on a novel set in the Heian court of the tenth century. He began writing *Shigemoto's Mother* as soon as he completed his move to an estate near the Shimogamo Shrine in Kyoto in April, 1949, and completed it before serialization began in November. This was a remarkably short time for Tanizaki, who often lamented that he could write no more than two or three pages a day.

Tanizaki's interest in the Heian period was nothing new. His first published work, the play *Tanjō* (*Birth*, 1910), is based on eleventh-century sources and set in the Heian court, and a number of stories and plays that he wrote between 1911 and 1918 have Heian settings. Reminders of Heian culture also figure in several works from the early 1930s—*Arrowroot*, *The Secret History of the Lord of Musashi*, and *The Reed Cutter*. It was probably around this time that the idea for *Shigemoto's Mother* began to germinate. One of Tanizaki's principal sources for *Shigemoto* was discovered in 1931—*Heichū monogatari*, also known as *Heichū nikki* (*Tales of Heichū*, *Diary of Heichū*), a tenth-century work similar to other *uta nikki* or *uta monogatari* (poem-diaries or poem-tales) such as *Ise monogatari* and *Yamato monogatari* (*Tales of Ise*, *Tales of Yamato*). It was also around this time that Tanizaki told Satō Haruo he wanted to write a novel in the form of an *uta nikki*. In 1935 he began his first modern-Japanese translation of *Genji monogatari* (*The Tale of Genji*), which was followed by *The Makioka Sisters*, with its many reminders of court culture. Just before *Shigemoto's Mother* he published "Fujitsubo," a translation of passages he had omitted from his first *Genji*; and right after completing *Shigemoto* he began his second *Genji* translation.

Before *Shigemoto's Mother*, Tanizaki had already offered imaginative, alternative "histories" in *Arrowroot*, *A Tale of Chrysanthemums in Chaos*, "A Blind Man's Tale," *The Secret History of the Lord of Musashi*, "A Portrait of Shunkin", *Kikigakishō*, and *The Makioka Sisters*. Each but the last of these takes the form of an historical novel, but, as Tanizaki admitted, they are largely the products of his imagination. The relationship of his material to actual events varies in these works, one extreme being represented by "A Blind Man's Tale," an imaginative elaboration on people and events that every Japanese pupil would have been familiar with, and the other extreme by *The Secret History of the Lord of Musashi*, which is pure fabrication. Tanizaki points out in his introduction to *Chrysanthemums in Chaos* that the tale takes place in the late fifteenth and early sixteenth centuries, a period that few people know anything about. "The author set his eye on this era," he writes, "not because he wanted to uncover unknown historical facts or characters, but because the age leaves free room for his imagination." "Tokugawa *gesaku* writers made Koremori the adopted son of a sushi-shop keeper," he continues. "I doubt that I will be able to muster that kind of audacity, but I hope that I can be uninhibited, even if it means that historians will scold me a little."

Captain Shigemoto's Mother differs from earlier Tanizaki works in its relationship to the historical background.

"While striving to be faithful to historical facts," Tanizaki admitted, "I seek out the gaps in the historical record and there unfold my own world"; but he does not identify the "gaps" in the story of Shigemoto's mother, and his "own world" is so skillfully woven into the historical fabric that most readers will cross the line between documented and imaginative history without realizing that a line exists. In his preface to the 1951 edition of *Shigemoto's Mother*, Tanizaki explains, "For the most part this work is derived from classics of the Heian period. The author has named each of them and made it clear which sections are drawn from these sources. . . . The name of one fictional document—a 'source' fabricated by the author—is also included, however, and the passages relating to it are products of the author's imagination. This is already clear to those who know the name of the document, and the question has nothing to do with the literary value of this work. In consideration of the general reader's interest, therefore, the author has chosen not to identify the fictional source here."

All of the major characters—Shigemoto's mother (the central figure) and the men in orbit around her (her lover Heijū, her first husband Kunitsune, her second husband Shihei, her sons Shigemoto and Atsutada)—appear in authentic Heian texts, which are cited in the novel; but one of the "sources," *Shigemoto no nikki* (*Shigemoto's Diary*), is indeed fabricated. Most developments in the last four chapters of the novel—Shigemoto's encounters with his father Kunitsune and the reunion with his mother—are "based" on Shigemoto's diary and so are of Tanizaki's invention, while the events of the earlier chapters follow classical sources more or less faithfully. Heijū's theft of Jijū's toilet box, for example, is adapted closely from *Konjaku monogatarishū* (*Tales of Times Now Past*; twelfth century).

The fictitious *Shigemoto's Diary* is slipped in among authentic sources so that the transition is natural and plausible. The summary in Chapter 7 of the fate of Shihei and his progeny concludes with a discussion of Atsutada, Shihei's son by Shigemoto's mother; and Chapter 8, logically enough, proposes to tell what became of Kunitsune and *his* progeny. At the end of Chapter 7, the personality and love affairs of Shigemoto's half-brother Atsutada are described and a number of his poems are quoted; the discussion of Atsutada refers to no fewer than six classical sources and quotes six poems from Heian collections. This much attention might be excessive, since Atsutada himself never appears in the novel, but a great deal more is known about him than about Shigemoto—Atsutada serves as a relatively solid foundation upon which to fabricate Shigemoto. More important, the authentic classical citations at the end of Chapter 7 prepare the reader for the introduction of *Shigemoto's Diary* in Chapter 8. As Chapter 7 ends with examples of Atsutada's poetry, Chapter 8 begins with several of Shigemoto's, gleaned from *Tales of Yamato* and the *Gosenshū* (*Later Selection of Poetry*), both from the tenth century. "These references are commonly known," says the narrator, "but there is another, which is not so widely read, a manuscript in the collection of the Shōkokaku Library called *Shigemoto's Diary*." It hardly occurs to the reader to question the authenticity of this new source, when the narrator cites more than thirty authentic sources. The subsequent paraphrases of *Shigemoto's Diary* seem plausible precisely because earlier paraphrases of authentic sources are accurate, and because *Shigemoto's Diary* is presented in the same learned style. The reader is further beguiled by the fact that the first episode based on *Shigemoto's Diary*, in which Heijū writes a poem on Shigemoto's arm, can be partially verified in authentic sources. The episode has already been mentioned briefly in Chapter 6, where the source of the story (the headnote to *Gosenshū* no. 711) is quoted, and its reappearance in the context of *Shigemoto's Diary* helps prepare the reader to accept the purely fictional material that follows.

In fact, the headnote says simply "a child of the lady's"; the novel specifies that the child was Shigemoto. There is a good deal of fiction even in the first seven chapters of **Shigemoto's Mother**, the chapters based on authentic sources. Passages that appear to be straight exposition often embellish upon, or even deviate from, the sources. There is no evidence, for example, that either Shigemoto or his mother was still alive in 944, the year they are reunited in the novel. One fairly reliable source has Shigemoto dying in 931. In the world of the novel, however, Shigemoto cannot meet his mother until his half-brother Atsutada is dead. Atsutada is known to have died in 943, and so Shigemoto and his mother must be kept alive at least that long.

The clearest example of Tanizaki's adapting the historical past to his fictional world is Kunitsune's surrender of his wife to Shihei. Kunitsune—old, impotent, and therefore, he believes, unable to make his young wife happy—feels guilty for monopolizing her and yields her to his nephew Shihei. The episode is adapted from an account in *Tales of Times Now Past*, but in Tanizaki's hands it becomes another manifestation of the common Tanizaki motif in which a man yields a woman to a younger man. Often the man is unable to satisfy the woman sexually; the woman is usually, but not always, his wife. Citing a passage in Tanizaki Matsuko's memoirs, some commentators have assumed that the theme originated in Tanizaki's feelings for her; but it appears in his work as early the 1914 novella **Jōtarō**. Jōtarō, the title character, takes his former student and rival Shōji to see Otama, the woman they both love. Simultaneously attracted to both Shōji and Otama, Jōtarō grovels before them. "Many times he had tried to love this boy with the same passion as he would a woman and always failed. But now he became aware of an indescribable feeling of love and worship gradually overcoming the anger within him. The more strength and arrogance the youth [Shōji] displayed the greater was Jōtarō's masochistic feeling of joy in being overcome."

In this motif, then, the older man typically allows himself to be "overcome"—succeeded, superseded—by a younger man (or, in *Quicksand*, a woman) with whom he identifies and to whom he may be attracted. There is a wide range of examples. Kaname (in *Some Prefer Nettles*), having lost interest in his wife sexually, encourages her to have an affair. In *Quicksand*, Kakiuchi condones his wife's

lesbian relationship with Mitsuko, to whom he, too, is attracted. Seribashi (in **The Reed Cutter**) teaches his son to love Oyū as he has loved her. The ailing professor in *Kagi* (*The Key*, 1956), believing that he is inadequate to his wife's sexual demands, encourages her relationship with the handsome young Kimura, both to assuage his sense of guilt and to enflame his jealousy and sex drive; and his wife, addressing her husband through her diary, observes that "[Kimura] is identified with you, you are part of him, the two of you are really one." The dying father in **"The Bridge of Dreams"** passes the baton, both psychological and carnal, to his son. Finally, the impotent old man of *Fūten rōjin nikki* (*Diary of a Mad Old Man*, 1961-1962) pushes his daughter-in-law, to whom he is powerfully attracted, into an affair with his nephew. The old man is explicit about the process by which he derives vicarious enjoyment: "I can be near a beautiful woman without arousing suspicion. And to make up for my own inability, I can get her involved with a handsome man, plunge the whole household into turmoil, and take pleasure in *that*. . . . Now that I can't enjoy the thrill myself any more, I can at least have the pleasure of watching someone else risk a love affair." In **Shigemoto's Mother**, Tanizaki shapes the episode from *Tales of Times Now Past* to fit the pattern of an older man yielding his wife to a younger, and Shihei becomes the first of Kunitsune's alter egos.

Judiciously chosen images accentuate the relationship between Kunitsune and his other alter ego, Shigemoto. The novel describes two memorable encounters between father and son. The first is set in Kunitsune's garden, where the old man teaches his son to recite verses by Po Chü-i that express his longing, and the second, at a riverbed burial ground where Kunitsune practices the Contemplation of Impurity in an attempt to forget his wife. Kunitsune's preoccupations, Chinese poetry and Buddhism, are foreign and conventionally masculine. Both encounters between father and son take place in autumn, the season of melancholy, decline, and impending death. The sensory imagery associated with Kunitsune is cold, harsh, and colorless: the morning after giving away his wife, he wakes up cold; Shigemoto is chilled by the cold ground under his feet and by the dew on his collar as he follows his father to the burial ground; and the cold, white moonlight that ruthlessly illuminates the corpses looks like frost on the ground—a simile that recalls a well-known verse by Li Po:

> The moon shines brightly before my bed—
> I took it for frost on the ground.
> Raising my head I gaze at the moon;
> Bowing my head I think of my home.

The imagery reinforces the foreign associations that have already been established for Kunitsune. References to Buddhist treatises and *setsuwa* collections give the passage a cerebral quality that is in keeping with Kunitsune and his attempts to escape his grief and so contributes to the effect of the image cluster.

The old man reminds one of the priest in Ueda Akinari's *Aozukin* (*The Blue Hood*), who goes mad with grief and devours the corpse of a beloved acolyte, then tries to free himself from his obsession by meditating on a couplet from a T'ang religious poem. Kunitsune emerges from the burial ground a complex figure: grotesque yet appealing; cerebral yet emotional; distant, but sympathetic because he is so humanly weak. Through the imagery deployed around him, he is relentlessly associated with harsh light, foreign poetry and religion, cold, decline, decay, and death.

Kunitsune's Buddhist practices offer Shigemoto one way to overcome the loss of his mother. The imagery, as Shigemoto follows his father under the clear, cold moon, their shadows sharp against the white ground, echoes imagery in **"Longing for Mother,"** *The Secret History of the Lord of Musashi*, and *The Reed Cutter*. In a dream, the narrator of **"Longing for Mother"** searches for his mother through just such a moonlit landscape. As a boy, the man in the reeds in *The Reed Cutter* has followed his father on long walks in the moonlight to Oyū's villa, where they peer at her through a hedge. Hōshimaru, in *The Secret History*, twice moves furtively through bright moonlight: first, when he follows an old woman on a cold, winter night to the storehouse where he sees the scene that will dominate his fantasy life; and second, when he slips out of the castle a few nights later to try to enact his fantasy for the first time: "It was about two o'clock in the morning when the boy started down the path. The moon that had cast its pale glow on his nightly visits to the attic rested now on the ridge of Mount Ojika and inscribed his shadow sharply on the ground. He held a thin veil over his head so that he would look like a woman fleeing the castle; as he walked he saw its tremulous shadow float across the ground like a jellyfish." The imagery in the burial-ground scene suggests that Shigemoto, like these other characters, is approaching a liminal experience, perhaps the catalyst for an obsession. Crossing a bridge over a stream (an image repeated in **"The Bridge of Dreams"**) on the way to the burial ground, Kunitsune and Shigemoto enter a world apart, and "[t]he sight of his father kneeling like a solitary shadow in these surroundings made Shigemoto feel that he had been drawn into a weird dream world." Shigemoto seems to be on the brink of discovering "in the innermost recesses of his heart," as Hōshimaru does, "a deep well of a different constitution, beyond the reach of his self-discipline." In a different novel, Shigemoto might have become a necrophiliac. But the dream that Kunitsune offers is the wrong dream at the wrong time—Shigemoto "was summoned back willy-nilly to the world of reality by the putrid smell that assaulted his nostrils." As he listens to his father's explanation of the Contemplation of Impurity, Shigemoto wants to cry out, "Father, please don't make Mother into something dirty." Hōshimaru goes back to the storehouse night after night, but one such night is enough for Shigemoto; he never accompanies his father to the burial mounds again.

Shigemoto's reunion with his mother in the next chapter contrasts sharply with the burial-ground scene. The latter has an intellectual tone, but the reunion is lyrical and, though the story originates with Tanizaki, almost every detail has precedents in Heian literature. The setting, at the western foot of Mount Hiei, is rich in literary associations. The full moon softened by the spring mist is the *oborozuki* of Heian poetry and of the *Genji*, not the ominous, cold moon of Kunitsune's autumn. It shines warmly on cherry blossoms and on the *yamabuki*, two of the favorite flowers of court poets, and under the cherry tree stands a nun veiled in white. The result is to associate Shigemoto's mother with the familiar and the traditional—native poetry, spring haze, cherry blossoms, the lingering fragrance of incense, soft, reassuring shadows, and the promise of life held by spring and by motherhood.

The image of a beautiful woman under a tree echoes countless Japanese works from ancient times to *The Makioka Sisters*. The familiar poem by Ōtomo no Yakamochi (718-785) is an early example:

> Haru no sono kurenai niou
>> momo no hana shitateru michi ni idetatsu
>>> otome

> A garden in spring—blossoming in fragrant pink
> The flowers of the peach color the path beneath
>> them where now steps forth a maiden.
>>> (*Man'yōshū* XIX:4139)

Tanizaki's fiction routinely associates cherry blossoms with motherhood and continuity. The narrator of *Arrowroot*, for example, recalls his mother showing him the blossoms at Yoshino, and the Makiokas' annual visits to the blossoms at the Heian Shrine reinforce their ties with the past and give order to their lives. The close association of the cherry tree with Shigemoto's mother is unmistakable. When Shigemoto sees her from a distance, standing in the moonlight under the blossoms, he mistakes her at first for a drooping, flower-laden branch. When he realizes that the figure is human, he imagines that she is the fairy of the uncannily beautiful tree. His mother does not simply appear: she emerges from the blossoms as though created from them by some wonderful alchemy.

The image of a woman under a tree has Buddhist associations as well, because of the tradition that Maya gave birth to Siddhartha under a tree, and so is doubly appropriate for Shigemoto's mother, who has become a Buddhist nun. The theme of Buddhism is common to both the burial-ground scene and the reunion; but Kunitsune's Buddhism is ascetic, harsh, and cerebral, while Shigemoto's mother's is a gentler, more compassionate, more domesticated—in a word, more maternal—form. The full moon, a common symbol of Buddhist enlightenment, is a spring moon here; the full moons of **"Longing for Mother,"** *The Secret History*, *The Reed Cutter*, and the burial ground are autumnal. Even her incense has both Buddhist and secular, even romantic, connotations. A famous love poem, already cited in connection with *Arrowroot*, comes to mind when Mother's incense reminds Shigemoto of the past.

> Satsuki matsu hanatachibana no ka o kageba
> mukashi no hito no sode no ka zo suru

> The orange blossoms that wait for early summer
> Bear the fragrance of the sleeves of the one of
> old.
>
> (*Kokinshū* no. 139, anonymous)

The narrative gradually prepares the reader to accept Shigemoto's mother as an ideal figure capable of embodying both the maternal and the Buddhist. Her full name is never given; she is always "principal wife" (*kita no kata*), "the Ariwara lady," "Shigemoto's mother," or simply "mother." Her face is described as "mysterious," "beautiful," and "small," but individual traits are omitted. Shigemoto cannot see her face clearly when he visits her as a young child, and she is already described in transcendent terms—"It was like peering reverently at an image of the Buddha ensconced deep in a shrine, and he never had a full, satisfying look." She takes no action and rarely speaks.

Classical sources, however, reveal more about the lady and her family than the novel does. The narrator provides detailed information on her son Atsutada, but neglects to say that her brother Motokata was (like Atsutada) one of the Thirty-six Sages of Poetry, and that her elder sister is mentioned in *Tales of Yamato* and *Gosenshū*. The narrator also suppresses a report that Shigemoto's mother was "flirtatious, and she was not at all pleased at finding herself married to an elderly husband."

The idealization of Shigemoto's mother is enhanced by the points of view from which she is described—those of the men who love her and who are least likely to be objective. When Kunitsune peers at her, wondering what feelings lie hidden in her heart, he finds her face "mysterious" and "enigmatic." To the child Shigemoto, she is at first a sweet fragrance, then a beautiful face wreathed in soft spring light. After their separation, Shigemoto believes that she is too remote for him to approach—almost a being of another world. When he finally does meet her after forty years and looks up at her face, it is "blurred by the light of the moon filtering through the cherry blossoms; sweet and small, *it looked as though it were framed by a halo*" (emphasis added). The events of the last four chapters, based on *Shigemoto's Diary*, are seen through a child's eyes, and the most memorable pictures of both Kunitsune and his wife are sketched by Shigemoto from his childhood memories. A child's eye being an effective filter on events, all but a few essential details are blurred, while those that are remembered are endowed with the mystery, the beauty, or the horror most likely to impress a child. Shigemoto's fragmentary childhood memories are, in turn, filtered through the intelligence of the narrator, who selects and interprets. To Kunitsune and Shigemoto, then, Shigemoto's mother is not an individual woman with distinctive traits, but an idealization of womanhood and motherhood.

In their longing for Shigemoto's mother, father and son are one. The same trio—a dead or dying father, a beloved wife-mother, and a young son who eagerly assumes his father's role in adoring her—appears in *The Reed Cutter* and **"The Bridge of Dreams"** as well. On the one hand, Kunitsune has qualities of a child—"the eighty-year-old Major Counselor wanted to wail, like a child calling for his mother" when he realizes that his wife is gone; and he is scolded like a child by Shigemoto's nurse. On the other hand, Shigemoto is Kunitsune's emotional heir. He perpetuates his father's longings for many years after his father's death, and when he is reunited with his mother at the end of the novel, he is both his mother's son and his father's surrogate. This is one reason the reunion scene is so powerful.

In longing for Mother, then, Shigemoto is Kunitsune's alter ego, but father and son respond differently to the lady's departure. Kunitsune turns to drink, Chinese poetry, and Buddhist sūtras to help him forget his wife, and tries to neutralize and purge his love by forcing himself to think of her as a decomposing corpse, but his attempts to forget her—or to turn her into something dirty, as Shigemoto puts it—fail. Shigemoto idealizes his mother and thereby avoids his father's misery:

> "Mother," to him, was nothing more than the memory of a tearful face that he had glimpsed in his fifth year and the sensory awareness of her fragrant incense. For forty years, memory and awareness were cherished, gradually beautified into an ideal, and purified, until they had become something vastly different from the reality.

Even after all obstacles have disappeared, Shigemoto lets years go by before he visits her, because he prefers his beautiful memories.

> It seems likely that Shigemoto wanted to go on forever adoring his mother just as he had seen her in his childhood. He had been angry with his father, deploring the desecration of his mother's image when the old Counselor practiced the Contemplation of Impurity, and during forty years of separation he had cherished an idealized version of his mother, which he had constructed from the image that lingered vaguely in his memory. What would she look like now, forty years later, having left the world after so many changes and become a servant of the Buddha? The mother Shigemoto remembered was an aristocratic woman of twenty or twenty-one, with long hair and full cheeks, but his mother the nun, living alone in a hut at Nishi-Sakamoto, was an old woman past sixty years of age. The thought must naturally have caused Shigemoto to shrink from facing cold reality. It may have seemed far better to embrace forever the image of the past, savoring his memories of her gentle voice, the sweet fragrance of her incense, and the sensation of her brush caressing his arm, rather than to drink rashly from the cup of disillusionment.

Shigemoto's approach is the opposite of the holy men so skilled in the Contemplation of Impurity that "a living beauty will come to look revolting, not only in the subjective view of the ascetic himself but in the eyes of onlookers as well"; instead, Shigemoto's imagination turns an elderly nun into a beautiful young woman. Like Sasuke (in **"A Portrait of Shunkin"**), he is able to render time and age irrelevant: he clings to an idealization of his mother, rather than trying to "erase her lovely image from the depths of his heart," as his father does, or seeking to interact with the woman herself. He admires Atsutada fondly from a distance because his half-brother resembles their mother. Even when Shigemoto finally does meet his mother again, he sees not the face of an old woman who has taken the tonsure, but a face "blurred by the light of the moon filtering through the cherry blossoms" that looks "as though it were framed by a halo," and so he is able to maintain his idealized image. Shigemoto himself ceases to be a middle-aged man: "in an instant he felt as though he had become a child of five or six," and "like a child secure in his mother's love, he wiped his tears again and again with her sleeve." Shigemoto's solution is far more gentle than Sasuke's, but finally he is like Sasuke in preferring a private, idealized version in place of the woman herself.

The apotheosis of Shigemoto's mother has precedents in Tanizaki's work but is nevertheless unusually explicit and complete. Shunkin is likened to "the Buddha Amida, coming to lead a devout believer to the Pure Land," but Shigemoto's mother actually becomes a religious figure. When Shigemoto asks her if she is the mother of the late Middle Counselor (Atsutada), she replies, "I was as you say, before I left the world [i.e., before taking Buddhist vows]." Having "left the family" (*shukke*), in the standard Japanese expression, and become a nun, she is no longer Atsutada's or Shigemoto's mother. She has become even more than a nun. An ethereal, indistinct figure illuminated by the full moon and standing under a blossoming cherry tree, she represents the simultaneous realization of Eternal Mother and of Buddhist enlightenment.

FURTHER READING

Criticism

Hibbett, Howard. Introduction to *Seven Japanese Tales,* translated by Howard Hibbett, pp. v-ix. New York: Alfred A. Knopf, 1963.

Highlights story elements in the collection *Seven Japanese Tales* that recur elsewhere in Tanizaki's fiction.

Mayer, David R. "Outer Marks, Inner Grace: Flannery O'Connor's Tattooed Christ." *Asian Folklore Studies* 42, No. 1 (1983): 117-27.

Compares Tanizaki's story "The Tattooer" with Flannery O'Connor's "Parker's Back," which is about the effect that a distinctive tattoo has upon its owner.

Miyama Ochner, Nobuko. "History and Fiction: Portrayals of Confucius by Tanizaki Jun'ichirō and Nakajima Atsushi." In *Literary Relations: East and West,* edited by Jean Toyama and Nobuko Ochner, pp. 68-79. Honolulu: University of Hawaii Press, 1990.

Contrasts the depiction of Confucius in the short story "Kirin" by Tanizaki and the novella *Deshi* by Nakajima Atsushi.

Peterson, Gwen Boardman. "Tanizaki Jun'ichir." In *The Moon in the Water: Understanding Tanizaki, Kawabata, and Mishima,* pp. 44-120. Honolulu: The University Press of Hawaii, 1979.

Survey of Tanizaki's career. During the course of her study, Boardman discusses "The Tattooer," "Portrait of Shunkin," *Ashikari,* and "Bridge of Dreams" as exemplars of Tanizaki's literary themes and style.

Yamanouchi, Hisaaki. "The Eternal Womanhood: Tanizaki Jun'ichirō and Kawabata Yasunari." In *The Search for Authenticity in Modern Japanese Literature,* pp. 107-36. Cambridge, England: Cambridge University Press, 1978.

Discusses Tanizaki's works, including "The Tattooer" and "Searching for Mother."

White, Edmund. "Shadows & Obsessions." *The New York Times Book Review,* (July 18, 1982): 8, 22-3.

Discusses the theme of "obsessive sexuality" in *Bushuko Hiwa (The Secret History of the Lord of Musashi).*

Additional coverage of Tanizaki's life and career is contained in the following sources published by Gale Research: *Contemporary Authors,* Vols. 25-28 (rev. ed.), 93-96; and *Contemporary Literary Criticism,* Vols. 8, 14, 28.

William Trevor
1928-

(Full name William Trevor Cox) Irish short story writer, novelist, and dramatist.

INTRODUCTION

Trevor is acknowledged as one of Ireland's finest contemporary short story writers. Often compared to James Joyce and Frank O'Connor, he skillfully blends humor and pathos to portray the lives of people living on the fringe of society. While many of his early works are set in England, his most recent fiction incorporates the history and social milieu of his native Ireland. In works such as *The Ballroom of Romance, and Other Stories*, Trevor explores the importance of personal and national history as he focuses on lonely individuals burdened by the past.

Biographical Information

Born in Country Cork to Protestant parents, Trevor moved frequently while growing up and attended thirteen different schools before entering St. Columba's College in Dublin in 1942. Shortly after graduating from Trinity College, Dublin, he left Ireland to accept a position teaching art in England, where he currently resides. While he was in his mid-thirties, he abandoned a successful career as a sculptor to pursue writing full-time. His first novel, *A Standard of Behaviour*, was generally dismissed as imitative and pretentious. *The Old Boys*, proved significantly more successful, winning the Hawthornden Prize for literature in 1964. In the years that followed, Trevor continued to write novels and also produced a number of well-received plays. However, it is as a writer of short fiction that he has received the most critical and commercial attention. The publication of his first collection of short stories, *The Day We Got Drunk on Cake*, was soon followed by the highly popular works *The Ballroom of Romance* and *Angels at the Ritz, and Other Stories*. One story in particular—"The Ballroom of Romance"—established Trevor's reputation as a talented short fiction writer, inviting comparisons to works by Evelyn Waugh, Graham Greene, and Muriel Spark. Trevor's most recent short fiction collections, *The News from Ireland, and Other Stories*, *Family Sins, and Other Stories* and *Two Lives: Reading Turgenev; My House in Umbria* continue to generate popular and critical acclaim.

Major Works of Short Fiction

In his works Trevor typically focuses on eccentric individuals isolated from mainstream society. For example, in

"The General's Day" a retired British army officer living in a shabby apartment falls victim to his housekeeper who exploits his loneliness and steals from him. Many of Trevor's characters are imprisoned by the past, such as the title character of the short story, "In Love with Ariadne" who cannot bear the shame of her father's suicide and rumors of his pedophilia. As a result, she enters the convent, refusing a future with a man who loves her. Other Trevor characters, dissatisfied with their present lives, relive the past. In "Virgins," two women who are unhappy in their marriages recall their youth when they fell in love with the same man, while the protagonist of *My House in Umbria* confuses memories from her past with the present. Trevor's recent short fiction incorporates these thematic concerns with the history and political turmoils of Ireland. *Beyond the Pale, and Other Stories* and *The News from Ireland, and Other Stories* address more directly the troubles in Ireland and its tenuous relationship with England. For instance, in the title story of *Beyond the Pale, and Other Stories* English tourists are exposed to terrorist violence while staying at an isolated resort in Northern Ireland. While initially rationalizing the event, the vacationers are eventually forced to confront their own roles in perpetuating the Anglo-Irish conflict.

Critical Reception

While some critics have praised Trevor's emphasis on the past, others have found his subject matter tiresome. Anatole Broyard lamented: "Too many of Trevor's characters are haunted by the past. After a while, when I grew tired of them, they reminded me of the sort of people who sentimentalize in attics. Although nothing demands deftness so much as nostalgia, Mr. Trevor is sometimes content just to shamble around it." Despite the often bleak tone of his work, Trevor has been lauded for his compassionate characterizations; in particular, many commentators have noted and commended his sensitive treatment of female characters. Trevor's restrained writing style and subtle humor have also received favorable attention. The last few years have seen the publication of several full-length studies of Trevor, expanding critical analysis of his work to include such topics as gender relations, religious symbolism and the context of Irish literature.

PRINCIPAL WORKS

Short Fiction

The Day We Got Drunk on Cake, and Other Stories 1967
The Ballroom of Romance, and Other Stories 1972
Angels at the Ritz, and Other Stories 1975
Old School Ties (short stories and memoirs) 1976
Lovers of Their Times, and Other Stories 1978
The Distant Past, and Other Stories 1979
Beyond the Pale, and Other Stories 1981
The Stories of William Trevor 1983
The News from Ireland, and Other Stories 1986
Nights at the Alexandra (novella) 1987
Family Sins, and Other Stories 1990
Two Lives: Reading Turgenev; My House in Umbria (novellas) 1991
The Collected Stories 1992

Other Major Works

A Standard of Behaviour (novel) 1958
The Old Boys (novel) 1964
The Boarding House (novel) 1965
The Love Department (novel) 1966
Mrs. Eckdorf in O'Neill's Hotel (novel) 1969
Miss Gomez and the Brethren (novel) 1971
* *The Old Boys* (play) 1971
Going Home (play) 1972
Elizabeth Alone (novel) 1973
The Fifty-Seventh Saturday (play) 1973
A Perfect Relationship (play) 1973
Marriages (play) 1974
The Children of Dynmouth (novel) 1976
Other People's Worlds (novel) 1980
Scenes from an Album (play) 1981
Fools of Fortune (novel) 1983
A Writer's Ireland: Landscape in Literature (nonfiction) 1984
The Silence in the Garden (novel) 1988
Excursions in the Real World (memoirs) 1994

Felicia's Journey (novel) 1994
Juliet's Story (juvenilia) 1994

*Adapted from Trevor's novel *The Old Boys*.

CRITICISM

Michael Standen (essay date 1967)

SOURCE: A review of *The Day We Got Drunk on Cake*, in *Stand*, Vol. 9, No. 2, 1967, p. 56.

[*In the following mixed review, Standen discusses the uneven quality of* The Day We Got Drunk on Cake.]

William Trevor's ***The Day We Got Drunk on Cake,*** comes in a jacket so swinging and irrelevant that one is eventually forced to the conclusion that there was a muddle in Bodley Head's design cloakroom. Mr. Trevor's characters are in fact mostly ageing and/or lonely—certainly characters of England before the Flood. There are twelve stories of middle-class life—nearly all the private tragedies of people who would expect to keep up appearances but whose lives have dipped wildly and uncontrollably beneath the surface.

Often objects (an antique table, the furnishings of a luxury penthouse) play a crucial part and this may be generally true of the short story form which forces a writer to coalesce rather than develop his characters. [Yukio] Mishima does the same thing, using thermos flasks, a wardrobe, a pearl. Objects (and 'servants') are part of the trap that William Trevor's characters live in. His method is clinical although he is less truly detached than the Japanese writer—in fact it is those stories where his sympathy breaks through which are the best. Of the twelve **"The General's Day"** is probably the most satisfying and **"A School Story"** is finely done. The overall impression though is one of unevenness. In **"In at the Birth"** for example a lady who goes to babysit for a couple, who are in fact childless, ends up herself in a cot—the child they never had. Here there is not much of sympathy and too much of formula. One is left wondering if William Trevor isn't working a very narrow seam.

Auberon Waugh (essay date 1972)

SOURCE: "Brief Cases," in *The Spectator*, May 13, 1972, pp. 733-34.

[*Waugh is an English novelist, journalist, and nonfiction writer. In the following laudatory assessment of* The Ballroom of Romance, *he examines the characters in Trevor's short stories, asserting that characters "who in ordinary life would merely be depressing suddenly become objects of compassion, and as such afford keen enjoyment."*]

All Mr Trevor's characters are people whom any sane man would wish to avoid. The English have an admirable convention that we never talk to strangers—in railway carriages, bars or anywhere else—unless to request or convey precise information. The reason for this is the fear that we will find strangers boring or unsympathetic in some other way, and in ninety-nine cases out of a hundred we are surely right. People who are shy, or lonely, or have some secret sorrow are, generally speaking, best left alone unless one is consciously trying to be charitable. Nothing is more dismal than the half-drunk man in a bar who wishes to show you photographs of the children from whom he is separated by some matrimonial indiscretion on his own part. Spinsters whose characters have been warped by a revulsion from sex do not make the best company, nor even do those heroic people who devote their lives to looking after an elderly parent.

Madwomen, incurable masturbators, public school headmasters, drunks, all Mr Trevor's characters are social or emotional cripples. One looks down from the Press Gallery of the House of Commons from time to time on the heads of exactly such a collection, without ever experiencing the faintest twinge of sympathy, or amusement, or interest in the personal tragedy behind each wreck of a human being. The sad truth is that life must go on, and these people are best left to be looked after by nuns and others who specialise in that sort of work.

It is part of Mr Trevor's genius that he manages to make these cases appear if not sympathetic at any rate pathetic. People who in ordinary life would merely be depressing suddenly become objects of compassion, and as such afford keen enjoyment. It is not usual to devote whole articles to a single volume of short stories nowadays, but then it is very rare to find work of Mr Trevor's high standard in any field. One can say without hesitation that at least three of the short stories in this collection are as excellent as it is possible for a short story to be—as well written, meticulously observed, ingeniously constructed, generously conceived—deserving to be treated as classics of the form. They may even result in a certain amount of moral uplift, encouraging us to be more considerate to the drunks, bores and emotional cripples we meet in the course of our daily lives. The tragedy is that so few people want to read short stories nowadays. Before Mr Trevor and I can hope to improve the moral tone of the nation in this way, we must persuade people to buy his volume. I can only say it is easy to read, packed with laughs and with pleasurable feelings of compassion.

The first story, **'Access to the Children'** describes a man going to seed. Divorced by his wife after an affair with an American lady, he is deserted by his mistress and realises he was deeply in love with his beautiful wife all along. Distraught and lonely, he takes to drink and is sacked from his job. Every Sunday he takes his children out for the day, cherishing the glimpse of his wife and deceiving himself that a smile from her means she has forgiven him and is prepared to take him back. One Sunday he gets drunk and declares himself, to learn (what the reader already knew) that his wife has not the slightest wish to

have him back and plans to remarry. We leave him with his drunken optimism. It is profoundly moving in its contrast between the warmth, security and happinesss of married life and the bleak squalid loneliness of its alternative—a highly moral tale for husbands who are tempted to stray.

The second story, **'Nice Day at School'** is again highly moral. A fourteen-year-old working-class schoolgirl, the only virgin in her age group, child of hopeless parents, dreams of a happier life, where a kind man with delicate hands will take her away to her honeymoon in Biarritz by Air France. Her immediate prospects are of furtive, rabbit-like coupling out of doors with a blubbery-faced butcher's boy who fancies her. Eventually, she agrees to this—"I wanted to be done, 'cause it's the Class Two fashion"—changing her mind at the last moment and resigning herself to a life of embittered spinsterhood. The pathos of this story lies in the hopelessness of her inability to communicate with her unintelligent, unthinking parents. Its error, I suppose, is to imagine that anyone born into such a background would have the same sensitivies as Mr Trevor or the reader, but there is no reason why we should not lavish our middle-class sensitivities on her plight, and, as I have said, it makes a good read.

Another excellent story describes a happy family in which the mother goes mad; another the yearnings of a middle-aged Irish spinster dedicated to looking after her father; another the infatuation of a sweet, pathetic twenty-seven-year-old girl for a hopelessly selfish man of fifty-five, who visits her every Saturday for a few hours and then leaves her until the next Saturday to go to the cinema; another returns to the frustrations of a thirty-eight-year-old under-matron at a boys' prep school, comparing her lot with that of an emotionally deprived schoolboy at the same school; another describes the loneliness and sexual fantasies of a fifteen-year-old boy in a small Irish town; another tells how a brutal, boring headmaster and his poor wife meet their former headboy and his young bride on their honeymoon in an Irish hotel. The partition between their rooms is thin, and the headmaster hears his head boy unsuccessfully trying to penetrate his bride. When the headmaster and the boy go fishing, the headmaster's wife unsuccessfully advises the young bride to run away before it is too late, citing her own life as a terrible example.

All the stories are about people who are deprived in one way or another, people who are missing out on the good and happy life we must suppose they might enjoy if they were not deprived. Only one of them seems to be a complete failure—when Mr Trevor tries to put himself in the shoes of a deprived secretary who takes a trip on LSD under the influence of her boss. The key story, which sums up the burden of all the others, is the last one called **'O Fat White Woman,'** in which Mr Trevor explores the image conjured by Lear's memorable couplet:

> Why do you walk through the field in gloves
> O fat white woman whom nobody loves?

The fat white woman is, needless to say, the frustrated wife of a prep school headmaster, who turns out to derive sexual satisfaction from punishing the boys at his school. She only wanted to do well, to come up to scratch as his wife. Now she has stopped caring. Things might have been different. But they aren't. It is a bleak world which Mr Trevor asks us to explore with him, but he makes it worth the journey. Perhaps he will even make better people of us all: kinder, more considerate to those who are emotionally or socially deprived. If not, at least he has given us a highly enjoyable day's reading.

Paul Theroux   (essay date 1972)

SOURCE: "Miseries and Splendours of the Short Story," in *Encounter*, Vol. XXXIX, No. 3, September, 1972, pp. 69-75.

[*Theroux is an American fiction writer, critic, and travel writer who, since 1963, has lived outside the United States, first traveling to Africa with the Peace Corps and later settling in England. Many of his novels and short stories have foreign settings—Kenya in* Fong and the Indians *(1968), Malawi in* Girls at Play *(1969) and* Jungle Lovers *(1971), Singapore in* Saint Jack *(1973)—and feature characters whose conflicting cultural backgrounds, as well as their personal conflicts, provide the substance of the story. Critics often find Theroux's fictional works to be sardonic expositions of chaos and disillusionment presented with wit, imagination, and considerable narrative skill. Theroux has also produced several nonfiction accounts of his travels, including* The Great Railway Bizarre *(1975) and* The Old Patagonian Express *(1979). As a critic, he has written a study of Trinidadian novelist and essayist V. S. Naipaul and frequently reviews books for several major English and American periodicals. In the following essay, he offers a favorable assessment of the short stories comprising* The Ballroom of Romance.]

The English short story writer resembles the Russian writer whose work is considered hateful and disaffected by the Kremlin. Both men have to send their stories abroad to be published and appreciated. The half-dozen outlets for short stories in England, only one or two of them monthly magazines, can hardly accommodate story writers of the achievement of Angus Wilson, L. P. Hartley, William Sansom, V. S. Pritchett, Gabriel Fielding, Francis King, Muriel Spark, William Trevor, Elizabeth Taylor—and there must be many more. The short story is being written as vigorously in this country as it always has, but it is seldom published here with any vigour. Typically, the English writer's story appears in an American magazine; it is collected and the volume of stories receives a cursory notice, an abbreviated paragraph simply indicating its publication and a lightning glance at its contents. It is discouraging, and publishers have begun to consider short stories an obligatory but uncommercial philanthropy, a gesture for culture for which they will be respected but not rewarded. It is an attitude the poet knows well, and it has something to do with the decline of the monthly magazine which welcomed poetry and stories; now both poet and short story writer are regarded as cranks, hobbyists, part-timers.

A short story is a twenty-minute read, but surely the pleasure of the short story is not the collection, for no collection can be read straight through like a novel. One stops and ponders after each story, and with the best stories one feels like closing the book and saving the rest for later. It is uniquely suited, like a poem, for a magazine where on its discovery the reader gets a little thrill. Few English readers are ardent magazine subscribers; that they are regular library-goers (unlike Americans, who are members of book clubs) must account for the unpopularity of English monthlies and the appearance of stories in collections. And that new phenomenon, the televised story, has grown out of the public's indifference to the magazine story.

So William Trevor, an immensely gifted short story writer, is known as a writer of television plays, though all the plays he has written have been adaptations of his short stories. But you can hardly blame him. His new collection, *The Ballroom of Romance*—two or three of the stories have appeared on television—confirms the reputation he gained on the publication of his previous collection, *The Day We Got Drunk On Cake* (best since *The Wrong Set*, best since the war, critics said). Last year, in a reflective piece on English writers in general, a literary editor suggested that Mr Trevor might try travelling to some equatorial outpost, a former colony or infant tropical republic, and writing about it. The suggestion was well-intended and may have been prompted by a suspicion that having turned up such surprising creatures in what were thought to be rather ordinary London suburbs, he might do the same in, say, Tunapuna, Kandy or the suburbs of Lahore. Ivy Eckdorf caused quite a bit of talk in O'Neill's hotel, but what if she had taken her camera to Raffles in Singapore! In places that are familiar and unremarkable Mr Trevor has acquainted us with the strange and startling: consider those excitable geriatrics in *The Old Boys,* the odd assortment of residents in *The Boarding House*, Mrs Eckdorf, Miss Gomez.

> **Mr Trevor's achievement has been to create, by means of the clearest and most original prose in this generation and a compassionate balance of fascination and sympathy, real people of flesh and blood out of characters another writer would dismiss as goons or drudges.**
>
> **—Paul Theroux**

The stories in *The Ballroom of Romance* are set in England and Ireland, and look who he has found: Miss Awpit, Mrs Maugham, Mr Gipe and Mr Belhatchet, Wragget, Dympna and Mr Dicey. You don't have to know much more than their names. It is plain that Miss Awpit looks after mad old Mrs Maugham; Gipe is a handyman; and Belhatchet is the man in **"Kinkies"** who drugged a poor girl's orange juice. Wragget—who else? —was beaten at Digby-Hunter's school, and died, and Dympna the serving girl is going to tell the police. Mr Dicey is the postman who steams letters open.

"'Wragget' is a terrifying name," I said to a man. His reply was, "You scare easily." Maybe so, but it would be hard to find a better one for this poor wretch. When a Trevor character is sympathetic he is awarded a sympathetic name, like Malcolmson in **"Access to the Children"**, or Eleanor who appears in two stories, first as a schoolgirl in **"Nice Day at School"** and then as Belhatchet's victim (she is ten years older) in **"Kinkies."** Mr Trevor's style matches the ingenuity of his naming; it is spare and filled with suggestion—the sentence "'*vederci,*' said Mr Belhatchet, replacing his green telephone" is worth a whole page of description. But the characters are more than their names, weirdness is not their only attribute, and though the characters in Mr Trevor's novels are quite different from his short story characters (the former are several degrees more perverse than the latter, as well as—usually—from a different social class), Mr Trevor's achievement has been to create, by means of the clearest and most original prose in this generation and a compassionate balance of fascination and sympathy, real people of flesh and blood out of characters another writer would dismiss as goons or drudges.

It is for the women in this collection that one feels most deeply. Indeed, the thread that runs through all the stories is of brittle or urgent femininity thwarted by rather boorish maleness. Mr Trevor's men are feckless, or else malicious snobs, or drunkards, or comradely and exclusive old boys; his women are victims of, at once, their own strength and the men's weakness, isolated by their longings or by the perversity of their husbands or lovers. Malcolmson in **"Access to the Children"** has forced a separation on his wife while he lived briefly with his American girlfriend Diana; but the story is of his decline, of his wife's fortitude, and at the point when one believes there might be a reconciliation one realises how his wife's love permitted his infidelity, and how, having taken unfair advantage of this love, he has risked and lost everything, including the attention of his children. Eleanor in **"Nice Day at School"** and Bridie in the title story cling to an idea of love and romance while understanding that they will have to face a life with louts. Mavie tries hard to please Mr McCarthy in **"The Forty-seventh Saturday"**, but he remains a visitor, almost a client, and will not let her love shake him out of the routine of his fantasy. And so it goes, wives and lovers getting short shrift, and even accepting it when they are warned away from it as in **"The Grass Widows."** This is one of the best in the collection; here, a woman late in life realises how boring and trivial her husband is, and in ironic circumstances attempts to save a newly-married woman from the same fate; but the younger woman is offended by the warning and finally chatted into accepting her husband's immaturity and inattention.

Some of the stories are heartrending, but Mr Trevor writes with a light touch, without sentimentality and always with humour. There is a crotchety precision about his narration; what other writer would be able to get away with the sentence, "No alcoholic liquor was ever served in the Ballroom of Romance, the premises not being licensed for this added stimulant"? He is the master of exasperation, of the person speaking at length in tones of formal annoyance; and he is at his best when dealing with a condition of lucidity one has always thought of as madness. His real skill lies in his ability to portray this behaviour as a heightened condition of life; in his work there is no madness, but there is much suffering.

Peter Ackroyd   (essay date 1975)

SOURCE: A review of *Angels at the Ritz,* in *The Spectator,* Vol. 235, No. 7689, November 8, 1975, pp. 604-05.

[*An English biographer, critic, nonfiction writer, poet, and editor, Ackroyd is known for his novels that focus upon the interaction between artifice and reality and emphasize the ways in which contemporary art and life are profoundly influenced by events and creations of the past. In the following excerpt, he offers a positive assessment of the stories comprising* Angels at the Ritz.]

Angels at the Ritz is one of the most imaginative and substantial books I have read this year; the fact that it is a volume of short stories is probably beside the point, although it may be an indication of the way good English writing is going. Perhaps the most interesting writer of my own generation, for example—Ian McEwan—has gained a reputation through just one volume of short stories.

Mr Trevor is a very accurate, not to say painstaking writer and it is the particular virtue of his writing that he should be the observer rather than the fantasist, and that his prose should characteristically be one of definition and description rather than of image and metaphor. In **'In Isfahan'**, the first story of the book, a middle-aged man knows the truth about himself but will not share it, even with a stranger in a strange country. In **'The Tennis Court'**, a tennis party is held in an old lady's ramshackle house, in the interval between two wars; from such small beginnings, a story of life and power grows beyond the dreams of a hundred serious novelists. In **'Office Romances'**, it is seen to be better to suffer from illusions than to have none at all. Trevor, through all of these stories, manages that combination of a dispassionate prose style with some highly sentimental and even inflammatory content. In **'Mrs Silly'** a young boy disowns his mother in one of those small acts of treachery that will last a lifetime. The story is so perfectly modulated, the boy's unspoken life so accurately conveyed, and each scene so carefully arranged that Trevor, perhaps despite himself, emerges as the master of the short story in its English guise.

But a short story can be merely a story, and Trevor brings to his form a number of larger issues. **'Angels at the**

Ritz', the title-story, is a study of men and women who grope blindly towards an understanding of themselves in their middle age. There is always that large question in Trevor's stories which remains unanswered: When did everything change for the worse? He is adept at conveying the loneliness of people, the intractability of their plight and the suffering which can be caused from living without illusions. It is this which makes Trevor's direct and sometimes neutral prose so effective, since it seems to record all of those events which cannot be explained and are always endured. Life simply goes on, and Mr Trevor represents it. He never admits to anything so general as this, of course, and it must be said that it is the small touches—the local details, the brief moments of insight, even the names of his characters—which make Trevor so outstanding a writer:

> She felt ashamed of herself for having tea with him, for going to see him when she shouldn't, just because Poppy was dead and there was no one else who was fun to be with. Leo Ritz and his Band were playing 'Scatterbrain' as she left the dance-rooms. The middle-aged dancers smiled as they danced, some of them humming the tune.

V. S. Pritchett   (essay date 1979)

SOURCE: "Explosions of Conscience," in *The New York Review of Books,* Vol. 26, No. 6, April 19, 1979, p. 8.

[*Pritchett, a modern British writer, is respected for his mastery of the short story and for what critics describe as his judicious, reliable, and insightful literary criticism. In the following essay, he considers the "obscure dignity" of characters in* Lovers of Their Time, and Other Stories.]

The excellent short story depends so much on alerting immediate doubts and acute expectations; we are alerted by a distinctive style and self; yet there are one or two writers who cunningly insinuate an abeyance of the self, a quiet in the inquiry that, for the moment, calms the nerves. To this class William Trevor belongs. He is one of the finest short story writers at present writing in the Anglo-Irish modes. His people are those who, in the course of their lives, are so humdrum in their ordinariness, so removed from the power of expressing themselves that he has to efface himself in order to speak for them. They appear to be confused by experience and in moral judgment, but they live by an obscure dignity and pride which they are either too shy or too unskilled to reveal at once: his art is to show they have their part in an exceptional destiny and even in a history beyond the private. Impartially he will justify them.

In one of his Irish stories, a bustling tippling priest speaks half pityingly, half in exasperation, of his brother, the timid manager of a provincial hardware store: the man is fatally married to the memory of his domineering mother—a banal and common Irish dilemma—yet the timid, inarticulate man is in the midst of a momentous, devastat-

ing religious crisis. The two brothers have made the ritual visit to Jerusalem and the timid one experiences a violent shock not only to his faith but to his understanding and conscience. For him the early Christian legend and especially the sight of the Stations of the Cross in the Via Dolorosa are unimaginable, meaningless outside the Irish Christianity of Co. Tipperary. He has become a victim of the indignity of History.

The mother of the two men dies while the brothers are away. The timid one will not recover his faith unless he gets back home at once to the proprieties of his mother's funeral. A petty, pathetic dilemma? No, for him an earthquake. And there is more to it than that: for it was he, he now knows, who was by nature a priest; it was the bustling priest, the organizer of Catholic pilgrimages, who has the devious habits of the shopkeeper. This is a story of frustration, and on such a level it may seem dim even in its pathos; but notice—the timid brother will become the master; his conscience is reborn. He forces his priestly brother to give up the tour and return: Galilee and Bethlehem are travesties.

In nearly all Trevor's stories we are led on at first by plain unpretending words about things done to prosaic people; then comes this explosion of conscience, the assertion of will which in some cases may lead to hallucination and madness. In that disordered state the victim has his or her victory; these people are not oddities but figures crucified by the continuity of evil and cruelty in human history, particularly the violent history of, say, the wars and cruelties of the last sixty years of this century. Theirs is a private moral revolt. The point is important, for Trevor has sometimes been thought of as the quiet recorder of "out of date" lives living tamely on memories of memories, as times change.

Tragically (comically too) he is aware of the seismic shock that history, even the ignorance of it, has prepared for the dumb or the successful. The obvious ironies are not laughed off; he goes deeper and more ruthlessly than that. The Irish in him—one would guess—faces the horrors, the English dismays at having to accept circumstance by putting on the best face available. He moves easily in the idiom of the appalling children in **"Broken Homes,"** who, in the interest of Community Spirit, wreck the house of an eighty-seven-year-old woman and daub her kitchen with paint and fuck in her bedroom; or in the jocose mixture of "refined" and vulgar accents in the boozy office party; in the hearty, classy voices of middle-aged friends, remembering their schooldays—the time bomb here is the exposure of their homosexual goings on at school and of a hushed-up suicide—or in the dialect of the Carnaby Street Sixties and the Beatles; he notes the illiterate English of a young lesbian's touching proposal:

> Well Im a les and I thought you was as well. I'm sorry Sarah I didnt' mean to ofend you I didnt' no a thing about you.

The voices of 1914, 1940, 1970 define lives, a matter of importance to a writer whose people live through and among one another for years on end. (It is not common to find this diffusion in the short story, in which a writer is tempted to economize on everything except his drama). Trevor quietly settles into giving complete life histories, not for documentary reasons, but to show people changing and unaware of the shock they are preparing for themselves. When we begin on the novella in three parts, *Matilda's England,* we sleepily enjoy the happiness of the farm children who are taken up by the grand Mrs. Ashburton at the Manor whose husband—how sad it is—let the place go after being shell-shocked in the First World War. She has kindly lured the kids into cutting the grass on her tennis court which has been overgrown and lets them play there.

So far an idyll. But now we are alerted when the children are grown up and another father and a brother are killed in the next war. The Manor house is empty. Matilda, the narrator, and a vulgar friend discover that lovers are using the summer house. History now strikes a third blow: Matilda's own mother, widowed by the Second War, has a lover, a mean little draper from the town; she is defiling the summer house.

As his master Chekhov did, William Trevor simply, patiently, truthfully allows life to present itself, without preaching; he is the master of the small movements of conscience that worry away at the human imagination and our passions.

—*V. S. Pritchett*

Now the childish pastoral is done for. Matilda becomes odd. Odder still when she marries—politely but without love—the fastidious young businessman who has too perfectly renovated the Manor, sacred to poor dead Mrs. Ashburton and her confidences about the horrors her husband went through in his war. Surely the transfiguration of the Manor will appease Maltida's morbid imaginings? Not at all: human cruelty is continuous, Mrs. Ashburton had taught her: the cruelty of two wars has, so to say, moved into Matilda's own heart. She wrecks her husband's life, utters her hatred with all the clarity of the obsessed as she sits embroidering a peacock on a drawing room cushion, and he leaves her for good. She is Mrs. Ashburton reborn. Mad? No. Iced is the word. At the end of Matilda's story, Matilda is older and alone. Her erring mother and stepfather are dead, her husband Ralphie will never return; but Matilda is able to say:

> But if Ralphie walked in now I would take his hand and say I was sorry for the cruelty that possessed me and would not go away, the cruelty she used to talk about, a natural thing in wartime. It lingered and I'm sorry it did.

This will not avail her.

The most powerful story in this collection is **"Attracta"**; it is set in today's Northern Ireland and after the usual quiet beginning, assaults us with the tale of two terrible political murders, the decapitating of an English officer and the rape and murder of his English wife who has joined the Women's Peace Movement there. A newspaper report affects an elderly Protestant woman schoolteacher who, in her childhood, had gradually become aware that her own parents were killed "by mistake" in an ambush. She discovers one of the perpetrators is now a harmless old man. Quietly she stands in her schoolroom and insists on telling the children about the soldier's murder and how the killers sent his head to his wife.

> "Can you see that girl?" [she asks.]

> "Can you imagine men putting a human head in a tin box and sending it through the post? Can you imagine her receiving it? The severed head of the man she loved?"

> "Sure, isn't there stuff like that in the papers the whole time?" one of the children suggested.

The purpose of the teacher's grim questioning is to awaken imagination and conscience, and teach that God doesn't forever withhold His mercy. Those men who exacted a vengeance may one day for all we know keep bees, budgerigars, serve in shops, be kind to the blind and deaf, till their gardens in the evenings, and be good fathers. It is not impossible.

The sickened children are Protestants—they are stupified by her attempt to stir a moral reflection. The outraged parents demand that the old teacher shall be retired. What is more remarkable even than the tale is that it conveys what is going on in the backs of the minds of all the people in the town, of whatever faction: of how all, except one or two bigots, are helplessly trying to evade or forget the evils that entangle them. As his master Chekhov did, William Trevor simply, patiently, truthfully allows life to present itself, without preaching; he is the master of the small movements of conscience that worry away at the human imagination and our passions.

Julian Gitzen   (essay date 1979)

SOURCE: "The Truth Tellers of William Trevor," in *Critique: Studies in Modern Fiction,* Vol. XXI, No. 1, 1979, pp. 59-72.

[*In the following excerpt, Gitzen offers a thematic analysis of Trevor's early short stories.*]

Since the appearance of his first novel, *A Standard of Behavior* (1958), William Trevor has published a total of eleven volumes of fiction. Despite the popularity of *The Old Boys* (1964), *The Boarding House* (1965), and *The Ballroom of Romance* (1972), extensive analysis of his writing is as yet in short supply. Reviewers, on the other hand, have neither ignored Trevor nor hesitated to classify him. With virtual unanimity, they have labeled him a comic writer, differing only in their terms of references, which vary from "black comedy" to "comedy of humor" to "pathetic" or "compassionate" comedy. As a satirist, he is most frequently compared with Evelyn Waugh, although Muriel Spark, Angus Wilson, Kingsley Amis, and Ivy Compton-Burnett are also mentioned. Additional points of comparison could readily be suggested: Trevor's ear for humorously banal small talk is reminiscent of Pinter; what has been referred to [by Jonathan Raban, *New Statesman*, October 15, 1971] as "the incredulous, stuffy exactitude . . . the fustily elegant grammar" of his language recalls Beckett; his ruthless undeviating pursuit of a grubby, shabby verisimilitude evokes the work not only of Graham Greene but of such contemporaries as Edna O'Brien, John Updike, and David Storey. In addition, his interest in psychological questions and his preference for the traditional short story and novel allies him with writers as diverse as Henry James and Saul Bellow.

If Trevor is a comic writer, however, he with Beckett is assuredly among the most melancholy, as reflected in his character's surroundings, in their situations and activities, and particularly in the theme of loneliness and hunger for love which more than any other feature distinguishes his writing. As a preface to exploring this theme, let us review Trevor's typical locales and representative features of the people who inhabit them. Consistently, his interest has focused on the marginal setting: a gaudy pub in a seedy district being demolished for reconstruction; a threadbare boarding house, its brown wallpaper and cheap furnishings unchanged for forty years; a deteriorating and unfrequented hotel in a Dublin backstreet; a tract house enveloped in tall weeds and grass, smelling of home-brewed beer and home-grown mushrooms. These are appropriate backgrounds for the lonely and forgotten, far removed from centers of purposeful activity and social ferment. Despite feeble resorts to the public media, these characters, described as "survivors, remnants, dregs" [Valentine Cunningham, *Times Literary Supplement*, October 24, 1975], find little to which they may attach themselves. They are unenamored of the images on their television screens and cannot or will not be gathered into the collective mindlessness of popular culture. Most typical are those at the social fringes: the timid and ineffectual middle-aged bachelor reduced to an insignificant job, the homely spinster alone with memories of dead parents, the petty criminal, ever dodging but seldom unscathed. Many are orphans in search of surrogate families; others are so old that they have outlived both family and friends. Though many are married, not a single couple is conspicuously happy or contented; indeed, distorted or frustrated sexuality abounds. With divorce almost epidemic, numerous separated characters drift into solitary middle age. The majority are more notable for weakness or failure than for strength or success, which contributes to the choice they are usually forced to make: either to recognize (and forgive) cruelty or unfaithfulness in those they love or limitations in themselves, or to cultivate comforting illusions, ranging from harmless daydreams and fantasies to compulsive and profound convictions. According to their dif-

fering temperaments and needs, some accept the truth, while others find illusions the only bearable remedy. Indeed, furnished as they often are with active capacities for fantasy and reverie, and given to daydreaming or imagining themselves in situations contrary to actuality, Trevor's characters are peculiarly well fitted for creating and sustaining illusions.

With its constriction of form, the short story highlights Trevor's thematic concerns. Each of his three collections of stories centers on a common theme, and the themes of each are notably similar. The first, *The Day We Got Drunk on Cake* (1967), carries no epigraph, but a fitting motto would be Mrs. Fitch's: *in vino veritas*. Characteristically, the setting is the pub or cocktail party, where excessive consumption loosens the tongue of one character, causing him to make blunt statements offensive to his companion. Tension increases as the unpalatable truth emerges. Alternatively, the truth about their situations occurs spontaneously to the leading characters, although the reactions of others toward them may trigger their awareness. **"The General's Day"** is typical, especially since it involves heavy drinking as a medium for truth. At seventy-eight, General Suffolk is among the extremely old people for whom Trevor has a particular fondness, no doubt because of their conspicuous loneliness but possibly also because he considers them the least afraid of truth and, therefore, the most refreshingly blunt of speech. On the day of the story, the General is frustrated in his attempts to carry on his favorite practices of drinking congenially with friends and seducing middle-aged women. Late at night, bitterly disappointed and very drunk, he suddenly realizes that he has grown unwelcome and even repulsive to others and thinks with lucid horror, "My God Almighty, I could live for twenty years."

The Ballroom of Romance (1972) concerns love unrequited, unequally shared, or selfishly taken for granted. Again loneliness becomes a source of anxiety, bringing with it the choice between truth and illusion. The heroine of the title story is thirty-six-year-old Bridie, whose one entertainment through the laborious years on her father's farm has been the Saturday night dance in a building named "The Ballroom of Romance." But romance has eluded Bridie, despite her faithfulness as a customer. At sixteen she fell in love with a young man whom she met at the ballroom, only to see him marry another. Having abandoned her quest for love, Bridie now aims only for a companionable marriage, centering her current hopes on the dance-band drummer. On the evening of the story, however, Bridie becomes conscious of the desperately predatory gestures of Madge Dowding, a spinster three years older; noticing the amusement of younger women at Madge's expense, Bridie realizes that she cannot return again to the ballroom, lest she too become a figure of the fun. Surrendering all further thoughts of the drummer, she resigns herself to eventual marriage to the wastrel, Bowser Egan, whom she will accept—since, after her father's death, she will be lonely. Thus Madge's loneliness betrays her into an illusion from which Bridie escapes in the cause of self-esteem, while recognizing that loneliness will in time drive her to an unpalatable compromise.

"**The Grass Widows**" elaborates the theme by demonstrating how features of character or age may screen out sudden truth, condemning one generation to relive the mistakes of another until it, too, gradually acquires self-awareness. While on a yearly fishing trip with her husband, the headmaster of a public school, Mrs. Angusthorpe recognizes a kindred spirit in the honeymooning bride, Mrs. Jackson, whose husband is one of Mr. Angusthorpe's former head boys. Seeing the two men behaving so compatibly, Mrs. Angusthorpe realizes that they are similarly domineering, inconsiderate, and selfish. In hopes of sparing Mrs. Jackson an unhappiness like her own, she calls the bride's attention to the "cruelty, ruthlessness, and dullness" of their two husbands. Not surprisingly, Mrs. Jackson rejects Mrs. Angusthorpe's advice that she should leave her husband and loyally protests that he is loving and considerate. With resignation Mrs. Angusthorpe concludes that, just as young Mr. Jackson is the successor to his old headmaster, so Mrs. Jackson is her own heir, locked into the guileless confidence which marked her own entry upon marriage and fated to discover in her own painful way that she is the victim of an unequal love. "**An Evening with John Joe Dempsey**" and "**Office Romances**" also treat the premise that the young often repeat the mistakes of their elders.

If Trevor is a comic writer, however, he with Beckett is assuredly among the most melancholy, as reflected in his characters' surroundings, in their situations and activities, and particularly in the theme of loneliness and hunger for love which more than any other feature distinguishes his writing.

—*Julian Gitzen*

The Ballroom of Romance is distinguished from the other volumes of stories in offering the additional illuminative device of variations played on the mirror-image. In nearly every story the central figure is confronted by another person whose situation parallels or highlights his own. The protagonist's eventual recognition of such a parallel may engender increased self-awareness; alternately, the failure to perceive a manifest parallel creates dramatic irony. Thus Bridie's sense of her impending resemblance to Madge Dowding inspires her resolution to stop attending the ballroom in a futile search for romance. On the other hand, Mrs. Angusthorpe finds similarities enough between herself and Mrs. Jackson but fails to draw the full moral, for she remains ironically oblivious that her advice to the bride to leave her husband is even more applicable to herself. A third mirror-image appears in "**An Evening with John Joe Dempsey**," where a fifteen-year-old boy with greater astuteness than Mrs. Angusthorpe draws the latent parallel between himself and Mr. Lynch, the celibate but lustful middle-aged bachelor, a regular drinker at the village pub. Mr. Lynch has never left his jealous and righteous old mother, but he has lived with her at the price of lies and deception, knowing that she would be outraged if he were to act on or even confide to her his secret longings. Instead, he escapes from her to the pub, where he tells melancholy sexual anecdotes, intended, he insists, as a "warning" to lads of the town. Young John Joe, too, lives in the shadow of an overly protective widow-mother from whom already he must conceal his adolescent sexual fantasies and from whom, he wearily recognizes, he must continue to hide his desires so long as he remains, like Mr. Lynch, the willing hostage of a mother's possessive devotion.

In *Angels at the Ritz* (1975), Trevor's characters continue to be subjected to unpleasant truths, with the opportunity to display strength in accepting or reconciling themselves to them. In the title story, Polly Dillard confronts two bitter and closely related truths: at thirty-six she can never again recapture the exuberant frivolity with which she and her friends celebrated her twenty-second birthday at the Ritz; second, what was unthinkable in those sparkling days is about to happen: her husband will soon sleep with her life-long friend. These circumstances she accepts as the legacy of middle age. For characters with less sturdy powers of resignation than Polly's, illusions *can* offer a comforting means of alleviating loneliness and reducing suffering. But as illustrated by "**In Isfahan**," illusion lacks the "quality" of truth. Iris Smith, discontentedly married to an Indian and living in Bombay, meets the Englishman Normanton on a day-tour of Isfahan. In another instance of *in vino veritas,* she consumes enough liquor to stimulate the confession that she has no desire to return to India. Clearly, she conceives Normanton as the gallant companion who will reprieve her from an unpleasant fate. Despite her candor, Normanton remains reserved and affects to ignore her tentative advances, though he does not correct her romantic speculation that he is a married architect. After her departure, he inwardly reviews his own unhappy past—including two failed marriages which have discouraged him from trying again. He perceives that their encounter has at least provided her with the comforting illusion of having "met a sympathetic man." She will never know his personal shortcoming, "a pettiness which brought out cruelty in people." Their exchange has been unequal, for his impression of her represents what she actually is, while her memory of him is composed of imagined details. He is deprived of a vital dimension: "He was the stuff of fantasy. She had quality, he had none."

William Trevor with Mira Stout (interview date 1989)

SOURCE: An interview in *The Paris Review,* Vol. 31, No. 110, Spring, 1989, pp. 118-51.

[*In the following interview, Trevor discusses his background, the creative process, and the influences on and major themes of his fiction.*]

[Stout]: *What did you do after leaving university?*

[Trevor]: When I left Trinity Dublin, I tried to get a job, and it was very difficult in those days—in the 1950s in

Ireland. Eventually I found an advertisement in a newspaper that said someone's child needed to be taught. "Would suit a nun" it suggested at the end of it, which was interesting, and I actually got that job. So I used to leave Dublin every day on the bus, go about twenty-five miles into the country, and teach this rather backward child. Her mother brought in the neighbor's children, and a little academy was formed.

Why had they asked for a nun?

Because nuns sometimes have time on their hands. It was half a day's work, which was enough to live on, and this went on for about a year. I wasn't interested in writing in those days. I left that job when I got married, and then worked in a school in Northern Ireland for about eighteen months, before the school went bankrupt. We had to leave Ireland after that because I couldn't get another job. I taught in a school in England for two years or so—in the Midlands near Rugby—before deciding to try and make a living as a sculptor. I came down to the west country and set myself up, rather like Jude the Obscure, as a church sculptor, and existed like that for seven years. Then, when our first child was about to be born, it was clear that the money couldn't be spread between three people, so I gave that up, and got a job writing advertisements—which I was very lucky to get because I knew nothing about it. I was thirty. We moved to London, and I wrote advertisements for some years, always on the point of being sacked.

Why?

Because I was extremely bad at it. It was then that I began to write short stories. I was given a typewriter and endless cups of tea. I was always allowed to spend days and days over an advertisement, because they were regarded as so very important. If I was writing, for instance, four lines about paint, they wouldn't expect to see any copy for two days. I couldn't take that seriously so I began to write stories. I wrote *The Old Boys* while I was there, and two other novels I think.

On company time?

Not entirely. But I did photocopy one of my novels on the company machine. The poet Gavin Ewart, who also was at the agency, refers to that in one of his poems: "Later we both worked at Notley's—where no highbrow had to grovel / and I remember Trevor (with feminine help) xeroxing a whole novel. / 'I see you're both working late,' the Managing Director said / as he went off to his routine gin and tonics and dinner and bed." In the end I persuaded them to allow me to work two days a week, but I abused that privilege. Jane and I went to Bruges one weekend and didn't come back. I'd left some firm in the Midlands in the lurch. I resigned just as I was on the point of being sacked. I've always had an uneasy relationship with employers.

Did you enjoy any aspect of working in an ad agency?

Only in retrospect. But all experience is good for writers—except physical pain. Office life is interesting. People behave quite differently from the way they behave at home with their families. I had to visit a factory near Birmingham, I remember, that manufactured screws. I'd never have met people who made screws otherwise, and I happen to be particularly interested in the work people do. And I was always seriously frightened that I was going to be sacked, and that, too, is a useful feeling to remember.

Did you produce good copy?

Oh, no. I produced very bad copy. I found it difficult to write convincingly about boat propellers or beer or airlines. I could never think of slogans. But advertising wasn't a very big part of my life—I was a teacher for just as long, and if ever I had to earn a salary again I'd prefer to teach, I think.

What did you teach?

More or less everything really. I liked teaching math best because I don't have a natural way with figures and therefore had sympathy with the children who didn't either. And I greatly respected the ones who did possess that aptitude. My skill in art and English made me impatient, and I found those subjects rather dreary to teach as a result. "Why are the art room walls covered with pictures of such ugly women?" a headmaster asked me once. "And why have some of them got those horrible cigarette butts hanging out of their nostrils?" I explained that I had asked the children to paint the ugliest woman they could think of. Unfortunately, almost all of them had looked no further than the headmaster's wife. I like that devilish thing in children.

Were you really a chicken farmer too?

No, I was never a chicken farmer; I'm sorry to have to say I wasn't. I read in an American newspaper once that I was a very good polo player which pleased me enormously. I've never played polo in my life.

When did you first want to be a writer?

I wanted to be a writer when I was very young. I was a great reader of thrillers. When I was ten I wanted to write thrillers. And I went on wanting to be a writer for a long time, and then, under the influence of an art master, I discovered sculpture. So I stopped wanting to write, and in fact didn't take up writing seriously until quite late in life. I didn't write at all during the time I was a student.

What were you reading around the time that you began to get serious about writing?

I had graduated from thrillers and detective stories, and begun to read A. J. Cronin and Francis Brett Young, Cecil Roberts—middlebrow authors like that. I thought them marvelous, but later I moved on from them to Somerset Maugham, whom I've always admired—in particular his short stories—and then I began to read the Irish writers whom I'd never read, because we didn't in Ireland for some reason. We ignored them, perhaps because they were homegrown produce. I probably began with Joyce; and at some point I read Dickens and the Victorians. I read hungrily and delightedly, and have realized since that you can't write unless you read.

Your own style of writing is very steady—were you experimenting at all with form at that time? Do you think your writing has changed much?

No, I think all writing is experimental. The very obvious sort of experimental writing is not really more experimental than that of a conventional writer like myself. I experiment all the time but the experiments are hidden. Rather like abstract art: you look at an abstract picture, and then you look at a close-up of a Renaissance painting and find the same abstractions.

When you wrote The Old Boys, *were you friends with other writers and artists?*

Up to that time my friends were mostly from the art world rather than from the world of literature; I didn't really know any other writers. But I've never gone in for the business of belonging to sets of people. For some reason I'm not drawn by that. I have friends because I like them. I hate the idea of groups.

Was A Standard of Behavior *your first novel?*

That's really a fragment which was written for profit when I was very poor. Strictly speaking it is my first novel, written some time before *The Old Boys,* but *The Old Boys* was the first serious thing I ever wrote.

Did you have any difficulty getting published?

Oddly enough, no. Everything else had been difficult— trying to get space in galleries, for instance. A couple of my short stories were published in magazines—*The London Magazine* and the *Transatlantic Review,* and one or two glossy magazines—and then an editor was shown them, or read them, and he suggested the writing of a novel. He actually gave me £50 to start writing *The Old Boys.* I was very lucky with that novel because it was turned into a television play and a radio play, and somehow or other people found it funny, and I began to do a bit of reviewing, and wrote a stage play. It was just chance or good fortune, and at least it made up for the fact that it had been so very difficult to make a living of any kind for the ten or fifteen years before then.

How old were you when The Old Boys *came out?*

I think it came out in 1964, so I must have been thirty-six.

I read that Evelyn Waugh gave The Old Boys *his imprimatur . . . how did that come about?*

He read it, said that he liked it, and because of that he was quoted on the jacket.

Did you have much self-confidence starting out?

I don't think so. I think self-confidence is a very dangerous thing for writers. I tend to write in a fragile, edgy, doubtful sort of way, trying things out all the time, never confident that I've got something right.

Do you think of yourself as being part of an Irish literary tradition?

That's a question that usually irritates Irish writers very much because they feel it implies an Irish writer is rather like a writer from, say, Liverpool or Yorkshire, suggesting a local and regional authority.

Isn't it the contrary?

It is, in fact, the contrary. I always call myself an Irish writer. I'm one of the few Irish writers who actually likes the phrase. Since I am an Irishman, I feel I belong to the Irish tradition. I don't really feel that being Irish is the important thing. What is important is to take Irish provincialism—which is what I happen to know about because it's what I come from—and to make it universal.

Heroes don't really belong in short stories. . . . I find the unheroic side of people much richer and more entertaining than black-and-white success.

—*William Trevor*

When you were growing up did you have heroes who were Irish writers? Have you ever been aware of trying to emulate anyone in particular?

If I thought of Irish heroes at all I thought of Irish political leaders. In those days Irish writers weren't as established as they are now. Yeats and Bernard Shaw were very much alive when I was a child, and they hadn't the stature that they have since acquired. All the poetry I remember learning, apart from "The Lake Isle of Innisfree," was English or Scottish poetry. I'm very fond of Joyce, especially *Dubliners.* But I have never thought in terms of literary heroes.

Do you feel a sense of duty or obligation to address the political situation in Ireland in your work? Sometimes you do address it—as in Fools of Fortune *and in* The News from Ireland, *where political tyranny is the underpinning of the narrative—but you also write with equal intensity about the strife of a suburban housewife and her carefully-applied lipstick.*

I don't feel it as a duty. If you are an Irishman, and if you have lived through this particular period in Irish history—

the very recent period of Irish history—it's bound to involve you. You reflect and dwell upon it a great deal. It will therefore creep into what you write whether you like it or not; and you just let it creep in where it seems to be right. It's exactly as you said, you've really answered the question: sometimes it's there and it suggests something to you, and sometimes something else suggests itself. I feel exactly the same intensity about the housewife with the lipstick as I do about some family that has suffered in the Ulster crisis. The only reason Ireland comes into it is because Ireland is my country and I'm familiar with it. I mean, I'm as horrified about a bomb in Bologna as I am about a bomb in Derry. And I am as heartbroken by the death of innocent Italians or Americans as by anything that happens in Ireland.

It's difficult to know to what extent one is engaged or involved, especially indirectly, in the troubles of one's country—what you say about responsibility "creeping in" seems quite right.

You are involved as a person. But quite often the way you are involved as a person doesn't make for good writing. The writer and the person are two very separate entities. You think as a person in a way that is not the same as the way you think as a writer. It is only when you actually feel, as a writer, "*this* has got the makings of a story in it," that you will use it. Otherwise it really has no interest to you as a writer. You may feel strongly about something, but there may be nothing you can do with that intensity of feeling, no story to tell. Whereas you can tell a story just because it makes a good story. And you tell it, because that's how you communicate. It's better to tell a good story than to feel more strongly as a person while you tell a bad one. It's a foggy area, this—it's almost impossible to talk about it. People like me write because otherwise we are pretty inarticulate. Our articulation is our writing. All of this—for me at least—is particularly difficult to analyze. As soon as I begin to analyze I feel myself becoming some kind of academic who's examining what I'm doing, and that's most uncomfortable. It's a strange trinity—the person, the writer, the analyst. I try to keep the first and the last out of what I do.

Do you think the well-developed sense of tragedy in your work is informed by the crisis-bound state of Ireland, on any level, or by your exposure to the suffering of the Irish?

It's hard to winkle out an answer to that. I've got a feeling that I'm not affected in that particular way. I don't know that I soak up something that then goes through an artistic net and comes out the other end. I think it's more likely that my sense of tragedy probably comes from childhood. And I say that because countries—one's own country—haven't anything to do with human relationships, whereas something you observed in childhood so often has. That is where I think both tragedy and comedy come from. The struggle in Ireland, and the sorrow, is a very good backdrop for a fiction writer, but I don't think, certainly not for me, that it is any sort of inspiration. Possibly another writer would react differently.

Why do you think that?

Well, what seems to nudge me is something that exists between two people, or three, and if their particular happiness or distress exists for some political reason, then the political reason comes into it—but the relationship between the people comes first. I'm always trying to get rid of a big reason—a political one, for instance—but sometimes it's difficult. Human reasons, for me, are more interesting than political ones.

You once said, "You have to get out of Ireland before you can really know it." What did you mean by that?

It's really a question of being too close to something. I'd never been outside the country until my early twenties, and I think if I'd remained there in a town like Skibbereen, in County Cork, I wouldn't have seen it the way you should see it—like looking down the wrong end of a telescope. I'd not be able to see Ireland in terms of other countries. I think that applies to any country, not just to Ireland. Most writers benefit from exile.

Then there isn't something special about Ireland, some peculiar quality about it that drove you away with all the other famous exiles?

No; the only thing that drove me away from Ireland was the fact that I couldn't get work there. I didn't want to leave Ireland. I would have stayed there. I wasn't ambitious to go away in order to "see Ireland correctly from a distance"; it's just that the accident of going away has caused me to see it. Had I remained there, and had I begun to write there, I then might have shovelled myself out. I might have said, "You've got to get out because you can't see the place properly," or perhaps I wouldn't have been able to write about it at all. I don't know what would have happened. I didn't write about Ireland for a very long time. I wrote books which were thought to be very English, especially in America, and that, of course, was because I was writing about a country that was totally strange to me, and very fascinating to me. I didn't know England very well, so it was rather the same thing in reverse: I wasn't too close, I was at a considerable distance away. I found English society very strange, but I was able to pick it up reasonably accurately. Then, after several books, I realized that Ireland was falling into perspective, so I began writing about Ireland.

Did growing up as a Protestant in southern Ireland make you examine religious belief in an intense sort of way?

No. What is now apparent to me is that being a Protestant in Ireland was a *help*, because it began the process of being an outsider—which I think all writers have to be—and began the process of trying to clear the fog away. I didn't belong to the new post-1923 Catholic society, and I also didn't belong to the Irish Ascendancy. I'm a small-town Irish Protestant, a "lace-curtain" Protestant. Poor Protestants in Ireland are a sliver of people caught between the past—Georgian Ireland with its great houses and all the rest of it—and the new, bustling, Catholic state.

Without knowing any of this, without its ever occurring to me, I was able to see things a little more clearly than I would have if I had belonged to either of those worlds. When I write about, say, a Catholic commercial traveler, I can almost feel myself going back to those days—to an observation point. And when I write about the Ascendancy I am again observing. Elizabeth Bowen writes of her family employing boys from the local town, Mitchelstown, where I was born, to stand round the tennis court collecting the balls. I would have been one of those little Protestant boys, had I been the right age. There was a certain amount of "cutaway-ness" that has been a help. Certainly it feels like that, looking back at this very small group of not well-off Irish Protestants. Displaced persons in a way—which is really very similar to what a writer should be, whether he likes it or not.

You've spoken about religion in a social context, but not about religion as religion.

I didn't come from what you'd call a particularly religious background. But Ireland is a religious country, and in those days everyone went to mass or church. It was just all taken for granted. It didn't really impinge in any sort of way, except that one felt different as a Protestant.

There are a lot of priests in your books.

There are a lot of priests in Ireland—and a lot of nuns. The first school I went to was a convent, and I liked the nuns very much. I had quite a lot to do with the Catholic Church, although I've never been seriously tempted to join it. English writers like Graham Greene, for instance, and Evelyn Waugh, became Catholics because they were frustrated. But Ireland being a religious country, the religious side of people is satisfied more naturally than it is in England.

Are you religious?

I don't really think of myself as religious . . . I only ever go to church in Ireland. I don't like the Church of England. I feel much more drawn towards Catholicism when I'm in England—not that I'd do anything about it. I always feel that Protestantism in England is strangely connected with the military. All the cathedrals here are full of military honors. It's part of an establishment with the armed forces; tombs, rolls of honor, that sort of thing. It's a strange combination. The Protestant Church of Ireland is a shrunken, withered little church that I'm quite attracted by.

There is a strong element of faith in your work, of people coping, enduring, of being borne along in their lives. Is it humanist or spiritual faith?

I don't think it is humanist; I think it is just a kind of primitive belief in God. I think that certainly occurs in my books. I'm always saying that my books are religious; nobody ever agrees with me. I think there is a sort of God-bothering that goes on from time to time in my books. People often attack God, say what an unkind and cruel figure he is. It is outside formal religion; the people who talk about it aren't, generally speaking, religious people, but there is a bothering, a gnawing, nagging thing.

Other People's Worlds was like that, with Julia's worry for Francis's daughter, Joy.

That's the sort of thing I mean.

What do you think of other contemporary writers?

I don't read a lot of contemporary writing. I reread Dickens and George Eliot, and Jane Austen. I've always been attracted by American writers, particularly American short-story writers. I admire F. Scott Fitzgerald, Hemingway, Faulkner, John Updike. And I like Carson McCullers, Mary McCarthy, and Tennessee Williams—his prose rather than his plays. Of Irish writers, I'm particularly fond of George Moore and James Stephens, and the stories of Joyce, whom I've already mentioned. I rarely read anything in translation because I feel I'm missing so much. But I do reread Proust. And Mauriac.

What quality do you admire in American writers?

A kind of freshness, and directness.

What about contemporary English writers?

I'm a great admirer of the late Elizabeth Taylor. Of Graham Greene, Ivy Compton-Burnett, Anthony Powell, the short stories of V. S. Pritchett. The test of literary admiration is whether or not you reread. I reread all those writers, and Henry Green and Evelyn Waugh. They've all created characters that have become hooked into my imagination, like real people. Of contemporary Irish writing, I read mainly short stories—by almost everyone writing them.

Has England had any particular effect on your writing?

I don't think I'd write in quite the same way if I hadn't moved to England. I think English eccentricity is what first attracted me in terms of writing—it was that that made me wonder and muse about this country.

How did you get to know about the eccentricity in The Old Boys? *Had you taught at a public school?*

I really had to imagine—by a process which is part of a fiction writer's paraphernalia—what boys I remembered at school would be like when they were old. I found it very amusing to wonder what So-and-so would become like. They became something like what they *were* . . . little boys sitting at desks. I have never believed in the axiom that a writer should first and foremost write about what he knows. I think it's a piece of misinformation.

What's the difference between an Irish eccentric and an English eccentric?

That's difficult to say—it's like asking what the difference is between English humor and Irish humor. It's a dry quality that you get with English eccentricity at its best;

Irish eccentricity is much more outlandish. Crazier. English eccentricity is something you hardly notice until all of a sudden you realize that you're in the presence of an eccentric mind. It's not like that at all with an Irish eccentric; you know about it all very easily and quickly. English eccentricity has a suburban quality—it's like a very neatly-trimmed garden in which you suddenly realize that the flower beds aren't what they seem to be. There's a kind of well-turned-out quality about English eccentricity, whereas the Irish equivalent is higgledy-piggledy, and sometimes even noisy. The marvel of the English version is that it's almost secretive. I've never quite believed in the obvious English eccentric, the man who comes into the pub every night and is known to be a dear old eccentric. I always suspect that that is probably self-invention. What I do believe in is the person who scarcely knows he's eccentric at all. Then he says something so extraordinary and you realize he perhaps lives in a world that is untouched by the world you share with him.

What is your definition of a short story?

I think it is the art of the glimpse. If the novel is like an intricate Renaissance painting, the short story is an Impressionist painting. It *should* be an explosion of truth. Its strength lies in what it leaves out just as much as what it puts in, if not more. It is concerned with the total exclusion of meaninglessness. Life, on the other hand, is meaningless most of the time. The novel imitates life, where the short story is bony, and cannot wander. It is essential art.

Do you think your Irish stories differ fundamentally from your English and Italian stories?

Yes, I do. There is a sense of community in the Irish short stories that doesn't exist in the others. In the Irish stories people tend to talk to each other, whereas in the English ones people talk *at* each other. The English are much more oblique; we Irish are more direct. This is not meant as any profound observation, but it is often those little things about people of different nationalities that tell so much and are so effective in fiction. Ireland is so old-fashioned that it almost belongs to another age. It is about fiit than that: fo England—and at the same time it is a Third World country, where it snows in winter. Things happen there very quickly, and the old values, alongside those changes, form a fascinating mixture.

You have never created a hero. Why is that?

Because I find them dull. Heroes don't really belong in short stories. As Frank O'Connor said, "Short stories are about little people," and I agree. I find the unheroic side of people much richer and more entertaining than black-and-white success.

Time plays a part in both your stories and your novels— the things that have happened to characters in the past, the effect of time passing. How important is that past?

A huge amount of what I write about is internal, a drifting back into childhood, based on a small event or a moment.

By isolating an encounter and then isolating an incident in the past you try to build up an actual life, and you cannot build up a life without using time in that sense. I think of a short story very much as a portrait.

Is time a destroyer or a preserver?

Both. It both heals and destroys, depending on the nature of the wound; it actually reveals the character. There is either bitterness or recovery: neither can take place without time. Time is the most interesting thing to write about besides people—everything I write about has to do with it. Time is like air; it is there always, changing people and forming character. Memory also forms character— the way you remember things makes you who you are. People struggle to share a very private side of themselves with other people. It is that great difficulty that I often write about.

Why?

I don't know, and I say that because I don't want to get it wrong. Truth is the most important thing that there is, and if you lose sight of it, your writing will be destroyed in the end.

You have done quite a number of adaptations of your works for the stage, television and radio. How do you feel about the imposition of actors' faces and voices on your characters?

The actual physical appearance of people creates a "jerk" in the communication of the story, it changes the gear of the story. The audience has to work much less hard, and you cease to address a vital part of their imagination. The part of their imagination engaged by reading a description lies completely dormant. You let the audience off the hook. Radio, on the other hand, works much better for me since it is only the actor's voice that comes between the audience and its imagination.

Has moving down here to Devon changed the way you work at all?

Not really. It hasn't made any difference at all. It doesn't matter to me where I live and work. I work in the mornings, and I'd do that anywhere—hotels, or anywhere.

When do you get up?

Well, I used to get up at four o'clock and do most of my work—expecially in the summer—between half-past four and breakfast-time. But I stopped doing that some time ago—it had become just straightforward punishment. I now start work at about twenty minutes to eight and work until about twelve, and I might do a little more later in the day.

Do you work on a typewriter?

Yes, I do, and also in longhand. I do a lot of rewriting. I find that the more versions you see of, say, the beginning of a chapter—blue paper, white paper, typed, longhand—the more you get it right in the end. This is a tremendously longwinded way of saying you have to become familiar with what you're doing, so that in the end you practically know the whole thing by heart. After a certain time it becomes so familiar that you know exactly where to look for this bit or that bit and you know at once if it's wrong. But more importantly, really, you know the characters inside out. You know what day it is when he did such and such a thing, what her favorite flowers are, the pattern of wrinkles on her face. I can't do that unless I've spent ages with a novel, or a story. One of the big differences between the two is that the novel is a very different subject for me to *see round,* to the end of it. But you can see round a short story long before it's finished, and feel what it's going to be like. I have to create for the novel a tremendous amount of raw material, and then cut the novel out of it. I write novels the way films are made. I literally cut with a pair of scissors. In *Fools of Fortune* there is a character who disappears for years; I know where he went, and I've written all that and abandoned it. But I couldn't have written the novel without knowing what he'd done, and where he was. But that's an extreme example. A better one is knowing, say, what someone has done during a week it doesn't tell you about in the book.

You actually write all that down and throw it out?

I write incidents and scenes over and over again until eventually they are completely clear to me. For a reader it would be boring to know all those details, so the details in the end just wither away, after you've picked out the ones that you want . . . but *you* know how he's perambulated round a particular room, and what she does after he goes, or whatever it happens to be. And, of course, the bits that *aren't* there are just as important as the bits that *are* there, because they're deliberately left out. You keep back from the reader the fact that she went down to the kitchen and boiled an egg. You don't want to say so because it is somehow important that that is left for the reader to imagine.

Do readers write to you often and tell you what they think of your stories?

Yes, they do.

Do you keep up a correspondence with them?

You can't, really; it's too time-absorbing. It's very difficult to keep up a correspondence with a lot of people.

What is your own favorite among your works?

My favorite work is always the last one that I've done. I suppose it's the same thing as a new-born child being your favorite for a short time because it's so fragile. The other ones are hardened old things by now, and they can get about on their own. I don't really have any favorites. But if I keep on disliking a story or being unhappy about it, it generally means that the story isn't any good.

Do you find it difficult to write from a woman's point of view?

No, I don't find it difficult. It's the same thing as writing about elderly people when you're not elderly yourself—I was quite young when I wrote *The Old Boys*. It would seem to me very dull to write only about personal experience. I wrote about elderly people out of a sense of curiosity. I want to know what it's like to be old, what it's like to cross a room when your limbs are all seized up. And similarly, I want to know what it's like to be woman, so again I write out of a sense of curiosity. Now, as I'm getting older myself, I tend to write more about children, because it's been such a long time since I was a child. It's a slightly different process, but it does belong to the same obsession.

> **There is a sense of community in the Irish short stories that doesn't exist in the others. In the Irish stories people tend to talk to each other, whereas in the English ones people talk *at* each other**.
>
> —*William Trevor*

Do you ever feel you're trying to stretch too far, or get in over your head with characters and find yourself unable to discover what it is that makes them tick?

Yes, I do do that, quite often. In fact, I become involved in a story which doesn't seem to be working, and it's usually not working for that very reason. The character I've invented simply won't be explored, and there's nothing I can do about it. I find that I'm saying to myself, "I can't find anything interesting in this man. He belongs to somebody else." What generally happens then is that man becomes a tiny walk-on part. And I realize that the story—or some other character in it—interests me more than the man I started out with.

It's almost disturbing the way in which you are able to get inside such a varied cast of characters, regardless of their age, sex, or background. It seems somewhat diabolical, the way you're able to enter so easily into these characters' thoughts; how could you know so much about the way all these different people live? It seems a bit like a ventriloquist who is able to throw his voice into anything. Is it the case that the better you become as a writer the more you feel a need to stretch yourself in more difficult ways, the more bizarre and complex a character you must create? I've always wondered how you came to understand the character, at what point you understood his motivations, why a woman wore the color cherry red, what it was that illuminated their world. How do you get there?

Well, it does seem to me that the only way you can get there is through observation. I don't think there is any other route. And what you observe is not quite like just meeting someone on a train, having a conversation and then going away. I mean, really, it's a kind of adding up of people you notice. I think there's something *in* writers of fiction that makes them notice things and store them away all the time. You *notice* the cherry red. Writers of fiction are collectors of useless information. They are the opposite of good, solid, wise citizens who collect good information and put it to good use. Fiction writers remember tiny little details, some of them almost malicious, but very telling. It's a way of endlessly remembering. A face comes back after years and years and years, as though you've taken a photograph. It's as though you have, for the moment, thought: "I know that person very well." You could argue that you have some extraordinary insight, but actually it's just a very hard-working imagination. It's almost like a stress in you that goes on, nibbling and nibbling, gnawing away at you, in a *very* inquisitive way, wanting to know. And of course while all that's happening you're stroking in the colors, putting a line here and a line there, creating something which moves further and further away from the original. The truth emerges, the person who is created is a different person altogether—a person in their own right.

You've said that when you start a story, rather than starting with language, the story often begins with a physical event, something you see or overhear which ignites something in you.

Often it does occur like that, but the truth is that stories begin in all kinds of ways. With a remembered schoolteacher, or someone who might later have had something to do with your life, or some unimportant occurrence. You begin to write and in the process of writing it is often the case that whatever it was that started you off gets lost. On other occasions, stories simply come out of nowhere: you never discover the source. I remember being on a train and I was perhaps walking down to the bar when I noticed a woman and a boy traveling together. He was in his school uniform and she was clearly in charge of him. I can remember now the fatigue on her face. Afterwards—probably years afterwards—I wrote a story called **"Going Home."**

Do you know how a story is going to end before you write it?

That's what I mean by being able to see round it. I can see approximately—but only very approximately—how it will be. With a novel I can't even do that. A novel is like a cathedral and you really can't carry in your imagination the form a cathedral is to take. I like the inkling, the shadow, of a new short story. I like the whole business of establishing its point, for although a story need not have a plot it must have a point. I'm a short-story writer, really, who happens to write novels. Not the other way around.

Have you been particularly pleased with any of your novels?

No, I'm not terribly pleased with anything.

Have you surprised yourself with the way any of them have turned out?

Yes, mainly because there are an awful lot of changes. Your own standpoint, and the importance of certain characters, seem to change as you write a novel; some characters become very big, and some characters become very small, and some incidents don't occur at all. None of that happens so much with short stories. Short stories tend to be more predictable because you know approximately where you're going, so there's not so much alteration. You surprise yourself only when you realize that you've been doing it wrong. That's what I mean by experimenting, and also by lack of confidence—if you don't allow yourself to be wrong, you're not going to get anywhere. In a way, you're always trying to be wrong. You're trying to do it in a wrong way in order to find the right way of doing it, so you can then say, "*That*, at least, is not possible." It's all very exhausting.

Do you have to concentrate very hard when you try to gauge the motivations or imagine the interior workings of some particularly complex character—for example, the teenage boy in The Children of Dynmouth—*or does it come easily?*

No, I don't think that that is a matter of concentration at all. I think in fact, that oddly enough, if you try to concentrate and are too intense about it, you lose it. I think you have to be much more relaxed and loose about it. It's instinctive, and I'm an instinctive writer anyway. I think if I sat down and screwed my eyes up and *thought* too hard about what a psychopath is like, it wouldn't work. I prefer to let things take me by surprise. It's rather like wondering casually why a friend suddenly behaves in a strange way, or in a way you didn't imagine him capable of.

You're very good at middle-aged women, their daydreams and so on. Sometimes I wonder if you weren't a middle-aged woman in a former life.

I don't know if you've noticed that when middle-aged women talk they are particularly revealing. And I'm quite a good listener. I sometimes become fascinated by what a woman is telling me—something which, in fact, is rather dull and mundane. It's her selection of detail that's interesting, why she chooses this rather than that, and why she wants to tell a stranger. Men do exactly the same thing, of course. Well, the thing is, the people are there. They are there to be seen, all you have to do is wonder about them. I think you can understand a psychopath. It's not particularly that I'm interested in that stratum of society; it's just I've always found heroes, and perhaps glamorous people, to be too glittery. Quite often, in fact, I do write about people who are rather glamorous—middle-aged women very heavily made-up—but that glamor is a false one: I find it interesting because of that.

If I may reduce your work to being about *something, it seems to be about people coming to terms with things. I wonder if you think that's right, first of all, and if you think that is the ultimate thing that can be done with what we have, a coming to terms, or an acceptance?*

Do you mean a sort of settling for second best?

Sometimes that could be the way it's taken, but at other times indeed much more than that, that it is in fact a tremendous act of bravery to accept in this way.

Yes, I suppose that does come in a bit. I don't think on my part it's a conscious conclusion. I don't think I ever think like that when I'm writing the piece of a story which implies that people come to terms with something. I'm still working out what they would do, still believing that this is what happens because I know it happens. That is probably the difference between an instinctive writer—I don't know what other word to use—and an intellectual writer. I have no messages or anything like that; I have no philosophy and I don't impose on my characters anything more than the predicament they find themselves in. That seems to me to be quite enough to go along with. I'm known for not commenting very much, for keeping myself fairly quiet. Even that is not a choice; it is not something I have chosen to do, it is just the way I do it. If I tried to do it some other way, I think it would be a mess. I simply stick to my own particular piece of knitting.

Do you agree with what some critics have called a sense of "hopelessness" in your characters?

Well, some characters are pretty hopeless in themselves. Others find themselves in hopeless situations. There doesn't seem to be very much going for them, as it were; that's also true. But generally speaking that's true in life. There is a certain amount of hope, not an endless supply. It's not as rose-tinted a world as most people would like it to be. But the people in my stories and novels are not ragingly desperate; they have, as you said a moment ago, come to terms, and coming to terms in itself is quite an achievement. There's not a total absence of hope there. It's not an entirely pessimistic view, I think. In fact, it's even faintly optimistic.

I read somewhere that you describe yourself as a melancholic; how does this manifest itself? Is it a state, a temperament through which you write?

I don't ever recall referring to myself as a melancholic— I would rephrase that, with the chicken farming too. A melancholic chicken farmer suggests suicide to me. I don't think you can write fiction unless you know something about happiness, melancholy—almost everything which human nature touches. I doubt that an overwhelmingly jolly, optimistic person has ever been an artist of any short. You are made melancholy, more than anything, by the struggle you have with words—the struggle you have with trying to express what sometimes resists expression. It can be a melancholy business. As a fiction writer, every time you go out into the day you've also got to experience the bleakness of night. If I were purely a melancholic I don't think I'd write at all. I don't think writers can allow themselves the luxury of being depressives for long. Writers are far less interesting than everyone would have them. They have typewriters and will travel. They sit at desks in a clerk-like way. What may or may not be interesting is

what we write. The same applies to any artist; we are the tools and instruments of our talent. We are outsiders; we have no place in society because society is what we're watching, and dealing with. Other people make their way in the world. They climb up ladders and get to the top. They know ambition, they seek power. I certainly don't have any ambitions, nor am I in the least interested in power. I don't think fiction writers tend to be. Certainly not as a civil servant may be, or an engineer. Fiction writers don't *want* in the same way; their needs are different. Personally, I like not being noticed. I like to hang about the shadows of the world both as a writer and as a person; I dislike limelight, and the center of things is a place to watch rather than become involved in. I dwell upon it rather than in it; I wonder about what occurs there and record what I see because that seems to be my role. I get matters down onto paper and impose a pattern, and all of that is a fairly ordinary activity, or so it seems to be. If I could analyze all this, if I could really talk about it, I don't think I'd be writing at all. It's invading the gray-haired woman, the child, the elderly man, that keeps me going and delights me; but I don't know how I do it. And I believe that mystery is essential. Again, if you now ask me why, I won't be able to tell you.

Archibald MacLeish once accused both Fitzgerald and Hemingway of behaving like glorified journalists dancing around outside of what they saw as being "ultimate reality" and taking notes. MacLeish claims that the important thing for a writer is not curiosity and observation, but deep knowledge of one's self. What do you make of that?

What is very interesting about that is when he talks about making notes he makes it sound rather ridiculous; but in fact notes are made simply because people forget things. I don't use notes very often, but writers have at all times made notes in order to remind themselves of something. When he talks about "dancing around the outside" he actually describes *exactly* what fiction writers have to do. You've got to be like a journalist from a newspaper, and personally the last person I want to know about is myself. I always think a very good example of an artist is Henry Moore. Henry Moore was somebody who disliked being in the limelight. Even to look at him, you felt that he seemed to be pressing backwards, always in a hurry to get back to his work. He was opposed to the artist as represented by the flamboyant, noisy figure. I am totally uninterested in myself.

Critics have been incredibly supportive and enthusiastic about your work. How do you react to that? Do you trust them?

When I was younger, like all young writers, I used to read the critics, but I don't read them much anymore. So if you told me that they'd all turned savagely against me, I wouldn't have known. If I'm abroad and a batch of notices arrives, then it's quite fun to read them all, but I never go out now and buy a newspaper specially on the day something is published. Sometimes when critics say a lot of nice things they have actually got hold of the wrong end of the stick, just as somebody who is very hostile may have too. But that doesn't mean that the sweet critic is any better than the other one. There are particularly good critics who are not always favorable, who are very balanced, and sharp, and know what they're doing, and you know they're quite right. But nearly always you would have been more severe yourself.

What do you think are your own shortcomings as a writer?

That tends to bring us back to analysis. I most certainly have shortcomings, but I don't particularly want to identify them.

Are you writing at full throttle at the moment?

Oh, no. I would never use that description. A very, very *slow* throttle of some sort. No, you can never tell, actually, whether or not you might have lost your grasp entirely. Only time can tell you that. I'm a great believer in looking back on things. In retrospect, experiences, like everything else, change; it's the same with writing. I write very swiftly, but also very slowly, because I hold on to things for a very long time. I will put away a short story when I've written it, and not look at it for months and months. When I take it out again and read it, it's sometimes as though I am just another reader. I'll do some rewriting and put it away again. That's where confidence works the other way round. You must have confidence in your skill as a craftsman, I think. Not confidence that you're going to be right every time; but you have to be confident in saying to yourself, "Only I really know how this works, because I made it."

Do you think it takes anything different to become a writer now than it did when you were starting out?

It shouldn't. If you've got something to say as a writer, as James Thurber would put it, it somehow should come out. I don't really think that it's become any more difficult for writers, rather the opposite, really.

So you don't think literature has been much diminished by the glare of TV, cinema, video, and by entertainment hunger?

I think there is a danger of that. In a way it depends on your mood how you answer that question; if you're cross about it then you tend to say, "I wish there was more seriousness about." And by serious writing I mean everything from Thomas Hardy to P. G. Wodehouse, from Chekhov to Sean O'Faolain. Instead of that, there's now the pressure of fashion in literature, and I imagine that is something that's demanded by your entertainment-hungry public. Fashion belongs on a coat hanger. In literature—in any art—it's destructive. Some of the prizes that have crept on to the British literary scene have made rather a circus of literature. It's nice to win them, and all money freely given to the arts is a good thing. But prizes and best-seller lists and fashion tend to *tell* people what to read, and it's discovering what to read for yourself that lends reading half its pleasure. Glamor and glossiness are not what literature is about. Literature is Thomas Hardy, who wasn't fashionable in the least. He ate his guts out in Dorset, and was miser-

able, and produced marvelous books; in the end, only the books matter. Nowadays, books tend to be shoveled into a chat-show wheelbarrow, more talked-about than read.

Has there been any time when you've been able to figure out what it is that you want to do as a writer, what you're aiming at?

Well, to be completely honest, I wouldn't have any such aim at all. I don't have any general ambition. I don't really want to make any statement. I see the writing of a story as creating an impression, and that impression is going to communicate itself to somebody else. That's all I seek to do.

Robert E. Rhodes   (essay date 1989)

SOURCE: "'The Rest is Silence': Secrets in Some William Trevor Stories," in *New Irish Writing: Essays in Memory of Raymond J. Porter,* edited by James D. Brophy and Eamon Grennan, Twayne Publishers, 1989, pp. 35-53.

[*Rhodes is an American educator and literary critic with a special interest in Irish literature. In the following excerpt, he explores the theme of secrecy in Trevor's stories, asserting that it is "a means of directing our attention to his most important fictional concern: the mystery of human personality, behind which may also preside some assumptions, conscious or otherwise, about dimensions of the Irish personality."*]

Prior to the 1986 collection *The News from Ireland and Other Stories,* William Trevor had published five collections of short stories. The first collection (1967) contained a single Irish story, **"Miss Smith."** The four succeeding volumes had an average of four Irish stories each. In *News,* seven of the twelve are Irish: the title story, **"The Property of Colette Nervi," "Bodily Secrets," "Virgins," "Music," "Two More Gallants,"** and **"The Wedding in the Garden."** Published almost simultaneously in the *New Yorker* were two thus far uncollected Irish stories, **"The Third Party"** and **"Kathleen's Field,"** and not many months later, **"Events at Drimaghleen"** appeared in *Grand Street.*

In these recent Irish works, Trevor has dropped a former major preoccupation, stories of the contemporary Troubles seen largely from an Anglo-Irish perspective, though the title story of *News* is an Anglo-Irish story, telling of the Great Famine and exploring something of the antecedents for the modern conflict. But for the most part these recent stories continue the types of settings, characters, and themes that are familiar to Trevor's regular readers: class and religious stress, rural isolation and loneliness, provincial drabness, thwarted love, the persistence of the past into the present, imaginations fed by films and shallow fiction, the vanity of human wishes.

On the whole, most reviewers of *News* found the collection admirable and frequently singled out one or more of the Irish stories for something that distinguishes them from the English stories. Virtually alone amongst the reviewers, John Dunne had serious reservations, noting that "generally [Trevor's] work ambles along in a pleasant nondescript manner which, for me at any rate, seldom elicits any emotional response at all ["Good and Averagely Good," *Books Ireland,* September, 1986].

It is true that Trevor's stories are usually understated. For example, one will search in vain in *News* for striking or even memorable tropes, their stock being pretty much depleted by the following: "His hair was like smooth lead . . . ," ". . . his face . . . exploding like a volcano . . . ," "The moon that was Thelma's face . . . ," "his rounded hill of a stomach . . . ," and ". . . short hair as spiky as a hedgehog's." Nor is Trevor the exegete's dream in being a technical experimenter in point of view, for example. He's almost always in total charge as narrator and takes us where we need to go either through omniscience or through easy access to the consciousness of one character or another, with occasional irony deflecting a straightforward view of things. The reader seldom has problems with structure: Trevor stories ordinarily begin in a present and move without interruption to a conclusion; sometimes they open in a present and return to a past; sometimes they alternate between the present and the past; but very seldom do they give us difficulty in knowing where we are and when and why we are there.

But this very lack of difficulty—what Dunne calls "a pleasant nondescript manner"—a certain reticence on Trevor's part, leads, upon consideration, to an important motif that ties these several stories together—his use of secrets as a plot device and as a means of directing our attention to his most important fictional concern: the mystery of human personality, behind which may also preside some assumptions, conscious or otherwise, about dimensions of the Irish personality. Thus, "plot" and "character" and "style" are somewhat congruent and work together toward the presentation of theme. Secrets are of course not exclusive to Trevor, nor are they new to these stories; a quick review of Trevor's earlier Irish stories turns up, for example, **"Autumn Sunshine," "Beyond the Pale," "Saints," "Attracta," "Mr. McNamara," "The Raising of Elvira Tremlett," "The Time of Year," "Miss Smith," "Death in Jerusalem,"** and **"Teresa's Wedding,"** among others that are activated by secrets. But their persistence in the present set of stories finally claims extended attention and a firm reason for reading Trevor more carefully than may have been the case in the past.

On the face of it, "secrets" are basic to almost any story; indeed, simple plot hinges upon secrets—we keep reading because we want to know what happens next. Not every story has secrets—more ordinarily considered—kept or disclosed by characters. Those that do, however, probably involve readers more than those that do not; as insiders, when a secret is shared with a character or characters or the reader, there is compelling dramatic irony, and the tension that is part of the story communicates itself readily to readers. Certainly secrets in a story can generate tremendous energy by giving, for example, an added erot-

ic charge to the secrecy of a love affair. And secrets may be part of the dramatization of deceit, discretion or indiscretion, the role of knowledge, the problem of communication, the conflict of illusion and reality.

To go an important step further, they add to the stories something of the mystery of human character, a quality that is at the heart of the two most important stories considered here, **"The News from Ireland"** and **"Events at Drimaghleen,"** both works that probe the difficult and perhaps the impossibility of one's ever truly penetrating the enigma of others, especially, perhaps, if the others are Irish. Thus, the title story, **"The News from Ireland,"** about news that is only partially or imperfectly conveyed, serves admirably if ironically as a representative title for the seven Irish stories of the collection and the three additional stories; and **"Events at Drimaghleen,"** the most recent of the stories, concludes the framing introduced by **"News."** Before turning to these two stories, a handful of observations on variations that Trevor has rung on the theme in the other stories will suggest its ubiquity and importance to Trevor.

Of the eight stories, four dramatize events in which secrets are kept. **"Kathleen's Field,"** a title richly evocative of the possibilities of an allegorical reading for a story predicated on a characteristic Irish land hunger, tells of the innocent Kathleen, held hostage to the lechery of her employer by her fear that revelation of his lechery will mean that her father will forfeit the land he covets. The other three stories of this set have stories that end in marriages. In **"The Property of Colette Nervi,"** Trevor reprises his familiar Irish rural isolation and emotional deprivation, and ends with a marriage under the shady circumstances of secrets kept about the stolen property of the French Colette Nervi, whose brief intrusion into an Irish backwater precipitates events. With a strong subtext of class and religious differences as the source for secrecy, **"The Wedding in the Garden"** sees maid Dervla remaining in the service of the family of her lost love after he marries another so that she may haunt his happiness with her daily presence and the secret of what had been between them. Like **"The Wedding in the Garden," "Bodily Secrets"** has deterrents to marriage in religious and class differences, but they are overcome by the middle-aged couple's maturity, intelligence, and determination, traits that also enable them to negotiate secrets and to secure a workable conspiracy of silence over the husband's hidden homosexuality and Norah, the wife's, unwillingness to expose her aging body's loss of beauty.

In all of these stories, by having secrets remain concealed, Trevor has sacrificed at least one dramatic confrontation scene in each that might have eventuated in climax, resolution, and easing of conflict. Instead, secrets—Kathleen's guilty one, for example, or Norah's vain one—remain intact; we share Kathleen's silent despair and perhaps Norah's relief, and whatever tension is generated by the secrets becomes all the more powerful for remaining untold.

"Two More Gallants," the first of four stories in which secrets are revealed—and Trevor's contribution to the

James Joyce centenary observances—is perhaps the slightest of Trevor's recent Irish stories. It dramatizes the clandestine means by which a prideful student, Heffernan, exposes the pretensions of a Joycean scholar, Professor Flacks, himself hubris-ridden enough not to have penetrated the secret scheme against him. Given the love triangle suggested by its title, **"The Third Party"** is charged with secrets—the very conduct of the affair itself, the concealed natures of the lovers from one another, the revelation by the husband of his wife's true nature (or is it?) to her lover, the conundrum of the wife's ability to bear a child, for example—we are left pondering, even after certain revelations. In **"Music"** thirty-three-year-old Justin has built a fantasy life on the fiction of a musical talent fostered by a kindly surrogate mother, Aunt Roche, and father—a priest, Father Finn—as he in turn provides them with a surrogate son and pretext for a family, the existence of which has been kept secret from Justin's real family. When guilt drives Aunt Roche to confess the subterfuge to Justin, he pushes away her imploring hands and curses her as he leaves. In **"Virgins"** Trevor knits with elaborate care the friendship of two adolescent girls in a provincial Irish town. He then intrudes into their relationship the delicate but powerfully vain Ralph de Courcy, whose manipulation of the feelings of both girls causes them to keep secrets from one another, then to reveal them, and then, even forty years later, when they meet again, to part with wordless regret and "shrugging smile."

In these four stories where secrets are revealed, Trevor gains some of the dramatic confrontation scenes and sense of climax that he sacrifices when secrets remain concealed. For example, Heffernan's revelation of his manipulation of Professor Flacks results in Flacks's public disclosure and humiliation; and Aunt Roche's confession leads to Justin's private agony. Interestingly, revelation of secrets is no more of a guarantee of a happy ending than their being kept intact, a conclusion that accords with Trevor's persistent rueful appraisal of human affairs.

After several stories about the contemporary troubles in Ireland, very often told from an Anglo-Irish viewpoint, Trevor appeared to write a coda in the 1983 novel, *Fools of Fortune,* where the Anglo-Irish are anomalies in an Ireland they had ruled for 300 years, vestiges only, anachronisms, but therefore all the more reason for them to have won Trevor's understanding, compassion, and even admiration. With **"The News from Ireland,"** however, he again takes up their story, this time becoming more judgmental of the Ascendancy Anglo-Irish and finding in their lives greater responsibility for Ireland's present ills than he had earlier. Additionally, the story provides Trevor with the opportunity to deploy subtly the uses and effects of secrets in a more complex fashion than we have yet seen.

In **"News,"** we are with the Pulvertaft family at an unnamed Anglo-Irish Big House, one not much different in kind and significance from the restored Glencorn Lodge of Trevor's **"Beyond the Pale"** or the Carraveagh of his **"The Distant Past"** or the Kilneagh of *Fools of Fortune,* for example. This is familiar territory to Trevor, except that it takes place in 1847-48, near the end of the Great Famine, the single most important fact—and source of the most important mystery—at the heart of the story.

The Pulvertafts of Ipswich had come to Ireland in 1839, on the death of old Hugh Pulvertaft, to assume responsibility for the estate and to restore the derelict house, symbol both of British dominance and British distance from actual Irish circumstances. Relative newcomers to Ireland, the Pulvertafts have moved from "surprise and dismay at the Irish" to "making allowances for the natives" to "coming to terms" and—a leitmotiv in the story—"learning to live with things," stages more or less followed by protagonist Anna Maria Heddoe, freshly arrived in Ireland in 1847 as family governess on her own journey to accommodation with Ireland and the Irish.

For the most part, the Pulvertafts, decent and wishing to be responsible but undiscerning—much of the Irish situation is simply a closed case, a "secret" to them—and therefore ineffective at relieving local distress, live as if they were still in Ipswich. Indeed, much of the energy and tension in the story are generated and sustained by the contrast between the naive mentality of the Pulvertafts and the Irish realities outside. The contrast is between what Mrs. Pulvertaft thinks of as "dear, safe, uncomplicated England," reembodied in their Irish estate, and the physically proximate but psychically remote, untidy, and very complicated mass starvation outside the estate precincts.

A high stone wall surrounds Big House and grounds. A typical drawing-room scene discovers the Irish maids fastening the shutters and drawings the blinds, further isolating and insulating the family. Within, three marriageable daughters ponder possible husbands. The sole son, young George Arthur, considers an army career in distant India while innocently but ignorantly wondering if the Irish "poor people," not far removed, eat their babies. Mrs. Pulvertaft, "round and stout," has a daily nap. Mr. Pulvertaft, with gleaming boots, presides at table and painful piano recitals. And Trevor ironically limns starvation without by repletion within: Mrs. Pulvertaft's daily bouts of indigestion, for example, or the leftover food sometimes dispatched down the lavatory or the champagne at daughter Charlotte's wedding to Captain Roche.

Underpinning the essential uselessness of the Pulvertafts' role in alleviating famine starvation is the first of two major symbols in the story. Historically accurate in type, weaving its way throughout the story is a symptomatic and symbolic road under construction, the Pulvertaft contribution to the usually useless work projects under British aegis that proliferated by thousands throughout the Famine years. Its purpose (other than providing make-work) a mystery, it circles the estate within its walls, both further enclosing the Big House and replicating the circle that Anna Maria traces in moving from one kind of stranger in Ireland to another. This road that goes nowhere occupies the thoughts of the Pulvertafts as they plan scenic vistas and "ornamental seats" on its circular route. "What could be nicer," muses Mr. Pulvertaft, ". . . than a picnic of lunch by the lake, then a drive through the silver birches, another pause by the abbey, continuing by the river for a mile, and home by Bright Purple Hill? This road, Miss Heddoe, has become my pride." But Fogarty, the astute butler, knows the truth of it; "the useless folly of the road," he exclaims. And of Erskine, the one-armed former British army officer who hates the Irish but as estate manager has the job of overseeing the roadwork, we are told: "Leading nowhere, without a real purpose, the estate road is unnecessary and absurd, but he accepts his part in its creation. It is ill fortune that people have starved because a law of nature has failed them, it is ill fortune that he has lost a limb and seen a military career destroyed; all that must be accepted also."

Under all these circumstances, with a family nearly dedicated to not getting the truth, it would be difficult enough for anyone wanting to receive the real news from Ireland, and Anna Maria Heddoe wants to. To the difficult situation is added Fogarty, nearly the presiding genius in the story; more than a little sinister, moving always in secrecy and penetrating the secrets of others while husbanding his own; Protestant but still inimical to both the family and to Anna Maria. For example, he keeps from the Pulvertafts what he wishes he might say to them: "that their fresh decent blood is the blood of the invader though they are not themselves invaders, that they perpetuate theft without being theives." Spying on the governess, he then keeps his thoughts about her from his one confidante, his sister, the cook. After he has read some of Anna Maria's own secrets about the family, her role in the house, Ireland and the Irish, committed to her journal, and Anna Maria discovers that he has, he asks her to keep his invasion of her privacy secret from the Pulvertafts, to which she rejoins that she has no wish to share secrets with him. And it is Fogarty, as we shall see, who mediates, only to confound rather than to clarify, between both Pulvertafts and Anna Maria and the key episode—and symbol—in the story, the Irish infant with Christ's stigmata.

Governess Anna Maria Heddoe, twenty-five or six, with "nervous" features, "severe" hair, and "dowdy" clothes, is a "young woman of principle and sensitivity, stranger and visitor to Ireland," we are told almost at once. That Anna Maria wants to learn—to hear and understand the news from Ireland—is clear enough. That gimlet-eyed observer of her life, Fogarty, tells her that her "fresh sharp eye has needled" things out. But journal entries of 17 and 20 October 1847 suggest Anna Maria's limitations and presage her eventual acceptance of enigma without understanding it. Her opening observation on 20 October is: "I am not happy here. I do not understand this household, neither the family nor the servants. This is the middle of my third week, yet I am still in all ways at a loss." Yet later, under the same date, while reporting Mrs. Pulvertaft's insistence that she get to know the family better, she confides that, "I felt, to tell the truth, that I knew the Pulvertafts fairly well already."

Anna Maria's unconscious confusion about what she does or does not know establishes the context for introducing—in her journal entries for both 17 and 20 October—the second major, much more ambiguous, even mysterious, symbol, one that comes from beyond this local pale

in a piece of news from Fogarty. With "grisley smile" and seeming "faintly sinister" to Anna Maria, he reports to her of an Irish child born with Christ's stigmata on hands and feet; and he tells her the local priest's opinion is that "so clearly marked a stigma has never before been known in Ireland. The people consider it a miracle, a sign from God in these distressful times". But a sign—a symbol—of what? "Stigmata" clearly suggests one thing; the priest's word, "stigma," another. Have we a sign of God's displeasure with the Irish or a mark of His benign concern for His Irish children?

Anna Maria is "amazed" that the news does not even surprise Fogarty, not because he believes in God's visitations to papists but because he believes that the distraught parents, driven to blasphemy and barbarity by the starvation deaths of their seven other children, have themselves inflicted the marks of the stigmata in the hope of obtaining food for themselves. Given its immense significance to Anna Maria, she is early on upset that the Pulvertafts never so much as mention the occurrence, and that when they do learn of it they are totally untouched and accept Fogarty's explanation of a hoax.

On the one hand, Anna Maria seems to accept the stigmata as a sign of God's presence; on the other, when the child dies and Fogarty reports that people in the soup line and on the road are "edgy" because they feel "that Our Lord has been crucified again," Anna Maria retorts "ridiculous!" Five months later, she thinks again of an "infant tortured with Our Saviour's wounds," a seeming acceptance of Fogarty's theory of cruel fraud. Wondering what the Irish have done to displease God—in a way she would not have done only months before—she admits to herself that the Irish have not been easy to rule, that they have not obeyed the laws, and that their superstitious worship is a sin.

These acknowledgments complete a desensitization process and ready Anna Maria to accept the marriage proposal of the insensitive Erskine, British estate manager, and to move closer to the company of the Pulvertafts. At the very end, bringing the story full circle in its language, within which are enclosed many mysteries—never mind "news"—Trevor writes: "Stranger and visitor, she has written in her diary the news from Ireland. Stranger and visitor, she has learned to live with things." Weeping and sick at heart because of her perceived loss of her sensitivity and, perhaps, the will to try to penetrate the mystery of the child and thus the mystery of her situation in Ireland; because of her compromise of principle by marriage to an unprincipled man; and because of her symbolic union with the Pulvertafts by an expected invitation to dine at their table as Mrs. Erskine, Anna Marie capitulates and rejects further pursuit of understanding.

Reminding us of "news," the "events" of **"Events at Drimaghleen"**—three violent deaths in the McDowd and Butler families and their discovery and first report—occur on the night of Tuesday and the morning of Wednesday, 21 and 22 May 1985. But the "truth" of them is ultimately as much a mystery, a secret, as the circumstances surrounding the infant bearing Christ's stigmata. As the local folks in **"News"** are seized by that confounding occurrence, the neighboring folks in **"Events"** find these three deaths more appalling and shocking and horrible than anything that has ever occurred in their area.

A newsworthy event in a sparsely populated area, one version of it is deduced by local garda Superintendent O'Kelly, supported by the people of Drimaghleen, and reported in the Irish media. A second, more lurid version later appears in an English newspaper's Sunday supplement. Both versions are suspect. Skeptical readers may well be meant by Trevor to ponder the truth of both versions, to examine the evidence themselves, and to ask, as the evidence or lack thereof suggests they should, what Trevor's reasons might be for continuing rather than revealing the mystery at the heart of events. The speed with which Superintendent O'Kelly reaches his conclusions is based on much less than complete observation and his reading of relatively simple personalities, this relative lack of complexity perhaps deepening the mystery rather than simplifying it. What we know of the three dead people is not complex: Mrs. Butler is fiercely possessive of her son, who is spoiled and weak and who has formed a relationship with the passive Maureen. The Sunday supplement version is based on new evidence, which may or may not be valid, some faulty observation, and a different rendering of personalities.

As Trevor lays out his story, personality and locale suggest something of the difficulty in getting at the truth. For example, in describing the unwillingness of Mr. McDowd, the father of one of the victims, to speak to an outsider photographer, Trevor provides much of the deterrence to arriving at the truth: "He lifted a hand and scratched at his grey, ragged hair, which was his way when he wished to disguise bewilderment. Part of his countryman's wiliness was that he preferred outsiders not to know, or deduce, what was occurring in his mind," and we as readers also remain outsiders in many ways.

McDowd's reticence, indeed, distrust—his wife shares it abundantly and, we may assume, the other countryfolk do as well—has been nurtured in his isolation from his neighbors. Trevor is on familiar and sure ground here and establishes it as firmly as he ever has: "Drimaghleen, Kilmona and Mountcroe," he writes, "formed a world that bounded the lives of the people of the Drimaghleen farms. Rarely was there occasion to venture beyond it to the facilities of a town that was larger—unless the purpose happened to be a search for work or the first step on the way to exile." Each area's particulars are set out to underscore isolation of families from one another and from the larger world of Ireland and beyond, isolation that creates wariness. Mountcroe, the largest, has the school, the creamery, the butcher shop, the hardware store and a grocery store, an abandoned cinema, and it is where the area men get drunk, though they may have a few bottles of stout in the bar adjoining the grocery in smaller Kilmona, where the church is also located. Drimaghleen itself is merely a townland marked only by a crossroads, and the small farms of the area are scattered miles apart over the boglands.

Wednesday, 22 May 1985, begins like most days for the sixtyish older McDowds. He dresses and goes out to fetch the cows for milking; she washes, puts on the kettle, and calls their twenty-five-year-old daughter, Maureen, the only one of five children still at home. Repeated callings jar McDowd into awareness that Maureen's bicycle is not in its usual place; and when his wife announces that Maureen's bed has not been slept in they know without saying so that she has not come back from the Butler farm, where she'd gone the evening before to see Lancy Butler, spoiled son of a widowed mother, and each fears that Maureen has run off with the feckless Lancy. And since everyone in the area knows—knowledge essential to local acceptance of the official version of events—that Lancy has been spoiled to the point of uselessness by a stereotypical possessive Irish mother, there is apparently good reason for the McDowds to have opposed the relationship as much as Mrs. Butler has. And so they set off to the Bulter farm four miles away.

What they find in the Butler farmyard is revealed serially. Mrs. McDowd sees Maureen's dead body by the pump, her bicycle and two dead rabbits nearby. Mr. McDowd discovers the dead Mrs. Butler in a doorway several yards off, her face blown away. Then, near Maureen's body but behind two barrels, Mrs. McDowd finds Lancy's body with the Butler shotgun nearby. Neither now nor later are specific distances given—only "another part of the yard" or "a yard or so away" (twice) or "nor far from it"—so that more exact knowledge of the physical relationships of the bodies and thus possible fuller knowledge of the course of events is withheld. We learn eventually that Lancy and Maureen had often taken the shotgun and, with Lancy peddling Maureen's bicycle—Lancy having none of his own—and Maureen riding sidesaddle on the rear carrier, holding, we might reasonably infer, as does the Sunday supplement account, the shotgun, gone off to shoot rabbits; so that when they returned to the farmyard from the evening's expedition it was entirely probable that Maureen carried both the rabbits found near her and the shotgun.

"O'Kelly of the garda arrived at a swift conclusion," Trevor tells us. Knowing, as do the people in the area, of Mrs. Butler's possessiveness of her son, her determination that no one should take her from him, and her reputed oddness and rages, O'Kelly concludes that Mrs. Butler had shot Maureen; that Lancy had then wrenched the gun from her and by accident or design had discharged it and killed his mother; that Lancy, never a strong man and unable to face what has happened, killed himself. These conclusions, "borne out by the details of the yard, satisfied O'Kelly . . ." Drimaghleen folk arrived at the same conclusion, and the matter is settled. It will not do.

In 1985, even in remote rural Ireland, a case of this magnitude would surely result in certain standard procedures. However, there are no autopsies; there is no ballistics test; there is no clarification of distances; there is no reenactment of events; there is no information on the proximity and trajectory of the three shots; there are no data on what an examination of the wounds might reveal; there is no revelation to us—or, as far as we know, to O'Kelly—about the possibility of Lancy having shot himself—where?

—with the shotgun. There is no consideration of finger-prints or their location on the gun, though later we learn that those of all three victims are there, blurred and in several different locations, this discovery seeming to be the sole concession to normal procedures in such cases. This discovery is also natural enough since Maureen carried the gun, Lancy used it to shoot rabbits, and, since it was the Butler family gun, Mrs. Butler would have had occasion to handle it even apart from O'Kelly's deduction that she handled it to shoot Maureen. Even setting aside the absence of forensic ballistics, chemistry, medicine, and psychiatry, there are problems with the officials story.

This version holds that Mrs. Butler shot Maureen. If so, how did the gun come into her possession on this occasion? Presumably from Lancy, who, in this account, shot his mother, whether by accident or design, when he was wrestling it from her after she'd shot Maureen. But why would Lancy have taken the gun from Maureen, who would have been holding it after the rabbit hunt, and walk—how far? —to his mother with it and allow her to take it and shoot Maureen—how far away? Even if, for some unknown reason, he did let her take it, then take it back and shoot her, why would he walk back to near where Maureen lies dead and shoot himself there? None of these questions is asked by Trevor, and, so far as we know, by O'Kelly either. And none is answered by Trevor.

And so the case is closed, and after mention of the events in the media, quiet again descends on Drimaghleen. For the McDowds, there are letters of sympathy, neighbors call in briefly, and Father Sallins places himself on call. But heartbroken, inconsolable, haunted, the McDowds retreat into their customary silence and isolation. May passes into October, when strangers come into the farmyard in a red car.

Trevor's words are right for this intrusion—the car "edged its way"; it is like "some cautious animal"; it has a "slow creeping movement"—because the McDowds do not welcome outsiders and are not only reticent but belligerent and threatening. Doubtless, they would have reacted this way with any strangers but these and their mission are charged with provocation. Jeremiah Tyler, from Dublin, and Hetty Fortune, from England, are photographer and Sunday supplement writer, respectively, and they have come to reopen the case. Trevor's details for them are the right ones to elicit the McDowds' distrust and belligerence. Tyler, seedy and unkempt, "was florid-faced, untidily dressed in dark corduroy trousers and a gabardine jacket. His hair was long and black, and grew coarsely down the sides of his face in two brushlike panels. He had a city voice . . ."

Hetty is somber-faced, wears sunglasses and matching blue shirt and trousers, smokes, speaks with an English accent, and strikes Mrs. McDowd as insincere, an acute appraisal.

Having spent time at the Butler place, they say, and in the area talking with a number of people, they declare repeatedly that the truth of the case has not been established, that they want to talk with the McDowds to help them settle it and have it published together with color pictures. Characteristically, the McDowds resent and resist—until

Hetty mentions a payment in excess of £3,000, when the McDowds, realizing what could be done with the sum to ease their lives, capitulate and agree to talk.

There follows Hetty Fortune's version of events in the Sunday supplement, together with "fashionably faded pictures," interspersed with information supplied by Trevor about the pictures and something of the conduct of the interview and then with the reactions of the McDowds when Father Sallins brings them the newspaper.

This version of events, placed by Hetty Fortune in the context of Ireland's sensational Kerry babies mystery and the Flynn case, suggests that the mystery of this case is typical of what occurs all over Ireland in "small, tucked away farms like the Butlers' and the McDowds'," where "These simple folk . . . of Europe's most western island form limited rural communities that all too often turn in on themselves." Maureen is pictured as "helpful," "special," gentle, sweet-natured, considered by her parents a perfect daughter, a near saint—nothing that we have ever learned of her and somewhat different from the "bitch" her father had called her before the discovery of her body; indeed, "The Saint of Drimaghleen . . . never missed mass in all her twenty-five years."

But, the account adds, she was "young, impetuous, bitterly deprived of the man she loved" and ripe for any action to keep Lancy. Additionally, the newspaper quotes a letter purportedly written by Maureen to Lancy a week before the shootings and found behind a drawer in a table of the Butlers sold at auction, in which she admits that the relationship may be at an end because of the objections of all parents. Deduced from this by Hetty Fortune is Mrs. Butler's knowledge that the affair would soon be over so there would be no reason for her to kill Maureen. If Mrs. Butler did not kill Maureen because she did not need to, who did and what really happened?

> **It seems reasonable to conclude that in the Irish circumstances and characters he has chosen to explore, Trevor has found an unusually rich and natural matrix from which to develop his understated— and sometimes unstated—dramas of character.**
>
> **—Robert Rhodes**

In the revised scenario, Mrs. Butler, rather than acting in jealous rage and shooting Maureen, is instead shot by a Maureen determined not to lose her man. Maureen then shoots Lancy and then herself. This will not do, either. Setting aside, as before, the whole question of forensics and a complete investigation, and setting aside much, if not most, of the revelation of Maureen's saintly character as serving some purpose other than the truth, there are as many flaws in this version as in the original.

Chastising Superintendent O'Kelly on the issue of fingerprints on the gun, Hetty Fortune concludes that Maureen's are there because she carried the gun on returning from hunting rabbits, a reasonable conclusion but one that undercuts her further view that the prints are part of the evidence that Maureen shot Mrs. Butler. There is the question of Maureen's letter to Lancy. Was there in fact such a letter? If so, was it proven—and how and to whom—to be Maureen's? Who, exactly, discovered it and turned it over to Hetty Fortune? Hetty Fortune deduces from this letter that Mrs. Butler knew that the affair was over and thus had no need to kill Maureen, but there is no evidence that Mrs. Butler, knew of the purported letter, one hidden away at that. "It is known," writes Hetty Fortune as part of her scenario, "that Maureen McDowd wept shortly before her death," but we do not in fact know this any more than we know the things claimed to be in the victims' minds. Is the state of Maureen's wound consonant with what is expected in self-inflicted wounds? We do not know. Finally, if Maureen shot Mrs. Butler, then Lancy, and finally herself, how did the gun come to be beside Lancy's body? Did she shoot herself and then toss it there?

On the basis of what we know, this version of events will not wash any more than O'Kelly's and we must ask why Hetty Fortune told it at all. Part of the answer is simply to boost her paper's circulation through the sensationalism of the case—like the Kerry babies and Flynn case. Part seems to be simply to indict O'Kelly and the rural Irish in a particularly invidious fashion. The people are reputed in the article—there is no evidence that this is so—to believe, along with the older McDowds, in Maureen's "unblemished virtue." Thus believing, Hetty Fortune writes, they swept O'Kelly into a similar belief publicly stated, a part, in fact, of a conspiracy of silence to protect against revelation that their saint was only a plaster saint: "Had he publicly arrived at any other conclusion Superintendent O'Kelly might never safely have set foot in the neighborhood of Drimaghleen again, or the village of Kilmona, or the town of Mountcroe. The Irish do not easily forgive the purloining of their latter-day saints."

The story moves to its conclusion amid the spoils purchased with the £3,000, electric stove, carpets, radio, television. Mr. McDowd remains silent. Father Sallins fears that more than household goods have been purchased—more magazine articles, more strangers, perhaps a film, Maureen's nature argued over in books, "the mystery that had been created becoming a legend." And Mrs. McDowd shrills scream after scream.

Having wondered why Superintendent O'Kelly and Hetty Fortune, whose jobs are ostensibly to report accurately "the news from Ireland," arrive at flawed versions, in some ways transparently so, we must also ask why Trevor has withheld the truth not only from his characters but from us. Similarly, we might well ask why the truth about the child with Christ's stigmata is reversed not only from the casual curiosity of the Pulvertafts but from Anna Maria Heddoe, who, up to a point, seeks it assiduously, and from readers.

In the several other stories briefly noted, the truth behind secrets is either known to readers almost from the outset or is eventually plainly displayed or can be divined with some certainty. If Trevor in these other stories has wandered at will in and out of the minds of his characters and has assumed the omniscience that explains and clarifies, why has he not done so with these two? Some obvious answers suggest themselves. For example, Trevor is under no obligation to be consistent in his techniques. Similarly, he is not required to have the same purpose in every story. Again, he as well as we would soon weary of all matters plainly put. Taking this a step further, readers have an obligation to remain alert and to join Trevor in his pursuit of what is elusive in human experience.

This point opens up what may be one reasonably satisfactory reason for Trevor's strategies in these two stories and at least the tentative conclusion that these strategies have helped create the two most interesting of this whole set of stories and some of the best of his work.

Generous in granting interviews, in at least three of them Trevor has marked out his consistent fictional concerns. In [an April 23] 1983 interview for the *Guardian*, Hugh Hebert reports two relevant Trevor observations. First he says, "I think you have to know a tremendous amount about your characters that you never put down on paper. I love cutting things, it's the short story writer in me, and I love taking chances with readers." And then, "I've never been interested in politics. What I'm interested in is what happens to people." A later 1983 interview conducted by Amanda Smith and appearing in *Publishers Weekly* finds Trevor using his novel *Fools of Fortune* to make his point: "I don't really have any heroes or heroines. I don't seem to go in for them. I think I am interested in people who are not necessarily the victims of other people, but simply the victims of circumstance, as they are in *Fools of Fortune*. I'm very interested in the sadness of fate, the things that just happen to people." Finally, in a 1985 interview with Sean Dunne in the *Sunday Tribune*, Trevor says, "I don't like to think too much about where my stories are set—I think they're about people."

There we have some of it: "What I'm interested in is what happens to people"—"I think I am interested in people. . . ."—"I think [my stories are] about people." Secrets, in ways suggested early in this essay, work very well as springs of motivation and action in several ways, and many of these are illustrated in all the stories discussed. But in **"News"** and **"Events"** Trevor has complicated matters because, as he says, he knows more than he says, because he likes to cut things, because, finally, he loves to take "chances with readers."

For the writer who is more interested in people than in, say, plot, and who likes to take chances by "cutting things," chancing that readers will involve themselves, stories in which secrets are revealed give us one level for probing and pondering. Stories in which secrets remain unrevealed by an omniscient narrator and/or by characters and/or lack of evidence force us to some deeper level of thought and, if the chance has succeeded, some profounder sense of human personality and conduct. Perhaps we might say that by mystery—in the case of **"Events"** quite literally a murder mystery—Trevor wishes to illustrate by technique the enigma of human personality that is at the heart of the stories' substance. For instance, why does Superintendent O'Kelly not reveal all that might be revealed? Or, for example, why would Fogarty the butler in **"News"** not tell all that he might and why does Anna Maria Heddoe abort her search for the truth? And so the questions multiply and we touch more deeply than if we were not required to ask because we have been told. Beneath the ordinarily unadorned and plain style of Trevor's stories there are often human enigmas that might give up revelation to those who take Trevor's dare.

The persistence of secrets—of several kinds and at different levels of interpretation—in Trevor's Irish stories leads inevitably to the question: Does Trevor mean that there is something in the Irish personality that is more predisposed to secrecy than in that of other peoples or something in Irish circumstances that create this predisposition?

One possible answer is that Trevor does not find the Irish any more inclined to secrecy than any other people. The closest that he comes to an outright suggestion that there is such an inclination is in **"Events,"** as we have seen, when he tells us of Mr. McDowd that "Part of his countryman's wiliness was that he preferred outsiders not to know, or deduce what was occurring in his mind"; but the same wiliness might be attributed to the Slavic peasant, for example. And Trevor has made some effort to claim universality for at least some of his Irish stories. For example, in an "Author's Note" to *The Distant Past and Other Stories,* Trevor's own selection of his Irish stories, he says of one of them, "Miss Smith," that it "might perhaps have come out of anywhere, but in fact is set in a town in Munster. . . ." Similarly, in the 1985 *Sunday Tribune* interview, he observes, "Even '**The Ballroom of Romance,'** and this might sound strange"—as indeed it does to those who think of **"Ballroom"** as a quintessentially Irish story of isolation, deprivation, and loneliness— "I don't think of as a particularly Irish story—the film [of the story] seems to have gone down just as well in places like Israel and Norway. It has a universality." And there are traits of jealousy and possessiveness, for example, everywhere, and Ireland has no corner on stultifying provincial towns or the yen for more land.

On the other hand, to begin with, the particular circumstances of some of the stories place them ineluctably in Ireland. Some facts of the Great Hunger may be similar to those of other famines, but some of the facts of Ireland's and its consequences are intractably Irish, some analysts even having argued that they have marked the contemporary Irish character. Similarly, for instance, one might argue that it is typical strictly of the Irish-English relationship that a Hetty Fortune would invidiously attack the rural Irish; or that Protestants in Ireland occupy a position utterly unique; or that Ireland's geography and the history of land ownership are sufficiently singular to have created exceptional attitudes toward ownership.

Furthermore, despite what might appear as Trevor's at least implicit wish for a kind of universality to his characters,

and even without an extensive analysis of the Irish personality in search of a penchant for secrecy, we can draw briefly on a handful of commonly held views of the Irish and their uses or nonuses of language to suggest that "secrecy" in its many forms is engrained in the Irish nature.

For example, we can draw on the very fact of the physical isolation of many Irish communities, families, and individuals as a means of explaining—as Hetty Fortune does—a kind of tribal reticence that does not readily yield up its secrets even to other Irish. Carried a step further, it is a commonplace that the Irish as a whole, as a people so long dominated by the British, have been driven to a conspiratorial mode of life in dealing not only with the British but with one another. Thus, in both **"News"** and **"Events,"** for instance, to cite only the Irish authority figures, Fogarty the butler and Superintendent O'Kelly do not tell all that they might to either the other Irish or to the British outsiders.

Taking an antithetical but complementary tack, we can observe that rather than being characterized by reticence, the Irish are more often and more traditionally marked by their loquacity, and loquacity not merely as small talk and chatter, though it is often enough that, too, but as a wondrous if sometimes manipulative way with words, a trait that often manifests itself in talk as performance. And with talk as performance—in addition to the truism for all peoples that merely the existence of verbal fluency has never been a guarantee of its veracity—Irish loquacity, in some of its flights of fancy often takes the form of indirectness, obfuscation, obscurity, ambiguity, innuendo, exaggeration and/or understatement—to say nothing of outright lies—all with the same practical effect of secrecy more strictly conceived.

In a fascinating 1982 essay, "Irish Families," in the collection, *Ethnicity and Family Therapy,* a compendium of studies designed to assist therapists in dealing with family problems by introducing the therapists to the characteristics of different ethnic families, Monica McGoldrick writes:

> The paradox of the general articulateness of the Irish and their inability to express inner feelings can be puzzling for a therapist who may have difficulty figuring out what is going on in an Irish family. . . . Family members may be so out of touch with their feelings that their inexpressiveness in therapy is not a sign of resistance, as it would be for other cultural groups, but rather a reflection of their blocking off inner emotions, even from themselves. Thus, although the Irish have a marvelous ability to tell stories, when it comes to their own emotions, they may have no words. The Irish often fear being pinned down and may use their language and manner to avoid it. The affinity of the Irish for verbal innuendo, ambiguity, and metaphor have [sic] led the English to coin the phrase "talking Irish" to describe the Irish style of both communicating and not communicating at the same time. Some have suggested that, in the extreme, this style of communication is responsible for the high rate of schizophrenia found among the Irish. . . .

It would probably be unwise for a literary study to pursue too far—to say nothing of uncritically accepting—the clinical implications and conclusions of these observations, at least for Trevor's stories, but there is no escaping that a study such as McGoldrick's helps us to understand how and why, perhaps even without his full awareness but simply as something taken as a given, Trevor has infused so many of his characters and situations with the kinds of secrecy we have found. At bottom then, it seems reasonable to conclude that in the Irish circumstances and characters he has chosen to explore, Trevor has found an unusually rich and natural matrix from which to develop his understated—and sometimes unstated—dramas of character.

Francis Doherty   (essay date 1991)

SOURCE: "William Trevor's 'A Meeting in Middle Age' and Romantic Irony," in *Journal of the Short Story in English,* No. 16, Spring, 1991, pp. 19-28.

[*In the following essay, Doherty determines the influence of James Joyce's "A Painful Case" on Trevor's "A Meeting in Middle Age."*]

Many Irish writers have worked the theme of isolation, and William Trevor is one of the present masters. In his novel of 1965, *The Boarding House* (1968), he has his central character, Mr. Bird, the man who runs the boarding house (an analogue for the creative artist as he creates the boarding house as his own work and to suit himself), admit to a specialist's interest in loneliness:

> Mr. Bird said he had studied the conditions of loneliness, looking at people who were solitary for one reason or another as though examining a thing or an insect beneath a microscope. The memory of Mr. Bird was bitter at that moment, and the words he spoke in her mind were unwelcome there, for they were cruel in their wisdom.

About the same time he published a story in *Transatlantic Review* in 1966, **'A Meeting in Middle Age',** which was later published in *The Day We Got Drunk On Cake* in 1967 (and later still selected by Malcolm Bradbury for inclusion in *The Penguin Book of British Short Stories,* 1987, from which quotations will be taken). Here William Trevor seems to bring together his Irishness—in spite of the story's being set in England with English characters—his concern with isolation and a tribute to Joyce.

Close reading of the story shows how some of the effects of this little story come from the suggestions which carry the reader back to Joyce's story from *Dubliners,* 'A Painful Case'. That original story had made its own the use of romance and irony to create a saddened tale of the inability to love and the anguish of despair, as all readers are aware. The multiple ironies which surround and suffocate the central offending figure, Mr Duffy, are now, in turn, called on subtextually to enrich and deepen a later tale on the same theme.

A specialist in isolations, Trevor is able to use a variety of devices to persuade the reader of the ways in which

an individual is locked into his or her world, aching often to escape but condemned to their loneliness. So, it is a little pleasure to watch the invasion of irony in the first paragraph of the story when the verbal forms used suggest, comically enough, that these two complete strangers are singularly united in attitude of mind and commonalty of purpose:

> They did not speak as they marched purposefully: they were strangers to one another, and in the noise and bustle, examining the lighted windows of the carriages, there was little that might constructively be said.

Brought together by the common activity and united in the 'they', this makes them a pair or a couple paradoxically at one in their strangerliness and purposefulness as the sisters in the opening paragraph of, say D.H. Lawrence's *Women in Love*:

> Ursula and Gudrun Brangwen sat one morning in the window-bay of their father's house in Beldover, working and talking. Ursula was stitching a piece of brightly-coloured embroidery, and Gudrun was drawing upon a board which she held on her knee. They were mostly silent, talking as their thoughts strayed through their minds.

Here Lawrence succeeds in giving some sense of how the sisters share certain qualities in common and how close they are in their ability to be at ease and together in this shared 'they'. Trevor, on the other hand, establishes his pair as both parallel and somehow opposite, qualities symbolically represented in their hand luggage:

> They carried each a small suitcase, Mrs da Tanka's of white leather or some material manufactured to resemble it, Mr Mileson's battered and black.

There is comic delight in making the luggage so eloquent, and the speaker's inability or reluctance to distinguish the pretence or factitious in Mrs da Tanka from what might be real is characteristically comic and at the time suggestive of the mystery, eventually unfathomable, in all our encounters with others. But, as in all love stories, there is a meeting of minds, of bodies, of expectations, fantasies, desires, and, taking our cue from the title, we should feel comfortable with verbs which showed us common or shared experiences, thoughts and attitudes. We might even say that we should be more prepared for the joint verbal union of 'they' at the end of the story where two strangers had been brought into a love affair than at the beginning of a non-love story which will turn out to be the enactment of a charade affair which is paid for, a technicality which can subsequently be invoked in divorce proceedings as 'adultery'. So, the fitting union of this couple in all the various ways employed by the first paragraph parodies what we expect of a love story.

The element of parody seems to be intensified when we relate this pair of middle-aged pseudo-lovers to what I take to be their originals, Mr Duffy and Mrs Sinico of 'A Painful Case'. Both men are careful bachelors living in one room, both tidy and orderly men who are at the same time non-sexual and who have a fear of sex. Indeed, Joyce gives us one of the jottings which his hero had written in the 'sheaf of papers which lay in his desk':

> One of his sentences, written two months after his last interview with Mrs Sinico, read: Love between man and man is impossible because there must be no sexual intercourse, and friendship between man and woman is impossible because there must be sexual intercourse.

Mr Mileson's condition is similar, but Trevor's handling of it is lighter, more jocular, with comic undertones:

> In 1931 Mr Mileson had committed fornication with the maid in his parents' house. It was the only occasion, and he was glad that adultery was not expected of him with Mrs da Tanka. In it she would be more experienced than he, and he did not relish the implication. The grill-room was lush and vulgar. 'This seems your kind of place,' Mr Mileson repeated rudely.

The women in both stories are victims of their sexuality. Mrs Sinico is merely an appendage to her husband's life. She is someone in great need of affection, a lonely, sexually empty woman, yet someone whose sexuality is made plain to the reader (and Mr Duffy)—'her astrakhan jacket, moulding a bosom of a certain fullness'—and yet a woman whom her husband has undramatically rejected.

> He had dismissed his wife so sincerely from his gallery of pleasures that he did not suspect that anyone else would take an interest in her.

In a comic version of this, we hear how Mr da Tanka's back had often been turned on Mrs da Tanka (his 'broad back, so fat it might have been padded beneath the skin' had been 'often presented to her' 'he was that kind of man'), and we hear her alliterative account of how weeks passed 'without the exchange of a single significant sentence'. To the hearer, Mr Mileson, again with intended authorial irony, both of the lady's husbands merge into the same man, 'shadowy, silent fellows who over the years had shared this woman with the well-tended hands'.

Drink, too, is a common bond between the stories, tragic in Joyce, comic in Trevor. Mrs Sinico's taking to drink and dying, either by suicide or by accident, under the wheels of a train, is directly related to Mr Duffy's failure to show her any real affection (being a man who reduces intimate conversations which have real potentiality for progression to sexual intercourse to his 'last interview', how could he?). But drink is also part of the configuration of Mr Duffy himself; it is, first, part of his social context, and then, by turning to it after reading the account of the Inquest in the evening paper, it becomes his ironic and unacknowledged tie to Mrs Sinico. Not only is the view from his flat a view 'into the disused distillery', as we hear at the beginning of the story, but we are reminded, after he has read the report, that he gazed into the 'cheer-less evening landscape' where 'the river lay quiet beside the empty distillery'. We are conscious of the intended pain in the Joycean parody of two lovers lying together in peaceful tranquillity, as the writer cashes in some of the ironic value which he has invested in placing in the loca-

tion of Mr Duffy's flat in *Chapelizod*, 'the Chapel of Isol-de', drawing attention, as this indirectly does, to the tragic loves of Tristan and Isolde. More than this, Mr Duffy takes to drink that evening (though genteelly taking two hot punches—which one might take for a cold, 'medici-nally' perhaps—rather than 'huge pint tumblers' which the crude and spitting working-men drink). In the gloom of his reflections in the public-house on Chapelizod Bridge, no doubt affected by the alcohol acting as a depressant, he sympathizes for the first time with the loneliness of the dead woman only to absorb that sympathy instantly into his own self-pity in which he bathes:

> He understood how lonely her life must have been, sitting night after night, alone in that room. His life would be lonely too until he, too, died, ceased to exist, became a memory—if anyone remembered him.

Mr Duffy's internalized self-pity is taken by Trevor and externalized in a comic version when Mrs da Tanka de-flates Mr Mileson:

> 'You should write your memoirs, Mr Mileson. To have seen the changes in your time and never to know a thing about them! You are like an occasional table. Or a coat-rack in the hall of a boarding-house. Who shall mourn at your grave, Mr Mileson?'

Mrs da Tanka drinks, but much more openly, with much more verve and determination, not from desperation or to blot out reality as a substitute for suicide:

> 'Gin and lemon, gin and lemon,' said Mrs da Tanka, matching the words with action: striding to the bar.

The couple sit on 'while she drank many measures of the drink', and, as Mr Mileson's measures are not being count-ed, we presume that he makes do with his single glass of rum, a drink he chose, 'feeling it a more suitable drink though he could not think why'. Both ladies drink; both men are, in theory, non-drinkers.

It might be noted in all this that both authors keep to a formal system of naming their characters, never trans-gressing against the 'Mr' and 'Mrs' formula, the one shocking exception being when Mrs Sinico's Christian name, Emily, is given for the first and only time in the newspaper report of the Coroner's Inquest. In more sub-stantial ways, however, the two stories come together at several crucial points in the story, one of them being the time spent together by each couple in the dark, a dark which promises sex but which can never accomplish it. For instance, in Joyce's story one of the powerful images which carries Mr Duffy's thoughts of death and destruc-tion is the image of the 'good train winding out of Kings-bridge Station, like a worm with a fiery head winding through the darkness, obstinately and laboriously'. This powerful image, which seems to catch up into itself so much of the story, is transposed downwards into a comic version in the later story. There it becomes the image of Mrs da Tanka's cigarette's tip glowing in the darkness which leads to panicstricken but comically treated re-

flections on death threatening to result from her careless-
ness with her cigarettes:

> Sleep was impossible: one cannot sleep with the thought
> of waking up in a furnace, with the bells of fire brigades
> clanging a death knell.

Mrs da Tanka's mockery of Mr Mileson's sexual inexpe-
rience makes the bed heave 'with the raucous noise that
was her laughter, and the bright spark of her cigarette
bobbed about in the air', while Mr Duffy had heard the
train's noise and had wound Mrs Sinico's name into it (a
Joycean musical favourite of two dactyls, 'Emily Sinico',
like 'Malachi Mulligan', itself modelled on 'Oliver Gogarty'), after he had registered the image of the 'fiery head'
in the darkness.

It is in the darkness that both couples are at their most
intimate and yet at their most separate, though separate
for their different reasons. In Joyce's story the moments
in the dark between the man and the woman are flooded
with irony. What unites the couple is 'the music that still
vibrated in their ears' as they sit quite alone in the dark in
her little cottage outside Dublin when:

> Many times she allowed the dark to fall upon them,
> refraining from lighting the lamp. The dark discreet
> room, their isolation, the music that still vibrated in
> their ears united them.

This, of course, is picked up and turned into self-punishing
reflections by Mr Duffy at the end of the story, music being
replaced by the 'laborious drone' of the engine, and so on.
But, more immediately, Joyce uses ironic allusions to comment implicitly on Mr Duffy's reflections as he sits in these
moments of intimacy in the dark with Mrs Sinico:

> and, as he attached the fervent nature of his companion
> more and more closely to him, he heard the strange
> impersonal voice which he recognized as his own,
> insisting on the soul's incurable loneliness.

This is too close to a primary Romantic text for chance,
and too full of verbal echoes to be an accident. We seem
to be close to Shelley's early poem, *Alastor; or The Spirit
of Solitude,* where the words which are limitated in Joyce
are being used for a characteristically Shelleyan consummation of physical love in a dream, a combination of
solitude in the dream-state and the ecstasy of sexual union
with another. The Poet dreams:

> a veilèd maid
> Sate near him, talking in low solemn tones.
> Her voice was like the voice of his own soul
> Heard in the calm of thought.

But this maid makes music which has a very different
effect on the Poet:

> wild numbers then
> She raised, with voice stifled in tremulous sobs
> Subdued by its own pathos: her fair hands

> Were bare alone, sweeping from some strange harp
> Strange symphony, and in their branching veins
> The eloquent blood told an ineffable tale.
> The beating of her heart was heard to fill
> The pauses of her music, and her breath
> Tumultuously accorded with those fits
> Of intermitted song.

She reveals herself to the poet who sees her 'glowing limbs
beneath the sinuous veil / Of woven wind' and so on, and:

> He reared his shuddering limbs and quelled
> His gasping breath, and spread his arms to meet
> Her panting bosom . . .

This is followed by sleep which 'Like a dark flood suspended in its course/Rolled back its impulse on his vacant
brain'. Joyce enfolds Mr Duffy in Shelley's ecstatic verse
to ironize and judge the pusillanimity of his hero.

In his turn William Trevor uses his allusions to Joyce's
story to deepen the pain within this ostensibly comic tale.
Yet we cannot deny the comedy, nor the ironic devices by
which the author remains at a decent remove from his
characters. One of these devices is the language which he
finds for his couple to speak, or rather to share. They
communicate with one another in an idiom only this particular pair, you feel, could speak. It is as though they had
spent a lifetime together to fall into the same idiolect,
stylistically formal, a little stilted, certainly sounding contrived, and almost like a rehearsed script. There is no
allowance for hesitation, evasion, none of the fractures of
ordinary social discourse between almost total strangers.
They become public and open in their assaults on one
another though treating each other as strangers, and their
tone is rather like that of long-married partners well-versed
in hurting one another.

> 'How servile waiters are! How I hate servility, Mr
> Mileson! I could not marry that waiter, not for all the
> tea in China.'

> 'I did not imagine you could. The waiter does not
> seem your sort.'

> 'He is your sort. You like him, I think. Shall I leave
> you to converse with him?'

> 'Really! What would I say to him? I know nothing
> about the waiter except what he is in a professional
> sense. I do not wish to know. It is not my habit to go
> about consorting with waiters after they have waited
> on me.'

> 'I am not to know that. I am not to know what your
> sort is, or what your personal and private habits are.
> How could I know? We have only just met.'

> 'You are clouding the issue.'

> 'You are as pompous as da Tanka. Da Tanka would
> say issue and clouding.'

'What your husband would say is no concern of mine.'

The reader is steadily made aware in many other ways of how this pair really belong together as complementaries, as so much folk-lore about relationships would have it. Only the reader will ever know this, and they will inevitably remain locked within their private worlds, unable ever beyond the confines of the story to recognize or receive one another. We see them as truly complementary, but we also see them as truly opposites and antagonistic, never one nor the other simply. So, for instance, they share a common past interest in the countryside, as we learn that he collected birds' eggs on the common when a boy, and she loved the countryside of Shropshire where she was brought up. Her love, however, was wordless, a love without a need for names, 'without knowing, or wishing to know, the names of flowers, plants or trees.' His was a codified knowledge, accurate and without emotion. They also have entirely different ways of dealing with the past: she 'had kept nothing. She cut off the past every so often, remembering it when she cared to, without the aid of physical evidence,' while he had a present dominated by the past. He had inherited a house which brought its own symbolic death with it (the termination of its lease), and his grasp on procreation and its denial seems happily symbolized in his collection of birds' eggs which he still possessed.

The author enjoys many ways of balancing the characters, so that not only is the single fornication weighed against a sexuality of which the lower limit is the two husbands, and whose higher limit we are never to learn, but he amusingly balances these two husbands against two unwashed plates:

> She thought of da Tanka and Horace Spire, wondering where Spire was now. Opposite her, he thought about the ninety-nine-year lease and the two plates, one from last night's supper, the other from breakfast, that he had left unwashed in the room at Swiss Cottage.

But just before the story ends, at the most ironically inappropriate moment, we have the most surprising and moving coupling of the pair through the word 'cowparsley'. This word involves a disclosure of the interior of the individual, of that hidden and secret world which has been locked away since childhood, that world of pre-puberty, of the pre-self-consciousness. The trigger word slips out of him unbidden and almost unnoticed in response to her heavily sarcastic question about his possible preferences for flowers on his coffin.

> 'When you die, Mr Mileson, have you a preference for the flowers on your coffin? It is a question I ask because I might send you off a wreath. That lonely wreath. From ugly, frightful Mrs da Tanka.'

Mr Mileson's automatic response is 'cowparsley'. Against what the discourse seems to expect, the hidden and secret worlds of each of the speakers lie within reach, if only they knew the right key, and accidentally the keys have been pressed. Mr Mileson responds not to the 'flowers' part of the question but, characteristically for someone so

against life, we feel, he responds to the image of himself in the coffin, 'an image he often saw and thought about'. 'Cowparsley' comes out unregistered by its speaker. Mrs da Tanka picks on the right key 'coffin' and gets rewarded by the trigger word 'cowparsley'. This in turn prompts an uncensored and defenceless set of her imagistic memories which flood back from Shropshire:

> 'Cowparsley?' said Mrs da Tanka. Why did the man say cowparsley? Why not roses or lilies or something in a pot? There had been cowparsley in Shropshire; cowparsley on the verges of dusty lanes; cowparsley in hot fields buzzing with bees; great white swards rolling down to the river. She had sat among it on a picnic with dolls. She had lain on it, laughing at the beautiful anaemic blue of the sky. She had walked through it by night, loving it.

Her memories are more powerful and involve evocatively sensuous imagery, including all the senses; and she can even recapture an image of herself almost like a photograph in the past.

> She could smell it again: a smell that was almost nothing: fields and the heat of the sun on her face, laziness and summer. There was a red door somewhere, faded and blistered, and she sat against it, crouched on a warm step, a child dressed in the fashion of the time.

He, by contrast, had seen it only once (analogous to his unique sexual experience) 'on a rare family outing to the country', 'had seen it and remembered it', and 'he remembered, that day, asking the name of the white powdery growth'. Drily the author matches Mr Mileson's dryness:

> He had picked some and carried it home; and had often since thought of it, though he had not come across a field of cowparsley for years.

So, this pair, balanced, complementary, matched, opposite, part, and the balanced relationship which has been comically and pathetically given to us in the story is shown in its ironic parting, 'moving in their particular directions' (almost a standing parody of Milton's famous ending for the fallen Adam and Eve who 'hand in hand with wandring steps and slow, / Through *Eden* took thir solitarie way.'):

> She to her new flat where milk and mail, she hoped, awaited her. He to his room; to the two unwashed plates on the draining board and the forks with egg on the prongs; and the little fee propped up on the mantelpiece, a pink cheque for five pounds, peeping out from behind a china cat.

This comic ending is entirely appropriate to the story and its tone, but I believe that its tragic predecessor still operates in the body of the work to deepen the feelings at times and to allow the echoes to reverberate from Joyce, as he had let the echoes of Shelley reverberate in his story. William Trevor may not have been conscious of reworking 'A Painful Case', but it hardly matters. These things have a way of being triggered unconsciously.

Julia O'Faolain   (essay date 1991)

SOURCE: "The Saving Touch of Fantasy," in *The Times Literary Supplement,* No. 46005, May 31, 1991, p. 21.

[O'Faolain is an English novelist and short story writer. In the following review, she examines the tension between reality and fantasy in Trevor's Two Lives.*]*

William Trevor's fictions swing between realism and the escape-hatch of fantasy and the process is symbiotic, for it is his characters' plausibility which earns credence for their excesses. Like real people, they can commit cartoonish follies without becoming cartoonish. Reality dogs them. Realism delivers them up to scrutiny and we, like Peeping Toms, may even feel an uneasy shiver at its verisimilitude. Humour rarely distances his subjects for long. Just as we settle to the release of laughter, a twitch of the plot hauls them back in for another shock of recognition. They are apt to be close to the end of their tether and are often very like ourselves. Trevor's empathy finds poignancy in the plainest lives.

It is this generosity of vision which makes the publication of his twenty-first book an occasion for celebration. So does his feel for a reality spliced with dreams. He is a writer attuned to this secular age which is full of hype and hope, when many are tantalized and fantasy is not only an escape but also a coping mechanism. Some of his most moving narratives pivot on the way their dreams nerve people to snatch at a happiness beyond their means. Thus, in his 1960s tale, **"Lovers of Their Time"**, a couple, who have nowhere to be alone, take to sneaking into an Edwardian bathroom in the Great Western Royal Hotel, where they make love in a tub whose Great Western spaciousness was not meant for their sort. Nemesis, to be sure, catches up. Beneath the fizz of farce is a desperation kept, precariously, at bay.

There is a fair bit of that in Ireland, where Trevor has lately been setting more stories, no doubt because of the way the past there acts on the present—one of his themes. Able, when he chooses, to make realism levitate, he can, by subverting it, show up the shiftiness and dangers of truth. The title story of a recent collection, **Family Sins,** does just that. At first it seems to be a tale from rural stock about a possessive mother turning a gun on the girl her son wants to marry. Sadly, when all seems over, the girl's parents accept their bereavement. They are small farmers, and wrenching a living from poor land leaves scant time for brooding. Then, a journalist from the city writes an article which destroys their self-respect. Baffled at seeing themselves described as "disadvantaged", they are shamed by innuendo about their dead daughter and by the shock of seeing their lives through alien eyes. Interestingly, the story counterpoints a classic one on the same theme. Frank O'Connor's "In the Train" shows villagers returning from perjuring themselves in court so as to shield a murderess whom they would now punish in their own way. There, the alien consciousness is recognized as inimical and outfaced. Half a century later, it is harder to resist. Writing, truthful or not, is an intrusion

Caricature of Trevor.

and it is typical of Trevor's seriousness that he should turn his scrutiny on his own craft. His latest book does this again.

Two Lives is the umbrella title for a brace of novellas which turn on a common theme: fantasy filtering into a woman's life to replace, and perhaps redeem it. The lives are harsh and the dream-doses powerful. Side-effects wreak havoc and the women end up a little mad. The question left simmering is whether this is a mercy. The first of the two, *Reading Turgenev,* belongs to the author's chronicle of Anglo-Irish decline. This time we are far from the Yeatsian glories of the great houses whose fall Trevor has dramatized with such panache in earlier books. Ordinary people too get trapped by history, and Mary Louise, whose blue eyes "had a child's wild innocence", belongs to a poor Protestant community whose "very life was eroded by the bleak economy of the times". The times are the 1950s and she, stuck on a lonely farm, yearns for the lights of the local town. Unable to find work, she settles for marriage with "the only well-to-do Protestant for miles around". Elmer Quarry owns the town drapery, is fourteen years older than she, "square-looking" and "attired invariably in a nondescript suit".

The stale vocabulary—"attired" rather than "dressed"—sets the tone. Elmer, in keeping with family custom, has given his best years to his shop before thinking of "the securing of the line". When he does, he invites Mary Louise to the cinema, without bothering to find out what is on. It is *The Flame and the Flesh*: elements with which he has not reckoned, and it is, he will find, "about a woman in Italy, with a number of men interested". The subdued term for erotic arousal has a ring of the counting-house . . . where his true passions lie.

Clearly, the marriage is a mistake which Trevor, persuasively, turns into a destiny. Detail after coercive detail is hammered home until the couple are helpless. The proposal made and—after a month—accepted, "Elmer passed his tongue over his lips, dried them with a handkerchief and announced that he was going to kiss her." He was "decent and reliable"; Miss Mullover, the school-teacher and chorus, takes a "sanguine view".

What no one will know is that Elmer is also impotent. In rural communities, a woman caught in such a plight does not shame her man by trying to escape it. Their joint misery drives him to drink and her to seek out an invalid cousin who reads Turgenev to her, tells her he was in love with her as a boy, then dies. Their few trysts are in a graveyard where she will later yearn to lie with him. Memory will turn to fantasy and fiction become her refuge. Reading to her "had been her cousin's courtship, all he could manage, as much as she could accept". Now, rather than grapple with realities, she frightens her sour sisters-in-law and poor, soft stick of a husband by openly buying rat poison, then colouring their rissoles with green ink. Committed to an asylum for the mad, she is happy "in a refuge where her love affair could spread itself". From dream, to macabre prank, to possibly feigned madness: her shifts have the mutually reinforcing coherence of metaphor. Rooted in a helpless community, they allegorize its fate while Trevor's precision—the brand of ink used is Stephen's, as it would have been in those years—guarantees authenticity. Our last glimpse of her recalls a remark from a previous novel: "in Ireland it happens sometimes that the insane are taken to be saints of a kind". And indeed there is something devotional about her cult of her dead cousin. "'I dress for him,' she says. 'I make up my face in our graveyard.'" The opium of the people has, it would seem, been privatized.

As often now with Trevor, he is reworking an old theme. In **"The Raising of Elvira Tremlett,"** an unhappy boy fantasizes about a dead girl and ends, with relief, in an asylum. A girl in *Fools of Fortune* becomes a saint "of a kind" and, in *Nights at the Alexandra,* another yearner retreats into the memory of someone dead. However, the last two of these have more buoyancy than *Reading Turgenev,* in which unalloyed realism is bleakly deterministic and lacks leavening. There was complexity and humour in *Fools of Fortune*, while in *Nights at the Alexandra* the redemptive memory was more magical, perhaps because its dream-source was a cinema whose romance and scarlet seats and "rosy gloom" offered a counterpoise to the drabness outside. Turgenev's world provides a less effective contrast with provincial Ireland, since his very name evokes a parallel to it: a sluggish society full of tragic destinies. Moreover, *On the Eve,* the particular novel which Mary Louise keeps reading, is about a lover who dies.

Despite the shared theme, the second novella here is very different. Mrs Delahunty, narrator of **My House in Umbria,** is quite without roots, constructs her identity as she goes along, and possesses several aliases. She was born fifty-eight years ago in an English seaside town to parents who owned a Wall of Death around which her father rode a motorbike with her mother on the pillion. They sold their daughter forthwith to foster-parents whom she left on her sixteenth birthday because the man kept forcing himself on her in the back-yard shed. Later adventures led to a brothel in Africa where she made the money to buy a house in the Umbrian countryside, in which she and her dubious Irish factotum, Quinty, now take paying guests. Meanwhile, she writes money-making romances which improve greatly on life as she has known it. Boozy and big-hearted, she has the common touch.

On a trip to Milan, her train compartment is blown up by a bomb. Later, in hospital, she is a prey to "ugly" memories, which she tries to baffle by planning a new romance and wondering about those around her. A champion survivor, she now has fellow survivors to care for and invites three to her villa. One, Aimee, and eight-year-old American girl orphaned by the explosion, becomes the particular object of her concern, and no doubt stands in for the abused child of Mrs. Delahunty's memories. Cared for by Doctor Innocenti, whose name echoes the one usually put on foundling hospitals in Italy, Aimée's mind is in a precarious state. So is Mrs Delahunty's. Her fantasies darken as she wonders who could have wanted to slip a bomb into the travellers' luggage. Ingenious explanations occur to her and she begins to see Aimée as an agent of redemption.

Back at the house, farce and oddity take over as Quinty, the con-man, imports into its genteel surroundings something of the brothel where he and Mrs Delahunty first met. Expecting to inherit from her, he seems a likelier bomber than the suspect on whom her fantasies have fixed. She has now begun to believe that she sees into the minds and pasts of other people and as this conviction grows more compelling, the narrative we are reading becomes increasingly unreliable.

When Aimée's uncle, an American professor, whose speciality is ants, turns up to take her home with him, there are farcical scenes in which Mrs Delahunty pleads ardently with him not to do so. Unfortunately, her manner is that of the brothel, and the ant-expert is repelled. Eaversdropping on his telephone conversations, she comes to the conclusion that he lacks the warmth which Aimée needs. In one of these overheard conversations, he distresses her by describing her fiction as "trash". "'Her imagination has consumed her,' he said. From his tone he could have been referring to an ant." Two years later, she learns that Aimée has been put in a home. Though her romances may be "trash"—and evidence is provided to show them to be pretty much that—her intuitions were right. Her unreliable fantasies contained a core of wisdom.

Trevor has frequently been praised for allowing life to present itself without preaching, but this time Mrs Delahunty sermonizes on his behalf. The preoccupations of these two novellas—the use and abuse of the imagination—are old concerns of his but they have not elicited his usual verve. The first is a grim threnody. Strangely for Trevor, the second is lacking in particularity: Umbria is picture-postcard, and Mrs Delahunty a bit of a rattle. Graceless though it may be to quarrel with a writer who has so often provided marvels of entertainment, he is not here at the top of his form.

Bernard O'Donoghue   (essay date 1992)

SOURCE: "The Plain People of Ireland," in *The Times Literary Supplement,* No. 4676, November 13, 1992, p. 19.

[*O'Donoghue is an Irish poet, critic and editor. In the following favorable review of* The Collected Stories, *he discusses the defining characteristics of Trevor's short stories.*]

Graham Greene said that William Trevor's **Angels at the Ritz** (1975) was "one of the best collections, if not the best collection since Joyce's *Dubliners*". Leaving aside the extravagance of this (Greene is bound to like Trevor: the **Collected**'s opening story, **"Meeting in Middle Age",** is like Greene without the metaphysics), the *Dubliners* parallel—unavoidable as it is in a collection of Irish stories with major claims—is misplaced. The stories of *Dubliners* are in the romantic mode and focus on the individual; the narrative is taken over by the characters ("Lily, the caretaker's daughter, was literally run off her feet").

Trevor is no romantic; his stories, like Frank O'Connor's, are social observations. Even in the shortest of them, the context in which the characters operate is evoked with absolute sureness. There is no question of one story in Trevor acting as a gloss or extension of a previous one, as happens in *Dubliners* or in George Moore's *The Untilled Field*. Every Trevor story is a totally new beginning. Most reviewers of John McGahern's recent *Collected Stories* have commented that his tales return with concentrated absorption to the same themes. He is in the Moore-Joyce tradition rather than the O'Connor-Trevor one: the novelist writing short stories rather than the short story specialist.

In fact, Trevor's relation to the tradition of the modern short story is oblique. Most of the contrivances associated with the form do not occur in his. They don't begin with an over-arching thematic statement; they don't have a twist in the tail (indeed the absence of this is almost their hallmark); they are not for the most part concerned with groups marginalized in their societies ("the lonely voice"); above all, they don't have recourse to narrative special effects ("free indirect speech" and its by-products). His telling never risks overshadowing the tale. The prose has an extraordinary transparency which is all the more remarkable because the medium varies subtly from story to story, according to the setting, without losing any of its perspicuity.

This transparency is most reminiscent of the master of the Irish short story, Frank O'Connor. The similarity is reinforced by the fact that the celebrated success of television versions of Trevor (**"Access to the Children"**, **"The Ballroom of Romance"** and **"Events at Drimaghleen"**) is only matched among Irish short stories by adaptations of O'Connor, such as "The Mad Lomasneys". It is stories like the latter, with its descriptive precision and pointed brevity, that are most brought to mind here.

But Trevor's settings do invite comparison with the worlds of other novelist-short-story-writers such as Elizabeth Bowen, J. G. Farrell, Greene and Evelyn Waugh. If there is one world which predominates it is that of Molly Keane: the well-behaved battleground of female stoicism. This is not confined (as it tends to be in Keane) to the narrative terrain of small-town Protestant Ireland; the women who behave well as a relic of old decency in Trevor's works are not only the distressed minor gentlefolk of Keane and Farrell but the plain people of Ireland too. And they are nearly all women; it is not so much that men do not behave well in Trevor; they hardly behave at all. There are some exceptions; for example, Davy, the orphaned servant-boy of **"Honeymoon in Tramore",** displays the same clear-eyed modesty as Trevor's most memorable women: Bridie in **"The Ballroom of Romance"**; Kathleen in **"Kathleen's Field"**; Dervla in **"The Wedding in the Garden".**

Trevor is no romantic; his stories, like Frank O'Connor's, are social observations. Even in the shortest of them, the context in which the characters operate is evoked with absolute sureness.

—Bernard O'Donoghue

But his ease and authority in the world of well-behaving Irish women does not mean that he is confined to it. Like Elizabeth Bowen, he is as comfortable with English home-counties decencies as with Ireland. The eighty-five stories in this collection (a modest advance on the previous Penguin **Collected**) range in length from seven pages to the sixty pages of the slightly unconvincing war-triptych, *Matilda's England*. In tone they range from the grave pathos of the wonderful **"The Distant Past"** to the viciously accurate comedy of **"The Grass Widows"**. The even-toned beginning of the latter is a good example of Trevor's coverage and style: "The headmaster of a great English public school visited every summer a village in County Galway for the sake of the fishing in a number of nearby rivers." The humorous archness of the narrative voice—for example in the almost inverted word-order of "visited every summer a village"—surrounds two registers: the pompous "great" and the conciliatory Irish "for the sake of".

This is Trevor's greatest skill: the tact and precision with which he manoeuvres between societies and dialects, especially between Ireland and Anglo-Ireland. This is mag-

nificently done in **"The Distant Past"**, a desolating evocation of the gradual ostracizing of a fading Irish Protestant couple because of the Troubles. It is typical of
Trevor's steady-eyed recording of the devastations of
everyday hardship that the ostracism is caused by awkwardness as much as by principle. Stangely, his vision is
ultimately optimistic in its humanism, celebrating the
minor heroics of this acceptance of suffering as the centre of life. In this way, Trevor's *Collected*—to adapt
Greene's tribute—has claims to be seen as the best full
collection since O'Connor.

Bruce Allen   (essay date 1993)

SOURCE: "William Trevor and Other People's Worlds,"
in *The Sewanee Review,* Vol. CI, No. 1, Winter, 1993, pp.
138-44.

[*In the following mixed assessment of* Two Lives *and* The
Collected Stories, *Allen derides the pedantic, overly-po-
litical nature of Trevor's short fiction set in and around
Northern Ireland.*]

Aficionados of the contemporary short story could undoubtedly summon up a dozen or so names if asked to identify
the best living practitioners of the form. For me there are
three now writing in English who dominate this genre: the
Canadian Alice Munro, America's Peter Taylor, and the
Anglo-Irish master William Trevor. (I'm tempted to expand
the list to include John Updike, and I would add Eudora
Welty and Hortense Calisher were there evidence that either is still writing short fiction.)

Munro, Taylor, and Trevor all possess the ability to suggest the contour of a whole life in a single transfiguring
incident, and each writes of people inextricably bonded
with a culture and community, shaped by environment
and ever responsive to its stimulations and inhibitions.
In Trevor's case the physical place is Ireland—especially in its embattled relations with neighboring, contrasting England—and a parallel context arises from the often explosive antagonism between Catholic and Protestant communicants.

Born and educated in Ireland, Trevor has lived and worked
in Italy and England (where he has resided for many years),
and his books have "traveled" equally successfully. A member of the Irish Academy of Letters and a winner of several English literary prizes and of the *Hudson Review's*
Bennett prize, he has also been named a commander of
the British Empire.

In his fiction Trevor has ventured to explore (as he has
elsewhere put it) other people's worlds, while remaining
essentially focused on the divided nature of his native
country and its people. His early novels (such as *The Old
Boys,* 1964, and *Mrs. Eckdorf in O'Neill's Hotel,* 1970)
and his many plays written for radio, stage, and television
most frequently portray repressed or disappointed solitar-
ies whose drab daily lives contrast tellingly and painfully

with their romantic imaginings. One feels they're not unlike romantic Ireland (in Yeats's phrase) itself, enduring a
diminished, impoverished here and now by concentrating
on soothingly grandiose visions of a glorious—and perhaps imagined—past.

Since the early 1980s William Trevor has deliberately
become a more socially and politically committed writer.
Probing examinations of Northern Ireland's volatile discontent and its spreading effects—from the potato famine
of the mid-nineteenth century through the terrorist bomb-
ings and genocidal bombast of recent decades—have frequently taken center stage, especially in the novels *Fools
of Fortune* (1983) and *The Silence in the Garden* (1989)
and in the last three short-story collections. The results, in
my opinion, have been distinctly mixed.

Yet, even when his fiction feels most argumentative, Trevor
remains one of the quietest of all contemporary writers.
He writes the plainest prose imaginable, devoid of ostentatious metaphors or modifiers, dedicated to the accurate
rendering of place and revelation of character. Precise
phrasing and superbly realistic dialogue distinguish his
characteristic double focus—on individuals and on the
surrounding influences upon them of families, colleagues,
religious instructors, and fellow townspeople. His stories
exfoliate outward from simple beginnings and contexts,
showing us how even singular and lonely people participate in a reality larger than themselves. He interests us in
the quotidian by probing gently and insistently beneath
the surfaces of common experiences and familiar things.

Trevor has two new books, the paired novels **Reading
Turgenev** and **My House in Umbria,** published together
as **Two Lives** (1991), and the augmented **Collected Stories** (1992). This latter is a huge omnibus volume containing the stories that appeared in Trevor's seven previous
collections published between 1967 and 1990, plus four
heretofore uncollected stories: there are 85 to 90 in all,
occupying more than twelve hundred pages. It offers satisfying evidence of Trevor's continuing productivity, as it
follows by less than a decade the **Stories** (1983), which
reprinted his first five collections.

Trevor's earliest stories (from **The Day We Got Drunk on
Cake,** 1967, and **The Ballroom of Romance,** 1972) are
comic and ironical studies of failures or misfits mired in
stultifying environments or disappointing relationships:
children cramped by domineering parents, or older people
exploited and victimized by the rapacious young ("**The
Hotel of the Idle Moon**" is an especially vivid expression of what will become a recurrent Trevor theme); adolescents hesitantly daring sexual discovery; lonely wom-
en disappointed or humiliated by the very men with whom
they expect to find perfect happiness.

Comedies of social misunderstanding ("**The Penthouse
Apartment**") or embarrassment ("**The Introspections of
J. P. Powers**") alternate with more ambitious productions
like "**The General's Day,**" an incisive character study of
"an elderly man with a violent past" in which Trevor
manages to make a pompous and deceitful old lecher

vulnerably and appealingly human (this story, which was successfully dramatized for BBC television, made a magnificent vehicle for the late Alastair Sim).

There are darker stories, concerned with sexual irregularity and sadism in marriage (**"O Fat White Woman"**), disturbed behavior in seemingly neutral settings (in **"A School Story,"** a boy preys on an unfortunate schoolmate's neurosis; in **"Miss Smith,"** a schoolboy's crush on an unresponsive teacher cripples him emotionally), even the occasional Kafkaesque tale (for example **"In at the Birth,"** in which a babysitter is engaged to care for a strange married couple's imaginary child).

Trevor expertly evokes the inchoate passions flickering briefly up in the lives of his withdrawn dreamers. But he avoids monotony by giving fair hearing to multiple viewpoints, opening up stories that initially appear focused on isolated individuals (**"Raymond Bamber and Mrs. Fitch"** and **"The Forty-Seventh Saturday"** are exemplary—especially for the latter story's surprisingly sympathetic penetration into the psyche of a middle-aged Lothario whom we had believed no more than a boorish seducer).

Angels at the Ritz (1976) and *Lovers of Their Time* (1979) contain Trevor's best work in the short story thus far. Graham Greene called the former volume "one of the best collections, if not the best collection, since Joyce's *Dubliners.*" I would bestow that encomium on Hemingway's *Men without Women* or Frank O'Connor's *Domestic Relations,* but Greene was not far wrong.

The stories in these volumes are unusually generously plotted and detailed, and handle the tactic of ending a narrative with a brief authorial overview or commentary as skillfully as has anyone since Chekhov. Familiar subjects are observed with deepening intensity. **"Torridge,"** another among several stories about boarding-school boys, brings a living ghost from the tangled pasts of several schoolmates back to haunt them into an acknowledgement of fears and desires they've hidden away for years. Both **"Broken Homes"** and **"A Dream of Butterflies"** pursue the theme of alien forces impinging on cautious, conservative householders, their action clearly suggesting the plight of a complacent England grown increasingly defenseless against unruly outsiders.

Sexual roundelays are depicted with increasingly elegant economy and irony (in **"Angels at the Ritz,"** primal matters are interpreted as social niceties; and **"Lovers of Their Time"** wittily surveys the economics, as well as the ethics, of adultery). **"Death in Jerusalem,"** which J. F. Powers might well envy, is a beautifully plotted story about an innocent priest's awakening to moral laxity and callousness when he had expected spirituality. Several stories explore the emotions of "Protestants in what had become Catholic Ireland"—**"The Distant Past,"** **"Another Christmas,"** and, most memorably, **"Attracta,"** in which a Protestant woman teacher struggles to understand a recent atrocity in northern Ireland and also the legacy of violence that has dogged her own family. Her complex conviction, hard earned and rooted in powerfully specific memories, that reparation and

recovery are possible, that "it mattered when monsters did not remain monsters for ever," make her one of Trevor's most fully realized and vibrant characters.

The realistic skill and moral force displayed by such stories—and of others as variously well-fashioned as **"A Complicated Nature,"** **"Last Wishes,"** and the moving **"Mrs. Acland's Ghosts"**—combine for a level of achievement which Trevor has not, in my opinion, reached since.

His collection *Beyond the Pale* (1981), for example, shows us both the older Trevor and a newer one (turned spokesman, it seems) coexisting in a most uneven balance. Stories of moral and sexual dissension (**"Mulvihill's Memorial,"** **"The Teddy-Bears' Picnic,"** **"The Paradise Lounge"**) add nothing to earlier treatments of their now-familiar themes, and they reveal a seeming bitterness and ennui that remind me of Angus Wilson (who does this sort of thing much better than Trevor).

Stories that presume to minister to the diseased mind and heart of divided Ireland suffer from the same weakness that marred the otherwise limpid *Fools of Fortune* (1983)— underdevelopment. Trevor tends increasingly in his adversarial fictions to assume as données the melodramatic circumstances and twists of plot that imprison his characters, declining to show the origin or development of forces only gradually brought thus into collision. **"Autumn Sunshine"** and **"Beyond the Pale"** are little more than essayistic presentations of sensitive or insensitive attitudes toward "the troubles" ("It isn't nice, the truth in northern Ireland. None of it is nice"). Of course the feeling seems genuine, but the presentation can only be called inartistic. Characters who realize how destructive the continuing violence and hatred are, are presented as almost preternaturally self-controlled and wise; they're naked projections of their author's own stance.

Trevor's recent collections *The News from Ireland* (1986) and *Family Sins* (1990) contain twenty-four stories set variously in Ireland, England, and Italy. If they are concentrated too numbingly on people "familiar with defeat" and are resolved too predictably in failure or resignation, they're notable nevertheless for the masterly economy with which the finest of them render long sweeps of time and gradual processes of decay. **"The Property of Colette Nervi,"** **"The Wedding in the Garden,"** and **"The Third Party"** offer refreshing perspectives on religious and social incompatibility. **"The News from Ireland,"** a family chronicle that ranges from the famine of 1847 through much of the twentieth century, and **"Family Sins,"** about an inheritance of shame borne by a son whose parents died drunk in a car crash, offer remarkably compact explorations of individuals and generations mutually in extremis. And in the moving **"Kathleen's Field"** (almost matched by its virtual companion piece **"Honeymoon in Tramore"**), Trevor again proves that when he concentrates on closely sympathetic portrayals of timid beaten people unable or unwilling to resist their oppressors, he is unexcelled.

The four uncollected stories are a decidedly mixed lot. **"Memories of Youghal"** makes of its central situation—

"a detective going on about his past to an elderly woman on the terrace of an hotel"—a thin but affecting contrast between two companion spinsters. **"The Death of Peggy Meehan"** mingles sexual curiosity, religious tension, and the runway imagination of a fledgling novelist in a fascinating tale whose very promising materials aren't kept fully under control.

"The Smoke Trees of San Pietro" is a limp, forgettable tale of a possibly adulterous intimacy observed, and not understood till long afterward, by a "delicate," sensitive boy. **"Mags,"** easily the best of the four, subtly examines the effect on an unstable couple of the wife's self-effacing best friend, who while living with them and without ever meaning any offense, quietly "consumes" their marriage. It's one of the best of Trevor's studies of the repressed life, and of the paradoxical power withdrawn and lonely people can exert over more outwardly secure and confident ones.

Two Lives shows Trevor working at close to the peak of his ability. *My House in Umbria* is the story of Emily Delahunty, a woman with a compromised past who has secured respectability and wealth as the "author of a series of fictional romances." She operates a kind of pensione in Italy aided by a seedy intimate named Quinty who seems an alter ego perversely reminiscent of her less circumspect days.

The novel describes the "singular summer" of 1987; specifically, the bombing of a train (it is believed by terrorists—the case remains unsolved) in which several passengers are killed and a few, including Emily Delahunty, survive. Emily thereafter plays host, at her house in Umbria, to an elderly English general, a young German whose fiancée perished with her family aboard the train, and an orphaned American girl who does not speak and draws with crayons tortured expressionistic pictures of slaughter and suffering.

We need Trevor writing about what he surely knows best and feels most keenly: the individual at war with himself, his nearest and dearest, his community, and what, in a more innocent time, we might have called his soul.

—Bruce Allen

The summer consists of Emily's complex relationships with her guests, and with her own writerly urge to make discordant things cohere—the latter especially stimulated by the appearance of the girl Aimée's American uncle, a reserved academic to whom Emily passionately attempts to communicate her conviction that the world is not an ordered and logical place, that "there was evidence, all around us, of what each and every one of us is capable of."

There are narrative and rhetorical imperfections. For example Emily's "delirium" following "the outrage" is rendered so clinically that the reader is more often confused than drawn in. And generally the tale teeters so between reality and fantasized embroiderings on it that we grow impatient for the conflicts set forth to move toward their resolution. They eventually do so, stunningly, and Trevor brings all these convoluted matters to a powerfully convincing conclusion. The novel is memorable for its ambitious mixture of themes and tones, and for the virtuosity, if not formally perfect success, with which they're interwoven.

Reading Turgenev (a wan title) is a sad story of frustrated devotion forged in Trevor's very best vein. In parallel stories, set in different time periods and handled with magnificent economy and tact, he tells the story of Mary Louise Dallon, a docile Protestant country girl who marries the draper Elmer Quarry, a dozen years her senior, and comes to live with him and his flinty, disapproving unmarried sisters Rose and Matilda.

Her marriage unconsummated, her needs ignored or denied, Mary Louise begins secretly visiting her "invalid cousin" Robert, whom she believes she must have loved as a child. They meet in a graveyard, where he reads aloud to her from the stories of Turgenev. The idyll cannot last, and the strain of her double life leads Mary Louise to take refuge in fantasy, and eventually she goes to the "institution" from which (in the present-day narrative, chapters of which alternate with the past story) we learn she'll be "released"— with devastatingly ironic consequences.

Though not without sentimentality and contrivance, this is a powerfully affecting story, charged with emotion and rich in subtle metaphor. As usual Trevor eschews heightened language, instead placing well-timed emphasis on familiar objects and subjects—a collection of toys stored away, a pocket watch, a heron wading in a pond, a girl's rapturous fascination with Joan of Arc—that vibrate with suggestiveness.

There are several virtuoso sequences (the Quarrys's honeymoon trip, and an awkward encounter in a hotel bar; a wedding scene in which for pages on end we anticipate that the truth about Mary Louise's secret life will be revealed), and some astonishingly specific and intricate analyses of temperament and motivation. Most important is Trevor's mastery with understatement and suggestion— never better employed than here, quietly and firmly involving us in the lives of people whom we'd have thought unable, perhaps even unwilling, to elicit our sympathy. By the story's end we are sorry for the oafish Elmer Quarry, even for his two dreadful sisters. To have brought us to feel thus is no small triumph.

The news from William Trevor, then, remains encouraging. I'm hopeful that in his future work he will leave political statement to the activists and proselytizers and till the field that he has made his own. We need Trevor writing about what he surely knows best and feels most keenly: the individual at war with himself, his nearest and dearest, his community, and what, in a more innocent time, we might have called his soul.

Reynolds Price   (essay date 1993)

SOURCE: "A Lifetime of Tales from the Land of Broken Hearts," in *The New York Times Book Review,* February 28, 1993, pp. 125-7.

[*Price is a well-respected American novelist, poet, short story writer, and critic. In the following positive review of* The Collected Stories, *he examines the scope and major themes of Trevor's short fiction, praising the "range of knowledge and depth of feeling" of the short stories in the collection.*]

The voices of extraordinary writers like William Trevor are almost as quickly recognizable as those of great singers. Any lover of song will know a Pavarotti, a Leontyne Price, in an opening phrase—often in a single note. The genuinely sizable writers of fiction announce their presence almost as early. Some, like Conrad or Hemingway, speak in timbres distinctive enough to declare their makers in a single sentence. More often the novelist or short-story writer quietly names himself or herself, not by actual words or syntax but by an almost immediate revelation of what might be called his primal scene.

Even the voices of writers as wide-gauged as Tolstoy or Proust are grounded in a single scene, most often a lingering sight from childhood or early youth. And that scene is almost always one that a seasoned reader may well suspect lies near the start of a given writer's reason for writing—the physical moment in which a single enormous question rose before a watchful child and fueled the life-long search for an answer.

In Tolstoy, it's the terrible moment in a bright country house when a boy barely 2 years old hears the news of his mother's death and senses that he stands alone, doomed to the orphan's endless starvation for perfect love. In Proust it's the scented and breathless young man poised at the bolted thick glass door of a salon teeming with human monsters he's powerless not to adore and struggle to capture, though he knows they'll despise him if he breaches the threshold that rightly divides them. In Virginia Woolf it's the silent instant in a high-ceilinged room when, after her first attack of madness, a beautiful, lean girl understands that in all her world no other person shares her eyes and the other senses that make the world so uniquely dazzling and awful a sight for her alone, demanding her witness.

And though William Trevor is very much alive and at work— his *Collected Stories* consists of more than a thousand pages, many of them recent—it's seldom possible to move past the first page of any story from his broad array without detecting a boy, of 12 say, at the edge of a lush field or patchy lawn in a country far from the great world's noise, his gray eyes fixed in a just and merciless (though not unkind) gaze at a

family in evening light some yards beyond him, thirsty faces taut with the pain of hiding their most urgent needs and the dread of loosing their long-hid yearnings.

As with most large writers, that primal scene with its set of fixed eyes and its destined angle has proved to be Mr. Trevor's most valuable gift and his only impediment. Long before he sensed his profession—he spent long years as a painter and sculptor before deciding to write his first story—that half-concealed boy's eyes and mind had stored several remade worlds as rich in meaning as the actual earth. They'd likewise broken his heart too soon. For his one great lack as a writer is hope, the clear stream, however slight and easily stemmed, that runs on past private loss and ruin in the worlds of writers even as near desperation as Kafka or James Joyce, Mr. Trevor's huge predecessor.

William Trevor was born in 1928, a son of the troubled marriage of middle-class Protestant parents with roots in the farmland of Catholic Ireland. He moved restlessly in childhood about that small, cold, white-hot country, smaller than most American states. The atmosphere of a miserable home and the rootlessness of a vagabond childhood may have saved him from an ordinary career of balked melancholia. Mr. Trevor's distinctly alien qualities as a Protestant child without firm grounding in a particular village or city may have rescued him from the curse of self-loathing that might otherwise have silenced him or, worse, sent him forward as one more pale ventriloquist's doll worked by the strings of his dead ancestors—such giant figures as Shaw, Synge, the protean Yeats, O'Casey and the coiled reptilian exile Joyce, all natives of the same small room and perilously near at the time of his birth.

It was a peril of birth that Mr. Trevor shares with many of his fellows in other brands of fiction—American Southerners born in the wake of Faulkner, Porter, Welty and O'Connor; American Jewish males in the wake of Bellow, Malamud and Roth; most of the dozens of hapless souls born lately in any big Western city—the atmospheres of Paris, London, New York and Los Angeles that are now as nearly worked out as a sharecropper's cotton field in south Alabama or a beauty parlor in suburban Nashville.

But Mr. Trevor's apparently effortless triumph is to have taken a world worn nearly smooth by long and splendid handling and through pure intensity of attention and care to have found a nearly endless new set of subjects and tones. Almost as surprising, he has managed the greater part of his work in an all but total avoidance of the sourness of spirit, the meanness of outlook and the treacherous grandiloquence that has often afflicted those writers who inherit the bitter divisions of a small and brutally torn homeplace—Yeats and Joyce, even Faulkner in the wake of our Civil War, are not as free as William Trevor of that blight.

Yet Mr. Trevor has found a deeper chill, a core of defeat as pure and compelling in its ultimate sadness as that at the heart of Euripides—the unbroken spectacle of worthy men, women and children frozen by genetic inheritance and the warp of history. Among these 80-odd stories from

30 years, the most haunting, in their range of knowledge and depth of feeling, all focus on an action that with nearly invisible speed moves a small clutch of figures toward the instant when fate uncovers before their eyes in a silent rush the bleak denying future that they've either earned or been endowed with by family and home.

For me, among the stories that promise to last are the famous **"Ballroom of Romance," "An Evening With John Joe Dempsey," "O Fat White Woman," "Death in Jerusalem," "The Paradise Lounge," "Honeymoon in Tramore," "In Love With Ariadne"** and **"Kathleen's Field."** Of these best, only **"O Fat White Woman"** is set outside Ireland (in rural England); only **"In Love With Ariadne"** is set in a city; all the others are deeply socketed in the Irish countryside of small towns and villages.

Such a hard limitation on place and type of character might, in different hands, threaten monotony and quick exhaustion. But just as a reader thinks "He's told me this more than once already; he's badly stuck," Mr. Trevor's sheer intensity of entry into the lives of his people stalls the complaint and proceeds to uncover new layers of yearning and pain, new angles of vision and credible thought—layers that most readers would never have guessed in men, women and lone unassisted children whose home and history would seem to have left them as mute as Galway ponies in the rain.

The father and daughter in **"Kathleen's Field"** have frames of reference as narrow as paleolithic man's, but the depth of their hunger for that very life eventually lends them a sturdy heroism of pain endured. In **"In Love With Ariadne,"** the medical student who falls for the daughter of his Dublin landlady is almost literally ignited by the heat of his need for union with the beautiful girl and so fails to guess how terrifying his courteous longing is for someone with a past where love has proved truly lethal; yet the texture of the student's need and Ariadne's fear are brought as close to the reader's face as deep-cut words on a stark gravestone.

Mr. Trevor's apparently effortless triumph is to have taken a world worn nearly smooth by long and splendid handling and through pure intensity of attention and care to have found a nearly endless new set of subjects and tones.

—*Reynolds Price*

"An Evening With John Joe Dempsey" comes as close as Mr. Trevor allows himself to affectionate hope for a character's life—a boy just turned 15 and trembling on the brink of sex—but by the end of a simple happy evening,

we hear again the barely audible leak of sadness assert itself and press in on him, now and for good: this boy's chances of meeting a mate to his own patient sweetness are virtually nil.

Such pain and defeat are so clearly drawn in the best of Mr. Trevor's stories, so memorably sounded in a prose as plain and natural as daylight, that reading them in quantity would take more appetite for suffering than most readers bring to a book. If, that is, Mr. Trevor weren't offering abundant parallel compensations—the invisible nearness of eyes and a mind as watchful as his own, as steadily concerned with human feeling; the lucid prose that works its aims with no obvious effort; and almost everywhere the faintly rising scent of laughter.

For like most other sizable writers who choose country life as the field of their work and whose brand of country is stocked with people—the farmers of Ireland and, say, our own South—who've endured the forces of nature firsthand, forces more exacting than the dangers of cities, Mr. Trevor's vision is deeply, though never entirely, comic. However bleak the present and future of a given human life, the salient nearness of a vital ongoing world of rocks and fields, ocean and shore, will throw an enormous inhuman yardstick up against that one sad life and let us see the unreadable smile of time and fate that shines through even a child's unanswerable hope or need.

Only in his urban stories—and most of them are set in an England populated by the upper middle class—does Mr. Trevor's comic sense go savage. In a story like **"Raymond Bamber and Mrs. Fitch,"** in which he starts with a character whose boringness has a gruesome charm, the thrust of vicious laughter is turned at the final moment, and a comprehending tolerance rises. But in an awful excursion like **"The Teddy-Bears' Picnic,"** no single person from a group of young wealthy twits persuades Mr. Trevor inward for a closer look; and the story itself ends in a mocking laughter that praises itself as it executes the prose equivalent of a mass death sentence on all in sight (and none too soon).

That shallowness—Mr. Trevor's only recurrent fault but a luckily rare one—proceeds from both the vapidity of so much urban life, its hectic obsession with saving one's face in an endless string of pointless social risks, and from what seems Mr. Trevor's refusal or inability to wade as deeply into city life as he always manages when he stands on home ground. Confined as the meanness is to his English urban stories, a reader may wonder if the well-to-do English aren't the only possible resting place for Mr. Trevor's considerable powers of hate and destruction (he's lived in England for many years). With Irish countryfolk, even Anglo-Irish gentry, his perfect sense of pitch and sympathy can lay out the full implications of tragic or merely foolish choices; but a native tenderness spares them his malice.

In whatever country—and he's often written about Italy— his crafty skills never desert him, and now and then he manages a city story of airless dry brilliance to equal Maupassant or John O'Hara. In his novel *Other People's*

Worlds, he has enough space and a big enough cast to string a web of masochism, psychopathy, eager self-delusion, and pathos (but only in the very old and young) that awaits readers with the horror of a Jacobean melodrama—but, as well as the horror, the shallowness of a well-made teaspoon precisely filled to the rim with water, then frozen hard.

The little that Mr. Trevor reveals in interviews about his life suggests that his desert years of work in England from the early 1950's on as a teacher and sculptor, then—of all things—as an advertising copywriter in a London agency may partly account for the sharp division of feeling in the fiction he finally turned to a decade later. That and perhaps a natural scorn for the people whose ancestors lorded over Ireland for more than three centuries. More crucially, I suspect, and despite the lean results they've brought him, he's continued his sporadic raids on the heartless English because he only encountered them in numbers after his childhood and because the short story permits him to do a quick turn at their expense and exit grinning.

In the hands of a writer as practiced as Mr. Trevor, occasional failures are far more likely to be the results of dangers inherent in a chosen form than of some weakness in the writer's equipment—a good writer's short stories fail, when they fail, mostly because the form is short. It can often deprive the writer of time and space in which to burrow beneath the gloss of worlds that don't lie near his old knowledge or engage his care; it goads him into quick and readily salable effects that do slim credit to him or his subjects.

Again such stories are a small minority of what Mr. Trevor offers; and a serious look at the best of his novels confirms that when he works nearer home and gives himself sufficient room, his hand will almost automatically feel its way very deeply indeed into minds and actual summoned places (towns and houses) that open at his touch and show their intricate, amazing cores—an Irish village on market day in a William Trevor story can come to life with the crowding abundance of Dickens's London. For despite the wider fame of his stories and his own recent and thoroughly wrong remark to *The New Yorker* that his novels are "a lot of linked-up short stories," it's in the later novels of the 10 he's published that Mr. Trevor stakes an unimpeachable claim for the size and very high value of his work.

No novels written in British English since the final trance-intensities of Virginia Woolf feel more likely to hold a long-term claim on human attention than William Trevor's most recent three—*Fools of Fortune, The Silence in the Garden* and **Reading Turgenev** (which he calls a novella in the volume, **Two Lives,** though it has both the length and weight of a novel).

Each of the three is set in Ireland; each studies an ample stretch of time, a life span at least; two of the three are grounded in the wake of the murderous rebellion of 1919-21 that expelled British power, unseated a resident English gentry (most of them stayed on in their ample holdings) and left a vital continuing legacy of sworn vendetta by the native rebels or the loathed Black and Tans. Such

arcs of history are hardly fit subjects for short fiction, though Joyce embalmed scraps of the early struggle in his *Dubliners*; but Joyce's genius, like his understanding, was for the overwhelming moment of bleak revelation or the vast tessellated mosaic in which sharp fragments form a larger scene for the reader prepared to donate a large part of life and time to dogged decipherment.

Mr. Trevor's knowledge—despite his disclaimer—proves deeper, broader and longer-winded than Joyce's, yet far less showy in its calm refusal to follow Joyce in the strangling pursuit of a handmade new tongue able to do more than language can. And the language of Mr. Trevor's best work, of whatever length, proves its modest but entire adequacy in telling us all he seems to know or means to tell us (he most frequently inhabits the mind of women, plainly because for him women possess the more complex and subtle thoughts and feelings). And in lean and audaciously elliptical prose, he makes wide leaps over years and actions that often seem too urgent to skip; then he lands in the darkened room of the present to lay out quietly all the years have failed to tell us, such awful truths as:

Your father waited in silence for decades, then crossed the Irish Sea to England, killed the man who'd killed his own father in the time of the Troubles and now must live in anonymity, far from us. That fact explains the agony of your life till now.

You've entered a loveless village marriage; your husband will prove to be kind but impotent; your in-laws are vicious. You'll turn to the cousin you loved in school; the two of you will flourish in secret till he dies young. Then at last you'll face a literally unlivable life. Choose long years of madness instead; then return to your changed home, peaceful at last.

You'll live a whole life in the presence of lovers yet never know love. Many millions of humans, for thousands of years, have done just that. Expect no pity. Bear your load.

There are living writers, in the United States and Latin America (to go no farther), who possess a more complicated knowledge of a wider range of human life and of how that life enacts itself beneath the hand of individual will and the weight of a wider history. There are living writers of the short story to contend mightily with the recent claims of literary couturiers that Mr. Trevor is now the premier story writer in the language—in the United States alone we have Eudora Welty, William Maxwell, John Updike and Joyce Carol Oates, to name an irresistible few. Each of these four has matched the breadth of Mr. Trevor's skills and, what is more, has found occasions for glimpsing feasible routes through the real world's thickets toward at least a modicum of human fulfillment.

But crowns or garlands in the world of fiction—however fervently readers and journalists fling them at this head or that—are meaningless to the point of hilarity. No two good writers have ever agreed to enter the same race. Some admittedly enter more races; some enter races that are more worth winning. Occasionally one performs with a grace that's overwhelming and momentarily blanks the field, as the thrillingly beautiful late work of Raymond Carver briefly held the local scene.

With this new immense collection, William Trevor has filed in serene self-trust the results of years of work of impeccable strength and a piercing profundity that's very seldom surpassed in short fiction. Seasoned admirers of his stories alone should know, however, that his long fiction is stronger still—not merely for length but resonance: the sound of a voice that with near-inaudible dignity earns its place in the narrow circle of excellence, that ragged secular communion of saints who watch our lives with unblinking care, then give us our human names and ranks, our just rewards.

Kristin Morrison   (essay date 1993)

SOURCE: "The Garden and Trevor's 'System of Correspondence,'" in *William Trevor,* Twayne Publishers, 1993, pp. 9-18.

[*Morrison is an American educator and critic with a special interest in Irish literature. In the following excerpt, she analyzes "The News from Ireland" from a cosmological perspective, maintaining that Trevor attempts to connect past and present in his fiction through a complex series of mutual interrelationships.*]

When Mr. Erskine, the Pulvertaft's estate manager, begins courting Miss Heddoe, the English governess, in **"The News from Ireland,"** he invites her "to stroll about the garden" and boasts that he "reclaimed the little garden [that surrounds his own house], as the estate was reclaimed." In the Ireland of 1848 this vast walled demesne of hills, lakes, trees, shrubbery and flower gardens, orchards and kitchen gardens contrasts starkly with the famine outside. Thus in purely secular terms this estate is an Eden, a garden of abundance in the midst of want. Any poor governess would find so elevating a marriage as this offered her to be socially and economically its own kind of paradise. But Trevor allows these obvious metaphors to go unstated and instead introduces allusions to the original Eden through his reference to the Legend of the True Cross (connected ultimately with the Tree of the Knowledge of Good and Evil growing in the center of Paradise). By associating a typical Irish estate and actual historical events with the Garden of Eden and the central Judeo-Christian myths about sin and redemption, Trevor has combined in this one important short story a configuration of themes and ideas that appear in virtually all his fiction.

Behind each of Trevor's gardens lies that original garden, all of them connected by a conceptual system in which not only gardens but also all people, events, points of space, and moments of time are related to one another. The garden is one of Trevor's chief recurrent metaphors. His "system of correspondences" is the operative principle of that world, that cosmos, in which the garden occurs.

Trevor writes not only about his fictional gardens, characters, and events but even about political and historical matters from what could be called a cosmological perspective: events remote from each other in time or space are linked in such a way as to suggest that the apparent barriers of past and present, as well as of physical distance, are illusory, that connections exist among the various parts of his universe that make it a cosmos, an orderly (though often damaging) series of mutual interrelationships. According to the concept that dominates his work, past and present are, actually, the same moment; apparently separate realms (e. g., the public and the private, or the political and the domestic) inevitably overlap; all the various elements of space and time are intrinsically interrelated, comprising an elaborate and powerful "system of correspondences" which shapes the world. Such a habit of mind is indicated by the metaphors Trevor uses to describe the relationship between Irish myth and the Christian story: "The convolutions of ancient myth, the honeycomb of anecdote nestling within the major plot, the layers of fresh invention: all of it, when it was at last recorded, created an effect not unlike the elaborations of the decorated gospels" [*A Writer's Ireland: Landscape in Literature,* 1984]. This mode of thought is very like the academically familiar one described by E. M. W. Tillyard in *The Elizabethan World Picture,* though not so neat and regular: not now kings and suns and eagles and whales all conjoined by their rulership of their respective realms but English and Irish, lovers and haters, planters and dispossessed, the well-fed and the starving, each aspect of the complex, multicentury Anglo-Irish history exerting strange and powerful influences on various counterparts.

And although now, in the twentieth century, there are those who see political and moral spheres as quite different, in Trevor's system of correspondences (as also indeed in that medieval and Renaissance one) questions of good and evil are unavoidably bound up with political and secular issues. If the king was wicked, inevitably the land declined and the people suffered. So too now, in Trevor's world, the immoral behavior of individuals necessarily wounds the whole social fabric, and, conversely, rottenness in the body politic has its inevitable analogue in private lives and personal character. In Trevor's fiction the relatedness of microcosm and macrocosm is not a quaint concept from the past but a fact of human life in the present, a fact to be taken seriously.

It is in this light that the observations of the butler in **"The News from Ireland"** must be seen, as he waits on the current occupants of the reclaimed estate, the reclaimed garden: "Serving them in the dining-room, holding for them a plate of chops or hurrying to them a gravy dish, he wishes he might speak the truth as it appears to him: that their fresh, decent blood is the blood of the invader though they are not themselves invaders, that they perpetrate theft without being thieves." These nineteenth-century residents of the big house, the Pulvertafts of Ipswich, are both innocent and guilty because the intervening years since Elizabeth granted their family the land have not mitigated that usurpation, despite their personal sense of duty in caring for estate and tenants. Their aged and poor Irish Protestant butler, Fogarty, is not simply a crank as, reflecting on history, he considers the various invaders to be "visitors": "the Celts, whose ramshackle gipsy empire expired in this same landscape, St. Patrick with his holy shamrock, the outrageous Vikings preceding the wily Normans, the adventurers of the Virgin Queen." Such linkage and juxtaposition virtually annihilate time, implicate all groups in responsibility for the current distress, and deny any group, whether an invading people or a single resident family, intrinsic claim to the land, whether this particular garden or all Ireland. Yes, Fogarty *is* a crank, but he is also a vehicle for a concept that dominates all Trevor's fiction.

A closer look at **"The News from Ireland"** will help illustrate this point. Set in an Irish estate in 1847-48, the narrative shows private and public worlds held severely apart and yet impinging on each other irrevocably. The public is the world of famine; the private is the world of privileged domesticity (drives in the estate park, picnics, music lessons, weddings in the garden). Both worlds are flawed, perhaps in some essential, irreparable way. Although the English family, the Pulvertafts, who now inhabit this estate are aware of the suffering "outside," although they give alms, distribute soup, and even contrive a program of work for the neighborhood, they live a lie. As their Irish Protestant butler has said to himself, they perpetrate theft without being thieves. The lie they live is quite simply their assumption that this estate, this garden, is theirs; that they can live safely within its walls; that their obligations outside are a matter of charity and not justice. Trevor uses the presence of a stranger, the most recent visitor, to establish a norm of values in the story: the new English governess is horrified by what she sees, by the Pulvertafts themselves, by their inherent lack of honesty, a lack so profound that they are unaware of it. The butler aids her critical perspective by telling her the news of the starving peasant child with the stigmata (the wounds of Christ in its hand and feet). Either explanation of this phenomenon shocks her: if the wounds are authentic, it is a sign not to be ignored; if the wounds were inflicted by the parents as a strategy of survival, that too is an event to be reckoned with. She cannot understand why the big house has no interest.

For the reader, of course, this child is clearly an emblem of the peasantry itself, crucified by the ascendancy, the poor crucified by the rich. And within the world of the story the child also serves as an explicit emblem, a focus of discontent for the starving masses and for the butler, who tells the governess his dream that one day descendants of these hungry people will destroy this estate, burning house and gardens. But she does not heed the warnings given her, to act on her outrage and leave the estate to its decay, to avoid participating in its immorality; instead she becomes an accomplice. Her critical perspective as a stranger, allowing her to see both public and private worlds irrevocably interconnected, gives way to the same lie the Pulvertafts live. "I do not know these things," she says with determination to the butler, denying awareness of the observations that had earlier troubled her. She turns her back on the public world; she chooses the private

world and the illusion that she can live well and safely in its garden. She accepts the estate manager's proposal despite the butler's vision of his house in flames.

At the center of her corruption is a lie, the kind of lie that makes ordinary life possible. It is innocently exemplified in the story by the piano recital of one of the Pulvertaft daughters: "She really plays it most inelegantly," the new governess observes to herself. "Yet in the drawing-room no frown or wince betrayed the listeners' ennui." Such polite deception keeps everyone in the story, not only the butler, from speaking "the truth as it appears to him." There is a lie in the way the governess takes her meals: before returning her tray to the kitchen, the butler flushes down the toilet what she does not eat so that the cook will not be offended. And there is a lie in her marriage: not love but considerations of social position and compromise sway her decision.

The story is in fact full of lies, just as these two worlds, public and private, are full of flaws. The works project of the Pulvertafts, though intended to be beneficial, is a lie that insults the workers, a road that goes nowhere. The old abbey is now "a lady's folly, a pretty ruin that pleases and amuses." The stigmata itself is *called* a lie by the big house, wishing to dismiss it, and—with that complexity Trevor often gives to his deceptively simple details—the lie-calling is itself a lie, missing the real truth of the child's wounds, whatever their source.

But how is one to live in such a world, go on with ordinary piano lessons, marriages, and strolls in the garden? Only by doing what the governess has done—weep into her pillow, be sick at heart, write in her diary her news from Ireland (her diary: a private, not a public, medium), and then learn "to live with things." Yes, of course, Trevor's story condemns her with this concluding line. And yet not entirely. "The wickedness here is not intentional," the butler had said. That does not make it any less wicked but does mitigate the guilt and point to the difficulty of solution.

Where is the source of the evil? As always in Trevor's work, far, far in the past. In response to the butler's news about the child's stigmata the governess tells him the Legend of the True Cross: that a seed falling into Adam's mouth sprouted from his body when he died and grew into a great tree on which, centuries later, Christ was crucified. This ancient legend presents a classic paradigm of the kind of thinking that is behind the correspondences inherent in Trevor's fiction. It is not enough that the act of original sin in the Garden of Paradise and the act of redemption centuries later in Palestine should both have been merely *associated* with trees. No, these trees must themselves be related to each other, intrinsically connected, just as the Savior and the Sinner are connected. Jesus is called the new Adam because there is a profound metaphysical connection between him and the first Adam (as Saint Paul puts it in 1 Corinthians 15:22, "For as in Adam all die, even so in Christ shall all be made alive," and several verses later Paul underscores the equation between the two by explicitly calling them by the same name, one "the first man Adam" and the other "the last Adam").

Christian tradition, liturgy, and poetry extend this equation: "As sin and death and entered the world by the Tree in the Garden, so by a Tree the redemption of the world was achieved. Nay, the Tree of the Garden had been miraculously preserved, and from its wood, by the poetic justice of God, was formed the Cross, that Tree which bore a better fruit for the healing of the nations" [F.J.E. Raby, *A History of Christian-Latin Poetry from the Beginnings to the Close of the Middle Ages,* 2nd ed., 1953]. These commonplace notions of Christian theology and piety need no elaboration here. But it is important to note that Trevor himself suggests by his repeated reference to the Legend of the True Cross that he wants his readers explicitly to associate such correspondences with the events in this story. Indeed, the governess herself seems to recount her telling of the legend to the butler as if it were a correlate of his story of the starving child, as if this religious legend and that political event were intrinsically connected, just as in another context she matches story with story "because the subjects seemed related."

In the public world of famine a child is marked with the wounds of Christ. In the private world of domestic privilege and fruitful gardens the governess speaks of the cross on which Christ died. These two events of present starvation and past crucifixion are no more remote from each other in time and space than the events of Christ's passion and Adam's sin. In fact, the whole point of that ancient Christian legend is to annihilate time and space, to show the cross of salvation and the tree of transgression to be significantly one. And now, by this same mode of thinking, this starving population in nineteenth-century Ireland is also one with Christ crucified, not in some vague, poetic, metaphoric sense but quite powerfully, intrinsically one.

The conjunction of these two stories—about the stigmatic child and about the True Cross—clearly establishes this connection between various supposedly separate worlds in Trevor's skillfully structured narrative. So too does the grim pun accompanying these accounts. In its etymology the word *starve* means "to die" and is thus found in many medieval poems and carols that refer to "Christ who starf on food." The word eventually became restricted to one specialized form of death, the meaning we use now, "to die from lack of food." Hence the pun makes all the more appropriate Trevor's association of starvation in Ireland with the death of Christ, through references to stigmata and the True Cross. The pun even seems to reinforce Trevor's implicit system of correspondences by showing that language itself partakes of the process.

It is precisely this kind of association, with its implied complex of correspondences, that at times makes Trevor's work seem grotesque to some modern readers; often in reviews his characters and situations are described as too bizarre to be generally appealing. But the point is that these seemingly odd conjunctions are in fact pertinent: that there does exist an old and abiding tradition, a view of the universe asserting that acts in one realm reverberate in another, that, for example, the physical damage of one person is re-created in the spiritual damage of a second, or vice versa.

What is striking in all Trevor's work is how frequent and elaborate these various connections and analogues are, so pervasive that it does not seem an overstatement to call them a *system* of correspondences. One of his earliest stories, **"The Original Sins of Edward Tripp,"** presents its titular character as feeling the present so dominated by the past that his own earlier childish mischief in Ireland and the recent horrendous murder of eight nurses in Chicago become kindred events; the sister with whom he shares this vision declares, "we know about the deceased. They're everywhere, Edward. Everywhere," and she means that quite literally. In the much later story **"Beyond the Pale"** Cynthia, the English visitor who "is extremely knowledgeable about all matters relating to Irish history," makes her companions uncomfortable by discerning the past alive in the present of the Antrim coast where they so blithely holiday: "'Can you imagine,' she embarrassingly asked, 'our very favourite places bitter with disaffection, with plotting and revenge? Can you imagine the treacherous murder of Shane O'Neil the Proud?'" When a suicide occurs at their idyllic hotel, she will not let its implication be ignored: the violence, terroism, and murder that precipitated the suicide are not "beyond the pale" of this garden resort but a symptom of its very existence, a present manifestation of evils going back to "the Battle of the Yellow Ford . . . , the Statutes of Kilkenny. The Battle of Glenmama," and so on through a long recital. Their landlord's furious rejection of her associating past events with present realities is itself unwittingly phrased in terms that suggest connection: "You are trying to bring something to our doorstep which most certainly does not belong there." Yes, this is a metaphor, but one that in context seems almost palpable: a real "something," a real "doorstep," just as there was and still is an actual "pale" holding back the starving from the well fed, protecting the complacent from the desperate, suggesting, deceptively, that private worlds of vacationing adulterers can be kept discreetly separate from the grander cruelties of history.

In addition to correspondences involving time and space are many other components of Trevor's system, ones related to plot, characterization, setting, imagery, theme, narrative technique—in fact, to all the various elements that help make up fiction. For example, it is not accidental that references to love and war are often justaposed in *Fools of Fortune*; these are not simply "standard thematic abstractions" of literature (though, as "love and death," they are also that), but their repeated, varied, and complex conjunction shapes this novel and helps constitute its point. Early in the narrative Willie notices that "all around us there seemed to be this unsettling love," and then he begins the next section of his memories with the observation that "the men of the village came back from the war." This juxtaposition of love and war is presented but not remarked on and indeed would not necessarily be noted in retrospect by the reader were there not so many other instances of it, not only of the actual words *love* and *war* but of incidents related to them. For example, gazing out a window one night as a young boy, Willie "pretended that a Black and Tan was lurking among the mass of rhododendrons" and that he apprehends him with his father's shotgun. But in the next moment what he actually sees is an erotic scene between Tim Paddy and the Sweeney girl, private, so they think, in the bushes.

The boy then and the aged narrator he has now become make no conscious connection between the subject of his fantasy and what he really witnesses, but the novel demonstrates that there is a most important connection, that one is virtually an emblem of the other. Both violent attack and erotic congress, in these two particular scenes, are shrouded in darkness, attempting concealment in "the garden," or at least in the bushes that grow in that garden; both sets of actors intend something good from one point of view and something bad from another (the Black and Tan would protect the English hold on Ireland, good or bad, depending on one's allegiance; Tim Paddy and the Sweeney girl would have their pleasure for the moment but thus betray their real interest in other people); and both events are frustrated, as in fantasy the soldier is apprehended and in real life the erotic tumble is interrupted by the arrival of others. More important than these similarities of detail is that both events are witnessed and recounted by a character who will grow up to become a person for whom the fantasy of "war" will overshadow even the actuality of "love" and whose mix of these two realities will literally become incarnate in his own child, conceived in love and born into war.

Suzanne Morrow Paulson   (essay date 1993)

SOURCE: "Stories about Courtship: Bachelors/Spinsters, Fathers/Daughters," in *William Trevor: A Study of the Short Fiction,* Twayne Publishers, 1993, pp. 57-82.

[*In the following excerpt, Paulson commends Trevor's sensitive and realistic portrayal of gender relations in "The Ballroom of Romance," "Kathleen's Field," and "The Wedding in the Garden."*]

While codes governing courtship and marriage are changing in some parts of the world, in most places feminine and masculine gender identities are governed by two antagonistic codes of behavior—purity for women, promiscuity for men. Certainly Trevor's stories about courtship—such as **"The Ballroom of Romance," "Teresa's Wedding,"** and **"The Property of Colette Nervi"**—reflect these codes. In these stories young women driven by a fear of spinsterhood marry undesirable suitors in communities governed by men. Economic concerns override considerations of love or happiness in marriage. **"Kathleen's Field"** tells the story of a farmer's daughter so submissive to her father she does not even recognize she is being condemned to a lifetime of servitude and spinsterhood. **"The Wedding in the Garden"** traces the development into manhood of an initiate whose "progress" is partly responsible for the "regress" of at least two women in his community. The deprivation of servants and the deprivation of women go hand in hand. Such deprivation deems certain women as appropriate targets for male lust and certain others as marriageable.

Although the setting for stories in this vein is frequently Ireland, the universality of prizing sons and conditioning deprived daughters to be submissive to fathers is most important. Trevor's sensitivity to the suffering of women is evident in the many stories that culminate either in a wedding motivated by economic concerns or permanent spinsterhood. Destructive gender codes as represented in Trevor's stories discourage fidelity, discourage sensitive men who nurture, and encourage frigidity and submissiveness in women.

Trevor's stories focused on gender should be seen not only in relation to the nineteenth-century British novel of manners and morals, courtship and marriage, but also to the eighteenth-century Augustan tradition. Writers in this latter tradition directed satiric barbs toward men but not with the same relish that they excoriated the folly of women (e. g., Pope and Swift).

When Trevor deals with gender he directs his ire toward the folly of men—not exclusively but emphatically. He portrays women—even the most neurotic (as in **"Raymond Bamber and Mrs. Fitch"**)—with an inordinate amount of compassion and tenderness. [In her *Toward a Recognition of Androgyny,* 1973] Carolyn Heilbrun explains female neurosis in relation to sexual repression as follows: "A woman must enjoy the full cycle of experience, or she would become riddled with complexes like a rotting fruit." Terrible barriers between men and women in the nineteenth century caused wives to envision sexual freedom as the freedom to say no to their husbands. I am not suggesting in any way that promiscuity on the part of women should be encouraged, but as Dorothy Dinnerstein [in *The Mermaid and the Minotaur,* 1976], among others, has shown, conditioned responses to feminine stereotypes result in "the special muting of woman's erotic impulsivity," which is a tragic development underlying the cause of the "midlife crisis" serving the older man so well when he wishes to abandon his wife for a younger woman.

Men and women indeed suffer when faced with only two viable models of womanhood: whore or Holy Mother. The consequences of this ancient predicament are self-hatred in the case of women, distaste for the body in the case of men as well as women. Gender codes in a patriarchal society privilege men and objectify women. Few can overcome such social conditioning that so profoundly governs relationships between men and women.

In Ireland gender codes are further complicated by colonialism. In her work on Joyce, Suzette Henke points out [in *James Joyce and the Politics of Desire,* 1990] that "unconsciously emulating their English masters, the Irish assert a specious manhood through blustering claims to patriarchal privilege, making infantile demands that frustrate and feminize those already demeaned by colonial subjugation." Irish women—but also women everywhere—bear the brunt of blustering husbands and fathers. Subjugation because of gender, then, is the most important factor in the stories to be addressed here.

The best example of Trevor's sensitive rendering of women is **"The Ballroom of Romance,"** although given the preponderance of overbearing and narcissistic fathers in the Trevor canon, the father in this story is an anomaly. Even though Bridie's father *does* care about his daughter, he must be understood in the context of a society endorsing fathers, husbands, brothers, and womanizers who are insensitive to the suffering of girls trying to salvage their floundering self-respect in a world that targets them as sex objects or ignores them; of submissive wives; of middle-aged women desperately trying to maintain their physical appearance; and of elderly women marginalized because they are alone—treated like children because physically fragile and suffering from an inferiority complex not unlike that of adolescents. Understanding the subtleties of **"The Ballroom of Romance"** and the stories depicting elderly women is crucial to understanding Trevor's many stories about courtship, sexuality, and gender.

The mother dies before we enter the lives of Bridie, the ballroom spinster, and her crippled father, who is not obviously narcissistic or domineering. Nonetheless, the gender codes governing Bridie's exaggerated, self-sacrificing nature are indirectly but poignantly revealed in the way she interacts with other members of this Irish community—the conforming spinsters and brides as well as the rebelling mothers; the womanizers of the dancehall in hot pursuit; the "father" representing the voice of the Church; and the businessmen, exemplified in Mr. Dwyer, the dancehall owner.

Bridie's father is apparently admired by his community and loved by his devoted daughter; despite his concern about Bridie's subservience, however, his handicap clearly requires that she spend most of her time meeting his every need. This physically crippled father—through no fault of his own—requires so much "mothering" that he "smothers" his emotionally crippled daughter, a plot line that inverts the more common scenario of a son entangled in his mother's apron strings.

Of course, gender codes in every society dramatically determine whether a daughter or son develops autonomy by separating from both parents. As Jessica Benjamin and other gender critics have argued, the son's individuation from the mother is more readily accomplished than the daughter's individuation from either parent. The son's idealization of and identification with the father is untainted by submission because cultural constructions of maleness incorporate concepts of power, thus encouraging independence from and actual authority over the mother. On the other hand, the daughter "idealizes deprivation" and submission to the father [Jessica Benjamin, *Feminist Studies* 8 (1982)].

The daughter cannot identify with the father and thereby establish an identity independent of the mother. Indeed, the mother is not a figure encouraging individuation for either child. To teach sons to be like the mother stereotypically conceived—affectionate, nurturing, sensitive, and tender—is to castrate them. Mothers may therefore inculcate in their sons an unfeeling stoicism, competitive independence, and "natural" aversion for nurturing to ensure their access to the power lines of a phallocentric world. Mothers likewise indoctrinate their daughters to be submissive and attractive to men. Furthermore, daughters are conditioned to develop what Benjamin identifies as "an

adoration of heroic men, who sacrifice love for freedom"— heroic men like those found in American wild west novels, Bridie's father's preferred entertainment.

Bridie is indeed radically limited, nervously worried whenever she "abandons" her father, which is only twice each week: on Sunday to attend Mass and on Saturday to attend "a wayside dancehall" where she hopes to "[drum] up" a husband, perhaps Dano Ryan, the drummer in the band. Bridie struggles to snag a husband without regard for her own needs or her own suffering.

In the first paragraph an understated, matter-of-fact narrator casually highlights Bridie's *father's* woes from "having had a leg amputated after gangrene had set in." The farm pony's death is mentioned before the mother's—the latter death related in one sentence and with the same intensity as the former's. The narrator flatly outlines in a shopping-list tone the routine comings and goings of the central characters as well as the usual visitors to the family farm—that is, three "in-comers" to Bridie's world: Canon O'Connell, the milk lorryman, and the grocer Mr. Driscoll. Bridie is a limited "out-goer."

The discourse of routine at the start of this story masks Bridie's suffering—her fear of growing old without a husband, her despair over her mother's death, her isolation. The absence of eulogy, a more appropriate response to the death of a parent, clarifies the neglect of Bridie by everyone in her community except the undesirable bachelors whose motives are suspect.

[In *The Dialogic Imagination*, edited by Michael Holquist, 1981] Bakhtin explains the subtlety at issue here when he discusses the reflexive nature of language and its tendency to distort, idealize, or mask the tragedies of life. The prominence of routine in Trevor's stories has already been mentioned; the discourse of routine in this story most emphatically "weatherizes," as Bakhtin imagines it, adjacent texts defining Bridie's struggle.

A pattern of subtexts conveys Bridie's entrapment by societal norms. The discourse of routine functions as an underlying refrain in many of Trevor's stories. Here this discourse marks the malaise of Bridie's life and the inevitability of her fate. On the first page alone we learn what was done "Sundays," "Mondays," "two years later," "not long after," "by the week," "daily," "during the week," "weekly," "once each month," "on a Friday afternoon," "by now," "often," "at night," and "in the evenings." Trevor demonstrates that Bridie functions "in time," with little freedom to develop the self.

Bridie is defined by her routine activities—domestic chores, the hard farm labor, the mothering of her father, and regular cycling to the nearest town (11 miles from the farm) to shop. She buys "for herself, material for a dress, knitting wool, stockings, a newspaper, and paper-backed Wild West novels for her father." The masculine communal voice relegates women to domestic tasks such as knitting and men to pioneering the wild west—adventures demanding that men be courageous "out-goers" and rescuers of helpless females, who foolishly presume they can survive a life beyond domesticity. There is an unhappy gap between the realms of women and men in this Irish community. When reading wild west novels, women less readily than men identify with masculine heroes and less easily feel vicarious enjoyment when aggressive men assert their will in gun battles and their freedom in the exploration of new frontiers, arenas closed to women.

Elaine Showalter quotes Louise Bogan to clarify the limitations of female domesticity in a similar context:

> Women have no wilderness in them.
> They are provident instead.
> Content in the tight hot cell of their hearts
> To eat dusty bread.

Bridie's dry domesticity, passivity, and entrapment, then, are subtly conveyed by reference to the wild west and a literary genre sentimentalizing the heroic feats of men. The father's reading of such novels is only one clue that we should be looking, as Annette Kolodny puts it [in *The New Feminist Criticism,* edited by Elaine Showalter, 1985] with "an acute attentiveness to the ways in which power relations, usually those in which males wield various forms of influence over females, are inscribed in the texts (both literary and critical) that we have inherited."

Trevor in fact manipulates many different voices so that the dialogue of others tells the *real* story of Bridie's plight with a tragic tone. The point is the absence of feminine power in the Irish community, the silencing of women. When Bridie converses with "some of the [town] girls she'd been to school with, girls who had married," she notes enviously that "most of them had families." But a rebelling feminine "they" tells Bridie, "You're lucky to be peaceful in the hills . . . instead of stuck in a hole like this." The narrator then relates Bridie's feelings of "surprise" that the girls "envied her life" because this aging spinster longs to conform to gender codes that place more value on the *fact* of being married than on the importance of marriage based on love.

It is an ironic, authorial voice that counters Bridie's wish to marry at any cost by defining married Irish women as "tired . . . from pregnancies and their efforts to organize and control their large families." The authoritarian voice of the Church urges women to have "large families" and to be happy despite the difficulties of "controlling" children when child-rearing is accomplished by mothers alone. The women characters in this story either assume mindlessly the proper female role or rebel by complaining about being "stuck" as mother-women exclusively—a role that is tiring. Nonetheless, Bridie and the other spinsters doggedly conform and romanticize the wife/mother role.

Bridie is "usually" thinking about how best to serve her father, "mending clothes or washing eggs." She agonizes over the possibility of becoming "a figure of fun in the Ballroom"—that is, a spinster like Madge Dowling, the hopeless case still chasing middle-aged bachelors. Bridie is radically determined by societal norms, first perpetuated by her father and later by the various men she imagines as rescuing her from spinsterhood. She deludes herself about the romantic potential of these bachelors: Dano Ryan, Eyes Horgan, Bowser Egan. Also, metonymy works to hilarious effect as "the guy with the long arms" appears and reappears, further darkening the romantic horizons of the spinsters.

Bowser most clearly conveys the masculine view of marriage: "he'd want a fire to sit at and a woman to cook food for him"—a woman "great at kissing." On the other hand, Bridie's fantasies about marriage do not include a sexual element. Benjamin argues that "daughters [reject] sexuality as a component of woman's autonomy." Nonetheless, the authorial voice describes Bridie physically and suggests a certain "masculine" vitality—an anomaly given Bridie's conformity to asexual feminine roles but a promising factor.

Bridie's repressed energy has the potential to counter her malaise. The narrator says that Bridie is "tall and strong," qualities more commonly attributed to men; "the skin of her fingers and her palms [are] stained and harsh to touch. The labor they'd experienced had found its way into them, as though juices had come out of vegetation and pigment out of soil: since childhood she'd torn away the rough scotch grass that grew each spring among her father's mangolds." Her "hands daily [root] in the ground. . . . Wind had toughened the flesh on her face." Rooted here in nature, Bridie tragically cannot fulfill the "natural" functions of wife and mother except by assuming the role of both wife and mother to her own father.

The same mindless dialogues grind up Bridie's day: the ballroom owner, Justin Dwyer, has been promising "for twenty years" he would visit Bridie's father. We are told that Bridie "never minded" "cycling" to either the ballroom or Mass. But the fact that "she'd grown quite used to all that" assumes the reality of a potent time past when she minded it "all" very much.

Furthermore, the dialogue of others tells the *real* story with a tragic tonality that must be reconstructed. Again at the start, after mention of Bridie's mother's death, we see Canon O'Connell's response, not Bridie's. He tells her not to "worry about it all." The narrator tells us that the good Canon here refers to "the difficulty of transporting her father to mass" because her mother is no longer there to help. The public rhetoric of this authority figure provides soothing evasions that ignore Bridie's suffering over the death of her mother. Surely "it all" encompasses more than getting her father to church.

Bridie suffers the loss of her mother. She worries about growing old, about becoming a spinster, about being isolated on a farm with a crippled father, about properly performing the domestic chores inside and the hard labor outside, and about fulfilling the duties of errand girl, daughter, wife, and mother to her father. Bridie's father sympathetically articulates the problem: "It's a terrible thing for you, girl." It is easier for her female friends to see the problem. Cat Bolger asks, "Are you on your own, Bridie?" Dano Ryan orders, "Tell your father I was asking for him" when she wishes he'd be asking for her instead.

Patty Byrne asks, "Are you O.K., Bridie?" A nameless youth asks, "Is there sense in it, Bridie?"

This nameless youth is also isolated, supporting his uncle until he can earn enough money to emigrate. The emigration of men owing to a poor rural economy in fact has limited Bridie's choices. Men are free to move "to Dublin or Britain, leaving behind them those who became the middle-aged bachelors of the hills"—leaving behind the women. Emigration is defined as escape from the mother country. Abandoning one's country seems as inevitable as abandoning one's parent, but abandoning one's parent is the first and necessary step toward autonomy. Women are limited in terms of emigration because of economics and in terms of independence because gender codes demand the dependence of wives, mothers, and daughters on husbands, fathers, and brothers—a painful dependence requiring no small measure of self-sacrifice.

Bridie suffers but behaves "as though nothing had happened." Her suffering is more evident when we consider not only how Wayne Booth perceives it but also how perspective is refined and clarified by Bakhtin. Authorial, narrative, character, communal male, and communal female voices vie with one another in Trevor's stories to form an underlying grid of relationships poignantly impinging on women characters. In this case aggressive forces oppress Bridie's personal freedom. She is habituated to behavior more appropriate for mother and wife than for a young maid seeking a husband.

Thus Bridie rides her mother's bicycle, the "old Rudge" digging deeper ruts in the same old track that forces her subservience to her father, who still calls his 36-year-old daughter "girl," even though it is *he* who depends on *her*. Bridie's father declares that he would "be dead without *the* girl [my daughter?] to assist [him]." We should notice that the father's comment implies the reverse of the usual case: parents ordinarily sustain the life of the child, not vice versa.

Unaware of her oppression, Bridie looks forward to being controlled by a husband. She daydreams about "when she was just sixteen" and had anticipated that Patrick Grady "would *lead* her into sunshine, to the town and the Church of Our Lady Queen of Heaven, to marriage and smiling faces" (my italics). Appropriately, given the inspiration of **"The Ballroom of Romance,"** Bridie romanticizes the social and religious codes demanding that men lead, women follow. When contemplating marriage, Bridie does not fantasize a husband who assumes the role of helpmate as expected but a husband who takes part in an oddly formulated threesome. The father-in-law and son form a pair: "two men working together" outside in the fields. Bridie thus attends "to things in the farmhouse." Her ideas of courtship and marriage are based on communal fantasies, not on reality (cripples don't work fields), and the inadequacy of these communal fantasies is implied as the story progresses.

Community codes condition women to be self-sacrificing, but Bridie sees her father, not herself, as a martyr, believing that he "had more right to weep, having lost a leg," a sort of castration. Even though the father's helpless "hobbling" de-

serves some sympathy, still the authorial voice solicits the largest measure of sympathy for Bridie, whose passivity and de-centered relation to the community is common enough.

All of the women at **"The Ballroom of Romance"** assume their proper "places on upright wooden chairs" and "[wait] to be asked to dance." These women are furthermore "too embarrassed to do anything about" the men who dance too close. Bridie is so conditioned by societal and religious codes regulating proper female behavior that she does not really belong anywhere and cannot escape her possessive father, who also suffers because he is unable to fulfill masculine norms of independence and freedom of movement.

Neither the father nor the daughter can openly express their suffering. Bridie feels it "improper" to weep "in the presence of her father," which also suggests that gender identity is inappropriately conditioned behavior—and that Bridie's response to such conditioning is confused. Societal codes in the Irish community and elsewhere require that men stoically repress tears, women weep or threaten to weep in order to control men. Bridie sublimates her own needs, and her "tears" are seen as "a luxury." Trevor amazingly presents weeping in a positive light. When men cry in this story, however, their tears are associated with an ailment, with disease. Dano develops "a watering of the eyes that must have been some kind of cold." Bridie, of course, tries to *mother* Dano by suggesting he take "Optrex," which she uses to bathe her father's eyes when he has similar trouble.

Unfortunately, Bridie is not aware enough to identify what she subconsciously wants—recognition as a subject. [In *Modern Fiction Studies* 35 (1989)] Margot Norris discusses Joyce's "The Dead" in a similar context and posits a reason for a wife's wish to be controlled by her husband: "Being treasured as a valued and cherished object—that is, relations more proper to the parent-child relation—is easier to achieve than recognition and significance as a subject."

Trevor's story about Bridie's plight finally identifies failures of male-female and parent-child relationships owing to the pressures of gender codes in a materialistic society idealizing the conventions of romance and mandating the subservience of women. The point emerges most clearly when readers relate the romantic delusions of Bridie's daydreams to those of aspiring brides everywhere.

At the root of male-female conflicts in the modern world is the failure of "romance" to result in meaningful relationships. **"The Ballroom of Romance"** has no humanity. The misanthropic capitalist, Dwyer, hates "the middle-aged bachelors who . . . came down from the hills like mountain goats, released from their mammies and from the smell of animals and soil." Indeed, Dwyer reduces love, the "evening rendezvous," to "business." His wife counts the "evenings takings" and raises turkeys rather than children. . . .

"Kathleen's Field" is [a very sinister story]—a vivid and painful portrait of feminine vulnerability and parental narcissism. Hagerty, the father in this story, unknowingly drives his daughter to despair as surely as he drives three bullocks to market in a futile attempt to muster enough money to purchase a lush field adjacent to his farm. Establishing his son's financial security is the father's goal. He worries that his eldest son's inheritance of the farm and land will be inadequate to attract a good wife. He worries about being abandoned by the three younger of his 10 children, the elder seven having already emigrated because of the poor rural economy. Con is his only remaining son, Biddy and Kathleen the last of his daughters.

Thus Hagerty justifies his scheme to ensure that his remaining son and two daughters remain within his grasp; his son especially must be restrained "from being tempted by Kilburn or Chicago." He manipulates "his youngest daughter," the 16-year-old Kathleen, whom he rationalizes as "his favorite," until she agrees to work for the pretentious owners of Shaughnessy's Provisions and Bar. Her wages are applied against the father's debt so that Con "would be left secure" and the mentally defective Biddy "would be provided for." This father unwittingly sells his daughter Kathleen into slavery. Mrs. Shaughnessy clarifies the arrangement when she tells her husband that Hagerty "has a girl for us," as if claiming her "property." The father reassures the lady of the pub that her efforts to train his daughter will not be wasted: she will not "go off to get married."

When her father explains that her "wages . . . would be held back and set against the debt" as a "convenience," Kathleen notices her father's relief: "the fatigue in his face had given way to an excited pleasure." She responds by agreeing with his plan. His suffering is over, hers just started.

This is yet another case of the daughter nurturing her father: the daughter here is focused on the father's pain—on his needs rather than her own. It does not seem to matter to the father that the son's welfare is won as the daughter's welfare is sacrificed. The loan for the land and the "loan" of a daughter are both reduced to a matter of doing business. Whereas purchasing the field expands the borders of her father's farm, the daughter's "field" of existence is radically circumscribed. This conforming daughter suffers unbearable working conditions and an overbearing taskmaster, Mrs. Shaughnessy, who deems Kathleen "raw," resolves "to train every inch of her," and complains about her "country accent." Worse, the child-molesting husband abuses the inexperienced young girl. This devious molester "liked the style" of having a servant because it afforded him the opportunity to sexually harass Kathleen.

Mrs. Shaughness expresses to Kathleen's father her worry that after spending a year training his daughter she'd "go off and get married." A cruel irony obtains when Hagerty assures his investor that "Kathleen wouldn't go running off, no fear of that"—exactly the fear that inspired his scheme in the first place to prevent her from leaving *him.*

The first view of Kathleen on the job focuses on her alarm and the fact that Mrs. Shaughnessy renames her new servant "Kitty," the name of the servant Kathleen has replaced. Mrs. Shaughnessy thus strips Kathleen of her identity and avoids the bother of herself adjusting to change. That this overbearing woman wants to call her new servant according to the name of a past one testifies to her regressive traits. Mrs. Shaughnessy complains that her last "girl" was "queer" because she ate raw onions, but the reader suspects this was the young woman's ploy to escape the clutches of Mr. Shaughnessy, who "liked to have a maid about the house" to molest.

Mrs. Shaughnessy trains Kathleen to set the table, cut kindling, dust "all the places where grime would gather," and rake the yard. Kitty's uniforms do not fit Kathleen well, making her uncomfortable. She is restricted to using the outhouse. And Mrs. Shaughnessy refers to her abusive husband as Kathleen's "master." Kathleen works six days, going home only on Sundays. During one visit she explains to her parents that she doesn't want to return, but her mother expresses her fears that the farm will consequently fail, the family will end up "no better than tinkers." The good daughter returns to the Shaughnessy establishment despite Mr. Shaughnessy's bold advances: "his hands passing over her clothes." His attentions only deepen an old track—her memories of rejection because boys her own age never tried to kiss her. Mr. Crawley, the butcher, often asks her if she's "going dancing," but "no one displayed any interest in her whatsoever." The shame that Kathleen feels over what becomes in her mind a "surreptitious relationship" with Mr. Shaughnessy is worsened by the shame of not being courted, of a future most certainly that of the spinster maid abused by "a grey-haired man" (Mr. Shaughnessy? her father?) because "a bargain was a bargain," as her mother puts it in the last line of the story.

> When Trevor deals with gender he directs his ire toward the folly of men— not exclusively but emphatically. He portrays women—even the most neurotic—with an inordinate amount of compassion and tenderness.
>
> —*Suzanne Morrow Paulson*

Those who labor in fields or work as servants of the great house in Trevor's stories would seem at odds with those who celebrate weddings in gardens. As in **"Kathleen's Field,"** however, the son's inheritance is a central issue in **"Wedding in the Garden,"** and it is a vulnerable young woman who suffers because of this concern. Moreover, we also again explore the terrible rift between men and women owing to differing attitudes toward sexuality and marriage.

Gender differences in **"The Wedding in the Garden"** are complicated by class differences. Gender and class codes determine not only *whether* one marries but also *who* one marries. Although Mrs. Congreve "married beneath her" and indeed the Protestant British aristocracy would normally shun Mr. Congreve, the middle-class proprietor of the Royal Hotel, still her son, Christopher, must seek a higher level. The plot, then, centers on an appalling event from the perspective of the Congreves, who focus strictly on economic concerns: Christopher seduces their servant girl, Derval. These parents worry that because of this indiscretion the "stylish" family pretense will not be maintained.

This story most suitably ends this discussion of gender and marriage because it subtly raises issues related to the covert nature of the double sex standard: the code that encourages the promiscuous behavior of men worried about their manhood and the frigidity of "ladies" worried about their virginity—with servant girls somewhat exempted.

The authority of the Church and the aristocracy are represented by the "clerical sombreness" of Mr. Congreve's "clothes" and the "ladylike" nature of Mrs. Congreve mentioned right at the start. Social hierarchies are then undercut when this paragraph ends with a superb double entendre. The voice of the young heir's lust merges for an instant with a voice expressing lower-class values, which have been determined by the pretentious upper class. More precisely, Derval's lower-class father defines aristocratic virtue: "The Congreves have great *breeding* in them." The "breeding" that takes place between Derval and Christopher would certainly not meet with her father's approval. The elevated discourse of the upper class sometimes imitated by the working class encourages the reader's disdain for such considerations as not just "good" but "great breeding."

The proprietors of the Royal Hotel are concerned with improprieties of class that would undermine their stature in the community. They "naturally" condemn Christopher's affair with the maid. Such socioeconomic concerns as class—Mrs. Congreve's "stylishness" and that of her children "imbued with this through the accident of their birth"—are, in Trevor's view, superficial differences. Nonetheless, the Congreves demand that Christopher marry an affluent Protestant minister's daughter. Derval is condemned to the life of a servant/spinster devastated by lost love.

Class codes coincide with gender codes as this story develops. In a typical phallocentric and classist society, women and servants are often invisible. Christopher does not apparently notice the new servant, Derval, for "a year or so," perhaps not until he reaches puberty. She appears at first as "a solitary figure in a black coat"; Christopher "didn't [even] know her name or what her face was like." Servants are faceless. She is simply "the girl." His sense of Derval is so vague that he "couldn't remember the first time he'd been aware of her." Likewise, his sisters "paid her no attention," even though she was "a child as they were." Finally, Christopher, while wandering about town, "had never noticed Thomas MacDonagh Street," Derval's neighborhood. When he does finally notice the young and physically attractive servant, he "[follows] with his eyes . . . the movement of Derval's hips beneath her black dress." This sort of attention is of course suspect.

Derval's invisibility is most subtly conveyed when Trevor represents Christopher's return from boarding school. Greeted by "a great fuss," "excited" sisters, and his father, apparently anxious to hear his son's "tale of the long journey from Dublin," Christopher recalls his experiences at boarding school to an eager audience, which at first seems to include only the family. The presence of the servants is only evident halfway through the paragraph when abruptly one line of direct dialogue intrudes: "Like the game of tennis it would be," the yardman Artie here responding to Derval's inquiry about "what cricket was." This snatch of dialogue, the second half of the exchange, then transfers the reader's attention from Christopher's story of boarding-school exploits to Derval's "excited" interest, and the second half of the paragraph relates Derval's vicarious living of Christopher's experiences.

This "turn" in a single paragraph effectively conveys the invisibility of the servant class, yet at the same time it infers Derval's interest in the event, although the Congreves ignore her. Her inspired imaginings reprocess Christopher's story of "the big grey house . . . and bells always ringing, and morning assemblies, and the march through cloisters to the chapel." The breathlessness inferred by the sequence of "and . . . and . . . and" approaches a sense of awe, which is also felt by Christopher's sisters, who stand on the sidelines and are also generally ignored.

Women and servants *are,* on the other hand, noticed if they behave as if they do not know their proper place, if they do not observe "the formalities," as Mr. Congreve puts it. Mary, the elderly and "rheumaticky" maid Derval replaces, refuses Mr. Congreve's offer for her to rest on her long way to her attic bedroom: "'It was unseemly,' Derval had heard old Mary saying in the kitchen," that servants should sit on the furniture. Voice becomes complicated in this passage as we are told by a narrator what Derval heard old Mary and Mr. Congreve say. Sequence provides a clue as to whose voice we hear: Mr. Congreve complains that "it took [Mary] half a day . . . to mount the stairs to her bedroom at the top of the hotel, and the other half to descend it." This criticism darkens the atmosphere of the next sentence, the cheery claim (probably the servants' misconception) that Mr. Congreve "was fond of" Mary.

Similarly, this paragraph ends with another suspect conclusion that "Mr. Congreve was devil-may-care about matters like that." This sentence continues with a series of elitist and chauvinist considerations surely meant to represent Mr. Congreve's ambitious perspective on proprieties governing the servants—"but what would a visitor say if he came out of his bedroom and found a uniformed maid in an armchair? What would Byrne from Horton's say, or Boylan the insurance man?" The "visitors" who would be disturbed by a servant overstepping her bounds are presumed to be men. The next paragraph represents Mr. Congreve's concern over "the formalities." Surely his attention to Mary's infirmities are insincere, not only because she is a servant but also because she is a woman.

Mr. Congreve charms Dervla with the same pretense of interest as he does all the servants when he seems to care about the infirmities of the old maid, Mary. The master of the house tries to converse with the younger maid by "asking how her father was." Dervla is "somehow—in front of him . . . embarrassed" and later suffers "a nightmare . . . that [Mr. Congreve] was in *the* house on Thomas MacDonagh Street and that her mother was on her knees, scrubbing the stone floor of the scullery" (my italics). Reluctant to claim her home as "my house," she realizes the disparity between her family and Christopher's.

Disparities owing to class are clear when we consider the differences between Dervla's and Christopher's families. Disparities owing to gender are clear as Christopher relates to Dervla and also to his sisters. Sons are given preferential treatment over daughters early in their development and emphatically so when they approach manhood. In this case Christopher avoids his sisters because he wants "to be alone at that time of his growing up"; "his sisters [are] too chattery." Indeed, Christopher's puberty is defined in terms of romanticized notions of a boy's initiation into manhood, his need to be "alone"—that is, not in the company of girls—and to explore the world beyond the home. His "wanderings about the town" end with the shops where as a child he bought sweets but now buys *Our Boys, Film Fun,* and *Wide World.*

Whereas Christopher enjoys "lingering by the shops that sold fruit and confectionery" and Christopher's sisters enjoy playing games in the garden, Dervla seems to work at least a 12-hour day, "arriving before breakfast, cycling home again in the late evening." The difference here depends on class differences more than those of gender, but of course aristocratic attitudes toward the working class often involve drawing boundaries according to what is "natural." "Nature" likewise limits women economically and physically. Christopher knows it is not "natural in any way at all" for him to sit with Dervla on a rug in the sun or "to wheel the bicycle of the dining-room maid." Trevor appropriately allows much more space to define Dervla's awareness of class difference than to define Christopher's, whose awareness of such differences eventually causes him to abandon the maid.

Dervla in fact is "fascinated" by the status, "stylishness," and wealth of her employers, whose worth is measured according to their possessions. Christopher's "grand" initialed "green trunk" captures her imagination each time he returns home from boarding school. She imagines the Congreves in "their motor-car, an old Renault," surely in a state of grace when they "[make] the journey to the Protestant church" and "the bell ceased to chime" upon their arrival.

Despite the Congreves' conformity to theological dogma on regular church attendance here, other transgressions seem less weighty. Trevor relates Dervla's seduction by Christopher in a very few lines, affording this event very little space in comparison with other passages—say, those focused on status symbols, which are developed at some length. The seduction, the first tender tryst, encompasses six sentences strategically positioned to follow Dervla's

father's litany of her marriage prospects—Buzzy Carroll, who worked in Catigan's hardware; Flynn; Chappie; Butty; Streak; and the nameless "porter . . . [whose] toes joined together in such a peculiar way that he showed them to people." Trevor's concision suggests the ease with which Christopher initiates the affair by declaring, "I'm fond of you, Dervla," and then leading "her upstairs to Room 14, a tiny bedroom." There follows a brief discussion of how the seduction developed into a routine. In the seventh sentence of this sequence we learn that "after that first afternoon they met often to embrace in Room 14." In the eighth sentence Christopher declares, "They would marry [and] live in the hotel, just like his parents."

The promise of this loving relationship is also all-to-briefly developed in the bat of an eye when "the warmth of their bodies [becomes] a single warmth." Christopher's "love" for Dervla changes his attitude toward his community, which he had previously seen as "a higgledy-piggledy conglomeration of dwellings, an ugly place." After the affair he sees his community as "Dervla's town, and . . . his own; together they belonged there." That basic human need for a sense of belonging is central to the story. Christopher envisions his future: "in middle age [he walks] through [the town's] narrow streets . . . returning to the hotel and going at once to embrace the wife he loved with a passion that had not changed"—again, a fleeting embrace.

Trevor here does celebrate the potential of love to nurture the lovers' sense of belonging—to each other and to their community. Love does stave off the ravages of time, does overcome the adolescent's sense of alienation. The promise of Dervla and Christopher's love, however, cannot last. Dervla's father first intrudes. Trevor frames the seduction passage by the paternal voice urging his daughter to accept suitors of her own class. The frame is completed by her father's insistence, "Not a bad fella at all. . . . Young Carroll." And Dervla wonders "what on earth [her father would] say if he knew about Room 14."

The need to belong reappears when Mother Congreve develops five reasons to convince Dervla to relinquish Christopher. She admonishes Dervla to consider "propriety" given certain social hierarchies ("there are differences between you and Christopher that cannot be overlooked. . . . Christopher is not of your class, Dervla. He is not of your religion"). She shames Dervla by appealing to her sense of honesty and duty (she blames the poor maid for "betraying" their trust). She clarifies the relationship of the powerful ruling class to the servant class in terms of economics (she threatens that Dervla will lose her job, Christopher his inheritance). She tries to instill a feeling of obligation in Dervla ("We have trained you, you know. We have done a lot")—obligation that should yield to authority. Most cleverly, she targets the adolescent's need to belong when she asks, "Don't you feel you belong in the Royal, Dervla? . . . You will not be asked to leave."

The Church further undermines Dervla's determination to defend her love. Dervla considers that "it was a sin" and reluctantly writes to Christopher, conforming to his mother's wish that the maid be the one to break off the affair.

After he receives Dervla's letter written in "tidy, convent handwriting" and declaring the affair over, Christopher's "bewilderment turned to anger," a conditioned masculine response to loss. Before he can confront Dervla, his father confronts him, chastizing him for "messing about with maids" and then exhibiting the typical masculine perspective on sexual violations of women: "it's a bit of a storm in a tea-cup." Only after having a clear sense of his parents' attitudes does Christopher confront Dervla with, "Is it priests?" and "Did my mother speak to you?" Dervla answers in the affirmative—"Your mother only said a few things"—but Christopher is unresponsive to her reply. The moment of opportunity to seize love and retrieve his ethical sense is lost. He does not question Dervla enough and all too quickly becomes "reconciled to the loss of their relationship [because] between the lines of her letter there had been a finality." The "finality," however, is based on class lines.

When the no-longer-maiden maid finally confesses to "the priests" about "the sinning that had been so pleasurable in Room 14," the priest, like Christopher's father, sees the servant's affair as a "misdemeanour." Dervla herself comes to realize that her lover "would *naturally* wish to forget it now: For him, Room 14 must have come to seem like an adventure in indiscretion, as *naturally* his parents had seen it" (my italics).

Dervla remains in the Royal Hotel and is forced to observe the development of Christopher's interest in the archdeacon's beautiful daughter. The maid listens to stories told by the more suitable maiden, who converses during dinner about her past. Dervla feels abandoned while "expertly disposing of chop bones or bits of left-behind fat." She herself was as easily disposed of and has become "leftovers." Her realization "that this was the girl who was going to take her place, in [Christopher's] life" is more poignant on Christopher's wedding day, when "a new maid with spectacles" appears, probably to replace Dervla just as Dervla replaced Mary.

The reality of what was lost fades because the routine of "Dervla [clearing] away the dishes" no longer calls attention to young love. The servant is again invisible. Dervla's previous prayers—ironically, to "the Virgin's liquid eyes"—that Christopher's "little finger might accidentally touch her hand" are soon eclipsed by confessions. By the time of his wedding, in fact, the ritual of confession and the ritual of the wedding toast have lost meaning. Pretense causes the "excess of emotion in the garden, an excess of smiles and tears and happiness and love" expressed by "glasses . . . held up endlessly, toast after toast."

Indeed, the marriage celebration is really "a business arrangement," like the archdeacon's agreement "as convention demanded" to pay for the reception to be held at the hotel. Christopher realizes that Dervla "was not beautiful" even though "once, not knowing much about it, he had imagined she was." When he acknowledges that there "was something less palpable [than physical beauty] that distinguished her," we are left to ponder exactly what the groom has in mind. What is it that finally distinguishes the uni-

formed maid? It was precisely Dervla's "palpability" or physical attractiveness that first caused Christopher to notice his "servant."

The priests finally "get" Dervla; the archdeacon's daughter "gets" Christopher. And yet a sense of less permeates this outcome. The bride's unnaturally beautiful "skin like the porcelain of a doll's skin" causes us to question her humanity. Routine, ritual, convention, the civility of shared memories, and "speeches . . . made in the sunshine" round out our days. The cliché-ridden voices of various community members resound throughout the garden as guests share fond memories of the past to affirm that they truly "belong" in this elegant present.

Whereas Dervla's father had admired his wife for having "the strength of an ox," thereby surviving childbirth and producing Dervla at the age of 42, Christopher's bride is virginal, her hand "as delicate as the petal of a flower." The point of the story, nevertheless, is that few women possess the strength to emerge from an affair without scars—sometimes wounds that eclipse any possibility for wedded bliss. Dervla's vulnerability is clear when Christopher realizes, "She would indeed not ever marry," and then turns away.

The vulnerability of women emerges most emphatically at the end of the story when we are surprised to discover that Christopher's sexual adventures may not have been limited to his purported love for Dervla. The best man, Tom Gouvernet, declares that "Christopher had been "a right Lothario" with a "shocking reputation at school," then encourages the bride to remember her groom's best man when she gets "tired" of her new husband. The mood here changes; actually it is not much different from the mood of the best man in **"Teresa's Wedding"** (no harm done by his "great bloody ride"). This jubilant mood is ominous: the groom more likely will tire of the bride.

Finally, the disparity between Dervla's and Christopher's perceptions of their "romance" and the conventions of "Ancient Romance," as Bakhtin explains it, may sharpen the reader's conception of the circumstances in this story. In ancient romance the boy and girl are expected to be "exceptionally chaste." At the end of this story the best man casts doubt on Christopher's chastity when he seduced Dervla—also on his pretense of romantic feeling. Dervla, on the other hand, retains her innocence because she maintains her fidelity to her lover, like the classic case of the romantic heroine.

In ancient romance the lovers are beset with "obstacles that retard and delay their union," as Bakhtin explains it. The deft lover here wins Dervla's immediate submission. The hero and heroine do not know their lineage in ancient romance: "The first meeting of hero and heroine and the sudden flare up of their passion for each other is the starting point for plot movement; the end point for plot movement is their successful union in marriage." Their "love remains absolutely unchanged . . . their chastity is preserved." In this story Dervla and Christopher, conversely, are all too aware of their lineage. Their first meeting is a nonevent. The plot develops around the dramatic change of events when Dervla is confronted by Christopher's mother.

In ancient romance the heroine withstands trials and tests while maintaining her fidelity, which proves her triumph over her humble origins. Dervla is tested but never rises above her class. The "maid" is not transformed into "lady," and in fact she is fallen, no longer a "maiden." The hero of ancient romance does not give in to materialistic temptations as Christopher does when conforming to parental authority in order to preserve "his inheritance," which Trevor ironically defines early in the novel in terms of a "greenish . . . threadbare" carpet.

Christopher realizes that he must endure a lifetime of pretense and suffer the constant gaze of his faithful servant: "while he and his parents could successfully bury a part of the past, Dervla could not. It had never occurred to him that because she was the girl she was she did not appreciate that some experiences were best forgotten. . . . [Such] subtleties had *naturally* eluded the dining room maid." Christopher wishes he had told his bride about Dervla and realizes he cannot because the Archdeacon's daughter would certainly dismiss her servant. Poignant irony obtains in the groom's scruples here as the reader conflates "a promise made to a dining-room maid [that] must be honoured" with the promise to marry Dervla that was not honored.

Marriages are not likely to succeed if based on secrets and determined by business "arrangements"—the Congreves' conniving a case in point. Although gender codes are central to the stories addressed here, the force of "business as usual" also has been a constant undercurrent.

FURTHER READING

Criticism

Broyard, Anatole. "Radical Comes from Root." *The New York Times Book Review* (31 October 1972): 43.
    Derides the traditional style of *The Ballroom of Romance, and Other Stories.*

Craig, Patricia. "The Pressure of Events." *The Times Literary Supplement*, No. 4530 (26 January 1990): 87.
    Observes three recurrent themes in Trevor's short fiction: domestic scandals, acrimony in marriages, and recollecting the past.

Gordon, Mary. "The Luck of the Irish." *The New York Review of Books* (22 December 1983): 53-4.

Studies the influence of Trevor's middle class, Irish Protestant background on his work.

Heyward, Michael. "Domestic Terrors." *The New Republic* CCIII, No. 14 (1 October 1990): 40-1.
    Praises Trevor's narrative technique in *Family Sins, and Other Stories.*

Morrison, Kristin. *William Trevor.* New York: Twayne Publishers, 1993, 196 p.
    Full-length critical study of Trevor's novels, plays, and short stories. Morrison includes a selected bibliography.

Paulson, Suzanne Morrow. *William Trevor: A Study of the Short Fiction.* New York: Twayne Publishers, 1993, 214 p.
    Book-length critical study of Trevor's stories and novellas. Paulson endeavors to "spotlight representative masterpieces of human insight—masterpieces demanding that Trevor be recognized in America for his singular understanding of personality and his major contributions to the short-story form."

Rhodes, Robert E. "William Trevor's Stories of the Troubles." In *Contemporary Irish Writing*, ed. James D. Brophy and Raymond J. Porter, pp. 83-113. Boston: Iona College Press and Twayne Publishers, 1983.
    Examines the treatment of the Anglo-Irish conflict in Trevor's short fiction.

Schirmer, Gregory A. *William Trevor: A Study of His Fiction.* New York: Routledge, 1990, 180 p.
    Offers an extensive survey of Trevor's short stories.

Solataroff, Ted. "The Dark Souls of Ordinary People." *The New York Times Book Review* (21 February 1982): 7, 34.
    Lauds Trevor's sympathetic portrayals of banal and restricted lives in *Beyond the Pale, and Other Stories.*

Towers, Robert. "Gleeful Misanthropy." *The New York Times Book Review* (2 October 1983): 1, 22-4.
    Surveys the shift from "harsh comedy" to empathic humor in Trevor's fiction.

————. "Good News." *The New York Review of Books* (26 June 1986): 32-5.
    Discusses the pressure of the past in *The News from Ireland, and Other Stories.*

————. "Short Satisfactions." *The New York Review of Books* (17 May 1990): 38-9.
    Mixed review of *Family Sins and Other Stories.*

Trevor, William. "Some Notes on Writing Stories." *London Magazine* IX, No. 12 (March 1970): 10-12.
    Trevor briefly comments on his own short story technique.

Additional coverage of Trevor's life and career is contained in the following sources published by Gale Research: *Contemporary Authors*, Vols. 9-12 (rev. ed); *Contemporary Authors New Revision Series*, Vols. 4, 37; *Contemporary Literary Criticism*, Vols. 7, 9, 14, 25, 71; *Dictionary of Literary Biography*, Vols. 14, 139; and *Major 20th-Century Writers*.

Giovanni Verga
1840-1922

Italian short story writer, novelist, and dramatist.

INTRODUCTION

Verga is a major figure both in Italian literature and in the evolution of modern Western literature. During the era of his mature genius he was the leading voice of *verismo*, an Italian movement of literary realism roughly corresponding to the school of Naturalism originated by French novelist Émile Zola. Verga employed a unique style in which the story is told completely through direct and indirect speech of the characters. The form, diction, and tone of the story mirror the attitudes and consciousness of its characters, both individually and collectively. This method was particularly effective in Verga's depictions of Sicilian peasant life. One of his most successful examinations of this peasant world was "Cavalleria rusticana," which the author wrote as both a short story and a drama, and which was adapted as the libretto for Pietro Mascagni's well-known opera of the same title.

Biographical Information

Verga was born in Sicily into an upper-class family, and for a time he studied law at the University of Catania. His interests, however, were resolutely literary, and after publishing some undistinguished early novels he decided to leave Sicily in 1869 and pursue his career in the more cosmopolitan centers of Florence and Milan. The novels he produced during the next few years were fashionable romances dealing with the passions of the rich, and they did not yet display his ultimate style. While living in Milan, Verga's artistic concerns altered dramatically, from romanticism to realism, and from the culture of high society to the rural life that surrounded him when he was growing up in Sicily. By 1879 Verga had returned completely to his Sicilian roots and moved into his childhood home in Catania. He died there in 1922 after twenty years of literary silence.

Major Works of Short Fiction

"Nedda," which Verga subtitled "A Sicilian Sketch," is one of the earliest stories to exhibit the cultural and stylistic focus of his later genius. With the publication of this story in 1874, Verga truly began to develop his style of *verismo*. In his later work Verga sought to efface the author's identity and allow the fictional subject to dictate the form of the work. Thus, in his later short stories and novels Verga let the dialects and idioms of his characters permeate every level of his narrative. Some of the stories that best exemplify Verga's mature style are "Cavalleria rusticana," "The

She-Wolf," "Gramigna's Mistress," and "Rosso Malpelo," all of which are included in his major collections: *Vita dei campi* (*Cavalleria Rusticana, and Other Tales of Sicilian Peasant Life*) and *Novelle rusticane* (*Little Novels of Sicily*). Verga writes each in the *style indirect libre,* or "free indirect style," where the characters seem to narrate themselves with no intrusion from the author. In these stories, Verga anticipates such modernist artistic devices as interior monologue and stream of consciousness.

Critical Reception

Critics agree that Verga's genius is most brilliantly displayed in his development of *verismo*. His gift for letting action and dialogue relate the story, with never a word wasted, is universally lauded. Commentators consider him the first Italian writer to accurately represent the language of the Sicilian people and the peculiar subtleties of their dialects. Critics debate whether Verga's method of *verismo* developed independently of others with similar styles, but his mastery of the technique is rarely questioned. Although he produced the body of his work in the nineteenth century, Verga is perhaps best understood in terms of twentieth-century modernist literature and the search for new forms of expression.

PRINCIPAL WORKS

Short Fiction

Vita dei campi [*Cavalleria Rusticana, and Other Tales of Sicilian Peasant Life*, 1893; also published as *Cavalleria Rusticana, and Other Stories*, 1928] 1880
Novelle rusticane [*Little Novels of Sicily*, 1925] 1883
Per le vie 1883
Vagabondaggio 1887
Don Candeloro e c' [*Don Candeloro and Co.*, 1958] 1894
Pane nero, and Other Stories 1962
The She-Wolf, and Other Stories 1973

Other Major Works

Una peccatrice (novel) 1866
Storia di una capinera (novel) 1871
Eva (novel) 1873
Tigre reale (novel) 1873
Eros (novel) 1875
I Malavoglia: Romanzo [*The House by the Medlar-Tree*, 1890] (novel) 1881
Il marito di Elena: Romanzo (novel) 1881
Cavalleria rusticana (drama) 1884
Mastro-don Gesualdo: Romanzo [*Master Don Gesualdo*, 1893] (novel) 1889
La Lupa. In portinaio. Cavalleria rusticana. Drammi (dramas) 1896
La caccia al lupo. La caccia alla volpe. Bozzetti scenici (dramas) 1902

CRITICISM

D. H. Lawrence (essay date 1928)

SOURCE: A preface to *Cavalleria Rusticana, and Other Stories*, by Giovanni Verga, translated by D. H. Lawrence, 1928. Reprint by Greenwood Press, 1975, pp. 7-33.

[*Lawrence was an English novelist, poet, and essayist noted for his introduction of the themes of modern psychology to English fiction. In his lifetime he was a controversial figure, both for the explicit sexuality he portrayed in his novels and for his unconventional personal life. Much of the criticism of Lawrence's work concerns his highly individualistic moral system, which was based on absolute freedom of expression, particularly sexual expression. In the following excerpt, Lawrence notes Verga's interest in peasant characters as they exemplify the* passion, naivete, and spontaneity lacking in urban-dwelling sophisticates. Lawrence argues that Verga did not glorify his peasant characters or glamorize their impoverished state.]

Cavalleria Rusticana is in many ways the most interesting of the Verga books. The volume of short stories under this title appeared in 1880, when the author was forty years old, and when he had just "retired" from the world.

The Verga family owned land around Vizzini, a biggish village in southern Sicily; and here, in and around Vizzini, the tragedies of Turiddu and La Lupa and Jeli take place. But it was only in middle life that the drama of peasant passion really made an impression on Giovanni Verga. His earlier imagination, naturally, went out into the great world.

The family of the future author lived chiefly at Catania, the seaport of east Sicily, under Etna. And Catania was really Verga's home town, just as Vizzini was his home village.

But as a young man of twenty he already wanted to depart into the bigger world of "the Continent," as the Sicilians called the mainland of Italy. . . . A true provincial, he had to try to enter the *beau monde*. He lived by journalism, more or less: certainly the Vizzini lands would not keep him in affluence. But still, in his comparative poverty, he must enter the *beau monde*.

He did so: and apparently, with a certain success. And for nearly twenty years he lived in Milan, in Florence, in Naples, writing, and imagining he was fulfilling his thirst for glory by having love-affairs with elegant ladies: most elegant ladies, as he assures us.

To this period belong the curiously unequal novels of the city world: *Eva, Tigre Reale, Eros*. They are interesting, alive, bitter, somewhat unhealthy, smelling of the 'seventies and of the Paris of the Goncourts, and, in some curious way, abortive. The man had not found himself. He was in his wrong element, fooling himself and being fooled by show, in a true Italian fashion.

Then, towards the age of forty, came the recoil, and the *Cavalleria Rusticana* volume is the first book of the recoil. It was a recoil away from the *beau monde* and the "Continent," back to Sicily, to Catania, to the peasants. . . .

Cavalleria Rusticana marks a turning-point in the man's life. Verga still looks back to the city elegance, and makes such a sour face over it, it is really funny. The sketch he calls **"Fantasticheria"** (**"Caprice"**) and the last story in the book, **"Il Come, il Quando, et il Perchè"** (**"The How, When, and Wherefore"**) both deal with the elegant little lady herself. The sketch **"Caprice"** we may take as autobiographical—the story not entirely so. But we have enough data to go on.

The elegant little lady is the same, pretty, spoilt, impulsive, emotional, but without passion. The lover, Polidori, is only half-sketched. But evidently he is a passionate man who *thinks* he can play at love and then is mortified to his very soul because he finds it is only a game. The tone of mortification is amusingly evident both in the sketch and in the story. Verga is profoundly and everlastingly offended with the little lady, with all little ladies, not for taking him absolutely seriously as an amorous male, when all the time he doesn't quite take himself seriously, and doesn't take the little lady seriously at all.

Nevertheless, the moment of sheer roused passion is serious in the man: and apparently not so in the woman. Each time the moment comes, it involves the whole nature of the man and does not involve the whole nature of the woman: she still clings to her social safeguards. It is the difference between a passionate nature and an emotional nature. But then the man goes out deliberately to make love to the emotional elegant woman who is truly social and not passionate. So he has only himself to blame if his passionate nose is out of joint.

It is most obviously out of joint. His little picture of the elegant little lady jingling her scent-bottle and gazing in nervous anxiety for the train from Catania which will carry her away from Aci-Trezza and her too-intense lover, back to her light, gay, secure world on the mainland is one of the most amusingly biting things in the literature of love. How glad she must have been to get away from him! And how bored she must have been by his preaching the virtues of the humble poor, holding them up before her to make her feel small. We may be sure she didn't feel small, only nervous and irritable. For apparently she had no deep warmth or generosity of nature.

So Verga recoiled to the humble poor, as we see in his **"Caprice"** sketch. Like a southerner, what he did he did wholesale. Floods of savage and tragic pity he poured upon the humble fisherfolk of Aci Trezza, whether they asked for it or not;—partly to spite the elegant little lady. And this particular flood spreads over the whole of his long novel concerning the fisherfolk of Aci-Trezza: *I Malavoglia.* It is a great novel, in spite of the pity: but always in spite of it.

In *Cavalleria Rusticana,* however, Verga had not yet come to the point of letting loose his pity. He is still too much and too profoundly offended, as a passionate male. He recoils savagely away from the sophistications of the city life of elegant little ladies, to the peasants in their most crude and simple, almost brute-like aspect.

When one reads, one after the other, the stories of Turiddu, La Lupa, Jeli, Brothpot, Rosso Malpelo, one after the other, stories of crude killing, it seems almost too much, too crude, too violent, too much a question of mere brutes.

As a matter of fact, the judgment is unjust. Turiddu is not a brute: neither is Alfio. Both are men of sensitive and even honourable nature. Turiddu knows he is wrong, and would even let himself be killed, he says, but for the thought of his old mother. The elegant Maria and her

Erminia are never so sensitive and direct in expressing themselves; nor so frankly warm-hearted.

As for Jeli, who could call him a brute? or Nanni? or Brothpot? They are perhaps not brutal enough. They are too gentle and forbearing, too delicately naïve. And so grosser natures trespass on them unpardonably; and the revenge flashes out.

His contemporaries abused Verga for being a realist of the Zola school. The charge is unjust. The base of the charge against Zola is that he made his people too often merely physical-functional arrangements, physically and materially functioning without any "higher" nature. The charge against Zola is often justifiable. It is completely justifiable against the earlier D'Annunzio. In fact, the Italian tends on the one hand to be this creature of physical-functionary activity and nothing else, spasmodically sensual and materialist; hence the violent Italian outcry against the portrayal of such creatures, and D'Annunzio's speedy transition to neurotic Virgins of the Rocks and ultra-refinements.

But Verga's people are always people in the purest sense of the word. They are not intellectual, but then neither was Hector nor Ulysses intellectual. Verga, in his recoil, mistrusted everything that smelled of sophistication. He had a passion for the most naïve, the most unsophisticated manifestation of human nature. He was not seeking the brute, the animal man, the so-called cave-man. Far from it. He knew already too well that the brute and the cave-man lie quite near under the skin of the ordinary successful man of the world. There you have the predatory cave-man of vulgar imagination, thinly hidden under expensive cloth.

What Verga's soul yearned for was the purely naïve human being, in contrast to the sophisticated. It seems as if Sicily, in some way, under all her amazing forms of sophistication and corruption, still preserves some flower of pure human candour: the same thing that fascinated Theocritus. Theocritus was an Alexandrine courtier, singing from all his "musk and insolence" of the pure idyllic Sicilian shepherds. Verga is the Theocritus of the nineteenth century, born among the Sicilian shepherds, and speaking of them in prose more sadly than Theocritus, yet with some of the same eternal Sicilian dawn-freshness in his vision. It is almost bitter to think that Rosso Malpelo must often have looked along the coast and seen the rocks that the Cyclops flung at Ulysses; and that Jeli must some time or other have looked to the yellow temple-ruins of Girgenti.

Verga was fascinated, after his mortification in the *beau monde,* by pure naïveté and by the spontaneous passion of life, that spurts beyond all convention or even law. Yet as we read, one after the other, of these betrayed husbands killing the co-respondents, it seems a little mechanical. Alfio, Jeli, Brothpot, Gramigna ending their life in prison: it seems a bit futile and hopeless, mechanical again.

The fault is partly Verga's own, the fault of his own obsession. He felt himself in some way deeply mortified, insulted in his ultimate sexual or male self, and he enacted over and over again the drama of revenge. We think to ourselves, ah, how stupid of Alfio, of Jeli, of Brothpot, to have to go killing a man and getting themselves shut up in prison for life, merely because the man had committed adultery with their wives. Was it worth it? Was the wife worth one year of prison, to a man, let alone a lifetime?

We ask the question with our reason, and with our reason we answer No! Not for a moment was any of these women worth it. Nowadays we have learnt more sense, and we let her go her way. So the stories are too old-fashioned.

And again, it was not for love of their wives that Jeli and Alfio and Brothpot killed the other man. It was because people talked. It was because of the fiction of "honour."— We have got beyond all that.

We are so much more reasonable. All our life is so much more reasoned and reasonable. *Nous avons changé tout cela.*

And yet, as the years go by, one wonders if mankind is so radically changed. One wonders whether reason, sweet reason, has really changed us, or merely delayed or diverted our reactions. Are Alfio and Jeli and Gramigna utterly out of date, a thing superseded for ever? Or are they eternal?

Is man a sweet and reasonable creature? Or is he, basically, a passional phenomenon? Is man a phenomenon on the face of the earth, or a rational consciousness? Is human behaviour to be reasonable, throughout the future, reasoned and rational?—or will it always display itself in strange and violent phenomena?

Judging from all experience, past and present, one can only decide that human behaviour is ultimately one of the natural phenomena, beyond all reason. Part of the phenomenon, for the time being, is human reason, the control of reason, and the power of the Word. But the Word and the reason are themselves only part of the coruscating phenomenon of human existence; they are, so to speak, one rosy shower from the rocket, which gives way almost instantly to the red shower of ruin or the green shower of despair.

Man is a phenomenon on the face of the earth. But the phenomena have their laws. One of the laws of the phenomenon called a human being is that, hurt this being mortally at its sexual root, and it will recoil ultimately into some form of killing. The recoil may be prompt, or delay by years or even by generations. But it will come. We may take it as a law.

We may take it as another law that the very deepest quick of a man's nature is his own pride and self-respect. The human being, weird phenomenon, may be patient for years and years under insult, insult to his very quick, his pride in his own natural being. But at last, oh phenomenon, killing will come of it. All bloody revolutions are the result of the long, slow, accumulated insult to the quick of pride in the mass of men.

A third law is that the naïve or innocent core in a man is always his vital core, and infinitely more important than his intellect or his reason. It is only from his core of unconscious naïveté that the human being is ultimately a responsible and dependable being. Break this human core of naïveté—and the evil of the world all the time tries to break it, in Jeli, in Rosso Malpelo, in Brothpot, in all these Verga characters—and you get either a violent reaction, or, as is usual nowadays, a merely rational creature whose core of spontaneous life is dead. Now the rational creature, who is merely rational, by some cruel trick of fate remains rational only for one or two generations at best. Then he is quite mad. It is one of the terrible qualities of the reason that it has no life of its own, and unless continually kept nourished or modified by the naïve life in man and woman, it becomes a purely parasitic and destructive thing. Make any human being a really rational being, and you have made him a parasitic and destructive force. Make any people mainly rational in their life, and their inner activity will be the activity of destruction. The more the populations of the world become only rational in their consciousness, the swifter they bring about their destruction pure and simple.

Verga, like every great artist, had sensed this. What he bewails really, as the tragedy of tragedies, in this book, is the ugly trespass of the sophisticated greedy ones upon the naïve life of the true human being: the death of the naïve, pure being—or his lifelong imprisonment—and the triumph or the killing of the sophisticated greedy ones.

This is the tragedy of tragedies in all time, but particularly in our epoch: the killing off of the naïve innocent life in all of us, by which alone we can continue to live, and the ugly triumph of the sophisticated greedy.

It may be urged that Verga commits the Tolstoyan fallacy, of repudiating the educated world and exalting the peasant. But this is not the case. Verga is very much the gentleman, exclusively so, to the end of his days. He did not dream of putting on a peasant's smock, or following the plough. What Tolstoi somewhat perversely worshipped in the peasants was poverty itself, and humility, and what Tolstoi somewhat perversely hated was instinctive pride or spontaneous passion. Tolstoi has a perverse pleasure in making the later Vronsky abject and pitiable: because Tolstoi so meanly envied the healthy passionate male in the young Vronsky. Tolstoi cut off his own nose to spite his face. He envied the reckless passionate male with a carking envy, because he must have felt himself in some way wanting in comparison. So he exalts the peasant: not because the peasant may be a more natural and spontaneous creature than the city man or the guardsman, but just because the peasant is poverty-stricken and humble. This is malice, the envy of weakness and deformity.

We know now that the peasant is no better than anybody else; no better than a prince or a selfish young army officer or a governor or a merchant. In fact, in the mass, the peasant is worse than any of these. The peasant mass is the ugliest of all human masses, most greedily-selfish and brutal of all. Which Tolstoi, leaning down from the gold bar of heaven, will have had opportunity to observe. If we have to trust to a *mass,* then better trust the upper or middle-class mass, all masses being odious.

But Verga by no means exalts the peasants as a class: nor does he believe in their poverty and humility. Verga's peasants are certainly not Christlike, whatever else they are. They are most normally ugly and low, the bulk of them. And individuals are sensitive and simple.

Verga turns to the peasants only to seek for a certain something which, as a healthy artist, he worshipped. Even Tolstoi, as a healthy artist, worshipped it the same. It was only as a moralist and a personal being that Tolstoi was perverse. As a true artist, he worshipped, as Verga did, every manifestation of pure, spontaneous, passionate life, life kindled to vividness. As a perverse moralist with a sense of some subtle deficiency in himself, Tolstoi tries to insult and to damp out the vividness of life. Imagine any great artist making the vulgar social condemnation of Anna and Vronsky figure as divine punishment! Where now is the society that turned its back on Vronsky and Anna? Where is it? And what is its condemnation worth, to-day?

Verga turned to the peasants to find, *in individuals,* the vivid spontaneity of sensitive passionate life, non-normal and non-didactic. He found it always *defeated.* He found the vulgar and the greedy always destroying the sensitive and the passionate. The vulgar and the greedy are themselves usually peasants: Verga was far too sane to put an aureole round the whole class. Still more are the women greedy and egoistic. But even so, Turiddu and Jeli and Rosso Malpelo and Nanni and Gramigna and Brothpot are not humble. They have no saint-like, self-sacrificial qualities. They are only naïve, passionate, and natural. They are "defeated" not because there is any glory or sanctification in defeat; there is no martyrdom about it. They are defeated because they are too unsuspicious, not sufficiently armed and ready to do battle with the greedy and the sophisticated. When they do strike, they destroy themselves too. So the real tragedy is that they are not sufficiently conscious and developed to defend their own naïve sensitiveness against the inroads of the greedy and the vulgar. The greedy and the vulgar win all the time: which, alas, is only too true, in Sicily as everywhere else. But Giovanni Verga certainly doesn't help them, by preaching humility. He does show them the knife of revenge at their throat.

And these stories, instead of being out of date, just because the manners depicted are more or less obsolete, even in Sicily, which is a good deal Americanized and "cleaned up," as the reformers would say; instead of being out of date, they are dynamically perhaps the most up-to-date of stories. The Tchekovian after-influenza effect of inertia and will-lessness is wearing off, all over Europe. We realize we've had about enough of being null. And if Tchekov represents the human being driven into an extremity of self-consciousness and faintly-wriggling inertia, Verga represents him as waking suddenly from inaction into the stroke of revenge. We shall see which of the two visions is more deeply true to life.

"Cavalleria Rusticana" and "La Lupa" have always been hailed as masterpieces of brevity and gems of literary form. Masterpieces they are, but one is now a little sceptical of their form. After the enormous diffusiveness of Victor Hugo, it was perhaps necessary to make the artist more self-critical and self-effacing. But any wholesale creed in art is dangerous. Hugo's romanticism, which consisted in letting himself go, in an orgy of effusive self-conceit, was not much worse than the next creed the French invented for the artist, of self-effacement. Self-effacement is quite as self-conscious, and perhaps even more conceited than letting oneself go. Maupassant's self-effacement becomes more blatant than Hugo's self-effusion. As for the perfection of form achieved—Mérimée achieved the highest, in his dull stories like *Mateo Falcone* and *L'Enlèvement de la Redoute.* But they are hopelessly literary, fabricated. So is most of Maupassant. And if *Madame Bovary* has form, it is a pretty flat form.

But Verga was caught up by the grand idea of self-effacement in art. Anything more confused, more silly, really, than the pages prefacing the excellent story "Gramigna's Lover" would be hard to find, from the pen of a great writer. The moment Verga starts talking theories, our interest wilts immediately. The theories were none of his own: just borrowed from the literary smarties of Paris. And poor Verga looks a sad sight in Paris ready-mades. And when he starts putting his theories into practice, and effacing himself, one is far more aware of his interference than when he just goes ahead. Naturally! Because self-effacement is, of course, self-conscious, and any form of emotional self-consciousness hinders a first-rate artist: though it may help the second-rate.

Therefore in "Cavalleria Rusticana" and in "La Lupa" we are just a bit too much aware of the author and his scissors. He has clipped too much away. The transitions are too abrupt. All is over in a gasp: whereas a story like "La Lupa" covers at least several years of time.

As a matter of fact, we need more looseness. We need an apparent formlessness, definite form is mechanical. We need more easy transition from mood to mood and from deed to deed. A great deal of the meaning of life and of art lies in the apparently dull spaces, the pauses, the unimportant passages. They are truly passages, the places of passing over.

So that Verga's deliberate missing-out of transition passages is, it seems to me, often a defect. And for this reason a story like "La Lupa" loses a great deal of its life. It may be a masterpiece of concision, but it is hardly a masterpiece of narration. It is so short, our acquaintance with Nanni and Maricchia is so fleeting, we forget them almost at once. "Jeli" makes a far more profound impression, so does "Rosso Malpelo." These seem to me the finest stories in the book, and among the finest stories ever written. Rosso Malpelo is an extreme of the human consciousness, subtle and appalling as anything done by the Russians, and at the same time substantial, not introspective vapours. You will never forget him.

And it needed a deeper genius to write **"Rosso Malpelo"** than to write **"Cavalleria Rusticana"** or **"La Lupa."** But the literary smarties, being so smart, have always praised the latter two above all others.

This business of missing out transition passages is quite deliberate on Verga's part. It is perhaps most evident in this volume, because it is here that Verga practises it for the first time. It was a new dodge, and he handled it badly. The sliding-over of the change from Jeli's boyhood to his young manhood is surely too deliberately confusing!

But Verga had a double motive. First was the Frenchy idea of self-effacement, which, however, didn't go very deep, as Verga was too much of a true Southerner to know quite what it meant. But the second motive was more dynamic. It was connected with Verga's whole recoil from the sophisticated world, and it effected a revolution in his style. Instinctively he had come to hate the tyranny of a persistently logical sequence, or even a persistently chronological sequence. Time and the syllogism both seemed to represent the sophisticated falsehood and a sort of bullying, to him.

He tells us himself how he came across his new style:

> I had published several of my first novels. They went well: I was preparing others. One day, I don't know how, there came into my hands a sore of broadside, a halfpenny sheet, sufficiently ungrammatical and disconnected, in which a seacaptain succinctly relates all the vicissitudes through which his sailing-ship has passed. Seaman's language, short, without an unnecessary phrase. It struck me, and I read it again; it was what I was looking for, without definitely knowing it. Sometimes, you know, just a sign, an indication is enough. It is a revelation. . . .

This passage explains all we need to know about Verga's style, which is perhaps at its most extreme in this volume. He was trying to follow the workings of the unsophisticated mind, and trying to reproduce the pattern.

Now the emotional mind, if we may be allowed to say so, is not logical. It is a psychological fact, that when we are thinking emotionally or passionately, thinking and feeling at the same time, we do not think rationally: and therefore, and therefore, and therefore. Instead, the mind makes curious swoops and circles. It touches the point of pain or interest, then sweeps away again in a cycle, coils round and approaches again the point of pain or interest. There is a curious spiral rhythm, and the mind approaches again and again the point of concern, repeats itself, goes back, destroys the time sequence entirely, so that time ceases to exist, as the mind stoops to the quarry, then leaves it without striking, soars, hovers, turns, swoops, stoops again, still does not strike, yet is nearer, nearer, reels away again, wheels off into the air, even forgets, quite forgets, yet again turns, bends, circles slowly, swoops and stoops again, until at last there is the closing-in, and the clutch of a decision or a resolve.

This activity of the mind is strictly timeless, and illogical. Afterwards you can deduce the logical sequence and the time sequence, as historians do from the past. But in the happening, the logical and the time sequence do not exist.

Verga tried to convey this in his style. It gives at first the sense of jumble and incoherence. The beginning of the story **"Brothpot"** is a good example of this breathless muddle of the peasant mind. When one is used to it, it is amusing, and a new movement in deliberate consciousness: though the humorists have used the form before. But at first it may be annoying. Once he starts definitely narrating, however, Verga drops the "muddled" method, and seeks only to be concise, often too concise, too abrupt in the transition. And in the matter of punctuation he is, perhaps deliberately, a puzzle, aiming at the same muddled swift effect of the emotional mind in its movements. He is doing, as a great artist, what men like James Joyce do only out of contrariness and desire for a sensation. The emotional mind, however apparently muddled, has its own rhythm, its own commas and colons and full-stops. They are not always as we should expect them, but they are there, indicating that other rhythm.

Everybody knows, of course, that Verga made a dramatized version of **"Cavalleria Rusticana,"** and that this dramatized version is the libretto of the ever-popular little opera of the same name. So that Mascagni's rather feeble music has gone to immortalize a man like Verga, whose only *popular* claim to fame is that he wrote the aforesaid libretto.—But that is fame's fault, not Verga's.

Thomas Goddard Bergin (essay date 1931)

SOURCE: "Nedda," in *Giovanni Verga,* Yale University Press, 1931, pp. 38-45.

[*In the following excerpt, Bergin studies the themes, characters, and technique of "Nedda," demonstrating that it is the first example of Verga's more accomplished, mature style.*]

Placed demurely and inconspicuously in the middle of the *romanzi giovenili,* flanked, as it were, by the exotic *Tigre Reale* and the passionate *Eros,* the story **"Nedda,"** containing the germ of the author's later and more famous tales, made its unassuming appearance. The year is 1874, seven years before *I Malavoglia*; but many of the characteristics destined to make of the latter volume a rallying ground for the *veristi* and a point of attack for their opponents are already present in **"Nedda."**

When we, who have the good fortune to be able to view his work in retrospection, consider the results that Verga eventually achieved in this new style, it is rather amusing to read contemporary comment on the work. The *Nuova antologia,* while praising the courage of Signor Verga, cannot but warn him that "proseguendo per questo via egli deve giungere fino al punto che il lettore debba chiuder gli occhi e turarsi il naso." It evidently seemed strong stuff. It will be worth our while to examine in some detail the elements of **"Nedda"** and to consider more thoroughly those new details which were apparently viewed with such great distaste by his contemporaries.

The plot, as almost invariably with Verga, is extremely simple. To an English reader the general outline would immediately recall *Tess of the D'Urbervilles*. It is the story of a poor *contadina siciliana* who is compelled to work in the fields to support her widowed mother. On the death of the latter she yields to the advances of Compare Janu, who promises to marry her when he has saved enough to make a home for her. This he apparently intends to do, but he is accidentally killed, leaving Nedda with an illegitimate child which dies shortly after its birth. The story closes with Nedda entirely alone and disgraced, thankful only that her child has not lived to suffer as she has. It will be apparent immediately that the formula of the youthful novels is sadly altered in this tale. The protagonist is no longer a version of the hero, neither the young Sicilian artist that was Lanti, nor the cynical man of the world that was Alberti. The peasant girl is as remote as possible from the aristocratic actors of the early novels. The background is no longer the theater, club, or *salotto* of the great northern cities but the bleak Sicilian countryside. With the loss of this background goes of necessity the loss of tone of the other romances for the details added to give realism are essentially gross where formerly they were elegant. Perhaps even more important is the disappearance of the sensual element. There is no glorification of the flesh in **"Nedda."** Indeed far from being beautiful is the heroine for the author informs the reader that, as a result of hard work and privations, she has almost ceased to look like a human being. There is, furthermore, no moralizing. Paradoxically enough, with **"Nedda"** the real moral force of Verga's cycle begins, but it lies in the story, perhaps even in the reader. Certainly neither author nor characters do any moralizing.

So much for what is lost in the formula. Are there any new elements to replace these losses? Doubtless even Verga himself must have been conscious of the fact that artistically **"Nedda"** was his first success. It possesses a concentration and a unity that his other works had lacked. This concentration might almost be called impact, so striking it is in its effect. I have indicated already that for the effeminate artist there has been substituted the less complex but undoubtedly more robust figure of the peasant. The people are coming into their own. It is diverting to see in what a confused state of mind this leaves the critics. They object to Janu's "gross" manifestations of affections and shake their heads over the love scene which is interrupted by the braying of an ass. There is nothing more offensive from a prudish point of view in these scenes than there is in the numerous unpleasant details of the *ménage* of Lanti and his mistress. And it seems odd also that they should object to Nedda indicating her love by boxing Janu's ears while Narcisa and Tigre Reale are allowed to bite their lovers with impunity. The reviewers are not conscious of their own attitude. They claim to be objecting to offensive and vulgar details; as a matter of fact they are objecting to the social class of Verga's heroine.

Another novelty, introduced perforce with the character of the peasant, is the rôle of nature. Nature ceases to be a casual background and begins to take a very definite part in the story. Not only is it a hot summer day which causes Nedda to yield to Janu, but far more deeply than that natural forces shape the destiny of the characters. The *contadini* depend for their very existence on the whims of the weather. When it rains Nedda is unable to work in the fields, hence her mother gets no money for medical attention. If the *annata* is good, all is well; if not, then those on the margin of society pay the price. It is no one's fault, as Nedda herself says; it is starkly inevitable. This sense of an irresistible destiny created by elemental forces differs somewhat from the rather vague, romantic fatalism that . . . frequently creeps out in the early novels; but it represents the same attempt of the author, much more logically supported, to assume an impersonal attitude. There arises from this latter fatalism a curious, perhaps unconscious, anti-Christian feeling which is to grow stronger during the later period of Verga's work. God is as remote and impersonal as nature. He may do us good but he is more likely to do us harm. His Church turns away from the sinner; Nedda, carrying her illegitimate child, is not allowed to enter the church on Easter Day. And the irony seems to become almost bitter at one point. When Janu leaves Nedda she bids him take care of himself, as he is all she has in the world. "God will take care of me," he replies, and in a few weeks he is dead.

To resume then these new elements. There is a change in background and in the social type of story. The author makes an evident and quite successful attempt to be impersonal. The emphasis on nature brings into his art a pagan pessimistic philosophy. . . .

For a time it seemed that this little story—which would hardly have deserved so much of our attention were it not for its close connection with other and greater works—was to remain unique in Verga's production. It was followed by *Eros*, in 1875, and *Primavera ed altri racconti* a year later. It seemed for a while as if the author had gone back definitely to the early type of novel. After the publication of the latter of these above mentioned, there ensued a period even more puzzling to friend and critic alike. For four years he published nothing at all and there were all sorts of rumors abroad concerning him, the consensus of them being that he had nothing more to say and had definitely given up writing.

But with the publication of *Vita dei campi,* in 1880, Verga returned to the literary world. And he returned unmistakably as the Verga of **"Nedda."** With these *novelle* he reiterates his creed and initiates the series of tales that were to mark him as Italy's foremost novelist. *Vita dei campi* contains nine stories of which one, **"Il come, il quando ed il perchè,"** is a survival of the old manner, illicit love among the upper classes being the subject; and another, **"Fantasticheria,"** is not, strictly speaking, a story at all; but the other seven may be said to represent artistically a development of the theories that were indicated in **"Nedda."**

All the characters in these tales come from the lowest division of the social scale. One of them—"La Lupa"—is compared quite vividly to a she-wolf; another—"Jeli il pastore"—sniffs at new ideas with the diffidence of a colt; and a third—"Rosso Malpelo"—is compared to the poor half-blind asses who work in the mines. He happens to have hands so he comes out once a week; the asses do not enjoy this occasional holiday: that is the only difference. The conception of fate from which it is impossible to flee because this fate is so necessarily a part of nature reappears. Horses are made to be sold, cattle are created only to be led to the butchers; even the birds, who seem to have nothing to do but sing, starve in the winter when snow covers the ground. What then can man expect in such a universe? The impersonality of the author is carried even farther, if possible, than in "Nedda." Pathetic though some of the stories may be, it is an objective pathos aroused by the mere presentation of a situation; the author himself expresses no opinion and seems as callous as nature itself. It is this utter impersonality that has made the tales of *Vita dei campi* immortal.

Little Novels of Sicily presents a veritable panorama of poverty. Individually, each tale has its own lights and shadows, but together they form a dun-coloured vista, like the vegetation along the dust-choked roads of southern Italy.

—*in* The Dial, *July, 1925.*

There is an extremely significant development in style. In "Nedda" we have seen how the story is divested of all ornament and told as simply as possible. Here he goes a little farther and adopts the language of his creatures as the vehicle for his story. In "Nedda" the effect was attained by the frequent use of dialogue; here, even where there is no dialogue and the author is telling a story, the vocabulary is that of the peasants. The first paragraph of "Cavalleria rusticana" will serve as an example:

> Turiddu Macca, il figlio della gnà Nunzia, come tornò da fare il soldato, ogni domenica si pavoneggiava in piazza coll' uniforme da bersagliere e il berretto rosso, che sembrava quello della buona ventura, quando mette su banco colla gabbia dei canarini. Le ragazze se lo rubavano cogli occhi, mentre andavano a messa col naso dentro la mantellina, e i monelli gli ronzavano attorno come le mosche.

Not only does this little passage contain a number of extremely colloquial expressions but the first sentence, in its looseness of construction, might indeed be called ungrammatical. Furthermore, the author seems to assume that the reader has a certain knowledge of the background. He tries to give the impression of one *paesano* telling a story to another. He even inserts occasionally "they say," as if disclaiming final responsibility for the story as merely gossip.

These stories are not behind "Nedda" in concentration. If anything, there is even more condensation. "Cavalleria rusticana" is told in ten pages, "La Lupa" in eight. Indeed the insistence on the essential points of the story to the exclusion of irrelevant details has made Tonelli think of Mérimée; and it must be admitted that in this respect there is a great similarity between Verga and the author of *Matteo Falcone*.

In short, the characteristics of "Nedda" are continued and even intensified. There are also one or two precise reminiscences of "Nedda" which, in spite of their apparent triviality, I feel obliged to cite, for they indicate an important element in what is to be the author's later inspiration. There are, then, a few scenes that are dangerously close to imitations of what has been found in "Nedda." The lovers Mara and Jeli begin their affair with the same gross manifestations of affection that had taken place between Nedda and Janu. Santuzza, in "Cavalleria rusticana," confesses—with dire results—at Easter time; her plight recalls Nedda's. Indeed Easter seems to be a favorite day for tragedy with Verga; La Lupa's story reaches its climax on that day. This trick of our author's of drawing on his own previous work for inspiration is more marked in the later phases of his development . . . but it is found— though overlooked by the critics—even in *Vita dei campi*. There are not only reminiscences of "Nedda," but the little book *Vita dei campi*, like Jules Verne's ship, depends on itself for fuel. "Pentolaccia," in the character of the protagonist and the outline of the action, is another "Jeli" and "Cavalleria rusticana" is closely related to the group. I say nothing of the fact that jealousy is the theme of these tales taken as a whole; that, after all, is legitimate and gives a certain unity to the collection, as [Luigi] Russo has sagaciously observed. But it is at least worth noting that three of these stories match in general outline, and of these three, two are furthermore united by a similarity of the protagonist.

Such then, to return to our muttons, is the general character of these tales. Realistic, full of authentic local color, told in a very intimate and highly specialized language, with an impersonal attitude well maintained throughout, they are worthy successors of "Nedda." The difference is that they were welcomed. [Luigi] Capuana and [Edouard] Rod laud them; none seems to object to their excessive realism, though they go beyond "Nedda." The public taste has changed in six years; in France the *Rougon-Macquart* are going ponderously on their way, while in Italy the efforts of Capuana and his coterie, together with an intangible but none the less obvious change in artistic attitude, have made Verga's undertaking a little more comprehensible, a little more *simpatico* to the Italian reader. The time is now ripe for a definite statement of program; the leader of the *veristi* is about to come into his own. *I Malavoglia* appeared in 1881.

Luigi Pirandello (essay date 1931)

SOURCE: "Appendix: Pirandello on Verga," in *Verga's Milanese Tales,* by Olga Ragusa, S. F. Vanni, 1964, pp. 106-26.

[*In the following excerpt, part of a speech that was first presented to the Royal Academy of Italy celebrating the fiftieth anniversary of the publication of* I Malavoglia *in 1931, Pirandello investigates the concept of reality in art and takes issue with the claim that Verga wrote objective, realist fiction.*]

It is probable that every nation produces two human types from its stock: the builders and the adaptors, the necessary beings and the beings of luxury; the former endowed with a "style of objects" and the latter with a "style of words." These two great families or categories of men, living contemporaneously within every nation, are quite distinct and easily recognizable in Italy, perhaps more so than anywhere else. But only for someone who knows our situation well and is able to analyze it with understanding. Because inattentive observers, be they Italian or non-Italian, are easily deceived by the noise, the pomp, the frequent self-display of those whom I have called of the "style of words," and think that this type only exists in Italy. It is easy to be deceived, first of all, because these individuals are much more numerous, more sociable, more accessible than the others, and also, because Italy actually seems to have been created for them, to give vividness, color, and meaning to their showy manifestations, their grand gestures, their beautiful words, their decorative passions, and their solemn celebrations. So much so, that when one thinks of Italy, of its natural beauty and its traditions, it is almost impossible, especially for a foreigner, not to picture all Italians living the life of the senses, intoxicated by sun, light and color, exulting in song, each one playing some easy musical instrument, having in him a little of the adventurer, a little of the actor, created for love and luxury, even if abjectly poor. And the men who best represent Italy are pictured as imaginative men of letters speaking a sonorous tongue, magnificent adorners and evokers of the glories of the past. All in all, a people that lives off the bliss of a wonderful natural setting and the dignity of a great past—lives off it and even makes a profit, as though all were a game or a fantastic pageant where everything is dream-like and there are no needs, and everything is easy and already accomplished, and nothing is difficult or still to be done.

Of course this is not so. There are the others in Italy, too: those who shine less and contribute more, those whom I have called of the "style of objects."

For the first, a thing is valuable not so much in itself as for how it is said; the writer, the seducer always shines through, the actor who wants to prove how good he is at saying it even if he does not actually show his hand. For the second, the word states the thing and has no independent value as a word; so that, between the thing and the person who is to see it, the word as word disappears and only the thing itself remains. There we have the showy structure of carefully chosen musical words that are intended to have their own value besides the value of the thing named; but in the long run the artifice is apparent and they satiate and tire. Here we have an inner construction; things that appear and place themselves before you so that you walk among them, breathe among them, touch them: stones, flesh, those particular leaves, those eyes, this water.

Throughout the whole course of our literature there have been two categories of writers, each quite distinct but almost parallel to the other. We can follow them, proceeding together and yet opposing one another, from the earliest period to the present: Dante and Petrarch, Machiavelli and Guicciardini, Ariosto and Tasso, Manzoni and Monti, Verga and D'Annunzio.

It is sufficient to recall that Dante died in exile and that Petrarch was crowned on the Campidoglio; that Machiavelli spent his last years in the condition he himself described in a famous letter; that Ariosto was turned from poet into "a rider of horses"; that only insanity deprived Tasso of the benefits of good fortune and that in spite of everything he too was finally named for the high honor of coronation on the Campidoglio. It is sufficient to remember that *I Promessi Sposi* was at first received with disappointment and that Leopardi died almost unknown, while lofty honors were attained by Monti. In the light of all this we cannot but recognize that in this Italy of ours, with its historical memories, its wealth of sweet, full and strong verbal sonorities, its pure formal beauty, its natural magnificence—in this Italy of ours, which is a miracle of the senses and a temple to values, the man able to say more words than things has a greater right to citizenship. We cannot but recognize how cruel, difficult and unbearable must appear the lucid effort endured by the writer whose aim is to say nakedly the things he has to say, outlining their harsh contours: objects and not words, tyrannical objects that demand our absolute respect for their naked innocence.

But though the years pass, and even the centuries, it is to those who are capable of this effort that we return. We return to Dante. We return to Machiavelli, to Ariosto, to Leopardi, and to Manzoni. And we return to Giovanni Verga.

[. . . .]

Where we have not the object, but the words that name it; where we want to be applauded for how we speak about it; there we have not creation, but literature. And even as far as literature is concerned, we have not art but adventure, a wonderful adventure that we wish to live through writing about it, or that we wish simply to live so that we can write about it.

Not even the young Verga was exempt from this desire. His early works are the expression of his romantic and sensual sentimentality: a world created from the outside and—what may seem paradoxical—without any direct feeling on his part. Not because at the time he did not actually have those feelings, but because he had too many and they were too close to him. Consequently, he was unable to clothe reality from within, unable to see it and place it objectively in a character, in the very character that as a story-teller he aspired to create. In other words, Verga's ambition was to live these novels while writing them; and only artifice could be the result. His aspirations remained muddy and confused, and never became purified in the filter of art.

But it was an experience necessary to his passionate nature which was trying to incarnate itself in art, trying to find its novel, and which began by forming it artificially, lodged within models that came to him from France. All this romantic dross had to burn so that the gold could flow more pure. Verga had first to reach that conclusion which we read in his youthful work *Eros*: "All knowledge of life lies in simplifying human passions and reducing them to their natural proportions." That is to say, it lies in the small area that must be dug in depth, so that the oak's roots may reach as far down as its branches grow in height and firmness into the sun. It does not lie in the vast field to be tilled on the surface only, so that the plants of one season may sprout in it merely to be beaten down by the first blast of wind. In brief, the fire of art, having burned the dross, had to sweep over him to the very marrow of living matter.

But when this happened, when Verga was through with living his adventure and began the toil and labor of creation, the work that was born no longer had any resonance. It was mute. Mute, in a time that was already beginning to echo with the literary adventure of a quite different conjurer, who with his continuous fascinating dazzle captured and held the public's attention for many years. He was a man qualified to do so and magnificent, born for adventure in art as in life, and in an admixture of life and art such that it was impossible to say how much of his art was in his life, and how much of his life in his art. But this confusion led to the only salvation possible, that of the luxurious cloak of never-ending literary production. I speak of Gabriele d'Annunzio.

Giovanni Verga is the most unliterary of writers.

It was impossible that, in an age that was re-echoing with that new and great literary adventure, the work and art of Giovanni Verga should receive more than an absent-minded hearing. No greater antithesis could be imagined. In d'Annunzio, all the fickleness of propitious occasions. In Verga, the static monotony of a desperate and resigned dejection. In d'Annunzio, the pompous opulence of a prose style all turgid flesh and skilful color; and even the material opulence of the things portrayed, villas and idle hours, the whims and the proud arrogance of the upper classes. In Verga, terse emaciation and naked poverty of words and things; always the same square and the old houses of a humble village; the sea (but not the divine poetic sea), the covetous and cruel sea of the fishermen; the deserted countryside infested by malaria; privations and needs; the strange, jealous and suspicious passions of the lowest classes, intent on rising, or already risen and tired, restless, and unable to find peace and consolation.

Let us look again at those two races or categories of writers, running parallel and yet opposite one another with regard to the eternal question of the language as well—language, which has always been considered from an external point of view and not what it is: creation. For the one group, langauge is the composed, written, literary language. For the other, beginning with Dante who saw the common tongue embedded in all the dialects and not in this or that specific one, there is its idiomatic, dialectal flavour. All the richness of the literary language is in d'Annunzio. Verga is dialectal. Dialectal, but in a manner suited to a nation that lives the varied life and therefore uses the varied languages of its many regions. The "dialecticism" of Verga is truly a formal creation, which cannot be considered part of "the question of the language," in the usual manner, noting its often strictly Sicilian syntactical structure and its idioms.

In the case of Verga, "idiomatic" means "right." The life of a region in the reality that Verga gave it, as he saw it, as it took form and movement in him, that is to say, as it created itself in Verga, could not be expressed differently: that language is the very creation of that region. And if Italian writers create the region in its language, this is not a defect in their literature, nor evidence of its feebleness, but rather proof of its merit and richness.

The direct testimony of someone like myself may be of interest. As a young man I was present at the passionate discussions that took place during Giovanni Verga's artistic maturity and dealt with certain esthetic ideas, schools and methods of art, with certain notions of the evolution of form, and with literary forms in particular. This may be of interest not so much for the things I may have to say, which are already well known to those acquainted with the vicissitudes of our recent literary history, but because at that time I was close to Luigi Capuana. Indeed, ours was the intimacy of the most cordial friendship. Capuana was the valiant and tireless defender of the school to which Verga belonged, of the method that Verga applied, of the reason and, indeed, necessity of adopting that method in attempting a narration no longer historical but contemporary, of the fruits that that school and method bore first in France and then in Italy, and especially of the work of his close friend and fellow worker, Giovanni Verga.

I don't know how consistently Capuana was praised for his accomplishments and merit as a critic, and especially for the good he did in lighting the path of art for Giovanni Verga. Later, those same critical insights were denounced as the first root of his failure as a writer. This is a great injustice, and to the man who loved Capuana it is a source of great bitterness. Thus I want to remember him here in order to speak of the shortcoming of his work as a critic and of the value of his art. To the latter, numerous admirable peasant stories and many pages of pure beauty in the *Marchese di Roccaverdina* and in *Profumo* bear eloquent witness.

Capuana set forth the reasons why, in wanting to narrate events and passions not of the past but of the present, he thought that, since there were no indigenous models, it

Verga with his close friend and fellow writer Luigi Capuana.

themselves, pointing to models and prescribing the rules and method by which a certain type of narrative is to be conducted, we make the same intellectual error made by rhetoric, whose other error was in the external search for expression. But language, meant to express what is in us, cannot be looked for elsewhere. It is something that takes shape within us with thought itself; it is indeed that very thought that sees itself in all its aspects clearly within us. Moreover, we in Italy already had the model of a living, effective prose, suited to expressing the most delicate and secret recesses of passion and thought, although it was used in a narration of past events, Manzoni's *Promessi Sposi*: a prose that was the result of the agony of three revisions. Finally, as far as the question of that famous "impersonality" or objectivity of narrative art is concerned, it should not have been difficult to see that it was essentially nothing more than a question of two different attitudes of the imagination in the act of representation. Art, as awareness of the subject, can never be objective except if we place what is our creation outside of ourselves; as though it were not ours but some independent reality that we had but to portray faithfully, without showing any sympathy for it; in brief, as diligent and dispassionate spectators.

Like all critics that belonged to *verismo,* Capuana, through lack of esthetic discernment, fell into the same error that had led Manzoni to condemn his masterpiece; with the only difference that Manzoni erred esthetically because he was too scrupulous to depart from history, while Capuana and the naturalists erred because they were too attentive to science as understood in their day.

To show or not to show awareness of one's own creation: this is the crux of the matter. To take a lyrical position, that is, to express oneself through the subjective elements of the spirit: feeling and will; or to take an historical position, that is, to express oneself through the objective element of the spirit: the intellect. The perfect work of art is extremely rare because infrequently does the whole spirit act in the harmonious union of its various elements, without allowing one or the other to prevail. Through unexpected actions and reactions, instead, one or the other element always ends by prevailing. Indeed, accompanying or following upon every new literary movement, we have always had a new orientation in philosophic thinking. As a reaction to intellectualism—whose poetic expression was classicism—we had the break-through of two subjective elements, wild and blind in their rebellion against the light of the intellect by which they had been held in check: feeling and will power, the two elements whose poetic expression was to be romanticism. And later, as a reaction to romantic idealism, we had materialism and experimental positivism whose poetic expression was literary naturalism with its program of giving us "human documents" and *tranches de vie,* drowning art in science. There was a reaction to this movement too. Fogazzaro in one sense, D'Annunzio in another and much more so, proposed to be—more than they actually were—the champions of this reaction. At present, tired and satiated with forms excessively polished and resounding, we are returning to "pure fragments" and *tranches de vie.* Humbly, we are returning

was indispensable to turn to France, where after a long period of elaboration, the two genres of the novel and the short story had reached their ultimate development. And he often spoke of the agonizing search for a "living prose" capable of expressing the "almost imperceptible nuances of modern thought." And to the very end he strove to uphold the so-called impersonality of narration and the objectivity of narrative art.

Up to the novel *Eros* Verga had followed the old narrative formulas of Romanticism, modernizing them somewhat in accordance with the taste and tone of a certain French literary fashion. But eventually he made Capuana's ideas and propositions about art his own.

But to speak of tradition in art as of something on which the work of art depends and without which it could not or could only with great difficulty be born is, as usual, to state the problem badly; while it should be stated, and consequently resolved, otherwise. Every true work of art is and should be "unique" and therefore have no models. There is no such thing as the form "novel" or the form "short story" existing by itself in the abstract, evolving independently here and there, reaching a more advanced stage of development here and a less advanced stage there. There are only certain novels, certain short stories, each with its own form, impossible to be mistaken for any other if they are truly works of art. When we consider forms by to the great art of Verga; who fortunately had little understanding for these theoretical matters, and relied on Capuana's exposition only insofar as it aided him to see clearly the basic strength given him by his attachment to his land, his subject matter, and encouraged him to find for it powerful, frank and closely adherent expression. Those who think that the work of Verga's maturity was intentionally patterned on an artistic method suggested by others and imported from outside Italy, without having developed within him as his own living subject matter, are mistaken. That method was Verga's, not because it came to him from the French naturalist school, but because it was his, the intimate law of his being as a writer, the free and spontaneous expression of his own personal image of life that being free and spontaneous could take no other form than the form it took. So much so that now, after so much time has elapsed, Verga's work survives whole and perfect, with all its unique elements marvelously interrelated and cooperating with one another to form a living body. And there is no reason to think that the form of any of these elements is what it is because of the artist's desire to conform to any of the canons of the French naturalist school, canons that we do not even remember.

> **Those who think that the work of Verga's maturity was intentionally patterned on an artistic method suggested by others and imported from outside Italy, without having developed within him as his own living subject matter, are mistaken. That method was Verga's, . . . the free and spontaneous expression of his own personal image of life that being free and spontaneous could take no other form than the form it took.**
>
> —*Luigi Pirandello*

Sicilians, almost all of them, have an instinctive fear of life; they shut themselves up within themselves, apart from others, content with the little they have, as long as it gives them security. They note with diffidence the contrast between their own closed personalities and the nature that surrounds them, wide-open and flooded by the sun. And they withdraw even further within themselves, distrusting the openness about them, the sea that isolates them, cuts them off, leaving them lonely and alone. Each one becomes an island to himself and enjoys his small share of pleasures—if he has any—soberly, by himself. Alone, silent, without seeking comfort, he suffers his often desperate unhappiness.

But there are those who escape. Those who not only literally cross the sea but, defying their instinctive fear, break loose (or think they break loose) from the little they have

that makes them islands to themselves; and go forth, hungry for life, wherever their imaginative sensuality takes them, giving free rein to their feelings; or rather, suppressing and betraying their true hidden passion by this aspiration to live an ephemeral life.

The young Verga was one of these. Therefore he was in principle neither passionate nor austere, as some have wanted to define him. As a matter of fact he was never austere or, to be more exact, moralistic. His attitude towards life and his feelings in general indicate as much. For no one who sympathizes with and excuses contrasting passions and is always ready to recognize the other's point of view can be called austere or moralistic.

It has also been said that Verga "sees the world realistically, as it actually is, and recognizes that it cannot be any different from what it is."

I don't know what the value of such a statement is.

The world has no reality in itself except if we give it one. Consequently, if we have given it that reality, we cannot expect it to be otherwise. To do so would be to distrust ourselves, to distrust the reality that we ourselves have given the world. Luckily for him Verga did not distrust the reality of his world, and therefore he is not, nor can he be, a humorist in the true and proper meaning of the word.

We must be clear about all this, because it is a basic point for a school that, like the naturalist school, proposed to exclude the "personality" of the writer from the portrayal of the so-called "truth."

Fundamentally the fiction of art and the fiction that we all construct with the data of our senses is one and the same thing.

Yet we call the representation of our senses "true" and the representation of art "false." But if we look closer we notice that here we are dealing not with a question of "reality" but with a question of "will." For the fiction of art is always "willed," not in the sense that it is sought intentionally for an extraneous purpose, but because it is sought for itself, loved for itself, disinterestedly. The fiction produced by the data of our senses, instead, is not dependent on our intentions; it occurs simply because we are endowed with senses. The former, then, is free; the latter is not free. The one is the image or form of sensations; the other—the fiction of art—is the creation of a form. In effect the esthetic fact begins to exist only when a fiction acquires will in us "for itself alone"—that is, when it "wills itself," by this alone inspiring the act that is to bring it to life outside ourselves. If the fiction lacks this will which—as I have already stated—is the very act forming the image, it is a common psychic fact: an image that is not formed intentionally but a spiritual-mechanical combination that we cannot control, the response to a simple sensation.

There is in all of us more or less a will that inspires the formation of the images that create our life. This creation that each one of us makes of himself for himself needs the collaboration of all the activities and functions of the spirit, of the intellect and the imagination as well as of the will. The more richly endowed are able to construct more freely, creating a higher, vaster, more vigorous life. The difference between this creation and the creation of art lies in one fact alone (which, however, renders the former banal and the latter unique): the common creation is "interested," the creation of art is "disinterested." This means that the former has a practical objective, a usefulness; while the latter has no objective, being its own objective. The one is willed to a purpose; the other is willed for itself. And proof of this can be found in a phrase that we all repeat, whenever we fail to attain the practical end to which we were striving, whenever our interests suffer a setback: "I toiled for the sake of art."

And the tone in which this phrase is said explains why the majority of men, who work with a practical end in mind and have no appreciation for what is disinterested, are accustomed to thinking of poets as crazy. For in the poet the representation is an end in itself, and poets want it to be exactly as it forms itself.

This total disinterestedness, and this alone, constitutes the "impersonality" of the writer with respect to the reality that he has created. Everywhere else he is present, the more so where he is most hidden.

Reality exists only in the feelings that create it for us. We would live it blindly if it were not lit up for us by the intellect, more so in some cases and less in others, according to each man's temperament and situation. Created by our feelings, reality needs the intellect in order to see itself, but it needs the will if it is to start living in us, for us and with us.

Art is art, because what is reality—that is, this composition of our feelings, lighted by the intellect and triggered by the will; an infinitely varied and constantly changing thing, conditioned as it is by the changing circumstances of space and time—is fixed forever by the imagination in one or more crucial moments, outside of multiplicity (that is, of space and time). Reality in art is one and eternal. But it is not fixed absolutely as an abstraction; it is eternal because it belongs to all times; it is one because it is *that* particular reality whose life stems from the consensus of all, though in each it takes a particular form. Reality in art is free of all that is banal, self-evident, transient; free of all the obstacles that in the creation of our own lives distract us, thwart us, deform us.

Therefore one cannot say that a writer—a writer such as Capuana wanted him to be, such as he thought Verga was, or such as any impersonal writer might be, Flaubert, Zola, Maupassant, Capuana himself—"sees the world realistically, as it actually is, and recognizes that it cannot be any different from what it is." Instead we should try to determine what particular feelings give a writer—any writer, and in the present case Verga—his own reality, the reality of his world, lighted by his intellect, and triggered by his will.

Now Verga—as he developed within the history of his own time, in his particular way of being, conditioned by his time and changing with it—had no active faith, no norm and direction in his life; nor did he seek one, for he thought that none existed. Actually he did have one but it was hidden, obscure as are all things that reside in feeling and not in intellect. Verga's faith had to do with his affections, his immediate affections: his family, his land, the customs of his people, their interests and their passions. And, indeed, it was only in this area that he was able to set "a reality" for himself. Thus he did not create a world ideologically; he was not able to construct it to correspond to an abstract idea, from the outside, within a reality going beyond it, that is, beyond himself. He accepted the world within that obscure reality which his feelings dictated, from within himself piecemeal; and he said that reality was as it was because that is how it was. Naturally, since his feelings took this form by chance and without the aid of the intelligence, they became progressively sadder, drying up bit by bit, like a mechanism governed by some anguished destiny. He pictured the almost fatal existence of those feelings in realities that can only be exactly as they are, because those feelings are what they are and cannot be otherwise—so sad, so implacably sad!

And so we have *Vita dei campi,* and the *Novelle rusticane,* and *Per le vie,* and *Vagabondaggio,* and *I Malavoglia,* and *Mastro don Gesualdo.* And yet Verga thought that the restlessness of his vagabond imagination could find peace quietly "in the serenity of sweet, simple feelings, succeeding one another calmly and regularly from generation to generation." He thought that he could find peace by considering worthy of the deepest respect the tenacious attachment of a poor people to the rock on which fate had decreed that they be born, their resignation to a life of hardship, the religion of the family casting its sober light on their work and home, on the stones that surround that home. But instead of finding peace in all this, he perceived something like a fatal necessity in the tenacious affections of the weak, in the instinct of the humble to band together in order to protect themselves against the storms of life; and he tried to decipher the modest and nameless drama that defeats the plebeian actors of his masterpiece, *I Malavoglia.* The essence of this drama he himself described: "When one of those humble ones tries to leave the group, either because he is attracted by the unknown, or because he desires to improve his lot, or because he is curious about the rest of the world, the world, hungry fish that it is, swallows him and those closest to him as well."

This is the idea that lights up his feelings. But what a sad light it is! And the feelings—his love for those humble ones, for those weak ones, for those poor beings—become passion in that light, and the passion becomes torment. Quite the contrary of sweet peacefulness! Quite the contrary of serene peace! Quite the contrary of gentle, simple feelings, of a calm succession of events, unchanged from generation to generation! This is a world, a poor world of fundamental necessities, of basic affections, intimate, primitive, naked, a world of naked things, of elemental simplicity, abandoned to some fatal necessity. He is the first to suffer because of it, but the light of the intellect immediately convinces him that it can only be thus, that there is no escaping into any other reality—a reality that would be different if one were to look at it from another angle, if the feelings of the characters were to mirror themselves even just fleetingly in the reflection of someone standing on the outside, as so often happens in Manzoni. No, Verga looks at this reality steadily, always from within, with the eyes of his characters, continually identifying with them. And reality is only that reality, as the feelings of his characters create it, implacably, inexorably, always that reality. Not that it is not sometimes comic, or that it may not turn an ironic glance upon itself, in the comments of the other actors on the scene, or in the contrasts—often cruel and awkward—of life in the provinces or life in the country. But here too that necessity is always present, turning even irony into melancholy and awkwardness into sadness, as is the case in **"Malaria,"** and in **"Il Reverendo,"** and in **"Cos'è il Re,"** or in **"Licciu Papa,"** and a bit everywhere in the short stories, and in *I Malavoglia* and *Mastro don Gesualdo*. One must come to terms with this impending fate, and woe to him who doesn't do so, or doesn't want to do so; he will have the damage and the scorn. This is the nature of Verga's resignation and it is so bitter. Not "rationality" then, which gives the idea of a mechanical rigidity, but resignation to a fatal necessity that vanquishes all and allows no one to rebel.

This is why Verga is Verga and not Manzoni. As Manzoni loved the humble, so he pictured their life; and Manzoni, long outliving his work as a writer, had the enviable fortune of being assured of the immortal life of that work, tested by his long silence. But how different is the light of the one, nourished by the faith that consoles and sustains, from the other that barely succeeds in making less bitter (because somehow comforted) that squalid resignation to impending fate, by gathering it about the domestic hearth. Because for Verga, as for all Sicilians, the domestic hearth is sacred. Death and damnation to those who attack it, death and damnation to those who betray it, to those who forget it. In almost all of Verga's work there is not other sacred pivot than this. Verga always looks at it through the eyes of his characters with veneration, nostalgia, and tenderness. He is filled with pity for those who have no hearth, for those condemned to leave it or to lose it, because of want and poverty. "To each bird its nest is beautiful." Oh the proverbs of Padron 'Ntoni Malavoglia, for whom men are made like the fingers of a hand! Oh unforgettable house of the Medlar Tree! And all the hardships to win it back only to end up dying far away, in the poorhouse in the city, with eyes glued to the door to see if no one is coming to take one back to where one can no longer live but one could at least die! And what is saddest for Mastro don Gesualdo is to have to die like a dog in his daughter's palace, he who in his eagerness "to amass things" had never allowed himself a moment's rest.

But don Gesualdo Motta is inferior to Padron 'Ntoni Malavoglia. Not because don Gesualdo's figure doesn't stand out powerfully in full relief, nor because his deeds, his feelings, his every smallest act, and those of the others about him, aren't portrayed even more skilfully than in the

first novel. But don Gesualdo's story is already constructed with elements that obviously go beyond him, without the compact and sincere naturalness of the other novel, so much more admirable and almost miraculous. For we do not know how all the life of that fishing village can be so tightly knit around the house of the Medlar, and how this novel, whose plot is non-existent and whose events occur almost by chance, can be so full of passion.

One cannot claim that all this was not intentional, for it was part of Verga's aspiration, as he revealed it in dedicating the short story **"L'amante di Gramigna"** to Salvatore Farina. In that dedication he wrote that the triumph of the novel would occur "when the affinity and the cohesion of its every part will be so complete that the process of creation remains a mystery, like the development of human passions; when the harmony of its forms will be so perfect, the sincerity of its reality so evident, its mode and reason for being so necessary that the hand of the artist will remain absolutely invisible. Then the novel will have the stamp of a real happening, and the work of art will seem to *have produced itself,* to have matured and grown spontaneously like a fact of nature without maintaining any point of contact with its author. . . . it will stand by itself, by the simple reason that it is as it should be and it is necessary that it be, palpitating with life, and immutable like a bronze statue whose author had the divine courage of stepping aside, disappearing into his own immortal work."

The secret of the miracle lies in the author's total vision, that endows what seems scattered and haphazard in the work with that intimate, vital unity that never dominates from the outside, but is transfused into and lives in the single actors of the drama. It is true that they are many, but they all know one another, and each one knows everything about the other, and understands every voice and every aspect of the little village; knows from what church the bell he hears is ringing; hears a cry, and knows who cried and why; all of them united by every slightest event that forthwith becomes common to them all.

And thus the work of art is held firmly together from beginning to end by innumerable threads that move not this character or that, but are themselves moved by the impending fatal necessity. And it is marvelously joined in almost Homeric primitiveness to that rock, that sea, the ancient solemn rectitude of that old sea-wolf. But over all there hangs a feeling of the fatalism of ancient tragedy, for the ruin of one is the ruin of all. And a lofty lesson derives from this, amid our dismayed pity for the fate of the vanquished.

The work is admirable, but the commitment from which it springs is even more admirable. Its new and inevitable style keeps it alive forever as a work of art, more alive today than ever before, as a model of action and faith, and even aside from any literary considerations, as an act of life. I am referring to the commitment that at one point Verga imperiously felt called upon to make, perhaps at the very moment when he was furthest and most forgetful of his origins. The voice of his land and all that was religious in his spirit called him—he who had already triumphed in public opinion with the easy things, the things that pleased the readers of his day—to the exigent, humble and sad task of expressing things. Things, difficult things, things as they appear to us. This in a certain sense means to do, to act, and no longer to desire and contemplate.

All intellectual concepts of life resulting from works of art must be evaluated judiciously. Nothing is more foolish than to ask the artist to defend them in the name of practical life. And, indeed, it is not the intellectual concept of life which results from this admirable work that helps us—a concept that may well appear depressing, or at least opposed to our present state of mind (for we no longer have the attitude of the defeated) to which another, different concept seems fitting and exulting—but what helps us is the very divesting oneself of all that is superfluous in order to live a reality that is still to be created, the very force that is actively at work, the very return to our origins, of which Verga gives us the example. Neccessities that are fundamental and unique, whether in the creation of a true work of art, or in the affirmation of a human personality in life, or in the life itself of a whole people. This divesting oneself, this constructive force, this return to origins, that lead the way to the only conquest necessary to men and nations: the conquest of one's style.

Robert Weaver (essay date 1953)

SOURCE: A review of *Little Novels of Sicily,* in *The Canadian Forum,* Vol. XXXIII, No. 393, October, 1953, p. 161.

[*In the review below, Weaver praises the modern qualities of Verga's stories and the author's deft combination of sympathy for and detachment from his characters.*]

His two novels and handful of stories about Sicily are enough to make Giovanni Verga rank as an important writer. In many respects, it seems to me, Verga should seem as important to us as, say, Balzac or Zola. And for some modern readers Verga will have an advantage over many of the writers of his own time: for although he belongs to the nineteenth century, his work has a strong contemporary flavor. There are few digressions in his novels, little moralizing, no heavy undergrowth of description. His dialogue is quick and revealing, his narrative prose firm, rapid and vigorous. His descriptive passages and metaphors are fresh, vivid, closely related to the life of the people he is writing about. Perhaps Verga's contemporary feeling owes something to D. H. Lawrence, who translated three of his books (how Lawrence must have loved this task!); but the novel which Lawrence did not translate, *The House by the Medlar Tree,* also seems very modern, if you read it in the translation which was published two or three years ago.

Verga was born in Sicily in 1840, and he died there in 1922. For a time he made a career in Italy as a popular romantic writer; then he went home, and began to write about his own people. He planned a trilogy, to be called *The Defeated,* and wrote one novel about a family of poor fishermen and another about the rise and fall of a small landowner; but the third book, which was to have dealt with the upper class, was never completed. For the last half of his life he appears to have written nothing, and, says Lawrence, "He kept apart from all publicity, proud in his privacy . . ."

When he went back to Sicily as a mature person and a writer, Verga was returning to a society which must have been as harsh, violent and isolated as any in Europe. It was a land as hard and pitiless as the everlasting sunlight; the people were drenched in superstition, cruelty and pride. Small landowners and landless peasants worked the thin, rocky fields, or sickened in the richer, malaria-choked lowlands. In Verga's novels and stories a whole people and a way of life seem to have fallen out of time and history, and any standard of judgment we apply to them seems inadequate and invalid.

In this society, as we might expect, Verga discovered an existence and an attitude which are profoundly tragic. Yet he did not become a remorseless or a pitying observer; he did not exploit or sentimentalize the tragedy, he merely recorded it. He combines an intense detachment with an intense sympathy. What makes this possible is the degree to which he shares in the sad, violent, yet astonishingly varied life of the village. He touches all of them; the priests and the officials, the landowners and the peasants, the children, the idiots and the senile aged . . . (Even the animals: perhaps the most powerful sketch in this book is **"Story of the Saint Joseph's Ass."**) By becoming so wholly a part of the village, Verga is able to share the gift for irony and even robust humor which somehow makes life still bearable. As an artist, he concerns himself with the exact cadence of speech and the precise description of incident and actuality. And so he wrote four books which, for the most part, avoid rhetoric and indignation and self-pity.

There are a dozen sketches and stories in ***Little Novels of Sicily,*** and they provide a good cross-section of the sort of writing which readers will find in Verga's other books. The new edition is a handsome book, and for anyone who hasn't read Verga, it would make a good place to start. And if you haven't read Verga, you've missed a writer who is well worth your time and attention.

Giovanni Cecchetti (essay date 1957)

SOURCE: "The Last Stories of Giovanni Verga," in *Italian Quarterly,* Vol. 1, No. 2, Summer, 1957, pp. 8-14.

[*In the following essay, Cecchetti examines Verga's last collection of stories,* Don Candeloro e Compagni, *which is often overlooked by critics.*]

The English-speaking readers of Italian literature know of four books by Giovanni Verga: two novels—*I Malavoglia*

(*The House by the Medlar Tree*) and *Mastro Don Gesu-aldo*—and two volumes of short stories—*Vita dei Campi* (*Cavalleria Rusticana and Other Stories*) and *Novelle Rusticane* (*Little Novels of Sicily*). These four books are unquestionably Verga's masterpieces, the ones which have placed him among the great European writers of the last century. They were all written between 1878 (the approximate date when Verga began to work seriously on *I Malavoglia,* after having thought about the subject for three years) and 1889, when the second and final version of *Mastro Don Gesualdo* was published.

In this period Verga's creativity was at its peak. Before then, during his youth, he had devoted himself to writing sentimental novels mostly dealing with love affairs between hot-blooded southern Italian men transplanted in the Florentine aristocratic world and the sexually rapacious women whom they were pursuing. These works are now read mainly by scholars who want to delve into his formative years.

After *Mastro Don Gesualdo* he brought out two volumes of short stories: *I Ricordi del Capitano d'Arce* (*Captain d'Arce's Memoirs*) and *Don Candeloro e Compagni* (*Don Candeloro & Co.*). Except for a short novel of no great importance printed in 1906, they are his last two books. If we further take into account the fact that some of the stories contained in the first had already appeared in 1884 under different title, then *Don Candeloro e Compagni* becomes the only collection written by Verga after his second great novel, *Mastro Don Gesualdo,* and before he abandoned narrative art almost completely.

The critics have generally neglected *Don Candeloro e Compagni*. A few mention it in their monographs, but for the purpose of acknowledging its existence rather than of appraising its significance. It undoubtedly deserves more attention than it has been given so far.

The book is uneven, but some of the stories are very good. In them one still finds the hand of the man who had written so many masterpieces about the lives and the struggles of poor Sicilians, and one is reminded of both his unmistakable way of portraying humanity and his uniquely unadorned and direct style.

The first two short stories of *Don Candeloro e Compagni* are connected to the extent of being two chapters of the same story. The protagonist is Don Candeloro, the owner of a puppet show; he lives in a remote Sicilian town and manages to make his living with his puppets. But slowly he begins to lose his public; the people's imaginations cannot be satisfied simply with puppets: what they want is real actors and succinctly dressed actresses. Soon Don Candeloro begins to travel from town to town, taking along his show and his family. But nowhere, not even in the most distant villages, does he find the attention and the sympathy he needs. Finally, in order to please the public and to earn his daily bread, he decides to become a clown. But the public still scorns him. Meanwhile, his daughter runs away with his helper and apprentice, Martino. Don Candeloro does all he can to defend the reputation of his

family, but slowly the material necessities of life make him indulgent and at the end he finds himself eating at the tables of his daughter's occasional lovers.

The two stories are tight and powerful. Verga presents his people in the hands of a ruthless destiny that never relaxes its grip. They are the real puppets, whose movements are always determined by a superior and inescapable force: the necessity of survival, for which they struggle with all the means at their disposal. The puppet show is therefore the counterpart of the characters, and at the same time it can be viewed as the symbol of all mankind.

Don Candeloro e Compagni **is uneven, but some of the stories are very good. In them one still finds the hand of the man who had written so many masterpieces about the lives and the struggles of poor Sicilians, and one is reminded of both his unmistakable way of portraying humanity and his uniquely unadorned and direct style.**

—*Giovanni Cecchetti*

The first part of the book contains also two stories dealing with big-city actresses: **"La Serata della Diva"** (**"The Star's Great Night"**) and **"Il Tramonto di Venere"** (**"The Setting of Venus"**). They are related in the sense that they portray two strikingly different periods in an acting career. The stars have their short hour of fame, but life cannot be a continuous triumph and success is quickly followed by the long hours of misery. The great star who once seemed to be the mistress of her destiny, now, while she clings to all possible means of survival, reveals her true identity: like everybody else, she has been vanquished by life.

In what one can call the second part, the volume has many other noteworthy characters and "scenes:" an ambitious peasant who, by his Machiavellian shrewdness, becomes first a friar and then the head of a monastery in order to be able to rule others and behave the way he wants to (**"Papa Sisto"**); the turmoil caused among the nuns by two handsome priests who have come to preach in their convent (**"L'Opera del Divino Amore"**); a girl who is forced to become a nun and slowly convinces herself that she has done so of her own free will (**"La Vocazione di Suora Agnese"**); the effect of the exaggerations of a histrionic preacher on a narrow-mindedly religious woman who is expecting a child, and consequently on her husband (**"Il Peccato di Donna Santa"**); and other lesser stories.

The whole book is intended to represent various human dramas as they develop in different environments, or, rather, on the different stages of the theater of life. As a conclusion Verga wrote a piece consisting of a series of sketches tied together by the same idea. At the beginning he states: "How often in the dramas of life, fiction is so mixed with reality as to be confused with it and to become tragic, and the man who is forced to play his part becomes deeply identified with it, just as if he were a great actor." This concept was later to become one of the basic principles of Pirandello's theater. It is very doubtful that Pirandello derived his philosophy from Verga's last book of stories, yet we could almost say that the former began where the latter left off.

In all of Verga's mature works, the characters are slowly overcome and destroyed by life, by their needs, their passions, and their ambitions. The Malavoglias are victims of an inexorable fate that they themselves help to create, and so is Mastro Don Gesualdo, who dies in the desperate solitude which seems to be the natural end of all his labor and his toiling. And so are the protagonists of the short stories, who are generally led to their destruction by their own actions.

In *Novelle Rusticane,* the best of Verga's collections of stories, circumstances bring about not only the misery of the people but also the progressive disintegration of their moral values, which are their strongest defense. Slowly everything seems to collapse under the weight and the pressure of everyday needs. The same happens fairly often in *Don Candeloro e Compagni.*

Verga's conception of life is characterized by a virile pessimism, which stems directly from his realism and embraces all human manifestations. His people are constantly striving to improve their material conditions, but in so doing they sink into deeper misery. If they are sustained by dreams, these dreams are inevitably submerged by the waves of reality. In his last book his conception of life is still gloomier, because it begins to lose its dynamism. The unavoidable and unchangeable conclusions often weigh heavily on his stories from the very beginning. This might be a reason why Verga, after *Don Candeloro e Compagni,* could not continue writing; his work was finished.

From Verga's pessimistic version of life springs his humor. It is a bitter humor, which in his greatest works generates deep human compassion; in other instances, instead, it appears motionless, something like the gelid smile of a man who observes human events with impassive eyes.

In *Don Candeloro e Compagni* there is this kind of humor, and it is such that at times it borders on cynicism. Some of the stories (**"Papa Sisto"** and **"L'Opera del Divino Amore"**) have a Boccacesque flavor, but they lack the warm laughter of Boccaccio: Verga views the various happenings with too much detachment, and as a consequence his characters tend to acquire the qualities of caricatures; they are really like the marionettes of Don Candeloro's puppet show.

"Il Peccato di Donna Santa" (**"Donna Santa's Sin"**), which is presented here in English for the first time, is a

combination of social satire and psychological analysis, and certainly stands as one of the best stories of the book. The first part, in which the author portrays the whole village in church and gives brief sketches of the lives and inclinations of so many people, is a remarkable piece in itself. One cannot help admiring the ease with which Verga handles a great mass of characters at once. On the other hand, some readers may feel that the satirical element is so prevalent that it seems to have become the only preoccupation of the writer. And there is a certain disproportion between the introductory part and the rest, which actually constitutes the story; in fact the main character, Doctor Brocca, appears a little too late.

The second part is centered around the mental sufferings of the Doctor, who suspects he has been cuckolded by his unattractive wife, but cannot obtain a confession. Again one may have the impression that the author is ridiculing his character, rather than inspiring deep human sympathy and compassion, as he does in his great works. **"Donna Santa's Sin"** is a sort of jest: Doctor Brocca is deceived, since the sin does not exist, and has to carry the cross of a man who thinks that he is, and is believed to be, dishonored. There is something Pirandellian about this conclusion: what counts is not what we really are, but what we think we are or are thought to be.

The theme of poverty and of the resulting struggle for survival, as well as the theme of the compulsive desire for earthly possessions, which provide the common ground for almost all of Verga's best known narratives, are absent from the story. There is, however, the theme of conjugal honor, and therefore of the supreme necessity of defending what to a southern Italian is more important than daily bread and property. This theme had produced swift and powerful tragedies in **"Cavalleria Rusticana"** and in **"Jeli il Pastore"** (**"Jeli, the Shepherd"**). Here it is treated rather sardonically, and in such a different way that comparison is not possible.

In Verga, as in all true writers, the question of style is particularly important. He declared that short stories and novels should appear as if they had created themselves, and the presence of the author should remain completely undiscoverable. This was the theory of the impersonality of art; it came to Verga from his faith in realism, which he believed to be the only road to literary creation. Actually, however, realism was for him an external stimulus to discover himself and to realize his potentialities. Even if impersonality cannot exist, that principle helped him to free himself from all the superficialities of his early novels and to create a profoundly original style.

After 1874, he worked for years trying to develop a prose which should be one and the same with the people he portrayed and in which nothing should derive from virtuosity or stylistic brilliance; every word was to be indispensable and originate directly in the inner world of the characters. Thus he eliminated descriptive passages and adopted a vocabulary that is comparatively limited and generally popular in quality—but every expression is newly enriched with suggestive meanings each time it occurs.

Above all, he had his characters "narrate themselves," that is, he told the story in their own words.

One of the main characteristics of Verga's style is the continuous use of what today is technically called *style indirect libre,* or "free indirect style." Whenever he mentions a person he also repeats that person's words, merely placing the tenses in the past and without other changes. It would be enough to recall, by way of example, the paragraphs in **"Donna Santa's Sin"** where the thoughts and words of Doctor Brocca automatically become the substance of the narration, without any direct indication that he is thinking or speaking. It is preferable, however, to quote another passage, which reproduces the thoughts of a minor character, Donna Orsola, in her own words; starting with "since," at least, we are listening to her comments:

> Donna Orsola held her nose, disgusted by the scandal that Caolina brought to church, since for women of that sort men neglect even the sacrament of matrimony and let your daughters grow moldy at home; and then there are the other troubles that come from all this: the girls, who to help themselves even latch on to a penniless tramp without ways or means, like Nini Lanzo; the men with families, who still go gallivanting when they are fifty years old . . .

By making such an extensive use of "free indirect style," Verga gave his narration an exceptional vivacity, and at the same time made all the details extremely concrete. But this is only one of the main characteristics of prose that at every reading discloses new richness and depth. The writers of our century have adopted and expanded many of the devices that had been employed by Verga; and this renders his prose still more vital.

It must be said that although Verga's last stories do not measure up to his masterpieces and do not possess their extraordinary insight and poetic power, they are not only good but also worthy of a great writer.

Olga Ragusa (essay date 1964)

SOURCE: "Critical Assessment of Verga's Milanese Tales," in *Verga's Milanese Tales,* S. F. Vanni, 1964, pp. 1-6.

[*In the following excerpt, Ragusa examines the critical dismissal of Verga's Milanese tales, finding that the lasting reputation of these stories is based largely on the opinions of critic Luigi Russo.*]

The works of Verga that do not reflect the Sicilian peasant world have rarely been considered favorably by critics. The so-called mundane narratives that belong to his youthful production, stories peopled by idle aristocrats and budding young artists with their typical *fin de siècle* anxieties, have indeed received some measure of attention, if only because of their importance for the artist's formative years. But the Milanese tales, almost all written during Verga's maturity, have been completely overshadowed by the more numerous and more successful works set in Sicily. The impoverished working people, the low-class prostitutes, the starving music-hall entertainers, the crooks, invalids, consumptives, unemployed—the urban derelicts, in short—who appear in most of Verga's Milanese tales, have elicited little sympathy and have been brushed aside as figures inspired almost exclusively by his desire to vie with the popular naturalist novels of France. This negative judgement, due largely to Luigi Russo's 1919 groundbreaking work on Verga [*Giovanni Verga*] has up to now precluded more than a superficial examination of this segment of Verga's production. As a consequence, besides more serious errors, it is not unusual to find in critical studies devoted to the novelist, inexactitudes of all kinds, including the incorrect labelling of stories as Milanese, while others that properly belong to the category are overlooked.

Russo's book on Verga marked the latter's official entry into the history of Italian literature. Though in many respects indebted to Croce's more balanced and incisive essay of 1903 ["Giovanni Verga," *La Critica,* I, 1903], Russo's study outshone its precursor completely and remained *the* work on Verga down to the post-World War II period. Rewritten in parts and thoroughly revised for several different editions, enriched by complementary studies of a scholarly, popular, and scholastic nature, Russo's *Giovanni Verga* has the comprehensiveness and the authority of a life-work. But it is also a Sicilian's interpretation of the Sicilian Verga's world, and though the author's personal involvement lends the work warmth and eloquence, it marks at the same time its limitations. The early editions bore a dedication that disclosed from the beginning the spirit in which the study was conducted: "Alla memoria di mio padre e di mia madre dedico questo libro che, nell'opera mi ha dato il loro vecchio cuore, con le pene, i disegni, le travagliate speranze, l'umiltà laboriosa, della nostra vita e della nostra casa laggiù" [I dedicate this book to the memory of my father and mother, for in writing it I recaptured their ancient hearts, with the sorrows, the projects, the troubled hopes, the industrious simplicity of our lives and our home down there]. These words of filial reverence were later modified to: "Dedico questo libro alla memoria dei miei genitori Giuseppe Russo e Diega Meo, la cui pia immagine è accorsa e mi ha accompagnato più assidua e pungente descrivendo l'arte di un mondo che fu la loro realtà biografica" [I dedicate this book to the memory of my parents, Giuseppe Russo and Diega Meo, whose loving image accompanied me with assiduousness and poignancy as I described the art of a world that had been a living reality to them]. But the change, as indeed other changes in the later editions, was more of tone and emphasis than of substance and point of view. Russo himself confirms this in the preface to the 1934 edition, saying that he rewrote the book not because he wished to retract any of his initial judgements, but because the climate of opinion on Verga had changed and "un tono più storico e critico, meno polemico e difensivo" [a more historical and critical, less polemic and defensive tone] seemed in order.

Russo's work would have carried little weight had only sentiment dictated his judgement. But his critical method, which he himself objectively defined in the 1934 preface as a combination of Croce's esthetic and De Sanctis' historical criticism, served to reinforce rather than attenuate his opinions. The two aspects of the method: a critical reading of the text with the object of distinguishing the artistically successful from the artistically unsuccessful (Croce's method), and the reconstruction of the artist's development so as to arrive at the formulation of the essential characteristic or central idea of his total production (De Sanctis' procedure), both separately and in conjunction with one another, led Russo to dismiss Verga's non-Sicilian tales as weak and colorless, as artistic failures: "Quelle volte che il Verga si allontana da quel *locus sacer* (i.e., the family hearth, singled out by Russo as the basic myth around which Verga's production evolves), il suo racconto si fa più fiacco, la sua anima si distrae e anche il suo malinconico umorismo cede il posto a un (*sic*) analisi esatta ma senza colore deciso" (1st ed., p. 113) [Whenever Verga moves away from that *locus sacer,* his narrative weakens, his attention wanders, and even his melancholy sense of humor is replaced by analysis. His analysis is precise but without distinguishing color].

In the first edition, Russo cited **Per le vie** (1883), **Vagabondaggio** (1887), and the dramatic sketch *In portineria* (performed 1885, an adaptation of "Il canarino del n. 15" which had appeared in *Domenica letteraria,* May 21, 1882, before being included in **Per le vie**) as among the works in which Verga moves furthest from the *locus sacer.* Russo described the protagonists of these works as "vagabondi delle vie di Milano e vagabondi delle vie del mondo" [vagabonds of the streets of Milan and vagabonds of the streets of the world], and maintained that in telling of them, Verga, in spite of a masterful display of psychological analysis, was unable to make use of the dramatic and elegiac elements of "psicologia domestica" (1st ed., p. 115). By "domestic psychology" Russo means that religion of home and family which dominates his own study and is centered in a specific geographic locale: "laggiù," that is, in Sicily. Though the later editions of *Giovanni Verga* are more precise in their attention to chronology and detail, separating the discussion of **Per le vie** from that of **Vagabondaggio,** the identification of the *locus sacer* not only with the domestic hearth but more particularly with the Sicilian hearth persists.

Yet, uncomfortably aware that in the age of triumphant esthetic criticism he might incur censure for giving undue importance to content, Russo takes pains to make a rather tenuous distinction whereby the artistic merit of the Sicilian tales can be attributed to something else than the intrinsic superiority of their subject matter. He states axiomatically that "l'arte grande non nasce mai da osservazione programmatica della vita, ma è piuttosto impellente e saliente ricordo di esperienze patite senza scopo" [great art never springs from an intentional observation of life, but is rather the resurgent and impellent memory of experiences lived through to no practical purpose at all], and tries to show in Verga's different psychological attitude to the Sicilian and non-Sicilian worlds the reason for the artistic perfection of the Sicilian tales and for the failure of the others:

. . . . il mondo siciliano era come tramato nella mente dell'artista, era fuso nel suo sangue, nella sua educazione, nei suoi ricordi, ed egli rispetto ad esso, si trovava in una situazione nostalgica: si aveva quella tale visione a distanza, quel covare nella memoria, che è la prima condizione della poesia, quella capacità di sogno sul mondo che ieri è stato anche il nostro mondo. L'arte non è *amor vitae. . . .* ma l'amore dell'amore della vita, desiderio del desiderio. Davanti a questo mondo della città, il Verga non è un nostalgico, ma piuttosto un curioso, un osservatore puro, uno scrittore desideroso di allargare i particolari di una sua antica provata esperienza, di ritrovare a sè nuovi documenti e testimonianze umane (6th ed., p. 238).

[. . . . the Sicilian world was as though woven into the artist's mind; it was fused with his blood, with his education, with his memories, and he was homesick for it. In this case, there existed that certain distant vision, that brooding in memory, which is the first condition of poetry, that ability to dream about the world that but a short while ago has been our world too. Art is not love of life. . . . but it is love of the love of life, desire of desire. With respect to the world of the city Verga feels no nostalgia, but rather curiosity; he is the pure observer, the writer wishing to enrich an old experience of his with new details, to discover new documents and new facts of human life.]

By thus turning the *locus sacer* from a spot in space (Sicily and the family hearth) to a spot in time (memory of Sicily and of the family hearth), Russo is able to give as the basic reason for the inferiority of the Milanese tales Verga's insufficient psychological penetration of the northern milieu, which had not become "fused with his blood, with his education, his memories," for which he felt no nostalgia, and toward which he consequently had no artistic disposition.

Giovanni Cecchetti (essay date 1973)

SOURCE: An introduction to *The She-Wolf, and Other Stories*, by Giovanni Verga, translated by Giovanni Cecchetti, revised edition, University of California Press, 1973, pp. v-xx.

[*In the following excerpt, Cecchetti probes the motivating forces behind Verga's characters. The critic then describes Verga's search for a new, completely impersonal narrative form, which, Cecchetti argues, "helped [Verga] to reject worn-out expressive patterns, approach reality more directly, and achieve an often naked but always lyrical prose."*]

One of the recurrent themes in the writings of Verga's second period is economic. His people are constantly engaged in a struggle for the most elementary means of survival. Their incessant need for material security often determines their actions and leads them to tragedy and ruin.

The novel *I Malavoglia* tells of a family of Sicilian fishermen prompted to speculate on a cargo of lupins to better their lot. But unfortunate circumstances bring about the loss of the cargo, the death of the oldest son, the eventual loss of the family house, and the disintegration of the family itself. The theme of poverty is equally evident in the short stories. In **"Cavalleria Rusticana,"** Lola jilts Turiddu because Alfio is better off; in **"Malaria,"** the disease seems to prostrate only the poor because they cannot afford to move away from the infested region; in the **"Story of the Saint Joseph Donkey,"** the animal is of some use as long as it produces financial benefits for its owners, but its misery becomes identified with the misery of the people who are trying to make a living with its help; in **"The Orphans,"** Meno cries over his wife's death because with her he has lost her dowry, and can finally find some comfort in the possibility of marrying Alfia, who owns property; in **"Black Bread,"** Santo and the Redhead fight constantly because they are poor ("The trouble is we aren't rich enough to love each other all the time. When chickens don't have anything to peck at in the coop, they peck at each other"), Pino the Tome marries the crippled widow and abandons the beautiful Lucia only because the widow is well off ("It was for love of bread," he says), Lucia gives in to Don Venerando because he gives her money for her dowry, her fiancé pushes her into the affair because he wants the dowry, and her brother and sister-in-law forget all moral considerations as soon as they realize that she has earned it; in **"Consolation,"** poverty drives Arlia from one delusion to another until she sinks into stupefied resignation; in **"The Last Day,"** the protagonist resorts to suicide because he cannot support himself; and in **"Nanni Volpe,"** Raffaela marries the old man only because he has property.

But even when Verga's characters have accumulated considerable wealth, they retain the psychology of the poor with its feeling of insecurity: they are driven by a compulsive desire for more wealth and thus unconsciously nourish the drama of their emptiness. Such a person is Mastro Don Gesualdo. By laboring day and night he acquires a large fortune. Then, to improve his social status, he marries a penniless aristocratic girl, but is disliked by his wife's relatives as well as by the people of his former class. Finally he dies alone, in the palace of his son-in-law, neglected by his daughter and laughed at by the servants. Similar is the story of Nanni Volpe. He spends the best years of his life making money and buying property; when he feels that he has enough to start a family, he gets married, but it is too late, and his marriage is a total failure. All he is able to do is to try to get out of his money whatever personal advantage he can, by playing wife and nephew against each other. Still more tragic is the story of Mazzarò in **"Property"**: all his life he has done nothing but amass money and buy land, until everything in sight belongs to him; he has no children, no grandchildren, no relatives of any kind, he has only property. But as he realizes that death is near and sees the inadequacy of his riches, he goes mad with despair. Verga's rich are in truth poorer than the poor.

But for Verga poverty is also a deterministic factor in an environment where passions may explode with unexpected violence. Love and jealousy, the two main passions of his characters, are as prominent in his world as the struggle for survival and the desire for wealth.

Love enables him to portray the fundamental gentleness inherent in humble people, as in the section of **"Jeli,"** where he beautifully recreates the childhood idyll of the two protagonists. Sometimes, however, he sees love as a dark passion ruling human lives inexorably. In **"The She-Wolf,"** Nanni falls under the spell of his mother-in-law and has no way of freeing himself except by killing her. Pina is depicted as invincible, as the symbol of the inescapability of the flesh, in whose presence even religion loses its effectiveness. **"The She-Wolf,"** which Verga called "the most accentuated" of the stories of *Vita dei Campi,* is a drama of unusual power. It has been compared to the tragedies of incest found in Greek literature. The closing paragraph is certainly one of the most impressive passages in all of Verga's stories.

A different treatment appears in **"Gramigna's Mistress."** Peppa falls in love with a bandit because he is her ideal of strength and manhood; she ignores all conventional rules of respectability and follows him. When Gramigna is captured, she lives by her memories of him, working near the jail and doing little jobs for the policemen. She moves within a dream of love which has become the only reality of her life.

Although love may have its tender, poetic moments, jealousy either generates tragedy or tortures a man with unreasonable suspicions. In **"Cavalleria Rusticana,"** Turiddu feels betrayed by Lola and wants to make her jealous in order to win her back; by so doing he makes Santa jealous, and tragedy ensues. Jeli, in the story that bears his name, cannot believe that his old friend has taken Mara away from him; after a long period of revery, during which he refuses to accept the facts, he suddenly sees the truth and kills Don Alfonso without a moment of hesitation. What happens to **"Stinkpot"** is not very different. Jealousy seems to spring up as an integral part of the psyche of these characters.

"Cavalleria Rusticana" and **"Jeli"** also reveal a primitive moral code by which Verga's people live. If they offend, they know that they must pay; if they are offended, they know that they are entitled to justice, and are ready to take the law into their hands in order to get it. Turiddu is conscious that he has offended Alfio ("I know I've done wrong") and that he deserves to be killed. Jeli instinctively feels that he must kill the man who has defiled his home. And after the crime, he is sure that it was the least he could do; when they arrest him, he exclaims candidly: "What! I shouldn't even have killed him? . . . But he'd taken Mara! . . ."

Jealousy is a basic passion that prompts these men to protect their families and their honor, and therefore their own lives. But of course there are times when it may be only the product of unfounded suspicions and may consequently cause unnecessary mental suffering. This is the theme of **"Donna Santa's Sin,"** in which Doctor Brocca becomes the humorous and yet pathetic victim of his own apprehensions—

fostered as they are by the delirious utterances of his wife and the unscrupulous insinuations of his friends.

Like all human beings, Verga's people are simple and complex at the same time. We can single out some major traits, some stronger impulses, but these are merely elements in a total picture. The only way to perceive the full humanity of these characters—as of the characters in any work of art—is to follow the continuous interplay of their actions and aspirations, their drives and passions, their sorrows and joys.

With *Vita dei Campi* (1880), not only did Verga discover and recreate a world which was in sharp contrast with the one of his early work, but he also forged a style by which that world could be brought to life in the most direct and unmistakable way. Before publishing that book, he had spent many years in search of a "form," as he called it, which was to be "one and the same with the subject matter." And by form he meant language, images, structure, and everything these terms imply. His objective was to attain that ideal of impersonality, set forth in the preface to **"Gramigna's Mistress,"** whose main tenet was that the work of art should appear to have "matured and come into being spontaneously, like a fact of nature." Obviously Verga's impersonality, like Flaubert's *impassibilité,* does not exist. The author can never efface himself: the very choice of a subject matter, the particular manner of approaching the characters, and the preference for certain means of expression unavoidably bear the imprint of his personality. But the pursuit of such an impossible and nonexistent goal helped him to reject worn-out expressive patterns, approach reality more directly, and achieve an often naked but always lyrical prose.

What Verga actually wanted to do was to interpret his Sicilian world not in literary terms but in the terms that were ideally those of that world itself. For this purpose he adopted a very limited vocabulary, which consisted of words that were popular in quality, or would sound so in a given context. He condensed the narration as much as possible, eliminating everything except what seemed absolutely indispensable and could not be suggested between the lines. His syntax became linear, and kept some traces of the syntax of Sicilian dialect—the language most of his characters would have spoken in real life. His sentences acquired certain peculiarities of everyday speech. The conjunction "e" ("and") was employed repeatedly to connect coördinate clauses and sentences, as is common in popular narration.

Most of all—and this may be the primary source of all the characteristics of Verga's style—he had his people "narrate themselves," without apparent intrusions on his part; that is to say, he told the story with the words of his characters, or of a chorus of villagers who witnessed, or participated in, the action. The stories and novels of his second period, in fact, seem to be told by the very people the author writes about; they are all written in *style indirect libre,* or "free indirect style." In the first page of **"Cavalleria Rusticana,"** for instance, we find this sentence: "As soon as Turiddu found out, damn it! he was

going to tear that Licodian's guts from his belly, he was!" Here Verga relates the words of Turiddu, without omitting either his curse or his habitual repetition, and inserts them into the narrative stream, merely changing the personal pronouns and placing the verbs in the past tense, giving no indication that Turiddu might be speaking. Generally, in Verga's stories, when a character is mentioned, his speech follows. This technique was remarkably original for the time and contributed greatly to the power and freshness of Verga's prose. In our century it has been adopted by most major writers.

The speech of the chorus can be heard almost everywhere. In some cases Verga makes it evident by introducing such popular phrases as "God save us!" "God forbid!" and similar utterances. But it is usually discoverable through the language, the syntax, and the references to local customs and beliefs. Nearly all of **"Stinkpot,"** for example, is related in the words of the villagers or the spectators.

This strict adherence to the world of his characters leads Verga to eliminate conventional description. He treats nature and all external elements as integral parts of his people. The grueling Sicilian sun that scorches the countryside, and the fogs and rains that destroy the crops, are never considered for their own sake, but are felt as components of the toil and struggle of his men and women. One of the best examples of this approach to nature can be found toward the end of **"Jeli."** Jeli asks Mara to go with him to Salonia, where he works as a shepherd, but Mara answers "that she wasn't born to be a shepherdess." Her words immediately suggest to Jeli how hard the life of a shepherd is, and convince him that it is better for Mara to stay home:

> In fact, Mara wasn't born to be a shepherdess, and she wasn't used to the north wind of January when your hands stiffen on the staff and your fingernails seem to be falling out, and to the furious rainstorms when the water goes through to your bones, and to the suffocating dust of the roads when the sheep move along under the burning sun, and to the hard bed on the ground and to the moldy bread, and to the long silent and solitary days when in the scorched countryside you can see nothing but a rare sun-blackened peasant driving his little donkey silently ahead of him on the white, endless road.

These are Jeli's thoughts; they spring from his everyday life and from his feelings for Mara. Through them we become aware of what the deserted countryside at Salonia looks like, and of the changing of the seasons, but we see these facts as part of the life of the protagonist.

In the **"Story of the Saint Joseph Donkey,"** the writer goes even so far as to look at the surrounding fields through the very eyes of the poor animal:

> His eyes [were] lifeless, as if he were tired of looking at that vast white countryside which was clouded here and there with dust from the threshing floors and seemed made only to let you die of thirst and to make you trot around on the sheaves.

In the opening pages of **"Malaria,"** the apparent description of the Plain of Catania is in reality the picture of the disease itself, of the desolation it causes, and of the people who cannot escape it:

> In vain Lentini, and Francofonte, and Paternò try to climb like stray sheep up the first hills that break loose from the plain . . . malaria snatches up the villagers in the deserted streets and nails them in front of the doors of their houses . . .

At the beginning of **"Property,"** our eyes do not rest on the orange orchards, the huge storehouses, the immense vineyards and olive groves, the endless lines of oxen, and the herds filling the pastures of Canziria, but on Mazzarò, who becomes instantly identified with all of them. From the very first lines of that truly "symphonic" beginning, we know that all that property *is* Mazzarò, and that Mazzarò is nothing but his property.

Thus in Verga external factors are interiorized and charged with the inner life of his characters; they are, in other words, transformed into images and symbols. This is the essence of his lyricism.

Only a few words are sufficient for Verga to present a psychological situation in all its richness and suggestiveness. Who can forget the two sentences that introduce the She-Wolf? Her figure, her eyes, her red, devouring lips give us her picture and suggest the symbol she embodies. How delicately, on the contrary, the writer says that Santa had fallen in love with Turiddu: "The tassel of the *bersagliere*'s cap had tickled her heart and was always dancing before her eyes"—which is, among other things, an admirable way of expressing the most common of human events. And of Peppa, when asked by Gramigna if she wants to stay with him, Verga writes only that she nodded "avidly"; and of the dejected protagonist of **"The Last Day"** he mentions a pair of shoes that are falling apart. In **"War Between Saints,"** the misery of the whole town is evoked in a sentence depicting the women, immobile in their despair: "It was one of those long years when the famine begins in June, and the women, with stunned eyes, stand idle and disheveled at the doorways."

The beginning of **"Rosso Malpelo"** is especially vivid from this point of view: "He was called Malpelo because he had red hair; and he had red hair because he was a mean and bad boy, who promised to turn into a first-rate scoundrel." Here Verga uses a touch of popular psychology: the traditional prejudices of the people join to introduce the unfortunate victim, who will be forced to become an outcast, if he wants to be an individual in a hostile environment. A beginning like this would be considered striking even today.

With his tightly knit prose, his immediacy and directness, his powerful conciseness, and his lyricism, Verga was ahead of his time. This might be the reason why his major works did not enjoy much popularity during an era when the general public was used to fiction of a Victorian type. The only work of his that became widely known was **"Cavalleria Rusticana,"** thanks to the theater version and to Mascagni's opera. Fame was to come to Verga after World War I, when readers and critics finally realized his greatness. Since then he has been a profound influence on contemporary Italian literature. This should not be surprising, for most of the narrative devices of twentieth-century fiction were already his.

Verga's style, at its best, as is often the case in *Novelle rusticane*, is immediate and unmistakable. Though the medium is Italian, Sicilian ways of thought and feeling provide the sinews of the narrative. The stories are rich in *modi di dire*, emphatic colloquialisms and in expressions with a proverbial ring.

—*D. Maxwell White, in a review of* Little Novels of Sicily, *translated by D. H. Lawrence, in* The Modern Language Review, *July, 1975*.

Ann H. Hallock (essay date 1982)

SOURCE: "*Fantasticheria*: Verga's Declaration of Transition," in *Italian Culture,* Vol. II, 1982, pp. 91-102.

[*In the following essay, Hallock champions "Fantasticheria" as Verga's "statement of transition" from "decadent romanticism" to the* verismo *school of writing.*]

Of all Giovanni Verga's works, **"Fantasticheria"** is most singular for its special content and the scant critical attention it has received. Scholars have historically regarded it as a peripheral work in their studies of Verga's poetics or have used it in reference to their investigations of *I Malavoglia*. However, **"Fantasticheria"** does not deserve such superficial treatment, for it is a serious work of art in its own right. Moreover, it establishes the beginning of Verga's changed literary focus. In fact, the 1879 **"Fantasticheria"** is Verga's structural and stylistic masterpiece with which he denounces his previous voguish literary concern—decadent romanticism—and declares his return to his Sicilian roots as the source of his new orientation. As such, **"Fantasticheria"** is Verga's declaration of transition in the evolution of his writing.

It is easy to understand why **"Fantasticheria"** has not been recognized as such a crucial work in Verga's writing. On the surface it appears to be merely a superficial, appropriately-entitled reminiscence which records his memories of a brief, romantic sojourn he and an elegant Continental companion spent in Aci Trezza. Thus, precisely because of the frivolity immediately associated with **"Fantasticheria"**'s title and content and reinforced by its utterly conspicuous and, seemingly, incongruous appearance in the very midst of **"Cavalleria Rusticana," "La Lupa," "Jeli il Pastore"** and **"Rosso Malpelo,"** critics have brushed aside **"Fantasticheria"** as whimsical and have found it significant only because it contains a schematic prelude to *I Malavoglia* and nascent signs of Verga's *verismo.*

"Fantasticheria," however, is in its entirety a very serious, sustained *double-entendre* wherein structure, language, imagery and tone brilliantly function on two levels of meaning. Its second connotation at once epitomizes and renounces the superficial Continental life foreign to the profound Sicilian world. Thus, while on one level **"Fantasticheria"** is a frivolous tale, on the other it is Verga's statement of transition from Continental romance to Sicilian reality.

On Verga's stylistic development:

In the early work, [Verga] attempted to write in Tuscan, and the attempt, for all the popularity that some of these novels achieved, was a failure: the style as much a matter of the outsider listening and reading, as the situations were of the outsider looking—neither more sharply nor fully than an outsider could. At any rate, he was no more satisfied with the attempt at literary migration than we may assume that he was with the attempt at social migration, for suddenly, in 1874, as if in imaginative exasperation with the manner that he had developed and the matter that he was still to exploit, he burst out with **"Nedda,"** the true promise. This Sicilian *Tess,* with its abrupt shift in subject matter, expelled at a blow every affectation of syntax and figure that he had cultivated, and the story, told swiftly and baldly and with a certain brutality, takes its stylistic color from the dialogue of its peasant characters. Yet two more works in the old manner were to follow, and then, in 1876, after the beginning of the author's own return to Catania, four years of silence, and then the revolutionary triumph in the *Cavalleria* volume of 1880, which brings to its fulness every promise of **"Nedda"** in new style, new method, new subject, and which was to alter the history of Italian fiction.

Mark Schorer, "The Fiction of Giovanni Verga," in The Arts at Mid-Century, *edited by Robert Richman, Horizon Press, 1954.*

Ironically, the *novella*'s dual nature is immediately apparent in its very title. Verga employs the word *fantasticheria* as a *double-entendre* signifying both "reverie" and, more importantly, "serious consideration." However, the only meaning critics have seen in the title is "reverie," a word which immediately—and purposefully—invites comparison between **"Fantasticheria"** and the much-acclaimed 1874 **"Nedda."** The *fantasticheria* in **"Nedda,"** namely, Verga's "peregrinazioni vagabonde dello spirito" before the embers of his fireplace, is, however, just a simple device to introduce the reader to the other fire he had seen "ardere nell'immenso focolare della fattoria del Pino." The drawing-room fire before which the cosmopolitan author muses in Milan—far from his native land, immersed in the

elegance of the elitist lifestyle he had chosen and assimilated, languishing in the "voluttuosa pigrizia del caminetto," sunk in the familiar comfort of his armchair "col sigaro semispento, cogli occhi socchiusi, le molle fuggendovi dalle dita allentate"—evokes the emergence of his suppressed desire to return to his Sicilian homeland.

In reverie, nearly mesmerized by the flickering fire, he watches the released, Sicilian "other part" of himself "andar lontano, percorrere vertiginose distanze," taking him and his thoughts back to that other fire, similar yet so distant in miles and culture to the one which had elicited it. Clearly, **"Nedda"** records Verga's first stirrings of recognition of the undeniable Sicilian essence of his being. It documents his subconscious return to his native Sicily. However, this reverie can hardly be considered the conscious statement of a critical moment in his artistic development. Thus, **"Nedda"** merely preludes the heretofore unplumbed **"Fantasticheria."**

The other connotation of his *double-entendre* title, to wit, "serious consideration," announces the true significance of this *novella,* namely, that it is something more than reminiscences of a romantic interlude. **"Fantasticheria"**'s "serious consideration" is Verga's deliberate statement of transition in which, as a person and as a writer, he abandons his adopted worldly Continental existence and returns to the simple life of Sicily which from his childhood had nourished his innermost self. **"Fantasticheria"** thereby heralds his transition from conventional Continental romanticist to nonconformist Sicilian *verista.*

The fact that **"Fantasticheria"** was intended to be the manifesto of his new artistic focus is substantiated by his treatment of this work from its very inception. Indeed, he published **"Fantasticheria,"** chronologically the first *novella* of *Vita dei Campi,* in the August 24, 1879 issue of *Fanfulla della Domenica* while he was writing *Vita dei Campi* and *I Malavoglia* for publication scarcely a year later. As such, **"Fantasticheria"** was his literal public *"avviso"* declaring the new course his writing was to take. Furthermore, in his original, 1880 edition of *Vita dei Campi,* **"Fantasticheria"** appears immediately after the two *novelle* which Verga correctly intuited were to become his most acclaimed and well known—**"Cavalleria Rusticana"** and **"La Lupa"**—and just before those which he also correctly discerned would be the collection's less popular *novelle.* In this pivotal position it serves as an explanatory commentary on the radical shift in his literary orientation which is evident in these two dramatically powerful works and also functions as a preface for the remainder of the collection by declaring his allegiance to the new perspective also sustained in the subsequent *novelle* of *Vita dei Campi*—beginning with **"Jeli il Pastore."** Thus, while **"Fantasticheria"** appears to be capriciously placed in *Vita dei Campi,* its flagrant inclusion and deliberate positioning provide the key to understanding the revolutionary significance of the collection as a whole.

Moreover, in his definitive, 1897 Treves edition, which required new typesetting and provided Verga an unexpected opportunity to revise *Vita dei Campi,* he conclusively substantiated **"Fantasticheria"**'s role as the manifesto of his literary transition. To this edition he added the herald of his new literary horizons, **"Nedda."** Significantly, he placed this almost subconscious draft of his inner leanings immediately before **"Fantasticheria,"** and therefore, by literal placement, designated **"Nedda"** as the prelude to **"Fantasticheria"**'s conscious statement of his return to his basic Sicilian world and his rejection of his voguish cosmopolitan interests.

The final proof that he considered **"Fantasticheria"** to be such a statement is found in the fact that, although he radically altered the content and style of all the other *novelle* of *Vita dei Campi* in order to achieve the stylistic fluidity demanded by his new artistic tenets, he adamantly left **"Fantasticheria"** and **"Nedda"** virtually unchanged except for punctuation. The variants of **"Fantasticheria"** reveal that he replaced commas with dashes to create greater pauses—which become chasms between the Sicilian and Continental worlds—and substituted the past absolute for the imperfect tense, thereby creating maximal remoteness between himself and the cosmopolitan world of his female companion. Thus the variants demonstrate that he clearly considered his other *novelle* in *Vita dei Campi* to be *lit-*

Portrait of Verga by Amedeo Bianchi, 1912.

erary in nature and revised them accordingly. By the same token, his almost complete disinterest in changing the artistic expression of his inseparably-coupled **"Nedda"** and **"Fantasticheria"** attest to his radically different view of these works as literary manifestos.

Internal analysis substantiates **"Fantasticheria"**'s reality as Verga's statement of transition. It also reveals that this statement of transition orders all aspects of the *novella*'s design. Verga deliberately chooses the first person narrative form in a blatant, rare move, thereby allowing himself as author a wry *double-entendre* in which he assumes the dual role of narrator of a collage-like series of memories and expositor of his own manifesto. Thus the *novella* becomes on two levels an autobiographical confession of his metamorphosis.

In fact, on the surface his tale appears to be simply a reminiscence of the forty-eight hours he spent in Aci Trezza with his companion. With tongue in cheek he addresses this work to her, painting as it were a souvenir portrait in words to satisfy for the moment her vain desire to be the protagonist of a book. She seems at first glance to be another of the Continental heroines of his prior novels, such as *Eva* and *Tigre Reale,* which had won him international acclaim and had established him among the leading European authors of his age. For the first time in his writings, however, significant differences appear. From the *novella*'s very outset she is merely a memory of the past. He has literally said goodbye to her. She has left by train to return to her cosmopolitan life, and he has remained in Sicily, immersed in his origins. Thus, in the *novella*'s first eleven lines Verga allegorically states the actuality of his definitive separation from his previous Continental being and his return to Sicily. These eleven lines also exemplify the manner in which **"Fantasticheria"**'s structure and style are in themselves a brilliant artistic statement of this transition.

The entire progression of the *novella* subtly reiterates this statement of transition. At the beginning of the *novella,* his female protagonist holds center stage, a position befitting the prima donna that she is. As the story evolves, however, although she seems to be its protagonist, she gradually fades until all that is left of her is the memory of her footprint. As she pales before the reader's eyes, the Sicilian peasants, who were an anonymous background at the outset, take shape and acquire heroic proportions as they advance to become the *novella*'s true protagonists. With his almost imperceptible inversion of his protagonists, Verga literally and allegorically makes the transition from Continental to Sicilian complete.

Paralleling its structure, **"Fantasticheria"**'s *double-entendre* language also unmistakenly transmits Verga's intense, conscious awareness of his transition. Ever so deftly his unrelenting, ironic language reduces his lofty lady to a sham. His carefully selected, key words describe her as "stanca"; "impaziente"; arrogant ("Un bel quadretto davvero! e si indovinava che lo sapeste anche voi dal modo in cui vi modellaste . . ."); "ingenua"; "centomila lire di entrata"; "pretesto" and "parer meritevole"; aimlessly seeking to fill her life ("vi affannate"), and, ultimately, the passive antithesis of the active Sicilian world which is for her merely a "spettacolo." Significantly, as his narrative of his memories evolves, the Sicilian characters of this "spettacolo" grow in stature as he increasingly exposes their rich inner world and epic heroism, culminating in his statement that their lives seem to him "seriissime e rispettabilissime." Thus, the very nature and progression of his words delineating the protagonists of these two worlds are literally and figuratively Verga's statement of transition from the hollow Continental life of his paramour to the full humanity of the Sicilians.

Close analysis of the *novella*'s second paragraph, which I believe is one of the sublime moments in Verga's writings, epitomizes the brilliant artistry of structure, language, imagery, mood and tone with which he makes this statement throughout **"Fantasticheria."** The scene opens with that magnificent dawn which had concluded a romantic evening by surprising the couple atop the *faraglione*. He describes his chic companion standing on a cliff above the deep-green sea in the midst of the violet dawn caressing Aci Trezza, "quel gruppetto di casuccie che dormivano quasi raggomitolate sulla riva." Elegantly wrapped up in her own world, she poses in the spotlight of the sunrise behind her. Verga's verbal portrait must have made her smile with delight at herself:

> . . . in cima allo scoglio, sul cielo trasparente e profondo, si stampava netta la vostra figurina, colle linee sapienti che vi metteva la vostra sarta, e il profilo fine ed elegante che ci mettevate voi.—Avevate un vestitino grigio che sembrava fatto apposta per intonare coi colori dell'alba.—Un bel quadretto davvero! e si indovinava che lo sapeste anche voi dal modo in cui vi modellaste nel vostro scialletto, e sorridendo coi grandi occhioni sbarrati e stanchi a quello strano spettacolo, e a quell'altra stranezza di trovarvici anche voi presente.

A second reading reveals, however, that his irony and *double-entendres* present her in all her vanity—utterly estranged from the life of the background. He does not depict her as a person, but, rather, as the flat, superficial silhouette of an elegant mannequin. He completes his reduction of her to a lifeless portrait with his conclusion, "Un bel quadretto davvero!" His *double-entendre* imagery reinforces her lifelessness. She sees through tired, staring eyes. Moreover, she is shrouded in grey silk and shawl and has become a mere shade—a black spectre before the dawn's light. In the final, unique *double-entendre* image, "quadretto," she is encased forever within the four wooden sides of a rectangle. The imagery thus clearly confirms the figurative death of this woman who represents his former life. Her only words, "Non capisco come si possa viver qui tutta la vita," confess that she could not survive in the midst of such a vital environment. With this observation Verga gives the kiss of death to his former Continental life.

In this scene, as in the other scenes constituting **"Fantasticheria"**'s narrative and forming its strategy, he makes the decisive statement of his transition also through the ingenious technique of at once superimposing and contra-

posing the images of its two worlds. Indeed, as we have noted, he upheld his lifeless protagonist against the backdrop of that symbolic sunrise caressing Aci Trezza and evoking his first revelation of his inner being as he completely responds to its beauty and radiance. He thus announces the dawning of his new life as the *novella*'s Sicilian world and his identification and kinship of spirit with it begin to come to the foreground. In his reply to her observation, the irony of his language and tone at once so sympathetic toward the Sicilians and derogatory toward her reveals that she, the supreme example of all Continental life, is moribund, while the Sicilians, who by comparison seem to have nothing, are vital:

> . . . la cosa è più facile che non sembri: basta non possedere centomila lire di entrata, prima di tutto; e in compenso patire un po' di tutti gli stenti fra quegli scogli giganteschi, incastonati nell'azzurro, che vi facevano battere le mani per ammirazione. Così poco basta perché quei poveri diavoli . . . trovino fra quelle loro casipole sgangherate e pittoresche . . . tutto ciò che vi affannate a cercare a Parigi, a Nizza ed a Napoli.

With his subsequent statement, he definitively divorces her from this Sicilian world to which he has so lyrically responded when he says, "È una cosa singolare; ma forse non è male che sia così—per voi e per tutti gli altri come voi."

After this second paragraph, Verga enunciates with increasing clarity throughout the remainder of the *novella* his complete severance from his former world and affirmation of the primacy of his Sicilian origins. In fact, whereas Continental situations had evoked Sicilian scenes in his previous writings, now the Sicilian ambiance elicits memories of his Continental life. Moreover, he uses irony to stamp the memories of his Continental past with a markedly negative tone and also underscores the fact that he recalls them only because of their Sicilian associations. We note this new mood of reverie, which functions as yet another stylistic medium for the statement of his manifesto, in the following passage. He candidly declares to this alter-Eva that her capricious wish that he dedicate some pages to her was evoked in him by

> quella povera donna cui solevate fare l'elemosina . . . ed io, girellando, col sigaro in bocca [an obvious reminder of the antithetical reverie in **"Nedda"**], ho pensato che anche lei, così povera com'è, vi aveva vista passare, bianca e superba.

He unequivocally affirms the new Sicilian inspiration of his thought with his admonishment to her: "Non andate in collera se mi son rammentato di voi in tal modo, e a questo proposito." He undauntedly pursues his testimony of his diametric change of perspective, confessing that she was also evoked by the *shawl* of the poor, shivering woman, which prompts an even more pregnant superimposition of images, biting *double-entendre* and tone exposing the dramatic antithesis between the quintessential Sicilian world and her satiety:

> . . . la mantellina di quella donnacciola freddolosa, accoccolata, poneva un non so che di triste, e mi faceva

pensare a voi, sazia di tutto, perfino dell'adulazione che getta ai vostri piedi il giornale di moda, citandovi spesso in capo alla cronaca elegante—sazia così da inventare il capriccio di vedere il vostro nome sulle pagine di un libro.

He ultimately seals this indelible statement of transition with his ironic observations on that would-be protagonist and her eternal carnival from which the Sicilian realities ordering his thought are utterly and irrevocably alienated:

Quando scriverò il libro, forse non ci penserete più; intanto i ricordi vi mando, così lontani da voi, in ogni senso, da voi inebbriata di feste e di fiori, vi faranno l'effetto di una brezza deliziosa, in mezzo alle veglie ardenti del vostro eterno carnevale.

Throughout the remainder of **"Fantasticheria"** Verga insistently reveals that reality for him is Sicily, not Milan or Florence or the woman symbolizing their cultures. In fact, by now she has become merely the *mise en scène* for his lyrical observations on the inhabitants of Aci Trezza. As he sharpens his focus on them, his irony, tone and language increasingly lay bare his genuine admiration and affection for the epic Sicilians while continuing his now blatant derision of her. His tone has clearly changed from that of a fond lover to a harsh critic; thereby it, too, sounds his statement of transition. We witness these decisive shifts of emphasis reinforced by his new tone in the following passage, which typifies the second half of **"Fantasticheria"**:

L'altro, quell'uomo che sull'isolotto non osava toccarvi il piede per liberarlo dal lacciuolo teso ai conigli, nel quale v'eravate impigliata da stordita che siete, si perdè in una fosca notte d'inverno, solo, fra i cavalloni scatenati, quando fra la barca e il lido . . . c'erano sessanta miglia di tenebre e di tempesta. Voi non avreste potuto immaginare di qual disperato e tetro coraggio fosse capace per lottare contro tal morte quell'uomo che lasciavasi intimidire dal capolavoro del vostro calzolaio.

Moreover, at the conclusion of **"Fantasticheria,"** Verga openly declares his absolute respect and sympathy for the substance and character of his Sicilians. As they now command the stage, he eloquently defends their heroic and eternal values, which became central in his own life and work, in his rebuttal to her predictable condescending, trite observation:

—Insomma l'ideale dell'ostrica!—direte voi—Proprio l'ideale dell'ostrica! e noi non abbiamo altro motivo di trovarlo ridicolo che quello di non esser nati ostriche anche noi.

Per altro il tenace attaccamento di quella povera gente allo scoglio sul quale la fortuna li ha lasciati cadere, mentre seminava principi di qua e duchesse di là, questa rassegnazione coraggiosa ad una vita di stenti, questa religione della famiglia, che si riverbera sul mestiere, sulla casa, e sui sassi che la circondano, mi sembrano—forse pel quarto d'ora—cose seriissime e rispettabilissime anch'esse.

With these words, Verga also affirms that the Sicilian world is not to be viewed as a farcical stage spectacle from a box seat through opera glasses. Instead, it is a profound human drama in which he is now an active participant, as he indicates with his emphatic repetition of *questa,* not *quella.*

Ultimately, in his subsequent, last superimposition of images from his two worlds (which are now epitomized and antithetical to the extreme), Verga himself represents the Sicilian antithesis of the Continental world. He literally and figuratively states his identity with the Sicilian world as he frankly proclaims his total immersion in it. "Sembrami," he says,

che le irrequietudini del pensiero vagabondo s'addormenterebbero dolcemente nella pace serena di quei sentimenti miti, semplici, che si succedono calmi e inalterati di generazione in generazione.—Sembrami che potrei vedervi passare, al gran trotto dei vostri cavalli, col tintinnìo allegro dei loro finimenti e salutarvi tranquillamente.

Here, in the climax of the *novella,* Verga's statement of transition is thus consummate. He has moved from subjective involvement in the world of romance to a stance so securely rooted in Sicily that he can view the epitome of his former life with utter indifference. In this culmination all the *double-entendre* stylistic and structural devices of **"Fantasticheria"** have achieved their relentless 180° turn and complete their statement of his transition.

In conclusion, there can be no doubt that **"Fantasticheria,"** written and published five years after **"Nedda"** while Verga was residing in Sicily and writing *Padron 'Ntoni,* is the manifesto of his new literary direction. Moreover, it marks the first, crucial step—"farci piccini anche noi"—toward the realization of his theoretical premises elaborated in his 1878-1880 letters to Capuana and in his manifesto of *verismo* prefacing the *novella* now entitled **"L'amante di Gramigna."** Verga's *verismo,* as Croce so accurately perceived, is a moment in the spiritual evolution of the writer—the decisive moment. **"Fantasticheria"** is Verga's declaration of that definitive moment of transition.

Myriam Yvonne Jehenson (essay date 1983)

SOURCE: "Verga's *La Lupa*: A Study in Archetypal Symbolism," in *Forum Italicum,* Vol. 17, No. 2, Fall, 1983, pp. 196-206.

[*In the following essay, Jehenson reads "La Lupa" as a cyclical tale of classic archetypal symbolism, with the She-Wolf acting as the primordial goddess.*]

In his discussion of the effectiveness of the great realistic novelists, Georg Lukács predicates two essential aspects of their art. It has a poetic quality which "manifests itself precisely in the ability to overcome the unpoetic nature of their world," and it has as its central category and criterion the literary type. By "type" Lukács means a peculiar synthesis which "organically binds together the general and the particular," thereby rendering concrete, "the peaks and limits of men and epochs." Lukács' description is especially appropriate to Giovanni Verga's novella **"La lupa."**

"La Lupa" or **"The Shewolf"** is included in Verga's 1880 collection of short stories, *Vita dei campi*. In **"The Shewolf,"** Verga rises above the stiflingly oppressive setting of a conventional Sicilian village by giving it the timelessness and universality of true poetry. In his description of the Shewolf herself, however, Verga goes beyond Lukács' description of the type and evokes the even more universal archetype. Thus Verga taps deep human reactions in the reader, who is moved on both conscious and the unconscious level.

"The Shewolf" is, on the first level, the depiction of a typical agrarian village with its limitations and parochial mores. Verga, whose **"Cavalleria rusticana"** was to be the basis for Mascagni's well-known operatic version, creates settings of primitive passions which lead inexorably to tragedy. In **"The Shewolf,"** a woman stands out for her defiance of Sicilian convention. The villagers call her the Shewolf "because she never had enough—of anything." Verga describes her through association, thereby giving us both a physical portrayal of her and, more importantly, an immediate awareness of how the villagers perceive her:

> The women made the sign of the cross when they saw her pass, alone as a wild bitch, prowling about suspiciously like a famished wolf; with her red lips she sucked the blood of their sons and husbands in a flash, and pulled them behind her skirt with a single glance of those devilish eyes . . .

Consistently alone, "without saying a word," the Shewolf lives her own life ignoring their customs and mores: "the Shewolf never went to church," and appears stronger in her appeal and fascination than their Christian beliefs: "Father Angiolino of Saint Mary of Jesus, a true servant of God, had lost his soul on account of her." The Shewolf is, in fact, a foil to the entire community. This includes her daughter Maricchia who is "like every other girl in the village," and who "cried in secret because she was the Shewolf's daughter, and no one would marry her, though . . . she had her fine linen in a chest and her good land under the sun"; and the peasant Nanni whom the Shewolf loves, but who rejects her for "appropriate" Sicilian values: "And I want your daughter, instead, who's a maid."

Yet Verga underscores the fact that it is the Shewolf, and not Maricchia his young wife, who fills Nanni's life and thoughts. The Shewolf "came to the threshing floor again and more than once, and Nanni did not complain. On the contrary, when she was late, in the hours between nones and vespers, he would go and wait for her at the top of the white, deserted path, with his forehead bathed in sweat."

Verga presents Nanni as consistently fearful. When the affair between him and the Shewolf becomes known, he immediately fears her as "the temptation of hell," and rejects her because "now the whole town knows about it."

Nanni is essentially passive in his reactions throughout the novella. He wants *to be* killed, *to be* removed from the house where the woman who fascinates him lives: "For God's sake, Sergeant, take me out of this hell. Have me killed, put me in jail; don't let me see her again, never! never!" The Shewolf becomes a "spell" which he must exorcize through the conventional methods of the village: "He paid for Masses for the souls in purgatory and asked the priest and the Sergeant for help. At Easter he went to confession, and in penance he publicly licked more than four feet of pavement, crawling on the pebbles in front of the church. . . ." It is all in vain. The Shewolf's hold on him is too powerful.

Verga depicts the Shewolf, on the other hand, as wholly natural and uninhibited. She simply informs Nanni that she wants him. In the circumscribed setting wherein she moves, she defies all convention. She "was the only living soul to be seen wandering in the countryside . . . in those hours between nones and vespers when no good woman goes roving around," and she "went into the fields to work with the men, and just like a man too, weeding, hoeing, feeding the animals, pruning the vines, despite the northeast and levantine winds of January." Nanni immediately succumbs to the Sergeant's mandate that he leave the Shewolf's presence, the Shewolf, on the contrary, forthrightly refuses to be ordered around: "No! . . . It's my house. I don't intend to leave it."

The end of the novella portrays the Shewolf as sanguine about death as she has been about life. When Nanni resorts to his ultimate and desperate way of freeing himself of her fascination, she calmly responds to his threat: "Kill me, . . . I don't care; I can't stand it without you."

There is a second and much more interesting level on which **"The Shewolf"** operates. It is the unconscious and archetypal one. The unconscious, as psychologists describe it, is composed of two layers. The personal unconscious, which was Freud's discovery, is particular to each individual and houses our subjective and lived experiences. The collective unconscious, Jung's contribution to Freud's psychological findings, is of a "collective, universal, and impersonal nature identical in all individuals. This collective unconscious does not develop individually but is inherited." According to Jung, archetypes derive from the layer of the collective unconscious, and seem to emerge from patterns of the human mind that are transmitted by tradition and heredity. Archetypes operate on an independent basis from an individual's life and have little to do with the individual's subjective experience:

> The archetypes of the collective unconscious are manifested . . . in the "mythological motifs" that appear among all peoples at all times in identical or analogous manner and can arise just as spontaneously—i.e., without any conscious knowledge—from the unconscious of modern man. [Erich Neumann, *The Great Mother: An Analysis of the Archetype*, trans. by Ralph Manheim, 1955, rpt. 1972]

Archetypes are divided into two categories. The first consists of personified archetypes like the Good or Wise

Mother, The Child-hero, which abound in mythology. The second category deals with situations, places or processes, and is concerned with themes of transformation such as journeys and death-resurrection motifs. One of the most compelling archetypes, and one explored in depth by Jungians, is that of the Feminine Principle or the Primordial Goddess. Second-generation Jungians like Erich Neumann have been greatly helped in their exploration of the archetype of the Primordial Goddess by archeological excavations and the art forms these have uncovered. During the past one hundred years, over one thousand female figurines have been found from the Paleolithic era dating from about 30,000 B.C.E. to 9,000 B.C.E. The manifestations of the Primordial Goddess archetype have been found in the concrete form of sculpture, cave paintings, and bas reliefs of the Upper Paleolithic period. Archetypes like the Primordial Goddess continue to find expression today as they did in the past. It is through symbol, myth and art, that these archetypes become visible, that the unconscious is brought to the conscious level. Works of literature and art constitute the bridge between the sensible world and the realm of the collective unconscious where the Primordial Goddess exists, ever ancient and ever new. In the words of Erich Neumann,

> The Primordial Goddess, combining elementary and transformative character in one, is an "eternal presence"; wherever the original traits of the elementary or the transformative character appear, her archaic image will be constellated anew, regardless of time and space.

In Verga's novella, the Shewolf evokes the two categories of the archetype. She personifies the Primordial Goddess Demeter, and she reenacts Demeter's ancient fertility rites, the agricultural mysteries of death and resurrection which ensured a rich harvest. The symbolic structure of Verga's novella helps make the archetype visible on a conscious level. **"The Shewolf"** is cyclical. It ends as it begins, dominated by the Shewolf as The Great Round, the Primordial Goddess who contains within herself the principles of life and of death, the insight that "the world lives on death."

Verga begins his narrative by presenting the Shewolf through the rhetorical process of *pars pro toto,* the part being given importance over the whole:

> She was tall, thin; she had the firm and vigorous breasts of the olive-skinned—and yet she was no longer young; she was pale, as if always plagued by malaria, and in that pallor, two enormous eyes, and fresh red lips which devoured you.

Verga always describes the Shewolf in this way, as a composite of parts. He underscores her breasts: the "firm and vigorous breasts of the olive-skinned," her "arrogant breasts." He stresses her pallor—like a White Goddess she is always "pale," with a "pallor . . . as if always plagued by malaria," and her black, penetrating eyes—"two enormous eyes," "devilish eyes," "coal-black eyes," "eyes as black as coal," and scarlet lips: in the deathly pallor of her face, what stands out are her "red lips," her

"fresh red lips which devoured you." It is the same manner of presentation that archeologists have pointed out in the representation of the Primordial Goddess figures of the Paleolithic period. For Marija Gimbutas, the "symbolic synecdoche" used in the figures of the Upper Paleolithic female figurines is functional. It calls attention to essential meanings associated with the artist's emphasis on the breasts, and vulvar region, namely, the symbolic aspects of her fertility and power of regeneration [*The Gods and Goddesses of Old Europe, 1000-3500 B.C.: Myths, Legends and Cult Images,* 1974]; for Erich Neumann, "a goddess represented in this way is never a goddess only of fertility but is always at the same time a goddess of death and the dead. She is the Earth Mother, the Mother of Life, ruling over everything . . .". The level of abstraction implied by such a synecdochal representation of these female figurines suggests to Alexander Marshack also that the significance of the Primordial Goddess figures must be explored away from the realm of mere anatomic references and specifically within the realm of myth and of religion [*The Roots of Civilization,* 1972]. I would like to show that it is within this realm, that of myth and of ancient religious practices, that the deeper level of Verga's **"The Shewolf"** can be most effectively displayed.

In his initial description of the Shewolf, Verga highlights three colors which he consistently uses in depicting her: the pale *whiteness* of her face, the *redness* of her lips, the *blackness* of her eyes. She is thereby immediately given the attributes of the Triad Goddess, one of those powerful archetypes which, for Jung, "may be considered the fundamental element[s] of the conscious mind, hidden in the depths of the psyche . . ."; and for Robert Graves is essential to all creative works: ". . . a true poem is necessarily an invocation of the White Goddess . . . the Mother of all Living, the ancient power of fright and lust . . . whose embrace is death" [*The White Goddess,* 1948, rpt. 1966]. The Goddess the Shewolf immediately evokes is Demeter, the "Barley Mother." Mythographers have shown, however, that Demeter is the Triad Goddess because she is often depicted in her three ages as Moon Goddess. She is Kore or Maiden, the age wherein Demeter reigns over the new corn and her color is white for the new moon. She is Persephone or Nymph, the age wherein Demeter reigns over the ripe corn, and her color is red for the harvest moon. The unfortunate confusion that results from Persephone's becoming separate from Demeter is a later one. Demeter's third age is that of Hecate or Crone wherein she reigns over the harvested corn, and her color is black for the moon that has waned.

In **"The Shewolf,"** time is factored according to agricultural phases. June is mentioned as the month in which the Shewolf falls in love with Nanni while they are mowing the hay. Verga presents the Shewolf to us as a veritable Demeter in the fields: ". . . as the sun hammered down overhead, the She-wolf gathered bundle after bundle, and sheaf after sheaf, never tiring, never straightening up for an instant." The description is intensely sensual: "she fell in love in the strongest sense of the word feeling the flesh afire beneath her clothes; and staring him in the eyes, she suffered the thirst one has in the hot hours of June deep in the plain." The scene evokes the seasonal and solemn sex orgies of the Eastern Mediterranean. This is the fertility rite to which the adventures of the Goddess Demeter in the thrice-ploughed field refers, the open coupling of the Corn Priestess and her consort in order to ensure a good harvest. The Shewolf initiates the encounter, beckoning to Nanni who is "beautiful as the sun and sweet as honey." But Nanni rejects her for her virgin daughter. Demeter-like in her anger, the Shewolf abandons the fields: "The She-wolf thrust her hands into her hair, scratching her temples, without saying a word, and walked away. And she did not appear at the threshing floor any more."

We do not hear from her until she sees Nanni in October. Again he rejects her for Maricchia. It is not until Winter, the time for the mythological and agricultural burying of the seed which will sprout in the Spring, that the Shewolf becomes really active. She "went into the fields to work with the men, and just like a man too, weeding, hoeing . . . despite the northeast and levantine winds of January." It is just before the Harvest, at the time of the "August sirocco," that the Shewolf couples with Nanni in the fields, and Verga once more describes her through "symbolic synecdoche," thereby evoking meanings beyond the immediate act. She comes to him, "pale, with her arrogant breasts and her coal-black eyes, [and] he stretched out his hands gropingly."

In the sprouting early spring, "in the green wheat fields," the Shewolf returns as Nanni is "hoeing the vineyard." The terrified Nanni takes an axe from the elm tree near by, and confronts the Shewolf, now presented as a synecdochal vision of Demeter's principal colors, red and black: "her hands laden with red poppies, her black eyes devouring him." Verga ends the novella with the line: "'Ah! damn your soul!' stammered Nanni."

This ending, however elliptical, is especially significant if we want to conclude our archetypal reading. The Demeter-Kore myth always accounted for the winter burial of a female Corn doll which was uncovered in the early Spring. Its symbolic value was the fruitful death of the grain. In order to "resurrect" Kore, a mattock or axe had to break open Mother Earth's head, thereby ritually freeing Kore and ensuring the regeneration of the fields. In late antiquity, Porphyry reminds us, the word for Kore, was still explained as the feminine form of the word for Sprout, *kóros.* These agricultural mysteries of pre-Hellenic times survived late into Classical times as the vase paintings of Kore's "resurrection" shows.

Verga's placing of the red poppies in the Shewolf's hands, for the first and only time at the end of his novella, is indicative. It evokes the same Demeter-associated theme of transformation, the death and resurrection motif. The Spring equinox encounter of the Goddess and her consort ritually ended with the annual death which guaranteed the rich harvest in late summer. It is "in the green wheat fields" that the final encounter between Nanni and the Shewolf takes place. The poppies in her hands are her attributes as Demeter, the Corn Goddess. Poppies are well-known symbols of death. They and the spotted toadstool, the *amanita muscaria,* are often featured in scenes of the underworld

or afterlife. They become the promise of resurrection when held in the hands of the Goddess Demeter-Persephone. To quote Robert Graves [in *The Greek Myths,* 1955, rpt. 1960]:

> Poppies are naturally associated with Demeter, since they grow in cornfields; Core picks or accepts poppies because of the sopophoric qualities and because of their scarlet colour which promises resurrection after death.

Nanni, and not the Shewolf, is terrified at the end of Verga's novella. She is in complete control, aware of the significance of the archetypal situation that she is about to reenact. The red poppies become an integral part of the death-resurrection process she will initiate:

> The Shewolf saw him come, pale and wild-eyed, with the ax glistening in the sun, but she did not fall back a single step, did not lower her eyes; she continued toward him, her hands laden with red poppies, her black eyes devouring him.

At the end of **"The Shewolf,"** we have come full archetypal circle. Verga ends the story as he began it, with minor but significant differences. Demeter-like, the Shewolf still dominates. The redness of her lips is now transferred to the sopophoric red poppies at the end. She devours not with her lips, as at the beginning, but with her black eyes—the color of the Phigalian Black Demeter Δημήτηρ Μελαίνᾳ—whom she now personifies. As Goddess of Death and Resurrection, the Shewolf is the Goddess Demeter in her Hecate aspect of Goddess of the Underworld.

The ring composition of Verga's literary structure has paralleled the archetypal symbolism of the story, they are both cyclical. The Shewolf ends as the Primordial Triad Goddess who rules the Upper, Middle, and Lower Worlds. She is the Great Round. All things come from and return to her. She "not only bears and directs life as a whole . . . but also takes everything . . . back into its womb of origination and death" [Erich Neumann, *The Great Mother*].

Gregory L. Lucente   (essay date 1988)

SOURCE: "The Historical Imperative: Giovanni Verga and Italian Realism in the Light of Recent Critical Trends," in *Neohelicon,* Vol. XVI, No. 2, 1988, pp. 149-74.

[*In the following essay, Lucente offers a critical overview of Verga's work as an Italian realist.*]

Nineteenth century Italian realism in general (or *verismo*) and Giovanni Verga's works in particular have received a great deal of critical attention over the past three decades. From the biographically and thematically oriented idealist treatments of the 1950s and 1960s through the post-1968 Marxist reinterpretations of the 1970s, Verga criticism has remained in the forefront of Italian literary debates. This has been the case in large part because of the representational slant of *verismo*'s aesthetic and because of the extraordinary complexity that any adequate theory of literary representation necessarily involves.

In recent years, two trends have dominated Verga studies: on the one hand, an interest in textual criticism, in the establishing and re-editing of Verga's major texts; and on [the] other an interest in the details of Verga's historical milieu, in recapturing the nineteenth century Sicilian environment that Verga's realist narratives endeavor, in literary terms, to re-create. While the first of these trends is a matter of editorial refinement within Verga studies, the second, in its openly historicizing tendencies, has implications that extend well beyond Verga studies as such. This critical concern for the material particulars of everyday life within a specific sociocultural milieu furnishes an important analogy to recent American critical interest regarding the nature of literary representation, especially as that interest is manifest in the "new historicist" critical enterprise currently under way in the United States. Before suggesting how and why such a parallel is germane to the study of literary realism overall, however, it may prove useful to sketch the primary characteristics of Verga's *verismo* and, albeit in summary fashion, the history of *verismo*'s critical "fortune."

Verga, along with his fellow Sicilian Luigi Capuana, was one of the founding fathers of the realist movement that was known as *verismo*. While Capuana's importance as a *verista* derives primarily from his critical tracts written to explain and propagate Italian realism, Verga's significance lies in the literary *praxis* of his realist narratives, along with the prefaces and introductions that he used as discursive preambles to his novels and short stories. Verga's major realist works include two volumes of short stories, *Vita dei campi* (1880) and *Novelle rusticane* (1883), and two novels, *I Malavoglia* (1881) and *Mastro-don Gesualdo* (1888-89). The vast preponderance of these narratives focuses on the lives of the rural lower classes in Verga's native Sicily. At one and the same time, this choice of subject matter demonstrates the affinity of Verga's *verismo* with contemporaneous realist movements throughout Europe and Verga's marked divergence from earlier nineteenth century trends in Italian literature, which, in general, had remained highly romantic and elegantly stylized.

Any description of Verga's realist practice as either directly or naively representational falls short, however, on at least two counts. First, although Verga often sympathetically adopted the perspective of the Sicilian peasantry, he also developed a series of literary techniques permitting him not only to describe but also to criticize his subjects' views of the events in which they participate, in a way that brings to mind [Georg] Lukács' notion of critical realism (as distinct from both classical bourgeois realism and modern socialist realism). Second, whereas the realistic elements of Verga's narratives—such as the accurate representation of local scenes, the seemingly simple language, and the clarity of character motivation—serve Verga's goal of portraying the historical life and times of his subjects, in the view of many of his characters, as well as in Ver-

ga's own perspective, at the heart of history lay not just day-to-day reality but also the shaping force and feeling of myth. This striking combination of both critical and mythic effects within an essentially realistic narrative frame distinguishes all of Verga's major narratives, and it helps to place him in the company of the great and often surprisingly heterodox realist authors of other nineteenth century European traditions, such as Balzac, Dickens, Hardy, Clarín, and Tolstoy, to mention only a few.

In terms of representational technique, Verga's selection of the objects of representation brought with it a particularly difficult linguistic problem, since the everyday language of the Sicilian populace is a regional dialect quite different from Italian. To solve this problem, beginning with the story "Nedda" of 1874, Verga transposed the locutions, rhythms, and syntax peculiar to Sicilian dialect into standard Italian in descriptive passages as well as in dialogue. In his major works, Verga also made extensive use of the *style indirect libre,* or free indirect discourse, in which the distinctions between the narrator and the characters are blurred to such an extent that the work of art, at least in appearance, "sembr[a] essersi fatta da sé"; "seem[s] to have made itself," as Verga says in the introduction to the story **"L'amante di Gramigna"** (in *Vita dei campi*). The two-fold effects of Verga's linguistic mastery are, therefore, immediacy and objectivity. Since Verga's stories are related from what appears in part to be the perspectives of the characters themselves, moreover, the narratives seem to bear the stamp of authenticity in their very narration, as though the world created by the fiction were indeed "real."

It is also worth noting that Verga's seeming objectivity creates another effect in his narratives, this, too, evident from **"Nedda"** on. It is clear in the course of the story that Nedda, who experiences first the loss of her lover and then that of her child, suffers from her situation but does not finally understand it. If there is to be understanding, it must come from the reader. This sort of implicit appeal to the reader (which, I must stress, is only implicit, owing to Verga's objectivist aesthetics) proves to be characteristic of all of Verga's most accomplished works, and it contributes both to the power of their starkly objective presentation and to the remarkably consistent sympathy that they elicit for the plight of their protagonists.

One of the more notable historical aspects of this plight is the way in which society and the institution of the family come together in Verga's view of nineteenth century Italian social history. In this regard, Verga's regular focus on Sicily is especially telling, since it was precisely in the early period of national unity, following the success of the Risorgimento and the politics of unification during the 1860s and '70s, that the nation's interest in the social life of the various little-known regions, and especially those of the south, rose considerably. This new attention, which made itself felt in politics and in journalism as well as in literature proper, was also evidenced by the 1876 report on the conditions and problems of the Sicilian region submitted to the Italian Parliament by Leopoldo Franchetti and Sidney Sonnino. Verga's view of the development of Sicilian social life paralleled a number of the findings of the Franchetti-Sonnino report, at times in remarkably close fashion. As set forth throughout Verga's major realist works, his view of that development was far from sanguine. For Verga, the family itself was the basic unit of society and of labor, as is concisely demonstrated at the outset of *I Malavoglia* by Padron 'Ntoni's "five-finger" metaphor encompassing both the familial hierarchy and the organization of the work force: "'Per menare il remo bisogna che le cinque dita s'aiutino l'un l'altro. . . . Gli uomini son fatti come le dita della mano: il dito grosso deve far da dito grosso, e il dito piccolo deve far da dito piccolo'"; "'To pull an oar, the five fingers must work together. . . . Men are made like the fingers of a hand: the thumb must act like a thumb, and the little finger must act like a little finger.'" In regard to this conception of the family as the unit of labor there are numerous examples in *I Malavoglia*. One of the most interesting, in thematics as well as style, occurs at the beginning of Chapter 10 when the force and sincerity of young 'Ntoni's activities in the fishing boat are compared to the powers of the sea itself:

> 'Ntoni andava a spasso sul mare tutti i santi giorni, e gli toccava camminare coi remi, logorandosi la schiena. Però quando il mare era cattivo, e voleva inghiottirseli in un boccone, loro, la *Provvidenza* e ogni cosa, quel ragazzo aveva il cuore più grande del mare.

> Il sangue dei Malavoglia! diceva il nonno; e bisognava vederlo alla manovra, coi capelli che gli fischiavano al vento, mentre la barca saltava sui marosi come un cefalo in amore.

> 'Ntoni took a stroll on the sea every blessed day, and he had to travel on his oars, breaking his back. But when the sea was rough and threatened to gulp all of them down in one big mouthful, them, the *Provvidenza* and all the rest, that boy had a heart greater than the sea.

> It's the Malavoglia blood! his grandfather said; and you had to see him maneuvering the boat, with his hair whistling in the wind, while the boat leapt over the billows like a mullet in love.

It is true that the stylistic elements of this passage should not be overlooked (i.e., the linking repetition of the opening phrase, which ties the beginning of this chapter to the end of the previous one in the typical concatenation of popular discourse; the actively anthropomorphic metaphorization of nature and of natural vitality; the subtle play of perspective in the initially choral effect of padron 'Ntoni's interjection). It is also true, in terms of narrative thematics, that this passage leads shortly thereafter in the chapter to a massive storm at sea, in symbolic reaffirmation of Verga's overall pessimism. Nonetheless, the joy of physical labor *within* the familial setting is if anything all too evident in these paragraphs. Even the background threat of the sea, which would devour the remaining working members of the familial clan in one bite, is countered both by human value (the heart of young 'Ntoni) and by the comparison to another, more positive aspect of nature (the

mullet in love). How different these valuations are, then, from those of such realist writers as Zola, for whom the mechanism of human passion meant also the downfall of all humanity (a phenomenon most obviously at work in the scenes of passionate outburst—libidinous, bibibulous, gustatory—regularly preceding the disastrous scenes of *L'Assommoir*), or, regarded from another angle, from those of Dickens, for whom the toil of the workhouse was just that: labor in the key of exhaustion, pain, exploitation.

In Verga's judgment, however, the developing economic and social system then on the rise in Italy, with its roots in capitalist aspiration and competition, brought with it not only the disruption of the social order of the family, as symbolized by the cherished *focolare*, or familial hearth, but also the loss of the traditional codes of honor and labor that the family had always sustained. In this historical context, it is worthy of note that Verga's two major novels are in many respects family sagas, evocative of the concern in nineteenth century fiction for genealogy and familial well-being. Indeed, they were to be just the first two installments in a (never completed) five-part cycle tracing the rise and disconcertingly concurrent fall of a group of families and family protagonists. It is also significant that the overall title for the cycle was "I vinti", or "The Defeated," since even though the positive aspects of Verga's view of human life are undeniably in evidence, they are thoroughly subsumed within the all-embracing pessimism of his view of contemporary Italian history.

When taken together, *I Malavoglia* and *Mastro-don Gesualdo*, buttressed by the less substantial but no less meaningful support of Verga's short stories, show that Verga's attitude was not merely a celebration of the joys of labor and the ideal unity of the family, a perspective that had been so apparent in Giuseppe Mazzini's influential treatise on "The Duties of Man." But neither do Verga's works constitute a materialist polemic against the ruin of family life by an economic system that effectively turns the dependent members of the unit into slaves, as is the case in Marx's *Capital*, 1.4.15. Verga's position is, once again, utterly heterodox, divergent from the philosophies of both nineteenth century idealism and materialism, since no solution to these social problems is seen as possible in his texts. History continues its march of "progress", and human suffering remains in force. But in terms of Verga's narratives, no worldly solution to these difficulties can be found, as is indicated by the novels' constant criticism of socialism as well as capitalism. Verga's realist aesthetic obliged him to represent what he regarded as historical reality, but, to put matters bluntly, it did not require him to like it. To approach this point from a different angle, although Verga believed in the reality of historical change—as his narratives repeatedly demonstrate—he refused to the end, in a fashion strikingly different from Lukács' view of the major realists, to believe in the future of social progress. As the desires of the competitive marketplace broke the family apart, they also destroyed any hope for the positive outcome of Italian social history.

Verga's realism, which in the theory of *verismo* should have been objective, random, unbiased, combined in his fictional practice with the closed, predetermined, given components of myth in such a way as to lend both realistic authenticity *and* symbolic depth to his narrative portrayal of social life. This is not, however, a question of simple oppositions like openness as opposed to closure, randomness as opposed to predictability, objective representation as opposed to subjectively determined truth. In Verga's narratives, these categories become thoroughly mixed rather than achieving oppositional stability, and this is the case because all such oppositions are finally subordinate, in Verga's fictional practice, to the one great overriding *and* predetermined system, history itself. That the motions of history take on the aura of fate in Verga's texts should not surprise us, given their author's ideological view of nineteenth century Italian social life. In *I Malavoglia* the destiny at work in Sicilian life when capitalist desire enters society is clear both on the level of the individual and the family, as Padron 'Ntoni, spurred by what in the novel's often discussed preface Verga terms "le prime irrequietudini pel benessere . . . la vaga bramosìa dell'ignoto"; "the first anxious desires for material well-being . . . the vague yearning for the unknown," makes the deal for the transport and sale of the lupins that will lead to the death of his son, the sinking of the family's fishing boat, and eventually the loss of the familial house by the medlar tree, the "casa del nespolo," with its pure natural redolence in what is now a sadly corrupt world. A similar historical process of loss and exclusion can be seen in the fate of Mastrodon Gesualdo, who pays for his extraordinary economic success both with his separation from the joys of affective life and with his suffering from the symbolic yet also undeniably real cancer eating away at him from inside. As in *I Malavoglia,* the signs of capitalist desire in *Mastrodon Gesualdo* carry the added burden of the social sins of capitalist exchange, all arrayed, for Verga, within the overarching system of history from which, once entered, there was no escape. In this regard, it should perhaps be recalled that the name of the Malavoglia's ill-starred familial fishing boat, which set Verga's realist cycle in motion, was nothing other than the "Provvidenza".

Within the realm of *verismo* Verga and Capuana had important contemporaries, among them the southerner Federico De Roberto and the northerner Emilio De Marchi; and Verga's realism influenced subsequent generations of writers in a variety of ways, including the young Pirandello and D'Annunzio and, half a century later, the Italian neorealists working in literature and in film. But it might be more useful at this point to trace Verga's reception in critical circles rather than his influence on literary developments as such. Verga's critical reception over the course of this century has had to do, as might be expected, with the problematics of literary representation, which is to say with questions of literary style as they come together with questions of historical content.

It would be convenient, if nothing else, had Francesco De Sanctis been of particular influence in the criticism of Verga or of *verismo,* since a "return" to De Sanctis, as advocated by Gramsci among others in critical matters, is often a useful way to begin historical considerations of Italian critical evaluation over the last century and a half.

But De Sanctis, while openly expressing interest in his public lectures in the anthropological realism of Darwin and in the literary realism of Zola, had little demonstrable interest in nineteenth century Italian realist literature. Nor does the next critical giant in Italian literary circles offer much assistance, since Benedetto Croce, though thoroughly conversant with Verga studies, was, predictably, far from being sympathetic either to *verismo*'s aesthetic or to Verga's representational goals. When evaluated within the critical perspective of Croce's idealist formalism, as explained in his major essay on Verga ["Giovanni Verga," *La letteratura della nuova Italia,* 1915], the program of *verismo* was not so much wrong as simply wrongheaded. Any recourse to such a general term as *"verismo",* and especially to a term linked not to the imaginative spirit of the author and/or his work but to the material objects of representation, merely masks the genuine expressive nature of the individual work of art. *Verismo* is thus a slogan, to be considered as "un'etichetta", or "a label", one finally to be rejected in favor of the quality of the actual aesthetic artifact, which will then succeed or fail in relation to criteria that are completely different from those posited by the realist aesthetics of *verismo*. In Croce's view, perhaps fortunately for further generations of Verga's critics and readers given the dominance of Crocean aesthetics in Italy up to and through the 1960s, Verga's works did in fact succeed in aesthetic value precisely because they did not slavishly follow their professed realist program (a program inherited, somewhat inappropriately in Croce's view, from French and English forebears). Verga's *verismo* was thus seen by Croce as a sort of poorly aimed but inevitable parting shot, a way to get things going in a new mode, or, as Croce says of Verga's practice of *verismo,* insightfully albeit dismissively: "fu soltanto una spinta liberatrice"; "it was only a liberating push."

Croce had many followers, of course, but his was not the only line taken by Italian literary critics and philosophers in the period between the two wars. One polemically non-Crocean thinker, Antonio Gramsci, was, somewhat surprisingly, even less sympathetic to Verga's aims and procedures than Croce had been. Despite his usual perspicacity, Gramsci was unwilling or unable either to grasp the meaning or to feel the force of Verga's literary/historical critique. Of those critics who were heavily influenced by Croce and Crocean aesthetics during these years, one of the most interesting evaluations of Verga was that of Attilio Momigliano, who faulted Verga on several of the same points as Croce (while placing particular emphasis on Verga's overall failure in novelistic organization) but who also saw Verga, in a collection of essays published later, as deserving of comparison with such other obviously imperfect authors as Dante and Manzoni. Not bad company, all things considered.

During the revaluation of Verga and *verismo* after World War II, a large number of important biographies, literary histories, and anthologies of Verga criticism appeared. The one genuinely new aspect of this criticism in Italy, however, was the examination of Verga's formal innovations in the use of the *style indirect libre*. This scrutiny of

Verga's language had begun in Italy with Luigi Russo's 1941 additions to his earlier landmark study, *Giovanni Verga* (1919-20). While I have treated this topic in some detail elsewhere (as a debate that eventually involved quite a diverse group of critics, among them Vittorio Lugli, Giacomo Devoto, Nicola Vita, Leo Spitzer, Ivo Franges, Hans Sørensen, Giulio Herczeg, Francesco Nicolosi, Giovanni Cecchetti, Antonio Lanci, and Olga Ragusa), it might be useful in this context at least to point out that there is a sort of final consensus in Verga studies that the technical achievement of Verga's prose is its distinctive mixture of (in Russo's term) "choral" discourse, indirect discourse, and the *style indirect libre*.

Along with fostering interest in Verga's style, Russo's work has also served as a touchstone for subsequent treatments of the historical context of Sicilian *verismo*. Discussions of history *and* ideology in Verga's work have been most common in the recent decades. It is true that there were attempts to focus on these issues as early as the 1940s (and studies by Natalino Sapegno and Gaetano Trombatore come immediately to mind). But in the eyes of the generation of politically committed, post-1968 materialist critics, such prior studies, including Russo's—even though often written by critics politically on the left—erred in repeating many of the idealist assumptions of their more conservative and/or adamantly apolitical colleagues. Indeed, this same idealizing tendency can be seen in the specifically *artistic* "revaluation" of Verga's works in the early postwar years, in the form of Luchino Visconti's openly socialist recasting of *I Malavoglia* as "La terra trema" (1948), a film in which the characters—contrary to those of the novel—seem both to understand the nature of socioeconomic oppression and to aspire to do something about it.

Early post-1968 criticism of Verga had a notable rallying point to which any subsequent examination is obliged to return, the 1972 collection of essays edited by Alberto Asor Rosa bearing the title *Il caso Verga* (or, roughly, "the debate over Verga"). The majority of these essays and responses—by Asor Rosa, Giuseppe Petronio, Vitilio Masiello, Romano Luperini, and Bruno Biral—had appeared previously, beginning in point of fact in 1968, in the pages of Petronio's periodical, *Problemi*. It would be misleading to claim that the contributors are all in agreement (for good or ill, such accord would belie the actual nature of Italian literary criticism); but their pieces do share a common concern for narrative content and for the ideological underpinnings of Verga's fiction, and they all reveal the influence of the thought of Gramsci, Lukács, Marcuse, and more recent theorists on the left, though here and there in the form of opposition rather than endorsement.

The intent of much of the criticism in this volume, as well as of other contemporary writing by similarly committed critics, is twofold: to come to terms with Verga's notion of social history as expressed in his works and to examine both that notion and its implications from a critical perspective. Verga thus remains an undoubtedly powerful and accomplished artist, but one to be viewed within the context of the historical limits of his class, his region, and his

century. It is this second step that, for these critics, seemed missing from the idealizing leftist criticism of prior decades, which, due to this failing, tended not just to regard Verga as a great author but also to miss the socio-historical import of his extraordinarily bleak view of the progression of Italian social history, a view that I have attempted to sketch out above. In other words, this more recent criticism is against any supposedly "historical" recuperation of nineteenth century Italian realism if such recuperation means little or nothing more than ahistorical praise masked as criticism.

Due to the detailed treatment of such problems as individual versus social destiny, sentimental versus critical realism, and the social status of the individual artist in the late nineteenth century, the essays and responses in *Il caso Verga* made up an important volume for realist studies in Italy. It is true, of course, that the collection displays obvious failings. As is the case for much socially oriented criticism in Italy (and as Petronio himself laments), the sense of the literary text is often lost in the course of highly speculative and on occasion emotionally tinged social or historical "analysis." *Il caso Verga* also suffers from the limitations that characterized so many of the discussions about Italian culture in the turbulent years of the late 1960s and on into the '70s, which is to say, not only is the work in the volume *engagé,* it is also strikingly one-sided.

These failings, however, are not inevitable ones, and there were a number of critics working on realist topics in the 1970s who were more successful in integrating prior stylistic and biographical material into sociohistorical analysis. I would like to concentrate on two of these critics, Vittorio Spinazzola and Romano Luperini, because, taken together, they demonstrate two notably fruitful lines of inquiry into nineteenth century realism overall and especially into Verga's œuvre. These lines have to do, first, with the power of symbolism in realist literature and, second, with the question of historical fidelity. To take the question of the thrust and the intent of symbolic effects in Verga's realist narratives, it might be best to begin by considering the critical groundwork laid in Spinazzola's *Verismo e positivismo* of 1977, and more specifically in the chapter "Legge del lavoro e legge dell'onore nei *Malavoglia*," originally published in a shorter form in 1973. In this and several companion pieces on Verga's works, Spinazzola discusses the interrelations of Verga's conceptions of individual sexuality, family organization, social law and repression, rising capitalism, historical pessimism, and literary style. By tracing *verismo*'s roots in nineteenth century positivism, Spinazzola demonstrates the seemingly "scientific" rationalist bias of *verismo*'s aesthetic. But at the same time he shows how this bias—so apparent in the movement's theoretical tracts—is in fact undercut by *verismo*'s literary practice. *Verismo* has two faces then, not just one. Vitalism combines with positivism to produce the heterodox mixture of *verismo*'s discourse. As Spinazzola's treatment suggests, at the heart of Verga's realism, we find the power of symbol. But Spinazzola's analysis does not stop with that conclusion since, perhaps surprisingly, at the heart of the symbol we find history itself. Such archetypal figures of Verga's narrative as the *mater dolorosa,* the prodigal son, the dutiful daughter, Neptune and the sea itself—which earlier critics, and in particular the brilliant, Jungian-oriented Giacomo Debenedetti, had considered as elements of stability and mythic presence in *verismo's* discourse—are treated by Spinazzola, too, but in a different vein. Indeed, Spinazzola sees such textual archetypes not so much as universal literary and psychological phenomena but, more to the point, as indicators of the ways in which the roles of men and women and the powers of destiny are viewed in Verga's works and in the broader Sicilian society that these works claim to represent.

To focus on a concrete example of Spinazzola's critical strategy, we might consider his treatment of a passage from the conclusion of *I Malavoglia's* second chapter. In this passage Mena, one of the family's marriageable young women, has just said goodnight to her friend Alfio, the impoverished carter; and, as she awaits her grandfather on the balcony of the familial home, she is lost in thoughts of the local environs, the sea, the road, and the wide world, "il quale è tanto grande che se uno potesse camminare e camminare sempre, giorno e notte, non arriverebbe mai"; "which is so large that even if you could walk and walk forever, day and night, you'd never get to the end of it." Because of the play of perspective and the stylistic mastery in this section of the chapter, this passage has been singled out for discussion in a host of stylistic and psychological studies of Verga's work, and the influence of these earlier treatments is clearly evident in Spinazzola's analysis. But the central discovery of Spinazzola's discussion lies elsewhere. For Spinazzola, the crucial element of the passage is a curious lacuna, in Mena's reluctance to invoke the name of Alfio despite the sound of the cart or carts passing nearby. Spinazzola's discussion of Mena's sublimation of her own desires and her resort to a fantasy played out only indirectly ("fantasticheria giocata sul sottinteso"), in her imagining of a constant worldly journey without ever attaining any desired end, is more than just an inquiry into psychological subtlety or linguistic refinement. As Spinazzola perceives, the entire passage contributes to the portrayal of Mena as an imaginative yet essentially passive and obedient family member. In fact, through no fault of her own, Mena's unhappiness is eventually sacrificed to the requirements of the laws of the *patriarcato,* and, like her symbolic namesake, the virginal martyr "sant'Agata"—the name by which the villagers call her— she never does find social fulfillment either in marriage or in motherhood.

As Spinazzola shows here and elsewhere in regard to narrative symbolism and narrative representation, the historical tensions in late nineteenth century Sicily between the opportunities of incipient capitalism and the old rules of honor and work produced both the subject of Verga's text and the energy giving rise to its "realistic" discourse. It is also true, of course, that the symbolic *and* real conflicts between the sublimations required by the old social codes and the desires fostered by the new ones cannot be satisfactorily resolved within the world of Verga's narratives. But even though Verga's vast historical pessimism formed an implicit denunciation of the course of social life in nineteenth century Italy, it did not—in contrast to the literary effects of many of his realist confreres in France and England—preclude narrative sympathy for his characters at the level of the individual.

Significantly, what is masked by this sympathy for individual characters and families as distinct from larger social groups acting more or less in concert (as in the reckless and ultimately tragic rebellion in the story **"Libertà"** from *Novelle rusticane*) is precisely the motivated interest of class. Verga sees that the Sicilian peasantry's inheritance from the decaying southern aristocracy consists both in economic oppression (fostered now by the rising bourgeoisie) and in attempted continuing adherence to the old feudal codes of honor and work. But again, Verga's only solution to this predicament is made up by the nurturing stability of the family and by the joys of labor, as organized human activity beneficial in and of itself with regard to subsistence, certainly, yet *without* regard to notions of profit or advancement. On the individual and familial plane, therefore, Verga can value the irrational force of passion—a valuation exactly opposite, for example, that of Zola—*as long as* that force itself is ultimately turned back within the social system to the family's good.

It is not difficult to see that this idealizing ahistorical view of the family and of labor, when circumscribed by Verga's overriding pessimism, derives in part from Verga's own social position as a southern, land-based aristocrat writing after the Risorgimento and the unification, a member of a class in some ways as marginalized as the peasantry, cut off from the sociopolitical and economic future of a country now run with ever increasing authority by the gradually industrializing northern bourgeoisie. In certain respects, the great pathos of Verga's realist narratives stems from his remarkable ability, enhanced by his use of symbolism, to remain at the two furthest poles of human life, the individual and the universal, thus turning his regionalism into a universe of its own, in which what should historically be questions of class seem to become questions of caste. This is one of the ways in which history attains the overall semblance of destiny. As Spinazzola's analysis demonstrates, this intricate representational ploy evidences the ideological underpinnings of Verga's texts even as it adds symbolic power to his "historical" critique, which remains tenaciously constant throughout the period of his realist production all the way up until his famous final silence, in which, in his last years, he reacted to Italian history in the one way he could: he turned his back on it and effectively stopped writing in the process. For Verga, the future of the *patriarcato,* and of all Italian society with it, was going along only one path, to wrack and ruin. And throughout his realist works, he was not hesitant, in terms of narrative symbolism as well as narrative realism, to say so.

The second question to be addressed, that of the historical accuracy of Verga's narratives, has arisen in many guises over the decades since his works appeared, but it has been treated most recently and most suggestively by Romano

Luperini. This is, to be sure, the criterion by which *verismo*, in common with other nineteenth century realist programs, intended to be judged. As Verga announced in the concluding sentence of the preface to *I Malavoglia*, his purpose was to offer the representation of historical reality "as it was" ("la rappresentazione della realtà com'è stata"), which meant in this context to depict local Sicilian life with the greatest fidelity possible. True, Verga was fully aware that such representation was *only* a goal, that historical accuracy was, in fictional terms, an impossibility, as is indicated by his inclusion at the end of his introduction's final sentence of his artistic caveat: "o come [la realtà] avrebbe dovuto essere"; "or as [reality] should have been". But in spite of Verga's profound understanding of the cleverly illusionist nature of realist aesthetics, he did take the representational aims of *verismo*'s program with unquestionable seriousness, and evidence of the commitment to historical fidelity—in spirit even more than in fact—shows up again and again in his major works.

As Luperini has pointedly demonstrated in his monograph on **"Rosso Malpelo"** (one of the best known stories in *Vita dei campi*), the study of the historical accuracy of Verga's *verismo* has a privileged locus in the Franchetti-Sonnino parliamentary report of 1876. This report, which contains hundreds of pages of information on the socioeconomic conditions of nineteenth century Sicilian life, including that of the peasantry, was based on the observations of Franchetti and Sonnino during an extended period of local investigation. Verga almost certainly knew the text of the report well, since his works reflect many of the report's findings and since, as Luperini has shown, the preface to *I Malavoglia* repeats some of the sentiments as well as some of the language of the report's introduction, dated December 20, 1876. Along with providing general information on the characteristics of the region (which, of course, Verga also knew from first-hand experience), the report contains a wealth of detail regarding not only local social tensions and social comportment but also criminality and banditry (the topic of one of Verga's major stories, **"L'amante di Gramigna"**); and it offers special insights into the working conditions in the Sicilian mines, which form the background for **"Rosso Malpelo"**, the short story that, following Russo's study, has usually been considered to be Verga's most important.

Along with such matters as the payment and the treatment of workers, the report is interesting in relation to **"Rosso Malpelo"** for what it says about the use and the abuse of child labor in the mines. These comments are found in the report's concluding section, entitled "Il lavoro dei fanciulli nelle zolfare siciliane". This part of the report describes the children's miserable and extremely hazardous working conditions as well as the damage occasionally done thereby to familial relations, a topic of primary import in **"Rosso Malpelo"** (in which the central family's destruction is graphically portrayed). The authors of the report, to a certain extent similar to Verga, lay the blame for the miners' situation on a single group, the *padronizz*. It is true that Franchetti and Son-

nino, as politicians with parliamentary responsibility, were reform-minded (and goal-oriented) in a way that Verga was not. Indeed, they mention contemporary legislation in Germany—thus indicating the extraordinary importance that the issue of child labor had throughout the industrializing West—and they propose a possible route toward rectification of conditions in Italy by way of national legislation. Significantly enough, along with the many political problems that such reforms encountered, they also faced, in the case of the mines, entrenched opposition on practical (i.e., economic) grounds: because the underground galleries had been designed and constructed specifically with child labor in mind, they were too low for fully grown adults to move about in. It is possible that if the proposed reforms went through, the physical structures would have had to be completely redone, at nothing less, it was feared by the owners, than huge expense.

The Franchetti-Sonnino report is thus useful in coming to terms both with material particulars of the world of Verga's narratives and with the broader economic, social, and political climate of the times; and Luperini is right to insist on its relevance for Verga studies. On almost every page, it reminds us how pressing these issues were for national life in the previous century. Verga's narratives, rather than merely serving as examples of narrative eccentricity or "local color", were thus part and parcel of their times. This is not to say that there is or should be a naively drawn, positivistic, one-to-one correspondence between the world within the realist text and the historical world of its creation. As a matter of fact, what is often most to the point in this sort of inquiry is to see not only what is included in the literary text but also what is either notably slanted or even left out altogether. In Verga's realist texts (as opposed to his earlier novels), what is left out is often, oddly enough at first glance, the bourgeois world of elegant style, industrial development, and economic advancement against which his critique is so consistently directed. However, since Verga's polemic is aimed not so much at the rising bourgeoisie itself as at the underlying socioeconomic values this rise at once implies and fulfills, the fact that his texts "speak" by silence makes them all the more forceful. In other terms, by not giving substantive voice to the objects of his critique (with the major exception of the later chapters of *Mastro-don Gesualdo*) Verga avoids the possibility that his victims might be able, at least to some extent, to speak back. In the end, one of the more instructive lessons to be gained from the sort of historical investigation proposed and carried out by Luperini and his colleagues in Italy is that imaginative considerations of historical studies, fully as much as considerations of narrative symbolism, lead, if followed assiduously, to considerations of ideology as well as of thematics and form, which is to say, to the generating mechanisms that reside at the deepest, prenarrative levels of the realist text.

This brand of historical endeavor is no doubt always germane in one sense or another to literary studies, but it is of greatest moment in the critical analysis of realist narrative, the one mode of literary representation which attempts most openly and most consistently to re-create the historical objects of its discourse. Recuperation of such extra-literary phenomena permits a fuller reading of these texts than would otherwise be available, a reading that includes the objective truths of social conflict, social oppression, and social aspiration as well as the subjective truths of individual psychology and literary craft. In short, we as critics should be doing more, rather than less, of this type of work.

The other major trend in current realist studies in Italy, as I mentioned at the outset, has to do with editorial and bibliographical work. However, because this material is widely available, and because it is of interest primarily within specialized Verga studies, it might be best, by way of conclusion, to move on to a consideration of what the recent trends in Italian realist criticism have to tell us about realist studies in a comparative context, one that includes current critical studies in the United States. It does not require a great deal of imagination to see that the sorts of historically oriented inquiries that Luperini's work represents are remarkably similar to those of the new historicist criticism in America and the current revival of marxist criticism as regards nineteenth-century studies in England. In the United States, such relatively recent journals as *New Literary History, October, Social Text,* and *Representations* attest to these historical interests in a fashion, *sensu lato,* analogous to that of Luperini's newly founded *L'ombra d'Argo.* Moreover, the exceptionally enthusiastic reception of Fredric Jameson's *The Political Unconscious* further attests to the rise of these social/historical concerns in literary studies in the United States. True, the often idealizing and on occasion politically conservative slants of some of this criticism in America is, generally speaking, antithetical to both the philosophical and the ideological thrusts of the recent historically attentive criticism in Italy, but despite such various exceptions the parallels remain genuine and functional.

Why, it should be asked, are these sorts of studies currently of such importance in these countries? One part of the answer is linked without doubt to the critical traditions preceding these approaches, in terms of the natural reaction of critical trends not only to engulf but also to work against prior elements in the cycle of critical developments, which is to say, in Italy, against Crocean idealism, and, in America, against both New Critical and structuralist formalism and against the idealist program of (imported) Derridean deconstruction. But there is another aspect of this question that is, it seems to me, still more significant. This has to do with the nature of artistic representation and with the necessity of considering both style and content, not as mutually exclusive entities but as they blend, in order to come to terms with what representation is all about. Neither the bracketing of questions of style to concentrate solely on historical content in positivistic fashion, nor the shunting aside of elements of historical content and context to focus solely on aspects of textuality in "weak" or strong deconstructive fashion, permits the kind of rich reading of historical intertextuality suggested above. That neither one nor the other of these approaches is adequate as an end in and of itself is why, I think, Jameson insists in his formulaic shorthand on the study not just of ideology or just of form but of the ideology *of* form.

In what I have said so far I hope it is clear that to my mind the current opposition in Anglo-American critical circles between something concrete known as "history" and something abstract known as "theory" is a bogus one. Theory always tends toward the concrete as it is placed in critical praxis. History, on the other hand, is not available to us outside of textuality, although it is a text to be read *differently* from other texts, the master-narrative to be read in the key of necessity rather than contingency. The sort of theoretical apparatus required to keep such a literary, historical project going, it should be apparent, would be the most sophisticated and broadly based possible, one that would depend on theoretical-historical integration rather than opposition or exclusion. In the present setting, a project like this would have two goals: first, to see nineteenth century realist texts in their own contexts, in regard to the aesthetics of representation and social history; and, second, to attempt to see why and in what form the basic issues at stake in the works of writers like Verga as well as Dickens and Zola—i.e., the organization of the family, the social effects of rising capitalism, and the alienation of the individual subject—remain in force *as* problems in the literature of the West today.

Finally, to return for just a moment to a consideration of Verga as a regionalist writer (but one seen from the comparative perspective just outlined), it might be of some use to regard his depiction of Sicily from the point of view of dependency theory. In certain respects, his mixture of realistic and mythic effects within a representational framework, along with the trenchant social critique carried out from the perspective of a socially marginalized and economically dependent region, brings to mind the literary aspirations, reactions, and effects of such other authors creating literary worlds in economically and politically dependent climates as Faulkner, Vargas Llosa, and García Márquez. In all these texts, be they *I Malavoglia* and *Mastro-don Gesualdo,* or *Absalom, Absalom!* and the Snopes trilogy, or *La casa verde* and *La guerra del fin del mundo,* or *Cien años de soledad,* the historical fact of dependency—economic, social, and in often oblique ways cultural—becomes the valued myth, in the perspective of the texts' subjects, of either socioeconomic self-sufficiency, independence, or indeed at times superiority. This *myth* of *history* is represented in the fiction of these authors, but not apart from its concomitant critique. The myth and the critique are both powerful, but neither is fully comprehensible without the other, nor are they understandable even together without a consideration of their differing historical components. The many-layered effects of realism and myth combine, then, to describe and condemn a situation that is not only historically "verifiable" but also, in the end, tellingly unacceptable, at least in fictional terms. But we should not make light of this sort of fictional description and statement. From a literary *and* historical perspective,

Verga's works and the fictional worlds they re-create may turn out to be much closer to our own—but on their deepest levels, not on superficial ones—than we would have suspected. When all is said and done, that is why we are, or should be, still reading and thinking about them.

FURTHER READING

Biography

Alexander, Alfred. *Giovanni Verga.* London: Grant & Cutler, 1972, 252 p.
> Biography compiled with the assistance of Verga's nephew; includes letters and photographs.

Cattaneo, Giulio. *Verga.* Torino: UTET, 1963.
> An Italian monograph regarded by many scholars as the definitive Verga biography.

Criticism

Biasin, Gian-Paolo. "The Sicily of Verga and Sciascia." *Italian Quarterly* 9, Nos. 34-5 (Summer-Fall 1965): 3-22.
> Discusses the region of Sicily as portrayed in Verga's stories. Biasin calls Verga "the first and best writer who brought his native land to the fore."

Cecchetti, Giovanni. *Giovanni Verga.* Boston: Twayne Publishers, 1978, 172 p.
> Critical study of the author's work by a noted scholar in Verga studies. Cecchetti includes a selected bibliography.

De Vito, Anthony J. "Politics and History in the Work of Giovanni Verga." *Forum Italicum* III, No. 3 (September 1969): 386-403.
> Identifies correspondences between political references in Verga's work and contemporary political events in Italy.

Erickson, John D. "A Milanese Tale by Giovanni Verga." *Symposium* XX, No. 1 (Spring 1966): 7-12.
> A stylistic and thematic study of "L'ultima giornata" ("The Last Day"). The critic argues that, in this story, "Verga brings to near perfection the objective writing method."

Joyce, Wendy, and Schächter, Elizabeth Mahler. "Giovanni Verga and Emile Zola: A Question of Influence." *Journal of European Studies* VII, No. 28 (December 1977): 266-77.
> Studies "examples of direct mutual influence" between Verga and Zola. The authors argue that Zola benefited more from the authors' relationship than did Verga.

Lucente, Gregory L. "The Ideology of Form in Verga's 'La Lupa': Realism, Myth, and the Passion of Control." *Modern Language Notes* 95, No. 1 (January 1980): 104-38.
> A close reading of the original Italian text of "La Lupa," concentrating on the story as a transitional work in Verga's developing *verismo* style.

————. "Critical Treatments of Verga and *Verismo*: Movements and Trends (1950-1980)." *Modern Language Notes* 91, No. 1 (January 1983): 129-36.
> Addresses developments in the criticism of Verga's technical achievements in *verismo, style indirect libre*, "choral" discourse, and indirect discourse.

————. "'What's in a Name?': Symbolic Meaning and the Play of Narrative Perspective in Verga's 'Rosso Malpelo.'" In *Beautiful Fables: Self-consciousness in Italian Narrative from Manzoni to Calvino*, pp. 68-97. Baltimore: Johns Hopkins University Press, 1986.
> Detailed explication of "Rosso Malpelo."

Ruderman, Judith G. "Lawrence's *The Fox* and Verga's 'The She-Wolf': Variations on the Theme of the 'Devouring Mother.'" *Modern Language Notes* 94, No. 1 (January 1979): 153-65.
> Explores Verga's influence on D. H. Lawrence. The critic argues that Lawrence's reading of Verga's "The She-Wolf" had a profound effect on his redrafts of the story *The Fox*, especially in the number and intensity of violent episodes.

Russo, Luigi. *Giovanni Verga.* Bari: Laterza, 1947.
> A valued Italian-language study of Verga's work.

Schorer, Mark. "The Fiction of Giovanni Verga." In *The Arts at Mid-Century*, edited by Robert Richman, pp. 137-45. New York: Horizon Press, 1954.
> Brief overview concentrating on Verga's literary reputation, his stylistic development, and his innovative techniques.

Selig, Karl-Ludwig. "Reading Verga's *Rosso Malpelo*." *Teaching Language through Literature* XXVI, No. 2 (April 1987): 33-9.
> Stylistic and thematic analysis of "Rosso Malpelo."

Weisstein, Ulrich. "Giovanni Verga's 'Cavalleria rusticana': A Translator's Nightmare?" In *Comparative Literature East and West: Traditions and Trends*, pp. 91-106. Honolulu: College of Languages, Linguistics and Literature, University of Hawaii and the East-West Center, 1989.
> Compares several English translations of "Cavalleria rusticana" in order to highlight variations among translations of the original text.

White, D. Maxwell. Introduction to *Pane nero, and Other Stories*, by Giovanni Verga, pp. 1-10. Manchester, England: Manchester University Press, 1962.
> Overview of Verga's life and selected works.

Woolf, D. "Three Stories from *Novelle rusticane*." In *The Art of Verga: A Study in Objectivity*, pp. 30-52. Sydney: Sydney University Press, 1977.
> Structural and thematic study of a selection of stories from *Novelle rusticane*.

Additional coverage of Verga's life and career is contained in the following sources published by Gale Research: *Contemporary Authors*, Vols. 104, 123; and *Twentieth-Century Literary Criticism*, Vol. 3.

Angus Wilson
1913-1991

English short story writer, novelist, critic, playwright and essayist.

INTRODUCTION

Wilson was recognized as a prominent figure in both fiction and literary criticism in post World War II England. He began his career as a short story writer, and these tales—laced with violence and satire—are considered by numerous critics to be precursors of the social protest works by the Angry Young Men of the 1950s and 1960s. Many of Wilson's stories are semiautobiographical, analyzing dysfunctional family relationships and depicting postwar society in flux. Wilson criticized traditional middle-class aspirations and values while focusing on the shortcomings of his characters and the collapse of social structure. Critics contend that his works serve as a detailed social history of the times, due to his painstaking recreation of time and place as well as his considerable talent for mimicry. Wilson gained immediate acclaim for his collections of short fiction, but eventually abandoned this form once he began writing novels in the 1950s.

Biographical Information

Wilson was born in England to parents from wealthy families. Largely due to his father's gambling, however, the family was forced into genteel poverty, and Wilson spent much of his boyhood living in hotels. The family's somewhat nomadic existence, combined with the fact that Wilson was much younger than his siblings, led him to feel insecure and isolated; these feelings were compounded with his mother's death when he was fifteen; subsequently, themes of childhood, family dynamics, and loss often presented themselves in his short fiction and novels. Wilson took up writing in his thirties as a form of therapy after a nervous breakdown. Despite the success of his first volume of stories, Wilson's writing was confined to weekends and limited to short fiction because of the demands of his full-time job at the British Museum Library. After several collections of short stories and a novel were published, Wilson decided to leave his job and devote himself to literary matters. After writing several novels, he experimented with nontraditional form and also produced highly regarded works of criticism. Wilson was knighted in 1980 for his literary achievements and contributions to arts and services organizations.

Major Works of Short Fiction

In 1949 Wilson published his first volume of short fiction, titled *The Wrong Set and Other Stories.* This collection yielded one of his most controversial stories, "Raspberry Jam," in which a young boy is confronted with cruel and untrustworthy adults in the form of two women who torture a bird in his presence. *Such Darling Dodos and Other Stories* appeared the following year; the title story, which uses terminal illness to symbolize the death of 1930s liberal ideals, was lauded for keenly portrayed psychological and historical details. Wilson's third collection, *A Bit Off the Map and Other Stories,* was distinguished by its softened stance toward the characters, mixing the pathos and comedy that often marks his writings with more subtle satire. It was at this time that *Hemlock and After,* Wilson's first novel, appeared. Subsequently, only different collections of his early stories were published, with the occasional piece of short fiction appearing in literary magazines. His *The Wild Garden or Speaking of Writing,* based upon university lectures, delves into the major influences on his writing and is considered a candid look at his creative process.

Critical Reception

When Wilson's first stories were published, reviewers were impressed with the technical skill displayed by the fledgling author. They praised his work for its attention to detail, expert mimicry, and accurate representation of the English social scene. One element that evoked negative comments was the violence exhibited in his fiction. A critic of Wilson's first collection expressed surprise at the horror and cruelty depicted in the stories, but acknowledged that it aptly reflected the "sickness" of the postwar period. In general, however, most commentators judged Wilson's stories as innovative and bold, taking some pleasure in the sometimes humorous unpleasantness of the tales. Wilson's reputation grew with the publication of several popular novels, but his experimentation with nontraditional form in subsequent works drew mixed reactions. Indeed, some of his later novels were deemed inaccessible, but renewed interest in—and appreciation of—his work was sparked shortly before his death in 1991.

PRINCIPAL WORKS

Short Fiction

The Wrong Set and Other Stories 1949
Such Darling Dodos and Other Stories 1950
A Bit Off the Map and Other Stories 1957
Death Dance: Twenty-Five Stories 1969
The Collected Stories of Angus Wilson 1987

Other Major Works

Emile Zola: An Introductory Study of His Novel (criticism) 1952
Hemlock and After (novel) 1952
For Whom the Cloche Tolls: A Scrapbook of the Twenties (fictional journal) 1953
The Mulberry Bush (play) 1955
Anglo-Saxon Attitudes (novel) 1956
The Middle Age of Mrs. Eliot (novel) 1958
The Old Men at the Zoo (novel) 1961
The Wild Garden or Speaking of Writing (essay) 1963
Late Call (novel) 1964
No Laughing Matter (novel) 1967

The World of Charles Dickens (criticism) 1970
As if by Magic (novel) 1973
The Strange Ride of Rudyard Kipling (criticism) 1977
Setting the World on Fire (novel) 1980

CRITICISM

Rosemary Carr Benét (essay date 1950)

SOURCE: "On the Way Up or Down," in *The Saturday Review of Literature*, Vol. XXXIII, No. 11, March 18, 1950, p. 15.

[*In the following review, Benét praises* The Wrong Set, *noting that Wilson's writing "is marked by sharp detail and a keen eye and ear."*]

These are very good short stories. I was surprised at how good they are, for I did not know the author's name. I was even more surprised to read that he has worked since 1937 on the staff of the British Museum Library, for that staid atmosphere is not reflected here. It is only fair to warn that the stories [in *The Wrong Set*] are not always pleasant ones. If you are squeamish you may object to some of the emotions for there is a queer, morbid vein running through them, but I doubt if you will forget them. Angus Wilson has been compared to Saki—"the sudden round-the-corner surprise of Saki"—and at least one story here reminded me of Katherine Mansfield's method. His writing is his own but like Saki's and Mansfield's it is marked by sharp detail and a keen eye and ear. The emotional content is high. I thought I was a case-hardened reader, but I felt a pricking and my hair standing on end over one called **"Raspberry Jam,"** about a little boy who has tea with two crazy ladies—insane-crazy.

The stories often have a savage intensity and Mr. Wilson can write with equal knowledge and accuracy about a professor of English poetry at Oxford or a pianist in a London night club. The background is very English; that is, what is called the frame of reference, is English. We get things like "her mind was intent upon the cultivation of a Knightsbridge exterior with a Kensington purse," which needs to be interpreted for us, but, on the other hand, the human values translate well. A case in point is **"Union Reunion,"** the story that reminded me of Katherine Mansfield. It has a South African setting—Mr. Wilson has lived in South Africa—but it centers about an English family group. In this terrible picture of a family reunion the details are undoubtedly accurately African, the "crimson bougainvillea and the boundless panorama of the Umgeni valley," but the emotions are universal. We have the American equivalent of that family, just as we have the counterpart of the London night club. In general these stories are about people on their rapid way up or down the

K. W. Gransden on the characteristics of Wilson's satire:

The success of Wilson's early stories lies in their sharp, vivid satirical analyses of people's vulnerability, failure and self-deception. His technique is to show a character as he wishes to appear to others, and as he has succeeded in appearing to himself, and to interpose ironic deflationary comments which reveal the resentments and true motives hidden behind the veneer. . . .

A character frequently satirized in this way is the ex-officer, the gentleman down on his luck, the professional cadger with his sentimental reminiscences of better days. He recurs with minor variations throughout Wilson's work and may be compared with the portrait of the author's father in *The Wild Garden*. . . .

Many of the early stories revolve round . . . snubs or humiliations. In **'Realpolitik'** the pushing newly-appointed administrator-head of an art-gallery snubs his staff; only his admiring secretary remains loyal, but even she punctuates his self-esteem and his final thought is 'perhaps a graduate secretary would really be more suitable now'. Other stories which end with a snub are **'Learning's Little Tribute'**, **'Et Dona Ferentes'** and **'Christmas Day in the Workhouse'**.

Many of the stories begin on a quiet realistic note and are then pushed deliberately over the edge of realism into a climax of farce, hysteria or violence: the author contrives a situation in which the characters lose control. . . . The most violent climax is the famous ending of **'Raspberry Jam'** in which two crazy drunken old women tear a live bird to pieces in front of a child.

K. W. Grandsden, in his Angus Wilson, *Longmans, Green & Co., 1969.*

Edmund Wilson on the repellent quality of Wilson's satire:

[The pieces in ***The Wrong Set and Other Stories***] are fundamentally satirical. There is evidently in Mr. Wilson a strain of the harsh Scottish moralist who does not want to let anybody off and does not care if his sarcasm wounds. This is nowadays an unusual element to find in a British writer. The smart school of fiction in England, though it cultivates bitter implications and sometimes invokes religion, has come to perfect a cuisine of light, appetizing dishes, good for one dinner and easily digestible, which— much though it would have surprised George Moore or Henry James if anyone had prophesied it to them—almost rivals that of the French in the early nineteen-hundreds. It is true that these stories, too, from the point of view of neatness and brevity and of the avoidance of emotionalism, are products of the same cuisine, but they are carried to lengths of caricature that prevent them from being so pleasantly assimilable as the usual British product. The book becomes a sort of thriller, for one goes on from one horror to another, beginning to hold on to one's seat as one wonders what uncomfortable, ignoble thing Mr. Wilson will think up next. Yet one shares in the malevolent gusto with which he invents detail, for he is a master of mimicry and parody and is as funny as anyone can be who never becomes exhilarated. It is rather like a combination of Sinclair Lewis with the more biting side of Chekhov, and Mr. Wilson's dreadful people may affect us in the long run a little like the caricatures of Lewis (the up-and-coming museum curator of the story called **"Realpolitik"** is an incipiently American type who might easily have been imagined by Lewis). We end by being repelled and feeling that it is not quite decent to enjoy so much ugliness. There ought to be some noble value somewhere.

Emund Wilson, "Bankrupt Britons and Voyaging Romantics," in The New Yorker, *Vol. XXVI, No. 8, April 15, 1950.*

ladder of fame, beauty, social success, academic prestige, sexual normality, and, in one case at least, of sanity. Almost always we are concerned with the loss of the quality.

This is brilliant, bitter work. It is sophisticated and can sometimes be horrifying. It is also fresh and skilful and full of excellent dialogue. Four of the thirteen stories have come out in magazines, according to the credit line here; three in *Horizon* and one in *The Listener*. I should think other magazines searching for new discoveries in this vein might look this way. Though he has been well received in England, this is the author's first appearance here [in the United States]. It will be interesting to see what Mr. Wilson does next, which way his violent talent veers.

The Times Literary Supplement **(essay date 1957)**

SOURCE: "Human Frailty," in *The Times Literary Supplement*, No. 2903, October 18, 1957, p. 62.

[*In this mixed review of* A Bit Off the Map, *the critic approves of Wilson's "accurate" and "kindly" fictional observations but speculates that the stories might become dated due to their emphasis on contemporary society.*]

His new collection of short stories proves that Mr. Angus Wilson's ear and eye are no less acute than they were eight years ago, when his first volume appeared;

the implied condemnation of vulgarity, hypocrisy, complacency and second-rate behaviour on both the moral and social levels is as stern as before; but there are indications that his sympathy with human frailty—which perceptive readers may have recognized as controlling, from a distance, even his earlier work—has taken a more prominent place in his writing, and adds considerably to its effect. This softening of heart involves no blurring of outline, and if the satire is less savage than it was it is now more deadly because more subtle; also, the prose in which it is expressed, hitherto the least impressive part of Mr. Wilson's equipment as a writer, has become more polished and controlled. The stories, needless to say, are as readable as ever.

The first, which gives the collection its title, is as brilliantly funny as anything he has yet written. This is pure satire, feeding on its own exuberance, fearlessly generalizing and disdaining qualifications, punishing by exaggeration certain modern pretensions that have not been properly recognized, let alone ridiculed, before. The psychopathic juvenile delinquent, moronically searching for "the truth" and meaninglessly repeating empty phrases he has learnt, no doubt, from articles in the popular Press about angry young men, is a devastating comment on the James Dean cult; while the seedy group of coffee-bar philosophers who adopt him, spouting their sad re-hash of dated Fascist clichés with a pathetic air of discovery, bring to mind, whether intentionally or not, certain other literary phenomena. It is for stories such as this, which convey an eminently sane judgment in the attractively crazy guise of his original comic gift, that we should be deeply grateful to Mr. Wilson.

Some of the shorter pieces in *A Bit off the Map* are comparatively slight, but all contain accurate and, for Mr. Wilson, almost kindly observation. Of the two other long stories, **"After the Show"** is scarcely satire at all, and shows that the author does not need to be indignant to be absorbing. **"More Friend than Lodger"** is fascinatingly complex, but only partially successful; the narrator, a completely amoral young woman, emerges as a character invented rather than observed, but the incidental social satire in this story, particularly in the treatment of her really deplorable lover, is outstandingly clever.

Mr. Wilson is a writer difficult to judge objectively. So much of his work is concerned with fashions of thought and behaviour, potentially dangerous moral platitudes, which are current to-day, that it is impossible to tell whether or not it will preserve its relevance when these have been dispersed and forgotten. The social satirist, of necessity obsessed with superficiality, is in danger of becoming superficial himself. A certain gravity about this book promises, perhaps more than the rather hysterical virtuosity of his novels, that his intelligence and humour will be preserved beyond their immediate entertainment value by the moral conviction behind them. In the meantime, he is almost alone among English creative writers to be bold enough to describe what is actually happening at the time of going to press.

Michael Millgate (essay date 1957)

SOURCE: "Angus Wilson's Guide to Modern England," in *The New Republic,* Vol. 137, No. 2244, November 25, 1957, pp. 17-18.

[*In the following excerpt, Millgate finds* A Bit Off the Map *to be more compassionate than Wilson's earlier story collections. The critic also believes that the book is an insightful guide to the English social structure after World War II.*]

It is, of course, the characters in Angus Wilson's new book of short stories who are off the map, hopelessly lost in a land of shifting values and changing class-lines—not the author himself. He, indeed, sits squarely in the middle of the contemporary English scene, like a supersensitive radar scanner sweeping the horizon on every side. With one exception, the stories in *A Bit Off the Map* are set in the post-1945 period, and, with his references to Suez, Elvis Presley and the Angry Young Men, Wilson contrives to seem as up-to-date as this morning's newspaper. He even manages to make the Angry Young Men themselves look old-fashioned: for he is more aware than most of that group seem to be of the political and social forces at work in Britain today, and much better equipped to convey this awareness in terms of human relationships.

Wilson's newest novel, *Anglo-Saxon Attitudes,* took a great sweep through English life at many levels; one was always conscious of the social structure which conditioned the words and actions of the characters, and even their very emotions. The new stories, in a sense, complement the novel. There are eight of them (three long, four short, and one in-between), and they deal with, for example, young civil servants and their wives living on the dreary outskirts of a "new town," a rich and ennobled business family, working-class and lower middle-class village life, a wealthy Jewish family and its less opulent connections, the London half-world of "Teddy boys" and espresso bars. It is a wide range, and, altogether with *Anglo-Saxon Attitudes, A Bit Off the Map* could safely be recommended as probably the best and certainly the most enjoyable short guide to contemporary English life—with none of the nastiness shirked and just a little of the niceness suggested.

Although Wilson remains a collector of bugs rather than butterflies (there are, after all, a great many more species of them), this is a much warmer book than *The Wrong Set* or *Such Darling Dodos*, Wilson's two previous volumes of short stories. He puts his characters in the pillory still, all their weakness and wickedness exposed, but he invites us to pity rather than pelt them. Some readers may regret this partial mellowing, for satire, with its uncomplicated viewpoint, often makes for greater incisiveness: the characters may turn out to be caricatures, but most of us are suckers for monsters anyway.

Perhaps none of these stories has quite the kick of, say, **"The Wrong Set"** from Wilson's first collection—but then Wilson, who began writing rather late (at the age of 33), sprang suddenly and fully-armed upon the literary scene, and some of those first stories are almost perfect of their kind. Wilson has advanced in the present volume in his greater humanity, his fuller, rounder characterization, which may also be a product of his experience as a novelist, and his readiness to tackle new kinds of characters and new areas of society.

Not that there is any falling off in technical skill here. One or two of the shorter stories seem makeweights, but most of the book is right up to Wilson's own high standards. The title story is quite masterly. Of *novella* length, it is told partly objectively and partly through the mouth of a character Nathanael West might have created—a fantasy-crammed "Teddy boy," with skin-tight jeans, lacquered hair and a face that is "a mixture of John Keats and cretinism," who prowls the London espresso bars in search of the Truth. This is Kennie Martin, a modern grotesque if ever there was one—yet frighteningly true to life. Wilson, with his uncannily accurate ear for dialogue (does he carry a tape-recorder in his inside pocket?), catches the tone and manner exactly: "See, some people go about like it doesn't matter why we're here or what it's all for, but I'm not like that. I want to get at the Truth.". . .

All the stories illustrate in one way or another the blurring of class-lines in contemporary England, the break-down of the old social patterns. In some of them Wilson seeks in addition to expose the essential falsity of the old philosophies to which people are currently turning in the attempt to recover some sense of being recognizably "on the map." **"A Bit Off the Map"** does this for Nietzscheanism.

"More Friend than Lodger," the funniest of these new stories, is a first-person account by a thorough-going bitch, the young wife of a rather stuffy publisher, of her calculated adultery with a high-grade confidence man. Her answer to the unsatisfactoriness of life is an utterly selfish and ruthless hedonism which leads her to betray, in effect, both her husband and her lover.

Since 1949 Angus Wilson has published two novels (with a third promised us early next year), three volumes of short stories, a play (*The Mulberry Bush*) which has been successfully performed in London and on television, a much admired study of Zola, and a lively skit on the twenties (*For Whom the Cloche Tolls*). It is a remarkable achievement.

C. B. Cox (essay date 1963)

SOURCE: "Angus Wilson: Studies in Depression," in *Critical Essays on Angus Wilson*, edited by Jay L. Halio, G. K. Hall & Co., 1985, pp. 81-7.

[*In this essay, originally published in Cox's 1963 book* The Free Spirit, *the critic argues that Wilson's short stories represent a liberal humanist attitude but that the author's pessimism about human life makes his humanist sentiments less idealistic than those of authors like English novelist E. M. Forster.*]

The fiction of Angus Wilson provides evidence for the great changes that have taken place in the thinking of liberal humanists during the last hundred years. In fact George Eliot would have found him a very odd humanist indeed. Particularly in the early short stories, his attitude towards human life appears to be one of disgust. There is a revulsion from the body in all his writing, and this saps his work of full vitality. For example, in **"Union Reunion"** he dwells upon the fat, bloated flesh of the whites in South Africa. The women are like "so many brightly painted barrels," and their eating dinner is "a deliberate locust-like advance that finally left the table a battlefield of picked bones, broken shells, dry skins and seeds." Minnie's once attractive small hands and feet now only look absurd on her mountainous body, and her attempts at foot-play under the table with her old admirer, Harry, make her an object of contempt. This kind of physical nausea occurs repeatedly. Trevor squeezing blackheads from his nose in **"The Wrong Set,"** the young technician spitting fragments of potato as he talks to his girl friend in **"Christmas Day in the Workhouse,"** or Tom Pirie spitting on Meg's arm as they chat together in *The Middle Age of Mrs. Eliot,* are all typical examples. The frequency with which such details occur suggests a squeamish refinement in Wilson. It is significant that in his stories there are many women, such as Mrs. Carrington in **"Mother's Sense of Fun,"** who find the physical side of marriage repulsive.

This disgust is not only hardly suitable for a humanist, but also seriously affects Wilson's values. A. O. J. Cockshut has argued in a most intelligent essay [in *Essays in Criticism,* Vol. IX, 1959] that Wilson's "fiercest moral condemnations are mingled with aesthetic and intellectual distaste; we cannot tell where one begins and another ends." Cockshut uses Celia Craddock in *Hemlock and After* as an example, blamed in the same way for being a half-baked intellectual as she is for being selfish. And in the depiction of Minnie in **"Union Reunion"** the physically and the morally repellent are curiously muddled together. In his early work Wilson is fighting against an emotional conviction that human beings, with a few rare exceptions, are in every way contemptible, and moral action useless. Rage at human inadequacy pervades his early writing, and his values are confused by the passionate intensity of this feeling. At times he is very close to complete despair.

Living in the post-1945 world, Wilson has lost much of Forster's assurance, and this appears most clearly in his irony. Where Forster is evasive, Wilson is savage and uncompromising. His short stories are peopled by lonely hypocrites, who try desperately to hide from themselves their own futility. He is particularly successful in caricaturing middle-class affectation, and in his treatment of this expresses fundamental attitudes to character which are hard to square with his humanism. He repeatedly depicts personality as a mask, a cover for either deep-seated insecurity or egotism. His novels parade before us the self-righteous, the smugly conventional, the followers of cliques, in a great tableau of debased humanity.

Language itself among the middle classes has become a means of evading reality. With delightful irony, Wilson captures the exact intonations of that middle-class drawl which places other people at a distance and leaves the speaker in a superior, detached position. In **"Raspberry Jam"** Grace recounts the sins of the Miss Swindales, but does nothing to remove her child from their influence: "You've heard the squalid story about young Tony Calkett, haven't you? My dear, he went round there to fix the lights and apparently Dolly invited him up to her bedroom to have a cherry brandy of all things and made the *most* unfortunate proposals."

This type of speech makes the experience of others a curiosity for drawing-room gossip; it is a game played by the middle classes to avoid recognition of the real pain and evil that surrounds them. And this evasive use of words is also brilliantly caught in the conversation of Dr. Early, in **"Learning's Little Tribute,"** who speaks of his daughters as "his girlies," and "always in so arch a manner that one might have fancied him master of a seraglio."

More important, Wilson suggests that a large part of human personality is built upon this false assumption of rôles. Many of his characters are mere ragbags of pretence and affectation; they have no unique individuality but have become merely a series of poses. This frightening sense that personality is fashioned entirely by pretence is shown vividly in a story such as **"What Do Hippos Eat?"** Greta is a typical Wilson figure, whose real identity has become lost in a series of social gestures. Wilson describes ironically her "virtues as a real good pal; her Dead End Kid appeal that went through the heart." She has created this shadowy conventional figure in order to get on with other people. Her reward is the attention of Maurice, a broken-down gentleman who only wants her money and nearly murders her as they watch the hippos at the zoo. The scene is treated in a mood of farce, and the actions of such humans appear suited only to this medium.

Wilson's irony is at its most severe in condemning these false substitutes for real living. In **"A Flat Country Christmas"** Carola likes the thought that she is her husband's "funny little mouse." And at the Christmas gathering in this story, each character can be merry only when he assumes his "party" face. Eric tries to bridge the underlying conflicts by being "at the top of his Max Miller form." And this false gaiety is typical of all the ghastly parties to which Wilson's characters submit themselves. In **"Saturnalia," "Christmas Day in the Workhouse,"** or **"Totentanz,"** the party atmosphere shows in extreme form all that is meaningless in the day-to-day lives of the participants. The party masks and games are not the exceptions, but in their fantasies an expression of the poses typical of human relations.

Evasion is seen again among the Cockshuts in **"Crazy Crowd,"** whose eccentric manners are a great game by which they hide from themselves their own egotism; and in **"A Visit in Bad Taste"** a pair of humanists, intelligent and cultured, cannot stretch their tolerance sufficiently far to accept into their home the homosexual relation just out of prison. It is interesting that the sin most talked about in these stories is self-pity. This blurs the honest acceptance of reality which is Wilson's own ideal.

This unmasking process is expressed by the prevailing ironic tone. In common with many other post-war novelists, Wilson often writes in a flat, banal manner which contrasts sharply with the forced gaiety or supposedly deep emotions of the characters being described. A good example is the account of the New Year's dance in **"Saturnalia"**: "The pretty waitress Gloria had gone very gay. 'Take it away' she cried to the band. Her shoulder strap was slipping and a bit of hair kept flopping in her eyes. It was difficult to snap your fingers when your head was going round. She and young Tom the porter were dancing real *palais de danse* and 'Send me, darling, send me' she cried." Here the simple sentences act as a means of deflation. This is a style deliberately made bare of all emotional overtones. Its casual ordinariness works in opposition to the jargon of Gloria, forcing home the triviality of her feelings. There is no emphasis, for nothing is worthy of emphasis here. This passage makes an interesting comparison with E. M. Forster's portrayal of Kingcroft in *Where Angels Fear to Tread*. Forster still delights in the absurdity of his comic creations; he is still in sympathy with the English comic tradition which can laugh at fools because they are the exception from the norm, and he is not altogether aware of the new notes of uncertainty that are creeping into his style. Angus Wilson does not suffer his fools gladly. He is depressed by their futility and feels only the pathos of their condition.

In the short stories in *The Wrong Set* (1949) the deliberately unpretentious style often debases all action to a meaningless animal-like series of gestures: "Then he sat in his pants, suspenders, and socks squeezing blackheads from his nose in front of a mirror. All this time they kept on rowing. At last Vi cried out 'All right, all right, Trevor Cawston, but I'm *still* going.' 'O.K.' said Trevor, 'how's about a nice little loving?' So then they broke into the old routine." And **"Significant Experience"** is a sort of parable to illustrate what so-called "significant" experiences are made up of in reality. The pompous Loveridge talks romantically about the value for a young man of an affair with a mature woman. Jeremy remembers the actuality of his summer affair with Prue—her neuroses, her temper, her sexual promiscuity, his own inadequacy. And Wilson's style deflates the oldest source of romantic joy. Even when Jeremy and Prue are happy together, the style makes their love appear a pretence: "Their fingers entwined more closely. It was such a *happy* evening." There are times when for Wilson all happiness is illusion; depression is the natural state for the humanist of our times.

It would be wrong to say that Wilson's attitude is wholly contemptuous, for there is compassion in his treatment of these lost people. Also, he feels that loneliness, and its compensatory illusions, are in part a necessary result of modern conditions. His people are always a prey to anxiety, psychological breakdown, even lunacy. The reasons for this are often obvious. In the aftermath of war his stories are full of girls and widows whose men have been killed, of refugees and people who can never completely suppress their fear of a nuclear cataclysm. . . .

For Wilson, pessimism is realistic and self-confidence a delusion. The power of evil now invades every corner of the humanist world, and Wilson's imagination is obsessed by breakdown and violence. The burden of modern conditions makes his characters easily irritated and a prey to moods. Their feelings shift rapidly from anger to affection, as with people who live under stress. The violence that threatens in the outside world is reflected in the characters themselves. There are constant outbreaks—the drunken scene at the end of **"Fresh Air Fiend,"** for example, or Kennie striking the mad Colonel Lambourn in **"A Bit Off the Map."** Much of the writing conveys a feeling that civilized conduct is an uneasy pose above a threatening abyss. In **"What Do Hippos Eat?"** the animals are part of the destructive element that human beings try to forget. The hippopotamus pool is slimy and smells abominably: "Every now and again the huge black forms would roll over, displacing ripples of brown, foam-flecked water, and malevolent eyes on the end of stalks would appear above the surface for a moment." This horror is ever present in the stories, a vision of meaningless evil that haunts the imagination of the sensitive characters and at times imposes itself as the only possible view of reality on this planet.

In the short story, **"The Wrong Set,"** and in *Anglo-Saxon Attitudes,* there are hints that an honest vitality still exists among the working classes, but no effort is made to study such people in detail. Wilson's imagination is taken up by the dead lives of the middle classes. On the one hand there are characters such as Vi in **"The Wrong Set"** who, amidst night-club squalor, still believes she is carrying on a genteel tradition; on the other, there are characters in **"A Flat Country Christmas"** who have deliberately emancipated themselves from their conventional backgrounds. Carola, Ray, and Sheila have left behind them various set types of upbringing—in a Baptist family, the working classes, and rich Guildford business society respectively; but they are left without any way of life at all in the wilderness of a new housing estate. The liberal ideal of freedom, examined so relentlessly by Henry James, brings these characters to complete emptiness. On their way to the party Carola and Ray can see the by-pass, "its white concrete line of shops shining in the dying light—the snack bar, the Barclay's bank, the utility furniture shop, Madame Yvonne's beauty parlour"; the bareness of this scene is a comment on their romantic illusions. Similarly in **"Higher Standards,"** Elsie, the school-teacher, has been educated out of her class. She is unmarried, longing for the days before her scholarship to the "County" cut her off from the village community. Her escape from the dull village routine has brought her only isolation and neurosis. Wilson is more conscious of the psychological problems arising out of the education of the working classes than of the benefits in a widening of cultural horizons. Progress through education, the ideal held so fervently by many Victorian humanists, for Wilson has problems of its own and offers no final solutions.

These violent changes in class structure, the breakdown of traditional beliefs, and the threat of war have brought other writers to complete abandonment of humanist beliefs. Wilson courageously fights against his own despair and tries to rebuild the broken fragments of optimistic humanism. As he develops, he becomes more compassionate towards his misfits and failures. But he insists that humanists must take into account the facts of modern life, the suffering, the power of evil, and the failure of most human aspirations. He tries to be completely honest and he rejects the illusions which seduced Forster. He believes that human beings must accept their essential loneliness. No personal relationship, not even marriage, can overcome separateness. The whole of middle-class convention is a structure built to avoid these facts; and for Wilson Christian idealism is a form of sentimental evasion.

In many stories Wilson insists that human life does not permit any perfect solutions, and he often satirizes misguided enthusiasts who try to sort out a tangled human situation. In **"Fresh Air Fiend"** Miss Eccles visits the Searles in the hope of straightening out their broken marriage and of infusing Professor Searle with the energy needed to start his long-delayed study of Mary Shelley. She believes in absolute sincerity, and by honest outspokenness hopes to let fresh air into the poisoned atmosphere. But the result is a complete breakdown in Professor Searle. We must live with the muddle of our private miseries and accept inadequacy as the common lot. This explains an apparent ambiguity in Wilson's treatment of the possessive mother. He often writes of lonely children, dominated by a mother, as with the Middletons in *Anglo-Saxon Attitudes*; but in **"Mother's Sense of Fun"** and **"A Sad Fall"** he brings out the irony of the situation. To love is to make demands on another person, to possess, and often it is better to accept such servitude than to be free. So after the death of his mother, which he welcomes with relief, Donald in **"Mother's Sense of Fun"** is suddenly overwhelmed by loneliness. And in **"A Sad Fall"** Mrs. Tanner wants to love without "holding," but knows this is almost impossible. Freedom, travelling light, is no easy solution for Wilson as it is for Forster.

These ironies and ambiguities are most clearly seen in the controversial story **"Raspberry Jam."** The two old women, Dolly and Marian, are the only ones who care for the boy, Johnnie, entering into his fantasy world and trying to give him the affection denied to him by his parents. Also they are repeatedly concerning themselves with lost causes, defending the broken and the worn-out with true kindness. But both are mad, Dolly obsessed by sex and Marian by the reputation of her father. The implication, repeated in so many stories, is that to *live,* to feel deeply and realistically about the human condition, is to face the danger of breakdown and perhaps lunacy. And so the two old ladies have taken to drink, and Wilson makes no concessions to sentimentality. They have invited Johnnie to tea but have been drunk for so many days that the raspberries have been eaten by the birds: "The awful malignity of this chance event took some time to pierce through the fuddled brains of the two ladies, as they stood there grotesque and obscene in their staring pink and clashing red, with their heavy pouchy faces and bloodshot eyes show-ing up in the hard, clear light of the sun." With insane delight in revenge, they let Johnnie watch them as they put out the eyes of a bird. This ending is not just a sen-sational trick. The most sympathetic of the adults in this story have been driven by their neuroses into the most horrible act of cruelty. Wilson deliberately shocks the reader to force home the danger of the sentimental, ideal-istic view of human goodness. The humanist must act in this type of muddled situation, and he can never escape into a world of clear-cut decisions and moral absolutes.

Although Wilson uses all his intelligence to find new ways of satisfying conduct for the humanist, he often suggests that true humanism is dying, its representatives growing old and being replaced by a younger generation whose values he deplores. In **"Realpolitik"** Sir Harold, the "last of the humanists," has been replaced at the Art Gallery by John Hobday, the ruthless careerist; and a comparable change is the theme of one of the most successful satires, **"Such Darling Dodos."** Priscilla and Robin are typical left-wing intellectuals who have been involved in all the political campaigns of the 'thirties. Wilson laughs at their naïve idealism, at the ugly fashions of Priscilla, and their curiously typical behaviour; but these two did care for people, and their pathetic idealism contrasts with the dead conservatism of the modern generation. Michael, the un-dergraduate, does not find chapel a bore; Harriet believes responsibility is what matters in India, not freedom, and that the abolition of the death penalty is an easy luxury in the face of social duty. Priscilla's cousin Tony, who is conservative, Roman Catholic, and reactionary, feels for the first time very much at home with young people. This arraignment of the new post-war generation is repeated in the portrayal of Miss Eccles in **"Fresh Air Fiend,"** of Maurice in **"After the Show,"** and of John Appleby in **"A Sad Fall."** Appleby takes a statistical view of people; for him it does not matter if Roger dies after his fall from the roof, for there are millions more like him. Wilson still cares above all for the individual case, and in **"Ten Min-utes to Twelve"** he sums up this feeling that a new au-thoritarianism is perverting modern youth. The old man, Lord Peacehaven, has lived in the Victorian tradition of individual enterprise, a great man whose energetic self-confidence hid an essential fear and anxiety and whose career ended in madness: ". . . their certainty was so lim-ited. . . . There was only a bottomless pit beneath their strength of will." But the young man, Geoff, is like his grandfather. "Why shouldn't people be ordered about . . . ," he says, "if they get in the way and don't pull their weight. What's the good of being in charge if you don't give orders." With a few exceptions, the younger generation are like James and Sonia in *Hemlock and After,* with no sense of the danger of their own assertive wills. The hu-manists in the novels—Bernard Sands, Gerald Middleton, Meg Eliot, and David Parker—are all older people, fight-ing to keep alive their values in a society increasingly unsympathetic. Whether Wilson is right to think that hu-manist values are in decline in England can only be a matter for conjecture and the comparison of personal impressions; but it is worthy of note that his depression appears to be characteristic of those artists whose early

manhood was spent in the atmosphere of the last war. Such writers usually find difficulty in understanding those whose memories are not crammed with scenes of violence and killing.

Wilson on his female protagonists:

I like writing about women, and I like having women as my central figures. This is a very curious thing, I don't know how to explain it. It is to do with my feeling, for all that it might look today as though it were not so—maybe it comes from my mother and so on, but I feel that women have had a very bad deal in life, and I feel on the side of my woman characters very strongly indeed. It always interests me that people say, 'Oh, your awful portraits of women,' as though I was malicious towards women. This is quite the opposite of the case. If in the short stories, at the beginning, there are some rather formidable and awful women, this is because I rather disliked the sort of woman who becomes immensely feminine, you know the way that things used to be.

But in general I have enormously strong feelings for women, and I like writing inside them and about them. I have no difficulty in making that jump and I don't think it's just me who thinks it, because I do get a lot of women writing to me and saying: 'I can't understand how you understand her so well.'

Angus Wilson, in an interview with Robert Robinson on "The Book Programme" on BBC-2, in The Listener, *Vol. 95, No. 2447, March 4, 1976.*

Angus Wilson   (essay date 1963)

SOURCE: An excerpt, in *The Wild Garden or Speaking of Writing,* University of California Press, 1963, pp. 23-55.

[*In this excerpt from his book-length commentary regard-ing his development as a writer, Wilson discusses the manner in which events and characters from his life in-fluenced his short fiction.*]

An analysis of the making of [my first short story, **'Rasp-berry Jam'**] may suggest some of the ways in which a novelist unconsciously comes to make one moral state-ment while supposing that he is making another. The sto-ry, the first fictional work of my life, was written in fever-ish excitement in one day. I proposed earlier that the present book should contain no estimation of my own work, but I pause to say that the failure of English masters, at all the schools I attended, to give me any comprehension of the purpose of punctuation is splendidly evident in that story. It tells of a boy of thirteen, the lonely son of con-ventional, self-centred upper middle class parents in an English village. He has only two friends in the village: two old sisters of gentle birth, now impoverished, drunken and the subject of village scandal. While an adult group at his mother's house gossip about the two old women, ostensibly asking whether they are suitable friends for the boy, Johnnie returns in his mind to the episode that, unknown to his family, has brought his friendship with them to an end, a terrible and traumatic episode for him. The two old women had invited him to tea. When he arrived they were clearly half-tipsy and they plied him with drink. They then brought in a bullfinch—'the prisoner'—and tortured it to death in front of him. The act, of course, though to the boy it is just an incredible horror, is in fact a culmination of rising paranoia produced in the simple, imaginative, generous old women by the narrow-minded malice, jealousy and frightened detestation that their originality has aroused in the village. The irony is that in their drunken craziness they destroy their friendship with Johnnie which alone gave any natural play to their generosity and childlike imaginative needs, perhaps destroy for ever the innocence of the boy himself.

When I wrote this story I saw the two old women as the embodiment of that saintliness which the mediocrity of the world seeks to destroy; by this reading, their craziness and their destruction of their young friend's peace of mind is not their 'fault' but that of the world which has failed to cherish them. Yet, as I have subsequently thought of the story, I have felt this to be a disturbingly illogical pattern, at variance with the shape of the story as it unfolds. I see now that what the story *says,* as opposed to what I thought I was saying, is that those, who like my old women, seek to retain a childlike (childish) innocence, and in particular a childlike (childish) ignorance, however 'good' their conscious motives, will inevitably destroy themselves and in all probability those they love. It is not insignificant, perhaps, that Johnnie, who at the age of thirteen might reasonably live in a world of childlike (childish) fantasy, is shown, without my realizing it as I wrote, using this fantasy to protect himself from the reality of his parents' demands upon him to grow up—although their conception of growing up, of course, is an inadequate one.

The character was drawn directly from myself as I had been at that age, but I felt only sympathy with my childhood self as I wrote, and did not notice the sting in the tale. Further, the old women, intended to strengthen the concept of childlike (childish) goodness, but really undermining it, were taken from two old women I knew much later in my life, at the age of twenty or so. And with these women, far from successfully creating an imaginative bond, I rather seriously failed to make any *rapport* at all, whereas a brother of mine was beloved by them. This was the brother next to me who at the age of thirteen had endured his nose being put out of joint by my unexpected birth. He was a saintly and exceedingly selfless man, and I only fear that the old ladies' preference for him showed a greater insight than I granted them; for in real life I regarded them not as receptacles of sanctity, but, like the village in the story, thought of them solely as a crazy nuisance, the more crazy since they did not respond to my charms. I seem in fiction to have righted any disappointment I may have felt by making them the intimates of my own starved affections at a much earlier age.

Such falsification in fact, unconscious at the time of writing (I had no conscious memory of the old women and was only vaguely aware that Johnnie came out of myself) suggests the way in which fiction can be constructed out of protective falsehood. The moral truth of the story was still deep in my unconscious; the conscious mind was soothed with fact unconsciously rearranged to propose a more flattering, untrue moral thesis. But the shape of the narrative defies this falsification.

Implicit in this first story also was the observation of the English social scene as it had changed since 1939. This social aspect coloured the larger part of the stories that I wrote for my first two books in 1949 and in 1950. I was struck then by the fact that a mild social revolution had taken place in England overnight, although its novelists had not yet noticed this. Readers and critics alike responded to this aspect of my stories. Indeed it earned me a reputation for being a 'social satirist', which seems to me only an aspect of my writing. The stories had indeed a sort of *à la page* assessment that 'placed' many things in the new English society that had not yet been mapped. I think that I could not have done this if I had not come from a family and a social background that was so essentially a part of the older disappearing England. The very small-scale *rentier* and professional group to which my family belonged had no place in Labour's England and was subsequently to prove the most expendable element of the Tory Party's supporters when the Conservatives began to convert social-welfare England into an affluent opportunity society. My attitude to this social revolution was inevitably ambivalent, my affections often in conflict with my reason; this is reflected in the stories. Yet I doubt if I could have imagined fictions concerning this social change with any intensity, even though the world of my family was condemned by it, had I not myself been forced at that very same moment to make a similar change-over from long preserved childhood ways to some acceptance of an adult world.

Beneath many of these stories, most of which bear a far more social-seeming surface than the first story, **'Raspberry Jam,'** that I have analysed, there lies the same attack on the falsity of preserved innocence or ignorance. This false innocence is embodied in the heroes and heroines and in all these characters I believed as I wrote that I was describing true simplicity. It would be tedious to detail other examples in addition to the old ladies of **'Raspberry Jam,'** but for those interested I would point to Vi, the night club pianist in **'The Wrong Set,'** to the young civil servant hero of **'Crazy Crowd,'** and to the haunted lady of **'A Little Companion.'** I do not, of course, say that the social statement in these satirical short stories is not rightly the centre of interest. Nor would it be true to say that the conflict between emotion and reason embodied in the social aspect of the stories is altered by the personal conflict that lies behind it—my affection and dislike for my youthful self about equalled the affection and dislike I felt for the dodo classes I described—but I emphasize the personal impulse here because I know that without it I should not have written the stories at all, and I also believe that it is this underlying personal motive which injects into them the fierceness that is their strength.

A change comes with the title story of my second book, *Such Darling Dodos*. This story more openly lays a charge against the preserved innocence of the genuinely good, but blinkered, left-wing don and his wife. I had become by then somewhat more conscious of my hostility to cherished illusions, at any rate in the political sphere. Yet in a way, too, once more the attack shifts to a new, deeper, unconscious level. It is clearly in this story no longer possible to judge on a purely social level. If, for the moment, the sympathies of the educated youth of England have swung against the left-wing causes of Priscilla and Robin (ironically at the moment of Labour's triumph at the polls), no reader (and certainly not the writer) can suppose that these causes have become the less worthwhile in themselves. This is not, as my earlier satire on the *nouveau pauvre* or the *lumpen-bourgeoisie,* an attack on *false* standards, but an attack on *insufficient* standards. Robin and Priscilla lack some deeper personal convictions, some poetry to illumine them when history has temporarily turned against them. Even so Robin is given a dignity superior (though no more touching, I think) to the 'pluckiness' of the *nouveau pauvre*. Yet in the long run, for all their superior intellect and better morality, my new liberal targets had failed to realize themselves quite as much as the raffish flotsam of *The Wrong Set*. This attack on insufficient good-works liberalism was to be the conscious theme of the play I wrote called *The Mulberry Bush* with an equally dignified target—the Padleys. . . .

. . . . .

What of the context in which [the themes of my short stories and early novels] were placed, from what part of my life have I taken the material of my fiction? Often, as in **'Raspberry Jam,'** the events from two parts of my life fuse to make one imaginative whole. I have already suggested, in the case of this story, why these two episodes should have been brought together. In these early stories, in any case, I found material by deliberately surveying my youth and adolescence, by using the incidents that I recalled and mingled in order to reflect ironically upon the position that the middle classes had reached ten or twenty years later. Typical of such stories is **'Saturnalia,'** a potpourri of hotel types, assembled for the servants' ball on New Year's Eve 1931. The story somewhat confounded American critics, since the idea of a mixed servants' and guests' dance is a typical product of British class snobbery. American status snobbery finds, no doubt, other occasions, office parties for instance, which indeed have become more typical in an England now more committed to a status society. I chose 1931 deliberately both for its direct reflection upon the relations of the classes in the opening years of the depression, and for its ironic reflection in contrast with the changed position of 1947 (the year in which it was written) although overtones of the future are present in the story as they were in 1931.

Nevertheless the stories never came to me by selection from a past lying open ready as a book from which to take appropriately didactic selections. Most of these short stories came from a remembered phrase or word that in ret-

rospect seemed to have a curiously ironic ring. For instance, *The Wrong Set* stuck in my mind because it had been used by a Church of England dignitary to describe the world in which his daughter, to his great distress, was moving. As she lived in the eminently respectable British South Coast town of Bournemouth, I had been puzzled. But it later emerged that to his horror she had become friendly with 'Chapel people'. The anecdote and the expression became a part of the stereotyped private language which I shared with my friends. There was a legion of other such phrases and stories which circulated in my family circle. It was such expressions, with their ironic overtones transposed into quite other scenes, in part derived from other areas of my experience and in part purely imagined, that were the starting-points of stories. Such established private jokes may be a very powerful source of imagination, for long use has made all their overtones familiar. They are, so to speak, the personal epics from which more sophisticated literature descends. Their dangers, either of a preserved nursery immaturity, or of a failure to generalize that condemns the work to coterie communication, are obvious. Much of the 'provincialism' of the English novel derives from this, but so also does its strength, its unstated tensions.

The hotel world of my childhood had been the foundation of these early stories. One by-product of this hotel world appears in what seems to many modern critics the neo-Dickensian caricature of my characters, for the inhabitants of those Kensington hotels tended towards the eccentricity that comes with penurious old age. Such a larger-than-life picture of human beings is inevitably the child's one; in my childhood it was in great degree objectively justified. It was certainly reinforced by my days much later as Deputy to the Superintendent of the British Museum Reading Room. But it is not only the scale of many of my characters in the stories that disturbs my readers, it is also the tone of their speech and behaviour. All writers know aspects of life that they take very much for granted, that yet to their readers appear peculiar, special. Of such a kind, I think, is the pervasive raffishness that hangs around many of my earlier stories and novels. It is the more peculiar, or, at any rate, unacceptable to respectable middle-class readers, because these raffish characters lay claim to, indeed can claim purely by class, social positions and ranks that the middle-class reader prefers to associate with less vulgar, less meretricious, more disciplined, more 'responsible' morality. I suspect my experience of a middle class with its skeletons taken from the cupboard and exposed to public exhibition is not so special as people make out. It reveals a truth about the between-the-wars English middle class when the sanctions that made for Victorian hypocrisy had weakened. At any rate it was my experience from my family, which was strongly reinforced by the atmosphere of my hotel childhood.

To this I can directly relate, I think, one of my greatest difficulties of communication. Vulgarities, lack of discrimination, weaknesses, which appear to me widespread and no more than venial beside the real wickedness of life, so disturb and repel readers that they seem unable to exercise charity toward 'such unpleasant characters'. I have noticed that quite discriminating readers have supposed me to have a puritanical revulsion from the human body, because, for example, in my earlier stories some of my characters spit when they talk or suffer from blackheads. It is rather that my strong sensual pleasure in physical beauty makes me acutely aware of whatever diminishes it. I think that such ways of looking at people, of expectation of human behaviour, remain, even though judgements and understanding may mature or change. That I grew up in a world where the discretion with which the English middle classes once disguised their grosser failures had largely broken down through the desperations of genteel poverty has probably given my picture of middle-class life a permanent colouring.

Finally with this hotel life I should connect one of the chief preoccupations of my earlier work, of the short stories. I mean the ambiguous tone, somewhere between satirical and admiring, with which I describe the resistance of many of my middle-class characters, particularly women, to economic and social decline and the empty disappointment of a life that is going downhill. I suppose that this portrayal is deeply embedded in my attitude to my mother, whose life, to say the least, was hard and heartbreaking. This courage, to which the period and class English expression 'pluck' most satisfactorily applied, commanded my deep admiration and compassion; nevertheless it also commanded my irony because it is associated with assumptions of class superiority, and indeed expectations from society, that reveal both an implacable fear and hatred of the poor and a snobbish envy of the rich. If, throughout my childhood, I knew my mother's 'pluck' to be what stood between us and disaster, I also knew it to be the chilling barrier that cut us off from happy communication with others. We could not know the A's because they were common, we must not know the B's because we could not pay back their hospitality. My mother clung to her 'class' as the only sure rock of a shipwrecked existence.

This 'pluck' I met in the greater part of 'the new poor' ladies (as they would have called themselves) that I knew so well in my youth. It is impossible to say how far such a quality can have a general significance sufficient to make it a subject for serious literature which is not purely social satire. I am inclined to suppose that the social trappings here are enough superficial to allow the underlying emotion to reach a reader unfamiliar with the social scene. However the ambiguities in this moral courage that I had observed as a child affected me enough to become a central theme in my novel *The Middle Age of Mrs Eliot*. Here I have tried to explore the general moral validity of what I have observed in a particular class by making my central characters, Meg Eliot and her brother, conscious critics of their own courage in face of disaster, and by contrasting them with various types of 'plucky' middle-class women of a more conventional, unselfcritical kind. I have also tried to extend my communication by making my heroine as little familiar with the small hotel world which suddenly confronts her as most of my readers must be. Nevertheless I owe the moral theme—can someone be courageous in sudden adversity without bitterness, without losing their

compassion, without losing their humanity?—to these hotel ladies, and I believe it to be one rich in overtones. I offer the case as one example of how novelists—even, I suppose, the nineteenth-century giants who could command a far wider social experience in a far more compact society than any of us can hope for now—have to seek means to generalize and extend the emotions that they know only in more narrow contexts of class or nation.

However, increasingly as I wrote these early short stories, these *aperçus,* derived from the ironies of private language and the disordered philistine middle-class world in which I had spent my youth, began to prove less satisfactory to me, as did the short story form with its snap ending echoing the ironic title. As I have already suggested, my own personal dilemma, the attack upon contented innocence, that unconsciously lay beneath these social stories was sharpening into the conflict between the twin necessary hells of society and solitude to which the blinkered innocence had to awake. This presented itself to me in two main theses, adumbrated in certain short stories, but demanding, I knew, a fuller treatment.

It is clear to me that as my underlying themes developed so my memory was forced to move on to a later section of my past life in order to find the right stimulation. Stories like **'Fresh Air Fiend,' 'Crazy Crowd'** and **'Et Dona Ferentes'** still challenge blinkered innocence and still satirize the middle classes; but the blinkered innocent is no longer a child, like Johnnie in **'Raspberry Jam,'** or uneducated like Vi in **'The Wrong Set'**; he or she is now a more intellectual person although often without self-criticism. On occasion, even, as in what I believe to be my best short story, **'A Visit in Bad Taste,'** the fake innocence becomes instead a calculated refusal of imaginative compassion: the sister who can find no place for her vulgar ex-convict brother disguises her selfishness neither with false simplicity nor with thoughtless amorality but with deliberation masked as a superior realism, a refusal of sentimentality. Yet apart from its move towards a more intelligent, cultivated, self-inquiring anti-heroine, this story's theme was not developed in my later writing; perhaps because it was successfully realized in the shorter form.

'Et Dona Ferentes' and **'Fresh Air Fiend'** directly pose the evasion of personal relationship by cultivated, liberal-minded people, and also the absurdity of those who think that such delicate situations can be resolved by honest and frank broadsides. This difficulty was to be developed in *Hemlock and After* (where Bernard and Ella Sands represent the two opposite poles) and in *Anglo-Saxon Attitudes* (where Gerald Middleton unites more subtle conceptions of both approaches in a single person). The more complex note of the novels, however, was imposed upon me as I increasingly felt that the depths of this chasm between the liberal intention in personal relationships and its actual failure were to be found neither in falsely innocent evasion (Ingeborg Middleton), nor even in concern with the externals of tolerant acceptance masking a deeper self-deception (as with Bernard Sands), but in the existence side by side of constant intellectual self-inquiry and emotional blindness (Bernard Sands, Gerald Middleton, Meg

Eliot); leading me in the end to the tragic paradox that the self-knowledge necessary to bridge the chasm is itself the agent of the stultified will (Simon Carter, the anti-hero of *The Old Men at the Zoo*). An allied but less fruitful, more simple theme was adumbrated in **Such Darling Dodos** where liberal beneficent public activity is contrasted with failure in private relationships. This was extended in my play, *The Mulberry Bush,* some part of the failure of which may lie in the fact that I had already solved the artistic presentation of its essential theme at least adequately in the earlier story. In any case, it is a theme that has probably been artistically solved once for all by Henrik Ibsen.

I have said that this new development in my imaginative interest drew its material from a different phase of my life. The world of my family and of the small hotels was essentially the world of the comedy (and of the pathos) of manners. Contrasts of behaviours, slang, modes and *idées reçues* of the various older generations of a section of the British middle class actively in decline, and of the younger generations conscious of this decline, were the points of interest that the world of my childhood presented to the aware observer. The strength of the stories I wrote about them lies perhaps in the deeper, more sympathetic overtones of wasted talents, lost hopes, unrealized dreams that I inevitably imparted to a picture of people I knew so well, a world to which, after all, I owed my existence. But the new themes that were developing could not be adequately fed upon this material. I sought for a more apparently coherent, more self-conscious world of middle-class values—one, perhaps, that I could take more seriously, both in love and hate, than the philistine bourgeoisie; one that would offer both more sympathetic and tougher targets than those 'natural' innocents—drunk majors, 'fast' middle-class ladies, amateur pros (off tarts), sugar daddies of male tarts, and so on—that were my first targets, all people for whom I had emotional sympathy, but no intellectual regard.

I found my new targets—and thus attacked my own fostered innocence more deeply—in the world of cultured, upper middle class supporters of Left Wing causes, the well-to-do Socialists of the 'thirties. It is often said that these people no longer exist in post-war England. I do not believe that this is true, although, of course, the emotional (and just) source of their political allegiance has been removed with the disappearance of gross economic indecency; such as remain show up less in a more affluent and, superficially at any rate, more liberal-minded society. The old pre-war upper middle class Left, however, was a more homogeneous body, although it contained many different strands, and was not, as it is often represented now, a simple offshoot of what is called 'Bloomsbury'. But whatever the road by which they came to the Left, these professional or business families shared many of the same virtues and defects. They had, I realized about 1950 or so, to share both in the triumph and the failure of Welfare England. It had also become quite clear that they were rapidly proving as much out of touch with the new post-war England as the more stupid middle-class 'dodos' I had satirized in the earlier stories; indeed at certain moments they have been more out of touch. I tried now to place this whole middle-class Left world. In doing so I was dealing with a group of people to whom I had more intense intellectual loyalties, and emotional ties less atavistic no doubt, but to all my conscious sense at least as strong as those that bound me to the world of my family. The change, of course, pressed upon me in two ways, as a change of artistic concentration no doubt must do—in the constant presence of the 'idea', of all that generally connected with the strengths and weaknesses of a class dedicated by ethical duty or intellectual belief to bringing about the end of its own supremacy; but far more than the 'idea' was the constant crowding into my memory of the people and places in my life connected with that idea. I found it, in fact, suddenly difficult to remember my childhood, almost impossible not to recall my late adolescence. The progression copied life, for when my mother died in my fifteenth year I sought and in some degree found substitutes for her affections among the mothers of my friends. These families, unconnected but not wholly dissimilar, differed from my own by being more cultivated, richer, more elegant and, above all, more liberal politically. It was they who, altered indeed out of all recognition, became the centre of my attack upon the deficiencies of a liberal socialism to which I still give my own moral and cultural allegiance. This attack reflects my slow and gradual realization of the many evasions, the failures of imagination and the coldnesses of heart, that marred the ideals of the families of my adoption. It is perhaps a more killing attack than the blunt sallies of my early stories against the Kensington of my childhood, but then disillusionment with an environment one has chosen is more bitter than the natural and inevitable reaction against the environment into which one has been born. The atmosphere of these families (and especially of these mothers) of my adoption was at its fullest in *Hemlock and After,* but still hangs over *Anglo-Saxon Attitudes,* although in the main the characters and incidents of that novel are more completely touched by fancy and, where taken from life, come from more various parts of my experience than in my earlier novel. With my last volume of short stories, **A Bit Off the Map,** and the novels that have followed it, the need to regroup the events of my childhood and adolescence seems to have been worked out; the themes of my nervous crisis—the unthroning of innocence, man's two hells—also reached their climax in *Mrs Eliot* and have given way to other themes less apparently connected with my life, or at present still too close to me to yield to my analysis.

If, as I suggest, my early life had been exhausted as a source, I have to ask myself why certain events should apparently have played so little part in my writing. A good example is the death of my mother. In any event a mother's death is important to a son; my mother's death was very sudden, a culmination of her sad life, her strained relations with my father and, above all, happening as it did in a boarding-house which she felt to be a 'social come-down', a culmination of the genteel poverty and loss of privacy that had increasingly made her life miserable. Certainly this was how my brothers saw it and how I saw it at that time. I have tried to rationalize the absence of my mother as a character, and of her death as an incident, from my writing by supposing that this indicates how little important she was to me. Such a conclusion seems to defy all likelihood, and indeed it does not agree with the fact that throughout my life, although I think of her seldom, if I shut my eyes it is usually her image that comes immediately before me. What I have observed, however, in my writing is perhaps more interesting—deaths that are connected with hers occur in three of my stories, none of them part of my attempted major themes, none of them in my novels. The first, **'A Story of Historical Interest,'** is an almost direct relation of my father's death, in which I have cast myself in the role of a daughter. My relationship to him was emotionally much that of the daughter he would have liked to have had. The father-daughter relationship is more conventionally acceptable to readers. However I was not aware of either of these motives when I transposed the sex. More interesting is the fact that I have transcribed the events exactly as they happened except for setting them in a small hotel with all the attendant humiliations of the proprietress's annoyance, legal regulations about dead bodies in hotels and so on. Now my father did not die or even come near to death in a hotel. My mother *did* die in a hotel. My distress at the time of her death, like the heroine's in the story, was aggravated by this circumstance, by similar humiliations. Removal to hospital to die is, of course, one of the stereotyped horrors of the impoverished middle class. Critics of this story have told me that the hotel scenes seem the most deeply felt, yet I certainly had no sense as I wrote it that I was introducing an episode from my mother's death. Indeed I was mainly concerned with the special distress we suffer when great public events overshadow our private griefs. My father died as Hitler marched into Prague. My mother's death in early 1929 was too early even to be overshadowed by the economic crisis.

Twice again, I think, my mother's death has entered my work by a side road. Each time it has been masked behind the death of my country landlady of 1949. In the first, a story called **'Heart of Elm'** included in *Such Darling Dodos,* the incident is mixed with the account I received second-hand of the death of the matron of my school. The story is mainly concerned to contrast the natural acceptance (one might almost say welcome) of the death of an old servant by her mistress, with the overcharged grief of the adolescent children who do not want to grow up. My two fellow-lodgers pointed out to me when the story was published that they, who with considerable changes figured as the two children, were no more, probably less, sentimentally attached to our landlady, and were certainly less concerned to treat her as a surrogate mother than I had been. I had in fact once again unconsciously attributed 'plucky' life-loving acceptance of death to myself as in **'A Story of Historical Interest'.** When I came to write a second time about the death of this landlady, I did so consciously and with what I have just analysed in my mind. This time the central figure of a television play, *The Stranger,* was a lodger, and his brutal treatment by the old woman's family after her death is shown as a direct result of his carefully fostered innocence. The fiction, being consciously related to the fact, was less indulgent to myself. My landlady's death had something of the same traumatic suddenness for me as my mother's. I opened the door of her cottage one Saturday afternoon to find her lying on the floor in an apoplexy from which she later

died. But what strikes me most is the social element by which, in both stories, the deaths are given an extra pathos derived from the ignorance, simplicity and peasant wisdom of the dying woman. This element in **'Heart of Elm'** is so marked that an American reviewer could compare the story to a satire on the relations of a Southern family with their old negro mammy. My landlady and, to a less degree, my school matron did have exactly these qualities; to herself and to most observers my mother was far from such a person, yet for me, even at fifteen, she had, through her disappointed shabby genteel life, acquired exactly this pathos. The altered social element stands, I feel sure, for those angers and reflections of her own sense of humiliation that I felt on her behalf at her death when the boarding-house proprietress and the other boarders treated it as something faintly demeaning to the name of the hotel.

So much for examples of particular subjects and incidents which seem to derive directly if unconsciously from my life, or of incidents which perhaps were too traumatic even for unconscious use, but appear obliquely in my writings. More curious perhaps is the relation of an author's life to what can be called the atmosphere of his novels, the flavour given to it by recurring subjects, symbols and places.

If, as I suspect, the creation of atmosphere is the least reasoned, most unconscious and automatic part of a novelist's art, it is likely also to be the most difficult for him to analyse, even when the particular fiction is a completed work of art, removed from his creative process and, as happens with finished works, appearing to be no longer connected with him. For this reason the oddly assorted *milieux,* objects and activities which I have been able to assemble as recurring, or possessing an apparently mysterious stress or significance, in my novels are probably fewer than another reader could detect; indeed some of those I shall describe were brought to my attention by readers or critics. Such associative objects, too, come so easily as I write, play so little part in the conscious planning that precedes the writing of my books, that they remain, even reviewed in tranquillity, obstinately unsusceptible to analysis. Yet this very material which the author's conscious mind rejects is in great degree the most idiosyncratic aspect of his work, and it would seem desirable that he should throw what small light upon it he can, if only by describing its associations with his own life.

I shall start with gardens and flowers. Their recurrence in my work seems particularly to strike readers—indeed, for those unfamiliar with garden flowers, often to irritate them. Some part they play in my fictions is stated in the first short story in my first book, **'Fresh Air Fiend'** (in the U.S. **'Life and Letters'**). Miranda Searle, the embittered, neurotic but clever and once beautiful, aristocratic wife of Professor Searle, uses her garden as an exercise in thwarted power to decree that this plant shall be scrapped and that encouraged; it is also clearly her last desperate attempt at communication, for if she can no longer 'hear' people, she has a real feeling for the flowers she tyrannizes over. When I wrote this story I had never gardened, although it has since become my chief hobby. I had only one woman friend who was a devoted gardener at that time (1946). Had I been told then that she resembled my character Miranda Searle I should have rejected the idea, and so I think would others who knew her. Ten years later when my friend died she had become an unhappy neurotic not so unlike Miranda Searle. I should not scout the idea that I could have drawn a character in this apparently prophetic manner. I have known too many instances of such apparent prophecy to be sceptical about this aspect of character creation. Nor do I think that the phenomenon defies rational explanation. If a novelist has the insight to create a character by the fusion of two or three real people, or by a combination of observation and fancy, it does not seem improbable that he may be able, in the process of creation, to foreshadow in people he knows degenerations or changes of character that he is not consciously aware of at the time. In the case of Miranda Searle, I certainly had no conscious sense of drawing from my friend. The character seemed to me, as I wrote, a transposition into quite other circumstances of what I imagined Lady Ottoline Morell to have been, itself something quite imaginary for I never knew her nor at that time had met anyone who knew her. As to the effects on Miranda Searle of her gardening activities, these were to a large extent drawn from what I felt would be the influence, good and bad, that gardening would have on my character should I take it up as a hobby—something which at that time seemed quite out of the question. Yet I must suppose that the character was much more drawn from what my subconscious told me were the hidden qualities of my friend; for little though I may have had her in my conscious mind, she was my principal association in life with the activity I was describing; and this, despite the fact that she did not, like Miranda Searle, exhibit her desperate possessiveness in her gardening, but found in it her only release from the tensions of her egoistic desperately willed life.

Jay L. Halio (essay date 1964)

SOURCE: *"The Wrong Set* and *Such Darling Dodos,"* in *Angus Wilson,* Oliver and Boyd, 1964, pp. 13-26.

[*In this chapter from his book-length study of Wilson, Halio discusses the author's first two collections of short stories and outlines the characters, situations, and constructs employed in his fiction.*]

The original, enthusiastic response to Wilson's first two collections of short stories, **The Wrong Set** and **Such Darling Dodos,** unquestionably owed much to their refreshing wit and vigorous satire. Causing this response, too, was the brilliant way that they treated the problems of contemporary life, particularly the difficulties of social re-adjustment in post-war England. They offered no panaceas, of course, but as John Wain has observed [in *The New Yorker,* XXXV, No. 11, April, 1959] they had the merit of telling their readers something about the world they were then living in. If, a decade and a half later, they still hold both our interest as well as our admiration, we may have to look further to find some

more solid basis for judgment. We shall see then, perhaps, that their ultimate appeal lies in a fundamental concern with recurrent human predicaments, like defeated pride or divided loyalty, rather than in an obvious ability to amuse or in an expert detailing of time and place. Finally, in their development of the short story form we may discover still another reason why these stories tend to remain among the more significant accomplishments of recent fiction.

For all the variety of individual experience, a number of rather clearly defined character types and situations emerge from among the twenty-three stories contained within these volumes. There is, for example, the Raffish Old Sport who appears in various stages of increasing decrepitude, like Trevor in the title story, **"The Wrong Set,"** or Mr Nicholson in **"Rex Imperator."** Many of these studies seem to be modelled upon Wilson's own father and reflect a mixed attitude of affection and contempt. This ambivalence is typical of Wilson's attitude to many other characters, whose weaknesses he tries to understand without at the same time absolving them of blame for the evil they cause. Elspeth Eccles, the Intense Young Woman of **"Fresh Air Fiend,"** Hamish Cockshutt and Donald Carrington, the Young Intellectuals in **"Crazy Crowd"** and **"Mother's Sense of Fun,"** are other cases in point. Many of the characters deserve to be grouped under the semi-opprobrium of the titles of these collections, and often the titles of individual stories themselves provide ironic commentaries—**"Saturnalia," "Realpolitik," "Sister Superior."** But the characters are not really very far removed from what we may like to believe is normal, or at any rate actual, life. The titles of these collections, like the stories they are taken from, cut two ways.

Among the many character types, Wilson's interest is keenest where the type is most varied. Most significant is the Widow Who Copes. She reappears frequently, though not quite so often as the Raffish Old Sport; her experiences, however, are both more varied and more serious. Often, like Mrs Graham in **"Heart of Elm"** or Mary in **"Sister Superior,"** she has children, a boy and a girl: but occasionally she is alone, like Thea in **"Christmas Day at the Workhouse."** Her experiences usually have much to do with the problem of fulfilling what remains of her life. Sometimes she shows an extreme possessiveness about her children (Mrs Carrington in **"Mother's Sense of Fun"**); at others she doggedly carries on in lonely but useful work (Thea's War service). In *The Middle Age of Mrs Eliot,* Wilson's most searching novel, the lives of three or four such widows enlighten Meg's, whose existence alters abruptly with the sudden loss of her husband. It thus becomes possible to treat Wilson's short stories as merely preliminary sketches for his novels—a temptation to which we easily enough succumb. But there is a question whether Wilson would ever have written novels had it not been for the success of his stories—a success which, . . . he had neither anticipated nor planned on. In any case, though the novels may, and in fact do, grow naturally out of the stories, the latter still have a strong claim to be judged on their own merits.

Throughout *The Wrong Set* and *Such Darling Dodos,* no matter what kind of characters he portrays, Wilson seems primarily interested in the success or failure—or sheer unwillingness—of people to understand what they are and what they are doing. Because of this psychological or consciously analytical bias, symbolism is not one of his basic literary techniques. Where symbols appear, they are almost always explicitly translated, usually by the character whom they most concern. In **"Significant Experience,"** for example, when Jeremy goes for a walk with Prue during the last day of their affair in the south of France, he sees in front of a villa an especially ornate garden whose rich flowers look faded, dust-covered, and dry. On the veranda sits an old woman in black; she, too, looks wan and dessicated. For Jeremy, this scene resembles the end of his exotic affair with an older woman, someone who is still quite attractive and very adept at love-making, but whose increasing possessiveness has begun to stifle him. When the description is over, explication follows directly: "The whole deadened spectacle connected in [Jeremy's] mind with his thoughts about Prue and he shuddered." This is quite at the other extreme, say, from Joyce's technique in *Dubliners.* Elsewhere, the explication of symbolism may be part of an interior monologue; it is typical of Wilson's more alert characters that they should try to interpret their experiences to themselves in this way. Where Wilson's symbols remain unexplained, as in the storm that gathers over the picnickers in **"Et Dona Ferentes,"** they are either so obvious or so deeply-rooted in the story that an explanation would seriously hamper their function—to say nothing of affronting the reader.

The situations Wilson treats of are invariably dramatic and often, as in Ibsen's plays, begin at a point just before a crisis. A visit or some other intrusion into the normal relationships of the characters—the loss of a job, reorganisation of an office, death—usually precipitates the crisis. Because of the limitations of its form, the short story can present only the most important events leading up to the crisis, the crisis itself, and the resulting shock: it has not the scope, as Wilson uses it, for a follow-through, a gradual reconstruction of attitudes or any other sustained denouement. And since Wilson is most concerned with the dramatic impact of these situations upon his central characters, he frequently employs the interior monologue to investigate its consequences. He does not adopt the stream-of-consciousness style of *Ulysses,* however, nor even the variation of it that Virginia Woolf uses, although there are closer similarities to her technique, perhaps, than to anyone else's. Basically, Wilson's use of interior monologue derives from such nineteenth-century writers as Émile Zola, an admitted influence. In **"Mother's Sense of Fun,"** Donald Carrington's meditation as he lies in bed listening to his mother talk with their cook illustrates how versatile the form can be, notwithstanding its presentation in the third person. In the space of a few sentences, the narrator blends a report of information with scraps of dialogue and even the direct personal address of his main character. In other stories, like **"Et Dona Ferentes"** and **"Heart of Elm,"** Wilson introduces the interior monologues of several characters. By contrasting the ways in which they all respond to a central event, he develops a kind of psycho-logical drama that underlies or reinforces the surface drama carried forward by the dialogue.

Typically, Wilson's characters belong to either the declining middle classes between the Wars, or the rising lower classes and ascendant bureaucracies—academic bureaucracies included—of the nineteen-forties. What happens to such people is therefore his special concern, though not his limitation. **"A Story of Historical Interest,"** for example, deals with shabby-genteel Lois Gorringe's self-sacrificing efforts to care for her widowed father, a Raffish Old Sport. When the old man suffers a stroke, Lois's efforts to nurse him reveal not only her own clumsiness and futility, but also her father's basic ingratitude for everything she has tried to do for him. Lois is deeply wounded, especially when Mr Gorringe prefers to stay in a cheap and rather unlikely nursing home rather than remain with her: but the shock is salutary. At the end, as his illness takes a serious turn for the worse, Lois refuses to come to his side; she looks forward instead to a party that evening and "the hundreds of interesting new people" she hopes to meet before going on to dinner with friends.

Lois Gorringe's response to her father's impending death may strike some readers as remarkably cold-blooded, particularly if they fail to see the bitterness that underlies her decision and the real effort that her bravado costs. But it is towards life that Lois turns, not towards the quagmires of sentimentality that have characterised her earlier experience. Her decision thus foreshadows the action of Wilson's later and more fully developed heroines. Living sometimes involves renunciation of what we have previously held dear, Wilson seems to say, especially when that something or someone—like Mr Gorringe—has tended to drain rather than fulfill our highest potentialities for existence. But not all of the people in these stories are able to withstand the shock of such revelations. In **"Fresh Air Fiend,"** Professor Searle collapses before the spectacle of his marriage that a pupil, Miss Eccles, has drawn for him. In **"The Wrong Set,"** an unhappy Vi, surrounded by the misery and squalor provided by her lover, who is off on a drunk, and a seedy nightclub job, from which she has just been fired, tries to get some of her own back. She telegraphs her sister that her son, who has earlier rebuffed Vi's attempts to be friendly, has fallen into the hands of communists, conchies, and Jews—the "wrong set," as she with unintended self-irony describes them. Even Rex Palmer's meagre triumph in **"Rex Imperator"** is seriously qualified by his emotional breakdown at the end of the story; it is left for his admiring wife to take charge and with calm matter-of-factness restore their household's equilibrium.

This element of pathos amidst disaster clearly attests to Wilson's generally humane point of view, and would seem to soften the misanthropy that many of his critics once charged him with (some still do). In the complex fabric of his design, pathos plays an important part, as it seldom does in the stories and novels of Evelyn Waugh, to whom he has most often been compared. Even in farcical situations—and in these stories Wilson, like Waugh, proves to be an excellent maker of farce—other dimensions, or depths, sometimes appear beneath the predominant hilarity. The farce that makes up almost the whole of **"Saturnalia"** is touched in this way as well as by more pointed stabs of satire. For example, when the hotel manageress, Mrs Hennessy, discharges a waitress because she is jealous of the attention Bruce Talfourd-Rich has shown her, she reveals a poverty of spirit not only in herself, but in her whole *milieu,* since Bruce is the shallowest sort of ladies' man—and a cad besides. A more sombre pathos darkens the uproarious family dinner in **"Union Reunion"** when the way Laura's son died finally becomes known. In **"Totentanz"** the farcical, the pathetic, and the grotesque all merge in the culminating disaster of Isobel Capper's first—and last— London entertainment, as suicide, murder, and other acts of despair rapidly follow one another to the end.

The violence at the end of **"Totentanz"** is, however, only an outward manifestation of the psychological violence that occurs frequently among Wilson's stories. In **"The Wrong Set"** or **"Rex Imperator"** no one actually dies or is killed, but a series of psychological outrages takes place that causes severe injuries of another order. A snub, among Wilson's characters, may be every bit as damaging as its physical counterpart, the knife wound. It is certainly intended to be. Stephanie's involuntary cruelty and Thea's retaliation in **"Christmas Day at the Workhouse"** are instances of such psychological warfare. If the violence is withstood—and sometimes it is ironically misunderstood, as at the end of **"What Do Hippos Eat?"**—the characters may come off stronger for having been subjected to it, toughened by the experience and often embittered by it, but at least better prepared for the ways of this world. Disaster lies either in being unaware of the violence taking place (Mary in **"Sister Superior"**), or in surrendering to it (John Hobday's staff in **"Realpolitik"**). But standing up to the revelation of violence has a danger of its own— the danger dramatised by Margaret Tarrant's ruthless pronouncement about her brother at the end of **"A Visit in Bad Taste."** There exists a frontier, Wilson suggests, on each side of our humanity: confronting reality too boldly, or not confronting it boldly enough, is to become either more or less than human.

But when everything else has been said, what emerges as Wilson's most salient characteristic in these stories is his histrionic sensibility, as demonstrated primarily by his use of dialogue. His ability to capture the sound of the human voice has justly been acclaimed by critics; only slightly less acclaimed is his ability to grasp the way people think. He is most successful with the types of people he has lived among: the dons of his Oxford and British Museum days, the professional and mercantile classes of his childhood, civil servants from the Foreign Office, and the rest of the people—actors, writers, editors—who make up his personal acquaintance. It is the varied voice of middle-classdom, but occasionally a lower-class accent appears, a cockney's, an East Anglian farmer's, or some other. The settings of his stories are never important in themselves, but are strictly limited to introducing his characters' personalities. Thus the main character in **"Realpolitik,"** the new chief of a provincial art gallery, is quite briefly presented, sitting at the edge of his desk waiting for his staff

Wilson early in his writing career.

to give him their attention. Dialogue immediately follows, and in John Hobday's opening remarks we soon recognise the accents of the huckster, the Young Bureaucrat on the Make. Through a series of slight interruptions by his audience, we become aware almost as quickly that a tense situation is developing between them. The effect of this presentation, as in most of Wilson's stories, is exactly that of a curtain rising in a theatre. We are propelled at once into a dramatic event, picking up whatever information we need to understand it mainly from the dialogue, but with the advantage, too, of liberally supplied internal monologues. This is certainly at the other extreme not only of Joyce, but of Joseph Conrad or William Faulkner, who often share the exposition and the action of their stories equally between dialogue and description. In stories that deal chiefly with the inner conflict of a single character, as in **"Raspberry Jam,"** Wilson also seems to prefer a rather theatrical presentation. Thus before proceeding to Johnnie's recollection of past events, he shows the boy in the company of his mother and her circle, who play only secondary roles in the story. Even in **"A Little Companion,"** the objective, omniscient narrator passes quickly from a few preliminary remarks to describe his subject, Miss Arkwright, as she first appears during a cocktail party.

To introduce his stories, Wilson chooses such social gatherings as staff meetings, parties, family picnics or dinners, because they offer many opportunities for dialogue with which to begin at once the play and counterplay of human personality. His technique of defining a character or a group of characters by their reaction to a common event or to other characters is both quickly and easily employed. Here he seems to be following Joyce and Virginia Woolf, but of course earlier writers, such as Jane Austen and Dickens, whom Wilson much admires, developed the device as well. Thus the encyclopaedists of **"Learning's Little Tribute"** first appear at the graveside of a deceased colleague, as each one manœuvres to profit from the sudden gap in their ranks. Later they reappear, trying to prevent their chief from making the situation serve his own interest. Finally, all of them are brought face to face with their colleague's widow, whose honest and independent spirit, together with her genuine feelings of bereavement, baffles their condescension and frustrates the aims of their charity. Such an arrangement of incidents suggests a dance-like movement, or structure, which becomes still more apparent in **"Totentanz,"** as the title partly suggests. A less ordered dance, thoroughly in keeping with its theme, appears in **"Saturnalia."** In **"A Flat Country Christmas"** (first published in 1950 as **"Old, Old Message"** but not collected until later), this analogy between the sequence of events and a dance is made explicit. But the intricacies of a dance do not justify the rather mechanical arrangement of incidents in **"Realpolitik"** or the serial re-telling of events in **"Mother's Sense of Fun"**—stories which depend much more for their effect than the others upon a final ironic twist or shock. In *For Whom the Cloche Tolls: A Scrap-Book of the Twenties* (1953), Wilson achieves his *tour de force,* complete with drawings by Philippe Jullian. He again begins with a death, but unlike **"Learning's Little Tribute,"** here the dead person becomes the central figure. In the story, related mainly by letters, Maisie's children, friends, and others record their reactions to her death but more importantly to her life, especially those aspects of her life which appear to epitomise the spirit of her age. The technique is of course Jamesian, which may have something to do with the heroine's American birth as well as her name. At the end, her own voice is briefly heard—in excerpts from a diary—but brief as it is, it becomes the fitting culmination for the whole presentation of her character and her epoch.

At his best, then, Wilson presents an intricate drama of tense personal relationships. These often may be diagrammed (though not without violence to the closely-woven fabric of his design) by a triangular pattern, or several superimposed triangular patterns. At the base of the triangle is usually a couple in a relationship of either harmony or tension, as in **"Fresh Air Fiend"** or **"A Visit in Bad Taste."** At the apex, exerting pressure upon either or both of the principals at the base, is a third person—or group of persons, as in **"A Story of Historical Interest"** or **"What Do Hippos Eat?"** As conflict grows, the triangle may be seen to invert itself, the point of the apex now becoming a wedge forcing apart the couple at the base. In more complex situations, the number of triangular situations usually increases. The essential thing, however, is to recognise the human drama of these stories, whether it involves the almost wholly in-

troverted conflict of **"Necessity's Child,"** or the outward conflicts of a large group of people. In those stories which deal with a few people—no more than three or four—Wilson appears to probe most deeply, using his most incisive irony. Very possibly his greatest achievements in fiction lie in this direction. But no one can deny his other achievements, especially his handling of farce, which invariably requires the management of many more persons; and in his novels an important part of the action—like the hilarious opening of Vardon Hall in *Hemlock and After* or Marie-Hélène's "do" in *Anglo-Saxon Attitudes*—reaches its climax in this way.

A detailed analysis of one of the stories may be useful here. **"Heart of Elm"** is a likely choice since it deals with characteristic themes and situations, and since its structure falls somewhere between the single triangular pattern described above and the more complex structure of stories having a larger cast of persons. It begins with the dialogue of Constance Graham, a widow, and her two children, Thomas and Katherine. In a room upstairs the children's old nurse, Ellen, lies dying. Constance is busy preparing sandwiches for the three or four members of Ellen's family who will presently arrive, separately, to pay their last—and almost only—respects to their sister. The children deeply resent this intrusion into their household; they are afraid that at the last moment they will be displaced in the affections of their dear nurse. This is especially true of Katherine, the intense young teen-ager whose tight-lipped heroism is almost more than her older brother can bear: for Thomas, "capacity for self-expression is not incompatible with true feeling." But the narrator's comments swiftly undercut the pretensions of both children, directing our sympathies instead towards their mother, who actually looks forward to Ellen's death. She longs to sell the house which has been a veritable prison to her, and in the ten years or so that remain of her middle age, she wants to live by herself in London. As for her offspring, Constance resents their lingering adolescence. She believes that Ellen is mainly responsible for it, although she recognises that she must share in the responsibility too, partly because of her initial blindness, and partly because of her unwillingness afterwards to alter the situation by hurting others. The time has come, however, when she must act decisively—or lose everything. Summoning up courage to take her stand, she confronts the children with her plans before the guests arrive. Thomas and Katherine are, in their own ways, naturally shocked by the decision; then they are almost horrified by the revelations about themselves and their relationship with Ellen that Constance is forced to make. Before this conflict can be resolved, or, indeed, proceed further, the first visitor drives up to the house.

So far, the general pattern of relationships is fairly simple. Ellen, representing the life of their childhood, lies in harmonious but now delicate balance with Katherine and Thomas. Constance, at the apex of the triangle, appears to exert pressure downwards on either side, when suddenly, as Ellen is dying, she becomes a wedge-like force breaking up the relationship at the base. The arrival of Jack Gilmore, Ellen's black-sheep brother, inaugurates a series of new relationships which not only increases the complexities of the drama, but culminates in the ironic turn of events at the end.

Jack's success in cheering Ellen up at once poses a double threat: bringing out the coarser side of Ellen's nature, he transforms the image the children wish to retain of their simple old nurse; and Thomas, at least, suspects that Mr Gilmore will try to inveigle whatever he can of Ellen's property—a threat real enough, but of only secondary importance in the story. Gilmore thus momentarily replaces Constance at the apex of the triangle, forcing apart the children's bond with Ellen, and suggesting a regrouping of relationships that will eventually lump all the Grahams together as against the members of Ellen's own family.

The second guest is Mrs Temple, Ellen's younger sister, who arrives with her son, Len. Mrs Temple's comic, genteel affectation somewhat reduces the tension generated so far, as Ellen receives her shortly and immediately pretends to sleep. At this point, Constance asks her son to take charge of their guests. He delights in putting himself over these people, and climaxes his "performance" with the invention of an appropriate epithet for Ellen: "She is, you know, a real heart of oak." The histrionics, the sentimentality of the phrase, immediately unite everyone in a splendid show of appreciation (Constance of course is absent, and we are not sure where Katherine is). But the feeling is short-lived. Lottie, Ellen's older, unmarried sister, arrives and at once takes full command of things, leaving Constance, Thomas, and Katherine to sit alone in the hall, waiting for the end.

When the end does come, it introduces a new and thoroughly ironic perspective. For it is in Constance's arms that the old nurse chooses to die, mumbling, "My dearie, my lovie." The effect upon Mrs Graham is one of complete horror. Ellen's last gesture would seem to defeat her again, destroying at one stroke her hard won determination to escape: "it was clearly she whom Ellen had adored," she says to herself, "she could not deceive herself about that, however stiffly she had held the dying woman, she knew that she was holding the person who had loved her more than anyone ever would, and that calculatedly she must betray that love." This love, invisible even to its chief object, has underlain all the others. But Constance, like many of Wilson's heroines, shows strength enough to maintain her earlier resolve. Her renunciation of Ellen's love reveals a tragic awareness that may seem harsh, cruel, and bitter: yet it must also seem brave. The story tries to make this point explicit. At the end, in a deliberate anticlimax of mingled farce and pathos, Constance seizes upon the undertaker's recommendation to use elm wood for Ellen's coffin. She begins to laugh and explains, "I was only just thinking—not heart of *oak*, you know, at all, heart of *elm*." When Katherine tries to interpret the remark favourably, describing Ellen as "a great elm under which we all sheltered," Constance does not allow her to be entirely deceived. "Oh! yes," she says, "she was like an elm tree. But understand this, there aren't any more elm trees, no more hearts of elm."

Some years ago, in a review article for *The Spectator* [1954], Wilson surveyed the development of the short story in the twentieth century. Against the "classic" story of Somerset Maugham's era, he contrasted Katherine Mansfield's attempts to inject "greater subtlety of mood and deeper levels of consciousness" into a form that had hitherto emphasised narrative and surprise. The result was almost to destroy the short story by reducing it to a "sketch." More recently, writers have tried to combine these elements into a single form. Novelists have faced a similar problem, but Wilson believes that, on the whole, the short story writers have been more successful "in restoring shape without losing subtlety." However we may agree or disagree with these conclusions, especially the last, one fact about Wilson's own stories remains clear. He certainly has contributed much towards restoring the classic form of the earlier era. His influence is especially significant in the use of dramatic techniques to convey his narrative, as we have seen. His influence in the novel is similar, although there he succeeds somewhat more perfectly in keeping the balance between narrative action and deeper levels of consciousness.

Malcolm Bradbury (essay date 1966)

SOURCE: "The Short Stories of Angus Wilson," in *Studies in Short Fiction*, Vol. III, No. 2, Winter, 1966, pp. 117-25.

[*An English man of letters, Bradbury is best known as the author of such satiric novels as* Eating People Is Wrong *(1959) and* Stepping Westward *(1965). He has also, as a literary critic, written extensively on English and American literature, especially the works of E. M. Forster. In this analysis, he discusses Wilson's unusual mix of moral realism and absurd, grotesque characters.*]

Many of the critics who have commented on Angus Wilson's fiction appear to have seen him as a direct inheritor of a central tradition in English fiction—the socio-moral tradition, which concerns itself with the moral analysis of life in society. Seen in this light, Wilson is a writer who carries on the habitual concerns of storytellers from Jane Austen to Forster into the world of post-Second World War uncertainty. He is a writer of intense moral concern, a moral realist devoted to the analysis of man in his social context. He is a writer of liberal humanist sympathies, seeking honest conduct and exploring the dilemmas of modern humanism under conditions of extreme strain and tension. He is a novelist of manners, his social world that of the English upper middle classes and their associated intelligentsia, a world with elaborated social forms and distinct social types, a world the standards of which the welfare state and Suez, the new town and the end of Empire have nonetheless challenged. This social world, set at some distance by Wilson's characteristic irony, yet relished for its manners and styles, is judged in terms of its capacities for personal relationships, and for its capacities to face present history. Because Wilson exercises his irony generously, and because he is particularly attentive to extreme states of mind, critics who see him in this way would admit to finding it hard, often, to pin down his exact moral perspective; but they tend to see it as essentially a liberal-radical one, speaking for tolerance and social decency— its ideal achievement personal sanity, honest conduct in human relationships, and emotional fulfillment within the available conditions of history. And so by this view Wilson emerges as a moral realist, exacting in his judgment on his characters, expert at presenting their states of self-delusion, devastating in his analysis of the terms of the liberal dilemma.

But at the same time critics have recognized that there is another strain in his work, and one that does not sit easily with the first. This is the strain indicated by the fact that Wilson himself has confessed a debt not only to Austen and Forster but also to Dickens. Dickens, too, is of course a social novelist, but one who works with rather different assumptions both about what society is and how it may be rendered from those of novelists like Jane Austen or George Eliot or Forster or the other central figures of Leavis' Great Tradition (though Leavis includes Dickens, somewhat guardedly, in it). Dickens tends to see society as an elaborated complex of persons and institutions in which individual control and moral mastery are rare and improbable. Society is a prison or a fog, a pattern of interconnections by family and class and profession whose meaning is difficult to shape and whose impact on the individual is often confining. There is, in Dickens, social range but also social simplification. The engagement of the individual with any role or style tends to be heightened toward the absurd; and in Dickens' concern with the grotesque and with caricature, we sense a shrillness of tone, which is also a sense of absurdity, of the odd distortion given to men by their daily life. Dickens' comedy is not ironic, not comedy of manners so much as comedy of human observation. And Wilson himself has pointed out how anarchic Dickens' social world is, how he deals repeatedly with plots of pursuit and flight, how he sees home as prison and makes his mode of picaresque a mode of psychological search for existence. The gothic instinct of Dickens, his sense of haunting wrongs, family secrets, depredations on innocence, runs deep in his work and has much to do both with his human judgment and his comic dimensions. The debt to Dickens that Wilson himself calls attention to is in fact reasonably evident; the way in which Wilson plans his novels over a broad scope, with large casts of characters, with the same sense of the tension and the hopelessness of family life, the same sense that society is a maze, the same sense of human motivation deriving from guilts and tensions, the same patterns of pursuit and flight, the same sense of comedy, must throw into some question the account of him as the novelist of manners, the rigorous analyst of delusion and folly.

In fact, of course, both of the debts co-exist; and they consort oddly in Wilson's work, giving it a distinct kind of strangeness that seems to have proved troubling to a considerable number of his critics. For Wilson does have the dimension of a moralist, along with all the running inventiveness he has acquired from the more gothic tradition. Essentially a comic writer, he has various moods of

comic procedure. Thus we often find ourselves encountering a mode of moral analysis we are familiar with in Austen and Forster, while at the same time becoming aware that Wilson's characters are of a different order, are potential grotesques—so that they evade the insistences of moral judgment by their tincture of unreality, by their touch of the absurd. We are invited, indeed, to put the test of moral realism to personages whose moral reality Wilson's mode of creation throws into doubt. We think we observe in one of his personages the features of snobbery or social cruelty; and then we find, as we proceed, that the cruelty is better than the progressive rationalism that would challenge it. Or we see the familiar ties of parents to children, of husbands to wives, of relative to relative, exposed as exploitation; we think we know how to judge that, but then exploitation comes to seem in this world the only possible relationship, seems part of Wilson's essential perception of what relationships are. Or again, Wilson the liberal seems persistently to offer hopes of social betterment: finer relations between man and man, happier orders of society, greater tolerance. But history, so active a force in his writing, is never so regenerative as the promise seems to suggest; and we come to find that the prevailing world is one of degeneration, of new convolutions of cruelty, new possibilities in self-deception, new kinds of strain.

The difficulty is evident enough in his novels; and it is present, too, in the stories, though the stories do have to some extent their own modes and styles. Nonetheless they are an important and central part of Wilson's endeavor; in fact he is one of the few postwar English writers who have made much of their reputation in the form. Wilson's satirical and comic talents are fully exercised in them; and so are some of his most persistent themes. In this form he touches on both of the modes mentioned, and encourages the same kind of critical uncertainty. For example, many of the stories turn on a moment of moral realism, a moment of truth—a moment when, often, he reveals the grotesque as the grotesque. In **"Fresh Air Fiend"**—the first story in Wilson's first collection, *The Wrong Set*—time and history have turned Mrs. Searle, the wife of an Oxford professor, into a "grotesque"; and Wilson takes a characteristic delight in rendering her manners and style, while at the same time introducing an agent, Miss Eccles, a research student of Professor Searle's, who sees through her. But when the girl tries to "let a breath of fresh air into a very fetid atmosphere," her act is only destructive; it produces a breakdown in Professor Searle, whom she has been trying to help. The moment of truth, then, does not sustain the need for reality; rather it discloses the danger. And the satirical victim of the story is not the grotesque Mrs. Searle, or her husband, but the fresh air fiend herself. The grotesque is not in fact a comic mode that Wilson necessarily used for satirical assault on the character. Indeed, it is often an achieved condition of life, a form of human balance the more appreciated because of its essential style.

The style is not, of course, spared acute analysis, but the comedy that creates it is often appreciative of it. We relish by invitation Mrs. Searle's triumphs over the girl's inhuman simplicity, her inability to appreciate the finely balanced tensions of the marital relationship—Searle is impotent, guilty about his marriage, attracted by the girl but more committed than she can see to his wife, an incubus on her as well as she on him. And the same is true of the two mad old ladies in **"Raspberry Jam"** (*The Wrong Set*), whom the young boy in the story relishes:

> In a totally unselfconscious way, half crazy as they were and half crazy even though the child sensed them to be, the Misses Swindale possessed just those qualities of which Johnnie felt most in need. To begin with they were odd and fantastic and highly coloured, and more important still, they believed that such peculiarities were nothing to be ashamed of, indeed were often a matter for pride.

At times, of course, the grotesquerie, the craziness, does indeed become discreditable—as it does in **"Crazy Crowd"** or **"The Wrong Set"** (both in *The Wrong Set*). It becomes the voice of extreme snobbery, of spoiled personality, of Fascism; it advances into the terrifying, the aggressive, and the possessive; and Wilson sketches alternatives against it—Peter's innocent openness in **"Crazy Crowd,"** and more firmly Mrs. Thursby's left-wing, pacifist household in **"The Wrong Set."** But though the grotesquerie is identified, as quite often it is, with the sensibility of social arrogance exacerbated into oddity by the democratic pressures of the new England, though it is in fact a *social* grotesquerie, Wilson can be involved as much with it as against it; and we may not simply identify him as a democratic satirist who is exposing the unreality of a disinherited class. Some critics have tried to locate him in this way, and it is true that from time to time he appeals to the procedure. But that Wilson is, like Dickens, too much involved in the unrealities, is, in fact, too psychologically curious, seems so evident as to make this an incomplete way of characterizing the essential quality of his work.

Of course it is perfectly evident that Wilson is concerned very precisely with the social process, and with the deprivation from central social experience that social change can bring about. The very titles of his three volumes of stories—*The Wrong Set, Such Darling Dodos,* and *A Bit Off the Map*—carry the implication. One can see that the volumes if taken together draw upon the social developments in England from the 1930's to the 1950's; the pressure toward democracy in the 1930's, the tense democracy of the war, the austerity of the Labor Government in the immediate postwar period, the rise of the Welfare State and a more planned and bureaucratized social order with levelling implications in the period thereafter, the rise of youth culture and the tension of Suez. Wilson gives a good deal of attention to these developments; he often defines the characters in their politics; their crises coincide with radical political changes—thus **"A Story of Historical Interest"** (*The Wrong Set*) *is* of historical interest, being located just on the outbreak of war; and the financial and social consequences of such changes are part of the data of most of the tales. And Wilson does, repeatedly, deal with the socially dispossessed; his characteristic milieu is that of frayed-at-the-heels upper-middle class gentility, and it would seem true to say that nowhere in

recent English letters has the cry of dispossession and impoverishment been so shrilly sounded. And indeed the extravagance and the oddity of so many of Wilson's characters, their patterns of stylishness and selfishness, of snobbery and arrogance, their class and sexual jealousies, direct us specifically to social sources—to the way in which the life-style of a class can become exaggerated and even menacing when the conditions that served the style are threatened. We can indeed take Wilson's stories as a kind of elaborated portfolio of the decline of the English upper middle class, of a whole order pinned and placed—except that Wilson's relationship to his material is neither totally detached nor totally involved, but a complicated mixture of the two responses.

For at times Wilson presents this social world with a comic detachment resembling Waugh's; morally uninterested, socially curious, the writer renders the world as a total impression. The comedy derives from a sense of the social world as an unreal one, a "lurid nightmare," as Paul Pennyfeather sees it in *Decline and Fall,* in which justice and order break down, and the bounder and cad prevail. But, as Jay Halio points out [in *Angus Wilson,* 1964], there is a difference between Waugh and Wilson in their handling of this sort of comedy, for Wilson, repeatedly, is engaged with the emotion of pathos. His characters have much of the outrageousness of Waugh's, but they exist in a much more probable context; they have more direct appeal to authenticity than do Waugh's, and we are engaged with them in terms of reasonably recognizable experience: they call up our sense of the "frightful"—the frightful, bad weekend in the country, the frightful, impecunious relative. They are not beyond our experience; and our experience is heightened in recognizable ways. For if Wilson is, like Waugh, essentially a sophisticated observer, his sophistication is a kind of metropolitan urbanity about our situation. Families are really hell; his characters readily break affectionate relationships; the springs of relationship are tension and guilt and sexuality; behind gentility lies vulgarity. The degree to which Wilson appeals to our sense of the rather frightful and the very vulgar is consonant with the degree to which he appeals to our sense of the essential pathos of most human roles and relationships. In fact, then, his sense of social unreality—which one is tempted to read politically—is part of the conditioning material of a larger assumption: that disintegration, social and psychological, is the fundamental condition; that to be socially insecure and financially unsafe and in the power of the tough hotel manageress is within the order of normal experience; that sexuality burns long and love is short-lived; and that, therefore, the inadequate posturings that are on the one hand feasible objects of satire are also the assertion of some grit or energy by means of which life continues possible.

For Wilson's "dodos" are in fact rarely the weak but usually the strenuous: aging hostesses, fading Edwardian roués, professional spongers, well-trained survivors of old struggles. Their past has never been secure; there is no comfortable, conservative idyll behind them; they are the longterm products of an hotel civilization. Their sexual sophistication and resource are vast, and they are old hands at shoring the fragments against their ruins. As Halio points out, there are repeated types among them to which Wilson seems to have a special literary attachment: the Raffish Old Sport, the Widow Who Copes, the Fresh Air Fiend, the Social Oxbridge Academic, the New Bureaucrat—often types both frightful and with strong capacities for endurance and domination. Wilson is attentive to their individual styles, to their modes of conversation and intercourse; and he often presents them with a kind of joyful creativity independent of moral implications. He has himself spoken of the state of creative "possession" involved in the act of writing, where the writer becomes engaged with his material to the point of debilitating any rigorous moral perspective upon it; and we can see that the process must often work for him. There are instances—as in the story **"Such Darling Dodos"**—where the moral and indeed the political judgment seem plain, but more often that is not the effect. Rather there is a blurring of the moral implication in the interest of sensations and judgments of different kinds. Thus in most of the early stories—at least he works by providing large numbers of personages within the story, and a constant variation of point of view, which detaches us from a direct involvement. In one of the novellas of *A Bit Off the Map*, **"More Friend Than Lodger,"** Wilson tells a story through a single character, the story emerging as a superb piece of self-exposure—a self-exposure that is also self-awareness on the part of the first-person narrator. But usually such awareness as we have about a character's weaknesses and how they should be judged derives from the use of inner monologue counterpointed with external observation and the manipulation of other points of view, to produce what is finally an ambiguous effect. In the case of the more strenuous and grotesque characters, this seems often to derive from the novelist's attraction to the view of the universe from which they derive, his attraction for recognizing that the world is a collocation of exploitative relationships, that humanism is simply another mode of self-deception, that the cool, cruel wrongs perpetrated by one character upon another provide the only viable assertion of selfhood he may possess. Thus Wilson's urbanity, despite an often devastating satire, seems designed to create in us a regard for his extreme grotesques, especially when they are efficient manipulators of a debased environment.

Many of Wilson's characters seem in fact to be in the grip of a kind of depraved romanticism—the only mode of romanticism available to them. And it would seem that Wilson is in some sense a "romantic" writer in that he is concerned with a psychological mode of notation; and his intricate dramas of personal relationships are contests in the pursuit of freedom. The impression of his work is that to have lived and formed relationships is to have entered a world of imprisonment, a world from which the individual can escape only by the repossession of some long-deprived romantic joy. But the joy, so often hinted at—in the unachieved homosexual relationship of **"Et Dona Ferentes,"** in the release from the mother in **"Mother's Sense of Fun,"** in the attraction of the tartish Sylvia in **"After the Show"**—is itself likely to be deceptive; Wilson's romanticism rarely goes so far as to propose success. (In this respect, his stories show some similarities to those of Forster, which, too, have strong romantic overtones, but a surer attitude toward the positive worth of freedom, of escape from convention and lovelessness and smugness.) For Wilson, the sought freedom has an air of unreality, and he exploits not the possibilities of it but the irony of the pursuit. For Wilson's characters are usually caught in the psychoanalytic trap; the dream of freedom is an irony. They live out their social roles, as representatives of a family function or a class, while thirsting for more; they are, so often, part of an architectured social structure of disappointment. At times, Wilson enforces his point by a directly "gothic" rendering of the situation. **"Totentanz"** is a dance of death in a world in which the sinister is of the atmosphere. The ominous names of the characters—Todhunter, Professor Cadaver—the gruesome memorial in the living room, the final dance of death of the guests, drives home with an unusually surrealistic indulgence a kind of perception implied in many of the other stories, in which funereal domination generally plays a singularly large part. **"A Little Companion"** exploits a more familiar "gothic" mode—it is a psychological ghost story; and so, too, is **"Mummy to the Rescue,"** with its recourse to madness. Wilson's modern supernatural is never very far from the scene, in fact; and his sensibility unites—as Dickens' does—the comic, the grotesque and the pathetic, taking the comic as a main mode of modern experience.

Wilson's essential capacity as a writer of fiction is, I think, to disquiet us by distinguishing the resources of selfishness, cruelty, violence, and unfulfilled ambition that lie within our family experience; and in the service of this approach he uses, I suggest, modes other than those of familiar social comedy. A writer who draws heavily on the identifiable social world, on contemporary history, on recognizable tones of voice and on the familiar objects of present-day England, he nonetheless manages to create a surrealistic landscape and a surrealistic society, a special kind of fantasy which is his distinctive world. It is, I think, limiting and unsatisfactory to describe him—as many critics do—simply as a social satirist, since the mode of comic procedure is extremely complex, having a less direct relation with "familiar reality" than we are often encouraged to think. Wilson is in fact an inventive and indeed sometimes an indulgent writer, yet one who guides his effects, though broad, by what is very much a "gothic" sensibility. His comedy, though socially observant, is not, I think, adequately defined for us unless we recognize in it the elements of exaggeration that this kind of sensibility invites; nor is it defined unless we say that it involves us in ironic ambiguities that contain distinctive kinds of hope and despair. It is comedy not just of social surface but of psychological conflict, in which he reveals passionate urgencies in every heart, and in which he presents the spectacle of decadence or misery with a brilliance that makes it both amusingly absurd and engagingly pathetic. Wilson's writing never engages him with the alternatives sufficiently for us to feel the pathos too deeply to enjoy the comedy. He is never fully involved in urging the view of freedom, rarely suggesting that his characters are trapped in a situation from which they might escape. Consequently, though it is possible to regard him as a "hard" or "cruel" writer, he is not concerned to offer to us a sense that there is a better world beyond our own decadent sensibilities. A writer substantially fed by the culture in which he lives, and attentive to the forces at work in it, he is nonetheless much less the meliorative social satirist than the collector of grotesqueries which, because they are culturally and psychologically grounded, come to us with ominous recognition.

Joyce Carol Oates (essay date 1969)

SOURCE: A review of *Death Dance: Twenty-five Stories,* in *The Saturday Review,* New York, Vol. LII, No. 27, July 5, 1969, pp. 33-4.

[*Oates is an American fiction writer and critic who is perhaps best known for her novel* Them *(1969), which won a National Book Award in 1970. Her fiction is noted for its exhaustive presentation of realistic detail as well as its striking imagination, especially in the evocation of abnormal psychological states. As a critic, Oates has written on a remarkable diversity of authors—from Shakespeare to Herman Melville to Samuel Beckett—and is appreciated for the individuality and erudition that characterize her critical work. In this favorable review, Oates comments on the preoccupation with death that plagues many of Wilson's characters.*]

Here are stories from Angus Wilson's *The Wrong Set, Such Darling Dodos,* and *A Bit Off the Map*—masterful, concise, rather macabre tales of postwar England. The collection is aptly named, for most of the characters in this volume are involved in dances of death of one kind or another, consciously or unconsciously celebrating the doom of their civilization.

Wilson is a master of what we now call the Chekhovian short story: beginning with an immediate involvement in the consciousness of a central character, giving us details which, like dabs of color in an impressionist painting, suggest a whole that is never quite seen but is fully sensed. Wilson's people are generally well-educated, middle-class Anglo-Saxons, human enough but at times rather cruel, sterile, played-out.

The earliest stories in the book deal with characters whose sense of themselves is theatrical and whose attempts at living, especially at love, are fraudulent. The hard-drinking, overly sophisticated, shallow Tories of **"The Wrong Set"** engage in spiritless defamatory remarks about "Reds and Jews," drift through the years immediately following World War II, and feel that "Life was hell anyhow." In **"Saturnalia"** a New Year's Eve party at a private hotel mixes tenants and staff in a sleazy comedy of pseudo-amorous gestures. **"Crazy Crowd,"** a looser, more extravagant story, deals with the relationship between a young woman and her lover, who is brought with her to visit her "crazy" family. Occasionally, when Wilson descends into the human, the colorful, for its own sake, his stories read like Frank O'Connor's, though his unique touch of wit is always present, rather ominously.

These stories, written in the late Forties and Fifties, demonstrate Wilson's increasing awareness of his craft. Though the concern with individuals as actors, acting out rather pathetic, vapid roles, is still uppermost in his imagination, Wilson gradually warms to his characters, giving us an increasing sense of their human dilemma. But even in so familiarly moving a story as **"Mother's Sense of Fun,"** which presents a bachelor-professor's terrible loneliness after his mother's death, Wilson cannot resist a macabre pun. The story concludes: "'My poor boy will be lonely,' she had said. She was dead right."

"Totentanz," which lends the collection its title, brings together various obsessions—the snobbery of these icy Anglo-Saxons, perhaps too well-educated for their own good fortune; the capriciousness of fate (an inheritance that promises much but brings little); the morbid conclusion of an ostentatious reception. Thomas Mann himself would not have imagined so preposterous an illustration of bourgeois decadence as the "Totentanz" costume party, celebrating various aspects of death: a fireplace got up as a crematorium, waiters dressed as skeletons, guests as corpses, hearses to carry them back home. The grotesque deaths of three prized guests follows immediately, perhaps logically.

Violence and death, the attraction toward disintegration and dissolution, the loss of vitality in even the young—these are Wilson's preoccupations. In the fine story **"After the Show,"** published first in 1957, the eerie dissociation of human beings from their feelings, even their feelings about love and death, is explored in terms of theatrical events, with an attempted suicide as a kind of act, an event that fails but fails even more mysteriously to involve true feelings. Wilson's "younger generation" are contemptuous of their elders, anxious to break free into their own adulthood and into power; but a kind of premature paralysis limits them. Their imaginations are as narrow as their parents' after all:

> They had discussed it so often, schooled themselves for the task of leadership which would fall to their generation—leadership out of the desert of the television world, out of the even more degrading swamps of espresso-bar rebellion. They had fed themselves on high purposes and self-discipline . . . Now for the first time he was called upon to control a situation . . . and yet the situation seemed to drift by while he stood like a night stroller . . . He was emerging not as the hero leader but as that feeble figure, the *homme moyen sensuel*—the "hero" type of all the literature that he and his friends most despised. And he saw no way out of it.

And indeed there seems no way out. These decent godless people know all the right words; they are witty, civilized, attractive connoisseurs of what is left of their world; they are perhaps more in control of their lives than they should be if their lives are to be real, and yet they are obviously failures. Their obsession with death points up their essential failure. And when they actually die, their deaths are troublesome rather than tragic.

Robert Kirsch (essay date 1969)

SOURCE: "*Death Dance: 25 Stories Designed to be Dipped Into*," in *Los Angeles Times*, August 25, 1969, p. 8.

[*In this mixed review of* Death Dance: Twenty-Five Stories, *Kirsch criticizes Wilson's detachment in his stories and his overemphasis on English class relations, traits that often result in one-dimensional characters.*]

Death Dance: Twenty-five Stories by Angus Wilson should not be read straight through but rather dipped into. I suspect that the first procedure produces a response similar to the presence of a weekend guest: he is interesting at times but an intense exposure produces moments of ennui.

The fact is that too much of Wilson, with his coolness and detachment, his concern with the nuance of class, caste and condition, results in an impatience.

In fairness, however, it must be said that just when you want to put the book down, you run into a story such as **"More Friend Than Lodger,"** a superb and knowing tale about a poseur and a parasite in the world of publishing, or **"After the Show,"** which reveals the coming of age of a young man who finds in the sordid circumstances of his elders an almost irresistible romantic appeal.

There are others: **"A Little Companion,"** the story of a middle-aged spinster haunted by the apparition of a vulgar and whining little slum child, whose appearance might be of psychotic or psychic origin: **"Christmas Day in the Workhouse,"** in which the loneliness and solitude of girls working in wartime offices produce cruelty and humiliation.

At his best he is reminiscent of Maugham, at his narrowest there are also echoes of Maugham. Yet a situation which would be a subtheme in, say, Maugham's "P. & O.," is the whole matter in **"Saturnalia"** where a once-a-year dance to which the staff is invited points up the unhappiness and pretention of class: "'Well, after all,' drawled Claire, 'if one can't put oneself out for the servants for one evening. It isn't very much to ask. Only one evening in the whole year.'"

For Americans, enjoyment of such stories as **"The Wrong Set"** or **"A Visit in Bad Taste"** must be an acquired taste. The importance of these attitudes is likely to be diminished. The result is that irony, the strongest element in Wilson's writing, falters in some of the slighter tales.

Not so in **"Totentanz"** the title story. Here Wilson is at his best in convincing us that such things are important.

He is aided by the use of elements which generate importance a great, though strange, bequest of money which enables a provincial university professor and his socially ambitious wife to escape from the death-in-life condition of academic life remote from London, only to find themselves in another sort of death-in-life.

"Well I shall catch my death of cold if I stay here," a lady teacher says. The master's wife says "No one would notice the difference." These are intelligent, feeling people trapped in the corset of tradition and situation; we are at once aware of the source of eccentricity in British character. It is a defensive response. "Boredom had given the Master's wife a conviction of psychic as well as psychological powers and she suddenly 'felt aware of evil.'"

But the power that is generated in these tales is often the very force which makes us impatient with them. These are lonely people concerned with form, occasionally rebelling. Wilson's detachment doesn't really help; it is part of the same condition.

Only when he uses a narrator such as in **"More Friend than Lodger"** or **"A Bit Off the Map"** or occasionally in a deeply felt story such as **"After the Show"** do we feel his characters as something more than caricatures. Most of the time Wilson shares the same trap as his characters.

Angus Wilson with Frederick P. W. McDowell (interview date 1971)

SOURCE: "An interview with Angus Wilson," in *The Iowa Review*, Vol. 3, No. 4, Fall, 1972, pp. 77-105.

[*In the following excerpt, taken from an interview conducted in the fall of 1971, Wilson discusses various writers that have influenced his work, including Charles Dickens, Fedor Dostoevsky, and Samuel Beckett.*]

[McDowell]: *You have presented your views on Dickens at considerable length in* The World of Charles Dickens. *. . . Like Dickens you tend to have one or two characters presented in some detail (especially with respect to their moral choices), surrounded by a group of characters presented from the outside. Dickens illustrates this principle in surrounding Pip, Arthur Clennam, Esther Summerson, and David Copperfield by externally conceived characters. Do you admit to such a principle of organization in your fiction?*

[Wilson]: Yes. I have read Dickens since I was very young, and I suppose I have read him more often than any other author; and he inevitably goes very deep into my work. Apart from the humor of Dickens which lies very close to a good deal of my humor, what is vital to his approach and to mine is that he sees his central figures always in relation to, first of all, a group and then in relation to the whole of society. Frequently with him the direction in his novels is, rather, outward from society and inwards toward the group and the central figure but always in connection with a great number of other people; he sees the central figures internally and the others are presented externally. On the whole, this has been my method. It has been the only way, I think, in which I can present my sense of man's total isolation, his working out of his problems within himself but also in terms of the other human beings whom he comes across. I would say, however, that

I am an agnostic and Dickens is a Christian. Therefore our view of man's potentiality is obviously different; but insofar as we are dealing with this world, I think Dickens was very concerned, whatever his beliefs in the future life, to see what man could do with himself. He frequently wrote about what had gone wrong with a man's life. *Little Dorrit* is a very good example of this preoccupation. How can an individual face up to failure, to seeming guilt, to a heavy burden of responsibility, how can he free himself? My books are very much about the freedom that is available to man and what he does with it. I think that both Dickens and I have a rather limited view of what that freedom is, of how much freedom is left to a man. Nevertheless, I start from the same kind of temperament as Dickens', that is to say, I am a person who is almost immediately drawn to people. I like very much being with people, I like individual people, I am excited by them; but I am also liable to fall into a deep sort of boredom. There is in my love/hate for people (save a very few with whom I have made secure contact) a manic-depressive kind of love/hate that is liable, uncontrolled by reason and social ethic, to pivot violently. I think it would be much truer to say that it pivots between a strong vitalism and a sense of emptiness and resignation. And this dichotomy, I believe, is also true of Dickens' work.

In an interview a few years ago you mentioned the great influence on you of Richardson's Clarissa. *You have implied more recently in conversation that Stendhal's* La Chartreuse de Parme *is such another seminal book for you.*

They are two novels which I admire very greatly indeed. I read *Clarissa* first when I was about eighteen, and I have read it a number of times since then. It has influenced me, I think, in two ways. One, I think there is no novel in which that sort of building up of realistic detail into what is finally a grotesque or fantastic form occurs so firmly— something which you find in Dickens when he speaks of *Bleak House* being the romantic side of everyday things. Richardson had this capacity to create by lots of realistic details what is finally the appearance of realism but which is, in fact, something extraordinarily fantastic. The power to imprison both his characters and his readers is something that I have always aimed to do, because my books are about people imprisoned and how they break out of prison. My characters have to break out with what is left to them in this life, whereas Clarissa triumphantly and wonderfully, in what I think is the greatest Christian novel ever written, breaks out and goes to her heavenly bridegroom. But I would also say that *Clarissa* has influenced me in another way. I have always felt that I am concerned deeply in my books with the hopeless, the lost, those who don't matter. All my books are about the necessity of taking these people into account. And it seems to me that even these days women belong to this group of the disregarded. They are still the victims of society, not of course to the same extent that they were; and, indeed, many of the great feminists are very good examples of what happens as a result of victimization. I think that *Clarissa* has influenced me enormously as the supreme representation of this understanding of women as victims. I am always interested that women readers of my books fall into two categories, those who state that I have understood women very well (because I do see this tragic denial of their full rights) and those who say that I am very horrible to women (because, in portraying the denial of their rights, I do show them in the shabby lights in which they can appear when they try to evade or accept their imprisonment). And I think that some of the ambiguity of *Clarissa,* of women seen as both victors and victims, arises in this way. But I would really say that *Clarissa* is a superb book to me because, finally, with the certain defects that Clarissa has, she is a great woman who breaks out of her bonds without artifices which are unworthy of her—very, very differently, for example, to Pamela. *La Chartreuse de Parme* is also a novel that I love and reread often. I wish I could say that it had influenced me in the same degree in my writing. I fear that I have never been able to attain in my novels that sense of the totality of passion found in it: I mean by that totality both love and sexual passion, romantic love when people are deeply, deeply attracted to one another. No one, I think, has understood so well as Stendhal the supremacy of passion, the way in which such abandonment to emotion can create a sort of happiness that transcends absolutely everything. Further, he understood how this transcendent passion can quite suddenly, as at the end of *La Chartreuse de Parme,* collapse into a strange kind of dust. This sense of collapsed passion perhaps I have been able to convey. Also I would say that just as Clarissa represents woman triumphant and victorious but, of course, a martyr, so Sanseverina represents woman using her femininity: not using it in a manipulative way but enjoying it and her sensuality to the full—tragic also, but the other side of triumphant woman. I wish that I had created a Sanseverina; certainly she is one of the great characters of all fiction. The only heroine in the English novel, I think, that approaches Sanseverina is Clara Middleton in *The Egoist.* She combines intelligence, youth, vitality in a way which Jane Austen achieved in Catherine Morland but never captured again. Clara seems to me to live, untrammeled by her author, as, say, Dorothea Brooke or Gwendolen Harleth or Isabel Archer never do. In her spiritual authority and largeness of nature she is the heiress of Clarissa.

You once said that Dostoevsky is the greatest of the European novelists. This statement would imply that he has influenced your view of human beings and their psychology, possibly also the themes developed in your novels and the techniques used in them.

Before I begin to talk this time, I should say that my pleasure in discussing great names like Dickens, Richardson, Stendhal, and Dostoevsky by no means implies that my work ought to be compared to theirs. But I do think that a writer can legitimately define his own views, the contours of his work, and his technical problems by considering them in relation to the novels of those by whom he has been most deeply moved and impressed. Perhaps a serious writer can think of his own art and the issues it raises in no other way. And it would hardly avail, out of deference to greatness, to discuss, instead, writers of lesser importance, those who have failed to capture one's imagination. So please regard these great writers as representing standards of excellence hardly to be attained by anyone now writing and their works as points of reference for discussion of the art of literature. As for Dostoevsky's psychology, I am interested in it very much and I think that it is very remarkable. I don't know that I have ever successfully captured it: that is to say, this extraordinary capacity for the emotions to change suddenly in a person, this apparent lack of relation between their actions and their words, this all but total rejection of logical motivation, and so on. I am impressed by his insight into human unpredictability, but I am not quite so impressed by it as I used to be. I do think sometimes that it's a bit of a trick. I think that sometimes, as in D. H. Lawrence, what Dostoevsky succeeds in making us think is a natural and extraordinary impulse is, in fact, a very carefully worked artifact. But still it is true that I wish my work were more influenced by this sense of the unpredictable and were less deterministic. It has been my fear that the influence of Zola, for example, whom I admire greatly in other ways, has led to too great a determinism of my characters. But where Dostoevsky has influenced me enormously is in his concept of the relationship existing between society and chaos. He thought, as indeed I do, that society and civilization rest on a very thin ice. This view led him to be very reactionary in politics. It hasn't led me to be so, but I do think that there are (and we have seen them in recent times very greatly) malevolent forces at work, unhappy people who, through being twisted, are really concerned more to break up civilization than to do anything particular with it. And this kind of growing hysteria that you get in his novels—markedly in *The Idiot* and in *The Possessed* but in all the novels where they begin, you know, so frequently in the province of X, with reports that there have been recently a number of senseless crimes and so on—this sense that there is some kind of chaos at work somewhere, which can usually be traced to one or two characters in the book (Pyotr Verhovensky notably in *The Possessed*), and which culminates usually in some public gathering in which all chaos breaks loose and the forces of good, the forces of humanistic duty, and so on are for the moment routed—this has been a pattern enormously present in my books. It conveys, often, the sense of the individual alone in a crowd of people (and of hostile forces) if you like; and it's particularly, I suppose, to be seen at Vardon Hall in *Hemlock and After.* . . .

In a talk which I recently heard you give, you said that Samuel Beckett is the greatest writer of our time and you also mentioned that, among contemporary novelists, you admire Nabokov, Borges, and Montherlant. I wonder if you would care to comment briefly on what each of these writers has meant to you.

Yes, I think that there is a distinction to be made between Beckett and the others. Beckett is usually counted as anti-humanist, but I don't see him in that light. I've written some reviews suggesting that he is, in fact, a considerable humanist but a humanist of man at his stage of final disintegration. He still thinks man worthwhile enough to make him the center of such novels as *Malone Dies* and so on, where you get just what is left when man is finally nothing much more than a body. I think he takes on from the

humanism of Joyce, in the wonderful representation of Leopold Bloom who is one of the great figures in fiction to me. And I have felt that some of my tendency to try to bolster up the humanism of my characters in my novels with what are, after all, the accidentals of culture, of natural perception, of talent and so on has been corrected by this viewing of man in a reduced way as Beckett does. Beckett's rigor has been a corrective to what I feel to be the rather false humanism which I inherited from E. M. Forster's novels, a humanism derived from one segment of middle-class civilization and not from humanity in general. I have tried in my later novels, at any rate, to work somewhat from Beckett's position. Even in my early stories I always, as I hoped, balanced everything as much against my characters as for them, so that there would be no patronage, so that when they came through they'd come through on their own account and everything that could be said against them had been said. But I think that I wasn't always scrupulous enough with them; and I have increasingly tried— and Beckett has influenced me greatly here—to let them stand alone as perhaps Sylvia Calvert (*Late Call*) does, divested of all that contemporary society has given them but still able to win through in some degree. Now the other three—Borges, Nabokov, and Montherlant—are, I think, anti-humanists. I admire their work technically and, indeed, the power of their minds and their wit; but I don't admire their particular kind of aristocratic disdain of man. However, they have been again great correctives to any sentimentality that I have (and I am sure that I have got it) in my treatment of human beings. Particularly, I have taken from them the elements of parody, the use of parody of civilization, of culture as it is handed down to us in literature. Parody becomes a means of alienating the reader, of ensuring that he does not become over fond of the characters, of preventing him from regarding the book as a "good read" and from being unable to see where he's going because he's too absorbed in it. I think that *Tristram Shandy* is a great beginner of this willed alienation of the reader, and it is a technique that we can't afford to do without now. I think we must be prepared to alienate our readers at times so that they shall not go through our books as by rote, feeling comfortable and happy and feeling that they are reading warm, moving books.

Peter Faulkner   (essay date 1980)

SOURCE: "To 1950: *The Wrong Set* and *Such Darling Dodos,*" in *Angus Wilson: Mimic and Moralist,* Secker and Warburg, 1980, pp. 1-21.

[*In this excerpt from his book-length study of Wilson, Faulkner analyzes the stories in Wilson's first two collections of short stories, noting the author's developing style.*]

The title [of Wilson's first collection] ***The Wrong Set*** is a highly appropriate one for the whole volume, as well as for the [title] story, for Wilson's central concern is with characters who find themselves with wrong sets of relationships; can there be relationships, the volume asks, which allow and help all concerned to grow and develop, or are they necessarily props for some and prisons for others? The sombreness which underlies the wit comes from the fact that the answer suggested is negative.

Those who think they can helpfully reshape other people's lives are sharply criticised in the first story, **"Fresh-Air Fiend"**. The earnest Elspeth Eccles aims to restore her former supervisor, Professor Searle, to his proper academic eminence by letting fresh air into his relationship with his alcoholic wife Miranda. But the scheme fails—as do those of the interfering idealists in Ibsen's *The Wild Duck* and O'Neill's *The Iceman Cometh*. The result of the fresh air is to cause Professor Searle to have a breakdown. We are not shown Elspeth's reaction to the news of this, so that we do not know whether she is capable of learning from the experience. There has been a strong implication that jealousy of Miranda has played a part in her motivation. At all events, the placing of the story first suggests the writer's reminder to himself that relationships are complex and his urge to "interfere" through the medium of his art may well have its own dangers. Insight in these cases needs to be reached through sensitivity and intelligence.

Does the implication of this attitude lead to the kind of detachment shown in someone like Mrs Rackham in **"Et Dona Ferentes"**? "Fond as I am of Monica, I wouldn't be able to help, whatever may be wrong . . . She turned to her book, then laughed out loud as it came to her how little even she had profited from her reading. Let me remember Miss Woodhouse's folly in interfering in the affairs of others, she said, and began her twenty-third reading of *Emma*." Here, as often in these stories, the reader is given little help in deciding on the merits of the attitude described. But Mrs Rackham's detachment is mirrored in her grandson Richard, busy with *The Possessed,* who sees himself unable to help his mother when the crisis occurs: "I've failed again, thought Richard. When I was reading about Stefan Trofimovich's death, I wanted to be there so that I could make him happy, to tell him that for all his faults I knew he was a good man. But when my own mother is in trouble I can't say anything." In this crisis Mrs Rackham behaves decisively and effectively, but she has no awareness of the real situation, while Richard feels powerless to help in real life—"No, I must always be shut in like this." There is a suggestion that human beings *ought* to be able to help one another through their problems, but an even stronger sense of the difficulty of doing so.

Nevertheless there is a strong urge towards judgement in these stories—mostly the satirist's negative judgement on the patterns of life he sees around him. This is usually only implicit, though it sometimes becomes explicit, as in **"Saturnalia",** with the statement, "The Colonel's lady and Lily O'Grady were both 'lumpen' under the skin." In **"The Wrong Set",** the whole narrative moves into Vi's final judgement on what has happened to her student nephew, Norman, which she expresses in her warning telegram to his mother: "Terribly worried. Norman in the Wrong Set. Vi." The fact that the reader has seen that it is the unfortunate Vi, trying to keep up a "Mayfair" front when dismissed from her job as pianist at the Passion Fruit Club, who is in a bad set, exploited by all around her, creates an

effective irony. But this does not totally undermine the possibility of right judgement—after all, the reader could not enjoy the irony if he were not making a different judgement of his own: it serves rather to show again the necessity for intelligent and sensitive discrimination.

The reader is led to participate in such a process in the deepest of these stories—**"A Story of Historical Interest"**, **"Crazy Crowd"**, **"Mother's Sense of Fun"**, and **"Et Dona Ferentes"**. The first of these is perhaps the best, in the series of readjustments which the reader is led to make to his judgements. At first we are nearest to Lois Gorringe's point of view. The story is told from close to her consciousness, which has the effect of giving initial authority to her responses. As she travels in the ambulance with her seriously ill father and her brother Harold, we share her recollections of the terrible three days since her father's stroke had brought her back from the office to the hotel where she had been looking after him, and how her awkwardness as a nurse had caused him pain and anger. At this stage we see Lois as determinedly unselfish, feeling for her father "a deep, almost maternal love", but prevented from expressing it effectively by her clumsiness. She has looked after the old man since her mother's death, deliberately cultivating a gaiety which has made him call her "Daddy's Little Pal". We share her sense that it is unfair that the jolly young Irish nurse should have gained her father's approval so easily with her gentle plump hands. We are made more sympathetic to Lois by her evidently painful memories of Mr Gorringe's unfaithfulness to her mother, and by her effort to be kind to the nurse. As she goes over in her mind the story of how she is looking after her father, while her brother Harold begrudges the money he sends and wants to take the old man off to live with him in Tunbridge Wells ("he would have hated it, away from the West End, his poker and his racing, treated like an old dependent"), Lois appears humane and unselfish.

But Lois's reaction to the discovery that the note the nurse had asked her to give to the doctor contains a declaration of love to him—"My God, how disgusting!"—seems excessive, and we begin to reassess our view of the situation. Nevertheless she retains our sympathy in the next two scenes, with the manageress of the hotel where they have been living, and with the doctor, mainly because in both cases Lois is the victim of arrogance. Mrs Cooper is ruthless in getting rid of her now unwanted guests—"Shall we say not later than a week from today?"—and Dr Filby is off-hand and unconcerned. (Wilson always writes strongly against the inconsiderateness or cruelty of those in positions of power.) As the ambulance moves away from London into the country, we discover that Harold is uneasy about the arrangement he has made for his father to go to live with a Miss Wheeler, who normally looks after unwanted babies. Harold does not disguise the fact that he has chosen this because the nursing homes were too expensive, and again we share something of Lois's indignation. We also share her impatience in the next scene, when she is delayed in going to bed by the vacuous conversation of her enormous and greedy sister-in-law Daisy. Daisy's insensitivity is conveyed by the tone of her remark, "Poor old Lois . . . too bad, my dear. Never mind, we'll be taking the burden on now."

The story then moves rapidly to its end. The next morning Mr Gorringe is found to be much better, spruce and cheerful. He is on good terms with Miss Wheeler ("She cuts my beard and I give her the winner of the 2.30") and is even enjoying the babies' company. He talks affably to Daisy, and is puzzled by Lois's suggestion that she will help him to get away if he doesn't like it: "Don't you worry your head, girlie . . . the old woman's a very decent sort. You ought to be cutting back to town, you don't want to upset them at the office." There is nothing for Lois to do except leave. By this time our view of the whole situation has changed. We are inclined now, with hindsight, to think of Lois's *ménage* with her father as something she had created for her own benefit rather than his. When we see Mr Gorringe settling down happily with Miss Wheeler, we realise that Lois had exaggerated his need for London—had even perhaps encouraged his independence from Harold and Daisy in order to give herself a satisfying social role.

The story ends with Lois back in London, about to go out with a friend. Daisy telephones to say that Mr Gorringe is probably dying, and is surprised that Lois does not want to go down to see him unless he definitely asks for her. Rather, she wants to go out: "I'm rather in the mood to meet hundreds of interesting, new people." We may partly share Daisy's puzzlement, even shock, at Lois's apparent callousness—"It's really only of historical interest." But the story is subtle enough for us also to feel relief and hope on Lois's part. In one sense her looking after her father had been an emotional prop; in another it had been a prison, from which she may now be emerging into life. Looking back at the whole story we can see that neither Lois nor Harold is heroic, but neither is evil. Harold had chosen Miss Wheeler partly for her cheapness, though it has worked out fortunately. Lois had done her duty as she understood it, though it was contrary to some of her inclinations and made for an arid self-righteousness. Simple judgements are inadequate because those involved are human beings with complex needs and potentialities. The changing pattern of the reader's feelings about Lois is a kind of moral education. This process is characteristic of reading the best of the longer stories in the volume.

Wilson suggested in *The Wild Garden* that the main preoccupation of these stories was "the falsity of preserved innocence or ignorance"—in Vi's thoughtless evaluations in **"The Wrong Set"**, in the hero's detached superiority in **"Crazy Crowd"**, in the deliberate childishness of the sisters, shared to some extent by the real child Johnnie, in **"Raspberry Jam"**. In this story Wilson felt that his conscious intention had been to draw a simple contrast between the innocence of the old ladies and the philistinism of the surrounding world, a kind of "protective falsehood", but that in the event "the shape of the narrative denies this falsification". Perhaps the violence of the story, which has shocked many readers, especially because it concerns the torturing of a bullfinch, is related to the sisters' refusal to

grow up. In fact, the bright worldliness of the conversation in Johnnie's home and the child's ignored sensitivity initially lead one to favour the old ladies, who are sympathetic to him. But the horrific dénouement does suggest that the villagers' suspicion of and hostility to them has some justification. On the other hand, what disturbs the reader most is not even the hideous death of the bird so much as Johnnie's response to it. The narrative neatly separates the two, so that before the latter is described we have Johnnie's ashamed reflections:

> Johnnie had sworn to himself to stand by them and to fight the wicked people who said they were old and useless and in the way. But now, since that dreadful tea-party, he could not fight for them any longer, for he knew why they had been shut up and felt that it was justified. In a sense, too, he understood that it was to protect others that they had to be restrained, for the most awful memory of that terrifying afternoon was the thought that he had shared with pleasure for a moment in their wicked game.

Here Wilson touches on a deep and disturbing level of human response to the infliction of pain, a sadism which he discerns within a particularly sensitive child. The shortness of the story does not allow the development which he gives to this theme in Bernard Sands in *Hemlock and After,* and so leaves the reader with the unpleasant taste of human cruelty which, though not condoned, is shown to have its own appalling appeal. The sisters can be taken off to some kind of hospital, but what about Johnnie's future? The story shows Wilson's early preoccupation with the problem of evil, and so links with much of his later writing.

It may well be argued, however, that the short story is not a suitable form for exploring so profound an area. Wilson himself sees the form in *The Wild Garden* as limiting, referring to "the short story with its snap ending echoing the ironic title", having suggested that his stories mostly took their origin in a phrase or word remembered for its "ironic ring", like "the wrong set" itself. The short story has not always been used in this way—Chekhov, Lawrence and Virginia Woolf, for instance, all used it more freely—though no doubt the discipline was helpful to Wilson as someone beginning his writing career. But the neatness of the titles does sometimes have restrictive effects which contradict the flexibility of mind which is called for in response to the best of them. This is more the case when the title seems imposed on the experience rather than growing—like "the wrong set" or "crazy crowd"—from the vocabulary of the characters themselves. For it is in his ability to register with accuracy the speech habits of his characters that Wilson's basic talent as a novelist lies—he himself calls it, . . . his "impressionistic mimicry . . . my principal natural asset as a writer".

This is particularly emphasised in **"Mother's Sense of Fun"**, when Donald Carrington's resentment of the maternal bonds from which he feels unable to escape is conveyed through his memories of her vocabulary and turns of phrase:

It always "rained cats and dogs", that is if the rain did not "look like holding off"; Alice Stockfield was "a bit down in the mouth", but then "she let things get on top of her"; Roger Grant was "certainly no Adonis", but she had "an awfully soft spot in her heart for him". At the end of a tiring day he would often wait for one of these familiar phrases, for he knew that criticism would be met by wounded silence, or the slow, crushing steam-roller of her banter, the terrible levelling force of her sense of humour. She and Cook were having a "good old laugh" at that very moment.

Donald feels that the words his mother uses "were surely specially designed to rob the English language of any pretensions to beauty it might possess". But it may be felt that Wilson is employing a dangerous procedure when he allows what amounts to moral discrimination to depend on such a matter as the use of clichés; is he merely implying, as some critical readers have felt, that "the right people", those who can use language conventionally and have a smart life-style to match, are justified in looking down on those who don't? It would be a very serious criticism if valid, but I do not feel that it is. Wilson is not criticising people who use language in an uneducated or uncultured way; he is attacking those who, by whatever methods, impose themselves unscrupulously on others. In this story we are made to feel very strongly Mrs Carrington's selfishness, unsuccessfully screened by her jollity of manner. But we do not feel much respect either for Donald, her twenty-five-year-old son, back from a six-month lecture tour in America, who makes no effort to free himself from the bondage of their relationship. His use of language may be superior to hers, but he refrains altogether from using it to break up the situation, from which he is partially "rescued" only by her death.

The mimicry, then, enables Wilson to make his characters speak in impressive variety. In **"Saturnalia"**, describing a New Year's Eve dance in a "bright" South Kensington hotel in 1931, the staff and guests are mixed. Their speech varies from Mrs Hennessy's drawling, "What shall I do with this man of yours? He keeps saying the most impossible things", through Bruce Talfourd Rich's "Pipe down, kiddie, pipe down" and Sir Charles' senile quotation of Francis Thompson: "Fear wist not to evade as love wist to pursue", to Tom the porter's blarneying, "I think it is that beautiful look of yours in your lovely white dress that's brought out the lilt in me", and the waitress Gloria's "You silly old cow. You won't send me away, you won't, not on your ruddy life." All these tones contribute to the creation of a story which successfully embodies the tensions of the English class situation at the beginning of the Thirties (the only story clearly set earlier is **"Union Reunion"**, which takes place in 1924). John Mander in *The Writer and Commitment* (1961) saw Wilson as a writer similar to those of the Thirties, like Auden, who based their values on Marx and Freud in an unstable combination, but he felt that **"Saturnalia"** was successful in fusing the social and psychological elements which remained separate in other stories. For him, "Mr Wilson's shabby Kensington hotel is England's class-war in miniature." Certainly Wilson succeeds in conveying the tensions of a divided culture in vivid relief.

Mr Mander suggests that "Mr Wilson's own values in these stories are . . . very much those of the Thirties", even when the subject-matter is post-war. Wilson is certainly critical of the young son Hamish in **"Crazy Crowd"**, with his ultra-traditionalist rhetoric: "We have privileges and we must act accordingly by setting an example to our inferiors." One feels his sympathy for Mrs Thursby in **"The Wrong Set"**, "the little dowdy bright-eyed woman" with her pacifist husband and belief in the Labour Government. But basically Wilson's values are those of the liberal, siding with those who are exploited whether socially or psychologically. Two of the best and shortest stories are **"Realpolitik"** and **"A Visit in Bad Taste"**. In the former, Wilson shows a new curator taking over a provincial gallery and, with his administrative ability and ruthless determination, brilliantly defeating the opposition of his three more highly principled assistants in a single meeting. He carries all the weapons necessary for success: self-confidence, business support, insensitivity. But the story makes us feel that well-meaning if muddled enthusiasts and scholars like the discomfited staff of the gallery are less dangerous than the new men, the meritocracy, which was busily taking over the running of that institution—and so much else since. Finally, in **"A Visit in Bad Taste"**, Wilson gives a chilling picture of how high principles can blend into selfishness. Malcolm and Margaret Tarrant are well-off and read "the progressive weeklies". When Margaret's brother Arthur comes out of prison for offences against children he comes to them, his nearest relations. Margaret sees the incongruity:

> "This isn't his kind of house." She thought with pleasure of all they had built up—the taste, the tolerance, the ease of living, the lack of dogmatism . . . Arthur had no place here.

The uneasy Arthur, with his over-pressed suit, his too "club" tie, his over-brilliantined hair, does not fit into this décor, and so must be asked to leave. The ending of the story is brilliant. Malcolm tries to comfort his conscience with the suggestion that Arthur will "find happiness somewhere", but Margaret denies this, saying they must face the truth that he is rotten and dead:

> Malcolm stared at his wife with admiration—to face reality, that was obviously the way to meet these things, not to try to escape. He thought for a few minutes of what she had said—of Arthur's rottenness—socially and personally—and of all that they stood for—individually alive, socially progressive. But for all the realism of her view, it somehow did not satisfy him. He remained vaguely uneasy the whole evening.

Wilson is powerfully critical of the "realism" which ignores individual human beings and culminates in *realpolitik*: this is one of his consistent themes. But he is also devastating in his exposure of those liberals and progressives who, whether wittingly or unwittingly, show by their deeds that their values are no better than those of the people whom they despise.

The success of *The Wrong Set*—the first impression was exhausted in a fortnight and the reviews were largely favourable—meant that Secker & Warburg had no hesitation in publishing a second volume of short stories, *Such Darling Dodos,* in the following year, 1950. Of these eleven stories, three had been previously published. It is not surprising that within so short a period of time there should be a marked similarity between the two volumes, both containing a high proportion of stories dealing with family situations, and with the way in which human relations can become forms of bondage. Wilson has suggested in *The Wild Garden* that he was moving in these years from concern with experiences deriving from his childhood and youth in the raffish world of seedy hotels and struggling clubs to the "blinkered innocence" of more intellectual characters. The raffish hotel would survive in *Such Darling Dodos* off-stage, as it were, but it is no longer the focus of attention. The two most immediately impressive stories for their social and psychological insight are the title story and **"What Do Hippos Eat?"**. Mr Mander states that in the latter Wilson achieves "a depth and delicacy of social analysis that no left-wing writer of the Thirties approaches", and he thinks even more highly of the former.

"Such Darling Dodos" is certainly an excellent story, whose brevity encompasses a great deal of accurate social observation. Basically the story concerns the changes of attitude that marked the post-war years. The elderly bachelor Tony represents everything that his Oxford cousins, Robin and Priscilla Harker, had despised in the left-wing atmosphere of the Thirties. Now he has come to visit his cousins, responding to a hysterical letter from the normally sensible Priscilla, shocked at news of her husband's terminal illness. A Roman Catholic, Tony has come to do his spiritual duty so that, absurd as he is, we cannot wholly despise him. At the heart of the story is the contrast between his values and those of his progressive cousins, expressed at one point in open discussion:

> "I'm afraid, though, Tony, that I remain satisfied not with the amount I have done, God forbid, but with the kind."

> "Satisfied with drains and baths and refrigerators?" Tony asked.

> "Yes," said Robin, "only with more of them and better ones, and with sickness benefits and secure old age and works committees and," here he smiled again, "the just wage. Strangely enough I did re-read William James the other day, but I'm sorry to say that in all the welter of religious experience I could find nothing to accord with anything I had ever known. I'm sorry, Tony."

However, when an ex-service couple, now students, come to lunch, it is the Harkers' turn to be discomfited, while Tony discovers to his surprise and pleasure that it is he who is now up-to-date: "at last *he* was on youth's side". He can afford to patronise his outmoded cousins in the phrase that gives the story its title.

In *The Wild Garden* Wilson reminds us that his attack here is once again on "preserved innocence", but that the

Harkers represent "not false standards, but *insufficient* standards"—although right, they and their view of life lack "poetry". While this is no doubt true, it is doubtful whether the reader feels that the Harkers are being severely criticised in the story. They are clearly people of good will whose main fault is a kind of puritanical joylessness, and the sense of the pathos of their condition—they are presented as lonely survivors of the Thirties in a world contemptuous of their cherished beliefs—is stronger than any criticism of them. We cannot hold them responsible for the direction events have taken, and they appeal to us more than the sybaritic and rather silly Tony, and the rigid young Ecclestons.

The impressiveness of **"Such Darling Dodos"** is located partly in the convincing quality of the social observation, including the North Oxford setting and the principal characters. We are convinced by Wilson's account of these people that we are being shown a piece of social history. But this view of the story must be regarded with caution, for it is easy to jump from the convincingness of the Ecclestons to a belief in their representativeness. Yet that is a matter open to dispute—many ex-servicemen were keen Labour supporters, in fact: how many, only social investigation could establish. This is only to say that we must not allow the quality of Wilson's social reporting to mislead us into thinking that it possesses objective status. The quality by which the story finally stands is a matter of its internal consistency: Priscilla in "her blue linen dress with its long full skirt", Tony, "almost a slim young man in his wellcut tweeds", but for "a strange stiffness in the legs", Robin, emaciated, "even his feet looked pitifully long in their leather sandals"—each is totally convincing, as is Tony's youthful background reading of Richard Le Gallienne, Beardsley's *Volpone* and Dowson's poems. It is because such references are accurate that we are convinced by the story. And the final crystallisation—Tony "hadn't felt so modern since the first production of *L'Après-Midi*"—is a perfect and witty fulfilment of the reader's expectations.

"What Do Hippos Eat?" is equally accurate in its social observation of the ex-officer of the Great War and his youngish Earls Court landlady having a day out at the zoo, but the main interest is in the relationship of the incongruous couple. Each is seeking to gain from the situation, Maurice financially and Greta in having a socially superior man who can teach her manners that will help her climb up the economic ladder. But the story is not simply that of two tough people ruthlessly exploiting each other. Rather do we see two lonely people needing help and affection. That the quality of what each can offer, and so receive, is tarnished, does not totally discredit it. Indeed, we are led to reflect, all human relationships have their elements of mutual need. But a relationship so largely based on different expectations is bound to produce misunderstandings, and the story is neatly ended by an almost poignant example. In humiliation and anger, Maurice is only just able to restrain himself from pushing Greta into the hippo's pool; Greta, thinking the gesture an amorous one, "was really rather touched". The story does not possess particularly striking sociological significance, though it could be said to exemplify two criss-crossing types of social mobility. But it is a convincing and interesting story in human terms, and it shows that Wilson does not have to depend for his success on presenting characters whose despicableness he can complacently demonstrate.

"Learning's Little Tribute" does have elements of satire, especially in the first part, at the funeral of Hugh Craddock, contributor on Art to Mr Brinton's grand encyclopaedia. Wilson is unable to restrain his dislike of the assistant editor, Dr Earley, with his "unctuous Cockney whine" and his two Chadband characteristics—"his morbid curiosity and his histrionic moralising". The rest of the staff of the encyclopaedia, including its proprietor, can hardly fail to seem agreeable if grotesque by comparison. But it is in the person of Hugh Craddock's widow that ordinary humanity enters the story, rapidly dissipating the staff's mood of condescending and calculating commiseration by her common sense. The offer of an appointment for her daughter is rapidly dismissed—"You see . . . really good qualifications are so important in scholarly work today"—and similarly one for her son. As for the suggestion that she should herself help out as a part-time secretary, this is not even proposed since she has already explained her intention of turning her house into lodgings for students. Mr Brinton is disgusted at having his plans pushed aside and is rude to her, but she is equal to him:

> "Well, of all the mean things," she said, "now I know why Hugh looked so low sometimes." She was about to add something more sharp, when she cried out "Oh! Lord, what's the good?" and gathering her handbag to her she went quickly out of the room, leaving behind her a trail of Californian Poppy.

As we are left with Dr Earley's self-deceiving and pompous remarks at the end, our thoughts return with relief to Mrs Craddock, "with her common accent and her flashy clothes", who nevertheless embodies human values which we must respect. This story is important evidence of the fact that Wilson distinguishes clearly between intellectual, social and moral qualities.

A group of stories in **Such Darling Dodos** introduces a note of macabre fantasy hardly noticeable in the earlier volume. The short story has often been used by English and American writers for supernatural effects that could not be sustained in longer works, and Wilson follows this tradition in **"A Little Companion"** and **"Totentanz"**. Two other stories, **"Necessity's Child"** and **"Mummy to the Rescue"**, also introduce a new, more deliberately poetic and subjective note. **"Necessity's Child"**—referred to by Wilson as "self-pitying" [in *The Wild Garden*]—is unusual for him in being a first-person narrative, that of a lonely thirteen-year-old boy who resembles the sensitive Johnnie of **"Raspberry Jam"**. Rodney is an imaginative child, a great reader of stories, despised in the family for his inability to swim and play games. ("'I'm not having Rodney on our side,' she said, 'I want to win.'") His well-meaning Aunt Eileen is too foolish to be much of an ally, and it is not surprising that he should make up fantastic stories about people he meets during the day. An old gentleman

who talks to him enthusiastically about books is described to the credulous aunt as having shown him "horrible, beastly pictures". The story ends with one of the few passages in these stories that is not immediately obvious in meaning. In it Rodney is describing, in lavish prose, his survival on a raft in the Pacific Ocean, after Mummy and Daddy have gone down with the ship. In the previous episode we have learnt that they are planning to go to Paris, leaving Rodney with his house-master at Uppingham, an arrangement which he deeply resents. Now he has his revenge, for what it is worth:

> Mummy and Daddy have gone down with the ship. It crashed and broke against the glass-green wall [we are now in the Atlantic], the name *Titanic* staring forth in red letters as it reared into the air. Mummy's black evening dress floated on the surface of the water and her shoulder showed white as she was sucked down. But I am left alone, tied to the raft, numbed, frozen, choking with the cold, or again, as it sails relentlessly on towards the next floating green giant, dashing me to pieces against ice as I fight with the ropes too securely tied.

These "ropes too securely tied" neatly represent one aspect of human relationships as Wilson presents them, but in **"Necessity's Child"** the effect is one of contrivance and strain, which is not felt in the more objective accounts of social experience.

Yet that Wilson was impelled at this stage to seek a more inward method is suggested by the parallel, though more appalling, events of **"Mummy to the Rescue"**. Even in the first, more normal, part of this story the grotesque element is noticeable. Nurse Ramsey—"an incongruous figure in her friend Marjorie's dainty room"—draws her legs apart, "displaying the thick grey of her winter knickers", while the dainty Marjorie busily wipes a chocolate stain from "her pretty *crêpe de Chine* frock, liberally soaking her little lace-bordered hanky with spittle to perform the task". Then we meet Nurse Ramsey's even more grotesque charge, Celia, clutching the doll she calls Mummy and, in her determination never to be separated, passing the doll's arms round her neck and knotting them to the bedpost behind her. Below, her grandparents, nearing senility, are considering whether they can afford to look after her any longer. In the next terrifying short section Celia is on the deck of a ship (her mother had left her to go on a ship all those years before). As the waves suddenly come to pull her down, she goes to Mummy for protection: "But Celia's Mummy's arms folded right round her neck, tighter and tighter." The physical pain is extreme as "the hands closed more and more tightly around her neck, crushing and pulping." Here Wilson is again giving an inward rendering of experience, rather than the observation which is his usual—and more successful—mode. The story ends by returning to the comparative normality of Nurse Ramsey, but does not let us off without describing the grotesque creature whose life has just come to an end. The characteristically neat rounding-off of the story seems less than appropriate here, for the disturbing feelings released by the narrative cannot be so easily controlled. Again, Wilson is attempting to express more powerful feelings than heretofore, but he has yet to find a successful way of doing so.

The two stories with more marked non-natural elements show Wilson extending his range in another way. **"A Little Companion"** is comparatively short, and concerns the arrival in the life of the apparently ordinary Miss Arkwright, a popular village spinster, of a "child" which addresses her as Mummy and refuses to leave her alone. The child's appearance is squalid—it has a "sickly, cretinous face"—quite unsuited to Miss Arkwright's "home of quiet beauty, unostentatious comfort, and restrained good taste". The woman is intelligent enough to see the child as "an emanation from the sick side of herself", but this does not make up for "dribble marks on her best dresses or for sticky finger marks on her tweed skirts". So she takes steps to get rid of the child, praying, asking the Bishop's help, going to London, trying Christian Science, taking purgatives, visiting spiritualists, travelling: she is only "saved" by a chance event in September 1939, but ironically finds that life without the unhealthy child is of no interest to her. Wilson again rounds his story off neatly with the vicar's verdict: "just another war victim". This leads us to consider the real causes of her decline, but the narrative does not offer a satisfactory answer. It could be said this is because the kind of rational, psychological answers one is expecting are being shown as inadequate. Wilson wants to suggest the presence in human experience of some disturbing elements which cannot be simply explained. But the reader is inclined to feel that he is being offered a neat supernatural story rather than something deeper. Again, perhaps, the short story form is responsible for this, since it allows little development.

"Totentanz" begins in Wilson's social world, with satirically observed academic types and their wives reacting to the news that the Cappers are to leave the remote Scottish university for London. The tone is highly sardonic:

> On such a day even the most mildewed and disappointed of the professors, the most blue and deadening of their wives, felt impulses of generosity, or at any rate a freedom from bitterness, that allowed them to rejoice at a fellow-prisoner's release. Only the youngest and most naïve research students could be deceived by the sun into brushing the mould off their *own* hopes and ideals, but if others had found a way back to their aims, well, good luck to them!—in any case the Cappers, especially Mrs Capper, had only disturbed the general morass with their futile struggles, most people would be glad to see them go.

The imagery of mildew and the morass gives a totally negative impression, and the Cappers emerge from it already somewhat blighted, Brian with his "hard, boyish charm" leaping a deck-chair to speak to an influential businessman, Isobel with her "combination of chic and Liberty artiness". At first the Cappers do well in London, Isobel working hard to cultivate the right people and ending with Professor Cadaver, authority on tombs, Lady Maude, the greedy aesthete, and Guy Rice, the clever "camp" decorator. When the grotesque will of the uncle who has left her the large Portman Square house which is

to be the centre of her social success is proved, a crisis occurs: memorials of the deceased aunt and uncle, each seven foot high in white marble "in the most exaggeratedly modern good taste by an amateur craftsman, a long way after Eric Gill" must be set in the room in which they entertain their friends. Guy's bright idea to cope with that is that their first party should be a Totentanz, with "everything morbid and ghostly".

The final movement of the story opens impressively: "The Totentanz was Isobel's greatest, alas! her last, triumph." Wilson describes the décor with entertaining panache, and the costumes of the guests live up to expectations: Mrs Mule is a Vampire, Lady Maude Marie Antoinette, shaved for the guillotine, Professor Cadaver a Corpse Eater, Guy the Suicide of Chatterton. It is Guy's comment which points towards the conclusion of the story: "I mean all this fun *is* rather hell when it comes to the point, isn't it?" The Totentanz leads in reality to the death it had been trying to render amusing: Guy takes an overdose, Lady Maude is assaulted with an axe by a burglar, Professor Cadaver falls into a freshly dug grave and breaks his neck. As a result, Isobel's social career is finished. She survives in a house increasingly filled with Brian's students, occasionally looking at the statues "with a look of mute appeal" that is not answered. A final commentary from Scotland emphasises the deathliness of it all. **"Totentanz"** is the blackest of all Wilson's comic stories, and for all its macabre verve it remains an uneasy combination of the grotesque and the realistic. We are not interested enough in any of the characters to see it as more than the *tour de force* which it undoubtedly is.

Yet **"Totentanz"** and the other stories in the volume in which the grotesque plays a larger role suggest the presence in Wilson's sensibility of an element which criticism cannot ignore. In Mr Mander's view it is to be regretted as confusing Wilson's aims, leading him away from the firm political discriminations which his satirical powers enable him to enforce. This is a cogent view, but it may be felt to narrow Wilson's world. More persuasive now is Malcolm Bradbury's argument in "The Short Stories of Angus Wilson" [in *Studies in Short Fiction* III, Winter 1966] that Wilson's creative energy is bound up with the co-existence in him of the liberal moralist and the celebrator of the grotesque. Professor Bradbury suggests that Wilson's depiction of the grotesque is not satirical because "he appeals to our sense of the essential pathos of most human roles and relationships", so that "the inadequate posturings that are on the one hand feasible objects of satire are also the assertion of some grit or energy by means of which life continues possible." This is excellently said, as is the remark that "his comedy is not . . . defined unless we say that it involves us in ironic ambiguities that contain distinctive kinds of hope and despair." Wilson's sensibility exhibits kinship here with those modern dramatists whom we associate with J. L. Styan's definition of "dark comedy" [as stated in *The Dark Comedy*, 1962]. The co-existence of these attitudes may sometimes make the stories confusing, but usually the energy which seems to consort in Wilson with his skilled mimicry of tones of voice animates the observed world. The world is one in which freedom is valued but seldom enjoyed, and in which human ingenuity is exerted more often in self-defeating strategies of self-protection than in successful creative activities of any kind. The moralist in Wilson regards this world with sardonic compassion, the mimic with delighted awareness of the chance it offers for his talents.

Satire or Social Comedy?:

Angus Wilson's *The Wrong Set* (1949), a collection of thirteen stories only three of which had previously been published in magazines, signaled the arrival of a major new talent. Wilson's forte, an abbreviated comedy of manners, is ultimately predicated on the social upheavals that occurred in Britain after World War II. Wilson (1913-) presents us with an array of vulgar or eccentric people, all of them, however, totally believable; the tone is generally one of slightly amused detachment, . . . but readers will, to varying degrees, discern some acidulous commentary beneath the flat, precise tones. Certainly Wilson is not on the side of vulgarity, sham, pretension, decadence, and hypocrisy; but the question remains open whether the moral bias is sufficiently present so that Wilson should be classified a satirist. Whether he is writing satire or social comedy, however, the accuracy of his work, combined with a ruthless irony, results in some of the most consistently witty stories of the period [1945-1950].

> Dennis Vannatta, in The English Short Story
> 1945-1980: A Critical History,
> *Twayne Publishers, 1985.*

Although short stories are not usually highly regarded in England, the volumes were well received. It was a period still dominated by older writers like Graham Greene, Evelyn Waugh and L. P. Hartley, and a ready welcome was available to a new generation—as became clearer with the reception of Kingsley Amis, John Osborne and Colin Wilson a few years later. Kenneth Allsop, in his account of the Fifties, *The Angry Decade* (1958)—a perceptive if melodramatic work—saw Wilson, like Anthony Powell and V. S. Pritchett, as an acute but detached observer of the period:

> Wonderfully accurate and authentic though he is, Wilson watches from the outside, from the liberal-humanist view point of someone born in 1913 and brought up in a home where there were servants and music and bank accounts.

But whatever the extent of his detachment, Wilson struck readers in 1949 and 1950 as a new voice representing a new attitude which was generally welcomed in the bland cultural world of the time. The influential American critic, Edmund Wilson [writing in *The New Yorker*, 15 April 1950], saw him as a possible successor to Evelyn Waugh, though focusing on a poorer and therefore more aggressive social group, and described him as not "so pleasantly assimilable as the usual British product":

> He seems, for better or worse, to represent something

that is quite distinct from the well-bred and well-turned entertainment that we have lately been getting from England.

Perhaps Wilson was fortunate to begin being published at that particular time, when there was a dearth of new British writers; certainly he soon began to establish his literary reputation, and to become an accepted reviewer and contributor to the BBC's Third Programme. Seán O'Faoláin had welcomed *The Wrong Set* with high praise in *The Listener* [XLI (7 April 1949)], suggesting that Wilson was bound for success. He also noted that some of Wilson's writing belonged "rather to the expansiveness of the novel than the compressed absorption of the short story". It was by turning to the novel that Wilson was next to try to solve the problem of expressing in fiction his sense of evil and his feeling for society.

Averil Gardner (essay date 1985)

SOURCE: "'Trifle Angus Wilson': Two Volumes of Short Stories" in *Angus Wilson*, Twayne Publishers, 1985, pp. 12-34.

[*Gardner is an English-born Canadian educator and critic. In this excerpt from her book-length study of Wilson, she discusses* The Wrong Set *and* Such Darling Dodos.]

"Mr. Wilson is a satirist," roundly declared an anonymous reviewer when *The Wrong Set* appeared in 1949. Since many of its stories, and many of those in *Such Darling Dodos* (1950), are lively, sharp, observant, and particularly concerned with social relationships and social class, it is not very surprising that they should have prompted a reviewer, pressed for time and space, to use this convenient label. "Satire" is also a term that Wilson himself employs quite frequently in *The Wild Garden* when discussing his early work.

At the same time, however, Wilson has denied any idea that satirizing people is the whole of his intention and it is apparent that he attaches little theoretical weight to his use of the term *satire*. As he indicated to Michael Millgate in 1957, satire for him "implies an abstract philosophy that I don't have" [Wilson, in an interview by Michael Millgate, *Paris Review*, 1957]. Though an acute commentator on human behavior, he is neither out to change it nor is he in general malicious about it. Wilson himself prefers to think of his work as "comedy of manners" [Millgate interview] and it would be a strange reader who rarely found anything to laugh at in the short stories; but they often mingle pathos with their comedy, sometimes provoking a nice mixture of distaste and sympathy in response to one and the same character or situation. And there are times when his chosen term "comedy of manners" cannot be accepted at all: stories like **"Raspberry Jam," "Mummy to the Rescue,"** and **"Necessity's Child"** are not in the least funny.

Most of Wilson's short stories, which are largely a fictional expression of elements in his learning and working life up to the end of World War II, belong to the first few years of his life as a writer from 1946 onwards. He turned first to the short story for the simplest of practical reasons: as a full-time official of the British Museum he lacked the leisure for extended production. Short stories could be written in a weekend and even, as in the case of **"Raspberry Jam,"** in a day. A sense of glibness and falsity is rarely, however, the impression these quickly written stories create. Rather, one has the feeling of an imaginative ferment, of material saved up for years and suddenly brought into focus.

In a review, published in 1954, of the work of other short-story writers Wilson indicated clearly the kind of short story, in a technical sense, that he himself had been trying to write. A keen admirer of Elizabeth Bowen, he agreed with her contention that the short story, as a form, is nearer to the play and the poem than to the novel. Like the play, it needs to be compressed, and involves "climax, surprise and other directly artful methods of presentation"; like the poem, it uses "allusion, symbolism and overtone." While admitting the influence of this view from the mid-1930s onwards, Wilson felt bound to point out that the situation in the first three decades of the century had been otherwise, the short story following the novel in changing from a storytelling medium into a vehicle for interior consciousness:

> The classic short story of Mr. Maugham's era, with its emphasis on narrative and surprise, proved too tight to convey the flow of sensitivity which to Katherine Mansfield was the essence both of art and life. By injecting greater sublety of mood and deeper levels of consciousness, she almost succeeded in destroying the form and reducing short stories to "sketches" [*Spectator* 198 (1 October 1954)].

The efforts of short-story writers since 1939, Wilson said, had been directed to "trying to tie the two threads together"—the two threads being narrative form and significant emotional content. Thus, in effect, the view of the short story expressed by Elizabeth Bowen almost as an article of faith was in fact the hard-won result of a shift in literary taste, of which Wilson's short stories are a part. They mix, in varying proportions, the devices of drama and poetry, and attempt to combine the forward movement of story with the revelation of personality by means of thought processes.

The Wrong Set (1949)

Angus Wilson also spoke, in the review already referred to, of the need for a collection of short stories to hang together, to have some sort of unity. Of the collections he was reviewing, he singled out Louis Auchincloss's *The Romantic Egoists* as the best in this respect. Wilson, a liberal humanist, did not approve of Auchincloss's "arrogant, neo-aristocratic" outlook, but it had had a good effect artistically, producing a book of stories with "a strict social framework and a convinced social standpoint." The coherence of Wilson's own earliest collections, both *The*

Wrong Set and *Such Darling Dodos,* is equally recognizable, though his middle-class framework is fluid rather than strict, and his social standpoint, that of a convinced liberal with an instinct for tolerance, allows for the inspection and questioning of values rather than for their dogmatic presentation. A characteristic conformation of Wilson's stories was pointed out by Kingsley Amis in 1957: "his subject is most often the explosions and embarrassments touched off when people of different class, training or culture are made to confront one another" [*Spectator,* 18 October 1957]. There is also in his work a clash of generations: on the personal level, between child and adult; on the public level, brought about by the social and political changes that gradually took place as the middle-class world in which Wilson grew up emotionally was displaced by the postwar triumph—as it then seemed—of the left-wing ideas he had espoused intellectually.

The unity of Wilson's short stories lies essentially in their atmosphere and their milieu, which are characterized by personal uncertainty, social precariousness, and an emotional ambivalence that allows incidents and persons to be funny and pathetic at the same time. A further cognate element in them, commented on by Wilson himself in 1963 [in *The Wild Garden*], is a "pervasive raffishness," the source of which was his own experience of "reduced" gentlewoman in Kensington hotels and "old school tie" men down on their luck. (One of Wilson's brothers had had to sell vacuum cleaners door to door after World War I.). . .

"Saturnalia," set at a staff-and-residents' dance in a small hotel in South Kensington on New Year's Eve, 1931, indicates the loosening effects of drink on the prewar class structure. The social spectrum ranges from a retired Colonial governor who quotes Greek and unsuccessfully pursues a good-looking page, down to Gloria, the pretty waitress who gets fondled by Bruce Talfourd-Rich, and Tom, the handsome Irish porter who almost succeeds in "making" Bruce's "injured wife," Claire, a woman tempted by thoughts of Lady Chatterley's lover while trying to maintain "a Knightsbridge exterior with a Kensington purse." The precarious pivot of this not-very-merry social roundabout is Stella Hennessy, who has "buckled to" after the economic crash and manages the hotel in order to maintain her son at public school. The cost to her of her sacrifice and "drudgery," in terms of internal coarsening, is economically suggested by the contrast between the "dove grey tulle" she wears and the hardness of her eyes, like "boot buttons," when she snubs Tom's blarneying advances: her new position, on the edge of gentility, seems too close to his for comfort. The claustrophobia and increasing heat of the evening are well conveyed by the dense look on the page of its long paragraphs, packed with snatches of dialogue and fleeting thoughts—a technique that Wilson also employs in **"Crazy Crowd"** to express Peter's sexual tension, trapped among the uncongenial Cockshutts. In both stories, as in several others, there is explosive release of the built-up tension in verbal violence which gives an almost orgasmic pleasure to the reader: in **"Crazy Crowd"** Peter attacks his lover Jenny's self-satisfied approval of the "crazy" quality of her family by rejecting it as repellent, so furiously that she can only silence him by pulling him on top of her in a direct sexual advance. In **"Saturnalia"** Gloria rejects the high moral tone taken by Stella who, jealous of Gloria's greater success with Bruce, takes the opportunity of her drunkenness to dismiss her from the hotel: "You silly old cow . . . you won't send me away, you won't, not on your ruddy life. I know too much about you, my treasure, old Mother have me if you like Hennessy." At the end of **"Saturnalia"** a measure of order is restored when Claire dances with her husband, but the frustrations and antipathies of the crumbling social system have emerged unmistakably.

Wilson wrote **"Saturnalia"** in 1947, but set it in 1931 partly in order to exploit an ironic contrast between the past, when the middle classes and their protective social distinctions still had some meaning, and the present, in which they were becoming obsolete. The title story, **"The Wrong Set,"** is placed in the gray postwar Socialist world of clothing coupons and restricted foreign travel, in which earnest young students like Norman Hackett take part in Communist demonstrations and the faded remains of the old guard, represented by the moustached and monocled sponger, Major Trevor Cawston, eke out their existence between bed-sitting rooms in Earl's Court and sleazy Soho nightclubs in which they can tell snide stories about Prime Minister Attlee.

Though not hostile to either Norman or the disreputable Major, who at least know which social "set" they belong to, Wilson reserves most of his sympathy for the confused and good-hearted Vi, the pianist at the Passion Fruit Club, who is Norman's aunt and Trevor's mistress (and provider). Vi really belongs to neither set: to her working-class relatives she appears disreputable because she is not married to Trevor, while she aspires to the propriety of "wife" and clings to outmoded middle-class notions that "class told." Vi is in fact a social victim, expendable; but even when she loses her job—just after she has treated the club's Italian-cockney owner to a drink—she cannot perceive this. There is obvious irony in her telegraphed message to her sister that Norman is "in the Wrong Set," but she does not send it "to get some of her own back," as Jay L. Halio [in *Angus Wilson,* 1964], with uncharacteristic imperceptiveness, has written. Set adrift by the loss of her job, she may be seen as hanging on to a sense of her own identity by asserting her responsible role as aunt; she herself, in a semi-drunken mood of desperation that is both comical and moving, sees it as her "duty" as a "Conservative" to try to keep Norman out of "the hands of the Reds," and her final "Mayfair" attempts at dignity are impressive as well as pathetic.

"The Wrong Set" is a triumph of compression: its span of action covers only twenty-four hours, but its use of significant, sharply observed detail—not only at Vi's club but in Earl's Court and at Norman's lodgings in northwest London—enables Wilson to create in the space of ten pages a microcosm of changing British society. Even briefer, but also less comprehensive, is **"Realpolitik,"** which reveals in its title and its neat, dramatic form the cold winds blowing through the postwar world. John Hobday, a newly appointed art gallery curator, confronts with careerist efficiency the old department heads who despise his manner and methods. "Hardboiled" as these scholarly idealists are, their poor committee methods are no match for Hobday's ruthless incisiveness, a quality made worse by the false geniality that accompanies it.

A more moving clash of opposites occurs in the triangular situation of **"Fresh Air Fiend."** Here again, as with **"The Wrong Set"** and **"Realpolitik,"** a cliché of speech is taken as a title and given an ironic dimension in the story that follows. It is Elspeth Eccles, former pupil and now research assistant of Professor Searle, who wishes to open windows and let in some air; but though, unlike John Hobday, she does not inspire simple dislike, the unexpected result of her action, announced by a similar twist at the end, proves how disastrous, indeed how counterproductive, can be the attempts of the younger generation to cut through the protective facades maintained by their elders.

Professor Searle is perhaps the first example in Wilson's work of the liberal whose decent principles and instincts do not enable him to cope with family problems: Bernard Sands of *Hemlock and After* and Gerald Middleton of *Anglo-Saxon Attitudes* are more fully drawn versions of the type. Wilson's sympathy for him is conveyed partly in a private code—part of his research, shared with Elspeth, is on Shelley, who was "a much-loved hero figure" in Wilson's own "mythology"—but it is also evident in the guilt feelings that Searle expresses about his wife, Miranda, whose secret drinking is a consequence of her son's death and of the uncongenial life she has had to lead as the wife of an Oxford don. For Elspeth, the important problem is Searle's work, which he should be free to concentrate on: she hero-worships her professor and cannot bear to think of him as chained to the wreck of a former society beauty.

The tensions between Elspeth and Miranda, beautifully caught in their barbed, mutually patronizing exchanges in the garden, come to a head in the evening after dinner. Utterly drunk, Miranda interrupts her husband's tête-à-tête with Elspeth, making unworthy insinuations and accusing him of being "no great cop" in bed. The provocation results in Elspeth's slapping her face, Miranda's collapsing in tears, and, as is ironically revealed at the end, in Searle's subsequent nervous breakdown. The cause of this, we are left to infer, is not simply his own embarrassment, but distress that his wife's state should have been witnessed by a third party. His feelings had not "become hardened to the routine."

One is sorry for Searle; but Wilson's most instinctive sympathies seem to lie with Miranda, whose thwarted appetite for life has been channeled into gardening, and whose outrageous shocking of the "wretched middle-class norm" of other dons' wives he reports with relish. In Elspeth's attempts to draw her out—to get her, as Miranda scornfully puts it, to "share"—there is rather too much of the condescension of a social worker. Certainly her retort to Elspeth's new-fangled psychoanalytic jargon about a "well-adjusted view of life" carries a merited old-world sting: "'Adjusted' never connects with —'life' for me, only with —'shoulder strap.'"

The *Times Literary Supplement* review of *The Wrong Set* noted "passages strongly reminiscent of Virginia Woolf" [*Times* (London) *Literary Supplement*, March 26, 1949], and there is much truth in the observation. Wilson read a great deal of her work in adolescence, and though he said in 1957 [in the Millgate interview] that he was "in great reaction against" her, he also admitted that such reading could go very deep. His recurrent use of interior monologues, short or long, of the third-person and, less commonly, the first-person variety, indicates that it did. The first paragraph of **"Fresh Air Fiend"**—the first thing that a reader of Angus Wilson in 1947 would have encountered—is a good example, particularly in view of its telling use of the Woolfian pronoun "one." Miranda Searle, explicitly linked with Bloomsbury by being compared to Lady Ottoline Morrell, is discovered musing among her flowers: Woolfian style is used to describe a characteristic posture of the Virginia Woolf heroine.

Virginia Woolf's influence can also be felt in the long third-person interior monologues of Laura and Flo in the South African story **"Union Reunion."** In this story influence shades into literary parody in the first-person monologue of Minnie, which makes use of the "simple sentence" technique of *The Waves* in order to present a character who would be more at home in the pages of a Harlequin Romance:

> "If the Kaffirs attacked 'The Maples'" thought Minnie, "I should have no man to defend me. Flo has Stanley and Laura has Harry, and Edie has her boys. I have no man. No woman was made to be petted and cared for more than me and yet I have no one. My hair is a lovely corn colour and my figure is beautiful . . . I trace figures in the sand with the tip of my cream lace parasol, but I do not look up. I am playing with him as Woman must."

Another example of Wilson's tendency to mimic, perhaps unconsciously, a writer against whom he is in conscious reaction, occurs in **"Significant Experience,"** set in the South of France which Wilson himself had visited a number of times in the 1930s. This time the writer is Aldous Huxley, whose early heroes the "aesthetic" Jeremy somewhat resembles—though in his "very English intellectual, very Pirates of Penzance" clothes he is also a product of a strong "camp" vein in Wilson himself. Jeremy's aspirations, as he tries to disentangle himself from Prue, the sensual "older woman" with whom he has had an affair, have distinct overtones of the "sophisticated" novels that Aldous Huxley published in the 1920s and that Wilson read as a Westminster schoolboy:

> His thoughts leapt forward all the time to his future, to his freedom—he would visit Aigues Mortes and Montpellier, wander up through Arles and Nimes, perhaps see the Burgundian tombs at Auxerre, he would read the new Montherlant he had bought in Paris, he might even write some poems again.

The interior monologue method associated with Virginia Woolf is used in one of Wilson's most directly personal stories, **"A Story of Historical Interest,"** which he has

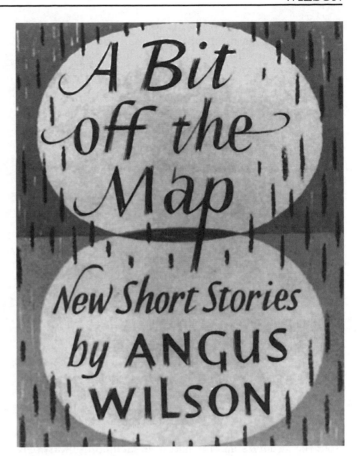

Dust jacket for Wilson's 1957 collection.

described as "an almost direct relation of my father's death in which I have cast myself in the role of a daughter" [as he explained in *Wild Garden*]. Interior monologue is, however, used in a regular pattern of alternation with narrative. The method has affinities with that of **"Mother's Sense of Fun,"** its thematic mirror-image: this consists of two large blocks, separated by some weeks, each of which proceeds internally by means of flashback; the story concluding, in the present, with a substantial shift of emotional perspective. But **"A Story of Historical Interest"** is longer and more complex, its sequence of internal flashbacks digging deeply into the personality of Lois Gorringe and her last days with her paralyzed father in a Kensington hotel, while she sits beside him in the ambulance on its bumpy way to her brother's house in Tunbridge Wells and the children's home in which he finally dies. The gradual deathward movement of Lois's father is paralleled in the public world by Neville Chamberlain's delaying tactics to prevent war—a fact which gives an ironic ring to the title, though of course this also refers to the story's biographical aspect. . . .

Emotional ambivalence, related to the need Angus Wilson himself felt to emerge from the protective yet stifling companionships of his early life, gives many of his stories what he has called "the fierceness that is their strength" [in *The Wild Garden*]. Many of them are concerned with a quality he refers to as "preserved innocence"—an innocence (or ignorance) properly associated with childhood, but becoming harmful when retained in adult life. The self-satisfied insularity of the Cockshutt family in **"Crazy Crowd"** is a satirical example of it, the "uneducated" class-loyalties of Vi in **"The Wrong Set"** a more touching one. But the quality is most powerfully investigated in Wilson's first story, **"Raspberry Jam,"** and with a fierceness that shocked early reviewers, one of them calling its conclusion—the torturing of a bullfinch by two drunken old ladies—"blood-curdling" [review of *The Wrong Set, Times* (London) *Literary Supplement,* March 26, 1949], another seeing it as an illustration of Wilson's "taste for brutality" [J. D. Scott, review of *The Wrong Set, New Statesman and Nation,* April 30, 1949].

The ending of **"Raspberry Jam"** is indeed unpleasant, the more so because it involves the momentary, horrified complicity of Johnnie, the boy on the verge of puberty who witnesses it; Johnnie, Wilson has said, is "drawn directly from myself as I had been at that age," and Wilson had admitted being "barbarously cruel to insects," and burning moths in a candle flame at fifteen [*The Wild Garden*]. But such sadistic impulses, however deplorable, are hardly rare; what is more important—indeed the moral point of the story—is the incident's shock-value for Johnnie, in terminating abruptly his friendship with the two old ladies, whose congeniality as companions in imagination is now seen to be rooted in a failure to grow up, an inability to cope with an uncongenial adult world.

Both the structure and the narrative method of **"Raspberry Jam"** are extremely ingenious. The emotional force of the tale derives from its sticking for much of the time to Johnnie's own view of events and the three worlds in which he lives: his anthropomorphic, book-influenced games with his toy animals; his "love-starved" homelife among "unimaginative adults" who on the one hand urge him to grow up into their duller world and, on the other, like pompous, romantic Mr. Codrington, advocate retaining "the fantasies, the imaginative games of childhood, even at the expense of a little fear"; his friendship with the two colorful, upper-class old ladies, Marian and Dolly Swindale, who "were the first people he had met who liked what he liked and as he liked it." One is led to sympathize with Johnnie in his loneliness, his reluctance to grow up ("one always seemed to be getting too old for something"); and his delight in the company of the two sisters, who share his imaginative games, enlarge his horizons by their recollections, and value the "odd" and the "fantastic." Interwoven with Johnnie's impressions, however, and with his intense protectiveness toward the old ladies, whom their Sussex village neighbors think "old and useless and in the way," are recurrent suggestions from Wilson's authorial voice that their engaging dottiness is not far from insanity, that their kindness to Johnnie is a form of mental retardation, and that their enlisting of his protective instincts proceeds from persecution mania. (They have, in fact, previously been "put away.") Yet the authorial voice, though judicial, is also compassionate, revealing the sisters—the gruff, soldierly Marian, the painted, "naughty" Dolly, who makes eyes at bus conductors—as pathetic survivals of a former age: they outrage their

neighbors, but can also be seen as misunderstood and rejected by them.

Wilson's structuring of the story, which inverts its time sequence, also creates a complex emotional reaction in the reader. From Johnnie's point of view, the terrible climax has already taken place; from the reader's, it has still to come. Thus Johnnie is perceived adjusting to life without his friends, and to his new vision of them as dangerous, before the reader knows why. Johnnie's memories of his pleasure in their company serve the double purpose of creating suspense and enlisting sympathy, a sympathy both widened and edged with tension as the week leading up to the fateful Thursday is described in terms of the sisters' experience: their village quarrels, their uncharacteristic mutual falling-out, and the separate drinking bouts that follow it. When, therefore, Wilson's elaborate flashback reaches Johnnie's visit, the torturing of their bullfinch "prisoner" is both understandable from their crazed point of view (to them it is a thief of the raspberries they had intended for their beloved guest and a captured "spy" from the hostile village), and horrifying from Johnnie's.

The relation of climax and flashback carries the reader in an ever-renewed circle from the "end" of the story to the beginning. Johnnie's attempt to expunge the incident from his mind by stamping the dead bullfinch into "a lump of raspberry jam" on the farmhouse floor explains his nightmares (reported by his mother soon after the story opens) and his screams when she offers him raspberry jam for tea. And his realization, in such a violent way, of the sisters' essential madness makes understandable his leaving the room when Mr. Codrington concludes his well-meaning eulogy of them by referring to "the imaginative games of childhood," as the "true magnificence of the Springtime of life." For Johnnie, the innocence of childhood has exacted too high a price.

"Preserved innocence" is not always so sympathetic as Johnnie's rococo fantasy-world with his animals, or even as the Swindale sisters' inability to move beyond memories of their Victorian father, the General. In some cases it can become what Wilson calls "a calculated refusal of imaginative compassion," as in **"A Visit in Bad Taste,"** which he thinks of as his best story. It is also his shortest, and in it the touch of poetic symbolism of **"Raspberry Jam"** is replaced by a quasi-dramatic approach: the story is like a one-scene play, covering hardly more than an hour, in which speeches are counterpointed, with unobtrusive cunning, against actions that reveal their hollowness.

Margaret and Malcolm Tarrant, two apparent liberals who have built up in their carefully furnished home a place of "taste, . . . tolerance, . . . ease of living, . . . lack of dogmatism," are faced with the presence of Margaret's brother Arthur, a former bank manager and ex-public-school man who has, at sixty, just finished a prison term for "offences against children." With his air of "military precision" and his "overpressed" suit, Arthur belongs to the type of "old sport" represented by Mr. Gorringe and Major Cawston; but though his unease with his chilly relatives reveals him in a momentarily sympathetic light,

Wilson chooses to play him down as a person in order to emphasize the lack of ordinary charity in Margaret's and Malcolm's response to him as a case.

Malcolm's "Covenanting ancestry" makes it impossible for him to forgive Arthur's crime, though on his own he might treat Arthur himself kindly. The more decisive hostility to Arthur comes from Margaret, whose unwillingness to have him in the house proceeds from a kind of aesthetic snobbery: Arthur's manner is "servile," his style of speech displeases her, she cannot stand his right-wing prejudices about her servants—while herself loathing the kind of working-class people with whom his offenses have involved him. At Arthur's trial Margaret enjoyed a "Dostoevskeyan mood" of high-flown literary suffering; but now that Arthur is physically present again she wants no more of him and even suggests—in a dramatic manner now reminiscent of Hedda Gabler's exhortations to Eilert Lövborg to "do it beautifully"—that he may find suicide the best way out. Her liberalism is nothing more than a set of self-flattering gestures, a suite of mental furniture that Arthur does not "go with."

Her rejection of Arthur on grounds such as these comes over as cold and despicable. Malcolm's attitude, at least intellectually, seems to merit some respect. But the story's last phrase—"He remained vaguely uneasy the whole evening"—conveys, along with its tautological pointer to the reader, the implication that Malcolm, who feels culturally superior to his wife and thus should behave better, is at least equally to blame: his qualms will be forgotten so very quickly. His underlying unity with Margaret, despite his not-identical opinions, is suggested by Wilson's use of telling movements, as of actors on a stage. Just as Margaret, while talking, "rustled and shimmered across the room to place a log on the great open fire" and "speared a crystallised orange from its wooden box," so Malcolm "replaced his glass of port on the little table by his side" and "moved his cigar dexterously so that the long grey ash fell into the ashtray rather than onto his suit." For all their liberal "lack of dogmatism," they share an instinctive taste for gracious living which the presence of Arthur, awkward and vulgar, can only spoil. More bleakly than most of Wilson's stories, **"A Visit in Bad Taste"** has "a kind of immediate ethical text" [Millgate interview], and its clarity is much aided by the use of such silent gestures.

"Et Dona Ferentes," written a month after **"Raspberry Jam"** and printed at the end of the collection, is perhaps the richest story in *The Wrong Set*. It combines all the aspects of Wilson's method as a short-story writer, revealing its six characters through the barbed exchanges of dramatic dialogue as well as through detailed interior monologues, and moving the five-section narrative forward against an unusual background for early Wilson, that of external nature. It also suggests the interpersonal tensions of the basic situation—Monica Newman's jealousy and embarrassment at her husband's interest in a Swedish boy—by means of a brewing storm which bursts in lightning and subsides in rain. The story, presenting three generations of an English middle-class family and the disruptive stranger in their midst, anticipates the larger canvases of Wilson's novels.

The story's title, a reference to the famous line in Virgil's *Aeneid,* "Timeo Danaos et dona ferentes" (I fear the Greeks, especially when they bring gifts), encapsulates Monica Newman's viewpoint: the pendant that she rejects at the end is bought for her by her homosexually inclined husband, Edwin, at the malicious instigation of their teenage Swedish visitor, Sven Sodeblom, to whom he has taken a fancy and with whom he has disappeared from the family picnic. It is the possibility that Edwin will, through Sven's presence, succumb to powerful past temptations that partly explains Monica's edginess at the beginning of the story and entirely explains her waspishness toward Sven, whom she despises for his materialism and vanity, but also fears for his physical attractiveness and animal charm. Her edginess, however, is accompanied by guilt: in recently cutting down sex with Edwin, who is depicted as extremely youthful, she "had withdrawn her sympathy at the very moment Edwin needed it most," and feels that if anything happens she will be to blame. Edwin's disappearance from the picnic is followed by the bursting of the storm, whose flashes of lightning both cause and mimic Monica's rising hysteria.

Despite her love for Edwin, and her guilt feelings, which win the reader's sympathy, Monica's inability to relax outdoors, and her view of nature as "patterns of shape and colour" to be completed and improved by man, together with her basic lack of interest in sex, make it understandable that Edwin should feel stifled in her company. A lack of direct confrontation with life is also perceived by Edwin—and by the reader—in his daughter Elizabeth, who is going through a "priggish" religious phase, and in her bookish son Richard, whose sensitive involvement with Dostoevsky's *The Possessed* cannot yet translate itself into easy or tactful communication with real people. Mrs. Rackham, Edwin's mother-in-law, comes over as pleasant enough, in her detached way, and at the end gives useful practical help to enable Edwin and Monica to patch up their marriage at their London flat; but she is also presented as someone who (unlike "one of those Virginia Woolf mothers") cannot fathom the emotions of others and indeed prefers to plunge into "her twenty-third reading of *Emma*"—a book that Wilson, generally an admirer of Jane Austen, sees as recommending self-satisfied insularity.

Edwin's attempt to communicate with Sven does not, in the event, work out. What starts as a genuine wish to make amends to Sven for Monica's and his children's inhospitality by showing him some Saxon remains, develops into a wish to "get to know" him better by means of an overnight stay in a nearby town. Edwin's romantic attraction to Sven is seen both as a sympathetic wish to "break out" and renew his youth, and as slightly ridiculous. His hinting advances are too easily "placed" by Sven's sexual sophistication, which sees in them only the opportunity to acquire a present and to get his own back for Monica's "bitchiness" by alarming her. As it happens, Sven is a rampant heterosexual, and in turning out the contents of his shallow mind Wilson shows him as incapable of much emotion beyond a repellent narcissism: thinking of his earlier female conquests Sven sees himself as "so handsome he felt that sometimes he almost wanted himself."

The wry conclusion of this skillful, involving story—a story reminiscent of E. M. Forster in its picture of various "undeveloped hearts" and even more in its sense of landscape as a challenging force and its portrayal of the disturbing Sven as like Pan—shows Edwin reunited with Monica after his sudden return from Milkford bearing placatory gifts. Whether Sven's sexual unwillingness, or Edwin's thinking better of his wild impulse, has aborted the intended night in a hotel we are not told. In a sense, Edwin is well out of it: someone like Sven will find greener pastures back home, and Monica's feelings are still important to her husband. Nevertheless, the mixture of relief and regret in the final paragraph conveys the cost to Edwin of his return to the orthodoxy of the family fold:

> Safe, thought Edwin, safe, thank God! But the room seemed without air, almost stifling. He threw open one of the windows and let in a refreshing breeze that blew across from the hills.

Such Darling Dodos

After this fairly detailed treatment of *The Wrong Set,* it is not necessary to spend quite so much time on Wilson's second collection. The feelings, recollections, and social ambience out of which both volumes spring are to a large extent the same, though the stories in *Such Darling Dodos* sometimes have a certain emotional thinness (as in "Sister Superior") and an element of exaggeration and contrivance (as in "A Little Companion") that suggest an imagination working at reduced pressure while the conscious mind makes a story out of an interesting idea.

"Rex Imperator," which derives its claustrophobic emotional atmosphere from the many vacations Wilson spent in the 1930s at his elder brother's house at Seaford, is a fictional version of that brother's relationship to the rest of the Wilson family: martyred by his relatives' parasitic dependence on him, Rex Palmer is also their "King Emperor" by virtue of having money for their support at his disposal. Offering a sharp study of the perverse operations of "Bourgeoisie Oblige," the story finely balances dislike of Rex's domineering ways and of the ingratitude they provoke in his relatives, with pained admiration for Rex's self-torturing sense of duty and a degree of sympathy for the pretensions by means of which his relatives cling to their human dignity: old Mr. Nicholson, Rex's garrulous father-in-law, is based on Wilson's own father, the archetypal "raffish old sport."

"Necessity's Child," like "Raspberry Jam," goes further back in Wilson's life, being a "near autobiography . . . of my last childhood years" at Bexhill. Rodney, unable to swim and poor at games, is presented as both unpleasantly sly and much to be pitied: excluded by his parents' closeness from the love he needs, he makes up stories in which he cuts a good figure and tells lies in order to gain notice and sympathy. His pathetic lies about his dependent invalid mother, which he tells to a friendly old couple encountered on the seafront, and the near-criminal lies that he later tells his aunt about them, both win him the same tribute: "I shall always think of you as a very brave boy." But the story ends with a nightmare vision of isolation no less powerful for deriving from Rodney's reading of *Moby Dick* and stories of the *Titanic* disaster. The story's final version of Rodney's ambivalent dependence on his "vanished" parents, as he struggles on a raft "with the ropes too securely tied" is given a more horrible, if melodramatic, twist at the end of "Mummy to the Rescue," in which the retarded Celia, having tied herself to the bed with the blue cardigan she associates with her drowned mother, chokes to death while dreaming that her mother is strangling her.

The attractive story "What Do Hippos Eat?" which is printed last in the volume, has affinities with "The Wrong Set," though it is placed in the 1930s: Maurice Legge's better days as an ex-officer, embroidered by sentimental memory, seem to be well in the past. Like Trevor Cawston, he is now down on his luck in a boardinghouse in Earl's Court, but ever hopeful that something will turn up. In fact, something has: his landlady and mistress, Greta, twenty years younger than himself, who has risen from working-class origins but finds in Maurice a gentleman in whose company she can further polish her manners and feel a lady: "she was ready to forgive him anything as she watched him finger the knot of his old school tie whilst he studied the menu, and heard him refer to her as 'madam' when he finally gave the order." In being genuinely fond of the man she supports, Greta resembles Vi; but she is tougher-minded, not to be sponged on more than she wishes and not averse to putting Maurice in his financial place. The intricate interplay in their relationship of affection, self-interest, and class snobbery is shown in the course of a visit to the zoo, which brings out in both of them a vulgar, patronizing attitude to the animals, behavior of which Wilson disapproves [as he explains in *Wild Garden*], but which also probes the uneasiness and hostility that lurk beneath his showing-off and her "dopey jokes."

In the zoo, a series of incidents reveals Greta's money-emboldened vulgarity and Maurice's poverty-undermined snobbishness, both of which taint their genuine affection. These incidents culminate in Maurice's mad impulse to push Greta into the hippo pool. He is only restrained by the realization that to fail in his grand gesture of feeding Greta to the hippos, and thus set her completely against him, would be worse than to succeed. Ironically, the "childlike" Greta interprets his hands on her waist as a "touching" gesture, a public show of affection such as Maurice has taught her is "just not done." The misunderstanding turns potential melodrama into near-farce; but the incident crystallizes very successfully the tensions inherent in a changing society where those on the way down attempt communication with those on the way up.

A new element enters *Such Darling Dodos* in the title story. As well as being concerned to show, in his short stories, what he has called the "false standards" of the genteel or "new poor" middle classes—the type he knew from the Kensington hotels of his youth—Wilson also felt dissatisfaction with the "insufficient standards" [*Wild Garden*] of the kind of middle-class liberals, or Fabian socialists, whom he had known as an undergraduate at Oxford and during his prewar years at the British Museum.

The precise cause of his disenchantment is not clear: **"Such Darling Dodos,"** with its dense accumulation of small cultural details—the "oatmeal fabrics and unpolished oak" of "Courtwood," the puffed wheat and strong Indian tea which Tony is offered for breakfast, and the "sensible" clothes of his relatives, Priscilla and Robin, suggests that it may have been a distaste for the Fabians' personal style as much as any sense that their policies had failed. Wilson did not, in fact, turn away from a concern for social justice: in *The Wild Garden* he makes it clear that "the left-wing causes of Priscilla and Robin," for all their unfashionableness to the young, still seemed to him no less "worth-while in themselves," and after he settled in Suffolk in 1955 he earned a local reputation as a "radical" by canvassing for the Labour Party. One is left to infer in Wilson's postwar questioning of the way of life he had once espoused some sense that the whole pattern of prewar life had let him down—both his close involvement with his own Imperialist family and his friendships with substitute families in whose Socialism he had perhaps hoped to find a personal as well as a political panacea.

One hint Wilson does give of the reason for his dissatisfaction with a "progressive" life devoted to good causes, saying in *The Wild Garden* that "Robin and Priscilla lack . . . some poetry to illuminate them." The lack is indicated, cattily, in Tony's reaction to the large, awkward Priscilla as she hovers by his bedroom door: "Surely . . . there must be some delinquent child or unmarried mother to claim her attention even at this hour of the morning." For Tony, an aesthete who grew up with his "ears full of Stravinsky and his eyes full of Bakst," it is pitiful that Priscilla can still "believe in this illusory paradise of refrigerators for all." Her type, worthy but gray, is immediately recognizable, and though Tony's opinions about her are undercut by our view of him in bed—a wrinkled pansy in a hair-net, wearing cold cream—an early authorial comment aims at our less equivocal assent, pointing to Priscilla's taste for human "pathos" and the committee and clinic work that expresses it as things that "fixed her emotionally as a child playing dolls' hospitals." Not only "poetry" but family piety takes second place to such a life of good works: Robin is dying, but he and Priscilla have decided this does not justify summoning their son Nick back from Germany, involved as he is in the important task of "reorganising the whole teaching syllabus at the Hochschule."

It is the approaching death of Robin, Socialist economics don but born a Catholic, that has brought Tony, with all the zeal of a Catholic convert, to his relatives' house in North Oxford. He has been prompted to come by an emotional letter from Priscilla in which she spoke of her fear of future loneliness. Tony, whose faith is vital to him but who has also, in the past, felt he has "missed the essentials of life" and envied his left-wing relatives' easy rapport with the politically minded young, has seen in Priscilla's uncharacteristic uncertainty a chance to demonstrate the superiority of his own values by convincing Robin and Priscilla of the greater importance of eternity and bringing Robin back to the faith. For Tony, their decision not to call their son home is a deep shock: with a sort of Catholic romanticism he has idealized their relationship as one that approaches "Christian marriage," and sees in this an achievement far greater than their good works and likely to outlast them.

Tony's visit does not succeed in its purpose, though in stating the case for faith and for "God's infinite mercy," he attains a real eloquence that transcends any self-interest in his motives. For Priscilla, and for Robin, it is what people achieve in life, for others, that matters, not how they face the "squalid" irrelevance of death: human works, not religious faith. Their side of the case, too, is put with an equivalent, if bleak, impressiveness, particularly by the cadaverous Robin: rereading William James's *The Varieties of Religious Experience* he has been able to find "nothing to accord with anything I had ever known."

In terms of its arguments, or rather its statements, **"Such Darling Dodos"** reaches an honest impasse: one is left uncertain which set of values is right; and choice between the two comes to depend on individual taste, style, or predisposition. The ironic conclusion of the story gives a kind of verbal victory to Tony; but it is an irony that cuts both ways. Michael and Harriet Eccleston, visiting "Courtwood" at the end, do not share the attitudes of Priscilla and Robin; they find something "theatrical" and inadequate in the "famous rally" to feed the Hunger Marchers from Jarrow, think the photographs of people "relaxing at Fabian summer schools" and carrying "incredible banners" something of a joke, prefer right-wing concepts of "responsibility" and order to left-wing notions of freedom, and feel some attraction toward religion. With such postwar new-style young people Tony at last feels at home, and in their company refers to Robin and Priscilla, with a slight touch of malice, as "dodos . . . but . . . such darling dodos." It is the last phrase of the story. Perhaps they are, and one feels some pity for their outmodedness. Just before the end, however, Tony has told the young people that "a good many of us thought quite differently" from Robin and Priscilla, and in Michael's reply there is a subtle indication that, all the same, Tony resembles them in one inescapable detail: "'Oh naturally, Sir,' said Michael, he loved old world manners." Tony, too, is a dodo: the failures in communication, stemming from honestly held opinions, between members of the same generation are displaced, in the process of history, by the inevitable differences between one generation and the next.

The difficulty of escaping from the past, indeed from what seems almost the preordained shape of one's fate, is an important theme in **"Totentanz,"** one of three stories that derive from Wilson's Bletchley years. (The other two are **"Christmas Day in the Workhouse"** and **"Heart of Elm."**) It also embodies on a grand scale the element of the supernatural that is peculiar to *Such Darling Dodos,* finding expression elsewhere in Celia's nightmare in **"Mummy to the Rescue"** and, more whimsically, in the mischievous alter-ego figure that haunts Miss Arkwright, the spinster of **"A Little Companion."** In its malevolent academic framework **"Totentanz"** has something in common with **"Learning's Little Tribute,"** which depicts with minute, acidulous care the petty hypocrisies and meanness of a group of academic hacks and pretentious litterateurs.

The origin of **"Totentanz"** lay in a visit Wilson made, for therapeutic purposes, after his nervous breakdown at Bletchley Park in 1944. He went to Scotland, to the small university town of St. Andrews; apart from Oxford, it was the only university town he had encountered. The place struck him as a very closed-in society, and one likely to be especially stifling to the wife of an academic there. His eventual story, set in 1949, erects on this basic feeling—sympathy for a woman trapped in a constricting place—a construction that is very much larger than life, a kind of Northern Gothic fantasy in which initial exaggeration ("subarctic isolation . . . continual mists . . . perpetual northeast gales") gives place to inventions more and more bizarre and macabre, as if Wilson were writing out of his system the pressures of his nervous breakdown and his wartime sense of claustrophobia.

For Brian Capper, newly appointed to a Chair of Art History at London University, and his wife Isobel, who has simultaneously come into a legacy of half a million pounds, rescue from their stifling, provincial environment seems to have come only just in time. He is escaping from "the waters of Lethe" which are turning him from an academic "infant phenomenon" into a dull, pipe-wielding automaton, she from "the flames of hell," a burning consciousness of frustrated social ambition in a place unappreciative of her fashionable artistic taste. Neither of the Cappers is attractive, but Wilson's depiction of the smug mannerisms of local academic society makes it possible to sympathize with them in their stroke of luck, and in the summer weather of the university town even Brian's colleagues are able to forgive him for it, to "rejoice at a fellow-prisoner's release." At first, in London, both the Cappers find the smart kind of success they want, Brian's name carrying weight "at the High Tables of All Souls and King's," Isobel cultivating such (decidedly odd) luminaries as Professor Cadaver, the expert on ancient tombs; Lady Maude, the rich art-connoisseur; Guy Rice, the homosexual interior decorator and expert on chic taste in clothes and people; and Tanya Mule, the ravaged ex-beauty who knows all the illegal ways of managing well in austerity Britain.

If the names of Isobel's friends suggest, correctly, the influence on **"Totentanz"** of the black comedy of Evelyn Waugh, to whose *Decline and Fall* it bears a distinct resemblance, a short interlude passage set in Scotland brings in overtones of *Macbeth,* as the Master's wife and Miss Thurkill, described as "an evil bat" and "a barking jackal" respectively, express a sense of foreboding that (like the prophecies of the Weird Sisters) is difficult to distinguish from ill-wishing. And in fact the Cappers' new life soon goes awry: the bequest to Isobel, from her drowned aunt and uncle, contains a condition. The Cappers not only have to live in their benefactors' house,

they must also live with two seven-foot-high statues of them, to be kept permanently in "that room in which they entertain their friends."

Having begun in a mode not too far from realism, **"Totentanz"** moves at this point into the world of grotesque fable—the "dead hand of the past" in white marble sculpture—and of sinister literary archetype: Macbeth and Lady Macbeth at the feast with Banquo's ghost visible for all to see. Guy Rice's clever suggestion that their first big reception be a *Totentanz*—a "Dance of Death" with the guests dressed in all variations of costume from Vampire and Corpse Eater to "the suicide of Chatterton"—seems the way to accommodate Isobel's ambitions as a hostess with the strange demand of her relatives. Unfortunately, Isobel's "greatest triumph" proves the end of her hopes, followed as it is by the actual suicide of Guy Rice, who is being blackmailed, the decapitation of Lady Maude by a burglar, and the death of Professor Cadaver as he tries to break open a grave in Brompton Cemetery—all of these events being described with ghoulish, operatic panache. Isobel declines into a state of apathetic communion with "the two great monuments," hardly noticing that her husband has turned into the hearty, hollow academic stereotype he was threatening to become before he left his job in Scotland. There, where it began, the story ends, with a malevolent exchange between the Master's wife, a "huge, squat toad," and Miss Thurkill, a "writhing . . . malicious snake." Having visited London in a vain attempt to get a post herself, Miss Thurkill has noticed that the Capper house is apparently shut up; the Master's wife replies "Got the plague, I expect . . . took it from here."

In psychological terms this may well be the explanation: in the Scottish university town "at least we know we're dead"; and the Cappers, in trying to escape something outside themselves, seem only to have discovered it was inside all along. But Wilson's gross, blackly comic inventiveness, worthy of Evelyn Waugh at his most destructive, turns this rueful insight into a fiction that exists brilliantly for its own sake, and it is easy to understand why, in his *Spectator* review of 1954, he should have said: "There is nothing more satisfactory, as I know from experience, than writing a macabre or a morbid short story."

Wilson as a Short-Story Writer

Wilson's satisfaction with **"Totentanz"**—whose heartless yet zestful extravagance gives it a unique place among his short stories—is a feeling his readers have generally experienced toward his two earliest collections as a whole. They are a most distinguished contribution to the genre, and display such versatility of technique and variation of detail that no story seems merely to repeat another, even though they proceed from a mental world recognizably Wilson's own and thus characterized, like that of any writer, by recurrent patterns and underlying assumptions. The world of Wilson's short stories assumes a close emotional link (whether present or desired) between children and parents, an "apprehension of moral ambiguity in relationships" [The Wild Garden], a sense of the comedy and pathos of human life, and a preference for the near-at-hand of the observer rather than for the remote distances of the visionary.

Lying behind all these aspects is the central reality of Wilson's short stories: they present a world of people. Nature is not of much importance in them, and the divine or the eternal even less. It is noticeable that the people in Wilson's short stories are rarely alone; when they are, it is because their relationships are giving them trouble, not because they are seeking solitude. Through interior monologue Wilson is adept at presenting their inner worlds, but his even more striking gift is for the personal or social exchange of dialogue, which in his stories is revealingly specific and sharply credible to the ear. Similarly acute is Wilson's eye for the betraying detail of dress, decor, or behavior. Both his dialogue and his description present the seething, unregenerate vitality and the failings of human beings—not "types," as a reviewer of *Such Darling Dodos* [in *Times* (London) *Literary Supplement*, July 28, 1950] felt, but individuals—with an honesty that gave many of his original readers a sense of release. In Wilson's stories they recognized with delighted shock the little eccentricities, the irritating mannerisms of speech and attitude, that other writers had ignored or failed to spot. But Wilson's concern to balance failings with virtues, or at least to contrast the faults of one person with those of another, insures an overall atmosphere of tolerance and fairness: he is a writer who notices, unsparingly, but not one who despises. Only occasionally does his presentation of people fail to ring true, as when for instance, in **"Learning's Little Tribute,"** he puts into the mouth of the chief encyclopedist Mr. Brunton a contextually incredible tirade against the decent Mrs. Craddock.

On *The Collected Stories of Angus Wilson*:

With one exception, published in 1980, these short stories all come from the first decade of Sir Angus Wilson's forty-year career. Indeed, twenty-three of the thirty-two stories appeared in the first two volumes, in 1949 and 1950. This book is therefore an opportunity to experience that remarkable début once again. It is easy, given the hindsight provided by subsequent achievement, to feel that a writer's early work already possesses an out-of-the-ordinary quality, but with Angus Wilson this is really so. The aggression of his satire, backed as it was by remarkable powers of mimicry and insight, was noted at the time (the early Angus Wilson was described as a "human killer"), but perhaps what stands out now is the force and self-definition of his narrative persona: here was a writer who had found his voice and his subject.

Mark Casserly, in a review of The Collected Stories of Angus Wilson, *in* The Times Literary Supplement, *No. 4414, November 6-12, 1987.*

The majority of Wilson's stories reveal individual situations at some point of crisis or decision, the classic formula of the short story which concentrates on only a short period of time or a small group of people. Some, howev-

er, imply a possibility of expansion: **"Union Reunion"** and **"Et Dona Ferentes,"** with their larger casts; **"A Little Companion"** and **"Totentanz,"** with their longer timescales; **"Heart of Elm"** with its mention of Constance Graham's ten-year past relationship with her faithful retainer Ellen. There is, also, in **"Such Darling Dodos,"** the suggestion of material lying between past and present that could be explored at greater length. Though with his first two volumes Wilson demonstrates a remarkable mastery of the short story, his turning after 1950 to the larger and more complex form of the novel comes as no surprise.

J. H. Stape   (essay date 1987)

SOURCE: "The Unknown Angus Wilson: Uncollected Short Stories from the Fifties and After," in *Twentieth Century Literature*, Vol. 33, No. 1, Spring, 1987, pp. 80-97.

[*In this essay, Stape analyzes a number of Wilson's lesser-known stories. The critic focuses on the incidents from the author's life that contributed to the tales and discusses the manner in which the characters and themes of the stories are reflected in Wilson's subsequent novels.*]

A number of stories published in the 1950s and excluded from Angus Wilson's three short-story collections throw considerable light on the discovery and development of his distinctive voice and on his exploration of the genre. These early stories published in London newspapers, in periodicals specializing in short fiction, and in thematic anthologies, though they share to a certain extent the tone and themes of those collected in *The Wrong Set* (1949) and *Such Darling Dodos* (1950), belong neither in those books nor in *A Bit off the Map* (1957), despite their common focus on displacement, self-deception, and irresponsible innocence. While they differ from the first collections partly in scale, their exclusion from *A Bit off the Map* can be accounted for by that collection's self-conscious attempt at mid-Fifties topicality.

Two later stories—a self-sustained fragment from an abandoned novel, **"My Husband Is Right,"** published in 1961 in an issue of *The Texas Quarterly* devoted to contemporary British writing, and a Christmas story, **"The Eyes of the Peacock,"** commissioned by the *Sunday Times* and published in 1975—largely serve a preparatory function, rehearsing ideas given full-scale treatment in novels. **"My Husband Is Right"** anticipates some of the thematic interests of *No Laughing Matter* (1967), and **"The Eyes of the Peacock"** contains in embryo the characters and principal motifs of *Setting the World on Fire* (1980). The early stories and the later ones demonstrate a continuity of interest and treatment, confirming Wilson's obsession with the wellsprings of his imagination in his childhood and adolescence and reiterating his fascination with certain human types.

Although the recovery of the stories published in the 1950s allows for a more complete view of Wilson's development as a writer, a reading of them does not encourage a revaluation of his contribution to the short story, nor do the stories depart radically either in method or concern from his other works of the 1950s: penetrating psychological insight abets a commitment to humane values and sharp social observation establishes and provides a context for character. And as do a number of the stories collected in *The Wrong Set* and *Such Darling Dodos,* these fictionalize aspects of Wilson's own life and experiences. Rodney in **"Aunt Cora"** and Julia in **"The Men with Bowler Hats"** recall the emotional tensions and economic realities of Wilson's fraught and insecure childhood as do the tensions developed in **"Aunt Mathilde's Drawings"** and **"Her Ship Came Home."** **"Who for Such Dainties?"** mocks the intellectual cocktail-party set that lionized Wilson after the immediate success of *The Wrong Set* and *Such Darling Dodos.* And while superficially more distanced from his own experience, **"Unwanted Heroine"** and **"An Elephant Never Forgets"** evoke the psychology and behavior of highly self-conscious but painfully self-deceived women—a Wilson forte—characters all in some way recalling his mother, whose egotistic self-sacrifice he presents full-length in *No Laughing Matter* (1967). Loneliness, alienation, and brutality, themes that dominate Wilson's early work, are forcefully developed in **"Animals or Human Beings"** and **"Mrs. Peckover's Sky . . . ,"** stories that share a pattern whereby fascination becomes disillusion and, ultimately, rejection.

In short, the uncollected stories of the 1950s point to positions Wilson later elaborated in *The Wild Garden,* the most extended exegesis of his writings: that his life, transformed, forms the basis of his art, and, indeed, in some ways gives it shape and coherence, and since life and art are for the artist inseparable, that criticism of a writer's work must take into account a writer's biography, a position elaborated in his critical works on Zola, Dickens, and Kipling. At the same time, as, in the main, a realist, Wilson attempts to convince his reader of the validity of a presented world. The dual necessity of personal revelation, however disguised or distanced, conjoined with an engagement of the "actual" world (re-created and transformed by the imagination) creates a tension that informs and animates much of Wilson's early work, giving it its "period" vividness as well as its more enduring significance as an exploration of the human—and humanist—dilemma.

Wilson's concern with self combined with its apparent contradiction—a fascination with others—is most directly evidenced in **"Aunt Cora," "The Men with Bowler Hats,"** and **"Mrs. Peckover's Sky . . . ,"** stories patently autobiographical in inspiration. More a character sketch than a story, **"Aunt Cora"** (1950) presents a vivid recollection of an eccentric old woman through the sympathetic eyes of her "highly strung" young nephew. An Edwardian figure in manner and dress, and immensely rich, Aunt Cora with "her rose-decked picture hats, her hour-glass figure and her lace parasols" is an exotic visitor to the boy's "quiet Weybridge home." The figure of family legend—an invented operatic career explains her "retinue of young tenors and teachers of the tango"—in the mid-1920s she drops young men to take up spiritualism, the new but enduring interest about which the sketch's two incidents revolve. An afternoon luncheon party "on a rather hot June afternoon in 1933" concludes with a search for her valuable ruby ring spirited away by "malign influences," which, to the embarrassment of Rodney's parents, are found to be incarnated by Lady Grackle, a fellow guest in whose handbag the ring is found.

The second major incident—Rodney's visit to her flat at age fifteen, a visit that consists largely of "an exhausting afternoon of table turning, clairvoyance and every other psychic performance in which her histrionic powers could shine"—plays up her delicate sense of manners. He fails to realize that her knock upon a door as they leave the parlor for tea in the library, far from being yet another psychic exhibition, primly indicates the room where he should "wash his hands." And her legacy to him recalls his indiscretion: abroad in the forces when she dies, he inherits an Edwardian etiquette book with the chapter "How to Enter and Leave the Room" carefully marked.

Cora's is a kind of fantasy world carefully created and maintained as a means of escaping harsh and insistent reality, and while her "period" quality makes her an exotic—almost, perhaps, a grotesque—it engenders the boy's affectionate attitude to her. Rodney, however, already showing signs of a greater commitment to the actual world, feels considerably less positive about her psychic explorations, activities that, nonetheless, ally her to the theatrical and dramatic and represent an intrusion of the imagination (albeit not of the highest kind) into his everyday existence. Cora as a neurotic type symbolizes the dangers of imaginative engagement with its invitation to escapism, and Rodney's affectionate but ultimately distanced reaction to her signifies his ability to discern the imagination as a potentially devouring force. The story, then, dramatizes the artist's dual and simultaneous attraction to the inner and outer worlds, cautioning that total engagement in either negates the possibility of creating art.

As social comment, **"Aunt Cora"** explores the collision between the manners and morals of distinct historical moments. Cora the Edwardian survives to see her values and habits superseded by another, less delicate age, maintaining them in the face of change and even attempting their perpetuation by the symbolic legacy she leaves her nephew. In a way, the story metaphorically summarizes the situation of postwar England not yet fully convinced of the profound alteration of its social landscape, attempting to ward off the consequences of change by repeating fixed habits that had lost their force and significance (much as Wilson's own parents, living beyond their needs and means, attempted to maintain a facade of "normality" in the face of declining social status and income).

Although **"Aunt Cora"** lacks the polish of the best of Wilson's early work, it provides a rare and valuable glimpse of his fictional apprenticeship, allowing the sympathetic reader to observe more directly than in Wilson's mature writings the transformation of autobiography into art. The story plays an obvious role as apprentice work exorcising familial ghosts that might have hindered the development of Wilson's craft and imagination. The title character, in later guises the Miss Rickard of *No Laughing Matter* and Great-aunt Cara of **"The Eyes of the Peacock,"** apparently conflates aspects of his own "very histrionic" mother with a more distant relation by marriage who as her late husband's parrot sat upon her shoulder claimed it embodied his departed spirit [Angus Wilson, *The Wild Garden*]. The story may also recollect the two friends who served as sources for the Misses Swindale of **"Raspberry Jam,"** lonely women who befriended a lonely boy and in turn received his sympathetic understanding, though the boy in question was not Wilson himself but one of his brothers. However, the depiction of Rodney (the name is also used in **"Necessity's Child,"** an acknowledged self-portrait) clearly resumes autobiographical elements, and the figure of the lonely and sensitive individual who escapes a banal environment by a fantasizing capacity recurs throughout Wilson's fiction.

The long story **"An Elephant Never Forgets"** (1951) focuses sharply on conflict, loneliness, egotism, and false pretenses. The friendship between Mildred Vereker, the "uncrowned queen" of a seaside resort town, and the newcomer Delice, the title's "elephant" who dabbles in clairvoyance but whose actual stock-in-trade lies in overblown emotionalism and a self-consciously created "exotic" atmosphere, is observed by Constance, an old friend of Mildred's just returned from a two-year absence abroad. Set in 1921 with a sequel in 1926, the story allows Wilson to evoke 1920s mores and fashions through the eyes of a waspish middle-aged woman, a voice he uses to great comic and ironic effect in *For Whom the Cloche Tolls* (1952).

The story is essentially a character study and a drama of types: the observant Constance is at times subtly undercut by her own society voice; Delice serves as a kind of dry run for the monstrous egotism and lack of self-awareness of Inge in *Anglo Saxon Attitudes*; Mildred takes on the role of queen bee in provincial society; and her son Reggie, the lady's man on the make, even succumbs briefly to Delice's faded charms (though he calls her "Jumbo" behind her ample back). Detailed description abets and sometimes substitutes for characterization:

> Her rather stoutly-built but erect figure swam towards me through the sea of occasional tables, grand pianos, curio cases, Japanese screens, bowls of sweet peas and pots of hydrangeas that still marked her drawing room as a backwater of the Edwardian era. She was always well dressed but, after the more modish Parisian chic, her tight-skirted cornflower blue shantung coat and skirt with its rows of large buttons at the sides and the large tongued, buckled, white linen shoes, though highly suitable for the hot weather, carried a suggestion of a war-time fashion that was now well on the way out.

The story's central interest lies in detailing Delice's decline and fall; Mildred's eyes are gradually opened, Delice becomes increasingly possessive and extravagant (there is a slight suggestion of lesbianism), Reggie and Constance fail to take to Mildred's new acquisition, and finally Delice is expelled from Seastone society. Five years

later she takes her revenge as she arrives—unexpectedly and uninvited—at a pre-matinee luncheon attended by Reggie's fiancée and her parents—Sir Eric and Lady Stetson—and, of course, Constance. Delice is a triumph of vulgarity, patronizing everyone, and pretending to great intimacy with the Verekers. In short, the moral in the story's title becomes a reality.

"An Elephant Never Forgets" succeeds as a nuanced rendering of a social world but fails to connect that world with larger issues so that the story remains only a clever character sketch of its arch and observant narrator and her circle, a study of sensibilities through the eyes of a limited narrator. The story's moral comment is muted: such types call down their own condemnation, but they are, after all, the "darling dodos" that Wilson depicts with such force in the collection of that name.

The "darling dodo" theme also dominates two of Wilson's *Evening Standard* stories—**"Aunt Mathilde's Drawings"** (1952) and **"Silent Pianist"** (1952)—both of which focus on old women caught in harsh new realities. Aunt Mathilde, in her youth a famous French artist's model and mistress, lives now on her relatives' sufferance while her colorful past gives her a certain cachet as does the "portfolio of drawings done by the great painter" which "everyone agreed must be worth a very good deal." Living beyond their means, the Templetons, her long-suffering relations, seek a valuation only to learn that Aunt Mathilde's "engravings" prove to have been "a famous and good series in their day," but are not, in fact, worth very much. The story closes with an ironic twist as a neighbor robbed of her jewels becomes the object of Aunt Mathilde's contempt: "My dear," she said, "how stupid to have real jewels and furrs in the home. She should have lettle copies made," a comment that causes Mrs. Templeton "almost to hate her aunt."

The uncovering of deception forms the story's core as Wilson dissects familial relationships based on an absence of feeling and a lack of scruples. Again, the family is posited as a cruel and heartless social structure, a reaction, in part, against its sentimental treatment in much popular fiction. The Templetons and Aunt Mathilde are equally unsympathetic, and this minor story gives shape to an almost Balzacian vision of the predatory character of human relationships.

"Silent Pianist," like many of Wilson's stories, targets moral failure and self-deception as the out-of-date Mrs. Ramsay (a stab at Virginia Woolf, whose work Wilson then saw unsympathetically) attempts to maintain a vanished world by means of too much make-up and an overly dramatic manner. Lonely and desperate for attention, she tries first to interest the waitress in the "stuffy, beer-fumed saloon bar dining-room" where she takes her lunch and next seeks to engage in conversation Stephen, a man at the next table. Her false manner bores and slightly irritates him while she makes unoriginal observations on the food and the weather before finally proclaiming the negative effect television has had on the cinema. She herself had played the piano at the cinema before "those ugly harsh talkies" came along, she informs him, and in unself-conscious contradiction has to hurry along to an afternoon film—"It doesn't do to be late for the cinema, does it? Always such long queues."

The story has two targets: the "dodo" world Mrs. Ramsay lives in and the callous modern one that the waitress and Stephen inhabit. An early version of Rose Lorimer in *Anglo-Saxon Attitudes,* Mrs. Ramsay simultaneously invites sympathy and criticism in her preference for fantasy to reality. But the waitress and Stephen alike are victims of self-absorption, finally symbolizing its passive cruelty. Although principally the portrait of an old woman as self con-artist, the story's moral aim gives it more than simple period interest as Wilson's observant eye gleams with the satirist's intention.

The brief story **"Who for Such Dainties?"** (1952), also typical of Wilson's early work in its precise social observation and multilayered ironic treatment of manners, develops two characters—Harriet Mackenzie, a snob whose comeuppance provides the story's main action, and Maurice Neaves, "the greatest Shakespearean actor in England," himself a bit of a poseur. A third character, Pamela Vaughan, a "mountainous, pink blancmange-like woman, with her strident blue dress, purple hair and glittering bangles and brooches," author of a play about smuggling in eighteenth-century Truro, forms the pivot about which the minimal action and central irony turn.

The opening cocktail party, a device to establish mood and character, prepares for the principal incident—a disastrous lunch for Harriet at Pamela's flat. The final scene—a conversation between Harriet and Maurice about this luncheon—occurs "many weeks" later. The luncheon at Pamela's is characteristically detailed: the "good" sherry followed by a "good" borsch soup form the prelude to a Rumanian stew gone amiss: "Pamela's meat ration would not allow for more than lumps of fat in the stew, whilst the olives and plums had stuck to the saucepan and were burned." The dessert—stewed guavas served in treacle—irritates Harriet's teeth, which are "badly in need of stopping." The topic of conversation is, inevitably, Maurice Neaves, and Harriet, annoyed by the food and with her teeth on edge, in the end decides that "such a woman" should never be helped. In the final episode she maliciously serves up Maurice a description of that "terrible woman's" lunch, which in her version consists only of the borsch soup. And Maurice, surprised to hear of Harriet's ill-luck, for Pamela had treated him to "the most delicious of stews with all the produce of the East in it, and guavas, lovely guavas, cooked excellently in treacle," announces coolly that he is planning to produce Pamela's play, *Cornish Cream,* in the spring.

"Who for Such Dainties?" contains all the elements of a clever and well-told joke, but suffers from being overly concise. Wilson nonetheless manages, even in so confined a space, to depict convincingly the moral atmosphere of snide and overly self-concerned individuals. The deftly sketched characters, self-conscious surprise ending, and richly ironic title evidence the same thorough mastery of craft found in *The Wrong Set* and *Such Darling Dodos.* Although in either of these collections the story might appear slight, on its own it remains an amusing if barbed pleasantry. Typically, none of its characters escape criticism: Pamela, obviously on the make to advance her career, plays up both her guests; Harriet's thinly disguised social pretensions serve only to assuage a rather crude need for one-upmanship; and Maurice, the actor-manager, succumbs to Pamela's obvious flattery, a victim less of good food than of his own oversized ego. The self-deception Harriet and Maurice practice lays them open to Pamela's cynical machinations, and, although she perhaps deserves to succeed, the world in which she does is the unpleasant one delineated in Wilson's first two collections: that of a rationing Britain shaken by political and economic changes with their attendant social consequences.

Like **"Who for Such Dainties?," "The Men with Bowler Hats"** (1953) treats the dispossessed middle class and its compulsive need to maintain appearances, and, if possible, get ahead. The social setting, what Malcolm Bradbury has called "frayed-at-the-heels upper-middle class gentility" [*Studies in Short Fiction* III, No. 2, Winter, 1966], is, however, less important for its own sake than for the opportunity it provides Wilson to explore the antagonism between adult life—existence circumscribed by class, economic circumstances, and acute self-awareness—and the imaginative world, represented frequently in his fiction by children or the childlike. The story's protagonist, Julia, a girl of eight, whose contact with adult reality is fraught and only partially understood, unwittingly engineers yet another change of circumstances for herself and her affectionate but irresponsible father, Mr. Chalpers, another "Raffish Old Sport," a type patently based on Wilson's own father.

After a brief introduction of characters, the story focuses on a single dramatic situation: the new relationship between Mr. Chalpers and Mrs. Gregoby, an American widow with a nine-year-old son, Timmie. (Mrs. Gregoby, similarly a Wilson type, the "Widow Who Copes," has analogues in other stories—**"Heart of Elm," "Sister Superior," "Christmas Day in the Workhouse"**—as well as in *The Middle Age of Mrs. Eliot* and *Late Call*; the American widow in England also appears in *Hemlock and After* and *Setting the World on Fire,* another evidence of Wilson's obsession with certain types, this possibly based on autobiographical sources.) Mr. Chalpers envisages how much this friendship will alter his economic condition, while Mrs. Gregoby, "Auntie Rosemary" to Julia, herself looks forward to an improved economic condition after marrying "Daddy." The classic misunderstanding, rendered with ironic as well as comic touches, moves forward to its logical and inevitable conclusion as the children's games reveal the truth. Timmie's dress-up imitation of "waiters and porters, and the ladies in curl-papers" turns out to be no less knowledgeable than Julia's, and when the adults discover their offspring "wearing black paper hats on their heads and pretending to drink tea out of mugs," the children's imaginative re-creation of an unpleasant reality occasions the now predictable end of the adult "friendship." On their way home Julia explains to Daddy that she and Timmie were playing "the men in bowler hats that come to people's houses" (bailiffs), adding that Timmie remembered them as having come four times to his. The whole adult fictional structure of mutual deception and self-deception collapses with her revelation, and the story ends with Mr. Chalpers informing the hotel porter that he will always be out when Mrs. Gregoby calls, an, of course, unnecessary precaution.

A transparent reworking of Wilson's own early life, like Julia's economically strained and passed in a string of London residential hotels, **"The Men with Bowler Hats"** is especially interesting for the unresolved conflict between pleasure and responsibility, a theme fully treated in *Hemlock and After*. The story's underlying structure sees adult concerns—sex, money, class—overturned by the children's "innocence." As Julia and Timmie's make-believe world forces the adults to confront their true situation, Mr. Chalpers' repeated confrontations with the bowler hat—on the one hand, the symbol of social respectability and financial success, and, on the other, of his personal failure—always result in the unmaking of his dreamworld.

The children's appropriation of this symbol is not only an accusation of failure aimed at the parental figures for their unwillingness to make a contract with the adult world, but also represents their premature adulthood. The knowing child corrupted by experience and the childlike or childish adult unable to disentangle himself from the charms of childhood are figures Wilson typically uses to focus on the commitment and responsibility necessary to a fully adult, moral life. But such maturity, he realizes, is achieved all too frequently at the expense of the imagination. (This tension, particularly acute for some artists, might be seen as coming to a head in Wilson's breakdown during the war, the result, in part, of his having to confront a situation in which his previous adaptation to life—a talent for mimicry and capacity for fantasy—proved wholly inadequate to the demands wartime realities placed on him.) As Julia and Timmie in **"The Men with Bowler Hats"** don adult clothing and ape adult manners, the imagination (the children's make-believe) reveals itself ironically as a means of apprehending reality (adult responsibility).

Aside from the reworking of autobiographical materials, the story's interest lies in its handling of point of view. Julia's naive language and limited apprehension, conveyed through a perfectly adapted free indirect style, expose the disharmony between the meaning of event and experience and her interpretation of them:

> Once when they were living in very dingy rooms in a street near the Oval a lady came from the Ministry to ask why Julia was not at school. Daddy seemed very pleased to see her and laughed and talked a lot. When the lady went away she said she was so glad she had been able to help. But after she had gone Daddy was very angry and they had moved the next day.

The rendering of the child's limited cognitive and linguistic capacities, the means through which the narrative is filtered, heightens the reader's awareness of the gap between the storyteller's acute and full understanding of his tale and the deliberate naïveté of its telling. As in **"Raspberry Jam"** the story's center articulates a sympathetic and compassionate rendering of a child's vulnerability to the adult world. At the same time Wilson creates this sympathy, the comic treatment of the "misunderstanding" Mr. Chalpers and Mrs. Gregoby arrive at through their self-centeredness and cynicism—character traits that yield a limited apprehension of "the world" while nonetheless pretending to a masterful manipulation of it—modulates and perhaps even slightly undercuts it. The children's miming of a world beyond their apprehension mirrors the adults' insufficient knowledge of each other, and, ultimately, of themselves.

"Unwanted Heroine" (1954) depicts the slow coming-to-awareness of the self-dramatizing Rosalind, who decides to put off marriage with James, a Cambridge history lecturer, for the sake of her stepmother, Anne. As it turns out, Anne has her own plans to marry Reggie Sinclair, who Rosalind sees as a "rich son of a rich business man . . . unbearably vulgar with his flashy good looks and sports cars." Finding her sacrifice unwanted, Rosalind does marry James, whose maturity helps her to see her self-preoccupation, but the Joycean epiphany occurs only in the final scene as Anne's attitude and comments reveal that role-playing and egotism masquerading as concern for others have no purchase in adult life and relationships. Although the story hits on major Wilson preoccupations, the absence of distancing devices—the bittersweet humor and irony characteristic of his best work—tends to undermine its potential force. Rosalind's egotism and neurotic self-concern are depicted on too small a canvas, and the other characters, perhaps appropriately given her self-absorption, remain peripheral and sketched in. As so often with Wilson, the protagonist's moral education is worked out in the confrontation between the world of self (and selfishness) and the adult world of awareness and responsibility. The major metaphor of the story—the theater—that sustained illusion where self-gratification is essential for the actor—functions as a moral yardstick: Rosalind's heroics are not only unwanted by Anne but ought to be unwanted by Rosalind herself.

"Her Ship Came Home" (1955), another story featuring the tensions of childhood's partial awareness of adult realities, dissects a failed adult relationship. During his 1922 Christmas holidays spent with an aunt at the Osprey Court, a residential hotel "—"on the other side of the Park,'" the narrator is befriended by the Lestelles, a couple past their prime living in the hope that Mr. Lestelle's Uncle Ted in Australia will die so that they can inherit. In order to prick his wife's social pretensions and those of the Osprey Court set, Mr. Lestelle announces that their ship has come home: Uncle Ted has died. Later when Mr. Lestelle reveals that his announcement is a practical joke his wife spirits away the narrator's plasticine, making with it "a great wax doll" into whose head she sticks Mr. Lestelle's hair and through whose left side she has thrust "a long hat pin." Mr. Lestelle dies not from drink, as might be expected, but suddenly of a heart attack. By one of fate's ironies, Uncle Ted dies a week later. A mixture of naïveté and insight allows the narrator to conclude that, "In any case, Mrs. Lestelle's ship came home."

Although preoccupied with family and surrogate family relationships, the autobiographical elements of **"Animals or Human Beings"** (1955) are more distanced. Deliberately evoking generic conventions, the story fully realizes Wilson's argument that the modern horror story ought to abandon the practice of its nineteenth-century antecedents in placing horror in the unknown and find it instead in "the hysteria, the melancholy, the bitterness turned to malevolence that lie in our homes." Fräulein Partenkirchen, a familiar Wilson type, an outsider with a marginal existence in the great world and a tenuous hold on it—a kind of child—is sent to England by her family under the pretense of her acquiring English to obtain a secretarial post. But in reality they hope she finds herself a husband, and, in trust, they simply want "to be rid of her." Destined, then, to serve as housekeeper to a Miss Alice Ingelow living in the Welsh marshes, an animal lover quite "crazy" about the subject of vivisection, Fräulein Partenkirchen first encounters her new employer through Mrs. Gosport, a Jamesian intermediary who greets the German girl in London. Their conversation gives the story its title as Mrs. Gosport focuses on Miss Ingelow's partiality for animals in preference to "so much *human* material in need of help . . . ." On her arrival, the Fräulein is immediately introduced to Maria, delivered of a litter of which their father, Rufus, is "jealous." Jealousy and partiality for birds force "Auntie" to confine him to a cage, but to Fräulein Partenkirchen, who, she hopes, *likes* animals she praises his "beautiful coat," "fine tail," and "magnificent whiskers." Walking downstairs alone, the Fräulein leaves a note saying she does not like animals, and as she leaves the decaying house through its neglected garden hears "two loud shrieks" announcing Miss Ingelow's fate:

> Upstairs, Miss Ingelow lay on the floor with her throat torn open. An enormous buck rat was hissing and scratching at the wires of a cage. It wanted to get its doe and devour the young ones. Soon it would have eaten all the raw meat that Miss Ingelow had brought with her; and as she had closed the door of the room behind her, there would be nothing then for Rufus to devour except Miss Ingelow herself. But the little bells she had put on his cage jangled merrily.

Returning home "more reserved and her skin more sallow," Fräulein Partenkirchen tells a story that, to her relatives' distress, even lessens her chances of making a match. Suggesting that "there was always the chance that she had seen ghosts," they attempt to console themselves with her "echt Deutsch quality uniting her with all the old Legenden and Märchen. But hardly if all she could see was ghost rats!"

The pattern of rejection followed by violence is common enough in Wilson's work, operating powerfully, for example, in **"A Bit off the Map"** and *Hemlock and After,* but the violence is displaced here: although the placid Fräulein takes no revenge herself upon her family for her isolation and abandonment, the story's action does so: the mother surrogate is devoured by her own obsession, a retribution for her neglect of human beings. (Indeed, the neglected garden—always a significant metaphor in Wilson—also serves to symbolize both her lack of interest in and alienation from a world outside her own.) The family complex is also embodied in the rat family with Rufus, the "jealous" father, wanting to eat his own young. At the end, the unlikelihood of the Fräulein's finding a husband may serve partly as her unstated refusal to participate in the brutalities of the family situation itself—although the penalty of refusing is that she, like Miss Ingelow, becomes an eccentric in her indifference as the older woman had by her cloying and ultimately self-destructive sentimentalism.

In common with **"The Men with Bowler Hats,"** the story succeeds by its manipulation of a naive and not wholly aware heroine. And the management of tone, achieving emotional distance from character and event, reserves the ending's full horror for the reader alone. Even the reader's initial assumption that Rufus and Maria are cats is a narrative deception permitted because of the limitations of the Fräulein's interest in life: she chooses neither animals nor human beings, while Miss Ingelow's horrific death, obliterating the choice the title offers, forces the reader into emotional response—repulsion and disgust for the animals, and some measure of pity and sympathy, despite their irresponsible innocence, for the eccentric women. Wilson's stated aim in his early stories was to deprive both his characters and his readers of emotional response; here, without uniting brutality of action and symbol, he allows it and has diminished the story's effect.

"Mrs. Peckover's Sky . . ." (1955) also features a self-obsessed heroine. The story opens as the anonymous narrator down for a weekend with a rather boring but rich Oxford colleague is initiated into one family circle. Roy's sister Joan proves uninteresting, and Roy's father, "a very amateurish local historian," a bore, but the exquisite home pleasures his aesthetic sense and its hostess charms and fascinates him, even enlivening the other members of the Peckover family. Mrs. Peckover's is an unkind spell, however, for it rests on a thoroughgoing egotism: "everything—animal, mineral and vegetable—in that place, including her family and servants, was hers." Her possessiveness extends not only to the view but even to the sunset itself. Later, informed of rumors of war, she claims "I shouldn't allow such a messy, unpleasant thing." Visiting Bugloss Hall in 1944, the narrator sees only Mrs. Peckover—Roy is away with the forces, Mr. Peckover has been killed in a tank, Joan has married. The sunset and sky still cooperate, but Mrs. Peckover's bright manner cannot mask the fact that she is "old and miserable," and to the narrator's expression of sincere happiness at seeing her there, she brutally replies: "I'm not. I wish I was dead." Her wish comes true enough; when the narrator is in Cairo, Mrs. Peckover is "killed with a lot of other old ladies by a bomb that fell on a Knightsbridge hotel."

"Mrs. Peckover's Sky . . ." contains in embryo a number of motifs Wilson develops in *Anglo-Saxon Attitudes*: the young Gerald Middleton's fascination with Elvira Portway, the sense of surrogate family, the local historian, Elvira's attempt to ward off ugliness and death by brightness and charm. The story's link to **"Aunt Cora"** is also obvious. What is, however, particularly noteworthy is its displaced violence: the title character's death related in that final, brutal sentence callously dismisses it, Mrs. Peckover's saccharine-sweet vision, and the mother-surrogate relationship. Somewhat in the manner of Waugh's *Brideshead Revisited,* disillusion lurks behind the narrator's rejection of the Peckovers, and his greater maturity and experience allow him a complete appreciation of the inadequacy of Mrs. Peckover's vision. But here insight fails to become compassion, and the narrator's rhetoric ultimately reveals only his own moral failure.

"My Husband Is Right" (1961), although it contains echoes of **"Ten Minutes to Twelve,"** represents a marked shift in tone from most of Wilson's later stories, differing as well in its original purposes as the prologue—one of his favored devices—to an abandoned novel, *Goats and Compasses,* of which only it and one chapter was completed. Although it has a vignette quality, the piece possesses sufficient weight to stand alone. Set in Bruges, it focuses exclusively on a few hours in the life of an anonymous middle-aged couple who have gone abroad in an attempt to preserve the husband's sanity. Again, Wilson's own family context replete with his parents' histrionic quarrels provides part of the story's personal background, and *No Laughing Matter* obviously takes up some of the fragments dropped here. (Wilson's own nervous breakdown in 1944, caused partly by a disastrous love affair, contributes to the authentic note of desperation and of a relationship gone awry.) Although momentarily "unfaithful" to her husband's needs in her own selfish preoccupation, the wife affirms her commitment to him when she collects their belongings from the hotel in which he has just made a "scene": *"Mon mari a raison."* The statement allies her to his "correct" attitude toward the concierge and porter, but ironically underlines the entire situation's problem: her husband's "reason," his sanity, *is* indeed in question. The detailing of action and the precise observation of social realities, at times indulged in for their own sake in some of the early stories, is never less than purposeful here, displaying a technical maturity won through working in the more extended form of the novel.

"The Eyes of the Peacock" (1975), which Wilson has called a "children's story," recalls Wilde's excursions in the same genre, particularly "The Canterville Ghost," but aside from relying on some children's literature conventions—a fairy godmother figure incarnated here by a formidable but benevolent great-aunt (an obvious reworking of the Aunt Cora figure), a boy hero, and a ghost—the story addresses itself to an exclusively adult audience. Set "once upon a time when King George the Fifth and his gracious Queen Mary ruled in England, and a big dark man like a bullfrog called Mussolini ruled in Italy," a significant blending of fantasy and realism, the tale moves rapidly from Armistead Castle—which Stephen takes particular delight in exploring—to his Great-aunt Cara's "glorious Venice." As Cara, a former opera singer, nourishes Stephen's imagination in opposition to his practical parents, the boy comes to dream of presenting a ballet when he grows up. The tale closes with Cara's disappearance in

the Venice of the black shirts. (Has she too been a ghost, like the one she and Stephen are alone privileged to see at Armistead Castle?) Thanks to a legacy from her Stephen accomplishes his childhood dream, putting on *The Eyes of the Peacock,* and "although it wasn't put on at Covent Garden or anywhere important, it *was* performed."

Crowded with incident to the bursting point, the story is primarily interesting for its parallels with *Setting the World on Fire* (1980), published some four years later. **"The Eyes of the Peacock"** anticipates the novel's characters, situations, and themes: Great-aunt Cara evolves into Lady Mosson; Stephen becomes Piers, and his parents play the role of Tom; Armistead Castle becomes Tothill House; the ballet becomes Lully's opera *Phaeton.* Even the novel's opposition between imagination and practicality and its political atmosphere of anarchism and terrorist activity are rehearsed here. Weighed down by its artist-parable thesis, however, the tale lacks a genuinely fictional inspiration, although, as always, Wilson adeptly conveys mood, and in Cara offers a brilliant caricature of the world of the late Twenties and early Thirties in the manner of *For Whom the Cloche Tolls.* Stephen, the child hero whose alienation from the actual world permits rich compensation in the world of fantasy, a figure met repeatedly (Julia in **"The Men with Bowler Hats,"** Johnnie in **"Raspberry Jam,"** the Matthews children in *No Laughing Matter*), affirms the centrality of the theme of the imagination and the child symbol in Wilson's fiction. As in other stories or in the novels, the isolated central figure accompanies his search for self-affirmation and balance, the quest to resolve the conflicting claims of "life" and "art," against a background of threat or actual brutality (here the black shirts). Although neither fully worked out nor convincingly portrayed, Stephen's uncertain status in the real world (indicated mostly by his Oedipal game leg) is balanced by the reality of his inner one, which is constellated as he achieves his dream: "it *was* performed."

"The Eyes of the Peacock" represents a double return to childhood in method and subject, and confirms again by its narrative displacements the sources of Wilson's art in his own early life. The legacy of these years—a dramatizing imaginative capacity—finds its embodiment in an appropriately domestic (if distinctly undomesticated) muse—Great-aunt Cara/Aunt Cora. And the portrait of artist tutored and protected by his *femme inspiratrice* (revealingly neither a beloved nor a wife but an aunt, a parental relation) gains strength and resonance from reference to archetypal situations. Even if the story remains largely a rehearsal for the longer work that followed, its wounded hero who conquers loneliness and fear (the black shirts) by aspiring to Art transcends Wilson's personal crises and history, speaking powerfully to the artist's condition and to his eternal battle with the twin demons of conformity and bourgeois life. Given the concerns and method of **"The Eyes of the Peacock,"** it is hardly surprising that Wilson's next imaginative work, *Setting the World on Fire,* should be a full-scale retelling of myth.

These uncollected stories, though separated widely in time, nonetheless occupy a confined and delimited space. Indeed, their main value may lie in suggesting the essential fact that however wide the grasp of Wilson's imagination and the range of his social interests they possess a kind of homing instinct that finally returns them to their origins in his early life. Even in the later novels where echoes of his childhood and adolescence seem more distant, where academics and students, the aristocracy, the extremely wealthy are "done"—social situations and character types that extend his range in truly Dickensian fashion—the bedrock remains much the same. To say this, however, is not to diminish Wilson's considerable achievement either in the short story or the novel. But revealing this essential situation highlights the necessity of Wilson's turning to the more extended form, a form that his creative exuberance inevitably came to demand as, for example, the over-crowded landscape of **"The Eyes of the Peacock"** amply demonstrates. Moreover, this realization also serves to increase our appreciation of the tautness and concision of his early work.

A focus on the uncollected stories of the 1950s, whatever their individual interest and value, puts into relief the formal mastery and almost startling social and psychological realism of the stories collected in *The Wrong Set* and *Such Darling Dodos*. And by calling attention to the disjunctions between the opposed worlds of fairy tale and fascist politics, **"The Eyes of the Peacock"** serves to expose Wilson's fundamental optimism, which continues to insist, despite overwhelming evidence to the contrary, that fantasy and the imagination are as real and as strong as the forces opposing them.

John Bayley   (essay date 1988)

SOURCE: "Last Words," in *London Review of Books,* Vol. 10, No. 1, January 7, 1988, p. 16.

[*An English poet, novelist, and critic, Bayley is best known for his critical studies of Thomas Hardy, Alexander Pushkin, and Leo Tolstoy. In this review, Wilson's stories are compared to the work of English authors D. H. Lawrence and Rudyard Kipling, though Bayley finds that Wilson's early stories, in particular, are "in a class of their own."*]

There is certainly a hint of [D. H.] Lawrence in Wilson's verbal exuberance and zest, and in his ruthless geniality, although the Wilson world is all his own. Lawrence, like [Rudyard] Kipling, makes extensive use of what might be termed the ambiguous event, or non-event, and Wilson does it too, in his own masterly way. In **'The Captain's Doll'** and **'The Fox'** things happen—a wife's defenestration and a lesbian lady's execution by a falling tree—which strike one as taking place less in the world of action than in that of wish-fulfilment: the husband's and the young soldier's desire to do, or to see done, what then appears actually to take place. Even 'The woman who rode away' is perhaps best read in this light, as Lawrence's half-sardonic, half-wistful play with the theme of foolish modern romance and true primitive energy. In rather the same spirit, Angus Wilson plays with his vividly-realised con-

temporary types, placing them in situations in which the life of the mind cannot be distinguished from the comic-dreadful thing that happens, embarrassing situations which actually occur.

The agitation that blows like a comic gale through the stories of *The Wrong Set* and *Such Darling Dodos* is as strong as ever today. As in the cases of Kipling and of Lawrence, the heart of the story is the relief it affords to the author, a relief in which its art makes the reader share with irresistible abandonment. The sense of creation is as fresh as paint, and the characters are not so much turned inside out for our amusement as enlisted in a wild party in which everyone can do their thing, the author most of all. Wilson's characters are openly created, as Mary Postgate ambiguously was, in terms of the inner shock brought about by the need for sustaining an outward persona. Kipling is in deep sympathy with this, and so is Wilson: neither shares Lawrence's compulsive need to put his characters down. With Wilson as with Kipling we are all in the same boat—in fact, one of Kipling's titles.

Wilson marshals the inner life of his characters like a conductor encouraging an orchestra, and the composition is always superbly organised. He orchestrates human wickedness, his own included, in terms of its inner drives, the unacted desires which throw people out of windows, or drop trees on them, or leave them to die in agony. **'Realpolitik'** is a continuous virtuoso performance: the enactment, mostly in dialogue, of a staff meeting at an imaginary provincial art gallery, with a new Machiavellian and philistine director seeking to get rid of the honourable old figures who have been running the place according to custom and tradition. Although the exchanges are masterly on the page, and supposed as taking place, their real location is in the head, the place where the most wounding utterance is planned in advance, or perfected afterwards in the mood of *l'esprit d'escalier*. After the meeting, with the staff driven before him in disarray, the director gloats with his secretary and ally, who is none the less doubtful about the wisdom of what he has done, and says: 'It's not those misfits I'm worrying about, it's you.'

> 'Me?' said John. 'Why?'
>
> 'You're getting too fond of bullying,' said Veronica, 'it interferes with your charm, and charm's essential for your success.' She went out to make the coffee.
>
> What Veronica said was very true, thought John, and he made a note to be more detached in his attitude. All the same these criticisms were bad for his self-esteem. For all her loyalty Veronica knew him too well, got too near home. Charm was important to success, but self-esteem was more so.

Not only does she understand him, but her understanding and criticism are conveyed to John not so much by words as by his own intuition of what she is thinking about him. The story ends with John planning to get rid of her.

In **'Mother's Sense of Fun'** there is a subtle gradation between what is actually said, and the impression it is designed, almost unconsciously, to produce. Mother contrives to make her son's friends sound ridiculous, to themselves and to him. Her warm jokey goodsport manner paralyses them like a spider wrapping up a fly: simple as she is, her jealousy gives her an extraordinary range of diplomatic finesse. She even manages to shoot down her son's most valued and most sophisticated woman friend by refusing to be shocked by the kind of stories she tells, whereupon the stories themselves lose all point and merely look silly. The upshot of the tale is brilliant, and moving. Mother catches a cold, giving the son a 'treat' outing, and it turns to pneumonia. As she dies, he can just hear her murmur: 'My poor boy will be very lonely without mother.' The sense of freedom and release is wonderful, and he plans all sorts of things for himself, but one night he has a nasty dream, with no one to turn to as he wakes up from it:

> He felt dreadfully lonely, so lonely that he began to cry. He told himself that this sense of solitude would pass with time, but in his heart he knew that this was not true. He might be free in little things, but in essentials she had tied him to her and now she had left him for ever. She had had the last word in the matter as usual. 'My poor boy will be lonely,' she had said. She was dead right.

The story goes to the heart not just of its own situation but of all social and family life. Boredom and exasperation are necessary to our sense of belonging: we are lonely without the people who provoke them. Mother's last word reverberates through the social universe. ' "Ah well, thank God for a sense of humour, without it the evening might have been very dull." How he had longed to say that even with it the evening had not been very interesting.' The sense of fun is social collusion, being one of us, and Jane Austen would have appreciated the special twist of the knife that Wilson gives it here. Being 'one of us' is no fun if someone—in this case mother—forces the relationship possessively and purposefully upon us. But even that is better than being lonely. Wilson's style shows to particular advantage in the last words of the story, where the simple and moving cliché language ('would pass with time, but in his heart . . . ') is brought up with a snap against a brisker catchphrase: 'She was dead right.'

In **'Significant Experience', 'Crazy Crowd',** and **'Et Dona Ferentes',** the real subject appears suddenly behind the back, as it were, of the narrative: always a sign of the best kind of short story. The first is about an undergraduate who is picked up by a rich older woman in Paris and has a good time until her tantrums and her impossibleness begin to get him down. He escapes coldbloodedly from the hotel in the South of France where they are staying, and on the way to the station is pursued and teased by a lithe male adolescent. It is this which he later mentions to his friends as the vac's 'significant experience'. Less Somerset Maugham and more purely Wilson is the marvellous evocation of a family in **'Crazy Crowd',** when a bright young academic from a humble background goes with his fiancée for the weekend to her Cambridgeshire home. Her stiflingly lively family reduce him to a state of misery and rage, she herself becoming with them a quite different person, and only the last resort of her physical caresses can calm him down. Although a social point is made—the daunting charm of an upper class—the real point is how individuals and communities frighten each other without meaning to, or do they really mean to? Involuntary social cruelty is in any case worse than the real thing in this effervescent pre-*Lucky Jim* story.

Wilson's great strength as a narrator is the way in which his sense of camp flows without effort or warning into an area of pain or grief, or simple wickedness, which are all described with robust and resolute honesty. In **'Et Dona Ferentes'** we encounter misery head-on in the first sentences—that of Monica, the chain-smoking wife scourged by invisible furies, the ghosts of handsome boys for whom her much-loved husband has so often fallen. In this story pain is far more real than sex: although sex, in the person of the young Swede who is staying with them, her son's pen-friend, is more in the foreground. Sensing the wife's tension, and resenting her rudeness to him, the handsome Swedish boy offers himself to her husband, who dreams of a situation in which they could spend the night together in a hotel, and in which he could buy the boy expensive presents. But nothing happens, except that the wife is condemned more closely to her prison of fear, and the husband to his dreams of liberation. 'He threw open one of the windows and let in a refreshing breeze that blew across from the hills.' Love, like sex, is with most of us no more than a persistent fantasy. And yet there is an almost intolerably moving moment in **'Heart of Elm',** when the old servant, from whom her employer has been longing to escape for years, dies in her arms with a last cry of 'My dearie, my lovie.' Dying, she can reveal what she hardly knew she had felt, and the employer wakes from her dream of liberation from her tyranny to a bleak realisation of what it had really meant.

After the mid-Fifties Angus Wilson launched himself as a novelist, and the later stories, comparatively few in number, seem to have in miniature the preoccupations of the larger form rather than the special features of the short story. They openly discuss political and social questions, and are uncompromisingly on the side of the Labour Government, which the early stories are only by implication. Like Zola, of whom Wilson had made a study, they are full of facts and observations about facts, and they have a kind of intelligent looseness about them which is very original. They have some resemblance to Pushkin's short studies for novels, but at story length. **'A Bit off the Map'** is a good example of this odd and interesting genre. In terms of impact, however, the early stories in *The Wrong Set* and *Such Darling Dodos* are in a class of their own. **'Raspberry Jam'** must certainly be one of the wickedest stories in the world, and all the more so because, as with 'Mary Postgate', wickedness does not attach itself to any motive or person, but is horribly present in the directions the words themselves seem to be taking. And there is no doubt in that story that the climactic horror really does happen.

FURTHER READING

Criticism

Admas, Stephen. *The Homosexual as Hero in Contemporary Fiction.* New York: Barnes & Noble Books, 1980, 181 p.
  Examines Wilson's portrayal of homosexual characters.

Allen, Walter. "Wilson." In *The Short Story in English*, pp. 289-95. New York: Oxford University Press, 1981.
  Survey of several of Wilson's short stories and their social criticism.

Bowen, Elizabeth. "The Wrong Set." In *The Mulberry Tree*, pp. 171-72. San Diego: Harcourt Brace Jovanovich, Publishers, 1986.
  States that Wilson's first collection of stories shows talent, but finds them filled with excessive detail and little humor.

Fletcher, Mary Dell. "Wilson's Raspberry Jam." *The Explicator* 40, No. 3 (July 1950): 49-51.
  Discusses the plot and meaning of one of Wilson's most famous short stories.

Green, Martin. "Artist Astray." *Chicago Review* 12, No. 3 (Autumn 1985): 76-9.
  Deems Wilson's stories grotesque and pornographic.

Mander, John. "A House Divided: The Short Stories of Angus Wilson." In *The Writer and Commitment*, pp. 111-38. London: Secker & Warburg, 1961.
  Describes Wilson's short fiction as influenced by Freud and Marx and argues that Wilson is a "committed" artist.

Millgate, Michael. "The Art of Fiction: Angus Wilson." *Paris Review* 5, No. 17 (Autumn-Winter 1957): 89-105.
  Explores how Wilson has been influenced by other writers and how he views his characters.

Moorcock, Michael. "Angus Wilson Talks to Michael Moorcock." *Books and Bookmen* 18, No. 8 (May 1973): 22-8.
  Outlines Wilson's writing style and various influences on his work.

Sexton, David. "My Family and Other Monsters." *Spectator* 259, No. 8319-8320 (19-26 December 1987): 71-2.
  Remarks that Wilson's stories are a "compendium of monsters."

Additional coverage of Wilson's life and career is contained in the following sources published by Gale Research: *Contemporary Literary Criticism*, Vols. 2, 3, 5, 25, 34; and *Dictionary of Literary Biography*, Vols. 15, 139, 155.

Appendix:

Select Bibliography of General Sources on Short Fiction

BOOKS OF CRITICISM

Allen, Walter. *The Short Story in English*. New York: Oxford University Press, 1981, 413 p.

Aycock, Wendell M., ed. *The Teller and the Tale: Aspects of the Short Story* (Proceedings of the Comparative Literature Symposium, Texas Tech University, Volume XIII). Lubbock: Texas Tech Press, 1982, 156 p.

Averill, Deborah. *The Irish Short Story from George Moore to Frank O'Connor*. Washington, D.C.: University Press of America, 1982, 329 p.

Bates, H. E. *The Modern Short Story: A Critical Survey*. Boston: Writer, 1941, 231 p.

Bayley, John. *The Short Story: Henry James to Elizabeth Bowen*. Great Britain: The Harvester Press Limited, 1988, 197 p.

Bennett, E. K. *A History of the German Novelle: From Goethe to Thomas Mann*. Cambridge: At the University Press, 1934, 296 p.

Bone, Robert. *Down Home: A History of Afro-American Short Fiction from Its Beginning to the End of the Harlem Renaissance*. Rev. ed. New York: Columbia University Press, 1988, 350 p.

Bruck, Peter. *The Black American Short Story in the Twentieth Century: A Collection of Critical Essays*. Amsterdam: B. R. Grüner Publishing Co., 1977, 209 p.

Burnett, Whit, and Burnett, Hallie. *The Modern Short Story in the Making*. New York: Hawthorn Books, 1964, 405 p.

Canby, Henry Seidel. *The Short Story in English*. New York: Henry Holt and Co., 1909, 386 p.

Current-García, Eugene. *The American Short Story before 1850: A Critical History*. Twayne's Critical History of the Short Story, edited by William Peden. Boston: Twayne Publishers, 1985, 168 p.

Flora, Joseph M., ed. *The English Short Story, 1880-1945: A Critical History*. Twayne's Critical History of the Short Story, edited by William Peden. Boston: Twayne Publishers, 1985, 215 p.

Foster, David William. *Studies in the Contemporary Spanish-American Short Story*. Columbia, Mo.: University of Missouri Press, 1979, 126 p.

George, Albert J. *Short Fiction in France, 1800-1850*. Syracuse, N.Y.: Syracuse University Press, 1964, 245 p.

Gerlach, John. *Toward an End: Closure and Structure in the American Short Story*. University, Ala.: The University of Alabama Press, 1985, 193 p.

Hankin, Cherry, ed. *Critical Essays on the New Zealand Short Story*. Auckland: Heinemann Publishers,

1982, 186 p.

Hanson, Clare, ed. *Re-Reading the Short Story*. London: MacMillan Press, 1989, 137 p.

Harris, Wendell V. *British Short Fiction in the Nineteenth Century*. Detroit: Wayne State University Press, 1979, 209 p.

Huntington, John. *Rationalizing Genius: Ideological Strategies in the Classic American Science Fiction Short Story*. New Brunswick: Rutgers University Press, 1989, 216 p.

Kilroy, James F., ed. *The Irish Short Story: A Critical History*. Twayne's Critical History of the Short Story, edited by William Peden. Boston: Twayne Publishers, 1984, 251 p.

Lee, A. Robert. *The Nineteenth-Century American Short Story*. Totowa, N. J.: Vision / Barnes & Noble, 1986, 196 p.

Leibowitz, Judith. *Narrative Purpose in the Novella*. The Hague: Mouton, 1974, 137 p.

Lohafer, Susan. *Coming to Terms with the Short Story*. Baton Rouge: Louisiana State University Press, 1983, 171 p.

Lohafer, Susan, and Clarey, Jo Ellyn. *Short Story Theory at a Crossroads*. Baton Rouge: Louisiana State University Press, 1989, 352 p.

Mann, Susan Garland. *The Short Story Cycle: A Genre Companion and Reference Guide*. New York: Greenwood Press, 1989, 228 p.

Matthews, Brander. *The Philosophy of the Short Story*. New York, N.Y.: Longmans, Green and Co., 1901, 83 p.

May, Charles E., ed. *Short Story Theories*. Athens, Oh.: Ohio University Press, 1976, 251 p.

McClave, Heather, ed. *Women Writers of the Short Story: A Collection of Critical Essays*. Englewood Cliffs, N. J.: Prentice-Hall, 1980, 171 p.

Moser, Charles, ed. *The Russian Short Story: A Critical History*. Twayne's Critical History of the Short Story, edited by William Peden. Boston: Twayne Publishers, 1986, 232 p.

New, W. H. *Dreams of Speech and Violence: The Art of the Short Story in Canada and New Zealand*. Toronto: The University of Toronto Press, 1987, 302 p.

Newman, Frances. *The Short Story's Mutations: From Petronius to Paul Morand*. New York: B. W. Huebsch, 1925, 332 p.

O'Connor, Frank. *The Lonely Voice: A Study of the Short Story*. Cleveland: World Publishing Co., 1963, 220 p.

O'Faolain, Sean. *The Short Story*. New York: Devin-Adair Co., 1951, 370 p.

Orel, Harold. *The Victorian Short Story: Development and Triumph of a Literary Genre*. Cambridge: Cambridge University Press, 1986, 213 p.

O'Toole, L. Michael. *Structure, Style and Interpretation in the Russian Short Story*. New Haven: Yale University Press, 1982, 272 p.

Pattee, Fred Lewis. *The Development of the American Short Story: An Historical Survey*. New York: Harper and Brothers Publishers, 1923, 388 p.

Peden, Margaret Sayers, ed. *The Latin American Short Story: A Critical History*. Twayne's Critical History of the Short Story, edited by William Peden. Boston: Twayne Publishers, 1983, 160 p.

Peden, William. *The American Short Story: Continuity and Change, 1940-1975*. Rev. ed. Boston: Houghton Mifflin Co., 1975, 215 p.

Reid, Ian. *The Short Story*. The Critical Idiom, edited by John D. Jump. London: Methuen and Co., 1977, 76 p.

Rhode, Robert D. *Setting in the American Short Story of Local Color, 1865-1900*. The Hague: Mouton, 1975, 189 p.

Rohrberger, Mary. *Hawthorne and the Modern Short Story: A Study in Genre*. The Hague: Mouton and Co., 1966, 148 p.

Shaw, Valerie. *The Short Story: A Critical Introduction*. London: Longman, 1983, 294 p.

Stephens, Michael. *The Dramaturgy of Style: Voice in Short Fiction*. Carbondale, Ill.: Southern Illinois University Press, 1986, 281 p.

Stevick, Philip, ed. *The American Short Story, 1900-1945: A Critical History*. Twayne's Critical History of the Short Story, edited by William Peden. Boston: Twayne Publishers, 1984, 209 p.

Summers, Hollis, ed. *Discussion of the Short Story*. Boston: D. C. Heath and Co., 1963, 118 p.

Vannatta, Dennis, ed. *The English Short Story, 1945-1980: A Critical History*. Twayne's Critical History of the Short Story, edited by William Peden. Boston: Twayne Publishers, 1985, 206 p.

Voss, Arthur. *The American Short Story: A Critical Survey*. Norman, Okla.: University of Oklahoma Press, 1973, 399 p.

Walker, Warren S. *Twentieth-Century Short Story Explication: New Series, Vol. 1: 1989-1990*. Hamden, Conn.: Shoe String, 1993, 366 p.

Ward, Alfred C. *Aspects of the Modern Short Story: English and American*. London: University of London Press, 1924, 307 p.

Weaver, Gordon, ed. *The American Short Story, 1945-1980: A Critical History*. Twayne's Critical History of the Short Story, edited by William Peden. Boston: Twayne Publishers, 1983, 150 p.

West, Ray B., Jr. *The Short Story in America, 1900-1950*. Chicago: Henry Regnery Co., 1952, 147 p.

Williams, Blanche Colton. *Our Short Story Writers*. New York: Moffat, Yard and Co., 1920, 357 p.

Wright, Austin McGiffert. *The American Short Story in the Twenties*. Chicago: University of Chicago Press, 1961, 425 p.

CRITICAL ANTHOLOGIES

Atkinson, W. Patterson, ed. *The Short-Story*. Boston: Allyn and Bacon, 1923, 317 p.

Baldwin, Charles Sears, ed. *American Short Stories*. New York, N.Y.: Longmans, Green and Co., 1904, 333 p.

Charters, Ann, ed. *The Story and Its Writer: An Introduction to Short Fiction*. New York: St. Martin's Press, 1983, 1239 p.

Current-García, Eugene, and Patrick, Walton R., eds. *American Short Stories: 1820 to the Present*. Key Editions, edited by John C. Gerber. Chicago: Scott, Foresman and Co., 1952, 633 p.

Fagin, N. Bryllion, ed. *America through the Short Story*. Boston: Little, Brown, and Co., 1936, 508 p.

Frakes, James R., and Traschen, Isadore, eds. *Short Fiction: A Critical Collection.* Prentice-Hall English Literature Series, edited by Maynard Mack. Englewood Cliffs, N.J.: Prentice-Hall, 1959, 459 p.

Gifford, Douglas, ed. *Scottish Short Stories, 1800-1900.* The Scottish Library, edited by Alexander Scott. London: Calder and Boyars, 1971, 350 p.

Gordon, Caroline, and Tate, Allen, eds. *The House of Fiction: An Anthology of the Short Story with Commentary.* Rev. ed. New York: Charles Scribner's Sons, 1960, 469 p.

Greet, T. Y., et. al. *The Worlds of Fiction: Stories in Context.* Boston, Mass.: Houghton Mifflin Co., 1964, 429 p.

Gullason, Thomas A., and Caspar, Leonard, eds. *The World of Short Fiction: An International Collection.* New York: Harper and Row, 1962, 548 p.

Havighurst, Walter, ed. *Masters of the Modern Short Story.* New York: Harcourt, Brace and Co., 1945, 538 p.

Litz, A. Walton, ed. *Major American Short Stories.* New York: Oxford University Press, 1975, 823 p.

Matthews, Brander, ed. *The Short-Story: Specimens Illustrating Its Development.* New York: American Book Co., 1907, 399 p.

Menton, Seymour, ed. *The Spanish American Short Story: A Critical Anthology.* Berkeley and Los Angeles: University of California Press, 1980, 496 p.

Mzamane, Mbulelo Vizikhungo, ed. *Hungry Flames, and Other Black South African Short Stories.* Longman African Classics. Essex: Longman, 1986, 162 p.

Schorer, Mark, ed. *The Short Story: A Critical Anthology.* Rev. ed. Prentice-Hall English Literature Series, edited by Maynard Mack. Englewood Cliffs, N. J.: Prentice-Hall, 1967, 459 p.

Simpson, Claude M., ed. *The Local Colorists: American Short Stories, 1857-1900.* New York: Harper and Brothers Publishers, 1960, 340 p.

Stanton, Robert, ed. *The Short Story and the Reader.* New York: Henry Holt and Co., 1960, 557 p.

West, Ray B., Jr., ed. *American Short Stories.* New York: Thomas Y. Crowell Co., 1959, 267 p.

Short Story Criticism Indexes

Literary Criticism Series
Cumulative Author Index

SSC Cumulative Nationality Index
SSC Cumulative Title Index

How to Use This Index

The main references

Calvino, Italo
1923-1985.....CLC 5, 8, 11, 22, 33, 39,
73; SSC 3

---

list all author entries in the following Gale Literary Criticism series:

BLC = *Black Literature Criticism*
CLC = *Contemporary Literary Criticism*
CLR = *Children's Literature Review*
CMLC = *Classical and Medieval Literature Criticism*
DA = *DISCovering Authors*
DC = *Drama Criticism*
HLC = *Hispanic Literature Criticism*
LC = *Literature Criticism from 1400 to 1800*
NCLC = *Nineteenth-Century Literature Criticism*
PC = *Poetry Criticism*
SSC = *Short Story Criticism*
TCLC = *Twentieth-Century Literary Criticism*
WLC = *World Literature Criticism, 1500 to the Present*

The cross-references

See also CANR 23; CA 85-88;
obituary CA 116

---

list all author entries in the following Gale biographical and literary sources:

AAYA = *Authors & Artists for Young Adults*
AITN = *Authors in the News*
BEST = *Bestsellers*
BW = *Black Writers*
CA = *Contemporary Authors*
CAAS = *Contemporary Authors Autobiography Series*
CABS = *Contemporary Authors Bibliographical Series*
CANR = *Contemporary Authors New Revision Series*
CAP = *Contemporary Authors Permanent Series*
CDALB = *Concise Dictionary of American Literary Biography*
CDBLB = *Concise Dictionary of British Literary Biography*
DLB = *Dictionary of Literary Biography*
DLBD = *Dictionary of Literary Biography Documentary Series*
DLBY = *Dictionary of Literary Biography Yearbook*
HW = *Hispanic Writers*
JRDA = *Junior DISCovering Authors*
MAICYA = *Major Authors and Illustrators for Children and Young Adults*
MTCW = *Major 20th-Century Writers*
NNAL = *Native North American Literature*
SAAS = *Something about the Author Autobiography Series*
SATA = *Something about the Author*
YABC = *Yesterday's Authors of Books for Children*

Anouilh, Jean (Marie Lucien Pierre)
1910-1987 . . . . . . **CLC 1, 3, 8, 13, 40, 50**
See also CA 17-20R; 123; CANR 32;
MTCW

Anthony, Florence
See Ai

Anthony, John
See Ciardi, John (Anthony)

Anthony, Peter
See Shaffer, Anthony (Joshua); Shaffer,
Peter (Levin)

Anthony, Piers 1934- . . . . **CLC 35**
See also AAYA 11; CA 21-24R; CANR 28;
DLB 8; MTCW

Antoine, Marc
See Proust, (Valentin-Louis-George-Eugene-)
Marcel

Antoninus, Brother
See Everson, William (Oliver)

Antonioni, Michelangelo 1912- . . . . . **CLC 20**
See also CA 73-76; CANR 45

Antschel, Paul 1920-1970
See Celan, Paul
See also CA 85-88; CANR 33; MTCW

Anwar, Chairil 1922-1949 . . . . **TCLC 22**
See also CA 121

Apollinaire, Guillaume . . **TCLC 3, 8, 51; PC 7**
See also Kostrowitzki, Wilhelm Apollinaris
de

Appelfeld, Aharon 1932- . . . . **CLC 23, 47**
See also CA 112; 133

Apple, Max (Isaac) 1941- . . . . **CLC 9, 33**
See also CA 81-84; CANR 19; DLB 130

Appleman, Philip (Dean) 1926- . . . . . **CLC 51**
See also CA 13-16R; CAAS 18; CANR 6,
29

Appleton, Lawrence
See Lovecraft, H(oward) P(hillips)

Apteryx
See Eliot, T(homas) S(tearns)

Apuleius, (Lucius Madaurensis)
125(?)-175(?) . . . . **CMLC 1**

Aquin, Hubert 1929-1977 . . . . **CLC 15**
See also CA 105; DLB 53

Aragon, Louis 1897-1982 . . . . **CLC 3, 22**
See also CA 69-72; 108; CANR 28;
DLB 72; MTCW

Arany, Janos 1817-1882 . . . . **NCLC 34**

Arbuthnot, John 1667-1735 . . . . **LC 1**
See also DLB 101

Archer, Herbert Winslow
See Mencken, H(enry) L(ouis)

Archer, Jeffrey (Howard) 1940- . . . . **CLC 28**
See also BEST 89:3; CA 77-80; CANR 22

Archer, Jules 1915- . . . . **CLC 12**
See also CA 9-12R; CANR 6; SAAS 5;
SATA 4

Archer, Lee
See Ellison, Harlan (Jay)

Arden, John 1930- . . . . **CLC 6, 13, 15**
See also CA 13-16R; CAAS 4; CANR 31;
DLB 13; MTCW

Arenas, Reinaldo
1943-1990 . . . . **CLC 41; HLC**
See also CA 124; 128; 133; DLB 145; HW

Arendt, Hannah 1906-1975 . . . . **CLC 66**
See also CA 17-20R; 61-64; CANR 26;
MTCW

Aretino, Pietro 1492-1556 . . . . **LC 12**

Arghezi, Tudor . . . . **CLC 80**
See also Theodorescu, Ion N.

Arguedas, Jose Maria
1911-1969 . . . . **CLC 10, 18**
See also CA 89-92; DLB 113; HW

Argueta, Manlio 1936- . . . . **CLC 31**
See also CA 131; DLB 145; HW

Ariosto, Ludovico 1474-1533 . . . . **LC 6**

Aristides
See Epstein, Joseph

Aristophanes
450B.C.-385B.C. . . . . **CMLC 4; DA;
DAB; DC 2**

Arlt, Roberto (Godofredo Christophersen)
1900-1942 . . . . **TCLC 29; HLC**
See also CA 123; 131; HW

Armah, Ayi Kwei 1939- . . . . **CLC 5, 33; BLC**
See also BW 1; CA 61-64; CANR 21;
DLB 117; MTCW

Armatrading, Joan 1950- . . . . **CLC 17**
See also CA 114

Arnette, Robert
See Silverberg, Robert

**Arnim, Achim von (Ludwig Joachim von
Arnim)** 1781-1831 . . . . **NCLC 5**
See also DLB 90

Arnim, Bettina von 1785-1859 . . . . **NCLC 38**
See also DLB 90

Arnold, Matthew
1822-1888 . . . . . **NCLC 6, 29; DA; DAB;
PC 5; WLC**
See also CDBLB 1832-1890; DLB 32, 57

Arnold, Thomas 1795-1842 . . . . . . **NCLC 18**
See also DLB 55

Arnow, Harriette (Louisa) Simpson
1908-1986 . . . . **CLC 2, 7, 18**
See also CA 9-12R; 118; CANR 14; DLB 6;
MTCW; SATA 42; SATA-Obit 47

Arp, Hans
See Arp, Jean

Arp, Jean 1887-1966 . . . . **CLC 5**
See also CA 81-84; 25-28R; CANR 42

Arrabal
See Arrabal, Fernando

Arrabal, Fernando 1932- . . . **CLC 2, 9, 18, 58**
See also CA 9-12R; CANR 15

Arrick, Fran . . . . **CLC 30**
See also Gaberman, Judie Angell

Artaud, Antonin 1896-1948 . . . . . **TCLC 3, 36**
See also CA 104

Arthur, Ruth M(abel) 1905-1979 . . . . **CLC 12**
See also CA 9-12R; 85-88; CANR 4;
SATA 7, 26

Artsybashev, Mikhail (Petrovich)
1878-1927 . . . . **TCLC 31**

Arundel, Honor (Morfydd)
1919-1973 . . . . **CLC 17**
See also CA 21-22; 41-44R; CAP 2;
CLR 35; SATA 4; SATA-Obit 24

Asch, Sholem 1880-1957 . . . . **TCLC 3**
See also CA 105

Ash, Shalom
See Asch, Sholem

Ashbery, John (Lawrence)
1927- . . . . . . **CLC 2, 3, 4, 6, 9, 13, 15, 25,
41, 77**
See also CA 5-8R; CANR 9, 37; DLB 5;
DLBY 81; MTCW

Ashdown, Clifford
See Freeman, R(ichard) Austin

Ashe, Gordon
See Creasey, John

Ashton-Warner, Sylvia (Constance)
1908-1984 . . . . **CLC 19**
See also CA 69-72; 112; CANR 29; MTCW

Asimov, Isaac
1920-1992 . . . . . . **CLC 1, 3, 9, 19, 26, 76**
See also AAYA 13; BEST 90:2; CA 1-4R;
137; CANR 2, 19, 36; CLR 12; DLB 8;
DLBY 92; JRDA; MAICYA; MTCW;
SATA 1, 26, 74

Astley, Thea (Beatrice May)
1925- . . . . **CLC 41**
See also CA 65-68; CANR 11, 43

Aston, James
See White, T(erence) H(anbury)

Asturias, Miguel Angel
1899-1974 . . . . **CLC 3, 8, 13; HLC**
See also CA 25-28; 49-52; CANR 32;
CAP 2; DLB 113; HW; MTCW

Atares, Carlos Saura
See Saura (Atares), Carlos

Atheling, William
See Pound, Ezra (Weston Loomis)

Atheling, William, Jr.
See Blish, James (Benjamin)

Atherton, Gertrude (Franklin Horn)
1857-1948 . . . . **TCLC 2**
See also CA 104; DLB 9, 78

Atherton, Lucius
See Masters, Edgar Lee

Atkins, Jack
See Harris, Mark

Atticus
See Fleming, Ian (Lancaster)

Atwood, Margaret (Eleanor)
1939- . . . . . **CLC 2, 3, 4, 8, 13, 15, 25, 44,
84; DA; DAB; PC 8; SSC 2; WLC**
See also AAYA 12; BEST 89:2; CA 49-52;
CANR 3, 24, 33; DLB 53; MTCW;
SATA 50

Aubigny, Pierre d'
See Mencken, H(enry) L(ouis)

Aubin, Penelope 1685-1731(?) . . . . **LC 9**
See also DLB 39

Auchincloss, Louis (Stanton)
1917- . . . . **CLC 4, 6, 9, 18, 45**
See also CA 1-4R; CANR 6, 29; DLB 2;
DLBY 80; MTCW

Auden, W(ystan) H(ugh)
  1907-1973 ...... CLC 1, 2, 3, 4, 6, 9, 11,
      14, 43; DA; DAB; PC 1; WLC
  See also CA 9-12R; 45-48; CANR 5;
      CDBLB 1914-1945; DLB 10, 20; MTCW

Audiberti, Jacques 1900-1965 ...... CLC 38
  See also CA 25-28R

Audubon, John James
  1785-1851 .... NCLC 47

Auel, Jean M(arie) 1936- .... CLC 31
  See also AAYA 7; BEST 90:4; CA 103;
      CANR 21

Auerbach, Erich 1892-1957 .... TCLC 43
  See also CA 118

Augier, Emile 1820-1889 .... NCLC 31

August, John
  See De Voto, Bernard (Augustine)

Augustine, St. 354-430 ..... CMLC 6; DAB

Aurelius
  See Bourne, Randolph S(illiman)

Austen, Jane
  1775-1817 ..... NCLC 1, 13, 19, 33, 51;
      DA; DAB; WLC
  See also CDBLB 1789-1832; DLB 116

Auster, Paul 1947- .... CLC 47
  See also CA 69-72; CANR 23

Austin, Frank
  See Faust, Frederick (Schiller)

Austin, Mary (Hunter)
  1868-1934 .... TCLC 25
  See also CA 109; DLB 9, 78

Autran Dourado, Waldomiro
  See Dourado, (Waldomiro Freitas) Autran

Averroes 1126-1198 .... CMLC 7
  See also DLB 115

Avicenna 980-1037 .... CMLC 16
  See also DLB 115

Avison, Margaret 1918- .... CLC 2, 4
  See also CA 17-20R; DLB 53; MTCW

Axton, David
  See Koontz, Dean R(ay)

Ayckbourn, Alan
  1939- .... CLC 5, 8, 18, 33, 74; DAB
  See also CA 21-24R; CANR 31; DLB 13;
      MTCW

Aydy, Catherine
  See Tennant, Emma (Christina)

Ayme, Marcel (Andre) 1902-1967... CLC 11
  See also CA 89-92; CLR 25; DLB 72

Ayrton, Michael 1921-1975 .... CLC 7
  See also CA 5-8R; 61-64; CANR 9, 21

Azorin .... CLC 11
  See also Martinez Ruiz, Jose

Azuela, Mariano
  1873-1952 .... TCLC 3; HLC
  See also CA 104; 131; HW; MTCW

Baastad, Babbis Friis
  See Friis-Baastad, Babbis Ellinor

Bab
  See Gilbert, W(illiam) S(chwenck)

Babbis, Eleanor
  See Friis-Baastad, Babbis Ellinor

Babel, Isaak (Emmanuilovich)
  1894-1941(?) ...... TCLC 2, 13; SSC 16
  See also CA 104

Babits, Mihaly 1883-1941 .... TCLC 14
  See also CA 114

Babur 1483-1530................. LC 18

Bacchelli, Riccardo 1891-1985 ..... CLC 19
  See also CA 29-32R; 117

Bach, Richard (David) 1936- .... CLC 14
  See also AITN 1; BEST 89:2; CA 9-12R;
      CANR 18; MTCW; SATA 13

Bachman, Richard
  See King, Stephen (Edwin)

Bachmann, Ingeborg 1926-1973..... CLC 69
  See also CA 93-96; 45-48; DLB 85

Bacon, Francis 1561-1626 .... LC 18
  See also CDBLB Before 1660; DLB 151

Bacon, Roger 1214(?)-1292 ...... CMLC 14
  See also DLB 115

Bacovia, George................. TCLC 24
  See also Vasiliu, Gheorghe

Badanes, Jerome 1937-............ CLC 59

Bagehot, Walter 1826-1877 ...... NCLC 10
  See also DLB 55

Bagnold, Enid 1889-1981........ CLC 25
  See also CA 5-8R; 103; CANR 5, 40;
      DLB 13; MAICYA; SATA 1, 25

Bagritsky, Eduard 1895-1934 ..... TCLC 60

Bagrjana, Elisaveta
  See Belcheva, Elisaveta

Bagryana, Elisaveta............... CLC 10
  See also Belcheva, Elisaveta
  See also DLB 147

Bailey, Paul 1937- .... CLC 45
  See also CA 21-24R; CANR 16; DLB 14

Baillie, Joanna 1762-1851 .... NCLC 2
  See also DLB 93

Bainbridge, Beryl (Margaret)
  1933- .... CLC 4, 5, 8, 10, 14, 18, 22, 62
  See also CA 21-24R; CANR 24; DLB 14;
      MTCW

Baker, Elliott 1922- .... CLC 8
  See also CA 45-48; CANR 2

Baker, Nicholson 1957- .... CLC 61
  See also CA 135

Baker, Ray Stannard 1870-1946 ... TCLC 47
  See also CA 118

Baker, Russell (Wayne) 1925-...... CLC 31
  See also BEST 89:4; CA 57-60; CANR 11,
      41; MTCW

Bakhtin, M.
  See Bakhtin, Mikhail Mikhailovich

Bakhtin, M. M.
  See Bakhtin, Mikhail Mikhailovich

Bakhtin, Mikhail
  See Bakhtin, Mikhail Mikhailovich

Bakhtin, Mikhail Mikhailovich
  1895-1975 .... CLC 83
  See also CA 128; 113

Bakshi, Ralph 1938(?)-............ CLC 26
  See also CA 112; 138

Bakunin, Mikhail (Alexandrovich)
  1814-1876 .... NCLC 25

Baldwin, James (Arthur)
  1924-1987 ...... CLC 1, 2, 3, 4, 5, 8, 13,
      15, 17, 42, 50, 67, 90; BLC; DA; DAB;
          DC 1; SSC 10; WLC
  See also AAYA 4; BW 1; CA 1-4R; 124;
      CABS 1; CANR 3, 24;
      CDALB 1941-1968; DLB 2, 7, 33;
      DLBY 87; MTCW; SATA 9;
      SATA-Obit 54

Ballard, J(ames) G(raham)
  1930- .... CLC 3, 6, 14, 36; SSC 1
  See also AAYA 3; CA 5-8R; CANR 15, 39;
      DLB 14; MTCW

Balmont, Konstantin (Dmitriyevich)
  1867-1943 .... TCLC 11
  See also CA 109

Balzac, Honore de
  1799-1850 ..... NCLC 5, 35; DA; DAB;
          SSC 5; WLC
  See also DLB 119

Bambara, Toni Cade
  1939- .... CLC 19, 88; BLC; DA
  See also AAYA 5; BW 2; CA 29-32R;
      CANR 24, 49; DLB 38; MTCW

Bamdad, A.
  See Shamlu, Ahmad

Banat, D. R.
  See Bradbury, Ray (Douglas)

Bancroft, Laura
  See Baum, L(yman) Frank

Banim, John 1798-1842......... NCLC 13
  See also DLB 116

Banim, Michael 1796-1874 ...... NCLC 13

Banks, Iain
  See Banks, Iain M(enzies)

Banks, Iain M(enzies) 1954-....... CLC 34
  See also CA 123; 128

Banks, Lynne Reid .... CLC 23
  See also Reid Banks, Lynne
  See also AAYA 6

Banks, Russell 1940- .... CLC 37, 72
  See also CA 65-68; CAAS 15; CANR 19;
      DLB 130

Banville, John 1945-.............. CLC 46
  See also CA 117; 128; DLB 14

Banville, Theodore (Faullain) de
  1832-1891 .... NCLC 9

Baraka, Amiri
  1934- .... CLC 1, 2, 3, 5, 10, 14, 33;
          BLC; DA; PC 4
  See also Jones, LeRoi
  See also BW 2; CA 21-24R; CABS 3;
      CANR 27, 38; CDALB 1941-1968;
      DLB 5, 7, 16, 38; DLBD 8; MTCW

Barbauld, Anna Laetitia
  1743-1825 .... NCLC 50
  See also DLB 107, 109, 142

Barbellion, W. N. P................ TCLC 24
  See also Cummings, Bruce F(rederick)

Barbera, Jack (Vincent) 1945-...... CLC 44
  See also CA 110; CANR 45

Barbey d'Aurevilly, Jules Amedee
  1808-1889 .... NCLC 1; SSC 17
  See also DLB 119

Barbusse, Henri 1873-1935 . . . . **TCLC 5**
See also CA 105; DLB 65

Barclay, Bill
See Moorcock, Michael (John)

Barclay, William Ewert
See Moorcock, Michael (John)

Barea, Arturo 1897-1957 . . . . **TCLC 14**
See also CA 111

Barfoot, Joan 1946- . . . . **CLC 18**
See also CA 105

Baring, Maurice 1874-1945 . . . . **TCLC 8**
See also CA 105; DLB 34

Barker, Clive 1952- . . . . **CLC 52**
See also AAYA 10; BEST 90:3; CA 121;
129; MTCW

Barker, George Granville
1913-1991 . . . . **CLC 8, 48**
See also CA 9-12R; 135; CANR 7, 38;
DLB 20; MTCW

Barker, Harley Granville
See Granville-Barker, Harley
See also DLB 10

Barker, Howard 1946- . . . . **CLC 37**
See also CA 102; DLB 13

Barker, Pat 1943- . . . . **CLC 32**
See also CA 117; 122

Barlow, Joel 1754-1812 . . . . **NCLC 23**
See also DLB 37

Barnard, Mary (Ethel) 1909- . . . . **CLC 48**
See also CA 21-22; CAP 2

Barnes, Djuna
1892-1982 . . . **CLC 3, 4, 8, 11, 29; SSC 3**
See also CA 9-12R; 107; CANR 16; DLB 4,
9, 45; MTCW

Barnes, Julian 1946- . . . . **CLC 42; DAB**
See also CA 102; CANR 19; DLBY 93

Barnes, Peter 1931- . . . . **CLC 5, 56**
See also CA 65-68; CAAS 12; CANR 33,
34; DLB 13; MTCW

Baroja (y Nessi), Pio
1872-1956 . . . . **TCLC 8; HLC**
See also CA 104

Baron, David
See Pinter, Harold

Baron Corvo
See Rolfe, Frederick (William Serafino
Austin Lewis Mary)

Barondess, Sue K(aufman)
1926-1977 . . . . **CLC 8**
See also Kaufman, Sue
See also CA 1-4R; 69-72; CANR 1

Baron de Teive
See Pessoa, Fernando (Antonio Nogueira)

Barres, Maurice 1862-1923 . . . . **TCLC 47**
See also DLB 123

Barreto, Afonso Henrique de Lima
See Lima Barreto, Afonso Henrique de

Barrett, (Roger) Syd 1946- . . . . **CLC 35**

Barrett, William (Christopher)
1913-1992 . . . . **CLC 27**
See also CA 13-16R; 139; CANR 11

Barrie, J(ames) M(atthew)
1860-1937 . . . . **TCLC 2; DAB**
See also CA 104; 136; CDBLB 1890-1914;
CLR 16; DLB 10, 141, 156; MAICYA;
YABC 1

Barrington, Michael
See Moorcock, Michael (John)

Barrol, Grady
See Bograd, Larry

Barry, Mike
See Malzberg, Barry N(athaniel)

Barry, Philip 1896-1949 . . . . **TCLC 11**
See also CA 109; DLB 7

Bart, Andre Schwarz
See Schwarz-Bart, Andre

Barth, John (Simmons)
1930- . . . . . . **CLC 1, 2, 3, 5, 7, 9, 10, 14,
27, 51, 89; SSC 10**
See also AITN 1, 2; CA 1-4R; CABS 1;
CANR 5, 23, 49; DLB 2; MTCW

Barthelme, Donald
1931-1989 . . . . . . **CLC 1, 2, 3, 5, 6, 8, 13,
23, 46, 59; SSC 2**
See also CA 21-24R; 129; CANR 20;
DLB 2; DLBY 80, 89; MTCW; SATA 7;
SATA-Obit 62

Barthelme, Frederick 1943- . . . . **CLC 36**
See also CA 114; 122; DLBY 85

Barthes, Roland (Gerard)
1915-1980 . . . . **CLC 24, 83**
See also CA 130; 97-100; MTCW

Barzun, Jacques (Martin) 1907- . . . . **CLC 51**
See also CA 61-64; CANR 22

Bashevis, Isaac
See Singer, Isaac Bashevis

Bashkirtseff, Marie 1859-1884 . . . **NCLC 27**

Basho
See Matsuo Basho

Bass, Kingsley B., Jr.
See Bullins, Ed

Bass, Rick 1958- . . . . **CLC 79**
See also CA 126

Bassani, Giorgio 1916- . . . . **CLC 9**
See also CA 65-68; CANR 33; DLB 128;
MTCW

Bastos, Augusto (Antonio) Roa
See Roa Bastos, Augusto (Antonio)

Bataille, Georges 1897-1962 . . . . **CLC 29**
See also CA 101; 89-92

Bates, H(erbert) E(rnest)
1905-1974 . . . . . . **CLC 46; DAB; SSC 10**
See also CA 93-96; 45-48; CANR 34;
MTCW

Bauchart
See Camus, Albert

Baudelaire, Charles
1821-1867 . . . . . **NCLC 6, 29; DA; DAB;
PC 1; SSC 18; WLC**

Baudrillard, Jean 1929- . . . . **CLC 60**

Baum, L(yman) Frank 1856-1919 . . . **TCLC 7**
See also CA 108; 133; CLR 15; DLB 22;
JRDA; MAICYA; MTCW; SATA 18

Baum, Louis F.
See Baum, L(yman) Frank

Baumbach, Jonathan 1933- . . . . . . **CLC 6, 23**
See also CA 13-16R; CAAS 5; CANR 12;
DLBY 80; MTCW

Bausch, Richard (Carl) 1945- . . . . . . **CLC 51**
See also CA 101; CAAS 14; CANR 43;
DLB 130

Baxter, Charles 1947- . . . . **CLC 45, 78**
See also CA 57-60; CANR 40; DLB 130

Baxter, George Owen
See Faust, Frederick (Schiller)

Baxter, James K(eir) 1926-1972 . . . . **CLC 14**
See also CA 77-80

Baxter, John
See Hunt, E(verette) Howard, (Jr.)

Bayer, Sylvia
See Glassco, John

Baynton, Barbara 1857-1929 . . . . . . **TCLC 57**

Beagle, Peter S(oyer) 1939- . . . . **CLC 7**
See also CA 9-12R; CANR 4; DLBY 80;
SATA 60

Bean, Normal
See Burroughs, Edgar Rice

Beard, Charles A(ustin)
1874-1948 . . . . **TCLC 15**
See also CA 115; DLB 17; SATA 18

Beardsley, Aubrey 1872-1898 . . . . . **NCLC 6**

Beattie, Ann
1947- . . . . **CLC 8, 13, 18, 40, 63; SSC 11**
See also BEST 90:2; CA 81-84; DLBY 82;
MTCW

Beattie, James 1735-1803 . . . . **NCLC 25**
See also DLB 109

Beauchamp, Kathleen Mansfield 1888-1923
See Mansfield, Katherine
See also CA 104; 134; DA

Beaumarchais, Pierre-Augustin Caron de
1732-1799 . . . . **DC 4**

**Beauvoir, Simone (Lucie Ernestine Marie
Bertrand) de**
1908-1986 . . . . **CLC 1, 2, 4, 8, 14, 31, 44,
50, 71; DA; DAB; WLC**
See also CA 9-12R; 118; CANR 28;
DLB 72; DLBY 86; MTCW

Becker, Jurek 1937- . . . . **CLC 7, 19**
See also CA 85-88; DLB 75

Becker, Walter 1950- . . . . **CLC 26**

Beckett, Samuel (Barclay)
1906-1989 . . . . . . **CLC 1, 2, 3, 4, 6, 9, 10,
11, 14, 18, 29, 57, 59, 83; DA; DAB;
SSC 16; WLC**
See also CA 5-8R; 130; CANR 33;
CDBLB 1945-1960; DLB 13, 15;
DLBY 90; MTCW

Beckford, William 1760-1844 . . . . **NCLC 16**
See also DLB 39

Beckman, Gunnel 1910- . . . . **CLC 26**
See also CA 33-36R; CANR 15; CLR 25;
MAICYA; SAAS 9; SATA 6

Becque, Henri 1837-1899 . . . . **NCLC 3**

Beddoes, Thomas Lovell
1803-1849 . . . . **NCLC 3**
See also DLB 96

Bedford, Donald F.
See Fearing, Kenneth (Flexner)

Berne, Victoria
See Fisher, M(ary) F(rances) K(ennedy)

Bernhard, Thomas
1931-1989 .... CLC 3, 32, 61
See also CA 85-88; 127; CANR 32;
DLB 85, 124; MTCW

Berriault, Gina 1926- .... CLC 54
See also CA 116; 129; DLB 130

Berrigan, Daniel 1921- .... CLC 4
See also CA 33-36R; CAAS 1; CANR 11,
43; DLB 5

Berrigan, Edmund Joseph Michael, Jr.
1934-1983
See Berrigan, Ted
See also CA 61-64; 110; CANR 14

Berrigan, Ted .... CLC 37
See also Berrigan, Edmund Joseph Michael,
Jr.
See also DLB 5

Berry, Charles Edward Anderson 1931-
See Berry, Chuck
See also CA 115

Berry, Chuck .... CLC 17
See also Berry, Charles Edward Anderson

Berry, Jonas
See Ashbery, John (Lawrence)

Berry, Wendell (Erdman)
1934- .... CLC 4, 6, 8, 27, 46
See also AITN 1; CA 73-76; DLB 5, 6

Berryman, John
1914-1972 ...... CLC 1, 2, 3, 4, 6, 8, 10,
13, 25, 62
See also CA 13-16; 33-36R; CABS 2;
CANR 35; CAP 1; CDALB 1941-1968;
DLB 48; MTCW

Bertolucci, Bernardo 1940- .... CLC 16
See also CA 106

Bertrand, Aloysius 1807-1841 .... NCLC 31

Bertran de Born c. 1140-1215 ..... CMLC 5

Besant, Annie (Wood) 1847-1933 ... TCLC 9
See also CA 105

Bessie, Alvah 1904-1985 .... CLC 23
See also CA 5-8R; 116; CANR 2; DLB 26

Bethlen, T. D.
See Silverberg, Robert

Beti, Mongo .... CLC 27; BLC
See also Biyidi, Alexandre

Betjeman, John
1906-1984 ... CLC 2, 6, 10, 34, 43; DAB
See also CA 9-12R; 112; CANR 33;
CDBLB 1945-1960; DLB 20; DLBY 84;
MTCW

Bettelheim, Bruno 1903-1990 ...... CLC 79
See also CA 81-84; 131; CANR 23; MTCW

Betti, Ugo 1892-1953 .... TCLC 5
See also CA 104

Betts, Doris (Waugh) 1932- .... CLC 3, 6, 28
See also CA 13-16R; CANR 9; DLBY 82

Bevan, Alistair
See Roberts, Keith (John Kingston)

Bialik, Chaim Nachman
1873-1934 .... TCLC 25

Bickerstaff, Isaac
See Swift, Jonathan

Bidart, Frank 1939- .... CLC 33
See also CA 140

Bienek, Horst 1930- .... CLC 7, 11
See also CA 73-76; DLB 75

Bierce, Ambrose (Gwinett)
1842-1914(?) .... TCLC 1, 7, 44; DA;
SSC 9; WLC
See also CA 104; 139; CDALB 1865-1917;
DLB 11, 12, 23, 71, 74

Billings, Josh
See Shaw, Henry Wheeler

Billington, (Lady) Rachel (Mary)
1942- .... CLC 43
See also AITN 2; CA 33-36R; CANR 44

Binyon, T(imothy) J(ohn) 1936- .... CLC 34
See also CA 111; CANR 28

Bioy Casares, Adolfo
1914- ... CLC 4, 8, 13, 88; HLC; SSC 17
See also CA 29-32R; CANR 19, 43;
DLB 113; HW; MTCW

Bird, Cordwainer
See Ellison, Harlan (Jay)

Bird, Robert Montgomery
1806-1854 .... NCLC 1

Birney, (Alfred) Earle
1904- .... CLC 1, 4, 6, 11
See also CA 1-4R; CANR 5, 20; DLB 88;
MTCW

Bishop, Elizabeth
1911-1979 ...... CLC 1, 4, 9, 13, 15, 32;
DA; PC 3
See also CA 5-8R; 89-92; CABS 2;
CANR 26; CDALB 1968-1988; DLB 5;
MTCW; SATA-Obit 24

Bishop, John 1935- .... CLC 10
See also CA 105

Bissett, Bill 1939- .... CLC 18
See also CA 69-72; CAAS 19; CANR 15;
DLB 53; MTCW

Bitov, Andrei (Georgievich) 1937- ... CLC 57
See also CA 142

Biyidi, Alexandre 1932-
See Beti, Mongo
See also BW 1; CA 114; 124; MTCW

Bjarme, Brynjolf
See Ibsen, Henrik (Johan)

Bjornson, Bjornstjerne (Martinius)
1832-1910 .... TCLC 7, 37
See also CA 104

Black, Robert
See Holdstock, Robert P.

Blackburn, Paul 1926-1971 ...... CLC 9, 43
See also CA 81-84; 33-36R; CANR 34;
DLB 16; DLBY 81

Black Elk 1863-1950 .... TCLC 33
See also CA 144; NNAL

Black Hobart
See Sanders, (James) Ed(ward)

Blacklin, Malcolm
See Chambers, Aidan

Blackmore, R(ichard) D(oddridge)
1825-1900 .... TCLC 27
See also CA 120; DLB 18

Blackmur, R(ichard) P(almer)
1904-1965 .... CLC 2, 24
See also CA 11-12; 25-28R; CAP 1; DLB 63

Black Tarantula, The
See Acker, Kathy

Blackwood, Algernon (Henry)
1869-1951 .... TCLC 5
See also CA 105; DLB 153, 156

Blackwood, Caroline 1931- .... CLC 6, 9
See also CA 85-88; CANR 32; DLB 14;
MTCW

Blade, Alexander
See Hamilton, Edmond; Silverberg, Robert

Blaga, Lucian 1895-1961 .... CLC 75

Blair, Eric (Arthur) 1903-1950
See Orwell, George
See also CA 104; 132; DA; DAB; MTCW;
SATA 29

Blais, Marie-Claire
1939- .... CLC 2, 4, 6, 13, 22
See also CA 21-24R; CAAS 4; CANR 38;
DLB 53; MTCW

Blaise, Clark 1940- .... CLC 29
See also AITN 2; CA 53-56; CAAS 3;
CANR 5; DLB 53

Blake, Nicholas
See Day Lewis, C(ecil)
See also DLB 77

Blake, William
1757-1827 .... NCLC 13, 37; DA; DAB;
PC 12; WLC
See also CDBLB 1789-1832; DLB 93;
MAICYA; SATA 30

Blake, William J(ames) 1894-1969 ... PC 12
See also CA 5-8R; 25-28R

Blasco Ibanez, Vicente
1867-1928 .... TCLC 12
See also CA 110; 131; HW; MTCW

Blatty, William Peter 1928- .... CLC 2
See also CA 5-8R; CANR 9

Bleeck, Oliver
See Thomas, Ross (Elmore)

Blessing, Lee 1949- .... CLC 54

Blish, James (Benjamin)
1921-1975 .... CLC 14
See also CA 1-4R; 57-60; CANR 3; DLB 8;
MTCW; SATA 66

Bliss, Reginald
See Wells, H(erbert) G(eorge)

Blixen, Karen (Christentze Dinesen)
1885-1962
See Dinesen, Isak
See also CA 25-28; CANR 22; CAP 2;
MTCW; SATA 44

Bloch, Robert (Albert) 1917-1994 ... CLC 33
See also CA 5-8R; 146; CAAS 20; CANR 5;
DLB 44; SATA 12; SATA-Obit 82

Blok, Alexander (Alexandrovich)
1880-1921 .... TCLC 5
See also CA 104

Blom, Jan
See Breytenbach, Breyten

Bloom, Harold 1930- .... CLC 24
See also CA 13-16R; CANR 39; DLB 67

Bloomfield, Aurelius
See Bourne, Randolph S(illiman)

Blount, Roy (Alton), Jr. 1941- ..... **CLC 38**
See also CA 53-56; CANR 10, 28; MTCW

Bloy, Leon 1846-1917............ **TCLC 22**
See also CA 121; DLB 123

Blume, Judy (Sussman) 1938-... **CLC 12, 30**
See also AAYA 3; CA 29-32R; CANR 13,
37; CLR 2, 15; DLB 52; JRDA;
MAICYA; MTCW; SATA 2, 31, 79

Blunden, Edmund (Charles)
1896-1974 .... **CLC 2, 56**
See also CA 17-18; 45-48; CAP 2; DLB 20,
100, 155; MTCW

Bly, Robert (Elwood)
1926- .... **CLC 1, 2, 5, 10, 15, 38**
See also CA 5-8R; CANR 41; DLB 5;
MTCW

Boas, Franz 1858-1942........... **TCLC 56**
See also CA 115

Bobette
See Simenon, Georges (Jacques Christian)

Boccaccio, Giovanni
1313-1375 .... **CMLC 13; SSC 10**

Bochco, Steven 1943-............. **CLC 35**
See also AAYA 11; CA 124; 138

Bodenheim, Maxwell 1892-1954 ... **TCLC 44**
See also CA 110; DLB 9, 45

Bodker, Cecil 1927- .... **CLC 21**
See also CA 73-76; CANR 13, 44; CLR 23;
MAICYA; SATA 14

Boell, Heinrich (Theodor)
1917-1985 .... **CLC 2, 3, 6, 9, 11, 15, 27,
32, 72; DA; DAB; WLC**
See also CA 21-24R; 116; CANR 24;
DLB 69; DLBY 85; MTCW

Boerne, Alfred
See Doeblin, Alfred

Boethius 480(?)-524(?) .... **CMLC 15**
See also DLB 115

Bogan, Louise
1897-1970 ...... **CLC 4, 39, 46; PC 12**
See also CA 73-76; 25-28R; CANR 33;
DLB 45; MTCW

Bogarde, Dirk .... **CLC 19**
See also Van Den Bogarde, Derek Jules
Gaspard Ulric Niven
See also DLB 14

Bogosian, Eric 1953- .... **CLC 45**
See also CA 138

Bograd, Larry 1953-.............. **CLC 35**
See also CA 93-96; SATA 33

Boiardo, Matteo Maria 1441-1494 .... **LC 6**

Boileau-Despreaux, Nicolas
1636-1711 .... **LC 3**

Boland, Eavan (Aisling) 1944-... **CLC 40, 67**
See also CA 143; DLB 40

Bolt, Lee
See Faust, Frederick (Schiller)

Bolt, Robert (Oxton) 1924-1995 .... **CLC 14**
See also CA 17-20R; 147; CANR 35;
DLB 13; MTCW

Bombet, Louis-Alexandre-Cesar
See Stendhal

Bomkauf
See Kaufman, Bob (Garnell)

Bonaventura.................... **NCLC 35**
See also DLB 90

Bond, Edward 1934-....... **CLC 4, 6, 13, 23**
See also CA 25-28R; CANR 38; DLB 13;
MTCW

Bonham, Frank 1914-1989........ **CLC 12**
See also AAYA 1; CA 9-12R; CANR 4, 36;
JRDA; MAICYA; SAAS 3; SATA 1, 49;
SATA-Obit 62

Bonnefoy, Yves 1923-........ **CLC 9, 15, 58**
See also CA 85-88; CANR 33; MTCW

Bontemps, Arna(ud Wendell)
1902-1973 .... **CLC 1, 18; BLC**
See also BW 1; CA 1-4R; 41-44R; CANR 4,
35; CLR 6; DLB 48, 51; JRDA;
MAICYA; MTCW; SATA 2, 44;
SATA-Obit 24

Booth, Martin 1944-.............. **CLC 13**
See also CA 93-96; CAAS 2

Booth, Philip 1925-............... **CLC 23**
See also CA 5-8R; CANR 5; DLBY 82

Booth, Wayne C(layson) 1921- ..... **CLC 24**
See also CA 1-4R; CAAS 5; CANR 3, 43;
DLB 67

Borchert, Wolfgang 1921-1947 ..... **TCLC 5**
See also CA 104; DLB 69, 124

Borel, Petrus 1809-1859......... **NCLC 41**

Borges, Jorge Luis
1899-1986 ... **CLC 1, 2, 3, 4, 6, 8, 9, 10,
13, 19, 44, 48, 83; DA; DAB; HLC;
SSC 4; WLC**
See also CA 21-24R; CANR 19, 33;
DLB 113; DLBY 86; HW; MTCW

Borowski, Tadeusz 1922-1951...... **TCLC 9**
See also CA 106

Borrow, George (Henry)
1803-1881 .... **NCLC 9**
See also DLB 21, 55

Bosman, Herman Charles
1905-1951 .... **TCLC 49**

Bosschere, Jean de 1878(?)-1953... **TCLC 19**
See also CA 115

Boswell, James
1740-1795 ...... **LC 4; DA; DAB; WLC**
See also CDBLB 1660-1789; DLB 104, 142

Bottoms, David 1949-............. **CLC 53**
See also CA 105; CANR 22; DLB 120;
DLBY 83

Boucicault, Dion 1820-1890...... **NCLC 41**

Boucolon, Maryse 1937-
See Conde, Maryse
See also CA 110; CANR 30

Bourget, Paul (Charles Joseph)
1852-1935 .... **TCLC 12**
See also CA 107; DLB 123

Bourjaily, Vance (Nye) 1922- .... **CLC 8, 62**
See also CA 1-4R; CAAS 1; CANR 2;
DLB 2, 143

Bourne, Randolph S(illiman)
1886-1918 .... **TCLC 16**
See also CA 117; DLB 63

Bova, Ben(jamin William) 1932-.... **CLC 45**
See also CA 5-8R; CAAS 18; CANR 11;
CLR 3; DLBY 81; MAICYA; MTCW;
SATA 6, 68

Bowen, Elizabeth (Dorothea Cole)
1899-1973 ...... **CLC 1, 3, 6, 11, 15, 22;
SSC 3**
See also CA 17-18; 41-44R; CANR 35;
CAP 2; CDBLB 1945-1960; DLB 15;
MTCW

Bowering, George 1935-........ **CLC 15, 47**
See also CA 21-24R; CAAS 16; CANR 10;
DLB 53

Bowering, Marilyn R(uthe) 1949-... **CLC 32**
See also CA 101; CANR 49

Bowers, Edgar 1924- .... **CLC 9**
See also CA 5-8R; CANR 24; DLB 5

Bowie, David .... **CLC 17**
See also Jones, David Robert

Bowles, Jane (Sydney)
1917-1973 .... **CLC 3, 68**
See also CA 19-20; 41-44R; CAP 2

Bowles, Paul (Frederick)
1910- .... **CLC 1, 2, 19, 53; SSC 3**
See also CA 1-4R; CAAS 1; CANR 1, 19;
DLB 5, 6; MTCW

Box, Edgar
See Vidal, Gore

Boyd, Nancy
See Millay, Edna St. Vincent

Boyd, William 1952-........ **CLC 28, 53, 70**
See also CA 114; 120

Boyle, Kay
1902-1992 ..... **CLC 1, 5, 19, 58; SSC 5**
See also CA 13-16R; 140; CAAS 1;
CANR 29; DLB 4, 9, 48, 86; DLBY 93;
MTCW

Boyle, Mark
See Kienzle, William X(avier)

Boyle, Patrick 1905-1982......... **CLC 19**
See also CA 127

Boyle, T. C. 1948-
See Boyle, T(homas) Coraghessan

Boyle, T(homas) Coraghessan
1948- .... **CLC 36, 55, 90; SSC 16**
See also BEST 90:4; CA 120; CANR 44;
DLBY 86

Boz
See Dickens, Charles (John Huffam)

Brackenridge, Hugh Henry
1748-1816 .... **NCLC 7**
See also DLB 11, 37

Bradbury, Edward P.
See Moorcock, Michael (John)

Bradbury, Malcolm (Stanley)
1932- .... **CLC 32, 61**
See also CA 1-4R; CANR 1, 33; DLB 14;
MTCW

Bradbury, Ray (Douglas)
1920- .... **CLC 1, 3, 10, 15, 42; DA;
DAB; WLC**
See also AAYA 15; AITN 1, 2; CA 1-4R;
CANR 2, 30; CDALB 1968-1988; DLB 2,
8; MTCW; SATA 11, 64

Bradford, Gamaliel   1863-1932..... **TCLC 36**
See also DLB 17

Bradley, David (Henry, Jr.)
1950- .... **CLC 23; BLC**
See also BW 1; CA 104; CANR 26; DLB 33

Bradley, John Ed(mund, Jr.)
1958- .... **CLC 55**
See also CA 139

Bradley, Marion Zimmer   1930-..... **CLC 30**
See also AAYA 9; CA 57-60; CAAS 10;
CANR 7, 31; DLB 8; MTCW

Bradstreet, Anne
1612(?)-1672 ...... **LC 4, 30; DA; PC 10**
See also CDALB 1640-1865; DLB 24

Brady, Joan   1939- .... **CLC 86**
See also CA 141

Bragg, Melvyn   1939- .... **CLC 10**
See also BEST 89:3; CA 57-60; CANR 10,
48; DLB 14

Braine, John (Gerard)
1922-1986 ....**CLC 1, 3, 41**
See also CA 1-4R; 120; CANR 1, 33;
CDBLB 1945-1960; DLB 15; DLBY 86;
MTCW

Brammer, William   1930(?)-1978 .... **CLC 31**
See also CA 77-80

Brancati, Vitaliano   1907-1954..... **TCLC 12**
See also CA 109

Brancato, Robin F(idler)   1936- ..... **CLC 35**
See also AAYA 9; CA 69-72; CANR 11,
45; CLR 32; JRDA; SAAS 9; SATA 23

Brand, Max
See Faust, Frederick (Schiller)

Brand, Millen   1906-1980 .... **CLC 7**
See also CA 21-24R; 97-100

Branden, Barbara .... **CLC 44**
See also CA 148

Brandes, Georg (Morris Cohen)
1842-1927 .... **TCLC 10**
See also CA 105

Brandys, Kazimierz   1916- .... **CLC 62**

Branley, Franklyn M(ansfield)
1915- .... **CLC 21**
See also CA 33-36R; CANR 14, 39;
CLR 13; MAICYA; SAAS 16; SATA 4,
68

Brathwaite, Edward Kamau   1930-... **CLC 11**
See also BW 2; CA 25-28R; CANR 11, 26,
47; DLB 125

Brautigan, Richard (Gary)
1935-1984 .... **CLC 1, 3, 5, 9, 12, 34, 42**
See also CA 53-56; 113; CANR 34; DLB 2,
5; DLBY 80, 84; MTCW; SATA 56

Braverman, Kate   1950- .... **CLC 67**
See also CA 89-92

Brecht, Bertolt
1898-1956 ...... **TCLC 1, 6, 13, 35; DA;**
DAB; DC 3; WLC
See also CA 104; 133; DLB 56, 124; MTCW

Brecht, Eugen Berthold Friedrich
See Brecht, Bertolt

Bremer, Fredrika   1801-1865 ..... **NCLC 11**

Brennan, Christopher John
1870-1932 .... **TCLC 17**
See also CA 117

Brennan, Maeve   1917-............. **CLC 5**
See also CA 81-84

Brentano, Clemens (Maria)
1778-1842 .... **NCLC 1**
See also DLB 90

Brent of Bin Bin
See Franklin, (Stella Maraia Sarah) Miles

Brenton, Howard   1942-........... **CLC 31**
See also CA 69-72; CANR 33; DLB 13;
MTCW

Breslin, James   1930-
See Breslin, Jimmy
See also CA 73-76; CANR 31; MTCW

Breslin, Jimmy .... **CLC 4, 43**
See also Breslin, James
See also AITN 1

Bresson, Robert   1901-............ **CLC 16**
See also CA 110; CANR 49

Breton, Andre   1896-1966... **CLC 2, 9, 15, 54**
See also CA 19-20; 25-28R; CANR 40;
CAP 2; DLB 65; MTCW

Breytenbach, Breyten   1939(?)- .. **CLC 23, 37**
See also CA 113; 129

Bridgers, Sue Ellen   1942- .... **CLC 26**
See also AAYA 8; CA 65-68; CANR 11,
36; CLR 18; DLB 52; JRDA; MAICYA;
SAAS 1; SATA 22

Bridges, Robert (Seymour)
1844-1930 .... **TCLC 1**
See also CA 104; CDBLB 1890-1914;
DLB 19, 98

Bridie, James.................... **TCLC 3**
See also Mavor, Osborne Henry
See also DLB 10

Brin, David   1950-................ **CLC 34**
See also CA 102; CANR 24; SATA 65

Brink, Andre (Philippus)
1935- .... **CLC 18, 36**
See also CA 104; CANR 39; MTCW

Brinsmead, H(esba) F(ay)   1922- .... **CLC 21**
See also CA 21-24R; CANR 10; MAICYA;
SAAS 5; SATA 18, 78

Brittain, Vera (Mary)
1893(?)-1970 .... **CLC 23**
See also CA 13-16; 25-28R; CAP 1; MTCW

Broch, Hermann   1886-1951....... **TCLC 20**
See also CA 117; DLB 85, 124

Brock, Rose
See Hansen, Joseph

Brodkey, Harold   1930-............ **CLC 56**
See also CA 111; DLB 130

Brodsky, Iosif Alexandrovich   1940-
See Brodsky, Joseph
See also AITN 1; CA 41-44R; CANR 37;
MTCW

Brodsky, Joseph .. **CLC 4, 6, 13, 36, 50; PC 9**
See also Brodsky, Iosif Alexandrovich

Brodsky, Michael Mark   1948- ..... **CLC 19**
See also CA 102; CANR 18, 41

Bromell, Henry   1947-............. **CLC 5**
See also CA 53-56; CANR 9

Bromfield, Louis (Brucker)
1896-1956 .... **TCLC 11**
See also CA 107; DLB 4, 9, 86

Broner, E(sther) M(asserman)
1930- .... **CLC 19**
See also CA 17-20R; CANR 8, 25; DLB 28

Bronk, William   1918-............. **CLC 10**
See also CA 89-92; CANR 23

Bronstein, Lev Davidovich
See Trotsky, Leon

Bronte, Anne   1820-1849......... **NCLC 4**
See also DLB 21

Bronte, Charlotte
1816-1855 .... **NCLC 3, 8, 33; DA;**
DAB; WLC
See also CDBLB 1832-1890; DLB 21

Bronte, Emily (Jane)
1818-1848 .... **NCLC 16, 35; DA; DAB;**
PC 8; WLC
See also CDBLB 1832-1890; DLB 21, 32

Brooke, Frances   1724-1789 .... **LC 6**
See also DLB 39, 99

Brooke, Henry   1703(?)-1783 .... **LC 1**
See also DLB 39

Brooke, Rupert (Chawner)
1887-1915 .... **TCLC 2, 7; DA; DAB;**
WLC
See also CA 104; 132; CDBLB 1914-1945;
DLB 19; MTCW

Brooke-Haven, P.
See Wodehouse, P(elham) G(renville)

Brooke-Rose, Christine   1926-...... **CLC 40**
See also CA 13-16R; DLB 14

Brookner, Anita
1928- .... **CLC 32, 34, 51; DAB**
See also CA 114; 120; CANR 37; DLBY 87;
MTCW

Brooks, Cleanth   1906-1994 ..... **CLC 24, 86**
See also CA 17-20R; 145; CANR 33, 35;
DLB 63; DLBY 94; MTCW

Brooks, George
See Baum, L(yman) Frank

Brooks, Gwendolyn
1917- ...... **CLC 1, 2, 4, 5, 15, 49; BLC;**
DA; PC 7; WLC
See also AITN 1; BW 2; CA 1-4R;
CANR 1, 27; CDALB 1941-1968;
CLR 27; DLB 5, 76; MTCW; SATA 6

Brooks, Mel...................... **CLC 12**
See also Kaminsky, Melvin
See also AAYA 13; DLB 26

Brooks, Peter   1938-.............. **CLC 34**
See also CA 45-48; CANR 1

Brooks, Van Wyck   1886-1963...... **CLC 29**
See also CA 1-4R; CANR 6; DLB 45, 63,
103

Brophy, Brigid (Antonia)
1929- .... **CLC 6, 11, 29**
See also CA 5-8R; CAAS 4; CANR 25;
DLB 14; MTCW

Brosman, Catharine Savage   1934-.... **CLC 9**
See also CA 61-64; CANR 21, 46

Brother Antoninus
See Everson, William (Oliver)

Broughton, T(homas) Alan   1936- ... **CLC 19**
See also CA 45-48; CANR 2, 23, 48

Broumas, Olga   1949-.......... **CLC 10, 73**
See also CA 85-88; CANR 20

Brown, Charles Brockden
1771-1810 . . . . NCLC 22
See also CDALB 1640-1865; DLB 37, 59, 73

Brown, Christy 1932-1981 . . . . CLC 63
See also CA 105; 104; DLB 14

Brown, Claude 1937- . . . . CLC 30; BLC
See also AAYA 7; BW 1; CA 73-76

Brown, Dee (Alexander) 1908- . . CLC 18, 47
See also CA 13-16R; CAAS 6; CANR 11, 45; DLBY 80; MTCW; SATA 5

Brown, George
See Wertmueller, Lina

Brown, George Douglas
1869-1902 . . . . TCLC 28

Brown, George Mackay 1921- . . . . CLC 5, 48
See also CA 21-24R; CAAS 6; CANR 12, 37; DLB 14, 27, 139; MTCW; SATA 35

Brown, (William) Larry 1951- . . . . . . CLC 73
See also CA 130; 134

Brown, Moses
See Barrett, William (Christopher)

Brown, Rita Mae 1944- . . . . . CLC 18, 43, 79
See also CA 45-48; CANR 2, 11, 35; MTCW

Brown, Roderick (Langmere) Haig-
See Haig-Brown, Roderick (Langmere)

Brown, Rosellen 1939- . . . . CLC 32
See also CA 77-80; CAAS 10; CANR 14, 44

Brown, Sterling Allen
1901-1989 . . . . CLC 1, 23, 59; BLC
See also BW 1; CA 85-88; 127; CANR 26; DLB 48, 51, 63; MTCW

Brown, Will
See Ainsworth, William Harrison

Brown, William Wells
1813-1884 . . . . NCLC 2; BLC; DC 1
See also DLB 3, 50

Browne, (Clyde) Jackson 1948(?)- . . . CLC 21
See also CA 120

Browning, Elizabeth Barrett
1806-1861 . . . . . NCLC 1, 16; DA; DAB; PC 6; WLC
See also CDBLB 1832-1890; DLB 32

Browning, Robert
1812-1889 . . NCLC 19; DA; DAB; PC 2
See also CDBLB 1832-1890; DLB 32; YABC 1

Browning, Tod 1882-1962 . . . . CLC 16
See also CA 141; 117

Brownson, Orestes (Augustus)
1803-1876 . . . . NCLC 50

Bruccoli, Matthew J(oseph) 1931- . . CLC 34
See also CA 9-12R; CANR 7; DLB 103

Bruce, Lenny . . . . CLC 21
See also Schneider, Leonard Alfred

Bruin, John
See Brutus, Dennis

Brulard, Henri
See Stendhal

Brulls, Christian
See Simenon, Georges (Jacques Christian)

Brunner, John (Kilian Houston)
1934- . . . . CLC 8, 10
See also CA 1-4R; CAAS 8; CANR 2, 37; MTCW

Bruno, Giordano 1548-1600 . . . . LC 27

Brutus, Dennis 1924- . . . . CLC 43; BLC
See also BW 2; CA 49-52; CAAS 14; CANR 2, 27, 42; DLB 117

Bryan, C(ourtlandt) D(ixon) B(arnes)
1936- . . . . CLC 29
See also CA 73-76; CANR 13

Bryan, Michael
See Moore, Brian

Bryant, William Cullen
1794-1878 . . . . . . NCLC 6, 46; DA; DAB
See also CDALB 1640-1865; DLB 3, 43, 59

Bryusov, Valery Yakovlevich
1873-1924 . . . . TCLC 10
See also CA 107

Buchan, John 1875-1940 . . . TCLC 41; DAB
See also CA 108; 145; DLB 34, 70, 156; YABC 2

Buchanan, George 1506-1582 . . . . LC 4

Buchheim, Lothar-Guenther 1918- . . . CLC 6
See also CA 85-88

Buchner, (Karl) Georg
1813-1837 . . . . NCLC 26

Buchwald, Art(hur) 1925- . . . . CLC 33
See also AITN 1; CA 5-8R; CANR 21; MTCW; SATA 10

Buck, Pearl S(ydenstricker)
1892-1973 . . . . CLC 7, 11, 18; DA; DAB
See also AITN 1; CA 1-4R; 41-44R; CANR 1, 34; DLB 9, 102; MTCW; SATA 1, 25

Buckler, Ernest 1908-1984 . . . . CLC 13
See also CA 11-12; 114; CAP 1; DLB 68; SATA 47

Buckley, Vincent (Thomas)
1925-1988 . . . . CLC 57
See also CA 101

Buckley, William F(rank), Jr.
1925- . . . . CLC 7, 18, 37
See also AITN 1; CA 1-4R; CANR 1, 24; DLB 137; DLBY 80; MTCW

Buechner, (Carl) Frederick
1926- . . . . CLC 2, 4, 6, 9
See also CA 13-16R; CANR 11, 39; DLBY 80; MTCW

Buell, John (Edward) 1927- . . . . CLC 10
See also CA 1-4R; DLB 53

Buero Vallejo, Antonio 1916- . . . CLC 15, 46
See also CA 106; CANR 24, 49; HW; MTCW

Bufalino, Gesualdo 1920(?)- . . . . CLC 74

Bugayev, Boris Nikolayevich 1880-1934
See Bely, Andrey
See also CA 104

Bukowski, Charles
1920-1994 . . . . CLC 2, 5, 9, 41, 82
See also CA 17-20R; 144; CANR 40; DLB 5, 130; MTCW

Bulgakov, Mikhail (Afanas'evich)
1891-1940 . . . . TCLC 2, 16; SSC 18
See also CA 105

Bulgya, Alexander Alexandrovich
1901-1956 . . . . TCLC 53
See also Fadeyev, Alexander
See also CA 117

Bullins, Ed 1935- . . . . CLC 1, 5, 7; BLC
See also BW 2; CA 49-52; CAAS 16; CANR 24, 46; DLB 7, 38; MTCW

Bulwer-Lytton, Edward (George Earle Lytton)
1803-1873 . . . . NCLC 1, 45
See also DLB 21

Bunin, Ivan Alexeyevich
1870-1953 . . . . TCLC 6; SSC 5
See also CA 104

Bunting, Basil 1900-1985 . . . . CLC 10, 39, 47
See also CA 53-56; 115; CANR 7; DLB 20

Bunuel, Luis 1900-1983 . . CLC 16, 80; HLC
See also CA 101; 110; CANR 32; HW

Bunyan, John
1628-1688 . . . . . . LC 4; DA; DAB; WLC
See also CDBLB 1660-1789; DLB 39

Burckhardt, Jacob (Christoph)
1818-1897 . . . . NCLC 49

Burford, Eleanor
See Hibbert, Eleanor Alice Burford

Burgess, Anthony
. CLC 1, 2, 4, 5, 8, 10, 13, 15, 22, 40, 62, 81; DAB
See also Wilson, John (Anthony) Burgess
See also AITN 1; CDBLB 1960 to Present; DLB 14

Burke, Edmund
1729(?)-1797 . . . . LC 7; DA; DAB; WLC
See also DLB 104

Burke, Kenneth (Duva)
1897-1993 . . . . CLC 2, 24
See also CA 5-8R; 143; CANR 39; DLB 45, 63; MTCW

Burke, Leda
See Garnett, David

Burke, Ralph
See Silverberg, Robert

Burney, Fanny 1752-1840 . . . . NCLC 12
See also DLB 39

Burns, Robert 1759-1796 . . . . PC 6
See also CDBLB 1789-1832; DA; DAB; DLB 109; WLC

Burns, Tex
See L'Amour, Louis (Dearborn)

Burnshaw, Stanley 1906- . . . . . CLC 3, 13, 44
See also CA 9-12R; DLB 48

Burr, Anne 1937- . . . . CLC 6
See also CA 25-28R

Burroughs, Edgar Rice
1875-1950 . . . . TCLC 2, 32
See also AAYA 11; CA 104; 132; DLB 8; MTCW; SATA 41

Burroughs, William S(eward)
1914- . . . . CLC 1, 2, 5, 15, 22, 42, 75; DA; DAB; WLC
See also AITN 2; CA 9-12R; CANR 20; DLB 2, 8, 16, 152; DLBY 81; MTCW

Burton, Richard F. 1821-1890 . . . . NCLC 42
See also DLB 55

Author Index

Busch, Frederick 1941- . . . **CLC 7, 10, 18, 47**
See also CA 33-36R; CAAS 1; CANR 45;
DLB 6

Bush, Ronald 1946- . . . . **CLC 34**
See also CA 136

Bustos, F(rancisco)
See Borges, Jorge Luis

Bustos Domecq, H(onorio)
See Bioy Casares, Adolfo; Borges, Jorge
Luis

Butler, Octavia E(stelle) 1947- . . . . . **CLC 38**
See also BW 2; CA 73-76; CANR 12, 24,
38; DLB 33; MTCW

Butler, Robert Olen (Jr.) 1945- . . . . . **CLC 81**
See also CA 112

Butler, Samuel 1612-1680 . . . . **LC 16**
See also DLB 101, 126

Butler, Samuel
1835-1902 . . . . . . **TCLC 1, 33; DA; DAB;
WLC**
See also CA 143; CDBLB 1890-1914;
DLB 18, 57

Butler, Walter C.
See Faust, Frederick (Schiller)

Butor, Michel (Marie Francois)
1926- . . . . **CLC 1, 3, 8, 11, 15**
See also CA 9-12R; CANR 33; DLB 83;
MTCW

Buzo, Alexander (John) 1944- . . . . . . **CLC 61**
See also CA 97-100; CANR 17, 39

Buzzati, Dino 1906-1972 . . . . **CLC 36**
See also CA 33-36R

Byars, Betsy (Cromer) 1928- . . . . **CLC 35**
See also CA 33-36R; CANR 18, 36; CLR 1,
16; DLB 52; JRDA; MAICYA; MTCW;
SAAS 1; SATA 4, 46, 80

Byatt, A(ntonia) S(usan Drabble)
1936- . . . . **CLC 19, 65**
See also CA 13-16R; CANR 13, 33;
DLB 14; MTCW

Byrne, David 1952- . . . . **CLC 26**
See also CA 127

Byrne, John Keyes 1926-
See Leonard, Hugh
See also CA 102

Byron, George Gordon (Noel)
1788-1824 . . . . . **NCLC 2, 12; DA; DAB;
WLC**
See also CDBLB 1789-1832; DLB 96, 110

C. 3. 3.
See Wilde, Oscar (Fingal O'Flahertie Wills)

Caballero, Fernan 1796-1877 . . . . . **NCLC 10**

Cabell, James Branch 1879-1958 . . . **TCLC 6**
See also CA 105; DLB 9, 78

Cable, George Washington
1844-1925 . . . . **TCLC 4; SSC 4**
See also CA 104; DLB 12, 74

Cabral de Melo Neto, Joao 1920- . . . **CLC 76**

Cabrera Infante, G(uillermo)
1929- . . . . **CLC 5, 25, 45; HLC**
See also CA 85-88; CANR 29; DLB 113;
HW; MTCW

Cade, Toni
See Bambara, Toni Cade

Cadmus and Harmonia
See Buchan, John

Caedmon fl. 658-680 . . . . **CMLC 7**
See also DLB 146

Caeiro, Alberto
See Pessoa, Fernando (Antonio Nogueira)

Cage, John (Milton, Jr.) 1912- . . . . . **CLC 41**
See also CA 13-16R; CANR 9

Cain, G.
See Cabrera Infante, G(uillermo)

Cain, Guillermo
See Cabrera Infante, G(uillermo)

Cain, James M(allahan)
1892-1977 . . . . **CLC 3, 11, 28**
See also AITN 1; CA 17-20R; 73-76;
CANR 8, 34; MTCW

Caine, Mark
See Raphael, Frederic (Michael)

Calasso, Roberto 1941- . . . . **CLC 81**
See also CA 143

Calderon de la Barca, Pedro
1600-1681 . . . . **LC 23; DC 3**

Caldwell, Erskine (Preston)
1903-1987 . . . . **CLC 1, 8, 14, 50, 60;
SSC 19**
See also AITN 1; CA 1-4R; 121; CAAS 1;
CANR 2, 33; DLB 9, 86; MTCW

Caldwell, (Janet Miriam) Taylor (Holland)
1900-1985 . . . . **CLC 2, 28, 39**
See also CA 5-8R; 116; CANR 5

Calhoun, John Caldwell
1782-1850 . . . . **NCLC 15**
See also DLB 3

Calisher, Hortense
1911- . . . . **CLC 2, 4, 8, 38; SSC 15**
See also CA 1-4R; CANR 1, 22; DLB 2;
MTCW

Callaghan, Morley Edward
1903-1990 . . . . **CLC 3, 14, 41, 65**
See also CA 9-12R; 132; CANR 33;
DLB 68; MTCW

Calvino, Italo
1923-1985 . . . . . **CLC 5, 8, 11, 22, 33, 39,
73; SSC 3**
See also CA 85-88; 116; CANR 23; MTCW

Cameron, Carey 1952- . . . . **CLC 59**
See also CA 135

Cameron, Peter 1959- . . . . **CLC 44**
See also CA 125

Campana, Dino 1885-1932 . . . . **TCLC 20**
See also CA 117; DLB 114

Campbell, John W(ood, Jr.)
1910-1971 . . . . **CLC 32**
See also CA 21-22; 29-32R; CANR 34;
CAP 2; DLB 8; MTCW

Campbell, Joseph 1904-1987 . . . . **CLC 69**
See also AAYA 3; BEST 89:2; CA 1-4R;
124; CANR 3, 28; MTCW

Campbell, Maria 1940- . . . . **CLC 85**
See also CA 102; NNAL

Campbell, (John) Ramsey
1946- . . . . **CLC 42; SSC 19**
See also CA 57-60; CANR 7

Campbell, (Ignatius) Roy (Dunnachie)
1901-1957 . . . . **TCLC 5**
See also CA 104; DLB 20

Campbell, Thomas 1777-1844 . . . . **NCLC 19**
See also DLB 93; 144

Campbell, Wilfred . . . . **TCLC 9**
See also Campbell, William

Campbell, William 1858(?)-1918
See Campbell, Wilfred
See also CA 106; DLB 92

Campos, Alvaro de
See Pessoa, Fernando (Antonio Nogueira)

Camus, Albert
1913-1960 . . . . **CLC 1, 2, 4, 9, 11, 14, 32,
63, 69; DA; DAB; DC 2; SSC 9; WLC**
See also CA 89-92; DLB 72; MTCW

Canby, Vincent 1924- . . . . **CLC 13**
See also CA 81-84

Cancale
See Desnos, Robert

Canetti, Elias
1905-1994 . . . . **CLC 3, 14, 25, 75, 86**
See also CA 21-24R; 146; CANR 23;
DLB 85, 124; MTCW

Canin, Ethan 1960- . . . . **CLC 55**
See also CA 131; 135

Cannon, Curt
See Hunter, Evan

Cape, Judith
See Page, P(atricia) K(athleen)

Capek, Karel
1890-1938 . . . . . . **TCLC 6, 37; DA; DAB;
DC 1; WLC**
See also CA 104; 140

Capote, Truman
1924-1984 . . . . . . **CLC 1, 3, 8, 13, 19, 34,
38, 58; DA; DAB; SSC 2; WLC**
See also CA 5-8R; 113; CANR 18;
CDALB 1941-1968; DLB 2; DLBY 80,
84; MTCW

Capra, Frank 1897-1991 . . . . **CLC 16**
See also CA 61-64; 135

Caputo, Philip 1941- . . . . **CLC 32**
See also CA 73-76; CANR 40

Card, Orson Scott 1951- . . . . **CLC 44, 47, 50**
See also AAYA 11; CA 102; CANR 27, 47;
MTCW; SATA 83

Cardenal (Martinez), Ernesto
1925- . . . . **CLC 31; HLC**
See also CA 49-52; CANR 2, 32; HW;
MTCW

Carducci, Giosue 1835-1907 . . . . **TCLC 32**

Carew, Thomas 1595(?)-1640 . . . . **LC 13**
See also DLB 126

Carey, Ernestine Gilbreth 1908- . . . . **CLC 17**
See also CA 5-8R; SATA 2

Carey, Peter 1943- . . . . **CLC 40, 55**
See also CA 123; 127; MTCW

Carleton, William 1794-1869 . . . . . . **NCLC 3**

Carlisle, Henry (Coffin) 1926- . . . . . . **CLC 33**
See also CA 13-16R; CANR 15

Carlsen, Chris
See Holdstock, Robert P.

Chandler, Raymond (Thornton)
1888-1959 .... TCLC 1, 7
See also CA 104; 129; CDALB 1929-1941;
DLBD 6; MTCW

Chang, Jung 1952- .... CLC 71
See also CA 142

Channing, William Ellery
1780-1842 .... NCLC 17
See also DLB 1, 59

Chaplin, Charles Spencer
1889-1977 .... CLC 16
See also Chaplin, Charlie
See also CA 81-84; 73-76

Chaplin, Charlie
See Chaplin, Charles Spencer
See also DLB 44

Chapman, George 1559(?)-1634 ...... LC 22
See also DLB 62, 121

Chapman, Graham 1941-1989 ...... CLC 21
See also Monty Python
See also CA 116; 129; CANR 35

Chapman, John Jay 1862-1933 ..... TCLC 7
See also CA 104

Chapman, Walker
See Silverberg, Robert

Chappell, Fred (Davis) 1936-.... CLC 40, 78
See also CA 5-8R; CAAS 4; CANR 8, 33;
DLB 6, 105

Char, Rene(-Emile)
1907-1988 .... CLC 9, 11, 14, 55
See also CA 13-16R; 124; CANR 32;
MTCW

Charby, Jay
See Ellison, Harlan (Jay)

Chardin, Pierre Teilhard de
See Teilhard de Chardin, (Marie Joseph)
Pierre

Charles I 1600-1649 .... LC 13

Charyn, Jerome 1937- .... CLC 5, 8, 18
See also CA 5-8R; CAAS 1; CANR 7;
DLBY 83; MTCW

Chase, Mary (Coyle) 1907-1981 ...... DC 1
See also CA 77-80; 105; SATA 17;
SATA-Obit 29

Chase, Mary Ellen 1887-1973 .... CLC 2
See also CA 13-16; 41-44R; CAP 1;
SATA 10

Chase, Nicholas
See Hyde, Anthony

Chateaubriand, Francois Rene de
1768-1848 .... NCLC 3
See also DLB 119

Chatterje, Sarat Chandra 1876-1936(?)
See Chatterji, Saratchandra
See also CA 109

Chatterji, Bankim Chandra
1838-1894 .... NCLC 19

Chatterji, Saratchandra .... TCLC 13
See also Chatterje, Sarat Chandra

Chatterton, Thomas 1752-1770 .... LC 3
See also DLB 109

Chatwin, (Charles) Bruce
1940-1989 .... CLC 28, 57, 59
See also AAYA 4; BEST 90:1; CA 85-88;
127

Chaucer, Daniel
See Ford, Ford Madox

Chaucer, Geoffrey
1340(?)-1400 .... LC 17; DA; DAB
See also CDBLB Before 1660; DLB 146

Chaviaras, Strates 1935-
See Haviaras, Stratis
See also CA 105

Chayefsky, Paddy .... CLC 23
See also Chayefsky, Sidney
See also DLB 7, 44; DLBY 81

Chayefsky, Sidney 1923-1981
See Chayefsky, Paddy
See also CA 9-12R; 104; CANR 18

Chedid, Andree 1920-............. CLC 47
See also CA 145

Cheever, John
1912-1982 ...... CLC 3, 7, 8, 11, 15, 25,
64; DA; DAB; SSC 1; WLC
See also CA 5-8R; 106; CABS 1; CANR 5,
27; CDALB 1941-1968; DLB 2, 102;
DLBY 80, 82; MTCW

Cheever, Susan 1943-.......... CLC 18, 48
See also CA 103; CANR 27; DLBY 82

Chekhonte, Antosha
See Chekhov, Anton (Pavlovich)

Chekhov, Anton (Pavlovich)
1860-1904 ..... TCLC 3, 10, 31, 55; DA;
DAB; SSC 2; WLC
See also CA 104; 124

Chernyshevsky, Nikolay Gavrilovich
1828-1889 .... NCLC 1

Cherry, Carolyn Janice 1942-
See Cherryh, C. J.
See also CA 65-68; CANR 10

Cherryh, C. J. .... CLC 35
See also Cherry, Carolyn Janice
See also DLBY 80

Chesnutt, Charles W(addell)
1858-1932 .... TCLC 5, 39; BLC; SSC 7
See also BW 1; CA 106; 125; DLB 12, 50,
78; MTCW

Chester, Alfred 1929(?)-1971....... CLC 49
See also CA 33-36R; DLB 130

Chesterton, G(ilbert) K(eith)
1874-1936 .... TCLC 1, 6; SSC 1
See also CA 104; 132; CDBLB 1914-1945;
DLB 10, 19, 34, 70, 98, 149; MTCW;
SATA 27

Chiang Pin-chin 1904-1986
See Ding Ling
See also CA 118

Ch'ien Chung-shu 1910-........... CLC 22
See also CA 130; MTCW

Child, L. Maria
See Child, Lydia Maria

Child, Lydia Maria 1802-1880 .... NCLC 6
See also DLB 1, 74; SATA 67

Child, Mrs.
See Child, Lydia Maria

Child, Philip 1898-1978 .... CLC 19, 68
See also CA 13-14; CAP 1; SATA 47

Childress, Alice
1920-1994 .. CLC 12, 15, 86; BLC; DC 4
See also AAYA 8; BW 2; CA 45-48; 146;
CANR 3, 27; CLR 14; DLB 7, 38; JRDA;
MAICYA; MTCW; SATA 7, 48, 81

Chislett, (Margaret) Anne 1943-.... CLC 34

Chitty, Thomas Willes 1926-....... CLC 11
See also Hinde, Thomas
See also CA 5-8R

Chivers, Thomas Holley
1809-1858 .... NCLC 49
See also DLB 3

Chomette, Rene Lucien 1898-1981
See Clair, Rene
See also CA 103

Chopin, Kate
.... TCLC 5, 14; DA; DAB; SSC 8
See also Chopin, Katherine
See also CDALB 1865-1917; DLB 12, 78

Chopin, Katherine 1851-1904
See Chopin, Kate
See also CA 104; 122

Chretien de Troyes
c. 12th cent. - .... CMLC 10

Christie
See Ichikawa, Kon

Christie, Agatha (Mary Clarissa)
1890-1976 ...... CLC 1, 6, 8, 12, 39, 48;
DAB
See also AAYA 9; AITN 1, 2; CA 17-20R;
61-64; CANR 10, 37; CDBLB 1914-1945;
DLB 13, 77; MTCW; SATA 36

Christie, (Ann) Philippa
See Pearce, Philippa
See also CA 5-8R; CANR 4

Christine de Pizan 1365(?)-1431(?) .... LC 9

Chubb, Elmer
See Masters, Edgar Lee

Chulkov, Mikhail Dmitrievich
1743-1792 .... LC 2
See also DLB 150

Churchill, Caryl 1938-... CLC 31, 55; DC 5
See also CA 102; CANR 22, 46; DLB 13;
MTCW

Churchill, Charles 1731-1764........ LC 3
See also DLB 109

Chute, Carolyn 1947-.............. CLC 39
See also CA 123

Ciardi, John (Anthony)
1916-1986 .... CLC 10, 40, 44
See also CA 5-8R; 118; CAAS 2; CANR 5,
33; CLR 19; DLB 5; DLBY 86;
MAICYA; MTCW; SATA 1, 65;
SATA-Obit 46

Cicero, Marcus Tullius
106B.C.-43B.C................ CMLC 3

Cimino, Michael 1943-............. CLC 16
See also CA 105

Cioran, E(mil) M. 1911-........... CLC 64
See also CA 25-28R

Cisneros, Sandra 1954-...... CLC 69; HLC
See also AAYA 9; CA 131; DLB 122, 152;
HW

Clair, Rene.................... CLC 20
See also Chomette, Rene Lucien

Clampitt, Amy   1920-1994 . . . . CLC 32
See also CA 110; 146; CANR 29; DLB 105

Clancy, Thomas L., Jr.   1947-
See Clancy, Tom
See also CA 125; 131; MTCW

Clancy, Tom. CLC 45
See also Clancy, Thomas L., Jr.
See also AAYA 9; BEST 89:1, 90:1

Clare, John   1793-1864 . . . . . . NCLC 9; DAB
See also DLB 55, 96

Clarin
See Alas (y Urena), Leopoldo (Enrique
Garcia)

Clark, Al C.
See Goines, Donald

Clark, (Robert) Brian   1932- . . . . CLC 29
See also CA 41-44R

Clark, Curt
See Westlake, Donald E(dwin)

Clark, Eleanor   1913- . . . . CLC 5, 19
See also CA 9-12R; CANR 41; DLB 6

Clark, J. P.
See Clark, John Pepper
See also DLB 117

Clark, John Pepper
1935- . . . . CLC 38; BLC; DC 5
See also Clark, J. P.
See also BW 1; CA 65-68; CANR 16

Clark, M. R.
See Clark, Mavis Thorpe

Clark, Mavis Thorpe   1909- . . . . CLC 12
See also CA 57-60; CANR 8, 37; CLR 30;
MAICYA; SAAS 5; SATA 8, 74

Clark, Walter Van Tilburg
1909-1971 . . . . CLC 28
See also CA 9-12R; 33-36R; DLB 9;
SATA 8

Clarke, Arthur C(harles)
1917- . . . . . . CLC 1, 4, 13, 18, 35; SSC 3
See also AAYA 4; CA 1-4R; CANR 2, 28;
JRDA; MAICYA; MTCW; SATA 13, 70

Clarke, Austin   1896-1974. . . . . CLC 6, 9
See also CA 29-32; 49-52; CAP 2; DLB 10,
20

Clarke, Austin C(hesterfield)
1934- . . . . CLC 8, 53; BLC
See also BW 1; CA 25-28R; CAAS 16;
CANR 14, 32; DLB 53, 125

Clarke, Gillian   1937- . . . . CLC 61
See also CA 106; DLB 40

Clarke, Marcus (Andrew Hislop)
1846-1881 . . . . NCLC 19

Clarke, Shirley   1925- . . . . CLC 16

Clash, The
See Headon, (Nicky) Topper; Jones, Mick;
Simonon, Paul; Strummer, Joe

Claudel, Paul (Louis Charles Marie)
1868-1955 . . . . TCLC 2, 10
See also CA 104

Clavell, James (duMaresq)
1925-1994 . . . . CLC 6, 25, 87
See also CA 25-28R; 146; CANR 26, 48;
MTCW

Cleaver, (Leroy) Eldridge
1935- . . . . CLC 30; BLC
See also BW 1; CA 21-24R; CANR 16

Cleese, John (Marwood)   1939- . . . . . CLC 21
See also Monty Python
See also CA 112; 116; CANR 35; MTCW

Cleishbotham, Jebediah
See Scott, Walter

Cleland, John   1710-1789 . . . . LC 2
See also DLB 39

Clemens, Samuel Langhorne   1835-1910
See Twain, Mark
See also CA 104; 135; CDALB 1865-1917;
DA; DAB; DLB 11, 12, 23, 64, 74;
JRDA; MAICYA; YABC 2

Cleophil
See Congreve, William

Clerihew, E.
See Bentley, E(dmund) C(lerihew)

Clerk, N. W.
See Lewis, C(live) S(taples)

Cliff, Jimmy. . . . . CLC 21
See also Chambers, James

Clifton, (Thelma) Lucille
1936- . . . . CLC 19, 66; BLC
See also BW 2; CA 49-52; CANR 2, 24, 42;
CLR 5; DLB 5, 41; MAICYA; MTCW;
SATA 20, 69

Clinton, Dirk
See Silverberg, Robert

Clough, Arthur Hugh   1819-1861 . . NCLC 27
See also DLB 32

Clutha, Janet Paterson Frame   1924-
See Frame, Janet
See also CA 1-4R; CANR 2, 36; MTCW

Clyne, Terence
See Blatty, William Peter

Cobalt, Martin
See Mayne, William (James Carter)

Cobbett, William   1763-1835 . . . . . NCLC 49
See also DLB 43, 107

Coburn, D(onald) L(ee)   1938- . . . . . . CLC 10
See also CA 89-92

Cocteau, Jean (Maurice Eugene Clement)
1889-1963 . . . . CLC 1, 8, 15, 16, 43; DA;
DAB; WLC
See also CA 25-28; CANR 40; CAP 2;
DLB 65; MTCW

Codrescu, Andrei   1946- . . . . CLC 46
See also CA 33-36R; CAAS 19; CANR 13,
34

Coe, Max
See Bourne, Randolph S(illiman)

Coe, Tucker
See Westlake, Donald E(dwin)

Coetzee, J(ohn) M(ichael)
1940- . . . . CLC 23, 33, 66
See also CA 77-80; CANR 41; MTCW

Coffey, Brian
See Koontz, Dean R(ay)

Cohan, George M.   1878-1942 . . . . . TCLC 60

Cohen, Arthur A(llen)
1928-1986 . . . . CLC 7, 31
See also CA 1-4R; 120; CANR 1, 17, 42;
DLB 28

Cohen, Leonard (Norman)
1934- . . . . CLC 3, 38
See also CA 21-24R; CANR 14; DLB 53;
MTCW

Cohen, Matt   1942- . . . . CLC 19
See also CA 61-64; CAAS 18; CANR 40;
DLB 53

Cohen-Solal, Annie   19(?)- . . . . CLC 50

Colegate, Isabel   1931- . . . . CLC 36
See also CA 17-20R; CANR 8, 22; DLB 14;
MTCW

Coleman, Emmett
See Reed, Ishmael

Coleridge, Samuel Taylor
1772-1834 . . . . NCLC 9; DA; DAB;
PC 11; WLC
See also CDBLB 1789-1832; DLB 93, 107

Coleridge, Sara   1802-1852 . . . . . . NCLC 31

Coles, Don   1928- . . . . CLC 46
See also CA 115; CANR 38

Colette, (Sidonie-Gabrielle)
1873-1954 . . . . . . TCLC 1, 5, 16; SSC 10
See also CA 104; 131; DLB 65; MTCW

Collett, (Jacobine) Camilla (Wergeland)
1813-1895 . . . . NCLC 22

Collier, Christopher   1930- . . . . CLC 30
See also AAYA 13; CA 33-36R; CANR 13,
33; JRDA; MAICYA; SATA 16, 70

Collier, James L(incoln)   1928- . . . . . CLC 30
See also AAYA 13; CA 9-12R; CANR 4,
33; CLR 3; JRDA; MAICYA; SATA 8,
70

Collier, Jeremy   1650-1726 . . . . LC 6

Collier, John   1901-1980 . . . . SSC 19
See also CA 65-68; 97-100; CANR 10;
DLB 77

Collins, Hunt
See Hunter, Evan

Collins, Linda   1931- . . . . CLC 44
See also CA 125

Collins, (William) Wilkie
1824-1889 . . . . NCLC 1, 18
See also CDBLB 1832-1890; DLB 18, 70

Collins, William   1721-1759 . . . . LC 4
See also DLB 109

Colman, George
See Glassco, John

Colt, Winchester Remington
See Hubbard, L(afayette) Ron(ald)

Colter, Cyrus   1910- . . . . CLC 58
See also BW 1; CA 65-68; CANR 10;
DLB 33

Colton, James
See Hansen, Joseph

Colum, Padraic   1881-1972. . . . . CLC 28
See also CA 73-76; 33-36R; CANR 35;
CLR 36; MAICYA; MTCW; SATA 15

Colvin, James
See Moorcock, Michael (John)

Colwin, Laurie (E.)
1944-1992 .... CLC **5, 13, 23, 84**
See also CA 89-92; 139; CANR 20, 46;
DLBY 80; MTCW

Comfort, Alex(ander) 1920-......... CLC **7**
See also CA 1-4R; CANR 1, 45

Comfort, Montgomery
See Campbell, (John) Ramsey

Compton-Burnett, I(vy)
1884(?)-1969 ...... CLC **1, 3, 10, 15, 34**
See also CA 1-4R; 25-28R; CANR 4;
DLB 36; MTCW

Comstock, Anthony 1844-1915 .... TCLC **13**
See also CA 110

Conan Doyle, Arthur
See Doyle, Arthur Conan

Conde, Maryse 1937-............ CLC **52**
See also Boucolon, Maryse
See also BW 2

Condillac, Etienne Bonnot de
1714-1780 .... LC **26**

Condon, Richard (Thomas)
1915-............ CLC **4, 6, 8, 10, 45**
See also BEST 90:3; CA 1-4R; CAAS 1;
CANR 2, 23; MTCW

Congreve, William
1670-1729 .... LC **5, 21; DA; DAB;**
DC 2; WLC
See also CDBLB 1660-1789; DLB 39, 84

Connell, Evan S(helby), Jr.
1924-.................. CLC **4, 6, 45**
See also AAYA 7; CA 1-4R; CAAS 2;
CANR 2, 39; DLB 2; DLBY 81; MTCW

Connelly, Marc(us Cook)
1890-1980 .... CLC **7**
See also CA 85-88; 102; CANR 30; DLB 7;
DLBY 80; SATA-Obit 25

Connor, Ralph .... TCLC **31**
See also Gordon, Charles William
See also DLB 92

Conrad, Joseph
1857-1924 .... TCLC **1, 6, 13, 25, 43, 57;**
DA; DAB; SSC 9; WLC
See also CA 104; 131; CDBLB 1890-1914;
DLB 10, 34, 98, 156; MTCW; SATA 27

Conrad, Robert Arnold
See Hart, Moss

Conroy, Pat 1945-............ CLC **30, 74**
See also AAYA 8; AITN 1; CA 85-88;
CANR 24; DLB 6; MTCW

Constant (de Rebecque), (Henri) Benjamin
1767-1830 .... NCLC **6**
See also DLB 119

Conybeare, Charles Augustus
See Eliot, T(homas) S(tearns)

Cook, Michael 1933- .... CLC **58**
See also CA 93-96; DLB 53

Cook, Robin 1940- .... CLC **14**
See also BEST 90:2; CA 108; 111;
CANR 41

Cook, Roy
See Silverberg, Robert

Cooke, Elizabeth 1948- .... CLC **55**
See also CA 129

Cooke, John Esten 1830-1886 ..... NCLC **5**
See also DLB 3

Cooke, John Estes
See Baum, L(yman) Frank

Cooke, M. E.
See Creasey, John

Cooke, Margaret
See Creasey, John

Cooney, Ray .... CLC **62**

Cooper, Douglas 1960-............ CLC **86**

Cooper, Henry St. John
See Creasey, John

Cooper, J. California .... CLC **56**
See also AAYA 12; BW 1; CA 125

Cooper, James Fenimore
1789-1851 .... NCLC **1, 27**
See also CDALB 1640-1865; DLB 3;
SATA 19

Coover, Robert (Lowell)
1932- .. CLC **3, 7, 15, 32, 46, 87; SSC 15**
See also CA 45-48; CANR 3, 37; DLB 2;
DLBY 81; MTCW

Copeland, Stewart (Armstrong)
1952- .... CLC **26**

Coppard, A(lfred) E(dgar)
1878-1957 .... TCLC **5; SSC 21**
See also CA 114; YABC 1

Coppee, Francois 1842-1908 ...... TCLC **25**

Coppola, Francis Ford 1939-....... CLC **16**
See also CA 77-80; CANR 40; DLB 44

Corbiere, Tristan 1845-1875 ..... NCLC **43**

Corcoran, Barbara 1911-.......... CLC **17**
See also AAYA 14; CA 21-24R; CAAS 2;
CANR 11, 28, 48; DLB 52; JRDA;
SAAS 20; SATA 3, 77

Cordelier, Maurice
See Giraudoux, (Hippolyte) Jean

Corelli, Marie 1855-1924........ TCLC **51**
See also Mackay, Mary
See also DLB 34, 156

Corman, Cid....................... CLC **9**
See also Corman, Sidney
See also CAAS 2; DLB 5

Corman, Sidney 1924-
See Corman, Cid
See also CA 85-88; CANR 44

Cormier, Robert (Edmund)
1925- .... CLC **12, 30; DA; DAB**
See also AAYA 3; CA 1-4R; CANR 5, 23;
CDALB 1968-1988; CLR 12; DLB 52;
JRDA; MAICYA; MTCW; SATA 10, 45,
83

Corn, Alfred (DeWitt III) 1943-.... CLC **33**
See also CA 104; CANR 44; DLB 120;
DLBY 80

Corneille, Pierre 1606-1684.... LC **28; DAB**

Cornwell, David (John Moore)
1931-..................... CLC **9, 15**
See also le Carre, John
See also CA 5-8R; CANR 13, 33; MTCW

Corso, (Nunzio) Gregory 1930-... CLC **1, 11**
See also CA 5-8R; CANR 41; DLB 5, 16;
MTCW

Cortazar, Julio
1914-1984 ...... CLC **2, 3, 5, 10, 13, 15,**
33, 34; HLC; SSC 7
See also CA 21-24R; CANR 12, 32;
DLB 113; HW; MTCW

CORTES, HERNAN 1484-1547..... LC **31**

Corwin, Cecil
See Kornbluth, C(yril) M.

Cosic, Dobrica 1921-.............. CLC **14**
See also CA 122; 138

Costain, Thomas B(ertram)
1885-1965 .... CLC **30**
See also CA 5-8R; 25-28R; DLB 9

Costantini, Humberto
1924(?)-1987 .... CLC **49**
See also CA 131; 122; HW

Costello, Elvis 1955-.............. CLC **21**

Cotter, Joseph Seamon Sr.
1861-1949 .... TCLC **28; BLC**
See also BW 1; CA 124; DLB 50

Couch, Arthur Thomas Quiller
See Quiller-Couch, Arthur Thomas

Coulton, James
See Hansen, Joseph

Couperus, Louis (Marie Anne)
1863-1923 .... TCLC **15**
See also CA 115

Coupland, Douglas 1961-.......... CLC **85**
See also CA 142

Court, Wesli
See Turco, Lewis (Putnam)

Courtenay, Bryce 1933-........... CLC **59**
See also CA 138

Courtney, Robert
See Ellison, Harlan (Jay)

Cousteau, Jacques-Yves 1910-...... CLC **30**
See also CA 65-68; CANR 15; MTCW;
SATA 38

Coward, Noel (Peirce)
1899-1973 .... CLC **1, 9, 29, 51**
See also AITN 1; CA 17-18; 41-44R;
CANR 35; CAP 2; CDBLB 1914-1945;
DLB 10; MTCW

Cowley, Malcolm 1898-1989 .... CLC **39**
See also CA 5-8R; 128; CANR 3; DLB 4,
48; DLBY 81, 89; MTCW

Cowper, William 1731-1800....... NCLC **8**
See also DLB 104, 109

Cox, William Trevor 1928- ... CLC **9, 14, 71**
See also Trevor, William
See also CA 9-12R; CANR 4, 37; DLB 14;
MTCW

Coyne, P. J.
See Masters, Hilary

Cozzens, James Gould
1903-1978 .... CLC **1, 4, 11**
See also CA 9-12R; 81-84; CANR 19;
CDALB 1941-1968; DLB 9; DLBD 2;
DLBY 84; MTCW

Crabbe, George 1754-1832....... NCLC **26**
See also DLB 93

Craig, A. A.
See Anderson, Poul (William)

Deloria, Vine (Victor), Jr. 1933-.... CLC 21
    See also CA 53-56; CANR 5, 20, 48;
    MTCW; NNAL; SATA 21

Del Vecchio, John M(ichael)
    1947- .... CLC 29
    See also CA 110; DLBD 9

de Man, Paul (Adolph Michel)
    1919-1983 .... CLC 55
    See also CA 128; 111; DLB 67; MTCW

De Marinis, Rick 1934-.......... CLC 54
    See also CA 57-60; CANR 9, 25

Demby, William 1922-....... CLC 53; BLC
    See also BW 1; CA 81-84; DLB 33

Demijohn, Thom
    See Disch, Thomas M(ichael)

de Montherlant, Henry (Milon)
    See Montherlant, Henry (Milon) de

Demosthenes 384B.C.-322B.C. ... CMLC 13

de Natale, Francine
    See Malzberg, Barry N(athaniel)

Denby, Edwin (Orr) 1903-1983..... CLC 48
    See also CA 138; 110

Denis, Julio
    See Cortazar, Julio

Denmark, Harrison
    See Zelazny, Roger (Joseph)

Dennis, John 1658-1734........... LC 11
    See also DLB 101

Dennis, Nigel (Forbes) 1912-1989.... CLC 8
    See also CA 25-28R; 129; DLB 13, 15;
    MTCW

De Palma, Brian (Russell) 1940-.... CLC 20
    See also CA 109

De Quincey, Thomas 1785-1859 ... NCLC 4
    See also CDBLB 1789-1832; DLB 110; 144

Deren, Eleanora 1908(?)-1961
    See Deren, Maya
    See also CA 111

Deren, Maya .... CLC 16
    See also Deren, Eleanora

Derleth, August (William)
    1909-1971 .... CLC 31
    See also CA 1-4R; 29-32R; CANR 4;
    DLB 9; SATA 5

Der Nister 1884-1950............ TCLC 56

de Routisie, Albert
    See Aragon, Louis

Derrida, Jacques 1930-........ CLC 24, 87
    See also CA 124; 127

Derry Down Derry
    See Lear, Edward

Dersonnes, Jacques
    See Simenon, Georges (Jacques Christian)

Desai, Anita 1937- ...... CLC 19, 37; DAB
    See also CA 81-84; CANR 33; MTCW;
    SATA 63

de Saint-Luc, Jean
    See Glassco, John

de Saint Roman, Arnaud
    See Aragon, Louis

Descartes, Rene 1596-1650 .... LC 20

De Sica, Vittorio 1901(?)-1974 ..... CLC 20
    See also CA 117

Desnos, Robert 1900-1945....... TCLC 22
    See also CA 121

Destouches, Louis-Ferdinand
    1894-1961 .... CLC 9, 15
    See also Celine, Louis-Ferdinand
    See also CA 85-88; CANR 28; MTCW

Deutsch, Babette 1895-1982 .... CLC 18
    See also CA 1-4R; 108; CANR 4; DLB 45;
    SATA 1; SATA-Obit 33

Devenant, William 1606-1649 .... LC 13

Devkota, Laxmiprasad
    1909-1959 .... TCLC 23
    See also CA 123

De Voto, Bernard (Augustine)
    1897-1955 .... TCLC 29
    See also CA 113; DLB 9

De Vries, Peter
    1910-1993 .... CLC 1, 2, 3, 7, 10, 28, 46
    See also CA 17-20R; 142; CANR 41;
    DLB 6; DLBY 82; MTCW

Dexter, Martin
    See Faust, Frederick (Schiller)

Dexter, Pete 1943-............ CLC 34, 55
    See also BEST 89:2; CA 127; 131; MTCW

Diamano, Silmang
    See Senghor, Leopold Sedar

Diamond, Neil 1941- .... CLC 30
    See also CA 108

Diaz del Castillo, Bernal 1496-1584.. LC 31

di Bassetto, Corno
    See Shaw, George Bernard

Dick, Philip K(indred)
    1928-1982 .... CLC 10, 30, 72
    See also CA 49-52; 106; CANR 2, 16;
    DLB 8; MTCW

Dickens, Charles (John Huffam)
    1812-1870 ...... NCLC 3, 8, 18, 26, 37,
                     50; DA; DAB; SSC 17; WLC
    See also CDBLB 1832-1890; DLB 21, 55,
    70; JRDA; MAICYA; SATA 15

Dickey, James (Lafayette)
    1923- .... CLC 1, 2, 4, 7, 10, 15, 47
    See also AITN 1, 2; CA 9-12R; CABS 2;
    CANR 10, 48; CDALB 1968-1988;
    DLB 5; DLBD 7; DLBY 82, 93; MTCW

Dickey, William 1928-1994 ..... CLC 3, 28
    See also CA 9-12R; 145; CANR 24; DLB 5

Dickinson, Charles 1951-........... CLC 49
    See also CA 128

Dickinson, Emily (Elizabeth)
    1830-1886 .... NCLC 21; DA; DAB;
                     PC 1; WLC
    See also CDALB 1865-1917; DLB 1;
    SATA 29

Dickinson, Peter (Malcolm)
    1927- .... CLC 12, 35
    See also AAYA 9; CA 41-44R; CANR 31;
    CLR 29; DLB 87; JRDA; MAICYA;
    SATA 5, 62

Dickson, Carr
    See Carr, John Dickson

Dickson, Carter
    See Carr, John Dickson

Diderot, Denis 1713-1784 .... LC 26

Didion, Joan 1934-..... CLC 1, 3, 8, 14, 32
    See also AITN 1; CA 5-8R; CANR 14;
    CDALB 1968-1988; DLB 2; DLBY 81,
    86; MTCW

Dietrich, Robert
    See Hunt, E(verette) Howard, (Jr.)

Dillard, Annie 1945-............ CLC 9, 60
    See also AAYA 6; CA 49-52; CANR 3, 43;
    DLBY 80; MTCW; SATA 10

Dillard, R(ichard) H(enry) W(ilde)
    1937- .... CLC 5
    See also CA 21-24R; CAAS 7; CANR 10;
    DLB 5

Dillon, Eilis 1920-1994............ CLC 17
    See also CA 9-12R; 147; CAAS 3; CANR 4,
    38; CLR 26; MAICYA; SATA 2, 74;
    SATA-Obit 83

Dimont, Penelope
    See Mortimer, Penelope (Ruth)

Dinesen, Isak.......... CLC 10, 29; SSC 7
    See also Blixen, Karen (Christentze
    Dinesen)

Ding Ling....................... CLC 68
    See also Chiang Pin-chin

Disch, Thomas M(ichael) 1940-... CLC 7, 36
    See also CA 21-24R; CAAS 4; CANR 17,
    36; CLR 18; DLB 8; MAICYA; MTCW;
    SAAS 15; SATA 54

Disch, Tom
    See Disch, Thomas M(ichael)

d'Isly, Georges
    See Simenon, Georges (Jacques Christian)

Disraeli, Benjamin 1804-1881 .. NCLC 2, 39
    See also DLB 21, 55

Ditcum, Steve
    See Crumb, R(obert)

Dixon, Paige
    See Corcoran, Barbara

Dixon, Stephen 1936-..... CLC 52; SSC 16
    See also CA 89-92; CANR 17, 40; DLB 130

Dobell, Sydney Thompson
    1824-1874 .... NCLC 43
    See also DLB 32

Doblin, Alfred .... TCLC 13
    See also Doeblin, Alfred

Dobrolyubov, Nikolai Alexandrovich
    1836-1861 .... NCLC 5

Dobyns, Stephen 1941-............ CLC 37
    See also CA 45-48; CANR 2, 18

Doctorow, E(dgar) L(aurence)
    1931- ..... CLC 6, 11, 15, 18, 37, 44, 65
    See also AITN 2; BEST 89:3; CA 45-48;
    CANR 2, 33; CDALB 1968-1988; DLB 2,
    28; DLBY 80; MTCW

Dodgson, Charles Lutwidge 1832-1898
    See Carroll, Lewis
    See also CLR 2; DA; DAB; MAICYA;
    YABC 2

Dodson, Owen (Vincent)
    1914-1983 .... CLC 79; BLC
    See also BW 1; CA 65-68; 110; CANR 24;
    DLB 76

Doeblin, Alfred 1878-1957........ TCLC 13
    See also Doblin, Alfred
    See also CA 110; 141; DLB 66

du Gard, Roger Martin
See Martin du Gard, Roger

Duhamel, Georges 1884-1966 .... **CLC 8**
See also CA 81-84; 25-28R; CANR 35;
DLB 65; MTCW

Dujardin, Edouard (Emile Louis)
1861-1949 .... **TCLC 13**
See also CA 109; DLB 123

Dumas, Alexandre (Davy de la Pailleterie)
1802-1870 .. **NCLC 11; DA; DAB; WLC**
See also DLB 119; SATA 18

Dumas, Alexandre
1824-1895 .... **NCLC 9; DC 1**

Dumas, Claudine
See Malzberg, Barry N(athaniel)

Dumas, Henry L. 1934-1968 ..... **CLC 6, 62**
See also BW 1; CA 85-88; DLB 41

du Maurier, Daphne
1907-1989 .... **CLC 6, 11, 59; DAB;**
SSC 18
See also CA 5-8R; 128; CANR 6; MTCW;
SATA 27; SATA-Obit 60

Dunbar, Paul Laurence
1872-1906 ...... **TCLC 2, 12; BLC; DA;**
PC 5; SSC 8; WLC
See also BW 1; CA 104; 124;
CDALB 1865-1917; DLB 50, 54, 78;
SATA 34

Dunbar, William 1460(?)-1530(?) .... **LC 20**
See also DLB 132, 146

Duncan, Lois 1934-............... **CLC 26**
See also AAYA 4; CA 1-4R; CANR 2, 23,
36; CLR 29; JRDA; MAICYA; SAAS 2;
SATA 1, 36, 75

Duncan, Robert (Edward)
1919-1988 .... **CLC 1, 2, 4, 7, 15, 41, 55;**
PC 2
See also CA 9-12R; 124; CANR 28; DLB 5,
16; MTCW

Duncan, Sara Jeannette
1861-1922 .... **TCLC 60**
See also DLB 92

Dunlap, William 1766-1839 ...... **NCLC 2**
See also DLB 30, 37, 59

Dunn, Douglas (Eaglesham)
1942-...................... **CLC 6, 40**
See also CA 45-48; CANR 2, 33; DLB 40;
MTCW

Dunn, Katherine (Karen) 1945-..... **CLC 71**
See also CA 33-36R

Dunn, Stephen 1939- .... **CLC 36**
See also CA 33-36R; CANR 12, 48;
DLB 105

Dunne, Finley Peter 1867-1936.... **TCLC 28**
See also CA 108; DLB 11, 23

Dunne, John Gregory 1932-........ **CLC 28**
See also CA 25-28R; CANR 14; DLBY 80

Dunsany, Edward John Moreton Drax
Plunkett 1878-1957
See Dunsany, Lord
See also CA 104; 148; DLB 10

Dunsany, Lord................ **TCLC 2, 59**
See also Dunsany, Edward John Moreton
Drax Plunkett
See also DLB 77, 153, 156

du Perry, Jean
See Simenon, Georges (Jacques Christian)

Durang, Christopher (Ferdinand)
1949-.................... **CLC 27, 38**
See also CA 105

Duras, Marguerite
1914- ...... **CLC 3, 6, 11, 20, 34, 40, 68**
See also CA 25-28R; DLB 83; MTCW

Durban, (Rosa) Pam 1947-........ **CLC 39**
See also CA 123

Durcan, Paul 1944-........... **CLC 43, 70**
See also CA 134

Durkheim, Emile 1858-1917 ...... **TCLC 55**

Durrell, Lawrence (George)
1912-1990 .... **CLC 1, 4, 6, 8, 13, 27, 41**
See also CA 9-12R; 132; CANR 40;
CDBLB 1945-1960; DLB 15, 27;
DLBY 90; MTCW

Durrenmatt, Friedrich
See Duerrenmatt, Friedrich

Dutt, Toru 1856-1877........... **NCLC 29**

Dwight, Timothy 1752-1817...... **NCLC 13**
See also DLB 37

Dworkin, Andrea 1946- .... **CLC 43**
See also CA 77-80; CAAS 21; CANR 16,
39; MTCW

Dwyer, Deanna
See Koontz, Dean R(ay)

Dwyer, K. R.
See Koontz, Dean R(ay)

Dylan, Bob 1941- ...... **CLC 3, 4, 6, 12, 77**
See also CA 41-44R; DLB 16

Eagleton, Terence (Francis) 1943-
See Eagleton, Terry
See also CA 57-60; CANR 7, 23; MTCW

Eagleton, Terry .... **CLC 63**
See also Eagleton, Terence (Francis)

Early, Jack
See Scoppettone, Sandra

East, Michael
See West, Morris L(anglo)

Eastaway, Edward
See Thomas, (Philip) Edward

Eastlake, William (Derry) 1917-..... **CLC 8**
See also CA 5-8R; CAAS 1; CANR 5;
DLB 6

Eastman, Charles A(lexander)
1858-1939 .... **TCLC 55**
See also NNAL; YABC 1

Eberhart, Richard (Ghormley)
1904-.............. **CLC 3, 11, 19, 56**
See also CA 1-4R; CANR 2;
CDALB 1941-1968; DLB 48; MTCW

Eberstadt, Fernanda 1960-........ **CLC 39**
See also CA 136

Echegaray (y Eizaguirre), Jose (Maria Waldo)
1832-1916 .... **TCLC 4**
See also CA 104; CANR 32; HW; MTCW

Echeverria, (Jose) Esteban (Antonino)
1805-1851 .... **NCLC 18**

Echo
See Proust, (Valentin-Louis-George-Eugene-)
Marcel

Eckert, Allan W. 1931- .... **CLC 17**
See also CA 13-16R; CANR 14, 45;
SATA 29; SATA-Brief 27

Eckhart, Meister 1260(?)-1328(?) .. **CMLC 9**
See also DLB 115

Eckmar, F. R.
See de Hartog, Jan

Eco, Umberto 1932-........... **CLC 28, 60**
See also BEST 90:1; CA 77-80; CANR 12,
33; MTCW

Eddison, E(ric) R(ucker)
1882-1945 .... **TCLC 15**
See also CA 109

Edel, (Joseph) Leon 1907-...... **CLC 29, 34**
See also CA 1-4R; CANR 1, 22; DLB 103

Eden, Emily 1797-1869 .... **NCLC 10**

Edgar, David 1948-............... **CLC 42**
See also CA 57-60; CANR 12; DLB 13;
MTCW

Edgerton, Clyde (Carlyle) 1944- .... **CLC 39**
See also CA 118; 134

Edgeworth, Maria 1768-1849... **NCLC 1, 51**
See also DLB 116; SATA 21

Edmonds, Paul
See Kuttner, Henry

Edmonds, Walter D(umaux) 1903-.. **CLC 35**
See also CA 5-8R; CANR 2; DLB 9;
MAICYA; SAAS 4; SATA 1, 27

Edmondson, Wallace
See Ellison, Harlan (Jay)

Edson, Russell.................... **CLC 13**
See also CA 33-36R

Edwards, Bronwen Elizabeth
See Rose, Wendy

Edwards, G(erald) B(asil)
1899-1976 .... **CLC 25**
See also CA 110

Edwards, Gus 1939-.............. **CLC 43**
See also CA 108

Edwards, Jonathan 1703-1758.... **LC 7; DA**
See also DLB 24

Efron, Marina Ivanovna Tsvetaeva
See Tsvetaeva (Efron), Marina (Ivanovna)

Ehle, John (Marsden, Jr.) 1925-..... **CLC 27**
See also CA 9-12R

Ehrenbourg, Ilya (Grigoryevich)
See Ehrenburg, Ilya (Grigoryevich)

Ehrenburg, Ilya (Grigoryevich)
1891-1967 .... **CLC 18, 34, 62**
See also CA 102; 25-28R

Ehrenburg, Ilyo (Grigoryevich)
See Ehrenburg, Ilya (Grigoryevich)

Eich, Guenter 1907-1972 .... **CLC 15**
See also CA 111; 93-96; DLB 69, 124

Eichendorff, Joseph Freiherr von
1788-1857 .... **NCLC 8**
See also DLB 90

Eigner, Larry...................... **CLC 9**
See also Eigner, Laurence (Joel)
See also DLB 5

Eigner, Laurence (Joel) 1927-
See Eigner, Larry
See also CA 9-12R; CANR 6

Eiseley, Loren Corey 1907-1977 . . . . . **CLC 7**
See also AAYA 5; CA 1-4R; 73-76;
CANR 6

Eisenstadt, Jill 1963- . . . . **CLC 50**
See also CA 140

Eisenstein, Sergei (Mikhailovich)
1898-1948 . . . . **TCLC 57**
See also CA 114

Eisner, Simon
See Kornbluth, C(yril) M.

Ekeloef, (Bengt) Gunnar
1907-1968 . . . . **CLC 27**
See also CA 123; 25-28R

Ekelof, (Bengt) Gunnar
See Ekeloef, (Bengt) Gunnar

Ekwensi, C. O. D.
See Ekwensi, Cyprian (Odiatu Duaka)

Ekwensi, Cyprian (Odiatu Duaka)
1921- . . . . **CLC 4; BLC**
See also BW 2; CA 29-32R; CANR 18, 42;
DLB 117; MTCW; SATA 66

Elaine . . . . **TCLC 18**
See also Leverson, Ada

El Crummo
See Crumb, R(obert)

Elia
See Lamb, Charles

Eliade, Mircea 1907-1986 . . . . **CLC 19**
See also CA 65-68; 119; CANR 30; MTCW

Eliot, A. D.
See Jewett, (Theodora) Sarah Orne

Eliot, Alice
See Jewett, (Theodora) Sarah Orne

Eliot, Dan
See Silverberg, Robert

Eliot, George
1819-1880 . . . . . **NCLC 4, 13, 23, 41, 49;**
DA; DAB; WLC
See also CDBLB 1832-1890; DLB 21, 35, 55

Eliot, John 1604-1690 . . . . **LC 5**
See also DLB 24

Eliot, T(homas) S(tearns)
1888-1965 . . . . . **CLC 1, 2, 3, 6, 9, 10, 13,**
15, 24, 34, 41, 55, 57; DA; DAB; PC 5;
WLC 2
See also CA 5-8R; 25-28R; CANR 41;
CDALB 1929-1941; DLB 7, 10, 45, 63;
DLBY 88; MTCW

Elizabeth 1866-1941 . . . . **TCLC 41**

Elkin, Stanley L(awrence)
1930-1995 . . . . . **CLC 4, 6, 9, 14, 27, 51;**
SSC 12
See also CA 9-12R; 148; CANR 8, 46;
DLB 2, 28; DLBY 80; MTCW

Elledge, Scott . . . . **CLC 34**

Elliott, Don
See Silverberg, Robert

Elliott, George P(aul) 1918-1980 . . . . . **CLC 2**
See also CA 1-4R; 97-100; CANR 2

Elliott, Janice 1931- . . . . **CLC 47**
See also CA 13-16R; CANR 8, 29; DLB 14

Elliott, Sumner Locke 1917-1991 . . . **CLC 38**
See also CA 5-8R; 134; CANR 2, 21

Elliott, William
See Bradbury, Ray (Douglas)

Ellis, A. E. . . . . **CLC 7**

Ellis, Alice Thomas . . . . **CLC 40**
See also Haycraft, Anna

Ellis, Bret Easton 1964- . . . . **CLC 39, 71**
See also AAYA 2; CA 118; 123

Ellis, (Henry) Havelock
1859-1939 . . . . **TCLC 14**
See also CA 109

Ellis, Landon
See Ellison, Harlan (Jay)

Ellis, Trey 1962- . . . . **CLC 55**
See also CA 146

Ellison, Harlan (Jay)
1934- . . . . **CLC 1, 13, 42; SSC 14**
See also CA 5-8R; CANR 5, 46; DLB 8;
MTCW

Ellison, Ralph (Waldo)
1914-1994 . . . . **CLC 1, 3, 11, 54, 86;**
BLC; DA; DAB; WLC
See also BW 1; CA 9-12R; 145; CANR 24;
CDALB 1941-1968; DLB 2, 76;
DLBY 94; MTCW

Ellmann, Lucy (Elizabeth) 1956- . . . . **CLC 61**
See also CA 128

Ellmann, Richard (David)
1918-1987 . . . . **CLC 50**
See also BEST 89:2; CA 1-4R; 122;
CANR 2, 28; DLB 103; DLBY 87;
MTCW

Elman, Richard 1934- . . . . **CLC 19**
See also CA 17-20R; CAAS 3; CANR 47

Elron
See Hubbard, L(afayette) Ron(ald)

Eluard, Paul . . . . **TCLC 7, 41**
See also Grindel, Eugene

Elyot, Sir Thomas 1490(?)-1546 . . . . . **LC 11**

Elytis, Odysseus 1911- . . . . **CLC 15, 49**
See also CA 102; MTCW

Emecheta, (Florence Onye) Buchi
1944- . . . . **CLC 14, 48; BLC**
See also BW 2; CA 81-84; CANR 27;
DLB 117; MTCW; SATA 66

Emerson, Ralph Waldo
1803-1882 . . . . . **NCLC 1, 38; DA; DAB;**
WLC
See also CDALB 1640-1865; DLB 1, 59, 73

Eminescu, Mihail 1850-1889 . . . . . **NCLC 33**

Empson, William
1906-1984 . . . . **CLC 3, 8, 19, 33, 34**
See also CA 17-20R; 112; CANR 31;
DLB 20; MTCW

Enchi Fumiko (Ueda) 1905-1986 . . . . **CLC 31**
See also CA 129; 121

Ende, Michael (Andreas Helmuth)
1929- . . . . **CLC 31**
See also CA 118; 124; CANR 36; CLR 14;
DLB 75; MAICYA; SATA 61;
SATA-Brief 42

Endo, Shusaku 1923- . . . . . **CLC 7, 14, 19, 54**
See also CA 29-32R; CANR 21; MTCW

Engel, Marian 1933-1985 . . . . **CLC 36**
See also CA 25-28R; CANR 12; DLB 53

Engelhardt, Frederick
See Hubbard, L(afayette) Ron(ald)

Enright, D(ennis) J(oseph)
1920- . . . . **CLC 4, 8, 31**
See also CA 1-4R; CANR 1, 42; DLB 27;
SATA 25

Enzensberger, Hans Magnus
1929- . . . . **CLC 43**
See also CA 116; 119

Ephron, Nora 1941- . . . . **CLC 17, 31**
See also AITN 2; CA 65-68; CANR 12, 39

Epsilon
See Betjeman, John

Epstein, Daniel Mark 1948- . . . . **CLC 7**
See also CA 49-52; CANR 2

Epstein, Jacob 1956- . . . . **CLC 19**
See also CA 114

Epstein, Joseph 1937- . . . . **CLC 39**
See also CA 112; 119

Epstein, Leslie 1938- . . . . **CLC 27**
See also CA 73-76; CAAS 12; CANR 23

Equiano, Olaudah
1745(?)-1797 . . . . **LC 16; BLC**
See also DLB 37, 50

Erasmus, Desiderius 1469(?)-1536 . . . . **LC 16**

Erdman, Paul E(mil) 1932- . . . . **CLC 25**
See also AITN 1; CA 61-64; CANR 13, 43

Erdrich, Louise 1954- . . . . **CLC 39, 54**
See also AAYA 10; BEST 89:1; CA 114;
CANR 41; DLB 152; MTCW; NNAL

Erenburg, Ilya (Grigoryevich)
See Ehrenburg, Ilya (Grigoryevich)

Erickson, Stephen Michael 1950-
See Erickson, Steve
See also CA 129

Erickson, Steve . . . . **CLC 64**
See also Erickson, Stephen Michael

Ericson, Walter
See Fast, Howard (Melvin)

Eriksson, Buntel
See Bergman, (Ernst) Ingmar

Ernaux, Annie 1940- . . . . **CLC 88**
See also CA 147

Eschenbach, Wolfram von
See Wolfram von Eschenbach

Eseki, Bruno
See Mphahlele, Ezekiel

Esenin, Sergei (Alexandrovich)
1895-1925 . . . . **TCLC 4**
See also CA 104

Eshleman, Clayton 1935- . . . . **CLC 7**
See also CA 33-36R; CAAS 6; DLB 5

Espriella, Don Manuel Alvarez
See Southey, Robert

Espriu, Salvador 1913-1985 . . . . **CLC 9**
See also CA 115; DLB 134

Espronceda, Jose de 1808-1842 . . . **NCLC 39**

Esse, James
See Stephens, James

Esterbrook, Tom
See Hubbard, L(afayette) Ron(ald)

Estleman, Loren D. 1952- . . . . **CLC 48**
See also CA 85-88; CANR 27; MTCW

Author Index

Gale, Zona 1874-1938 . . . . **TCLC 7**
See also CA 105; DLB 9, 78

Galeano, Eduardo (Hughes) 1940- . . . **CLC 72**
See also CA 29-32R; CANR 13, 32; HW

Galiano, Juan Valera y Alcala
See Valera y Alcala-Galiano, Juan

Gallagher, Tess 1943- . . . . **CLC 18, 63; PC 9**
See also CA 106; DLB 120

Gallant, Mavis
1922- . . . . **CLC 7, 18, 38; SSC 5**
See also CA 69-72; CANR 29; DLB 53;
MTCW

Gallant, Roy A(rthur) 1924- . . . . **CLC 17**
See also CA 5-8R; CANR 4, 29; CLR 30;
MAICYA; SATA 4, 68

Gallico, Paul (William) 1897-1976 . . . **CLC 2**
See also AITN 1; CA 5-8R; 69-72;
CANR 23; DLB 9; MAICYA; SATA 13

Gallup, Ralph
See Whitemore, Hugh (John)

Galsworthy, John
1867-1933 . . . . . . **TCLC 1, 45; DA; DAB;**
WLC 2
See also CA 104; 141; CDBLB 1890-1914;
DLB 10, 34, 98

Galt, John 1779-1839 . . . . **NCLC 1**
See also DLB 99, 116

Galvin, James 1951- . . . . **CLC 38**
See also CA 108; CANR 26

Gamboa, Federico 1864-1939 . . . . . . **TCLC 36**

Gandhi, M. K.
See Gandhi, Mohandas Karamchand

Gandhi, Mahatma
See Gandhi, Mohandas Karamchand

Gandhi, Mohandas Karamchand
1869-1948 . . . . **TCLC 59**
See also CA 121; 132; MTCW

Gann, Ernest Kellogg 1910-1991 . . . . **CLC 23**
See also AITN 1; CA 1-4R; 136; CANR 1

Garcia, Cristina 1958- . . . . **CLC 76**
See also CA 141

Garcia Lorca, Federico
1898-1936 . . . **TCLC 1, 7, 49; DA; DAB;**
DC 2; HLC; PC 3; WLC
See also CA 104; 131; DLB 108; HW;
MTCW

Garcia Marquez, Gabriel (Jose)
1928- . . . . **CLC 2, 3, 8, 10, 15, 27, 47, 55,**
68; DA; DAB; HLC; SSC 8; WLC
See also AAYA 3; BEST 89:1, 90:4;
CA 33-36R; CANR 10, 28; DLB 113;
HW; MTCW

Gard, Janice
See Latham, Jean Lee

Gard, Roger Martin du
See Martin du Gard, Roger

Gardam, Jane 1928- . . . . **CLC 43**
See also CA 49-52; CANR 2, 18, 33;
CLR 12; DLB 14; MAICYA; MTCW;
SAAS 9; SATA 39, 76; SATA-Brief 28

Gardner, Herb . . . . **CLC 44**

Gardner, John (Champlin), Jr.
1933-1982 . . . . . **CLC 2, 3, 5, 7, 8, 10, 18,**
28, 34; SSC 7
See also AITN 1; CA 65-68; 107;
CANR 33; DLB 2; DLBY 82; MTCW;
SATA 40; SATA-Obit 31

Gardner, John (Edmund) 1926- . . . . . **CLC 30**
See also CA 103; CANR 15; MTCW

Gardner, Noel
See Kuttner, Henry

Gardons, S. S.
See Snodgrass, W(illiam) D(e Witt)

Garfield, Leon 1921- . . . . **CLC 12**
See also AAYA 8; CA 17-20R; CANR 38,
41; CLR 21; JRDA; MAICYA; SATA 1,
32, 76

Garland, (Hannibal) Hamlin
1860-1940 . . . . **TCLC 3; SSC 18**
See also CA 104; DLB 12, 71, 78

Garneau, (Hector de) Saint-Denys
1912-1943 . . . . **TCLC 13**
See also CA 111; DLB 88

Garner, Alan 1934- . . . . **CLC 17; DAB**
See also CA 73-76; CANR 15; CLR 20;
MAICYA; MTCW; SATA 18, 69

Garner, Hugh 1913-1979 . . . . **CLC 13**
See also CA 69-72; CANR 31; DLB 68

Garnett, David 1892-1981 . . . . **CLC 3**
See also CA 5-8R; 103; CANR 17; DLB 34

Garos, Stephanie
See Katz, Steve

Garrett, George (Palmer)
1929- . . . . **CLC 3, 11, 51**
See also CA 1-4R; CAAS 5; CANR 1, 42;
DLB 2, 5, 130, 152; DLBY 83

Garrick, David 1717-1779 . . . . **LC 15**
See also DLB 84

Garrigue, Jean 1914-1972 . . . . **CLC 2, 8**
See also CA 5-8R; 37-40R; CANR 20

Garrison, Frederick
See Sinclair, Upton (Beall)

Garth, Will
See Hamilton, Edmond; Kuttner, Henry

Garvey, Marcus (Moziah, Jr.)
1887-1940 . . . . **TCLC 41; BLC**
See also BW 1; CA 120; 124

Gary, Romain . . . . **CLC 25**
See also Kacew, Romain
See also DLB 83

Gascar, Pierre . . . . **CLC 11**
See also Fournier, Pierre

Gascoyne, David (Emery) 1916- . . . . . **CLC 45**
See also CA 65-68; CANR 10, 28; DLB 20;
MTCW

Gaskell, Elizabeth Cleghorn
1810-1865 . . . . **NCLC 5; DAB**
See also CDBLB 1832-1890; DLB 21, 144

Gass, William H(oward)
1924- . . . **CLC 1, 2, 8, 11, 15, 39; SSC 12**
See also CA 17-20R; CANR 30; DLB 2;
MTCW

Gasset, Jose Ortega y
See Ortega y Gasset, Jose

Gates, Henry Louis, Jr. 1950- . . . . . . **CLC 65**
See also BW 2; CA 109; CANR 25; DLB 67

Gautier, Theophile
1811-1872 . . . . **NCLC 1; SSC 20**
See also DLB 119

Gawsworth, John
See Bates, H(erbert) E(rnest)

Gaye, Marvin (Penze) 1939-1984 . . . **CLC 26**
See also CA 112

Gebler, Carlo (Ernest) 1954- . . . . **CLC 39**
See also CA 119; 133

Gee, Maggie (Mary) 1948- . . . . **CLC 57**
See also CA 130

Gee, Maurice (Gough) 1931- . . . . **CLC 29**
See also CA 97-100; SATA 46

Gelbart, Larry (Simon) 1923- . . . **CLC 21, 61**
See also CA 73-76; CANR 45

Gelber, Jack 1932- . . . . **CLC 1, 6, 14, 79**
See also CA 1-4R; CANR 2; DLB 7

Gellhorn, Martha (Ellis) 1908- . . **CLC 14, 60**
See also CA 77-80; CANR 44; DLBY 82

Genet, Jean
1910-1986 . . . **CLC 1, 2, 5, 10, 14, 44, 46**
See also CA 13-16R; CANR 18; DLB 72;
DLBY 86; MTCW

Gent, Peter 1942- . . . . **CLC 29**
See also AITN 1; CA 89-92; DLBY 82

Gentlewoman in New England, A
See Bradstreet, Anne

Gentlewoman in Those Parts, A
See Bradstreet, Anne

George, Jean Craighead 1919- . . . . . . **CLC 35**
See also AAYA 8; CA 5-8R; CANR 25;
CLR 1; DLB 52; JRDA; MAICYA;
SATA 2, 68

George, Stefan (Anton)
1868-1933 . . . . **TCLC 2, 14**
See also CA 104

Georges, Georges Martin
See Simenon, Georges (Jacques Christian)

Gerhardi, William Alexander
See Gerhardie, William Alexander

Gerhardie, William Alexander
1895-1977 . . . . **CLC 5**
See also CA 25-28R; 73-76; CANR 18;
DLB 36

Gerstler, Amy 1956- . . . . **CLC 70**
See also CA 146

Gertler, T. . . . . **CLC 34**
See also CA 116; 121

Ghalib 1797-1869 . . . . **NCLC 39**

Ghelderode, Michel de
1898-1962 . . . . **CLC 6, 11**
See also CA 85-88; CANR 40

Ghiselin, Brewster 1903- . . . . **CLC 23**
See also CA 13-16R; CAAS 10; CANR 13

Ghose, Zulfikar 1935- . . . . **CLC 42**
See also CA 65-68

Ghosh, Amitav 1956- . . . . **CLC 44**
See also CA 147

Giacosa, Giuseppe 1847-1906 . . . . . . **TCLC 7**
See also CA 104

Gibb, Lee
See Waterhouse, Keith (Spencer)

Gibbon, Lewis Grassic . . . . TCLC 4
  See also Mitchell, James Leslie

Gibbons, Kaye 1960- . . . . CLC 50, 88

Gibran, Kahlil
  1883-1931 . . . . TCLC 1, 9; PC 9
  See also CA 104

Gibson, William 1914- . . CLC 23; DA; DAB
  See also CA 9-12R; CANR 9, 42; DLB 7;
  SATA 66

Gibson, William (Ford) 1948- . . . CLC 39, 63
  See also AAYA 12; CA 126; 133

Gide, Andre (Paul Guillaume)
  1869-1951 . . . . TCLC 5, 12, 36; DA;
  DAB; SSC 13; WLC
  See also CA 104; 124; DLB 65; MTCW

Gifford, Barry (Colby) 1946- . . . . CLC 34
  See also CA 65-68; CANR 9, 30, 40

Gilbert, W(illiam) S(chwenck)
  1836-1911 . . . . TCLC 3
  See also CA 104; SATA 36

Gilbreth, Frank B., Jr. 1911- . . . . CLC 17
  See also CA 9-12R; SATA 2

Gilchrist, Ellen 1935- . . CLC 34, 48; SSC 14
  See also CA 113; 116; CANR 41; DLB 130;
  MTCW

Giles, Molly 1942- . . . . CLC 39
  See also CA 126

Gill, Patrick
  See Creasey, John

Gilliam, Terry (Vance) 1940- . . . . CLC 21
  See also Monty Python
  See also CA 108; 113; CANR 35

Gillian, Jerry
  See Gilliam, Terry (Vance)

Gilliatt, Penelope (Ann Douglass)
  1932-1993 . . . . CLC 2, 10, 13, 53
  See also AITN 2; CA 13-16R; 141;
  CANR 49; DLB 14

Gilman, Charlotte (Anna) Perkins (Stetson)
  1860-1935 . . . . TCLC 9, 37; SSC 13
  See also CA 106

Gilmour, David 1949- . . . . CLC 35
  See also CA 138, 147

Gilpin, William 1724-1804 . . . . NCLC 30

Gilray, J. D.
  See Mencken, H(enry) L(ouis)

Gilroy, Frank D(aniel) 1925- . . . . CLC 2
  See also CA 81-84; CANR 32; DLB 7

Ginsberg, Allen
  1926- . . . . . . CLC 1, 2, 3, 4, 6, 13, 36, 69;
  DA; DAB; PC 4; WLC 3
  See also AITN 1; CA 1-4R; CANR 2, 41;
  CDALB 1941-1968; DLB 5, 16; MTCW

Ginzburg, Natalia
  1916-1991 . . . . CLC 5, 11, 54, 70
  See also CA 85-88; 135; CANR 33; MTCW

Giono, Jean 1895-1970 . . . . CLC 4, 11
  See also CA 45-48; 29-32R; CANR 2, 35;
  DLB 72; MTCW

Giovanni, Nikki
  1943- . . . . . . CLC 2, 4, 19, 64; BLC; DA;
  DAB
  See also AITN 1; BW 2; CA 29-32R;
  CAAS 6; CANR 18, 41; CLR 6; DLB 5,
  41; MAICYA; MTCW; SATA 24

Giovene, Andrea 1904- . . . . CLC 7
  See also CA 85-88

Gippius, Zinaida (Nikolayevna) 1869-1945
  See Hippius, Zinaida
  See also CA 106

Giraudoux, (Hippolyte) Jean
  1882-1944 . . . . TCLC 2, 7
  See also CA 104; DLB 65

Gironella, Jose Maria 1917- . . . . CLC 11
  See also CA 101

Gissing, George (Robert)
  1857-1903 . . . . TCLC 3, 24, 47
  See also CA 105; DLB 18, 135

Giurlani, Aldo
  See Palazzeschi, Aldo

Gladkov, Fyodor (Vasilyevich)
  1883-1958 . . . . TCLC 27

Glanville, Brian (Lester) 1931- . . . . . . CLC 6
  See also CA 5-8R; CAAS 9; CANR 3;
  DLB 15, 139; SATA 42

Glasgow, Ellen (Anderson Gholson)
  1873(?)-1945 . . . . TCLC 2, 7
  See also CA 104; DLB 9, 12

Glaspell, Susan (Keating)
  1882(?)-1948 . . . . TCLC 55
  See also CA 110; DLB 7, 9, 78; YABC 2

Glassco, John 1909-1981 . . . . CLC 9
  See also CA 13-16R; 102; CANR 15;
  DLB 68

Glasscock, Amnesia
  See Steinbeck, John (Ernst)

Glasser, Ronald J. 1940(?)- . . . . CLC 37

Glassman, Joyce
  See Johnson, Joyce

Glendinning, Victoria 1937- . . . . CLC 50
  See also CA 120; 127; DLB 155

Glissant, Edouard 1928- . . . . CLC 10, 68

Gloag, Julian 1930- . . . . CLC 40
  See also AITN 1; CA 65-68; CANR 10

Glowacki, Aleksander
  See Prus, Boleslaw

Glueck, Louise (Elisabeth)
  1943- . . . . CLC 7, 22, 44, 81
  See also CA 33-36R; CANR 40; DLB 5

Gobineau, Joseph Arthur (Comte) de
  1816-1882 . . . . NCLC 17
  See also DLB 123

Godard, Jean-Luc 1930- . . . . CLC 20
  See also CA 93-96

Godden, (Margaret) Rumer 1907- . . . CLC 53
  See also AAYA 6; CA 5-8R; CANR 4, 27,
  36; CLR 20; MAICYA; SAAS 12;
  SATA 3, 36

Godoy Alcayaga, Lucila 1889-1957
  See Mistral, Gabriela
  See also BW 2; CA 104; 131; HW; MTCW

Godwin, Gail (Kathleen)
  1937- . . . . CLC 5, 8, 22, 31, 69
  See also CA 29-32R; CANR 15, 43; DLB 6;
  MTCW

Godwin, William 1756-1836 . . . . . . NCLC 14
  See also CDBLB 1789-1832; DLB 39, 104,
  142

Goethe, Johann Wolfgang von
  1749-1832 . . . . NCLC 4, 22, 34; DA;
  DAB; PC 5; WLC 3
  See also DLB 94

Gogarty, Oliver St. John
  1878-1957 . . . . TCLC 15
  See also CA 109; DLB 15, 19

Gogol, Nikolai (Vasilyevich)
  1809-1852 . . . . NCLC 5, 15, 31; DA;
  DAB; DC 1; SSC 4; WLC
  See also CA 103

Goines, Donald
  1937(?)-1974 . . . . CLC 80; BLC
  See also AITN 1; BW 1; CA 124; 114;
  DLB 33

Gold, Herbert 1924- . . . . . . CLC 4, 7, 14, 42
  See also CA 9-12R; CANR 17, 45; DLB 2;
  DLBY 81

Goldbarth, Albert 1948- . . . . CLC 5, 38
  See also CA 53-56; CANR 6, 40; DLB 120

Goldberg, Anatol 1910-1982 . . . . CLC 34
  See also CA 131; 117

Goldemberg, Isaac 1945- . . . . CLC 52
  See also CA 69-72; CAAS 12; CANR 11,
  32; HW

Golding, William (Gerald)
  1911-1993 . . . . CLC 1, 2, 3, 8, 10, 17, 27,
  58, 81; DA; DAB; WLC
  See also AAYA 5; CA 5-8R; 141;
  CANR 13, 33; CDBLB 1945-1960;
  DLB 15, 100; MTCW

Goldman, Emma 1869-1940 . . . . TCLC 13
  See also CA 110

Goldman, Francisco 1955- . . . . CLC 76

Goldman, William (W.) 1931- . . . . CLC 1, 48
  See also CA 9-12R; CANR 29; DLB 44

Goldmann, Lucien 1913-1970 . . . . . . CLC 24
  See also CA 25-28; CAP 2

Goldoni, Carlo 1707-1793 . . . . LC 4

Goldsberry, Steven 1949- . . . . CLC 34
  See also CA 131

Goldsmith, Oliver
  1728-1774 . . . . . . LC 2; DA; DAB; WLC
  See also CDBLB 1660-1789; DLB 39, 89,
  104, 109, 142; SATA 26

Goldsmith, Peter
  See Priestley, J(ohn) B(oynton)

Gombrowicz, Witold
  1904-1969 . . . . CLC 4, 7, 11, 49
  See also CA 19-20; 25-28R; CAP 2

Gomez de la Serna, Ramon
  1888-1963 . . . . CLC 9
  See also CA 116; HW

Goncharov, Ivan Alexandrovich
  1812-1891 . . . . NCLC 1

Goncourt, Edmond (Louis Antoine Huot) de
  1822-1896 . . . . NCLC 7
  See also DLB 123

Goncourt, Jules (Alfred Huot) de
  1830-1870 . . . . NCLC 7
  See also DLB 123

Gontier, Fernande 19(?)- . . . . CLC 50

Goodman, Paul 1911-1972 . . . . CLC 1, 2, 4, 7
  See also CA 19-20; 37-40R; CANR 34;
  CAP 2; DLB 130; MTCW

Gordimer, Nadine
    1923- .... **CLC 3, 5, 7, 10, 18, 33, 51, 70;**
        DA; DAB; SSC 17
    See also CA 5-8R; CANR 3, 28; MTCW

Gordon, Adam Lindsay
    1833-1870 .... **NCLC 21**

Gordon, Caroline
    1895-1981 ... **CLC 6, 13, 29, 83; SSC 15**
    See also CA 11-12; 103; CANR 36; CAP 1;
        DLB 4, 9, 102; DLBY 81; MTCW

Gordon, Charles William 1860-1937
    See Connor, Ralph
    See also CA 109

Gordon, Mary (Catherine)
    1949- .... **CLC 13, 22**
    See also CA 102; CANR 44; DLB 6;
        DLBY 81; MTCW

Gordon, Sol 1923-................. **CLC 26**
    See also CA 53-56; CANR 4; SATA 11

Gordone, Charles 1925- .... **CLC 1, 4**
    See also BW 1; CA 93-96; DLB 7; MTCW

Gorenko, Anna Andreevna
    See Akhmatova, Anna

Gorky, Maxim........ **TCLC 8; DAB; WLC**
    See also Peshkov, Alexei Maximovich

Goryan, Sirak
    See Saroyan, William

Gosse, Edmund (William)
    1849-1928 .... **TCLC 28**
    See also CA 117; DLB 57, 144

Gotlieb, Phyllis Fay (Bloom)
    1926- .... **CLC 18**
    See also CA 13-16R; CANR 7; DLB 88

Gottesman, S. D.
    See Kornbluth, C(yril) M.; Pohl, Frederik

Gottfried von Strassburg
    fl. c. 1210-................. **CMLC 10**
    See also DLB 138

Gould, Lois .... **CLC 4, 10**
    See also CA 77-80; CANR 29; MTCW

Gourmont, Remy de 1858-1915.... **TCLC 17**
    See also CA 109

Govier, Katherine 1948-.......... **CLC 51**
    See also CA 101; CANR 18, 40

Goyen, (Charles) William
    1915-1983 .... **CLC 5, 8, 14, 40**
    See also AITN 2; CA 5-8R; 110; CANR 6;
        DLB 2; DLBY 83

Goytisolo, Juan
    1931- .... **CLC 5, 10, 23; HLC**
    See also CA 85-88; CANR 32; HW; MTCW

Gozzano, Guido 1883-1916 .... **PC 10**
    See also DLB 114

Gozzi, (Conte) Carlo 1720-1806 .. **NCLC 23**

Grabbe, Christian Dietrich
    1801-1836 .... **NCLC 2**
    See also DLB 133

Grace, Patricia 1937-............. **CLC 56**

Gracian y Morales, Baltasar
    1601-1658 .... **LC 15**

Gracq, Julien................. **CLC 11, 48**
    See also Poirier, Louis
    See also DLB 83

Grade, Chaim 1910-1982 .... **CLC 10**
    See also CA 93-96; 107

Graduate of Oxford, A
    See Ruskin, John

Graham, John
    See Phillips, David Graham

Graham, Jorie 1951-............. **CLC 48**
    See also CA 111; DLB 120

Graham, R(obert) B(ontine) Cunninghame
    See Cunninghame Graham, R(obert)
        B(ontine)
    See also DLB 98, 135

Graham, Robert
    See Haldeman, Joe (William)

Graham, Tom
    See Lewis, (Harry) Sinclair

Graham, W(illiam) S(ydney)
    1918-1986 .... **CLC 29**
    See also CA 73-76; 118; DLB 20

Graham, Winston (Mawdsley)
    1910-................... **CLC 23**
    See also CA 49-52; CANR 2, 22, 45;
        DLB 77

Grant, Skeeter
    See Spiegelman, Art

Granville-Barker, Harley
    1877-1946 .... **TCLC 2**
    See also Barker, Harley Granville
    See also CA 104

Grass, Guenter (Wilhelm)
    1927- ..... **CLC 1, 2, 4, 6, 11, 15, 22, 32,**
        49, 88; DA; DAB; WLC
    See also CA 13-16R; CANR 20; DLB 75,
        124; MTCW

Gratton, Thomas
    See Hulme, T(homas) E(rnest)

Grau, Shirley Ann
    1929- .... **CLC 4, 9; SSC 15**
    See also CA 89-92; CANR 22; DLB 2;
        MTCW

Gravel, Fern
    See Hall, James Norman

Graver, Elizabeth 1964-.......... **CLC 70**
    See also CA 135

Graves, Richard Perceval 1945- .... **CLC 44**
    See also CA 65-68; CANR 9, 26

Graves, Robert (von Ranke)
    1895-1985 ...... **CLC 1, 2, 6, 11, 39, 44,**
        45; DAB; PC 6
    See also CA 5-8R; 117; CANR 5, 36;
        CDBLB 1914-1945; DLB 20, 100;
        DLBY 85; MTCW; SATA 45

Gray, Alasdair (James) 1934- ...... **CLC 41**
    See also CA 126; CANR 47; MTCW

Gray, Amlin 1946- .... **CLC 29**
    See also CA 138

Gray, Francine du Plessix 1930-.... **CLC 22**
    See also BEST 90:3; CA 61-64; CAAS 2;
        CANR 11, 33; MTCW

Gray, John (Henry) 1866-1934 .... **TCLC 19**
    See also CA 119

Gray, Simon (James Holliday)
    1936- .... **CLC 9, 14, 36**
    See also AITN 1; CA 21-24R; CAAS 3;
        CANR 32; DLB 13; MTCW

Gray, Spalding 1941-............. **CLC 49**
    See also CA 128

Gray, Thomas
    1716-1771 ...... **LC 4; DA; DAB; PC 2;**
        WLC
    See also CDBLB 1660-1789; DLB 109

Grayson, David
    See Baker, Ray Stannard

Grayson, Richard (A.) 1951-....... **CLC 38**
    See also CA 85-88; CANR 14, 31

Greeley, Andrew M(oran) 1928-.... **CLC 28**
    See also CA 5-8R; CAAS 7; CANR 7, 43;
        MTCW

Green, Brian
    See Card, Orson Scott

Green, Hannah
    See Greenberg, Joanne (Goldenberg)

Green, Hannah .... **CLC 3**
    See also CA 73-76

Green, Henry.................... **CLC 2, 13**
    See also Yorke, Henry Vincent
    See also DLB 15

Green, Julian (Hartridge) 1900-
    See Green, Julien
    See also CA 21-24R; CANR 33; DLB 4, 72;
        MTCW

Green, Julien................ **CLC 3, 11, 77**
    See also Green, Julian (Hartridge)

Green, Paul (Eliot) 1894-1981...... **CLC 25**
    See also AITN 1; CA 5-8R; 103; CANR 3;
        DLB 7, 9; DLBY 81

Greenberg, Ivan 1908-1973
    See Rahv, Philip
    See also CA 85-88

Greenberg, Joanne (Goldenberg)
    1932- .... **CLC 7, 30**
    See also AAYA 12; CA 5-8R; CANR 14,
        32; SATA 25

Greenberg, Richard 1959(?)-....... **CLC 57**
    See also CA 138

Greene, Bette 1934-.............. **CLC 30**
    See also AAYA 7; CA 53-56; CANR 4;
        CLR 2; JRDA; MAICYA; SAAS 16;
        SATA 8

Greene, Gael .... **CLC 8**
    See also CA 13-16R; CANR 10

Greene, Graham
    1904-1991 .... **CLC 1, 3, 6, 9, 14, 18, 27,**
        37, 70, 72; DA; DAB; WLC
    See also AITN 2; CA 13-16R; 133;
        CANR 35; CDBLB 1945-1960; DLB 13,
        15, 77, 100; DLBY 91; MTCW; SATA 20

Greer, Richard
    See Silverberg, Robert

Gregor, Arthur 1923-.............. **CLC 9**
    See also CA 25-28R; CAAS 10; CANR 11;
        SATA 36

Gregor, Lee
    See Pohl, Frederik

Gregory, Isabella Augusta (Persse)
    1852-1932 .... **TCLC 1**
    See also CA 104; DLB 10

Gregory, J. Dennis
    See Williams, John A(lfred)

Haley, Alex(ander Murray Palmer)
    1921-1992 .... **CLC 8, 12, 76; BLC; DA;**
                                            DAB
    See also BW 2; CA 77-80; 136; DLB 38;
    MTCW

Haliburton, Thomas Chandler
    1796-1865 .... **NCLC 15**
    See also DLB 11, 99

Hall, Donald (Andrew, Jr.)
    1928- ....**CLC 1, 13, 37, 59**
    See also CA 5-8R; CAAS 7; CANR 2, 44;
    DLB 5; SATA 23

Hall, Frederic Sauser
    See Sauser-Hall, Frederic

Hall, James
    See Kuttner, Henry

Hall, James Norman 1887-1951 ... **TCLC 23**
    See also CA 123; SATA 21

Hall, (Marguerite) Radclyffe
    1886(?)-1943 ....**TCLC 12**
    See also CA 110

Hall, Rodney 1935- .... **CLC 51**
    See also CA 109

Halleck, Fitz-Greene 1790-1867 .. **NCLC 47**
    See also DLB 3

Halliday, Michael
    See Creasey, John

Halpern, Daniel 1945- .... **CLC 14**
    See also CA 33-36R

Hamburger, Michael (Peter Leopold)
    1924- ....**CLC 5, 14**
    See also CA 5-8R; CAAS 4; CANR 2, 47;
    DLB 27

Hamill, Pete 1935- .... **CLC 10**
    See also CA 25-28R; CANR 18

Hamilton, Alexander
    1755(?)-1804 .... **NCLC 49**
    See also DLB 37

Hamilton, Clive
    See Lewis, C(live) S(taples)

Hamilton, Edmond 1904-1977....... **CLC 1**
    See also CA 1-4R; CANR 3; DLB 8

Hamilton, Eugene (Jacob) Lee
    See Lee-Hamilton, Eugene (Jacob)

Hamilton, Franklin
    See Silverberg, Robert

Hamilton, Gail
    See Corcoran, Barbara

Hamilton, Mollie
    See Kaye, M(ary) M(argaret)

Hamilton, (Anthony Walter) Patrick
    1904-1962 .... **CLC 51**
    See also CA 113; DLB 10

Hamilton, Virginia 1936-.......... **CLC 26**
    See also AAYA 2; BW 2; CA 25-28R;
    CANR 20, 37; CLR 1, 11; DLB 33, 52;
    JRDA; MAICYA; MTCW; SATA 4, 56,
    79

Hammett, (Samuel) Dashiell
    1894-1961 .... **CLC 3, 5, 10, 19, 47;**
                                            SSC 17
    See also AITN 1; CA 81-84; CANR 42;
    CDALB 1929-1941; DLBD 6; MTCW

Hammon, Jupiter
    1711(?)-1800(?) .... **NCLC 5; BLC**
    See also DLB 31, 50

Hammond, Keith
    See Kuttner, Henry

Hamner, Earl (Henry), Jr. 1923- ... **CLC 12**
    See also AITN 2; CA 73-76; DLB 6

Hampton, Christopher (James)
    1946- .... **CLC 4**
    See also CA 25-28R; DLB 13; MTCW

Hamsun, Knut............. **TCLC 2, 14, 49**
    See also Pedersen, Knut

Handke, Peter 1942- .. **CLC 5, 8, 10, 15, 38**
    See also CA 77-80; CANR 33; DLB 85,
    124; MTCW

Hanley, James 1901-1985 ...**CLC 3, 5, 8, 13**
    See also CA 73-76; 117; CANR 36; MTCW

Hannah, Barry 1942-....... **CLC 23, 38, 90**
    See also CA 108; 110; CANR 43; DLB 6;
    MTCW

Hannon, Ezra
    See Hunter, Evan

Hansberry, Lorraine (Vivian)
    1930-1965 ...... **CLC 17, 62; BLC; DA;**
                                            DAB; DC 2
    See also BW 1; CA 109; 25-28R; CABS 3;
    CDALB 1941-1968; DLB 7, 38; MTCW

Hansen, Joseph 1923-............. **CLC 38**
    See also CA 29-32R; CAAS 17; CANR 16,
    44

Hansen, Martin A. 1909-1955..... **TCLC 32**

Hanson, Kenneth O(stlin) 1922-.... **CLC 13**
    See also CA 53-56; CANR 7

Hardwick, Elizabeth 1916- .... **CLC 13**
    See also CA 5-8R; CANR 3, 32; DLB 6;
    MTCW

Hardy, Thomas
    1840-1928 ...... **TCLC 4, 10, 18, 32, 48,**
                        53; DA; DAB; PC 8; SSC 2; WLC
    See also CA 104; 123; CDBLB 1890-1914;
    DLB 18, 19, 135; MTCW

Hare, David 1947- .... **CLC 29, 58**
    See also CA 97-100; CANR 39; DLB 13;
    MTCW

Harford, Henry
    See Hudson, W(illiam) H(enry)

Hargrave, Leonie
    See Disch, Thomas M(ichael)

Harjo, Joy 1951- .... **CLC 83**
    See also CA 114; CANR 35; DLB 120;
    NNAL

Harlan, Louis R(udolph) 1922-..... **CLC 34**
    See also CA 21-24R; CANR 25

Harling, Robert 1951(?)-.......... **CLC 53**
    See also CA 147

Harmon, William (Ruth) 1938-..... **CLC 38**
    See also CA 33-36R; CANR 14, 32, 35;
    SATA 65

Harper, F. E. W.
    See Harper, Frances Ellen Watkins

Harper, Frances E. W.
    See Harper, Frances Ellen Watkins

Harper, Frances E. Watkins
    See Harper, Frances Ellen Watkins

Harper, Frances Ellen
    See Harper, Frances Ellen Watkins

Harper, Frances Ellen Watkins
    1825-1911 .... **TCLC 14; BLC**
    See also BW 1; CA 111; 125; DLB 50

Harper, Michael S(teven) 1938- .. **CLC 7, 22**
    See also BW 1; CA 33-36R; CANR 24;
    DLB 41

Harper, Mrs. F. E. W.
    See Harper, Frances Ellen Watkins

Harris, Christie (Lucy) Irwin
    1907- .... **CLC 12**
    See also CA 5-8R; CANR 6; DLB 88;
    JRDA; MAICYA; SAAS 10; SATA 6, 74

Harris, Frank 1856(?)-1931....... **TCLC 24**
    See also CA 109; DLB 156

Harris, George Washington
    1814-1869 .... **NCLC 23**
    See also DLB 3, 11

Harris, Joel Chandler
    1848-1908 .... **TCLC 2; SSC 19**
    See also CA 104; 137; DLB 11, 23, 42, 78,
    91; MAICYA; YABC 1

Harris, John (Wyndham Parkes Lucas)
    Beynon 1903-1969
    See Wyndham, John
    See also CA 102; 89-92

Harris, MacDonald................. **CLC 9**
    See also Heiney, Donald (William)

Harris, Mark 1922- .... **CLC 19**
    See also CA 5-8R; CAAS 3; CANR 2;
    DLB 2; DLBY 80

Harris, (Theodore) Wilson 1921-.... **CLC 25**
    See also BW 2; CA 65-68; CAAS 16;
    CANR 11, 27; DLB 117; MTCW

Harrison, Elizabeth Cavanna 1909-
    See Cavanna, Betty
    See also CA 9-12R; CANR 6, 27

Harrison, Harry (Max) 1925-...... **CLC 42**
    See also CA 1-4R; CANR 5, 21; DLB 8;
    SATA 4

Harrison, James (Thomas)
    1937- .... **CLC 6, 14, 33, 66; SSC 19**
    See also CA 13-16R; CANR 8; DLBY 82

Harrison, Jim
    See Harrison, James (Thomas)

Harrison, Kathryn 1961-.......... **CLC 70**
    See also CA 144

Harrison, Tony 1937-............. **CLC 43**
    See also CA 65-68; CANR 44; DLB 40;
    MTCW

Harriss, Will(ard Irvin) 1922-...... **CLC 34**
    See also CA 111

Harson, Sley
    See Ellison, Harlan (Jay)

Hart, Ellis
    See Ellison, Harlan (Jay)

Hart, Josephine 1942(?)-.......... **CLC 70**
    See also CA 138

Hart, Moss 1904-1961 .... **CLC 66**
    See also CA 109; 89-92; DLB 7

Harte, (Francis) Bret(t)
  1836(?)-1902 . . . . TCLC 1, 25; DA;
                                        SSC 8; WLC
  See also CA 104; 140; CDALB 1865-1917;
  DLB 12, 64, 74, 79; SATA 26

Hartley, L(eslie) P(oles)
  1895-1972 . . . . CLC 2, 22
  See also CA 45-48; 37-40R; CANR 33;
  DLB 15, 139; MTCW

Hartman, Geoffrey H. 1929- . . . . CLC 27
  See also CA 117; 125; DLB 67

Hartmann von Aue
  c. 1160-c. 1205 . . . . CMLC 15
  See also DLB 138

Haruf, Kent 19(?)- . . . . CLC 34

Harwood, Ronald 1934- . . . . CLC 32
  See also CA 1-4R; CANR 4; DLB 13

Hasek, Jaroslav (Matej Frantisek)
  1883-1923 . . . . TCLC 4
  See also CA 104; 129; MTCW

Hass, Robert 1941- . . . . CLC 18, 39
  See also CA 111; CANR 30; DLB 105

Hastings, Hudson
  See Kuttner, Henry

Hastings, Selina . . . . CLC 44

Hatteras, Amelia
  See Mencken, H(enry) L(ouis)

Hatteras, Owen . . . . TCLC 18
  See also Mencken, H(enry) L(ouis); Nathan,
  George Jean

Hauptmann, Gerhart (Johann Robert)
  1862-1946 . . . . TCLC 4
  See also CA 104; DLB 66, 118

Havel, Vaclav 1936- . . . . CLC 25, 58, 65
  See also CA 104; CANR 36; MTCW

Haviaras, Stratis . . . . CLC 33
  See also Chaviaras, Strates

Hawes, Stephen 1475(?)-1523(?) . . . . . LC 17

Hawkes, John (Clendennin Burne, Jr.)
  1925- . . . . . . CLC 1, 2, 3, 4, 7, 9, 14, 15,
                                         27, 49
  See also CA 1-4R; CANR 2, 47; DLB 2, 7;
  DLBY 80; MTCW

Hawking, S. W.
  See Hawking, Stephen W(illiam)

Hawking, Stephen W(illiam)
  1942- . . . . CLC 63
  See also AAYA 13; BEST 89:1; CA 126;
  129; CANR 48

Hawthorne, Julian 1846-1934 . . . . . TCLC 25

Hawthorne, Nathaniel
  1804-1864 . . . . . . NCLC 39; DA; DAB;
                                         SSC 3; WLC
  See also CDALB 1640-1865; DLB 1, 74;
  YABC 2

Haxton, Josephine Ayres 1921-
  See Douglas, Ellen
  See also CA 115; CANR 41

Hayaseca y Eizaguirre, Jorge
  See Echegaray (y Eizaguirre), Jose (Maria
  Waldo)

Hayashi Fumiko 1904-1951 . . . . . . TCLC 27

Haycraft, Anna
  See Ellis, Alice Thomas
  See also CA 122

Hayden, Robert E(arl)
  1913-1980 . . . . . CLC 5, 9, 14, 37; BLC;
                                         DA; PC 6
  See also BW 1; CA 69-72; 97-100; CABS 2;
  CANR 24; CDALB 1941-1968; DLB 5,
  76; MTCW; SATA 19; SATA-Obit 26

Hayford, J(oseph) E(phraim) Casely
  See Casely-Hayford, J(oseph) E(phraim)

Hayman, Ronald 1932- . . . . CLC 44
  See also CA 25-28R; CANR 18; DLB 155

Haywood, Eliza (Fowler)
  1693(?)-1756 . . . . LC 1

Hazlitt, William 1778-1830 . . . . . . NCLC 29
  See also DLB 110

Hazzard, Shirley 1931- . . . . CLC 18
  See also CA 9-12R; CANR 4; DLBY 82;
  MTCW

Head, Bessie 1937-1986 . . . CLC 25, 67; BLC
  See also BW 2; CA 29-32R; 119; CANR 25;
  DLB 117; MTCW

Headon, (Nicky) Topper 1956(?)- . . . CLC 30

Heaney, Seamus (Justin)
  1939- . . . . CLC 5, 7, 14, 25, 37, 74; DAB
  See also CA 85-88; CANR 25, 48;
  CDBLB 1960 to Present; DLB 40;
  MTCW

Hearn, (Patricio) Lafcadio (Tessima Carlos)
  1850-1904 . . . . TCLC 9
  See also CA 105; DLB 12, 78

Hearne, Vicki 1946- . . . . CLC 56
  See also CA 139

Hearon, Shelby 1931- . . . . CLC 63
  See also AITN 2; CA 25-28R; CANR 18,
  48

Heat-Moon, William Least . . . . CLC 29
  See also Trogdon, William (Lewis)
  See also AAYA 9

Hebbel, Friedrich 1813-1863 . . . . . NCLC 43
  See also DLB 129

Hebert, Anne 1916- . . . . CLC 4, 13, 29
  See also CA 85-88; DLB 68; MTCW

Hecht, Anthony (Evan)
  1923- . . . . CLC 8, 13, 19
  See also CA 9-12R; CANR 6; DLB 5

Hecht, Ben 1894-1964 . . . . CLC 8
  See also CA 85-88; DLB 7, 9, 25, 26, 28, 86

Hedayat, Sadeq 1903-1951 . . . . TCLC 21
  See also CA 120

Hegel, Georg Wilhelm Friedrich
  1770-1831 . . . . NCLC 46
  See also DLB 90

Heidegger, Martin 1889-1976 . . . . . . CLC 24
  See also CA 81-84; 65-68; CANR 34;
  MTCW

Heidenstam, (Carl Gustaf) Verner von
  1859-1940 . . . . TCLC 5
  See also CA 104

Heifner, Jack 1946- . . . . CLC 11
  See also CA 105; CANR 47

Heijermans, Herman 1864-1924 . . . TCLC 24
  See also CA 123

Heilbrun, Carolyn G(old) 1926- . . . . . CLC 25
  See also CA 45-48; CANR 1, 28

Heine, Heinrich 1797-1856 . . . . . . NCLC 4
  See also DLB 90

Heinemann, Larry (Curtiss) 1944- . . CLC 50
  See also CA 110; CAAS 21; CANR 31;
  DLBD 9

Heiney, Donald (William) 1921-1993
  See Harris, MacDonald
  See also CA 1-4R; 142; CANR 3

Heinlein, Robert A(nson)
  1907-1988 . . . . CLC 1, 3, 8, 14, 26, 55
  See also CA 1-4R; 125; CANR 1, 20;
  DLB 8; JRDA; MAICYA; MTCW;
  SATA 9, 69; SATA-Obit 56

Helforth, John
  See Doolittle, Hilda

Hellenhofferu, Vojtech Kapristian z
  See Hasek, Jaroslav (Matej Frantisek)

Heller, Joseph
  1923- . . . . CLC 1, 3, 5, 8, 11, 36, 63; DA;
                                         DAB; WLC
  See also AITN 1; CA 5-8R; CABS 1;
  CANR 8, 42; DLB 2, 28; DLBY 80;
  MTCW

Hellman, Lillian (Florence)
  1906-1984 . . . . . . CLC 2, 4, 8, 14, 18, 34,
                                         44, 52; DC 1
  See also AITN 1, 2; CA 13-16R; 112;
  CANR 33; DLB 7; DLBY 84; MTCW

Helprin, Mark 1947- . . . . . CLC 7, 10, 22, 32
  See also CA 81-84; CANR 47; DLBY 85;
  MTCW

Helvetius, Claude-Adrien
  1715-1771 . . . . LC 26

Helyar, Jane Penelope Josephine 1933-
  See Poole, Josephine
  See also CA 21-24R; CANR 10, 26;
  SATA 82

Hemans, Felicia 1793-1835 . . . . . . NCLC 29
  See also DLB 96

Hemingway, Ernest (Miller)
  1899-1961 . . . . CLC 1, 3, 6, 8, 10, 13, 19,
  30, 34, 39, 41, 44, 50, 61, 80; DA; DAB;
                                         SSC 1; WLC
  See also CA 77-80; CANR 34;
  CDALB 1917-1929; DLB 4, 9, 102;
  DLBD 1; DLBY 81, 87; MTCW

Hempel, Amy 1951- . . . . CLC 39
  See also CA 118; 137

Henderson, F. C.
  See Mencken, H(enry) L(ouis)

Henderson, Sylvia
  See Ashton-Warner, Sylvia (Constance)

Henley, Beth . . . . CLC 23
  See also Henley, Elizabeth Becker
  See also CABS 3; DLBY 86

Henley, Elizabeth Becker 1952-
  See Henley, Beth
  See also CA 107; CANR 32; MTCW

Henley, William Ernest
  1849-1903 . . . . TCLC 8
  See also CA 105; DLB 19

Hennissart, Martha
  See Lathen, Emma
  See also CA 85-88

Henry, O. .... TCLC 1, 19; SSC 5; WLC
See also Porter, William Sydney

Henry, Patrick 1736-1799 .... LC 25

Henryson, Robert 1430(?)-1506(?).... LC 20
See also DLB 146

Henry VIII 1491-1547............. LC 10

Henschke, Alfred
See Klabund

Hentoff, Nat(han Irving) 1925- ..... CLC 26
See also AAYA 4; CA 1-4R; CAAS 6;
CANR 5, 25; CLR 1; JRDA; MAICYA;
SATA 42, 69; SATA-Brief 27

Heppenstall, (John) Rayner
1911-1981 .... CLC 10
See also CA 1-4R; 103; CANR 29

Herbert, Frank (Patrick)
1920-1986 ...... CLC 12, 23, 35, 44, 85
See also CA 53-56; 118; CANR 5, 43;
DLB 8; MTCW; SATA 9, 37;
SATA-Obit 47

Herbert, George
1593-1633 .... LC 24; DAB; PC 4
See also CDBLB Before 1660; DLB 126

Herbert, Zbigniew 1924- .... CLC 9, 43
See also CA 89-92; CANR 36; MTCW

Herbst, Josephine (Frey)
1897-1969 .... CLC 34
See also CA 5-8R; 25-28R; DLB 9

Hergesheimer, Joseph
1880-1954 .... TCLC 11
See also CA 109; DLB 102, 9

Herlihy, James Leo 1927-1993 ...... CLC 6
See also CA 1-4R; 143; CANR 2

Hermogenes fl. c. 175- .... CMLC 6

Hernandez, Jose 1834-1886 ...... NCLC 17

Herrick, Robert
1591-1674 ..... LC 13; DA; DAB; PC 9
See also DLB 126

Herring, Guilles
See Somerville, Edith

Herriot, James 1916-1995 .... CLC 12
See also Wight, James Alfred
See also AAYA 1; CA 148; CANR 40

Herrmann, Dorothy 1941-......... CLC 44
See also CA 107

Herrmann, Taffy
See Herrmann, Dorothy

Hersey, John (Richard)
1914-1993 .... CLC 1, 2, 7, 9, 40, 81
See also CA 17-20R; 140; CANR 33;
DLB 6; MTCW; SATA 25;
SATA-Obit 76

Herzen, Aleksandr Ivanovich
1812-1870 .... NCLC 10

Herzl, Theodor 1860-1904 .... TCLC 36

Herzog, Werner 1942-............ CLC 16
See also CA 89-92

Hesiod c. 8th cent. B.C.- .... CMLC 5

Hesse, Hermann
1877-1962 .... CLC 1, 2, 3, 6, 11, 17, 25,
69; DA; DAB; SSC 9; WLC
See also CA 17-18; CAP 2; DLB 66;
MTCW; SATA 50

Hewes, Cady
See De Voto, Bernard (Augustine)

Heyen, William 1940- .... CLC 13, 18
See also CA 33-36R; CAAS 9; DLB 5

Heyerdahl, Thor 1914-............ CLC 26
See also CA 5-8R; CANR 5, 22; MTCW;
SATA 2, 52

Heym, Georg (Theodor Franz Arthur)
1887-1912 .... TCLC 9
See also CA 106

Heym, Stefan 1913-.............. CLC 41
See also CA 9-12R; CANR 4; DLB 69

Heyse, Paul (Johann Ludwig von)
1830-1914 .... TCLC 8
See also CA 104; DLB 129

Heyward, (Edwin) DuBose
1885-1940 .... TCLC 59
See also CA 108; DLB 7, 9, 45; SATA 21

Hibbert, Eleanor Alice Burford
1906-1993 .... CLC 7
See also BEST 90:4; CA 17-20R; 140;
CANR 9, 28; SATA 2; SATA-Obit 74

Higgins, George V(incent)
1939-................. CLC 4, 7, 10, 18
See also CA 77-80; CAAS 5; CANR 17;
DLB 2; DLBY 81; MTCW

Higginson, Thomas Wentworth
1823-1911 .... TCLC 36
See also DLB 1, 64

Highet, Helen
See MacInnes, Helen (Clark)

Highsmith, (Mary) Patricia
1921-1995 .... CLC 2, 4, 14, 42
See also CA 1-4R; 147; CANR 1, 20, 48;
MTCW

Highwater, Jamake (Mamake)
1942(?)-..................... CLC 12
See also AAYA 7; CA 65-68; CAAS 7;
CANR 10, 34; CLR 17; DLB 52;
DLBY 85; JRDA; MAICYA; SATA 32,
69; SATA-Brief 30

Higuchi, Ichiyo 1872-1896....... NCLC 49

Hijuelos, Oscar 1951- ...... CLC 65; HLC
See also BEST 90:1; CA 123; DLB 145; HW

Hikmet, Nazim 1902(?)-1963....... CLC 40
See also CA 141; 93-96

Hildesheimer, Wolfgang
1916-1991 .... CLC 49
See also CA 101; 135; DLB 69, 124

Hill, Geoffrey (William)
1932-................. CLC 5, 8, 18, 45
See also CA 81-84; CANR 21;
CDBLB 1960 to Present; DLB 40;
MTCW

Hill, George Roy 1921-........... CLC 26
See also CA 110; 122

Hill, John
See Koontz, Dean R(ay)

Hill, Susan (Elizabeth)
1942-.................... CLC 4; DAB
See also CA 33-36R; CANR 29; DLB 14,
139; MTCW

Hillerman, Tony 1925-............ CLC 62
See also AAYA 6; BEST 89:1; CA 29-32R;
CANR 21, 42; SATA 6

Hillesum, Etty 1914-1943 .... TCLC 49
See also CA 137

Hilliard, Noel (Harvey) 1929-...... CLC 15
See also CA 9-12R; CANR 7

Hillis, Rick 1956-................ CLC 66
See also CA 134

Hilton, James 1900-1954......... TCLC 21
See also CA 108; DLB 34, 77; SATA 34

Himes, Chester (Bomar)
1909-1984 .... CLC 2, 4, 7, 18, 58; BLC
See also BW 2; CA 25-28R; 114; CANR 22;
DLB 2, 76, 143; MTCW

Hinde, Thomas .... CLC 6, 11
See also Chitty, Thomas Willes

Hindin, Nathan
See Bloch, Robert (Albert)

Hine, (William) Daryl 1936-....... CLC 15
See also CA 1-4R; CAAS 15; CANR 1, 20;
DLB 60

Hinkson, Katharine Tynan
See Tynan, Katharine

Hinton, S(usan) E(loise)
1950- .... CLC 30; DA; DAB
See also AAYA 2; CA 81-84; CANR 32;
CLR 3, 23; JRDA; MAICYA; MTCW;
SATA 19, 58

Hippius, Zinaida .... TCLC 9
See also Gippius, Zinaida (Nikolayevna)

Hiraoka, Kimitake 1925-1970
See Mishima, Yukio
See also CA 97-100; 29-32R; MTCW

Hirsch, E(ric) D(onald), Jr. 1928-... CLC 79
See also CA 25-28R; CANR 27; DLB 67;
MTCW

Hirsch, Edward 1950- .... CLC 31, 50
See also CA 104; CANR 20, 42; DLB 120

Hitchcock, Alfred (Joseph)
1899-1980 .... CLC 16
See also CA 97-100; SATA 27;
SATA-Obit 24

Hitler, Adolf 1889-1945.......... TCLC 53
See also CA 117; 147

Hoagland, Edward 1932-.......... CLC 28
See also CA 1-4R; CANR 2, 31; DLB 6;
SATA 51

Hoban, Russell (Conwell) 1925- .. CLC 7, 25
See also CA 5-8R; CANR 23, 37; CLR 3;
DLB 52; MAICYA; MTCW; SATA 1,
40, 78

Hobbs, Perry
See Blackmur, R(ichard) P(almer)

Hobson, Laura Z(ametkin)
1900-1986 .... CLC 7, 25
See also CA 17-20R; 118; DLB 28;
SATA 52

Hochhuth, Rolf 1931-........ CLC 4, 11, 18
See also CA 5-8R; CANR 33; DLB 124;
MTCW

Hochman, Sandra 1936-.......... CLC 3, 8
See also CA 5-8R; DLB 5

Hochwaelder, Fritz 1911-1986...... CLC 36
See also CA 29-32R; 120; CANR 42;
MTCW

Hochwalder, Fritz
See Hochwaelder, Fritz

Kantor, MacKinlay 1904-1977 ...... **CLC 7**
See also CA 61-64; 73-76; DLB 9, 102

Kaplan, David Michael 1946- ...... **CLC 50**

Kaplan, James 1951- .... **CLC 59**
See also CA 135

Karageorge, Michael
See Anderson, Poul (William)

Karamzin, Nikolai Mikhailovich
1766-1826 .... **NCLC 3**
See also DLB 150

Karapanou, Margarita 1946- .... **CLC 13**
See also CA 101

Karinthy, Frigyes 1887-1938 ...... **TCLC 47**

Karl, Frederick R(obert) 1927- ..... **CLC 34**
See also CA 5-8R; CANR 3, 44

Kastel, Warren
See Silverberg, Robert

Kataev, Evgeny Petrovich 1903-1942
See Petrov, Evgeny
See also CA 120

Kataphusin
See Ruskin, John

Katz, Steve 1935- .... **CLC 47**
See also CA 25-28R; CAAS 14; CANR 12;
DLBY 83

Kauffman, Janet 1945- .... **CLC 42**
See also CA 117; CANR 43; DLBY 86

Kaufman, Bob (Garnell)
1925-1986 .... **CLC 49**
See also BW 1; CA 41-44R; 118; CANR 22;
DLB 16, 41

Kaufman, George S. 1889-1961 ..... **CLC 38**
See also CA 108; 93-96; DLB 7

Kaufman, Sue .... **CLC 3, 8**
See also Barondess, Sue K(aufman)

Kavafis, Konstantinos Petrou 1863-1933
See Cavafy, C(onstantine) P(eter)
See also CA 104

Kavan, Anna 1901-1968 ...... **CLC 5, 13, 82**
See also CA 5-8R; CANR 6; MTCW

Kavanagh, Dan
See Barnes, Julian

Kavanagh, Patrick (Joseph)
1904-1967 .... **CLC 22**
See also CA 123; 25-28R; DLB 15, 20;
MTCW

Kawabata, Yasunari
1899-1972 ..... **CLC 2, 5, 9, 18; SSC 17**
See also CA 93-96; 33-36R

Kaye, M(ary) M(argaret) 1909- ..... **CLC 28**
See also CA 89-92; CANR 24; MTCW;
SATA 62

Kaye, Mollie
See Kaye, M(ary) M(argaret)

Kaye-Smith, Sheila 1887-1956 ..... **TCLC 20**
See also CA 118; DLB 36

Kaymor, Patrice Maguilene
See Senghor, Leopold Sedar

Kazan, Elia 1909- .... **CLC 6, 16, 63**
See also CA 21-24R; CANR 32

Kazantzakis, Nikos
1883(?)-1957 .... **TCLC 2, 5, 33**
See also CA 105; 132; MTCW

Kazin, Alfred 1915- .... **CLC 34, 38**
See also CA 1-4R; CAAS 7; CANR 1, 45;
DLB 67

Keane, Mary Nesta (Skrine) 1904-
See Keane, Molly
See also CA 108; 114

Keane, Molly .... **CLC 31**
See also Keane, Mary Nesta (Skrine)

Keates, Jonathan 19(?)- .... **CLC 34**

Keaton, Buster 1895-1966 .... **CLC 20**

Keats, John
1795-1821 .... **NCLC 8; DA; DAB;**
PC 1; WLC
See also CDBLB 1789-1832; DLB 96, 110

Keene, Donald 1922- .... **CLC 34**
See also CA 1-4R; CANR 5

Keillor, Garrison .... **CLC 40**
See also Keillor, Gary (Edward)
See also AAYA 2; BEST 89:3; DLBY 87;
SATA 58

Keillor, Gary (Edward) 1942-
See Keillor, Garrison
See also CA 111; 117; CANR 36; MTCW

Keith, Michael
See Hubbard, L(afayette) Ron(ald)

Keller, Gottfried 1819-1890 .... **NCLC 2**
See also DLB 129

Kellerman, Jonathan 1949- .... **CLC 44**
See also BEST 90:1; CA 106; CANR 29

Kelley, William Melvin 1937- ...... **CLC 22**
See also BW 1; CA 77-80; CANR 27;
DLB 33

Kellogg, Marjorie 1922- .... **CLC 2**
See also CA 81-84

Kellow, Kathleen
See Hibbert, Eleanor Alice Burford

Kelly, M(ilton) T(erry) 1947- .... **CLC 55**
See also CA 97-100; CAAS 22; CANR 19,
43

Kelman, James 1946- .... **CLC 58, 86**
See also CA 148

Kemal, Yashar 1923- .... **CLC 14, 29**
See also CA 89-92; CANR 44

Kemble, Fanny 1809-1893 .... **NCLC 18**
See also DLB 32

Kemelman, Harry 1908- .... **CLC 2**
See also AITN 1; CA 9-12R; CANR 6;
DLB 28

Kempe, Margery 1373(?)-1440(?) ..... **LC 6**
See also DLB 146

Kempis, Thomas a 1380-1471 .... **LC 11**

Kendall, Henry 1839-1882 .... **NCLC 12**

Keneally, Thomas (Michael)
1935- ...... **CLC 5, 8, 10, 14, 19, 27, 43**
See also CA 85-88; CANR 10; MTCW

Kennedy, Adrienne (Lita)
1931- .... **CLC 66; BLC; DC 5**
See also BW 2; CA 103; CAAS 20; CABS 3;
CANR 26; DLB 38

Kennedy, John Pendleton
1795-1870 .... **NCLC 2**
See also DLB 3

Kennedy, Joseph Charles 1929-
See Kennedy, X. J.
See also CA 1-4R; CANR 4, 30, 40;
SATA 14

Kennedy, William 1928-... **CLC 6, 28, 34, 53**
See also AAYA 1; CA 85-88; CANR 14,
31; DLB 143; DLBY 85; MTCW;
SATA 57

Kennedy, X. J. .... **CLC 8, 42**
See also Kennedy, Joseph Charles
See also CAAS 9; CLR 27; DLB 5

Kenny, Maurice (Francis) 1929- .... **CLC 87**
See also CA 144; CAAS 22; NNAL

Kent, Kelvin
See Kuttner, Henry

Kenton, Maxwell
See Southern, Terry

Kenyon, Robert O.
See Kuttner, Henry

Kerouac, Jack ..... **CLC 1, 2, 3, 5, 14, 29, 61**
See also Kerouac, Jean-Louis Lebris de
See also CDALB 1941-1968; DLB 2, 16;
DLBD 3

Kerouac, Jean-Louis Lebris de 1922-1969
See Kerouac, Jack
See also AITN 1; CA 5-8R; 25-28R;
CANR 26; DA; DAB; MTCW; WLC

Kerr, Jean 1923- .... **CLC 22**
See also CA 5-8R; CANR 7

Kerr, M. E. .... **CLC 12, 35**
See also Meaker, Marijane (Agnes)
See also AAYA 2; CLR 29; SAAS 1

Kerr, Robert .... **CLC 55**

Kerrigan, (Thomas) Anthony
1918- .... **CLC 4, 6**
See also CA 49-52; CAAS 11; CANR 4

Kerry, Lois
See Duncan, Lois

Kesey, Ken (Elton)
1935- ...... **CLC 1, 3, 6, 11, 46, 64; DA;**
DAB; WLC
See also CA 1-4R; CANR 22, 38;
CDALB 1968-1988; DLB 2, 16; MTCW;
SATA 66

Kesselring, Joseph (Otto)
1902-1967 .... **CLC 45**

Kessler, Jascha (Frederick) 1929- .... **CLC 4**
See also CA 17-20R; CANR 8, 48

Kettelkamp, Larry (Dale) 1933- .... **CLC 12**
See also CA 29-32R; CANR 16; SAAS 3;
SATA 2

Keyber, Conny
See Fielding, Henry

Keyes, Daniel 1927- .... **CLC 80; DA**
See also CA 17-20R; CANR 10, 26;
SATA 37

Khanshendel, Chiron
See Rose, Wendy

Khayyam, Omar
1048-1131 .... **CMLC 11; PC 8**

Kherdian, David 1931- .... **CLC 6, 9**
See also CA 21-24R; CAAS 2; CANR 39;
CLR 24; JRDA; MAICYA; SATA 16, 74

Khlebnikov, Velimir .... **TCLC 20**
See also Khlebnikov, Viktor Vladimirovich

Khlebnikov, Viktor Vladimirovich 1885-1922
See Khlebnikov, Velimir
See also CA 117

Khodasevich, Vladislav (Felitsianovich)
1886-1939 .... TCLC 15
See also CA 115

Kielland, Alexander Lange
1849-1906 .... TCLC 5
See also CA 104

Kiely, Benedict 1919- .... CLC 23, 43
See also CA 1-4R; CANR 2; DLB 15

Kienzle, William X(avier) 1928- .... CLC 25
See also CA 93-96; CAAS 1; CANR 9, 31;
MTCW

Kierkegaard, Soren 1813-1855 .... NCLC 34

Killens, John Oliver 1916-1987 ..... CLC 10
See also BW 2; CA 77-80; 123; CAAS 2;
CANR 26; DLB 33

Killigrew, Anne 1660-1685 .... LC 4
See also DLB 131

Kim
See Simenon, Georges (Jacques Christian)

Kincaid, Jamaica 1949- ... CLC 43, 68; BLC
See also AAYA 13; BW 2; CA 125;
CANR 47

King, Francis (Henry) 1923- ..... CLC 8, 53
See also CA 1-4R; CANR 1, 33; DLB 15,
139; MTCW

King, Martin Luther, Jr.
1929-1968 .... CLC 83; BLC; DA; DAB
See also BW 2; CA 25-28; CANR 27, 44;
CAP 2; MTCW; SATA 14

King, Stephen (Edwin)
1947- ...... CLC 12, 26, 37, 61; SSC 17
See also AAYA 1; BEST 90:1; CA 61-64;
CANR 1, 30; DLB 143; DLBY 80;
JRDA; MTCW; SATA 9, 55

King, Steve
See King, Stephen (Edwin)

King, Thomas 1943- .... CLC 89
See also CA 144; NNAL

Kingman, Lee .... CLC 17
See also Natti, (Mary) Lee
See also SAAS 3; SATA 1, 67

Kingsley, Charles 1819-1875 ..... NCLC 35
See also DLB 21, 32; YABC 2

Kingsley, Sidney 1906-1995 .... CLC 44
See also CA 85-88; 147; DLB 7

Kingsolver, Barbara 1955- ...... CLC 55, 81
See also AAYA 15; CA 129; 134

Kingston, Maxine (Ting Ting) Hong
1940- .... CLC 12, 19, 58
See also AAYA 8; CA 69-72; CANR 13,
38; DLBY 80; MTCW; SATA 53

Kinnell, Galway
1927- .... CLC 1, 2, 3, 5, 13, 29
See also CA 9-12R; CANR 10, 34; DLB 5;
DLBY 87; MTCW

Kinsella, Thomas 1928- .... CLC 4, 19
See also CA 17-20R; CANR 15; DLB 27;
MTCW

Kinsella, W(illiam) P(atrick)
1935- .... CLC 27, 43
See also AAYA 7; CA 97-100; CAAS 7;
CANR 21, 35; MTCW

Kipling, (Joseph) Rudyard
1865-1936 ...... TCLC 8, 17; DA; DAB;
PC 3; SSC 5; WLC
See also CA 105; 120; CANR 33;
CDBLB 1890-1914; CLR 39; DLB 19, 34,
141, 156; MAICYA; MTCW; YABC 2

Kirkup, James 1918- .... CLC 1
See also CA 1-4R; CAAS 4; CANR 2;
DLB 27; SATA 12

Kirkwood, James 1930(?)-1989 ...... CLC 9
See also AITN 2; CA 1-4R; 128; CANR 6,
40

Kirshner, Sidney
See Kingsley, Sidney

Kis, Danilo 1935-1989 .... CLC 57
See also CA 109; 118; 129; MTCW

Kivi, Aleksis 1834-1872 .... NCLC 30

Kizer, Carolyn (Ashley)
1925- .... CLC 15, 39, 80
See also CA 65-68; CAAS 5; CANR 24;
DLB 5

Klabund 1890-1928 .... TCLC 44
See also DLB 66

Klappert, Peter 1942- .... CLC 57
See also CA 33-36R; DLB 5

Klein, A(braham) M(oses)
1909-1972 .... CLC 19; DAB
See also CA 101; 37-40R; DLB 68

Klein, Norma 1938-1989 .... CLC 30
See also AAYA 2; CA 41-44R; 128;
CANR 15, 37; CLR 2, 19; JRDA;
MAICYA; SAAS 1; SATA 7, 57

Klein, T(heodore) E(ibon) D(onald)
1947- .... CLC 34
See also CA 119; CANR 44

Kleist, Heinrich von
1777-1811 .... NCLC 2, 37
See also DLB 90

Klima, Ivan 1931- .... CLC 56
See also CA 25-28R; CANR 17

Klimentov, Andrei Platonovich 1899-1951
See Platonov, Andrei
See also CA 108

Klinger, Friedrich Maximilian von
1752-1831 .... NCLC 1
See also DLB 94

Klopstock, Friedrich Gottlieb
1724-1803 .... NCLC 11
See also DLB 97

Knebel, Fletcher 1911-1993 .... CLC 14
See also AITN 1; CA 1-4R; 140; CAAS 3;
CANR 1, 36; SATA 36; SATA-Obit 75

Knickerbocker, Diedrich
See Irving, Washington

Knight, Etheridge
1931-1991 .... CLC 40; BLC
See also BW 1; CA 21-24R; 133; CANR 23;
DLB 41

Knight, Sarah Kemble 1666-1727 ..... LC 7
See also DLB 24

Knister, Raymond 1899-1932 ..... TCLC 56
See also DLB 68

Knowles, John
1926- .... CLC 1, 4, 10, 26; DA
See also AAYA 10; CA 17-20R; CANR 40;
CDALB 1968-1988; DLB 6; MTCW;
SATA 8

Knox, Calvin M.
See Silverberg, Robert

Knye, Cassandra
See Disch, Thomas M(ichael)

Koch, C(hristopher) J(ohn) 1932- ... CLC 42
See also CA 127

Koch, Christopher
See Koch, C(hristopher) J(ohn)

Koch, Kenneth 1925- .... CLC 5, 8, 44
See also CA 1-4R; CANR 6, 36; DLB 5;
SATA 65

Kochanowski, Jan 1530-1584 .... LC 10

Kock, Charles Paul de
1794-1871 .... NCLC 16

Koda Shigeyuki 1867-1947
See Rohan, Koda
See also CA 121

Koestler, Arthur
1905-1983 .... CLC 1, 3, 6, 8, 15, 33
See also CA 1-4R; 109; CANR 1, 33;
CDBLB 1945-1960; DLBY 83; MTCW

Kogawa, Joy Nozomi 1935- .... CLC 78
See also CA 101; CANR 19

Kohout, Pavel 1928- .... CLC 13
See also CA 45-48; CANR 3

Koizumi, Yakumo
See Hearn, (Patricio) Lafcadio (Tessima
Carlos)

Kolmar, Gertrud 1894-1943 .... TCLC 40

Komunyakaa, Yusef 1947- .... CLC 86
See also CA 147; DLB 120

Konrad, George
See Konrad, Gyoergy

Konrad, Gyoergy 1933- ...... CLC 4, 10, 73
See also CA 85-88

Konwicki, Tadeusz 1926- ..... CLC 8, 28, 54
See also CA 101; CAAS 9; CANR 39;
MTCW

Koontz, Dean R(ay) 1945- .... CLC 78
See also AAYA 9; BEST 89:3, 90:2;
CA 108; CANR 19, 36; MTCW

Kopit, Arthur (Lee) 1937- .... CLC 1, 18, 33
See also AITN 1; CA 81-84; CABS 3;
DLB 7; MTCW

Kops, Bernard 1926- .... CLC 4
See also CA 5-8R; DLB 13

Kornbluth, C(yril) M. 1923-1958 .... TCLC 8
See also CA 105; DLB 8

Korolenko, V. G.
See Korolenko, Vladimir Galaktionovich

Korolenko, Vladimir
See Korolenko, Vladimir Galaktionovich

Korolenko, Vladimir G.
See Korolenko, Vladimir Galaktionovich

Korolenko, Vladimir Galaktionovich
1853-1921 .... TCLC 22
See also CA 121

Korzybski, Alfred (Habdank Skarbek)
1879-1950 .... TCLC 61
See also CA 123

Kosinski, Jerzy (Nikodem)
1933-1991 .... CLC 1, 2, 3, 6, 10, 15, 53,
70
See also CA 17-20R; 134; CANR 9, 46;
DLB 2; DLBY 82; MTCW

Kostelanetz, Richard (Cory) 1940- .. CLC 28
See also CA 13-16R; CAAS 8; CANR 38

Kostrowitzki, Wilhelm Apollinaris de
1880-1918
See Apollinaire, Guillaume
See also CA 104

Kotlowitz, Robert 1924-........... CLC 4
See also CA 33-36R; CANR 36

Kotzebue, August (Friedrich Ferdinand) von
1761-1819 .... NCLC 25
See also DLB 94

Kotzwinkle, William 1938- ... CLC 5, 14, 35
See also CA 45-48; CANR 3, 44; CLR 6;
MAICYA; SATA 24, 70

Kozol, Jonathan 1936-........... CLC 17
See also CA 61-64; CANR 16, 45

Kozoll, Michael 1940(?)- .... CLC 35

Kramer, Kathryn 19(?)- .... CLC 34

Kramer, Larry 1935- .... CLC 42
See also CA 124; 126

Krasicki, Ignacy 1735-1801 .... NCLC 8

Krasinski, Zygmunt 1812-1859 .... NCLC 4

Kraus, Karl 1874-1936........... TCLC 5
See also CA 104; DLB 118

Kreve (Mickevicius), Vincas
1882-1954 .... TCLC 27

Kristeva, Julia 1941- .... CLC 77

Kristofferson, Kris 1936-......... CLC 26
See also CA 104

Krizanc, John 1956-............. CLC 57

Krleza, Miroslav 1893-1981........ CLC 8
See also CA 97-100; 105; DLB 147

Kroetsch, Robert 1927- ...... CLC 5, 23, 57
See also CA 17-20R; CANR 8, 38; DLB 53;
MTCW

Kroetz, Franz
See Kroetz, Franz Xaver

Kroetz, Franz Xaver 1946- .... CLC 41
See also CA 130

Kroker, Arthur 1945-............ CLC 77

Kropotkin, Peter (Aleksieevich)
1842-1921 .... TCLC 36
See also CA 119

Krotkov, Yuri 1917-............. CLC 19
See also CA 102

Krumb
See Crumb, R(obert)

Krumgold, Joseph (Quincy)
1908-1980 .... CLC 12
See also CA 9-12R; 101; CANR 7;
MAICYA; SATA 1, 48; SATA-Obit 23

Krumwitz
See Crumb, R(obert)

Krutch, Joseph Wood 1893-1970.... CLC 24
See also CA 1-4R; 25-28R; CANR 4;
DLB 63

Krutzch, Gus
See Eliot, T(homas) S(tearns)

Krylov, Ivan Andreevich
1768(?)-1844 .... NCLC 1
See also DLB 150

Kubin, Alfred 1877-1959 .... TCLC 23
See also CA 112; DLB 81

Kubrick, Stanley 1928-........... CLC 16
See also CA 81-84; CANR 33; DLB 26

Kumin, Maxine (Winokur)
1925- .... CLC 5, 13, 28
See also AITN 2; CA 1-4R; CAAS 8;
CANR 1, 21; DLB 5; MTCW; SATA 12

Kundera, Milan
1929- .... CLC 4, 9, 19, 32, 68
See also AAYA 2; CA 85-88; CANR 19;
MTCW

Kunene, Mazisi (Raymond) 1930-... CLC 85
See also BW 1; CA 125; DLB 117

Kunitz, Stanley (Jasspon)
1905- .... CLC 6, 11, 14
See also CA 41-44R; CANR 26; DLB 48;
MTCW

Kunze, Reiner 1933-............. CLC 10
See also CA 93-96; DLB 75

Kuprin, Aleksandr Ivanovich
1870-1938 .... TCLC 5
See also CA 104

Kureishi, Hanif 1954(?)-.......... CLC 64
See also CA 139

Kurosawa, Akira 1910-........... CLC 16
See also AAYA 11; CA 101; CANR 46

Kushner, Tony 1957(?)- .... CLC 81
See also CA 144

Kuttner, Henry 1915-1958........ TCLC 10
See also CA 107; DLB 8

Kuzma, Greg 1944-.............. CLC 7
See also CA 33-36R

Kuzmin, Mikhail 1872(?)-1936 .... TCLC 40

Kyd, Thomas 1558-1594....... LC 22; DC 3
See also DLB 62

Kyprianos, Iossif
See Samarakis, Antonis

La Bruyere, Jean de 1645-1696...... LC 17

Lacan, Jacques (Marie Emile)
1901-1981 .... CLC 75
See also CA 121; 104

Laclos, Pierre Ambroise Francois Choderlos
de 1741-1803 .... NCLC 4

La Colere, Francois
See Aragon, Louis

Lacolere, Francois
See Aragon, Louis

La Deshabilleuse
See Simenon, Georges (Jacques Christian)

Lady Gregory
See Gregory, Isabella Augusta (Persse)

Lady of Quality, A
See Bagnold, Enid

La Fayette, Marie (Madelaine Pioche de la
Vergne Comtes 1634-1693...... LC 2

Lafayette, Rene
See Hubbard, L(afayette) Ron(ald)

Laforgue, Jules
1860-1887 .... NCLC 5; SSC 20

Lagerkvist, Paer (Fabian)
1891-1974 .... CLC 7, 10, 13, 54
See also Lagerkvist, Par
See also CA 85-88; 49-52; MTCW

Lagerkvist, Par .... SSC 12
See also Lagerkvist, Paer (Fabian)

Lagerloef, Selma (Ottiliana Lovisa)
1858-1940 .... TCLC 4, 36
See also Lagerlof, Selma (Ottiliana Lovisa)
See also CA 108; SATA 15

Lagerlof, Selma (Ottiliana Lovisa)
See Lagerloef, Selma (Ottiliana Lovisa)
See also CLR 7; SATA 15

La Guma, (Justin) Alex(ander)
1925-1985 .... CLC 19
See also BW 1; CA 49-52; 118; CANR 25;
DLB 117; MTCW

Laidlaw, A. K.
See Grieve, C(hristopher) M(urray)

Lainez, Manuel Mujica
See Mujica Lainez, Manuel
See also HW

Lamartine, Alphonse (Marie Louis Prat) de
1790-1869 .... NCLC 11

Lamb, Charles
1775-1834 .. NCLC 10; DA; DAB; WLC
See also CDBLB 1789-1832; DLB 93, 107;
SATA 17

Lamb, Lady Caroline 1785-1828.. NCLC 38
See also DLB 116

Lamming, George (William)
1927- .... CLC 2, 4, 66; BLC
See also BW 2; CA 85-88; CANR 26;
DLB 125; MTCW

L'Amour, Louis (Dearborn)
1908-1988 .... CLC 25, 55
See also AITN 2; BEST 89:2; CA 1-4R;
125; CANR 3, 25, 40; DLBY 80; MTCW

Lampedusa, Giuseppe (Tomasi) di ... TCLC 13
See also Tomasi di Lampedusa, Giuseppe

Lampman, Archibald 1861-1899 .. NCLC 25
See also DLB 92

Lancaster, Bruce 1896-1963........ CLC 36
See also CA 9-10; CAP 1; SATA 9

Landau, Mark Alexandrovich
See Aldanov, Mark (Alexandrovich)

Landau-Aldanov, Mark Alexandrovich
See Aldanov, Mark (Alexandrovich)

Landis, John 1950-.............. CLC 26
See also CA 112; 122

Landolfi, Tommaso 1908-1979... CLC 11, 49
See also CA 127; 117

Landon, Letitia Elizabeth
1802-1838 .... NCLC 15
See also DLB 96

Landor, Walter Savage
1775-1864 .... NCLC 14
See also DLB 93, 107

Author Index

Landwirth, Heinz 1927-
See Lind, Jakov
See also CA 9-12R; CANR 7

Lane, Patrick 1939- .... **CLC 25**
See also CA 97-100; DLB 53

Lang, Andrew 1844-1912 .... **TCLC 16**
See also CA 114; 137; DLB 98, 141;
MAICYA; SATA 16

Lang, Fritz 1890-1976 .... **CLC 20**
See also CA 77-80; 69-72; CANR 30

Lange, John
See Crichton, (John) Michael

Langer, Elinor 1939- .... **CLC 34**
See also CA 121

Langland, William
1330(?)-1400(?) .... **LC 19; DA; DAB**
See also DLB 146

Langstaff, Launcelot
See Irving, Washington

Lanier, Sidney 1842-1881 .... **NCLC 6**
See also DLB 64; MAICYA; SATA 18

Lanyer, Aemilia 1569-1645 ...... **LC 10, 30**
See also DLB 121

Lao Tzu .... **CMLC 7**

Lapine, James (Elliot) 1949- .... **CLC 39**
See also CA 123; 130

Larbaud, Valery (Nicolas)
1881-1957 .... **TCLC 9**
See also CA 106

Lardner, Ring
See Lardner, Ring(gold) W(ilmer)

Lardner, Ring W., Jr.
See Lardner, Ring(gold) W(ilmer)

Lardner, Ring(gold) W(ilmer)
1885-1933 .... **TCLC 2, 14**
See also CA 104; 131; CDALB 1917-1929;
DLB 11, 25, 86; MTCW

Laredo, Betty
See Codrescu, Andrei

Larkin, Maia
See Wojciechowska, Maia (Teresa)

Larkin, Philip (Arthur)
1922-1985 .... **CLC 3, 5, 8, 9, 13, 18, 33,
39, 64; DAB**
See also CA 5-8R; 117; CANR 24;
CDBLB 1960 to Present; DLB 27;
MTCW

Larra (y Sanchez de Castro), Mariano Jose de
1809-1837 .... **NCLC 17**

Larsen, Eric 1941- .... **CLC 55**
See also CA 132

Larsen, Nella 1891-1964 ..... **CLC 37; BLC**
See also BW 1; CA 125; DLB 51

Larson, Charles R(aymond) 1938-... **CLC 31**
See also CA 53-56; CANR 4

Las Casas, Bartolome de 1474-1566 .. **LC 31**

Lasker-Schueler, Else 1869-1945 .. **TCLC 57**
See also DLB 66, 124

Latham, Jean Lee 1902- .... **CLC 12**
See also AITN 1; CA 5-8R; CANR 7;
MAICYA; SATA 2, 68

Latham, Mavis
See Clark, Mavis Thorpe

Lathen, Emma .... **CLC 2**
See also Hennissart, Martha; Latsis, Mary
J(ane)

Lathrop, Francis
See Leiber, Fritz (Reuter, Jr.)

Latsis, Mary J(ane)
See Lathen, Emma
See also CA 85-88

Lattimore, Richmond (Alexander)
1906-1984 .... **CLC 3**
See also CA 1-4R; 112; CANR 1

Laughlin, James 1914- .... **CLC 49**
See also CA 21-24R; CAAS 22; CANR 9,
47; DLB 48

Laurence, (Jean) Margaret (Wemyss)
1926-1987 .. **CLC 3, 6, 13, 50, 62; SSC 7**
See also CA 5-8R; 121; CANR 33; DLB 53;
MTCW; SATA-Obit 50

Laurent, Antoine 1952- .... **CLC 50**

Lauscher, Hermann
See Hesse, Hermann

Lautreamont, Comte de
1846-1870 .... **NCLC 12; SSC 14**

Laverty, Donald
See Blish, James (Benjamin)

Lavin, Mary 1912- ...... **CLC 4, 18; SSC 4**
See also CA 9-12R; CANR 33; DLB 15;
MTCW

Lavond, Paul Dennis
See Kornbluth, C(yril) M.; Pohl, Frederik

Lawler, Raymond Evenor 1922- .... **CLC 58**
See also CA 103

Lawrence, D(avid) H(erbert Richards)
1885-1930 .... **TCLC 2, 9, 16, 33, 48, 61;
DA; DAB; SSC 4, 19; WLC**
See also CA 104; 121; CDBLB 1914-1945;
DLB 10, 19, 36, 98; MTCW

Lawrence, T(homas) E(dward)
1888-1935 .... **TCLC 18**
See also Dale, Colin
See also CA 115

Lawrence of Arabia
See Lawrence, T(homas) E(dward)

Lawson, Henry (Archibald Hertzberg)
1867-1922 .... **TCLC 27; SSC 18**
See also CA 120

Lawton, Dennis
See Faust, Frederick (Schiller)

Laxness, Halldor .... **CLC 25**
See also Gudjonsson, Halldor Kiljan

Layamon fl. c. 1200- .... **CMLC 10**
See also DLB 146

Laye, Camara 1928-1980 ... **CLC 4, 38; BLC**
See also BW 1; CA 85-88; 97-100;
CANR 25; MTCW

Layton, Irving (Peter) 1912- ..... **CLC 2, 15**
See also CA 1-4R; CANR 2, 33, 43;
DLB 88; MTCW

Lazarus, Emma 1849-1887 .... **NCLC 8**

Lazarus, Felix
See Cable, George Washington

Lazarus, Henry
See Slavitt, David R(ytman)

Lea, Joan
See Neufeld, John (Arthur)

Leacock, Stephen (Butler)
1869-1944 .... **TCLC 2**
See also CA 104; 141; DLB 92

Lear, Edward 1812-1888 .... **NCLC 3**
See also CLR 1; DLB 32; MAICYA;
SATA 18

Lear, Norman (Milton) 1922- ...... **CLC 12**
See also CA 73-76

Leavis, F(rank) R(aymond)
1895-1978 .... **CLC 24**
See also CA 21-24R; 77-80; CANR 44;
MTCW

Leavitt, David 1961- .... **CLC 34**
See also CA 116; 122; DLB 130

Leblanc, Maurice (Marie Emile)
1864-1941 .... **TCLC 49**
See also CA 110

Lebowitz, Fran(ces Ann)
1951(?)- .... **CLC 11, 36**
See also CA 81-84; CANR 14; MTCW

Lebrecht, Peter
See Tieck, (Johann) Ludwig

le Carre, John .... **CLC 3, 5, 9, 15, 28**
See also Cornwell, David (John Moore)
See also BEST 89:4; CDBLB 1960 to
Present; DLB 87

Le Clezio, J(ean) M(arie) G(ustave)
1940- .... **CLC 31**
See also CA 116; 128; DLB 83

Leconte de Lisle, Charles-Marie-Rene
1818-1894 .... **NCLC 29**

Le Coq, Monsieur
See Simenon, Georges (Jacques Christian)

Leduc, Violette 1907-1972 .... **CLC 22**
See also CA 13-14; 33-36R; CAP 1

Ledwidge, Francis 1887(?)-1917 ... **TCLC 23**
See also CA 123; DLB 20

Lee, Andrea 1953- .... **CLC 36; BLC**
See also BW 1; CA 125

Lee, Andrew
See Auchincloss, Louis (Stanton)

Lee, Don L. .... **CLC 2**
See also Madhubuti, Haki R.

Lee, George W(ashington)
1894-1976 .... **CLC 52; BLC**
See also BW 1; CA 125; DLB 51

Lee, (Nelle) Harper
1926- ..... **CLC 12, 60; DA; DAB; WLC**
See also AAYA 13; CA 13-16R;
CDALB 1941-1968; DLB 6; MTCW;
SATA 11

Lee, Helen Elaine 1959(?)- .... **CLC 86**
See also CA 148

Lee, Julian
See Latham, Jean Lee

Lee, Larry
See Lee, Lawrence

Lee, Laurie 1914- .... **CLC 90; DAB**
See also CA 77-80; CANR 33; DLB 27;
MTCW

Lee, Lawrence 1941-1990 .... **CLC 34**
See also CA 131; CANR 43

Lee, Manfred B(ennington)
  1905-1971 . . . . CLC 11
  See also Queen, Ellery
  See also CA 1-4R; 29-32R; CANR 2;
  DLB 137

Lee, Stan 1922- . . . . CLC 17
  See also AAYA 5; CA 108; 111

Lee, Tanith 1947- . . . . CLC 46
  See also AAYA 15; CA 37-40R; SATA 8

Lee, Vernon . . . . TCLC 5
  See also Paget, Violet
  See also DLB 57, 153, 156

Lee, William
  See Burroughs, William S(eward)

Lee, Willy
  See Burroughs, William S(eward)

Lee-Hamilton, Eugene (Jacob)
  1845-1907 . . . . TCLC 22
  See also CA 117

Leet, Judith 1935- . . . . CLC 11

Le Fanu, Joseph Sheridan
  1814-1873 . . . . NCLC 9; SSC 14
  See also DLB 21, 70

Leffland, Ella 1931- . . . . CLC 19
  See also CA 29-32R; CANR 35; DLBY 84;
  SATA 65

Leger, Alexis
  See Leger, (Marie-Rene Auguste) Alexis
  Saint-Leger

Leger, (Marie-Rene Auguste) Alexis
  Saint-Leger 1887-1975 . . . . CLC 11
  See also Perse, St.-John
  See also CA 13-16R; 61-64; CANR 43;
  MTCW

Leger, Saintleger
  See Leger, (Marie-Rene Auguste) Alexis
  Saint-Leger

Le Guin, Ursula K(roeber)
  1929- . . . . . . CLC 8, 13, 22, 45, 71; DAB;
  SSC 12
  See also AAYA 9; AITN 1; CA 21-24R;
  CANR 9, 32; CDALB 1968-1988; CLR 3,
  28; DLB 8, 52; JRDA; MAICYA;
  MTCW; SATA 4, 52

Lehmann, Rosamond (Nina)
  1901-1990 . . . . CLC 5
  See also CA 77-80; 131; CANR 8; DLB 15

Leiber, Fritz (Reuter, Jr.)
  1910-1992 . . . . CLC 25
  See also CA 45-48; 139; CANR 2, 40;
  DLB 8; MTCW; SATA 45;
  SATA-Obit 73

Leimbach, Martha 1963-
  See Leimbach, Marti
  See also CA 130

Leimbach, Marti . . . . CLC 65
  See also Leimbach, Martha

Leino, Eino . . . . TCLC 24
  See also Loennbohm, Armas Eino Leopold

Leiris, Michel (Julien) 1901-1990 . . . CLC 61
  See also CA 119; 128; 132

Leithauser, Brad 1953- . . . . CLC 27
  See also CA 107; CANR 27; DLB 120

Lelchuk, Alan 1938- . . . . CLC 5
  See also CA 45-48; CAAS 20; CANR 1

Lem, Stanislaw 1921- . . . . CLC 8, 15, 40
  See also CA 105; CAAS 1; CANR 32;
  MTCW

Lemann, Nancy 1956- . . . . CLC 39
  See also CA 118; 136

Lemonnier, (Antoine Louis) Camille
  1844-1913 . . . . TCLC 22
  See also CA 121

Lenau, Nikolaus 1802-1850 . . . . . . NCLC 16

L'Engle, Madeleine (Camp Franklin)
  1918- . . . . CLC 12
  See also AAYA 1; AITN 2; CA 1-4R;
  CANR 3, 21, 39; CLR 1, 14; DLB 52;
  JRDA; MAICYA; MTCW; SAAS 15;
  SATA 1, 27, 75

Lengyel, Jozsef 1896-1975 . . . . CLC 7
  See also CA 85-88; 57-60

Lennon, John (Ono)
  1940-1980 . . . . CLC 12, 35
  See also CA 102

Lennox, Charlotte Ramsay
  1729(?)-1804 . . . . NCLC 23
  See also DLB 39

Lentricchia, Frank (Jr.) 1940- . . . . . . CLC 34
  See also CA 25-28R; CANR 19

Lenz, Siegfried 1926- . . . . CLC 27
  See also CA 89-92; DLB 75

Leonard, Elmore (John, Jr.)
  1925- . . . . CLC 28, 34, 71
  See also AITN 1; BEST 89:1, 90:4;
  CA 81-84; CANR 12, 28; MTCW

Leonard, Hugh . . . . CLC 19
  See also Byrne, John Keyes
  See also DLB 13

Leopardi, (Conte) Giacomo
  1798-1837 . . . . NCLC 22

Le Reveler
  See Artaud, Antonin

Lerman, Eleanor 1952- . . . . CLC 9
  See also CA 85-88

Lerman, Rhoda 1936- . . . . CLC 56
  See also CA 49-52

Lermontov, Mikhail Yuryevich
  1814-1841 . . . . NCLC 47

Leroux, Gaston 1868-1927 . . . . TCLC 25
  See also CA 108; 136; SATA 65

Lesage, Alain-Rene 1668-1747 . . . . . . LC 28

Leskov, Nikolai (Semyonovich)
  1831-1895 . . . . NCLC 25

Lessing, Doris (May)
  1919- . . . . . CLC 1, 2, 3, 6, 10, 15, 22, 40;
  DA; DAB; SSC 6
  See also CA 9-12R; CAAS 14; CANR 33;
  CDBLB 1960 to Present; DLB 15, 139;
  DLBY 85; MTCW

Lessing, Gotthold Ephraim
  1729-1781 . . . . LC 8
  See also DLB 97

Lester, Richard 1932- . . . . CLC 20

Lever, Charles (James)
  1806-1872 . . . . NCLC 23
  See also DLB 21

Leverson, Ada 1865(?)-1936(?) . . . . TCLC 18
  See also Elaine
  See also CA 117; DLB 153

Levertov, Denise
  1923- . . . . . . CLC 1, 2, 3, 5, 8, 15, 28, 66;
  PC 11
  See also CA 1-4R; CAAS 19; CANR 3, 29;
  DLB 5; MTCW

Levi, Jonathan . . . . CLC 76

Levi, Peter (Chad Tigar) 1931- . . . . . CLC 41
  See also CA 5-8R; CANR 34; DLB 40

Levi, Primo
  1919-1987 . . . . CLC 37, 50; SSC 12
  See also CA 13-16R; 122; CANR 12, 33;
  MTCW

Levin, Ira 1929- . . . . CLC 3, 6
  See also CA 21-24R; CANR 17, 44;
  MTCW; SATA 66

Levin, Meyer 1905-1981 . . . . CLC 7
  See also AITN 1; CA 9-12R; 104;
  CANR 15; DLB 9, 28; DLBY 81;
  SATA 21; SATA-Obit 27

Levine, Norman 1924- . . . . CLC 54
  See also CA 73-76; CANR 14; DLB 88

Levine, Philip 1928- . . CLC 2, 4, 5, 9, 14, 33
  See also CA 9-12R; CANR 9, 37; DLB 5

Levinson, Deirdre 1931- . . . . CLC 49
  See also CA 73-76

Levi-Strauss, Claude 1908- . . . . CLC 38
  See also CA 1-4R; CANR 6, 32; MTCW

Levitin, Sonia (Wolff) 1934- . . . . CLC 17
  See also AAYA 13; CA 29-32R; CANR 14,
  32; JRDA; MAICYA; SAAS 2; SATA 4,
  68

Levon, O. U.
  See Kesey, Ken (Elton)

Lewes, George Henry
  1817-1878 . . . . NCLC 25
  See also DLB 55, 144

Lewis, Alun 1915-1944 . . . . TCLC 3
  See also CA 104; DLB 20

Lewis, C. Day
  See Day Lewis, C(ecil)

Lewis, C(live) S(taples)
  1898-1963 . . . . . CLC 1, 3, 6, 14, 27; DA;
  DAB; WLC
  See also AAYA 3; CA 81-84; CANR 33;
  CDBLB 1945-1960; CLR 3, 27; DLB 15,
  100; JRDA; MAICYA; MTCW;
  SATA 13

Lewis, Janet 1899- . . . . CLC 41
  See also Winters, Janet Lewis
  See also CA 9-12R; CANR 29; CAP 1;
  DLBY 87

Lewis, Matthew Gregory
  1775-1818 . . . . NCLC 11
  See also DLB 39

Lewis, (Harry) Sinclair
  1885-1951 . . . . . TCLC 4, 13, 23, 39; DA;
  DAB; WLC
  See also CA 104; 133; CDALB 1917-1929;
  DLB 9, 102; DLBD 1; MTCW

Lewis, (Percy) Wyndham
  1884(?)-1957 . . . . TCLC 2, 9
  See also CA 104; DLB 15

Lewisohn, Ludwig 1883-1955...... TCLC 19
See also CA 107; DLB 4, 9, 28, 102

Lezama Lima, Jose 1910-1976 ... CLC 4, 10
See also CA 77-80; DLB 113; HW

L'Heureux, John (Clarke) 1934-.... CLC 52
See also CA 13-16R; CANR 23, 45

Liddell, C. H.
See Kuttner, Henry

Lie, Jonas (Lauritz Idemil)
1833-1908(?) .... TCLC 5
See also CA 115

Lieber, Joel 1937-1971............. CLC 6
See also CA 73-76; 29-32R

Lieber, Stanley Martin
See Lee, Stan

Lieberman, Laurence (James)
1935- .... CLC 4, 36
See also CA 17-20R; CANR 8, 36

Lieksman, Anders
See Haavikko, Paavo Juhani

Li Fei-kan 1904-
See Pa Chin
See also CA 105

Lifton, Robert Jay 1926-.......... CLC 67
See also CA 17-20R; CANR 27; SATA 66

Lightfoot, Gordon 1938-........... CLC 26
See also CA 109

Lightman, Alan P. 1948- .... CLC 81
See also CA 141

Ligotti, Thomas (Robert)
1953- .... CLC 44; SSC 16
See also CA 123; CANR 49

Li Ho 791-817.................... PC 13

Liliencron, (Friedrich Adolf Axel) Detlev von
1844-1909 .... TCLC 18
See also CA 117

Lilly, William 1602-1681.......... LC 27

Lima, Jose Lezama
See Lezama Lima, Jose

Lima Barreto, Afonso Henrique de
1881-1922 .... TCLC 23
See also CA 117

Limonov, Edward 1944-........... CLC 67
See also CA 137

Lin, Frank
See Atherton, Gertrude (Franklin Horn)

Lincoln, Abraham 1809-1865..... NCLC 18

Lind, Jakov .... CLC 1, 2, 4, 27, 82
See also Landwirth, Heinz
See also CAAS 4

Lindbergh, Anne (Spencer) Morrow
1906- .... CLC 82
See also CA 17-20R; CANR 16; MTCW;
SATA 33

Lindsay, David 1878-1945 .... TCLC 15
See also CA 113

Lindsay, (Nicholas) Vachel
1879-1931 .... TCLC 17; DA; WLC
See also CA 114; 135; CDALB 1865-1917;
DLB 54; SATA 40

Linke-Poot
See Doeblin, Alfred

Linney, Romulus 1930- .... CLC 51
See also CA 1-4R; CANR 40, 44

Linton, Eliza Lynn 1822-1898.... NCLC 41
See also DLB 18

Li Po 701-763................... CMLC 2

Lipsius, Justus 1547-1606 .... LC 16

Lipsyte, Robert (Michael)
1938- .... CLC 21; DA
See also AAYA 7; CA 17-20R; CANR 8;
CLR 23; JRDA; MAICYA; SATA 5, 68

Lish, Gordon (Jay) 1934-.. CLC 45; SSC 18
See also CA 113; 117; DLB 130

Lispector, Clarice 1925-1977...... CLC 43
See also CA 139; 116; DLB 113

Littell, Robert 1935(?)- .... CLC 42
See also CA 109; 112

Little, Malcolm 1925-1965
See Malcolm X
See also BW 1; CA 125; 111; DA; DAB;
MTCW

Littlewit, Humphrey Gent.
See Lovecraft, H(oward) P(hillips)

Litwos
See Sienkiewicz, Henryk (Adam Alexander
Pius)

Liu E 1857-1909................ TCLC 15
See also CA 115

Lively, Penelope (Margaret)
1933- .... CLC 32, 50
See also CA 41-44R; CANR 29; CLR 7;
DLB 14; JRDA; MAICYA; MTCW;
SATA 7, 60

Livesay, Dorothy (Kathleen)
1909- .... CLC 4, 15, 79
See also AITN 2; CA 25-28R; CAAS 8;
CANR 36; DLB 68; MTCW

Livy c. 59B.C.-c. 17 .... CMLC 11

Lizardi, Jose Joaquin Fernandez de
1776-1827 .... NCLC 30

Llewellyn, Richard
See Llewellyn Lloyd, Richard Dafydd
Vivian
See also DLB 15

Llewellyn Lloyd, Richard Dafydd Vivian
1906-1983 .... CLC 7, 80
See also Llewellyn, Richard
See also CA 53-56; 111; CANR 7;
SATA 11; SATA-Obit 37

Llosa, (Jorge) Mario (Pedro) Vargas
See Vargas Llosa, (Jorge) Mario (Pedro)

Lloyd Webber, Andrew 1948-
See Webber, Andrew Lloyd
See also AAYA 1; CA 116; SATA 56

Llull, Ramon c. 1235-c. 1316..... CMLC 12

Locke, Alain (Le Roy)
1886-1954 .... TCLC 43
See also BW 1; CA 106; 124; DLB 51

Locke, John 1632-1704 .... LC 7
See also DLB 101

Locke-Elliott, Sumner
See Elliott, Sumner Locke

Lockhart, John Gibson
1794-1854 .... NCLC 6
See also DLB 110, 116, 144

Lodge, David (John) 1935-........ CLC 36
See also BEST 90:1; CA 17-20R; CANR 19;
DLB 14; MTCW

Loennbohm, Armas Eino Leopold 1878-1926
See Leino, Eino
See also CA 123

Loewinsohn, Ron(ald William)
1937- .... CLC 52
See also CA 25-28R

Logan, Jake
See Smith, Martin Cruz

Logan, John (Burton) 1923-1987..... CLC 5
See also CA 77-80; 124; CANR 45; DLB 5

Lo Kuan-chung 1330(?)-1400(?)...... LC 12

Lombard, Nap
See Johnson, Pamela Hansford

London, Jack.. TCLC 9, 15, 39; SSC 4; WLC
See also London, John Griffith
See also AAYA 13; AITN 2;
CDALB 1865-1917; DLB 8, 12, 78;
SATA 18

London, John Griffith 1876-1916
See London, Jack
See also CA 110; 119; DA; DAB; JRDA;
MAICYA; MTCW

Long, Emmett
See Leonard, Elmore (John, Jr.)

Longbaugh, Harry
See Goldman, William (W.)

Longfellow, Henry Wadsworth
1807-1882 ...... NCLC 2, 45; DA; DAB
See also CDALB 1640-1865; DLB 1, 59;
SATA 19

Longley, Michael 1939-........... CLC 29
See also CA 102; DLB 40

Longus fl. c. 2nd cent. - .... CMLC 7

Longway, A. Hugh
See Lang, Andrew

Lopate, Phillip 1943- .... CLC 29
See also CA 97-100; DLBY 80

Lopez Portillo (y Pacheco), Jose
1920- .... CLC 46
See also CA 129; HW

Lopez y Fuentes, Gregorio
1897(?)-1966 .... CLC 32
See also CA 131; HW

Lorca, Federico Garcia
See Garcia Lorca, Federico

Lord, Bette Bao 1938-............ CLC 23
See also BEST 90:3; CA 107; CANR 41;
SATA 58

Lord Auch
See Bataille, Georges

Lord Byron
See Byron, George Gordon (Noel)

Lorde, Audre (Geraldine)
1934-1992 .... CLC 18, 71; BLC; PC 12
See also BW 1; CA 25-28R; 142; CANR 16,
26, 46; DLB 41; MTCW

Lord Jeffrey
See Jeffrey, Francis

Lorenzo, Heberto Padilla
See Padilla (Lorenzo), Heberto

Maclean, Norman (Fitzroy)
1902-1990 . . . . **CLC 78; SSC 13**
See also CA 102; 132; CANR 49

MacLeish, Archibald
1892-1982 . . . . **CLC 3, 8, 14, 68**
See also CA 9-12R; 106; CANR 33; DLB 4,
7, 45; DLBY 82; MTCW

MacLennan, (John) Hugh
1907-1990 . . . . **CLC 2, 14**
See also CA 5-8R; 142; CANR 33; DLB 68;
MTCW

MacLeod, Alistair 1936- . . . . **CLC 56**
See also CA 123; DLB 60

MacNeice, (Frederick) Louis
1907-1963 . . . . . . **CLC 1, 4, 10, 53; DAB**
See also CA 85-88; DLB 10, 20; MTCW

MacNeill, Dand
See Fraser, George MacDonald

Macpherson, James 1736-1796 . . . . . . **LC 29**
See also DLB 109

Macpherson, (Jean) Jay 1931- . . . . . . **CLC 14**
See also CA 5-8R; DLB 53

MacShane, Frank 1927- . . . . **CLC 39**
See also CA 9-12R; CANR 3, 33; DLB 111

Macumber, Mari
See Sandoz, Mari(e Susette)

Madach, Imre 1823-1864 . . . . **NCLC 19**

Madden, (Jerry) David 1933- . . . . **CLC 5, 15**
See also CA 1-4R; CAAS 3; CANR 4, 45;
DLB 6; MTCW

Maddern, Al(an)
See Ellison, Harlan (Jay)

Madhubuti, Haki R.
1942- . . . . **CLC 6, 73; BLC; PC 5**
See Lee, Don L.
See also BW 2; CA 73-76; CANR 24;
DLB 5, 41; DLBD 8

Maepenn, Hugh
See Kuttner, Henry

Maepenn, K. H.
See Kuttner, Henry

Maeterlinck, Maurice 1862-1949 . . . **TCLC 3**
See also CA 104; 136; SATA 66

Maginn, William 1794-1842 . . . . **NCLC 8**
See also DLB 110

Mahapatra, Jayanta 1928- . . . . **CLC 33**
See also CA 73-76; CAAS 9; CANR 15, 33

Mahfouz, Naguib (Abdel Aziz Al-Sabilgi)
1911(?)-
See Mahfuz, Najib
See also BEST 89:2; CA 128; MTCW

Mahfuz, Najib . . . . **CLC 52, 55**
See also Mahfouz, Naguib (Abdel Aziz
Al-Sabilgi)
See also DLBY 88

Mahon, Derek 1941- . . . . **CLC 27**
See also CA 113; 128; DLB 40

Mailer, Norman
1923- . . . . . . **CLC 1, 2, 3, 4, 5, 8, 11, 14,
28, 39, 74; DA; DAB**
See also AITN 2; CA 9-12R; CABS 1;
CANR 28; CDALB 1968-1988; DLB 2,
16, 28; DLBD 3; DLBY 80, 83; MTCW

Maillet, Antonine 1929- . . . . **CLC 54**
See also CA 115; 120; CANR 46; DLB 60

Mais, Roger 1905-1955 . . . . **TCLC 8**
See also BW 1; CA 105; 124; DLB 125;
MTCW

Maistre, Joseph de 1753-1821 . . . . **NCLC 37**

Maitland, Sara (Louise) 1950- . . . . . . **CLC 49**
See also CA 69-72; CANR 13

Major, Clarence
1936- . . . . **CLC 3, 19, 48; BLC**
See also BW 2; CA 21-24R; CAAS 6;
CANR 13, 25; DLB 33

Major, Kevin (Gerald) 1949- . . . . **CLC 26**
See also CA 97-100; CANR 21, 38;
CLR 11; DLB 60; JRDA; MAICYA;
SATA 32, 82

Maki, James
See Ozu, Yasujiro

Malabaila, Damiano
See Levi, Primo

Malamud, Bernard
1914-1986 . . . . . . **CLC 1, 2, 3, 5, 8, 9, 11,
18, 27, 44, 78, 85; DA; DAB; SSC 15;
WLC**
See also CA 5-8R; 118; CABS 1; CANR 28;
CDALB 1941-1968; DLB 2, 28, 152;
DLBY 80, 86; MTCW

Malaparte, Curzio 1898-1957 . . . . . **TCLC 52**

Malcolm, Dan
See Silverberg, Robert

Malcolm X . . . . **CLC 82; BLC**
See also Little, Malcolm

Malherbe, Francois de 1555-1628 . . . . . **LC 5**

Mallarme, Stephane
1842-1898 . . . . **NCLC 4, 41; PC 4**

Mallet-Joris, Francoise 1930- . . . . . . **CLC 11**
See also CA 65-68; CANR 17; DLB 83

Malley, Ern
See McAuley, James Phillip

Mallowan, Agatha Christie
See Christie, Agatha (Mary Clarissa)

Maloff, Saul 1922- . . . . **CLC 5**
See also CA 33-36R

Malone, Louis
See MacNeice, (Frederick) Louis

Malone, Michael (Christopher)
1942- . . . . **CLC 43**
See also CA 77-80; CANR 14, 32

Malory, (Sir) Thomas
1410(?)-1471(?) . . . . **LC 11; DA; DAB**
See also CDBLB Before 1660; DLB 146;
SATA 59; SATA-Brief 33

Malouf, (George Joseph) David
1934- . . . . **CLC 28, 86**
See also CA 124

Malraux, (Georges-)Andre
1901-1976 . . . . **CLC 1, 4, 9, 13, 15, 57**
See also CA 21-22; 69-72; CANR 34;
CAP 2; DLB 72; MTCW

Malzberg, Barry N(athaniel) 1939- . . . **CLC 7**
See also CA 61-64; CAAS 4; CANR 16;
DLB 8

Mamet, David (Alan)
1947- . . . . **CLC 9, 15, 34, 46; DC 4**
See also AAYA 3; CA 81-84; CABS 3;
CANR 15, 41; DLB 7; MTCW

Mamoulian, Rouben (Zachary)
1897-1987 . . . . **CLC 16**
See also CA 25-28R; 124

Mandelstam, Osip (Emilievich)
1891(?)-1938(?) . . . . **TCLC 2, 6**
See also CA 104

Mander, (Mary) Jane 1877-1949 . . . **TCLC 31**

Mandiargues, Andre Pieyre de . . . . . . **CLC 41**
See also Pieyre de Mandiargues, Andre
See also DLB 83

Mandrake, Ethel Belle
See Thurman, Wallace (Henry)

Mangan, James Clarence
1803-1849 . . . . **NCLC 27**

Maniere, J.-E.
See Giraudoux, (Hippolyte) Jean

Manley, (Mary) Delariviere
1672(?)-1724 . . . . **LC 1**
See also DLB 39, 80

Mann, Abel
See Creasey, John

Mann, (Luiz) Heinrich 1871-1950 . . . **TCLC 9**
See also CA 106; DLB 66

Mann, (Paul) Thomas
1875-1955 . . . . **TCLC 2, 8, 14, 21, 35, 44,
60; DA; DAB; SSC 5; WLC**
See also CA 104; 128; DLB 66; MTCW

Manning, David
See Faust, Frederick (Schiller)

Manning, Frederic 1887(?)-1935 . . . **TCLC 25**
See also CA 124

Manning, Olivia 1915-1980 . . . . . . **CLC 5, 19**
See also CA 5-8R; 101; CANR 29; MTCW

Mano, D. Keith 1942- . . . . **CLC 2, 10**
See also CA 25-28R; CAAS 6; CANR 26;
DLB 6

Mansfield, Katherine
. . . . . **TCLC 2, 8, 39; DAB; SSC 9; WLC**
See also Beauchamp, Kathleen Mansfield

Manso, Peter 1940- . . . . **CLC 39**
See also CA 29-32R; CANR 44

Mantecon, Juan Jimenez
See Jimenez (Mantecon), Juan Ramon

Manton, Peter
See Creasey, John

Man Without a Spleen, A
See Chekhov, Anton (Pavlovich)

Manzoni, Alessandro 1785-1873 . . **NCLC 29**

Mapu, Abraham (ben Jekutiel)
1808-1867 . . . . **NCLC 18**

Mara, Sally
See Queneau, Raymond

Marat, Jean Paul 1743-1793 . . . . **LC 10**

Marcel, Gabriel Honore
1889-1973 . . . . **CLC 15**
See also CA 102; 45-48; MTCW

Marchbanks, Samuel
See Davies, (William) Robertson

Marchi, Giacomo
See Bassani, Giorgio

Margulies, Donald . . . . **CLC 76**

Marie de France c. 12th cent. - . . . . **CMLC 8**

Marie de l'Incarnation 1599-1672 . . . . **LC 10**

Meaker, Marijane (Agnes) 1927-
See Kerr, M. E.
See also CA 107; CANR 37; JRDA;
MAICYA; MTCW; SATA 20, 61

Medoff, Mark (Howard) 1940- ... CLC 6, 23
See also AITN 1; CA 53-56; CANR 5;
DLB 7

Medvedev, P. N.
See Bakhtin, Mikhail Mikhailovich

Meged, Aharon
See Megged, Aharon

Meged, Aron
See Megged, Aharon

Megged, Aharon 1920-............. CLC 9
See also CA 49-52; CAAS 13; CANR 1

Mehta, Ved (Parkash) 1934-....... CLC 37
See also CA 1-4R; CANR 2, 23; MTCW

Melanter
See Blackmore, R(ichard) D(oddridge)

Melikow, Loris
See Hofmannsthal, Hugo von

Melmoth, Sebastian
See Wilde, Oscar (Fingal O'Flahertie Wills)

Meltzer, Milton 1915-............. CLC 26
See also AAYA 8; CA 13-16R; CANR 38;
CLR 13; DLB 61; JRDA; MAICYA;
SAAS 1; SATA 1, 50, 80

Melville, Herman
1819-1891 ..... NCLC 3, 12, 29, 45, 49;
DA; DAB; SSC 1, 17; WLC
See also CDALB 1640-1865; DLB 3, 74;
SATA 59

Menander
c. 342B.C.-c. 292B.C.... CMLC 9; DC 3

Mencken, H(enry) L(ouis)
1880-1956 .... TCLC 13
See also CA 105; 125; CDALB 1917-1929;
DLB 11, 29, 63, 137; MTCW

Mercer, David 1928-1980........... CLC 5
See also CA 9-12R; 102; CANR 23;
DLB 13; MTCW

Merchant, Paul
See Ellison, Harlan (Jay)

Meredith, George 1828-1909 ... TCLC 17, 43
See also CA 117; CDBLB 1832-1890;
DLB 18, 35, 57

Meredith, William (Morris)
1919-............... CLC 4, 13, 22, 55
See also CA 9-12R; CAAS 14; CANR 6, 40;
DLB 5

Merezhkovsky, Dmitry Sergeyevich
1865-1941 .... TCLC 29

Merimee, Prosper
1803-1870 .... NCLC 6; SSC 7
See also DLB 119

Merkin, Daphne 1954-............ CLC 44
See also CA 123

Merlin, Arthur
See Blish, James (Benjamin)

Merrill, James (Ingram)
1926-1995 .... CLC 2, 3, 6, 8, 13, 18, 34
See also CA 13-16R; 147; CANR 10, 49;
DLB 5; DLBY 85; MTCW

Merriman, Alex
See Silverberg, Robert

Merritt, E. B.
See Waddington, Miriam

Merton, Thomas
1915-1968 .. CLC 1, 3, 11, 34, 83; PC 10
See also CA 5-8R; 25-28R; CANR 22;
DLB 48; DLBY 81; MTCW

Merwin, W(illiam) S(tanley)
1927- ... CLC 1, 2, 3, 5, 8, 13, 18, 45, 88
See also CA 13-16R; CANR 15; DLB 5;
MTCW

Metcalf, John 1938-............. CLC 37
See also CA 113; DLB 60

Metcalf, Suzanne
See Baum, L(yman) Frank

Mew, Charlotte (Mary)
1870-1928 .... TCLC 8
See also CA 105; DLB 19, 135

Mewshaw, Michael 1943-........... CLC 9
See also CA 53-56; CANR 7, 47; DLBY 80

Meyer, June
See Jordan, June

Meyer, Lynn
See Slavitt, David R(ytman)

Meyer-Meyrink, Gustav 1868-1932
See Meyrink, Gustav
See also CA 117

Meyers, Jeffrey 1939-............ CLC 39
See also CA 73-76; DLB 111

Meynell, Alice (Christina Gertrude Thompson)
1847-1922 .... TCLC 6
See also CA 104; DLB 19, 98

Meyrink, Gustav................. TCLC 21
See also Meyer-Meyrink, Gustav
See also DLB 81

Michaels, Leonard
1933-............. CLC 6, 25; SSC 16
See also CA 61-64; CANR 21; DLB 130;
MTCW

Michaux, Henri 1899-1984 ...... CLC 8, 19
See also CA 85-88; 114

Michelangelo 1475-1564........... LC 12

Michelet, Jules 1798-1874....... NCLC 31

Michener, James A(lbert)
1907(?)-.......... CLC 1, 5, 11, 29, 60
See also AITN 1; BEST 90:1; CA 5-8R;
CANR 21, 45; DLB 6; MTCW

Mickiewicz, Adam 1798-1855 ..... NCLC 3

Middleton, Christopher 1926-...... CLC 13
See also CA 13-16R; CANR 29; DLB 40

Middleton, Richard (Barham)
1882-1911 .... TCLC 56
See also DLB 156

Middleton, Stanley 1919-........ CLC 7, 38
See also CA 25-28R; CANR 21, 46;
DLB 14

Middleton, Thomas 1580-1627........ DC 5
See also DLB 58

Migueis, Jose Rodrigues 1901-..... CLC 10

Mikszath, Kalman 1847-1910 ..... TCLC 31

Miles, Josephine
1911-1985 .... CLC 1, 2, 14, 34, 39
See also CA 1-4R; 116; CANR 2; DLB 48

Militant
See Sandburg, Carl (August)

Mill, John Stuart 1806-1873 ..... NCLC 11
See also CDBLB 1832-1890; DLB 55

Millar, Kenneth 1915-1983 .... CLC 14
See also Macdonald, Ross
See also CA 9-12R; 110; CANR 16; DLB 2;
DLBD 6; DLBY 83; MTCW

Millay, E. Vincent
See Millay, Edna St. Vincent

Millay, Edna St. Vincent
1892-1950 ...... TCLC 4, 49; DA; DAB;
PC 6
See also CA 104; 130; CDALB 1917-1929;
DLB 45; MTCW

Miller, Arthur
1915- .... CLC 1, 2, 6, 10, 15, 26, 47, 78;
DA; DAB; DC 1; WLC
See also AAYA 15; AITN 1; CA 1-4R;
CABS 3; CANR 2, 30;
CDALB 1941-1968; DLB 7; MTCW

Miller, Henry (Valentine)
1891-1980 .... CLC 1, 2, 4, 9, 14, 43, 84;
DA; DAB; WLC
See also CA 9-12R; 97-100; CANR 33;
CDALB 1929-1941; DLB 4, 9; DLBY 80;
MTCW

Miller, Jason 1939(?)-............ CLC 2
See also AITN 1; CA 73-76; DLB 7

Miller, Sue 1943-................ CLC 44
See also BEST 90:3; CA 139; DLB 143

Miller, Walter M(ichael, Jr.)
1923-..................... CLC 4, 30
See also CA 85-88; DLB 8

Millett, Kate 1934-................ CLC 67
See also AITN 1; CA 73-76; CANR 32;
MTCW

Millhauser, Steven 1943-........ CLC 21, 54
See also CA 110; 111; DLB 2

Millin, Sarah Gertrude 1889-1968 .. CLC 49
See also CA 102; 93-96

Milne, A(lan) A(lexander)
1882-1956 .... TCLC 6; DAB
See also CA 104; 133; CLR 1, 26; DLB 10,
77, 100; MAICYA; MTCW; YABC 1

Milner, Ron(ald) 1938-........ CLC 56; BLC
See also AITN 1; BW 1; CA 73-76;
CANR 24; DLB 38; MTCW

Milosz, Czeslaw
1911- ... CLC 5, 11, 22, 31, 56, 82; PC 8
See also CA 81-84; CANR 23; MTCW

Milton, John
1608-1674 ...... LC 9; DA; DAB; WLC
See also CDBLB 1660-1789; DLB 131, 151

Min, Anchee 1957-................ CLC 86
See also CA 146

Minehaha, Cornelius
See Wedekind, (Benjamin) Frank(lin)

Miner, Valerie 1947- .... CLC 40
See also CA 97-100

Minimo, Duca
See D'Annunzio, Gabriele

Minot, Susan 1956- .... CLC 44
See also CA 134

Minus, Ed 1938-................ CLC 39

Miranda, Javier
See Bioy Casares, Adolfo

Mirbeau, Octave 1848-1917...... **TCLC 55**
See also DLB 123

Miro (Ferrer), Gabriel (Francisco Victor)
1879-1930 .... **TCLC 5**
See also CA 104

Mishima, Yukio
...... **CLC 2, 4, 6, 9, 27; DC 1; SSC 4**
See also Hiraoka, Kimitake

Mistral, Frederic 1830-1914 ...... **TCLC 51**
See also CA 122

Mistral, Gabriela........... **TCLC 2; HLC**
See also Godoy Alcayaga, Lucila

Mistry, Rohinton 1952-........... **CLC 71**
See also CA 141

Mitchell, Clyde
See Ellison, Harlan (Jay); Silverberg, Robert

Mitchell, James Leslie 1901-1935
See Gibbon, Lewis Grassic
See also CA 104; DLB 15

Mitchell, Joni 1943-.............. **CLC 12**
See also CA 112

Mitchell, Margaret (Munnerlyn)
1900-1949 .... **TCLC 11**
See also CA 109; 125; DLB 9; MTCW

Mitchell, Peggy
See Mitchell, Margaret (Munnerlyn)

Mitchell, S(ilas) Weir 1829-1914 .. **TCLC 36**

Mitchell, W(illiam) O(rmond)
1914-....................... **CLC 25**
See also CA 77-80; CANR 15, 43; DLB 88

Mitford, Mary Russell 1787-1855.. **NCLC 4**
See also DLB 110, 116

Mitford, Nancy 1904-1973........ **CLC 44**
See also CA 9-12R

Miyamoto, Yuriko 1899-1951 ..... **TCLC 37**

Mo, Timothy (Peter) 1950(?)-...... **CLC 46**
See also CA 117; MTCW

Modarressi, Taghi (M.) 1931-...... **CLC 44**
See also CA 121; 134

Modiano, Patrick (Jean) 1945-..... **CLC 18**
See also CA 85-88; CANR 17, 40; DLB 83

Moerck, Paal
See Roelvaag, O(le) E(dvart)

Mofolo, Thomas (Mokopu)
1875(?)-1948 .... **TCLC 22; BLC**
See also CA 121

Mohr, Nicholasa 1935-...... **CLC 12; HLC**
See also AAYA 8; CA 49-52; CANR 1, 32;
CLR 22; DLB 145; HW; JRDA; SAAS 8;
SATA 8

Mojtabai, A(nn) G(race)
1938- .... **CLC 5, 9, 15, 29**
See also CA 85-88

Moliere
1622-1673 ..... **LC 28; DA; DAB; WLC**

Molin, Charles
See Mayne, William (James Carter)

Molnar, Ferenc 1878-1952....... **TCLC 20**
See also CA 109

Momaday, N(avarre) Scott
1934-........ **CLC 2, 19, 85; DA; DAB**
See also AAYA 11; CA 25-28R; CANR 14,
34; DLB 143; MTCW; NNAL; SATA 48;
SATA-Brief 30

Monette, Paul 1945-1995.......... **CLC 82**
See also CA 139; 147

Monroe, Harriet 1860-1936...... **TCLC 12**
See also CA 109; DLB 54, 91

Monroe, Lyle
See Heinlein, Robert A(nson)

Montagu, Elizabeth 1917-........ **NCLC 7**
See also CA 9-12R

Montagu, Mary (Pierrepont) Wortley
1689-1762 .... **LC 9**
See also DLB 95, 101

Montagu, W. H.
See Coleridge, Samuel Taylor

Montague, John (Patrick)
1929-.................... **CLC 13, 46**
See also CA 9-12R; CANR 9; DLB 40;
MTCW

Montaigne, Michel (Eyquem) de
1533-1592 ...... **LC 8; DA; DAB; WLC**

Montale, Eugenio
1896-1981 .... **CLC 7, 9, 18; PC 13**
See also CA 17-20R; 104; CANR 30;
DLB 114; MTCW

Montesquieu, Charles-Louis de Secondat
1689-1755 .... **LC 7**

Montgomery, (Robert) Bruce 1921-1978
See Crispin, Edmund
See also CA 104

Montgomery, L(ucy) M(aud)
1874-1942 .... **TCLC 51**
See also AAYA 12; CA 108; 137; CLR 8;
DLB 92; JRDA; MAICYA; YABC 1

Montgomery, Marion H., Jr. 1925-.. **CLC 7**
See also AITN 1; CA 1-4R; CANR 3, 48;
DLB 6

Montgomery, Max
See Davenport, Guy (Mattison, Jr.)

Montherlant, Henry (Milon) de
1896-1972 .... **CLC 8, 19**
See also CA 85-88; 37-40R; DLB 72;
MTCW

Monty Python
See Chapman, Graham; Cleese, John
(Marwood); Gilliam, Terry (Vance); Idle,
Eric; Jones, Terence Graham Parry; Palin,
Michael (Edward)
See also AAYA 7

Moodie, Susanna (Strickland)
1803-1885 .... **NCLC 14**
See also DLB 99

Mooney, Edward 1951-
See Mooney, Ted
See also CA 130

Mooney, Ted .... **CLC 25**
See also Mooney, Edward

Moorcock, Michael (John)
1939-.................... **CLC 5, 27, 58**
See also CA 45-48; CAAS 5; CANR 2, 17,
38; DLB 14; MTCW

Moore, Brian
1921- ...... **CLC 1, 3, 5, 7, 8, 19, 32, 90;**
DAB
See also CA 1-4R; CANR 1, 25, 42; MTCW

Moore, Edward
See Muir, Edwin

Moore, George Augustus
1852-1933 .... **TCLC 7; SSC 19**
See also CA 104; DLB 10, 18, 57, 135

Moore, Lorrie .... **CLC 39, 45, 68**
See also Moore, Marie Lorena

Moore, Marianne (Craig)
1887-1972 .... **CLC 1, 2, 4, 8, 10, 13, 19,**
47; DA; DAB; PC 4
See also CA 1-4R; 33-36R; CANR 3;
CDALB 1929-1941; DLB 45; DLBD 7;
MTCW; SATA 20

Moore, Marie Lorena 1957-
See Moore, Lorrie
See also CA 116; CANR 39

Moore, Thomas 1779-1852........ **NCLC 6**
See also DLB 96, 144

Morand, Paul 1888-1976.......... **CLC 41**
See also CA 69-72; DLB 65

Morante, Elsa 1918-1985........ **CLC 8, 47**
See also CA 85-88; 117; CANR 35; MTCW

Moravia, Alberto....... **CLC 2, 7, 11, 27, 46**
See also Pincherle, Alberto

More, Hannah 1745-1833 .... **NCLC 27**
See also DLB 107, 109, 116

More, Henry 1614-1687............. **LC 9**
See also DLB 126

More, Sir Thomas 1478-1535 .... **LC 10**

Moreas, Jean................... **TCLC 18**
See also Papadiamantopoulos, Johannes

Morgan, Berry 1919- .... **CLC 6**
See also CA 49-52; DLB 6

Morgan, Claire
See Highsmith, (Mary) Patricia

Morgan, Edwin (George) 1920-..... **CLC 31**
See also CA 5-8R; CANR 3, 43; DLB 27

Morgan, (George) Frederick
1922-....................... **CLC 23**
See also CA 17-20R; CANR 21

Morgan, Harriet
See Mencken, H(enry) L(ouis)

Morgan, Jane
See Cooper, James Fenimore

Morgan, Janet 1945- .... **CLC 39**
See also CA 65-68

Morgan, Lady 1776(?)-1859...... **NCLC 29**
See also DLB 116

Morgan, Robin 1941-.............. **CLC 2**
See also CA 69-72; CANR 29; MTCW;
SATA 80

Morgan, Scott
See Kuttner, Henry

Morgan, Seth 1949(?)-1990........ **CLC 65**
See also CA 132

Morgenstern, Christian
1871-1914 .... **TCLC 8**
See also CA 105

Morgenstern, S.
See Goldman, William (W.)

Moricz, Zsigmond 1879-1942 ..... **TCLC 33**

Morike, Eduard (Friedrich)
1804-1875 .... **NCLC 10**
See also DLB 133

Norton, Caroline 1808-1877...... NCLC 47
See also DLB 21

Norway, Nevil Shute 1899-1960
See Shute, Nevil
See also CA 102; 93-96

Norwid, Cyprian Kamil
1821-1883 .... NCLC 17

Nosille, Nabrah
See Ellison, Harlan (Jay)

Nossack, Hans Erich 1901-1978..... CLC 6
See also CA 93-96; 85-88; DLB 69

Nostradamus 1503-1566........... LC 27

Nosu, Chuji
See Ozu, Yasujiro

Notenburg, Eleanora (Genrikhovna) von
See Guro, Elena

Nova, Craig 1945-............. CLC 7, 31
See also CA 45-48; CANR 2

Novak, Joseph
See Kosinski, Jerzy (Nikodem)

Novalis 1772-1801 .... NCLC 13
See also DLB 90

Nowlan, Alden (Albert) 1933-1983 .. CLC 15
See also CA 9-12R; CANR 5; DLB 53

Noyes, Alfred 1880-1958.......... TCLC 7
See also CA 104; DLB 20

Nunn, Kem 19(?)-................ CLC 34

Nye, Robert 1939- .... CLC 13, 42
See also CA 33-36R; CANR 29; DLB 14;
MTCW; SATA 6

Nyro, Laura 1947- .... CLC 17

Oates, Joyce Carol
1938- ......CLC 1, 2, 3, 6, 9, 11, 15, 19,
33, 52; DA; DAB; SSC 6; WLC
See also AAYA 15; AITN 1; BEST 89:2;
CA 5-8R; CANR 25, 45;
CDALB 1968-1988; DLB 2, 5, 130;
DLBY 81; MTCW

O'Brien, Darcy 1939-............ CLC 11
See also CA 21-24R; CANR 8

O'Brien, E. G.
See Clarke, Arthur C(harles)

O'Brien, Edna
1936- ... CLC 3, 5, 8, 13, 36, 65; SSC 10
See also CA 1-4R; CANR 6, 41;
CDBLB 1960 to Present; DLB 14;
MTCW

O'Brien, Fitz-James 1828-1862... NCLC 21
See also DLB 74

O'Brien, Flann........ CLC 1, 4, 5, 7, 10, 47
See also O Nuallain, Brian

O'Brien, Richard 1942- .... CLC 17
See also CA 124

O'Brien, Tim 1946-......... CLC 7, 19, 40
See also CA 85-88; CANR 40; DLB 152;
DLBD 9; DLBY 80

Obstfelder, Sigbjoern 1866-1900... TCLC 23
See also CA 123

O'Casey, Sean
1880-1964 ...... CLC 1, 5, 9, 11, 15, 88;
DAB
See also CA 89-92; CDBLB 1914-1945;
DLB 10; MTCW

O'Cathasaigh, Sean
See O'Casey, Sean

Ochs, Phil 1940-1976............. CLC 17
See also CA 65-68

O'Connor, Edwin (Greene)
1918-1968 .... CLC 14
See also CA 93-96; 25-28R

O'Connor, (Mary) Flannery
1925-1964 .... CLC 1, 2, 3, 6, 10, 13, 15,
21, 66; DA; DAB; SSC 1; WLC
See also AAYA 7; CA 1-4R; CANR 3, 41;
CDALB 1941-1968; DLB 2, 152;
DLBD 12; DLBY 80; MTCW

O'Connor, Frank........... CLC 23; SSC 5
See also O'Donovan, Michael John

O'Dell, Scott 1898-1989........... CLC 30
See also AAYA 3; CA 61-64; 129;
CANR 12, 30; CLR 1, 16; DLB 52;
JRDA; MAICYA; SATA 12, 60

Odets, Clifford 1906-1963 .... CLC 2, 28
See also CA 85-88; DLB 7, 26; MTCW

O'Doherty, Brian 1934-........... CLC 76
See also CA 105

O'Donnell, K. M.
See Malzberg, Barry N(athaniel)

O'Donnell, Lawrence
See Kuttner, Henry

O'Donovan, Michael John
1903-1966 .... CLC 14
See also O'Connor, Frank
See also CA 93-96

Oe, Kenzaburo
1935- .... CLC 10, 36, 86; SSC 20
See also CA 97-100; CANR 36; DLBY 94;
MTCW

O'Faolain, Julia 1932-....... CLC 6, 19, 47
See also CA 81-84; CAAS 2; CANR 12;
DLB 14; MTCW

O'Faolain, Sean
1900-1991 .... CLC 1, 7, 14, 32, 70;
SSC 13
See also CA 61-64; 134; CANR 12;
DLB 15; MTCW

O'Flaherty, Liam
1896-1984 .... CLC 5, 34; SSC 6
See also CA 101; 113; CANR 35; DLB 36;
DLBY 84; MTCW

Ogilvy, Gavin
See Barrie, J(ames) M(atthew)

O'Grady, Standish James
1846-1928 .... TCLC 5
See also CA 104

O'Grady, Timothy 1951-.......... CLC 59
See also CA 138

O'Hara, Frank
1926-1966 .... CLC 2, 5, 13, 78
See also CA 9-12R; 25-28R; CANR 33;
DLB 5, 16; MTCW

O'Hara, John (Henry)
1905-1970 .... CLC 1, 2, 3, 6, 11, 42;
SSC 15
See also CA 5-8R; 25-28R; CANR 31;
CDALB 1929-1941; DLB 9, 86; DLBD 2;
MTCW

O Hehir, Diana 1922- .... CLC 41
See also CA 93-96

Okigbo, Christopher (Ifenayichukwu)
1932-1967 ..... CLC 25, 84; BLC; PC 7
See also BW 1; CA 77-80; DLB 125;
MTCW

Okri, Ben 1959- .... CLC 87
See also BW 2; CA 130; 138

Olds, Sharon 1942-......... CLC 32, 39, 85
See also CA 101; CANR 18, 41; DLB 120

Oldstyle, Jonathan
See Irving, Washington

Olesha, Yuri (Karlovich)
1899-1960 .... CLC 8
See also CA 85-88

Oliphant, Laurence
1829(?)-1888 .... NCLC 47
See also DLB 18

Oliphant, Margaret (Oliphant Wilson)
1828-1897 .... NCLC 11
See also DLB 18

Oliver, Mary 1935-............ CLC 19, 34
See also CA 21-24R; CANR 9, 43; DLB 5

Olivier, Laurence (Kerr)
1907-1989 .... CLC 20
See also CA 111; 129

Olsen, Tillie
1913- .... CLC 4, 13; DA; DAB; SSC 11
See also CA 1-4R; CANR 1, 43; DLB 28;
DLBY 80; MTCW

Olson, Charles (John)
1910-1970 ..... CLC 1, 2, 5, 6, 9, 11, 29
See also CA 13-16; 25-28R; CABS 2;
CANR 35; CAP 1; DLB 5, 16; MTCW

Olson, Toby 1937- .... CLC 28
See also CA 65-68; CANR 9, 31

Olyesha, Yuri
See Olesha, Yuri (Karlovich)

Ondaatje, (Philip) Michael
1943- .... CLC 14, 29, 51, 76; DAB
See also CA 77-80; CANR 42; DLB 60

Oneal, Elizabeth 1934-
See Oneal, Zibby
See also CA 106; CANR 28; MAICYA;
SATA 30, 82

Oneal, Zibby .... CLC 30
See also Oneal, Elizabeth
See also AAYA 5; CLR 13; JRDA

O'Neill, Eugene (Gladstone)
1888-1953 ...... TCLC 1, 6, 27, 49; DA;
DAB; WLC
See also AITN 1; CA 110; 132;
CDALB 1929-1941; DLB 7; MTCW

Onetti, Juan Carlos 1909-1994 ... CLC 7, 10
See also CA 85-88; 145; CANR 32;
DLB 113; HW; MTCW

O Nuallain, Brian 1911-1966
See O'Brien, Flann
See also CA 21-22; 25-28R; CAP 2

Oppen, George 1908-1984 .... CLC 7, 13, 34
See also CA 13-16R; 113; CANR 8; DLB 5

Oppenheim, E(dward) Phillips
1866-1946 .... TCLC 45
See also CA 111; DLB 70

Orlovitz, Gil 1918-1973.......... CLC 22
See also CA 77-80; 45-48; DLB 2, 5

Paton, Alan (Stewart)
1903-1988 . . . . . . **CLC 4, 10, 25, 55; DA;
DAB; WLC**
See also CA 13-16; 125; CANR 22; CAP 1;
MTCW; SATA 11; SATA-Obit 56

Paton Walsh, Gillian 1937-
See Walsh, Jill Paton
See also CANR 38; JRDA; MAICYA;
SAAS 3; SATA 4, 72

Paulding, James Kirke 1778-1860. . **NCLC 2**
See also DLB 3, 59, 74

Paulin, Thomas Neilson 1949-
See Paulin, Tom
See also CA 123; 128

Paulin, Tom . . . . **CLC 37**
See also Paulin, Thomas Neilson
See also DLB 40

Paustovsky, Konstantin (Georgievich)
1892-1968 . . . . **CLC 40**
See also CA 93-96; 25-28R

Pavese, Cesare
1908-1950 . . . . . **TCLC 3; PC 13; SSC 19**
See also CA 104; DLB 128

Pavic, Milorad 1929- . . . . **CLC 60**
See also CA 136

Payne, Alan
See Jakes, John (William)

Paz, Gil
See Lugones, Leopoldo

Paz, Octavio
1914- . . . . **CLC 3, 4, 6, 10, 19, 51, 65;
DA; DAB; HLC; PC 1; WLC**
See also CA 73-76; CANR 32; DLBY 90;
HW; MTCW

Peacock, Molly 1947- . . . . **CLC 60**
See also CA 103; CAAS 21; DLB 120

Peacock, Thomas Love
1785-1866 . . . . **NCLC 22**
See also DLB 96, 116

Peake, Mervyn 1911-1968 . . . . **CLC 7, 54**
See also CA 5-8R; 25-28R; CANR 3;
DLB 15; MTCW; SATA 23

Pearce, Philippa . . . . **CLC 21**
See also Christie, (Ann) Philippa
See also CLR 9; MAICYA; SATA 1, 67

Pearl, Eric
See Elman, Richard

Pearson, T(homas) R(eid) 1956- . . . . **CLC 39**
See also CA 120; 130

Peck, Dale 1967- . . . . **CLC 81**
See also CA 146

Peck, John 1941- . . . . **CLC 3**
See also CA 49-52; CANR 3

Peck, Richard (Wayne) 1934- . . . . . . **CLC 21**
See also AAYA 1; CA 85-88; CANR 19,
38; CLR 15; JRDA; MAICYA; SAAS 2;
SATA 18, 55

Peck, Robert Newton 1928- . . . . **CLC 17; DA**
See also AAYA 3; CA 81-84; CANR 31;
JRDA; MAICYA; SAAS 1; SATA 21, 62

Peckinpah, (David) Sam(uel)
1925-1984 . . . . **CLC 20**
See also CA 109; 114

Pedersen, Knut 1859-1952
See Hamsun, Knut
See also CA 104; 119; MTCW

Peeslake, Gaffer
See Durrell, Lawrence (George)

Peguy, Charles Pierre
1873-1914 . . . . **TCLC 10**
See also CA 107

Pena, Ramon del Valle y
See Valle-Inclan, Ramon (Maria) del

Pendennis, Arthur Esquir
See Thackeray, William Makepeace

Penn, William 1644-1718 . . . . **LC 25**
See also DLB 24

Pepys, Samuel
1633-1703 . . . . . **LC 11; DA; DAB; WLC**
See also CDBLB 1660-1789; DLB 101

Percy, Walker
1916-1990 . . . . **CLC 2, 3, 6, 8, 14, 18, 47,
65**
See also CA 1-4R; 131; CANR 1, 23;
DLB 2; DLBY 80, 90; MTCW

Perec, Georges 1936-1982 . . . . **CLC 56**
See also CA 141; DLB 83

Pereda (y Sanchez de Porrua), Jose Maria de
1833-1906 . . . . **TCLC 16**
See also CA 117

Pereda y Porrua, Jose Maria de
See Pereda (y Sanchez de Porrua), Jose
Maria de

Peregoy, George Weems
See Mencken, H(enry) L(ouis)

Perelman, S(idney) J(oseph)
1904-1979 . . . **CLC 3, 5, 9, 15, 23, 44, 49**
See also AITN 1, 2; CA 73-76; 89-92;
CANR 18; DLB 11, 44; MTCW

Peret, Benjamin 1899-1959 . . . . **TCLC 20**
See also CA 117

Peretz, Isaac Loeb 1851(?)-1915 . . . **TCLC 16**
See also CA 109

Peretz, Yitzkhok Leibush
See Peretz, Isaac Loeb

Perez Galdos, Benito 1843-1920 . . . **TCLC 27**
See also CA 125; HW

Perrault, Charles 1628-1703 . . . . **LC 2**
See also MAICYA; SATA 25

Perry, Brighton
See Sherwood, Robert E(mmet)

Perse, St.-John . . . . **CLC 4, 11, 46**
See also Leger, (Marie-Rene Auguste) Alexis
Saint-Leger

Perutz, Leo 1882-1957 . . . . **TCLC 60**
See also DLB 81

Peseenz, Tulio F.
See Lopez y Fuentes, Gregorio

Pesetsky, Bette 1932- . . . . **CLC 28**
See also CA 133; DLB 130

Peshkov, Alexei Maximovich 1868-1936
See Gorky, Maxim
See also CA 105; 141; DA

Pessoa, Fernando (Antonio Nogueira)
1888-1935 . . . . **TCLC 27; HLC**
See also CA 125

Peterkin, Julia Mood 1880-1961 . . . . **CLC 31**
See also CA 102; DLB 9

Peters, Joan K. 1945- . . . . **CLC 39**

Peters, Robert L(ouis) 1924- . . . . **CLC 7**
See also CA 13-16R; CAAS 8; DLB 105

Petofi, Sandor 1823-1849 . . . . **NCLC 21**

Petrakis, Harry Mark 1923- . . . . **CLC 3**
See also CA 9-12R; CANR 4, 30

Petrarch 1304-1374 . . . . **PC 8**

Petrov, Evgeny . . . . **TCLC 21**
See also Kataev, Evgeny Petrovich

Petry, Ann (Lane) 1908- . . . . . . **CLC 1, 7, 18**
See also BW 1; CA 5-8R; CAAS 6;
CANR 4, 46; CLR 12; DLB 76; JRDA;
MAICYA; MTCW; SATA 5

Petursson, Halligrimur 1614-1674 . . . . **LC 8**

Philips, Katherine 1632-1664 . . . . **LC 30**
See also DLB 131

Philipson, Morris H. 1926- . . . . **CLC 53**
See also CA 1-4R; CANR 4

Phillips, David Graham
1867-1911 . . . . **TCLC 44**
See also CA 108; DLB 9, 12

Phillips, Jack
See Sandburg, Carl (August)

Phillips, Jayne Anne
1952- . . . . **CLC 15, 33; SSC 16**
See also CA 101; CANR 24; DLBY 80;
MTCW

Phillips, Richard
See Dick, Philip K(indred)

Phillips, Robert (Schaeffer) 1938- . . . **CLC 28**
See also CA 17-20R; CAAS 13; CANR 8;
DLB 105

Phillips, Ward
See Lovecraft, H(oward) P(hillips)

Piccolo, Lucio 1901-1969 . . . . **CLC 13**
See also CA 97-100; DLB 114

Pickthall, Marjorie L(owry) C(hristie)
1883-1922 . . . . **TCLC 21**
See also CA 107; DLB 92

Pico della Mirandola, Giovanni
1463-1494 . . . . **LC 15**

Piercy, Marge
1936- . . . . **CLC 3, 6, 14, 18, 27, 62**
See also CA 21-24R; CAAS 1; CANR 13,
43; DLB 120; MTCW

Piers, Robert
See Anthony, Piers

Pieyre de Mandiargues, Andre 1909-1991
See Mandiargues, Andre Pieyre de
See also CA 103; 136; CANR 22

Pilnyak, Boris . . . . **TCLC 23**
See also Vogau, Boris Andreyevich

Pincherle, Alberto 1907-1990 . . . **CLC 11, 18**
See also Moravia, Alberto
See also CA 25-28R; 132; CANR 33;
MTCW

Pinckney, Darryl 1953- . . . . **CLC 76**
See also BW 2; CA 143

Pindar 518B.C.-446B.C. . . . . **CMLC 12**

Pineda, Cecile 1942- . . . . **CLC 39**
See also CA 118

Pinero, Arthur Wing 1855-1934 ... TCLC 32
See also CA 110; DLB 10

Pinero, Miguel (Antonio Gomez)
1946-1988 .... CLC 4, 55
See also CA 61-64; 125; CANR 29; HW

Pinget, Robert 1919- .... CLC 7, 13, 37
See also CA 85-88; DLB 83

Pink Floyd
See Barrett, (Roger) Syd; Gilmour, David;
Mason, Nick; Waters, Roger; Wright,
Rick

Pinkney, Edward 1802-1828 ..... NCLC 31

Pinkwater, Daniel Manus 1941- .... CLC 35
See also Pinkwater, Manus
See also AAYA 1; CA 29-32R; CANR 12,
38; CLR 4; JRDA; MAICYA; SAAS 3;
SATA 46, 76

Pinkwater, Manus
See Pinkwater, Daniel Manus
See also SATA 8

Pinsky, Robert 1940- .... CLC 9, 19, 38
See also CA 29-32R; CAAS 4; DLBY 82

Pinta, Harold
See Pinter, Harold

Pinter, Harold
1930- ..... CLC 1, 3, 6, 9, 11, 15, 27, 58,
73; DA; DAB; WLC
See also CA 5-8R; CANR 33; CDBLB 1960
to Present; DLB 13; MTCW

Pirandello, Luigi
1867-1936 ...... TCLC 4, 29; DA; DAB;
DC 5; WLC
See also CA 104

Pirsig, Robert M(aynard)
1928- .... CLC 4, 6, 73
See also CA 53-56; CANR 42; MTCW;
SATA 39

Pisarev, Dmitry Ivanovich
1840-1868 .... NCLC 25

Pix, Mary (Griffith) 1666-1709 .... LC 8
See also DLB 80

Pixerecourt, Guilbert de
1773-1844 .... NCLC 39

Plaidy, Jean
See Hibbert, Eleanor Alice Burford

Planche, James Robinson
1796-1880 .... NCLC 42

Plant, Robert 1948- .... CLC 12

Plante, David (Robert)
1940- .... CLC 7, 23, 38
See also CA 37-40R; CANR 12, 36;
DLBY 83; MTCW

Plath, Sylvia
1932-1963 ..... CLC 1, 2, 3, 5, 9, 11, 14,
17, 50, 51, 62; DA; DAB; PC 1; WLC
See also AAYA 13; CA 19-20; CANR 34;
CAP 2; CDALB 1941-1968; DLB 5, 6,
152; MTCW

Plato
428(?)B.C.-348(?)B.C. ..... CMLC 8; DA;
DAB

Platonov, Andrei .... TCLC 14
See also Klimentov, Andrei Platonovich

Platt, Kin 1911- .... CLC 26
See also AAYA 11; CA 17-20R; CANR 11;
JRDA; SAAS 17; SATA 21

Plick et Plock
See Simenon, Georges (Jacques Christian)

Plimpton, George (Ames) 1927- ..... CLC 36
See also AITN 1; CA 21-24R; CANR 32;
MTCW; SATA 10

Plomer, William Charles Franklin
1903-1973 .... CLC 4, 8
See also CA 21-22; CANR 34; CAP 2;
DLB 20; MTCW; SATA 24

Plowman, Piers
See Kavanagh, Patrick (Joseph)

Plum, J.
See Wodehouse, P(elham) G(renville)

Plumly, Stanley (Ross) 1939- ...... CLC 33
See also CA 108; 110; DLB 5

Plumpe, Friedrich Wilhelm
1888-1931 .... TCLC 53
See also CA 112

Poe, Edgar Allan
1809-1849 ..... NCLC 1, 16; DA; DAB;
PC 1; SSC 1; WLC
See also AAYA 14; CDALB 1640-1865;
DLB 3, 59, 73, 74; SATA 23

Poet of Titchfield Street, The
See Pound, Ezra (Weston Loomis)

Pohl, Frederik 1919- .... CLC 18
See also CA 61-64; CAAS 1; CANR 11, 37;
DLB 8; MTCW; SATA 24

Poirier, Louis 1910-
See Gracq, Julien
See also CA 122; 126

Poitier, Sidney 1927- .... CLC 26
See also BW 1; CA 117

Polanski, Roman 1933- .... CLC 16
See also CA 77-80

Poliakoff, Stephen 1952- .... CLC 38
See also CA 106; DLB 13

Police, The
See Copeland, Stewart (Armstrong);
Summers, Andrew James; Sumner,
Gordon Matthew

Polidori, John William
1795-1821 .... NCLC 51
See also DLB 116

Pollitt, Katha 1949- .... CLC 28
See also CA 120; 122; MTCW

Pollock, (Mary) Sharon 1936- ...... CLC 50
See also CA 141; DLB 60

Polo, Marco 1254-1324 .... CMLC 15

Pomerance, Bernard 1940- .... CLC 13
See also CA 101; CANR 49

Ponge, Francis (Jean Gaston Alfred)
1899-1988 .... CLC 6, 18
See also CA 85-88; 126; CANR 40

Pontoppidan, Henrik 1857-1943 ... TCLC 29

Poole, Josephine .... CLC 17
See also Helyar, Jane Penelope Josephine
See also SAAS 2; SATA 5

Popa, Vasko 1922-1991 .... CLC 19
See also CA 112; 148

Pope, Alexander
1688-1744 ...... LC 3; DA; DAB; WLC
See also CDBLB 1660-1789; DLB 95, 101

Porter, Connie (Rose) 1959(?)- ..... CLC 70
See also BW 2; CA 142; SATA 81

Porter, Gene(va Grace) Stratton
1863(?)-1924 .... TCLC 21
See also CA 112

Porter, Katherine Anne
1890-1980 ...... CLC 1, 3, 7, 10, 13, 15,
27; DA; DAB; SSC 4
See also AITN 2; CA 1-4R; 101; CANR 1;
DLB 4, 9, 102; DLBD 12; DLBY 80;
MTCW; SATA 39; SATA-Obit 23

Porter, Peter (Neville Frederick)
1929- .... CLC 5, 13, 33
See also CA 85-88; DLB 40

Porter, William Sydney 1862-1910
See Henry, O.
See also CA 104; 131; CDALB 1865-1917;
DA; DAB; DLB 12, 78, 79; MTCW;
YABC 2

Portillo (y Pacheco), Jose Lopez
See Lopez Portillo (y Pacheco), Jose

Post, Melville Davisson
1869-1930 .... TCLC 39
See also CA 110

Potok, Chaim 1929- .... CLC 2, 7, 14, 26
See also AAYA 15; AITN 1, 2; CA 17-20R;
CANR 19, 35; DLB 28, 152; MTCW;
SATA 33

Potter, Beatrice
See Webb, (Martha) Beatrice (Potter)
See also MAICYA

Potter, Dennis (Christopher George)
1935-1994 .... CLC 58, 86
See also CA 107; 145; CANR 33; MTCW

Pound, Ezra (Weston Loomis)
1885-1972 ...... CLC 1, 2, 3, 4, 5, 7, 10,
13, 18, 34, 48, 50; DA; DAB; PC 4; WLC
See also CA 5-8R; 37-40R; CANR 40;
CDALB 1917-1929; DLB 4, 45, 63;
MTCW

Povod, Reinaldo 1959-1994 .... CLC 44
See also CA 136; 146

Powell, Adam Clayton, Jr.
1908-1972 .... CLC 89; BLC
See also BW 1; CA 102; 33-36R

Powell, Anthony (Dymoke)
1905- .... CLC 1, 3, 7, 9, 10, 31
See also CA 1-4R; CANR 1, 32;
CDBLB 1945-1960; DLB 15; MTCW

Powell, Dawn 1897-1965 .... CLC 66
See also CA 5-8R

Powell, Padgett 1952- .... CLC 34
See also CA 126

Powers, J(ames) F(arl)
1917- .... CLC 1, 4, 8, 57; SSC 4
See also CA 1-4R; CANR 2; DLB 130;
MTCW

Powers, John J(ames) 1945-
See Powers, John R.
See also CA 69-72

Powers, John R. .... CLC 66
See also Powers, John J(ames)

Pownall, David 1938-............ **CLC 10**
See also CA 89-92; CAAS 18; CANR 49;
DLB 14

Powys, John Cowper
1872-1963 .... **CLC 7, 9, 15, 46**
See also CA 85-88; DLB 15; MTCW

Powys, T(heodore) F(rancis)
1875-1953 .... **TCLC 9**
See also CA 106; DLB 36

Prager, Emily 1952-............. **CLC 56**

Pratt, E(dwin) J(ohn)
1883(?)-1964 .... **CLC 19**
See also CA 141; 93-96; DLB 92

Premchand.................... **TCLC 21**
See also Srivastava, Dhanpat Rai

Preussler, Otfried 1923-........... **CLC 17**
See also CA 77-80; SATA 24

Prevert, Jacques (Henri Marie)
1900-1977 .... **CLC 15**
See also CA 77-80; 69-72; CANR 29;
MTCW; SATA-Obit 30

Prevost, Abbe (Antoine Francois)
1697-1763 .... **LC 1**

Price, (Edward) Reynolds
1933- .... **CLC 3, 6, 13, 43, 50, 63**
See also CA 1-4R; CANR 1, 37; DLB 2

Price, Richard 1949- .... **CLC 6, 12**
See also CA 49-52; CANR 3; DLBY 81

Prichard, Katharine Susannah
1883-1969 .... **CLC 46**
See also CA 11-12; CANR 33; CAP 1;
MTCW; SATA 66

Priestley, J(ohn) B(oynton)
1894-1984 .... **CLC 2, 5, 9, 34**
See also CA 9-12R; 113; CANR 33;
CDBLB 1914-1945; DLB 10, 34, 77, 100,
139; DLBY 84; MTCW

Prince 1958(?)-.................. **CLC 35**

Prince, F(rank) T(empleton) 1912- .. **CLC 22**
See also CA 101; CANR 43; DLB 20

Prince Kropotkin
See Kropotkin, Peter (Alekseievich)

Prior, Matthew 1664-1721........... **LC 4**
See also DLB 95

Pritchard, William H(arrison)
1932- .... **CLC 34**
See also CA 65-68; CANR 23; DLB 111

Pritchett, V(ictor) S(awdon)
1900- .... **CLC 5, 13, 15, 41; SSC 14**
See also CA 61-64; CANR 31; DLB 15,
139; MTCW

Private 19022
See Manning, Frederic

Probst, Mark 1925- .... **CLC 59**
See also CA 130

Prokosch, Frederic 1908-1989.... **CLC 4, 48**
See also CA 73-76; 128; DLB 48

Prophet, The
See Dreiser, Theodore (Herman Albert)

Prose, Francine 1947-............. **CLC 45**
See also CA 109; 112; CANR 46

Proudhon
See Cunha, Euclides (Rodrigues Pimenta) da

Proulx, E. Annie 1935- .... **CLC 81**

Proust, (Valentin-Louis-George-Eugene-)
Marcel
1871-1922 .... **TCLC 7, 13, 33; DA;
DAB; WLC**
See also CA 104; 120; DLB 65; MTCW

Prowler, Harley
See Masters, Edgar Lee

Prus, Boleslaw 1845-1912 .... **TCLC 48**

Pryor, Richard (Franklin Lenox Thomas)
1940- .... **CLC 26**
See also CA 122

Przybyszewski, Stanislaw
1868-1927 .... **TCLC 36**
See also DLB 66

Pteleon
See Grieve, C(hristopher) M(urray)

Puckett, Lute
See Masters, Edgar Lee

Puig, Manuel
1932-1990 ... **CLC 3, 5, 10, 28, 65; HLC**
See also CA 45-48; CANR 2, 32; DLB 113;
HW; MTCW

Purdy, Al(fred Wellington)
1918- .... **CLC 3, 6, 14, 50**
See also CA 81-84; CAAS 17; CANR 42;
DLB 88

Purdy, James (Amos)
1923- .... **CLC 2, 4, 10, 28, 52**
See also CA 33-36R; CAAS 1; CANR 19;
DLB 2; MTCW

Pure, Simon
See Swinnerton, Frank Arthur

Pushkin, Alexander (Sergeyevich)
1799-1837 ..... **NCLC 3, 27; DA; DAB;
PC 10; WLC**
See also SATA 61

P'u Sung-ling 1640-1715 .... **LC 3**

Putnam, Arthur Lee
See Alger, Horatio, Jr.

Puzo, Mario 1920-......... **CLC 1, 2, 6, 36**
See also CA 65-68; CANR 4, 42; DLB 6;
MTCW

Pym, Barbara (Mary Crampton)
1913-1980 .... **CLC 13, 19, 37**
See also CA 13-14; 97-100; CANR 13, 34;
CAP 1; DLB 14; DLBY 87; MTCW

Pynchon, Thomas (Ruggles, Jr.)
1937- ..... **CLC 2, 3, 6, 9, 11, 18, 33, 62,
72; DA; DAB; SSC 14; WLC**
See also BEST 90:2; CA 17-20R; CANR 22,
46; DLB 2; MTCW

Qian Zhongshu
See Ch'ien Chung-shu

Qroll
See Dagerman, Stig (Halvard)

Quarrington, Paul (Lewis) 1953-.... **CLC 65**
See also CA 129

Quasimodo, Salvatore 1901-1968 ... **CLC 10**
See also CA 13-16; 25-28R; CAP 1;
DLB 114; MTCW

Queen, Ellery................... **CLC 3, 11**
See also Dannay, Frederic; Davidson,
Avram; Lee, Manfred B(ennington);
Sturgeon, Theodore (Hamilton); Vance,
John Holbrook

Queen, Ellery, Jr.
See Dannay, Frederic; Lee, Manfred
B(ennington)

Queneau, Raymond
1903-1976 .... **CLC 2, 5, 10, 42**
See also CA 77-80; 69-72; CANR 32;
DLB 72; MTCW

Quevedo, Francisco de 1580-1645.... **LC 23**

Quiller-Couch, Arthur Thomas
1863-1944 .... **TCLC 53**
See also CA 118; DLB 135, 153

Quin, Ann (Marie) 1936-1973....... **CLC 6**
See also CA 9-12R; 45-48; DLB 14

Quinn, Martin
See Smith, Martin Cruz

Quinn, Simon
See Smith, Martin Cruz

Quiroga, Horacio (Sylvestre)
1878-1937 .... **TCLC 20; HLC**
See also CA 117; 131; HW; MTCW

Quoirez, Francoise 1935-........... **CLC 9**
See also Sagan, Francoise
See also CA 49-52; CANR 6, 39; MTCW

Raabe, Wilhelm 1831-1910 .... **TCLC 45**
See also DLB 129

Rabe, David (William) 1940-... **CLC 4, 8, 33**
See also CA 85-88; CABS 3; DLB 7

Rabelais, Francois
1483-1553 ...... **LC 5; DA; DAB; WLC**

Rabinovitch, Sholem 1859-1916
See Aleichem, Sholom
See also CA 104

Racine, Jean 1639-1699....... **LC 28; DAB**

Radcliffe, Ann (Ward) 1764-1823 .. **NCLC 6**
See also DLB 39

Radiguet, Raymond 1903-1923 .... **TCLC 29**
See also DLB 65

Radnoti, Miklos 1909-1944 .... **TCLC 16**
See also CA 118

Rado, James 1939-............... **CLC 17**
See also CA 105

Radvanyi, Netty 1900-1983
See Seghers, Anna
See also CA 85-88; 110

Rae, Ben
See Griffiths, Trevor

Raeburn, John (Hay) 1941-....... **CLC 34**
See also CA 57-60

Ragni, Gerome 1942-1991 .... **CLC 17**
See also CA 105; 134

Rahv, Philip 1908-1973 .... **CLC 24**
See also Greenberg, Ivan
See also DLB 137

Raine, Craig 1944-............... **CLC 32**
See also CA 108; CANR 29; DLB 40

Raine, Kathleen (Jessie) 1908- ... **CLC 7, 45**
See also CA 85-88; CANR 46; DLB 20;
MTCW

Rainis, Janis 1865-1929.......... **TCLC 29**

Rakosi, Carl..................... **CLC 47**
See also Rawley, Callman
See also CAAS 5

Raleigh, Richard
   See Lovecraft, H(oward) P(hillips)

Raleigh, Sir Walter   1554(?)-1618 .... **LC 31**
   See also CDBLB Before 1660

Rallentando, H. P.
   See Sayers, Dorothy L(eigh)

Ramal, Walter
   See de la Mare, Walter (John)

Ramon, Juan
   See Jimenez (Mantecon), Juan Ramon

Ramos, Graciliano   1892-1953 ..... **TCLC 32**

Rampersad, Arnold   1941-.......... **CLC 44**
   See also BW 2; CA 127; 133; DLB 111

Rampling, Anne
   See Rice, Anne

Ramsay, Allan   1684(?)-1758 .... **LC 29**
   See also DLB 95

Ramuz, Charles-Ferdinand
   1878-1947 .... **TCLC 33**

Rand, Ayn
   1905-1982 ...... **CLC 3, 30, 44, 79; DA;**
   WLC
   See also AAYA 10; CA 13-16R; 105;
   CANR 27; MTCW

Randall, Dudley (Felker)
   1914- .... **CLC 1; BLC**
   See also BW 1; CA 25-28R; CANR 23;
   DLB 41

Randall, Robert
   See Silverberg, Robert

Ranger, Ken
   See Creasey, John

Ransom, John Crowe
   1888-1974 .... **CLC 2, 4, 5, 11, 24**
   See also CA 5-8R; 49-52; CANR 6, 34;
   DLB 45, 63; MTCW

Rao, Raja   1909- .... **CLC 25, 56**
   See also CA 73-76; MTCW

Raphael, Frederic (Michael)
   1931- .... **CLC 2, 14**
   See also CA 1-4R; CANR 1; DLB 14

Ratcliffe, James P.
   See Mencken, H(enry) L(ouis)

Rathbone, Julian   1935- .... **CLC 41**
   See also CA 101; CANR 34

Rattigan, Terence (Mervyn)
   1911-1977 .... **CLC 7**
   See also CA 85-88; 73-76;
   CDBLB 1945-1960; DLB 13; MTCW

Ratushinskaya, Irina   1954- .... **CLC 54**
   See also CA 129

Raven, Simon (Arthur Noel)
   1927- .... **CLC 14**
   See also CA 81-84

Rawley, Callman   1903-
   See Rakosi, Carl
   See also CA 21-24R; CANR 12, 32

Rawlings, Marjorie Kinnan
   1896-1953 .... **TCLC 4**
   See also CA 104; 137; DLB 9, 22, 102;
   JRDA; MAICYA; YABC 1

Ray, Satyajit   1921-1992........ **CLC 16, 76**
   See also CA 114; 137

Read, Herbert Edward   1893-1968.... **CLC 4**
   See also CA 85-88; 25-28R; DLB 20, 149

Read, Piers Paul   1941- ...... **CLC 4, 10, 25**
   See also CA 21-24R; CANR 38; DLB 14;
   SATA 21

Reade, Charles   1814-1884 .... **NCLC 2**
   See also DLB 21

Reade, Hamish
   See Gray, Simon (James Holliday)

Reading, Peter   1946- .... **CLC 47**
   See also CA 103; CANR 46; DLB 40

Reaney, James   1926- .... **CLC 13**
   See also CA 41-44R; CAAS 15; CANR 42;
   DLB 68; SATA 43

Rebreanu, Liviu   1885-1944 .... **TCLC 28**

Rechy, John (Francisco)
   1934-......... **CLC 1, 7, 14, 18; HLC**
   See also CA 5-8R; CAAS 4; CANR 6, 32;
   DLB 122; DLBY 82; HW

Redcam, Tom   1870-1933 .... **TCLC 25**

Reddin, Keith.................... **CLC 67**

Redgrove, Peter (William)
   1932- .... **CLC 6, 41**
   See also CA 1-4R; CANR 3, 39; DLB 40

Redmon, Anne.................. **CLC 22**
   See also Nightingale, Anne Redmon
   See also DLBY 86

Reed, Eliot
   See Ambler, Eric

Reed, Ishmael
   1938- ... **CLC 2, 3, 5, 6, 13, 32, 60; BLC**
   See also BW 2; CA 21-24R; CANR 25, 48;
   DLB 2, 5, 33; DLBD 8; MTCW

Reed, John (Silas)   1887-1920 ...... **TCLC 9**
   See also CA 106

Reed, Lou....................... **CLC 21**
   See also Firbank, Louis

Reeve, Clara   1729-1807........ **NCLC 19**
   See also DLB 39

Reich, Wilhelm   1897-1957....... **TCLC 57**

Reid, Christopher (John)   1949-..... **CLC 33**
   See also CA 140; DLB 40

Reid, Desmond
   See Moorcock, Michael (John)

Reid Banks, Lynne   1929-
   See Banks, Lynne Reid
   See also CA 1-4R; CANR 6, 22, 38;
   CLR 24; JRDA; MAICYA; SATA 22, 75

Reilly, William K.
   See Creasey, John

Reiner, Max
   See Caldwell, (Janet Miriam) Taylor
   (Holland)

Reis, Ricardo
   See Pessoa, Fernando (Antonio Nogueira)

Remarque, Erich Maria
   1898-1970 .... **CLC 21; DA; DAB**
   See also CA 77-80; 29-32R; DLB 56;
   MTCW

Remizov, A.
   See Remizov, Aleksei (Mikhailovich)

Remizov, A. M.
   See Remizov, Aleksei (Mikhailovich)

Remizov, Aleksei (Mikhailovich)
   1877-1957 .... **TCLC 27**
   See also CA 125; 133

Renan, Joseph Ernest
   1823-1892 .... **NCLC 26**

Renard, Jules   1864-1910 .... **TCLC 17**
   See also CA 117

Renault, Mary.............. **CLC 3, 11, 17**
   See also Challans, Mary
   See also DLBY 83

Rendell, Ruth (Barbara)   1930- .. **CLC 28, 48**
   See also Vine, Barbara
   See also CA 109; CANR 32; DLB 87;
   MTCW

Renoir, Jean   1894-1979 .... **CLC 20**
   See also CA 129; 85-88

Resnais, Alain   1922-............. **CLC 16**

Reverdy, Pierre   1889-1960 .... **CLC 53**
   See also CA 97-100; 89-92

Rexroth, Kenneth
   1905-1982 ...... **CLC 1, 2, 6, 11, 22, 49**
   See also CA 5-8R; 107; CANR 14, 34;
   CDALB 1941-1968; DLB 16, 48;
   DLBY 82; MTCW

Reyes, Alfonso   1889-1959 .... **TCLC 33**
   See also CA 131; HW

Reyes y Basoalto, Ricardo Eliecer Neftali
   See Neruda, Pablo

Reymont, Wladyslaw (Stanislaw)
   1868(?)-1925 .... **TCLC 5**
   See also CA 104

Reynolds, Jonathan   1942- .... **CLC 6, 38**
   See also CA 65-68; CANR 28

Reynolds, Joshua   1723-1792....... **LC 15**
   See also DLB 104

Reynolds, Michael Shane   1937- .... **CLC 44**
   See also CA 65-68; CANR 9

Reznikoff, Charles   1894-1976 .... **CLC 9**
   See also CA 33-36; 61-64; CAP 2; DLB 28,
   45

Rezzori (d'Arezzo), Gregor von
   1914- .... **CLC 25**
   See also CA 122; 136

Rhine, Richard
   See Silverstein, Alvin

Rhodes, Eugene Manlove
   1869-1934 .... **TCLC 53**

R'hoone
   See Balzac, Honore de

Rhys, Jean
   1890(?)-1979 .... **CLC 2, 4, 6, 14, 19, 51;**
   SSC 21
   See also CA 25-28R; 85-88; CANR 35;
   CDBLB 1945-1960; DLB 36, 117; MTCW

Ribeiro, Darcy   1922- .... **CLC 34**
   See also CA 33-36R

Ribeiro, Joao Ubaldo (Osorio Pimentel)
   1941- .... **CLC 10, 67**
   See also CA 81-84

Ribman, Ronald (Burt)   1932- .... **CLC 7**
   See also CA 21-24R; CANR 46

Ricci, Nino   1959-................ **CLC 70**
   See also CA 137

Rice, Anne 1941- . . . . CLC 41
See also AAYA 9; BEST 89:2; CA 65-68;
CANR 12, 36

Rice, Elmer (Leopold)
1892-1967 . . . . CLC 7, 49
See also CA 21-22; 25-28R; CAP 2; DLB 4,
7; MTCW

Rice, Tim(othy Miles Bindon)
1944- . . . . CLC 21
See also CA 103; CANR 46

Rich, Adrienne (Cecile)
1929- . . . . CLC 3, 6, 7, 11, 18, 36, 73, 76;
PC 5
See also CA 9-12R; CANR 20; DLB 5, 67;
MTCW

Rich, Barbara
See Graves, Robert (von Ranke)

Rich, Robert
See Trumbo, Dalton

Richard, Keith . . . . CLC 17
See also Richards, Keith

Richards, David Adams 1950- . . . . . . CLC 59
See also CA 93-96; DLB 53

Richards, I(vor) A(rmstrong)
1893-1979 . . . . CLC 14, 24
See also CA 41-44R; 89-92; CANR 34;
DLB 27

Richards, Keith 1943-
See Richard, Keith
See also CA 107

Richardson, Anne
See Roiphe, Anne (Richardson)

Richardson, Dorothy Miller
1873-1957 . . . . TCLC 3
See also CA 104; DLB 36

Richardson, Ethel Florence (Lindesay)
1870-1946
See Richardson, Henry Handel
See also CA 105

Richardson, Henry Handel . . . . TCLC 4
See also Richardson, Ethel Florence
(Lindesay)

Richardson, Samuel
1689-1761 . . . . . . LC 1; DA; DAB; WLC
See also CDBLB 1660-1789; DLB 39

Richler, Mordecai
1931- . . . . CLC 3, 5, 9, 13, 18, 46, 70
See also AITN 1; CA 65-68; CANR 31;
CLR 17; DLB 53; MAICYA; MTCW;
SATA 44; SATA-Brief 27

Richter, Conrad (Michael)
1890-1968 . . . . CLC 30
See also CA 5-8R; 25-28R; CANR 23;
DLB 9; MTCW; SATA 3

Ricostranza, Tom
See Ellis, Trey

Riddell, J. H. 1832-1906 . . . . TCLC 40

Riding, Laura . . . . CLC 3, 7
See also Jackson, Laura (Riding)

Riefenstahl, Berta Helene Amalia 1902-
See Riefenstahl, Leni
See also CA 108

Riefenstahl, Leni . . . . CLC 16
See also Riefenstahl, Berta Helene Amalia

Riffe, Ernest
See Bergman, (Ernst) Ingmar

Riggs, (Rolla) Lynn 1899-1954 . . . . TCLC 56
See also CA 144; NNAL

Riley, James Whitcomb
1849-1916 . . . . TCLC 51
See also CA 118; 137; MAICYA; SATA 17

Riley, Tex
See Creasey, John

Rilke, Rainer Maria
1875-1926 . . . . TCLC 1, 6, 19; PC 2
See also CA 104; 132; DLB 81; MTCW

Rimbaud, (Jean Nicolas) Arthur
1854-1891 . . . . . NCLC 4, 35; DA; DAB;
PC 3; WLC

Rinehart, Mary Roberts
1876-1958 . . . . TCLC 52
See also CA 108

Ringmaster, The
See Mencken, H(enry) L(ouis)

Ringwood, Gwen(dolyn Margaret) Pharis
1910-1984 . . . . CLC 48
See also CA 148; 112; DLB 88

Rio, Michel 19(?)- . . . . CLC 43

Ritsos, Giannes
See Ritsos, Yannis

Ritsos, Yannis 1909-1990 . . . . . CLC 6, 13, 31
See also CA 77-80; 133; CANR 39; MTCW

Ritter, Erika 1948(?)- . . . . CLC 52

Rivera, Jose Eustasio 1889-1928 . . . TCLC 35
See also HW

Rivers, Conrad Kent 1933-1968 . . . . . . CLC 1
See also BW 1; CA 85-88; DLB 41

Rivers, Elfrida
See Bradley, Marion Zimmer

Riverside, John
See Heinlein, Robert A(nson)

Rizal, Jose 1861-1896 . . . . NCLC 27

Roa Bastos, Augusto (Antonio)
1917- . . . . CLC 45; HLC
See also CA 131; DLB 113; HW

Robbe-Grillet, Alain
1922- . . . . . . CLC 1, 2, 4, 6, 8, 10, 14, 43
See also CA 9-12R; CANR 33; DLB 83;
MTCW

Robbins, Harold 1916- . . . . CLC 5
See also CA 73-76; CANR 26; MTCW

Robbins, Thomas Eugene 1936-
See Robbins, Tom
See also CA 81-84; CANR 29; MTCW

Robbins, Tom . . . . CLC 9, 32, 64
See also Robbins, Thomas Eugene
See also BEST 90:3; DLBY 80

Robbins, Trina 1938- . . . . CLC 21
See also CA 128

Roberts, Charles G(eorge) D(ouglas)
1860-1943 . . . . TCLC 8
See also CA 105; CLR 33; DLB 92;
SATA-Brief 29

Roberts, Kate 1891-1985 . . . . CLC 15
See also CA 107; 116

Roberts, Keith (John Kingston)
1935- . . . . CLC 14
See also CA 25-28R; CANR 46

Roberts, Kenneth (Lewis)
1885-1957 . . . . TCLC 23
See also CA 109; DLB 9

Roberts, Michele (B.) 1949- . . . . CLC 48
See also CA 115

Robertson, Ellis
See Ellison, Harlan (Jay); Silverberg, Robert

Robertson, Thomas William
1829-1871 . . . . NCLC 35

Robinson, Edwin Arlington
1869-1935 . . . . TCLC 5; DA; PC 1
See also CA 104; 133; CDALB 1865-1917;
DLB 54; MTCW

Robinson, Henry Crabb
1775-1867 . . . . NCLC 15
See also DLB 107

Robinson, Jill 1936- . . . . CLC 10
See also CA 102

Robinson, Kim Stanley 1952- . . . . . . CLC 34
See also CA 126

Robinson, Lloyd
See Silverberg, Robert

Robinson, Marilynne 1944- . . . . CLC 25
See also CA 116

Robinson, Smokey . . . . CLC 21
See also Robinson, William, Jr.

Robinson, William, Jr. 1940-
See Robinson, Smokey
See also CA 116

Robison, Mary 1949- . . . . CLC 42
See also CA 113; 116; DLB 130

Rod, Edouard 1857-1910 . . . . TCLC 52

Roddenberry, Eugene Wesley 1921-1991
See Roddenberry, Gene
See also CA 110; 135; CANR 37; SATA 45;
SATA-Obit 69

Roddenberry, Gene . . . . CLC 17
See also Roddenberry, Eugene Wesley
See also AAYA 5; SATA-Obit 69

Rodgers, Mary 1931- . . . . CLC 12
See also CA 49-52; CANR 8; CLR 20;
JRDA; MAICYA; SATA 8

Rodgers, W(illiam) R(obert)
1909-1969 . . . . CLC 7
See also CA 85-88; DLB 20

Rodman, Eric
See Silverberg, Robert

Rodman, Howard 1920(?)-1985 . . . . . CLC 65
See also CA 118

Rodman, Maia
See Wojciechowska, Maia (Teresa)

Rodriguez, Claudio 1934- . . . . CLC 10
See also DLB 134

Roelvaag, O(le) E(dvart)
1876-1931 . . . . TCLC 17
See also CA 117; DLB 9

Roethke, Theodore (Huebner)
1908-1963 . . . . . . CLC 1, 3, 8, 11, 19, 46
See also CA 81-84; CABS 2;
CDALB 1941-1968; DLB 5; MTCW

Rogers, Thomas Hunton 1927- . . . . . CLC 57
See also CA 89-92

Rogers, Will(iam Penn Adair)
1879-1935 .... TCLC 8
See also CA 105; 144; DLB 11; NNAL

Rogin, Gilbert 1929-............. CLC 18
See also CA 65-68; CANR 15

Rohan, Koda .... TCLC 22
See also Koda Shigeyuki

Rohmer, Eric.................... CLC 16
See also Scherer, Jean-Marie Maurice

Rohmer, Sax .... TCLC 28
See also Ward, Arthur Henry Sarsfield
See also DLB 70

Roiphe, Anne (Richardson)
1935- .... CLC 3, 9
See also CA 89-92; CANR 45; DLBY 80

Rojas, Fernando de 1465-1541 ...... LC 23

Rolfe, Frederick (William Serafino Austin
Lewis Mary) 1860-1913...... TCLC 12
See also CA 107; DLB 34, 156

Rolland, Romain 1866-1944...... TCLC 23
See also CA 118; DLB 65

Rolvaag, O(le) E(dvart)
See Roelvaag, O(le) E(dvart)

Romain Arnaud, Saint
See Aragon, Louis

Romains, Jules 1885-1972 .... CLC 7
See also CA 85-88; CANR 34; DLB 65;
MTCW

Romero, Jose Ruben 1890-1952 ... TCLC 14
See also CA 114; 131; HW

Ronsard, Pierre de
1524-1585 .... LC 6; PC 11

Rooke, Leon 1934-............ CLC 25, 34
See also CA 25-28R; CANR 23

Roper, William 1498-1578.......... LC 10

Roquelaure, A. N.
See Rice, Anne

Rosa, Joao Guimaraes 1908-1967 ... CLC 23
See also CA 89-92; DLB 113

Rose, Wendy 1948-......... CLC 85; PC 13
See also CA 53-56; CANR 5; NNAL;
SATA 12

Rosen, Richard (Dean) 1949-....... CLC 39
See also CA 77-80

Rosenberg, Isaac 1890-1918....... TCLC 12
See also CA 107; DLB 20

Rosenblatt, Joe .... CLC 15
See also Rosenblatt, Joseph

Rosenblatt, Joseph 1933-
See Rosenblatt, Joe
See also CA 89-92

Rosenfeld, Samuel 1896-1963
See Tzara, Tristan
See also CA 89-92

Rosenthal, M(acha) L(ouis) 1917-... CLC 28
See also CA 1-4R; CAAS 6; CANR 4;
DLB 5; SATA 59

Ross, Barnaby
See Dannay, Frederic

Ross, Bernard L.
See Follett, Ken(neth Martin)

Ross, J. H.
See Lawrence, T(homas) E(dward)

Ross, Martin
See Martin, Violet Florence
See also DLB 135

Ross, (James) Sinclair 1908-....... CLC 13
See also CA 73-76; DLB 88

Rossetti, Christina (Georgina)
1830-1894 ..... NCLC 2, 50; DA; DAB;
PC 7; WLC
See also DLB 35; MAICYA; SATA 20

Rossetti, Dante Gabriel
1828-1882 ... NCLC 4; DA; DAB; WLC
See also CDBLB 1832-1890; DLB 35

Rossner, Judith (Perelman)
1935-................... CLC 6, 9, 29
See also AITN 2; BEST 90:3; CA 17-20R;
CANR 18; DLB 6; MTCW

Rostand, Edmond (Eugene Alexis)
1868-1918 ...... TCLC 6, 37; DA; DAB
See also CA 104; 126; MTCW

Roth, Henry 1906-........... CLC 2, 6, 11
See also CA 11-12; CANR 38; CAP 1;
DLB 28; MTCW

Roth, Joseph 1894-1939......... TCLC 33
See also DLB 85

Roth, Philip (Milton)
1933-...... CLC 1, 2, 3, 4, 6, 9, 15, 22,
31, 47, 66, 86; DA; DAB; WLC
See also BEST 90:3; CA 1-4R; CANR 1, 22,
36; CDALB 1968-1988; DLB 2, 28;
DLBY 82; MTCW

Rothenberg, Jerome 1931-....... CLC 6, 57
See also CA 45-48; CANR 1; DLB 5

Roumain, Jacques (Jean Baptiste)
1907-1944 .... TCLC 19; BLC
See also BW 1; CA 117; 125

Rourke, Constance (Mayfield)
1885-1941 .... TCLC 12
See also CA 107; YABC 1

Rousseau, Jean-Baptiste 1671-1741 ... LC 9

Rousseau, Jean-Jacques
1712-1778 ..... LC 14; DA; DAB; WLC

Roussel, Raymond 1877-1933 ..... TCLC 20
See also CA 117

Rovit, Earl (Herbert) 1927-........ CLC 7
See also CA 5-8R; CANR 12

Rowe, Nicholas 1674-1718........... LC 8
See also DLB 84

Rowley, Ames Dorrance
See Lovecraft, H(oward) P(hillips)

Rowson, Susanna Haswell
1762(?)-1824 .... NCLC 5
See also DLB 37

Roy, Gabrielle
1909-1983 .... CLC 10, 14; DAB
See also CA 53-56; 110; CANR 5; DLB 68;
MTCW

Rozewicz, Tadeusz 1921-........ CLC 9, 23
See also CA 108; CANR 36; MTCW

Ruark, Gibbons 1941- .... CLC 3
See also CA 33-36R; CANR 14, 31;
DLB 120

Rubens, Bernice (Ruth) 1923-... CLC 19, 31
See also CA 25-28R; CANR 33; DLB 14;
MTCW

Rudkin, (James) David 1936- ...... CLC 14
See also CA 89-92; DLB 13

Rudnik, Raphael 1933-............. CLC 7
See also CA 29-32R

Ruffian, M.
See Hasek, Jaroslav (Matej Frantisek)

Ruiz, Jose Martinez............... CLC 11
See also Martinez Ruiz, Jose

Rukeyser, Muriel
1913-1980 .... CLC 6, 10, 15, 27; PC 12
See also CA 5-8R; 93-96; CANR 26;
DLB 48; MTCW; SATA-Obit 22

Rule, Jane (Vance) 1931-.......... CLC 27
See also CA 25-28R; CAAS 18; CANR 12;
DLB 60

Rulfo, Juan 1918-1986.... CLC 8, 80; HLC
See also CA 85-88; 118; CANR 26;
DLB 113; HW; MTCW

Runeberg, Johan 1804-1877...... NCLC 41

Runyon, (Alfred) Damon
1884(?)-1946 .... TCLC 10
See also CA 107; DLB 11, 86

Rush, Norman 1933-.............. CLC 44
See also CA 121; 126

Rushdie, (Ahmed) Salman
1947- .... CLC 23, 31, 55; DAB
See also BEST 89:3; CA 108; 111;
CANR 33; MTCW

Rushforth, Peter (Scott) 1945- ..... CLC 19
See also CA 101

Ruskin, John 1819-1900......... TCLC 20
See also CA 114; 129; CDBLB 1832-1890;
DLB 55; SATA 24

Russ, Joanna 1937-.............. CLC 15
See also CA 25-28R; CANR 11, 31; DLB 8;
MTCW

Russell, George William 1867-1935
See A. E.
See also CA 104; CDBLB 1890-1914

Russell, (Henry) Ken(neth Alfred)
1927-........................ CLC 16
See also CA 105

Russell, Willy 1947-.............. CLC 60

Rutherford, Mark .... TCLC 25
See also White, William Hale
See also DLB 18

Ruyslinck, Ward 1929-............ CLC 14
See also Belser, Reimond Karel Maria de

Ryan, Cornelius (John) 1920-1974 ... CLC 7
See also CA 69-72; 53-56; CANR 38

Ryan, Michael 1946- .... CLC 65
See also CA 49-52; DLBY 82

Rybakov, Anatoli (Naumovich)
1911-..................... CLC 23, 53
See also CA 126; 135; SATA 79

Ryder, Jonathan
See Ludlum, Robert

Ryga, George 1932-1987 .... CLC 14
See also CA 101; 124; CANR 43; DLB 60

S. S.
See Sassoon, Siegfried (Lorraine)

Saba, Umberto 1883-1957 .... TCLC 33
See also CA 144; DLB 114

Sabatini, Rafael 1875-1950 .... TCLC 47

Shone, Patric
   See Hanley, James

Shreve, Susan Richards   1939-...... **CLC 23**
   See also CA 49-52; CAAS 5; CANR 5, 38;
      MAICYA; SATA 46; SATA-Brief 41

Shue, Larry   1946-1985............. **CLC 52**
   See also CA 145; 117

Shu-Jen, Chou   1881-1936
   See Lu Hsun
   See also CA 104

Shulman, Alix Kates   1932-...... **CLC 2, 10**
   See also CA 29-32R; CANR 43; SATA 7

Shuster, Joe   1914-............... **CLC 21**

Shute, Nevil..................... **CLC 30**
   See also Norway, Nevil Shute

Shuttle, Penelope (Diane)   1947-..... **CLC 7**
   See also CA 93-96; CANR 39; DLB 14, 40

Sidney, Mary   1561-1621.......... **LC 19**

Sidney, Sir Philip
   1554-1586.......... **LC 19; DA; DAB**
   See also CDBLB Before 1660

Siegel, Jerome   1914-............. **CLC 21**
   See also CA 116

Siegel, Jerry
   See Siegel, Jerome

Sienkiewicz, Henryk (Adam Alexander Pius)
   1846-1916.................... **TCLC 3**
   See also CA 104; 134

Sierra, Gregorio Martinez
   See Martinez Sierra, Gregorio

Sierra, Maria (de la O'LeJarraga) Martinez
   See Martinez Sierra, Maria (de la
      O'LeJarraga)

Sigal, Clancy   1926-................ **CLC 7**
   See also CA 1-4R

Sigourney, Lydia Howard (Huntley)
   1791-1865................... **NCLC 21**
   See also DLD 1, 42, 73

Siguenza y Gongora, Carlos de
   1645-1700.................... **LC 8**

Sigurjonsson, Johann   1880-1919... **TCLC 27**

Sikelianos, Angelos   1884-1951.... **TCLC 39**

Silkin, Jon   1930-............. **CLC 2, 6, 43**
   See also CA 5-8R; CAAS 5; DLB 27

Silko, Leslie (Marmon)
   1948-................. **CLC 23, 74; DA**
   See also AAYA 14; CA 115; 122;
      CANR 45; DLB 143; NNAL

Sillanpaa, Frans Eemil   1888-1964... **CLC 19**
   See also CA 129; 93-96; MTCW

Sillitoe, Alan
   1928-......... **CLC 1, 3, 6, 10, 19, 57**
   See also AITN 1; CA 9-12R; CAAS 2;
      CANR 8, 26; CDBLB 1960 to Present;
      DLB 14, 139; MTCW; SATA 61

Silone, Ignazio   1900-1978.......... **CLC 4**
   See also CA 25-28; 81-84; CANR 34;
      CAP 2; MTCW

Silver, Joan Micklin   1935-........ **CLC 20**
   See also CA 114; 121

Silver, Nicholas
   See Faust, Frederick (Schiller)

Silverberg, Robert   1935-.......... **CLC 7**
   See also CA 1-4R; CAAS 3; CANR 1, 20,
      36; DLB 8; MAICYA; MTCW; SATA 13

Silverstein, Alvin   1933-........... **CLC 17**
   See also CA 49-52; CANR 2; CLR 25;
      JRDA; MAICYA; SATA 8, 69

Silverstein, Virginia B(arbara Opshelor)
   1937-...................... **CLC 17**
   See also CA 49-52; CANR 2; CLR 25;
      JRDA; MAICYA; SATA 8, 69

Sim, Georges
   See Simenon, Georges (Jacques Christian)

Simak, Clifford D(onald)
   1904-1988.................. **CLC 1, 55**
   See also CA 1-4R; 125; CANR 1, 35;
      DLB 8; MTCW; SATA-Obit 56

Simenon, Georges (Jacques Christian)
   1903-1989....... **CLC 1, 2, 3, 8, 18, 47**
   See also CA 85-88; 129; CANR 35;
      DLB 72; DLBY 89; MTCW

Simic, Charles   1938-... **CLC 6, 9, 22, 49, 68**
   See also CA 29-32R; CAAS 4; CANR 12,
      33; DLB 105

Simmons, Charles (Paul)   1924-..... **CLC 57**
   See also CA 89-92

Simmons, Dan   1948-............. **CLC 44**
   See also CA 138

Simmons, James (Stewart Alexander)
   1933-...................... **CLC 43**
   See also CA 105; CAAS 21; DLB 40

Simms, William Gilmore
   1806-1870.................. **NCLC 3**
   See also DLB 3, 30, 59, 73

Simon, Carly   1945-............... **CLC 26**
   See also CA 105

Simon, Claude   1913-...... **CLC 4, 9, 15, 39**
   See also CA 89-92; CANR 33; DLB 83;
      MTCW

Simon, (Marvin) Neil
   1927-........... **CLC 6, 11, 31, 39, 70**
   See also AITN 1; CA 21-24R; CANR 26;
      DLB 7; MTCW

Simon, Paul   1942(?)-.............. **CLC 17**
   See also CA 116

Simonon, Paul   1956(?)-........... **CLC 30**

Simpson, Harriette
   See Arnow, Harriette (Louisa) Simpson

Simpson, Louis (Aston Marantz)
   1923-................. **CLC 4, 7, 9, 32**
   See also CA 1-4R; CAAS 4; CANR 1;
      DLB 5; MTCW

Simpson, Mona (Elizabeth)   1957-... **CLC 44**
   See also CA 122; 135

Simpson, N(orman) F(rederick)
   1919-...................... **CLC 29**
   See also CA 13-16R; DLB 13

Sinclair, Andrew (Annandale)
   1935-...................... **CLC 2, 14**
   See also CA 9-12R; CAAS 5; CANR 14, 38;
      DLB 14; MTCW

Sinclair, Emil
   See Hesse, Hermann

Sinclair, Iain   1943-.............. **CLC 76**
   See also CA 132

Sinclair, Iain MacGregor
   See Sinclair, Iain

Sinclair, Mary Amelia St. Clair   1865(?)-1946
   See Sinclair, May
   See also CA 104

Sinclair, May.................. **TCLC 3, 11**
   See also Sinclair, Mary Amelia St. Clair
   See also DLB 36, 135

Sinclair, Upton (Beall)
   1878-1968...... **CLC 1, 11, 15, 63; DA;**
                                    DAB; WLC
   See also CA 5-8R; 25-28R; CANR 7;
      CDALB 1929-1941; DLB 9; MTCW;
      SATA 9

Singer, Isaac
   See Singer, Isaac Bashevis

Singer, Isaac Bashevis
   1904-1991.... **CLC 1, 3, 6, 9, 11, 15, 23,**
              38, 69; DA; DAB; SSC 3; WLC
   See also AITN 1, 2; CA 1-4R; 134;
      CANR 1, 39; CDALB 1941-1968; CLR 1;
      DLB 6, 28, 52; DLBY 91; JRDA;
      MAICYA; MTCW; SATA 3, 27;
      SATA-Obit 68

Singer, Israel Joshua   1893-1944... **TCLC 33**

Singh, Khushwant   1915-........... **CLC 11**
   See also CA 9-12R; CAAS 9; CANR 6

Sinjohn, John
   See Galsworthy, John

Sinyavsky, Andrei (Donatevich)
   1925-...................... **CLC 8**
   See also CA 85-88

Sirin, V.
   See Nabokov, Vladimir (Vladimirovich)

Sissman, L(ouis) E(dward)
   1928-1976.................. **CLC 9, 18**
   See also CA 21-24R; 65-68; CANR 13;
      DLB 5

Sisson, C(harles) H(ubert)   1914-..... **CLC 8**
   See also CA 1-4R; CAAS 3; CANR 3, 48;
      DLB 27

Sitwell, Dame Edith
   1887-1964......... **CLC 2, 9, 67; PC 3**
   See also CA 9-12R; CANR 35;
      CDBLB 1945-1960; DLB 20; MTCW

Sjoewall, Maj   1935-............... **CLC 7**
   See also CA 65-68

Sjowall, Maj
   See Sjoewall, Maj

Skelton, Robin   1925-............. **CLC 13**
   See also AITN 2; CA 5-8R; CAAS 5;
      CANR 28; DLB 27, 53

Skolimowski, Jerzy   1938-......... **CLC 20**
   See also CA 128

Skram, Amalie (Bertha)
   1847-1905.................. **TCLC 25**

Skvorecky, Josef (Vaclav)
   1924-................. **CLC 15, 39, 69**
   See also CA 61-64; CAAS 1; CANR 10, 34;
      MTCW

Slade, Bernard................. **CLC 11, 46**
   See also Newbound, Bernard Slade
   See also CAAS 9; DLB 53

Slaughter, Carolyn   1946-.......... **CLC 56**
   See also CA 85-88

Slaughter, Frank G(ill) 1908- . . . . . . CLC 29
See also AITN 2; CA 5-8R; CANR 5

Slavitt, David R(ytman) 1935-. . . . CLC 5, 14
See also CA 21-24R; CAAS 3; CANR 41;
DLB 5, 6

Slesinger, Tess 1905-1945 . . . . TCLC 10
See also CA 107; DLB 102

Slessor, Kenneth 1901-1971. . . . . . . CLC 14
See also CA 102; 89-92

Slowacki, Juliusz 1809-1849 . . . . . NCLC 15

Smart, Christopher
1722-1771 . . . . LC 3; PC 13
See also DLB 109

Smart, Elizabeth 1913-1986. . . . . . . CLC 54
See also CA 81-84; 118; DLB 88

Smiley, Jane (Graves) 1949- . . . . CLC 53, 76
See also CA 104; CANR 30

Smith, A(rthur) J(ames) M(arshall)
1902-1980 . . . . CLC 15
See also CA 1-4R; 102; CANR 4; DLB 88

Smith, Anna Deavere 1950-. . . . . . . CLC 86
See also CA 133

Smith, Betty (Wehner) 1896-1972. . . CLC 19
See also CA 5-8R; 33-36R; DLBY 82;
SATA 6

Smith, Charlotte (Turner)
1749-1806 . . . . NCLC 23
See also DLB 39, 109

Smith, Clark Ashton 1893-1961 . . . . CLC 43
See also CA 143

Smith, Dave. . . . . CLC 22, 42
See also Smith, David (Jeddie)
See also CAAS 7; DLB 5

Smith, David (Jeddie) 1942-
See Smith, Dave
See also CA 49-52; CANR 1

Smith, Florence Margaret 1902-1971
See Smith, Stevie
See also CA 17-18; 29-32R; CANR 35;
CAP 2; MTCW

Smith, Iain Crichton 1928- . . . . CLC 64
See also CA 21-24R; DLB 40, 139

Smith, John 1580(?)-1631 . . . . LC 9

Smith, Johnston
See Crane, Stephen (Townley)

Smith, Lee 1944-. . . . . CLC 25, 73
See also CA 114; 119; CANR 46; DLB 143;
DLBY 83

Smith, Martin
See Smith, Martin Cruz

Smith, Martin Cruz 1942-. . . . . CLC 25
See also BEST 89:4; CA 85-88; CANR 6,
23, 43; NNAL

Smith, Mary-Ann Tirone 1944-. . . . . CLC 39
See also CA 118; 136

Smith, Patti 1946- . . . . CLC 12
See also CA 93-96

Smith, Pauline (Urmson)
1882-1959 . . . . TCLC 25

Smith, Rosamond
See Oates, Joyce Carol

Smith, Sheila Kaye
See Kaye-Smith, Sheila

Smith, Stevie . . . . CLC 3, 8, 25, 44; PC 12
See also Smith, Florence Margaret
See also DLB 20

Smith, Wilbur (Addison) 1933-. . . . . CLC 33
See also CA 13-16R; CANR 7, 46; MTCW

Smith, William Jay 1918- . . . . CLC 6
See also CA 5-8R; CANR 44; DLB 5;
MAICYA; SATA 2, 68

Smith, Woodrow Wilson
See Kuttner, Henry

Smolenskin, Peretz 1842-1885. . . . NCLC 30

Smollett, Tobias (George) 1721-1771 . . LC 2
See also CDBLB 1660-1789; DLB 39, 104

Snodgrass, W(illiam) D(e Witt)
1926- . . . . CLC 2, 6, 10, 18, 68
See also CA 1-4R; CANR 6, 36; DLB 5;
MTCW

Snow, C(harles) P(ercy)
1905-1980 . . . . . . CLC 1, 4, 6, 9, 13, 19
See also CA 5-8R; 101; CANR 28;
CDBLB 1945-1960; DLB 15, 77; MTCW

Snow, Frances Compton
See Adams, Henry (Brooks)

Snyder, Gary (Sherman)
1930- . . . . CLC 1, 2, 5, 9, 32
See also CA 17-20R; CANR 30; DLB 5, 16

Snyder, Zilpha Keatley 1927- . . . . . . CLC 17
See also AAYA 15; CA 9-12R; CANR 38;
CLR 31; JRDA; MAICYA; SAAS 2;
SATA 1, 28, 75

Soares, Bernardo
See Pessoa, Fernando (Antonio Nogueira)

Sobh, A.
See Shamlu, Ahmad

Sobol, Joshua. . . . . CLC 60

Soderberg, Hjalmar 1869-1941 . . . . TCLC 39

Sodergran, Edith (Irene)
See Soedergran, Edith (Irene)

Soedergran, Edith (Irene)
1892-1923 . . . . TCLC 31

Softly, Edgar
See Lovecraft, H(oward) P(hillips)

Softly, Edward
See Lovecraft, H(oward) P(hillips)

Sokolov, Raymond 1941-. . . . . CLC 7
See also CA 85-88

Solo, Jay
See Ellison, Harlan (Jay)

Sologub, Fyodor . . . . TCLC 9
See also Teternikov, Fyodor Kuzmich

Solomons, Ikey Esquir
See Thackeray, William Makepeace

Solomos, Dionysios 1798-1857 . . . NCLC 15

Solwoska, Mara
See French, Marilyn

Solzhenitsyn, Aleksandr I(sayevich)
1918- . . . . . . CLC 1, 2, 4, 7, 9, 10, 18, 26,
34, 78; DA; DAB; WLC
See also AITN 1; CA 69-72; CANR 40;
MTCW

Somers, Jane
See Lessing, Doris (May)

Somerville, Edith 1858-1949 . . . . . . TCLC 51
See also DLB 135

Somerville & Ross
See Martin, Violet Florence; Somerville,
Edith

Sommer, Scott 1951- . . . . CLC 25
See also CA 106

Sondheim, Stephen (Joshua)
1930- . . . . CLC 30, 39
See also AAYA 11; CA 103; CANR 47

Sontag, Susan 1933-. . . CLC 1, 2, 10, 13, 31
See also CA 17-20R; CANR 25; DLB 2, 67;
MTCW

Sophocles
496(?)B.C.-406(?)B.C. . . . . . CMLC 2; DA;
DAB; DC 1

Sordello 1189-1269. . . . . CMLC 15

Sorel, Julia
See Drexler, Rosalyn

Sorrentino, Gilbert
1929- . . . . CLC 3, 7, 14, 22, 40
See also CA 77-80; CANR 14, 33; DLB 5;
DLBY 80

Soto, Gary 1952-. . . . . CLC 32, 80; HLC
See also AAYA 10; CA 119; 125; CLR 38;
DLB 82; HW; JRDA; SATA 80

Soupault, Philippe 1897-1990 . . . . . CLC 68
See also CA 116; 147; 131

Souster, (Holmes) Raymond
1921- . . . . CLC 5, 14
See also CA 13-16R; CAAS 14; CANR 13,
29; DLB 88; SATA 63

Southern, Terry 1926- . . . . CLC 7
See also CA 1-4R; CANR 1; DLB 2

Southey, Robert 1774-1843 . . . . NCLC 8
See also DLB 93, 107, 142; SATA 54

Southworth, Emma Dorothy Eliza Nevitte
1819-1899 . . . . NCLC 26

Souza, Ernest
See Scott, Evelyn

Soyinka, Wole
1934- . . . . CLC 3, 5, 14, 36, 44; BLC;
DA; DAB; DC 2; WLC
See also BW 2; CA 13-16R; CANR 27, 39;
DLB 125; MTCW

Spackman, W(illiam) M(ode)
1905-1990 . . . . CLC 46
See also CA 81-84; 132

Spacks, Barry 1931-. . . . . CLC 14
See also CA 29-32R; CANR 33; DLB 105

Spanidou, Irini 1946- . . . . CLC 44

Spark, Muriel (Sarah)
1918- . . . . CLC 2, 3, 5, 8, 13, 18, 40;
DAB; SSC 10
See also CA 5-8R; CANR 12, 36;
CDBLB 1945-1960; DLB 15, 139; MTCW

Spaulding, Douglas
See Bradbury, Ray (Douglas)

Spaulding, Leonard
See Bradbury, Ray (Douglas)

Spence, J. A. D.
See Eliot, T(homas) S(tearns)

Theriault, Yves 1915-1983 . . . . **CLC 79**
See also CA 102; DLB 88

Theroux, Alexander (Louis)
1939- . . . . **CLC 2, 25**
See also CA 85-88; CANR 20

Theroux, Paul (Edward)
1941- . . . . **CLC 5, 8, 11, 15, 28, 46**
See also BEST 89:4; CA 33-36R; CANR 20,
45; DLB 2; MTCW; SATA 44

Thesen, Sharon 1946- . . . . **CLC 56**

Thevenin, Denis
See Duhamel, Georges

Thibault, Jacques Anatole Francois
1844-1924
See France, Anatole
See also CA 106; 127; MTCW

Thiele, Colin (Milton) 1920- . . . . **CLC 17**
See also CA 29-32R; CANR 12, 28;
CLR 27; MAICYA; SAAS 2; SATA 14,
72

Thomas, Audrey (Callahan)
1935- . . . . **CLC 7, 13, 37; SSC 20**
See also AITN 2; CA 21-24R; CAAS 19;
CANR 36; DLB 60; MTCW

Thomas, D(onald) M(ichael)
1935- . . . . **CLC 13, 22, 31**
See also CA 61-64; CAAS 11; CANR 17,
45; CDBLB 1960 to Present; DLB 40;
MTCW

Thomas, Dylan (Marlais)
1914-1953 . . . **TCLC 1, 8, 45; DA; DAB;
PC 2; SSC 3; WLC**
See also CA 104; 120; CDBLB 1945-1960;
DLB 13, 20, 139; MTCW; SATA 60

Thomas, (Philip) Edward
1878-1917 . . . . **TCLC 10**
See also CA 106; DLB 19

Thomas, Joyce Carol 1938- . . . . **CLC 35**
See also AAYA 12; BW 2; CA 113; 116;
CANR 48; CLR 19; DLB 33; JRDA;
MAICYA; MTCW; SAAS 7; SATA 40,
78

Thomas, Lewis 1913-1993 . . . . **CLC 35**
See also CA 85-88; 143; CANR 38; MTCW

Thomas, Paul
See Mann, (Paul) Thomas

Thomas, Piri 1928- . . . . **CLC 17**
See also CA 73-76; HW

Thomas, R(onald) S(tuart)
1913- . . . . **CLC 6, 13, 48; DAB**
See also CA 89-92; CAAS 4; CANR 30;
CDBLB 1960 to Present; DLB 27;
MTCW

Thomas, Ross (Elmore) 1926- . . . . . . **CLC 39**
See also CA 33-36R; CANR 22

Thompson, Francis Clegg
See Mencken, H(enry) L(ouis)

Thompson, Francis Joseph
1859-1907 . . . . **TCLC 4**
See also CA 104; CDBLB 1890-1914;
DLB 19

Thompson, Hunter S(tockton)
1939- . . . . **CLC 9, 17, 40**
See also BEST 89:1; CA 17-20R; CANR 23,
46; MTCW

Thompson, James Myers
See Thompson, Jim (Myers)

Thompson, Jim (Myers)
1906-1977(?) . . . . **CLC 69**
See also CA 140

Thompson, Judith . . . . **CLC 39**

Thomson, James 1700-1748 . . . . . . **LC 16, 29**
See also DLB 95

Thomson, James 1834-1882 . . . . . . **NCLC 18**
See also DLB 35

Thoreau, Henry David
1817-1862 . . . . . **NCLC 7, 21; DA; DAB;
WLC**
See also CDALB 1640-1865; DLB 1

Thornton, Hall
See Silverberg, Robert

Thurber, James (Grover)
1894-1961 . . . . **CLC 5, 11, 25; DA; DAB;
SSC 1**
See also CA 73-76; CANR 17, 39;
CDALB 1929-1941; DLB 4, 11, 22, 102;
MAICYA; MTCW; SATA 13

Thurman, Wallace (Henry)
1902-1934 . . . . **TCLC 6; BLC**
See also BW 1; CA 104; 124; DLB 51

Ticheburn, Cheviot
See Ainsworth, William Harrison

Tieck, (Johann) Ludwig
1773-1853 . . . . **NCLC 5, 46**
See also DLB 90

Tiger, Derry
See Ellison, Harlan (Jay)

Tilghman, Christopher 1948(?)- . . . . . **CLC 65**

Tillinghast, Richard (Williford)
1940- . . . . **CLC 29**
See also CA 29-32R; CANR 26

Timrod, Henry 1828-1867 . . . . **NCLC 25**
See also DLB 3

Tindall, Gillian 1938- . . . . **CLC 7**
See also CA 21-24R; CANR 11

Tiptree, James, Jr. . . . . **CLC 48, 50**
See also Sheldon, Alice Hastings Bradley
See also DLB 8

Titmarsh, Michael Angelo
See Thackeray, William Makepeace

**Tocqueville, Alexis (Charles Henri Maurice
Clerel Comte)** 1805-1859 . . . . . **NCLC 7**

Tolkien, J(ohn) R(onald) R(euel)
1892-1973 . . . . **CLC 1, 2, 3, 8, 12, 38;
DA; DAB; WLC**
See also AAYA 10; AITN 1; CA 17-18;
45-48; CANR 36; CAP 2;
CDBLB 1914-1945; DLB 15; JRDA;
MAICYA; MTCW; SATA 2, 32;
SATA-Obit 24

Toller, Ernst 1893-1939 . . . . **TCLC 10**
See also CA 107; DLB 124

Tolson, M. B.
See Tolson, Melvin B(eaunorus)

Tolson, Melvin B(eaunorus)
1898(?)-1966 . . . . **CLC 36; BLC**
See also BW 1; CA 124; 89-92; DLB 48, 76

Tolstoi, Aleksei Nikolaevich
See Tolstoy, Alexey Nikolaevich

Tolstoy, Alexey Nikolaevich
1882-1945 . . . . **TCLC 18**
See also CA 107

Tolstoy, Count Leo
See Tolstoy, Leo (Nikolaevich)

Tolstoy, Leo (Nikolaevich)
1828-1910 . . . . . . **TCLC 4, 11, 17, 28, 44;
DA; DAB; SSC 9; WLC**
See also CA 104; 123; SATA 26

Tomasi di Lampedusa, Giuseppe 1896-1957
See Lampedusa, Giuseppe (Tomasi) di
See also CA 111

Tomlin, Lily . . . . **CLC 17**
See also Tomlin, Mary Jean

Tomlin, Mary Jean 1939(?)-
See Tomlin, Lily
See also CA 117

Tomlinson, (Alfred) Charles
1927- . . . . **CLC 2, 4, 6, 13, 45**
See also CA 5-8R; CANR 33; DLB 40

Tonson, Jacob
See Bennett, (Enoch) Arnold

Toole, John Kennedy
1937-1969 . . . . **CLC 19, 64**
See also CA 104; DLBY 81

Toomer, Jean
1894-1967 . . . . . . **CLC 1, 4, 13, 22; BLC;
PC 7; SSC 1**
See also BW 1; CA 85-88;
CDALB 1917-1929; DLB 45, 51; MTCW

Torley, Luke
See Blish, James (Benjamin)

Tornimparte, Alessandra
See Ginzburg, Natalia

Torre, Raoul della
See Mencken, H(enry) L(ouis)

Torrey, E(dwin) Fuller 1937- . . . . **CLC 34**
See also CA 119

Torsvan, Ben Traven
See Traven, B.

Torsvan, Benno Traven
See Traven, B.

Torsvan, Berick Traven
See Traven, B.

Torsvan, Berwick Traven
See Traven, B.

Torsvan, Bruno Traven
See Traven, B.

Torsvan, Traven
See Traven, B.

Tournier, Michel (Edouard)
1924- . . . . **CLC 6, 23, 36**
See also CA 49-52; CANR 3, 36; DLB 83;
MTCW; SATA 23

Tournimparte, Alessandra
See Ginzburg, Natalia

Towers, Ivar
See Kornbluth, C(yril) M.

Towne, Robert (Burton) 1936(?)- . . . . **CLC 87**
See also CA 108; DLB 44

Townsend, Sue 1946- . . . . **CLC 61; DAB**
See also CA 119; 127; MTCW; SATA 55;
SATA-Brief 48

Townshend, Peter (Dennis Blandford)
1945- .... **CLC 17, 42**
See also CA 107

Tozzi, Federigo 1883-1920....... **TCLC 31**

Traill, Catharine Parr
1802-1899 .... **NCLC 31**
See also DLB 99

Trakl, Georg 1887-1914.......... **TCLC 5**
See also CA 104

Transtroemer, Tomas (Goesta)
1931- .... **CLC 52, 65**
See also CA 117; 129; CAAS 17

Transtromer, Tomas Gosta
See Transtroemer, Tomas (Goesta)

Traven, B. (?)-1969............ **CLC 8, 11**
See also CA 19-20; 25-28R; CAP 2; DLB 9,
56; MTCW

Treitel, Jonathan 1959- .... **CLC 70**

Tremain, Rose 1943-.............. **CLC 42**
See also CA 97-100; CANR 44; DLB 14

Tremblay, Michel 1942-........... **CLC 29**
See also CA 116; 128; DLB 60; MTCW

Trevanian........................ **CLC 29**
See also Whitaker, Rod(ney)

Trevor, Glen
See Hilton, James

Trevor, William
1928- ..... **CLC 7, 9, 14, 25, 71; SSC 21**
See also Cox, William Trevor
See also DLB 14, 139

Trifonov, Yuri (Valentinovich)
1925-1981 .... **CLC 45**
See also CA 126; 103; MTCW

Trilling, Lionel 1905-1975.... **CLC 9, 11, 24**
See also CA 9-12R; 61-64; CANR 10;
DLB 28, 63; MTCW

Trimball, W. H.
See Mencken, H(enry) L(ouis)

Tristan
See Gomez de la Serna, Ramon

Tristram
See Housman, A(lfred) E(dward)

Trogdon, William (Lewis) 1939-
See Heat-Moon, William Least
See also CA 115; 119; CANR 47

Trollope, Anthony
1815-1882 ..... **NCLC 6, 33; DA; DAB; WLC**
See also CDBLB 1832-1890; DLB 21, 57;
SATA 22

Trollope, Frances 1779-1863..... **NCLC 30**
See also DLB 21

Trotsky, Leon 1879-1940........ **TCLC 22**
See also CA 118

Trotter (Cockburn), Catharine
1679-1749 .... **LC 8**
See also DLB 84

Trout, Kilgore
See Farmer, Philip Jose

Trow, George W. S. 1943-........ **CLC 52**
See also CA 126

Troyat, Henri 1911-.............. **CLC 23**
See also CA 45-48; CANR 2, 33; MTCW

Trudeau, G(arretson) B(eekman) 1948-
See Trudeau, Garry B.
See also CA 81-84; CANR 31; SATA 35

Trudeau, Garry B................. **CLC 12**
See also Trudeau, G(arretson) B(eekman)
See also AAYA 10; AITN 2

Truffaut, Francois 1932-1984...... **CLC 20**
See also CA 81-84; 113; CANR 34

Trumbo, Dalton 1905-1976 .... **CLC 19**
See also CA 21-24R; 69-72; CANR 10;
DLB 26

Trumbull, John 1750-1831....... **NCLC 30**
See also DLB 31

Trundlett, Helen B.
See Eliot, T(homas) S(tearns)

Tryon, Thomas 1926-1991....... **CLC 3, 11**
See also AITN 1; CA 29-32R; 135;
CANR 32; MTCW

Tryon, Tom
See Tryon, Thomas

Ts'ao Hsueh-ch'in 1715(?)-1763....... **LC 1**

Tsushima, Shuji 1909-1948
See Dazai, Osamu
See also CA 107

Tsvetaeva (Efron), Marina (Ivanovna)
1892-1941 ....TCLC 7, 35
See also CA 104; 128; MTCW

Tuck, Lily 1938-................. **CLC 70**
See also CA 139

Tu Fu 712-770..................... **PC 9**

Tunis, John R(oberts) 1889-1975 ... **CLC 12**
See also CA 61-64; DLB 22; JRDA;
MAICYA; SATA 37; SATA-Brief 30

Tuohy, Frank..................... **CLC 37**
See also Tuohy, John Francis
See also DLB 14, 139

Tuohy, John Francis 1925-
See Tuohy, Frank
See also CA 5-8R; CANR 3, 47

Turco, Lewis (Putnam) 1934- ... **CLC 11, 63**
See also CA 13-16R; CAAS 22; CANR 24;
DLBY 84

Turgenev, Ivan
1818-1883 .... **NCLC 21; DA; DAB;
SSC 7; WLC**

Turgot, Anne-Robert-Jacques
1727-1781 .... **LC 26**

Turner, Frederick 1943-.......... **CLC 48**
See also CA 73-76; CAAS 10; CANR 12,
30; DLB 40

Tutu, Desmond M(pilo)
1931- .... **CLC 80; BLC**
See also BW 1; CA 125

Tutuola, Amos 1920- ... **CLC 5, 14, 29; BLC**
See also BW 2; CA 9-12R; CANR 27;
DLB 125; MTCW

Twain, Mark
..... **TCLC 6, 12, 19, 36, 48, 59; SSC 6;
WLC**
See also Clemens, Samuel Langhorne
See also DLB 11, 12, 23, 64, 74

Tyler, Anne
1941- .... **CLC 7, 11, 18, 28, 44, 59**
See also BEST 89:1; CA 9-12R; CANR 11,
33; DLB 6, 143; DLBY 82; MTCW;
SATA 7

Tyler, Royall 1757-1826.......... **NCLC 3**
See also DLB 37

Tynan, Katharine 1861-1931....... **TCLC 3**
See also CA 104; DLB 153

Tyutchev, Fyodor 1803-1873..... **NCLC 34**

Tzara, Tristan .... **CLC 47**
See also Rosenfeld, Samuel

Uhry, Alfred 1936-............... **CLC 55**
See also CA 127; 133

Ulf, Haerved
See Strindberg, (Johan) August

Ulf, Harved
See Strindberg, (Johan) August

Ulibarri, Sabine R(eyes) 1919- ..... **CLC 83**
See also CA 131; DLB 82; HW

Unamuno (y Jugo), Miguel de
1864-1936 .... **TCLC 2, 9; HLC; SSC 11**
See also CA 104; 131; DLB 108; HW;
MTCW

Undercliffe, Errol
See Campbell, (John) Ramsey

Underwood, Miles
See Glassco, John

Undset, Sigrid
1882-1949 ... **TCLC 3; DA; DAB; WLC**
See also CA 104; 129; MTCW

Ungaretti, Giuseppe
1888-1970 .... **CLC 7, 11, 15**
See also CA 19-20; 25-28R; CAP 2;
DLB 114

Unger, Douglas 1952-............. **CLC 34**
See also CA 130

Unsworth, Barry (Forster) 1930-.... **CLC 76**
See also CA 25-28R; CANR 30

Updike, John (Hoyer)
1932- ...... **CLC 1, 2, 3, 5, 7, 9, 13, 15,
23, 34, 43, 70; DA; DAB; SSC 13; WLC**
See also CA 1-4R; CABS 1; CANR 4, 33;
CDALB 1968-1988; DLB 2, 5, 143;
DLBD 3; DLBY 80, 82; MTCW

Upshaw, Margaret Mitchell
See Mitchell, Margaret (Munnerlyn)

Upton, Mark
See Sanders, Lawrence

Urdang, Constance (Henriette)
1922-....................... **CLC 47**
See also CA 21-24R; CANR 9, 24

Uriel, Henry
See Faust, Frederick (Schiller)

Uris, Leon (Marcus) 1924-....... **CLC 7, 32**
See also AITN 1, 2; BEST 89:2; CA 1-4R;
CANR 1, 40; MTCW; SATA 49

Urmuz
See Codrescu, Andrei

Urquhart, Jane 1949-............. **CLC 90**
See also CA 113; CANR 32

Ustinov, Peter (Alexander) 1921-.... **CLC 1**
See also AITN 1; CA 13-16R; CANR 25;
DLB 13

Voltaire
1694-1778 . . . . **LC 14; DA; DAB;
SSC 12; WLC**

von Aue, Hartmann   1170-1210 . . . **CMLC 15**

von Daeniken, Erich   1935- . . . . **CLC 30**
See also AITN 1; CA 37-40R; CANR 17,
44

von Daniken, Erich
See von Daeniken, Erich

von Heidenstam, (Carl Gustaf) Verner
See Heidenstam, (Carl Gustaf) Verner von

von Heyse, Paul (Johann Ludwig)
See Heyse, Paul (Johann Ludwig von)

von Hofmannsthal, Hugo
See Hofmannsthal, Hugo von

von Horvath, Odon
See Horvath, Oedoen von

von Horvath, Oedoen
See Horvath, Oedoen von

von Liliencron, (Friedrich Adolf Axel) Detlev
See Liliencron, (Friedrich Adolf Axel)
Detlev von

Vonnegut, Kurt, Jr.
1922- . . . . . . **CLC 1, 2, 3, 4, 5, 8, 12, 22,
40, 60; DA; DAB; SSC 8; WLC**
See also AAYA 6; AITN 1; BEST 90:4;
CA 1-4R; CANR 1, 25, 49;
CDALB 1968-1988; DLB 2, 8, 152;
DLBD 3; DLBY 80; MTCW

Von Rachen, Kurt
See Hubbard, L(afayette) Ron(ald)

von Rezzori (d'Arezzo), Gregor
See Rezzori (d'Arezzo), Gregor von

von Sternberg, Josef
See Sternberg, Josef von

Vorster, Gordon   1924- . . . . **CLC 34**
See also CA 133

Vosce, Trudie
See Ozick, Cynthia

Voznesensky, Andrei (Andreievich)
1933- . . . . **CLC 1, 15, 57**
See also CA 89-92; CANR 37; MTCW

Waddington, Miriam   1917- . . . . **CLC 28**
See also CA 21-24R; CANR 12, 30;
DLB 68

Wagman, Fredrica   1937- . . . . **CLC 7**
See also CA 97-100

Wagner, Richard   1813-1883. . . . . . . **NCLC 9**
See also DLB 129

Wagner-Martin, Linda   1936- . . . . **CLC 50**

Wagoner, David (Russell)
1926- . . . . **CLC 3, 5, 15**
See also CA 1-4R; CAAS 3; CANR 2;
DLB 5; SATA 14

Wah, Fred(erick James)   1939- . . . . . . **CLC 44**
See also CA 107; 141; DLB 60

Wahloo, Per   1926-1975 . . . . **CLC 7**
See also CA 61-64

Wahloo, Peter
See Wahloo, Per

Wain, John (Barrington)
1925-1994 . . . . **CLC 2, 11, 15, 46**
See also CA 5-8R; 145; CAAS 4; CANR 23;
CDBLB 1960 to Present; DLB 15, 27,
139, 155; MTCW

Wajda, Andrzej   1926- . . . . **CLC 16**
See also CA 102

Wakefield, Dan   1932- . . . . **CLC 7**
See also CA 21-24R; CAAS 7

Wakoski, Diane
1937- . . . . **CLC 2, 4, 7, 9, 11, 40**
See also CA 13-16R; CAAS 1; CANR 9;
DLB 5

Wakoski-Sherbell, Diane
See Wakoski, Diane

Walcott, Derek (Alton)
1930- . . . . **CLC 2, 4, 9, 14, 25, 42, 67, 76;
BLC; DAB**
See also BW 2; CA 89-92; CANR 26, 47;
DLB 117; DLBY 81; MTCW

Waldman, Anne   1945- . . . . **CLC 7**
See also CA 37-40R; CAAS 17; CANR 34;
DLB 16

Waldo, E. Hunter
See Sturgeon, Theodore (Hamilton)

Waldo, Edward Hamilton
See Sturgeon, Theodore (Hamilton)

Walker, Alice (Malsenior)
1944- . . . . **CLC 5, 6, 9, 19, 27, 46, 58;
BLC; DA; DAB; SSC 5**
See also AAYA 3; BEST 89:4; BW 2;
CA 37-40R; CANR 9, 27, 49;
CDALB 1968-1988; DLB 6, 33, 143;
MTCW; SATA 31

Walker, David Harry   1911-1992. . . . **CLC 14**
See also CA 1-4R; 137; CANR 1; SATA 8;
SATA-Obit 71

Walker, Edward Joseph   1934-
See Walker, Ted
See also CA 21-24R; CANR 12, 28

Walker, George F.
1947- . . . . **CLC 44, 61; DAB**
See also CA 103; CANR 21, 43; DLB 60

Walker, Joseph A.   1935- . . . . **CLC 19**
See also BW 1; CA 89-92; CANR 26;
DLB 38

Walker, Margaret (Abigail)
1915- . . . . **CLC 1, 6; BLC**
See also BW 2; CA 73-76; CANR 26;
DLB 76, 152; MTCW

Walker, Ted . . . . **CLC 13**
See also Walker, Edward Joseph
See also DLB 40

Wallace, David Foster   1962- . . . . **CLC 50**
See also CA 132

Wallace, Dexter
See Masters, Edgar Lee

Wallace, (Richard Horatio) Edgar
1875-1932 . . . . **TCLC 57**
See also CA 115; DLB 70

Wallace, Irving   1916-1990 . . . . **CLC 7, 13**
See also AITN 1; CA 1-4R; 132; CAAS 1;
CANR 1, 27; MTCW

Wallant, Edward Lewis
1926-1962 . . . . **CLC 5, 10**
See also CA 1-4R; CANR 22; DLB 2, 28,
143; MTCW

Walley, Byron
See Card, Orson Scott

Walpole, Horace   1717-1797. . . . . **LC 2**
See also DLB 39, 104

Walpole, Hugh (Seymour)
1884-1941 . . . . **TCLC 5**
See also CA 104; DLB 34

Walser, Martin   1927- . . . . **CLC 27**
See also CA 57-60; CANR 8, 46; DLB 75,
124

Walser, Robert
1878-1956 . . . . **TCLC 18; SSC 20**
See also CA 118; DLB 66

Walsh, Jill Paton . . . . **CLC 35**
See also Paton Walsh, Gillian
See also AAYA 11; CLR 2; SAAS 3

Walter, Villiam Christian
See Andersen, Hans Christian

Wambaugh, Joseph (Aloysius, Jr.)
1937- . . . . **CLC 3, 18**
See also AITN 1; BEST 89:3; CA 33-36R;
CANR 42; DLB 6; DLBY 83; MTCW

Ward, Arthur Henry Sarsfield   1883-1959
See Rohmer, Sax
See also CA 108

Ward, Douglas Turner   1930- . . . . **CLC 19**
See also BW 1; CA 81-84; CANR 27;
DLB 7, 38

Ward, Mary Augusta
See Ward, Mrs. Humphry

Ward, Mrs. Humphry
1851-1920 . . . . **TCLC 55**
See also DLB 18

Ward, Peter
See Faust, Frederick (Schiller)

Warhol, Andy   1928(?)-1987. . . . . **CLC 20**
See also AAYA 12; BEST 89:4; CA 89-92;
121; CANR 34

Warner, Francis (Robert le Plastrier)
1937- . . . . **CLC 14**
See also CA 53-56; CANR 11

Warner, Marina   1946- . . . . **CLC 59**
See also CA 65-68; CANR 21

Warner, Rex (Ernest)   1905-1986. . . . **CLC 45**
See also CA 89-92; 119; DLB 15

Warner, Susan (Bogert)
1819-1885 . . . . **NCLC 31**
See also DLB 3, 42

Warner, Sylvia (Constance) Ashton
See Ashton-Warner, Sylvia (Constance)

Warner, Sylvia Townsend
1893-1978 . . . . **CLC 7, 19**
See also CA 61-64; 77-80; CANR 16;
DLB 34, 139; MTCW

Warren, Mercy Otis   1728-1814. . . **NCLC 13**
See also DLB 31

Warren, Robert Penn
1905-1989 .... CLC 1, 4, 6, 8, 10, 13, 18,
39, 53, 59; DA; DAB; SSC 4; WLC
See also AITN 1; CA 13-16R; 129;
CANR 10, 47; CDALB 1968-1988;
DLB 2, 48, 152; DLBY 80, 89; MTCW;
SATA 46; SATA-Obit 63

Warshofsky, Isaac
See Singer, Isaac Bashevis

Warton, Thomas 1728-1790 .... LC 15
See also DLB 104, 109

Waruk, Kona
See Harris, (Theodore) Wilson

Warung, Price 1855-1911 .... TCLC 45

Warwick, Jarvis
See Garner, Hugh

Washington, Alex
See Harris, Mark

Washington, Booker T(aliaferro)
1856-1915 .... TCLC 10; BLC
See also BW 1; CA 114; 125; SATA 28

Washington, George 1732-1799 ...... LC 25
See also DLB 31

Wassermann, (Karl) Jakob
1873-1934 .... TCLC 6
See also CA 104; DLB 66

Wasserstein, Wendy
1950- .... CLC 32, 59, 90; DC 4
See also CA 121; 129; CABS 3

Waterhouse, Keith (Spencer)
1929- .... CLC 47
See also CA 5-8R; CANR 38; DLB 13, 15;
MTCW

Waters, Frank (Joseph) 1902- ...... CLC 88
See also CA 5-8R; CAAS 13; CANR 3, 18;
DLBY 86

Waters, Roger 1944- .... CLC 35

Watkins, Frances Ellen
See Harper, Frances Ellen Watkins

Watkins, Gerrold
See Malzberg, Barry N(athaniel)

Watkins, Paul 1964- .... CLC 55
See also CA 132

Watkins, Vernon Phillips
1906-1967 .... CLC 43
See also CA 9-10; 25-28R; CAP 1; DLB 20

Watson, Irving S.
See Mencken, H(enry) L(ouis)

Watson, John H.
See Farmer, Philip Jose

Watson, Richard F.
See Silverberg, Robert

Waugh, Auberon (Alexander) 1939- .. CLC 7
See also CA 45-48; CANR 6, 22; DLB 14

Waugh, Evelyn (Arthur St. John)
1903-1966 ...... CLC 1, 3, 8, 13, 19, 27,
44; DA; DAB; WLC
See also CA 85-88; 25-28R; CANR 22;
CDBLB 1914-1945; DLB 15; MTCW

Waugh, Harriet 1944- .... CLC 6
See also CA 85-88; CANR 22

Ways, C. R.
See Blount, Roy (Alton), Jr.

Waystaff, Simon
See Swift, Jonathan

Webb, (Martha) Beatrice (Potter)
1858-1943 .... TCLC 22
See also Potter, Beatrice
See also CA 117

Webb, Charles (Richard) 1939- ...... CLC 7
See also CA 25-28R

Webb, James H(enry), Jr. 1946- .... CLC 22
See also CA 81-84

Webb, Mary (Gladys Meredith)
1881-1927 .... TCLC 24
See also CA 123; DLB 34

Webb, Mrs. Sidney
See Webb, (Martha) Beatrice (Potter)

Webb, Phyllis 1927- .... CLC 18
See also CA 104; CANR 23; DLB 53

Webb, Sidney (James)
1859-1947 .... TCLC 22
See also CA 117

Webber, Andrew Lloyd .... CLC 21
See also Lloyd Webber, Andrew

Weber, Lenora Mattingly
1895-1971 .... CLC 12
See also CA 19-20; 29-32R; CAP 1;
SATA 2; SATA-Obit 26

Webster, John 1579(?)-1634(?) .... DC 2
See also CDBLB Before 1660; DA; DAB;
DLB 58; WLC

Webster, Noah 1758-1843 .... NCLC 30

Wedekind, (Benjamin) Frank(lin)
1864-1918 .... TCLC 7
See also CA 104; DLB 118

Weidman, Jerome 1913- .... CLC 7
See also AITN 2; CA 1-4R; CANR 1;
DLB 28

Weil, Simone (Adolphine)
1909-1943 .... TCLC 23
See also CA 117

Weinstein, Nathan
See West, Nathanael

Weinstein, Nathan von Wallenstein
See West, Nathanael

Weir, Peter (Lindsay) 1944- .... CLC 20
See also CA 113; 123

Weiss, Peter (Ulrich)
1916-1982 .... CLC 3, 15, 51
See also CA 45-48; 106; CANR 3; DLB 69,
124

Weiss, Theodore (Russell)
1916- .... CLC 3, 8, 14
See also CA 9-12R; CAAS 2; CANR 46;
DLB 5

Welch, (Maurice) Denton
1915-1948 .... TCLC 22
See also CA 121; 148

Welch, James 1940- .... CLC 6, 14, 52
See also CA 85-88; CANR 42; NNAL

Weldon, Fay
1933- .... CLC 6, 9, 11, 19, 36, 59
See also CA 21-24R; CANR 16, 46;
CDBLB 1960 to Present; DLB 14;
MTCW

Wellek, Rene 1903- .... CLC 28
See also CA 5-8R; CAAS 7; CANR 8;
DLB 63

Weller, Michael 1942- .... CLC 10, 53
See also CA 85-88

Weller, Paul 1958- .... CLC 26

Wellershoff, Dieter 1925- .... CLC 46
See also CA 89-92; CANR 16, 37

Welles, (George) Orson
1915-1985 .... CLC 20, 80
See also CA 93-96; 117

Wellman, Mac 1945- .... CLC 65

Wellman, Manly Wade 1903-1986 .. CLC 49
See also CA 1-4R; 118; CANR 6, 16, 44;
SATA 6; SATA-Obit 47

Wells, Carolyn 1869(?)-1942 ...... TCLC 35
See also CA 113; DLB 11

Wells, H(erbert) G(eorge)
1866-1946 .... TCLC 6, 12, 19; DA;
DAB; SSC 6; WLC
See also CA 110; 121; CDBLB 1914-1945;
DLB 34, 70, 156; MTCW; SATA 20

Wells, Rosemary 1943- .... CLC 12
See also AAYA 13; CA 85-88; CANR 48;
CLR 16; MAICYA; SAAS 1; SATA 18,
69

Welty, Eudora
1909- ...... CLC 1, 2, 5, 14, 22, 33; DA;
DAB; SSC 1; WLC
See also CA 9-12R; CABS 1; CANR 32;
CDALB 1941-1968; DLB 2, 102, 143;
DLBD 12; DLBY 87; MTCW

Wen I-to 1899-1946 .... TCLC 28

Wentworth, Robert
See Hamilton, Edmond

Werfel, Franz (V.) 1890-1945 ...... TCLC 8
See also CA 104; DLB 81, 124

Wergeland, Henrik Arnold
1808-1845 .... NCLC 5

Wersba, Barbara 1932- .... CLC 30
See also AAYA 2; CA 29-32R; CANR 16,
38; CLR 3; DLB 52; JRDA; MAICYA;
SAAS 2; SATA 1, 58

Wertmueller, Lina 1928- .... CLC 16
See also CA 97-100; CANR 39

Wescott, Glenway 1901-1987 .... CLC 13
See also CA 13-16R; 121; CANR 23;
DLB 4, 9, 102

Wesker, Arnold 1932- ... CLC 3, 5, 42; DAB
See also CA 1-4R; CAAS 7; CANR 1, 33;
CDBLB 1960 to Present; DLB 13;
MTCW

Wesley, Richard (Errol) 1945- .... CLC 7
See also BW 1; CA 57-60; CANR 27;
DLB 38

Wessel, Johan Herman 1742-1785 .... LC 7

West, Anthony (Panther)
1914-1987 .... CLC 50
See also CA 45-48; 124; CANR 3, 19;
DLB 15

West, C. P.
See Wodehouse, P(elham) G(renville)

West, (Mary) Jessamyn
1902-1984 . . . . **CLC 7, 17**
See also CA 9-12R; 112; CANR 27; DLB 6;
DLBY 84; MTCW; SATA-Obit 37

West, Morris L(anglo) 1916- . . . . . **CLC 6, 33**
See also CA 5-8R; CANR 24, 49; MTCW

West, Nathanael
1903-1940 . . . . . **TCLC 1, 14, 44; SSC 16**
See also CA 104; 125; CDALB 1929-1941;
DLB 4, 9, 28; MTCW

West, Owen
See Koontz, Dean R(ay)

West, Paul 1930- . . . . **CLC 7, 14**
See also CA 13-16R; CAAS 7; CANR 22;
DLB 14

West, Rebecca 1892-1983 . . **CLC 7, 9, 31, 50**
See also CA 5-8R; 109; CANR 19; DLB 36;
DLBY 83; MTCW

Westall, Robert (Atkinson)
1929-1993 . . . . **CLC 17**
See also AAYA 12; CA 69-72; 141;
CANR 18; CLR 13; JRDA; MAICYA;
SAAS 2; SATA 23, 69; SATA-Obit 75

Westlake, Donald E(dwin)
1933- . . . . **CLC 7, 33**
See also CA 17-20R; CAAS 13; CANR 16,
44

Westmacott, Mary
See Christie, Agatha (Mary Clarissa)

Weston, Allen
See Norton, Andre

Wetcheek, J. L.
See Feuchtwanger, Lion

Wetering, Janwillem van de
See van de Wetering, Janwillem

Wetherell, Elizabeth
See Warner, Susan (Bogert)

Whalen, Philip 1923- . . . . **CLC 6, 29**
See also CA 9-12R; CANR 5, 39; DLB 16

Wharton, Edith (Newbold Jones)
1862-1937 . . . . . . **TCLC 3, 9, 27, 53; DA;
DAB; SSC 6; WLC**
See also CA 104; 132; CDALB 1865-1917;
DLB 4, 9, 12, 78; MTCW

Wharton, James
See Mencken, H(enry) L(ouis)

Wharton, William (a pseudonym)
. . . . **CLC 18, 37**
See also CA 93-96; DLBY 80

Wheatley (Peters), Phillis
1754(?)-1784 . . . . **LC 3; BLC; DA; PC 3;
WLC**
See also CDALB 1640-1865; DLB 31, 50

Wheelock, John Hall 1886-1978 . . . . **CLC 14**
See also CA 13-16R; 77-80; CANR 14;
DLB 45

White, E(lwyn) B(rooks)
1899-1985 . . . . **CLC 10, 34, 39**
See also AITN 2; CA 13-16R; 116;
CANR 16, 37; CLR 1, 21; DLB 11, 22;
MAICYA; MTCW; SATA 2, 29;
SATA-Obit 44

White, Edmund (Valentine III)
1940- . . . . **CLC 27**
See also AAYA 7; CA 45-48; CANR 3, 19,
36; MTCW

White, Patrick (Victor Martindale)
1912-1990 . . **CLC 3, 4, 5, 7, 9, 18, 65, 69**
See also CA 81-84; 132; CANR 43; MTCW

White, Phyllis Dorothy James 1920-
See James, P. D.
See also CA 21-24R; CANR 17, 43; MTCW

White, T(erence) H(anbury)
1906-1964 . . . . **CLC 30**
See also CA 73-76; CANR 37; JRDA;
MAICYA; SATA 12

White, Terence de Vere
1912-1994 . . . . **CLC 49**
See also CA 49-52; 145; CANR 3

White, Walter F(rancis)
1893-1955 . . . . **TCLC 15**
See also White, Walter
See also BW 1; CA 115; 124; DLB 51

White, William Hale 1831-1913
See Rutherford, Mark
See also CA 121

Whitehead, E(dward) A(nthony)
1933- . . . . **CLC 5**
See also CA 65-68

Whitemore, Hugh (John) 1936- . . . . . **CLC 37**
See also CA 132

Whitman, Sarah Helen (Power)
1803-1878 . . . . **NCLC 19**
See also DLB 1

Whitman, Walt(er)
1819-1892 . . . . . **NCLC 4, 31; DA; DAB;
PC 3; WLC**
See also CDALB 1640-1865; DLB 3, 64;
SATA 20

Whitney, Phyllis A(yame) 1903- . . . . **CLC 42**
See also AITN 2; BEST 90:3; CA 1-4R;
CANR 3, 25, 38; JRDA; MAICYA;
SATA 1, 30

Whittemore, (Edward) Reed (Jr.)
1919- . . . . **CLC 4**
See also CA 9-12R; CAAS 8; CANR 4;
DLB 5

Whittier, John Greenleaf
1807-1892 . . . . **NCLC 8**
See also CDALB 1640-1865; DLB 1

Whittlebot, Hernia
See Coward, Noel (Peirce)

Wicker, Thomas Grey 1926-
See Wicker, Tom
See also CA 65-68; CANR 21, 46

Wicker, Tom . . . . **CLC 7**
See also Wicker, Thomas Grey

Wideman, John Edgar
1941- . . . . **CLC 5, 34, 36, 67; BLC**
See also BW 2; CA 85-88; CANR 14, 42;
DLB 33, 143

Wiebe, Rudy (Henry) 1934- . . . **CLC 6, 11, 14**
See also CA 37-40R; CANR 42; DLB 60

Wieland, Christoph Martin
1733-1813 . . . . **NCLC 17**
See also DLB 97

Wiene, Robert 1881-1938 . . . . **TCLC 56**

Wieners, John 1934- . . . . **CLC 7**
See also CA 13-16R; DLB 16

Wiesel, Elie(zer)
1928- . . . . . . **CLC 3, 5, 11, 37; DA; DAB**
See also AAYA 7; AITN 1; CA 5-8R;
CAAS 4; CANR 8, 40; DLB 83;
DLBY 87; MTCW; SATA 56

Wiggins, Marianne 1947- . . . . **CLC 57**
See also BEST 89:3; CA 130

Wight, James Alfred 1916-
See Herriot, James
See also CA 77-80; SATA 55;
SATA-Brief 44

Wilbur, Richard (Purdy)
1921- . . . . **CLC 3, 6, 9, 14, 53; DA; DAB**
See also CA 1-4R; CABS 2; CANR 2, 29;
DLB 5; MTCW; SATA 9

Wild, Peter 1940- . . . . **CLC 14**
See also CA 37-40R; DLB 5

Wilde, Oscar (Fingal O'Flahertie Wills)
1854(?)-1900 . . . . **TCLC 1, 8, 23, 41; DA;
DAB; SSC 11; WLC**
See also CA 104; 119; CDBLB 1890-1914;
DLB 10, 19, 34, 57, 141, 156; SATA 24

Wilder, Billy . . . . **CLC 20**
See also Wilder, Samuel
See also DLB 26

Wilder, Samuel 1906-
See Wilder, Billy
See also CA 89-92

Wilder, Thornton (Niven)
1897-1975 . . . . . . **CLC 1, 5, 6, 10, 15, 35,
82; DA; DAB; DC 1; WLC**
See also AITN 2; CA 13-16R; 61-64;
CANR 40; DLB 4, 7, 9; MTCW

Wilding, Michael 1942- . . . . **CLC 73**
See also CA 104; CANR 24, 49

Wiley, Richard 1944- . . . . **CLC 44**
See also CA 121; 129

Wilhelm, Kate . . . . **CLC 7**
See also Wilhelm, Katie Gertrude
See also CAAS 5, DLD 8

Wilhelm, Katie Gertrude 1928-
See Wilhelm, Kate
See also CA 37-40R; CANR 17, 36; MTCW

Wilkins, Mary
See Freeman, Mary Eleanor Wilkins

Willard, Nancy 1936- . . . . **CLC 7, 37**
See also CA 89-92; CANR 10, 39; CLR 5;
DLB 5, 52; MAICYA; MTCW;
SATA 37, 71; SATA-Brief 30

Williams, C(harles) K(enneth)
1936- . . . . **CLC 33, 56**
See also CA 37-40R; DLB 5

Williams, Charles
See Collier, James L(incoln)

Williams, Charles (Walter Stansby)
1886-1945 . . . . **TCLC 1, 11**
See also CA 104; DLB 100, 153

Williams, (George) Emlyn
1905-1987 . . . . **CLC 15**
See also CA 104; 123; CANR 36; DLB 10,
77; MTCW

Williams, Hugo 1942- . . . . **CLC 42**
See also CA 17-20R; CANR 45; DLB 40

Williams, J. Walker
See Wodehouse, P(elham) G(renville)

Williams, John A(lfred)
1925- .... CLC 5, 13; BLC
See also BW 2; CA 53-56; CAAS 3;
CANR 6, 26; DLB 2, 33

Williams, Jonathan (Chamberlain)
1929- .... CLC 13
See also CA 9-12R; CAAS 12; CANR 8;
DLB 5

Williams, Joy 1944- .... CLC 31
See also CA 41-44R; CANR 22, 48

Williams, Norman 1952- .... CLC 39
See also CA 118

Williams, Sherley Anne
1944- .... CLC 89; BLC
See also BW 2; CA 73-76; CANR 25;
DLB 41; SATA 78

Williams, Shirley
See Williams, Sherley Anne

Williams, Tennessee
1911-1983 ..... CLC 1, 2, 5, 7, 8, 11, 15,
19, 30, 39, 45, 71; DA; DAB; DC 4; WLC
See also AITN 1, 2; CA 5-8R; 108;
CABS 3; CANR 31; CDALB 1941-1968;
DLB 7; DLBD 4; DLBY 83; MTCW

Williams, Thomas (Alonzo)
1926-1990 .... CLC 14
See also CA 1-4R; 132; CANR 2

Williams, William C.
See Williams, William Carlos

Williams, William Carlos
1883-1963 .... CLC 1, 2, 5, 9, 13, 22, 42,
67; DA; DAB; PC 7
See also CA 89-92; CANR 34;
CDALB 1917-1929; DLB 4, 16, 54, 86;
MTCW

Williamson, David (Keith) 1942- .... CLC 56
See also CA 103; CANR 41

Williamson, Ellen Douglas 1905-1984
See Douglas, Ellen
See also CA 17-20R; 114; CANR 39

Williamson, Jack.................. CLC 29
See also Williamson, John Stewart
See also CAAS 8; DLB 8

Williamson, John Stewart 1908-
See Williamson, Jack
See also CA 17-20R; CANR 23

Willie, Frederick
See Lovecraft, H(oward) P(hillips)

Willingham, Calder (Baynard, Jr.)
1922-1995 .... CLC 5, 51
See also CA 5-8R; 147; CANR 3; DLB 2,
44; MTCW

Willis, Charles
See Clarke, Arthur C(harles)

Willy
See Colette, (Sidonie-Gabrielle)

Willy, Colette
See Colette, (Sidonie-Gabrielle)

Wilson, A(ndrew) N(orman) 1950- .. CLC 33
See also CA 112; 122; DLB 14, 155

Wilson, Angus (Frank Johnstone)
1913-1991 .. CLC 2, 3, 5, 25, 34; SSC 21
See also CA 5-8R; 134; CANR 21; DLB 15,
139, 155; MTCW

Wilson, August
1945- .... CLC 39, 50, 63; BLC; DA;
DAB; DC 2
See also BW 2; CA 115; 122; CANR 42;
MTCW

Wilson, Brian 1942- .... CLC 12

Wilson, Colin 1931- .... CLC 3, 14
See also CA 1-4R; CAAS 5; CANR 1, 22,
33; DLB 14; MTCW

Wilson, Dirk
See Pohl, Frederik

Wilson, Edmund
1895-1972 .... CLC 1, 2, 3, 8, 24
See also CA 1-4R; 37-40R; CANR 1, 46;
DLB 63; MTCW

Wilson, Ethel Davis (Bryant)
1888(?)-1980 .... CLC 13
See also CA 102; DLB 68; MTCW

Wilson, John 1785-1854.......... NCLC 5

Wilson, John (Anthony) Burgess 1917-1993
See Burgess, Anthony
See also CA 1-4R; 143; CANR 2, 46;
MTCW

Wilson, Lanford 1937-....... CLC 7, 14, 36
See also CA 17-20R; CABS 3; CANR 45;
DLB 7

Wilson, Robert M. 1944-........ CLC 7, 9
See also CA 49-52; CANR 2, 41; MTCW

Wilson, Robert McLiam 1964- ..... CLC 59
See also CA 132

Wilson, Sloan 1920-.............. CLC 32
See also CA 1-4R; CANR 1, 44

Wilson, Snoo 1948-............... CLC 33
See also CA 69-72

Wilson, William S(mith) 1932- ..... CLC 49
See also CA 81-84

Winchilsea, Anne (Kingsmill) Finch Counte
1661-1720 .... LC 3

Windham, Basil
See Wodehouse, P(elham) G(renville)

Wingrove, David (John) 1954-...... CLC 68
See also CA 133

Winters, Janet Lewis .... CLC 41
See also Lewis, Janet
See also DLBY 87

Winters, (Arthur) Yvor
1900-1968 .... CLC 4, 8, 32
See also CA 11-12; 25-28R; CAP 1;
DLB 48; MTCW

Winterson, Jeanette 1959-......... CLC 64
See also CA 136

Winthrop, John 1588-1649......... LC 31
See also DLB 24, 30

Wiseman, Frederick 1930-........ CLC 20

Wister, Owen 1860-1938 .... TCLC 21
See also CA 108; DLB 9, 78; SATA 62

Witkacy
See Witkiewicz, Stanislaw Ignacy

Witkiewicz, Stanislaw Ignacy
1885-1939 .... TCLC 8
See also CA 105

Wittgenstein, Ludwig (Josef Johann)
1889-1951 .... TCLC 59
See also CA 113

Wittig, Monique 1935(?)-......... CLC 22
See also CA 116; 135; DLB 83

Wittlin, Jozef 1896-1976 .... CLC 25
See also CA 49-52; 65-68; CANR 3

Wodehouse, P(elham) G(renville)
1881-1975 ... CLC 1, 2, 5, 10, 22; DAB;
SSC 2
See also AITN 2; CA 45-48; 57-60;
CANR 3, 33; CDBLB 1914-1945;
DLB 34; MTCW; SATA 22

Woiwode, L.
See Woiwode, Larry (Alfred)

Woiwode, Larry (Alfred) 1941-... CLC 6, 10
See also CA 73-76; CANR 16; DLB 6

Wojciechowska, Maia (Teresa)
1927- .... CLC 26
See also AAYA 8; CA 9-12R; CANR 4, 41;
CLR 1; JRDA; MAICYA; SAAS 1;
SATA 1, 28, 83

Wolf, Christa 1929- .... CLC 14, 29, 58
See also CA 85-88; CANR 45; DLB 75;
MTCW

Wolfe, Gene (Rodman) 1931-....... CLC 25
See also CA 57-60; CAAS 9; CANR 6, 32;
DLB 8

Wolfe, George C. 1954- .... CLC 49

Wolfe, Thomas (Clayton)
1900-1938 ..... TCLC 4, 13, 29, 61; DA;
DAB; WLC
See also CA 104; 132; CDALB 1929-1941;
DLB 9, 102; DLBD 2; DLBY 85; MTCW

Wolfe, Thomas Kennerly, Jr. 1931-
See Wolfe, Tom
See also CA 13-16R; CANR 9, 33; MTCW

Wolfe, Tom .... CLC 1, 2, 9, 15, 35, 51
See also Wolfe, Thomas Kennerly, Jr.
See also AAYA 8; AITN 2; BEST 89:1;
DLB 152

Wolff, Geoffrey (Ansell) 1937- ..... CLC 41
See also CA 29-32R; CANR 29, 43

Wolff, Sonia
See Levitin, Sonia (Wolff)

Wolff, Tobias (Jonathan Ansell)
1945- .... CLC 39, 64
See also BEST 90:2; CA 114; 117;
CAAS 22; DLB 130

Wolfram von Eschenbach
c. 1170-c. 1220 .... CMLC 5
See also DLB 138

Wolitzer, Hilma 1930-............ CLC 17
See also CA 65-68; CANR 18, 40; SATA 31

Wollstonecraft, Mary 1759-1797...... LC 5
See also CDBLB 1789-1832; DLB 39, 104

Wonder, Stevie .... CLC 12
See also Morris, Steveland Judkins

Wong, Jade Snow 1922-.......... CLC 17
See also CA 109

Woodcott, Keith
See Brunner, John (Kilian Houston)

Woodruff, Robert W.
See Mencken, H(enry) L(ouis)

Woolf, (Adeline) Virginia
1882-1941 . . . . . . **TCLC 1, 5, 20, 43, 56;**
DA; DAB; SSC 7; WLC
See also CA 104; 130; CDBLB 1914-1945;
DLB 36, 100; DLBD 10; MTCW

Woollcott, Alexander (Humphreys)
1887-1943 . . . . **TCLC 5**
See also CA 105; DLB 29

Woolrich, Cornell 1903-1968 . . . . . . **CLC 77**
See also Hopley-Woolrich, Cornell George

Wordsworth, Dorothy
1771-1855 . . . . **NCLC 25**
See also DLB 107

Wordsworth, William
1770-1850 . . . . **NCLC 12, 38; DA; DAB;**
PC 4; WLC
See also CDBLB 1789-1832; DLB 93, 107

Wouk, Herman 1915- . . . . **CLC 1, 9, 38**
See also CA 5-8R; CANR 6, 33; DLBY 82;
MTCW

Wright, Charles (Penzel, Jr.)
1935- . . . . **CLC 6, 13, 28**
See also CA 29-32R; CAAS 7; CANR 23,
36; DLBY 82; MTCW

Wright, Charles Stevenson
1932- . . . . **CLC 49; BLC 3**
See also BW 1; CA 9-12R; CANR 26;
DLB 33

Wright, Jack R.
See Harris, Mark

Wright, James (Arlington)
1927-1980 . . . . **CLC 3, 5, 10, 28**
See also AITN 2; CA 49-52; 97-100;
CANR 4, 34; DLD 5; MTCW

Wright, Judith (Arandell)
1915- . . . . **CLC 11, 53**
See also CA 13-16R; CANR 31; MTCW;
SATA 14

Wright, L(aurali) R. 1939- . . . . **CLC 44**
See also CA 138

Wright, Richard (Nathaniel)
1908-1960 . . . . **CLC 1, 3, 4, 9, 14, 21, 48,**
74; BLC; DA; DAB; SSC 2; WLC
See also AAYA 5; BW 1; CA 108;
CDALB 1929-1941; DLB 76, 102;
DLBD 2; MTCW

Wright, Richard B(ruce) 1937- . . . . . . **CLC 6**
See also CA 85-88; DLB 53

Wright, Rick 1945- . . . . **CLC 35**

Wright, Rowland
See Wells, Carolyn

Wright, Stephen Caldwell 1946- . . . . **CLC 33**
See also BW 2

Wright, Willard Huntington 1888-1939
See Van Dine, S. S.
See also CA 115

Wright, William 1930- . . . . **CLC 44**
See also CA 53-56; CANR 7, 23

Wroth, LadyMary 1587-1653(?) . . . . . **LC 30**
See also DLB 121

Wu Ch'eng-en 1500(?)-1582(?) . . . . **LC 7**

Wu Ching-tzu 1701-1754 . . . . **LC 2**

Wurlitzer, Rudolph 1938(?)- . . . **CLC 2, 4, 15**
See also CA 85-88

Wycherley, William 1641-1715 . . . . **LC 8, 21**
See also CDBLB 1660-1789; DLB 80

Wylie, Elinor (Morton Hoyt)
1885-1928 . . . . **TCLC 8**
See also CA 105; DLB 9, 45

Wylie, Philip (Gordon) 1902-1971 . . . **CLC 43**
See also CA 21-22; 33-36R; CAP 2; DLB 9

Wyndham, John . . . . **CLC 19**
See also Harris, John (Wyndham Parkes
Lucas) Beynon

Wyss, Johann David Von
1743-1818 . . . . **NCLC 10**
See also JRDA; MAICYA; SATA 29;
SATA-Brief 27

Yakumo Koizumi
See Hearn, (Patricio) Lafcadio (Tessima
Carlos)

Yanez, Jose Donoso
See Donoso (Yanez), Jose

Yanovsky, Basile S.
See Yanovsky, V(assily) S(emenovich)

Yanovsky, V(assily) S(emenovich)
1906-1989 . . . . **CLC 2, 18**
See also CA 97-100; 129

Yates, Richard 1926-1992 . . . . . **CLC 7, 8, 23**
See also CA 5-8R; 139; CANR 10, 43;
DLB 2; DLBY 81, 92

Yeats, W. B.
See Yeats, William Butler

Yeats, William Butler
1865-1939 . . . . . **TCLC 1, 11, 18, 31; DA;**
DAB; WLC
See also CA 104; 127; CANR 45;
CDBLB 1890-1914; DLB 10, 19, 98, 156;
MTCW

Yehoshua, A(braham) B.
1936- . . . . **CLC 13, 31**
See also CA 33-36R; CANR 43

Yep, Laurence Michael 1948- . . . . . . **CLC 35**
See also AAYA 5; CA 49-52; CANR 1, 46;
CLR 3, 17; DLB 52; JRDA; MAICYA;
SATA 7, 69

Yerby, Frank G(arvin)
1916-1991 . . . . **CLC 1, 7, 22; BLC**
See also BW 1; CA 9-12R; 136; CANR 16;
DLB 76; MTCW

Yesenin, Sergei Alexandrovich
See Esenin, Sergei (Alexandrovich)

Yevtushenko, Yevgeny (Alexandrovich)
1933- . . . . **CLC 1, 3, 13, 26, 51**
See also CA 81-84; CANR 33; MTCW

Yezierska, Anzia 1885(?)-1970 . . . . . **CLC 46**
See also CA 126; 89-92; DLB 28; MTCW

Yglesias, Helen 1915- . . . . **CLC 7, 22**
See also CA 37-40R; CAAS 20; CANR 15;
MTCW

Yokomitsu Riichi 1898-1947 . . . . . . **TCLC 47**

Yonge, Charlotte (Mary)
1823-1901 . . . . **TCLC 48**
See also CA 109; DLB 18; SATA 17

York, Jeremy
See Creasey, John

York, Simon
See Heinlein, Robert A(nson)

Yorke, Henry Vincent 1905-1974 . . . **CLC 13**
See also Green, Henry
See also CA 85-88; 49-52

Yosano Akiko 1878-1942 . . **TCLC 59; PC 11**

Yoshimoto, Banana . . . . **CLC 84**
See also Yoshimoto, Mahoko

Yoshimoto, Mahoko 1964-
See Yoshimoto, Banana
See also CA 144

Young, Al(bert James)
1939- . . . . **CLC 19; BLC**
See also BW 2; CA 29-32R; CANR 26;
DLB 33

Young, Andrew (John) 1885-1971 . . . . **CLC 5**
See also CA 5-8R; CANR 7, 29

Young, Collier
See Bloch, Robert (Albert)

Young, Edward 1683-1765 . . . . **LC 3**
See also DLB 95

Young, Marguerite 1909- . . . . **CLC 82**
See also CA 13-16; CAP 1

Young, Neil 1945- . . . . **CLC 17**
See also CA 110

Yourcenar, Marguerite
1903-1987 . . . . **CLC 19, 38, 50, 87**
See also CA 69-72; CANR 23; DLB 72;
DLBY 88; MTCW

Yurick, Sol 1925- . . . . **CLC 6**
See also CA 13-16R; CANR 25

Zabolotskii, Nikolai Alekseevich
1903-1958 . . . . **TCLC 52**
See also CA 116

Zamiatin, Yevgenii
See Zamyatin, Evgeny Ivanovich

Zamora, Bernice (B. Ortiz)
1938- . . . . **CLC 89; HLC**
See also DLB 82; HW

Zamyatin, Evgeny Ivanovich
1884-1937 . . . . **TCLC 8, 37**
See also CA 105

Zangwill, Israel 1864-1926 . . . . **TCLC 16**
See also CA 109; DLB 10, 135

Zappa, Francis Vincent, Jr. 1940-1993
See Zappa, Frank
See also CA 108; 143

Zappa, Frank . . . . **CLC 17**
See also Zappa, Francis Vincent, Jr.

Zaturenska, Marya 1902-1982 . . . . **CLC 6, 11**
See also CA 13-16R; 105; CANR 22

Zelazny, Roger (Joseph)
1937-1995 . . . . **CLC 21**
See also AAYA 7; CA 21-24R; 148;
CANR 26; DLB 8; MTCW; SATA 57;
SATA-Brief 39

Zhdanov, Andrei A(lexandrovich)
1896-1948 . . . . **TCLC 18**
See also CA 117

Zhukovsky, Vasily 1783-1852 . . . . **NCLC 35**

Ziegenhagen, Eric . . . . **CLC 55**

Zimmer, Jill Schary
See Robinson, Jill

Zimmerman, Robert
See Dylan, Bob

SSC Cumulative Nationality Index

SSC Cumulative Title Index

Title Index

See "Diálogo del espejo"

"The Dialogue of the Dogs" (Cervantes)
See "El coloquio de los perros"

Dialogues de bêtes (Colette) **10**:261, 272

Dialogues with Leucò (Pavese)
See *Dialoghi con Leucò*

"El diamante de Villasola" (Unamuno) **11**:312

"The Diamond as Big as the Ritz" (Fitzgerald) **6**:46-7, 58-60, 88, 92, 100-02

"A Diamond Guitar" (Capote) **2**:67

"The Diamond Maker" (Wells) **6**:383, 388, 408

"The Diamond Mine" (Cather) **2**:91-2

"The Diamond Necklace" (Maupassant)
See "La parure"

"The Diamond of Kali" (Henry) **5**:184

"Diary, 1900" (Hesse) **9**:230

"Diary of a Madman" ("A Madman's Diary"; "Notes of a Madman") (Gogol) **4**:82-3, 88, 91, 98, 100-01, 105-07, 122, 124, 126, 128-29

"Diary of a Madman" (Lu Hsun)
See *Kuangren riji*

"The Diary of a Madman" (Tolstoy)
See *Zapiski sumasshedshego*

"Diary of a Sixteen-Year-Old" (Kawabata)
See "Jūrokusai no Nikki"

"The Diary of a Superfluous Man" (Turgenev)
See "Dnevnik lishnego cheloveka"

"The Diary of an African Nun" (Walker) **5**:402, 404

"The Diary of Mr. Poynter" (James) **16**:223-24, 229-30, 232-33, 235, 249, 255

"A Diary of Sudden Death; By a Public-Spirited Observer on the Inside" (Bierce) **9**:83

"The Diary of the Rose" (Le Guin) **12**:230, 237-38

D'iavoliada (*Diaboliad, and Other Stories*) (Bulgakov) **18**:72-3, 91-2, 97-100

"Dichter und Komponist" (Hoffmann) **13**:191

"Dick Boyle's Business Card" (Harte) **8**:216, 252

"Dickon the Devil" (Le Fanu) **14**:223

"Did I Invite You?" (Pritchett)
See "Did You Invite Me?"

"Did You Invite Me?" ("Did I Invite You?") (Pritchett) **14**:285, 298

"Diddling Considered as One of the Exact Sciences" (Poe) **1**:407

"An die Musik" (Le Guin) **12**:211-12, 214, 219-20, 222-23, 245, 250

"The Die-Hard" (Benet) **10**:154

"Dieu d'amour" (Wharton) **6**:428

Different Seasons (King) **17**:262-67, 271-73, 275, 282, 284

Difficult Loves (Calvino)
See *Gli amori difficili*

"Difficult People" (Chekhov) **2**:155

"The Dilettante" (Mann) **5**:320, 323, 330, 335-37

"The Dilettante" (Wharton) **6**:424

"A Dill Pickle" (Mansfield) **9**:309-10

"Ding Dong" (Beckett) **16**:93

Ding Dong Bell (de la Mare) **14**:90, 92

"Dingle the Fool" (Jolley) **19**:223

"A Dinner at Poplar Walk" (Dickens) **17**:120

"Dinol and Crede" (Moore) **19**:299, 311

"The Dinosaurs" (Calvino) **3**:103, 109

"Díoltas" (O'Flaherty) **6**:287-88

"El dios de los toros" (Bioy Casares) **17**:68, 70

"Direction of the Road" (Le Guin) **12**:234

"The Discarded" (Ellison) **14**:103, 113-15, 117

"The Discarders" (Jolley) **19**:233

"The Disciple" (Aiken) **9**:4, 12-13

"Discord" (O'Faolain) **13**:284-286, 288, 293, 309, 315

"The Discounters of Money" (Henry) **5**:159

"Discourse of a Lady Standing a Dinner to a Down-and-out Friend" (Rhys) **21**:62

"Discourse on the *Tachanka*" (Babel) **16**:27, 55

"A Disgrace to the Family" (Boyle) **5**:64

"Disillusioned" (de la Mare) **14**:83, 86

"Disillusionment" (Mann) **5**:321, 330

"The Disinherited" (Bowen) **3**:33, 41, 45, 48-9, 51

"The Disintegration Machine" (Doyle) **12**:79

"The Dismissal" (Bowles) **3**:75, 80

Disorder and Early Sorrow ("Early Sorrow") (Mann) **5**:310-12, 323, 350

"The Displaced Person" (O'Connor) **1**:335-36, 338, 343-45, 347, 359

"Displaced Persons" (Sansom) **21**:90, 94

"Distance" ("Everything Stuck to Him") (Carver) **8**:4-5, 29, 42, 59

"Distance" (Oates) **6**:236-37

"Distance" (Paley) **8**:416-17

"The Distance of the Moon" (Calvino)
See "La distanza della luna"

"The Distances" (Cortazar)
See "Lejana"

"A Distant Episode" (Bowles) **3**:59, 61-2, 66-9, 72, 78

"Distant Music" (Beattie) **11**:4, 6-7, 17

"The Distant Past" (Trevor) **21**:248, 260-62

The Distant Past, and Other Stories (Trevor) **21**:253

"La distanza della luna" ("The Distance of the Moon") (Calvino) **3**:92, 103, 107, 109

Distortions (Beattie) **11**:2-5, 11-12, 15-16, 18-23, 26-8, 30-2,

"The Distracted Preacher" (Hardy) **2**:203, 205, 208, 213-15, 219-21

"The Disturber" (Villiers de l'Isle Adam)
See "L'inquiéteur"

"The Disturber of Traffic" (Kipling) **5**:283

"The Ditch" (O'Flaherty) **6**:265

"The Diver" (Dinesen) **7**:163, 167-68, 171

"The Diver" (Pritchett) **14**:260-61, 288-89, 299

A Diversity of Creatures (Kipling) **5**:275, 282-84

"Dividends" (O'Faolain) **13**:300

"The Division" (Turgenev) **7**:318

"A Division in the Coolly" (Garland) **18**:148, 160, 184

"Divorcing: A Fragment" (Updike) **13**:387

"Dixiong" ("Brothers") (Lu Hsun) **20**:149

"Dizzy-Headed Dick" (Dunbar) **8**:122

"D'javoliada" (Bulgakov)
See "Diaboliad"

"Djinn, No Chaser" (Ellison) **14**:127

"Djoûmane" (Merimee) **7**:285, 296-98

"Djuna" (Nin) **10**:300-01, 317

"Dnevnik lishnego cheloveka" ("The Diary of a Superfluous Man"; "The Journal of a Superfluous Man") (Turgenev) **7**:314, 318-20, 339

"Do the Dead Sing?" (King)

See "The Reach"

"Do You Like It Here?" (O'Hara) **15**:266

"Do You Want to Make Something Out of It?" (Thurber) **1**:428

"Doc Marlowe" (Thurber) **1**:414

"Doc Mellhorn and the Pearly Gates" (Benet) **10**:143, 154, 159-60

"Las doce figuras del mundo" (Bioy Casares) **17**:70

"The Dock-Witch" (Ozick) **15**:297, 300, 312-13, 326

"The Doctor" (Dubus) **15**:70, 77-9

"The Doctor" (Gallant) **5**:135, 139

"The Doctor and the Doctor's Wife" (Hemingway) **1**:208, 217, 234, 241, 245

Doctor Brodie's Report (Borges)
See *El informe de Brodie*

"Dr. Bullivant" (Hawthorne) **3**:164

"Doctor Chevalier's Lie" (Chopin) **8**:73

"Dr. Heidegger's Experiment" (Hawthorne) **3**:154, 178, 186-87

Doctor Jekyll and Mr. Hyde (Stevenson) **11**:265, 268-69, 282-83, 286-89, 291, 293, 295

See *The Strange Case of Dr. Jekyll and Mr. Hyde*

Doctor Martino, and Other Stories (Faulkner) **1**:180

"The Doctor of Hoyland" (Doyle) **12**:88

"A Doctor of Medicine" (Kipling) **5**:285

"Doctor Tristan's Treatment" (Villiers de l'Isle Adam)
See "Le traitement du docteur Tristan"

"The Doctors" (Barnes) **3**:9-10

"The Doctor's Case" (King) **17**:295

"The Doctor's Son" (O'Hara) **15**:247, 252, 256-57, 265-66, 286

The Doctor's Son, and Other Stories (O'Hara) **15**:249, 263, 264-67, 273-74

"A Doctor's Visit" (Chekhov) **2**:127, 156-58

"The Doctor's Wife" (Ozick) **15**:297, 300, 313-14

"Doe" (Coppard) **21**:29

"The Dog" (Turgenev) **7**:316, 321, 323-24, 326, 335-36, 338

"Dog Days" (Dixon) **16**:217

"The Dog Hervey" (Kipling) **5**:275, 284-85

"A Dog Named Trilby" (Hughes) **6**:122

"Dog Scent" (Zoshchenko) **15**:406

"Doge und Dogressa" (Hoffmann) **13**:183-84

"A Dog's a Dog" (Collier) **19**:111

The Dogs' Colloguy (Cervantes)
See "El coloquio de los perros"

"Dokutan" ("The German Spy") (Tanizaki) **21**:209-10

"Dolan's Cadillac" (King) **17**:294

"The Doll" (Chesnutt) **7**:17

Dollari e vecchie mondane (*Dollars and the Demi-Mondaine*) (Calvino) **3**:91

Dollars and the Demi-Mondaine (Calvino)
See *Dollari e vecchie mondane*

"Dolls" (Campbell) **19**:76, 85

"The Doll's House" (Mansfield) **9**:280, 282, 286, 301-05, 308, 311, 313

"Dolph Heyliger" (Irving) **2**:241, 247-48, 251, 254, 256, 259-60

"The Dolt" (Barthelme) **2**:38, 52

"A Domestic Dilemma" (McCullers) **9**:323, 331-32, 343, 353-54, 356, 359-60

"Domestic Life in America" (Updike) **13**:385-86, 388-89

Title Index

Title Index

Title Index

ISBN 0-7876-0753-3

90000

9 780787 607531